Contemporary
Literary Criticism

Guide to Gale Literary Criticism Series

For criticism on	Consult these Gale series
Authors now living or who died after December 31, 1959	*CONTEMPORARY LITERARY CRITICISM (CLC)*
Authors who died between 1900 and 1959	*TWENTIETH-CENTURY LITERARY CRITICISM (TCLC)*
Authors who died between 1800 and 1899	*NINETEENTH-CENTURY LITERATURE CRITICISM (NCLC)*
Authors who died between 1400 and 1799	*LITERATURE CRITICISM FROM 1400 TO 1800 (LC)* *SHAKESPEAREAN CRITICISM (SC)*
Authors who died before 1400	*CLASSICAL AND MEDIEVAL LITERATURE CRITICISM (CMLC)*
Black writers of the past two hundred years	*BLACK LITERATURE CRITICISM (BLC) AND BLACK LITERATURE CRITICISM SUPPLEMENT (BLCS)*
Authors of books for children and young adults	*CHILDREN'S LITERATURE REVIEW (CLR)*
Dramatists	*DRAMA CRITICISM (DC)*
Hispanic writers of the late nineteenth and twentieth centuries	*HISPANIC LITERATURE CRITICISM (HLC)*
Native North American writers and orators of the eighteenth, nineteenth, and twentieth centuries	*NATIVE NORTH AMERICAN LITERATURE (NNAL)*
Poets	*POETRY CRITICISM (PC)*
Short story writers	*SHORT STORY CRITICISM (SSC)*
Major authors from the Renaissance to the present	*WORLD LITERATURE CRITICISM, 1500 TO THE PRESENT (WLC)*
Major authors and works from the Bible to the present	*WORLD LITERATURE CRITICISM SUPPLEMENT (WLCS)*

ISSN 0091-3421

Volume 110

Contemporary Literary Criticism

Excerpts from Criticism of the Works
of Today's Novelists, Poets, Playwrights,
Short Story Writers, Scriptwriters, and
Other Creative Writers

Jeffrey W. Hunter
Deborah A. Schmitt
Timothy J. White
EDITORS

Tim Akers
Pamela S. Dear
Catherine V. Donaldson
Daniel Jones
John D. Jorgenson
Jerry Moore
Polly Vedder
Thomas Wiloch
Kathleen Wilson
ASSOCIATE EDITORS

GALE

DETROIT · LONDON

STAFF

Jeffrey W. Hunter, Deborah A. Schmitt, Timothy J. White, *Editors*

Tim Akers, Pamela S. Dear, Catherine V. Donaldson, Daniel Jones, John D. Jorgenson, Jerry Moore, Polly A. Vedder, Thomas Wiloch, and Kathleen Wilson, *Associate Editors*

Tracy Arnold-Chapman, Nancy Dziedzic, Linda Quigley, Paul Serralheiro and Fred Wheeler, *Contributing Editors*

Susan Trosky, *Permissions Manager*
Kimberly F. Smilay, *Permissions Specialist*
Steve Cusack, and Kelly Quin, *Permissions Associates*
Sandy Gore, *Permissions Assistant*

Victoria B. Cariappa, *Research Manager*
Julia C. Daniel, Tamara C. Nott, Michele P. Pica, Tracie A. Richardson,
Norma Sawaya, and Cheryl L. Warnock, *Research Associates*
Laura C. Bissey, Alfred A. Gardner I, and Sean R. Smith, *Research Assistants*

Mary Beth Trimper, *Production Director*

Barbara J. Yarrow, *Graphic Services Manager*

Randy Bassett, *Image Database Supervisor*
Robert Duncan and Mikal Ansari, *Scanner Operators*
Pamela Reed, *Imaging Coordinator*

Library of Congress Catalog Card Number 76-46132
ISBN 0-7876-2033-5
ISSN 0091-3421

Printed in the United States of America
10 9 8 7 6 5 4 3 2 1

Contents

Preface vii

Acknowledgments xi

Preface

A Comprehensive Information Source
on Contemporary Literature

Named "one of the twenty-five most distinguished reference titles published during the past twenty-five years" by *Reference Quarterly*, the *Contemporary Literary Criticism (CLC)* series provides readers with critical commentary and general information on more than 2,000 authors now living or who died after December 31, 1959. Previous to the publication of the first volume of *CLC* in 1973, there was no ongoing digest monitoring scholarly and popular sources of critical opinion and explication of modern literature. *CLC*, therefore, has fulfilled an essential need, particularly since the complexity and variety of contemporary literature makes the function of criticism especially important to today's reader.

Scope of the Series

CLC presents significant passages from published criticism of works by creative writers. Since many of the authors covered by *CLC* inspire continual critical commentary, writers are often represented in more than one volume. There is, of course, no duplication of reprinted criticism.

Authors are selected for inclusion for a variety of reasons, among them the publication or dramatic production of a critically acclaimed new work, the reception of a major literary award, revival of interest in past writings, or the adaptation of a literary work to film or television.

Attention is also given to several other groups of writers-authors of considerable public interest—about whose work criticism is often difficult to locate. These include mystery and science fiction writers, literary and social critics, foreign writers, and authors who represent particular ethnic groups within the United States.

Format of the Book

Each *CLC* volume contains about 500 individual excerpts taken from hundreds of book review periodicals, general magazines, scholarly journals, monographs, and books. Entries include critical evaluations spanning from the beginning of an author's career to the most current commentary. Interviews, feature articles, and other published writings that offer insight into the author's works are also presented. Students, teachers, librarians, and researchers will find that the generous excerpts and supplementary material in *CLC* provide them with vital information required to write a term paper, analyze a poem, or lead a book discussion group. In addition, complete bibliographical citations note the original source and all of the information necessary for a term paper footnote or bibliography.

Features

A *CLC* author entry consists of the following elements:

■ The **Author Heading** cites the author's name in the form under which the author has most commonly published, followed by birth date, and death date when applicable. Uncertainty as to a birth or death date is indicated by a question mark.

- A **Portrait** of the author is included when available.

- A brief **Biographical and Critical Introduction** to the author and his or her work precedes the excerpted criticism. The first line of the introduction provides the author's full name, pseudonyms (if applicable), nationality, and a listing of genres in which the author has written. To provide users with easier access to information, the biographical and critical essay included in each author entry is divided into four categories: "Introduction," "Biographical Information," "Major Works," and "Critical Reception." The introductions to single-work entries—entries that focus on well known and frequently studied books, short stories, and poems—are similarly organized to quickly provide readers with information on the plot and major characters of the work being discussed, its major themes, and its critical reception. Previous volumes of *CLC* in which the author has been featured are also listed in the introduction.

- A list of **Principal Works** notes the most important writings by the author. When foreign-language works have been translated into English, the English-language version of the title follows in brackets.

- The **Excerpted Criticism** represents various kinds of critical writing, ranging in form from the brief review to the scholarly exegesis. Essays are selected by the editors to reflect the spectrum of opinion about a specific work or about an author's literary career in general. The excerpts are presented chronologically, adding a useful perspective to the entry. All titles by the author featured in the entry are printed in boldface type, which enables the reader to easily identify the works being discussed. Publication information (such as publisher names and book prices) and parenthetical numerical references (such as footnotes or page and line references to specific editions of a work) have been deleted at the editor's discretion to provide smoother reading of the text.

- Critical essays are prefaced by **Explanatory Notes** as an additional aid to readers. These notes may provide several types of valuable information, including: the reputation of the critic, the importance of the work of criticism, the commentator's approach to the author's work, the purpose of the criticism, and changes in critical trends regarding the author.

- A complete **Bibliographical Citation** designed to help the user find the original essay or book precedes each excerpt.

- Whenever possible, a recent, previously unpublished **Author Interview** accompanies each entry.

- A concise **Further Reading** section appears at the end of entries on authors for whom a significant amount of criticism exists in addition to the pieces reprinted in *CLC*. Each citation in this section is accompanied by a descriptive annotation describing the content of that article. Materials included in this section are grouped under various headings (e.g., Biography, Bibliography, Criticism, and Interviews) to aid users in their search for additional information. Cross-references to other useful sources published by Gale Research in which the author has appeared are also included: *Authors in the News, Black Writers, Children's Literature Review, Contemporary Authors, Dictionary of Literary Biography, DISCovering Authors, Drama Criticism, Hispanic Literature Criticism, Hispanic Writers, Native North American Literature, Poetry Criticism, Something about the Author, Short Story Criticism, Contemporary Authors Autobiography Series,* and *Something about the Author Autobiography Series.*

Other Features

CLC also includes the following features:

- An **Acknowledgments** section lists the copyright holders who have granted permission to reprint material in this volume of *CLC*. It does not, however, list every book or periodical reprinted or consulted during the preparation of the volume.

- Each new volume of *CLC* includes a **Cumulative Topic Index,** which lists all literary topics treated in *CLC, NCLC, TCLC,* and *LC 1400-1800.*

- A **Cumulative Author Index** lists all the authors who have appeared in the various literary criticism series published by Gale Research, with cross-references to Gale's biographical and autobiographical series. A full listing of the series referenced there appears on the first page of the indexes of this volume. Readers will welcome this cumulated author index as a useful tool for locating an author within the various series. The index, which lists birth and death dates when available, will be particularly valuable for those authors who are identified with a certain period but whose death dates cause them to be placed in another, or for those authors whose careers span two periods. For example, Ernest Hemingway is found in *CLC,* yet F. Scott Fitzgerald, a writer often associated with him, is found in *Twentieth-Century Literary Criticism.*

- A **Cumulative Nationality Index** alphabetically lists all authors featured in *CLC* by nationality, followed by numbers corresponding to the volumes in which the authors appear.

- An alphabetical **Title Index** accompanies each volume of *CLC.* Listings are followed by the author's name and the corresponding page numbers where the titles are discussed. English translations of foreign titles and variations of titles are cross-referenced to the title under which a work was originally published. Titles of novels, novellas, dramas, films, record albums, and poetry, short story, and essay collections are printed in italics, while all individual poems, short stories, essays, and songs are printed in roman type within quotation marks; when published separately (e.g., T. S. Eliot's poem *The Waste Land),* the titles of long poems are printed in italics.

- In response to numerous suggestions from librarians, Gale has also produced a **Special Paperbound Edition** of the *CLC* title index. This annual cumulation, which alphabetically lists all titles reviewed in the series, is available to all customers and is typically published with every fifth volume of *CLC.* Additional copies of the index are available upon request. Librarians and patrons will welcome this separate index: it saves shelf space, is easy to use, and is recyclable upon receipt of the next edition.

Citing *Contemporary Literary Criticism*

When writing papers, students who quote directly from any volume in the Literary Criticism Series may use the following general forms to footnote reprinted criticism. The first example pertains to material drawn from periodicals, the second to material reprinted in books:

[1]Alfred Cismaru, "Making the Best of It," *The New Republic,* 207, No. 24, (December 7, 1992), 30, 32; excerpted and reprinted in *Contemporary Literary Criticism,* Vol. 85, ed. Christopher Giroux (Detroit: Gale Research, 1995), pp. 73-4.

[2]Yvor Winters, *The Post-Symbolist Methods* (Allen Swallow, 1967); excerpted and reprinted in *Contemporary Literary Criticism,* Vol. 85, ed. Christopher Giroux (Detroit: Gale Research, 1995), pp. 223-26.

Suggestions Are Welcome

The editors hope that readers will find *CLC* a useful reference tool and welcome comments about the work. Send comments and suggestions to: Editors, *Contemporary Literary Criticism,* Gale Research, 27500 Drake Rd., Farmington Hills, MI 48333-3535.

Acknowledgments

The editors wish to thank the copyright holders of the excerpted criticism included in this volume and the permissions managers of many book and magazine publishing companies for assisting us in securing reproduction rights. We are also grateful to the staffs of the Detroit Public Library, the Library of Congress, the University of Detroit Mercy Library, Wayne State University Purdy/Kresge Library Complex, and the University of Michigan Libraries for making their resources available to us. Following is a list of the copyright holders who have granted us permission to reproduce material in this volume of CLC. Every effort has been made to trace copyright, but if omissions have been made, please let us know.

COPYRIGHTED EXCERPTS IN *CLC*, VOLUME 110, WERE REPRODUCED FROM THE FOLLOWING PERIODICALS:

America, v. 136, March 26, 1977. © 1977. All rights reserved. Reproduced with permission of America Press, Inc.,106 West 56th Street, New York, NY 10019.—*The American Historical Review,* v. 102, February, 1997. Reproduced by permission.—*The American Poetry Review,* v. 20, May - June, 1991 for "Richard Wilber: An Interview" by Steve Kronen. Copyright © 1991 by World Poetry, Inc. Reproduced by permission of the author.—*The American Spectator,* v. 28, August, 1995. Copyright © *The American Spectator* 1995. Reproduced by permission.—*Annali d' Italianistica,* v. 7, 1989. Reproduced by permission.—*ANQ: A Quarterly Journal of Short Articles, Notes and Reviews,* v. 5, April-July, 1992. Copyright © 1992 Helen Dwight Reid Educational Foundation. Reproduced with permission of the Helen Dwight Reid Educational Foundation, published by Heldref Publications, 1319 18th Street, NW, Washington, DC 20036-1802.—*The Atlantic,* v. 258, September, 1986 for "Sex In Our Time" by Phyllis Rose. Copyright © 1986, by The Atlantic Monthly Company. Reproduced by permission of the author.—*Book World--The Washington Post,* v. V, January 24. 1971 for "In Sickness and in Wealth" by Edward Edelson. © 1971 Postrib Corp. Reproduced by permission of the author.—*Chasqui,* v. XVI, November, 1987. Reproduced by permission.—*The Chesterton Review,* v. XIX, May, 1993 for "Adam, Eve and Agatha Christie" by John Wren-Lewis. © 1993 The Chesterton Review. Reproduced by permission of the author.—*Chicago Tribune,* May 28, 1995 for "The Heat and the Intimacy: The Very Different Styles of Essayists Joseph Epstein and Barbara Ehrenreich" by Penelope Mesic. © copyrighted 1995, Chicago Tribune Company. All rights reserved. Reproduced by permission of the author.—*The Christian Science Monitor,* v. 81, September 11, 1989 for a review of "Fear of Falling: The Inner Life of The Middle Class" by Mary Warner Marien; November 30, 1989 for a review of "The Remains Of The Day" by Merle Rubin; November 4, 1995 for a review of "The Unconsoled" by Merle Rubin. © 1989, 1995 The Christian Science Publishing Society. All rights reserved. All reproduced by permission of the respective authors./ November 17, 1966. © 1966 The Christian Science Publishing Society. All rights reserved. Reproduced by permission from *The Christian Science Monitor.*—*Cineaste,* v. XX, 1993. Copyright © 1993 by Cineaste Publishers, Inc. Reproduced by permission.—*CLIO,* v. 24, Winter, 1995 for "The Shame of Memory: Blanchot's Self-Dispossession in Ishiguro's 'A Pale View of Hills'" by Cynthia F. Wong. © 1995 by Robert H. Canary and Henry Kozicki. Reproduced by permission of the author.—*Commentary,* v. 89, January, 1990 for "High Anxiety" by Wilfred M. McClay. Copyright © 1990 by the American Jewish Committee. All rights reserved. Reproduced by permission of the publisher and the author.—*Contemporary Literature,* v. XXX, Fall, 1989. © 1989 by the Board of Regents of the University of Wisconsin. Reproduced by permission of The University of Wisconsin Press.—*Contemporary Poetry,* v. II, Autumn, 1977 for "Richard Wilbur's Critical Condition" by Charles R. Woodard. © *Contemporary Poetry* 1977. Reproduced by permission of the author.—*Critica Hispanica,* v. VIII, 1986. Reproduced by permission.—*Critical Matrix: The Princeton Journal of Women, Gender and Culture,* v. 8, 1994 for "Crossing Games: Reading Black Transvestism at The Movies" by Hawley Russell. Reproduced by permission of Hawley Fogg Davis.—*Critical Survey,* v. 3, 1991. Reproduced by permission.—*Cross Currents,* Dobbs Ferry, v. 43, Summer, 1993. Copyright 1993 by Cross Currents Inc. Reproduced by permission.—*The Economist,* November 14, 1964. © 1964 The Economist Newspaper Group, Inc. Reproduced with permission. Further reproduction prohibited.—*European Studies Journal,* v. III, 1986. Reproduced by permission.—*The Explicator,* v. 50, Summer, 1991; v. 51, Fall, 1992; v. 55, Summer, 1996; v. 55, Winter, 1997. Copyright © 1991, 1992, 1996,

Cleanth Brooks
1906-1994

American critic and nonfiction writer.

The following entry presents an overview of Brooks's career. For further information on his life and works, see *CLC*, Volumes 24 and 86.

INTRODUCTION

Considered one of the most influential critics of the twentieth century, Brooks, along with John Crowe Ransom, Allen Tate, and Robert Penn Warren, was a principal proponent of the "New Criticism," a critical method that stressed analysis of a work based solely on the work itself, without consideration of the author's circumstances or previous writings. The subject of a book by Ransom (*The New Criticism,* 1941), this method was a radical departure from contemporary schools of criticism, which held that a work could only be properly interpreted in the context of the writer's life and times.

Biographical Information

Brooks was born October 16, 1906, in Murray, Kentucky. The son of a Methodist minister, he attended McTyeire School, a small Methodist preparatory school in McKenzie, Tennessee. Brooks continued his education at Vanderbilt University and Tulane University, and attended Oxford University as a Rhodes Scholar. In 1934, he married Edith Amy Blanchard. Brooks began his career as an educator in 1932 at Louisiana State University; he moved to Yale University in 1947, from which he retired in 1975. While at Louisiana State, Brooks edited the *Louisiana Review* with Warren from 1935 to 1941. From 1964 to 1966, Brooks served as the cultural attaché at the United States Embassy in London. He was also a Jefferson Lecturer at the Library of Congress and a member of the Library's council of scholars. Brooks also taught at the University of Texas, the University of Michigan, and the University of California at Los Angeles (UCLA). Brooks was widowed in 1986 and died on May 10, 1996, at his home in New Haven, Connecticut.

Major Works

Many of Brooks's writings were extensions of the critical philosophy he presented to his students. His first book of criticism, a college text co-edited with Warren and titled *Understanding Poetry* (1938), is considered part of the foundation of the New Criticism. His next book, *Modern Poetry and the Tradition* (1939), explained his philosophy of

evaluating poetry in the context of its place in the larger literary tradition. He expanded on the idea in *The Well Wrought Urn* (1947) and *A Shaping Joy* (1971), explaining and demonstrating a poem's "internal unity"—how well it succeeds in a unification of its forms and content as well as how it fits into the larger literary tradition. A controversial aspect of Brooks's critical theory, expounded in The Hidden God (1963), was the idea that the critic also had the responsibility of evaluating the moral aspect of a poem, taking a stand on the spiritual validity of a writer's work. Although Brooks developed his theory of criticism to further the understanding of poetry, he was also able to apply it to prose, principally in the study of William Faulkner. Brooks's *William Faulkner: The Yoknapatawpha Country* (1963), *William Faulkner: Toward Yoknapatawpha and Beyond* (1978), *William Faulkner: First Encounters* (1983), and *On the Prejudices, Predilections, and Firm Beliefs of William Faulkner* (1987) are listed among the most thorough and insightful critiques of Faulkner's work. Because Brooks stressed that a close reading and examination of the internal structure of a poem was the best evidence of the author's intent, and that criticism did not require an investigation of the poet's life, he was frequently accused of being oblivious to the historical significance of events which affected the poet. Partly in reply to this charge, Brooks wrote *Historical Evidence and the Reading of Seventeenth-Century Poetry* (1991). In this work, Brooks shows how the historical context of a poem can be used to uncover meanings which might be hidden by changes in the usage of words over time.

Critical Reception

The critical theory identified as the "New Criticism" was not initially well-received by the academic world. The individuals most closely associated with the "movement"—Brooks, Ransom, Tate, and Warren, did not see themselves as sharing a common theory of criticism. What they did share, according to Roger Kimball, "was a concern with the integrity of the literary object as such." The New Critics, as Allen Tate put it, were against "using social theories to prove something about poetry . . . trying to make an art respectable by showing that after all it is something else. Just this won them the undying hostility of the academic establishment." Kimball added, "What unites them is an insistence on the irreducibility of the aesthetic object: an insistence that literature, for example, is literature, not a covert species of politics." Other critics, however, saw the exclusion of the analysis of historical and social aspects of the writer's life as reactionary. They argued that keeping the focus within the poem itself, and ignoring the writer external to the work was a subtle means of preventing the examination of the effects of race, class, and gender on the arts. They also suggested that Brooks's focus on how a poem fits into the tradition— into the larger historical body of literature—emphasizes white male Europeans to the exclusion of newer, more diverse voices. Critics such as John N. Duvall said that Brooks's examination of the "inclusiveness" of a poem, the degree to which it participates in the literary and spiritual tradition, is in fact exclusive. "In his effort to discover the hidden unity of works and the tradition, Brooks's literary history omitted texts that were tainted with the secularization of politics. Thus Joyce and Faulkner are prized but not Dos Passos: Eliot and Yeats, but not Zukofsky (to say nothing of the proletarian poets from the 1930s). New Criticism was too ready to excuse the excesses either in a text's rhetoric or in the social system that a text represented, if one could read that text in a way that discovered unity or that celebrated community." Other critics acknowledged the spiritual component of Brooks's criticism, but did not see it as constraining. William Bedford Clark, comparing Brooks and Eliot, wrote, "Like Eliot, Brooks knows that literature inevitably reflects the values and beliefs, however implicit, of the author. Yet, once again in full accord with Eliot, Brooks would not make the reader's adherence to the author's values and beliefs a basis for experiencing or evaluating the work itself." In one area both champions and detractors of the New Criticism concurred: It is considered a foundation for all current forms of criticism. Anthony Tassin wrote, "Although a variety of new philosophies of literary criticism have come forward since the mid-century, the New Criticism is alive and well. For all purposes it has become a standard approach to teaching literature and is currently accepted by professors and students alike. When they speak of *criticism*, it is substantially the New Criticism to which they refer."

PRINCIPAL WORKS

The Relation of the Alabama-Georgia Dialect to the Provincial Dialects of Great Britain (nonfiction) 1935

Understanding Poetry: An Anthology for College Students [editor with Robert Penn Warren] (criticism) 1938; enlarged and revised edition, 1950

Modern Poetry and the Tradition (criticism) 1939

*Understanding Fiction [editor with Robert Penn Warren] (criticism) 1943

Understanding Drama [editor with Robert B. Heilman] (criticism) 1945; enlarged edition, 1948

The Well Wrought Urn: Studies in the Structure of Poetry (criticism) 1947; revised edition, 1968

Modern Rhetoric [with Robert Penn Warren] (nonfiction) 1949

Fundamentals of Good Writing: A Handbook of Modern Rhetoric [with Robert Penn Warren] (nonfiction) 1950

†Literary Criticism: A Short History [with William K. Wimsatt] (criticism) 1957

The Hidden God: Studies in Hemingway, Faulkner, Yeats, Eliot, and Warren (criticism) 1963

William Faulkner: The Yoknapatawpha Country (criticism) 1963

A Shaping Joy: Studies in the Writer's Craft (criticism) 1971

William Faulkner: Toward Yoknapatawpha and Beyond (criticism) 1978

William Faulkner: First Encounters (criticism) 1983

The Language of the American South (nonfiction) 1985

On the Prejudices, Predilections, and Firm Beliefs of William Faulkner (criticism) 1987

Historical Evidence and the Reading of Seventeenth-Century Poetry (criticism) 1991

*Abridged edition of this work was published as *The Scope of Fiction* in 1960.

†Part four of this work was published searately as *Modern Criticism: A Short History* in 1970.

CRITICISM

Robert Daniel (review date 1940)

SOURCE: A review of *Modern Poetry and the Tradition,* in *Sewanee Review,* Vol. 48, 1940, pp. 419-24.

[*In the following review, Daniel explains Brooks's theory of the evolution of poetic style.*]

In keeping with the critical principles that underlie **Understanding Poetry,** Cleanth Brooks makes in **Modern Poetry and the Tradition** a clear statement of the fundamental similarities between modernist verse and the metaphysical verse of the seventeenth century. "Modern poetry" means of course the work of Yeats, Eliot, Auden, Tate, and the others who have participated in the revolution that commenced about 1912 with the change in Yeats's style and the emergence of Pound—a revolution, Brooks maintains, comparable in importance to that which began in 1798 with the publication of the *Lyrical Ballads.*

The need for a new definition of metaphysical poetry has become apparent in the loose and conflicting usages of the term in much recent criticism, and in the application of it to modern poetry by such critics as John Crowe Ransom. Brooks's description of the metaphysical mode is exhaustive. Taking up one of the stock definitions, "the poetry of wit", he shows how it fits the work of Donne and his fellows on two levels. Wit in its present sense operates not only in the minor poetry of the time but in that of Shakespeare, Donne, and Milton—as is shown by their common fondness for puns, playful comparisons, and satirical thrusts. Wit in its older meaning of intellectual power presides over what all these poets wrote, developing and controlling the emotion. It led the metaphysical poet to regard his subject from all points of view, and thus to render an account of experience as complex as life itself. Hence Brooks derives a definition of wit as "a lively awareness of the fact that the obvious attitude toward a given situation is not the only possible attitude." The tone that wit produces in the poem Brooks call *irony,* meaning by it the total attitude resulting from a combination of the approbative and satirical attitudes—that is, by a mature mind fully commanding the situation and exploiting every aspect of it. Its presence accounts for the frequent occurrence of paradox in this poetry, and its habitual absence from the poetry of the next two centuries is the essential distinction between the two.

Because the intellect and not the emotions was sovereign in the writing of metaphysical verse, it recognized no class of words and objects as inherently "poetical". A thing was poetical only as it was successfully employed in a poem, and the poet was free to choose his subjects and his metaphors from the whole of life. At the same time, the metaphors were employed functionally rather than decoratively, for the figures cannot be removed from a metaphysical poem without demolishing it. "The comparison *is* the poem in a structural sense."

The different texture of the verse typical of the next two centuries resulted from the new conception of metaphor as an illustrative or decorative accessory, a point upon which both Samuel Johnson and A. E. Housman, writing as critics, are in complete agreement. These timid metaphors, which degenerate so readily into similes, may be removed without destroying the theme of the poem. It simply becomes less clear or less "beautiful". The fluid state in which such a poem exists is its radical difference from a metaphysical poem. From what seems to have been the older view of a poem as an object having a valid existence of its own, poets and critics turned to the notion that a poem was a statement intended to change the reader in some way. ". . . the test of the statement's value [was] its truth; and the success of the poet, his success as an expositor." The imagery and metrics were to be pleasant in themselves, apart from what was being said, and their only connection with what was being said was to make it more palatable.

> **The need for a new definition of metaphysical poetry has become apparent in the loose and conflicting usages of the term in much recent criticism, and in the application of it to modern poetry by such critics as John Crowe Ransom. Brooks's description of the metaphysical mode [in *Modern Poetry and Tradition*] is exhaustive.**
> **—Robert Daniel**

The reason for the change was the dominant position that rationalism and the new science assumed at this time under the leadership of Hobbes. Hobbes, who was so suspicious of metaphor that he excluded it entirely from prose, allowed it a place in poetry "only for pleasure or ornament". Poetry was believed to be, like science, a search for demonstrable truth. "For the imaginative act of fusing what in ordinary experience is inharmonious, the Hobbesian poet tended to substitute the rational act of sorting out the discordant and removing it from the context." A spirit of levity and paradox would impede the search for scientific truth, and since metaphor's only function was to make the demonstrated truth more agreeable, naturally the poet was not allowed to employ disagreeable words and images. "The first critical revolution in modern English poetry, then, may be described as a simplification of poetry." The poet sacrificed the totality of his vision: serious poetry had to be exclusively serious in tone, and satire was relegated to a secondary place. Abstractions and generalizations resembling those of science replaced the vivid particularity of Shakespeare and Donne.

The advent of Wordsworth, Coleridge, and their followers, Brooks maintains, produced only a demi-revolution; and the halfheartedness of their revolt from the eighteenth-century notions may be seen in a variety of ways. In the highest poetry, they supposed, materials that were technical, sharply realistic, and definite were to be avoided. The notion persisted of a limited class of objects that were intrinsically poetical, though the limits were extended and the objects changed. Simplicity was still preferred to complexity; and wit with its flashing conflict of attitudes was thought to be out of place. Either poets continued to kowtow to science and serve its ends or with "romantic irony" they wholly rejected its view of the world. In either case they failed to recapture the attitude that poetry is not in competition with science but complements it by offering a kind of knowledge that science does not know.

It is evident that on these disputed points the practice of the modernists is that of the metaphysicals. Wit, intellectual activity, and totality of vision, the inclusion of words and images of all kinds, the use of metaphor functionally rather than decoratively, the "reconciliation of warring elements", and the conception of poetry as a form of knowledge—all these characterize the work of Yeats and the rest. The obscurity of the moderns is of the same kind as that of Donne's verse and many of Shakespeare's Sonnets: it results from the poet's being once more a "maker" rather than an expositor, so that the experience his poem creates must inevitably contain something new and individual—that is, at least partially private. Brooks remarks that no-one blames Wordsworth for employing a leech-gatherer as the symbol for resolution and independence; yet it is a symbol at least somewhat private and obscure. Significantly enough, readers find obscurity not only in Donne on the one hand and Yeats on the other but also in the three intervening poets whose work (for example, in its untrammeled use of symbols) most resembles theirs: Blake, Emily Dickinson, and Gerard Manley Hopkins. Here the affinity between symbolists and metaphysical poetry becomes apparent—an affinity, Brooks shows, that caused the influence of French symbolists like Laforgue and Corbière to lead Eliot and the rest back to the principles underlying the metaphysical lyric.

Brooks's view of English literary history finds its firmest support in the chapter, "A Note on the Death of Elizabethan Tragedy"; and it is here that he shows himself most original and independent. The thesis is that tragedy fell a victim to the process that had changed the course of lyric poetry. The complexity of Shakespeare was replaced by the simplicity of Dryden, or else Shakespeare's plays themselves were simplified when they were revived. Like the Greek protagonist with his tragic flaw, the Elizabethan hero was hero and criminal at once; and from this ambiguity, together with the irony that the subject-matter was potentially comic if differently treated, there resulted the equilibrium, the tension, of great tragedy. After the Restoration, however, the subplot was condemned (though not even the neo-classicists could regard Lear's Fool as "affording comic relief"), and the result was

such an abstraction that, as Empson remarks, "one might almost say that the English drama did not outlive the double plot." Tragedy had come to envy science its ability to give answers; in order to do so the characters were simplified and made two-dimensional, that the audience might have a single attitude towards them, and the action became predictable and contrived. Comedy survived for a time because it allows of a single attitude; but it is significant that the most complex of Restoration comedies, *The Way of the World,* failed on the stage, and that Congreve retired from playwriting when he had scarcely reached his prime.

The novelty of this chapter indicates how the thesis of ***Modern Poetry and the Tradition*** has necessitated a revaluation of literary history, and in fact the last chapter is called, "Notes for a Revised History of English Poetry." In it Brooks makes plain his belief that eighteenth- and nineteenth-century poets wrote more alike than is commonly supposed, and that the work of Yeats and the rest is directly in the tradition of Shakespeare, Donne, and Milton. In this way Brooks shifts the burden of the proof from the modern poets to their assailants. The unity of the book results from the fact that the tradition is restated so as to include modern poetry, and thus the author fulfills his twin purposes of revaluating the work of the past and justifying that of the present; but it is to be regretted that he did not push on to particular analyses of non-metaphysical poems, to show how they are different and, as he believes, inferior. Even so, the importance of ***Modern Poetry and the Tradition*** in its aim can scarcely be overstated; and in the opinion of this reviewer the fulfillment of its aim is completely successful.

As Brooks himself acknowledges, his debt to such critics as Empson, Eliot, and Ransom is a large one; but by this means his book achieves a drawing-together and clarification of the principles basic to these most unsystematic and often puzzling writers. For example, the title of Allen Tate's book, *Reactionary Essays* is accounted for by Brooks's contention that Tate and the rest have not uprooted the tradition of English verse but rather have reacted from its perversion to an earlier age when it was in a state of health. ***Modern Poetry and the Tradition*** is particularly valuable for its illuminating analyses of *The Waste Land,* Yeats's mythology, and the verse of Ransom, Warren, Tate, MacLeish, Auden, and Frost (whose inclusion as a modern poet may surprise the dedicatee), so that the general comments on these poets are confirmed by detailed examinations of their achievements.

This book, it has been remarked, is not a manifesto of the kind that appears at the outset of a revolution. It is a work of elucidation the time for which arrives when the revolution is a *fait accompli.* For this reason readers familiar with Empson and the others will find much in it that is not new. It is, however, the most consistent and intelligible, statement of their position that has been made, and indeed it is not primarily addressed to the friends of modernist poetry.

Robert Daniel (review date January/March 1965)

SOURCE: "The Southern Community," in *Sewanee Review,* Vol. 73, No. 1, January/March, 1965, pp. 119-24.

[*Below, Daniel favorably reviews Brooks's* William Faulkner: The Yoknapatawpha Country. *Brooks's own southern heritage, Daniel argues, gives added clarity to his interpretations of Faulkner.*]

Faulkner's novels and stories have evoked studies the length of books by Campbell and Foster, Howe, O'Connor, Mrs. Vickery, Slatoff, Swiggart, Longley, and now Cleanth Brooks. (I may have overlooked a few, and on various grounds I have omitted Miner, Malin, Cooper, Coughlan, Meriwether, etc.) Despite the competition, Brooks's work has in general been well received—except by such implacable curmudgeons as Marvin Mudrick. Its admirers have had all sorts of reasons for admiring it, one of the most provocative being that it is the first such book to be written by "one who can speak from intimate but dispassionate knowledge of [Faulkner's] milieu": a point to which I must return. The reviews and the sales must be making the publisher look forward to bringing out the companion volume, which will be concerned with Faulkner's style and fictional technique, especially as analysis of his revisions may illuminate these.

It is a pleasure to agree with the praise that *William Faulkner: The Yoknapatawpha Country* has called forth. Brooks has indeed produced a most valuable guide to the meaning of Faulkner's major novels; and, what is more, once it gets really under way it is a joy to read. The analyses are generous with summary and quotation, presenting the substance of the novels with such discerning warmth as to rekindle the excitement one felt on one's first meeting with them. Yet I must at the same time sympathize with some of the reviewers' complaints: that Brooks writes as though Faulkner's characters led lives independent of his fictions; that the encomiums on every one of the fourteen Yoknapatawpha novels get monotonous, hardly discriminating between the worst and the best of them; that Brooks's thesis is vulnerable—viz., that to Faulkner the Southern community is "the field for man's action and the norm by which his action is judged and regulated," as Brooks formulates it on page 69. And the writing is sometimes absent-minded: "These instances of symbol-hunting . . . are only a little less absurd than much respectable commentary on Faulkner." For "less" read "more," surely.

I must add a few other cavils. Nearly half of the forty-two short stories in Faulkner's *Collected Stories* are set in the Yoknapatawpha country, and these have supplied some of our most memorable images of it. Yet Brooks mentions only six of the stories—mainly in his notes. (A full analysis of "Dry September," for instance, would have deepened his interpretation of *Light in August.*) His rather disjointed title seems intended to prepare for the whimsical structure of the book. Discussions of Faulkner's provincialism, his treatment of rustic characters, and the role nature plays in his work introduce the thirteen chapters on the Yoknapatawpha novels, *Sanctuary and Requiem for a Nun* being considered together. But the community with which the book is mainly concerned, as in the chapters on *Light in August* and *Intruder in the Dust,* resides in neither the countryside nor the wilderness. It resides in the town of Jefferson, and no introductory chapter treats of it. The discussions of the novels themselves occur neither in the order of their composition nor in that of history or geography. (Cf. the arrangement of the *Collected Stories.*) Brooks's arrangement, though his preface defends it, obscures the gradual evolution of Faulkner's major attitudes and his style, retards the expression of Brooks's thesis, and most unhappily—for it is an essentially sound thesis—robs it of the clarity that might have safeguarded it from attack.

> Although Brooks's stated intention [in *William Faulkner: The Yoknapatawpha County*] is "to determine and evaluate the meaning of the work in the fullness of its depth and amplitude," his method is very little that of the Formalist. Indeed, it is frequently moralistic, greatly concerned with the validity of Faulkner's judgments on his characters. And when this new development on Brooks's part is combined with his critiques of other approaches to Faulkner, some fine theoretical puzzles result.
>
> —*Robert Daniel*

For instance, it should not be necessary to deny, though it evidently is, that Brooks mistakes the Faulknerian community for a Utopia. He is showing only that it can nourish human relationships which, instead of being destructively competitive, are founded on disinterested kindliness and interdependence. Whoever wrote in a recent *New Republic* (hardly a reactionary journal) of "Southern California's vast, fragmented non-community, where . . . the rights of property remain the only constant value" (November 14, p. 6) would understand Faulkner's meaning without difficulty. But Faulkner did not discover this important theme all at once, and a critic can define it best if he traces its slow emergence in the novels. We may see Faulkner groping his way toward it in the Christmas Eve passage of *Sartoris;* with *As I Lay Dying* he brings it into sharper focus; and it flourishes even amid the horrors of *Light in August*—as Brooks finely shows at the conclusion of that chapter.

Although Brooks's stated intention is "to determine and evaluate the meaning of the work in the fullness of its depth and amplitude," his method is very little that of the Formalist. Indeed, it is frequently moralistic, greatly concerned with the validity of Faulkner's judgments on his characters. And when this new development on Brooks's part is combined with his critiques of other approaches to Faulkner, some fine theoretical puzzles result. Brooks makes war on two extremes: "sociologizing" and "symbol-mongering."(These are not counterparts, as he asserts, however, for the first reduces meaning, the second inflates it.) Of sociologizing, he remarks that "anything calculated to shake the reader's confidence in the literal accuracy of Faulkner's 'facts' is probably to be commended." Symbol-mongering is so calculated—and if Faulkner's fictitious situations are not true to life, what critical advantage is there in possessing "knowledge of how life is actually lived (and has been lived) in Mississippi"? Faulkner's European admirers doubtless lacked this knowledge, though they were among the first to appreciate his stature. It may be answered that, while Faulkner's best novels contain all that is needed for their understanding, the Southern critic will be alive to nuances that escape the outlander. Brooks implicitly claims more than this, though; e.g., "Peter Liska shows no knowledge of Southern mores when he assumes that the disclosure that Temple had been raped would be a 'socially acceptable' account." Here Brooks appeals to his own experience of Faulkner's milieu; and I wish he had somewhere addressed himself to the problem of how we can know when a novel is continuous, and when discontinuous, with the reality from which it has sprung.

The indictment of symbol-mongering also raises a problem of knowledge, which Brooks ignores, while effectively deriding various examples: the Compsons' Christmas dinner as a feast of atonement, Joe Christmas as Jesus, Ike Snopes as a Courtly Lover, Sutpen's mountain birthplace as an Eden. Some of these "discoveries" are merely silly; other symbolic readings, however, cannot be summarily rejected, unless they are shown to conflict with what seems the right interpretation of the whole novel. "Shall there be no more innocent consumption of pork chops and spareribs in Yoknapatawpha County," Brooks rightly asks, "because someone has read *The Golden Bough*?" But because Barbara Crossman has overinterpreted the Compsons' pig, shall there be no more archetypes? Is Neil Isaacs wrong, to take a recent example, in reading the murder of Sutpen as a kind of Götterdämmerung?

Brooks's own alertness to such implications produces one of the most compelling passages in his book: his account of

the mythic atmosphere of *The Hamlet*. Just so does his knowledge of the *facts* of Southern life make possible many of his other insights—despite his already quoted disclaimer. Two of the best examples are his suggestion that Sutpen's treatment of Clytie shows Sutpen lacking in "the usual Southern feeling" about Negroes, and the even more acute remark that the disintegration of the Compson family contrasts with, rather than represents, the general state of families in the South of 1910.

This knife, however, may cut both ways. A Southern critic may be both sensitive to the nuances of Faulkner's imaginary society and at the same time unduly defensive about the real society that underlies it. Brooks argues persuasively against the notion that Sutpen typifies the antebellum Southerner; and yet for all that, I think, *Absalom, Absalom!* excoriates the South by the motives it ascribes to Henry Sutpen, who is not the sympathetic character that Brooks would have him be. Henry's part of the story, as Brooks argues, is indeed what most affects Quentin—and it is Henry's actions that introduce ambiguity into Quentin's famous last words, "*I dont hate it!*"

Brooks presents Henry as "beset by conflicting claims . . . forced to make intolerably hard choices—between opposed goods or between conflicting evils." But what can "goods" mean in this sentence? Henry chooses to murder Charles Bon, his half-brother, rather than see him marry their sister, and the reason he finds himself in this apparent dilemma is that for six years he has been infatuated with Bon—so much so that during four of these years he has assented to the prospective marriage, knowing that Bon and Judith are half-brother and half-sister. (Much of all this derives from the conjectures of Quentin and Shreve; but, as Brooks shows, their conjectures have the same status as the rest of the novel's action.)

By suggesting that "Sutpen's unwillingness to acknowledge Charles Bon as his son does not spring from any particular racial feeling," Brooks obscures the biting ingenuity of Faulkner's plot. Sutpen's design, of course, has two parts: he wishes to make himself an aristocrat, and he wishes to found an aristocratic dynasty. In the incident of the Confederate camp, the ironist Bon offers himself as the fulfillment of the second wish; but his Negro blood means that if Sutpen acknowledged him he would frustrate the first one—and incidentally bastardize his white children. When Sutpen refuses, however, he removes the only obstacle to the marriage that Bon would recognize. Henry's choice is therefore not a true dilemma; to prevent the marriage he has only to proclaim his brotherhood with Bon. But he cannot entertain that alternative.

Quentin and Steve's conjectures, as Brooks summarizes them

on pages 434-435, make it all quite explicit, including Henry's silence at Bon's words, "*So it's the miscegenation, not the incest, which you cant bear.*" And surely the implication is that only when fifteen hundred miles away from Mississippi, and prodded by his Canadian roommate, can Quentin discern the truth about the South. While Sutpen is only a quasi-aristocrat, he has a genuine aristocrat for a son; and Henry, like Faulkner's other genuine aristocrats, is seldom guilty of treating other persons as mere instruments of his will. Yet both father and son are caught in an institution that makes the instrumental use of human beings peculiarly tempting, even to so amiable a character as Henry, who prefers murder to having a brother-in-law with Negro blood. It will not do to answer the question "Does Quentin hate the South?" by asking "Does Stephen Daedalus [*sic*] hate Dublin?" (Cf. p. 317.) The answer to that is Yes. The answer to the other question may be inferred from *Intruder in the Dust.*

Excoriates: the verb comes from one of Chick Mallison's reveries about Southerners, of which Brooks quotes several in arguing that Gavin Stevens should not be considered Faulkner's spokesman. Stevens' attitude toward the South is relatively tolerant; but what a re-reading of these passages makes plainer than ever is that Faulkner's deepest feelings are expressed by Chick. Does Chick hate Southerners? He burns with a "fierce desire that they should be perfect because they were his and he was theirs," and exhibits a "furious almost instinctive leap and spring to defend them from anyone anywhere so that he might excoriate them himself without mercy"—passions that he shares with Quentin. *Intruder in the Dust* does not end unhappily; what calls for excoriation is only an unrealized intention. In *Absalom, Absalom!*, however, Henry Sutpen carries a like intention into effect, and thereby destroys himself. Its last sentence represents Quentin's "furious almost instinctive leap and spring" of defense.

For Quentin, like Chick, is "theirs," and they are his. So was it also with Faulkner. Other interpreters of his work have inclined to abstract his excoriation of the South from the intricate web of emotions to which it belonged; and it is the abiding virtue of Brooks's study of Yoknapatawpha that it makes the positive values of Faulkner's community palpable to the reader, so that he may understand the rich ambiguity of Faulkner's feelings. Although one may doubt that Faulkner conceived of that community as always a dependable regulator of its members' actions, as Brooks sometimes implies, it is indisputably right to say, as he does in closing, that "Even lack of purpose and value take on special meaning when brought into Faulkner's world, for its very disorders are eloquent of the possibilities of order. . . . Faulkner's work speaks ultimately of the possibilities and capacities of the human spirit for finding and embodying meaning."

William Bedford Clark (review date 1982)

SOURCE: "Cleanth Brooks: Mr. Eliot's Christian Critic," in *Southern Review,* 1982, pp. 73-83.

[*In the following review, Clark examines several books and essays by Brooks, illustrating Brooks's belief that religion and art are complementary in man's search for truth and meaning.*]

An especially persuasive reading of the concluding lines of Pope's *The Dunciad* stresses the apocalyptic nature of the poet's gloomy account of the collapse of the Republic of Letters, and, by extension, of the imminent extinction of enlightened civilization itself:

> *Religion* blushing veils her sacred fires,
> And unawares *Morality* expires.
> Nor public *Flame,* nor *private,* dares to shine;
> Nor *human* Spark is left, nor Glimpse *divine,*
> Lo! thy dread Empire, CHAOS! is restored;
> Light dies before thy uncreating word:
> Thy hand, great Anarch! lets the curtain fall;
> And universal Darkness buries All.

Such a reading no doubt derives much of its force from the modern reader's awareness of the accelerated fragmentation of Western tradition in our own century, and, accordingly, I should like to suggest that there is something of the same sense of apocalyptic gloom and urgency in T.S. Eliot's essay "Religion and Literature." Writing nearly two hundred years after the publication of Pope's dismal prophecy of the demise of genuine humanism, Eliot likewise surveyed the literary scene of his time from an embattled and pessimistic perspective. Indeed, there is, beneath the authoritative urbanity characteristic of Eliot's mature prose style, an undercurrent of defensiveness about "Religion and Literature" that sets it apart from most of his earlier excursions into prose, and this fact suggests that it is, on one level at least, an intensely personal document in the guise of a public call for action.

Eliot is aware of the affective power of literature and of the fact that, though literature like any art is in one sense autotelic, it is impossible to insulate the literary experience from the moral dimension of man's being. Literature affects the whole man; what we read (or, more properly, how we assimilate what we read) manifests itself for better or worse in what we think and do. There is no "harmless" book, Eliot rather waggishly maintains, unless it be totally unreadable. Indeed, the more powerful writer has an almost demonic capacity to possess the weaker, less critical, consciousness of an inexperienced reader, a fact that poses an especially troublesome threat at a time when there is no solid moral center from which literature originates. As Eliot sees it, the state of contemporary literature is a kind of Babel of voices, a world in which each writer presents his private vision. Since few of these figures are blessed with truly Blakean powers, the result is literary confusion in a moral vacuum. The principal villain in this chaotic drama is "Secularism," with its insistence upon the cult of progress and democratic individualism, an unrealizable dream given the sad fact of man's imperfectibility. As a result, Eliot is deeply distrustful of the social consequences of much twentieth-century literature. He admits that certain "individual modern writers of eminence can be improving," but he nevertheless asserts that "contemporary literature as a whole tends to be degrading." Even the "better writers" can have a "pernicious" effect upon a reader who is ill-equipped to understand them in the proper light. Eliot confesses that his own work, improperly assimilated, might have such a negative influence.

Given this state of affairs, the role of the critic becomes crucial. In earlier essays like "Hamlet," Eliot had argued that the literary critic's "first business" was "to study a work of art." And in "The Perfect Critic" he had criticized the tendency of Coleridge to leave off literary criticism in favor of "a metaphysical hare-and-hounds." But in "Religion and Literature," Eliot insists that the critic's role is fraught with significant social responsibility. This seeming discrepancy in his portrayal of the ideal man of letters may well be essentially a matter of emphasis, yet it serves to underscore the extent to which the author moved from aesthetics to broader cultural concerns by the 1930's. The younger Eliot's search for unity, order, and tradition in art carried with it an awareness of the desirability of a similar wholeness in the social realm, a wholeness he saw as woefully absent in the modern world. However, things are not entirely hopeless. The critic, especially if he can ground himself in the firm stance of an integrated world-view like that offered by Christian orthodoxy, can learn to read and evaluate modern literature in a positive way. Eliot sees this as not only desirable, but necessary if traditional values are not to be totally engulfed by the materialism of modernity. Eliot cautions the Christian reader to be forever "conscious of the gulf fixed between ourselves and the greater part of contemporary literature" so that he is prepared to "extract from it what good it has to offer." Though he does not draw the analogy explicitly, Eliot is evoking here a modified version of the ancient patristic practice of reading the pagan authors in the light of Christian revelation—"despoiling the Egyptians." As early as 1930, Eliot had demonstrated such an approach in his discussion of Baudelaire, whose apparently godless world nevertheless held a valuable lesson for the discerning reader: "His [Baudelaire's] business was not to practice Christianity, but—what was much more important for his time—to assert its *necessity*." In short, Baudelaire's *malaise*, his visions of despair and disgust, argued powerfully for a return to healthy orthodoxy.

There are any number of practicing critics today who might aspire, consciously or otherwise, to Eliot's criteria for the Christian critic, but none, I believe, better realizes that role than Cleanth Brooks, who, as an active conservative layman in the Episcopal Church, shares Eliot's traditional theology, as well as many of his basic literary and social assumptions. Brooks too has felt, at times painfully, the cultural crisis confronting the man of letters in the contemporary world, where scientism and utility seem firmly in the saddle. Restating Eliot's denunciation of "Secularism" in more precise terms, Brooks attacks millennialism—the prevailing assumption that man can achieve perfection, realize the City of God as it were, on earth. Brooks's sense of human limitations, his religious awareness that fallen man cannot save himself, leads him to regard the pursuit of material utopias as folly. Yet, Brooks is aware that his position is a minority opinion; the work of the social engineers goes on.

In Brooks's view, among the inevitable by-products of millennial thinking and planning is the disruption of any genuine sense of community based upon the interaction of socially-responsible individuals. The traditional humanistic ideal of the social organism, the *body politic,* is thus replaced by a mechanistic surrogate. In a panel session at a conference on Southern literary study held at the University of North Carolina in 1972, Brooks decried the notion of a perfect society in which men and women would operate with the efficiency of IBM machines. Such a society, were it ever to be fully realized, would, he maintained, spell the "end of literature," for Brooks believes that poetic expression is directly related to a culture's grasp of its own humanity. In **"The Modern Writer and His Community"** (*A Shaping Joy*), Brooks paraphrases Yeats to the effect that the "plight of the poet" is a reliable "measuring stick for the health of the civilization," and for Brooks the state of poetry and the state of language are intimately interdependent. In **"The Uses of Literature"** (also a part of *A Shaping Joy*), he observes that "our generation inherits a language that has lost its hold on concrete reality, that is slack and imprecise, and that reflects a culture that lacks any commonly accepted value-system." A world in which the concreteness of language is eroded constantly by the abstracting tendency of scientism, statistics, and sociology is a world where literature and, presumably, the other arts must lose much of their force. By implication, it is incumbent upon the writer *and* the critic to fight what Brooks elsewhere calls a "rear guard action," not only in order for literature as we know it to survive, but in order to preserve man's sense of himself as man.

This predisposition on Brooks's part to connect the problematic future of society with that of poetry is nothing new, although recent developments in world history have no doubt served to focus his attention increasingly on the social sphere. Yet the misconception that Brooks is a critical "monist" with an ivory-tower obsession with the poem as a cold artifact existing in a kind of inviolable isolation (a misconception derived from a careless reading of his early books) persists even today in some circles. While it is true that Brooks has always insisted that the poem is a thing-in-itself, defying any biographical and historical reductionism, his criticism has never been limited to close analysis alone. Indeed, like Eliot, he often brings a rather sweeping perspective to bear on the interrelationships between art, the artist, and the age. His first book, *Modern Poetry and the Tradition* (1939), with its emphasis on metaphysical poetry and the understanding of modern writing within the context of what preceded it, can be read to advantage as an extended study in cultural history. Even *The Well Wrought Urn* (1947), in which Brooks established himself as the master explicator, is a book that assumes *a priori* that understanding the "poem as poem" is a matter which bears directly on the future of the humanities as a discipline. In an appendix to that book, **"Criticism, History, and Critical Relativism,"** Brooks makes the case for the relevance of his approach to literature unmistakably clear: "The Humanities have suffered under a variety of attacks which stem perhaps from the very nature of our age and of our civilization. But they have not been better defended, it seems to me—at least more effectively defended—because the teachers of the Humanities have tended to comply with the spirit of the age rather than to resist it." Instead of assimilating the methods and assumptions of the social reductionists under the aegis of critical relativism, the literary critic would do well, in Brooks's view, to insist upon the unique contributions to our intellectual and cultural life that he alone can make: "If the Humanities are to endure, they must be themselves—and that means, among other things, frankly accepting the burden of making normative judgements."

In *Literary Criticism: A Short History* (written in collaboration with William K. Wimsatt, Jr.), Brooks provides an extreme instance of how aesthetic questions can be confused with scientific concerns and distorted into something else altogether:

> . . . in the 19th century, the decay of metaphysics and the extraordinary growth of the physical sciences gave a special stress to affective theories of criticism. Gustav Fechner, for example, took the problems of aesthetics into the laboratory . . . The methods of investigation were to be empirical and inductive. There were to be "controlled" experiments to determine what percentage of human beings find the rectangle a more pleasing shape than the square or what percentage prefer rectangles proportioned to the golden section as compared to rectangles of other proportions.

However interesting the results of such tests might be in purely psychological terms, their significance in terms of understanding a given work of art is dubious at best. In stressing that a poem, like any other work of art, be understood on its own terms, Brooks is clearly assuming that literary criticism has a special role to fulfill, a role that cannot be subsumed under the banner of science. This explains his distrust of the more extreme instances of "psychologistic" tendencies in I.A. Richards' criticism, as well as his disapproval of Northrop Frye's efforts to make literary study "for the first time into a true science" so that it can at last take its place "among the other social sciences." Science has its uses, Brooks would admit, but to apply its methods to literature and to accept its insights uncritically is to surrender to the very forces that would render genuine "literature" impossible. Such a course of action represents an abdication of the literary critic's responsibilities as a humanist.

If criticism is not a science (at least not in the modern sense of the word), neither is it the handmaiden of religion. In "Religion and Literature," Eliot stresses the point that writing based upon theological and philosophical premises with which he is in substantial agreement is not, by virtue of that fact alone, literature of the first order. He cites the stories of G.K. Chesterton as an example. While he admits his delight in reading such fiction, Eliot nevertheless is unwilling to make great claims for its ultimate value in artistic terms. Brooks follows Eliot closely in this regard. Both critics are determined to keep the natures and functions of poetry and religion distinct. Thus Brooks, like Eliot, resists the temptation to make a religion of art along the lines envisioned by Matthew Arnold, who felt the need for literature to fill the vacuum created by the supposed death of traditional faith. Religion, like literature, may have a common enemy in the forces of modernism, but they are hardly interchangeable, and for Eliot and Brooks, faith is hardly dead. Yet religion and literature do have an important relationship with one another, which poses two important questions: What is the nature of that relationship? and, What is the proper role of the Christian critic?

Brooks addresses himself to the first of these questions in his own essay entitled **"Religion and Literature"** (*Sewanee Review:* Winter, 1974). While insisting that "it is in everybody's interest to maintain the distinctions between logic and ethics, science and religion, poetry and philosophy," he concedes that literature and religion "do overlap at points and they do have much in common." In earlier times, the roles of artist and priest were often merged in a single "spiritual leader of the people." This is natural enough, in Brooks's view, since both religion and literature are "suffused with terms that appeal to the human heart." Since "the literary artist brings together events and observations and moods into a pattern which has its coherence of attitude," the literary work provides the reader with "a value-structured experience" akin to that which is at the basis of religion. Yet, unlike religion, the coherent attitude provided by a poem, novel, or play need not make any "ultimate claim on our belief." One can read and respond to Herbert's poem "Love," Brooks suggests, without being "compelled to believe in Herbert's God of love." Like Eliot, Brooks knows that literature inevitably reflects the values and beliefs, however implicit, of the author. Yet, once again in full accord with Eliot, Brooks would not make the reader's adherence to the author's values and beliefs a basis for experiencing or evaluating the work itself.

Religion, by its own nature, does however make a very definite claim on our belief. In Brooks's words, "It demands a commitment" on the part of the believer. It requires "something more than a temporary suspension of disbelief." And herein lies the essential difference between the religious and the literary modes of human experience. Brooks thus implies that religion provides the reader with an absolute world-vision that has the power to inform his life, to enable him to translate attitude into action, whereas the literary experience does not necessarily require more than a momentary surrender of the reader's philosophical biases. While maintaining the separateness of religion and poetry, Brooks nevertheless insists upon a vital relationship between the two. Far from possessing the potential to replace religion, poetry, in fact, "needs religion" for "the relationship between religion and poetry is a polar relationship in something of the same sense in which we speak of the poles of an electric battery, one positive and the other negative, poles that mutually attract each other and thus generate a current of energy."

In keeping with his characteristic practice of reinforcing such a generalization with an appeal to concrete specifics, Brooks takes a close look at three poems by Yeats that illustrate to varying degrees the symbiotic interrelationship between religion and poetry, and he concludes that poetry needs religion in much the same way that it needs other concrete modes of human experience, "for poetry is a dramatization of, and thus an indirect commentary upon, characteristic human action." Furthermore, religion can free the poet from the burden of "justifying a particular course of action" rather than exploring, through his imagination, a broader range of alternatives. Throughout his essay, Brooks implicitly assumes that, based upon a hierarchical ranking, religion, with its demand for total commitment, must necessarily supersede poetry, yet he argues that "We need both of them." And this need is not merely personal, it also has important social and cultural dimensions. Literature takes on a special role in reflecting the society out of which it grows, for it reveals that society's relative state of health. It is "diagnostic," not "prescriptive." Religion, however, complements the work of the imaginative writer, for it provides us with "final commitments" and enjoins us to "specific actions."

Although Brooks does not specifically describe the role of the ideal Christian critic in "Religion and Literature," he has consistently assumed that role throughout his career, and a look at his methods reveals the extent to which he, like Eliot, can read literature from a Christian perspective without losing his objectivity or distorting an author's vision into something else in the name of orthodoxy. Indeed, Brooks has been a perennial enemy of propaganda art, whatever its ideological basis, preferring literature that embodies an "earned vision" like that extolled by his friend, colleague, and collaborator Robert Penn Warren—a literature that is metaphysical in the sense of utilizing tensions and ironies rather than excluding them. Thus, Brooks has less interest in a poet like Emerson who, in his view, has little awareness of the dialectical complexities that make great poetry than in a poet like Yeats, whose "saving physicality" acts as a check upon his tendency toward visionary abstraction. As a practicing Christian, Brooks naturally rejects both the romantic neo-Platonism of Emerson and the eccentric theosophy of Yeats. But as a critic, Brooks takes the work of literature on its own terms, evaluating its success or shortcomings on aesthetic, not moral or theological, grounds. This enables him to discuss Christian elements in Faulkner, for example, without making undue claims for the author's orthodoxy. He can resist the temptation many critics have felt to turn Joe Christmas into a full-blown Christ figure and point out the weaknesses of *A Fable* in spite of its explicit reliance upon the Christian *mythos*. He can say of the Catholic novelist Walker Percy, ". . . he takes seriously the metaphysical underpinnings of a society. He thinks dogma is important—and so do I." Yet, he refrains from tying his appreciation of Percy's fiction to their *shared vision.*

Nevertheless, like the critic Eliot calls for in "Religion and Literature," Brooks is especially skillful when it comes to determining the religious significance at the heart of avowedly secular, even consciously "anti-religious," fiction and poetry. Nowhere is this skill more in evidence than in *The Hidden God* (1963), a collection of lecture-essays on Hemingway, Faulkner, Yeats, Eliot, and Warren which bears the telling dedication "*In memoriam patris qui cum libros me docuit amare tum librum librorum.*" Acknowledging once more the shortcomings of modern secular society, Brooks, nevertheless, asserts that "a Christian looking at modern literature ought to find a great deal that is heartening and hopeful," and he proceeds to illustrate what he means by bringing a Christian consciousness to bear on writers who, with the notable exception of Eliot, are hardly Christian in a conventional sense. As we have seen, Eliot read Baudelaire's verse as a desperate dramatization of the need for religious values in a godless modern world. Similarly, Brooks, drawing upon the writings of Paul Tillich, sees Hemingway as reacting violently to the dehumanizing forces underlying our present technological society, and he further suggests that Hemingway demonstrates an essentially Augustinian awareness "that duration of time does not make a satisfactory life but that a satisfactory life is made rather by a complete satisfaction of spirit." In examining Faulkner's peculiar reliance upon certain tenets of Calvinism, especially the notion of Original Sin, Brooks quite significantly evokes the name of T. E. Hulme, whose defense of classicism over romanticism and faith over secularism had such a profound effect on the young T. S. Eliot. Similarly, Brooks places Yeats against the backdrop of intellectual history and views him as a man "robbed" of religious faith by Victorian skepticism. In Brooks's mind, the poet's subsequent interest in mysticism and private revelation represents a compensatory searching after God, a searching that results in an art that "asserts the dignity and power of the human spirit against the spiritual and intellectual corruption of our time." Warren, too, is portrayed as a searcher after the ultimate meanings at the core of human experience. Brooks sees a close analogy between the search for self-knowledge that is Warren's great theme and the Christian quest for redemption. Both represent an attempt to find a way out of the dilemmas confronting modern man.

One overriding aspect of Brooks's critical strategy that makes it peculiarly Christian stems from his temperamental distrust of abstractions, whether they be literary or ideological. In a special sense, the old Imagistic dictum "Go in fear of abstractions" and its poetic corollary "The natural object is always the *adequate* symbol" might well serve as epigraphs to a compendium of Brooks's thought.
—*William Bedford Clark*

Brooks's discussion of Eliot is, as might well be expected, especially insightful. Eliot, as a prime example of the Christian artist at work in an intellectually hostile environment, is praised for his "method of indirection." Since he cannot depend upon a receptive audience for his message in its most explicit terms, he is faced with the problem of how "revealed truth" is best "mediated to the gentiles." At a time when the traditional symbols of faith have lost much of their force and effectiveness, Eliot succeeds in evolving new symbols to embody ageless truths. Throughout his discussions of these writers, Brooks exemplifies the role of the Christian critic as Eliot conceived of it. He never seeks to impose an arbitrary set of theological assumptions upon the works in question; rather, he shows how they inevitably generate their own theological dimensions. Yet, free as they are from a restrictive sectarian bias, Brooks's observations are, nevertheless, the clear outgrowths and expressions of an unmistakably Christian sensibility. His criticism is informed by the kind of "final" commitments he describes in "Religion and Literature" and elsewhere.

One overriding aspect of Brooks's critical strategy that makes it peculiarly Christian stems from his temperamental distrust of abstractions, whether they be literary or ideological. In a special sense, the old Imagistic dictum "Go in fear of abstractions" and its poetic corollary "The natural object is always the *adequate* symbol" might well serve as epigraphs to a compendium of Brooks's thought. As early as *Modern Poetry and the Tradition,* Brooks had adopted John Crowe Ransom's distinction between the abstracting functions of science and speculative philosophy and the concreteness of religious and poetic modes of knowledge, and he has consistently maintained in his later writings that "poetry—whatever else it is—is incorrigibly concrete." To illustrate the extent to which this emphasis upon the concrete, an emphasis Brooks shares with Eliot and Allen Tate as well as with Ransom, is a manifestation of an essentially religious consciousness, I should like to appeal to the work of the distinguished Jesuit critic William F. Lynch. In *Christ and Apollo: The Dimensions of the Literary Imagination,* Father Lynch shows how many of the greatest writers, instinctively turning away from fantasy and vague symbolism, ground their visions in what he calls the "generative finite." His notion of the "literary process" as a "highly cognitive passage through the finite and definite realities of man and the world" is remarkably akin to Brooks's own. Father Lynch goes on to say that the concrete images born of human limitations "are in themselves the path to whatever the self is seeking," whether it be "insight," "beauty," or, ultimately, God. For Father Lynch, as for Brooks,

> This path is both narrow and direct; it leads . . . straight through our human realities, through our labor, our disappointments, our friends, our game legs, our harvests, our subjection to time. There are no shortcuts to beauty or insight. We must go *through* the finite, the limited, the definite, omitting none of it lest we omit some of the potencies of being-in-the-flesh. This does not mean that we should go through it violently, looking for a means to a breakthrough . . . The finite is not itself a generality to be encompassed in one fell swoop. Rather, it contains many shapes and byways and cleverness and powers and diversities and persons, and we must not go too fast from the many to the one.

This statement of the proper Christian approach to the world and (to use Ransom's phrase) to the "world's body" has its parallels throughout Brooks's writing, and it sheds light on the remarkable consistencies between Brooks's literary criticism and his social and religious pronouncements. Thus Brooks's disparagement of propaganda art and "pure" poetry is of a piece with his warnings against the abstracting trends at work in the modern world. Thus Brooks's early insistence that the careful study of a poem as "poem" bears upon the very future of humanism seems perfectly logical.

Near the end of *The Hidden God,* Brooks says that the role of the writer is "to give us an awareness of our world, not as an object viewed in clinical detachment, not as a mere mechanism, but of our world as it involves ourselves—in part a projection of ourselves, in part an impingement upon ourselves. In making us see our world for what it is, the artist also makes us see ourselves for what we are." In this same regard, it should be remembered that Eliot, in "Religion and Literature," suggests that the strength of the Christian critic is dependent upon his capacity to know not only what he is but what he should be. Cleanth Brooks is such a critic. Like Eliot, he is no apostle of "progress" and its attendant millennialism, but rather an orthodox believer who recognizes the necessity of maintaining a traditional set of values in the face of an increasingly relativistic secularism. Yet Brooks's attitude toward modern literature is more sanguine in the final analysis than is Eliot's. The Christian's position in the contemporary scene is an embattled one to be sure, but he can find powerful allies in a group of major writers who, while they may not always share his faith, share his awareness of man's absolute need for spiritual meanings beyond the constrictive limits of contemporary ideology. For Brooks, the best of modern writing is, or at least can be, an invaluable "religious" resource.

Richard S. Calhoun (essay date 1992)

SOURCE: "Formalistic Criticism," in *Critical Survey of Poetry,* edited by Frank N. Magill, Salem Press, 1992, pp. 3973-80.

[*In the following essay, Calhoun gives a concise history of the development of Formalistic Criticism, especially the New Criticism of Brooks and others.*]

The formalist approach to poetry was the one most influential in American criticism during the 1940's, 1950's, and 1960's, and it is still the one most often practiced in literature courses in American colleges and universities. Its popularity was not limited to American literary criticism. In France, formalism has long been employed as a pedagogical exercise in reading literature in the universities and in the lycées. In England in the 1940's and in the 1950's, formalism was associated with an influential group of critics writing for a significant critical periodical, *Scrutiny,* the most prominent of whom was F.R. Leavis. There was also a notable formalist movement in the Soviet Union in the 1920's, and, although championed by René Wellek in the United States, its influence at that time was primarily limited to Slavic countries.

The formalist approach in America was popularized by John Crowe Ransom, Allen Tate, Robert Penn Warren, and Cleanth Brooks, all four Southerners, all graduates of Vanderbilt University, and all, in varying degrees, receptive to the indirections and complexities of the modernism of T. S. Eliot, James Joyce, and William Butler Yeats, which their critical method—known as the "New Criticism"—was, in part, developed to explicate. A fifth critic, not directly associated with the Vanderbilt group, R. P. Blackmur, made important contributions to the formalist reading of poetry in *The Double Agent* (1935) and in essays in other books. He did not, however, develop a distinctive formalist method.

Formalism in the History of Literary Criticism

Formalism is clearly a twentieth century critical phenomenon in its emphasis on close reading of the literary text, dissociated from extrinsic references to the author or to his or her society. There had been formalist tendencies before in the history of literary criticism, but it did not, as in twentieth century formalism, approach exclusivity in its emphasis on the structure of the work itself. Aristotle's analysis in the *Poetics* (written sometime between 370 and 322 B.C.) of the complex tragic plot as having a tripartite division of reversal, recognition, and catastrophe is one of the most valuable formalist analyses of the structure of tragedy ever made. That Aristotle's approach to poetics was not intrinsic but extrinsic, however, has been made clear by his twentieth century followers, the Chicago Neo-Aristotelians, Ronald S. Crane and Elder Olson. They have been the harshest critics of what they regard as the limited critical perspective of modern formalists, pointing out that an Aristotelian analysis was characteristically in terms of four causes. These were the formal cause (the form that the work imitates), the material cause (the materials out of which the work is made), the efficient cause (the maker), and the final cause (the effect on the reader or audience). Crane charged in *Critics and Criticism: Ancient and Modern* (1952) that the New Criticism is concerned with only one of these causes, language, in order to distinguish poetic from scientific and everyday uses of language without being able to distinguish among the various kinds of poetry. It is true that formalism is largely concerned with literature as a verbal art. This single-mindedness has been its strength in explication as well as its weakness as a critical theory.

Two key concepts in the literary theory of the English Romantic period may have been influential on twentieth century formalism. Although the New Critics were professedly anti-Romantic following T. S. Eliot's call for impersonality in modern poetry, their stress on the meaning of the total poem rather than finding the meaning centered in a specific part probably owes something to the concept of organic form, assumed by most Romantics and stated explicitly by Samuel Taylor Coleridge in his defense of William Shakespeare. This is the concept that a poem grows like a living organism, its parts interrelated, its form and content inseparable; the total work is thus greater than the sum of its parts. This concept was assumed by all the New Critics except Ransom, who viewed "texture" as separate from structure.

The formalist view of creativity is of a "rage" brought to "order" through submission to the discipline of form. A good poem is characterized by tensions that are usually reconciled. The most detailed statement of this view by a New Critic is in Robert Penn Warren's essay "Pure and Impure Poetry," in which Warren gives a long list of resistances or "tensions" in a good poem. The origin of this idea lies in Romantic critical theory. Warren's statements, as well as Allen Tate's discussion of tension in his essay "Tension in Poetry," undoubtedly owe much to Chapter 14 of Coleridge's *Biographia Literaria* (1817), in which he describes the distinctive quality of the creative imagination of the poet as revealing itself "in the balance or reconciliation of opposite or discordant qualities."

The strongest twentieth century influences on formalism in America and in England were the early essays of T. S. Eliot, especially those in *The Sacred Wood* (1920), and two books by I.A. Richards, *Principles of Literary Criticism* (1924) and *Practical Criticism* (1929). Eliot, influenced by the anti-Romanticism of T. E. Hulme in *Speculations* (1924), called for a theory of the impersonal in the modernist view of poetry to rectify the personality cults of Romantic and Victorian poetry, and he even detailed how to impersonalize personal emotions through the use of "objective correlatives." Eliot's intention was to redirect critical attention from the poet to the work of art, which he declared to be "autotelic," self-contained, a fictive world in itself. It was this pronouncement of Eliot's, more than any statement in his essays in the 1920's, which had the strongest influence on the development of formalist criticism.

Eliot also devised his own version of a Cartesian "split" between logic and untrustworthy feelings, his theory that a dissociation of sensibility took place in English poetry in the late seventeenth century. John Donne had a unified sensibility capable of devouring any kind of experience. In the Metaphysical poets "there is a direct sensuous apprehension of thought": they could think feelings and feel thoughts. The New Critics were to develop a formalist approach to poetry that could show this kind of sensibility at work. To a formalist such as Cleanth Brooks in *Modern Poetry and the Tradition* (1939), Metaphysical poetry was the proper tradition in which to fit modern poetry, and critical techniques were needed in order to explicate the complexities of poetry in the tradition. He provided a model for formalist explication in a brilliant analysis of parallelisms and ironic contrasts utilized functionally by Eliot in *The Waste Land* (1922).

The Formalist Defense of Poetry

Formalism in America and England may have evolved in reaction to nineteenth century literary thought and practice as a method of understanding a modernist literature that was indirect, impersonal, complex, and "autotelic." As far as the New Critics were concerned, their formalism was a defense of poetry in an age of science. Their criticism can quite properly be regarded as an "apology" for poetry in the tradition of Sir Philip Sidney and Percy Bysshe Shelley. An "apology" is a formal defense of poetry in an age thought to be hostile to the poetry of its own time. Sidney "apologized" for poetry at a time when Puritans were attacking drama and voicing suspicions as to whether poetry could and did advance morality. Shelley defended the value of poetry in an age that was beginning to turn to prose, assuming that the golden age of poetry was over. In this tradition the New Critics "apologized" for poetry in an age of logical positivism, when scientific method was regarded as the sole means to truth and poetry was being limited to mere emotive effects.

In his *Principles of Literary Criticism,* I. A. Richards sought to find a place for poetry in an age of science by emphasizing the psychological effects of poetry on the personality of the reader. In *Practical Criticism* he documented the helplessness of his graduate students when confronted with an unidentified poem to explicate, and made a case for a literary criticism that specialized in explicating the text. Richards seemed, however, at least in the earlier book, to be in agreement with the positivistic view that poetry was a purely emotive use of language in contrast to science, which was the language of factual assertion. Although influenced by Richards, the New Critics attempted to counter his apparent denial of a cognitive dimension of poetry. They did this through their formalism, staying inside the poem in their explications and declaring it characteristic of the poet's use of language to direct the reader to meanings back inside the poem rather than to referents outside the poem.

Cleanth Brooks contended that poets actually block too direct a pinpointing to everyday referents outside the poem and that the meanings of a poem cannot be wrenched outside the context of the poem without serious distortions. He was making a case for meaning in the poem and at the same time was keeping poetry out of direct competition with science. In a poem, he asserted, apparently referential statements are qualified by ambiguities, paradoxes, and ironies so that the knowledge offered cannot stand as a direct proposition apart from the poem itself. This is why it does not matter that John Keats in a famous sonnet credits Hernando Cortes, not Vasco de Balboa, with the first sighting by a European of the Pacific Ocean. What Keats writes is true to the poem, not to historical fact, and he does not intend a truth claim to be taken outside the poem and examined for factual accuracy. Murray Krieger has argued quite plausibly in the *New Apolo-*

gists for Poetry (1956) that the New Critics might be called "contextualists" because of their insistence on getting meaning from and in the context.

Each major New Critic was in his own way trying to establish that poetry offers a special kind of knowledge and does not compete with the more referential knowledge that Richards found characteristic of scientific assertions. Their "apology" for poetry committed them to formalism, to directing critical attention intrinsically to the structure of the poem rather than extrinsically to referents outside. Ransom, *The World's Body* (1938) and *The New Criticism* (1941), even departed from the concept of organic form to argue that the main difference between scientific and poetic language was that while both had "structure," only the latter had "texture," details that are interesting in themselves. Through his "texture" the poet expresses his revulsion against the inclination of science to abstract and to categorize by giving his reader the particulars of the world, the "sensuous apprehension of thought" that Eliot had admired in the Metaphysical poets. To Ransom, this was knowledge of "the world's body." Ransom's single most important contribution to formalism was his often anthologized essay, "Poetry—A Note on Ontology."

The most philosophically inclined of the New Critics, Allen Tate, also made a specific claim that literature offers a special kind of knowledge, more complete than the knowledge of science; it is experiential knowledge rather than the abstracted, shorthand version of experience given by science. Tate argued that a special characteristic of poetic language is the creation of "tension," a kind of balance between the extremes of too much denotation and literalness and too much connotation and suggestiveness. A good poem possesses both a wealth of suggestiveness and a firm denotative base. In his essay "Tension in Poetry," he provided examples of tension as a kind of touchstone for critical judgments.

In "Pure and Impure Poetry," Robert Penn Warren presented his own version of the concept of "tension," one closer to Coleridge's than Tate's was. He was also influenced by Richards' concept of a "poetry of inclusion" (in turn derived from Coleridge), a poetry that contains its own oppositions. Warren believed that such an "impure" poet writing today must "come to terms with Mercutio," that is, use irony to qualify direct propositions, much as William Shakespeare used the realistic, bawdy jests of Mercutio to counter the sentimental love poetry in *Romeo and Juliet* (1954-1596). Such irony is accessible only through formalist analysis of the poem itself, a close reading of the text. As a formalist, Warren believed, as the other New Critics did, in a less assessable meaning beyond the usual public meaning.

The Practice of Formalism

Cleanth Brooks was the most consistent practicing formalist and the most influential as well, whether in collaboration with Robert Penn Warren, in their popular textbooks, *Understanding Poetry* (1946) and *Understanding Fiction* (1943) or in his own studies in formalism, *Modern Poetry and the Tradition* and *The Well Wrought Urn* (1947). In *Modern Poetry and the Tradition*, Brooks extended Eliot's concept of tradition to a selective history of poetry from seventeenth century Metaphysical poetry to twentieth century modernism. The proper tradition for the modern poet was the Metaphysical tradition because "hard" Metaphysical conceits conveyed both thought and feeling and maintained a proper balance, in contrast to the excessive emotion in much Romantic poetry and the excessive rationalism in much neoclassical poetry. Brooks wrote the book to show the relationship between Metaphysical and modern poetry and to explain modern poetry to readers whose understanding of poetry was primarily based on Romantic poetry.

> **Cleanth Brooks was the most consistent practicing formalist and the most influential as well, whether in collaboration with Robert Penn Warren, in their popular textbooks, *Understanding Poetry* (1946) and *Understanding Fiction* (1943) or in his own studies in formalism, *Modern Poetry and the Tradition* and *The Well Wrought Urn* (1947).**
> **—*Richard S. Calhoun***

His next book, *The Well Wrought Urn*, was slightly revisionist, expanding the tradition to include some of the best works of Romantic and Victorian poetry, and even a major poem of the neoclassical period, Alexander Pope's *The Rape of the Lock* (1712). The test for admission to the tradition is again a careful formalist analysis, revealing, in unexpected places, tensions and paradoxes—although the formalist technique has been refined and even expanded. Brooks contended that poetry is "the language of paradox," evident even in a poem such as William Wordworth's "Composed upon Westminster Bridge." The paradox central to the structure of the poem is that a city, London, is enabled to "wear the beauty of the morning," a privilege that Wordsworth usually reserves for nature. The city is also paradoxically most alive with this surprising beauty when it is asleep, as it is on this occasion. Brooks conceded that Wordsworth's employment of paradox might have been unconscious, something he was driven to by "the nature of his instrument," but paradox can also be conscious technique, as it was in John Donne's "The Canonization."

Brooks's analysis of "The Canonization" is a model of formalist method, as his analysis of Eliot's *The Waste Land* had been in his previous volume. The poem is complex but unified, an argument dramatically presented but a treatise on the important subject of divine and profane love as well. The tone, an important element of meaning, is complex, scornful, ironic, and yet quite serious. Also central in the poem is the "love metaphor," and basic to its development is the paradox of treating profane love as if it were divine love. Such a treatment permits the culminating paradox in the speaker's argument for his love: "The lovers in rejecting life actually win to the most intense life." In this poem, technique has shaped content: the only way in which the poet could say what the poem says is by means of paradox.

Brooks made another major contribution to formalist practice in *The Well Wrought Urn.* He demonstrated the importance of the dramatic context as the intrinsic referent for meaning in a poem. Even the simplest lyric has some of the drama of a play. There are within a poem a speaker, an occasion, sometimes an audience, and a conflict—in a lyric usually a conflict of attitudes. Brooks declared in **"The Problem of Belief and the Problem of Cognition"** that a poem should not be judged by the truth or falsity "of the idea which it incorporates, but rather by its character as drama. . . ." The formalist as New Critic, most fully represented by an explication according to Brooks's formula, is concerned with this drama in the poem, with how the conflict of attitudes is resolved, with paradox and how it is central to argument in poetry, with metaphor and how it may be the only permissible way of developing the thought of the poem. He is concerned with technique in a verbal art, and these techniques make possible the poetic communication of what becomes the content.

Ranking with *The Well Wrought Urn* as a major formalist document is René Wellek and Austin Warren's *Theory of Literature* (1949). When it was published, the intention of the book was to argue for the use of intrinsic approaches to literature, drawing on the New Criticism, Russian Formalism, and even phenomenology, in conjunction with literary history and the history of ideas, then the dominant approaches. Its value today is as a source book of formalist theory, just as Brooks's *The Well Wrought Urn* is a source book of formalist practice. Wellek and Warren make the distinction between the scientific use of language, ideally purely denotative, and the literary use of language, not merely referential but expressive and highly connotative, conveying the tone and attitude of speaker and writer. Form and content are regarded as inseparable: technique determines content. Reference to the Russian Formalists reinforces the New Critics on this point. Meter, alliteration, sounds, imagery, and metaphor are all functional in a poem. Poetry is referential but the references are intrinsic, directed back inside the fictive world that is being created.

The Decline of Formalism

The influence of formalism reached its peak in the 1950's and began to decline in the 1960's. In England, *Scrutiny* suspended publication; although F. R. Leavis continued to publish, his criticism became less formalistic and more Arnoldian. In America, the New Critics also became less formalistic, and their formalism was taken over by followers who lacked the explicative genius of Ransom, Tate, Brooks, and Warren.

Warren had always published less formal criticism than his colleagues, and in the 1960's he turned his attention even more to fiction and, especially, to writing poetry. Allen Tate, never as fond as the others of critical explications, continued to write essays of social and moral significance, moving in and out of Catholicism and the influence of Jacques Maritain. His best critical explication remained that of his own poem, "Ode to the Confederate Dead," an exploration of the creative process as well as a formalistic analysis. He died in 1979. Ransom continued to edit the most important new critical journal, *The Kenyon Review,* until his retirement from Kenyon College; then he returned to something he had put aside for many years—his poetry. In the few essays that he wrote in the years just before his death in 1974, his Kantian interests preoccupied him more and more. Cleanth Brooks wrote one more book that might be called formalistic, *A Shaping Joy* (1971), but he turned most of his attention to his two major books on William Faulkner, *William Faulkner: The Yoknapatawpha Country* (1963) and *Toward Yoknapatawpha and Beyond* (1978). In these works, Brooks brilliantly discusses Faulkner's novels, but it is clear that his interest is more in the relationship of Faulkner's fiction to his Southern society than in formalist analysis.

Newer critical approaches appeared, none of which was content to remain within the structure of the poem itself—the archetypal criticism of Northrop Frye, the phenomenological criticism of Georges Poulet and Hillis Miller, the structuralism of Roland Barthes, and the deconstruction of Jacques Derrida. The latter are influential, but more concerned with the modes of literary discourse than with the explication of texts, and better with fiction than with poetry. During the protest movement of the later 1960's, formalism fell into disrepute because of its lack of concern for the social and political backgrounds of literary works. Ironically, the New Critics were accused of empiricism and scientism in the analysis of literature.

Nevertheless, twentieth century formalism has had a seemingly permanent influence on the teaching of literature in the United States, just as it has in France. *Understanding Poetry* has stayed in print, and the only widely used introductions to literature are mostly formalistic in their approaches.

The New Critics taught a generation of students the art of close reading of the text. They warned readers against fallacies and heresies in reading and teaching poetry, and the lessons seem to have been widely learned. Although they used paraphrase masterfully themselves, they warned against "the heresy of paraphrase." The prose statement should not be regarded as the equivalent of the meaning of the poem. They attacked and seemingly permanently damaged the positivistic view that would limit poetry to the emotions only— what they called "The affective fallacy." As Brooks declared in *The Well Wrought Urn:* "Poetry is not merely emotive . . . but cognitive. It gives us truth . . ." Formalism did not prevent, but did restrict, practice of the biographical fallacy, studying the man instead of his works.

The most controversial fallacy exposed by the New Critics was the intentional fallacy, against which all the formalists warned. Monroe C. Beardsley and William K. Wimsatt, who stated (in *The Verbal Icon,* 1954) what was implicit in formalism all along, may have gone too far in seeming to exclude the poet from throwing any light at all on the meaning of his poem; they did, however, warn against finding the meaning of a work in some prose statement by the author before or after he wrote it. Formalism has made the point that the actual intention of a poem can be determined only from an explication of the poem itself. Few literary critics today would regard the poem as a fictive world that is sufficient unto itself. Poems have thematic and psychological contexts as well as verbal and dramatic contexts. Formalist analyses were too innocent of the linguistic structures of the language that poetry used. Nevertheless, no modern critical approach has revealed more of the richness of meaning potentially available within a poem.

Michael L. Hall (review date Spring 1992)

SOURCE: "Well Wrought Facts," in *Sewanee Review,* Vol. 100, No. 2, Spring, 1992, pp. xxxviii-xli.

[*In the following review, Hall favorably reviews the content and structure of* Historical Evidence and the Reading of Seventeenth-Century Poetry.]

Historical Evidence and the Reading of Seventeenth-Century Poetry will be especially rewarding, as the title suggests, for readers interested in the good minor poetry of the seventeenth century. Some familiarity with the poets collected by H. J. C. Grierson and Geoffrey Bullough in their once standard *Oxford Book of Seventeenth-Century Verse* (1934), a book earlier generations of English doctoral students studied in preparation for oral qualifying examinations, would be helpful, but is not essential. The more general sort of educated readers will be happy to learn, however, that with *Historical Evidence* Cleanth Brooks also continues his lifelong

project of teaching us how to read, understand, and appreciate literature.

Most obviously *Historical Evidence* may be approached as the demonstration Brooks claims it is of a method of reading old poems. In his introduction he remarks that his choice of seventeenth-century poetry was somewhat arbitrary, that he might just as well have performed his demonstrations with poems of a different period. He says he was "seriously tempted to choose poems printed between 1840 and 1890." He intends primarily to demonstrate that history is a valuable component of literary criticism: "Sometimes the biographer, the literary historian, and the lexicographer hold the keys necessary for unlocking a poem's full meaning, especially if the poem dates from an earlier time." Those startled to discover that Brooks still believes poems have meaning, full or otherwise, should be forewarned that he also speaks throughout this book of "literary value."

Brooks makes no effort, though, to join in recent critical debates. Nor is *Historical Evidence* a belated attempt, after more than forty years, to provide a corrective for the New Critical practices of *The Well Wrought Urn* (1947). In a brief epilogue Brooks notes connections between the two books and draws some obvious conclusions, but he makes no apologies. There remains, nevertheless, a complicated relationship between *Historical Evidence* and *The Well Wrought Urn* that should not be passed over lightly. Both books are, after all, demonstrations of interpretive practices that are usually applied to short lyric poems. Both begin with basic critical or theoretical assumptions but move quickly to specific examples. Both reprint the texts of the poems and rely heavily on close readings.

In other respects the two books offer contrasting mirror images. *The Well Wrought Urn* performs readings of some of the best-known poets of the canon: Donne, Shakespeare, Milton, Herrick, Pope, Gray, Wordsworth, Keats, Tennyson, and Yeats. In many ways Brooks intended his earlier book to show that New Critical methods would work in all periods and on all poets. With *Historical Evidence* he turns to minor poets of a single period and to poems nearly forgotten by everyone, save an older generation of literary scholars and a few specialists in the seventeenth century—poems by Henry King, Richard Corbett, James Shirley, Aurelian Townshend, Sir Richard Fanshawe, Lord Herbert of Cherbury, Sir Richard Lovelace, and Andrew Marvell. With the exception of Marvell's "To His Coy Mistress," "The Garden," and "Horatian Ode upon Cromwell's Return from Ireland," and perhaps not even excepting the last, these poems and poets will not be well known.

The Well Wrought Urn relies on familiarity and takes history and biography for granted, although not entirely. From time to time Brooks may remind us that "legend" "in

Donne's time meant 'the life of a saint,'" or recall that Herrick was an Anglican parson to complicate the irony of "Corrina's Going A-Maying," or allude to the allegoric figures "which clutter a great abbey church such as that at Bath or at Westminster" to explain references in Gray's "Elegy." But in *Historical Evidence* he expects unfamiliarity and performs virtuoso readings by means of detailed historical and biographical references, as well as frequent recourse to the OED and other sources for contemporary seventeenth-century meanings of a poem's words. His learned and sensible account of Marvell's use of the word *glew* in "To His Coy Mistress" should finally dispatch any lingering notion that the poet thought his young lady was coated in "youthful glue."

Despite these contrasts, however, the two books are finally much more alike than they are different. Both exhibit a range of address now almost absent from literary criticism. Both concentrate attention on literary qualities now more often ignored than illuminated. Both insist on the necessity to let the poem "speak for itself" even after the historical evidence is presented, even against this evidence. After a particularly effective reading of Henry King's "An Exequy To his Matchlesse never to be forgotten Friend," Brooks reminds us that the Anglican Bishop who so lamented the loss of his wife Anne, and who in the final stanzas of his most successful poem looks forward to his reunion with her in death, "I shall at last sitt downe by Thee," not only may have married again but certainly was not reunited with Anne in a common grave, since as bishop of Chichester he was buried in his cathedral. Then Brooks challenges us with a familiar question: "Let us suppose that some scholar should come upon documentary evidence that Bishop King had remarried. Ought we in that case to think less of "The Exequy'?" His answer comes as no surprise to readers of *The Well Wrought Urn.* After demonstrating that we cannot fully understand the meaning of King's "Exequy" without recourse to history and biography, Brooks reminds us that "this magnificent poem stands above and apart from all the vicissitudes of King's personal life" and "now enjoys a life of its own, not to be affected by what subsequently happened to its author or what he caused to happen."

Brooks's impressive range of address in *Historical Evidence* results in part from his allusions, often to poems that appeared in *The Well Wrought Urn,* but also to other poems both of the seventeenth century and afterward. The discussions of Hardy's poetry are a particular bonus, especially the comparison of "The Country Wedding" and John Hall's "On a Gentleman and His Wife," in which Brooks shows us why we may prefer Hardy to Hall, and why this is a poetic judgment on the relative success of the two poems as poems. Similarly his reading of James Shirley's "The glories of our blood and state" compares Shirley's poem to Gray's "Elegy," and then more briefly Gray's to Milton's "Il Penseroso," and

finally concludes with a reading of Hardy's "In Time of 'The Breaking of Nations.'" None of these allusions is incidental. Each helps to demonstrate connections between the specific historical context a poem may have grown out of and its ability to make contact with larger human universals.

Not that Brooks ignores differences. Noting contrasts is an important part of his method of reading, but his point is that the specific historical reading must give into a larger context that includes our knowledge of other periods and other styles of poetry. Brooks intends to demonstrate, finally, that his method of historical reading is not antiquarian but serves a larger purpose, and part of that purpose is to remind us why we would want to read these old poems, or any other works of literature, in the first place: "No one has ever doubted that poems (and novels and plays) are products of the culture out of which they came, and consequently at some level they must reflect that culture. But that fact does not prevent our assessing these literary documents on other levels, including what they can tell us about ourselves and about the universal human condition."

Coburn Freer (review date April-July 1992)

SOURCE: A review of *Historical Evidence and the Reading of Seventeenth-Century Poetry,* in *ANQ,* University of Kentucky Press, April-July, 1992, pp. 143-46.

[*In the following review, Freer contrasts* Historical Evidence and the Reading of Seventeenth-Century Poetry *with earlier writings by Brooks, asserting that "one of the chief subjects of this book is actually the evolution of Brooks's thought."*]

A collection of readings of ten poems by eight seventeenth-century poets, this volume [*Historical Evidence and the Reading of Seventeenth-Century Poetry*] brings together a number of essays that have appeared in various other collections and journals. Essays on King's "The Exequy," Corbett's "The Faeryes Farewell," Shirley's lyric beginning "The glories of our blood and state," Townshend's "To the Countess of Salisbury," Fanshawe's "The Fall," Herbert of Cherbury's "Ode upon a Question Moved," Marvell's "To His Coy Mistress" and "The Garden," Lovelace's "The Grasse-Hopper," and Marvell's "Horatian Ode" make up the body of the book; a brief Introduction and Epilogue tie these together.

Unfortunately there is no preface or acknowledgement page to indicate where and when the essays first appeared, and this is of more importance than it might seem at first. The book treats some familiar lyric poems that respond particularly well to the kind of close study that Brooks and others made the dominant form of analysis in the 1940s and 1950s, and the many essays that these ten poems inspired might comprise an index of the strengths and limitations of close reading. Further, styles in close reading have changed, for Brooks as for others, and knowing the original publication data, one could make comparisons that might illuminate this phase of modern criticism.

In the book at hand, Brooks has made many subtle but significant revisions in his original essays, responding to criticism (or defending himself more closely), and updating some of the readings. Most of the revisions are stylistic, but many go well beyond merely editorial changes, and the way the larger revisions change the rhetorical form of the essays can tell us almost as much about Brooks's attitude toward historical evidence as the argument he advances in the introductory and closing remarks. In other words, one of the chief subjects of this book is actually the evolution of Brooks's thought.

One illustration. On the Horatian Ode, much of what we have in the present volume is recast from Brooks's seminal English Institute lecture of 1946, published in 1947; that essay prompted a spirited exchange with Douglas Bush in the *Sewanee Review* in 1952 and 1953. The present essay makes a better defense against Bush (while not mentioning him) and deletes most of the paragraphs of throat-clearing that seemed to mark much criticism from that period. But some other more important changes reposition the essay as a study in literary history. The 1946 version of the essay ended with an afterthought: "Since completing this essay, I have come upon a further item which would suggest that the 'Horatian Ode' was circulating among Royalists—not Puritans—in the early 1650's." The evidence then offered (by correspondents to the [*Times Literary Supplement*]) concerns the stanza form adapted from Fanshawe and Tom May's translation of Lucan. Placed at the end of the essay as it is, with no comments following it, these historical notes convey only the sense that there was quite a curious collocation of minds there, a point well worth musing on. In the essay as revised for the present volume, these paragraphs of historical evidence are moved to the front of the essay and presented as necessary matter for reading the poem, even though the main outlines of the essay remain the same and the conclusion is essentially unchanged. Along the way, Brooks inserts references to Christopher Hill, John Wallace, Antonia Fraser, and others to reinforce the essentially unchanged thesis; a postscript returns to Hill, but with the primary purpose of reaffirming Brooks's familiar emphasis on the role of tension in poetry.

By this rearrangement in rhetorical structure and the more up-to-date citations, Brooks seems to concede more to history than he has before, but again his basic conclusions and above all his primary method of supporting his arguments remain unchanged. His chief source of historical evidence is linguistic—etymologies, derivations, and above all shifts in usage: the *OED* [Oxford English Dictionary] receives probably as many citations as all other sources together. But there is nothing wrong with that: Brooks was one of the first to insist on the importance of this kind of lexical play, and many of his revisions in these essays tease out still more latent and apt meanings in familiar words and phrases.

> **The achievement of [*Historical Evidence and the Readig of Seventeenth-Century Poetry*] thus lies first in its often brilliant readings of poems that vary considerably in subject and complexity, and second in its demonstration of a method that remains central to our criticism. It should be instructive for readers who have assumed the primacy of literary theory and have neglected attention to the history of English grammar and the English lexicon: as Brooks shows, only through this attention can we understand the subtleties of a poem's tone.**
>
> **—*Coburn Freer***

As for the other kinds of historical evidence appearing in the collection, most of it has a curious stumbled-over quality that distinguishes Brooks's work from that of the new historicists. In part this is simply a matter of presentation and organization. For example, after he has plugged in the Tom May material in his discussion of Marvell's ode, he signals a big shift we would never expect to see in the modern historicist idiom: "It is now time to turn more directly to the poem itself, and the poetic mode of expressing matters" (p. 137). That sentence does not appear in the first version of the essay, and it shows that Brooks remains unreconstructed in his critical values. Most of the time he will (in so many words) happen upon a curious woodcut, or puzzle over Strafford's burial site, or notice an odd anecdote or fragment. There is a certain accidental or casual quality with which the historical element is introduced into the argument, and this distinguishes the rhetoric of these essays from more recent historicist readings, in which the historical centerpiece—often an incident or artistic representation that is grotesque or outlandish—is presented up front, its significances peeled apart and then applied to the literary work. This is not to say that these critics have not found their evidence the same way Brooks does; they just display it differently. Brooks's diffidence in the way he handles what he calls extrinsic evidence is one element of the voice we hear speaking in these essays, which remains urbane, gracious, and tactful. While he is doubtless aware of new historicist readings of the poems he treats, he does not adopt either their rhetoric or manner of proceeding.

Indeed Brooks's self-conception seems on his mind, and occasionally he alludes to his reputation as a reader interested only in the text, referring to himself as "a literary critic reputed to be careless of, even hostile to, the biographical and historical background of a poem" (p. 122), and asserting "my own regard for the importance of establishing authorship, datings, biographical and historical references, and the specific and sometimes archaic uses of words that make up the poet's text" (p. 157). It is amusing that at a number of points in the book there surfaces that old bugbear of the poet's intention, but as the Epilogue says, "What finally counts are the achieved intentions, not prospective intentions. . . . The shaping impulses are indeed important, but *as manifest in the work*" (p. 158; Brooks's emphasis). Clearly this can apply to a critic as well as a poet.

The achievement of the book thus lies first in its often brilliant readings of poems that vary considerably in subject and complexity, and second in its demonstration of a method that remains central to our criticism. It should be instructive for readers who have assumed the primacy of literary theory and have neglected attention to the history of English grammar and the English lexicon: as Brooks shows, only through this attention can we understand the subtleties of a poem's tone. If he wants now to assert a stronger concern for historical fact than was sometimes imputed to him, that is his prerogative, although anyone familiar with his later work, particularly on Faulkner, would never have thought the matter in question.

Anthony Tassin (essay date Fall 1992)

SOURCE: "Cleanth Brooks and the Endurance of the New Criticism," in *The South Carolina Review,* Vol. 25, No. 1, Fall, 1992, pp. 33-43.

[*In the following essay, Tassin suggests that the New Criticism endures in its own right and as the bedrock upon which other schools of criticism are constructed.*]

The New Deal. The New Frontier. The New Criticism. They are no longer new, but each of these concepts in its day caught the attention of the public under the aegis of newness. In each case it was one man who conferred the name on the concept: Roosevelt, Kennedy, Ransom. And while these men have passed away, each has left his mark. Although a variety of new philosophies of literary criticism have come forward since the mid-century, the New Criticism is alive and well. For all purposes it has become a standard approach to teaching literature and is currently accepted by professors and students alike. When they speak of *criticism,* it is substantially the New Criticism to which they refer.

An inquiry into the literary criticism of every decade of the twentieth century reveals a constant re-examination of theory and methodology, new ways of thinking and talking about literature. In the early decades of our century, from various camps came new outlooks as scholars began seeking a study focused on the art object itself as opposed to the historical and genre approaches then in vogue. Rebels of a sort, the New Critics (broadly understood) rejected a number of criteria formerly espoused by earlier scholars. It was from such turmoil that the New Criticism took its origin. A 1941 book by John Crowe Ransom inadvertently bestowed a name upon the new trend, or at least provided a label whereby certain patterns of thinking might be referred to. As discussion and published essays manifested a certain new—though by no means homogeneous—philosophy, the movement came to be called (after the title of Ransom's book) the New Criticism. Among the pioneers of these new approaches to literature were poets, novelists, journalists, and critics. As time went on, most writers in the early group of Southern New Critics centered their efforts on poetry and fiction rather than criticism; thus, by the late 1940's, one of their number, Cleanth Brooks, came to be regarded as their primary critical spokesman.

The theory and criticism of which we speak has the firm foundation of a history reaching back more than seventy years. Indeed, its roots extend to a yet more distant past, to thinkers such as Coleridge, Hegel, Kant, and Kierkegaard. Therefore, it would seem that the phenomenon we are discussing deserves not only attention but a respect born of a wholesome maturation. Nevertheless, in the 1970's the prominence of the New Criticism waned. How did this come about? Some say the movement had run its course, delivered its message, and needed to retire to the wings. Perhaps a more accurate perception is not so much that the New Criticism had declined but that it had been upstaged by new ideologies, mostly European-born, which caught the fancy of some academic scholars. Upon the scene came structuralism, post-structuralism, deconstruction, semiotics, and reader response—all postmodern developments.

Now we must ask: What indeed is the status of the New Criticism in the decade of the 1990's? Is it altogether a thing of the past or is it alive and well? Anyone aware of the status of literary criticism in the past three decades knows that many scholars share the view cited by Rene Wellek that the New Criticism is "superseded, obsolete and dead" ("Pro and Contra" 87). Already thirty years ago, we were told "on all sides that the New Criticism is dead, that a reaction has set in against it" (Krieger 107). By 1981, the "New Criticism had been dead, . . . for a decade or more" (Higgins and Parker 27). H. M. Richmond, writing in *College English* in 1972, chose to title his essay "The Dead Albatross: 'New Criticism' as a Humanist Fallacy." Obviously, these voices strongly suggest a demise. But there are others who are equally strong in their conviction that the New Criticism lives on.

Critics of more recent decades tend to react with a certain skepticism toward the writing of the New Critics. It is interesting that two reviewers of Cleanth Brooks's *A Shaping Joy* (1971) declared that they experienced a generation gap in reading the essays in that anthology. The reviewer for *Choice* says, "For someone who attended graduate school and studied English after World War II and into the 1950's, this book of twenty-two essays of recent years will give pause, . . . a pang of nostalgia. Meaning, significance, form—what did they all amount to? . . . It all seems so worn out." The author of the *Times Literary Supplement* review of August 20, 1971, argues that "the shift of a decade . . . has left these essays high and dry." If Brooks's book gave the reviewer pause, the reviewer himself gives his readers pause. Granted that each age has a style and an ambience of its own, do we throw away the books of poetry and fiction we read twenty or forty years ago? Do we not name the time-tested works "classics" for the very reason that they have endured?

What indeed is the status of the New Criticism in the decade of the 1990's? Is it altogether a thing of the past or is it alive and well? Anyone aware of the status of literary criticism in the past three decades knows that many scholars share the view cited by Rene Wellek that the New Criticism is "superseded, obsolete and dead". . . . But there are others who are equally strong in their conviction that the New Criticism lives on.

—Anthony Tassin

One of the major strengths of the New Criticism, which has ensured its continuation, is that its prominent exponents taught students the methodology in such well-known textbooks as *An Approach to Literature, Understanding Poetry, Understanding Fiction,* and *Understanding Drama.* It should be noted further "that despite pleas from the social, psychological, and historical critics for greater recognition," the calls have gone unanswered in large measure because their proponents have failed to establish some form of practical pedagogy (Ray 1). Structuralism and Deconstruction have yet to produce their *Understanding Poetry.* Given the nature of their theory, it is hardly likely ever to come out in textbook form, with a specific set of dogmatic principles.

When Claire Hahn wrote her review of *A Shaping Joy,* she stated that "There are so many new-new critics hacking away

at the giant [Cleanth Brooks]. It is a sheer delight to see that [he] still stands, that his principles are just, that they can and do 'expose once more the living fibers of the imagination so that men might once again see who they are and where they were'" (91).

Just ten years ago Louis D. Rubin, Jr., re-affirmed the identity between the prime elements of the New Criticism and "criticism" in general, indicating a strength that many critics take for granted and leave unsaid. Rubin writes:

> If the New Criticism as a movement is concluded, it is because its job had been done: it had made us read poems closely and in their own right, so that we could gain access to poetry written in English during the first half of the twentieth century. But I remain convinced that it is not kaput, because I don't see its job as having been done. Certainly its faddishness is over; it is no longer a novelty. But in ceasing to be New it has not thereby become Old Criticism. Instead it has become simply criticism. (204)

It is most striking to note that in 1991, long after a number of American critics pronounced the demise of the New Criticism, an anthology of more than a dozen essays about Cleanth Brooks and his work was published in India. All of these essays are favorable and speak highly of Brooks's achievements. Perhaps a special note of integrity is to be found in the one essay by Bhagwati Singh dealing with Brooks's writings on Faulkner. Unlike many foreigners, or even non-Southerners in the U.S., Professor Singh has captured an accurate picture of the art and craft of Faulkner through Brooks's critical essays.

There is yet another voice to be heard in the current controversy—that of Brooks himself. We find a strong defense of the contemporary relevance of the New Criticism in the three lectures Brooks delivered in April 1982 at the University of Missouri. They are entitled "The Primacy of the Author," "The Primacy of the Reader," and "The Primacy of the Linguistic Medium." Why should these essays be considered relevant to the current status of the New Criticism? For several reasons. First of all, among the more recent writings of Cleanth Brooks, they are probably the most crucial in assessing Brooks's teaching on the nature of literature in our time. Secondly, the tripartite division of this series of essays—focused upon the author, the reader, and the linguistic medium—parallels the focal points of reference adopted by prominent theoreticians in the past three decades. In concentrating upon the author, we think of Harold Bloom. In focusing upon the text, we are reminded of Roman Jakobson. In placing the critical analysis with the reader, we come into the arena of Stanley Fish or perhaps Norman Holland.

In the first of these essays, "The Primacy of the Author," Brooks registers his earnest concern over the "disintegration of the very concept of literature." At this point he recalls that in his earlier days "the attack on literature came particularly from the historian and the biographer, who seemed bent on making literature simply the expression of the author or, more drastically, an expression through the author of a particular culture or a special climate of ideas" (*Rich Manifold* 29). Brooks's objection to the historian and the biographer usurping the role of literature is that history and biography deal with human actions more directly and factually than does literature, which is much more indirect and has the option of fictional content. Brooks goes on to cite Aristotle's dictum that literature is more philosophical than history because literature provides a more universal knowledge than does history. Brooks underscores the distinction between the factual, literal content of history and the freely organized, fictional, non-factual account rendered by literature. (Because the poet can "better observe the actual laws of human experience" Brooks concludes that literature is guaranteed an important humanistic role.) Next, Brooks recalls Descartes's "distinction between the truth that could be told about the spatio-temporal world in which man lives and that other world inside his own skull" (31). The matter here is one of objective truth and subjective truth.

Early in the second essay of this trilogy, "The Primacy of the Reader," Brooks indicates that even today there is a trend to see the literary work as "primarily the expression of its author" and cites Harold Bloom's last several books as presenting a renewed emphasis on the author in its most striking form. Noting Bloom's "intense interest in the writer as a man struggling to free himself from both literary conventions and the benumbing effects of an established tradition" (42), Brooks cites a statement from Dennis Donoghue: "Bloom's practical criticism is indifferent to the structure, internal relations, of the poem, or to its diction, syntax, meters, rhythm, or tone: it is chiefly concerned to isolate the primal gesture which the critical paradigm has predicted" (42).

Then Brooks turns "to an incursion into literary criticism from the other side—from an exaltation of the reader" by "the most vociferous proponent of this view of the critical process"—Stanley Fish (43-44). Brooks deplores the arbitrary norms that Fish accepts in seeking the most interesting interpretation of a poem over the one that gives a more nearly correct or adequate reading. Equally disconcerting is Fish's concept that "the process of reading is broken up into small units. It is not an unbroken flow—reading proceeds by jerks, in a process of starts and stops" (47). For Fish, reading is an indeterminate process and "the reader normally generates all kinds of out-of-the-way interpretations and meanings" (47). All of this amounts to a system of critical relativism.

Brooks's third essay deals with "The Primacy of the Linguistic Medium." Here he discusses what he considers "the most destructive encroachment of all upon literature"—the tendency of some linguistic theories (e.g. structuralism) to enlarge their scope to examine any kind of structure in all forms of human society, thus becoming entangled with anthropology and myths and all forms of social behaviors. Literature then becomes a secondary factor unto itself. A second defect of this approach is that the literary critic is more interested in his *method* than in any given literary work. What is beheld is seen as a system; whether literary or not is of little import. Related to the critic's fascination with method is the principle that the "structure" is generic and any linguistic model can be applied to any given text. Here again, the literary text undergoes undue subordination to an overruling frame of reference. Brooks provides the following explanation of deconstruction:

> Deconstruction . . . is an outgrowth of structuralism, but whereas structuralism attempts to reveal the deep structure that underlies the surface meanings of any literary construct, deconstruction, using a more radical analysis, deconstructs that very structure, revealing its lack of any relation to anything beyond itself. But upon one point both structuralism and deconstruction come to the same conclusion: namely, that literature is a self-enclosed system, referring to nothing outside and beyond itself. The consequences of any such conception of literature seem to me to be devastating to any concept of its humanistic value. (55)

William E. Cain shares this concern when he states:

> In one form or other, many at the present time are thus advancing one of the most unfortunate traditions of criticism—the belief that criticism cannot finally do what it claims to do, cannot make progress, cannot do more than recapitulate its mistakes and shortcomings. It is a striking fact, seen from the perspective of anti-critical history, that criticism has shunned analytical method or else, particularly since the dawn of the New Critical era, has refined methods while doubting their purposefulness. Criticism has, furthermore, consistently tied itself to social, cultural, and political values that it places in the realm of the unanalyzable. ("Anti-Criticism" 47)

After discussing the crippling if not devastating effects brought about by the relativistic approach of either structuralism or deconstruction, Brooks recalls a principle he enunciated early on regarding the relation of literature to philosophy and to history. He assigns to literature a certain value over philosophy in that the latter deals with abstractions and principles of a predictable nature, whereas literature affords writers a medium that engages human actions in a creative setting of concrete, dramatic narration. Literature enjoys a dynamism that philosophy, in principle, cannot afford. History, of course, deals with human actions, but these are already fixed by the record or chronicle of events. Again, history does not enjoy literature's prerogative of being either dynamic or dramatic; the script is already written and fixed. Brooks continues: "The truth provided by literature is not asserted or stated, but *rendered,* and the mode, I repeat, is essentially *dramatic*" (62). The content of the literary piece is in the text; it is not a relative thing nor is it clouded over with skepticism. It is as truly there as Beethoven's Seventh Symphony is "present" in the score "in the form of signs that are to be realized in musical tones" (63). Brooks goes on to note that these comparisons are not so much matters of competition but simply contrasts intended to illustrate the broad scope of literature.

One of the pitfalls of deconstruction is the Pandora's Box it opened upon itself in extending the proper study of literature to other areas of a non-literary nature. "Critical theory today, with its emphasis on textuality, discourse, and rhetoric," says Gregory S. Jay, "has once more forced us to ask what relation if any links literature to the referents of history, politics, psychoanalysis and the other human sciences" (970). Granted that history, psychology, and politics sometimes contribute substantial enrichments to literary productions, one must ask: Is it not incumbent upon the literary critic to be versed as well in the norms and criteria of history, sociology, psychology? And, if the norms of several disciplines are invoked simultaneously, how can an individual cope with such a plethora of standards?

Further, one might ask whether it is necessary for a literary work to conform to all the criteria of history, psychology, politics, etc., in order to qualify for excellence as literature. Allow me to illustrate with a simple example: historical fiction. Traditionally, readers allow the novelist a certain degree of poetic license in creating the scenario. On the other hand, some readers may be more discriminating and may get testy if some dates or sequence of events is altered or if the main characters do not conform to what is factually known about them. For example, the widely acclaimed play and movie *Amadeus* includes several major discrepancies concerning the character of Salieri and his relationship with Mozart. Suppose one revised the story so that the characters, events and dates were as close to known history as possible; what then? Would the resulting drama be interesting? Perhaps. But it would not be *Amadeus.* Has the liberty the author taken with the facts produced a defective work of art? Many critics and audiences seem to think not. If Alexander Pope was right that "the proper study of mankind is man," then perhaps the proper study of literary criticism is literature. It is hard to understand why a literary theoretician

would want to complicate his task to include a multitude of criteria from other fields. The adjunct sciences instead of being ancillary interpreters have become wayward intruders.

The contemporary critical scene might be described as a literary battlefield. Proponents of various forms of interpretation have not only sought to advance their new methodology. They also insist that what they say is right because some aspect of the New Criticism was wrong. Perhaps one of the most accurate descriptions of the embattled academy is given by David H. Hirsch when he states:

> The various strands of contemporary literary criticism and theory (reader responsism, or reception aesthetic; intentionalism, semiotics; deconstruction; interdeterminacy; and poststructuralism) all have in common an implacable enmity toward "the New Criticism." Each movement makes a broad dual claim: on the one hand to be moving inexorably forward into new realms of knowing, and on the other to be effecting this movement forward by means of a frontal assault on some aspect of New Critical error. (25)

The New Criticism speaks for itself through a large body of documents in the form of critical statements such as the "My Credo" series in the *Kenyon Review* (1950), countless essays explicating particular poems, college English textbooks prepared to guide students to understanding poetry and fiction and to writing clear and cogent rhetoric. The New Criticism stands self justified. However, as Hirsch has well observed:

> The fortress New Criticism under attack is actually a convenient house of straw constructed by the new metatheorists themselves. The kind of criticism against which they launch their most furious attacks was, by and large, not practiced by the major New Critics. Certainly such initiators of New Critical practice as T. S. Eliot, Cleanth Brooks, Robert Penn Warren, Allen Tate, and John Crowe Ransom were cognizant of author, reader, and historical background. (25)

Some articulate spokesmen who pose as adversaries of the New Criticism betray in their polemics a lack of acquaintance with the writings of the New Critics. Focusing upon, a few cliches, such as "the Intentional Fallacy," "the Affective Fallacy," and "Irony and Paradox," they proceed in true quixotic fashion to attack the windmills. Repeatedly one finds mention of "the autotelic text," described or referred to as some kind of incongruously imprisoned literary preserve of the New Critics. All the while they overlook the careful writings of most New Critics in relation to the role of the author and the reader. How can we make a fair evaluation of this situation? To begin with, we can turn to Cain for a resolution of the dilemma. "The New Criticism leads two lives. Or rather, it is dead in one sense and very much alive in another. It is dead as a movement, as many critiques and attacks demonstrate. But its lessons about literary study lead a vigorous life, setting the norms for effective teaching and marking the boundaries within which nearly all criticism seeks to validate itself" (*Crisis* 105).

In substance, Cain's essay, "The Institutionalization of the New Criticism," may serve as a manifesto for the New Criticism in the 1990's. This essay may well serve the same function as the several essays composed by New Critics for the *Kenyon Review* series "My Credo" (1950). But Cain's observation is not a recent discovery. Fifteen years ago Rene Wellek voiced a similar appraisal of the endurance of the New Criticism.

> I will not conceal my own conviction that the New Criticism has stated or reaffirmed many basic truths to which future ages will have to return: the specific nature of the aesthetic transaction, the normative presence of a work of art that forms a structure, a unity, coherence, a whole, which cannot be simply battered about and is comparatively independent of its origins and effects. The New Critics have also persuasively described the function of literature in not yielding abstract knowledge or information, message or stated ideology, and they have devised a technique of interpretation that often succeeded in illuminating not so much the form of a poem as the implied attitudes of the author, the resolved and unresolved tensions and contradictions: a technique that yields a standard of judgment that cannot be easily dismissed in favor of the currently popular, sentimental, and simple. ("Critic of Critics" 108)

In 1979 Grant Webster expressed a similar view: "Theoretically, Formalism is dead, but on the practical level, particularly in academic classrooms, it flourishes . . . One can say, generally, that Formalism lives now in the careers of its practitioners, many of whom have outlived the flowering of the movement, and of their students, and that it is likely to be believed in by, or to have been part of the development of, any literary person who came of age intellectually from 1935 to 1955" (205). Brian Higgins and Herschel Parker note that "although the New Criticism has been dead, folk say, for a decade or more, its legacy is omnipresent." They refer to critics of varying competence and aim their fire at those who are "unwilling or unable to evaluate and employ scholarly evidence" (27).

Another arena where one finds the New Criticism thriving is in the essays of such journals as the *Sewanee Review* and the *Southern Review*. Naturally it comes as no surprise that both these magazines should occasionally run reminiscent articles focusing upon the Fugitives and Agrarians and other well known literary figures of the past half century. But there is more than a retrospective monument here. There is also new New Criticism. One also finds *new* magazines edited by disciples of the New Critics, such as Radcliffe Squires's *Michigan Quarterly Review.*

Perhaps one of the strangest types of evidence testifying to the endurance of New Criticism is the quest of certain recent writers to clarify the *nature* of the New Criticism and to rename it in more precise terms. Undaunted by fifty years of usage, Grant Webster maintains that the term "New Criticism" is "both confusing and unenlightening," and insists it's time "to substitute a name which indicates the nature of what is basically a unified movement." And so he proposes "Tory Formalism" "as the term which best characterizes the charter group of men who believe in or wish for a social and intellectual world and a literature that express belief in tradition, order, hierarchy, the fallen nature of man, the war of good and evil, and the ultimate union of warring dualisms in the Word of God and the metaphors of poetry" (205).

E. D. Hirsch, Jr., in discussing "Some Aims of Criticism," consents to use the familiar term "New Criticism," but feels compelled to clarify that "the guiding principle of the movement was not formalism, or close analysis, or stylistics, but rather the programmatic idea that literature should be described and estimated in its own intrinsic categories." Hirsch holds that the notion that "literature should be dealt with as literature . . . still remains the dominant though not the only guiding principle for the teaching and criticism of literature" (124). We should also ponder this statement by Jonathan Culler: "It is important to recognize that what was once the aim of a particular critical movement now defines the general aims of criticism. Close reading of literary texts is the ground that nearly all theories and methods build upon or seek to occupy. And this holds true even for those that are explicitly set up in opposition to the New Criticism" (*Pursuit* 5).

In his essay "Beyond Interpretation," first published in 1976, Culler argued against the emphasis on "close reading" of texts and referred to it as the "insidious legacy" of the New Criticism. Culler sees the rejection (by the New Critics) "of possible external contexts, whether biographical, historical, psychoanalytic, or sociological," as a literary predestination of sorts to no choice of approach but interpreting the poem. One is taken aback, however, by Culler's rejection of the terminology so well known to those familiar with New Critical approaches: *ambivalence, ambiguity, tension, irony, paradox.* Surely any reader can readily see each of these terms as aspects of signs, significance, and semiotics. But that was early Culler. In his more recent work he suggests that there does not exist (as some might maintain) a diametrical opposition between inclusive structuralism and the New Criticism.

> The distinctiveness of an inclusive "structuralism" does not in fact lie in its cosmopolitan theoretical interests. The New Criticism, with which it is often contrasted, was by no means antitheoretical or provincial, as the discussions in Rene Wellek and Austin Warren's *Theory of Literature* show. . . . The interpretive projects of the New Criticism were linked to the preservation of aesthetic autonomy and the defense of literary studies against encroachment by various sciences. (*On Deconstruction* 20)

Culler takes pains to delineate the varieties of structuralism, not so much in terms of different models as in terms of what features are to be included in the "structure" or "structuralism" of a given literary piece: analysis which may include concepts from linguistics, philosophy, anthropology, psychoanalysis, Marxism, and so on. For some, such varied inclusion is objectionable and untenable. A second objection Culler cites is that structuralism "threatens the very raison d'etre of literary studies by foregoing the attempt to discover the true meaning of a work and by deeming all interpretations equally valid" (*On Deconstruction* 19).

We can conclude this overview by noting the endurance of the New Criticism on the basis of its insistence, not so much upon close reading or style, but upon the principle that literature should be approached and valued according to its own intrinsic categories. The New Criticism remains valid because it altered the course of teaching literature and brought the focus of literary pedagogy back to the text. Both in method and in theory, the New Criticism endures.

Lance Lyday (essay date Fall 1992)

SOURCE: "Faulkner Criticism: Will It Ever End?," in *The South Carolina Review,* Vol. 25, No. 1, Fall, 1992, pp. 183-92.

[*In the following excerpt, Lyday presents mixed opinions of Brooks's ideas.*]

Cleanth Brooks's *William Faulkner: The Yoknapatawpha Country* (1963) and *William Faulkner: Toward Yoknapatawpha and Beyond* (1978) have recently been reissued in twin paperback editions by Louisiana State University Press. The former volume was a kind of culmination of the literary wars between the Southern New Critics and the New York Intellectuals, who never really buried their differences as much as Schwartz implies. How does *The Yoknapatawpha Country* hold up after nearly thirty years? It has probably been the single most influential critical work on Faulkner ever published. It has certainly drawn more vigorous dissent than any other work on Faulkner, but that is largely because it refuses to fade into oblivion, as so many lesser books have done. It seems sentimental and backward-looking to many progressive-minded critics, yet it may provide more insight into the future than those critics would care to recognize. Indeed, some of those critics display more than a little of the "American innocence" that Brooks finds central to the meaning of one of Faulkner's greatest novels. Brooks's central theme in *The Yoknapatawpha Country* is the need for community. He argues that Faulkner's rural background provided him with a vantage point from which to criticize modern urban and commercial culture. In Faulkner's old-fashioned fictional world, the community is a powerful though virtually invisible force that constantly makes its presence felt. The individual finds his meaning in relation to the community, and the modern breakdown of traditional communal standards is responsible for our present disarray. The prophetic quality of *The Yoknapatawpha Country* is underlined by the fact that it was published at a time when the belief that eternal progress is America's destiny was at an all-time high.

How does *The Yoknapatawpha County* hold up after nearly thrity years? It has probably been the single most influential critical work on Faulkner ever published.
—*Lance Lyday*

Yet for many readers, Faulkner's community doesn't seem such a positive thing. It is dominated by white males, it contains plenty of bigotry, and it often stifles the individual's quest for personal fulfillment. Showing the influence of the Nashville Agrarians, Brooks attributes the positive qualities in Faulkner's world to his Southern background, but the negative qualities are "modern," "American," or simply universal. Brooks takes some Northern critics to task for "sociologizing" by assuming that Faulkner's more bizarre characters are typical Southerners, yet Brooks may be guilty of some sociologizing of his own by painting an overly rosy picture of the South. If Thomas Sutpen in *Absalom, Absalom!* is, as Brooks claims, an example of American innocence, why can't Emily Grierson in "A Rose for Emily" (which Brooks discusses in *Toward Yoknapatawpha and Beyond*) be an example of Southern decadence? Does Temple Drake's behavior in *Sanctuary* show that women have a secret rapport with evil, or is Temple's depravity partly rooted in the double standards of Southern society? Does Mrs. Compson deserve all the blame for her children's plight in *The Sound and the Fury,* and is her husband, the heir of the tradition, just an innocent victim? Is the tradition itself not to blame for many of the ills in Yoknapatawpha? Are the outsiders in *Light in August* all aliens by choice, or does the community itself decide whom it will and will not admit? Brooks's tendency to defend the South against stereotypical American attitudes is understandable, but Faulkner's South seems considerably more flawed than Brooks's version.

Brooks also criticizes what he calls "symbol-mongering" by critics who allegedly wrench details out of context to impose an abstract pattern on Faulkner's novels, thereby failing to treat them as fiction, and he seals his argument with the rhetorical question, "Shall there be no more innocent consumption of pork chops and spare ribs in Yoknapatawpha County because someone has read *The Golden Bough*?" Granted that there are bad examples of every type of criticism, but it is now well established that Faulkner did indeed read *The Golden Bough* and drew on it in his fiction. In his notes to *Toward Yoknapatawpha and Beyond,* Brooks includes a lengthy list of Faulkner's literary borrowings from writers such as Eliot, Housman, and Swinburne, but in his concluding chapter he argues against any direct influence on Faulkner by Bergson, even though Faulkner said he read Bergson. It is all right, the reader surmises, for Faulkner to draw on the writers of the Western literary tradition, but he must be protected from the newfangled ideas of Frazer, Freud, or Bergson, lest someone suspect that Faulkner was more of a modernist than Brooks believes. What seems most strange is that Brooks would deny Faulkner studies the very kind of exegesis he performed so well on *The Waste Land* when he showed how Eliot used Jessie Weston's *From Ritual to Romance.* Mythic and other patterns are just as prevalent in Faulkner's fiction, in only slightly more disguised form, as they are in Eliot's poetry.

In *Toward Yoknapatawpha and Beyond,* Brooks examines Faulkner's apprentice writings, the "non-Yoknapatawpha" novels, and selected short stories. As always, his commentaries shed abundant light on their subject, but Brooks clearly doesn't seem comfortable with these novels, and he sometimes engages in circular reasoning by arguing that the non-Yoknapatawpha novels are inferior because they are not set in Yoknapatawpha. Brooks may be vulnerable on these and other matters, but his point of view is also responsible for the tremendous wealth of insights that he brings to bear on Faulkner's work. These insights are nowhere better illustrated than in his comments on *Absalom, Absalom!*, a novel he analyzed brilliantly in *The Yoknapatawpha Country* and returns to in the Appendices to *Toward Yoknapatawpha and Beyond.* Though one may question some of Brooks's assertions about the antebellum South, what is perhaps most significant about his argument is that *Absalom, Absalom!* may be not merely a parable of the Southern past, but a prophecy of the American future. Always challenging and controversial, Brooks's work on Faulkner, particularly *The*

Yoknapatawpha Country, will stand as a monument long after most of Brooks's critics have been forgotten.

John N. Duvall (essay date Winter 1992/93)

SOURCE: "Eliot's Modernism and Brooks's New Criticism: Poetic and Religious Thinking," in *Mississippi Quarterly,* Vol. 46, No. 1, Winter, 1992/93, pp. 23-37.

[*In the following essay, Duvall argues that the spiritual values required by Eliot's Modernism and Brooks's New Criticism are fraught with contradiction and lead to a static literature.*]

Emerging as the dominant critical methodology in America after World War II during a time of enormous expansion in the American university, New Criticism apparently exemplified a democratic pedagogy: any student could learn the skills to become a close reader of literary works. Today, though, it might seem perverse to investigate a movement that repeatedly has been declared passe for at least twenty-five years. William Cain reminds us, however, that no matter what contemporary theoretical perspective from which one works, few would seriously question the usefulness of close reading as a tool of analysis: "So deeply ingrained in English studies are New Critical attitudes, values and emphases that we do not even perceive them as the legacy of a particular movement." In this regard, although Cleanth Brooks is no longer at the center of debates about theory and pedagogy, there are still things to learn from historical reflection on the role he played in popularizing T. S. Eliot's modernist poetics. Such reflection, for me, points to an intriguing intersection between two differing strains of Christianity—Anglo-Catholicism and fundamentalism. This intersection, which has shaped modern literary and cultural criticism, simultaneously clarifies the telos of New Critical close reading and helps us better understand the history of literary studies from the 1910s through the 1960s as a veiled ecclesiastical history. With this understanding, then, we may experience more directly the anti-democratic undertow of New Critical grounds.

A familiar charge against New Criticism of course is its lack of historical perspective. Yet René Wellek, in his role as apologist for New Criticism, maintains that it is unfair to accuse Cleanth Brooks's literary analyses of being ahistorical. If that is so, then what kind of history does Brooks write? He certainly writes a form of literary history, one that is repeatedly nostalgic for community. This nostalgia cannot be traced to a single source but in part may be teased out of the way the texts of T. S. Eliot pass through Nashville, Tennessee, during the 1920s. In this matrix we discover certain underlying assumptions—some acknowledged and some explicitly denied—regarding not only history but also religion, literature, and community. Taken together, this complex has affected not only what we read but how we read in American Departments of English.

It is hardly surprising to note that Eliot, high priest of modernist poetics, shaped Brooks, high priest of New Criticism. Cleanth Brooks's admiration of Eliot, both as poet and essayist, manifests itself in a myriad of ways. Eliot's "Tradition and the Individual Talent" echoes loudly in the opening sentences of Brooks's **Modern Poetry and the Tradition** (1939): "Every poet that we read alters to some degree our total conception of poetry. Most poets, of course, modify it in only a minute degree, and we continually talk as if our conception were not modified at all." Speaking in 1975 of the genesis of **Modern Poetry and the Tradition,** Brooks reflects: "I was particularly stimulated by two paragraphs in one of [Eliot's] essays on the metaphysical poets. In this brief passage, he suggested that the metaphysical poets were not to be regarded as a rather peculiar offshoot of the main course of English poetry, but that they had a deep, hidden connection with its central line of development." Brooks's rewriting of literary history in **Modern Poetry and the Tradition** by linking modern poetry's use of metaphor to that in metaphysical poetry and his arguments with eighteenth-century and Romantic poetics clearly depend on Eliot. But there are religious implications in Brooks's description of "a deep, hidden connection" that he sees in Eliot's essay on the metaphysical poets. This urge toward the hidden connection, which follows from Brooks's reading of Eliot, continually blurs the boundary between poetry and religion in New Critical practice. Both Eliot and Brooks employ religious language to express their overtly aesthetic and social concerns, and the words "unity" and "community" function particularly as God-terms, signs that authorize all other moves within their language-game.

The relationship between Eliot and Brooks, however, is not one-directional: if Brooks in a sense is produced by Eliot, Eliot is as much produced by Brooks, whose textbooks attempt to give the American undergraduate a consumable Eliot. Growing out of both the Fugitive and Agrarian movements, Brooks's reading of Eliot provides significant clues to the status of Brooks's history. Some historical sense of how Eliot enters Brooks's field of vision, therefore, proves a useful context.

The texts of Eliot, prior to his conversion to the Anglican Church in 1928, stand in much the same position to the Fugitives as the post-conversion Eliot's texts stand to the Agrarians, that is as sites of debate and contestation yet confirmation. In the foreword to the first issue of *The Fugitive,* published in April 1922. John Crowe Ransom announces that "a literary phase known rather euphemistically as Southern Literature has expired . . ." and that "THE FU-GITIVE flees from nothing faster than the high-caste Brahmins of the Old South." A key moment in Fugitive aesthetics was Allea Tate's championing of *The Waste Land* against the objections of Ransom and Donald Davidson. By the fourth issue of *The Fugitive,* Tate would write: "I think for all time—so important is *The Waste Land*—Mr Eliot has demonstrated the necessity, in special cases, of aberrant versification. For doubtless none assails the authenticity of his impersonal and increasingly abstract art. . . ." Eight years after this call to the modern, the introduction to the Southern Agrarian manifesto, *I'll Take My Stand,* in a voice as hortatory as *The Fugitive's* preface, takes a reactionary turn, warning that "Younger Southerners, who are being converted frequently to the industrial gospel, must come back to the support of the Southern tradition" or else the South will lose "its moral, social and economic autonomy." Cleanth Brooks attended Vanderbilt between 1921 and 1928 at a time when those literary rebels, the Fugitives, were moving in their separate artistic ways, yet at the same time were reforming in a more politicized avatar as the Southern Agrarians. Although Tate had left Vanderbilt before Brooks arrived, the Fugitive Tate insured that Eliot formed part of Brooks's course of study, even if Brooks's mentor would be Ransom. During his years at Vanderbilt. Brooks moved in circles that led to Southern Agrarianism, and although he did not participate in *I'll Take My Stand.* Brooks clearly took his stand with the Agrarian cause. Brooks finally met Tate in 1929 in Paris. The meeting proved fortunate for Brooks, who found in Tate a fellow Agrarian and a fellow traveler in Eliot's pessimistic reading of modernity. Tate, in fact, read drafts of material from Brooks's 1939 study, **Modern Poetry and the Tradition,** a book aptly dedicated to Tate.

In the transition from Fugitive aesthetics to Agrarian politics, Eliot remained a powerful cultural authority. It is not difficult to see why Eliot's essays of the 1930s would be read with care by one with an Agrarian world view. The social and literary criticism of Eliot, especially after his conversion to the Anglo-Catholic faith, richly resonates with the concerns of the Southern Agrarians. Both Eliot and the Agrarians fight a rear-guard action to preserve a community that they see slipping away. For the Agrarians, that community is the Southern community, specially conceived as the last best hope of preserving the European tradition of community life: the evil of modernity is primarily the encroachment of Northern industrial society into the South. Eliot's community is that of Christian believers, and, like the Agrarians, he is staunchly anti-communist. Eliot is also at least as wary of liberalism, which in his view ushered in the secularization of government, subsequently allowing a soulless technology to take the lead in organizing society.

Like his cultural hero Eliot, Brooks finally converts to Anglo-Catholicism, but from a different point of origin. Eliot was the grandson of a Unitarian minister. Brooks, the son of a Methodist minister, attended a small Methodist prep school that emphasized Greek and Latin, McTyeire School, in McKenzie, Tennessee. A question we might ask is "How does the religion of his father impinge on the force of the word 'community' for Cleanth Brooks?" It is precisely where religion informs Brooks's perspective that I see a contradiction arising within New Critical praxis. The locus of the contradiction in Brooks's attachment to Eliot occurs on the very topics—community, education, and the education of the community—where the Agrarian world picture seems to dovetail with Eliot's. The Agrarian nostalgia for the Southern community, however, is not the same as Eliot's nostalgia for those times in history when a writer could take for granted a community of Christian believers. But for Brooks as an Agrarian, the conflation of the two communities—the Agrarian community and Eliot's community of educated believers—is understandable, since both communities are based on exclusion: the Agrarian community's distrust of strangers is not unlike Eliot's disdain for those lacking classical training. However, Brooks's attraction to both Eliot's and the Agrarian exclusive community leads to an even more conflicted position on Brooks's vocation as literary exegete. The contradiction is that, in his New Critical witnessing for a fundamentalist unity of the centered text, Brooks draws on the same exclusionary tradition that Eliot developed to argue the necessity of Anglo-Catholicism to a civilized society. And so a question arises: is Brooks's community finally exclusive or expansionist?. As his work on Faulkner makes clear, Brooks's Southern community makes definite exclusions (it is, after all, the *white* community), but his sense of Christian community seems less closed. Certain cultural and literary criticism of Cleanth Brooks and T. S. Eliot from the 1930s helps us understand a tension in Brooks's vision of community and suggests that Eliot's modernist poetics and Brooks's New Critical practice intersect through their unacknowledged collapsing of the distinction between poetic and religious thinking.

In "Modern Education and the Classics" (1932). Eliot justifies hierarchical social organization by emphasizing unequal natural abilities among human beings, much as John Gould Fletcher does in his contribution to *I'll Take My Stand,* "Education Past and Present." Fletcher makes it clear from the outset that "all education can do in any case is to teach us to make good use of what we are if we are nothing to begin with, no amount of education can do us any good" (p. 93). Eliot expresses a similar opinion, though with a more elitist agenda: a "task of anyone who might be imagined as occupying a dictational position in the education of a country should obviously be to see that . . . no one received *too much* education, limiting the numbers treated to 'higher education' to a third (let us say) of those receiving the treatment today" (*Selected Essays.* p. 154). There is, of course, a note of irony in Eliot's use of the word "dictation," yet given the worldwide rise of fascism in the years following the essay's

publication, it is difficult not to be alert to the anti-democratic force of his playful suggestion. Eliot's essay, nominally a defense of teaching Greek and Latin, is highly critical of the American university's scale:

> America grew very rich, that is to say, it produced a considerable number of millionaires, and the next generation set itself to an equally mad programme of building, erecting within a short time a great variety of imposing, though in some places rather hastily built, halls and dormitories, and even chapels. And when you have sunk so much money in plant and equipment, when you have a large though not always well paid staff of men who are mostly married and have a few children, when you are turning out from your graduate schools more and more men who have been trained to become teachers in other universities, and who will probably want to marry and have children too, when your whole national system of higher education is designed for an age of expansion, for a country which is going to indefinitely increase its population, grow rich, and build more universities, then you will find it very difficult to retract.

Eliot's comments seem at odds with the economic reality of the depression, a time of retrenchment for most American universities: however, during Huey Long's term as governor, Louisiana State, which had recently hired Brooks, fits well the type of institution Eliot criticizes. How could Brooks, as one of these young men of whom Eliot speaks, forgive his cultural hero this attitude? Because quite apart from this strain in the essay there is another argument that resonates with Brooks's New Critical agenda. Eliot argues that if education is not to become technological (and hence without values), "we must derive our theory of education from our philosophy of life. The problem turns out to be a religions problem" (p. 152). The solution Eliot proposes is that "*all* education must be ultimately religious education" (p. 159): that is all education must be informed by transcendent values. Eliot is decidedly pessimistic about the chances of a Christian civilization grounded on the classics prevailing in the modern world and desires to "see a revival of the monastic life in its variety," since "the first educational task of the communities should be the *preservation* of education within the cloister, uncontaminated by the deluge of barbarism outside" (p. 160).

If we link Eliot's belief that education must be always religious education with his call in "Religion and Literature" (1935) for a "literature which should be *un*consciously, rather than deliberately and defiantly, Christian" (*Selected Essays,* p. 346), then we arrive, I think, at a better sense of the theological impulse in New Critical close reading as practiced by Cleanth Brooks. Eliot desires an unconscious

Christian literature because he believes that an openly Christian one cannot succeed "in a world in which it is assumed that Religion and Literature are not related" (p. 316). Just as Eliot had earlier called for education to be religious education here he calls for literary criticism to "be completed by criticism from a definite ethical and theological standpoint" (p. 343). Eliot's assertion of the inseparability of literary and religious judgment finds its fullest expression in the New Criticism of Cleanth Brooks, perhaps nowhere more clearly than in Brooks's reading of *The Waste Land* in **Modern Poetry and the Tradition,** a reading illuminated by Brooks's own Eliotic foray into social criticism.

On his way to rewriting English literary history and revising the way literature was taught in American universities, Brooks participated in the second Agrarian forum. *Who Owns America?* co-edited by Allen Tate and Herbert Agar, published in 1936. Brooks's contribution, **"A Plea to the Protestant Churches,"** posits an identity between poetic and religious thinking that is central to what I would call Brooks's textual fundamentalism. In this essay, Brooks reluctantly admits that fundamentalism has fallen into disrepute, yet he calls upon the Protestant establishment to renounce its infatuation with worldly schemes and to return—if it is not too late—to its proper mission, a mission that resurrects a key tenet of fundamentalism—a belief in the absolute. The somewhat coy rhetorical structure nearly obscures Brooks's point, for if the beginning of the essay suggests the death of fundamentalism, the end calls for its reexamination. One reason fundamentalism is dying, Brooks claims early on is that the Liberal Protestant (an abstraction Brooks critiques with irony) "has naturally found the cruder aspects of Fundamentalism repugnant." What precisely these aspects are Brooks does not say, but inasmuch as they might block "coveted intercourse with other intellectuals" (p. 323) it seems clear that biblical inerrancy is chief among them. Brooks's final plea for Protestants to reject Marxism echoes the ironic rhetoric of his opening: such a rejection "would not necessitate a return to the *crudities* of Fundamentalism, unless one believes, in an age of relativities, that belief in an absolute is crude" (p. 332). It is tempting to see an autobiographical element in his eliding the specific crudities of fundamentalism. Eventually moving from the content of his father's Methodist religion, Brooks apparently was no longer able to invest belief in the inerrancy of the biblical word: he nevertheless retained the form of his father's religion, now cathecting to and substituting the poetic word. This shift preserved for Brooks a sophisticated realm of the absolute—the infallible work of literature—in an age he sees as otherwise interested in a fundamentalist Christianity.

Liberal Protestantism, Brooks asserts in the body of his essay, is rapidly selling out to scientism on the one hand and secularism (particularly communism) on the other: these dilutions of Protestantism, he feels, lead to the end "of a *Christian* civilization" (p. 331). For Brooks, as for Eliot, to be a liberal is to be without values, and though Brooks is disdainful of communism, he sees in it a system of values that make it a religion, albeit "one of the materialistic religions and one of the religions of man, burdened with his infirmities" (p. 332). Also like Eliot, Brooks is wary of science, which he sees as an instrumentalism incapable of inculcating values.

> Science is quite properly the technician-in-chief in civilization: it defines the means to be employed by the attainment of various objectives. But it cannot be the pilot. It cannot as science—name the objectives. That is the function of religion, it religion is to have any function at all (p. 325)

At this moment in the essay, the structure appears clear. Science has been identified as the progressive, man-centered, value-free discipline of means, while Christianity, anchored in God's eternal values, is the discipline of ends. Brooks, one assumes, will now oppose religious and scientific knowledge. But instead, Brooks turns to art to exemplify what he means by religious thinking: "I am using *art* in the sense of a description of an experience which is concrete where that of science is abstract, many-sided where that of science is necessarily one-sided, and which involves the whole personality where science only involves one part, the intellect. These are qualities which are essential to worship, and a religion without worship is an anomaly" (p. 326). Brooks does claim that "religion is obviously more than art." But the only distinction seems to be that religion is based on supreme values while art is based on provisional values. He concludes his distinction between art and religion in a way that draws them back together: "But a religion which lacks the element of art is hardly a religion at all." Significantly, Brooks describes religious thinking entirely in terms of poetic thinking: "If there is to be a search [for God] . . . it will have to be a search in something of the sense in which the poet explores himself in relation to the truth, ordering it over, relating it to various sets of conditions, but returning to it and working back to it as to a center rather than regarding it as a point on a line along which he continually advances" (p. 327). Just as the Christian is centered in Christ, the poet is centered in the poem. The true Christian, it seems, always will be something of a poet.

Years later in **The Hidden God,** Brooks's image of the poetic Christian slides into a sense of the Christian poet through a description that has an almost prescriptive force in "T. S. Eliot: Discourse to the Gentiles": "The poet's task is not only to find new symbols for the central experiences but to reconstitute the old symbols, reclaiming them, redeeming them, setting them in contexts which will force us once again to confront their Christian meanings." This assertion leads us back in two directions simultaneously: first, to Eliot's call for an unconscious religious literature: and second, to

Brooks's reading of *The Waste Land* Brooks's close reading of *The Waste Land* in **Modern Poetry and the Tradition** is masterful: all paradox and tensions resolve themselves into pure orthodoxy: "Eliot's theme is the rehabilitation of a system of beliefs, known but now discredited" (p. 171). Because Eliot could not depend on a community of believers as Spenser and Dante could. "the only method is to work by indirection. The Christian material is at the center, but the poet never deals with it directly" (p. 174). "In this way," Brooks claims. Eliot's "statement of beliefs emerges *through* confusion and cynicism—not in spite of them" (p. 172). This is an interpretive tour de force. The student, Brooks, has mastered his cultural hero and in so doing has given back to Eliot precisely what he asked for—an unconscious Christian literature.

And now, having discovered the hidden Christian center in Eliot's great poem, Brooks never relinquishes it, for to do so would be to lose, as it were, a higher truth. The interpretation positing a hidden Christian center recurs whenever Brooks speaks of Eliot. The material I quoted above from **Modern Poetry and the Tradition** appears again in the commentary on *The Waste Land* in the 1950 revision of **Understanding Poetry**. And in **The Hidden God** the same spin is imparted to the later texts of Eliot when Brooks speaks of "Eliot's avoiding Christian terms and Christian symbols. One notices also that even in the avowedly Christian works, Eliot shows himself to be consistently aware of this problem of modern incomprehension" (p. 76). Although few readers today would agree with Brooks (Christian terms and symbols, after all, appear regularly in Eliot's "avowedly Christian works"), what is interesting about this assertion is its adherence to Eliot's own sense of modern incomprehension and its consistency within Brooks's larger reading of Eliot. Brooks argues that because modern readers do not belong to a community of believers. Eliot accommodates their lack of faith by presenting his Christian message in a way that does not privilege Christian discourse, a discourse that would doom his readers to refusing his message about human sin. Although Brooks first articulates this arguments in his reading of *The Waste Land,* we should remember that by 1939 he had available to him a great deal of poetry and criticism written by the post-conversion Eliot (texts that, I have suggested, urged Brooks toward the kind of reading he performs on *The Waste Land*). We can reconstruct then, the faulty syllogism apparently leads Brooks to his conclusion about *The Waste Land:* Eliot's openly Christian poetry avoids Christian terms and symbols (again a surprising position): Eliot's pre-conversion poetry also avoids Christian terms and symbols: therefore, Eliot's pre-conversion poetry is an unconscious Christian poetry. One local history, then, that Cleanth Brooks gives us about Eliot is a Christian teleology in which Eliot's conversion is the inevitable end.

Brooks's own position as a Christian critic may best be summarized by the now-familiar point he makes about Eliot in *A Shaping Joy.* Brooks's words become a kind of unacknowledged autobiography, if one substitutes the word *criticism* for poetry both times it occurs: "His community is the remnant of the Christian community in a post-Christian world. His [criticism]—including his specifically religious [criticism]—consistently addresses itself to the 'gentiles'— takes into account the reader's agnosticism." In light of this self-reflexive rhetoric, Brooks's quest for the organic unity in texts marked as poetic can be read as the displaced expression of his nostalgia for community and at the same time, as a manifestation of the hidden God. Again we see how Brooks's social and literary criticism employs a matrix of terms—unity, community, tradition—that each serve, at various moments, as tropes for God, or God-terms.

Brooks, professing his faith in the unitary meaning of texts in the context of the American university, deploys Eliot's words in a way that constantly pulls in directions antithetical to Eliot's. Eliot's tradition caters to an elitist, High-Church community. Because Eliot assumes that only a limited number of individuals can be educated, his Christian community, not surprisingly, is based on an exclusion— a fit few for the kingdom of God. His view implies pessimism and retreat (into a monastic community, if necessary). Brooks's community, however, oscillates in the space between his belief in exclusive community—whether Eliot's or the Agrarians—and his sense that all students are potentially worthy of poetical mysteries and thus, by extension, of God's grace. What Brooks's involvement in the various editions of **Understanding Poetry, Understanding Fiction, Understanding Drama,** and **An Approach to Literature** makes clear is that he is not afraid of an evangelical mission, even though that evangelism contradicts the very exclusivity of the tradition for which he proselytizes. So that although Brooks's discourse appears to duplicate the pessimism in Eliot's reading of modernity, Brooks's theological convictions cause him to speak, in a clear and common sense voice, what he sees as the difficult truths of poetry and belief.

Brooks's appropriation of Eliot, always filtered through a lens that is both Fugitive and Agrarian, most nearly unravels when he attempts to save Eliot from the charge of elitism. Speaking of instances of shifting and double meaning in the fourth section of the *Quartets.* Brooks writes: "They make the poetry more difficult to read, to be sure: but that difficulty has not been sought by Eliot. *The truth* of the matter *is that it could not be avoided*—it could not be avoided, that is if the poet were to be true to *his vision* and true to the circumstances under which that vision was vouchsafed" (**Hidden God.** p. 81, emphasis added). This vision, of course, is Eliot's Christian vision. Brooks asserts that the mysteries of the Christian vision cannot be articulated in plain language, which seems to validate Eliot's High Church view.

Brooks's reading, however, articulates his own more liberal Christian vision, thus affirming—through his own writing practice—what the content of his discourse denies, namely, that Christian faith can be spoken of without indirection and paradox. Clearly, *Four Quartets* embodies, through its complexity, Eliot's sense of truth. The Christian apparatus is of course, only one of the approaches (another being the artist and the word). Given the high level of generality in *Four Quartets'* Christianity, the differences between Eliot's and Brooks's specific varieties of Christianity perhaps are not identifiable in the poem. What is significant, however, is that Brooks's reading of the *Quartets* professes his faith through the New Critical God-term, unity. This theological impulse goes a long way toward explaining why critical judgment is so important to the New Critical project. Canon formation is crucial because one must judge what the good word is. Bad poetry isn't just bad: it's a form of heresy.

What, then, can we make of history in the Brooks-Eliot connection? The progressive narrowing of the canon of modernist poetry through the 1960s, based on a "disciplinary inclination to view the fragmented modernist text as a purely aesthetic object, its linguistic fragmentation purified of social influence and critique" (p. 211) has created large gaps in our cultural memory, as Cary Nelson's recent *Repression and Recovery* has so forcefully pointed out. In creating for Eliot the unconscious Christian literature that he called for, Brooks at that same time developed an unconscious Christian criticism even though certainly for Brooks himself it is quite conscious) that spawned a pedagogy with unmistakable theological undercurrents. To assume the organic unity of great poetry, drama, and fiction that one teaches and interprets is to practice a form of textual fundamentalism. This textual fundamentalism, as I argued earlier, already is implicit in Brooks's understated call for a return to a fundamentalism without crudity in **"A Plea to the Protestant Churches."** The critic who could not construct a reading that discovered the unity of an acknowledged masterpiece (no matter how conflicted and ambivalent that text might be) was at fault, never the text. If "all education is religious education," as Eliot claimed, we need always to ask what form of belief we may be promulgating when we turn to close reading in the classroom, even if today our historical and political awareness causes us to display to our students urns that are less well-wrought.

In another sense of the history of our discipline, New Criticism, in its theological urge, unconsciously writes itself as its own anti-history, emerging as its anathema, ideological criticism. (Complaints from New Critics that Marxist criticism has a political agenda assumed that New Criticism did not.) In his effort to discover the hidden unity of works and the tradition, Brooks's literary history omitted texts that were tainted with the secularization of politics. Thus Joyce and Faulkner are prized but not Dos Passos: Eliot and Yeats, but

not Zukofsky (to say nothing of the proletarian poets from the 1930s). New Criticism was too ready to excuse the excesses either in a text's rhetoric or in the social system that a text represented, if one could read that text in a way that discovered unity or that celebrated community. This devaluation of the secular leads to a quietism that we hear at the end of Eliot's "Literature and the Modern World" (1935), an essay included, we might note, in the 1939 edition of *An Approach to Literature,* edited by Brooks, Warren, and Purser. With the world poised on the brink of the second major war of our century, this essay, which argues that authors should not propagate social ideas in their writing, locates the threat in the present not with the rise of fascism but with the "secular revolution" of communism and urges a return to a Christian community:

> I think . . . that the passion for social righteousness will prove in the end not enough in itself. . . . An age of change, and a period of incessant apprehension of war do not form a favorable environment. There is a temptation to welcome change for its own sake, to sink our minds in some desperate philosophy of *action*. . . . We cannot effect intelligent change, unless we hold fast to the permanent essentials; and a clear understanding of what we should hold fast to and what abandon, should make us all the better prepared to carry out the changes that are needed. Thus we can look back upon the past without regret, and to the future without fear.

But if we look back only at the great tradition and ahead to the life to come, then the "action" primarily available in the present is a religio-poetical contemplation. At best, we can hope to become perfect critics reading perfects texts as solace in an all to imperfect world. Brooks's New Critical practice, as the ideological double of Eliot's modernism, only repeats a demand for politically disengaged reading. Brooks's history, thus, is problematic qua history because, as Christian telos of salvation, it operates in a timeless space, not unlike Eliot's tradition. A larger irony, the history lesson of the Brooks-Eliot matrix remains: the democratic method of reading that served us through much of the Cold War was founded on assumptions that were only marginally hospitable to democracy.

Roger B. Rollin (review date Fall 1994-Spring 1995)

SOURCE: "Apoligia Pro Vita Litteraria," in *The South Carolina Review,* Vol. 27, Nos. 1 & 2, Fall 1994-Spring 1995, p. 375.

[In the following review, Rollin praises Brooks's body of

work and its impact on criticism.]

This will be a personal kind of review. The news of Cleanth Brooks's death came while I was reading his book. I was surprised as well as saddened because I had seen him recently at two different professional meetings, looking fit and still wonderfully full of zest for the life of letters. The announcement of his passing reminded me how much my own life of letters owed to him. My undergraduate professors (I later came to understand) were New Critics, and their focus on the text not only taught me how to read but fired me with renewed enthusiasm for literature itself. (Years later, as a brand new assistant prof, and anxious to learn the trade, I asked a veteran English Ed professor how he would teach "L'Allegro/Il Penseroso"; when he replied, "First, I'd draw a map of Asia Minor on the blackboard," my heart sank, and I realized what had been wrong with my English education—and English education generally—prior to Cleanth Brooks.) In graduate school, I had the opportunity to take a seminar in Romantic Poetry with Professor Brooks, and on the first day he announced, "Ladies and gentlemen, I really don't know anything about Romantic Poetry, but we're going to learn together." That was modesty, of course, but a mark of the man, as were the courtesy and consideration he extended even to graduate students. One of the local sights was William K. Wimsatt, a hulking and rumpled six-foot five-inches looming over the dapper five-foot six-inch Brooks, as they ambled across campus, talking away about (we knew) momentous matters—perhaps their collaborative *Literary Criticism: A Short History,* which would become my bible. In the course of writing my dissertation, I discovered that one of the few articles on Robert Herrick that showed much understanding of that poet's special genius was "What Does Poetry Communicate?"—from *The Well-Wrought Urn,* of course. In my first teaching position I was assigned a course in reading poetry required of all English majors, and naturally I used Brooks and Warren's *Understanding Poetry.* And so it went, and so it still goes: Cleanth Brooks has been teaching me for over forty years and, while critical fashions come and go, he will continue to teach well into the next century through his students and his books.

Thus, I trust I will be understood to be praising *Historical Evidence and the Reading of Seventeenth-Century Poetry* when I say it has all the virtues of a series of superb undergraduate lectures. Each chapter is a graceful and lucid study of poems as familiar as Henry King's "An Exequy," Lovelace's "The Grasse-hopper," and Marvell's "The Garden" (how interesting and useful to study these very different poems together!) as well as "An Horatian Ode." Other chapters are bound to spark new interest in less well known poets, such as Richard Corbett ("The Faerys Farewell"), James Shirley ("The glories of our blood and state"), Aurelian Townshend (several poems), Sir Richard Fanshaw ("The Fall"), and Lord Herbert of Cherbury (also several

poems). Some of Brooks's readings are controversial; all illuminate.

> **I trust I will be understood to be praising *Historical Evidence and the Reading of Seventeenth-Century Poetry* when I say it has all the virtues of a series of superb undergraduate lectures.**
> —*Roger B. Rollin*

In essence, however, this book is an apologia pro vita litteraria. "I trust," says Brooks in his "Epilogue," "that the preceding chapters constitute solid testimony to my own regard for the importance of establishing authorship, datings, biographical and historical references, and the specific and sometimes archaic uses that make up the poet's text." And indeed, each chapter does show him bringing information "extrinsic to the text"—biographical documents, definitions from the *Oxford English Dictionary,* historical records, etc.—to bear upon his careful analyses of all that is intrinsic to the text.

That the New Critics religiously ignored biography and history was always, of course, a bum rap, a consequence of their efforts to unearth what had for so long been buried beneath layer upon stultifying layer of half-baked biographical criticism and misapplied historical criticism—the text itself and the possibilities of the literary experience. To do so did require deliberate downplaying of "the relevance of extrinsic evidence," as Brooks admits he did in *The Well-Wrought Urn.* But some readers may be as surprised as I was to learn that while he was completing that pioneering book of criticism he published a scholarly edition of *The Correspondence of Thomas Percy and Richard Farmer.* "The Republic of Letters," he notes, "needs both kinds of activity."

That may, of course, be regarded today as a non-issue. So too is Brooks's concern with the writer's "sincerity," which Northrop Frye settled long ago when he noted that all we can really mean by sincerity in literature is the effective communication of emotion. For all the formalists' efforts at a kind of rational criticism, they often began or concluded with the irrational—a work's "greatness" or lack thereof—and such personal aesthetic judgments elevated to absolutes are not absent from this book. So too is the tendency to rate poems and poets like baseball players, into "major" and "minor."

Nevertheless, whether read as an example of that all too rare phenomenon today, accessible literary criticism, or as a fascinating document in the history of twentieth-century criticism *Historical Evidence and the Reading of Seventeenth-Century Poetry* transcends its limitations. It instructs. It delights. It is an appropriate valediction from one who changed literary criticism and literary education for the better, forever.

Charlotte H. Beck and John P. Rhoades (essay date 1995)

SOURCE: "'Stanley Fish Was My Reader': Cleanth Brooks, the New Criticism, and Reader-Response Theory," in *The New Criticism and Contemporary Literary Theory,* edited by William J. Spurlin and Michael Fisher, Garland Publishing, New York City, 1995, pp. 211-26.

[*Below, Beck and Rhoades compare Brooks's New Criticism and Stanley Fish's Reader-Response theory.*]

The method of literary analysis which became known as the New Criticism began in meetings of the Nashville Fugitives during the 1920s, when John Crowe Ransom dominated the group. Between 1921 and 1925-1926, Ransom's students included Robert Penn Warren and Cleanth Brooks, who were to codify the "method" for use, first in their classes at LSU, and then in their critical essays and textbooks. Brooks, never a Fugitive and connected only briefly with Agrarianism, began to work out his own approaches to reading. He credits not only Ransom but also I. A. Richards and T. S. Eliot with having influenced him in the formulation of his critical theories (Interview). Like Ransom and Richards, Brooks used the classroom as a laboratory before codifying his methods in two collections of essays, ***Modern Poetry and the Tradition*** (1939) and ***The Well Wrought Urn*** (1947). Along with Warren, Brooks also combined theory with classroom experience in the structuring of textbooks which were to dominate literary pedagogy in the United States for the greater part of the twentieth century.

In 1947, Brooks moved to Yale University, where one of his graduate assistants was Stanley Fish, father-to-be of reader-response criticism. Although in recent letters to these authors, neither man professes to "remember" much about the other, that relationship of teacher and student, possibly problematic to both, may have played an indirect role in the evolution of Fish's approach, especially as a reaction to what Fish saw as the New Critical doctrine of the closed and autonomous literary text. Correspondingly, Brooks's dismissal of reader-response theory as an "anything goes" approach has served to over-dramatize the tension between the New Criticism and reader-response theories. In fact, the evolution of literature in general and criticism in particular may be viewed, after Harold Bloom, as a history of misreading, which has emerged in the two Bloomian modes of clinamen and kenosis; that is to say, the younger critic (Fish) both *misreads* and *breaks away from* his precursor. And although

Bloom's terminology refers specifically to poets (14-15), he finds it possible, with but a slight adjustment, to make room for anxieties of influence between critics:

> Poets' misinterpretations of poems are more drastic than critics' misinterpretations of criticism, but this is only a difference in degree and not at all in kind. There are no interpretations but only misinterpretations, and so all criticism is prose poetry. . . . For just as a poet must be found by the opening in a precursor poet, so must the critic. The difference is that a critic has more parents . . . poets and critics. (94-95)

Without presenting a detailed Bloomian analysis of the Brooks-Fish relationship (and who but Bloom himself could do *that*?), there are strong suggestions to be found in a parallel examination of the critical praxes of Cleanth Brooks and Stanley Fish that they are a case in point.

I. Cleanth Brooks and the New Criticism

Between 1922 and 1925, the group which called itself "The Fugitives" met in homes near the Vanderbilt campus, first for social and cultural interaction but later, under the leadership of John Crowe Ransom, as one of the first "workshops" in creative writing. These sessions became a laboratory in the close reading of the members' original poems, as well as a focus for the methods which Ransom used for a time in his Vanderbilt classes. When, in 1929, Ransom and his circle became Agrarians, turning their attention to other matters, he ceased even to demonstrate it in his classes. But before that change could occur, Ransom's students had included Robert Penn Warren and Cleanth Brooks.

Brooks, like Ransom, the son of a Methodist preacher, came to Vanderbilt in 1925 when the Fugitive movement was at its apex. In his freshman year, Brooks was too impressed to take advantage of Ransom's classes. He attributed this failure to "awe" brought on by "ignorance and innocence and my confused romanticism" (Young 3). He dropped Ransom's class as being too advanced for him, although, as T. D. Young remarks, "ironically, Ransom was merely submitting the literary texts to the kind of close, analytical, interpretive readings that Brooks would become justly acclaimed for later" (3). As Ransom later shrewdly commented, Brooks and he were "about as like as two peas from the same pod in respect to our native regions, our stock (we were sons of ministers of the same faith, and equally had theology in our blood), the kind of homes we lived in, the kind of small towns; and perhaps we were most like in the unusual parallel of our formal educations." In particular, both he and Ransom had heard a lot of Methodist Sunday sermons, during which "the preacher unpacked the whole burden of his theology from a single figurative phrase of Scripture taken out of context" (334). Ransom was, therefore, tailor-made to be Brooks's strong precursor in the evolution of Brooks's textual criticism. He decided to major in English, rather than become "a really shifty halfback," after hearing Donald Davidson's essay on a Kipling story read by his graduate assistant English teacher. Brooks recalled:

> This opened a new world for me. It revealed that you could look inside a story and see how it was put together, and could make sensible observations about it. . . . It showed me that the inner workings of a poem or a story were important. I'm sure that my prep school discipline in reading Latin and Greek—discussing the meaning of passages and parsing them—had prepared me rather directly for this new discipline of literary exploration. (Young 2)

During his senior year, Brooks read and became impressed with Ransom's poetry as well as with the "approach" to literature used in class by Ransom and Davidson. He seized on the concepts that "the sense of technique, the structure of a thing . . . [is] related to the life of the poem and then the life behind the poem" (Young 4).

After graduating from Vanderbilt in 1928, Brooks became connected briefly with Agrarianism by publishing one essay in *Who Owns America*? (1936), but criticism, not socio-politics, was to be his lifework. He began to work out his own approaches to reading apart from Ransom. The results were parallel and complementary production of his critical essays, soon collected in books, and a succession of textbooks beginning with a **"Poetry Manual"** (1935) (Brooks papers, Yale) for LSU students and *An Approach to Literature,* the four-genre predecessor to the vastly influential volumes *Understanding Poetry, Understanding Fiction,* and *Understanding Drama* (the latter with Heilman instead of Warren). These textbooks, themselves extensions of the analytical dialogue that Warren first encountered in the Fugitive group meetings, began as mimeographed exercises handed out to LSU students (interview).

Brooks remained at LSU for five years after Warren departed—and their involvement with *The Southern Review* ended—in 1942. Diverse teaching assignments intervened, such as Ransom's Kenyon summer schools of criticism (1948 to 1950), and the University of Michigan summer class (English 300k) in 1942, with whom Brooks, according to an acknowledgment to *The Well Wrought Urn,* worked out some of the analyses that were included in that collection of essays. Yale was to be Brooks's ultimate academic connection, where he taught for many years and, in his words, "overlapped" twice more with his old colleague Robert Penn Warren (interview). Brooks, Warren, and others (including the young Americanist R.W.B. Lewis) were to continue their careers of textbook and anthology production as they taught and also pursued active careers as practicing critics through another four decades.

II. "Stanley Fish was My Reader" (interview)

Unfortunately, Cleanth Brooks was unable to recall how Stanley Fish developed critical acumen during his graduate student days, when he for a time served as Brooks's assistant. Brooks remembered Fish as "an excellent reader, highly intelligent, [who] worked carefully and thoroughly. I have only commendation for what he did for me. But the little human interest things about him, quirks, special happenings, particular sayings—of these I have no record whatsoever" (letter to Beck, May 1990). Fish's fondest recollection of "Mr. Brooks" is of seeing him walk down the street with William Wimsatt "whom as you probably know was seven feet tall. Mr. Brooks was a low key and gentle instructor who exerted authority through his person and academic stature" (letter to Beck, May 1990). No doubt Fish was quietly formulating his own attitudes toward—or perhaps more accurately, *against*—what Brooks had theorized, since, like most post-structuralists, he defines his critical stance in large part as a reaction against the New Critics.

No subsequent interaction between Brooks and Fish appears to have been documented, except, in 1979, when they met at the University of Tennessee in Knoxville. This encounter occurred, significantly, just before the 1980 publication of *Is There a Text in This Class*?. The occasion was a symposium entitled "Three Critics/Three Poems," featuring Brooks, speaking on Thomas Hardy's "Channel Firing"; Hugh Kenner, on Charles Tomlinson's "The Way of a World"; and Stanley Fish, on two short poems, Ben Jonson's "To the Reader" and (according to Richard Kelly's report) "a found poem comprised of a random list of names of linguists" (UT *Newsletter* n.p.). This, obviously, was the classroom experience which Fish recounts in *Is There a Text in This Class?,* the seminal essay and core of *Text*. Brooks's and Kenner's presentations were extremely competent and by then orthodox examples of New Critical analysis. Fish's performance, which Kelly describes as follows, was something quite other:

> The first two speaker-magicians dazzled the audience by pulling unexpected rabbits out of old hats. The third magician, Stanley Fish, also extracted rabbits from his hat but with this difference: his hat was posted with a notice—"This hat contains rabbits; it is a trick hat with a concealed compartment; anyone can do this trick if he has the right hat." (Kelly n.p.)

According to Kelly, the University's English department, where Brooks was then visiting professor, was afterward buzzing with talk of "Brooks's and Kenner's incisive readings" and "Fish's challenge that all interpretations are accidents of history and personal subjectivity: the critic conditioned by his time and his background, creates his own structure, his own meaning." In recent correspondence, Fish did not profess to recall the incident, while Brooks remembered Fish's performance on that evening as "curious, even absurd." Brooks left this, his last recollected collaboration with his former student, astonished with Fish's apparent notion that "a charismatic teacher could make a class under his dominion believe anything that he told them about a text that he put up for them to discuss" (letter to Beck, April 1990). Clearly, the incident solidified Brooks's suspicion that his former pupil was and is a critical relativist, a philosophical position that Brooks had, throughout his career, consistently opposed.

III. Brooks and Fish: A Comparison

Because Cleanth Brooks and Stanley Fish, each having become exemplar for an important school of criticism, did interact as teacher and pupil for a time, it is useful to locate the apex of their division into apparently antipodal approaches to literature. As to their development, one "missing link" is surely to be found in I.A. Richards's "practical criticism." That both Brooks and Fish admit to having derived some primary elements of their theories from Richards's affective theory makes of their divergences a continuum.

René Wellek describes the New Critics as a group which rejects "the kind of metaphorical, evocative criticism practiced by the impressionists" and also as a group who "were united in their opposition to the prevailing methods, doctrines, and views of academic English literary scholarship" (146). C.E. Pulos, in *The New Critics and the Language of Poetry,* states that "I.A. Richards is commonly regarded as the founder of the new criticism," a claim Pulos admits "though not strictly true . . . is comprehensible" (49). Richards's book *The Principles of Literary Criticism* outlines his method of critical theory. Richards envisioned a system of criticism built on the twin pillars of "account of value" and an "account of communication" (25). Finally, Richards believed that criticism has to address two questions: "what gives the experience of reading a certain poem its value?" and "how is this experience better than another?" (5). Richards's contribution to the New Criticism was two-fold: his departure from interpreting literature through history—he believed that "the permanence of some art has often been an excuse for fantastic hypothesis"—and his emphasis on the organic nature of the poem. Richards believed that "every poem . . . is a strictly limited piece of experience, a piece which breaks up more or less easily if alien elements intrude" (78).

Despite his espousal of what were to be New Critical principles, Richards can be seen more properly as the founder of reader-response theory. Indeed, a 1980 compilation of post-structuralist writings states that "reader-response criticism could be said to have started with I.A. Richards's discussion of emotional response in the 1920s" (Tompkins x). Richards's critical theory places primary emphasis on the reader's experience, that "the reader must be required to wear no blinkers, to overlook nothing which is relevant, to shut off no part of himself from participation" (80). Richards views the genesis of experience as being communication: "an experience has to be formed . . . before it is communicated, but it takes the form it does largely because it may have to be communicated" (25). Richards later posits that the experiences one has in reading are "exactly the same kinds as those that come to us in other ways" (78). In "Literature in the Reader," the second chapter of Text, Stanley Fish admits that Richards's "principle article of faith," his "talk of readers and responses . . . sounds very much like mine" (52). In the final analysis, however, Richards supports New Critical positions by stating that "within racial boundaries, and perhaps within the limits of certain very general types, many impulses are common to all men" (190). Richards believes that common experiences are important to understanding poetry because they lead to similar readings of a poem. This difference between him and most of the post-structuralists, including Fish, may have influenced Brooks's belief in the integrity of the literary text. Through his dual emphases—on the text and on the reader—Richards was important to the development, first, of Cleanth Brooks's unitary theory of interpretation and, second, of Stanley Fish's reader-response hermeneutics.

We are left, then, with separate critical performances from Brooks and Fish as avenues to some understanding of the complementarity of their positions and practices. Both have described and demonstrated their critical strategies in *The Well Wrought Urn* and *Is There a Text in This Class?*, with such parallel components as complementary prefaces in Brooks's **"The Problem of Belief and the Problem of Cognition"** and Fish's "Demonstration and Persuasion." Both situate themselves in relationship, often defensive in tone, to precursor critics; and both make the reader, whether Brooks's scholarly one or Fish's common reader, a powerful medium between the literary text and the world.

Brooks's preface to *The Well Wrought Urn* presents as the plan of the book to examine, in terms of a common approach, a number of celebrated English poems, taken in chronological order from the Elizabethan period to the present, to which he adds the following defensive caveat: "*Whether or not the approach is really a common approach, and whether or not the examination reveals that the poems possess some common structural properties, are matters for the reader to determine*" (ix, italics added). These poems are to be "the concrete examples on which generalizations are to be based."

Technical explanations are relegated to the appendix. Brooks's method opposes two extremes, the reading of the poem "in terms of its historical context" and the "relativistic" "temper of our times" (x). He intends to ask whether or not a poem can be read *sub specie aeternitatis* and whether or not a critic "can make normative judgments" (xi). As with almost all of Brooks's criticism, his tone is defensive in reaction to earlier critics; indeed the New Criticism, like its successor schools of critical theory *and* praxis, came into being to counter the prevailing notions of how to read literary texts. For Brooks, those strong precursors are historical-biographical critics who attribute the poem to events in the life of the poet.

Brooks then presents essays on Donne, Shakespeare, Milton, Pope, Gray, Wordsworth, Keats, Tennyson, and Yeats, followed by three theoretical treatises: **"The Heresy of Paraphrase"** and his two appendixes, **"Criticism, History, and Critical Relativism"** and **"The Problem of Belief."** In the first appendix, Brooks chiefly reacts to the "old historicists" who would assert that since the critic is "plainly the product of his own day and time," he or she cannot judge the poems in universal terms. Brooks interestingly admits that "the foregoing discussions of poetry may, indeed, be hopelessly subjective" but that "for better or worse, the judgments are rendered . . . as if they were universal judgments" (217); indeed, the notion of universal norms and criteria is at the center of Brooks's theory then and now. I. A. Richards is left out of this chapter because Brooks's objective is not consciously to attack affective criticism. It is principally in the chapter on **"Wordsworth and the Paradox of the Imagination"** that Brooks really addresses Richards, but always in reference to specific readings of particular poems rather than to debate on any theoretical level (140-49). Suffice to say that by Brooks's own admission, Richards played, along with Ransom, an important role in the formulation of his (Brooks's) critical position and, in individual acts of reading, was always to be taken into consideration in regard to a unitary interpretation of any text.

Fish's debt to his important precursors is set forth in his critical *Bildungsroman, Is There A Text in This Class?*. Fish very methodically outlines the evolution of his critical philosophy, beginning with the introductory chapter, "How I Stopped Worrying and Learned to Love Interpretation" (the allusion to *Dr. Strangelove* a clue to the playfully satiric tone of the volume). Herein Fish relates how he first jousted with the theories of Wimsatt and Beardsley (to which Brooks also adhered), stating that "in order to dislodge the affective fallacy, for example, one would have to show first that the text was not the self-sufficient repository of meaning and, second, that something else was, at the very least, contributory" (2). For Fish, that "something else" is the reader. He recounts how he "substituted the structure of the reader's experience for the formal structures of the text on the grounds that while

the latter were the more visible, they acquired significance only in the context of the former" (2). A crisis that arose when he realized that he was arguing for a literary theory which was an amalgam of New Criticism and post-structuralism was resolved in the end by stating:

> Whereas I had once agreed with my predecessors on the need to control interpretation lest it overwhelm and obscure texts, facts, authors, and intentions, I now believe that interpretation is the source of texts, facts, authors, and intentions. (16)

Because Text is admittedly subjective and autobiographical, it is not surprising that Fish somewhat defensively recollects his departure from the New Criticism. If "How I Stopped Worrying" is a *Bildungsroman,* the final two chapters, "What Makes an Interpretation Possible" and "Demonstration versus Persuasion. . . ." are Fish's apologia for his anti-New Critical, anti-formalist, and anti-post-structuralist beliefs. He states that "the first thing one must do is not assume that he is preaching to the converted. That means that whatever the point of view you wish to establish, you will have to establish it in the face of anticipated objections" (368).

Ultimately Fish resembles Cleanth Brooks in his desire not to be labeled as a particular type of critic; but whereas Brooks was resisting only one label (that of being typed a New Critic), Fish tries to resist being thrice-branded, as New Critic, formalist, *and* post-structuralist. The first threat is repelled by his confession of faith in everything antithetical to New Criticism. Fish believes he successfully avoids the formalist label "by displacing attention from the text, in its spatial configurations, to the reader and his temporal experience" (4). Finally, in "Normal Circumstances and Other Special Cases," he attempts to dissociate himself "from a certain characterization (actually a caricature) of the post-structuralist or Derridian position," which holds that "the denial of objective texts and determinate meanings leads to a universe of absolute free play in which everything is indeterminate and undecidable" (268). By positioning himself in opposition to most major schools of critical theory, Fish demonstrates, though quite genially, that his own theories depend on distancing strategies, born in anxieties of influence, though in full awareness of their antithetical conception. In "How I Stopped Worrying . . .", Fish admits that in the development of his reader-response hermeneutic, insofar as he and the New Critics agreed on the "integrity of the text," he was "more dependent on new critical principles than I was ready to admit" (7). Although Fish does not mention Brooks by name, he does position himself in opposition to his former teacher elsewhere in *Text,* in his reading of Milton's "L'Allegro" and "Il Penseroso" (about which more later) and in "What Makes an Interpretation Acceptable." In the latter essay, Fish differentiates between "a classroom whose authority figures include David Bleich and Norman

Holland, [where] a student might very well relate a text to her memories of a favorite aunt" and "classrooms, dominated by the spirit of Brooks and Warren [where] any such activity would immediately be dismissed as nonliterary, as something that isn't done"; in other words, Fish ends by agreeing with most of his contemporary theoreticians, that Brooks stands for the "monolithic or stable," forever opposed to any situation wherein the "unwritten rules of the literary game" are multifarious and (playfully) fluid (343).

If, however, there is any convergence in the ways that Brooks and Fish pursue the task of critical praxis, it must be demonstrated in comparable critical performances. To that purpose, one may usefully place *Is There a Text in this Class?* alongside **The Well Wrought Urn,** both of which combine in a collection of loosely related, separate essays a demonstration and collaboration of their authors' approaches. The two volumes are similarly structured, with both authors beginning most essays by aggressively confronting previous commentators on the texts under consideration. Moreover, Brooks and Fish have, to a considerable degree, centered their commentary on seventeenth-century English poetry, with Milton coming in for significant attention from both critics. Their essays on Milton's "L'Allegro" and "Il Penseroso" form, in fact, an interesting bond between the two volumes of criticism. The fact that these are paired meditation poems makes them a suitable ground for encountering the anxiety that may exist between Fish and Brooks. "Il Penseroso," in that it demonstrates the thoughtful, or critical mind at work, might be regarded as a trope on the critical act; therefore, when Fish opens "What it's Like to Read . . ." (which he calls "the purest example" of reader-response criticism [116]) with "I have only one point to make and everything else follows from it: *L'Allegro* is easier to read than *Il Penseroso*" (112), he indirectly reflects that *challenging* dis-ease. Moreover, Fish's choice of the two poems not only indicates that he, like Brooks, needs a conveniently delimiting poem (if he is to engage Milton within the boundaries of *Text*), but also that he (Fish) wants at the same time to confront Cleanth Brooks.

Brooks's essay, **"The Light Symbolism in 'L'Allegro-Il Penseroso,"** begins in conventional fashion by placing his own reading in the context of earlier efforts by Samuel Johnson, who is said to be "about the critic's proper job": to "inspect the poems" but "not emote over them" (50), and in contrast to those after Johnson who merely express appreciation without calling for "careful reading" (51). His real point of departure is E.M.W. Tillyard, who, in Brooks's opinion, comes "close to the main matter" in "pointing our close connections" between Milton's companion poems. His own reading defends a unitary thesis, positing that "the light-shade imagery amounts to a symbolism" and that this symbolism is related ultimately to the "meaning of the poem, including its tone" (52-53). For Brooks, Milton has produced one

poem in which there is a "tension between two choices . . . which can appeal to the same mind" (rather than a contrast between two different minds) (53). The remainder of the essay develops in detail what Brooks sees as balancing qualities (positive-negative, involved-detached, etc.), by which "Milton's oppositions tend to come together" (56), as well as "cross over" tendencies, whereby antithetical elements bring the two poems together in less obvious ways (57-59). For Brooks, revealing Milton's overweening principle of unifying "patterns of opposites" undercuts critics' charges that Milton has thrown "materials into the double poem 'every which way'" and thereby undercut the "total effect" of one poem (57). The essay climaxes on an assertion that the light symbolism to be found in both poems in turn unifies the contrasting patterns of opposites, that one, not two, perceiving but detached individual undergoes an aesthetic experience both as happy and as pensive man:

If both poems are characterized by a leisurely flowing movement as the spectator in each case drifts from pleasure to pleasure, and if in both poems he is the detached spectator— not the participant in the world he wanders through—. . . the spectator moves through what are [in both poems] predominantly half lights. It is as if the half-lights were being used in both poems as a sort of symbol of the aesthetic distance which the cheerful man, no less than the pensive man, consistently maintains. (59)

The essay ends by positing intertexual relationships between the paradoxical light-dark symbolism of "L'Allegro-Il Penseroso" and *Paradise Lost* in the establishment of the central paradox in Milton's poetic vision (66). By the end of this masterful essay, not only the two companion poems but Milton's entire opus has become in effect a single "poem."

Brooks provides further insight into his method, or rather betrays its central vulnerability, when he observes in **"What Does Poetry Communicate?"** that the reader of convoluted poetry, the one capable of "untangling" Milton's complex imagery, or that of any paradoxical poet, is likely to be, not the common reader, but a highly erudite one, a professor of English like himself (75).

For Fish, the ground of his confrontation with Brooks resides, obviously, in his assumption that, in contrast to Brooks, he is dealing with two very different poems, one ("L'Allegro") which cannot be the object of critical analysis and another ("Il Penseroso") which must be. In the introduction to *Text,* he takes on all those precursor critics who have "mistakenly" attempted critical reading of "L'Allegro":

> . . . that as a poem whose parts are arranged in such a way as to exert no interpretive pressures it is unavailable to criticism insofar as interpretation is its

only mode. It follows then that since others who have written on the poem have to a man sought to interpret it, they are necessarily wrong. (6)

Brooks is, of course, among such critics; but interestingly enough, Fish is united with Brooks in his desire to protect the poems from the adverse comments of "the critics [who] are moved to fault the poem for a lack of unity," but Fish would—and here he means Brooks—also guard it from those who "supply the unity by supplying connections more firm and delimiting than the connections available in the text." They do this, not because they read differently, but because of "their critical preconceptions" (6). Looking back upon the time he wrote his essay on "L'Allegro," Fish is prepared to admit that at the time he had wanted to "posit an object in relation to which readers' activities could be declared uniform, and that object was the text; . . . but this meant that the integrity of the text was as basic to my position as it was to the position of the New Critics." He found that he could not both declare his "opposition to new critical principles and . . . the integrity of the text." Fish goes on to describe how he escaped this *cul de sac,* his primary enterprise being to distance himself from Brooks and his theories, thereby freeing the reader "from the tyranny of the text" (7).

In "What It's Like to Read L'*Allegro,*" Fish does not overtly make Brooks his point of departure; rather he goes farther back to an exchange in the TLS of Oct-Nov 1934 (about line 46, concerning who comes to the window) in order to maintain that all the readings concede to alternate readings, provide supporting details from the poem, then try to make sense of the ambiguity by rewriting the poem so as to "arrange the images and events into a sequence of logical action" (116). When he does mention Brooks by name, it is to declare, respectfully, that "Cleanth Brooks is not quite right when he declares that the unreproved pleasures of L'*Allegro* 'can be had for the asking'; they can be had *without* the asking" (118-119). Through this mild assertion, Fish denies overtly the text's dominance over the reader while covertly deflecting any dominance which Brooks, through his reading, might have over his (Fish's) critical enterprise. Fish agrees, however, that one task of the reader-critic is to deal with ambiguity, that his approach does not point to one "meaning" or "belief" (117); but he does not deny that the text has meaning (117). He does posit "a unity not of form but of experience" and a subject, "freedom" (124). These two admissions, that a unitary response is possible and that ambiguity exists, complement the most important principles in Brooks's theories.

In "Il Penseroso," Fish sees a [calculated?] "pressure" on the reader to interpret the poem which is absent from "L'Allegro" (128). "L'Allegro" is therefore easier to read than "Il Penseroso" (112-113) because, although they are companion poems,

1. their light-shadow imagery is an "opposing" pattern (Brooks calls it a shared pattern);

2. the poems proceed from two different mindsets, with "L'Allegro's" being careless and constant shifting, in an associated "series of discrete parts" (nobody's home), while "Il Penseroso's" is a melancholy "fixed mind" (Brooks's "observer" appears in both poems).

Fish concludes by stating that "'L'Allegro' and 'Il Penseroso' are the reader; that is, they stand for modes of being which the reader realizes in his response to the poems bearing their names," and that the formal and thematic features of each poem are intimately related to their meanings (132). At no other point in the essay is Fish closer to Cleanth Brooks, whose idea of an ideal reader likewise posits a unitary response when the poems are, as Brooks insists must be, read as one poem. Brooks's "spectator" thereby becomes Fish's reader! Fish remains adamant, however, in his belief that each reader can and will formulate a different reading of this or any literary text.

Close examination of these two essays—Brooks's **"The Light Symbolism in 'L'Allegro-Il Penseroso"** and Fish's "What It's Like to Read L'*Allegro* and *Il Penseroso*" suggests some similarities in method: close reading, often lifting discrete words and phrases out of context; stressing functional ambiguities in contexts; (with differing emphases) considering reading as an ongoing process; and insisting (again with differing emphasis) on the authenticity and primacy of the text. Not surprisingly, although Fish firmly asserts against Brooks and others that it is the reader who produces the text, the two critics come to some similar conclusions about what is occurring in the poems. We would agree with Ralph Rader, whom Fish answers in "A Reply to Ralph Rader," that Fish is very much a formalist and that his method is indebted to the New Criticism (142-43).

As key essays within their respective larger collections, the two essays on Miltonic texts underscore the underlying bond between Cleanth Brooks and Stanley Fish. Although neither Brooks nor Fish ceased to develop and practice his theories after (respectively) *The Well Wrought Urn* and Is *There A Text in This Class*?, these books occupy comparable positions in their development as critics. Both grew out of teaching situations; both demonstrate *and* defend basic hermeneutical strategies; both carry titles (*the* "Urn" and *a* "Text") which metaphorically signify the desired results of their critical enterprises.

At this point it is fitting to avoid closure by enlarging the scope of this study. We have attempted to demonstrate linkages between the allegedly antipodal positions of Cleanth Brooks and his former "reader" Stanley Fish. If Bloomian anxieties form only ephemeral linkages, surely similarities in style, graphic organization of their research, and similar fields of expertise create startlingly tangible connections. We have attempted to demonstrate that Fish's reader-response theory may be seen as an outgrowth of Brooks's New Criticism, with I.A. Richards forming an unlikely bond between the two. This continuum rubs against the thinking of those contemporary theorists who disavow any debt to the New Criticism by reasserting its continuing vitality. In common with Brooks's New Critical praxis, Fish's reader-response hermeneutic positions in the first act of reading an attempt to grasp the organicity of the text. That subsequent readings may discover flaws or fragments only reinforces the assumption that, for both critics, a self-supporting textual structure can exist, one upon which an informed or experienced reader may agree. In this context, the New Criticism clearly stands as the fountainhead of, if not all post-modern critical theory, certainly, through the unconscious bonds uniting Cleanth Brooks and Stanley Fish, the school of reader-response.

Cleanth Brooks with William J. Spurlin (interview date 1995)

SOURCE: "Afterword: An Interview with Cleanth Brooks," in *The New Criticism and Contemporary Literary Theory,* edited by William J. Spurlin and Michael Fisher, Garland Publishing, New York City, 1995, pp. 365-83.

[*In the following interview, Brooks and Spurlin discuss the response of other writers to the New Criticism.*]

The following conversation was conducted in the home of Cleanth Brooks in New Haven, Connecticut in October 1993. Prior to the meeting, Professor Brooks read the essays in Part III of this volume. Professor Brooks, after a distinguished writing and teaching career, died on May 10, 1994 at the age of eighty-seven. I am grateful for his comments and suggestions on the final draft of this interview.

[*Spurlin:*] *Professor Brooks, your work and the work of your fellow New Critics has not only influenced other literary critics, theorists, and scholars, but generations of literature students and teachers; indeed, the close reading of texts is a method that many of us have grown up with. But at the same time, you, René Wellek, and others have expressed concern about the difficulty of grouping together the New Critics as a monolithic group. For instance, you have pointed out that Allen Tate was interested in literary history and biography and I. A. Richards paid a great deal of attention to the reader. How did the New Criticism get its name? Could you talk about how it got started as a movement and what you specifically contributed to it? Did it, as far as you remember, have a common pursuit or agenda?*

[Brooks:] I can tell you that quite easily. John Ransom in 1941 published a book called *The New Criticism.* Its principal chapters deal with Yvor Winters, I. A. Richards, T. S. Eliot, Robert Penn Warren, William Empson, and the rest of us. If one reads with any care, one immediately sees that Ransom has several disagreements with these critics which he states in that book. His final chapter is called "Wanted: An Ontological Critic." I don't think he ever really gives a very clear definition of what he means by an ontological critic. "Ontological" here has to do with essence, the very being of literature. He thought that none of the critics with whom he was dealing in the book had really done that; one was too psychological, another was too historical, still another was too moralistic, and so on. The title of the essay implies that he has not found an ontological critic. What is it exactly that a New Critic does? Ransom never says.

Well, that book came out and the literary world was just aching for a name to attach to those names I just mentioned and to lesser folk like myself. We were all somehow out of line with how most graduate students had been trained. There was this funny thing going around and people asked, "What do you call this damn thing?" And they needed a term; no one at the time really knew what it meant, except that they didn't like what we were doing! Actually, had people been more careful about it, they would have noticed that these so-called New Critics differed among themselves.

As far as some sort of common pursuit is concerned, I think it is safe to say that these people generally took the text very seriously. One way to jump off of this is to assume that because of their *primary* interest in the text, the New Critics despised history. I don't despise history at all; I've written a hell of a lot of material on history as in my last book *Historical Evidence and the Reading of Seventeenth-Century Poetry* [University of Missouri Press, 1991]. When one looks at the last edition of *Understanding Poetry,* it is clear that Warren and I knew a lot of history and pointed out places where we thought it might be significant in relation to the text under study.

Ransom told me, not once but several times, that when he wrote *The New Criticism* he meant the kind of criticism that was being written by current critics of the time—Warren, Richards, Winters, Eliot, myself, and others. But the damage was done; I'm not blaming him for it, you understand. Anyway, he wrote a book called *The New Criticism,* and that's how the title got attached. It was not a name we used to describe ourselves. If one wants to attach a name to this group at all, then one must decide what are the things that bind it together; it's difficult because they're different in a lot of ways. I myself have felt for a long time, and still feel, that the term has done damage. It seems that none of us have ever claimed much about the *newness* or novelty of the New Criticism. What was so new about it? A lot of the things that we talked about are as old as Aristotle; for example, the worth of *Oedipus Rex,* or any play, is not in the artistic intentions of Sophocles or in the historical influences on him; the worth of the play is based on its cohesion, its complexity, its tightness, and so on. Now I don't say that everybody ought to agree with that. But my point is that this is not decidedly new if Aristotle also said these things, too. Also, it isn't fair to say that because the so-called New Critics didn't centrally address such factors as history, the socio-political influences on the author, and the effect of the work on the reader, it means that they were not at all interested in those things.

> **[John Ransom] wrote a book called *The New Criticism,* and that's how the title got attached. It was not a name we used to describe ourselves. If one wants to attach a name to this group at all, then one must decide what are the things that bind it together; it's difficult because they're different in a lot of ways. I myself have felt for a long time, and still feel, that the term has done damage.**
> **—*Cleanth Brooks***

Wasn't Ransom your teacher at Vanderbilt?

Yes, though I had only one course with him. Actually, I took a previous course with him and I found it was over my head; I wasn't ready for it, so I dropped out! The course I took with him later was a course in creative writing; I hope it improved my writing . . . I don't know . . . I wrote some poems for him. . . . He was not a flamboyant teacher. But it was not until I had long left Vanderbilt and was teaching myself that I at last got to know John and we then became very good friends. Actually, I would say that I didn't get to know John Ransom until well after I had published my first critical book. When I was at Oxford, he was in England for a year. He came to visit me at Oxford. But my critical position is much different from his. In reading John, one notices that he is constantly talking about the difference between meaning (or sense) and other rhetorical qualities in poetry. I think this is dualism and I reject it. In poetry, I think form and content become pretty thoroughly merged and I prefer not to split them apart; they define each other. A good poem is an object in which form and content can be distinguished but cannot really be separated. For example, a good metaphor is not really "decorating" the sense of the poem, it is conveying the sense in a special way. Anyway, this is a major difference between the critical positions of John Ransom and my own.

The New Criticism was mainly concerned with the detail of

the text which was very different from the kind of literary work that was going on before it. In one sense, perhaps, this is what made it so "new," but that needs to be further explored. The tone, rhythm, and the ways in which things are said convey meaning, too. Take Keats's *Ode on a Grecian Urn.* I have much respect for T. S. Eliot as a critic, but I don't agree with his interpretation of this poem. At the end of the poem, we get the lines "Beauty is truth, truth beauty,— that is all/Ye know on earth, and all ye need to know." To Eliot, Keats is becoming a philosopher and saying "Beauty is truth and truth is beauty," and in that sense that is all you're going to know about philosophy. And that's enough. But I think it is altogether different; that's too easy. The urn is the poem itself, from the beginning it is speaking to us. These last lines are not being spoken by Keats, but by the urn. What is a Greek urn, beautifully shaped, equipped to teach you? It will give you some perception of Greek culture and life, and perhaps of our own culture and life through its beautiful and accurate representation. This raises broader philosophical questions, such as what is the relationship between humankind and art. What can one expect to gain from art?

So as you have just illustrated with your reading of Keats's Ode on a Grecian Urn and Eliot's reading, it is possible to have more than one reading of a text. One reaction against the New Criticism is that it proliferated monolithic, unitary, singular readings of texts. . . .

Of course, there may be multiple readings. But of those multiple readings, you may find that some are much more satisfactory than others.

So, the notion of multiple readings doesn't imply that all readings are equally valid?

Oh, no. But as great a critic as Eliot was, I think my reading of the urn poem is better than his reading. It makes more sense in the poem, it sees it as a whole. I prefer to see it that way. I can make a good argument for that reading. I taught poems like this for many years starting at Louisiana State University. We were teaching LSU sophomores how to read poetry. But I couldn't claim as their teacher that I knew all the answers. I believe that as I went along I kept discovering things that I had earlier missed.

I think the decentering of the teacher's authority that you just mentioned is something that one doesn't normally associate with the New Criticism. This leads to my next question. Although the New Criticism has been under attack, which we will talk about shortly (and to which I am sure you have your own response!), the New Criticism began as a critique against the positivism of historical literary scholarship and the vagueness of impressionistic criticism. I think it is interesting that while many forms of current politically-

oriented criticism, such as feminist criticism, lesbian and gay studies, African-American criticism, and the work of other minorities, hope to democratize the study of literature, the New Criticism in its own time attempted to make literary study available to a broader range of students. There was, I think, a democratic impulse although now that impulse has come to be understood and represented as a hegemonic one. I was wondering, assuming that my assumptions, both historical and philosophical, are accurate, if you think the New Criticism achieved its democratic aim?

Well, we still have historical criticism today, don't we, although with perhaps more of a political focus. Some people cast Shakespeare as an imperialist, asking why he gave us a Caliban, for instance. To be sure, literary works can have political influences or effects and/or be read through specific political or sociological frameworks. This is very different from the way that I have spoken of literature because I am concerned not with the political effect, but with the literary effect of the work concerned.

Concerning the historicists and philologists, we never intended to displace historical literary study. This notion that some group, some conspiracy, some clan, some elite club is trying to over-run the academy is nonsense; we were a bunch of people trying to make a living! We weren't demanding power. I got my first job at LSU in 1932 and [Robert Penn] Warren joined me there in 1934. He said he was fired from Vanderbilt. It was difficult during the Depression to get any kind of work. My friends and I, there were maybe a dozen of us in all, enjoyed reading literature, especially poetry, and we were discovering new ways of reading it freshly, and perhaps more powerfully, and sharing this with other people.

But maybe the intention of the New Critics was not to displace historical literary scholarship or to change the course of literary study. But can't we look back and study its effects, how it shaped and influenced literary studies?

Sure, and you're quite right to raise that. I do know that Warren and I reached a lot of people through our books, especially through **Understanding Poetry.** Perhaps these were the vehicles of dissemination. The approaches taken by many of the teachers who had been influenced by the books may have opened up new doors and windows to the study of literature. It's hard to say for sure. . . .

But did the New Criticism, because it wasn't specifically geared to the literary specialist, enable people to read texts beyond the classroom so that perhaps the reading of literature became something more than just an academic exercise confined to the classroom, to the library, or to the university?

Yes, I think you're right. We didn't demand as much library

or technical or historical work as other teachers might have at the time.

And closely related to this, the New Criticism theorized a close relation to pedagogy and teaching . . .

Yes, of course it did.

William Cain remarks in the essay he has written for this volume that both you and your colleague, Robert Penn Warren, originally prepared **Understanding Poetry** *for your students at Louisiana State University, and that for Warren criticism was "an extension of teaching." But you have also written that the New Criticism has often been reduced or simplified to a classroom strategy. What are your thoughts on the relation between the critical disciplines of criticism and pedagogy?*

I would say this. All of us have strategies for teaching. I have always enjoyed teaching, I've done it for more than fifty years; I don't think it should be a drudging art. I admit that sometimes the way it is done, it is a drudging art! While the New Criticism has often been ridiculed as being elitist, I think the worst kind of elitism is to scorn careful reading. The teacher needs to be able to have an understanding of literature in its many and diverse forms in order to be able to teach it. While it is important to listen to how students respond to texts, it is not sufficient to simply toss a text to a class and ask students what they think of it and stop there. The teacher, too, has to struggle with *careful* reading him/herself. It is an oversimplification to assume, on the other hand, that just because the text is important, other things, such as context, social issues, history, the reader, the biography and intentions of the author, and so on, are not. It doesn't follow that we can simply ignore these things in order to make the point that the text is important. At the time we were writing, the text was not getting the attention we thought it should be receiving.

In my own training at Vanderbilt, my course work in English was mostly what we then called the old-fashioned criticism. We learned about the author, the historical background, and the ideas of the time. When I did the B.A. (Hons.) degree at Oxford, we had the same kinds of courses. Things were starting to change at Cambridge with Richards and Empson there, but not at Oxford. Empson was an interesting person; he was one of Richards's students initially. Empson was also different; earlier I pointed out that there were differences among us. He was much more radical. He once shared with Richards a book he had read written in America by Laura Riding and Robert Graves entitled *A Pamphlet Against Anthologies* [Garden City, NY: Doubleday, Doran and Company, 1928]. Riding and Graves had taken one of Shakespeare's sonnets to pieces and rebuilt it again to show how deep and how rich it was—in other words, they did what we might call a "New Critical" reading. But they didn't call it that, of course. Empson told Richards that he could do what Riding and Graves had done with one poem with any poem in the English language. Richards challenged him to go and do it, and three weeks later Empson had the groundwork for *Seven Types of Ambiguity* done!

Anyway, to get back to the point; I had a solid academic literary background, but something was missing. At Tulane, I was in a very good graduate class in eighteenth-century British literature. Once in a while, we had to write a paper on a particular author and off to the library we went to look up information about that author and his (or her, but, unfortunately, the authors we studied in this particular period were all men) work. At one point, I became friends with a very bright woman in the class. Sometimes she would ask me if I thought a particular author was a good author, if the works this particular person wrote were good or not. I suddenly realized that, as students, we were assuming that the only way to get to know if a work was a good one or not was to look up what other people had said about it or to depend on what the teacher told us about it in class. The classes we were attending were not providing us the opportunity to learn this for ourselves, to make judgments. I began to continually ask the question "What makes a good poem?" And if I liked it, I would then ask "Why do I like it?" "Why does it capture my attention?"

Perhaps the earlier way of teaching literature did not provide the opportunity, then, to ask these kinds of questions?

Well, you could, but no one was asking them then! And the books I was reading didn't address these questions.

Well, as you know, the topic for this volume is the connections and continuities between the New Criticism and contemporary theory. One connection that seems obvious to me, perhaps because of my own work in reader-oriented theories of literature, is the role of the reader in shaping, contributing to, or possibly configuring meaning. Do you, as you and your colleagues are often accused, consider the text to be autonomous in and of itself; is it an artifact to be contemplated with its own self-contained meaning, or is this an institutional simplification of the New Criticism (and, by implication, the affective fallacy)?

I think it is very interesting to ask how readings change over time and to try to account for the change. For example, the interpretations of a text, say, in the 1930s, may be dramatically different in the 1960s because of the influence of the social context in which the work is received. I can also imagine a situation where the writer comments on what he or she intended to convey through the work but the reader comes up with different readings. It is interesting to try to account

for this gap. But this does not, and should not, replace close and careful reading.

So, there does seem to be some space for the reader to freely imagine, then, in transacting with the text at least in the way that you are theorizing reading. Often people cite the affective fallacy as proof that the New Critics believed that the reader's role is very minimal—to extract a pre-existing meaning.

As with the intentional fallacy, I think that Bill Wimsatt's [and Monroe C. Beardsley's] essays ["The Intentional Fallacy" and "The Affective Fallacy"] aim to guard us from moving too far away from the text. They are not saying that authors don't have intentions and that we cannot try to study them, and they are certainly not implying that we are not affected by what we read. The reader's role is a very important one; it is to realize the work, to find a meaning, an experience, a judgment. And I would say that all three of these are interrelated, they don't exist separately. The text isn't realized as long as the words are just lying there on the page. The moment one looks at and tries to put it together, the moment when that transaction takes place, the process of realization begins.

I think a lot of the trouble and misunderstandings, like the one I just mentioned regarding the essays "The Intentional Fallacy" and "The Affective Fallacy," arise because people assumed that the New Criticism was a well-oiled machine that could crank out unproblematic meanings. I think many people still assume this about the New Criticism. But New Critical writing is more of a set of suggestions for reading.

Yes, and closely related to this point about the role of the reader, Patricia Clark Smith has identified her pedagogical space in the oscillation between teaching her students the tools of close reading and paying attention to detail, which she learned from the New Critics, and listening to the ideas and details students bring to the text, paying equal attention to what texts evoke in them. What do you think of her approach?

That's perfectly legitimate. As I've said, the reader's role is to realize the work. Often my own students would come to me and ask me what I thought of their interpretations and often I was surprised by the astuteness of their readings, of their seeing things that I had not seen before. But we have got to get out of the machine-age mentality. The New Criticism was not foolproof; there were plenty of opportunities for mistakes, errors, and omissions, which some of the work going on now has pointed out. The multicultural debates going on now are important, but I worry that they may run the risk of setting people apart rather than bringing them together. I would hate to think that we would get to the point where can no longer understand each other. We do see the world differently from our various perspectives, but we mustn't forget about how various groups may also be capable of more or less similar understandings.

Do you think that there is any risk of solipsism or an "anything goes" approach to literary study which is often the critique given to reader-oriented theories of literature and to classroom practices that attempt to create spaces for a more productive role on the part of the reader/student?

There is a risk to "anything goes" if we believe we can abandon altogether the text, history, and so on. Our technocratic world emphasizes means and how to get things done. We tend to think that we know what we want and it is just a matter of getting there; hence, the well-oiled machine of which I used to speak of the reception and use of the New Criticism earlier. But with this said, and getting back to this critique of reader-oriented theory as running the risk of an "anything goes" approach to reading and to literature, I believe that while we cannot discount the role of the text in reading, the text, at the same time, is not some kind of sanctified object outside of any relation to the world. That would be silly. What I'm trying to say is that we need to take the text seriously to avoid this "anything goes" you mention and then ask what responses are possible. We need to work *hard* and read *hard*.

This brings to mind an experience from my own teaching. For a while, after I had finished my undergraduate work, I taught Sixth Form English in Singapore. We were reading King Lear *and one of my students theorized that Cordelia was the villain of the play. The student's defense was based on the high value given to filial piety in Eastern cultures, which she felt Cordelia should have observed. Her interpretation was also a critique of the high value we place on the individual over the social in the West. Not yet having the critical discourse of theory, I was somewhat jarred by this interpretation, mostly because it was so eloquently argued, because it made sense in the context of an Eastern culture, and because it made me realize the role culture plays in reading. More importantly, it brought my pedagogical authority to crisis; I began to question my position as a teacher from a Western culture approaching the play from a humanist perspective whereby Cordelia is thought to be virtuous and the means and source of Lear's deterioration and regeneration. Are issues such as these important to consider?*

I've never heard that particular interpretation either. Culture does play a role and this is a point well worth making. If a culture places a high value on something such as piety to the parent, then this needs to be taken into account in terms of how people from that culture interpret the text.

Despite popular assumptions that deconstruction and the

New Criticism are antithetical, some contemporary critics, such as Frank Lentricchia in After the New Criticism, *Gerald Graff in* Professing Literature, *and in their essays in this volume, Paul Bové and William Cain, have commented on how deconstruction is not remarkably different from the New Criticism. In fact, Professor Cain has indicated in his essay that Robert Penn Warren accounted for the indeterminacy of language and the instabilities of poetic structures, and that these views would be used by later post-structuralists to contest New Critical authority. And a deconstructionist himself, J. Hillis Miller, in* The Ethics of Reading *and elsewhere, has argued that even though language is unstable and indeterminate, we are not exonerated from reading carefully, persistently, and patiently, which seems very similar to what you have said about reading a little while ago. How are the deconstructionists different from or similar to what you and your colleagues believed about language?*

Yes, in saying that one cannot find a perfect meaning of a poem, or to say that language is unstable and indeterminate, does not mean that one cannot perform an adequate or careful reading. I don't think any and all readings are valid as I've said before. The text may set limits, but that still leaves the reader plenty of room. We can say "I think this poem has this meaning," but in this very utterance, we are not saying what a text means *absolutely*. Give yourself twenty-five years, and you may discover, as I have, that you see the poem in an entirely different way. We need to be open to other readings but not accept them wholeheartedly and uncritically. People need to come together with their divergent readings and discuss them and argue them out. Actually, someone is interested in publishing some of my correspondence with Robert Penn Warren. In one of his letters, Warren told me that criticism for him was a social act; what he said he liked best was to get together with someone in a room who was different from him and read a play, novel, poem, or whatever, and talk about it, and argue over it, and fight over it, and see where they agree and disagree. That, for him, was criticism.

Yes, well, earlier you mentioned that one reaction to the New Criticism was one of suspicion and disturbance. A lot of people have also reacted to post-modern theory that way as well . . .

Yes, I'm disturbed by the deconstructionists. And that's exactly what I call it—disturbance. I've tried to read them, it's impossible to understand them, and therefore I'm disturbed!

I see. So, history may be repeating itself then? The audiences that first received you as the New Criticism was gaining influence were very much "disturbed" and perhaps a bit intimidated by you and what you were up to. . . .

But I'm such a mild little creature, really. A little white mouse . . .

But it wasn't you physically; what was frightening, perhaps, was the newness of your ideas which had tremendous influence. . . . Well, I did say we would get to some of the critiques! Reginald Martin, in his essay "New Criticism and New Black Aesthetic Criticism: Debts and Disagreements," has criticized the New Criticism as self-reifying in practice, that is, that the "universality" of literature in general or a text or set of texts in particular was appropriated by the New Critics themselves which simultaneously, though perhaps unintentionally, excluded alternative forms of expression such as texts by black writers, as well as the experiences of blacks and meanings evoked in texts by black readers. How do you respond to the notion that what is posited as "universal" or "common" may be culturally loaded, subject to the biases of, let us say, Anglo-Americans in the case of literatures by ethnic minorities?

Yes, I see the point. But I've never considered myself to be in a position of power. In fact, Warren and I challenged a lot of old-fashioned powerful figures. If I could live longer, I would like to be able to contribute to a broader idea of the universal. I understand the difficulty; we need more voices represented. I think it is coming about however. I'm pleased that Toni Morrison received the Nobel Prize in Literature last week. On the other hand, when I look over the list of English [course] offerings at Yale I am sometimes shocked. There is a lot in there that looks more like politics and sociology to me than literature.

But Virginia Woolf, for instance, in discussing Jane Austen in A Room of One's Own, *describes how difficult it was for women to write in the late eighteenth and early nineteenth century and how Austen herself was confined to writing in the sitting-room, hiding her manuscripts from others, as if there was something discreditable in writing. Perhaps she internalized a social attitude toward women writing; we don't know for sure. Yet, despite this, and given her domestic duties and her overseeing of the household and the servants, which were obligatory for women of her social class, she still found time to write. While Austen has obviously left her mark on the English canon, Woolf hints, I think, that Austen could perhaps have been even a better writer had she been able to overcome the narrow life imposed upon her. Or, to give a better example, Woolf mentions how difficult, how impossible, it would have been for a woman in Shakespeare's time who had Shakespeare's literary ability to write; the social conditions of the sixteenth century did not provide that kind of artistic space for women. Does the "literary" have some relation to the political then? Mightn't literary study be part of a socialization into the dominant culture? Is that what it should do?*

I'm not sure. We cannot dispute that mistakes have been made in the past. Two of my best friends were Eudora Welty and Katherine Anne Porter. They were both fine women writers. We tried to print as much of their work as we could in *The Southern Review* to help start their careers. I'm not taking credit for their success, you understand. But they were good writers and we were honored to have their work. We were not part of any conspiracy against women. . . .

Yes, but I'd like to come back to this notion of the universal so that you have the opportunity to address some of the critiques of the New Criticism, which I don't think are meant to be malicious attacks, but ways to get us to consider the limits of formalism, and how race and gender, for example, may become critical questions in the study of literature without necessarily becoming exclusively political and having no relevance to literary study. Can culture or cultural works be conceived of in the absence of the social and political? Annette Kolodny, in the essay we have reprinted in this volume, as well as other feminist work, has mentioned how students are being taught to read texts from points of view that are put across as "universal," but are often very particular in that they may be masculinist, Western, white, and/or heterosexist.

Well, at the time we were writing, to be honest, it didn't occur to us to write about race and gender. This does not mean, however, that we were racist or sexist. Warren was especially involved in many of the political movements in the South. We tried to get as many female authors as possible published in *The Southern Review*. In my classes and seminars at Yale, I generally found my female students to be much more articulate, much more savvy than my male students. But you are right, I think, that the term "universal" might be loaded culturally, socially, and so on, and we have to use these terms loosely. Regarding your point about certain ideas being put across to students as universal, I think we need to get back to the idea of critical pedagogy. Once again, I think teachers tend to simplify in the classroom because they are in search of that elusive well-oiled machine that the New Criticism or any other method of reading simply cannot provide. We have to help students get *really* close to a text, to help them find something over which to ponder.

I think the last point you made is an important one and I would like to come back to it. Coming back to some of these social and political issues, which are very much at the forefront of contemporary theory and literary and cultural studies, Michael Fischer, in his essay "The New Criticism in the New Historicism," speaks of Jerome McGann's implicit criticism of the New Criticism by arguing that if one pays attention primarily to the text, to its complexity, detail, and metaphorical richness, this could potentially mask certain other issues such as anti-Semitism, racism, fascism, and so on. Similarly, Patricia Clark Smith admits that as a student in 1959, she didn't have to think about Amy Lowell's lesbianism if texts existed independent of their authors; her New Critical training kind of got her "off the hook" in this regard. What are your thoughts on the idea that some texts may call for political rather than pure aesthetic responses?

That's a rather impossible thing to hand on anyone. Yes, in focusing on certain things, such as the complexity of a text, or the role of the reader, or the role of the author, and so on, we may neglect or not pay as close attention to other things. But the question is whether the masking that you mention is conscious or deliberate on the part of the critic. I think there is too much of an attempt to find as many things as possible wrong with this loose band of people we call the New Critics.

I don't think the issue is that the New Critics themselves consciously tried to mask political issues by arguing for close, careful readings of texts. But I think some people assume that if they focus, say, on the lesbianism of a poet, the New Critic will admonish them for committing the intentional fallacy. Mightn't this appeal to the intentional fallacy serve to effectively keep issues of race, gender, and sexuality safely out of discussion?

Of course the claim of lesbianism can be made. But one must argue, I think, how it operates in and relates to the *text* in question. We may learn much more about the author; we need to ask what more we learn about the poetry. It is too easy to slap labels on to things. Critical debates are not necessarily resolved by consulting the author. Years ago, in 1937, I wrote an account of Eliot's *Waste Land*. I wrote a letter to Eliot asking him to read it and to comment on it if he had the time. He wrote back and said that he thought my account was very good and that it was a good way to handle the poem. I decided not to print that letter because I did not want to bolster my interpretation by having the approval of the author. I also, quite honestly, didn't want to appear to be a young man riding on the coat-tails of this great poet. Many people still disagree with my reading of *The Waste Land,* and, for what it's worth, I've got the approval of the author. Do we necessarily resolve critical argument and debate by appealing to the author, his or her biography, and so on? It's an important question to ask.

Yes, I see your point. Throughout our discussion, you have mentioned that you do not undervalue the role of history in literary study. In their arguments over historicism in this book, Michael Fischer claims that you have minimized the importance of historical facts in poetry, and Jerome McGann has critiqued the historical determinacy of "facts" as "a function of the conceptual (ideological) frame in which they are viewed and manipulated." I was wondering if your views have in any way changed regarding the influence of the historical period in which the work was produced

in the positivist sense, and whether you think the act of criticism can transcend the historical (and therefore political, ideological, material, and cultural) contingencies of reading, which is a question a New Historicist might ask.

I'll be brief. History means a story, it is a narrative, a text; it isn't necessarily claiming to be the truth. Some people may think history is true in an absolutist sense, but I don't think this is what history has ever tried to claim. I agree that we can only see the past through our own biases and perspectives in the present. But this should not exonerate us from the attempt to try and understand past events.

I'd like to come back to a point you made a little earlier about helping students get close to a text and find something over which to ponder because it brings us once again back to pedagogy, to the classroom, which is where I'd like to end. Patricia Clark Smith pays tribute to her teacher, W.K. Wimsatt, for teaching her to pay attention to detail. Her essay is also about her transition from being a graduate student at Yale to a young faculty member at the University of New Mexico where she also taught Native American students on a Navajo reservation. She acknowledges that her training in the New Criticism at Yale, while valuable, was not sufficient for her to teach literature in a multicultural context. Smith says she had to abandon her "prissiness about various heresies and fallacies" (perhaps invoking your essay "The Heresy of Paraphrase" and the Wimsatt and Beardsley essays "The Intentional Fallacy" and "The Affective Fallacy"). What are your thoughts on the New Criticism with regard to the teaching of literature to culturally diverse student populations?

The teacher would have to decide for him or herself what may be valuable from the New Criticism. The New Criticism is not asking the teacher to make the sign of the cross every time he or she comes to that word. It is very much interested in you as the teacher finding out not just what the words in the text may mean to you as a person, but what they may *potentially* mean for audiences to whom they are addressed, in this case students. We need to tell students honestly that what is said in class about the text is not necessarily the poem, the realization of the work. That's what I was trying to say about the heresy of paraphrase, because for a long time no distinction was made between the realization of the work and a paraphrase of the text. We mustn't forget the reader's role in the process just because we're concerned with looking closely at the text. There is a difference between looking closely at the text and looking at it exclusively and seeing nothing else.

So, once again, New Critical work was not exclusively concerned with the text itself. Since this book is about how the New Criticism has influenced contemporary theory, what are your final thoughts on theory; do you as a New Critic feel that you have been influenced in any way by theory as it is practiced today or in general?

Oh, yes. But, remember theory is by no means a recent phenomenon. Actually, we could say that everything one does in the field of literary studies is based on some sort of theoretical orientation. Now, I did not intend to write theory per se, but certainly a theory of literature, as well as a theory of reading, history, authorship, and so on, is implied in my work as we have been discussing this afternoon. Others, such as René Wellek and Austin Warren, in their book *Theory of Literature* [New York: Harcourt, Brace and Company, 1942], dealt more directly with philosophical and theoretical issues pertaining to the nature and function of literature and the relation of literary study to sociology, psychology, aesthetics, stylistics, etc. But, speaking for myself, the books I wrote derived a theory of literature from careful readings of texts, as well as from the work of the people who most influenced me—I.A. Richards, Robert Penn Warren, and René Wellek. So, in this sense, the New Criticism was not devoid of "theory." I hope this is helpful.

Yes, and it has been a pleasure. Thank you.

FURTHER READING

Biography

Drake, Robert. "Cleanth Brooks." *Modern Age,* Vol. 37, No. 2 (Winter 1995): 166-68.
    Drake recounts a meeting and Brooks's comments on the state of criticism.

Gollin, James. "Cleanth Brooks Remembered." *The American Scholar,* Vol. 64, No. 2 (Spring 1995): 257-63.
    Personal recollections of Brooks are combined with a history of his writing.

McSween, Harold. "Cleanth Brooks, LSU, and the *Southern Review.*" *Sewanee Review,* Vol. 104, No. 2 (Spring 1996): 274-86.
    A concise history of Brooks's time at Louisiana State University and the political climate affecting the rise and fall of the *Southern Review.*

Rawson, Claude. "Cleanth Brooks: Some Personal Recollections." *Southern Review* (Spring 1995): 251-55.
    Rawson fondly remembers Brooks as a soft-spoken, consummate gentleman.

Simpson, Lewis P. "Cleanth Brooks: The Long Conversation," *Southern Review* (Spring 1995): 224-38.
    Simpson provides a record of some of the pivotal points in Brooks's life and career.

Criticism

Bush, Douglas. "Marvell's 'Horatian Ode.'" *Sewanee Review,* Vol. 60, No. 3 (July/September 1952): 363-76.
    Bush disagrees with Brooks's criticism of Marvell's poem. He cites several historical inaccuracies with Brooks's conclusions.

Kimball, Roger. "Cleanth Brooks and the New Criticism." *New Criterion,* Vol. 10, No. 2 (October 1991): 21-26.
    Kimball defends the New Criticism against the claims of "historical amnesia."

Additional coverage of Brooks's life and career is contained in the following sources published by Gale: *Contemporary Authors,* Vols. 17-20R and 145; *Contemporary Authors New Revisions Series,* Vols. 33 and 35; *Dictionary of Literary Biography,* Vols. 63 and 94; and *Major 20th-Century Writers.*

Alejo Carpentier
1904-1980

Cuban novelist, short story writer, poet, musicologist, librettist, composer, essayist, and journalist.

The following entry presents an overview of Carpentier's career. For further information on his life and works, see *CLC,* Volumes 8, 11, and 38.

INTRODUCTION

Alejo Carpentier is a critically acclaimed novelist and musicologist in his native Cuba, but his work is just beginning to gain recognition in North America and the rest of the world. His "magical realism" writing has influenced a number of better-known Latin-American writers including Gabriel García Márquez. A writer of varied interests and learning, Carpentier infuses his novels and short stories with references to music, history, politics, science, art, mythology, and other subjects. His novels are characteristically complex and detailed, particularly when describing the lush settings and exotic cultures of Latin America.

Biographical Information

Alejo Carpentier was born on December 26, 1904, in Cuba. His father, Georges Carpentier, was French, and his mother was Russian. The family was quite affluent and traveled extensively in Europe during Carpentier's childhood. For a time, the family settled in Paris where Carpentier studied at the Lycee Jeanson de Sailly and learned to speak French fluently. While a teenager, Carpentier moved with his family to the countryside outside of Havana. He was asthmatic and spent most of his time at home, writing and reading. In Cuba, Carpentier attended the Colegio Mimo and then Candler College, where he organized music concerts and wrote music reviews. He studied architecture at the Universidad de la Habana until his father abandoned the family; Carpentier then quit school to work and help support the family. Carpentier began writing articles for local magazines and newspapers and eventually became the chief editor for *Carteles,* an avant-garde weekly magazine. In the 1920s, he became involved in revolutionary political activities against the Cuban dictator Gerardo Machado y Morales, and was sent to prison for seven months in 1927. It was while he was in prison that he began writing his first novel, *¡Ecué-Yamba-O!,* which was published in 1933. After his release from prison, Carpentier was involved in a series of musical projects, including organizing concerts and composing music for ballets. In 1928 Carpentier again came under the suspicion of the Cuban government and fled to Paris where he spent the next eleven years working as a journalist and activist in the anti-fascist government. Carpentier returned to Cuba in 1939 and became the editor of the journal *Tiempo Nuevo.* He also worked for Cuban radio stations and as a musicologist for Cuba's National Conservatory of Music. He was divorced from his second wife in 1939 (his first marraige had left him a widower), and in 1941 he married a third time. He traveled to Haiti in 1943 and became fascinated with the country and its leader, Henri Christophe. The visit inspired the novel *El reino de este mundo* (*The Kingdom of This World;* 1949). Carpentier moved to Venezuela in 1945 and opened an advertising agency with a friend. He remained in Venezuela until Fidel Castro, whom he supported, came into power in Cuba in 1959. He served as the Cuban cultural attaché to France and continued to write until his death on April 24, 1980.

Major Works

Carpentier was influenced by surrealism, although he later split with the movement. His later work is referred to as "magical realism," derived from his term "lo real maravilloso" ("the marvelous real"). This technique influenced a generation of Latin-American writers. "Baroquism" is another term applied to Carpentier's style, referring to his abstruse vocabulary and the influence of music on his writing. *Ecué-Yamba-O!* shows the influence of surrealism on Carpentier's writing. The novel depicts the lives of black Cubans, including their magical folklore, rituals, and ceremonies. The novel also portrays the struggle of rural blacks to make their living from the land and includes a condemnation of the Machado government. *The Kingdom of This World* focuses on the magical country of Haiti and its legendary king, Henri Christophe. The novel shows how black slaves used their folklore to survive the inhumane treatment of their white masters. Carpentier used several of his recurring techniques in this novel, including history, time dislocations, free associations, and mythical allusions. *Los pasos perdidos* (1953; *The Lost Steps*) is considered by many to be Carpentier's masterpiece. The protagonist is a musicologist who travels to the jungles of Orinoco searching for ancient musical instruments. While there, he discovers a native group and becomes enchanted with their primitive lifestyle: He believes that he has found the origins of music. Carpentier's blending of the harmonious elements of the natural world and indigenous peoples with the technological focus of the modern world parallels the blending of the European and native worlds seen in most Latin-American cultures. Music played an important role in many of

Carpentier's works and often provided the structure of his novels, including *La consagración de la primavera* (1979), reminiscent of Igor Stravinsky's *Rite of Spring,* and *El acoso* (1956; *Manhunt, Noonday*), which was modeled on Ludwig van Beethoven's *Eroica* Symphony No. 3. *Concierto barroco* (1974) again follows Carpentier's interest in historical America and the role of music in culture. Carpentier based the novel on Antonio Vivaldi's opera *Motezuma,* but also drew on a variety of historical and literary sources. *El arpa y la sombre* (1979) employs Carpentier's main techniques: a blending of history and fiction; manipulation of time sequences; and symbolic language. The story centers on Christopher Columbus's discovery of the New World and portrays the impact of the mythological and natural lushness of Latin America on the European sensibility. Throughout his career, Carpentier also wrote several books on musical theory and history, including *La música en Cuba* (1946), and essays on literature collected in several books including *Literatura y conciencia política en América Latina* (1969).

Critical Reception

Many reviewers mention Carpentier's unique portrayal of time. Frances Wyers Weber said, "In *El acoso,* perfectly real and even ordinary events appear in such a way as to suggest that both for the author and his hapless protagonist, time and causality are purely phenomenal, without meaning in view of a fixed dramatic scheme." Critics also point out the way in which Carpentier builds fictional worlds on a foundation of historical fact. David H. Bost discussed Carpentier's *Concierto barroco* and his blending of history and fiction, asserting, "Carpentier's text, as expected, negates the formation of a singular historical truth. Instead he is more interested in exploring the dimensions of artistic truthfulness." Some critics complain that Carpentier's display of scholarship is excessive, but others consider this density a vital part of his craft. Florinda F. Goldberg stated, "To put it bluntly, in order to enjoy all the beauty of [*Kingdom of This World*], the reader has to know as much of history, religion, ethnology, music, art, and literature, as the author does. In this sense, undoubtedly, Carpentier is a writer for elites."

PRINCIPAL WORKS

Poemes des Antilles (poetry) 1931
¡Ecué-Yamba-O! (novel) 1933
Viaje a la semilla [*Journey Back to the Source*] (short story) 1944
La música en Cuba (music history) 1946
El reino de este mundo [*The Kingdom of This World*] (novel) 1949
Tristan e Isolda en Tierra Firme (novel) 1949

Los pasos perdidos [*The Lost Steps*] (novel) 1953; enlarged edition, 1976
El acoso [*Manhunt, Noonday*] (novel) 1956
Guerra del tiempo [*The War of Time*] (novel) 1958
El siglo de las luces [*Explosion in a Cathedral*] (novel) 1962
El derecho de asilo (novel) 1962
Tientos y diferencias (essays) 1964; enlarged editions, 1970 and 1973
Literatura y conciencia política en América Latina (essays) 1969
La cuidad de las columnas (nonfiction) 1970
Los convidados de plata (novel) 1972
Concierto barroco (novel) 1974
El recurso del método [*Reasons of State*] (novel) 1974
Novelas y relatos (novel) 1974
Crónicas. 2 volumes. [edited by José Antonio Portuondo] (articles) 1975
Razón de ser: Conferencias (essays) 1976
Cuentos (novel) 1977
La consagración de la primavera (novel) 1979
El arpa y la sombra (novel) 1979
Ese músico que llevo dentro. 3 volumes. [edited by Zoila Gómez García] (nonfiction) 1980
El adjetivo y sus arrugas (novel) 1980
La novelo latinamericana en vísperas de un nuevo siglo y otros ensayos (essays) 1981
Obras completas. 9 volumes. (collection) 1983-1986
Historia y ficción en la narrativa hispanoamerica (nonfiction) 1984
Conferencias 1987
Tientos, diferencias y otros ensayos 1987

CRITICISM

Frances Wyers Weber (essay date September 1963)

SOURCE: "*El Acoso:* Alejo Carpentier's War on Time," in *PMLA: Publications of the Modern Language Association of America,* Vol. 78, No. 1, September, 1963, pp. 440-48.

[*In the following essay, Weber discusses one of Carpentier's recurrent themes, "the representation, domination, or denial of time," as seen in his* El acoso.]

The protagonist of Alejo Carpentier's short novel **El acoso** is an informer fleeing from men who would avenge the deaths he has caused. The pursuit and punishment of an informer, not a new plot, is usually developed with rapid pacing and suspense. But Carpentier modifies this traditional story of the chase by breaking it into a mosaic of fragmentary incidents and remembrances arranged without chronological sequence. Adopting certain techniques of the stream-of-consciousness writers, he reduces external action to a minimum and uses interior monologues and confused shreds of memory to show the inner life of his characters. Yet his work is not primarily a psychological study: the combination of two apparently disparate approaches to the novel (one a story line based on a closely-knit, causal-temporal progression and the other a narrative structure determined in part by the flux and shift of consciousness) creates a static and almost allegorical depiction of Betrayal in its various modes and incarnations. This duality of presentation is also evident in the subject matter: definite historical happenings, tied to actual sites in the city of Havana, are the factual ingredients in a drama that seems to be just one possible version of a constant theme. Uniting the particular and the abstract, intertwining the external chain of events (shattered and rearranged according to noncausal principles) with pictures of internal chaos, Carpentier presents both the vision of a traitorous, degenerate world in which man plays out certain prescribed roles and the artistic or literary organization of this drama of the fall. Underlying these elements and binding them together is one of Carpentier's repeated themes—the representation, domination, or denial of time.

El acoso was first published separately and later included with three shorter works in a volume entitled *La guerra del tiempo.* The other tales are fantastic, either because of the narrative situation itself or because of the peculiar temporal distortions to which the author submits it. In **"El Camino de Santiago,"** a single man's self splits into two different roles played at successive periods in his life (Juan el Romero, Juan el Indiano), and they confront each other at the beginning and at the end of the story in identical, duplicated scenes, told from opposite points of view; in **"Viaje a la semilla,"** the normal passage from birth to death is simply reversed, as in a film run backwards; in **"Semejante a la noche,"** diverse avatars of the departing warrior are telescoped into a single person and scene. In all three stories, the unreality of the plot constitutes a negation of time as the medium of essential change: temporal succession reveals only varying combinations of changeless parts. In *El acoso,* perfectly real and even ordinary events appear in such a way as to suggest that both for the author and his hapless protagonist, time and causality are purely phenomenal, without meaning in view of a fixed dramatic scheme. A single episode, or even a simple physical gesture, may splinter into distinct images inserted at widely spaced sections of the narrative; past happenings are juggled and shuffled so that the reader must infer the action on the basis of dispersed clues and signals. The principal characters, the *Acosado* and the *taquillero,* see the course of their own lives not as a psychological unfolding but as a kind of timeless, mythical drama of primal innocence destroyed by the fall into sin.

The novel has three main parts, subdivided into eighteen unnumbered sections. But the progression of the narrative seems at first disordered and chaotic. Part I (first section) begins with a description of the thoughts of an unnamed ticket-taker during a concert intermission; next appears a torrential interior monologue in the mind of we know not whom (". . . ese latido que se me abre a codazos; ese vientre en borbollones; se corazón que se me supende . . ."). Only when the third section reintroduces the ticket-taker does the reader realize that the anguished inner voice was that of another person, one whose external shape will not become visible until Part II. Meanwhile, through the *taquillero's* memories, we piece together the story of a youth from a provincial village who has come to Havana to study music. For weeks he has been preparing himself for the evening's performance of Beethoven's *Eroica,* but no sooner does the orchestra begin than, giving in to a sexual impulse, he leaves the concert hall and hurries to the house of the prostitute Estrella. When she refuses him, he returns to the concert in time to catch the last nine minutes of the symphony.

The whole of Part II deals with the six previous days in the life of the novel's main character, the *Acosado.* Present action is interwoven with disordered recollections of past incidents in such a way that the reader must himself deduce the linking of causes and effects: by keeping careful track of fleeting allusions, of details charged with significance for the protagonist, by relating minute coincidences and mentally establishing a system of cross-references, one can recompose the biography of this other provincial student who had come to the capital to study architecture. The order of events is as follows: on arriving in Havana, he stays a short while with his aged former nurse; he joins the Communist Party, but after witnessing the violent police repression of a student demonstration, he goes over to the "bando de los impacientes." Although his terrorist acts begin idealistically enough ("Todo había sido justo, heroico, sublime en el comienzo"), the kangaroo trial of a student friend ("época del Tribunal") and his first political murder precipitate him into what he recognizes as a "burocracia del horror," a crime syndicate that cynically makes use of the idealistic fervor of its members. Finally, no better than a paid assassin, he accepts a salary to direct the elimination of the political foe of a certain *Alto Personaje.* Arrested the morning after the killing, he informs under threat of torture, and when he is released from prison, he finds himself hunted by his former associates. The present action of six days relates his hiding-out in his old nurse's house, his departure from that refuge, and his attempt to get help from the *Alto Personaje.* Spotted on the street by two of his pursuers, he has slipped into the concert hall just at the beginning of the *Eroica.*

The first section of Part III continues the *Acosado's* turbulent interior monologue as he listens to the concert; the second and final section returns to the *taquillero* and then concludes with the indirect reporting of the Hunted Man's execution.

In a narrative lacking normal time sequence, made up out of the subjectivity of the characters and jumbled bits of action described or merely alluded to, some unifying elements must serve as guide posts to the reader in his reconstruction of events. The order imposed upon this novel does not derive from causal plotting but from the disposition of motifs and the patterns of theme and structure. In the composition of any fiction we can distinguish between dynamic motifs that generate action and static motifs that effect no change of situation but contribute to the setting or mood. These last may or may not be directly related to the central action. In **El acoso** the numerous static motifs at first appear extraneous to the story, but gradually their true import emerges to reveal a system of chance connections and exchanges between *Acosado* and *taquillero;* they form a bundle of Ariadne threads that guide the reader through the narrative's cross-cutting paths. The delayed disclosure of the pertinence of these motifs weakens the sense of time, for a vision of the entire action must be suspended until all the elements can be coordinated; nonsequential articulation is an effective weapon in Carpentier's "guerra del tiempo."

Certain occurrences (which, however, do not come in chronological order) tie together the parallel lives of the informer and the ticket-taker: the yellow-papered cigarette butt, thrown out of Estrella's window by the taxi driver, burns the hand of the Hunted Man crouching against the wall of her house; a few hours later (though the passage is situated in the narrative some seventy-seven pages earlier), the ticket-taker finds Estrella's bed surrounded by "colillas de papel de maíz." The storm that the ticket-taker watches from the concert-hall lobby surprises the Hunted One with the *Becario* at the ocean shore. The screech of ambulance brakes that heralds the entrance of the hurried ticket buyer in Part I ("En aquel instante una ambulancia que llegaba a todo rodar pasó frente al edificio, ladeándose en un frenazo brutal") sounds again at the end of Part II when the fugitive darts in front of the speeding vehicle: "Una ambulancia, brutalmente frenada, había quedado entre su cuerpo y los gestos que estaban en suspenso a la altura del bolsillo del corazón." Other commonly perceived things and events indicate the physical proximity in which the two men have been living for the past two weeks: the old mansion next to the modern apartment house, the wake for the old woman. Alternately shared objects and experiences (the new bill, Estrella, and the Beethoven symphony) weld these two lives into a single action, a mechanism with rotating parts (or, to use the image of the *Acosado* in describing the third movement of the *Eroica,* "con algo de esos juguetes de niños muy chicos, que por el movimiento de varitas paralelas, ponen dos muñecos, a descargar martillos, alternativamente, sobre un mazo"). The new bill, a dynamic motif, appears now in the hands of one, now affects the life of the other, and these exchanges are vital to the plot's complication. The meshing of the visits paid by both to Estrella is a descriptive, static device, because the prostitute, as her name implies, is a fixed point of convergence, the motionless, timeless center in the lives of her clients and the pivot between *Acosado* and *taquillero.* Beethoven's *Eroica* not only determines the fictional time the narrative but also creates the strongest bond between the former architecture student and the music student. For days the man hiding on the roof-terrace hears the music played by his neighbor on the phonograph, at times almost unaware of its persistence, but finally convinced of its significance in his drama ("Estaba eso en la casa al lado, porque Dios quiso que as fuera . . .”). The symphony that accompanied him in his refuge and that now marks the temporal limits of his last anguish is one of the many signs of a divine plan.

Some motifs are connected with the *Acosado* alone and serve as directives for fitting together the story-line (frequently what appears first as a fragment of memory is later included as dramatic scene enacted in the present): the pistol; the explosive *Antología de oradores: de Demóstenes a Castelar;* the prayer book with the Cross of Calatrava on its cover; the *Alto Personaje* and the *Casa de la Gestión;* the attempted assassination in the graveyard; the fugitive's vomiting of the warm water drunk in desperation after three days of enforced fast; the learning of the Apostles' Creed; his torture. Other motifs, however, not only show the careful workings of the plot but are to the Hunted Man himself evidence of an unavoidable tragedy of sin and atonement. Thus, in the first interior monologue, he is horrified by an acne-scarred neck: "No mirar ese cuello: tiene marcas de acné; había de estar ahí, precisamente—único en toda la platea—, para poner tan cerca lo que no debe mirarse, lo que puede ser un Signo"; the explanation of this delirious obsession comes on pp. 242-243 when the *Acosado* recalls his first act of political terrorism. The dog that barked at him in the ruins of the *Casa de la Gestión* is yet another fixture in the divine plan of expiation, as are the Beethoven symphony, the overheard dialogue of a Sophoclean tragedy, and the words engraved in bronze on the façade of the University of Havana: *Hoc erat in votis.* This phrase, although taking on different connotations in different contexts, announces, in the first internal monologue, the protagonist's awareness of the ineluctability of his tragedy: it is the summary and prophetic declaration of a total and minutely detailed program of ensnarement. The terrible march of events is due neither to chance nor to the voluntary acts of the informer:

> [Era] Dios, que no perdonaba, que no quería mis plegarias, que me volvía las espaldas cuando en mi boca sonaban las palabras aprendidas en el libro de la Cruz de Calatrava; Dios que me arrojó a la calle y puso a ladrar un perro entre los escombros; Dios que puso aquí, tan cerca de mi rostro, el cuello con las horribles marcas; el cuello que no debe mirarse. Y ahora se encarna en los instrumentos que me obligó a escuchar, esta noche, conducido por los

truenos de su ira ... Sé ahora que nunca ofensor alguno pudo ser más observado, mejor puesto en el fiel de la Divina Mira, que quien cayó en el encierro, en la suprema trampa—traído por la inexorable Voluntad a donde un lenguaje sin palabras acaba de revelarle el sentido expiatorio de los últimos tiempos. Repartidos están lospapeles en este Teatro, y el desenlace está ya establecido en el *después—lhoc erat in votis*!—como está la ceniza en la leña por prender.

In this allegorical scheme of transgression and punishment, the old trunk containing the souvenirs of his student life, reminders of an uncorrupted youth ("mis cosas puras": books, architectural drawings, photographs of famous buildings, a Communist Party card, "la última barrera que hubiera podido preservarlo de lo abominable"), is to the Hunted One a symbol of man's innocence before original sin: "una figuración, sólo descifrable para él, del Paraíso antes de la Culpa."

Listening to the *Eroica* in the concert hall, the fugitive, only recently converted to a belief in God, sees the necessity of the episodes in his assigned role. Although this happens in Part I, the reader is not yet aware of the portentousness of the events recalled. The author scatters references to them throughout the text, sometimes in a very unobtrusive way, so that the realization of their importance, both in the make-up of the plot and in the emotional life of the protagonist, is acquired only gradually. Motifs that seem unrelated to the story—chance occurrences and apparently insignificant acts and objects—are eventually revealed as indispensable to its development. The reader retrospectively fits details into a meaningful unit and recognizes, along with the Hunted One, a rigorously preordained plan. This halting, piecemeal disclosure of an unchanging, inextricable web of facts divests a conventional dramatic plot of its normal pattern of suspense: tension arises not out of an evolving complication of the action but through the placement—counterpoint, shifts, juxtapositions—of anecdotal and descriptive fragments. By replacing the expected consecutive order with a discrete arrangement, the author destroys temporal progression and turns the narrative into a stable complex whose parts are simultaneously apprehended.

> **In addition to the intricate fretwork of concrete particulars, Carpentier unifies [*El aceso*] through a series of variations on the topic of betrayal and on the related theme of a world crumbling into moral and esthetic decay.**
> —*Frances Wyers Weber*

In addition to the intricate fretwork of concrete particulars, Carpentier unifies the novel through a series of variations on the topic of betrayal and on the related theme of a world crumbling into moral and esthetic decay. The *Acosado*'s traitorous acts are many: he abandons his studies, he defects from the Communist Party ("recordó que de eso tambiín habia renegado"), he refuses, out of cowardice, to stand up for a companion tried and sentenced by a kangaroo court, he becomes a criminal terrorist (thereby distorting his revolutionary ideals), and, finally, he steals his old nurse's meager food. The ticket-taker, whose function in the novel is to echo, as if in a minor key, the theme of the fall from original innocence, regards his surrender to sexual temptation as a betrayal of his high ideals ("la imagen de una prostituta bastara para apartarlo de lo Verdadero y lo Sublime"); his lost purity is personified by the old negro woman in the mansion ("Necesitaba saberla viva, en la noche, por rito de purificación"). All the other characters betray or deceive, some intentionally, some unwittingly: Estrella, the *Becario,* the taxi-driver, the police inspector. The very roles of delator and of expiatory victim are transferred indifferently from one man to another: the acne-marked dignitary who was once "el emplazado" ("el emplazado parecía feliz en el frescor mañanero") bequeaths the title to his murderer, the informer ("Una ambulancia llegaba a todo rodar ... el emplazado se arrojó delante de ella"). Thinking of his condemned friend, the *Acosado* remembers a corporeal image of guilt ("una miserable espalda se redondeaba en la sombra de los álamos") that the narrator applies to him a few pages later ("Miserable era ahora su espalda que se redondeaba en la sombra de los álamos"). A kind of chiasmus, whose terms must be held in mind by the reader, ties together the two men in the anonymity of the victim's role. Even the landscape across which the characters move is disintegrating: the former architecture student sees the decline of his epoch in the debasement of style and form: "Se asistía, de portal en portal, a la agonía de los últimos órdenes clásicos usados en la época."

The use of multiple, coexisting embodiments of a single theme reinforces the novel's static quality, for that which occurs only in time, the fall into corruption, is pictured as an invariable component in a repetitive design.

By interchanging the characters' roles Carpentier denies them individualized behavior; by excluding proper names he shows them to be mere actors in the play. All have abstract or generic titles ("el Acosado," "el taquillero," "el Becario," "el Alto Personaje"), with the single exception of Estrella, less a name than a sign for her function—the fixed point around which the others revolve. Not only does the narrator withdraw from his fictional creatures but they too disassociate themselves from their deeds: decisive acts appears as autonomous happenings not as the results of a conscious will. Both the *Acosado* and Estrella consider their treacheries in a curiously depersonified way: *Acosado:* "Había una fisura, ciertamente; un tránsito infernal. Pero, al considerar las peripecias de lo sucedido en aquel tránsito . . .”; Estrella: “Al medir el abominable alcance de lo dicho para quitarse de encima a los de la inquisición . . .”; “Un indicio, dado para desviar una amenaza sin mayor gravedad . . . había hecho de ella una puta.” The Hunted Man thinks of his original sin not as a deliberate act but as a mechanical response. He did not *kill,* he only made a certain gesture: “Jamás repetiría el gesto que le hiciera mirar tan fijamente un cuello marcado de acné.” The memory of his first murder is derationalized into a rapid succession of photographic images and interruptive sounds that impose themselves in a passive sensory apparatus: “la nuca, a poco, se le colocó tan cerca que hubieran podido contarse las marcas dejadas en ella por el acné. Luego fue un perfil, una cara empavorecida, dos ojos suplicantes, un aullido y una descarga.” His own death is reported with laconic indirectness: “Entonces, dos espectadores que habían permanecido en sus asientos de penúltima fila se levantaron lentamente, atravesaron la platea desierta . . . y se asomaron por sobre el barandal de un palco ya en sombras, disparando a la alfombra.” The event toward which the entire story moves, the Hunted One’s execution, becomes a secondary action, inserted as a modifying adverbial phrase—and the human target itself goes unmentioned.

Man, devoid of individuality and volition, is nothing but a congeries of automatic motions: “Un gesto resignado . . . apartó la cortina de damasco”; “La mano ha dejado la inservible brocha”; “Una mano crispada se hundió en la masa resquebrajada. . . . Y fue luego la lengua, ansiosa, presurosa, asustada de comer robando, la que limpié el plato con gruñidos de cerdo en las honduras de la loza, y saltó pronto al esparto de la silla, para lamer lo derramado. Levantóse luego el cuerpo sobre sus rodillas, y fue la mano, otra vez, en el envase del Cuáquero, escarbando con las uñas en la avena cruda”; “La boca se hundió en esa sopa de Domingos, resoplando y royendo antes de arrimarse al cartón del Cuáquero.” A mindless body motivates or performs the cowardly act: “su carne más irreemplazable se había encogido atrozmente ante la amenaza del tormento”; “Y hay que levantar la mano y sentenciar. . . . La mía permanece inerte, colgante, buscando un pretexto para no alzarse en el lomo de un perro . . . mi codo al fin se mueve, elevando dedos cobardes.” As for the occasion of his informing, the man remembers not the human semblance of his interrogators but their disembodied hands, gestures, voices: “Y luego de dos días de olvido, sin alimento . . . había sido la luz en la cara, y las manos que empuñaban vergajos y las voces que hablaban de llegarla a las raíces de las muelas con una fresa de dentista, y las otras voces que hablaban de golpearlo en los testículos.” The physical gesture is not only autonomous but at times its very import substantializes it, converting it into a material object: “Una ambulancia . . . había quedado entre su cuerpo y los gestos que estaban en suspenso a la altura del bolsillo del corazón.” Or it becomes

magnified into a divine revelation: “La portentosa novedad era Dios. Dios, que se le había revelado en el tabaco encendido por la vieja. . . . De súbito, aquel gesto de tomar la brasa del fogón y elevarla hacia el rostro . . . se la había magnificado en implicaciones abrumadoras.”

Estrella is aware of this mysterious independence of the flesh: “Hablaba de su cuerpo en tercera persona, como si fuese, más abajo de sus clavículas, una presencia ajena y enérgica, dotada, por sí sola, de los poderes que le valían la solicitud y la largueza de los varones. Esa presencia actuaba, de pronto, como por sortilegio, alentando prolongadas asiduidades por gentes de ámbitos distintos.” Her clients too are reduced to physical existence and appetite, “identificados en los mismos gestos y apetencias.” Indeed, Carpentier habitually presents people in the guise of pure corporality: the characters see each other as moving flesh: “Después del sofocante anochecer los cuerpos estaban como relajados”; “Más allá de las carnes era el parque de columnas”; flesh that the pursued man thinks of as a protective wall (“rodeado de gente, protegido por los cuerpos, oculto entre los cuerpos; de cuerpo confundido con muchos cuerpos”), or flesh that he has envied (“Yo envidiaba aquella carne ceñida a su contorno más viril”), or, in the case of his own, impersonally considered as bulk to be hidden (“cargado con el peso de un cuerpo acosado”). The man condemned by the revolutionary tribunal lives his last moments only in the automatic reactions of his body: “El cuerpo presente—presente ya ausente—se desprende el reloj de la muñeca . . . le da cuerda, por hábito conservado por el pulgar y el índice de su mano derecha.” In a sense the body, or more exactly the body’s sexuality, is held responsible for the parallel falls into sin of *Acosado* and *taquillero,* the fear of castration in the former, simple sensuality in the latter (“había dejado la Sublime Concepción por el calor de una ramera”). It is their sexual life, their commerce with Estrella, that provides one of the most important ties between these duplicating lives.

And the description of the body is usually purely sensory, frequently an optical impression: an ineradicable pictorial memory—the acne-scarred neck—afflicts the *Acosado.* Pictorial images are so insistent that physical qualities synecdochically replace their possessor. The characteristic of an object or person (which may be nominalized and subsequently modified by another adjective appropriate to the object) so predominate over the bearer that the latter disappears entirely behind an abstract construction: “Silencio ya en *lo después.* En lo que ya dejó de ser; pálpito y movimiento que ya saben del hierro arrojado a la rueda maestra, de la tierra que caerá sobre la todavía caliente inmovilidad de lo detenido.” Independent of its owner, the change in a human attribute signifies the death of a man: “lo que se movía, dejó de moverse; la voz enmudeció en la bocanada de sangre que ya viste, como un esmalte compacto, el mentón sin rasurar.” A further degree of abstraction is reached when the very substance of the cadaver is only circuitously alluded to: "Sobre el árbol del tronco más espeso se detienen las moscas, buscando los plomos que traspasaron." The body evaporates into a lingering warmth: "La casa estaba tibia aún de una presencia que demoraba en el desorden de la cama rodeada de colillas de papel de maíz."

Apposite to the dehumanized view of man is the sickly animation of the architectural setting. Buildings, pillars, decorative motifs and devices assume just enough life to suffer organic dissolution: "Había capiteles cubiertos de pústulas reventadas por el sol; fustes cuyas estrías se hinchaban de abscesos levantados por la pintura de aceite"; "Allí se afirmaba la condena impuesta por aquella ciudad a los órdenes que degeneraban en el calor y se cubrían de llagas, dando sus astrágalos para sostener muestras de tintorerías, barberías, refresquerías. . . ."

The disorder of the narrative's progress is, I have noted, only apparent, for scenes and evocations are actually carefully woven together through a system of clue-like motifs and a strict temporal arrangement. This last, however, is not immediately evident and the reader must reconstruct it on the basis of various references. We discover two time levels. The events of Parts I and II occur during the present-time frame of the Sunday evening concert, a period of about one hour—the action begins shortly before the performance of the *Eroica* (the correct interpretation of which, according to the *taquillero*, takes forty-six minutes) and ends shortly afterwards; the action of Part II begins, one gathers, on the previous Tuesday when, because illness has confined the old woman to her bed, the *Acosado* must hide in the belvedere of the decrepit mansion, and takes us up to a moment before the start of the symphony; the repeated screech of the ambulance brakes indicates the confluence of the two time periods. The two-week span of the action of Part II (concerned exclusively with the *Acosado*) corresponds to the two weeks during which the ticket-taker has studiously listened to recordings of the *Eroica*: "Le había observado [a la vieja] hacía dos semanas—dos semanas exactas, puesto que era el día de su compleaños, cuando, con el pequeño giro recibido del padre, se habiía regalado a sí mismo la *Sinfonia Heroica* en discos de mucho uso."

In terms of real chronology, the events of Part II are prior to those of Parts I and III, but instead of appearing as a remembrance in the consciousness of a character, a flashback illuminating previous material, they occur as present action that unfolds dramatically before the reader. Although they are the temporal and causal antecedents of what happens in Parts I and III, the narrative structure makes them seem independent and exclusive so that they do not truly constitute the preparation for the dénouement. Between Parts I and II is an unexplained time-shift reminiscent of the film-run-in-reverse device used in **"Viaje a la semilla."** At the end of

Part I the ticket-taker anxiously wonders if the wake in the old mansion is for the aged negro woman who symbolizes to him the lost purity of childhood: "Necesitaba saberla viva en la noche. Tanto lo necesitaba que correría a la casa del Mirador, en cuanto terminara el Final, para cerciorarse de que no era ella la persona de cuerpo presente." The first lines of Part II suddenly resuscitate this laid-out corpse: "La vieja se había recogido, encogida, en su estrecha cama de hierro . . . volviéndose hacia la pared."

The order of remembered events is determined by the emotional reactions of the protagonist. Part II reveals, albeit in a fragmentary way, the confession that led to the man-hunt; but this revelation lies submerged in the account of the fugitive's life in the old mansion, being postponed, in fact, until the end of the section and preceded by matters of more immediate concern to the character (his religious conversion, the memories of his revolutionary activities, etc.). For the Hunted One customarily considers his plight as the punishment for his original fall into sin—the betrayal of youthful ideals—rather than the necessary consequence of his cowardice in prison; his flight and suffering are part of a divinely decreed plan of atonement ("una perenne expiación por el tormento"; "fases de una expiación necesaria"). Because his crime is against God, not man, the recall of the "fisura," of the abominable gesture that makes him stare so fixedly at an acne-scarred neck, dissolves into a vision of penitent sinners: "Eran gemidos las palabras con que los atormentados, los culpables, los arrepentidos, se acercaban a la Santa Mesa, para recibir el Cuerpo del Crucificado y la Sangre del Sacrificio Incruento." The temporal rupture between Parts I and III on the one hand, and Part II on the other, is the literary reproduction of that psychological dissociation that divorces the denunciation of friends and comrades from its inevitable aftermath. For the reader, as well as for the *Acosado,* the pursuit is not directly linked to the informing.

This incision in the temporal continuity, this severing of determinants from results and the subsequent destruction of the normal causal relation between a crime and its punishment, transforms the episodes of a fast-moving suspenseful tale into the predictable stages of a ritual drama removed from time and the human world of motivation and will: "Sé ahora que nunca ofensor alguno pudo ser más observado, mejor puesto en el fiel de la Divina Mira, que quien cayó en la suprema trampa—traído por la inexorable voluntad." A man's deeds are nothing but the posturings of an actor playing an assigned role. "Repartidos están los papeles en este Teatro y el desenlace está establecido en el *después*." (At the close of his drama, the *Acosado* unsuspectingly comments on his own imminent disappearance from the stage: "Nadie se queda en un teatro cuando ha terminado el espectáculo. Nadie permanece ante un escenario vacío, en tinieblas, donde nada se muestra"). Human behavior does not evolve in time because the characters are cast as unvarying types.

The religious motifs woven into the story reinforce its representative quality, for they allude to what is timeless and archetypal. The action takes place during the first two weeks of Lent, the preparation for the great drama of betrayal and sacrifice ("el mayor de los dramas"). After his conversion, the fugitive reenacts the practice of the Christian catechumens in using this period to instruct himself for his initiation. Intrigued by the ceremonies of the mass that symbolically transpose the Mystery of salvation, he one day comes to understand how the liturgy of the Church, like architecture or any other art, gives form to man's experience: "Y ahora que se daba por enterado, hallaba en los simples movimientos que acompañaban el Gloria, el Evangelio, el Ofertorio, esa prodigiosa sublimación de lo elemental que, en la Arquitectura, había transformado el trofeo de caza en bucranio; la anilla de cuerdas que ciñe el haz de ramas del fuste primitivo, en astrégalo de puras proporciones pitagóricas." The liturgical references suggest not only the eternal but also the theatrical: religion becomes art.

The artist's conversion of the primary elements of his world (particularly of his perceptions of space and time) is schematically indicated in the novel by the pairing of the two characters, the student of architecture (the organization of spatial relations) and the student of music (the organization of temporal progression). The frame of their action is fiction, an image of time as memory. Music, Carpentier has written, is the achievement of human dominion over time, its submission to man's will. But the novel is also a manipulation of temporal sequence. The author successfully fuses these two modes in composing his narrative. Although he has destroyed normal chronology with the apparently illogical disposition of events, he carefully determines the duration of the action by the playing of the *Eroica,* thereby molding it to a musical order. The novel's abstractly executed plot is a literary parallel to the musical conformation of time.

The narrative display of esthetic transformation is evident not only in the ingenious temporal displacements but also in the story's strangely impersonal, hieratic quality; the passivity and powerlessness of the characters shows, as well as their human deficiency, their essential unreality, their literary nature. The author, precisely directing the paces of his actors according to a fixed program of betrayal and degradation, affirms human will in the very act of his novelistic contriving. Volition, so noticeably absent in the characters, is manifest in the shape and fact of the story itself. The informer's crime becomes a drama and, as artistic object, acquires value. The writer places his tragedy beyond the realm of incomprehensible motivations and unexpected changes, beyond the element in which these exist—beyond

time. Harassed and obsessed by time man seeks to subject it to his desired measure in music, religion, and narrative.

Ray Verzasconi (essay date March 1965)

SOURCE: "Juan and Sisyphus in Carpentier's 'El Camino de Santiago,'" in *Hispania,* Vol. XLVIII, No. 1, March, 1965, pp. 70-5.

[*In the following essay, Verzasconi discusses how Carpentier uses the myth of Sisyphus in his portrayal of Juan in "El Camino de Santiago."*]

"¿Qué capitán es este, qué soldado de la guerra del tiempo?" With this quotation from Lope de Vega, Alejo Carpentier prefaces *Guerra del tiempo,* a collection of three short stories and a novel. "Ese Capitán, ese Soldado," write the editors in the prologue to the volume, "es el Hombre, siempre semejante a sí mismo, inmensamente fiel a sus 'constantes,' aunque el Tiempo transcurra."

A concern for the essence of Man must necessarily be a fundamental part of any author whose work is worthy of critical evaluation. In at least two of the works of Alejo Carpentier, that Captain-Soldier, who represents the core of all that is Man, finds its expression through a re-interpretation of an ancient myth—the myth of Sisyphus. In the novel *Los pasos perdidos,* the Sisyphus theme is central and explicit, though no one, to my knowledge, has fully studied its significance. In **"El camino de Santiago,"** the first story in the volume cited above, the theme remains central, but it can only be established through a series of inferences. Nowhere does Carpentier specifically mention Sisyphus.

> **A concern for the essence of Man must necessarily be a fundamental part of any author whose work is worthy of critical evaluation. In at least two of the works of Alejo Carpentier, that Captain-Soldier, who represents the core of all that is Man, finds its expression through a re-interpretation of an ancient myth—the myth of Sisyphus.**
> **—Ray Verzasconi**

The Sisyphean label has been given most frequently to the man whose journey through life has consisted of an endless and fruitless task. This view of Sisyphus, representing futile and recurrent toil, comes not from his life on earth but from his punishment in the underworld. He is most often portrayed in Hades, where he must push a heavy stone over one mountain to another mountain. He never succeeds, however, because the weight of the rock overcomes him and he is forced to let it roll back to the plain, where he must then descend to begin his task anew.

Given Ernst Cassirer's judgment, however, that "the primitive mind was not aware of the meaning of its own creations," and that it is for us "to reveal this meaning," a belief which Carpentier has certainly followed, we will find that the protagonist of our story is not the traditional Sisyphus. If we are to understand the symbolism, if not the underlying principle of the myth as Carpentier portrays it, we must first examine certain primal experiences in Sisyphus' terrestrial life.

The great flaw in Sisyphus' character was produced by his dogmatic belief in a myth, which can have many names, but which was essentially the myth of *eternal terrestrial freedom*. He so loved life that he often chose to scorn the gods, and twice, to defy Death. Once he put Death in chains and only the god of war, on the order of Pluto, was able to free her from her conqueror. And once, after having obtained the permission of Pluto to make a brief return to the world in order to punish his wife—for a crime which he himself had ingeniously devised—Sisyphus decided to remain indefinitely. The anger and threats of the gods were of no avail. Finally, Hermes was sent to snatch Sisyphus away from his earthly pleasures. Before he was forced to begin his life of eternal slavery in the underworld, therefore, Sisyphus had successfully defied the gods and had temporarily obtained terrestrial freedom.

To understand another possible source for Carpentier's Sisyphean interpretation, a brief explanation of Camus' *Le Mythe de Sisyphe* will be helpful. As Camus views him, Sisyphus eventually triumphs over the unscrupulous gods who condemned him. As he stands briefly at the top of the mountain and watches his rock descend to the plain, Camus' Sisyphus finds happiness in his torment for it is the result of his own creation, which can have no more depth than that of human suffering. Happiness and hope are not synonymous for Sisyphus, however. Sisyphus is a tragic hero, according to Camus, because he realizes that there is no hope. But he finds happiness by self-deception and ends by concluding that "all is well." As he descends to the plain to begin his task anew, Camus believes that Sisyphus must accept his rock willingly, for in doing so, he not only acknowledges his wretched condition in the face of the gods, but ironically, he also acknowledges his triumph over their punishment.

Viewed in this light, Sisyphus can no longer represent futile and recurrent toil. For the accomplishment of his task, however trivial, is entirely of his own making, and his rock, however small in comparison to the universe, has become his own universe, governed entirely by his own capabilities.

Juan de Amberes, the symbolic protagonist of **"El camino de Santiago,"** is not, as I have stated, the ancient Sisyphus nor is he an exact replica of Camus' Sisyphus. Yet, as he wanders through time as Juan de Amberes, Juan el Romero, and Juan el Indiano he represents another interpretation of the principle behind the myth, an interpretation which espouses certain ideas from both of its predecessors.

Juan's mask, to begin with, is a modern one and more complex than that of his ancient counterpart and it is more detailed than the mask created by Camus. He lives in a Christian world, or more appropriately a Catholic world of sixteenth century Spain, whose implications must be taken into account. Moreover, as a mere soldier, Juan de Amberes must pay homage to a terrestrial king as well as to a divine ruler, whereas Sisyphus, as king of Corinth, had only to answer to the gods.

As a soldier, Juan de Amberes faithfully serves his king in Amsterdam. As a Spaniard, and thus a Catholic soldier, who has helped burn Protestants at the stake, he also served his God, despite the fact that he has not led a virtuous life. But his service to both his earthly and divine rulers does not long continue. The appearance of a plague changes the course of his life.

On the surface, Juan appears to react to the plague as a devout, sixteenth century Catholic; that is, he interprets it as a sign of divine punishment and he thus vows to make a pilgrimage to Santiago de Compostela in order to save his soul. But Juan, like the ancient terrestrial Sisyphus, loves life too much and his first concern is to save his body. He attempts to deceive his God by feigning illness, "para que Dios, compadecido de quien se creía enfermo, no le mandara cabalmente la enfermedad." Not until a visionary appearance of the Duque de Alba frightens him does Juan really decide to go to Santiago. One immediately recalls that it was Hermes, who as magician and messenger was qualified to guide the souls of the dead to Hades, who was sent to take Sisyphus away from his earthly pleasures. The Duque de Alba, for his relentless and ruthless persecution of the Lutherans in the Netherlands, acted likewise as a representative or messenger for both his Catholic king and Catholic god. Moreover, in his visionary appearance, the Duque de Alba displays his magical or supernatural powers.

To the heretic, of which Juan fears he might be suspect of being if he did not go to Santiago, Alba represents physical death; and to Juan, a Catholic, he also represents spiritual damnation. Santiago de Compostela offers him the possibility of saving both his body and soul. As the firmament brightens, symbolic perhaps of the presence of the Holy Ghost, Juan falls to his knees and cries out, "¡El Camino de Santiago!"

His intention is far from being sincere, or if it is, its meaningfulness is soon obliterated. Once Juan de Amberes leaves Amsterdam, he leaves behind him the plague and with it the fear of a physical death. Now, as Juan el Romero, he seemingly has defied, as the ancient Sisyphus had done, his worst enemy. His "calabaza" which first carries only "agua de arroyos" is soon filled with the spirit of Bacchus. The farther he is from Amsterdam and the plague, the more defiant he becomes of his God. He happily thinks of "aquellas mozas de Amberes, de carnes abundosas, que gustaban de los flacos españoles," and the wine in his "calabaza" is eventually replaced with "aguardiente."

By the time he reaches Burgos, which stands before Compostela like a beastly temptress who prevents the weak from reaching moral perfection, Juan completely forgets his vow to go to Santiago, for in Burgos "una moza le coge en su cama hasta mañana." As a Catholic who has continued to defy his God, despite the anger and threats presented in the form of a plague and a vision, Juan can expect his just retribution in an afterlife. In this fact, he is not unlike the ancient Sisyphus. But Juan's God is not as severe as were the ancient gods. Hope is never denied to him by his God.

In his search for absolute and eternal freedom, Juan temporarily rejects the "myth" of Santiago de Compostela and he is attracted to another myth, the "myth" of Santiago de Cuba, the "myth" of America. Though both Santiagos stand as the baptismal avenue to moral perfection and spiritual salvation, Juan creates a terrestrial burden for himself, a burden which can only offer him eternal damnation.

Juan is soon convinced that America will offer him everything he has ever desired: freedom from responsibility, freedom from the corruption of civil authority, and freedom from the corruption of divine authority for in America "la misma Inquisición tenía la mano blanda." But America, which could still offer him his freedom, his triumph over the corruptive forces of civil and divine authority, and his eventual moral perfection will become the mountain up which he will be condemned to push his self-created stone.

When Juan el Romero reaches Sevilla, one is given the first indication of the forthcoming torture, "porque Juan, en sus andanzas por el laberinto bético, se asombraba ante el gran portento de los humanos colores." The Andalusian countryside, swarming with American natives and other foreigners, stands as the entrance to the inescapable labyrinth which, like that built by Daedalus for the beastly Minotaur, would be responsible for the torture and downfall of all of those who entered it. Once Juan accepts the "myth" of America and enters into the labyrinth, he chooses eternal damnation for himself and his eventual repentance will be of no avail.

Juan presently begins his education—to contemplate his fate.

He discovers that even on the high seas he is not really free because his government will not allow him to go to Mexico.

> Juan recibió la nueva con pataleos y blasfemias. Pensó luego que era castigo de Dios por no haber llegado hasta Compostela. Pero a punto apareció el Indiano de la feria de Burgos en el albergue de viajeros, para decirle que una vez cruzado el Mar Océano, podría reírse de los oficiales del Consejo, pasando a donde mejor le viniera en ganas, como hacían los más cazurros. Y así, ya sin enojo, anda Juan.

By the time the ship approaches Cuba, "el ingrato camino para alcanzar la fortuna estaba cansando ya a Juan," as the weight of the rock must have begun to tire Sisyphus as he approached the top of the mountain. Now in America, where "todo es chisme, insidias, comadreros, cartas que van, cartas que vienen, odios mortales, envidias sin cuento," Juan is disillusioned. He curses the "indiano que le hiciera embarcar para esta tierra roñosa." How else indeed must Sisyphus have felt as he watched his rock descend to the plain for the first time? Now both Juan and Sisyphus, especially as Camus views the latter, can contemplate the absurdity of their fate in its entirety. Juan's effort to escape the corruption of civil and divine authority and Sisyphus' effort to push his stone upward have both ended in nothingness.

Juan is not prepared to accept the inevitable, however, as no man is after his first defeat. After he stabs a fellow adventurer, Juan escapes into the wilderness in order to hide from the justice of the governor. There in that wilderness, among the Calvinists, the Jew, and the Indians, all of them outcasts, Juan stands at the top of his mountain, turns and contemplates the world which stretches out before him on the plain below. Before he leaves that mountain retreat, he is offered salvation once more, and once again he will reject it.

His education continues with a confession. "¡Yo he matado!" he tells the Calvinist, "para tratar de descender en lo posible, al nivel de quien acaba de confesar el peor crimen." His immediate concern is still for his life because the Calvinist is pointing a firearm at him. But shortly the thought of his being a murderer will reoccur to him, and when it does he will think not of one murder, but many.

As the Calvinist describes to him the assassination of six hundred of his religious comrades in America, Juan realizes that such a punishment "le parecía un poco subido, y más aquí donde las víctimas, en verdad, en nada molestaban." Now Juan, "que ha visto enterrar mujeres vivas y quemar centenares de luteranos en Flandes, y hasta ayudó a arrimar la leña al brasero y empujar las hembras protestantes a la hoya, considera las cosas de distinta manera." It may be political and religious expediency in the Old World for man to fight over theological questions, he concludes, but in the New World, man, in his primitive state, has no need for either political or religious institutions.

And there in the wilderness, with his fellow outcasts, "ha encontrado Juan amparo contra la justicia del gobernador, y calor de hombres." Thus, for a brief moment, Juan finds happiness, not by accepting his burden, but by being allowed to taste briefly of the absolute freedom which he seeks.

But his education, or his own punishment, is not yet complete. Juan must return to the plain, as every man must eventually return to his burden. Or as Carpentier expresses it at the conclusion of *Los pasos perdidos,* "Hoy terminaron las vacaciones de Sísifo." In the lonely atmosphere of the wilderness, Juan, like all of his companions with the exception of the natives, is beset by melancholy. That melancholy leads him to believe that he is still a Christian, or that he should be, and he reaffirms his belief in his God.

He soon finds himself in the midst of another plague. "Juan se enfurece, patalea, grita, al verse envuelto por tantas mosquillas negras que zumban en sus oídos," and exhausted he falls asleep. His dream is symbolic as was the first dream in Amsterdam. Again, it appears as if his God is offering him the way to spiritual salvation. But this time, Juan finds the doors of the cathedral in Compostela closed to him. "Quiere entrar y no puede. Llama y no le oyen." But even though Juan has been allowed to contemplate the hopelessness of his fate, as a Catholic, he can cling stubbornly to the hope that was once given to him by the God that would now destroy it.

On his return to Spain, therefore, Juan again believes that he will carry out his original promise to go to Santiago. But as he approaches land, he suddenly feels "que el haber estado allá, en las Indias, le hace indiano. Así, cuando desembarque, será Juan el Indiano." And so, Juan el Indiano, completely lost in the labyrinth, does not reach Santiago de Compostela, and he never will.

When Juan el Indiano and the new Juan el Romero set out again for Sevilla, to complete anew the circular pilgrimage, the two represent the totality of Carpentier's Sisyphean character. Juan-Sisyphus is Man searching for eternal terrestrial freedom, but never being able to obtain it because he has failed to realize that freedom and moral perfection are synonymous. Though he could enjoy the fruit of that freedom in the American wilderness, which seems to symbolize the last vestige of the "Garden of Eden" before the "fall" of man, Juan continues to reject it and condemns himself eternally to his rock—his own immorality. That immorality, in turn, corrupts his only other opportunity for moral perfection and

spiritual salvation—his church-state, his civilization.

Despite his hopelessness, Juan, like Camus' Sisyphus, manages to triumph over the power of his God. By accepting the "myth" of Santiago de Compostela only when faced with death, Juan decides to shoulder his own burden, to create his own universe, however absurd his destiny may be. For a brief moment, which is his life-time, Juan curses the plague of death and deceives his God. But Juan is not the noble and tragic Sisyphus of which Camus speaks. Juan triumphs over his God only because that God has promised him eternal salvation. It is a triumph offered to him by the generosity of that God. Unlike Camus, Carpentier sees his Sisyphus as a contemptuous anti-hero, who triumphs at the expense of human dignity.

But by accepting the "myth" of Santiago, if only momentarily, Juan, too, acknowledges his weakness in relation to his God. He, too, confirms the fact that he is, after all, a slave, obeying the commands of his God. And thus, Santiago says what now must be obvious to Juan.

> Y cuando los Juanes llegan a la Casa de la Contratación, tienen ambos—con el negro que carga sus collares—tal facha de pícaros, que la Virgen de los Marcantes frunce el ceño al verlos arrodillarse ante su altar.
>
> —Dejadlos, Señora—dice Santiago, hijo de Zebedeo y Salomé, pensando en las cien ciudades nuevas que debe a semejantes truhanes. Dejadlos, que con ir allá me cumplen.

These two Juans, and others like them, will, despite their lack of human dignity, establish new shrines and new cities for their God in the New World. And in doing so, they will continue to offer hope, if not for themselves, for others who will follow them.

Though, in its essence, this hope has no limitations, and I do not believe that Carpentier intends for it to have such limitations, it appears in **"El camino de Santiago"** to be directed toward the completion of the great American adventure, which, in Latin America, has been and essentially remains a Spanish-Catholic venture. For in America, Man, in his primitive state, can yet realize that morality, though it distinguishes him from his beastly cousins, is part of his primal essence. And it is this primitive morality alone which can now relieve Juan-Sisyphus of his human burden. For Carpentier, it seems that moral perfection and spiritual salvation through Santiago de Compostela—an avenue closed by man's own corruption—will remain impossible until man realizes and accepts the true essence of Santiago de Cuba, of America, of his primitive and prehistorical being.

Alejo Carpentier with Klaus Muller-Bergh (interview date Fall 1976)

SOURCE: "Talking to Carpentier," in *Review,* No. 18, Fall, 1976, pp. 20-4.

[*In the following interview, Carpentier discusses his latest three novels,* Concierto barroco, El recurso del método, *and a work in progress.*]

The leaves on the chestnut trees are just beginning to turn yellow along the Avenue Foch and the Rue de la Faisanderie leading to the Cuban Embassy. A chilly wind announces the coming of autumn. I have not seen Alejo Carpentier for four years. My daughter Elena is with me, coloring book in hand, and is practicing her Spanish on the embassy's French receptionist.

Over the last decade, Carpentier has been working on three novels more or less simultaneously. He assures me that he is still in the habit of getting up at five or five-thirty in the morning to take advantage of the early hours for his writing. He doesn't believe in the Muse or inspiration, but in the progress of daily work. Obviously, he says, there are good and bad days, when you re-read the next morning and exclaim with disgust, "This is just terrible!" But no matter how bad it is, you always find something you can use. *Concierto barroco, El recurso del método,* and another novel as yet untitled are his three new books.

Carpentier considers *Concierto barroco* a novella, a sort of Summa Theologica of his style since it also contains all the mechanisms of "Baroquism." Some chapters are worked in different colors: the first begins with a silver frame, symbolic of the chief source of income in the Mexico of the Viceroys. All the early scenes are enveloped in this baroque atmosphere, in the style of Sor Juana Inés de la Cruz. A Mexican miner, grandson of Spaniards born "somewhere between Colmenar de Oreja and Villamanrique del Tajo," acquires wealth and decides to travel to Europe to enjoy himself. His Indian servant, Francisquillo, comes along: after all, what is a powerful man of the New World without an exotic servant? In the second chapter, shades of gold and sulphur take over when master and servant arrive in Havana in the midst of a yellow fever epidemic. The travelers flee the epidemic to Villa de Regla (a town across the bay from Havana), where there existed at that time a kind of concentration camp for Jesuits. The Indian servant dies of fever in Regla and is replaced by Filomeno, a young black, grandson of the black Salvador who cut off the head of Captain Gilberto Girón in the struggle against the French pirates, described in *Espejo de paciencia* by Silvestre de Balboa, the first work of Cuban literature. The third chapter begins in the dull Madrid of Philip V's reign, filthy, decadent, mutilated, with sordid brothel settings. It ends with the felicitous entrance of the two into Barcelona, an episode based on the forty-first chapter of the second part of the *Quijote.*

The fourth chapter, really the manifestation of Carpentier's esthetics, takes place during carnival time, an image of spectacles, mimes, and costumes which appears in the author's other novels. This is a Venetian carnival that takes place in a kind of non-Venice, free from all the themes and gratuitous associations usually given to this over-used Italian setting; here, the reader will look in vain for Harlequins chasing Columbines. The Mexican protagonist, dressed as Montezuma, gets involved in a drinking bout with a red-headed monk, a German, and a non-Venetian Italian he meets in a tavern. In chapter five the four revelers, accompanied by Filomeno, arrive at the Mercy Hospital, a semi-convent sheltering seventy female orphans, each of whom plays an instrument. The girls don't have ordinary names, they are addressed by the name of the instrument each of them plays: Pierina del Violino, Cattarina del Corneto, Bettina della Viola, Bianca Maria Organista, etc. Three of the visitors reveal themselves to be the composers Antonio Vivaldi, George Friedrich Händel, and Domenico Scarlatti, who met in Venice in the year 1709. The musicians played a funambulist concerto grosso, joined by the Negro servant with his improvised orchestra of pots, pans, and other kitchen utensils. Towards dawn the guests eat and disperse to rest.

In the first draft of *Concierto barroco,* finished in August, 1972, the action of the last two chapters took place in a Venetian cemetery. The protagonists seek out a quiet place to have breakfast: the ancient graveyard of the Capuchins, where each tells the story of his life. Filomeno's tale is the most extraordinary: it encompasses a time-warp, uniting two events in history: the struggles of his ancestors against the pirate Gilberto Girón, and the more recent events at the same site, Guacanayabo Gulf and the Bay of Pigs. The Negro begins by reciting tales from the early resistance of the people of Bayamo, a town in Oriente Province, and ends with the April, 1961, anti-Castro invasion that landed in the uninhabited mangrove swamps of Playa Girón. After that, the characters discover the name of Igor Stravinsky inscribed on a gravestone, and an animated discussion of his work ensues. (It will be remembered that the Russian composer, who died in New York on April 6, 1971, is buried in the San Michele cemetery in Venice.) Into this dream-like, Poe-like environment, a black gondola intrudes, the first overt allusion to the Venetian setting. The reference is to Wagner's funeral in 1883, when his coffin was transferred, first by gondola and later by train, from Venice to Bayreuth. In the original text Carpentier compares the Wagnerian locomotive with Turner's famous painting of 1844. *Rain, Steam and Speed: The Great Western Railway:* "Puffing in the fog, enveloped in its vapors, Turner's locomotive lay in wait, its Cyclopean eye already kindled." Among the first images of a train in nineteenth-century painting, its real theme is surely the effect of the beacon's swift light passing through the downpour. The novel ends with a new "baroque concert": a Duke Ellington jazz concert which the servant is about to attend.

The published version of **Concierto barroco** is significantly different. There are superficial changes in the first chapter; in the second, Carpentier develops the *Espejo de paciencia* and exploits Balboa's interesting poem: the third remains intact except for some polishing of the style, for example in the symbolism of the ferryman Caronte, now more subtly achieved. The sixth chapter is rather extensively rewritten to make time changes less obvious and to shorten the Playa Girón episode to connect it to the last chapter, creating a new revolutionary allusion with a different motive.

As for the last pages, the recent discovery of Alvise Giusti's libretto to Vivaldi's first opera, *Montezuma* (premiered in 1733), forced Carpentier to alter the ending, adding some forty pages and changing the dénouement slightly. The libretto, thought irrevocably lost, reveals that the opera's plot hinged on a naval battle in Texcoco Lake and the burning of a *teocali* (an ancient temple). Carpentier, following the trail of Roland Candé, a musicologist and Vivaldi specialist, found the Giusti libretto, which enabled him to add a seventh chapter about the *Montezuma* text and a new, long episode describing the opera's dress rehearsal. In their eighth and last chapter, he changed the ending by switching the jazz concert with Duke Ellington at the piano for the trumpet virtuosity of Louis Armstrong, thereby achieving in the narrative a closer analogy between the instrumentation of the famous air in Händel's *Messiah* "The Trumpet Shall Sound," and Louis Armstrong's trumpet playing Negro spirituals such as "Go Down Moses" and "Jonah and the Whale."

Carpentier insists that he is not a historian but a novelist, and that in confronting history he reserves the right to a behavior akin to Louis Aragon's *"place à l'imagination."* While a writer cannot falsify the date of the Battle of Waterloo or the Battle of Ayacucho, he ought, by presenting superfluous incidents, more interesting for their content than their form, to play with certain realities, using them as he pleases and according to his artistic vision.
—Klaus Muller-Bergh

Carpentier feels that discovering the libretto of Vivaldi's opera was crucial to finishing **Concierto barroco.** *Montezuma* is the first use of an American theme in opera, two years before the Inca setting of Jean Philippe Rameau's *Les Indes*

Galantes. Carpentier was also affected by the historical fact that Vivaldi, Händel, and Scarlatti met in Venice on December 26, 1709: December 26 is Carpentier's birthday, it is St. Stephen's Day, and it always has been a day of good luck for him. (No wonder the protagonist of **El siglo de las luces** [**Explosion in a Cathedral**] is named Esteban!)

The second novel, **El recurso del método,** has an ironic title punning on Descartes' *Discours de la Méthode:* resources (*recursos*) are a feature of Latin American countries and have played a role in their political reality since well before the nineteenth century, as Carpentier points out: "Dr. Francia, transcending his own adventure, instituted among us a method of governing whose resources, multiplied to infinity, are still in effect in the political life of many Latin American nations. Hence the title '*recurso del método*' given to this work, which is set in a country that is a *summa geographica* of the least Cartesian of all possible worlds." Thus without imitating any present or past book—Roa Bastos and Garcia Márquez have also written novels about dictatorship: *Yo, El Supremo* [I, The Supreme One] and *El otoño del patriarca* [*The Autumn of the Patriarch*]—Carpentier's book communicates with that introspective, analytical consciousness that is characteristic of the vanguard generation, and it fits into a Hispanic literary tradition that has its roots in "El matadero," *Tirano Banderas, El Señor Presidente,* and even *El acoso.*

El recurso del método is about the First Magistrate of the Nation (the title of most Latin American Presidents), mystical and flammarionesque dictator "overtaken by events," or as the author describes him "a reader, although not always well read, somewhat erudite, an occasional music lover, very given to the verbal baroque, implacable inside his country but excessively worried about what might be said about him outside of it." He is a sort of Latin American monster made up of the bits and pieces of real dictators: "Actually, a montage of elements which characterize many Latin American dictatorships of the past and present, faithfully incorporated into the *robot-portrait* in such a way that anybody reasonably well acquainted with our Latin American history could point out their source": Venezuela's Antonio Guzmán Blanco and Cipriano Castro; Mexico's Porfirio Diaz; Guatemala's Manuel Estrada Cabrera; Cuba's Gerardo Machado. Some contemporary historical figures are mentioned and allusions are made to "events which we continue to witness now." Thus Nehru appears in the novel's last chapter, which is entitled "1972." Carpentier notes: "Even though its actions extend over a period of fifteen years, and we know exactly what part of the history of this century those years are, the main character, by his omnipresence in the South American continent, breaks up his own chronology and exists simultaneously before and after the lifetime allotted him by the author." The technique of elaborating an American prototype with elements from different countries again reveals the universalist. American criterion typical of Carpentier's mature work. He intends for each reader to seek out the model for this or that passage in the novel, on his own and without the fetters of historical exactitude.

Carpentier insists that he is not a historian but a novelist, and that in confronting history he reserves the right to a behavior akin to Louis Aragon's *"place à l'imagination."* While a writer cannot falsify the date of the Battle of Waterloo or the Battle of Ayacucho, he ought, by presenting superfluous incidents, more interesting for their content than their form, to play with certain realities, using them as he pleases and according to his artistic vision. A good example of this technique is the second chapter of **El recurso del método,** where the First Magistrate attends—without understanding anything—a performance of *Pélleas et Mélisande* in 1914 in New York. The alert critic will observe that Debussy's opera did not have its première at the Metropolitan until 1921. But the main thing is the fact that the opera was heard at some point in New York, seven years' difference is not so important, and it certainly does not detract from the novel's credibility. Just as Carpentier tailors certain chronological elements to his imaginative needs, he does something similar in situating his characters in certain locales. At one time, various Latin American dictators lived in the Quartier de L'Etoile and one of Porfirio Diaz' ministers, Yves Limantour, had a house on the Rue Tilsit which, with the Rue de Presbourg, forms a circle around the Place d'Etoile. Thus Carpentier has the First Magistrate live out his days on the Rue Tilsit, in a house "from which Minister Limantour's mansion could be seen." And it is a historic fact that Porfirio Diaz' body rests almost directly across from Baudelaire's in the Montparnasse cemetery.

Carpentier plans to finish his third novel, as yet untitled, this year. He says the first part is divided into three sections and takes place in Paris and in Russia, at Baku on the Caspian Sea. Carpentier follows the life of his mother, a White Russian who eventually ended up teaching her native tongue in Cuba. We will find scenes, he says, from the decade following World War I, including the arguments spawned by Dadaism and Surrealism. Carpentier believes that in terms of the anguish of modern man as reflected in political and esthetic convulsions, the decade of the thirties was one of the most decisive in the twentieth century. It was then that for the first time the drama of the human condition was situated inside and not outside of man.

The second part of the novel develops during the Spanish Civil War, prelude to the most violent crisis in modern history. The memorable deeds of the Latin American volunteers in the international brigades, passed over in most accounts, form one of the most dramatic parts of the Civil War. In the brigades, people from the remotest places and backgrounds fought together: the Mexican painter David Alfaro Siqueiros,

nicknamed the "Coronelazo"; Evan Shipman, son of an American millionaire and friend of Robert Desnos; Pablo de la Torriente Brau, a Cuban who died under machine gun fire at the front; the Cuban trumpeter Cuevas who would play "La chambelona" to sound the charge for his comrades.

The third part of the novel takes place in Mexico during the *cristero* revolts. The fourth takes place in Cuba, ending with the Bay of Pigs. Carpentier tells the story through the impressions of fighters, wounded soldiers, and reports from Baragaño, a poet who died of a heart attack in 1962, whose artistic vision allowed him to narrate the historical events very differently from the other revolutionary activists. Into this novel of American events Carpentier incorporates bits and pieces of memories of living with the great ballet dancer Alicia Alonso in Venezuela and Cuba.

In early September, 1963, Carpentier met Igor Stravinsky in Brazil on the occasion of the International Festival of Music in Rio de Janeiro. The writer stayed at a hotel in the Copacabana not so much by taste—he would have preferred a more typical neighborhood—but because the hotel was near the Cuban Embassy. The Russian composer had come to conduct his Mass in memory of Pope John XXIII, which was performed at the Candelaria de Rio Church on September 8. One night Carpentier met Stravinsky by accident while out for a stroll on the Copacabana beach. They sat down on a bench on Avenida Atlántica, almost deserted at that hour, and talked about friends. Carpentier asked Stravinsky for permission to reproduce in his novel the first page of the manuscript of *Le sacre du printemps.*

Today, the novelist confesses that one of the mistakes of his book **La música en Cuba** was to believe too easily in nationalism. Now he realizes that it was a phase he had to go through, but that in the last analysis, it did not lead to anything concrete. That is, the idea held in those days that folklore would unite humanity in a single, immediate brotherhood, was too optimistic. Carpentier went into this problem in depth with arguments and examples in **Tientos y diferencias.** Years later, he attended a Czech ballet performed in Cuba and noted that part of the audience—some sixty Venezuelan peasants who were guests of the government—were bored to distraction. He decided that the reason Latin Americans so respect and appreciate first-rate folk guitarists and harpists is because they represent an institution, they are the custodians of a folk tradition that maintains its classic touches pure and unpolluted.

Carpentier does not think much of the thunder of the Boom in the Latin American New Novel. Actually he doesn't believe there has been a Boom as such, but rather the fortuitous coincidence, perhaps produced by the robust maturity, of a dozen or so writers, among whom are Miguel Angel Asturias, Jorge Luis Borges, Julio Cortázar, Carlos Fuentes, Gabriel García Márquez, Mario Vargas Llosa, etc. These writers, of different literary generations and different countries, have jumped to the fore by finding the formula to deprovincialize Hispanic American literature. One of the tasks confronting all Hispanic American artists continues to be the eternal problem of constantly watching over their craft while they discover new themes, new ideas, and to write in a simple, polished, and transparent style. This is one of the reasons Carpentier so admires Borges' prose.

As Cultural Adviser to the Cuban Embassy in Paris, the novelist continues to represent the revolutionary government at cultural events in Europe. At a symposium on Class Society and Racism (published as *Klassengesellschaft und Rassismus*), in Reda, Germany, he read a paper on "The Integration of the Afro-American Cultures in Latin America" and made some remarks that were taped and transcribed (unfortunately not very accurately). He continues to contribute to projects related to old friends. Shortly before his death, Pablo Picasso wrote a sixty-page poem entitled "The Burial of Count Orgaz," which was translated with an introduction by Carpentier. Picasso asked him to do it, and Michel Leiris, one of the last persons to visit Picasso frequently, brought him Carpentier's version, which Picasso approved. The poem is a surrealistic, cubist, very contemporary vision. It has been published by Gallimard in a bilingual edition, and other single poems will be published separately, in Carpentier's translation.

Lilia, his wife, interrupts us to say it is lunch time. My daughter demands her tourist's rights to climb into a Bateau Mouche. We say goodbye, I turn and wave. Elena and I walk toward the Trocadero while that "old and lovely lady that is the Tour Eiffel" appears, outlined against the Paris sky.

John M. Kirk (essay date Summer 1981)

SOURCE: "*Concientización:* Keystone to the Novels of Alejo Carpentier," in *The International Fiction Review,* Vol. 8, No. 2, Summer, 1981, pp. 106-13.

[*In the following essay, Kirk analyzes the theme of* concientización *or consciousness-raising as found in Carpentier's work, focusing on* El reino de este mundo, Los pasos peridios, *and* El siglo de las luces.]

Although Alejo Carpentier has referred on several occasions to the "major themes" encountered in his work, he has never explained precisely what he means by this term. For instance in an interview with Luis Harss, Carpentier expressed his disdain for what he termed "'the little psychological novel,' a pejorative term he seems to apply to any book involving situations—especially when subjective or emotional—that are not of direct public relevance." In their place he offered

the more relevant "epic substance" which he contends derives from the same "major themes": "I like big themes . . . they are the ones that confer the greatest richness to the characters and plot of the novel." To date several valuable attempts have been made to shed light both on the theory of Carpentier's understanding of these "grandes temas," and on their application in the Cuban writer's work. While most critics have made reference to Carpentier's obvious fascination with the Antillean and circum-Caribbean regions, and to his eloquent appraisal of that area's magical reality ("lo real maravilloso"), several interesting—and at times contradictory—hypotheses concerning these "temas" have also been advanced. At the risk of oversimplification, one can state that such interpretations have revolved around a core of related issues, namely Liberty-Revolution, War, Human Nature, and Time. While not disagreeing necessarily with these views, it does appear however that a further theme, *concientización,* can also be advanced, not only as one of the elusive "major themes" but also as a common denomination of all the novels of Alejo Carpentier.

> **In interpreting Carpentier's work much confusion has been engendered both by the Cuban writer's observations on the historical process, and by his setting of much of his work in an earlier era, essentially to illustrate the relevance of past occurrences to present-day situations.**
> **—John M. Kirk**

The terms *concientización* (or its occasional variant *concienciación*) are expressions which have only come into vogue in recent years and like the terms *politización* ("politicization") and *literatura comprometida* (best translated by the French, "littérature engagée") are occasionally misunderstood. *Concientización* may be loosely translated into English by the rather awkward phrase "consciousness-raising," although as one sociologist has shown, it also comprises other elements: "an amalgam of consciousness, conscience, conscientiousness, and commitment." In other words people who experience this process—generally in the spheres of social, political or moral questions—become more "conscious" or "aware," both of the external reality surrounding them and of the internal reality of their own character. Thus, *concientizados* of their nature, and of the surrounding conditions, they are able to perceive all from a new, enlightened, perspective. It is such a process of *concientización,* this paper maintains, that is one of the principal—if long ignored—*grandes temas* found in all the principal novels of Alejo Carpentier, three of which are discussed here: *El reino de este mundo* (*The Kingdom of This World*), 1949, *Los pasos peridios* (*The Lost Steps*), 1953, and *El siglo de las luces* (*Explosion in a Cathedral*), 1962.

engendered both by the Cuban writer's observations on the historical process, and by his setting of much of his work in an earlier era, essentially to illustrate the relevance of past occurrences to present-day situations. This decision was a deliberate one, since Carpentier's purpose, he has explained, was to "conjugar acciones en pasado-presente o en presente-pasado. Creo . . . que en el pasado pueden hallarse elementos que explican el presente." This observation, and many of a similar nature, have encouraged critics to assume that, for Carpentier, past and present times are totally interchangeable, and that—apparently by the novelist's own admission—the historical process must be viewed as embodying a repetitive, cyclical pattern.

At first glance the works of Carpentier would appear to bear out this interpretation. The best example to support such a thesis is probably *The Kingdom of This World,* where we continually encounter the theme of the exploitation of man. First we see the black slaves literally whipped into submission by the French settlers in Haiti. Later, when the novel's protagonist Ti Noël returns to his homeland after the overthrow of the white plantation owners and *colonos,* he confidently expects the seeds of liberty sown by the recent uprising to have borne fruit. Instead he is rudely disappointed, for he finds the reign of terror imposed by the new (black) overlord. Henri Christophe, to be even more despicable, since as he notes, "there was a limitless affront in being beaten by a negro as black as oneself, as thick-lipped and woolly-headed, as flat-nosed; as low-born; perhaps branded, too."

This second cycle of oppression is ultimately quashed, however, since once again the black rulers underestimate the spiritual powers of their subjects. (Despite his black heritage, Christophe rejects the whole concept of folk-religion and voodoo, preferring instead to nurture a facade of Christianity and of rather elaborate European trappings). Again, however, the exploited nation—after overthrowing Henri Christophe—fails to consolidate its position in victory, and as a result a new cycle begins, controlled this time by a different group, the "Republican mulattoes." Consequently the slaves find themselves, for the third time, at the mercy of heartless rulers: "Ti Noël learned from a fugitive that farm work had been made obligatory, and that the whip was now in the hands of Republican mulattoes, the new masters of the Plaine du Nord." The struggle for liberty has thus once again been aborted, resulting in a further round of dictatorship.

This rather depressing situation has been seen as the inevitable result of what many critics interpret as Carpentier's view of History in general, and in particular his conviction concerning the impossibility of effecting meaningful social change through revolution. Therefore, while the slaves succeeded twice in freeing themselves—briefly—from the tyr-

anny of their overlords, on each occasion they fell prey to a subsequent form of exploitation. In a thoughtful article Andrés Sorel underlines what he views as this circular, inherently pessimistic, view of the historical process held by Carpentier: ". . . el hombre camina por surcos que parecen distintos, que parecen llevar a un espacio situado más allá de su propio tiempo, y que te vuelve, cuando parecía llegar al final, al punto de partida. Todo tornará a repetirse, todo estará otra vez por hacer, todo vuelve a empezar justamente donde había terminado."

Such a reading however, seems somewhat precipitate, particularly if we consider the dramatic conclusion of the novel, and view the work in the context of all of Carpentier's other major works. Indeed, although Ti Noël is executed by his mulatto masters, his memory lives on to inspire his fellow slaves, just as the name of his predecessor in the liberating struggle, Mackandal, is *still* revered—Carpentier informs us in the novel's prologue—in contemporary Haiti. It is perhaps also worth mentioning the peculiar disappearance of Ti Noël who, after he is killed, ascends in the shape of a "*cross* of feathers" (my underlining). Emil Volek has emphasized, correctly, this point, claiming also that the name Noël ("Christmas," "the birth of Christ") symbolizes a degree of hope for future liberating attempts.

One could thus argue that, in their struggle against seemingly invincible foes, the black slaves—symbols of the oppressed around the world—eloquently reveal their determination to continue fighting to the death in order to obtain their eventual liberation. Moreover, it is worth noting that the fundamental "message" of Carpentier—found, as in all his work, toward the end of his novels—is underlined even more firmly by the moral and political development of his protagonist. Ti Noël. Prior to the ultimate confrontation with the Mulattoes, he has at all times participated in the revolutionary sallies in a rather lethargic, unconvinced fashion, fighting not out of personal conviction, but rather through loyalty to the revolutionary leaders Bouckman and Mackandal. Yet at the end of the novel his *concientización* has grown dramatically, for not only has he mastered the arts of voodoo and spearheaded the attacks of his fellow slaves against the new "cycle of oppression," but he has also found a purpose to his life. In a key introspective passage, Ti Noël shows precisely how his consciousness has been raised:

> Now he understood that a man never knows for
> whom he suffers and hopes. He suffers and hopes
> and toils for people he will never know, and who,
> in turn, will suffer and hope and toil for others who
> will not be happy either, for man always seeks a
> happiness far beyond that which is meted out to
> him. But man's greatness consists in the very fact
> of wanting to be better than he is. In laying duties
> upon himself. In the Kingdom of Heaven there is

no grandeur to be won, inasmuch as there all is an established hierarchy, the unknown is revealed, all is rest and joy. For this reason, bowed down by suffering and duties, beautiful in the midst of his misery, capable of loving in the face of afflictions and trials, man finds his greatness, his fullest measure, only in the Kingdom of This World.

It is thus "in wanting to be better than he is," in selflessly giving himself to his fellow humans, that man attempts to break out of this circular maze, struggling—as do Bouckman, Mackandal, and finally Ti Noël—to improve their human condition. It is worth noting in passing that Carpentier hints at the need for human talents to be used collectively, and not individually. Thus, as Raymond Souza has indicated, Ti Noël originally attempts to use his knowledge of voodoo for his personal use, and fails. Thereupon he "realizes that any powers he possesses must not be used to escape from man but to better man's condition." Accordingly Ti Noël issues the call to arms, enlightened now by the knowledge that, with every liberating attempt (tortuous but ultimately successful, he intimates), man is slowly inching his way forwards to liberty and self-realization.

On another level it is clear that while Mackandal, the Jamaican Bouckman, and finally Ti Noël are all executed, their revolutionary attempts completely quashed, there are nevertheless indications that definite progress has been accomplished, since in the aftermath of all three the cause of liberty espoused by them lives on, in each case stronger than before. To a certain degree, then, this novel can indeed be seen as reflecting what one critic has termed "to inmortal e invencible que son los anhelos y la lucha de un pueblo por la libertad y lo imposible que es detenerlos con la ejecución de uno o más lideres. Immediatamente aparecen otros que, en el momento culminante de su carrera llegan a ser . . . héroes en el sentido exacto de la palabra. Cumplen con su tarea histórica y desaparecen en la leyenda."

The view of Sorel expressed earlier would also—at first sight—appear applicable to Carpentier's next major work, *The Lost Steps,* since (on a superficial level, at least) the protagonist, a musician, encounters a similarly unhappy fate, and indeed "todo vuelve a empezar justamente donde había terminado." He leaves the spiritually arid ambience of a sprawling North-American city, in which he leads a Sisyphus-like existence, "ascending and descending the hill of days, with the same stone on my back, I kept going through a momentum acquired in jerks and spasms, but which sooner or later would end on a date that might be on this year's calendar." Eventually he reaches a remote area of Latin America where life finally seems to hold some meaning for him. Unfortunately he feels compelled to travel briefly to North America, and by the time he returns to the idyllic jungle setting and to his beloved Rosario, she has married. All now seems in vain for the unnamed protagonist, who sadly abandons Santa Mónica de los Venados and takes up residence again in "Civilization."

The cyclical structure is immediately obvious, since the narrator is quite clearly at the point from which his Odyssey started, with the one major difference being that he has now also lost the woman he loved. Yet the picture is not entirely black, since he has learned much of value during his pilgrimage, and has experienced many dramatic changes to his life. As a result many of his earlier ideas, and indeed many cultural works (earlier accepted unquestioningly by him,) "lay dead forever on the shelves of my library." Moreover, the experiences he underwent in the remote village of Santa Mónica de los Venados have clearly left a lasting impression on his music, which now appears to him far more original, and more authentic. Therefore as Raymond Souza has noted, like Ti Noël he will now consciously benefit from this purging experience, using his work as an illustration of man's potential: ". . . as a creative artist his task is to reveal to his contemporaries locked within an apocalyptic age the primal truths of the world of Genesis. He then becomes a mediator between the two realms, drawing from one to rejuvenate the other."

But perhaps the most convincing evidence to illustrate this *concientización* process is the attitude of the unnamed protagonist (thereby intended as a representative of modern society?) who, despite his tremendous disappointment at not being able to return to "the Fourth Day of Creation," nevertheless has learned much about himself and his society following the experiences in this "primitive" community. He can now see the pointless and rather sordid existence of his "advanced" society in the nameless North-American city where he lives: "I was amazed to see how the people around me came, went, passed one another on the wide pavement, in a rhythm that had nothing to do with their organic wills. If they walked at one pace rather than another, it was because their walking was linked to the idea of getting to the corner in time to see the green light go on to tell them they could cross the avenue." The end result of this process is a super-organized, selfish, and rather meaningless form of existence, Carpentier's protagonist suggests: "From these cement mazes emerged, exhausted, men and women who had sold another day of their time to the enterprises that fed them. They had lived another day without living, and would now restore their strength to live another day tomorrow which would not be lived either, unless they fled—as I used to do, at this same hour—to the din of the dance-hall or the benumbment of drink, only to find themselves the next sunrise more desolate, wearier, sadder than before." Consequently, while on a superficial level—as in *The Kingdom of This World*—the protagonist would appear to be facing inevitable defeat, there is indeed a message of hope extended for the future, one based precisely upon a profound awareness of the limits of "Civilization."

The relationship between rebellion and liberty . . . is perhaps the fundamental issue treated in Carpentier's *Explosion in a Cathedral*.
—John M. Kirk

The relationship between rebellion and liberty (a key theme in the Cuban writer's work) is perhaps the fundamental issue treated in Carpentier's *Explosion in a Cathedral*. Continually contrasted in this work are the differences between the characters' idealistic, and somewhat naive, concept of freedom, and the ensuing brutal revolutionary reality. On the one hand, then, while Victor Hugues offers to "liberate" people, extending to them the noble concepts of Freedom, Brotherhood, and Equality, on the other he protects these new-found liberties (and suppresses all forms of dissent) with the guillotine. The Uruguayan critic Emir Rodríguez Monegal not only views this situation as a fair reflection of the outcome of all revolutionary attempts during the past two centuries, but also considers this to be Carpentier's interpretation: "Cómo no pensar que Carpentier sabe que desde 1789 la Historia ha demostrado una y otra vez que las mejores revoluciones, las más justas, las más desinteresadas ideológicamente, acaban siendo utilizadas por minorías estratégicas en beneficio propio?"

As in the case of the other two novels, *Explosion in a Cathedral* does indeed appear—at first sight—to bear out the critic's remarks, particularly if we consider the revolutionary fervor of Victor Hugues. Esteban follows his *padre espiritual* to France, prepared to make an effective contribution to the revolutionary struggle. Disenchantment gradually sets in, however, followed by a refutation of the "liberating" doctrine. (At one dramatic moment he asks a companion what he would do if the struggle were to fail, to which his friend replied, "with a gesture of resignation: 'In spite of everything I shall go on the same. When you've worked at making a revolution, it's difficult to go back to what you did before.'" It would thus appear on the most obvious level at least, that the ideological inspiration lasted but a short time, being soon replaced by a vague form of inertia. Soon afterwards Hugues is sent to govern the island of Guadeloupe, where, as well as the doctrine of Liberty, Fraternity, and Equality, he also introduces the guillotine. Esteban's disillusionment continues to increase and in a very moving scene he finally confronts his mentor: "'I dreamed of such a different revolution,' murmured Esteban. 'And who authorized you to believe in what didn't exist?' Victor asked him. 'Anyway all this is just empty talk. . . . A revolution is not argued about, it's done.'"

This apparent failure—yet again—of the revolutionary process, and the resulting circular time structure found in the other novels of Carpentier, is studied in some detail by Luis Harss in his chapter on the Cuban (significantly subtitled "The Eternal Return") of his milestone of contemporary Latin-American criticism, *Into the Mainstream*. Basically he supports the view developed by Rodríguez Monegal, although Harss quite clearly understands a little better the ambivalent, subtle complexity of Alejo Carpentier's position: "Undoubtedly there is a duality in Carpentier: the political militant alternates, at unexpected moments with the ecumenic scholar for whom the essence of history—which can be annoyingly reactionary—is that it repeats itself. So it is, for instance, that revolutions become establishments, which eventually, rounding out the cycle, succumb to new revolutions. . . . On an absolute scale, outside time, there is no forward—or backward—movement, only the endless swing of a pendulum from a point suspended in space to its antipode." This view, however, ignores not only Carpentier's epigraph (taken from Zohar) to the novel ("words are not uttered in vain") but also what Carpentier himself has claimed to be the true sense of the novel—as typified by Sofía's eventual appreciation of the need for social change, despite the at times sordid reality of revolutionary society—and, finally, by her actions.

Both Sofía and Esteban agonize over the concept of revolution, passing from an initial heady atmosphere to a gloomy despair at the extremes of "revolutionary justice," for as Esteban notes, "the Age of the Scaffold had succeeded to the Age of the Tree of Liberty." Sofia condemns passionately the way in which the French Revolution, exported to Guadeloupe and Cayenne, has in many ways reverted to an orgy of wanton slaughter and subsequent exploitation—all carried out in the name of liberty. Yet at the same time she rationalizes that this particular corrupt "revolution" does not therefore mean that *all* revolutions necessarily had to follow this sorrowful path—something which most critics have chosen to overlook. Thus, despite her encounter with the disastrous Cayenne experience Sofía, like Ti Noël, realizes that man's greatness can only be reached after reading a path fraught with major (but essentially temporary) obstacles and setbacks. Once again we see one of Carpentier's characters stressing the need to adopt a long-term historical perspective, as the Cuban author describes the continuing struggle to reach a stage of *concientización:*

> One could not live without a political idea; the happiness of a whole people could not be achieved at the first attempt; grave errors had been made certainly, but these errors would serve as a useful guide for the future; she realized that Esteban had been through certain painful experiences—and she sympathized with him very much—but perhaps he had been the victim of an exaggerated idealism; she ad-

mitted that the excesses of the Revolution were deplorable, but great human victories could not be achieved without pain and sacrifice. To sum up: nothing big could be done in this world without blood being shed.

Following her disillusioning experience in Cayenne, Carpentier could easily have made Sofía follow Esteban's example, renouncing totally her earlier naive idealism. (In the same way as the novelist could have had Ti Noël resign himself to a life under the Mulatto Republicans, and the composer of *The Lost Steps* return to his earlier life style.) Yet Carpentier deliberately refuses to let her—and the other characters noted above—follow this course of action, instead electing to put her ideas to the test once again. Consequently many years later—and once again, it is interesting to note, towards the end of the novel—when both Sofía and Esteban are in Spain, we are shown explicitly how she overcomes her earlier disillusionment, returning to do battle for a cause in which she believes. Therefore, when Napoleon's troops enter Madrid on May 2, 1808, Sofia immediately picks up a sabre and tries to coax Esteban to join the popular struggle. He prefers not to become embroiled in the rebellion, and in fact cannot grasp Sofía's reasoning:

> It was at this moment that Sofía left the window: "Let's go down there!" she cried snatching down swords and daggers from the collection on the wall. Esteban tried to restrain her:
> "Don't be an idiot, they're shooting. You can't do any good with those bits of old iron."
> "Stay here if you want to. I'm going."
> "And who are you going to fight for?"
> "For the people who've run into the streets," cried Sofia.
> "We've got to do something."

Both are ultimately killed in the uprising but, like Bouckman and Mackandal, have risen above personal desires and, *concientizados,* have fought for the common good, in an attempt to fulfill their obligations in the "Kingdom of this World."

An overview of the weltanschauung of the three protagonists reveals characteristics common to all. Both Ti Noël and Sofía, for example, throw themselves wholeheartedly into the collective struggle against tyranny, knowing that, while they personally may die, their contribution to the common good will prevail, that they are important links in this process of developing *conciencia* among their peers. The case of the anonymous musician of *The Lost Steps* is somewhat different, since unlike the others he does not possess the same missionary zeal. Yet common to his struggle too is a determination to rise above both a temporary defeat (the loss of Rosario, and the impossibility of returning to live in Santa

Mónica), a refutation of what he now perceives as a meaningless existence, and a rejection of the apparent failure inherent in his return to the point of departure. What all these protagonists share is an awareness that, while they all appear as victims of a circular time structure, in fact they have learned something of value during the course of these experiences, and that therefore, despite setbacks, their lives have been irreversibly changed—in short, they have become *concientizados.* As a result, progress—in essence the result of human tenacity and a desire to improve one's material and spiritual conditions (both of which clearly derive from a reawakened *conciencia*)—is gradually achieved, as Salvador Bueno has correctly noted: ". . . esos círculos viciosos se rompen, la trayectoria cíclica de la historia es superada por el hombre que siempre se impone nuevas tareas; cada nuevo estado histórico, aunque parece repetir el ciclo anterior, lo supera, porque el hombre traza en la historia una espiral, lenta, difícil, pero segura, que constituye la trabajosa marcha de la humanidad en busca de una mayor felicidad en el Reino de este mundo."

This paper, studying three of Alejo Carpentier's major novels has attempted to show that the commonly-held view of many critics (who claim that Carpentier's work reveals his fascination with a circular time structure) is in fact a little simplistic. Instead, this essay contends that, while many of his characters do indeed return to the point from which they first departed, they are all very different now from their earlier condition. The fundamental difference is of course that they now possess *conciencia,* the result of learning from experiences (including errors), which allows them all—Ti Noël, the musician of *The Lost Steps,* and Sofía—to plot, by means of a conscious form of reasoning, their psychological and moral development.

Admittedly this determination to impose their will upon seemingly insoluble problems and to embark upon the resulting Odyssey along "una espiral lenta, difícil, pero segura" (to use Bueno's excellent analogy), does not come easily. Nevertheless, all of Carpentier's protagonists, following the process of *concientización,* throw themselves into this task with great energy, believing against all odds that they can make a lasting impression upon their environment. But then this should not surprise us, for as Ti Noël so eloquently puts it, "man's greatness consists in the very fact of wanting to be better than he is."

This same grandeur can also be seen clearly in the very life of Alejo Carpentier, whose untimely death on April 24, 1980, brought to a close one of the major chapters in the world of Hispanic letters. Like all his characters, Carpentier too underwent a process of *concientización,* including a period of imprisonment following his criticisms of the Machado tyranny, working for UNESCO, and supporting the government of Fidel Castro when it was fashionable for many intellectuals to abandon the Cuban cause. The common denominator of these activities was his conviction that, despite any temporary setbacks that might result from his stance, the mainstream advantages would make his position a justifiable one.

Arthur Natella Jr. (essay date 1986)

SOURCE: "The Great Theatre of the World: Alejo Carpentier and *Los Pasos Perdidos*," in *Crítica Hispánica,* Vol. VIII, No. 1, 1986, pp. 61-71.
[*In the following essay, Natella discusses the concept of "theatrum mundi," or "the idea that life is a stage and we are all its actors," as it applies to Carpentier's* Los pasos perdidos.]

Alejo Carpentier's famous novel of one man's attempt to retrace his roots back through the jungles of South America, *Los pasos perdidos,* is a brilliant evocation of the rootlessness of modern man. It is a novel that has received critical acclaim, and has been the subject of careful scrutiny by numerous scholars. Although the central themes of the work have been discussed many times, one of the main, allegorical themes of the novel has yet to receive, to the best of our knowledge, complete study even though it is an important, integral part of the novel and expresses a seminal aspect of the author's basic artistic vision. We refer to the baroque (or neo baroque) concept of the "theatrum mundi," the idea that life is a stage and that we are all its actors.

In an explanatory note at the end of *Los pasos perdidos,* Alejo Carpentier makes significant comment on the important characters of the jungle episodes of his novel. He states that he sees them as characters in a great drama: "El Adelantado, Montsalvatje, Marcos, Fray Pedro, son los personajes que encuentra todo viajero en el gran teatro de la selva." Of course, the reader of the novel, having reached this point, has already realized that these men are archetypal characters representing the generic, human types which first populated the South American continent during the earliest years of Spanish exploration. Yet when Carpentier calls these characters actors in "el gran teatro de la selva," he appears to be suggesting that they may be compared to the symbolic characters of the baroque, "autos sacramentales" of the Golden Age Spain. Indeed Salvador Bueno has already described the dramatically contrapuntal nature of the human types of *Los pasos perdidos* while Roberto González Echevarria has linked Carpentier's penchant for allegory with the thematic symbolism of the drama of Calderón de la Barca. Nevertheless, criticism so far has largely limited itself to viewing these characters in this light without linking them to the larger theme of the "theatrum mundi" which exists on many other levels of *Los pasos perdidos.*

Los pasos perdidos begins in the world of drama. In the very first page the protagonist describes his wife's role in a successful play in New York. The opening lines of the novel are extremely significant since they serve to introduce the book's basic theme: "Hacía cuatro años y siete meses que no había vuelto a ver la casa de columnas blancas, con su frontón de ceñudas molduras que le daban una severidad de palacio de justicia, y ahora, ante muebles y trastos colocados en su lugar invariable, tenía la casi penosa sensación de que el tiempo se hubiera revertido."

The passage introduces the central theme of the novel, namely the reversal of chronological time in a discovery of man's cultural roots in the past—a tension between past and present involving a baroque counterplay that is basic to the novel. Yet these opening lines have a double meaning since they refer directly to the protagonist's wife, Ruth, and indirectly to life as a whole. As an actress, Ruth must perform a never ending series of scenes which must be repeated with every performance. In a very real way, this is the novelist's first allegorical depiction of the world as a vast drama, for this "imprisonment" only foreshadows his own Sysphian punishment as an actor in the drama of life condemned to repeat an endless series of meaningless acts. It is for this reason that his description of Ruth's occupation is highly charged with symbolic meaning: here the meaninglessness of life as well as its intrinsic artificiality and falseness are reproduced in miniature within Ruth's world of drama: "Me consternaba pensando en lo dura que se había vuelto, para Ruth, esta prisión de tablas de artificio, con sus puentes volantes, sus telarañas de cordel y árboles de mentira." This punitive concept of the world of drama is further developed by the narrator as he views his wife as a veritable prisoner, "Así, para Ruth, lejos de ser una puerta abierta sobre el vasto mundo del Drama—un medio de evasión—este teatro era la Isla del Diablo." It is only as the first chapter continues to develop that we see that he himself is as much a prisoner as his wife. He also is condemned to repeat a series of meaningless acts. Worst of all, they are false since they betray the deepest part of his being. His words and his actions are mechanically reproduced simply to make the desired effect, for he too is an actor on the stage of life: "Mi esposa se dejaba llevar por el automatismo del trabajo impuesto, como yo me dejaba llevar por el automatismo de mi oficio."

On another level, Ruth herself is as much actress in real life as she is on the stage. When the narrator sees his wife change her appearance in order to begin her night's work, he notes the transformation that is worked in her, "Ruth se puso de pie, y me vi ante quien dejaba una vez más de ser mi esposa para transformarse en protagonista." This also, however, is a symbolic foreshadowing of the falseness that his wife will bring to their marriage. Indeed both in life and in her theatrical work, Ruth is false. She is nothing but an actress, and truth and fiction combine until it is impossible to distinguish one from the other. This becomes clear to the narrator on his return to the jungle when he notices that, "Mi esposa ha dejado el teatro para interpretar un nuevo papel: el papel de esposa." Playing the role of the dutiful wife, Ruth is more false than she is in the world of legitimate theater: "Y observo a Ruth, ahora, . . . y me parece que interpreta el mejor papel de su vida." Then married life itself becomes a living theater of falseness and insincerity, "De súbito, el sublime, teatro conyugal de mi esposa se hundia en el ridiculo."

In portraying his characters as timeless archetypes, Carpentier is employing, as he himself says, an age-old baroque device in creating a tension between one thematic extreme and another. On another level, however, this moulding of characters in rigidly defined "theatrical" roles portrays not only the illusory character of life but also one of the novel's main themes— namely the abolition of chronological time, for the basic human archetypes are eternal, and as such, they triumph over the divisory nature of time.
                                    —Arthur Natella Jr.

Nevertheless, this vision of the theatrical nature of human relations is only an introduction to a fuller, more general concept of the theatricality of existence as a whole which plays an important yet extremely subtle and complicated role in the basic messages of *Los pasos perdidos*.

We have seen how the author thematically connects the world of the legitimate theatre with a larger perspective on life as a whole. This, however, is but a foreshadowing of a more basic perception of the artificiality of life which appears in its most central form in his portrayal of the narrator's experiences in the South American jungle. Here the author sets his character among a timeless series of archetypes as he clearly evokes characters and events as being parts of an "autos sacramentales," "estampas" or prints or engravings, complete with generic, symbolic figures such as would be found in medieval and Renaissance church drama. This is true in chapter fifteen of the novel in which the narrator describes his visit to a small, jungle church. It is here that he finds himself called back to an appreciation of ancient mysteries of religion: "Así, rodeados más figuras de aleluya, los viejos santos que aparecen entregados a sus oficios, como si el templo fuese ante todo un taller . . . Ante el Cristo de madera negra que parecía desangrarse sobre el altar mayor, hallaba la atmósfera de auto sacramental, de misterio, de

hagiografía tremebunda." Before this, during his trip leading to the jungle, he sees a series of illuminated scenes that form an essentially theatrical depiction of the elements and generic human types that have constituted Latin American history. Here the narrator is conscious of the essential theatricality of the scene that he is witnessing: "Pero aquellos quince focos, siempre aleteados por los insectos, tenían la función aisladora de las luminarias de retablos, de los reflectores de teatros, mostrando en plena luz las estaciones del sinuoso camino que conducía el Calvario de la Cumbre." The narrator is more direct in depicting his life in the jungle as an interplay of generic, dramatic characters: "Como en los más clásicos teatros, los personajes eran, en este gran escenario presente y real, los tallados en una pieza del Bueno y el Malo, la Esposa Ejemplar o la Amante Fiel . . . Era evidente que Mouche estaba de más en tal escenario." Nor does he limit himself to viewing this symbolic, allegorical quality of human actions solely in others. In the first chapter, when he confesses his purposeless life to his old mentor, he is conscious of being part of a larger reality: "En el ser que se inscribía dentro del marco barroco del espejo actuaban en este momento el Libertino y el Predicador, que son los personajes primeros de toda alegoría edificante, de toda moralidad ejemplar."

In portraying his characters as timeless archetypes, Carpentier is employing, as he himself says, an age-old baroque device in creating a tension between one thematic extreme and another. On another level, however, this moulding of characters in rigidly defined "theatrical" roles portrays not only the illusory character of life but also one of the novel's main themes—namely the abolition of chronological time, for the basic human archetypes are eternal, and as such, they triumph over the divisory nature of time.

The novel also dwells on the theatrical interaction between nature and man in the jungle, as in the narrator's exclamation, "Por cuanto he pasado por nuevas Pruebas; por cuanto he visto el teatro y fingimiento en todas partes." Yet this fatalistic sense of the theatrical also gives way to a lyrical feeling that all of nature combines in its harmonious parts (as do the actors in a drama) to produce a result that has cosmic significance, "La creación no es algo divertido, y todos lo admiten por instinto, aceptando el papel asignado a cada cual en la vasta tragedia de lo creado. . . ."

This sense of the theatricality of existence involves a delineation of a sense of evolving and eternally repeated roles, both for nature and for man, within the framework of the natural world. Hence the Cuban author continues his description of "la vasta tragedia de lo creado," with the following observations:

> Pero es tragedia con unidades de tiempo, de acción
> y de lugar, donde la misma muerte opera por acción

de mandatarios conocidos, cuyos trajes de veneno, de escama, de fuego, de miasmas, se acompañan del rayo y del trueno que siguen usando, en días de ira, los dioses de más larga residencia entre nosotros. A la luz del sol o al calor de la hoguera, los hombres que aquí viven sus destinos se contentan de cosas muy simples, hallando motivo de júbilo en la tibieza de una mañana, una pesca abundante, la lluvia que cae tras la sequía, con explosiones de alegría colectiva, de cantos y de tambores, promovidos por sucesos muy sencillos como fue el de nuestra llegada.

The world of nature with its ancient, dramatic harmonies is reflected in the repetition of traditional events of human life which combine to create scenes from a primitive "drama" complete with songs and collective expressions of a primordial, ancestral dramatic ritual.

This sense of the archetypal theatricality of existence for man and nature becomes explicit in the use of the word "papel," a key word with which the novelist evokes a sense of admiration for the great drama of history and for each man and each society's role in it. Thus he considers life in the jungle in the following terms: "Me preguntaba ya si el papel de estas tierras en la historia humana sería el de hacer posibles, por vez primera ciertas simbiosis de culturas." Yet man himself has his own role in this theatre of life for each individual has his craft and skill which combines with others to form a harmonious whole in the great drama of life itself. The narrator admires this interchanging of social responsibilities in a "primitive" society in which each person's role is clearly defined, "La soberana precisión con que éste flechaba peces en el remanso, la prestancia de coreógrafo con que el otro embocaba la cerbatana . . . me revelaban la presencia de un ser humano llegado a maestro en la totalidad de oficios propiciados por el teatro de su existencia."

We have seen that music forms part of the drama of natural life in the jungle. As music is composed of the harmonious interchange of notes and instruments of an individual or of an orchestra or chorus, this harmonious interplay of parts can serve as a metaphor for the roles of a drama while at the same time the novelist is conscious of the musical elements of drama, especially those of classical, Greek drama.

Just as the jungle is portrayed as a drama in and of itself, it is also the scene for the correlation of a series of antifonal melodies that intertwine and mingle among themselves as profuse, baroque vegetation in sound. As in a musical theatrical presentation, here in the jungle, "la tormenta se lleva sus últimos rayos, tan pronto como los trajo, cerrando la tremenda sinfonía de su ira con el acorde de un trueno muy rodado y prolongado, y la noche se llena de ranas que cantan

su júbilo." Here the protagonist hears, "la ululante antifona de los canes," and the "más universal concierto de ladridos." This is the "sinfonía telúrica" the, "sinfonía que estamos leyendo al revés, de derecha a izquierda, contra la clave de sol, retrociendo hacia los compases del Génesis."

Here the disparate elements of drama in primitive culture—music, poetry and dance, are all components in the narrator's vision of the cosmos. As the protagonist listens he discovers a hidden beauty in the jungle: "He descubierto, de pronto, en un segundo fulgurante que existe una Danza de los Arboles. . . . Ninguna coreografía humana tiene la euritmia de una rama que se dibuja sobre el cielo. . . . Un día, los hombres descubrirán un alfabeto en los ojos de las calcedonias, en los pardos terciopelos de la falena, y entonces se sabrá con asombro que cada caracol manchado, era, desde siempre, un poema."

It is significant that Carpentier refers to "coreografía" and "escenografía" when speaking of the musicality of nature. These words, intimately connected with theatrical production, link the world of nature with the planned exactness of human theatricality: "estábamos en un lugar cuyos elementos componían una de esas escenografías inolvidables que el hombre encuentra muy pocas veces en su camino." The term appears again in a similar context: "me resultaban tan desconcertante y nuevo como los árboles enormes que comenzaban a cerrar las orillas y que, reunidos por grupos en las entradas de los caños, se pintaban sobre el poniente. . . . Yo identificaba los elementos de la escenografía, ciertamente."

In its fullest, most profound sense, this uniting of music and drama leads to the answer of the narrator's basic question about the true origins of music. Here it arises, (as the narrator will later learn) not from the imitation of natural sounds, as he had thought, but rather from the basic cries of nature which mix with the primordial expressions of human instinct to form elemental musical structures. Thus does the narrator realize (perhaps instinctively) the truth of Nietzsche's assertion in *The Birth of Tragedy* that drama, particularly tragedy, rose out of musical expression and is intrinsically linked to it. This is found to be true in **Los pasos perdidos** as scenes of the novel show us how music does indeed rise out of instinctive cries and shouts that express basic human needs. Just as Nietzsche has shown how drama arose from the spontaneous shouts of joy of the Dionysian revelers, the protagonist hears the cries of anguish at a native funeral where "Las mujeres rezaban en antifona en los dormitorios." Here he observes a primitive rite that links the past to the present: "Impresionado por la violencia de ese dolor, pensé, de pronto, en la tragedia antigua. . . . Frente al cadáver, esas campesinas clamaban en diapasón de coéforas, soltando sus cabelleras espesas, como velos negros. La persistencia de esa desesperación, el admirable sentido dramático con las nueve hermanas—pues eran nueve—fueron apareciendo por puerta derecha y puerta izquierda, preparando la entrada de una Madre que fue Hécuba portentosa, maldiciendo su soledad, sollozando sobre las ruinas de su casa, gritando que no tenía Dios, me hicieron sospechar que había bastante teatro en todo ello."

This significant passage clearly highlights many of the previously mentioned concepts of the "theatrum mundi," for the narrator perceives a true Greek tragedy as nine sisters group themselves as members of a classical chorus chanting over the death of a loved one. The reference to "aullantes troyanas," and "Hécuba Portentosa" are significant and thematically important. On another level, however, this is a "rito milenario" for as the narrator wisely says, "Pudieran sonreir algunos ante la tragedia que aquí se representaba. Pero, a través de ella, se alcanzaban los ritos primeros del hombre." Here in the jungle, man still performs age old rites and ceremonies, and Carpentier (in true baroque fashion) charges the word "tregedia" with a double meaning both as a tragedy in the death of a loved one and as the novelistic construction of a modern-day Greek tragedy complete with its own chorus. Here the protagonist feels that in the drama of existence there is a timeless uniting of past and present that gives meaning and substance to life.

A basic component of the baroque is a sense of contrived artifice. Inherent in this vision of life is a perception of reality as deceptive and illusory. Within Alejo Carpentier's novel there are often layers of reality, one hidden within another which are frequently not seen for what they are since ultimate reality is hidden under a false front or mask. Indeed the jungle itself is seen by Carpentier's narrator as a world of illusion and deception, a baroque profusion of forms where there is an "eterno barajarse de las apariencias y los simulacros, en esa barroca proliferación de lianas." The jungle, in a sense, wears a mask as does a character in a classical drama. Although it is true that the author refers to "el gran teatro de la selva" as a part of the great theatre of existence, he is more specific in delineating the jungle as a place of lies and illusion. Here reality is masked in a singular fashion: "Aquí todo parecía otra cosa, creándose un mundo de apariencias que ocultaba la realidad.... La selva era el mundo de la mentira ... allí todo era disfraz, estratagema, juego de apariencias.... Entre dos aguas se mecían grandes hojas agujereadas, semejantes a antifaces de terciopelo ocre...."

It is in this context that masks or "máscaras" and "disfraces" become symbols of the illusory character of life itself. This theme of mask-illusion begins during the first chapter of the novel while the narrator is living in New York. He comments significantly on his inability to sleep without a face mask, "Bebía y me holgaba de espaldas a los relojes, hasta que lo

bebido y holgado me derribara el pie de un despertador, con un sueño que yo trataba de espesar poniendo sobre mis ojos un antifaz negro que debía dejarme dormido, un aire de Fantomas al descanso...." Far more, however, than being simply a mask for sleeping, this face mask is the apparatus which ties him to the false reality of clocks and other machines; it is the symbolic representation of the artificiality of existence in the modern world. It is significant, then, that only in the natural world of South America can the narrator sleep without such a mask, "Y fue ésa la primera noche, en mucho tiempo, que dio descanso sin antifaz ni drogas." Here the narrator finds his true self as he once again comes to accept a harmonious existence in tune with the rhythms of nature. In other instances, masks appear to characterize various persons as belonging to the greater drama of life. So it is that the Adelantado is he who, "escucha con cazurra máscara, arrojando ramillas a la lumbre." This is also true when the narrator witnesses the turmoil of a Latin American revolution. Here the drama of life is metaphoric as each character assumes his mask, thus producing, in the words of Carpentier a theatrical scene making the whole episode smack of the unreal: "Con las máscaras antifases colgadas aún debajo de la barbilla ... parecía que sobre ellos se hubieran fijado, en coladas, borrones y pringues, las más negras exudaciones de la tierra.... Allí se producía un golpe de teatro ... habían aparecido mujeres en trajes de baile, con zapato de tacón y muchas luces en pelo y cuello ... me pareció alucinante."

If the jungle is the world of artifice and illusion, the narrator finds on leaving it that his own human relations are equally illusory. As we have seen, the narrator returns to his wife and to his home only to find once again that his role as husband is an artificial one, for his wife, far from being sincere in her marital relations, is only acting out her part. She too wears a mask that hides her true identity from others as well as from herself. The narrator realizes that there is often little difference between the roles performed on the legitimate stage and the social roles adopted in life. In both instances a character adopts a "mask" which hides his true identity, his true intentions. He learns that the essential mask behind which true reality lies is as deceptive here as it was in the jungle and so he speaks of Ruth observing that, "su cara parecía hecha de la materia yesosa de las máscaras trágicas."

In conclusion we may say that the baroque theme of the "theatrum mundi" appears on many diverse levels of this important novel. It is in itself a basic thematic motif which connects with the narrator's attempt to reverse the flow of chronological time in the realization of cultural and historical archetypes which transcend the limitations of temporal existence. Likewise, it is a basic and persistent metaphor of the illusory character of human and natural life. It is part of the baroque disillusionment with life and as such it characterizes man as a victim of a series of shifting realities which taunt and tempt him but which never give him knowledge of the ultimate truth, nor provide him the ultimate satisfaction.

David H. Bost (essay date May 1987)

SOURCE: "A Night at the Opera: *Concierto barroco* and *Motezuma*," in *Revista de Estudios Hispanicos,* Vol. 21, No. 2, May, 1987, pp. 23-38.

[*In the following essay, Bost asserts, "It is in* Concierto barroco *that Carpentier most imaginatively combines two of his principal concerns in his exploration of historical America: the play of fact with fictional exposition, and the role of music as a cultural force."*]

Alejo Carpentier's fiction often describes watershed events of Latin American history and culture. Novels such as *¡Ecué-Yamba-O!* and *El reino de este mundo* present vibrant images of the African impact in the Caribbean. *El recurso del método* portrays a dictatorship as a characteristically Latin American institution. Carpentier returns to the genesis of America in *El arpa y la sombra,* a novel about Columbus's first voyage to the New World and his contentious historical reception in the nineteenth century. *Concierto barroco* explores through the world of opera the fall of Aztec Mexico, one of the events that clearly gave Spain political and cultural hegemony in the New World during the sixteenth century. Viewed collectively, these examples of Carpentier's fiction form a thematic trilogy that symbolizes the historical evolution of Latin America: its discovery, conquest and colonization. These novels identify the critical historical strands that are interwoven throughout the tapestry of Latin American history. It is in *Concierto barroco* that Carpentier most imaginatively combines two of his principal concerns in his exploration of historical America: the play of fact with fictional exposition, and the role of music as a cultural force. Using Antonio Vivaldi's opera *Motezuma* as the centerpiece of the novel's exposition, Carpentier presents a hybrid fusion of documentary literature, opera, and fantasy in which textual sources become almost completely inseparable from the novel's narrative voice. *Concierto barroco* is both rigorously historical and unabashedly imaginative in its transformation of this material into fiction. In this sense, *Concierto barroco* is emblematic of Carpentier's last novelistic stage, a period in which he employs a bewildering number of literary styles and sources to create works that reflect a highly creative vision of Latin America's past. A trademark of Carpentier is to include brief commentaries in his novels that expose the textual sources that underpin the essential process of story-telling. Carpentier adds a note

at the conclusion of *Concierto barroco* which explains how he came across the opera *Motezuma,* and how Charles de Brosses's *Lettres italiennes* suggested the atmosphere for the novel's presentation of Vivaldi's home, the Ospedale della Pietà. These remarks provide a code for deciphering a number of allusions to musicology and various travel diaries. In addition to the texts Carpentier mentions, there are references within the novel to such works as Silvestre de Balboa's *Espejo de paciencia,* Rousseau's *Confessions,* Edward Wright's narrative of his travels through France and Italy, and John Mainwaring's biography of Handel, among others. By drawing together these various texts into his story, Carpentier composes a sort of baroque concerto. The novel harmonizes an irregular, uneven set of sources and characters through a series of musical performances which range from an impromptu jam session in the Ospedale to the elaborate staging of Vivaldi's *Motezuma.* Music is the unifying force of Western culture for Carpentier, a power that transcends time, place and nationality. *Motezuma,* as both literary text and musical event, binds together people of different races, countries and tastes. In this sense, the opera functions as the heart of the novel, its microcosmic center. The principal characters ultimately interact by means of the composition, production, performance and reception of this opera. *Concierto barroco* is a novel with a congeries of historical sources and literary influences; *Motezuma* is the primary work of this text of texts.

Carpentier's choice of this Vivaldian opera is, at first glance, a curious one. *Motezuma* is by no means among Vivaldi's better-known choral works. *Orlando Furioso* and *Griselda,* for instance, have enjoyed a great deal more attention over the years from critics as well as production companies. It is also likely that these works, among others, achieved a higher degree of success during Vivaldi's lifetime than *Motezuma.* Girolamo Giusti, *Motezuma*'s librettist, collaborated with Vivaldi on this opera only, and was relatively unknown when compared to more famous librettists Domenico Lalli, Pietro Metastasio and Grazio Braccioli. What separates *Motezuma* from the rest is that it deals solely with an American topic— the conquest of Mexico—some years before any other major European opera. So even though the music for *Motezuma* is lost and the libretto exists today only as an unedited manuscript, Carpentier has seen in the opera a special relevance. Carpentier assumes that Vivaldi shared his artistic vision when he writes in his concluding remarks:

> Tanto parece haber gustado el *Motezuma* de Vivaldi—que traía a la escena un tema americano dos años antes de que Rameau escribiera *Las Indias galantes,* de ambiente fantasiosamente incaico—que el libretto de Alvise (otros lo llaman Girolamo) Giusti, habría de inspirar nuevas óperas basadas en episodios de la Conquista de México a dos célebres compositores italianos: el veneciano Baldassare

Galuppi (1706-1785), y el florentino Antonio
Sacchini (1730-1786).

Motezuma thus represents for Carpentier a moment in the
history of music when composers began gazing abroad to
the New World for topics that would interest an audience
steeped in classical culture. In the eighteenth and nineteenth
centuries there were many operas in Europe and America
that dramatized the key figures of the New World experiences: Columbus, Cortés, Pizarro, Atahualpa and Ponce de
León, to name several. *Motezuma* marks the beginning of
an increased tendency in European arts to use America as a
foundational metaphor. The image of America from the sixteenth through the nineteenth centuries, primarily a product
of the European imagination, is one of wealth, natural beauty,
and noble races, as Ruland has noted.

Carpentier creates an historical ambience in **Concierto
barroco** that establishes a somewhat realistic context for the
creation and production of *Motezuma*. The opera was first
performed in Autumn of 1733 at the Teatro di Sant' Angelo
in Venice, which was probably Vivaldi's favorite theater. The
novel's main characters, the Indiano from Mexico and his
black servant Filomeno, come to the Sant' Angelo to watch
the dress rehearsal of *Motezuma*. Historically, Vivaldi had
been absent from Venice for several years prior to this production. His return to this theater with this opera marks a
moment of dramatic intensity in **Concierto barroco,** for it
is here that the Indiano views the world's first opera of his
country's violent history.

The festive mood of the visitors is highlighted by their celebration of the Venetian Carnival, a time when masks, mer-
rymaking and costumes were commonplace. The Indiano and
Filomeno fall easily into the atmosphere of revelry.
Carpentier's portrait of this scenario corresponds fairly
closely to several travel accounts of the period, as Müller-
Bergh has demonstrated. His depiction of the Venetian world
along these historical patterns creates a semblance of authenticity within the novel's more fictive occurrences. Carpentier
as well as his historical sources seem most fascinated by the
powerful mood of release that masks and disguises allow.
Carpentier suggests that anonymity allows people to lose
themselves in a joyous, if not totally pious, release of emotions: "Cada cual hablaba, gritaba, cantaba, pregonaba,
afrentaba, ofrecía, requebraba, insinuaba, con voz que no era
la suya. . . ." The custom of masking has a strangely democ-
ratizing effect upon the populace, for the strict social barriers are hidden behind the façades: "En cuanto al pueblo, la
marinería, las gentes de la verdura, el buñuelo y el pescado,
del sable, y del tintero, del remo y de la vara, fue una
transfiguración que ocultó las pieles tersas o arrugadas. . . ."
The English traveler Edward Wright observes that during the
Carnival the Venetians could hide not only their social rank
but also their gender: "For further variety, they sometimes

change sexes; women appear in men's habits, and men in
women's and so are now and then picked up, to the great
disappointment of the lover." Carpentier's black humor
twists this idea around as if to suggest that during Carnival
nothing is as it seems: ". . . en tanto que los maricones,
vestidos a la mitología o llevando basquiñas españolas,
aflautaban el tono de proposiciones que no siempre caían
en el vacío." When the Indiano finally sees a performance
of *Motezuma,* he is scandalized to discover that a male historical character is a woman in the opera, that a woman has
sung a male part, and that two of the women singers are off-
stage lovers. The world Carpentier has created in **Concierto
barroco** is topsy-turvy. The Indiano, initially sure of his own
identity and values, eventually emerges through his experiences in the Carnival with a new set of perspectives and values concerning his nationality and the history of his own
country.

The identity of the Indiano chooses for the festival is
Montezuma. His exotic dress immediately captures the attention of the unmasked Fraile Pelirrojo, Antonio Vivaldi.
The Indiano, between drinks and visits from Georg Friedrich
Handel and Domenico Scarlatti, narrates the story of the conquest of Mexico. Vivaldi listens attentively to the tale of the
daring Spaniards, bloodthirsty Indians and native temples.
During the course of the Carnival, the Indiano tells and retells the history of Montezuma to an increasingly fascinated
Vivaldi. The Indiano brings the story to life: ". . . llevado
por el impulso verbal, dramatizaba el tono, gesticulaba,
mudaba de voz diálogos improvisados, acabando por
posesionarse de los personajes." The Indiano begins a creative process that Vivaldi ultimately continues and completes
with his opera. Carpentier later reverses the role of performers and spectators when the Indiano watches the opera and
sees what Vivaldi has done to his story. Vivaldi is cast in
the novel as an enterprising impresario, a point of certain
historical accuracy. Vivaldi is concerned not only with the
music but also with the total dramatic possibilities: ". . .
pensando, de pronto, en los escenarios de ingenio, trampas,
levitaciones y *machinas,* donde las montañas humeantes,
apariciones de monstruos y terremotos con desplome de
edificios, serían del mejor efecto. . . ." But what attracts
Vivaldi most strongly to the Indiano's story is its freshness
and novelty. Vivaldi suspects that his audiences will soon
tire of the standard classical operatic repertoire and will want
to see works based on other lands and traditions. Vivaldi
senses a change in the artistic mood of Venice: "Soplan aires
nuevos." *Motezuma* thus represents a new creative possibility
for Vivaldi. He here has the chance to transform historical
material about America into an imaginative expression of
considerable originality. The audience will be able to turn
away from the characters of classical mythology, the
"pastores enamorados" and "ninfas fieles," and will look instead to the New World. But Vivaldi's choice of a historical
topic never presents serious artistic limitations. The Indiano

sadly learns that history, his nation's history, after all, is an extremely flexible creation capable of surprising mutations. He ultimately confronts the belief that the only truth about historical writing is its various interpretive possibilities.

The Indiano bases his objections to Vivaldi's treatment of history on his own reading of the *Historia de la conquista de México,* by Antonio de Solís, Vivaldi's source for *Motezuma.* It is not unusual that an educated subject of the Spanish Crown living in eighteenth-century Mexico would have a thoroughgoing knowledge of this historian. The *Historia de la conquista de México* is, in many regards, a literary elaboration of these famous historical events. Solís charts the early days of exploration and conquest, Cortés's initial negotiations with the Aztec nation, and his definitive triumph over the last defenders of the indigenous empire. The *Historia de la conquista de México* is more than a typical chronicle of events; it presents many of the customs, beliefs, and traditions of the native Mexicans. Solís's work was, in its day, the standard reference for the history of the Mexican conquest. By the time *Motezuma* was written and produced there were several Italian translations readily available to Giusti and Vivaldi.

Vivaldi and his librettist Giusti follow Solís's historical outline very loosely and broadly and focus on the last days of Montezuma's rule. The opera introduces new characters not present in the *Historia de la conquista de México* and changes the role of others. For example, in *Motezuma,* Cortés has a younger brother named Ramiro, and Teutile is not an Aztec general but Montezuma's daughter. Vivaldi uses many of the techniques that are commonplace in eighteenth-century operatic theater: a complex plot, characters hidden onstage, disguises and rapid changes in fate. The opening scenes of *Motezuma* present most of the conflicts that provide the opera's essential dramatic tension. Montezuma faces a critical dilemma: should he concede defeat to the Spanish and accept death, or should he fight on? His wife Mitrena encourages him to be strong and to search in his heart for courage: "Il corraggio, dov'è?" Teutile, too, must search for solutions to seemingly unresolvable problems. She has fallen in love with Ramiro, and because she frequently confided in him, she blames herself for the fall of the kingdom. Ramiro vacillates between his political and brotherly allegiance to Cortés and his obligations to Teutile. The younger soldier hides Montezuma, though his orders are to capture him. The Spaniards finally seize Montezuma and discuss his fate. Ramiro speaks on behalf of the Aztec ruler and implores his brother not to imprison him: "Dura legge mi par, e grave offesa." Fernando begins to suspect that Ramiro is struggling with a conflict between love and duty and begins to watch him more carefully. Montezuma, in chains, challenges Fernando to a fight, a defiance that Cortés cannot tolerate. In a series of highly improbable scenes the Aztecs and Spaniards reverse their fortune several times. The Indians

manage to capture Cortés and imprison him in a tower. Meanwhile, Teutile, Mitrena and an Aztec general named Asprano have conferred with the priests and decide that the gods have demanded some sacrifices. They then burn the tower Cortés was placed in. But they don't realize that in the meantime Ramiro has saved Cortés and Montezuma has taken refuge in the same tower. Believed dead, Montezuma miraculously returns in the last few scenes only to find Cortés in full control, victorious over the remaining Aztecs. Cortés attempts to consolidate his power totally by announcing to the people that they now have a new king and a new religion: "Nuovo Re ad adorar, e nuovi Numi." The people accept this proclamation and the chorus, presumably made up of Spaniards and Aztecs, offers Cortés a cry of praise and support: "Viva il Monarca Ispan, Fernando Viva."

In spite of its creative liberties, Vivaldi's opera follows a principal theme found in the *Historia de la conquista de México* and in earlier official chronicles of the conquest. The Spaniards had a mission in the New World, and their warfare with the Indians was, in their mind, politically, economically and religiously justified. Mitrena, perhaps created in the historical shadow of Malinche, recalls the arrival of Cortés to their land and suggests that their nation was ready for salvation. The Spaniards offered a superior culture to the Aztec world of myth and superstition. Mitrena uses traditional imagery of shadows and blindness to describe her people's state of ignorance:

> Vivea frà l'ombre ancora
> Di natia cecità, fuori de Mondo,
> Ignobile, negletta,
> Questa vasta Region.

She continues her long recitative saying that the Aztecs suffered for centuries under a cloud of darkness before Cortés's arrival:

> Per secoli si lunghi
> Furo i populi miei cotanto idioti
> Ch'anche i proprj tesor gl'erano ignoti
> Ma rischiarar tal nube
> Un di alfin si dovea.

Mitrena repeats traditional Aztec mythology by saying that the arrival of the Spanish had been long anticipated. Cortés and his men were fulfilling a prophetic expectation:

> Questo era scritto
> Nei decreti del Ciel, ne si potea
> Tanto esequir, se la natura, e il Cielo
> Non apriva l'arcano, onde potesse
> Un seminume al Mondo
> La linea trapassar co 'suoi elletti
> Per incogniti mar fin or negletti.

Mitrena's praises, however, are misleading. Though she appears to be justifying the Spanish conquest, she adds that Cortés betrayed their trust. Carpentier remarks that at this point her similarity to Malinche vanishes: "Una civilización de hombres superiores se había impuesto con dramáticas realidades de razón y de fuerza. . . . Pero, por lo mismo (y aquí se esfumaba el malinchismo de Mitrena en valiente subida del tono), la humillación impuesta a Montezuma era indigna de la cultura y el poderío de tales hombres." Mitrena's recitative is thus a clever rhetorical strategy designed to trap Cortés in a web of praise and admiration. Cortés suspects insincerity and interrupts her by saying: "Sensi d'adulation poco veraci." Mitrena viciously turns on him and claims that he violated their peaceful accord and illegally usurped the throne rightfully held by her husband. Mitrena continues to oppose the Spanish until Cortés, finally victorious, pardons his enemies and sanctions the marriage of Ramiro and Teutile. In this way, Cortés symbolically binds together the new and old regimes in a strong political *mestizaje.*

The Indiano in **Concierto barroco** becomes enraged with Vivaldi's unrestrained adaptation of Solís. Yet when the Indiano attempts to demonstrate his superior knowledge of Mexican history to Vivaldi, the Italian surprises his guest with a small sample of his own scholarly virtuosity:

> —"Pero . . . Nunca hubo tal emperatriz de México, ni tuvo Montezuma hija alguna que se casara con español."

> —"Un momento, un momento—" dice Antonio, con repentina irritación—: "El poeta Alvise Giusti, autor de este 'drama para música,' estudió la crónica de Solís, que en mucha estima tiene, por documentada y fidedigna, el bibliotecario mayor de la Marciana. Y ahí se habla de la Emperatriz, sí señor, mujer digna, animosa y valiente."

> —"Nunca he visto eso."

> —"Capítulo XXV de la Quinta Parte. Y también se dice, en la Parte Cuarta, que *dos o tres hijas* de Montezuma se casaron con españoles."

Vivaldi clearly knows his historical source, but he nevertheless feels no obligation to present the facts accurately. His interests are purely artistic: "Lo que cuenta aquí es la ilusión poética." Vivaldi feels that in art there are fewer restrictions than in history. Vivaldi and the Indiano confront the same reality—the *Historia de la conquista de México* by Solís— but each emerges from his reading with a strikingly different response. Both characters have concretized this text in opposing manners. The Indiano's concerns are text-bound. He feels that truth and judgment inhere objectively in the literary or historical work. But Vivaldi dismisses such dogmatic views. Vivaldi easily relativizes the history of the conquest and thus disrupts the stability and control of the primary text. Vivaldi is far more interested than the Indiano in the adaptation and artistic reception of the *Historia de la conquista de México.* He justifies his numerous departures from historical accuracy by putting on a good show, telling a good story. He is an exponent of what Wolfgang Iser identifies as the esthetic pole of the literary work. Iser notes: "The work is more than the text, for the text only takes on life when it is realized. . . ." *Motezuma* is thus a textual realization (*Konkretisation*) of Vivaldi's reading of Solís. Iser writes that "one must also take into account not only the actual text but also, and in equal measure, the actions involved in responding to the text." Vivaldi has had considerable experience in converting literary responses into esthetic expressions. The Indiano apparently feels that the written word should remain unchanged. His critical view of literary experience is manifestly opposed to Vivaldi's. Yet Vivaldi effortlessly deconstructs the Indiano's position by turning his knowledge and faith in the historical source against him. Vivaldi must forcefully remind the Indiano that the work of the Sant' Angelo is not to deal in matters of historical accuracy: "No me joda con la Historia en materia de teatro."

Telling and listening to tales occurs elsewhere in the novel with similar consequences. Earlier the Indiano listens to Filomeno's story of his great-grandfather, a subject in Balboa's *Espejo de paciencia.* The Indiano exhibits the same degree of impatience with Filomeno as with Vivaldi. Filomeno's tale has many digressions; the Indiano instructs his young servant in the proper narrative style: "Prosigue tu historia en línea recta, muchacho—interrumpe el viajero—, y no te metas en curvas ni transversales; que para sacar una verdad en limpio menester son muchas pruebas y repruebas." The Indiano speaks these words with the Master Solís in mind; the historian also presents a strong case for clarity and order in historiography. Filomeno finishes his story and later suggests to the composers that they write an opera about his ancestor. Handel and Vivaldi laugh at his proposal, a response that provokes the Indiano to come to his servant's defense: "No lo veo tan extravagante: Salvador Golomón luchó contra unos hugonotes, enemigos de su fe, igual que Scanderbergh luchó por la suya." This is an important step for the Indiano. By interceding on behalf of Filomeno, he is in effect championing an American topic over a European one.

The Indiano is eventually drawn into a more relativized form of literary response when he discovers that he has had an unexpected reaction to *Motezuma.* The Indiano admits to Filomeno that he was carried away by the opera's action and characters, and was surprised to find himself identifying more with the Indians than the Spaniards. He discovers a conflict within himself that is profoundly disturbing. He is a proud *criollo* whose grandparents came to America from Spain. Yet his sympathies are not with Cortés but with his antagonist. The Indiano is struggling with a nascent nationalistic consciousness. Since arriving in Europe he has felt out of place. He constantly compares the European sights, smells and sounds with America, which he ultimately prefers. He must view an Italian opera in Venice before he can make the following observation: "*A veces es necesario alejarse de las cosas,* poner un mar de por medio, *para ver las cosas de cerca*" (Carpentier's emphasis). He now sees he is from another world and does not belong in Italy or even Spain. Carpentier subtly presents a New World-Old World dichotomy throughout the novel. The Indiano's final posture implies that the Old World has exhausted itself creatively and must now look to America for inspiration. Europe is a parasite on America, a land of vitality that looks to the future, not the past. The Indiano concludes: "No entienden que lo fabuloso está en el futuro. Todo futuro es fabuloso." *Motezuma* allows the Indiano to see that his own destiny lies in the land of hope and promise—America.

The Indiano in **Concierto barroco** and Montezuma in Vivaldi's opera both experience moments of conversion. The Indiano ultimately accepts his American identity, while Montezuma finally admits that Mexico has changed forever. Each emerges from his ordeal with a new attitude concerning his country. The Indiano sees that his cultural formation is American: "Para mí es otro el aire que, al envolverme, me esculpe y me da forma." Montezuma, facing the irrevocable march of history, comes to view the Spanish faith more openly: "Ne vostri Dei gran verità si scorge. . . ." Montezuma seems to be aware of his own historical and literary destiny when he says that his misfortunes will be the "Argomento felice a nuove storie." Carpentier cites this passage from the opera as if to suggest that he is fulfilling the fallen king's prophecy. **Concierto barroco** presents another performance of *Motezuma* and thus becomes a "nuova storia" of the emperor's defeat. Montezuma and the Indiano are therefore present at crucial but opposing moments of Mexican history. Montezuma lives (in the opera, at least) to see his subjects accept Spanish rule. Cortés, ever faithful to his king, announces to the Aztecs that he cedes his throne to Spain, therefore maintaining the traditional lord-vassal relationship. Consequently, they all become part of the Spanish empire:

> Quel Soglio ove m'assido
> Non è Soglio per me. Or che lo prendo
> Alla Spagna lo cedo, e lo diffendo.

The Indiano, however, recognizes that his bond to this kingdom has slowly diminished. He has begun to see cracks in the cultural wall that Spain built around its New World empire. He discovers that he and his Spanish ancestors have little in common anymore. He began his journey as an

indiano, an entrepreneur who came to Europe to enjoy his new-found wealth. But he finds himself "deseando la ruina de aquéllos que me dieron sangre y apellido." He has no alternative but to return home. It is significant that at the end of the novel he is neither an *indiano* nor an *amo.* An *indiano* comes from America to Europe, a process he ultimately reverses. He also releases Filomeno, thereby extinguishing his rights as *amo.* He has turned his back upon much that he once held as sacred.

Carpentier's portrait of America is revealed through the new attitude of the Indiano. The Mexican knows that in his world new beginnings are possible; his land holds the hope of promise and perpetual renewal, as González Echevarrría has suggested. By contrast, Europe has grown old and decrepit: ". . . parecióle, de pronto, que la ciudad había envejecido enormemente." The Indiano's trip has given him the experience and perspective to realize that he cannot recover in Europe his sense of place and origin. Vivaldi's *Motezuma* has pointed him in the direction of Mexico, a land where he now knows he truly belongs. There is a hint of revolution in this moment of recognition, for it will not be long before the Mexicans begin to shake loose the harness of Spanish domination. Filomeno, who decides to stay in Europe, speaks openly and prophetically about such radical changes:

> —"En París me llamarán *Monsieur Philoméne,* así, con P.H. y un hermoso acento grave en le 'e.' En la Habana, sólo sería 'el negrito Filomeno.'"

> —"Eso cambiará algún día."

> —"Se necesitaría una revolución."

This will occur in the centuries following the Indiano's return. His new consciousness concerning his identity marks the beginning of the political and social uprisings that characterized the wars of independence, the Mexican Revolution, and the Cuban Revolution, three of the most definitive events in Spanish American history.

Concierto barroco is a novel that celebrates historical, literary and artistic change. The Indiano's attitude toward Mexican history is reflected by his response to the operatic performance. The Indiano unexpectedly becomes a spokesman for change. The importance of his trip to Europe is that he has experienced an awakening to the value of his own culture. Carpentier uses the device of the trip in many of his novels, often for the same purpose. The characters embark on a period of exploration that allows them to return home with an expanded view of the nature of their society: "Es que mucho se aprende viajando." The voyage allows them an extended period of psychological introspection during which they examine, often painfully, their life purpose. The Indiano's character development is one of political as well as psychological change. His view of society is initially quite conservative. His sharp reactions to the historical deviations of Filomeno and Vivaldi indicate a conservative stance toward the stability of society. But his gradual movement toward their respective interpretations indicates a more liberal perception of historical process. Hayden White writes about the characteristics of such ideological implications: ". . . Conservatives are inclined to imagine historical evolution as a progressive elaboration of the institutional structure that *currently* prevails. . . . By contrast, Liberals imagine a time in the *future* when this structure will have been improved, but they project this utopian condition into the *remote* future. . . ." Carpentier's repeated emphasis on the future suggests that the Indiano has abandoned his conservative ideals which venerated European society and ancestry. He now embraces a more liberal ideology which anticipates a world of immense social change.

From the point of view of character development, *Motezuma* is a powerful catalyst for change. The opera forces the Indiano to confront his anachronistic beliefs concerning his history. Though the Indiano is by no means a revolutionary at the end of the novel ("yo desconfío de las revoluciones"), he nevertheless has embraced a different set of values central to his life purpose. He now favors America over Europe; he comprehends the process of esthetic interpretation; and he anticipates (from a liberal posture) a time of radical changes in the world's economic structures. Carpentier dissolves all historical divisions in *Concierto barroco* by introducing symbols of an industrialized world: locomotives, electric guitars, and travelers' checks, icons of a new age.

Carpentier's interest in *Concierto barroco* is to examine the relationship between text and event. No one denies that history is an act of remembering, but it is also invention, as Vivaldi gladly demonstrates to his skeptical Mexican friend. Carpentier's *oeuvre* often critiques the uneasy symbiosis between history and fiction. His portrayal of Columbus in *El arpa y la sombra,* for example, wavers between the purely historical and the totally fictitious; the narrative depiction of this character incorporates the explorer's own words from his travel diary. Carpentier shares Vivaldi's attitude toward literary art spelled out in the prologue to *Motezuma:* "Tutto ciò, che di vero abbandono, e che di verisimile aggiongo è per adattarmi alla Scena. . . ." *Concierto barroco*'s adaptations to the scene evoke memories, future ones perhaps, of a uniquely Latin American context. Carpentier's text, as expected, negates the formation of a singular historical truth. Instead, he is more interested in exploring the dimensions of artistic truthfulness.

Sigrún A. Eiríksdóttir (essay date November 1987)

SOURCE: "Some Examples of Irony in Carpentier's Earlier Fiction," in *Chasqui,* Vol. XVI, No. 2, November, 1987, pp. 3-9.

[*In the following essay, Eiríksdóttir discusses Carpentier's use of irony in his earlier work.*]

La Consagración de la Primavera, Carpentier's most committed novel, seems not to have gained acceptance as the masterpiece its author clearly intended it to be. It has been suggested that among the reasons for this is that it lacks irony. To that extent it seems to bear out Barthes' comment that Marxist writing "aims at presenting reality in a prejudged form." It is as though Carpentier had resolved, or repressed, his earlier doubts about the process and speed of historical change and about the capacity of individuals to accept it. In consequence, *La Consagración de la Primavera,* for all its length and complexity, presents a tidy, unambiguous picture of reality, which contains certain reliably predictable features including the inevitability of progress through collective effort.

It was not always so. The fundamental tension identified by Muecke in what he terms simple ironies, where "one term is seen more or less immediately, as effectively contradicting, invalidating, exposing, or at the very least modifying the other" is more pronounced in Carpentier's fiction prior to *El siglo de las luces* (1962, but most probably written between 1956 and 1958) than later. This would accord with the view hinted at by Labanyi, in a seminal article, that we can discern in *El siglo de las luces* a certain shift in Carpentier's outlook towards a more positive, or as she calls it "dynamic" vision of historical progress, which was to triumph in *La Consagración de la Primavera.* According to Muecke, irony flourishes in "open ideologies," characteristically proposed by the "General Ironist [with his] distrust of systems, his acceptance of impermanence as normal, his ability to see 'that it might just as well have happened the other way around.'"

> *La Consagración de la Primavera,*
> **Carpentier's most committed novel, seems not to have gained acceptance as the masterpiece its author clearly intended it to be.**
> —*Sigrún A. Eiríksdóttir*

Irony as a general precept is not readily compatible with dogmatic or univocal thinking, and, in the words of Gurewitch, "entails hypersensitivity to a universe that is permanently out of joint . . . the ironist does not pretend to cure such a universe or solve its mysteries." As sentimentality is the mark of a tender-minded writer, who designedly presents a comforting vision of the world around us, so irony is the mark of a tough-minded writer who refuses to simplify and reassure. This is not to imply, of course, that Carpentier altered his stance totally after the late 1950s, but rather that there is a certain shift of emphasis, particularly after his return to Cuba.

However, it is noteworthy that even in his earliest fiction explicit irony, that is to say, verbal irony either in dialogue or through direct authorial commentary and the assumption of an intrusive authorial persona, is usually absent. Carpentier deals almost exclusively in impersonal, situational irony and in implied irony, which it is left to the alert reader to perceive and appreciate. Expectation is played off against event, the reader is presented with similarity where the author had prepared him to expect contrast and vice versa, and the writer stands detachedly aside without revealing any unqualified sympathies. In the body of the work to be discussed in this article, from the earliest writings up to and including *El reino de este mundo,* the main fount of such irony seems to be the author's awareness of the role played in human affairs by the need for belief.

As late as *La Consagración de la Primavera* itself, he is still insisting on the contrast between Vera's admission "Yo en nada tengo fe" and Gaspar Blanco's "sólida fe" in Marxism. Joseph Sommers identifies the beginning of this preoccupation, which is already endowed with ironic overtones, in the outer frame of Carpentier's first novel *Ecue-Yamba-O.* "La acción dramática," he writes, "se desenvuelve dentro de un marco de ironía, sugerido en primera instancia por el título mismo de la obra" (se traduce "Loado sea Dios"). Sommer's argument is that from the outset Menegildo, the hero, is confided to the care of the voodoo gods by magical rituals and observances. But such care neither assists him in his courtship of Longins nor protects him from imprisonment, subsequent relapse into criminality, and a violent death. Nonetheless his son is placed under the care of the same gods. The irony lies, at the primary level, in the discrepancy between the absolute faith of Menegildo and the total absence of protection which it affords him.

But it goes much deeper than that, and therein, in our view, lies much of the ironic ambiguity of the novel. Menegildo does not simply believe: he needs to believe in order to find his Black identity, that identity which allows him to credit himself with a deeper understanding of essential reality than the understanding enjoyed by the Whites. This has led to a division of opinion among critics about the inner meaning of the novel as a whole. Brushwood and González Echevarría suggest that Carpentier is affirming the superiority of "natural" (Black) values. Sommers argues that the reverse is really the case. In fact, the two stances co-exist uneasily side by side in the novel and the attentive reader

perceives a certain fluctuation on the part of Carpentier from one to the other. The irony, compounded of course by being found in a novel by a White writer about Black outlook, reveals an unresolved ambivalence on the author's part. The story is told from the Black point of view, that of Menegildo, who quite explicitly attributes to himself and to his race a special understanding of reality.

Some passages of authorial commentary, notably the key paragraph in Chapter XII in which Carpentier seems to endorse the "altísima sabiduría" underlying the Blacks' magical conception of the cosmos, at first lend credibility to the contention of González Echevarría and Brushwood. But they are offset not only by the ending, in which Menegildo dies in the course of a brawl between rival groups of voodoo initiates, but also by certain ironic juxtapositions which tend to devalue the authority of the magical beliefs on which Menegildo's presumption of his own superiority is based. We notice, for instance, that after his voodoo initiation some of the adepts present at the ceremony hurry off to watch a Catholic procession in which the image of the Virgin being carried along is described as dancing above the heads of the faithful exactly like the voodoo "Nazacó" during the initiation rite. A few pages later, the episode of the children visiting their den in an empty house in order to adore with "mágico respeto" a picture postcard of a naked woman, is strategically positioned so as to comment ironically on the enchantment of the voodoo ceremony which is the central episode of the novel. The general point, underlined by the drunken hymn-singing of the North Americans ("Borrachos evangélicos") in the Christmas scene and the comic presentation of the Salvation Army, is that both Blacks and Whites, Christians and voodoo adepts, derive their sense of superiority from belief (parodied in both cases) in supernatural powers. Carpentier indicates ironically that such belief, while commonly an important ingredient in coming to terms with a hostile cosmos, in fact betrays the believer. Faith is a form of hubris, a tragic assumption.

A similarly ironic treatment of magical ritual and Christian belief is visible in Carpentier's next work, the little-known, serio-comic short story in French **"Histoire de lunes."** A number of details connect the story to *Ecue-Yamba-O.* The pimp Radamés, whom Menegildo meets in prison, is here awaiting his naturalization papers: the girls wearing ribbons with the inscription "Viva la música" turn up afresh; above all the division of the voodoo adepts into "chivos" (here "boucs") and "sapos" reappears, once more with murderous consequences. In the story a number of village women are raped by the local boot-black who has been bewitched through his animal-double. When it is discovered that he rapes only the women of the rival voodoo brotherhood, the vigilantes' attempt to shoot him develops into a bloody feud which ends only when he is executed, not as a rapist but as a political subversive!

Here Carpentier adopts a more detached stance towards the Blacks' magical beliefs, with consequent benefit to the narrator's ironical approach, which becomes more explicit than in *Ecue-Yamba-O*. In the first part of the tale his ironic barbs appear to be directed against Catholicism, and we have a rare example in Carpentier of actual verbal irony, an authorial intrusion pointedly and disparagingly extending the terms of what Muecke would call "simple incongruity" or "minimal irony." The villagers, that is, are at Mass when they are summoned to the local sorcerer's dwelling by the voodoo drums. To satirize this Afro-Cuban mass, Carpentier describes how a china dove, representing the Holy Spirit, hangs ludicrously from the ceiling of the church on a piece of string. But the satire turns to irony when the sound of the drums, calling the faithful to their true spiritual allegiance in the middle of the church service, is compared deliberately to the "roucoulement d'un pigeon monstrueux." But lest we imagine that this implies the triumph of voodoo magic over Catholicism, Carpentier then nimbly shifts his stance to show the two brotherhoods mounting rival, apparently pious, Catholic processions which end in a riot at the church door. Just as he was to do later in *El reino de este mundo*, Carpentier stresses the stronger hold exerted by magical beliefs than by those of traditional Catholicism. But the ending of the story makes it clear he is not endorsing either. Rather, after separating them in the Mass episode, he then with equal ironic distance collapses the former back into the latter. Critics have taken too much at their face value Carpentier's famous assertions in the preface to *El reino de este mundo* about the role of "fe colectiva" in Haiti during the Black rebellions. His treatment of it in his second novel cannot be properly understood without taking into account the context provided by his earlier work.

In **"Oficio de tinieblas"** Carpentier again uses the device of an ironic interruption of the celebration of Mass. This tale is not told with the tone of slight amusement which we perceive in **"Histoire de lunes."** A macabre story of earthquake and plague, its theme is cosmic irony, nature's mockery of the vanity of human wishes, which contrasts the love of pomp and display typical of the colonial *criollos* of Cuba with the frightful forces of destruction which the tropics can suddenly unleash. Its title, like those of *Ecue-Yamba-O* and *El reino de este mundo,* is itself ironic and underlines the presence of such an attitude in nearly all the direct references to Catholicism in Carpentier's early work. Two features of the tale are relevant to the present study. One is the barbed notation which tells us that the prelude to the widespread destruction and death from cholera is a play performed by the wealthy *criollos,* the title of which is *La entrada en el gran mundo.* The second ironic effect is created at the climax as the defiant song of the common people, "Ahí va la Lola," incorporates itself into the Te Deum which celebrates the end of the epidemic. Janney rightly perceives that the story alludes to the "absurdity" of life in thrall to the arbi-

trary power of death. But he is wrong, in our view, to suggest that it is balanced by the "Choteo cubano" of the masses. The central figure, Panchón, is first seen carrying a double-bass on his head, and later carrying in the same way a corpse, which he lifts like a hat to salute the posters advertising the play—irony commenting on irony—before being carried off himself. The episode reveals that the technique of the tale is not merely one of humourous or satirical contrast, as Janney tends to imply. It is more a representation of the tragic fulcrum pointed out by Muecke, in which "irony regards assumptions as presumption and therefore innocence as guilt"—at least for the vindictive forces of the cosmos which make mockery of all human aspirations. Gurewitch comments, "Perhaps the fundamental distinction between irony and satire, in the largest sense of each, is simply that irony deals with the absurd, whereas satire treats the ridiculous." There is satire in **"Oficio de tinieblas,"** but the irony is more significant.

"Viaje a la semilla," Carpentier's next story, occupies a unique position among his earlier writings, because it is the only one into which what Gurewitch calls irony's preoccupation with "the morals of the universe" as distinct from "life's corrigible deformities" does not intrude. The story is concerned not with whether insight into human experience suggests the possible presence of "an incurable hoax of things," but with the quite different issue of the subversion of apparential reality. The thrust of the tale, that is, moves in a wholly different direction from that of the writings that surround it. In consequence, it may be excluded from this account. **"Los fugitivos,"** on the other hand, is described by Shaw as "intentionally ironic." His argument is that the second meeting of the two central characters, a tracker-dog and a slave, both runaways, contrasts ironically with the first. But this hardly does justice to the story as a whole. Man and dog are both initially slaves, fearing the same whip and chains. Both have escaped and returned to the wild. From this beginning Carpentier draws out a parallelism. For both slave and dog liberty means simply subjection to a different set of compulsions: the need for food and sexual activity. The technique of the story is based on the reader's surrender to this parallelism, rather than on the five elements identified by Shaw or the carnevalesque implications which González Echevarría unconvincingly reads into it. As the tale proceeds, the dog, whose sexual desire is more controlled and discontinuous than the slave's, predictably adjusts better to their new life-style. The slave, unable to control his body's demands, is recaptured in consequence, while the animal, toughened by life in the open, fights for and gains a bitch.

So far the ironic implications of the contrast thus established are banal and obvious. But at the climax these are suddenly and unexpectedly reversed. The dog, which hitherto has carried the associations of successful self-affranchisement from the experience of captivity, is confronted afresh by the newly-escaped slave. If the story had been, as González Echevarría suggests, essentially about the slave's condemnation by the "superfluity of his desires and actions," it would have ended with his recapture and the dog's successful incorporation into a pack. As it is, what the climax of the story emphasizes is the fact that, when the animal leaps at and kills the maroon, it is paradoxically because of its training and not because of its return to instinct. In this dashing of the reader's expectations, this sudden refutation of seemingly straightforward assumptions, lies the unlooked-for ironic aspect of this deceptive tale.

The elements of irony so far identified in Carpentier's earliest fiction matter both intrinsically and as a lead-in to cognate elements in his first major novel *El reino de este mundo.* For example, the episode in Part III, Chapter V of the latter, when the throbbing of ritual drums interrupts the Mass which King Henri Christophe is attending with his court, acquires a more emphatic meaning and greater effectiveness as a coded signal of impending conflict if we are aware that it is the third time in succession that Carpentier had employed this device of ironic juxtaposition. Granted, the context is rather different. The Masses alluded to in **"Histoire de lunes"** and **"Oficio de tinieblas"** are, in a sense, "genuine," whereas the Mass attended by Christophe symbolizes the betrayal of the "iglesia cimarrona" by aping the religion of the Whites. As in *Ecue-Yamba-O* there is a temptation to interpret the events of *El reino de este mundo* as indicative of the superiority of the Black culture pattern, which is based on real belief, over the White one with its ostentatious appeal to the mere external manifestations of faith. Indeed R. A. Young in his pithy Critical Guide to the text asserts confidently that "its central issue is the conflict between a dynamic culture and another in a state of decay. But at the same time he realizes that "The conventional view of history as a chain of consecutive events is . . . replaced by a view in which history . . . turns back on itself as if following the trajectory of a spiral." This is a superb scenario for irony. *El reino de este mundo* brings to an end the first phase of Carpentier's fictional work with a climax in the concluding chapter incorporating the often-quoted statement of his mature conviction that "la grandeza del hombre está precisamente en querer mejorar lo que es. En imponerse Tareas." Now, the basic irony of the novel lies in the contrast between the aspirations of the Blacks and their fulfillment. How are we to interpret the apparent discrepancy between this postulate and our recognition, along with Young but in contrast to those critics who have seen Carpentier's view of history as merely circular, that "history is not entirely static but remains open to the future?" The answer involves one of the least well-understood features of Carpentier's ideology, the clue to which appears in a crucially important remark in *La Consagración de la Primavera:* "Hay un inconciliable desajuste entre el tiempo

del Hombre y el tiempo de la Historia. Entre los cortos días de la vida, y los largos, larguísimos años del acontecer colectivo." It is precisely this awareness of a *desajuste,* of the inevitable but not insuperable setbacks to historical progress, which leaves open the possibility for irony in *El reino de este mundo.*

Young notices its presence in the novel, notably in the title itself and in the titles of some of the chapters. He remarks that it "is also a sign that Carpentier has not limited himself to identifying and simply reproducing the contexts of history." So indeed it must be, for irony is a comment on events. Discussing the episode of the wax heads and the calves' heads in Chapter I, Young concludes that there and elsewhere, the irony derives from "an inversion of conventional perspectives," "a juxtaposition of opposites." This is certainly the case, both here and in the episodes relating to Mlle. Floridor to which Young also refers. But his treatment, in our view, does not bring out the wider ironic implications of this story. The main thrust of the novel harks back to the contrast between Catholicism and voodoo already prominent in the **"Histoire de lunes."** When the Blacks triumph over the French planters, it seems as though what Carpentier calls "la viviente cosmogonía del negro" has vanquished the tepid beliefs of the Whites. But the triumph is ironic, for it leads to the tyranny of Christophe. When in turn, as the drums interrupting his Mass portend, he too succumbs to the superior force of Blacks beliefs, the result is the oppression of the Blacks by the mulattoes. The fact that the novel virtually ends with a completely unambiguous declaration by Carpentier of the need for man to "imponerse Tareas" in order to accelerate the slow onward march of history, does not alter the irony of the premise on which it is based. The premise is built structurally into the novel by the careful organization of the plot into two parallel cycles of events. In the first cycle White royal rule is overthrown, but is replaced by tyranny: in the second, Black royal rule is destroyed, but is again replaced by tyranny.

In the light of Carpentier's ambiguous presentation of the Blacks and their beliefs in *Ecue-Yamba-O,* it is hazardous to take his picture of them here at its seeming face value. Ti Noel, like Menegildo, believes unquestioningly in the superiority of the voodoo deities ("dioses verdaderos") over the Christian God of the Whites. At first sight they do appear to overcome. But Ti Noel's dream of Black "reyes de verdad" to replace the King of France finds ironic fulfillment in the rise of Christophe, a more savage, and repressive monarch than the White rulers had ever been—his construction, at a terrible human and material cost, of a fortress which in the end serves only as his tomb is thus an irony within an irony, qualifying the action on more than one level at once.

It is a simplification to suggest that what Carpentier is saying is that the Blacks had a "dynamic culture." What the novel implies is that belief, however grotesque (in this case belief in Mackandal's self-transformations), can be a powerful force in changing society; but more importantly, that lasting transformations come far more slowly than faith leads man to anticipate. In other words, the real message of *El reino de este mundo* is rooted in the ironic discrepancy between the effectiveness of the slaves' faith in fuelling their revolts and the extreme slowness with which these revolts approach their objective. It is Carpentier's refusal to gloss over this discrepancy which lends weight to his interpretation of history in *El reino de este mundo*. There, as in *El siglo de las luces,* the residual irony provides an indispensable counterbalance to the author's belief in the need for revolutionary commitment. As is characteristic of the ironic perception, even Carpentier's own worldly conviction is not entirely immune from ironic qualification.

Further study of irony in Carpentier's subsequent works would improve our critical perspective. In particular, one is struck by the fact that none of the critics of *El arpa y la sombra* whose essays appear in *Alejo Carpentier et son oeuvre* seems to have thought worthy of comment the reappearance of irony in Carpentier's outlook with that of a consistent verbal ironist, such as Borges, we perceive that the former is really a reluctant ironist. He is a writer whose honesty compels him to include irony as an ingredient of his response to reality, rather than one who enjoys it for its own sake. This is a significant aspect of his intellectual profile. It seems probable that the deeper level of his creative self tended to be uneasy with a detached, bifocal, paradoxical view of experience. Such uneasiness is of a piece with his gradual evolution towards the form of Marxist humanism which he eventually seems to have embraced. The thrust of his early work is more interrogative and based on a more "open" and ambiguous world view. His later development, especially after 1959, seems to have been towards the everlatent more declaratory stance and based on a more closed system of ideas.

Florinda F. Goldberg (essay date July-December 1991)

SOURCE: "Patterns of Repetition in *The Kingdom of This World*," in *Latin American Literary Review,* Vol. XIX, No. 38, July-December, 1991, pp. 23-34.

[*In the following essay, Goldberg traces the instances of repetition in Carpentier's* El reino de este mundo *and discusses what the repetition says about his conception of history.*]

Alejo Carpentier's conception of history as based on repetition was first expressed through structural patterns in *El*

reino de este mundo [*The Kingdom of This World*], at the levels of story, text and narration, as well as through explicit narrator-author declarations.

"Man never knows for whom he suffers and hopes. He suffers and hopes and toils for people he will never know and who, in turn, will suffer and hope and toil for others who will not be happy either, for man always seeks a happiness far beyond that which is meted out to him." In socio-political history, this basic pattern can be found in the dialectic alternation of *order and disorder:* any established social system constitutes an order that contains disruptive elements (internal disorder) which provoke its fall through external disorder. The latter, in turn, contains the chance for a better social arrangement, but also tendencies—such as the desire for power—which will make the new order faulty, and so on and on.

While this isotopy is signified in *KTW* along the diachronic axis of successive events, another isotopy moves vertically, from the particular-temporal to the universal-atemporal, through three levels of progressive abstraction: (1) the history of the island of Haiti between 1750 and 1820; (2) that history as metonymy of the specificity and difference of Latin American history as a whole—"a history impossible to locate in Europe"—; (3) this "otherness" as symbol of the ultimate sense of universal history.

Thus the ideology underlying the novel runs along two axes, the syntagmatic and the paradigmatic, each implying repetition, and each projected and repeated upon the other. The story of the novel is announced in Carpentier's prologue as "a succession of (. . .) events"; but the episodes, besides being 'successive', are linked by a pattern of *intratextual* repetition, i.e., the recurrence of components on all levels—unitary events, sequences, characters, words, images, symbols—which make each one reflect and reinforce the other.

Simultaneously, there are continuous references to a vast series of other texts, namely human experience as expressed in historical, religious, and artistic creations. This *intertextual* interplay (a repetition on another level) inserts the novel into universal culture. We shall not develop here the complex intertextualities of *KTW.* We merely mention that they include, among others, historical works like the *Description . . . de l'Isle de Saint Domingue* by Moreau de Saint-Méry and Carpentier's own *La música en Cuba,* the Old and New Testaments, and a full range of works from the literary, musical and plastic arts that constituted the cultural lot of the historical period covered by the novel, and which are also the sources of the quotations used as epigraphs.

Inter- and intratextual repetitions are interwoven when reference to a certain external text appears more than once. For instance, fragments from Racine's tragedies are quoted when the slaves are forced by their mistress to listen to her recitations. Shortly after, during an uprising, one of them rapes the lady "who, on those nights of tragic declamations, had displayed beneath the tunic with its Greek-key border breasts undamaged by the irreversible outrage of the years." This 'blind' quotation of *Atalie* exemplifies the technique by which the novel shapes its narrate as one capable of a very complex reading in which every interrelated detail and its sometimes hidden clues have to be decoded in all their richness. To put it bluntly, in order to enjoy all the beauty of *KTW,* the reader has to know as much of history, religion, ethnology, music, art, and literature, as the author does. In this sense, undoubtedly, Carpentier is a writer for elites.

A succession of episodes, weakly related by unity of space (a sector of the Caribbean islands), unity of time (some 70 years), and a character who can hardly be considered a hero (Ti Noel and, alternatively, Soliman), receive structural unity and significance by means of the repetition of an overall pattern, on the one hand, and the recurrence of sequences, characters, objects and words, on the other. During the actual process of reading, it is precisely the minor recurrent unities that gradually build the bigger structures (like the clay bricks with which Christophe's Citadel is slowly erected). We shall first identify the main motifs that run along the novel, and then analyze their concentration in the capital episodes.

The basic pattern, as stated earlier, is the dialectic alternation of order and disorder. Order is any stable state of social affairs, in which roles (economic, political, religious, and cultural) are perfectly established and delimited. This order contains its own disruptive components (again like the Citadel, attacked by fungi and thunderbolts), mainly despotism, injustice, disregard of the powerless by the powerful, etc. The disruptive components burst out at one point, provoking a revolt. This disorder may or may not succeed long enough to establish a new order: the Macandal revolt does not, Haiti's independence wars do. But the new order fatally repeats with variations the same old patterns, and different actors—individual or collective—fill in the same actantial roles: Christophe's rule is "a slavery as abominable as that he [Ti Noel] had known on the plantation of M. Lenormand de Mezy. Even worse, for there was a limitless affront in being beaten by a Negro as black as oneself." Power changes hands, but its rules are the same; and if some individuals or groups succeed in climbing up the scale, others, the Ti Noels, always remain at the bottom.

The novel opens with a perfectly clear division of power and submission between two collectives: the masters are white-European-Catholic-strong-despotic-violent; the slaves are black-African-pagan-weak-submissive. But the masters are weakened by their naiveté in believing their domination is absolute, and also by their indifference toward the culture of the blacks—and, as a consequence, their unawareness of its hidden energies and potential danger. In their turn, the slaves' strength lies in their hiding their beliefs and feelings, and, though they also despise the culture that is not their own, they are eager to learn the use of what they perceive as its true instruments of power: guns and, most significantly, writing.

The revolts bring about the social, economic and moral collapse of the political, social and cultural order established by the white masters: "All the bourgeois norms have come tumbling down." Settlers whose only purpose on the islands was to make profit abandon all productive activities and "give themselves over (. . .) to a vast orgy." When Negroes, in turn, attain power, they betray their own tradition and imitate the European imperial or republican states—instead of sticking to the dream of Macandal and restoring in America "the great kingdoms of Popo, of Arada, of the Nagos, of the Fulah."

The same process takes place with individual characters. At the start they clearly belong to one of the two basic collectives, but as the novel develops, some of the semes change fields. Ti Noel, Macandal, Henri Christophe and Soliman are black and slaves and hate whites. But while Ti Noel and Macandal remain loyal to their original codes, Christophe and Soliman are traitors that 'go over' to the enemy. Christophe acts like a European master, Soliman even reaches Europe; their death will symbolize the punishment for their disloyalty. Lenormand de Mezy and his wives, Pauline and Leclerc repeat all the characteristics of the European settler-tyrant in America; but Lenormand and Pauline will 'convert' to the Caribbean life, which for Pauline is a return to her original Corsican self carefully disguised by "the lies of the Directory."

In the Caribbean, Indians were completely exterminated soon after the Discovery, and in the period of *KTW* there was no native population in the islands. Both whites and blacks came from somewhere else, and were voluntary or involuntary exiles in a New World that itself came into historical being through a foundational expedition. Voyages and longing for the original land as Paradise Lost are recurrent motifs in the novel. Characters travel (or have travelled) continually, by various means of transportation (ships, horses, or on foot), along short or long distances: Europe-America, America-Europe, Africa-America, Haiti-Cuba, plains-mountains, etc. These voyages constitute the passage between qualitatively different spaces: from freedom to slavery, from culture to barbarism, from death to survival, and vice versa. But, paradoxically, the continent of forced or temporary residence becomes the real home for most of them, both when return is possible and when it is not. First is the case of Lenormand de Mezy: "But something strange had happened to him [in

Paris]. After a few months, a growing longing for sun, for space (. . .) made it plain to him that the 'return to France', to which he had looked forward for so many years, was no longer the key to happiness for him. After all his cursing of the colony (. . .) he returned to the plantation." The second is the Negroes' case. For Ti Noel, home is no longer in Africa but in "the former lands of Lenormand de Mezy, to which he was now returning like the eel to the mud in which it was born (. . .) feeling himself in a way the owner of that land." At the end, the missing symmetrical possibility of his return voyage to Africa is replaced by the symbolic flight of the vulture "into the thick shade of the Bois Caiman," the forest where the slaves exerted their will for freedom through their Solemn Pact.

The untamed power of the Caribbean climate and organic world turns out to be much more akin to Africa than to Europe, and therefore the slaves' adaptation to life in the islands is easier and more complete. As if in keeping with that fact, nature becomes an ally of the blacks in their political struggle. Macandal's revolt is based on the use of poisonous mushrooms unknown to the whites. The plague kills Leclerc, drives out Pauline and provokes turmoil in the colony. Fungi and thunderbolts attack the Citadel before it is finished. Insects corrode Sans-Souci, a palace built according to an architecture appropriate for another geography. In a milder way heat, the dominant natural force of the Caribbean, erodes the transferred European ways of life and culture: the "actresses from Paris (. . .) declaimed tragic alexandrines, pausing between hemistitches to wipe the sweat from their brows." During Pauline's voyage to the islands, "each change of wind carried off several alexandrines," and the heat will soon unfasten the officers' coats and strip Pauline herself naked. Her wardrobe, we are ironically informed, included "skirts of striped muslin that she planned to wear the first *warm* day" (our emphasis).

González Echevarría points out "the complicity between history and nature" in this novel, history being the struggle of the African culture (as part of the germinal tendencies of the genuine America-in-the-making) against the European establishment. Natural forces and human violence have the same effect of disrupting all that is European, and this collapse or regression becomes a symbolic motif. The first human victim of Macandal's poison "had suddenly dropped dead (. . .) dragging down in his fall the clock he was winding." Christophe's wife will use her fan "to quicken the slow-burning fire" on which she is preparing some "root brew" for her paralyzed husband, "with little thought for etiquette," and when running away from the palace she "discarded her slippers when the stones of the road wrenched off a heel." Fit-stricken Christophe is carried home in "a royal carriage drawn by six galloping horses"; but after his defeat and death, his body is hurriedly taken from the palace by a few men "carrying on their shoulders, *in the primitive way,* a

machete-trimmed branch from which hung a hammock" (our translation and emphasis).

Buildings function as an overall signifier for the European enterprise in the islands, both literally as concrete constructions, and metaphorically as a ruling system. Ruins are the consequence of that enterprise's failure, as an outcome of nature's or man's violence. The whites had cultivated the lands; after Macandal's poisoning "putrefaction had claimed the entire region for its own," and the Plaine becomes "the domain of the worms." Lenormand de Mezy's manor will turn into an unrecognizable ruin. On the social level, revolts and sickness disrupt morality and social rules: with each crisis comes social chaos, cruelty worsens, people devote themselves to sheer pleasure, the finest ladies sleep with Negroes, and so on. Pauline, dominated by Soliman, also becomes a ruin of herself—the only reversible case: she will return to the old Pauline during the inversely symmetrical voyage back to Europe.

Again, lines cross. A standing building can already be its own ruin, like the Citadel attacked by fungi creeping from below and by thunderbolts falling from above; or the Sans-Souci palace eaten by insects (again, metaphorically, like a social system with its internal disruptive components). A building becomes a potential ruin if it has been abandoned: the Sans-Souci palace without guards, the Palazzo Borghese without its masters. And the opposite is also true: ruins can become a home, like the one Ti Noel makes for himself by accumulating in what is left of the Mezy's manor all kinds of objects shifted to an unexpected use, as the "three volumes of the *Grande Encyclopédie* on which he was in the habit of sitting to eat sugar cane."

The motif of the statue is, in a wider sense, the relation between the living body and its artificial/artistic representation: "The substance was different, but the forms were the same." The motif will culminate in the Borghese episode, but its variations already appear in the first chapter, called *The Wax Heads.* While his master is at the barber's, Ti Noel contemplates the display counters of the town's shops. "The morning was rampant with heads": first he sees "four wax heads" bearing wigs; "by an amusing coincidence," the "tripe shop next door" exhibits "calves' heads (. . .) which possessed the same waxy quality," and in his refrained aggressivity he imagines "heads of white men" served for "an abominable feast." When the master comes out of the barber shop, "his face now bore a startling resemblance to the four dull wax faces that stood (. . .) smiling stupidly." On their way home, touching a calf head the master bought for lunch, Ti Noel will think "how much [its skull] probably resembled the bald head of his master hidden beneath the wig." There is also a series of prints showing the "bewigged heads" of the King of France, warriors and dignitaries; only one print shows fully-bodied people, an African king receiving the homage of a French ambassador. Therefore, this first chapter already raises the themes of the natural and the artificial, the authentic and the false, the full and the fragmented, and the pattern of repetition. There is also a subtle intertextual game: the time of the story is approximately 1755 and the European country of reference is France, which would soon find itself very busy with heads separated from their bodies and worth even less than a calf's skull.

The statue motif accompanies Pauline from her very entrance in the novel. On the ship that carries her to America, she enjoys exciting the officers and every morning stands "alongside the foresail, letting the wind ruffle her hair and play with her clothes, revealing the superb grace of her breasts." Even the most disciplined among Leclerc's men "found himself dreaming with open eyes before the statue that was her body, evoking in her honor the Galatea of the Greeks." As an intermediate reminder, at the Sans-Souci palace there is "a bust of Pauline Bonaparte which had once adorned her house at the Cap." The motif will culminate when Soliman encounters the Venus of Canova, which he will take for the actual corpse of Pauline: the theme that opened with a body that resembled a living statue will thus close with a statue seen as a dead body.

The tragic counterpart of this game between stone and flesh is when flesh becomes not a statue, but undifferentiated stone. Henri Christophe's corpse will be sunk into the fresh mortar of his fortress: he who wanted to be unique, to sit above everything, will remain on his heights, but shapeless and irreversibly lost.

The drum is the central material component of the African Voodoo culture in the novel. It accompanies the slaves' work, as well as their feasts and dances, always with religious connotations. Drums are the emblems of the gods and heroes on whom the slaves rely for delivery and victory: the horses of the Mandinga emperor in Africa "went (. . .) bearing the thunder of two drumheads that hung from their necks"; in the African kingdoms, in period of peace and abundance, "under palm-frond covers slept the giant drums, the mothers of drums, with legs painted red and human faces." The whites do not perceive the significance of drums, what makes them all the more effective. Only too late will Lenormand de Mezy "realize that, in certain cases, a drum might be more than just a goatskin stretched across a hollow log."

As religious symbols and instruments of communication in war, on story level drums alternate or join another primitive instrument, conch shells, and a non-human phenomenon, thunder, which is understood by Negroes as a drum-signal of supernatural origin. In his Messianic return, Macandal "would bring the thunder and lightning and unleash the cy-

clone." Bouckman's solemn pact is a secret conspiracy and so cannot be announced with drums, but tempest and thunders accompany the ceremony. Santiago (St. James), the Catholic saint of lightning, is assimilated to the African god Ogun Fai, Marshall of the Storms, and brings thunderbolts on Christophe's Citadel. On text level, thunder and drum serve as alternate metaphors for each other: "the thunder of two drumheads"; "thundering like the roll of a kettledrum."

Drums (conch shells, thunder) announce and accompany all the blacks' armed revolts. The signal to Bouckman's uprising is the most accomplished, symphonic development of the motif:

> From far off came the sound of a conch-shell trumpet. What was strange was that the slow bellow was answered by others in the hills and forests (. . .) It was as though all the shell trumpets of the coast, all the Indian lambies, all the purple conches that served as doorstops, all the shells that lay alone and petrified on the summit of the hills, had begun to sing in chorus. Suddenly, another conch raised its voice in the main quarters of the plantation. Others, high-pitched, answered from the indigo works, from the tobacco shed, from the stable. M. Lenormand de Mezy, frightened, hid behind a clump of bougainvillaea. All the doors of the quarters burst open at the same time, broken down from within.

The deaths of the four main Negro characters constitute the progressive climaxes of *KTW*. The first of them, the execution of Macandal, is a minor climax, because it happens very early in the novel and functions rather as a motivation of further developments, lacking the strong closure quality of the other three: the deaths of Henri Christophe and of Soliman, and the climactic death of Ti Noel with which the novel ends.

The motifs that have been running along the text cluster in these three episodes, potentiating and multiplying their significance as a result of cumulative repetitions, to reappear in the subsequent event, which in its turn will become a repetition with variations of the previous episodes.

This episode is built of three sequences: Cornejo Breille's execution and revenge; the death of Christophe; and Christophe's burial.

The story of Christophe's cruel condemnation of Archbishop Cornejo Breille is introduced by images in which buildings and men are metaphorically/metronymically equivalent:

> Ti Noel found the whole city in a death watch. It was as though all the windows and doors of the houses, all the jalousies, all the louvers, were turned towards the corner of the Archbishop's Palace with

an expectation so intense that it distorted the facades into human grimaces. The roofs stretched out their eaves, the corners peered sharply forward, the dampness painted only ears upon the walls.

A wall is precisely the instrument of Breille's execution, for he has been "buried alive in his oratory." That wall has "a small opening *like a cathole. Out of this hole, black as a toothless mouth, burst from time to time howls so horrifying . . .*" (our translation and emphasis). The howls gradually fade away to a "death-rattle" and to an ominous silence. In the next chapter, the royal family attends Mass at Breille's church, "against the advice of all." The melodic Latin prayers (carefully quoted) are sung against the background of drums heard from far off, "which he [Christophe] felt sure were not imploring a long life for him." Suddenly, a ghost appears, identified through the inversion of the previous metaphor: "And while his face was taking on contour and expression, from this lipless, *toothless mouth, as black as a cat-hole, a thundering voice emerged* which filled the nave . . ." (our emphasis). The Christian prayer becomes a thunder: "thundering like the roll of a kettledrum, there arose the words *Coget omnes ante thronus. . . .*" The fit that strikes Christophe is narrated by means of the same metaphors: "At that moment a thunderbolt that deafened only his ears struck the church towers (. . .) A rhythm was growing in the King's ears which might have been that of his own veins or that of the drums being beaten in the hills." Like thunder (divine punishment) and prayer in the church, drums (human revolt) and prayer will mix again at the palace where courtesans of weakening loyalty watch over a king condemned by men and gods:

> It was impossible to know whether the drums were really throbbing in the hills. But at moments a rhythm coming from the distant heights mingled strangely with the Ave Maria the women were saying in the Throne Room, arousing unacknowledged resonances in more than one breast.

In the next chapter, Christophe, barely recovered, listens to the "ruffle of eight military drums" that announce the change of guard. Suddenly the drum beat changes from the European "prescribed call" to a "syncopated tone in three beats, produced by hands against the leather. 'They are playing the *mandoucouman*', Henri Christophe screamed, throwing the bicorne to the floor." The revolt breaks out: "It was a general rout of uniforms to the sound of military drums beaten by fists."

The silence, Christophe's loneliness, and the insects "in the beamed ceilings which had never been heard before" turn the palace into the ruin it is to become: "It was the spoils of anyone that wanted to take it." A new relevant motif of rep-

etition appears: the mirrors, that reflect only a deserted king. Christophe enters the Throne Room:

> Two crowned lions upheld a shield displaying a crowned phoenix (. . .) Henri Christophe opened a heavy coffer (. . .) Then he threw on the floor, one after the other, several solid-gold crowns of different weight. One of them rolled to the door and went *thudding* down the stairway with a noise that reverberated through the palace" (our emphasis).

The crown motif has accompanied Christophe since his first appearance in the novel as the owner of an inn called Auberge de la Couronne, the sign of which was a "tin crown." After Bouckman's uprising, Lenormand de Mezy learns that Christophe "has given up the business for the uniform of the colonial artillery" and "the tin crown has been taken down." When he nominates himself as Emperor, his emblem is "in the shape of a crown and phoenix."

A digression is in order here. In his analysis of Carnival as a deep kernel of Western culture and literature, Mikhail Bakhtin says:

> The primary carnavalistic act is the mock crowning and subsequent decrowning of the carnival king (. . .) Under this ritual act of decrowning a king lies the very core of the carnival sense of the world— the pathos of shifts and changes, of death and renewal (. . .) Crowning/decrowning is a dualistic ambivalent ritual, expressing the inevitability and at the same time the creative power of the shift-and-renewal, the joyful relativity of all structure and order (. . .) And he who is crowned is the antipode of a real king, a slave or a jester (. . .) precisely in this ritual of decrowning does there emerge with special clarity the carnival pathos of shifts and renewal, the image of constructive death.

The Christophe story contains a full cycle: a tin crown is set up and "taken down," and then replaced by "solid-gold crowns" that are later symbolically thrown on the floor in an act of self-decrowning; the phoenix symbolizes "renewal [and] . . . constructive death." In fact, all of Christophe's absurd political project has something of the carnivalesque about it. When Ti Noel first sees the Sans-Souci palace, the Negroes dressed as French courtesans look very much like guests at a costume party. González Echevarría finds a deep carnivalesque structure in *KTW,* and indicates that chapter 5 of part II, which describes the decay of social rules among the white population after Bouckman's revolt—another form of Carnival—is the 13th in a sum total of 26 chapters and therefore the axis of the novel.

Drums and thunder close more and more upon Christophe, in a text that recalls the Bouckman conch shell symphony:

> At that moment the night grew dense with drums. Calling to one another, answering from mountain to mountain, rising from the beaches, issuing from the caves, running beneath the trees, descending ravines and riverbeds, the drums boomed, the radas, the congos, the drums of Bouckman, the drums of the Grand Alliances, all the drums of Voodoo. A vast encompassing percussion was advancing on Sans-Souci, tightening the circle. An horizon of thunder closing in. A storm whose eye at the moment was the throne without heralds or mace-bearers.

The mirror motif reappears with the fire that:

> lighted up the mirrors of the Palace, the crystal goblets, the crystal of the lamps, glasses, windows, the mother-of-pearl inlay of the console tables—the flames were everywhere, and it was impossible to tell which were flames and which reflections. All the mirrors of Sans-Souci were simultaneously ablaze. The whole building disappeared under this chill fire. . . .

Ironically, the drums cover the noise of the shot with which Christophe puts an end to his life.

In the following chapter, the family and a few loyal servants (Soliman among them) run away with the king's corpse, and their flight, as already mentioned, represents the dismissal of the useless European costume and habits. As they run, they see from above "a torch dance" in the palace as the looting begins, the same looting already witnessed at Lenormand's house. The Citadel's guard soon joins the rebels, and one of the soldiers asks for the Queen's head, showing "that the example set almost thirty years earlier by the idealists of the French Revolution was still vividly recalled," thus closing the head motif of the first chapter. The fortress "stood empty, taking on, with the vast silence of its rooms [the same silence of empty Sans-Souci] the funereal solemnity of a royal tomb." Christophe is buried in "his Escorial," sunk in a pile of mortar; he who immured Cornejo Breille, "became one with the stone."

The Night of the Statues brings together the main motifs related to Pauline Bonaparte (sculpture/body, and the misreading of cultures), the motifs clustered around Christophe's death (symbolic ruins, drums, mirrors, fires, and gods' vengeance), and the voyage towards salvation or death.

Christophe's family and servants have reached Rome, where the Mediterranean climate and some irrational traditions of Christian worship help ease their adaptation. Soliman is lead by his lover, a maid of the Palazzo Borghese, to the impressive residence, abandoned by its owners and neglected by its servants, that is already a potential ruin. As he reviews paintings and sculptures he is unable to understand, the limits between the living and its artistic reproduction become blurred: "It was a white, cold, motionless world, but its shadows took on life and grew under the light of the lantern (. . .) Soliman thought that one of the statues had lowered its arm a little." "After crossing a gallery adorned with mirrors," Soliman confronts the statue of "a naked woman lying on a bed and holding out an apple." "He knew that face, and the body, too; that whole body aroused a memory." He caresses the marble: "That voyage of his fingers refreshed his memory, bringing back distant images. He had known this contact before." Drunk and terrified, he takes the Venus of Canova for the corpse or the dying body of Pauline. He screams, "his heels stamped so strongly on the floor, turning the chapel beneath into a drumhead"; guards arrive, "the courtyard came ablaze with candles and lanterns." A second terrible memory awakes in him:

> As the mirrors were lighted up, the Negro turned sharply about. Those lights, the people crowding into the patio among the white marble statues, the unmistakable bicorns (. . .) brought back to him in a second's shiver the night of Henri Christophe's death.

He manages to escape, but overcome by malaria (the symmetrical equivalent of Leclerc's cholera), he dies praying to Papa Legba, Master of Roads—an amulet of whom he had once wrought "to open the paths of Rome for Pauline Bonaparte"—, one of the gods he (as Christophe) had forsaken to enter a culture that was not his own.

At the beginning of Part III, "old, but still steady on his bunioned, calloused feet" Ti Noel returns from Cuba to Haiti as a free man. After being forced to work in the construction of the Citadel, he settles in what is left of the house of his first and long-since dead master, Lenormand de Mezy. "Feeling in a way the owner of that land whose contours were meaningful only to him," he clears away some of the ruins and furnishes them with the spoils of Sans-Souci; for him, these become the attributes of his own "Royal Palace." He takes special pride in "a dress coat that had belonged to Henri Christophe (. . .) which he wore all the time, his regal air heightened by a braided straw hat that he had folded and crushed into the shape of a bicorne." Countryfolk come to his "palace" to dance and celebrate, "and Ti Noel, more majestic than ever in his green coat, presided over the feast, seated between a priest of the Savanna (. . .) and an old veteran, one of those who had fought against Rochambeau." Through this return of the carnavalesque, Ti Noel becomes both Lenormand and Christophe.

"But one morning the Surveyors appeared (. . .) the Republican mulattoes, the new masters from the Plaine du Nord." For Ti Noel, their 'new order' is but the threat of a new tyranny: "The old man began to lose heart at this endless return of chains, this rebirth of shackles." Remembering Macandal, he will procure lycanthropic escape among animals. But injustice reappears within communities of wasps, ants and geese, and Ti Noel finally understands that Macandal's message had been "to serve men, not to abjure the world of men." In a moment of illumination, he relives "the finest moments of his life" and feels in himself the whole of human history:

> He felt centuries old. A cosmic weariness, as of a planet weighted with stones, fell upon his shoulders shrunk by so many blows, sweats, revolts.

The meaning of human destiny becomes clear to him:

> Bowed down by suffering and duties, beautiful in the midst of his misery, capable of loving in the face of afflictions and trials, man finds his greatness, his fullest measure, only in the Kingdom of This World.

Raised to the universal Man and assimilated to Jesus Christ (a series of previous allusions connect him intertextually with episodes from the Gospels, such as the Sermon on the Mount and Palm Sunday), his death becomes a ritual sacrifice in which, in a symphonic manner, the whole of the novel's geography, motifs, and main episodes are brought together.

> Ti Noel climbed upon his table, scuffing the marquetry with his calloused feet. Toward the Cap the sky was dark with the smoke of fires as on the night when all the conch shells of the hills and coast has sung together (. . .) At that moment a great green wing, blowing from the ocean, swept the Plaine du Nord, spreading throughout the Dondon valley with a loud roar. And while the slaughtered bulls bellowed on the summit of Le Bonnet de l'Evêque, the armchair, the screen, the volumes of the Encyclopédie, the music box, the doll, and the moonfish rose in the air, as the last ruins of the plantation came tumbling down.

After this Apocalypse "nobody knew of Ti Noel" (our translation) except that "wet vulture," "a cross of feathers," "who turns every death to his own benefit," i.e., a variant of the phoenix, pointing to the eternal return within the cyclical history of mankind.

Frances Wyers (essay date June 1992)

SOURCE: "Carpentier's *Los pasos perdidos:* Heart of Lightness, Heart of Darkness," in *Revista Hispanica Moderna,* Vol. 45, No. 1, pp. 84-95.

[*In the following essay, Wyers discusses the influence of history, allegory, nature, and Joseph Conrad's* Heart of Darkness *on Carpentier's* Los pasos perdidos.]

Los pasos perdidos tells about a journey into the depths of the Orinoco jungle by a narrator-protagonist who wants to recover certain primitive musical instruments that he believes will explain the origins of music. But the quest is also an escape; he wants to free himself from the drudgery of modern life, from the alienation of the metropolis (presumably New York) and from his servitude to clock-time and calendar-time. He finds not only the instruments he seeks but also, deep in the jungle, an unexpected "heart of lightness," a world he sees (as do most critics and doubtless Alejo Carpentier himself) as a paradise, a world he eventually loses and to which he will be unable to return.

The narrator's journey is marked, at a few but significant moments, by his feeling that certain overarching laws determine his actions. These moments, as well as the historical reversal itself, suggest that the novel has an allegorical structure. As we shall see, what starts the trip backwards in time looks to him like a fateful occurrence, that is, an event outside of human time. The allegorical pattern, however, is only intermittent, never complete and it gives way to a reversal of one of the novel's primary mythic references, an "innocent" natural world untouched by humanity. Another novel of a journey up-river, Conrad's *Heart of Darkness* also looms behind this work. The explicit ideologies of both novels are quite different though we see certain curious coincidences.

Allegory and history, as everyone knows, figure in all of Carpentier's fictions, though if we look at them chronologically we see a shift in balance from the first to the second. Intertwined with these conceptual and organizational modes, are two central motifs: the opposition of culture to nature and the mimicry and changeability that pervade both. In some works these motifs contribute to a sense of allegorical law or historical design and in others they demolish those patterns. ***Los pasos perdidos*** wavers in a middle ground between these effects, but the whole of the work stresses the polarity of human history and natural metamorphosis. Nature becomes a world of ceaseless and inexplicable change, that overturns any kind of order. And history reverses itself as it moves towards a "paradise" that—unbeknownst to both the narrator and Carpentier—ironically repeats the outlines of the birth of civilizations, the beginning of an all too familiar repressive order.

Los pasos perdidos is characterized by the constant coincidence of anticipation and memory. Both, I believe, are purely formal. The narrative is a memoir that steadily pays heed to time but repeatedly negates change in the characters and in their world. The opening of the novel describes the setting of a play in which the narrator's wife is acting; the time is the U.S. Civil War; we learn exactly how long that play has run (four years and seven months). This ever-repeating bit of frozen past serves as a model for the novel's description of a history that goes backwards across a series of static tableaux. Time shifts back in jumps from one historical plateau to another. These shifts stand in place of continuity and progression. Throughout the narrator does not change. After fifteen days of travel in the jungle, and after having discovered the musical instruments, he says "algo dentro de mí, había madurado enormemente." But the reader does not see any maturing. In an interview, Carpentier spoke of his character's "momentary resurrection." I do not think there is any kind of resurrection. The character deludes himself, as does Carpentier and, it seems, very many readers.

Los pasos perdidos is characterized by the constant coincidence of anticipation and memory.
—Frances Wyers

The peculiar rigidity in the representation of time is emphasized by the narrator's occasional glimpses of a causal system that looks magical, as if ruled by supernatural powers. The first example is a chance meeting with the curator of the museum of musical instruments. The narrator is simply trying to get out of the rain, but the first drops on his face are "como si hubiesen sido la advertencia primera— ininteligible para mí entonces—del encuentro." The meaning of the encounter will only be revealed later in the web of its implications. "Debemos buscar el comienzo de todo, de seguro, en la nube que reventó en lluvia aquella trade, con tan inesperada violencia que sus truenos parecían truenos de otra latitud." The "annunciation" seems to refer to perfectly ordinary, even trivial events, but it stretches out to the tropical latitudes he will visit. The meeting with the curator is what sets the narrator on his journey and the text on its retrogressive course.

The first chapter is full to references to childhood memories, as well as later ones, that point ahead to future events, so that time takes on a kind of backwards-forwards sliding motion. He remembers the language of his childhood, the *Odyssey* that will play a symbolic part in his trip, his plan for a composition based on *Prometheus Unbound,* and, finally, Beethoven's Ninth Symphony with Schiller's "Ode to Joy." These artistic icons remind him of his father's unbounded admiration for all the products of European high culture; his father could not, of course, have foreseen the future that was part of the narrator's past, the rise of Nazism and the Second World War. In another glissade, the recollection of his mimetic-magical-rhythmic theory of the origin of music sends us forward towards the coming journey at the same moment that it makes us think of primordial time and of origins. Later, in the museum gallery, the chronological display of art works and implements allows the narrator to retrace humanity's past through the paleolithic and to "los confines del hombre." This voyage in time prefigures the whole of the novel's course.

In the midst of these trackings to and fro, before the above scene, the narrator watches and describes a film he had made, underwater views of "la llegada de las anguilas y el vasto viñedo cobrizo del Mar de los Sargazos. Y luego, aquellas naturalezas muertas de caracoles y anzuelos, la selva de corales y la alucinante batalla de los crustáceos, tan hábilmente agrandada, que las langostas parecían espantables dragones acorazados." This is the first of the novel's sightings of plants and animals that mimic others or evoke works of art and fantastic creatures. Such scenes are frequent in Carpentier's fictions. A set piece places characters or narrators before unknown and surprising plants, animals and minerals that change, entwine and create new symbiotic shapes. Although all descriptive passages interrupt the course of narrative, Carpentier's accounts of metamorphosis do not establish a background so much as a world that counters the human one. The positioning of these highly significant suspensions invariably comments on what comes before and after. But here the vision is an artificial one, produced by the skillful enlargements of the camera. And its aim is commercial. Yet placed among personal memories and historical references, the film contrasts the realm of natural mimicry and transmutation with that of human history. The scene prefigures later direct views of natural metamorphoses. It is placed in this first chapter between two different kinds of fixed systems: clock and calendar time that portion out the "daily tyrannies of modern life" and that hidden order announced by the drops of rain on the narrator's face.

Referring to the novel's many anticipations, Eduardo González has pointed out how the individual's most significant experiences are enclosed within an allegorical scaffolding and how Carpentier sees culture as "una acumulación de signos, redes o fuentes simbólicos de iluminación y de perplejidad para el sujeto." I would add that the doubling of scenes and thematic clusters also points to a level of hidden, magical principles. In his book on allegory, Angus Fletcher says that "any struggle between antithetical positions will arouse . . . formalized doubling." Antithetical pairings are central to the novel's plot and to the narrator's scheme of values. Among them are the valued past/the devalued present (or prehistory/history); authentic or integral culture / unauthentic or alienated culture; the origin of art /

the "end" or degeneration of art in commercialism (for example, the "theater" that originates in the funeral rites for Rosario's father / Ruth's commercial theatrical function). The narrator sets these oppositions before us and is generally aware of them. But he is often not aware of the symbolic unity behind them. Nor, as I have mentioned, does the author consistently maintain an allegorical subtext throughout the novel. Indeed, the narrative's figurative pattern is fragmentary, inconsistent and finally, as we shall see, reversible.

The mimesis that threads through the novel appears in different ways, the principal ones being mimicry in nature and mimicry in culture. Both are portrayed alternately in positive and negative terms. Cultural imitation can be a servile response to the social and economic power of the dominant world, an attempt to participate magically in its strength, beauty or prestige. It easily turns into falsification. Colonial culture attempts to appropriate the forms of the metropolis. The architectural jumble of the South American city, first stop on the journey, is a man-made anarchy of different period styles. The public attending an opera there duplicates a nineteenth century audience. As duplicate, it is a debasement, a sham on two different time levels. The narrator also looks down on other kinds of imitation: the way Mouche apes the intellectual fashions of St. Germain-des-Prés, and, in a country resort, the eagerness with which a white musician, an Indian poet and a black painter (surely an allegorical trio) seek information from Mouche so that they too might insert themselves in a foreign culture as faithful copyists.

Yet the novel's most significant—and positive—mimetic doubling occurs through the narrator's projection of European cultural history onto the different space-time periods of this American "Odyssey" (a reference he repeatedly uses to describe his travels). The first image in the creation of this palimpsest is the long forgotten "presencia de la harina en las mañanas . . . el pan que reparte el padre luego de bendecirlo." The almost religious allusion opens out to an earlier, even more exalted experience: "el gran sabor mediterráneo que ya llevaban pegado a la lengua los compañeros de Ulises." As he moves into the jungle and backwards in time, the narrator casts over each waystation a network of European references, from the nineteenth century through the Middle Ages to Homeric times (beyond that, in prehistoric eras, the importance of place, of continent, of Europe or America, quite naturally disappears). It is a curious lamination, convincing if one accepts the thesis that it was a medieval Spain that discovered and colonized the New World, but puzzling in view of the uniformly heroic portrayal of those times, especially when we remember that the narrator, telling about visits to European museums just before the outbreak of World War II, sees medieval art as the forerunner of the horrors of the Spanish Civil War and the rise of Nazism. "Ya no podía contemplarse un tímpano ilustre,

un campanil, gárgola o ángel sonriente sin oírse decir que ahí estaban previstas ya las banderías del presente. . . ." We do not know who "says" this but the narrator offers no disagreement. The "sin oírse decir" leads the reader to imagine a whole chorus of condemnation. That critique, however, does not cross the Atlantic. Quite the contrary, the narrator's enthusiasm for the marvelous transfer of European culture to the wilds of Latin America, might be described as a conceptual recolonization of that space. He never suggests or asks if this new world will follow the old one into the same inhumanity. By the end of the novel, the conflation of America and Europe appears as part of the narrator's unconscious confusion of notions of good an evil embedded in nature and civilization.

> *Los pasos perdidos's* **most significant—and positive—mimetic doubling occurs through the narrator's projection of European cultural history onto the different space-time periods of this American "Odyssey" (a reference he repeatedly uses to describe his travels).**
> —*Frances Wyers*

Conrad's merging of good and evil rests on different foundations: the evils of the European colonial enterprise become so entangled, through imagery and ideology, with the menace of the African landscape and population that in some passages we cannot tell which is which: "It was like the stillness of an implacable force brooding over an inscrutable intention. It looked at you with a vengeful aspect." If the reference is to the Congo, are we to think of nature, of the impenetrable jungle or of the people who live there?

When it takes the stance of turning away from cultural imitation, Carpentier's text must turn to the opposite, to creation. For the narrator, and for Carpentier, both enamoured of language, this means giving names to things. The narrator is scornful of Mouche because she sees all new things through the filter of European literature. As we have seen he does almost the same thing, though his range is broader. He proposes for himself "la única tarea que me pareciera oportuna en el medio que ahóra me iba revelando lentamente la índole de sus valores: la tarea de Adán poniendo nombre a las cosas." González Echevarría points out that this is one of the most frequently repeated commonplaces in Carpentier's work, identifying it with the desire to create an art free of the influence of Europe where everything is already named. Yet we have seen the narrator repeatedly places the social life of the New World under the template of European history. The only things to which he can give new names are features of the natural world.

Naming is a primary cultural act, involved with the making of tools and the transmission of that craft. Separated from toolmaking, it is the writer's special pride. We might related this enterprise to what Freud and Fenichel called "the magic of names" which, as Fletcher observes, dominates the allegorical work more than any other linguistic phenomenon. Although the weave of allegory is quite torn in this text, the treatment of language and the well-known idiosyncrasies of Carpentier's style show a basic allegorical orientation. Fenichel says that words are shadows of things, constituting a microcosm that reflects the macrocosm of things outside. "This-representations" (words) are "an attempt to endow the things with 'ego-quality' for the purpose of achieving mastery over them. He who knows a word for a thing masters the thing." Fletcher says the magic of names, the so-called "omnipotence of words," is explained as a superabstract withdrawal into a verbal universe. For Carpentier's narrator, as well as for Carpentier himself, words not only confer mastery but rescue things from namelessness, which is seen as a kind of non-existence: looking into a hallucinatory crater of demonic plants, the narrator forsees their disappearance from the planet without ever having been "recreated by the word." Carpentier's baroque style aims at both mastery and recreation. When confronted with realities already named he piles word upon word upon word in order to create anew the objects of his description, to bring into being an original, unique, linguistically crowded entity, thereby asserting his dominion over the "macrocosm of things."

The narrator's revelation about his task of naming is followed, a few pages later, by the first direct description that combines different orders of natural reality. He must now take on that "única tarea." Ascending the Andes he sees "peñas tristes como animales petrificados," where every night the organs of storm bellowed "en garganta y abismos." In this portentous environment he meets Rosario and learns about the members of a scientific expedition of fifty years ago who are congealed in transparent ice. Against this image of petrification, Rosario's physical features make him think of living change and transformation, the blending and mixing of races. Shortly afterwards, hearing Beethoven's Ninth Symphony on a radio, he thinks not of the accomplishments of Europe's high culture but of the shame and horrors of its history. Yet he describes the mourning for Rosario's father by reference to earlier monuments of that same culture; it is "una tragedia antigua," a "un rito milenario," an "auto sacramental"; all these command his deepest respect. The text repeatedly sets before us the narrator's ambivalence towards all culture, (especially that of the West), and repeatedly shows us that he is unaware of his contrary feelings.

In contrast to this narrator's admiration for racial mixing and in contrast to his reverent vision of the funeral rites for Rosario's father, Marlowe describes the Congo's inhabitants in the dehumanizing terms of fragmented body parts and frenzied gestures: "a burst of yells, a whirl of black limbs, a mass of hands clapping, of feet stamping, of bodies swaying, of eyes rolling . . ." He is "appalled" as "before an enthusiastic outbreak in a madhouse." Arguing that Conrad provides no alternative frame of reference for the actions and opinions of his characters, that there is no distance between Conrad and Marlowe, that "Marlowe seems to enjoy Conrad's complete confidence," Chinua Achebe has called the novel "an offensive and deplorable book." And if, as some students of Conrad claim, Africa is merely a setting for the disintegration of Kurtz's mind, then it becomes "a metaphysical battleground devoid of all recognizable humanity."

Aside from Rosario, Carpentier's narrative does not really refer much to the people of the Orinoco. One important exception is the tribe where he finds the musical instruments; he is impressed that Indians, whom he had previously seen only through more or less fantastic tales, live according to primordial rhythms, absolute "owners of the culture," their reality far from "the absurd concept of savage." They are human beings who master "la totalidad de los oficios propiciados por el teatro de su existencia." Another group of Indians, as we shall see, lives in the mire of pre-human squalor. But most of the narrative focuses on a mestizo, colonial culture that represents different stages of European culture set against an ever more astounding natural world.

Turning from one to the other—nature, culture, nature—the text always goes back to nature, a nature that copies not only its own creations but also those of man (culture in this text is invariably masculine). We see "bloques de granito en forma de saurios, de dantas, de animales petrificados." Enormous heaps of basalt look like "restos de una necrópolis perdida . . . los vestigios de una arquitectura creada con fines ignorados." If nature is cast in a man-made mold, so too is sexual experience; it is totally acculturated, fully circumscribed by a male scheme of domination and submission. The narrator will possess Rosario. Mouche may be dying, but he and Rosario exist in a world apart where he caresses her public hair "con mano de amo," the "master's hand." In this brave new world he discovers that the female "serves" the male "en el más noble sentido del término."

The shifting back and forth between scenes of a mineral world in metamorphosis (towards the animal, towards the architectural), references to human races also in metamorphosis, memories of the abominations of European history, archaic dramatic rituals and a sexual rite of masculine appropriation sets the predictability of human history—including the male ideology that informs it and that is clearly beyond any critical consciousness on the part of the narrator—against a natural world far from the human, even though it is portrayed by dint of man-made comparisons.

The confusion of natural forms grows in intensity as the voyage inland progresses. The river provides a "disorder of appearances" in a succession of "small mirages" that disconcert and disorient. Yet dawn brings "a primordial sensation of beauty"; while Rosario cleans his breakfast dishes, he feels "el orgullo de proclamarse dueño del mundo, supremo usufructuario de la creación." The "hombre-avispa," of the first chapter, the worker subjected to the schedules and rules of others turns into the supreme capitalist. The experience of nature becomes ownership. Its otherness is tamed and claimed in possession. Conrad sees this quite differently: "We could have fancied ourselves taking possession of an accursed inheritance." Of course Carpentier refers to esthetic possession, Conrad presumably to the appropriation of the material wealth of the Congo. Yet in the Carpentier text the esthetic is ominously linked with destructive power; it sets forth several inevitable historical sequences that tie art or language to annihilation, control, enslavement: the unstoppable progression from medieval art to the rise of Nazism is repeated by the memories awakened later on hearing Beethoven's Ninth; naming or the mastery over the "macrocosm of things" presents itself in another variation as the male's subjugation of the female. Linked images of control enclose the description of nature's awesome independence.

The natural world is bent to images of human fabrication: he sees twisted trees as anchored ships, more marble than wood, "emergían como los obeliscos cimeros de una ciudad abismada." A fertile vegetation is ensnared in lianas, bushes, vines, hooks and parasitical plants that jostle each other. What is most astonishing is "the endless mimetism of virgin nature": "Aquí todo parecía otra cosa, creándose un mundo de apariencias que ocultaba la realidad . . . La selva era el mundo de la mentira, de la trampa y del falso semblante; allí todo era disfraz, estratagema, juego de apariencias, metamorfosis." Plant, animal and insect forms combine; flowers are not flowers, fruit is the deceptive guise of some insectivorous plant. Even the sky lies at times, inverting its height in the quicksilver of ponds. This is the realm of an exuberant proliferation of lianas, an eternal shuffling of appearances and simulacra; we are back at the first chapters of Genesis. The pride of ownership gives way to an ethically loaded catalogue of the jungle's foreignness: lies, deceit, falsity. We are closer to Conrad's ambiguity. The narrator must feel that he can no longer domesticate nature through metaphors and imagery, so he denounces it even while expressing awe at its baroque inventiveness.

González Echevarría has observed that Carpentier's language echoes that of the mid-nineteenth century German explorer,

Robert Schomburgk who, in his *Travels in British Guiana,* struggled futilely to resist describing the landscape in Western terms. He finds traces in images, adjectives, similes but also in the coincidence of the unifying theme of the constant transformations of nature. He goes on to say that nature is a code, akin to that of writing in which meanings are always changing and "signs . . . engender other signs in perpetual multiplication." Therefore the narrator cannot 'read' it; he cannot get through the web of deception, subterfuge and metamorphosis. I would go further and point out how the narrator's own code, his ordered memoir—which ends with a neatly pointed moral about how "la única raza humana que está impedida de desligarse de las fechas es la raza de quienes hacen arte . . ."—contrasts with the disorder of a nature he ultimately come to see as rebellious and repellent. In Conrad's view, it was 'prehistoric' man who confounds the reading of signs: Marlowe cannot tell if the frenzied yells they hear are curses, prayers or forms of welcome.

From the entanglements of living forms the narrator's gaze moves to enormous rock formations, a world of Bosch and other painters of the fantastic. Everything is gigantic: a titanic city of multiple spacious buildings, cyclopean stairways reaching to the clouds; strange obsidian fortresses "defienden la entrada de algún reino prohibido al hombre." The capital of Forms asserts itself—a realm of the gods where some Final Judgement might be celebrated. In a small village he finds the primitive musical instruments that are the object of his search. Fray Pedro celebrates mass with simple religious artifacts and the narrator becomes acutely conscious of the backwards movement of time—from 1540 to the Middle Ages, to the birth of Christ, to the paleolithic. The past is made present; he touches it, breathes it. The reversal is swift, like the one in the final section of **"Viaje a la semilla":** "Perdió el Graal su relumbre, cayeron los clavos de la cruz, los mercaderes volvieron al templo, borróse la estrella de la Natividad y fue el Año Cero, en que regresó al cielo el Ángel de la Anunciación. . . . Estamos en la Era Paleolítica . . . intrusos, forasteros ignorantes . . . en una ciudad que nace en el alba de la Historia." In **"Viaje a la semilla,"** the reversal is magical. Here it takes place in the narrator's imagination where reeling sequences of objects mark different epochs. What is suggested throughout the text by spatial-temporal shiftings is here dramatically condensed in a cinematographic unravelling of the course of history. The effect (also suggested throughout the memoir) is the merging of historical and magical causation. Significantly, the history sighted is Western and Christian. The people without history do not appear. Only nature, with its amazing changes, stands as the contrast to this world of recorded human events.

History, inconceivable without writing or some form of visual recording system, is closely connected with the development of the state; it is, therefore, the story of hierarchical society. Such a society is the only one imagineable to the narrator, though others have imagined otherwise. For example, the anthropologist Salvatore Cucchiari has posited a pre-gender society unmarked by hierarchies and the rule of male over female, an era when social gender categories have not yet been constructed. Woman is not "other," not object and subordinate. (He situates the subsequent gender revolution in the Upper Paleolithic). Carpentier's narrator does not take us back to this pre-kinship social formation. Quite the contrary, he fancies an idealized world of total female subjugation. Rosario, as a "woman of earth," serves the male. She calls herself "your woman" and "en esa constante reiteración del posesivo encuentro como una solidez de concepto, una cabal definición de situaciones, que nunca me diera la palabra 'esposa.'" Rosario fulfills "un destino que más vale no analizarlo demasiado, porque es regido por 'cosas grandes' cuyo mecanismo es oscuro, y que . . . rebasan la capacidad de interpretación del ser humano." Are these "cosas grandes" part of that figurative realm that has almost vanished out of sight? Innocently, and with great delight, the narrator believes he has reached the absolute and "exact" definition of gender relations—mastery and servitude, ownership and unquestioning, happy slavery.

That slavery and debasement are part of this "return to paradise," or the move towards "momentary resurrection" appears in more ominous form in the next landing place, the habitat of a people with a culture much earlier than the one just seen. The travelers have left the paleolithic and entered "un ámbito que hacía retroceder los confines de la vida humana a lo más tenebroso de la noche de las edades," peopled by creatures who are barely human. The Adelantado shows him a muddy hollow, a kind of pig-sty filled with the captives of others who consider themselves a superior race, "the only rightful owners of the jungle." The prisoners look like living fetuses with white beards, wrinkled dwarfs with enormous bellies covered with blue veins who smile stupidly, fearfully, servilely." We have gone from the pleasures of oppression to its horrors, with no indication whatsoever that there might be some link between them. The narrator is unaware of the very connections he has put before us. And nothing in the sequence of plot—or in anything else—points to an ironic author behind the narrator.

Beyond this realm of infrahumanity, is a world prior to the creation of living beings: "Acaban de apartarse las aguas. . . . Estamos en el mundo del Génesis, al fin del Cuarto Día de la Creación," almost reaching the "terrible soledad del Creador." Then, repeating the forwards and backwards slidings of the first chapter, the plot line advances to the Adelantado's secret: he has founded a city. "Se puede ser Fundador de una Ciudad. Crear y gobernar una ciudad que no figure en los mapas, que se sustraiga a los horrores de la época, que nazca así, de la voluntad de un hombre, en este

mundo del Génesis. La primera ciudad, la ciudad de Henoch. . . ." The city turns out to be very similar to those built by the Spanish conquerors, with a Plaza Mayor, a Government House, the houses of the founder's children (the son's close to the center, the daughters' farther back) and behind, the Indians' settlement. The church will be built next. The city reproduces well-known distinctions between state, colonizers and Indians. Fray Pedro agrees that it is just like the cities founded by Pizarro, Diego de Losada and Pedro de Mendoza. It springs from the same impulse to impose one's designs on nature and on other human beings, especially on those who can be seen as racially or sexually inferior. It is the self-reflecting creation of a solitary man, "born out of the will of one man." The narrator marvels at the possibility of such an achievement; it fires his imagination. "Yo fundo una ciudad. Él ha fundado una ciudad. Es posible conjugar semejante verbo." The city, this compelling heart of darkness, is an expression of sheer willfulness. No wonder the Adelantado is no longer interested in searching for gold; he wants land and "el poder de legislar por cuenta propia." To rule over others and devise laws to control them, that is the Adelantado's Arcadian dream that the narrator so much admires. Arcadia turns out to be a city, *civis,* a nascent civilization. In miniature we see the establishment of class distinctions, racial separations, the state, church, and the inevitable structuring and reinforcement of gender divisions and roles. The conceptual recolonization effected by portraying Latin America through the stages of European history, here becomes a true recolonization, a real subjugation. Captivated by an order that he does not recognize as the roots of the very civilization from which he flees, the narrator decides to stay.

Fray Pedro takes him to see petroglyphs and, near those "Signs," on the side of the mountain, a crater filled with frightening, hallucinatory plants. This is the last long description of untouched, unruly nature, now perceived as a repugnant confusion of forms: "gramíneas membranosas, cuyas ramas tienen una mórbida redondez de brazo y de tentáculo. Las hojas enormes, abiertas como manos, parecen de flora submarina, por sus texturas de madrépora y de alga con flores bulbosas, . . . pájaros colgados de una vena, mazorcas de larvas, pistilos sanguinolentos, que les salen de los bordes por un proceso de erupción y desgarre, sin conocer la gracia de un tallo. Y todo eso, allá abajo, se enrevesa, se enmaraña, se anuda, en un vasto movimiento de posesión de acoplamiento, de incestos, a la vez monstruoso y orgiástico, que es suprema confusión de las formas." Fray Pedro calls these monstrous and orgiastic plants rebellious because they fled from man in the very beginning, refusing to serve as food. Here they hide in the last valley of prehistory. He explains that this diabolic vegetation surrounded the Earthly Paradise before the Fall. The whole cauldron is "demoniacal." These are the plants that the narrator says will disappear from the planet "without being named, without having been recreated by the word." The rebel plants will never be mastered or possessed by language.

Marlowe too refers to the absence of signs: "We were traveling in the night of first ages, of those ages that are gone, leaving hardly a sign—and no memories at all." But he is speaking not of the jungle but of those creatures who make him think "the worst of it—this suspicion of their not being inhuman."

In *Los pasos perdidos,* the vision of a vegetation now identified as incestuous, orgiastic, unheeding of man's wants and needs, stands in contrast to the orderliness of a man-made city with its hierarchies of racial, sexual and social privilege. By re-introducing these hierarchies and founding civilization anew, the text keeps at bay Marlowe's vision of savagery and cannibalism. It is the realm of plants, not of man, that becomes diabolical. The opposite of human history and human laws is the incomprehensible disorder of nature. First described as living and mineral forms that mimic each other, then as a scramble of appearances and simulacra, endless proliferations and metamorphoses, later as lies and deceits, nature finally appears as "demoniacal" and unnamable. Deep in the jungle, vegetation is the heart of darkness, the horrifying face of chaos. And, in a symmetrical reversal of terms, goodness, order and personal glory attach themselves to the newly founded city, which is, in reality, a perfect embryo of human repression. The narrative has turned itself inside out, deconstructing its forms and the myths to which it alludes.

González Echevarría speaks of how "en la mejor tradición de las confesiones, el texto traiciona a cada paso a su autor que pretende develar verdades sobre sí pero que sólo lo logra indirectamente." He adds that by placing Latin American reality within the framework of European history, the text establishes a marked contrast between what the narrator-protagonist says about himself and what he does. This fragmentation or multiplication "es irónica y socava la autoridad del narrador. No podemos fiarnos de la coherencia ideológica de su discurso, empedrado como está de una enorme cantidad de alusiones librescas. . . ." Eduardo González, reviewing this edition, also refers to the split between the protagonist's voice and "the ironic commentary which [his] actions and evasions weave around him. . . ." But not only bookishness and irony (the latter, in my view, disappearing in the second half of the book) make the reader stumble but also the presence of an underlying myth about nature and society that is barely stated and never explicitly affirmed or contested. Yet when it finally does take form in the text, we see that our cherished image of innocent nature vs. sinful metropolis has been turned topsy turvy. Whatever is left of the novel's allegorical and historical tapestry has been swallowed up in this reversal.

Not surprisingly, only back in the shelter of the new town, does the narrator recover the image of a placid landscape where bamboos dance in the breeze and where he can imagine a future time when men will discover "un alfabeto en los ojos de las calcedonias, en los pardos terciopelos de la falena, y entonces se sabrá con asombro que cada caracol manchado era, desde siempre, un poema." Most critics have been as misguided as the narrator in thinking that Santa Mónica de los Venados is a utopia (though many utopias are restrictive and rigid), a paradise beyond time and corruption. They confuse it with an idealized pristine landscape that only rarely makes an appearance in the work. People tend to read the novel as a voyage to the origin of things. When this critic says that the narrator-protagonist cannot "permanecer en el origen porque no puede suprimir su conciencia histórica," he ignores the fact that historical consciousness has embedded itself in the very town plan of Santa Mónica. In Conrad's original manuscript, Marlowe quite correctly says that comprehension of their surroundings "could only be obtained by conquest or surrender." History is the history of conquest. The beginning of a new life, what many critics have called simply "el origen," is tainted with all the discontents of civilization, with all its barbarisms. When Carpentier, in an interview, spoke of the "thesis" of his novel as a voyage "hasta las raíces de la vida," and of how his character had lost "la puerta de su existencia auténtica," he unwittingly (I suppose) situated authenticity in a class society that is racist and sexist. So strong is our cultural (romantic) paradigm of natural innocence and city wickedness that even so astute a reader as González Echevarría slides right past this radical reordering of the myth and speaks of "escape a la naturaleza, regreso a la civilización, intento fallido de regreso al mundo natural." Santa Mónica, as we have seen, is hardly natural. It is the creation of "the will of one man," cast in a mold of conquest and exploitation. In introducing "evil" in the form of the rape of a child by a leper, the author must be unaware that evil lies in the very heart and idea of the Adelantado's city. The rape and the bloody punishment that follow are gratuitous, melodramatic additions to the portrayal of a society whose unhappy future we can easily predict. We live in that future. The narrator tried to escape from it by going into the jungle. His return to the metropolis and his failed attempt to get back to Santa Mónica might look like the loss of paradise, but we know that it is simply a dream, a hallucination of good, just as the "diabolic crater" is a hallucination of evil. It is not, as Carpentier claimed, that his protagonist-narrator's resurrection is "momentary"; it is that it never happens. In moving from the immorality and exploitation of the modern metropolis to the innocence of nature in metamorphosis and then from the supposed virtues of a proto-metropolis that promises all the abuses of the world we know, to the "immorality" of an incestuously entangled, rebellious nature, the narrator—and the narrative (with its author)—confound all principles of good and evil, freedom and repression. The novel's title aptly expresses this profound disorientation.

Matthew C. Stewart (essay date 1993)

SOURCE: "Identity and Authenticity in Alejo Carpentier's *Reasons of State*," in *Imagination, Emblems and Expressions: Essays on Latin American, Caribbean, and Continental Culture and Identity,* edited by Helen Ryan-Ranson, Bowling Green State University Popular Press, 1993, pp. 75-87.

[*In the following essay, Stewart traces the dictator's struggle with identity in Carpentier's* Reasons of State.]

Ostensibly Alejo Carpentier's 1974 novel, **Reasons of State,** concerns itself with the political and military problems and actions of a mythical Latin American dictator who chooses to live in Paris as much as possible. The Head of State, as we know him, embodies nearly absolute power, as near as might be supposed possible in one man. Unsurprisingly political and military activities comprise the assertion of power and authority in this novel and also provide the series of events which propels the narrative forward. Nonetheless, these activities do not define and shape the novel's primary theme of identity; rather, they provide the background against which this topic is shown. Despite the implications of his title, Carpentier has not written a novel whose main enterprise is to examine the effects of power upon the autocrat who is its protagonist; nor has he examined at any length the consequences for the state, polity or population affected by the concentration of power in this one man. Nor yet does the novel concentrate on the mechanics or dynamics of political power in action. Indeed, except at the very basic level of event and fictional context **Reasons of State** can hardly be said to be an overtly political novel.

> **If Carpentier's main interest [in *Reasons of State*] is not in political explorations, then in what is it? Simply put, it is in the Head of State as a *letrado* [enlightened head] and more importantly, as a Latin American who incorporates a false identity because he rejects his own indigenous identity.**
> **—Matthew C. Stewart**

If Carpentier's main interest is not in political explorations, then in what is it? Simply put, it is in the Head of State as a *letrado* [enlightened head] and more importantly, as a Latin American who incorporates a false identity because he rejects his own indigenous identity. Beyond the simply intui-

tive apprehension that Carpentier's preoccupations (whether or not he is aware of them) are not politically oriented, textual analysis brings us to the same conclusion. Overtly political and military sections of the text pass quickly in that relatively large periods of time are devoted relatively few pages; thus such sections, because they do not demand extended attention and because they are not replete with detail or elaboration of theme, must be relegated to secondary status. Indeed, the most overtly and concentratedly political section of the novel—the section wherein the dictator crushes his erstwhile compatriot Hoffman's rebellion, reconsolidates power and tries to hold on to it in spite of increasingly active opposition—comprises 158 pages yet represents "several years," as we learn from his daughter, Ofelia. On the other hand, ten pages alone are devoted to a visit by the Distinguished Academician, which could not be thought to take more than an hour of the Head of State's time. Such dense sections as this all have as their central significance the question of identity and authentication, and it is upon such scenes that critical enquiry should focus if it wishes to penetrate the heart of the text's meaning. It should also be remarked that even the term used in the above paragraph, *concentratedly* political, must be taken as relative because even in that middle section, the novel's most overtly political, the theme of identity recurs many times, usually in the form of a "slow" scene or a motif appearing within the texture of the fast-moving political section.

Very early in the novel it becomes clear that the Head of State's chief pleasures are not brought about by the mundane duties of governing: "Happiness due to an empty agenda-tray, on the night-table beside the hammock, instead of a whole timetable of interviews, official visits, presentation of credentials, or ostentatious entry of soldiers. . . ." In fact the Head of State rarely seems to be a man who takes pleasure in the wielding or working of political power, who defines himself by the political and military power he embodies, who desires to exercise that power above all else. To be sure, his violent outbursts upon hearing of each of the rebellions with which he is confronted are based in part upon the betrayal and ingratitude he feels in the rebels. Yet an even larger element of his outrage comes from the fact that he is far from eager to return to his homeland, or, more properly put, to leave Paris. This regret is especially keen at Hoffman's rebellion: "He longed to stay here [in Paris], to get out of the magic circle, but just as if it really enclosed him he could not." The "magic circle" which he so wants to escape here is the Head of State's own conception of his country's history, with which, of course, he is inescapably involved.

What is this Paris which has or represents more attraction to the despot than his own country? The previous quotation seems to suggest that Paris's function in the text is symbolic, but it is so only in a very direct and emblematic way. Paris epitomizes the height of European culture, elegance and civility, but it is conceived differently in the minds of the reader and the dictator. For the Head of State, Paris is all that is marvelous in *La Belle Epoque,* but it is even more; it is the principal mediator of his desire, the means by which he defines himself. I am using *mediator* here in the sense put forth by Rene Girard in his model of triangular desire as elaborated in *Deceit, Desire and the Novel:* "The disciple pursues objects which are determined for him, or at least seem to be determined for him, by [a] model. . . . We shall call this model the mediator of desire." To discuss an authoritarian dictator as a disciple perhaps presses hard on the reader's credulity or expectations. Certainly the terms and orientation of discussion are far removed from those which are commonly associated with a dictator. Yet this is precisely how the novel asks to be read.

In a salubrious model of desire, no mediator is interposed between the subject and his object of desire so that the desiring subject wishes for the desired object without the "help" of any model he wishes to imitate or impress. The interposition of a mediator necessarily indicates a lack of ability to generate or find autonomous desire, that is, a lack of self-determination and authenticity. As the subject of triangular desire, the Head of State reveals and perpetuates his lack of self-definition and his misguided notions of identity. And, as we shall see, the dictator's lack of identity is also present in the country he governs. What precisely does the dictator desire? Not power, for he has power. Those parts of the text (and they are undeniably important) which treat the Head of State's relationship to power portray him trying to maintain the status quo, not to increase his power. Indeed, there are certain boundaries to and infringements upon his power to which he is content to resign himself, such as the towering presence of the United States as hemispheric giant. Yet no reader can fail to note the authentic, "home-grown" vitality which courses through the dictator prior to his return to quell the uprising of General Ataulfo Galvan:

> The Head of State . . . was pouring himself great swigs of Santa Ines rum—a rum that no longer seemed merely the nostalgic breath of patriotic feelings in *laissez-faire* Paris, but the rum of battle, hot and strong, foretelling hard rough marches and counter-marches in the near future, the smell of horses, soldier's armpits and gunpowder. And all at once, blotting out Jean-Paul Laurens' blessed Radegonde, Elistir's seascape and Gerome's gladiators, they were in the middle of a Council of War. Forgotten was the adolescent hero of the Arc de Triomphe. . . .

Epitomized here is the sort of exercise of authority which does truly pleasure the dictator. Only in his military endeav-

ors and in his bombastic speech-making do we see him "lose himself" to the moment—a paradoxical, yet true, metaphor in that at such infrequent moments the dictator is most truly himself and hence most genuinely happy.

If the dictator does not try to accumulate power, his desires must lie in another direction. This direction is apparent in the above quotation in the form of the works of art "blotted out" by the dictator's vision of the Council of War. But the works of art do not represent the object of desire; instead they epitomize the mediator of desire which in the fuller and more general form it takes throughout the text might best be called French culture. The real object of the dictator's desire is a sense of meaning, identity and legitimation for his life and activities. To fulfill his desires he repeatedly turns to models of European (particularly French) high culture and away from any models which his own Latin America might provide. In other words, he shuns desires which seem most nearly to arise spontaneously within him, such as those exemplified by the rum in the above quotation. Despite the fact that he had become more his true self during his return home to crush Galvan, upon his subsequent return to Paris, the dictator immediately and happily reimmerses himself in Parisian life, saying to his secretary Peralta: "We're better off here than in the Mummies' Cave," a statement which belies authentic desire and identity. Apparently the symbolic import of these native mummies, accidentally discovered by the Head of State while he briefly camped in their midst, is lost on him. He fails to see them as relics of an indigenous Latin American past. Shortly after this statement, the narrator remarks that the Head of State "[feels] something approaching an organic need to re-establish relations with the city." The language of this assertion at once conveys the depth ("organic") and the inauthenticity ("approaching") of the dictator's mediated desires.

To best understand the Head of State, it must be recalled that he is the leader of a nation which uses European models in its efforts to achieve beauty, culture, respectability or any sort of "improvements": "To make the resort more attractive, the municipality had constructed a cement pier with a casino at the end supported on piles, the whole affair copied from Nice . . . "; "Surveying instruments transformed flooded regions, waste land and goat pastures, dividing them into a number of marked-out squares, which having been since remote times 'The Lazar's small-holding,' 'Mexican farm' or 'Misia Petra's ranch,' suddenly *adopted* the names of 'Bagatelle,' 'West Side' or 'Armenonville' . . ." (my italics). Apparently, "sophisticated" citizens share their dictator's desire to replace indigenous ways by importing styles and names, however ludicrous their (mis) application The lamentable irony of this sort of imitation is that the nation has its own particular, often strange (from a European perspective) but rich, beauty and culture, as the novel makes abundantly clear.

Clearly not all the dictator's pretension and lack of self-knowledge can be blamed on him. Nor is this sort of mediated desire peculiar to him, though he exceeds the degree to which desire is mediated in his fellow countrymen because his powerful position enables him to do so. The dictator's own education was dominated by "text's in which more space was occupied—naturally enough—by the Soissons Vase than the battle of Ayacucho, and by Cardinal Balue's cage than the conquest of Peru, and which necessarily laid more stress on Saint Louis of the Crusades than on Simon Bolivar of Carabobo. . . ." As Girard has said, desires may be defined or generated according to "the Other in a movement which is so fundamental and primitive that [characters] completely confuse it with the will to be Oneself." This statement explains why the Head of State's school texts may have appeared "natural enough," but from a less Eurocentric posture, the domination of French history to the detriment of indigenous history could hardly appear more unnatural. As a native citizen of his country, the dictator is naturally in part a product of its self-perceived inferiority; as Head of State, he is in part responsible for the perpetuation of this mind-set.

The Head of State values culture above all else, though not always for mature or disinterested reasons. The relationship between the dictator and culture is impossible to summarize with terse quotations because it is complex and contradictory. On the one hand his pleasure in being asked to attend the Parisian sophisticate Madame Verdurin's musical evenings is surely not entirely grounded in savoring the evening's artistic endeavors. No small measure of his satisfaction stems from the sense of prestige and inclusion in influential European circles which the Head of State desires. The connection between high culture and high places in Paris is a happy one for the dictator. On the other hand, he *does* make sincere pronouncements about his attitudes toward culture. He is a ruthless tyrant only in the political arena: "Bullets and machetes for bastards. But complete liberty of criticism, polemics, discussion and controversy concerning art, literature, schools of poetry, classical philosophy . . . the concept of Beauty, and everything else in that line . . . that's culture."

The depth, and from his own perspective no doubt, the sincerity, of his attachment to French culture as mediator becomes apparent shortly after the dictator learns of the rebellion of Walter Hoffmann and the necessity of once again leaving Paris to reconsolidate his power. At this point, the Head of State conflates his present situation with that of Christ. He takes on several important Christ-like aspects and subsequently remembers the words declared by the Christ in a passion play he had once seen in his own country: "And if you take this from me, what shall I be? What will remain of me?" These words—originally spoken by the passion-play Christ to a distraught spectator who had come out to aid him on his trip to Golgotha—resound in the dictator's memory

because he feels deprived of that which he supposes to be his rightful destiny, that is, to live his version of the life of a cultured Parisian. Clearly the dictator sees his own identity as defined not by the functions of state he performs, not by the tremendous power he can yield, nor by his martial abilities, and least of all by the fact of his Latin American heritage and origin, but rather by this interaction with objects and persons who represent French culture and Parisian high society.

Peralta, sensing the thoughts of his *patrón,* suggests to him that he ought to abandon his duties and remain in his beloved Paris. "And suppose I get rid of *all that,*" the dictator replies, "what should I be? What would remain of me?" We should not suppose that this question reveals the dictator's awareness of, or any sudden awakening to, his genuine (or at least more authentic) identity. Indeed, quite the opposite is happening, as is revealed by the Head of State's next words: "Yes, I remember . . . thinking about the people who had turned against me because of that business at Nueva Cordoba, so that my personality had dwindled and become too small and helpless to play a part in this Apocalyptic world. I was taking on the Crusade for Latinity in order to reinstate my image." Here the dictator reveals that his feelings of self-worth are not generated from any desire to please his fellow countrymen or other Latinos, let alone from within himself. He hopes to recoup power only in order to regain his status in Paris, in order to become the *image* of Latinity he feels is required by the mediator, Paris. At this point the dictator has moved as far away from any desire for authentic identity as he will go in the novel. At this moment of potential crisis, he most explicitly states the falseness of his desires.

Later, when all is lost by the dictator in the United-States-backed coup and he is without power, he endures all sorts of ignominy within his own country, bears up under all manner of loss until he is made to think of the fact that he is not included in the *Petit Larousse:* "And that afternoon I wept. I wept because a dictionary—*Je seme a tout vent*—was unaware of my existence." Betrayal, utter powerlessness, disrespect for his authority, the hatred of his former polity, none of these break the dictator. Book six ends with him weeping because he will never be validated by French society in the way he has desired all his life.

The fact that the dictator blindly defines himself by European terms is further demonstrated after his first return to Paris when all his former "friends" (that is, his sources of legitimation) except the Academician spurn him. After the publication of the photographs of "that business at Nueva Cordoba" have changed his supposed image from that of the enlightened and encultured autocrat to that of the bloody tyrant, the dictator becomes depressed and angry. Yet instead of examining himself and searching for appropriate means of legitimation, the Head of State cynically turns toward Germanic models which function as no more than replacements for the equally false French models. His notable lack of concern about being a tyrant is, of course, hypocritical and despicable, but what is perhaps more noteworthy is the immediacy with which the dictator turns to another Old World model as a mediator of his desire for identity. The dictator, even here, refuses or is unable to return to his own origins for models of behavior. If he cannot define himself according to Frenchness, he will adopt a Germanic nature—just like that!—and in his eagerness to become Germanic we see too his sudden childish dislike and ill-will for things French. But this should not surprise us, for, as Girard has said, any:

> hostility [from the mediator] does not diminish his prestige but instead augments it. The subject is convinced that the model considers himself too superior to accept him as a disciple. The subject is torn between two opposite feelings for his model—the most submissive reverence and the most intense malice. This is the passion we call *hatred*. Only someone who prevents us from satisfying a desire which he himself has inspired in us is truly an object of hatred.

The events of **Reasons of State** clearly fit this pattern. As we have seen, Paris is the model of inspiration for the dictator, and Paris clearly rejects the bloody manifestations of his true self as exhibited at Nueva Cordoba. We have seen elsewhere the dictator's "submissive reverence" in his cynical Crusade for Latinity, and his "intense malice" displays itself as, among other things, the hopeful predictions that France will fare poorly in the war.

The dictator's flirtation with a Germanic identity does not last long, just long enough for the reader to assess the profundity of his lack of autonomous identity. This flirtation does not in fact seriously undercut the role of Paris as mediator. Nonetheless, part of **Reasons of State**'s brilliance lies in its desire to undercut or reverse its own structures. Such undercutting, or the willingness to depict and reveal paradox, however, does not mean that the text eventually fails to assert any consistent meanings. One of the prime examples of such self-undercutting is germane to our discussion, and that is the ability of the Head of State to take his friend the Academician with a grain of salt. As we have seen, the dictator desires identity and authentication and seeks it through the mediator epitomized in the word *Paris*. The Academician, by virtue of his position and status, ought to serve as an ideal representation of the mediator, but he does not. Just as the dictator is a false image of a Head of State—false because tyrannical, cruel, uninterested in his own people and nation—so is the Academician a spurious image of Old World reason and culture—self-important, chauvinistic, racist, opinionated.

The section wherein the Academician is introduced is the principal one concerning him, and this section is narrated by the dictator. Oddly it is through the Head of State, who is otherwise so blind to his devotion to French models, that the Academician's failures and shortcomings are revealed. He is both the central consciousness and the voice through which the Academician is at once presented and deflated. The dictator is knowing and indulgent. Only the reader, never the Academician, is privy to the dictator's parenthetical criticisms. Often the Head of State keeps his peace rather than contradict the Academician or defend his own people: "I remain silent rather than tell him how . . ."; "At this point I decide to remain silent. . . ." Later, when all of his other Parisian acquaintances have thrown him over because of the bloody debacle at Nueva Cordoba, only the Academician remains loyal to the dictator. However, the dictator receives little long-term comfort from this fact, although he is temporarily bucked up. At this point the Head of State feels the need for authentication by Paris so strongly that he feels "his strength of mind restored, and his mood made more aggressive by the conversation," but Peralta soon exposes the ignorance and chauvinism of the Academician in a justifiable outburst which restores the dictator's perspective concerning the Academician. Thus the narrator comments near the end of the scene: "And in the sole place in the Universe where other people's opinion had some importance to him, everyone was giving him the cold shoulder." Here, through the use of the word *everyone,* we see that the Academician is not truly regarded as important by the dictator. They use one another in times of crisis: the Head of State can supply money; the Academician can wield influence in the press.

At the height of the verbal confrontation between Peralta and the Academician, "the President silenced his secretary with an expression of fatigue." Once again the Head of State refuses to truly confront the Academician. These refusals to let that false embodiment of reason be deflated are partly due to the dictator's pragmatic streak, which allows him to recognize a useful ally. The refusal to defend his native land and people from the Academician's ignorant and racist onslaughts does little to endear the dictator to the reader. But more interesting is the fact that the Academician, even so potentially damaging a representative of the idealized, faultless culture of Paris as he, does nothing to dislodge or reshape Paris as the dictator's mediator. The Academician actually undercuts Old World culture: if his position of eminence marks him as a paragon and spokesman within that culture, then surely that culture has some serious flaws. The dictator would appear to ignore these flaws. He cannot afford to do otherwise since serious reflection on the mediator would necessarily involve the dictator in troubling questions about his own identity and about the worthiness and origins of his desire, and these sorts of questions the dictator never confronts. As Girard has said, "The obsessed man astounds us with his clear understanding of those like himself . . . and in his complete inability to see himself."

If this were a novel primarily concerned with exploring political power or systems, it would be unlikely to devote several pages to the preparation of lunch undertaken by the exiled dictator's live-in, the Mayorala Elmira, in book seven. It would certainly not have as its primary concern, as does **Reasons of State,** the dictator's movement toward (re) discovery of his authentic self. This last book begins with the epigram, "And deciding not to seek more knowledge than what I could find in myself . . ." and this is precisely the decision that the dictator makes, whether consciously or not, after his final disillusionment with France.

The adage, "you can't go home again" applies in every way to the overthrown dictator. Obviously he cannot return to his own country—he never even entertains hopes or illusions of doing so—nor is he at home in Paris, the false model through which he has striven to fulfill his desires his entire adult life. The Paris that the dictator returns to after his ouster is not the Paris fixed in his mind before his arrival, and he reacts with astonishment and dismay to the modernist works of art which have replaced the pieces that he had held so dear. His former friends and acquaintances, even his faithful *homme,* Sylvestre, are either dead or somehow so changed in circumstances (as is he) as to be socially unavailable to him: "I was afraid a princess—or someone with the presumptions of one—would scorn a man who was, after all, only a Latin-American president thrown out of his palace." This particular parenthetical aside concerning Madame Verdurin's possible presumption could never have been made by the Head of State in his previous Paris years because he was so blinded by his desire and self-deceit that he could not see the possibility of falseness in himself nor dare to admit its presence in the mediator. Logically the dynamics of mediated desire suggest that any devalorization of the mediator by the desiring subject would consequently necessitate a devalorization in the object of desire (and the inverse is also true). With an object of desire as vitally important as his very identity and worth, the dictator could not have afforded to ponder his chosen model too carefully, for the ramifications of unworthiness would have been unbearable.

But in his final return to Paris, the deposed tyrant's eyes are opened, and it would be a serious mistake not to recognize the depth of his change. Ironically, the dictator's epiphanic moment occurs in the brothel named *Aux glaces,* a name which suggests, of course, illusion and distortion, and which is full of prostitutes assuming false identities. But it is here that the dictator, or the *Ex* as he now prefers to be called, sees a true reflection of himself which he is ready to voice:

> Here, looking at what I am looking at, I feel I am witnessing the Arrest of Time. . . . I am . . . less of an exiled ruler, or actor in decline, and more identified with my own *ego,* still possessing eyes for looking, and impulses arising from the depths of vitality that is deliciously stimulated by something worth looking at—riches definitely preferable (I *feel* therefore I am) to those of a fictitious existence in the stupid ubiquity of a hundred statues in municipal parks, patios and town halls.

"Actor in decline," "fictitious existence," "stupid ubiquity"—the Head of State could never have made these remarks. The *Ex* Head of State can.

When the Ex speaks of "the Arrest of Time," he is saying more than he realizes. Inside the brothel, the Ex feels a timelessness, and the reader hearkens back to the previously quoted passage wherein the dictator professed his desire to escape time: "He longed to stay here, to get out of the magic circle, but just as if it really enclosed him he could not." As I have said, the magic circle from which the dictator wished to escape was his country's history, his involvement with his own origins. Ironically for him, the Ex does achieve this "timelessness," but he does so precisely when he is actually beginning to embrace his own origins and reject the model of Paris. Of course in one sense he has escaped his country's history in that he no longer wields power or influence there, but in the central sense of the novel, that of identity, he is reintegrated with the authentic aspects of his country's culture.

The word *sense* is a fortunate word here since it includes the concept of reason (the text's Cartesian component which is rejected finally by the *Ex*) as well as the signification found in the words *sensory* and *sensual,* which best characterize the experiences that lead the Ex back toward his origins ("I *feel* therefore I am"). The prime example of the *Ex's* unification with the authentic through the sensual is the Mayorala's meal—which even the ultimate fake and snob, Ofelia, cannot resist partaking in—that occurs shortly after the *Ex's* epiphanic moment in the brothel. By this time we recognize that food is a sign whereby cultural identity is displayed. Earlier during the campaign to crush Galvan's rebellion, the Head of State and his cronies dine on a medley of foods from Europe and their home country: "sardines, corned beef, baked bananas, *dulce de leche* and Rhine wine." This ethnic potpourri is matched to the dictator's level of authenticity at that time, and it marks the point when the dictator is most nearly his authentic self until his ultimate exile in Paris. Yet even on this campaign the staples are European, as is the wine with which the meal is washed down. Only the dessert and side-dish are native. This propensity of the dictator's for the food of others, like all his matters of identity, is mirrored by his fellow countrymen's habits during the boom-time coincident with World War I: "while only in Chinese eating houses could one eat the national dishes, now scorned as something connected with rope-soled shoes and ballads sung by the blind." However the Mayorala, whose unpretentiousness has been evident throughout the novel, had already pronounced her opinion of French food in a piece of foreshadowing which occurs long before her accompaniment of the dictator into Parisian exile: "She found a derogatory name for [it] all; the Burgundian snails were 'slugs'; the caviar, 'buckshot in oil'; the truffles, 'chips of charcoal'; the halva, 'nougat trying to be like turron from Jijona.'" Thus, long before the meal in exile, it is clear that in this text man is known by the food he eats, and the significance of the dictator feasting on his native cuisine is clear. Finally, ill in exile, the *Ex* convalesces on what he calls "a meal of our own sort—pancake, tamale . . . the only things that seem to me to taste of anything." The *Ex*'s movement toward authentic desire is clearly demonstrated by the foods he chooses to eat.

Girard has said that "the great novel does not succeed in shattering" ["the lie of spontaneous desire"] although it never ceases to denounce it." The dictator's slavish pretension toward Old World culture is clear enough, and while the objects of his desire (identity and feelings of self-worth) are not overt, they can be discovered through inference and textual analysis. Indeed, one of the lessons of the text is that the ostensibly enlightened despot is in fact quite in the dark in the most fundamental way; he is ignorant of himself. More than ignorant, he deceives himself with a mediated desire that at once reveals self-hatred, as well as stimulates and perpetuates his country's own lack of identity. To know all is most assuredly not to forgive very much in the present case, for no amount of explanation can excuse the sort of cruel, ruthless exploitation and tyranny which the dictator subjects his country to, and which is there for every reader to see.

I have said that *Reasons of State* is not primarily a political novel, and indeed the novel's major weakness is in its awkward and belated attempt in the final chapter to move the overtly political strand (represented in this chapter by the Student and other, newly introduced, revolutionary figures in Paris), which has been of a secondary nature up to this point, into the foreground with the primary material concerning the *Ex*'s identity. The belated appearance of this material is an intrusion which makes it seem as though Carpentier felt compelled to write a political novel, or at least to end his novel on an overtly political note, in spite of his own desires for his text.

To point out that the novel's main theme is identity is not to say, however, that the text has no political ramifications. The dictator and his countrymen clearly reflect an archetypal and actual problem of peoples from underdeveloped Latin-American countries, that is, the necessity of searching for a means by which their identity may be created or known, stan-

dards by which it may be measured and means by which it may be reinforced. A people that do not know who they are can hardly expect to know where they wish to go or how they intend to get there. It is from this level that the text's most important actual/historical lessons emerge from its largely mythical treatment of Latin-American particulars. To recognize and understand the ramifications of a lack of authentic identity in a figure of political power and the feelings of inherent inferiority in his polity is surely an important first step toward understanding a regrettable facet of Latin-American history and of Third World sociopolitical dynamics.

Mark I. Millington (essay date March 1996)

SOURCE: "Gender Monologue in Carpentier's *Los pasos perdidos*," in *Modern Language Notes,* Vol. 3, No. 2, March, 1996, pp. 346-67.

[*In the following essay, Millington asserts that "there is no doubt that what is achieved in* Los pasos perdidos *by the narrator is a masculist discourse of exclusion and manipulation, offset by some irony or counterpointed fragmentally when other voices become briefly audible."*]

In section XII in chapter 2 of **Los pasos perdidos,** the narrator reaches an area of the South American jungle which, in his calculation of his movement back through the stages of civilization, he calls "Tierras del Caballo." As always, his immediate reaction is highly wrought description—the construction of a complex semantic web to make sense of the unknown. This description of the "Tierras del Caballo" emphasizes physicality: the vivid sounds, smells and colours associated with horses and blacksmiths are invoked and also an imagined male rider's display of horse and self for a young woman. These romantic associations lead into a description of the "man" who inhabits this geographical-cum-temporal environment: "En las Tierras del Caballo parecía que el hombre fuera más hombre." And the passage continues through a celebratory characterization of this archetypal "man." His attributes are centred on control of the materials that he works, of the horse that he rides, and of the women whom he knows how to subdue:

> [El hombre] volvía a ser dueño de técnicas milenarias que ponían sus manos en trato directo con el hierro y el pellejo, le enseñaban las artes de la doma y la monta, desarrollando destrezas físicas de que alardear en días de fiesta, frente a las mujeres admiradas de quien tanto sabía apretar con las piernas, de quien tanto sabía hacer con los brazos. Renacían los juegos machos de amansar al garañón relinchante y colear y derribar al toro, la

bestia solar, haciendo rodar su arrogancia en el polvo.

It is not clear if these skills have any priority one over another, what seems important, however, is that the "man" is in charge: his skills give him power, and, by implication, he can perform his masculinity for his chosen audience: women. This is consistent with the earlier stress on physicality, since the relationship that women seem here to appreciate makes no mention of an emotional bond. "Tierras del Caballo" is a place for breaking horses, overwhelming bulls and possessing women, and these "juegos machos" are part of the proof of masculinity, the other part being the visible evidence. Or rather the visible parallel: it is the sexual organ of the horse, not the man, whose impressive presence is registered. Horse and man are identified via sexual power:

> Una misteriosa solidaridad se establecía entre el animal de testículos bien colgados, que penetraba sus hembras más hondamente que ningún otro, y el hombre, que tenía por símbolo de universal coraje aquello que los escultores de estatuas ecuestres tenían que modelar y fundir en bronce, o tallar en mármol, para que el corcel de buen ver respondiera por el Héroe sobre él montado, dando buena sombra a los enamorados que se daban cita en los parques municipales.

The link between man and horse is explicit and will be confirmed shortly after by a reference to "centauros." But the crude phallic assertion of the passage is doubly deflated. When it comes to the monumental sculpting of the rider and horse, the narrator becomes remarkably coy—he cannot name the symbol of power (the horse's penis) resorting rather weakly to euphemism, "aquello que los escultores [. . .] tenían que modelar." This sudden inhibition is compounded in its deflationary effect by the bathos of such assertive symbolism of phallic power being reduced to casting a shadow over lovers, not on the open plain, but in municipal parks. On one level, this reference undercuts the imaginary archetype of the "Héroe" (a rapid transformation from a mere "hombre"), whose sexual equipment is compared (in somewhat optimistic fashion) to that of the horse—hence the "mysterious" quality of the solidarity, one supposes. On another level, the reference figures the prevailing gender economy of everyday life, suggesting how heterosexual relations are dominated by such phallocentrism, and not without a certain banality.

The use of horses, bulls, and rather far-fetched archetypes to establish a definition of masculinity and male sexual behaviour is symptomatic of a certain strand in the novel. However, **Los pasos perdidos** does deploy a degree of irony to deflate some of this gender paradigm. And that irony is evident in the juxtaposition of the celebratory passage that I have just examined with the immediately preceding passage, which reveals a layer of self-doubt in the narrator concerning his sexual prowess. He feels insecure in the new location, especially as far as making advances to Rosario is concerned. He stresses cultural differences which he is still learning about, but he cannot disguise a fundamental sexual anxiety:

> hubiera querido acercarme más libremente a Rosario, cuya entidad profunda escapa a mis medios de indagación [. . .]. A cada paso temo ofenderla, molestarla, llegar demasiado lejos en la familiaridad o hacerla objeto de atenciones que puedan parecerle tontas o poco viriles. [. . .] Junto a ella me desasosiega continuamente el temor al ridículo, ridículo ante el cual no vale pensar que los otros "no saben," puesto que son ellos, aquí, los que saben.

In brief, the narrator does not know how to perform his sexuality for Rosario. The celebratory version of man, sex, and horses which follows is a crudely assertive counterweight to his fear of being thought more like a woman than a man. The sheer exuberance of the phallic assertiveness now begins to appear as a compensation for the moment of self-doubt: recourse to generalized archetypes offers imaginary salvation. However, the doubt is registered, and this interplay of insecurity and forceful assertion constitutes a potentially revealing moment in the discourse of the novel, since gender is a fundamental factor in the articulation of its meaning, albeit a factor which is hardly ever explicitly alluded to. Perhaps most revealing of all of the gender commitment of the narrator is the passage shortly after the insecurity/assertion oscillation when the narrator does finally make love to Rosario: when the moment arrives, he entertains no doubts but finds it in himself to act positively like all the men around him and the rider in his imagined scenario. All of which poses the question of how different the narrator's culture and that of the "Tierras del Caballo" really are when it comes to gender: the narrator insists that his journey takes him back through the stages of civilization, but he seems to know this element of cultural behaviour well. The further question here, therefore, concerns how much changes in the narrator's gender identity whilst (he claims) so much is changing in the other aspects of his identity.

There is here a contradiction in the narrator's presentation, for the jungle through which he travels is represented as alien to the world and culture that he has previously lived in. The customary view of the jungle accepts the narrator's characterization of its otherness. And this is underlined by the idealizing effect of his European cultural references: this tends to set up a neat binary. The jungle as Other is a strange, powerful force: in a word, it is "natural." It appears to be no accident that it is a sudden cloudburst that sets the whole expedition in motion: rain, of an almost tropical violence, "naturally" forces him to seek shelter in a concert hall, and this is a prelude to his meeting with his former mentor, the Curator. That meeting takes him to the jungle where he starts to live according to "natural" rhythms. The jungle, he claims, can totally disorientate him: the familiar clarity of perception is lost. Moreover, the people of the jungle are supposedly simply "what they are," perfectly adapted to their environment, with no need to intellectualize it (although the narrator intellectualizes their not intellectualizing it). The important point is that he produces the jungle as significant, in a structure of thought which seeks to articulate the quest for a new self. The jungle is other than New York, a "natural" space, one that allows him to re-establish contact with what he names as his roots. But the idea of this virgin territory, untouched and available as a space of self-discovery is highly questionable and naive. There is nothing natural about his version of the jungle: not only does he write a highly freighted version of it (full of Western cultural references), but this representation of the jungle only has meaning in the binary with the city. Hence this jungle is already a cultural projection, and largely the product of the narrator's alienation. Moreover, in one respect at least, life in the jungle is very similar to life in the city: the patriarchal gender economy in operation is similar in both locations. His relationships with women, especially in their sexual dimension, are fundamental in articulating his life in the city and also his renewal and self-discovery (insofar as these occur) in the jungle. This dependence remains the same. It is not insignificant that there are numerous other outsiders in the jungle engaged in quests—for diamonds, plants, religious converts—, and all are men articulating masculine desires for purpose and meaning. Not only does that coincide with the dominant cultural "imperative" in the West for men to identify with and manifest agency (men *do* things), but also the different kinds of quest in parallel with the narrator's suggest that he is not so different from his culture as he thought: where others seek the jungle's mineral, human and botanical resources, the narrator seeks first its musical resources and then its sheer geographical remoteness to pursue his own desires in it.

It is lack in the narrator that drives the narrative and the quest—it is the desire for "authenticity" which impels him. In sum, the jungle is a cultural construct that serves as the scenario for self-dramatization. On the surface, the narrator seeks renewal and change in himself, but it is not clear that he does change anything, despite his voluble claims. It is significant that he expresses admiration for all the other men on their quests in the jungle: despite his (apparent) reflexivity, one thing that he never puts in doubt is the gender dimension of his lack and his quest; he never tries to move out of his initial gender identity, nor does he raise the question as to why the others on their quests are all men. These

things are too close to him to be perceived. As a symptom of that blindness, the narrator produces representations of the women characters which constitute them in varied roles of otherness as a function of his narcissism.

What is striking in the deployment of the other characters is the sheer geometry of the system. There is a careful preparation of clearly defined and differentiated roles: each character helps delineate the narrator; he is the axial figure. Most important in this defining role are the women characters who are largely functions designed to articulate the different stages of the narrator's quest and to elicit reactions and values from him. They constitute possibilities or (mostly) obstacles on the narrator's path to self-realization. They are what the narrator uses to confirm who he is or is becoming, or what he needs to denigrate and abject. The use of the women characters in this way indicates the nature of the heterosexual economy of the novel: it is a patriarchal heterosexuality which exploits and contains women.

Ruth is referred to quite often in the novel but only appears near the end. As the narrator's wife she is shown as constituting an obstacle to him. She is an actress, but, symbolically, she is trapped in the unimaginative tedium of repeating her performance in a successful play. Her stultified creativity in New York parallels the narrator's own, but Ruth does nothing to alleviate it.

Significantly, it is Ruth who has the narrator brought back from the jungle by sparking the search for him. On his return, he finds himself caught in a blaze of publicity and expected to play the role of the grateful husband, which is not one that he has much experience of. At this point he starts to combine the two roles that he has ascribed to Ruth—wife and actress—and he projects her as playing her greatest part: the faithful wife. He demystifies this "play-acting," pointedly exposing what he sees as the fictional roles that Ruth and the media want them to play. In fact he insists on this inauthentic performance with elephantine excess, the ironic effect of which is to cast himself in the role of critical observer while all the others are taken in, though this example of *his* role-playing is not considered.

His ruthlessness is manifest in his disabusing Ruth about his future plans, in which she does not figure. When she learns that he has been in the jungle with another woman (Mouche), it is inevitable that he will represent her reaction as a performance of tragic proportions. Whilst Ruth articulates her response to his betrayal of their marriage, far from his expressing any regret, he insists on her skills as a tragedienne with their room serving as her stage. He implicitly accuses her of a monologue lasting half an hour, the irony being that it is the narrator who occupies the text with a monologue since he cannot remember what Ruth actually says and so contents himself with his own extensive words of deflationary sarcasm. He entertains no possibility that his betrayal of her might have caused her real hurt. In essence, he is contemptuous of his wife: the only truth of emotion or understanding is arrogated to himself. But the effect of his efforts is to concentrate attention on the supposed performance of Ruth who is implicitly accused of hypocrisy for her reaction, when the basic hypocrisy is the narrator's own since he committed the first wrong by having a relationship with Mouche. This double standard is reinforced during the divorce proceedings when the theatrical metaphor continues and the narrator finds himself cast in the role of unfaithful husband. This is doubly ironic: firstly because it is the narrator who normally casts others in roles to support his own ego; and secondly because this is no role since he has been a profligate husband. Nonetheless, he tries to manipulate events so that he can appear the victim and Ruth the guilty party: she is made responsible for bringing him out of the jungle when he willingly left it to acquire pens and paper, and to divorce Ruth. His desires were what mattered to his return, as they are dominant in his evaluation of all that he does. His representation of Ruth is a refusal to assume responsibility for his own actions and guilt, the result being that he frames Ruth in quite hypocritical fashion and shows no respect for her at all.

The narrator's view of Mouche shows her to be as much an obstacle to his desire as Ruth, but it is also clear that she is as necessary to the production of his own ego narrative. The negative depiction of Mouche operates consistently through the attribution to her of all that he wishes to cast off or leave behind as he penetrates the jungle: she is the repository for the cultural practices and values that he strives to jettison and which he vilifies. Hence the contrast between Mouche's and his reactions to Latin America is pivotal: the polarization begins as soon as they set foot off the plane, and is reinforced day after day. Whilst the narrator is overwhelmed and moved by the discovery of a new environment, Mouche is at best untouched, at worst hostile. And the hostility derives from the physical discomfort produced by the journey. The result is that her appearance deteriorates rapidly, rendering her less sexually attractive: if she cannot make up her face and dye her hair her beauty disappears—it is artificial. The narrator returns to this theme and spells out his disdain for her vanity in making up and falsifying the reality of her appearance, although those efforts obviously played a part in attracting him to her previously. Her current appearance alienates him and he finds her incapacity to adapt to her new context a severe limitation. The stress on Mouche's failing beauty and the minute dissection of her physical decline rely on the narrator's unexamined assumption that what matters most to a woman is her physical attractiveness. He even reaches the senseless extreme of criticizing Mouche for being the one to be bitten by a mosquito. Such crass unfairness is an example of the irony deployed by the implied author against the narrator:

> A dos jornadas del término de mi encomienda, cuando hollábamos las fronteras de lo desconocido y el ambiente se embellecía con la cercanía de posibles maravillas, tenía Mouche que haber caído así, estúpidamente, picada por un insecto que la eligiera a ella, la menos apta para soportar la enfermedad.

In such sweeping dismissals the narrator shows as little respect for Mouche as he does for Ruth. Mouche has been his mistress for two years when the journey starts, but there is no mention of his affection for her, on the contrary, theirs was a strongly physical relation. This is not uncharacteristic of the narrator. Mouche appears to have been useful to him in maintaining a certain gender profile: bored with his wife, he takes a mistress to whom he has no deep commitment. His representation of Mouche, while undercut in places by the irony of the implied author, reaches grotesque proportions: she can do no right, every attitude or value that she displays is declared anathema. So while he tries to fulfil his musical mission and his quest for identity, he presents Mouche as interested in tourism, and as quite prepared to forge the musical instruments which he seeks. Curiously, while the narrator is intent on leaving behind many aspects of Western civilization (all of which he castigates Mouche for displaying), he clings firmly to Western "High Art," and consequently when it comes to visiting the opera, in order to maintain the utterly negative view of Mouche it turns out that she is a "musical philistine" and is content to adopt the "fashionable pose" of rejecting opera as an art form. Whatever the narrator's commitment, it turns out that Mouche contradicts it, so rigid is the polarization. By contrast with her, his values and views are implied to be solid, healthy, and individual—though perhaps not entirely tolerant.

Not surprisingly, it is Mouche who is castigated for being unfaithful to the narrator. He claims to be deeply injured by her relation with Yannes and talks of punishing her, but he utterly fails to consider his own recent admission of desire for Rosario, or his long-standing betrayal of his wife precisely with Mouche. The implied author indicates this double standard by an undramatic reference to Ruth in the midst of the narrator's recriminations, although she is not relevant to the immediate context of his response to Mouche's "infamia." Blind to his own hypocrisy, the narrator soon starts to wrap himself in the severely patriarchal logic of the jungle culture, though he does not explain why two people who were formed elsewhere should now start to judge their personal relationship according to the rules of the local culture:

> Para los que con nosotros convivían ahora, la fidelidad al varón, el respeto a los padres, la rectitud de proceder, la palabra dada, el honor que obligaba y las obligaciones que honraban, eran valores

constantes, eternos, insoslayables, que excluían toda posibilidad de discusión. [. . .] Como en los más clásicos teatros, los personajes eran, en este gran escenario presente y real, los tallados en una pieza del Bueno y el Malo, la Esposa Ejemplar o la Amante Fiel, el Villano y el Amigo Leal, la Madre digna o indigna.

The attraction of such rigid stereotypes to the narrator must surely be that they safeguard male dominance, so that the alternative views of Mouche, and of women in general, can be ignored. "Hombría" holds sway here, and life and death are in its gift.

The problems and hypocrisy in the narrator's representation of Mouche reach their lowest point in dealing with her relationship with the Canadian woman painter. In this context, the narrator displays not just homophobia but a somewhat fevered imagination, since he makes "accusations" for which he has no evidence. Moreover, he cannot even name the "terrible reality" which he has imagined—his language becomes very prim:

> Yo sabía que cuando ella bebía se tornaba particularmente vulnerable a toda solicitud de los sentidos, y aunque esto no significaba una voluntad real de vilipendiarse, podía llevarla al lindero de las curiosidades más equívocas.

Later, he admits that he has no proof "against" Mouche, but that is insufficient to inhibit his mounting a sort of trial of her with the (still unnamed) charge of lesbianism. In the first place he sets up lesbianism as a despicable form of sexual behaviour and then he finds Mouche "guilty" of it. He observes her and the painter closely, vainly trying to detect a secret glance or phrase that will reveal the "truth" which he has decided is there. But his reaction is all about his own uncertainty and jealousy: it appears that the narrator fears a relationship that excludes him, one which is sufficient without a male component. His superfluousness inspires a kind of panic resulting in his petulant attempt to put the pair into a category which for him is (literally) unspeakable. For a man who constantly congratulates himself on his individuality and difference from the trivializing and unreflecting attitudes of his society, in this respect he displays extraordinarily narrow-minded conventionalism. But, all his gender and sexual commitments show the same unquestioned adherence to forms of exclusive, hegemonic masculinity.

After this damning treatment of Mouche in the jungle, the narrator continues his denigration on their separate returns to New York. He blames her for ruining his chance of capitalizing on media interest in his story: in fact, much of what Mouche tells the press is merely the truth about his affair with her and with Rosario and is no more than a corrective

to his own falsifying and self-promoting story. If it is true that Mouche is taking revenge for his flight with Rosario, she is successful and is doing no more than readjust the balance of power between them. Having vitiated his financial ambitions, Mouche becomes the one responsible for all his misfortunes as he slides down the ladder to destitution. She remains the figure on whom he casts out all the negative features of his life. For all that "monstering" and abjection, however, Mouche has regained her physical attraction for him and she now becomes a "devious temptress": she plies him with alcohol and he finds himself having sex with her. His subsequent hypocrisy—firstly in ascribing the role of seducer to her, and secondly in finding her efforts at love-making boring—is self-evident. Again the implied author leaves little doubt of the narrator's self-righteous behaviour. Indeed, the treatment of Mouche in New York is really rather crude, so crude in fact that the irony at the narrator's expense is largely ineffective. The implied author becomes complicit with this representation of Mouche because of enabling it in the first place and because of its sheer relish. The narrator is so obviously and coarsely ironized that the irony has little effect, and what remain are the shockingly thorough exploitation of Mouche as a device in the novel's gender economy and the suspicion that the relentlessness of Mouche's negativity exceed what is strictly necessary for the narrator's purposes and so express a patriarchal culture's desperate desire in relation to women.

Rosario's role in the narrator's account is captured in two paradigmatic moments very near the start of her arrival in the novel. One comes when the narrator is recalling the opening paragraph of *Don Quixote* but finds that he cannot complete the quotation. As he struggles to recall the text, the still unknown Rosario points to a hillside out of the bus window and speaks its name: La Hoya. This turns out to be a homonym for the key word in the forgotten sentence from *Don Quixote*: "Una olla." This coincidence releases what the narrator had forgotten. The lack in him is filled by Rosario, but as always the narrator is absorbed in literary allusions and Rosario is concerned with concrete reality. So while she helps him to retrieve what he had lost—not just the quotation, of course, but his roots in Latin America—, it is not a conscious process, indeed it is not one of which Rosario is in the least aware: she and the narrator exist on different cultural levels.

The other paradigmatic moment is her first sighting, and it is heavily overdetermined. She is sitting on a bridge over a deep chasm with a torrent audible at the bottom. The symbol of the bridge is an allusion to the narrator's transition back to his roots, and it is clear that Rosario only appears when that transition has already begun: he has had to return to Latin America and begin the journey into the interior before he can meet the symbolic figure of Rosario, representative of the Americas, halfway across the bridge. The narrator makes it clear that Rosario is a summation of the continent—all its races mix in her:

> Era evidente que varias razas se encontraban mezcladas en esa mujer, india por el pelo y los pómulos, mediterránea por la frente y la nariz, negra por la sólida redondez de los hombros y una peculiar anchura de la cadera [. . .].

At different points of his narrative, the narrator is also keen to stress Rosario's condition as a natural force, her closeness to rhythms of the natural world. Given this construction of Rosario, the contrast with Mouche and the narrator is obvious, although it is clear that, in this representation of Rosario, the "natural" is heavily involved with the social and cultural structures of patriarchy. The development of their relationship is rapid and its sexual dimension is called direct: the narrator bids for an elemental quality in it since Rosario has features which are supposed to precede social structures. Not surprisingly, therefore, the narrator describes his desire for her as the "incontenible apremio de un celo primordial."

In this respect, Rosario's role in the narrator's quest is clear. She is a focus of positive qualities which resuscitate forgotten areas in his inner life and which prompt him to take major steps out of superannuated social and cultural structures into the (re-)discovery of something vigorous and natural. It is, therefore, a culturally significant moment when the narrator "recognizes" that Rosario is beautiful. He has observed her intently for some hours and ascribed to her various qualities to do with nature and Latin America. In other words, he gradually crystallizes around her certain qualities which he now values. Simultaneously, after just one day's travelling by bus, Mouche has a headache and is feverish. Just as Mouche shows her weakness in the rigours of the natural world, Rosario shows her resilience and authenticity. As this geometry of rejection and desire falls into place, what for the narrator is inexplicable (but for the wary reader perhaps less so) dawns on him: "No sabía decir por qué esa mujer me pareció muy bella, de pronto [. . .]." This realization is "de rigueur" in the machista gender economy that the narrator (and frequently the implied author) subscribes to. And Rosario's beauty is restated as the journey progresses, and, more significantly, as Mouche's physical attraction fades— the inverse investment in the two women is obviously symmetrical. The narrator even spells this out:

> la joven crecía ante mis ojos a medida que transcurrían las horas, al establecer con el ambiente ciertas relaciones que me eran cada vez más perceptibles. Mouche, en cambio, iba resultando tremendamente forastera dentro de un creciente desajuste entre su persona y cuanto nos circundaba.

It is the identification (or lack of it) with the environment which is the decisive factor in his perception of the women's beauty (or loss of it).

Just as Mouche and Ruth are expressions of the narrator's unstable negative desire rather than portraits of independent characters, so Rosario is the object of positive desire, but still desire centred in a particular gender economy. There is arguably no comment made by the narrator about any of them which serves to establish a character that can be seen as separate from his needs and lacks. He is profoundly unreliable and blind to this projection of gender need: he needs these women characters to give him the illusion of definition. It is therefore not insignificant that Rosario is represented as conforming to a constricting patriarchy in the jungle. The journey that she is making is a return to help her dying father: in the early phase of the narrative she plays the role of the dutiful daughter. Just in time (for the narrator's purposes), her father dies allowing Rosario the freedom to carry on travelling with the narrator, although the point about filial duty has been made. It is but a short step from that to her passivity with him. Hence, even though it is Mouche who invites Rosario to accompany them upriver, Rosario waits for permission to do so from the narrator. More problematically, when she and he settle into a sexual relationship, Rosario casts herself in the role of servant. She calls herself "tu mujer," thus making herself an appendage of the male, and undertakes menial chores for him. He interprets Rosario's view of their relation in naturalizing terms, which makes it unnecessary (for him) to analyze what is (really) happening:

> se cumple un destino que más vale no andar analizando demasiado, porque es regido per "cosas grandes" cuyo mecanismo es oscuro, y que, en todo caso, rebasan la capacidad de interpretación del ser humano. Por lo mismo, [Rosario] suele decir que "es malo pensar en ciertas cosas."

This is somewhat convenient for the narrator. But there comes a moment when Rosario clearly has thought out an independent line and his dominant discourse falters. He is reluctant to consider marrying Rosario despite the urgings of Fray Pedro, but he guesses that Rosario would be happy to marry him—after all, it would confirm his view that she wishes to be dependent on him. To his surprise and annoyance, she firmly declares that she does not want marriage, and for clearly elucidated reasons:

> cuando creo que se va a agarrar de la oportunidad para hacerme el protagonista de un cromo dominical para uso de catecúmenos, la oigo decir, asombrado, que de ninguna manera quiere el matrimonio. Al punto se transforma mi sorpresa en celoso despecho.

Voy hacia Rosario, muy dolido, a pedirle explicaciones. Pero me deja desconcertado con una argumentación que es la de sus hermanas, fue sin duda la de su madre, y es probablemente la razón del recóndito orgullo de esas mujeres que nada temen: según ella, el casamiento, la atadura legal, quita todo recurso a la mujer para defenderse contra el hombre. El arma que asiste a la mujer frente al compañero que se descarría es la facultad de abandonarlo en todo momento, de dejarlo solo, sin que tenga medios de hacer valer derecho alguno. La esposa legal, para Rosario, es una mujer a quien pueden mandar a buscar con guardias, cuando abandona la casa en que el marido ha entronizado el engaño, la servicia o los desórdences del licor. Casarse es caer bajo el peso de leyes que hicieron los hombres y no las mujeres. En una libre unión, en cambio—afirma Rosario, sentenciosa—, "el varón sabe que de su trato depende tener quien le dé gusto y cuidado."

Yet again the double standard is in evidence: it is acceptable for him not to want to marry her but not vice versa. And the fact that Rosario produces an entirely coherent argument (which he cannot accept is hers but which he supposes borrowed from others) adds insult to his (self-inflicted) injury. He cannot resist trying to patronize her (though the word "sentenciosa" rings hollow uttered by him), but Rosario effectively silences him with her sophistication: "Confieso que la campesina lógica de este concepto me deja sin réplica." He attempts to continue condescending ("la campesina lógica"), but his attitude is undercut. For once, another voice (if only momentarily) registers its presence in the novel. Ultimately, however, it may be that Rosario's actions speak louder than her words, for the narrator learns that, after his absence in New York, Rosario has formed a relation with another man and is pregnant: she takes the decisive step which is an incisive commentary on his egocentric behaviour and attitudes.

The novel opens with the narrator in a crisis of identity and the repercussions of that crisis sustain the whole narrative. The question of the definition of the crisis and whether it finds any resolution is one of the novel's major focal points. That and a further question concerning the gender dimension of the crisis (of which the novel is, at best, only partially aware) are what concerns this analysis.

The narrator begins the novel suffering from a feeling of uneasiness about the freedom to think about himself with which he is presented. He has three weeks without obligations, but his capacity for self-determination is nil. He is led to reflect that life has been flowing over him without any real impact. When talking to the Curator of the museum, his mentor, the narrator paints an entirely negative picture of his recent life.

While the vehemence of this self-portrait can, in part, be ascribed to the fact of speaking to his role-model from earlier life with whom he has had no recent contact, there is no doubting the force of his self-denunciation:

"Además—gritabayo ahora—, ¡estoy vacío! ¡Vacío! ¡Vacío! ..." [...] Y así como el pecador vuelca ante el confesionario el saco negro de sus iniquidades y concupiscencias—llevado por una suerte de euforia de hablar mal de sí mismo que alcanza el anhelo de execración—, pinto a mi maestro, con los más sucios colores, con los más feos betunes, la inutilidad de mi vida, su aturdimiento durante el día, su inconsciencia durante la noche.

In particular, the narrator identifies a chasm between "el Yo presente" and "el Yo que hubiera aspirado a ser." This chasm amounts to a lack in being, a crisis in his ego and a recognition of a failure to sustain a desire for an ego-ideal. He suffers a total sense of self-distance, and begins to express it by an unremittingly bleak appraisal of New York and his circle of friends, and of his own work there. He accuses himself of sacrificing his gifts to commercial needs. This detailed self-condemnation is as much a symptom of his crisis as his anxiety, since the picture that begins to emerge is rather simplistically polarized: unnuanced blame attaches to those around him in New York and to his own activities, and seems to invoke a necessary counterbalancing positive project. The assessment is patently emotive and appears self-dramatizing.

In this state, the meeting with the Curator is fundamental: it not only forces an acutely negative self-confrontation (significantly, the narrator sees himself in a mirror as he lies about himself), but also offers the chance of self-renewal. It is as though in returning to the Curator the narrator had the chance to begin afresh, and this is clearly freighted with Oedipal connotations. The Curator is an obvious father-figure whose authority can be taken to signal the narrator's condition of castration: he accepts the position of child in the Curator's presence. And he catches sight of himself in the mirror in that guise: "Me veo con la tiesura de un niño llevado a visitas en la luna del conocido espejo que encuadra un espeso marco rococó." This image within an ornate frame is a sign of a particular containment: this is a self within a certain complex (rococo) cultural environment. And the project of reconstruction offered by the Father to the male child (the financing by the museum of the expedition to search for the rare musical instrument), when seen as part of the Oedipal process, comes to seem highly conformist: the narrator accepts the power of the Curator/Father and his own castration and so he takes on the mission set for him to find the instrument, as it were to assume the paternal inheritance, to strive to possess the phallus. In accepting this itinerary, he is not self-determining but dependent on symbolic structures. And those symbolic structures are bound up with hegemonic masculine imaginings. The opening lack is created by the perception of living a lie: the narrator has been untrue to what he conceives of as his "true self," the self that could have been a serious composer or musical scholar. The Curator/Father apparently provides the path to recover the self, to reconstruct its identity, This would supposedly fill his lack in being and recuperate the damaged ego. And the recuperation of the ego-ideal is particularly pregnant in that the narrator's mission takes him back to his Latin American roots and allows him to recover the Spanish language. This return to roots suggests that New York is an exile from the self and that it can be restored by an effort of will-power, by the affirmation of masculine agency. In the gender economy operative in the narrator's thinking, the self is to be revalidated by recourse to the traditional identification of men with action, preferably with heroic connotations. At this stage, therefore, *Los pasos perdidos* conforms to the classic paradigm of the Western Oedipal narrative in which the male child is transformed into a man.

The initial identity crisis and the route to escape it provided by the Curator/Father are deeply implicated in the dominant symbolic system of the West and in the narrator's way of thinking with humanist notions of the self and its capacity for (restored) homogeneity and wholeness. On the other hand, the novel can also be read against the grain as showing the narrator as constructing or dramatizing the self in a way which undermines such humanist convictions. The theatrical metaphor set up at the very start and later used by the narrator to criticize Ruth for the inauthenticity of her behaviour ironically applies to the narrator himself. His response to his identity crisis is precisely theatrical. In the first place, the crisis is expounded by the narrator in polarized terms which seek to dramatize the self. In the second place, the perceived lack in the self is to be covered up by the acting out of a particular mission, one full of gender presuppositions. That performative dimension is especially evident when the narrator wants to make sexual advances to Rosario but doubts his capacity to fulfil the expectations of virility within the local context. The point here is whether he will be *seen* adequately to perform the role of assertive, controlling male. The self-doubt is a form of gender panic in relation to the selected ego-ideal. Having chosen to recreate his identity via the encounter with the tough frontier culture of the jungle, does he know how to play the man with Rosario? Is his cosmopolitan sophistication not likely to be perceived as feminizing, a diminution of his masculine credentials? In short, anxiety reduces the narrator to the position of an adolescent with first night nerves. To live up to expectations, he plays the part of the protective male and fights Yannes when Mouche has foolishly encouraged the Greek's sexual advances, and the result is hardly a great success. Shortly after, in order to impress Rosario with his macho assertiveness, he plays the jealous lover in relation to

Mouche so as to mitigate the perceived effeminacy of his delicate shirt. For all the self-questioning in New York, there is no attention paid by him to the crucial point that at least part of what is in crisis is the masculine ego. His dilemma is largely the breakdown of masculine self-affection and it appears to trigger a narcissistic desire for self-regeneration and re-representation, a process which in practice means renewal as repetition of the self-same not as innovation or change.

It is the manner of reconstituting the narrator's ego after the early crisis which is crucial in uncovering the implicit gender economy in *Los pasos perdidos*. And in that regard, it is helpful to bear in mind the psychoanalytical view of the narcissistic ego which posits the ego not as an entity, agency or psychical content, but as constituted via the subject's relations with others. In this model, various libidinal investments in others are decisive for the ego's outline and features. As Lacan theorizes it, the ego is oriented and shaped around two functions, one being a joyful, affirmative self-recognition (in which the ego delights in a perceived unity of self-image), and the other being a paranoiac condition which issues from a divided, vulnerable subjectivity. On this view, the ego oscillates between a thirst for pleasure and self-aggrandizement, and the insecurity and frustration emerging from interpersonal relations. This duality is apparent in the narrator's relations with the women characters (as outlined above), insofar as he represents them as either utterly negative and damaging to him (Ruth and Mouche), or vital for his self-affirmation (Rosario). The point is that the construction of objects of aggression and otherness and of objects of desire is an inseparably dual process and part of the oscillating instability of ego constitution.

In the light of such a view of the ego and its libidinal investments, it is not surprising to see the mutations in the narrator's ego-ideal as circumstances change. The finding of the rare musical instrument which is his ostensible mission in the jungle releases a sense of fulfilment, of a self in control and in conformity with desire (the narrator lives up to his own and the Curator/Father's expectation). But once the narrator has decided to renounce the West and its values, he feels uncomfortable with the instrument that he has appropriated. Just as he switches his sexual desire from Mouche to Rosario in the course of the novel, so he now searches for another way to consolidate his ego and his object becomes a way of life in harmony with his surroundings. He stresses a kind of mythic quest for roots, a return from a decadent social being to a "natural" life in the jungle, and he praises himself for losing fat and overcoming his accumulated urban tensions: he affirms his physical and mental well-being, just as he rhapsodizes about Nature and silence in the jungle. The musical instrument becomes part of the rejected other—the West—which has so damaged him with its values and impositions. Here one sees precisely a process of affirmative desire being superseded by decisive othering as the narrator's ego slithers between identifications. But the West cannot be expunged so easily: the new attempt at self-recognition in the jungle is no more than the West's own fantasy of a pure object of desire—the "simple life." The truth of that delusion is manifest at the end when the narrator cannot return to Santa Mónica and cannot reappropriate Rosario, who is now another man's partner. Both aspects of this frustration disrupt his ideal and he reacts by seeking a defence: faced with the denial of his desire and the failure of the Oedipal narrative, a new image of the self is proposed which amounts to an affirmative misrecognition. The narrator's self-reconstruction consists in falling back on the Western myth of the archetypal cultural outsider: the frustration of self-fulfilment is transmuted into a revalorized isolation; being denied a return to the "prehistoric" world of Santa Mónica, he affirms his "tragic" identity as one of the select few who cannot escape his time:

> la única raza humana que está impedida de desligarse de las fechas es la raza de quienes hacen arte, y no sólo tienen que adelantarse a un ayer inmediato, representado en testimonios tangibles, sino que se anticipan al canto y forma de otros que vendrán después, creando nuevos testimonios tangibles en plena conciencia de lo hecho hasta hoy. Marcos y Rosario ignoran la historia. El Adelantado se sitúa en su primer capítulo, y hubiera podido permanecer a su lado si mi oficio hubiera sido cualquier otro que el de componer música—oficio de cabo de raza.

The narcissistic ego is thus reaffirmed via the myth of the creative artist destined to suffer, and it is notable that the mention of "raza" projects an identity over which the individual has no control: this is a self-affirmation in passivity, and that is a convenient alibi for failure with the previous image of the self. The effort at self-aggrandizement in the face of the frustrated desire appears even more fragile if one considers the grounds for the narrator's claim that his identity is constituted as that of "composer," for in what sense is he really a composer? He repudiates his professional musical life at the start of the novel, and in the jungle manages to write part of one piece of music. This is a rather flimsy basis on which to affirm an identity. The affirmation here is at best a partial misrecognition, but cannot lay claim to any totalizing unity. This is another imaginary device that, despite an earlier apparent turning against the West, is a reaffirmation of a central Western cultural myth of identity.

The reaffirmation is hardly surprising, however, as the West remains central to (if often negative in) his mode of thinking throughout. He rejects much of what is associated with the West as part of his effort to valorize the other and an-

other identity: the criticism of the West and the valorizing of Latin America are always paired. He dismisses the West as in terminal decline because of the loss of its authority in World War Two: Nazism is taken as a synecdoche for this decline, witnessed by him in travelling through Europe in the aftermath of the war. However, the decline of the West and the rejection of its values succumb to a rather gestural rhetoric—his insistence on ending and rupture are hardly in evidence in his own cultural performance. For, despite the rhetoric of rupture, there is a crucial continuity within his values and assessments. The narrator's discourse is saturated with cultural references to the West which seek to create a framework to understand the new. Western culture, far from being in decline and remote, is constantly reactivated in this process. There are detailed references not only to Western painting and to the Bible, but above all to Western literature and music. So frequent are the literary and musical allusions that they become rather mannered and predictable: no new encounter or experience can pass without being understood by some cultural analogy which comes to seem domesticating.

In clinging to Western music the narrator is repeating a process which is consistent in all aspects of his life. González Echevarría pinpoints this contradiction in him, relating it to Carpentier's writing:

> lo que Carpentier anhela es poder crear un arte que se escape de la influencia europea, donde las cosas ya tienen nombre. La dificultad de esta empresa comienza por el hecho de que la misma noción de escapar de Europa tiende a ser, como en este lugar común mismo, europea. El drama del protagonista-narrador de la novela se encuentra en este deseo que le resulta imposible satisfacer, y que lo traiciona a cada paso.

So, the narrator "goes back" in time only to set himself the task of composing "authentic" twentieth-century music. The same is true of his gender identity: for all his alienation from Western culture, the structure of masculine subjectivity acquired in it is never put at risk. The discourses of literature, music, philosophy and the Bible which saturate the writing of the narrator are a sign of his commitment to a certain imposing gender identity: his agency and power are heavily inscribed in the process of *making sense* with this material. This arrogant mastering almost obliterates the other, despite the rhetoric of renewal. The representation is monological—a totalitarian pretension seeks to control everything. This pretension appears to be a function of the masculine ego, such that the discourse deployed in the novel can be seen as entirely congruent with his mission to forge an identity: the perspective of the novel aims at narcissistic self-replication.

The narrator's voracious interpretation of the world is also manifest in his use of dialogue. It is not just that he hardly ever presents the actual words of his interlocutors, but that, in paraphrasing his own and others' words he constantly introduces explanations, interpretations, justifications and criticisms to diminish others and to enhance his own position. So he meets three young artists in Los Altos, but their conversation is obliterated beneath what matters more to him: his own opinions about them and modernist art. Or he admits to having forgotten what Ruth said to him in criticizing his selfish behaviour with other women but nonetheless delivers a wholly critical assessment of her "tragic performance" of betrayal, as though he had not been unfaithful to her. This way of treating the speech of interlocutors begins in the very first dialogue with the Curator, and it is clearly a manner of exercising power and consolidating his ego. He constantly interprets others and justifies himself, so that his ego virtually saturates the text. The voice of the other can hardly be heard to speak. Those very few occasions on which the direct words of others are presented are all highly revealing, showing a resistance to or incisive comment on the narrator. These are moments of truly dialogic potential, in the Bakhtinian sense. Hence, when Mouche says: "'Este viaje estaba escrito en la pared,'" it has a far-reaching resonance, and, as González Echevarría points out, it has a real relevance to the question of freedom or determinism for the whole of the narrator's enterprise. Similarly, Mouche's crazed cry of "'¡Cochinos!'" when she sees the narrator and Rosario making love openly in front of her, is an effective deflation of all of his words of self-justification for abandoning her for Rosario. When the narrator's discourse momentarily falters, a clear (if brief) critique of him is usually apparent. For example, his jealousy about Mouche's relation with the Canadian painter (whether sexual or not) leaves him incensed and full of homophobic accusations but utterly unable to say the word "lesbian." His coy circumlocutions and flimsy imaginings are ironic proof of his inability to tolerate the other. Such momentary interruptions of his discourse need to be very carefully noted in order to achieve perspective on his egocentric viewpoint.

There *are* multiple texts and references in *Los pasos perdidos,* but the question is: how are they deployed? The answer appears to me to be that they are deployed almost always within the mastering discourse of one voice. Truly polyphonic, dialogical moments are rare indeed.
—*Mark I. Millington*

Some of the difficulties in the novel concerned with the monologic gender and cultural blindness are encapsulated

in a description which the narrator makes of his musical composition, *Treno.* He says that he aims to combine polyphonic and harmonic writing:

> pensaba yo lograr una coexistencia de la escritura polifónica y la de tipo armónico, concertadas, machihembradas, según las leyes más auténticas de la música, dentro de una oda vocal y sinfónica, en constante aumento de intensidad expresiva, cuya concepción general era, por lo pronto, bastante sensata.

Now polyphonic music involves the combining of independent voices in a counterpoint: different lines sound together. In harmonic music one melodic line is complemented by other layers of sound which enhance or underpin its effect. The narrator's aim is to combine these two major types of writing and it is significant that they are described in gender terms as "machihembradas." It is not clear whether it is appropriate to assume that one of the compositional styles is inherently masculine, the other feminine. But the key issue would be whether such a compositional fusion would be possible. On the evidence of the narrator's *literary* writing, I would suggest that it is not. However, González Echevarría proposes in a footnote that the musical objective is achieved in the novel, maintaining that it is polyphonic:

> En varios sentidos esta descripción del *Treno* parece corresponder a la novela misma: polifonía de voces alrededor de la del protagonista-narrador. Es decir, muchos textos que se entretejen alrededor de su voz.

Unfortunately this assessment misconstrues the nature of polyphony, since, for other voices to be organized *around* that of the narrator, implies an harmonic relationship with a dominant voice. Moreover, González Echevarría does not mention here the role of harmonic writing, which in the narrator's theory is supposed to coexist with polyphony. In fact, the narrator perfectly describes the dominant format of the novel which *is* organized around a dominant voice: the narrator's own. And one might call that an harmonic (or monological) arrangement. There *are* multiple texts and references in *Los pasos perdidos,* but the question is: how are they deployed? The answer appears to me to be that they are deployed almost always within the mastering discourse of one voice. Truly polyphonic, dialogical moments are rare indeed. If one followed the narrator's own lead and saw the different compositional or writing styles in gender terms there is no doubt that what is achieved in *Los pasos perdidos* by the narrator is a masculist discourse of exclusion and manipulation, offset by some irony or counterpointed fragmentedly when other voices become briefly audible.

FURTHER READING

Criticism

Review of *The Lost Steps*. *Atlantic* 198, No. 5 (1956): 107-8.

> Questions Carpentier's belief in the virtues of primitive society, but asserts that "what is original and exciting about *The Lost Steps* is the way in which the action, sophisticated introspection, and powerfully evoked atmosphere are skillfully integrated."

Daruwalla, Keki N. "The Shadow of Power: Dictatorship and Human Destiny in the Novels of Marquez and Carpentier." In *Garcia Marquez and Latin America,* edited by Alok Bhalla, pp. 68-80. New Delhi: Sterling Publishers Private Limited, 1987.

> Compares Carpentier's depiction of dictatorship in *Reasons of State* to Gabriel García Márquez's approach to the same topic in *Autumn of the Patriarch.*

Díaz, Nancy Gray. "The Metamorphosis of Maldoror and Mackandal: Reconsidering Carpentier's Reading of Lautréamont." *Modern Language Studies* 21, No. 3 (Summer 1991): 48-56.

> Analyzes Carpentier's critique of the work of Isidore Ducasse, the Count of Lautréamont, in light of Carpentier's own novel, *El reino de este mundo.*

Emery, Amy Fass. "The 'Anthropological *Flaneur*' in Paris: *Documents, Bifur,* and Collage Culture in *¡Ecué-Yamba-O!*" *Hispanic Journal* 14, No. 2 (Fall 1993): 145-55.

> Discusses Carpentier's relationship to surrealism and its use of collage.

Harss, Luis, and Dohmann, Barbara. "Alejo Carpentier, or the Eternal Return." In their *Into the Mainstream: Conversations with Latin-American Writers,* pp. 37-67. New York: Harper & Row, 1967.

> Discusses Carpentier's career and the author's relationship to the Latin-American novel.

Huggan, Graham. "Anthropologists and Other Frauds." *Comparative Literature* 46, No. 2 (Spring 1994): 113-28.

> Analyzes the portrayal of anthropology in post-colonial literature using Carpentier's *Los pasos perdidos,* Yambo Ouologuem's *Le Devoir de violence,* and Albert Wendt's *Flying-Fox in a Freedom Tree.*

Martin, John, and McNerney, Kathleen. "Carpentier and Jolivet: Magic Music in *Los pasos perdidos.*" *Hispanic Review* 52, No. 4 (Autumn 1984): 491-98.

> Asserts that "The parallels between Carpentier's narrator in *Los pasos perdidos* and [André] Jolivet . . . seem to point to Jolivet as a source for the musical theories in the novel."

Matibag, Eugenio D. "Carpentier's Consecration of Stravinsky: The Avant-Garde after the Avant-Garde." *Journal of Interdisciplinary Studies* 5, No. 2 (1993): 299-322.

> Traces the influence of Igor Stravinsky on Carpentier's work.

Menton, Seymour. "Cuba's Hegemonic Novelists." *Latin American Research Review* 29, No. 1 (1994): 260-66.

> Compares the work of five Cuban novelists, including Carpentier's *Ombras Completas.*

Muller-Bergh, Klaus. "The Perception of the Marvelous: Paul Claudel and Carpentier's *El arpa y la sombra.*" *Comparative Literature Studies* 24, No. 2 (1987): 165-91.

> Analyzes the relationship between Carpentier's *El arpa y la sombre,* Paul Claudel's *Le Livre de Christophe Colomb,* and other historical documents which Carpentier incorporated into his novel.

Pastor, Beatriz. "Carpentier's Enlightened Revolution, Goya's Sleep of Reason." In *Representing the French Revolution: Literature, Historiography, and Art,* edited by James A. W. Heffernan, pp. 261-76. Hanover, NH: Dartmouth College, 1992.

> Discusses Carpentier's representation of the French Revolution and its effect on Latin America in his *El siglo de las luces.*

Shaw, Donald L. "Some Issues of Carpentier Criticism." *Revista Interamericana de Bibliografia* XXXV, No. 3 (1985): 297-304.

> Traces the different critical schools of thought concerning Carpentier's work.

——— "Columbus and the Discovery in Carpentier and Posse." *Romance Quarterly* (Summer 1993): 181-89.

> Discusses the portrayal of Christopher Columbus in Carpentier's *El arpa y la sombra* and Abel Posse's *Los perros del paraíso.*

Smith, V. A. "Carpentier's Journalism in Relation to his Works of Fiction." *Crítica Hispánica* VII, No. 2 (1985): 159-74.

> Asserts that there is a clear relationship between the subjects Carpentier tackled in his journalism and his fiction.

Tusa, Bobs M. "A Detective Story: The Influence of Mircea Eliade on Alejo Carpentier's *Los pasos perdidos.*" *Hispanofila* 30, No. 1 (September 1986): 41-65.

> Analyzes the influence of the work of Mircea Eliade, historian of religions, on Carpentier's *Los pasos perdidos.*

Additional coverage of Carpentier's life and career is contained in the following sources published by Gale: *Contemporary Authors*, Vols. 65-68 and 97-100; *Contemporary Authors New Revision Series*, Vol. 11; *DISCovering Authors Modules: Multicultural Authors; Dictionary of Literary Biography*, Vol. 113; *Hispanic Literature Criticism;* and *Hispanic Writers.*

Agatha Christie
1890-1976

(Full name Dame Agatha Mary Clarissa Christie. Also wrote as Agatha Christie Mallowan and under the pseudonym Mary Westmacott) English novelist, short story writer, dramatist, travel writer, and poet.

The following essay presents an overview of Christie's career. For further information on her life and works, see *CLC*, Volumes 1, 6, 8, 12, 39, and 48.

INTRODUCTION

Called the Grand Dame of mysteries, Agatha Christie is one of the most popular and best known writers in the world. Her books have been published in hundreds of languages, her sales are said to be rivaled only by Shakespeare and the Bible, and she is credited with developing several new components of the mystery genre. In addition to her mysteries, Christie wrote romance novels under the name of Mary Westmacott and penned several plays, one of which, *The Mousetrap* (1952), was the longest running show in British theater.

Biographical Information

Christie was born September 15, 1890, in Torquay, England to Frederick Alvah Miller, a wealthy American, and Clarissa Boehmer Miller. She was educated at home in an idyllic country setting similar to those of her novels. She left home to study piano and voice in Paris and met Colonel Archibald Christie, a member of the Flying Corps; the couple were married in 1914. Christie served as a nurse during World War I, first working for a Voluntary Aid Detachment in a Red Cross Hospital and later transferring to a local dispensary. During lulls in her work she began a detective novel in response to a challenge by her sister. *The Mysterious Affair at Styles* (1920) featured Hercule Poirot, inspired by the Belgian refugees near Torquay. Six publishers rejected it before it was accepted for the fee of twenty-five pounds, but the novel sold well. Christie followed her first success with several other moderately well-received works until the publication of *The Murder of Roger Ackroyd* (1926), which met with a sensational response. Christie's first marriage ended in divorce in 1928; the following year, she took the Orient Express to the Middle East, where she met and fell in love with archaeologist Max Mallowan. They married in September, 1930. During World War II, Mallowan served in North Africa and Christie returned to her work in a dispensary. During that time she wrote numerous novels, including some which were not published until the 1970s. She lived a quiet

life and continued writing after the war, producing a voluminous body of work. Christie died on January 12, 1976.

Major Works

Christie wrote nearly one hundred mysteries during her career, as well as numerous short stories, romances, plays, and poems. Her first work, *The Mysterious Affair at Styles,* which introduced her famous Belgian detective, Hercule Poirot, remains one of her most noted novels. In it she established many of the elements which she continued to employ for fifty years: a country setting, a formulaic structure in which all is not what it seems, and a detective who keeps clues to himself, making a startling revelation of guilt and innocence in a final meeting of all the characters. In *The Murder of Roger Ackroyd,* Christie introduced a new twist to the mystery genre by making the narrator the murderer. She introduced her second famous detective, Miss Marple, in *The Thirteen Problems* (1932). Miss Marple, an aged spinster aunt from the country village of St. Mary Mead, unravels crimes over her knitting, comparing suspects to her neighbors. The 1920s and 1930s are regarded as Christie's golden period, during which she wrote such classics as *The Murder at the Vicarage* (1930), *Murder on the Orient Express* (1934), *The A.B.C. Murders* (1936), and *Death on the Nile* (1937). She featured several detectives, some appearing in a single volume and others, such as Tommy and Tuppance Beresford and Harley Quinn, returning for several mysteries.

Critical Reception

Critics have disagreed over the quesion of which Christie novel is the best; in the running are *The Mysterious Affairs at Styles, The Murder at the Vicarage, Ten Little Indians* (1939), *Five Little Pigs* (1942), and *The Murder of Roger Ackroyd.* However, critics have agreed that Christie owes a debt to earlier crime writers such as Anna Katharine Green and Arthur Conan Doyle, who provided examples upon which Christie based her detectives and her story formulas. Scholars have also agreed that Christie had a tremendous influence on the crime novel genre. Stewart H. Benedict suggested that by allowing good people who kill bad people to escape the law in some of her cases, Christie may have created a tolerance for murder among hard-boiled writers. Gary Day argued that Christie legitimized and sanitized the readers' interests in murder: If Miss Marple, a well-bred and genteel woman, could delve into the misfortunes of others, then it was perfectly acceptable for the reader to observe them too. There is no consensus about the role Christie played in forwarding the cause of women. Such female characters as Tuppance, for instance, often exhibit spirit and independence during the investigation of a case, but conclude their adventures happily pursuing marriage and motherhood, and Miss Marple does not possess the arrogance and brilliance of her counterpart, Hercule Poirot. M. Vipond suggested that Christie's female characters represent a contradiction and reflect the changing views of the early twentieth century. Scholars and readers have also commented on the limitations and successes of the formulaic style of Christie's writing. Commentators critical of Christie's work describe her style as undistinguished, charge that her characters are stereotypical and lack depth, and lament the absence of any sociological analysis of the crimes. Some critics have also noted her less than tolerant views of other races and classes and her repeated use of the "least-likely-person" device, as well as her habit of concealing clues from the reader until the final scene.

PRINCIPAL WORKS

The Mysterious Affair at Styles (novel) 1920
The Secret Adversary (novel) 1922
The Murder on the Links (novel) 1923
The Man in the Brown Suit (novel) 1924
Poirot Investigates (short stories) 1924

The Secret of Chimneys (novel) 1925
The Road of Dreams (poetry) 1925
The Murder of Roger Ackroyd (novel) 1926
The Big Four (novel) 1927
The Mystery of the Blue Train (novel) 1928
Partners in Crime (short stories) 1929
The Under Dog (short story) 1929
The Seven Dials Mystery (novel) 1929
Black Coffee (drama) 1930
Giant's Bread [as Mary Westmacott] (novel) 1930
The Murder at the Vicarage (novel) 1930
The Mysterious Mr. Quin (short stories) 1930
The Sittaford Mystery [also published as *The Murder at Hazelmoor*] (novel) 1931
The Thirteen Problems (short stories) 1932; also published as *The Tuesday Club Murders*, 1933, and *Miss Marple's Final Cases*, 1972
Peril at End House (novel) 1932
The Hound of Death and Other Stories (short stories) 1933
Lord Edgeware Dies [also published as *Thirteen at Dinner*] (novel) 1933
Why Didn't They Ask Evans? (novel) 1934; also published as *The Boomerang Clue*, 1935
Murder on the Orient Express [also published as *Murder on the Calais Coach*] (novel) 1934
Unfinished Portrait [as Mary Westmacott] (novel) 1934
Parker Pyne Investigates [also published as *Mr. Parker Pyne, Detective*] (short stories) 1934
The Listerdale Mystery and Other Stories (short stories) 1934
Murder in Three Acts (novel) 1934; also published as *Three Act Tragedy*, 1935
Death in the Clouds [also published as *Death in the Air*] (novel) 1935
The A.B.C. Murders (novel) 1936
Cards on the Table (novel) 1936
Murder in Mesopotamia (novel) 1936
Murder in the Mews and Other Stories [also published as *Dead Man's Mirror and Other Stories*] (short stories) 1937
Death on the Nile (novel) 1937
Dumb Witness [also published as *Poirot Loses a Client*] (novel) 1937
Appointment with Death (novel) 1938
Hercule Poirot's Christmas (novel) 1938; also published as *Murder for Christmas*, 1939, and *A Holiday for Murder*, 1947
Murder Is Easy [also published as *Easy to Kill*] (novel) 1939
Ten Little Indians (novel) 1939; also published as *And Then There Were None*, 1940
The Regatta Mystery and Other Stories (short stories) 1939
One, Two, Buckle My Shoe (novel) 1940; also published as *The Patriotic Murders*, 1941
Sad Cypress (novel) 1940

Evil under the Sun (novel) 1941

N or M? (novel) 1941

The Body in the Library (novel) 1942

The Moving Finger (novel) 1942

Five Little Pigs [also published as *Murder in Retrospect*] (novel) 1942

Death Comes as the End (novel) 1942

Towards Zero (novel) 1944

Absent in the Spring [as Mary Westmacott] (novel) 1944

Sparkling Cyanide (novel) 1945

The Hollow (novel) 1946

Come, Tell Me How You Live [as Agatha Christie Mallowan] (travel) 1946

The Labours of Hercules (short stories) 1947

Witness for the Prosecution and Other Stories (short stories) 1948

The Rose and the Yew Tree [as Mary Westmacott] (novel) 1948

Taken at the Flood [also published as *There Is a Tide . . .*] (novel) 1948

Crooked House (novel) 1949

The Mousetrap and Other Stories (short stories) 1949

A Murder Is Announced (novel) 1950

They Came to Baghdad (novel) 1951

The Under Dog and Other Stories (short stories) 1951

They Do It with Mirrors [also published as *Murder with Mirrors*] (novel) 1952

Mrs. McGinty's Dead (novel) 1952

A Daughter's a Daughter [as Mary Westmacott] (novel) 1952

The Mousetrap (drama) 1952

After the Funeral [also published as *Funerals Are Fatal*] (novel) 1953

A Pocket Full of Rye (novel) 1953

Destination Unknown (novel) 1954; also published as *So Many Steps to Death*, 1955

The Spider's Web (drama) 1954

Hickory, Dickory, Dock [also published as *Hickory, Dickory, Death*] (novel) 1955

The Burden [as Mary Westmacott] (novel) 1956

Dead Man's Folly (novel) 1956

4:50 from Paddington [also published as *What Mrs. McGillicuddy Saw!*] (novel) 1957

Ordeal by Innocence (novel) 1958

Verdict (drama) 1958

The Unexpected Guest (drama) 1958

Cat among the Pigeons (novel) 1959

The Adventures of the Christmas Pudding, and Selection of Entrées (novel) 1960

Double Sin and Other Stories (short stories) 1961

The Pale Horse (novel) 1961

13 for Luck! A Selection of Mystery Stories (short stories) 1961

The Mirror Crack'd from Side to Side (novel) 1962; also published as *The Mirror Crack'd*, 1963

Rule of Three (drama) 1962

The Clocks (novel) 1963

A Caribbean Mystery (novel) 1964

Surprise! Surprise! (short stories) 1965

At Bertram's Hotel (novel) 1965

Star over Bethlehem and Other Stories [as Agatha Christie Mallowan] (short stories) 1965

Third Girl (novel) 1966

13 Clues for Miss Marple (short stories) 1966

Endless Night (novel) 1967

By the Pricking of My Thumbs (novel) 1968

Passenger to Frankfurt (novel) 1970

Fiddlers Three (drama) 1971

The Golden Ball and Other Stories (short stories) 1971

Nemesis (novel) 1971

Elephants Can Remember (novel) 1972

Akhnaton (drama) 1973

Postern of Fate (novel) 1973

Hercule Poirot's Early Cases (short stories) 1974

Miss Marple's Final Cases (short stories) 1974

Curtain: Hercule Poirot's Last Case (novel) 1975

The Mousetrap and Other Plays (dramas) 1978

The Harlequin Tea Set and Other Stories (short stories) 1997

CRITICISM

Stewart H. Benedict (essay date Winter 1962)

SOURCE: "Agatha Christie and Murder Most Unsportsmanlike," in *Claremont Quarterly*, Vol. 9, No. 2, Winter, 1962, pp. 37-42.

[*In the following essay, Benedict considers the culpability of Christie's murders, arguing that Christie may have paved the way for justifiable murders in mystery fiction.*]

Just as in politics the British offspring of an American mother became the symbol of Empire in a time of need, so too the most typically English mystery novels have come from the pen of an authoress who, although she can boast of almost a hundred million sales, cannot boast of one hundred percent pure U.K. blood. The lady in question is of course Agatha Christie, whose heraldry bears a transatlantic bar sinister, but who in her books has out-Harrowed the Harrovians and out-Blimped the Blimps.

Miss Christie launched her criminal career in 1920, with **The Mysterious Affair at Styles,** and, since this first case, has finished almost seventy others and has dispatched close onto two hundred fictional victims, incidentally becoming the world's best-selling authoress in the process.

Evidently fully convinced that nothing succeeds like success, Miss Christie at the start of her career relied on Sir Arthur Conan Doyle about as whole-heartedly as, say, V. I. Lenin did on Karl Marx. Her debt to the Sherlock Holmes stories can be seen in her choice of titles for novels (like *The Secret Adversary* and *The Big Four*) and short stories (like "The Adventure of the Cheap Flat," "The Tragedy at Marsdon Manor," and "The Mystery of Hunter's Lodge").

Indeed, the team of Hercule Poirot and Captain Hastings, as originally conceived, is a virtual carbon copy of Holmes and Watson. Poirot, like Holmes, is a convinced and convincing spokesman for the human rational faculty, has an unshakable faith in his own reason, uses his long-suffering Boswell as a sort of echo-chamber, and even has a mysterious and exotically named brother who works for the government. Captain Hastings, like Watson a retired military man, has much else in common with his prototype: he is a trusting, bumbling, superingenuous ex-soldier whose loyalty is touching but whose intellectual abilities, especially when turned loose on a problem of deduction, are so feeble as to be risible. Occasionally, though, the amanuensis wins applause from the master by making an observation which by its egregious stupidity illuminates some corner previously dark in the innermost recesses of the great mind.

Nor does the fumbling and ineffectual Inspector Lestrade lack a copy: Inspector Japp of the Christie novels is equally tenacious, incorruptible, and uninspired.

But the Baker Street influence permeates far deeper than these superficial features would indicate. Many scenes from Agatha's earlier works, especially those presenting conversations between the two principals, are considerably more Holmesian even than the literary collages constructed in imitation of the master by Adrian Conan Doyle and John Dickson Carr.

At the same time as she was writing by formula, Miss Christie was experimenting with a second type, in which she tried out various assorted detectives and crime-chasers, professional, semi-professional, and amateur.

In these novels she introduced a whole gallery of new sleuths: Tuppence and Tommy, Colonel Race, Superintendent Battle, Mr. Harley Quin and Mr. Satterthwaite, Parker Pyne, and Jane Marple. Some of the newcomers starred once and subsequently reappeared in supporting roles, some never moved out of short stories, while Miss Marple joined Poirot as a Christie regular.

Tuppence and Tommy Beresford, whose specialty was ferreting out espionage, made their debut in *The Secret Adversary,* showed up again in *Partners in Crime* and were resurrected in 1941 for *N or M?* Their frivolous and insouciant approach to detection, if something of a relief-giving contrast to the Holmes-Poirot methodology, nonetheless must have made them seem to their creatress too unreliable to cope with any subtle or complicated crime.

The enigmatic, laconic Colonel Race appeared first in *The Man in the Brown Suit* and sporadically thereafter. The Colonel, whose *locus operandi* was the colonies, did make it back to England for the fateful bridge party in *Cards on the Table,* but clearly his chief interest lay in shoring up the house that Rhodes built. Further, although not precisely what Miss Christie customarily refers to as "a wrong 'un," the Colonel gave the distinct impression of being willing to temporize on questions of ends and means, a point of view, we must assume, acceptable in the colonies but not in the Mother Country.

Superintendent Battle, stolid, dependable, hard-working, came onto the scene in *The Secret of Chimneys* and solved *The Seven Dials Mystery,* but his lack of color and elan must have been responsible for his being relegated to a subordinate role on later cases.

The most atypical product of the Christie imagination was the weird pair consisting of the other-worldly Harley Quin and his fussbudgety, oldmaidish "contact," Mr. Satterthwaite. The short stories in which they figured marked the authoress' closest approach to the occult.

Another unusual character who debuted during this experimental period was Parker Pyne. The ingenious Mr. Pyne specialized not in solving murders, but in manipulating the lives of others so as to bring them happiness and/or adventure. In some of these cases he was fortunate enough to have the assistance of Mrs. Ariadne Oliver, the mystery novelist. Just as it could not be proved that Willie Stark is Huey Long, so too it could not be stated flatly that Ariadne Oliver is Agatha Christie, but many of the clues seem to point in that direction. Mrs. Oliver's incessant munching on apples, her sartorial disorganization, and above all her theories on the art of the mystery novel make it difficult to avoid that conclusion.

It was in 1930, in *Murder at the Vicarage,* unquestionably the best-written Christie novel, that she first presented the character who became one of her two favorites. The attraction to Jane Marple is not hard to understand: she is one of those personified paradoxes in whom both authors and readers delight. Behind the antique, Victorian, tea-and-crumpets, crocheted-antimacassar facade, is a mind realistically aware of the frailty of all human beings and the depravity of some.

About 1935 there began to appear the third type, or what

might best be called the genuine Christie novel, with its numerous unique features.

Most publicized among these features, of course, is the use of an extraordinary gimmick: in *Murder in the Calais Coach* the murder is done with the connivance of a dozen people; in *The ABC Murders,* the highly suggestive suspect believes himself guilty of a series of crimes of which he is innocent and convinces the reader of his guilt; in *And Then There Were None,* the reader is led to believe that the killer has been a victim in a series of murders.

Less discussed, but really more significant, is the Christie ability to manage what may be called (to pirate a phrase from Sarcey) "the optics of the mystery." The successful mystery novel involves a special problem: the death(s) of the victim(s) must be made of interest, but not of deep concern, to the reader. The conventional, or, by now, hackneyed, methods of developing this special attitude in the reader are two: either the prospective corpse is presented so briefly that, living, he makes no impression at all, or he is depicted as so vicious that the audience looks forward eagerly to his demise.

Miss Christie, however, has evolved a completely different formula: she arranges a situation which is implausible, if not actually impossible and into this unrealistic framework places characters who act realistically for the most realistic of motives. In *Easy to Kill,* for example, four murders are committed in a minuscule town without any suspicions being aroused; in *A Murder Is Announced* the killer advertises in advance; in *What Mrs. McGillicuddy Saw*! the witness to a murder is a passenger in a train which travels parallel to another train just long enough for Mrs. McGillicuddy to see the murder. And, of course, some of the Christie Classics, especially *Murder in the Calais Coach, And Then There Were None,* and "Witness for the Prosecution," really test the ductility of coincidence.

The single characteristic which most stamps a whodunit as a Christie product . . . is the fate of the killer. Miss Christie sees murderers as being either good or bad individuals; the good ones dispose of evil victims, and vice versa.
—*Stewart H. Benedict*

As for the realistic elements, in only one instance (the short story **"The Face of Helen"**) does a murderer have recourse to a bizarre weapon; in every other case a completely pedestrian one is used: the poison bottle, the knife, the gun, the garrote, the bludgeon. The motive is always equally pedestrian: it is invariably either money or love.

The single characteristic which most stamps a whodunit as a Christie product, however, is the fate of the killer. Miss Christie sees murderers as being either good or bad individuals; the good ones dispose of evil victims, and vice versa. Further, the bad murderer is distinguished because he unvaryingly preys on people with inadequate defenses: he may be a doctor (and therefore *ipso facto* to be trusted, as contemporary folklore teaches us); or a handsome and clever lover who first uses, then kills, a woman who has been unlucky enough to fall in love with him; or an old and respected friend and confidant; or a man who selects a child, an old person, a physical or psychological cripple as a victim. This element, the victim's inadequate defenses against the criminal, puts the murderer beyond the pale—he is unsportsmanlike and consequently despicable. Over and over reference is made to the viciousness of those who betray faith and trust. Says Dr. Haydock in *Murder at the Vicarage* after he learns that the murderer has attempted to pin his crime on an innocent young curate who suffers from sleeping sickness and is not really sure of his own innocence: "The fellow's not fit to live. A defenseless chap like Hawes." In an analogous situation Hercule Poirot says to Franklin Clarke, who has actually succeeded in getting the suggestive epileptic Alexander Bonaparte Cust to believe himself a murderer: "No, Mr. Clarke, no easy death for you . . . I consider your crime not an English crime at all—not above-board—not sporting—. . ." He adds later, in analyzing the crime, "It was abominable—. . . the cruelty that condemned an unfortunate man to a living death. *To catch a fox and put him in a box and never let him go.* That is not *le sport.*"

Conversely, when the victim is completely unsympathetic and the murderer a decent person, it is very possible that the culprit will be revealed to be a sufferer from a far-advanced case of some incurable disease. If he is healthy, he usually has or is presented with the opportunity to commit suicide. On rare occasions such a person escapes any punishment at the hands of the law: in *Murder in the Calais Coach,* for instance, the victim turns out to have committed an especially unsportsmanlike crime and the otherwise tenacious Hercule Poirot simply steps out of the case, leaving it unsolved.

It is very clear, then, that Miss Christie is no moral absolutist where murder is concerned. In *Mr. Parker Pyne, Detective* Ariadne Oliver, speaking, we suppose, for the authoress, asks Poirot, "Don't you think that there are people who ought to be murdered?" The view that there are indeed such people seems to be sustained in *And Then There Were None,* in which no less than ten preeminently sleazy slayers are dispatched by a retired judge who escapes legal justice through suicide. The entire tone of this book gives the strong impression that Miss Christie is not sorry to see them go. It also suggests that there is a stratification of murderers, with special punishment due those whose crimes have been particularly un-British, i.e., heinous, even though the later Miss Christie can hardly be accused of advocating unrestrained *laissez-tuer*.

Since Miss Christie's prestige among her fellow mystery writers is towering, and since she has by implication espoused the quaint theory that a sportsmanlike murder doesn't really count, it is interesting to speculate as to whether this latitudinarian attitude has in any way influenced the writers of the hard-boiled school with their philosophy that it is all right to kill a killer. Paradoxical as it may seem, perhaps the literary godmother of bone-crushing Mike Hammer is none other than genteel Jane Marple.

M. Vipond (essay date Summer 1981)

SOURCE: "Agatha Christie's Women," in *The International Fiction Review,* Vol. 8, No. 2, Summer, 1981, pp. 119-23.

[*In the following essay, Vipond attempts to clarify Christie's representation of women, arguing that Christie's female characters are products of the time.*]

Agatha Christie's characters are stereotypes and caricatures, but they are not just that. They possess not simply two dimensions but two and a half. The little bit of fun gently poked at the "typical" figure, the slightly surprising or contradictory quality, the merest touch of real humanity—all make Christie's types just a bit more than cardboard puppets dancing to the choreography of the plot. In her characterization as in her puzzles, Christie found the perfect balance, the hallmark of the really skilled popular writer, between convention and invention. She gave her readers exactly what they anticipated, yet added just enough that was intriguingly new to keep them stimulated and absorbed. Her characters are recognizable and familiar individuals through whom escape and adventure can be enjoyable without being frightening.

There are a remarkable number of strong female characters in Christie's books, and only a very few of them are depicted negatively. Efficient, practical, and competent businesswomen, housekeepers and secretaries; successful and professional artists, actresses and authors; commanding, cultured, and intellectual headmistresses; the shrewd and courageous Miss Marple, on the surface a fluttery, dithering old maid but underneath ruthless in the cause of justice— these women, however briefly they pass through the stories, are essentially admirable types. In addition, Christie presented over the years a series of amateur heroines of "high spirits, daring, and imperturbability," from Prudence "Tuppence" Beresford, first introduced in *The Secret Adversary* in 1922 through Lady Eileen "Bundle" Brent of *The*

Secret at Chimneys (1925) and *The Seven Dials Mystery* (1929) and Lady Frances "Frankie" Derwent of *The Boomerang Clue* (1933) to Victoria Jones in *They Came to Baghdad* (1951), Hilary Craven in *Destination Unknown* (1954) and Katherine "Ginger" Corrigan in *The Pale Horse* (1961)—and quite a number of others. These young women all possessed similar attributes. Most importantly, they were thoroughly "modern." They were "plucky," "energetic," "impish," "boyish," "gamin," "spunky," "good sports," "spirited fillies," "alive," "courageous," "alert," "rakish," "minxes," "pert and saucy," "impudent," "gallant," "fighters," and "brimming over with life." They were typical 1920's flappers (right through to the books of the 1960's): they smoked, drank, and swore, and were regarded by their elders with a combination of outrage and envy. They were athletic enough to swing up and down the ivy when essential to the plot, skilled and audacious enough to drive bright little sports cars in a fashion which terrified everyone else on the road, brave enough to take more than their fair share of risks—and always they were admired for these qualities. In *N or M?* Tuppence Beresford, by now a middle-aged woman with a grown family, fakes a telephone call, hides in a cupboard, and beats her husband Tommy to the scene of a spy investigation in which she then plays a major role. Tommy's reaction to his wife's initiative and trickery is secret admiration, and his boss in British intelligence agrees: "She's a smart woman." When Ginger Corrigan in *The Pale Horse* insists on taking a grave personal risk to trap members of a murder-for-hire operation, the handsome and very eligible Mark Easterbrook promptly falls in love with "her red hair, her freckles, her gallant spirit." But the theme is perhaps best developed in *The Boomerang Clue* (British title: *Why Didn't They Ask Evans?*), in which Christie contrasted Lady Frances "Frankie" Derwent, an impish and very independent young woman with Moira Nicholson, gentle, "like a sad Madonna" and "terribly delicate." Bobby Jones, the rather bumbling but eminently nice young hero finds both women attractive, but for a while it looks like Moira is going to win him, because she brings out all his protective male instincts. "Bobby likes them helpless," complains the unhappy Frankie, "It's extraordinary how men like helpless women." Another character, Roger Bassington-french, tries to comfort Frankie: "The truth of the matter is that you've got guts and she hasn't." Of course Bobby eventually sees the light, and in the denouement admits to Frankie that while Moira's "face" had attracted him momentarily, Frankie had captured his heart because she was "so plucky about things," "so frightfully plucky." Just to provide the typical Christie double-twist, however, Moira's "weak and helpless" personality turns out to be a front; she is in fact a gang member and dope dealer, and has "the nerve to put any number of people out of the way without turning a hair!" Thus we are left with not one but two strong female characters, one good and one evil. And Frankie gets her man—as do Tuppence, Bundle, Ginger, and all the others of the type.

Here the complications begin. These peppy, modern young women are part of the romantic subplots of the novels in which they appear, and they are paired off at the end, married, and presumably live happily ever after. Frequently, and with conviction, Christie's characters speak of marriage as the goal and destiny of all womankind. Many of her female characters are employed, but whenever they have the chance, they throw up excellent jobs and careers for the sake of a man and a home. If they work after marriage, it is almost invariably because their husbands are invalids, wastrels, or deceased. Most explicitly described is the fate of Rosamund Darnley in *Evil under the Sun*. Hercule Poirot admires Rosamund very much from the moment he meets her, for she has brains, charm and *chic*. She is sensible, alert, and proud, and a very successful designer and businesswoman. Early in the book she has a rather ambiguous conversation with Poirot about her goals in life, but by the final paragraphs all doubt is dispelled. Kenneth Marshall, an old friend, proposes to her:

> "You're going to be the persecuted female, Rosamund. You're going to give up that damned dressmaking business of yours and we're going to live in the country."

> "Don't you know that I make a very handsome income out of my business? Don't you realize that it's My business—that I created it and worked it up and that I'm proud of it! And you've got the damned nerve to come along and say, 'Give it all up, dear.'"

> "I've got the damned nerve to say it, yes."

> "And you think I care enough for you to do it?"

> "If you don't," said Kenneth Marshall, "you'd be no good to me."

> Rosamund said softly; "Oh, my dear, I've wanted to live in the country with you all my life. Now— it's going to come true."

There can be little doubt, however, that after her marriage Rosamund remained sensible and successful—in her new job. For Tuppence Beresford, too, marriage was not "a haven, or a refuge, or a crowning glory, or a state of bondage." it was "a sport," and the glimpses we have of Tuppence as a married woman confirm that her marriage *was* like that. Christie presented marriages of partnership and companionship—"Joint Ventures"—in a positive light: the ones she showed more unfavorably were those in which either partner was weak or cowed by the other, although even in those cases she made it clear that she understood the human needs which led men and women into such relationships.

Often Christie illuminated character types by having them profess views on women which were typical of their class, age, and status: "Women tell a lot of lies," "All women fancy marriage, no matter how advanced and self-supporting they are," "Poison is a woman's weapon," "Women are ruthless," "If you want a thing broadcast, tell a woman," "Old maids are notoriously inquisitive," and so on. That Christie used such generalizations so frequently to delicate character reveals how pervasive and generally accepted some of them were, but one must resist the temptation to conclude that Christie herself necessarily agreed with them. Such statements were simply instantly and broadly recognizable clues which helped her readers to categorize the characters.

Agatha Christie's characters are stereotypes and caricatures, but they are not just that. They possess not simply two dimensions but two and a half. The little bit of fun gently poked at the "typical" figure, the slightly surprising or contradictory quality, the merest touch of real humanity—all make Christie's types just a bit more than cardboard puppets dancing to the choreography of the plot.
—M. Vipond

By other means, however, Christie did reveal that she herself had the somewhat "traditional" attitude to sex roles which was typical of her class and status. In her books, women's main mental capability seems to be intuitive; even Miss Marple, who is praised by her distinguished male admirers like Sir Henry Clithering for her wonderfully (and surprisingly) logical brain, is so discursive in speech that it seems unbelievable that she can think straight. On at least one occasion, the aging, fluffy-haired spinster explicitly denies solving a mystery by logical deduction but instead very femininely credits "feeling," "a kind of emotional reaction or susceptibility to—well . . . atmosphere." The spunky young heroines like Tuppence and Frankie, brave though they may be, are not really intelligent or sensible; they are over-inquisitive, headstrong, foolhardy, and thus are perpetually having to be rescued from some scrape or other. In several of her books, moreover, Christie implied that maternal love was one of the strongest possible motives for murder; if five characters all had motive and opportunity, but one is suspected of committing the crime for the sake of "her children," you can be fairly certain that she is the guilty party. As Poirot himself put it. "Mothers . . . are particularly ruthless when their children are in danger." Poirot, too, although usually fairly cynical about women, does have a soft spot for them when they are mothers—"Bonne mère, très femme." Although Christie biographer Derrick Murdoch goes much too far when he writes that Christie had "little feeling for sexual equality" and is quite wrong in insisting that "strong-willed wives receive unsympathetic treatment in all her books," there are certainly enough traces of such attitudes permeating Christie's works to explain how he has read them that way.

Christie thus presented seemingly contradictory images of women—the independent, self-sufficient, capable and courageous woman who is respected for those qualities and treated as an equal partner in adventure and in life coexisted with the silly, emotional woman who has no identity except through her husband and children. But the lines kept crossing; the independent young flapper heroines wanted to settle down to marriage and children, and the silly ditherers often turned out to be made of steel.

Christie herself lived a life of such ambivalences. Brought up to be a proper upper middle-class wife and mother, the natural pattern of her life was broken by service as a VAD nurse and dispenser during World War I, by the "accident" of her becoming a best-selling author, and by the failure of her first marriage. Whatever she might say about deferring to her husband, and no matter how she insisted that her occupation in life was not as author but as "Married Woman," she was in fact a professional, a considerable personality in her own right, and possessed of much independence of mind, not to mention income.

Christie reached maturity and began writing at a time when the image of women in England and North America had been tumbled from its Victorian pedestal, but had not been remodeled. The period between 1900 and the end of the 1920's was one of rapid transition in both the image and the role of women; it was in this period that Christie herself was formed, and her books describe that transition, directly and indirectly, at some length. While many of the traditional qualities of maternal love, gentleness, patience, and docility were still given lip-service, at the same time the needs of modern technological society (especially in wartime) demanded a different kind of woman—a capable, efficient, self-confident sort, who could perform a job as typist or nurse skillfully before marriage, and then settle down to being equally competent, self-sufficient, indeed "businesslike," as housewife and mother in an increasingly complex and demanding world. The popular literature of Christie's day glorified that contradictory and ambiguous mixture of qualities, and so did she, right through to her last books more than fifty years later.

Agatha Christie is credited with being the first major author to add the touches which opened up the classical mystery to a wide female readership. Her romantic subplots, thin as they were, helped that to occur. So did her quite deliberate attempt, especially in her early books, to provide vicarious adventure for the house-and duty-bound. But finally, it seems, her books appealed and continue to appeal to female readers because she possessed such an "accurate social eye"; because she succeeded so well in capturing the nuances and ambiguities of life in the twentieth century. Few of Christie's readers have had direct contact with the genteel upper middle-class life of the English village or country manor she so frequently described, nor, presumably, with murder. Like Miss Marple, however, they recognize typical people and behavior patterns, and thus can identify with them. Agatha Christie always liked to claim that she was a lowbrow; what she really meant was that she did not write down to her audience. She gave them back their own ambivalent image of what a woman is and does, because she shared it.

Agatha Christie is credited with being the first major author to add the touches which opened up the classical mystery to a wide female readership.
—M. Vipond

As Colin Watson, John Cawelti and others have pointed out, the enormous appeal of the classical mystery of the Golden Age of the 1920's and 1930's seemed to lie in its success in providing reassurance for its middle-class readers—reassurance that crime is an individual matter, not a social one, that it is logical and soluble, that it is neat and relatively painless, explicable, and not a matter for collective guilt. But Christie's books also reassured simply by the reiteration of familiar patterns and types. She did not delve very deeply into the souls of her characters, but in examining large numbers of them, and from various angles, she revealed just a few of the contradictions and complexities of real life. To generalize about sexual roles is to lose that touch of reality, and Christie never did that. Certain patterns emerge in her portrayal of women, but no simple typing or role-playing. Possibly one occasion when Christie *did* express her own opinion through the words of one of her characters was when she had Sarah King, a young doctor in *Appointment with Death,* remark: "I do hate this differentiation between the sexes. 'The modern girl has a thoroughly businesslike attitude to life!' That sort of thing. It's not a bit true! Some girls are businesslike and some aren't. Some men are sentimental and muddle-headed, others are clear-headed and logical. These are just different types of brains. Sex only matters when sex is directly concerned." Despite the fact that she wrote in a form which demanded stereotypes and caricatures, Christie was not a generalizer. She knew more of life than that. That is why her books give a surprisingly accurate picture of the life of twentieth-century women.

David I. Grossvogel (essay date 1983)

SOURCE: "Death Deferred: The Long Life, Splendid Afterlife, and Mysterious Workings of Agatha Christie," in *Art in Crime Writing: Essays on Detective Fiction,* St. Martin's Press, 1983, pp. 1-17.

[*In the following essay, Grossvogel explores why Christie's works remain popular today.*]

It is not uncommon for the demise of an author's popularity to coincide with his actual death, the chance of resurrection awaiting the archaeological whims of future scholars and critics. Not so Agatha Christie: even though she has been gone since 1976, even though the worlds she described are, for the most part, no longer with us, even though the very genre she helped fashion is largely obsolete—in great part because of the disappearance of those worlds—Dame Agatha, her worlds and her particular notion of a genre still seem to be defining for an exceptionally large readership.

Part of this anachronistic phenomenon seems to be due to the truly huge size of that readership developed by Agatha Christie during the course of a career that spanned well over half a century, a hundred titles (titles that number, in addition to her detective stories, plays, romantic novels written under the pseudonym Mary Westmacott, an autobiography, and so on), translations into more than a hundred languages: the size of that readership is impossible to evaluate accurately, but close to half a billion is the figure generally guessed at.

We are still tied to a past we never knew through a few strands that fray even as we hang on to them and, sooner or later, disappear: Agatha Christie is one of those strands. We believe that the detective story as we know it began with Edgar Allan Poe and, some forty years after his death, was popularized by Sir Arthur Conan Doyle. What we may be less aware of is that we are linked to these historical inceptions through the presence of Agatha Christie. The author of Sherlock Holmes was writing, and would still be writing for a number of years, when young Agatha Mary Clarissa Miller decided to try her hand at the genre. This was towards the end of the first world war: Agatha, born in 1890, was in her late twenties. For many years, she and her sister had been avid readers of Conan Doyle and they 'had always argued a lot about whether it was easy to write detective stories': challenged by her sister, Agatha began writing what was to be *The Mysterious Affair at Styles,* first published in 1920. From then on, and until 1973 when she wrote her last detective novel (*Postern of Fate*), Dame Agatha supplied an increasingly large and expectant audience with a steady flow of stories that owed to Conan Doyle two fundamental attributes which are unmistakably his even though they are not generally mentioned: a fondness for bucolic settings and a strong admixture of improbable occurrences (when one considers the supreme urbanity of Sherlock Holmes, it is strik-

ing to note how many of his adventures take place on distant moors and within halls of rural estates, drafty with an unurban otherness; and if one considers further that Sherlock Holmes is the child of that *esprit de finesse* Auguste Dupin, a reader of exceptional good will is required to grant their authors a criminal who turns out to be, against every rational expectation, an orangutan, as in *The Murders in the Rue Morgue,* or a trained snake, as in *The Adventure of the Speckled Band*). It was only after Conan Doyle that rules of fair play evolved, owing perhaps to an increasing desire of the genre to be the accurate reflector of a sociological scene (as with, for example, the 'hard-boiled' Americans).

When Agatha Christie began, she opted for a sunnier countryside than Doyle's, and one which she could people with the homey or homespun types that may have been the romanticizing of her own Devonshire youth. Its crystallization was the village of St Mary Mead (in the 1930 *Murder at the Vicarage*), with its representative spinster, Miss Jane Marple, who was to become, after Hercule Poirot, Agatha Christie's most ubiquitous detective. Miss Marple enjoyed from the very start an acuity and acquaintance with evil that belied her grand-auntish frailty. Over the long half-century of her author's writing, she became more and more that disabused acuity while the bucolic dream faded in England, as elsewhere, and the discontents of an industrial civilization reached from urban centre to urban centre across a dwindling rural space that had been able once to better conceal a less expected evil. (It was that undisguisable awareness that things were no longer what they had formerly been, however much they might still appear to be, that allowed Miss Marple to perform successfully in one of the more interesting of Agatha Christie's later stories, *At Bertram's Hotel,* in 1965. Even before that, in the 1950 *A Murder Is Announced,* Miss Marple had begun noticing what upward and other mobilities had done to traditional structures and how amenities and a security formerly taken for granted had systematically eroded.)

It is therefore in the nature of a cavil to note that, in a more enduring world, Miss Marple remained a sleuth in the tradition that assumed the unconditional omniscience of the detective and preserved that omniscience by imparting information to the heroine that had not necessarily been vouchsafed the reader, or by contriving circumstances so improbable as to be acceptable only to that heroine and her entourage of fictional listeners at the final disclosure.

Agatha Christie came to fame in 1926 with *The Murder of Roger Ackroyd,* and aroused the susceptibilities of such defenders of fair play as were already about by turning the narrator into the murderer; she ended Poirot by making *him* one of the killers-but by this time the defenders of fair play had all yielded to Dame Agatha, who had meanwhile turned the supposed victim into the assassin in *Peril at End House*

(1932), and done the same to a corpse in *Ten Little Niggers* (1939). In the words of Robert Barnard, 'When the time for a solution came round, the most unaccountable rabbits were produced from her hat: the murderer was the investigating policeman, he was a child, he was one we had thought already dead, he was all the suspects together. And all along, that inveterate gardener, Jane Marple, led uncomplaining generations of readers down primrose paths known only to her (usually by offering those readers a great diversity of paths, all but one of which they were supposed to pay any attention to).

And so did Poirot. But Poirot was also walking—even as was Jane Marple—a more interesting path, one leading, at least in the fiction, from Styles Court to Styles Court, through some fifty years and as many adventures, across the changing landscape of our times. On that long journey, moral notions evolved, social circumstances changed, what had once been clear markers became either difficult to read or were obliterated altogether, leaving the journeyer with the residual sense of our times, an anxiety that filtered at last beyond the covers meant to contain the adventure, and which transcended the spurious suspense of the detective genre.

I have analyzed elsewhere (*Mystery and Its Fictions,* 1979) the (relatively) innocent world of which, and within which, Agatha Christie first wrote. In that innocent world, the detective-story writer did not propose so much a solvable problem as a disposable one. Agatha Christie's first readers read her in order to purchase at the cost of a minor and passing disturbance the comfort of knowing that the disturbance was *contained,* and that at the end of the story the world they imagined would be continued in its innocence and familiarity.

The nature and consequences of that disturbance are crucial, for ultimately they are the key to Agatha Christie's huge popularity and her yet-enduring readership. A sense of Dame Agatha's climate in her early works will be obtained instantly through contrast with the hard-boiled variety mentioned in later chapters. In the latter, a relatively sordid private eye does battle with openly sordid forces loosed by the urban chaos. That private eye-Sam Spade, Philip Marlowe or Mike Hammer-encounter what is intended to be 'real' corruption, whether in a politician, a sexuality (most frequently a woman's, against which is successfully matched the demonstrative virility of the detective), a corpse. This 'reality' entails a specificity; the detective performs acts that particularize him even though they have nothing to do with the functional gestures required of him by the case he is on: he drinks, he makes love, he lets all and sundry know that he is 'tough'. He walks the back alleys of a city whose surfaces are fully analyzed. As Zola discovered a century before, such 'slice-of-life' realism not only entails specificity, it also assumes a burden of 'truth' which, more often than

not, it feels able to demonstrate only by exposing its seamier parts.

Agatha Christie was far more stylized. For her, the game was merely a puzzle (or a series of interlocking puzzles) told in the form of a story. The story required people, of course, but their creation was left largely to the imagination of the reader.

Writing in the years immediately after the end of the first world war, Agatha Christie was instinctively striving for a delicate balance, but one that was still possible at that time. It consisted in an intrusion upon the reader's ideal world, but an intrusion not so intense as to cast doubt on its eventual dissipation. She achieved this balance by identifying accurately her middle-class audience and its hankering for an Edwardian gentility.
—David I. Grossvogel

Writing in the years immediately after the end of the first world war, Agatha Christie was instinctively striving for a delicate balance, but one that was still possible at that time. It consisted in an intrusion upon the reader's ideal world, but an intrusion not so intense as to cast doubt on its eventual dissipation. She achieved this balance by identifying accurately her middle-class audience and its hankering for an Edwardian gentility. Dame Agatha offered these readers recognizable posters of a world which they had experienced only through posters: they were offered a journey to a land that they knew well, but only in the world of their social fantasizing and bygone dreams of empire. Poster and book served the selfsame purpose: they preserved the awareness of a world that must have exited for someone; it was a far better world than the known world and doubly comforting because of a suspicion that if it had indeed existed once, its days were now numbered.

In 1920, Styles Court was the province of the upper-middle class. Like most parts of the worlds which it supposed, it endured mainly in the reader's private storehouse of prides and prejudices. Styles Court was a functional set of lexical stimuli, never anything more precise than a 'fine, old house', with 'a broad staircase' which you descended in your mind's eye after having 'dressed' for 'supper . . . at half past seven' (due to wartime conditions, 'We have given up late dinners'). It had an 'open French window' in order to disclose 'the shade of a huge sycamore tree' beneath which 'tea' was ritualized in summer, and beyond which was located the leisured class's tennis court.

Part of the world adumbrated by Styles Court was a poster village, Styles St Mary, which was exactly like Jane Marple's St Mary Mead (ideal images being perforce identical), nestling in a small verdant world of scrubbed and loyal people—working or farming—with its quaint vicarage for an effortless accommodation of spiritual needs and a half-timbered inn for the mundane counterpart.

Through these postcards of rural England walked a few other stock types-a suitable clergyman for the vicarage, a jovial landlord or two for the pub, a third-generation solicitor for the competent handling of material vexations, servants whose starched surface hid a heart of gold, matrons on their way to the local flower show, elderly majors retired from colonial wars. The reader knew these people without having encountered them and they were therefore exactly suited to his expectations.

Murder within this English pastoral was not so much an evil act as one whose consequences would be unfortunate for a prescribed moment. Whereas a Mike Hammer or a Sam Spade might right their little piece of the corrupt, urban jigsaw puzzle while the complex itself remained corrupt and awaited the private eye's attention to the next area of his concern, murder upon the mead was more in the nature of a washable and cathartic stain. For a while, these good people would become each and every one suspect (Agatha Christie, who build her reputation early on a disregard for established rules, showed as little unwarranted sentimentality here: however much tradition might have endeared a particular type to the reader, none was above suspicion). Within this dream of rural England, murder was trivial enough; the corpse upon which Philip Marlowe stumbled might not have had quite the stench of Laius', but in St Mary Mead or Styles St Mary the murder itself was antiseptic—already a part of the cleansing process (there were always half a dozen compelling reasons to kill the victim—and as many evident suspects). It was the wake of the murder that made things momentarily disagreeable: the country inn would lose its ruddy bonhomie; the vicarage might be pressed uncomfortably close to moral quandaries; and, worst of all, aliens would walk the pristine land. For just as the reader was able to people fully a world to which he aspired, the reader would temporarily jeopardize through his own malaise the harmony of the world he had conjured from his fiction. And here again, Dame Agatha remained supremely aloof, giving the reader only such few and accurate stimuli as were needed.

In the shadow of evil, clean-shaven Styles St Mary would begin to see beards with all the unEnglish and other unfortunate implications of that facial indecorum. Alfred Inglethorp, who is only very nearly the villain of the piece, strikes 'a rather alien note', according to bland Hastings, the narrator (*The Mysterious Affair at Styles*). Hastings understands instantly why Inglethorp's son-in-law objected to the beard: 'It was one of the longest and blackest I have ever seen. . . . It struck me that he might look natural on the stage, but was strangely out of place in real life.' 'Real life' is of course Styles St Mary, and since Styles had never been under anything like the present cloud, the unnatural beard is contrary to what is normal and becomes a litmus of evil.

But that litmus comes from elsewhere as well, as demonstrated by another of the characters—Dr Bauerstein. Dr Bauerstein is merely here as a red herring—he turns out to be a spy who has nothing to do with the nasty business at Styles. But the early Christie readers thought they knew Bauerstein just as they thought they knew the Cavendishes and Styles St Mary itself. The way this red herring affected those readers was articulated by Hastings—even though Christie had done no more than name Bauerstein and mention that he was a 'tall bearded man': 'The sinister face of Dr Bauerstein recurred to me unpleasantly. A vague suspicion of everyone and everything filled my mind. Just for a moment I had a premonition of approaching evil.' Bauerstein is after all a Polish Jew—twice an alien. He comes by his beard naturally. The Polish Jew has no 'natural' place in the average reader's imaginings of Styles: Bauerstein brings to those fictional imaginings a parafictional unpleasantness from a world that is more intimate and habitual to that reader. Or so it was at least in 1920.

There was always a suspicion that Agatha Christie and Jane Marple had quite a bit in common. There were of course their moral and social beliefs; but there was also an acuity, a depth of *insight*. Just as Miss Marple was able to see the hidden snake lurking in Devonshire Edens, Agatha Christie was able to discern precisely what would give her reader the surest of twinges, though neither she nor that reader ever identified the causes to which they both referred. This being so, it might be unmannerly to repeat here that Dame Agatha was one to take unfair advantage of even such fundamental intuitions: in *Styles,* not only did the culprit turn out to be the most upright and prototypical of British stereotypes, but the author added insult to injury by hiding the culprit behind a (false) beard.

It was within a world distracted only momentarily by this kind of curable malaise that was born the detective destined to become one of the most famous of the genre: Poirot was able to dissipate the uneasiness, but he was also created and shaped by it to a great extent.

Like his prototypes, Dupin and Holmes, this sort of detective demonstrates a perfect intelligence within a multitude of flaws. The structural reason for this contrast results from a fundamental identity between the fictional detective and his circumstances: that detective is the reader's assurance that his expectation of an end to a number of small annoyances will be met-the detective's acuity is therefore absolute; but the reader's concession in that contract requires that a semblance of doubt be maintained for as long as it takes to tell the tale-all else in the detective is therefore flawed.

However, the strangeness of Dupin and Holmes confirmed their intelligence even as it removed them from the common world of mortals; Dupin and Holmes dwelt in remote worlds, isolated by books, drugs, laboratory or musical instruments-all awesome objects that extended the awesomeness of their brains. Poirot's flaws, on the other hand, represented a compendium of what marred the idyllic landscape once it became the temporary site of the somber event that brought Poirot into it. When Agatha Christie first described Poirot, he was in fact a part of the negative consequences that followed the transgression of the bucolic dream.

To start with, Poirot was a foreigner, another alien note within the pastoral harmony. The evidence of his foreignness was multiple, but because of the specific area of Poirot's first trespass, it was peculiarly unEnglish. Starting with his ridiculously short stature, most of his obvious traits were intended to amuse, but also to annoy, his English reader:

> Poirot was an extraordinary-looking little man. He was hardly more than five feet, four inches, but carried himself with great dignity. His head was exactly the shape of an egg, and he always perched it a little on one side. His moustache was very stiff and military. The neatness of his attire was almost incredible. I believe a speck of dust would have caused him more pain than a bullet wound. Yet this quaint dandyfied little man who, I was sorry to see, now limped badly, had been in his time one of the most celebrated members of the Belgian police.

Hastings' initial awareness and dismissal of the physical Poirot spoke for his reader, and Hastings' voice was subsequently echoed by countless others—villains, chambermaids, gardeners, romantic leads: just about everyone was to be taller than Poirot, treating him until the final moment of revelation and awe with either amused contempt or patronizing tolerance.

Lack of stature made Poirot's aping of British virtues something halfway between a joke and an affront: dignity sounded like an unseemly overstatement in one so short, while the military moustache became a ridiculous attribute. As for Poirot's sartorial fastidiousness, something that would have been praiseworthy in an Englishman of more normal size, could at best be quaintly dandifying in an undersized foreigner.

But Poirot added to even these shortcomings. Having been denied the grace of British birth, he compounded his misfortune by refusing to hide it, indulging an unBritish propensity for exuberance and exaggeration. He was from the first a boaster, one given to stressing the subject pronoun through the apposition of his own name, and using his hands with abandon for even greater emphasis. And to bring the picture to its full dejection, this master of the little grey cells never learned to speak English correctly. To the end, Poirot's sentences were marred by Gallicisms, even though they became more probable over a lifetime than the porcine 'Ah! Triple pig!' or 'you remain there like—how do you say it?—ah, yes, the stuck pig' that flavored his original speech.

Poirot's very intelligence, before even his unseemly boasting about it, was yet another exaggeration, and one which he displayed with equal lack of tact in his all too apparent egg-head. Aloof as ever, but knowing full well from which vantage point she observed her creation, Dame Agatha named him after the least favored of vegetables (*poireau:* the leek, which also means 'wart' in French) and then stressed the dismissiveness by pairing it with a singularly grandiloquent Christian name, Hercule—itself turned into still another over assertion by the diminutive size of its bearer.

Seemingly self-removed, Agatha Christie kept a gimlet eye on her reader at all times, knowing the disposition of his afferent nerves as accurately as might an acupuncturist. Where Mike Hammer's or Sam Spade's readers were drawn through a world which they either knew or knew to be there, Christie's readers were returned to their own imagination in order to flesh out the otherwise abstract puzzle. And though they only assumed that the enviable world of the fiction must exist, they tainted it for a while with fears that were as imaginary but which they knew to be real beyond the fiction. Preeminently, Christie knew how much her reader did not know: if that Edwardian world still existed for some in 1920, it is unlikely that it could ever have appeared as desirable or as easily jeopardized as it did to those for whom it was only a dream. For the latter, the bulk of Christie's readers, dream and jeopardy derived from aspirations and fears that the author intuited with unfailing accuracy. But as Agatha Christie wrote for a long time, and as her sense of her reader remained acute, the nature of those parafictional fears changed over the years.

Robert Barnard has called the quarter of a century of Agatha Christie's *maîtrise* (1925-50) her 'classic period': it is certainly true that by the time the euphoria of second-world-war victories evaporated, the delicate balance she had hitherto maintained could be maintained no longer. By the time of his end, it was possible to read in Poirot the deep alterations of the world upon which he had intruded only briefly at the start: Agatha Christie continued to write, but she and her readers were now affected by other fears and other longings.

At the end of the forties, Poirot and Hastings met in *Curtain* for the last time at the place of their first meeting, Styles. By now, Agatha Christie was writing with a sense of many deaths; not only was the writer aware of her own future death—from now on, an awareness of the passing of familiar worlds imparts an unmistakable shade to her writing. The war collapsed many social structures that wishful thinking had supported beyond their term: already in *Five Little Pigs* (1943), Poirot had gone back through memory lanes of better known and better liked times. So doing, he was starting to express Christie's growing sense of dismay at the assertion and vulgarity of new money, the deterioration of values formerly held, knowledge previously shared, the anxiety of exile from old assumptions into a world of rapid and radical change, where social contact could be only tentative and tenuous.

By the end of the forties, Styles stands for much more than simply its own demise. There is much to be read into the fact that it is now a 'guest house' whose once 'old-fashioned large bedrooms had been partitioned off so as to make several smaller ones'. Along with comfort, a style has gone: it is now 'furnished in cheap modern style'. The water is lukewarm, the towels thin, and Hastings muses.

> I remembered the clouds of steam which had gushed from the hot tap of the one bathroom Styles had originally possessed, one of those bathrooms in which an immense bath with mahogany sides had reposed proudly in the middle of the bathroom floor. Remembered too the immense bath towels, and the frequent shining brass cans of boiling hot water that stood in one's old-fashioned basin.

Styles can survive its eviction from Edwardian times only by becoming a part of the new mercantile world. The class structure that once supported it (and its hot-water basins) no longer exists. Nowhere is this loss more apparent than in the efforts of the author to sustain her stock characters. They are still there, but their presence is shadowy and unsure to the extent that their supporting world has largely vanished. Gone is the ideal working class that gave the village its solid and immaculate underpinnings. Gone, as a matter of fact, is the village itself: 'I realised the passage of years. Styles St Mary was altered out of all recognition. Petrol stations, a cinema, two more inns and rows of council houses.' The gardens are overgrown and the tennis court has presumably moved out of the private park and into the public playground. Class stereotypes have been replaced by others for which there is as yet no mythology; it is difficult to maintain the old mainstays within such a world:

> He looked as though he had led an out-of-doors life, and he looked, too, the type of man that is becoming more and more rare, an Englishman of the old

school, straightforward, fond of out-of-doors life, and the kind of man who can command.

> I was hardly surprised when Colonel Luttrell introduced him as Sir William Booyd Carrington. He had been, I knew, Governor of a province in India, where he had been a signal success. He was also renowned as a first-class shot and big game hunter. The sort of man, I reflected sadly, that we no longer seemed to breed in these degenerate days.

These 'degenerate' days extend into other ethical and social areas: a new rudeness is now currently permissible ('His manners were not what one would call polished to anyone'), the mere surface of a deeper and more pervasive corruption: 'Norton, the gentle-hearted, loving man, was a secret sadist. He was an addict of pain, of mental torture. There has been an epidemic of that in the world of late years—*L'appétit vient en mangeant.*'

The very family is disintegrating. Parental authority is flouted Hastings' daughter tells him, when he tries to warn her about an obvious cad, 'I think you have a perfectly filthy mind.' And the generations look at each other with pitying contempt across the gap that separates them: 'So vulnerable they are, these children! So ready, though they do not recognise it that way, to take a *dare!*'

This is the atmosphere of the times after the rural dream has ceased to be possible (or better, once it is no longer possible to write about it). It informs the present with a sense of failure: 'That's the depressing part of places like this. Guest houses run by broken-down gentle-people. They're full of failures—of people who have never got anywhere and never will get anywhere—who have been defeated and broken by life.'

The end of possibility is heightened by a pervasive sense of what used to be: 'To me there was a charm in his slightly old-fashioned way of putting things. It conjured a picture of old-world charm and ease.' 'I saw the scene in my mind's eye. I could imagine Daisy Luttrell with a young saucy face and that smart tongue—so charming then, so apt to turn shrewish with the years.'

The stock character hardest to sustain in this altered world is undoubtedly Poirot himself. Of necessity, he is still the little man who speaks gallicized English, who brags (a little), whose grey cells work as hard as ever. But constrained by the mood of the times, a new Poirot displaces much of the old caricature—a more 'living' character (as are many of the other characters similarly affected), one burdened by the darkened world, a longing for the past, an unstated apprehension of tomorrow.

The Poirot who brought disturbance in his wake (like Chaucer's Pandarus—through his *book*), and then disappeared Pied-Piperlike, taking the disturbance and its causes with him, that Poirot could no longer be effectual within the circumstances of which Agatha Christie was now so keenly aware. Though he could still solve the crime, Poirot could no longer return a world bereft of former bounds or norms to a definitive closure or normalcy: today's disturbances were simply not what they used to be. And as Agatha Christie's reader intuited that worlds formerly conjured from a putative reality could no longer be sustained by that reality, that same post-war reader also knew that former small and disposable irritations caused by the bearded alien, the foreign and quirky detective, the transitory interloper, the outlandish fashion, were no longer there to be disposed of in a world that now lacked the normative criteria against which these minor annoyances were once stated: they were now supplanted by the more insidious malaise of being in a world that lacked those normative criteria.

The last Poirot is therefore an awkwardness, a necessary aggregate of former traits that are without resonance once the codes of class structures, of social mores, of ethical modes, are no longer what they appeared to have been at the time of his creation. The functional caricature now throbs with a consciousness of the times, a nostalgia and a gloom. And the loss of that functional caricature causes the purity of the detective story to be lost as well. The deranged heiress, the pilfering solicitor, the two-timing butler may be removed at the end, but in a world of far more insidious threats, their removal does not return the world to a pristine innocence, and the non-functional reality of the former caricature endures in the reader's enduring anxiety.

After Poirot's premature passing, Agatha Christie would resurrect him, off and on, for still another quarter of a century, even as she would Miss Marple through the depletion of rural possibilities. Dame Agatha tried valiantly to have her people swing with the new, as in *They Do It with Mirrors* (Marple, 1952), *Hickory, Dickory, Dock* (Poirot, 1955), *The Mirror Crack'd from Side to Side* (Marple, 1962), *Third Girl* (Poirot, 1966), but she did not feel any easier in those new spheres than did her protagonists. The best of her later work shows people who feel themselves as she does to be spiritual outcasts and who may find in their marginality a new acuity of detection, reading a more accurate palimpsest through the modern surface. But, in general, the difficulties evidenced in *Curtain* were simply repeated.

Why then her continuing popularity? A part of the answer was intuited by the directors (Sidney Lumet, Don Guillermin, Guy Hamilton) who have recently turned into films *Murder on the Orient Express, Death on the Nile, The Mirror Crack'd,* peopling them with old-time actors now seldom seen on the screen Lauren Bacall, Richard Widmark, Bette

Davis, David Niven, Angela Lansbury, or, in a new, Queen-Motherish avatar, the enduring Elizabeth Taylor. These actors represent the cinema of a shinier moment, over a third of a century ago, before they were swept aside by the new forms of the present cinema. Seeing them once again on the screen, we re-enter that world briefly. This is especially felicitous casting for Agatha Christie, since we now regress through her books to something more real than the times she described: the period pieces that those descriptions themselves have become now attract us. There may have been a time when Agatha Christie mediated for her reader unattainable worlds: now her archaic books have become those worlds. We acknowledge our present discontent in retrospections that make us smile at what once constituted the measure of our passing cares, the sense of how comfortable we felt in a world of referable absolutes (after all, Dame Agatha herself tells us in her autobiography that she came to the detective story out of a comforting sense that Evil could be hunted down and that Good would triumph—an avowal that explains not a little her somber mood within, and tenuous grasp on, the world that followed the second world war).

In that world, our present one, a residual pull of psychological gravity draws us to the evidence that we once had faith in the possibility of control, of knowledge and of the power of reason against the irrational. We are still drawn to the old writings of Agatha Christie.

David A. Fryxell (essay date November 1984)

SOURCE: "All about Agatha," in *Horizon,* Vol. 27, No. 9, November, 1984, pp. 42-5.

[*In the following essay, Fryxell argues that Christie's works have not been successfully adapted for film.*]

"Everybody loves a gossip," Agatha Christie once said by way of explaining her phenomenal popularity. That's why she thought her mysteries have outsold everything but the Bible and Shakespeare: people love to snoop into other people's lives. Christie let her readers snoop into lives—and deaths—ranging from those of the tea-cozy denizens of quaint English villages to the upper crust on board the Orient Express. And what better topic for really juicy gossip than murder?

The Public Broadcasting Service knows how popular the subject of murder—especially of the Agatha Christie variety—can be, as evidenced in the popularity of its "Mystery" series. Beginning November 29 (check local listings for exact times), "Mystery" presents five adaptations of Christie's "Tommy and Tuppence" mysteries. James Warwick and Francesca Annis star in the London Weekend Television productions of "Partners in Crime." Tommy Beresford and Prudence "Tuppence" Crowley were two old chums who stumbled into detection and, later in their fictional careers, into matrimony. The *New York Times* called their escapades "the merriest collection of detective stories it has been our good fortune to encounter." The series begins with the couple's takeover of a detective agency, and each segment solves a different mystery. And this series only begins to tap the vast resources of Agatha Christie fiction.

Certainly, few "gossips" have been as prolific or profitable as Agatha Christie. In over fifty-five years, until her death in 1976, she penned nearly one hundred mystery novels and short-story collections, a half-dozen romantic novels under the name Mary Westmacott, twenty-one plays, and a two-volume autobiography. Her publishers claim to have long ago lost count of Christie's sales; American paperback editions of her works have easily topped half a billion books. *The Murder of Roger Ackroyd,* generally conceded to be the cream of Christie, has alone sold over a million copies. Fans have followed their beloved Agatha in more than one hundred languages.

Her play *The Mousetrap* nightly adds to its record as the longest-running production in English theatrical history. The play has outlived eight of the newspapers that originally reviewed it in 1952. Impresario Peter Saunders, who had predicted a six-month run, has since said, "Just about everybody in England has seen it except the Queen, and she thinks she's seen it."

The only media the queen of crime fiction was never quite able to crack were motion pictures and television. With a few exceptions—the Oscar-nominated *Witness for the Prosecution* and the box-office smash *Murder on the Orient Express*—Christie's works and her popularity have stubbornly resisted translation to the screen. To disappointed fans and dismayed producers, that failure remains the greatest single mystery in the career of Dame Agatha Christie.

Only Hercule Poirot could have detected the potential for greatness in this utterly conventional Englishwoman. Born Agatha Mary Clarissa Miller at a Devonshire seaside resort in 1890, she never attended school; her mother taught her at home. In 1914, Agatha showed the first clue of a taste for a life more thrilling than church fetes and tea on the lawn, marrying a dashing pioneer in the Royal Flying Corps named Archie Christie. World War I swept Archie off to the skies and Agatha to a military hospital, where she assisted in the dispensary.

Two years before, Agatha's elder sister Madge had challenged her to write a detective story. In the dispensary, surrounded by poisons, Agatha decided to take her up on it. In the years and books to come, she would knock off victims by such esoteric means as a kitchen skewer, a bronze figure of Venus, an electrified chessboard, a surgical knife, and an antique grain mill-but poison always remained her favorite. (At least one real-life poisoner modeled his crime on a Christie plot, *The Pale Horse.*) Her first poisoning was *The Mysterious Affair at Styles,* written in 1915 but not published until 1920. Therein she gave the world the inimitable Hercule Poirot.

Recalling a colony of Belgian refugees she encountered at Devonshire, she made her man a retired Belgian police detective. As a contrast to his stature—"hardly five-foot-four"—she named him for the mighty Hercules. "Poirot," she said, just popped into her head.

As far as Christie was concerned, Poirot's first case would also be his last. She'd met her sister's dare and that was that. But when the book finally saw print, it made enough money to prod her to try another. In the following six years, she published seven books and set the mystery world on its ear with the revolutionary *The Murder of Roger Ackroyd.*

That same year, 1926, Christie created a real-life mystery by vanishing without explanation for ten days. When she reappeared claiming amnesia, cynics decried it as a publicity stunt. Others have blamed a breakdown triggered by the death of her mother and the revelation of her husband's infidelity; she'd checked into a spa under the name of her husband's mistress. The mystery of those blank ten days, never unraveled, inspired a semifictional book and a 1978 movie, *Agatha.* Despite a stellar cast featuring Vanessa Redgrave and Dustin Hoffman, the film (true to Christie form) failed to shine either with critics or at the box office.

After several years of depression, Christie indulged her life-long love of trains and an interest in ancient ruins with a jaunt to the Near East on the Orient Express. That led to a novel, *Murder on the Orient Express,* and to her second marriage, to the assistant head of the archaeological digs, Max Mallowan.

The 1930s introduced readers to Christie's second great sleuth, the spinsterish Miss Marple—inspired by Christie's grandmother—whose constant flurry of knitting needles camouflaged her true hobby, "the study of human nature." And the decade produced some of Christie's best mysteries: *The ABC Murders, Death on the Nile,* and *Ten Little Indians.*

She would churn out at least a book a year until her death. Christie likened her prodigious production to "a sausage machine, a perfect sausage machine"—and the readers ate it up. In 1954, the Mystery Writers of America honored her with their first Grand Master of Crime Award. The next year, *Witness for the Prosecution* won the New York Drama Critics Circle award for best foreign play, the only mystery ever to do so. (*The Mousetrap,* amazingly, had flopped on Broadway.) Though Christie was already the grande dame of mystery, the Queen made it official in 1971 by naming her a Dame of the British Empire.

Yet Dame Agatha, still an English country girl at heart, chafed under the burden of fame. "I still have that overlag of feeling that I am *pretending* to be an author," she complained. Shy with strangers, she refused to make speeches and dodged interviews. When Britain's Detection Club elected her president, she made a deputy propose all the toasts and introduce guests. Her work seemed to decline as her fame rose: Dilys Winn, founder of Manhattan's Murder Ink bookstore, rates Christie's ***Elephants Can Remember*** (1972) as one of the ten all-time worst mystery novels. And Christie, like Conan Doyle before her, longed to be rid of her most famous detective. She finally wrote Hercule Poirot off in 1940 in ***Curtain,*** but the book didn't see print until 1975.

Most agree Christie was the master plotter of the age; as reviewer Will Cuppy put it, "She's probably the best suspicion scatterer and diverter in the business." And Margaret Miller, admiring the devious scheme of ***Witness for the Prosecution,*** perhaps said it best for all Christie peers in the profession: "I knew she really had a twisted little mind. I wished I had thought of it."

Most agree Christie was the master plotter of the age; as reviewer Will Cuppy put it, "She's probably the best suspicion scatterer and diverter in the business."
—David A. Fryxell

A few carpers found Christie's elaborate plots all too bloodless, like "animated algebra." In a famous essay entitled "Who Cares Who Killed Roger Ackroyd?" Edmund Wilson railed, "You cannot read such a book, you run through it to see the problem worked out; and you cannot become interested in the characters, because they never can be allowed an existence of their own, even in a flat two dimensions, but have always to be contrived so that they can seem either reliable or sinister, depending on which quarter, at the moment, is to be baited for the reader's suspicion."

Not even Christie's most fervent partisans would lay much claim for her strictly literary ability. Asked about her writing style, Otto Penzler, owner of the Mysterious Book Shop in Manhattan, sputtered, "Writing *what?* Writing *what?* I don't think she had much of a 'writing style.' A lot of best-selling writers would have trouble getting an 'A' on a college paper, but they strike a common chord that defies explanation."

Nonetheless, Penzler made a stab at explanation. "Agatha Christie wasn't threatening to anybody. Picking up an Agatha Christie book is like putting on cuddly old slippers." Similarly, Anthony Le Jeune concluded in *The Spectator:* "The real secret of Agatha Christie . . . lies not in the carpentering of her plots, excellent though that is, but in the texture of her writing. . . . In a literary sense, she doesn't write particularly well. But there is another sense which for a writer of fiction is perhaps even more important. The ability to buttonhole a reader, to make, as Raymond Chandler put it, 'each page throw the hook for the next,' is a separate and by no means uncommon art."

Translating that art from the page to the screen is no mean feat, though that hasn't stopped directors and screenwriters from trying. They began in 1928, when both movies and Christie's reputation were young. The first Christie adaptation, like the latest, brought to life her third-string sleuths, Tommy and Tuppence. Christie introduced the happy-go-lucky pair in her second book, ***The Secret Adversary*** (1922), which in 1928 was made into a German film titled *Die Abenteuer Gmbh* (Adventures Inc.), not a resounding success.

The first English-language stab at a Christie film was *The Passing of Mr. Quinn,* based on a minor short story. Filmmakers finally discovered Hercule Poirot in *Alibi* (1931), the first of three movies starring Austin Trevor as the Belgian sleuth. Trevor, much too tall for Poirot, was supposedly cast because he could do a French accent. Evidently that skill was not enough; none of the British-made films was released in the United States and they've vanished since from the archives. The third, *Lord Edgeware Dies,* would be the last attempt at portraying Poirot for thirty years.

A Christie film didn't cross the Atlantic until 1937, when *Love from a Stranger* paired Ann Harding and Basil Rathbone in an adaptation of the story "Philomel Cottage." Eight more years passed before anyone tried again.

Then, at last, Christie had something of a hit. *And Then There Were None,* adapted from ***Ten Little Indians,*** set ten familiar stars on a remote island and bumped them off one by one. Critics and audiences liked it enough to encourage two remakes (1965 and 1975), both titled *Ten Little Indians,* though with success that dwindled over time as rapidly as the number of survivors in the plot.

But back in the postwar years, it seemed as though the Christie puzzle had been cracked. When *The Mousetrap* hit pay dirt on the London stage, Romulus Films snapped up the movie rights—accepting the stipulation that ***The Mousetrap*** couldn't be made until six months after the play closed. They're still waiting. In the meantime, though, ***Witness for the Prosecution*** went from Broadway to Hollywood under the talented direction of Billy Wilder. He assembled an impressive cast: Charles Laughton, Marlene Dietrich, Tyrone Power, and Elsa Lanchester. To further boost interest, public relations flacks hung a Secrecy Pledge outside each movie house where the film opened; everyone who bought a ticket had to swear not to reveal whodunit. The ploy drew audiences and the picture drew six Oscar nominations.

Yet the only follow-up to this success was a minor film called *The Spider's Web,* also adapted from a Christie play. Made in England in 1960, it was never even released in the United States.

Moviemakers went back to square one in 1962, trying to break the jinx with a series of five movies about (at last) Miss Marple. The draw here was not Christie as much as it was the formidable Margaret Rutherford as Miss Marple. Though utterly wrong physically for the slim, spinsterish Marple (Christie said of Rutherford, "To me, she's always looked like a bloodhound"), Rutherford brought enough verve to the role to carry it through four of the planned five films. She made *Murder, She Said; Murder at the Gallop; Murder Most Foul;* and *Murder Ahoy!* before increasing silliness and decreasing ticket sales cut the series short. Only the first derived from an actual Miss Marple novel. Two were sleuth and sex-change operations from Poirot books; an offended Christie admitted, "I get an unregenerate pleasure when I think they're not being a success." The last was an original screenplay, of which Christie clucked, "It got very bad reviews, I'm pleased to say."

The movies finally returned to the real thing—Hercule Poirot as himself—in *The Alphabet Murders* (1966, based on *The ABC Murders*). Originally intended as a Zero Mostel vehicle, the production languished for two years because Christie, from bitter experience, objected to the script. It was finally made with Tony Randall heavily made up—though not heavily enough to shield him from the critics who branded the film a slapstick travesty.

After a non-Poirot flop titled *Endless Nights* (one reviewer wrote, "This movie wasn't released—it escaped"), Poirot and Christie finally made it big on-screen *with Murder on the Orient Express* in 1974. Director Sidney Lumet spared no expense in recreating the lavish look of a bygone era, constructing his own Orient Express at Elstree Studios near London. The all-star cast of suspects—Lauren Bacall, Richard Widmark, John Gielgud, Sean Connery, Wendy Hiller, Vanessa Redgrave, Ingrid Bergman (who won an Oscar as best supporting actress)—overshadowed Albert Finney as Poirot, which was perhaps just as well. *Murder on the Orient Express* made a killing; it was the most profitable wholly British-financed film to date.

The same producers hired director John Guillermin to make more box-office magic with *Death on the Nile.* He rounded up another cast of heavyweights, substituted Peter Ustinov as Poirot, and spent seven weeks on location in Egypt. The film's New York opening coincided with ticket sales for the Metropolitan Museum's King Tut show; then *Death on the Nile* went back in the can for two months until the Tut extravaganza actually opened. With a little help from Tut, it did well enough to inspire another Ustinov outing as Poirot, *Evil under the Sun*—more posh locales, more name actors, but also more labored.

In the meantime, director Guy Hamilton had taken another crack at bringing Miss Marple to the screen, this time with Angela Lansbury in *The Mirror Crack'd.* Elizabeth Taylor and Kim Novak, as rival movie stars, turned in their best work in years.

Television has since brought a few minor Christies to life in made-for-television movies and in a series of short stories on PBS's "Mystery." Amazingly, there has never been a commercial-network series based on Christie's characters.

Otto Penzler doesn't think the mysterious record of Christie works on screen is so strange at all. "To be fair, it's very difficult to put a good detective story on screen and make a good detective movie," he observed. "Most of what happens is cerebral—observing clues, making deductions—and that's hard to portray in an exciting manner on screen. It's just a different medium. You can't translate popularity to screen necessarily, and it's a mistake to try to make analogies between the two forms. A very ordinary book can be made into a great movie, and vice versa."

Christie herself wondered why she allowed her books to be ravaged on the screen. But, for Christie's fans, hope—like murder—springs eternal. They keep tuning in, knowing that every Christie puzzle is solved eventually—isn't it?

Earl F. Bargainnier (essay date Winter 1987)

SOURCE: "The Poems of Agatha Christie," in *Journal of Popular Culture,* Vol. 21, No. 3, Winter, 1987, pp. 103-10.

[*In the following essay, Bargainnier analyzes Christie's collection of poetry, discussing what her poems reveal about her personality.*]

In her autobiography Agatha Christie wrote, "The creative urge can come out in any form: in embroidery, in cooking of interesting dishes, in painting, drawing and sculpture, in composing music, as well as in writing books and stories. The only difference is that you can be a great deal more grand about some of these things than others." Christie was never "grand" about her detective fiction, and was even less so about her poetry. Yet in 1973, three years before her death, she permitted a small volume of her "collected" poems to be published. Christie's position as the most popular British writer ever deserves some analysis of her poems and their relationship, though slight, to her fiction.

She only gave a page and a half of over five hundred pages of *An Autobiography* to her poetry, but that small amount indicates both her modesty and pride. Saying that she wrote poetry early, she conceded that "some of my earlier examples are unbelievably awful." She then unfairly to herself quoted one written at the age of eleven:

> I know a little cowslip and a pretty flower too,
> Who wished she was a bluebell and had a robe of blue.

Christie's comment on those lines was "*Could* anything be more suggestive of a complete lack of literary talent?" (178-79). But she also wrote the following:

> By the age of seventeen or eighteen, however, I was doing better. I wrote a series of poems on the Harlequin legend: Harlequin's song, Columbine's, Pierrot, Pierrette, etc. I sent one or two poems to *The Poetry Review.* I was very pleased when I got a guinea prize. After that, I won several prizes and also had poems printed there. I felt very proud of myself when I was successful. I wrote quite a lot of poems from time to time. A sudden excitement would come over me and I would rush off to write down what I felt gurgling round in my mind. I had no lofty ambitions. An occasional prize in *The Poetry* Review was all I asked (179).

She then chose to quote in its entirety her poem "Down in the Wood," commenting that it "is not bad; at least it has something of what I wanted to express" (179).

First place in *Poems* is given to that "series of poems on the Harlequin legend": the ten which make up **"A Masque of Italy."** This work and twenty-five other poems constitute "Volume I," those originally published as *The Road of Dreams* in 1924. "Volume II" adds twenty-seven others, apparently written between then and 1960, for the last poem is entitled **"Picnic 1960."** The only other dates given are in Volume I: **"World Hymn 1914"** and **"Easter 1918."** However many poems Christie may have written, for her to have chosen for publication only sixty two from an entire lifetime, shows remarkable restraint, for by 1973 she could have published anything she wanted. Obviously she did not "work" at poetry as she did her detective fiction; poetry was a personal pleasure created by that "sudden excitement" that would come over her.

In form Christie's poems are traditional. There are sonnets and various stanzaic patterns, as well as freely metered works. Except for seven ballads, the poems are brief lyrics, nearly all between twelve and forty lines. She was fond of refrains, alliteration, and incremental repetition, and her favorite type of thyme was the couplet. She was equally adept at both short and long lines, but usually used tetrameter and pentameter. The general tone of the poems is reminiscent of such poets of the 1890s and early twentieth century as Ernest Dowson, Arthur Symons, Alfred Noyes, Walter de la Mare, and James Elroy Flecker—the last of whose "Gates of Damascus" provided the title of her last written novel: *Postern of Fate.* The ballads resemble those of G. K. Chesterton. With only one or two exceptions, Christie's poems could have been written before 1920. They are Romantic and Georgian in spirit: modernism is absent.

Her subjects are also Romantic. The majority of the poems fall into one of three broad subject areas. First are eighteen concerned with some form of the supernatural: magic, fairies, enchantment or dream worlds. The second group, her love poems, are, with the exception of those addressed to Sir Max Mallowan, her second husband, most often melancholy, and they number nineteen. (There is some overlapping between these two groups, as love is at times treated supernaturally, and the supernatural poems often have a romantic "plot.") Then there are six poems of place, particularly places in the Middle East, which she visited so often on Mallowan's archaeological expeditions. The other nineteen poems vary considerably, but most are reflective or meditative lyrics, ranging from thoughts on such huge topics as **"Beauty"** to the light **"Picnic 1960."** That gentle melancholy noted of her love poems, in fact, dominates most of the others as well; it is the single most distinguishing feature of Christie's poetry. On the other hand, a few show the wry humor evident in many of her novels; examples are **"In Baghdad"** and **"To a Beautiful Old Lady."** More of such works and less of such overly sentimental ones as **"Wild Roses"** and such obscurely allegorical ones as **"A Palm Tree in the Desert"** would be welcome—at least to this reader.

The supernatural poems range from such brief ones as **"Enchantment,"** a variation on "La Belle Dame Sans Merci," and another on the Undine legend to **"A Masque of Italy"** (to be considered later). There are three concerned with the world of dreams: **"The Dream Spinners," "The Dream City,"** and **"The Road of Dreams,"** the last of which provided the title for Christie's 1924 volume of poems. Of the three it most successfully captures the mysterious nature of the subject and has an appropriately "dreamy" tone. A poem that seems to echo the works of Sir James M. Barrie is **"From a Grown-up to a Child."** It is light verse, but its combination of baby girls and fairies is still too cute for comfort; for example, the last stanza:

The fairies stay awake all night
So little girls need take no fright,
For if the night light *does* go out
They know the fairies are about,
And they can heat their silky wings—
They *are* so kind, these darling things!

The two best of this group are **"Down in the Wood"** and **"Dark Sheila."** As already noted, Christie chose **"Down in the Wood"** as her only poem to appear in *An Autobiography.* It is also a dream poem, presenting a surrealistic world where "Beauty is left in the wood!," but *"naked Fear passes out of the wood!"* (It needs to be read in its entirety for its eeriness to be appreciated; see *Poems,* 53, or *An Autobiography,* 179.) **"Dark Sheila"** is one of Christie's most successful ballads presenting a brooding narrative of dark Sheila's grief at desertion by one lad who left her for another girl and the unexplained departure of a second lad who "loved you from the very hour he met you." Both now plead with her to let them return, but she does not answer, for she has found "a Shadow Lad"—quite clearly *death*—with whom to roam. The last stanza gives a partial idea of the Brontesque quality:

> But Sheila, dark Sheila, is out upon the moorland.
> She's out upon the moorland where the heather
>   meets the sky!
> And the lads shall never find her, for there's one
>   walks by her side there,
> A Stranger Lad, a Shadow Lad, who would not be
>   denied there . . .
> She turned her to his calling
> As the shades of night were falling,
> She turned her to his calling
> As the shades of night were falling.
> She turned her to his calling . . . and she answered
>   to his Cry.

Poems of love form the largest single group of Christie's poetry, especially if poems within the other two categories which deal with it in some way are also included. Most of these poems fit into four subgroups. Least important are those based upon historical or legendary figures, such as **"Count Fersen to the Queen"** (Marie Antoinette), **"Beatrice Passes,"** or the wistfully beautiful **"Isolt of Brittany."** Next are poems of dead or lost love, varying from the sentimental **"Wild Roses"** through the elegiac **"Love Passes"**—an excellent Italian sonnet—to the stoic **"The Wanderer."** Most original of these poems of dead love is the almost conversational **"I Wore My New Canary Suit":**

> I wore my new canary suit
> To go and meet my love,
> We talked and talked of everything
> In earth and heaven above.

> I went again to meet my love.
> The years had flitted by,
> I wore my old canary suit
> To bid my love goodbye.
> I took it to a jumble sale
> But brought it back once more
> And hung it on an inner peg
> Within my cupboard door.
> I shall not meet my love again
> For he is in his grave.
> So—I've an old moth-eaten suit
> And he is young and brave. . . .

The third type, and related to the second, might be called cries from the heart; they are somewhat surprising outbursts of passion. The two which stand out are **"Progression"** and **"The Lament of the Tortured Lover."** The first presents in very short lines, at times only one word, the development and end of a love affair through the progression of the seasons. The emotion may seem uncontrolled to some readers, but that was probably Christie's purpose. **"The Lament of the Tortured Lover"** is a plea from a lover who cannot express in mere words the depth of his feeling though his loved one demands overt statements. A poem that one hardly expects from the reticent Christie, it ranks among her most effective in paradoxically using words to state that words can never fully express love, as a few lines demonstrate:

> I have said I adore you;
> I have said it—I have said it.
> I am sick of words
> Of everlasting meaningless words.
> I love you—I love you—that parrot cry.
> Cannot flesh take flesh in silence?
> But no—you will not have it so.
> You were made for incense,
> For burning words,
> Words—words—words—going on through the
>   night . . .
> While I worship the pulse in your throat
> And the curve of your breast. . . .

Four other love poems by their placement together and their content indicate that they were written to Christie's second husband when he was away from her: **"To M.E.L.M. in Absence,"** **"Remembrance,"** **"A Choice,"** and **"My Flower Garden."** Each indicates her deep love for him and her anxious desire to be with him again. The most personal of her poems, they are testimony to over forty years of happy marriage, the nature of which is shown in lines five to twelve of the English sonnet **"To M.E.L.M.":**

> *Friendship* is ours, and still in absence grows.
> No dearer friend I own, so close, so kind.
> *Knowledge* is yours, from you to me it flows

And I have loved your wise and gentle mind.
Beauty we share, a white magnolia tree
Rooted in England brings you to my side,
And Roman columns rising from the sea
Must surely bring remembrance with the tide.

The six poems of place require little comment. **"Ctesiphon"** is an Italian sonnet on the ancient city, contrasting its "loneliness of naked beauty" seen on "one enchanted day" to the "Midget Man who wars and dies." **"The Nile"** is simply an evocation of a visit to Egypt, as **"Dartmoor"** is of that English region. **"In Baghdad,"** one of Christie's wry commentaries on human existence, uses first an image of melons covered with flies; then comes the barb:

God sees the world like a round green melon,
And then he see the flies
Buzzing and settling . . .
But, being merciful,
He looks away and says,
'I will try not to think of these human beings . . .'
Allah is very merciful.

Nearly as effective is **"To a Cedar Tree,"** in which she juxtaposes the cedar's Lebanese origin with its now being "in my garden by the Thames." Asking it, "Do you remember Lebanon", she writes,

Gracious you stand
With smooth clipped lawn all around you
And an English herbaceous border
Flaunting its bloom on a summer's day.
You are part of England now:
'Tea will be served on the lawn
Under the Cedar tree.'

When Christie was able to overcome the obvious and the sentimental through pointed humor or ironic reflection as in these last two poems, she could give readers that little shock that is poetry's essence.

Unfortunately that does not happen enough in the other miscellaneous poems. The sentimentality of **"The Bells of Brittany"** (a child is born, its mother dies) or the obviousness of **"World Hymn 1914"** ("The God of War is nigh! . . . Call to the God of Peace.") vitiate whatever actual feeling may be their motivation. Others that fail in similar ways are **"Spring," "The Sculptor,"** and **"Heritage,"** the last an example of the open-road school so popular in the early twentieth century. Differently unsatisfactory is the anti-miscegenation **"Racial Musings,"** which would better have been omitted—however Christie meant it. Just missing falling into that overly sentimental category, but still missing it, is **"Hawthorn Trees in Spring: A Lament of Women,"** apparently written during World War II. Contrast-ing the blooming trees to both human birth and wartime death, as well as the earthbound role of women as mothers versus the airborne freedom of men, the poem gently laments mankind's transience while affirming the continuity of natural existence. The first three sections read:

How heavy are the hawthorn trees,
Weighed down with blossom,
Laden with heavy perfume,
Like the bodies and souls of women
Heavy with fruit of men's desire
Or with their own desire in Spring.
Up in the sky, divorced from earth,
The aeroplanes pass
Roaring along on their gallent adventures;
They are the souls of men
Set free from earth,
Set free from the load of blossom
And the cloying perfumes of Spring.
They fly and are free.
Yet at the last they must return,
Fall back to earth,
Gliding down presently and skimming the ground
Or falling in vivid flame,
Yet still returning to earth.

A poem about World War I, **"Easter 1918,"** and another called **"A Passing"** also avoid the sentimental when it could easily be present, for they concern death. Both express a theme occasionally found in Christie's fiction: that death is not an end. The poems conclude almost identically, the first with "Which some call Death—and others name—Release!" and the second with "We call it—Death!/Nor dare to say—Escape!" Finally, two of the ballads demand mention. **"Elizabeth of England"** is a monologue in which the queen meditates on her heritage, her battles with Spain, her hatred of Mary Stuart, the glory of her reign, and her childlessness. It concludes: *"And I shall share in my Children's fame/Who have never a child of my own . . ."* Though less a psychological study than a survey of major elements of Elizabeth I's long reign, the tone is not rhetorical, but spirited, thus evoking the boisterous age it presents. **"The Ballad of the Flint"** is a rather bloodthirsty account of a Viking raid on a Celtic tribe, the stealing of the tribe's priestess, her rescue, and the retribution for the sacrilege, ending with the priestess executing the Viking chief, with whom she has fallen in love, and then committing suicide. It is essentially a short story told in forty-five hexameter-heptameter lines, with the unusual stanza rhyming pattern of *aabcb,* with every fourth line containing internal rhyme ("In confusion there we found them, and we seized and held and bound them").

It would be an exercise in futility to try to find many implicit or explicit relationships between these essentially personal poems and Christie's fiction. That poems such as

"Dark Sheila" or "Down in the Woods" deal with mysterious fear, an element often present in detective fiction, is hardly enough evidence on which to draw parallels, nor is the fact that there are poems on Baghdad, the Nile, and Dartmoor and also novels set in those places. "Hymn to Ra" in Volume I shows her early interest in ancient Egypt, but *Death Comes as the End* (1944), her mystery novel set in that world was first suggested to her by one of her husband's colleagues nearly twenty years later. The poems are filled with her interests, likes, and dislikes, and some of the same are bound also to appear in her fiction; that is all that need be said.

Poems is the least known of Agatha Christie's some eighty books. Few of the billions of readers of her fiction are even aware of its existence. Yet one can imagine her pleasure on its publication, a pleasure probably greater than that on the appearance of her fiftieth or sixtieth novel, for it is a distillation of her most private thoughts and emotions, as lyric poetry always is for its writer.
—*Earl F. Bargainnier*

There is one major exception, however, and that is the obvious connection between "A Masque of Italy" and the Harley Quin stories, for both have the same source: her childhood attendance at Christmas pantomimes. The characters of the Italian *commedia dell'arte* developed into stylized stage characters of English pantomime in the eighteenth century, and by the end of the nineteenth, Harlequin, Columbine, and their cohorts were standard figures of the annual Christmas pantomime: fairly-like creatures not bound by time or space. Thus the pantomime—"A Masque"—Quin link is clear. The immortal Harlequin of "A Masque of Italy" loses Columbine to the mortal Pierrot, but she in turn loses her immortality and dies. Pierrot is last seen as an old man living with an elderly Pierrette and awaiting his own death. The ten songs which recount the story are Christie the poet at her best, and it is not surprising that she won prizes for them. The songs are simple, direct, yet individualized for each character; that typical melancholy is ever-present; and the supernatural is accepted as a given without explanation or apology. Similarly, Harley Quin is a figure of the supernatural. He acts through the mortal Mr. Satterthwaite to help lovers and solve mysteries. In such stories as "Harlequin's Lane" and "The Harlequin Tea Set," Quin is presented as the messenger—if not the personification—of death, but death as a kind of ultimate fulfillment of life. The shadowy, all knowing Quin, who like his stage counterpart can appear or disappear at will, is a deliberately enigmatic figure. He is, without question, Christie's most

unusual detective; she wrote in *An Autobiography* that the Quin stories were her favorites and that she only wrote one when she felt like it, and added that Quin "was a kind of carryover for me from my early poems in the Harlequin and Columbine series" (420). Perhaps the Quin stories were her own favorite detective works because in them she came closer than in any others to writing like a poet.

Poems is the least known of Agatha Christie's some eighty books. Few of the billions of readers of her fiction are even aware of its existence. Yet one can imagine her pleasure on its publication, a pleasure probably greater than that on the appearance of her fiftieth or sixtieth novel, for it is a distillation of her most private thoughts and emotions, as lyric poetry always is for its writer. Christie was a very private person, and this little volume, whatever its faults, provides a new perspective on her personality—one quite different from the public image of "mistress of mystery."

Michele Slung (essay date 1988)

SOURCE: "Let's Hear It for Agatha Christie: A Feminist Appreciation," in *The Sleuth and the Scholar: Origins, Evolution, and Current Trends in Detective Fiction*, Greenwood Press, 1988, pp. 63-8.

[*In the following essay, Slung argues that the female characters in Christie's mysteries provide role models for women.*]

With all due respect to P. D. James and Ruth Rendell—to name two writers who have resisted inheriting the queenly mantle of Agatha Christie from over-eager blurb writers—there is no doubt in my mind that these women never should have been offered the honor in the first place. Bestsellerdom (in the case of James) or simply being British, acclaimed, and prolific (Rendell) just isn't enough to warrant succession to Christie's literary throne.

I should add here that in a recent *Time* magazine cover story (the international edition—it was Stephen King that week stateside), James has modified her previously stated distaste for Christie somewhat. "I write much better than she did" was how she'd once dismissed the comparison to Dame Agatha in an interview. Now, however, she has this to say: "She is a literary conjurer; she shuffles her cards with these clever hands and lays the cards face down. Each time you think you know the right one. And each time, you are wrong."

That's certainly diplomatic, carefully conveying admiration but indicating, nonetheless, how she perceives as *limited* the nature of Christie's achievement. What's wrong with her assessment, however, is that it, too, is limited. As she slips sidewise to prevent the royal Christie mantle from being draped on what *Time* refers to as "her unwilling shoulders," James, in an effort to protect herself, neglects the bigger picture.

By this I mean that Agatha Christie, with all her flaws intact, is *sui generis*. And P. D. James, for all her virtues, never will be. Around the world, in dozens of languages, for several generations of readers, the two words "Agatha Christie" are synonymous with "mystery story" or "detective fiction." I find I am even oddly moved when I think of this—that such an unlikely and private woman is writ so large in the minds of so many.

From Oz as a child, I moved on to River Heights, where Nancy Drew dwelled with Carson, Hannah Gruen, and the rest; but quite soon, there came a moment when old attics and crumbling castles lost their appeal, when I stopped caring about the next annual appearance of Carolyn Keene's plucky and boringly perfect heroine. (This isn't the moment to address the issue, but I want to go on record here as saying that taking away Nancy's frock and her roadster and giving her self-doubt, Calvin Klein jeans, and a Honda is as much of a defilement as putting a modern facade on any historic building, and I think the National Trust should have intervened.)

What happened was that I'd come upon a copy of *The Mysterious Affair at Styles*. In reading it, I'd entered a new stage. The following two or three years were spent tracking down the fifty or so Christie titles then available.

I also admit, without embarrassment, that, in the quarter of a century since, there have been almost no other authors—no matter how ardently I enjoy them or how avidly I seek out their various books—about whom that same thrilling joy accompanies the discovery of an unread volume by them.

And, of course, when I wasn't reading James or Proust, I went on from Christie to Doyle and Stout, Sayers and Allingham, Hammett and Chandler, Innes and Crispin, Lockridge and Rice, and so forth. Eventually, despite concerned college professors who steered my attention to Edmund Wilson's "Who Cares Who Killed Roger Ackroyd?" I turned my innocent amateur pastime into the sordid profession I demonstrate to you today: I became a commentator on the genre.

So I applaud Agatha Christie, and I'd even be willing to debate the proposition that we might not be convened here today had Agatha Christie never existed. Let me detail some of the reasons why I feel Agatha Christie is important to feminist readers and why I think it's so very wrong for seri-

ous critics to take a condescending or contemptuous tone when discussing her.

No one that I've ever come across has taken up the topic of role models in the work of Agatha Christie. Yet, in a rather obscure work of hers—I say "obscure" because it doesn't feature one of her series characters, such as Hercule Poirot, Miss Jane Marple, or Tommy and Tuppence Beresford, and because it contains no famous plot tricks—there's a heroine whose attitude and behavior, whose imaginative zest for life has continued to influence me in all the years since I first read about her. The book is *They Came to Baghdad*, the 1951 Christie; its heroine is the irrepressible Victoria Jones.

An adventuress in the making, now an unemployed typist with no outlet for her exotic yearnings, Victoria's "principal defect," Christie tells us, "was a tendency to tell lies at both opportune and inopportune moments. The superior fascination of fiction to fact was always irresistible to [her]. She lied with fluency, ease, and artistic fervour." (One is reminded of Saki's daughter of the house in "The Open Window." Romance at short notice was her specialty, too.)

The wonderful thing, when you think of Christie's retiring, matronly presence, her prim, perfected public self (like the Queen Mum—if the Queen Mum wrote best-selling thrillers), is that this opening portrait of the mendacious Victoria is affectionate and anticipatory of the fun to come, not at all disapproving. (And here I should add that it's not Victoria's fibs that inspired me, but rather, as Christie describes it, "her optimism and force of character.") What a flair for life Victoria has! And how beautifully flexible she is, when opportunity knocks. "One never knew, she always felt, what might happen."

This philosophy is definitely not that of a passive or retiring stay-at-home! And, since Victoria does wind up saving civilization as we know it, then settles herself being useful on an archeological dig—as Christie herself was, accompanying her second husband—it's very easy to imagine the sixty-one-year-old Agatha recasting her youth in the figure of such a heroine. "To Victoria an agreeable world would be where tigers lurked in the Strand and dangerous bandits infested Tooting." Now, isn't this just a penny-dreadful way of describing the world that Agatha Christie, living most of her life in luxurious suburban villas, could inhabit by writing thrillers?

Since Christie's notoriety, in 1926, when the strain of the breakup of her first marriage led to her mysterious disappearance, she shunned publicity and lived amazingly away from the claims of celebrity for someone of such global renown. Yet her books are filled with all manner of surrogates, highly active and ingenious female characters—no Nero

Wolfes they, sitting home and getting clues secondhand—whether the redoubtable Jane Marple (more about whom in a moment), clever Tuppence Beresford, or the booming-voiced Ariadne Oliver who writes mystery stories about a peculiar Finnish (read Belgian) sleuth. In fact, in the 1936 Christie, *Cards on the Table,* this selfsame Ariadne Oliver, who voices many of Christie's own sentiments about writing and the writer's life, is depicted as a "hot-headed feminist"—one who wishes, despairingly, that a woman was the head of Scotland Yard!

It's true, to contradict myself briefly, that when we first meet Miss Jane Marple, in 1928, in *The Thirteen Problems* (known in this country as *The Tuesday Club Murders*), the format in which she functions is a sedentary one. Not un-Wolfean, that is. An informal club of village friends is attempting to stump each other with curious outcomes to curious tales, and the placidly knitting Miss Marple, with her black lace mittens, fluffy white hair, and faded blue eyes, is only included as an afterthought, so as not to hurt her feelings. However, alert to every human foible, she outguesses her fellow members every time.

But, to look at this debut in another light, Agatha Christie herself, whom most of us now see only as the distinctly dowager type she was from the 1950s onwards, was just a mid-thirtyish young woman when the character of Jane Marple was forming in her mind. I find it distinctly praiseworthy that, for her, a true heroine was not bound by cliches of age or physical attractiveness. Christie also puts across the idea of Miss Marple's worth continually in sly ways, even letting Miss M. herself do a bit of horn-tooting from time to time. In "Miss Marple Tells a Story," written when Christie was in her forties and hardly tottering out to pasture, here's how the tale begins:

> "I don't think I've ever told you, my dears . . . about a rather curious little business that happened some years ago now. I don't want to seem *vain* in any way—of course I know that in comparison with you young people I'm not clever at all—Raymond writes those modern books all about rather unpleasant young men and women—and Joyce paints those very remarkable pictures of square people with curious bulges on them—very clever of you, my dear, but as Raymond always says (only quite kindly, because he is the kindest of nephews) I am hopelessly Victorian. . . . Now let me see, what was I saying? Oh yes—that I didn't want to appear vain—but I couldn't help being just a teeny weeny bit pleased with myself, because, just by applying a little common sense, I believe I really did solve a problem that had baffled cleverer heads than mine. Though really I should have thought the whole thing was obvious from the beginning. . . ."

Anna Katharine Green had Miss Amelia Butterworth; Dorothy L. Sayers, Miss Climpson; Patricia Wentworth, Miss Silver, and so forth. Jane Marple, thus, isn't—as my mother would say—the "only pebble on the beach." But isn't there something *enormous* about her? Just as Christie is for many millions of people synonymous with the mystery story, Miss Marple is the archetype of the elderly lady detective. And to move on from Nancy Drew to Jane Marple, as I did, so long ago, gave me something to grow up to. Not a flat earth up to seventy! With her own unfortunate experience—the faithless Archie Christie—in mind, Agatha Christie kept a cynical view toward men and marriage for most of her oeuvre. Yet in the first Miss Marple novel, *Murder at the Vicarage* (1930), Christie allows Miss Marple to reveal her method in these words: "It's really what people call intuition. Intuition is like reading a word without having to spell it out. A child can't do that, because it has had so little experience. But a grownup person knows the word because he's seen it before. You catch my meaning?"

Please notice that the word "women's" does not figure here. Her way of *knowing* is a human trait, regardless of sex but dependent on experience. Understanding people as she does she could be a shaman or a psychotherapist, but the seemingly conventional Agatha Christie was writing detective stories and so Jane Marple plies her perceptivity—that is, she detects—within those conventions.

Even if it's clear that the "psychopathology of everyday life" is what she's dealing with, still such case histories as **"The Bloodstained Pavement"** won't get the respect of "Combined Parapraxes," nor will **"The Affair at the Bungalow"** be accorded the stature of "Bungled Actions." Yet, if Sherlock Holmes could meet Freud, why not Jane Marple?

The problems of attempting to gain for Agatha Christie the vast honor I think she deserves—from feminists and misogynists alike, as well as Mr. and Ms. Intelligent Reader—are always being brought home to me. Just a few nights ago, I was at a dinner party and mentioned that I was working on this paper. But before I could explain, a Renaissance historian who was listening interrupted, claiming, "I can't read Agatha Christie. She's too tedious."

Sure, and for millions of others, she's anything but. And for many, many more, who've read her and thought about her work, their enthusiasm, if it exists, is often tempered by reservations about her blimpish social attitudes, her reliance on stereotypes when casting most of her parts, her less than limpid style, the repetition of some of her conjurer's tricks, her Never-Never Land of village teas and Blue Trains speeding through the night. Yet one *could* reply to those snooty folk who prefer Lord Peter to Hercule Poirot (and I grant you he's sexier, at least in his later incarnation) that Dorothy L. Sayers is only the Thinking Person's Agatha Christie!

I began this talk by deploring the comparison of such current writers as Ruth Rendell and P. D. James to Agatha Christie. They may believe it reflects ill on them; instead, I feel they should be so lucky. In regard to their series characters, Inspector Wexford and Adam Dalgliesh, I challenge anyone to be able to give me a really evocative word picture of either of these men. Will their first novels still be in print, translated into nearly as many languages as people speak, over half a century after original publication? I even have to ask, is it likely there'll be a cargo cult in Papua, New Guinea with either of them the object of Melanesian veneration? Finally, would anyone write an essay asking "Who Cares Who Killed . . . ?" Fill in the name of any victim in any of their books, if you can.

Moreover, no one can or need do again what Agatha Christie did in this century (something Anna Katharine Green is credited with doing in the previous one). She brought mass respectability to the genre, with an audience that ranged from presidents and queens to shop clerks, from nursery school teachers to university presidents.

I hope you understand that I'm not trying to equate ubiquity with quality, popularity with literary greatness. No, I'm talking about the kind of impact that's simply so large we can barely see it. Agatha Christie may not be Shakespeare, but then she's not Mary Roberts Rinehart or Judith Krantz either. She's a legend, not a mere phenomenon.

Rendell and James and their ilk, don't mistake me, are certainly truly talented writers, but in the end, genius, like murder, will out.

Nicholas Birns and Margaret Boe Birns (essay date 1990)

SOURCE: "Agatha Christie: Modern and Modernist," in *The Cunning Craft: Original Essays on Detective Fiction and Contemporary Literary Theory,* Western Illinois University, 1990, pp. 120-34.

[*In the following essay, the reviewers argue that Christie's writing is more complex than critics credit her.*]

Agatha Christie's position in the critical discourse surrounding the detective story is an anomalous one. While Christie is the best known and most popular writer of detective fiction in this century, she has rarely been analyzed with the kind of rigor and attention that such a position would ordinarily entail. Christie's relationship to modernism, the dominant discourse of the "high" literature of her day, has been particularly slighted. Christie's position as serious artist, as not only chronologically modern but aesthetically modern-ist, is obscured by the view of her work that has now become canonical. This normative position on Christie is crystallized in David Grossvogel's *Mystery and Its Fictions.* Grossvogel accuses Christie of a formulaic certainty, of a nostalgic love for a "bucolic . . . England" [43] and a controlled, cerebral puzzle-solving mentality. Writing with many of the presuppositions of the "critics of consciousness," Grossvogel opposes this to the unpredictable, truly existential mystery to be found in Sophocles, Dostoevsky, the Book of Job. Confining himself only to Christie's first book, ***The Mysterious Affair at Styles*** [1920] (in itself a misleading procedure, rather like analyzing the significance of Goethe by analyzing only *Götz von Berlichingen*), Grossvogel accuses Christie of "functional stylization", of creating characters who are only "shadows" and "do not exist" . Christie's characters, as individuals, hardly demonstrate the heart-wrenching range of psychological attributes, Grossvogel hints, to be found in such characters as Roquentin and Raskolnikov.

This existential denigration is transferred onto a more discursive level in other, self-consciously postmodern and poststructural treatments of Christie and the "classic" detective story paradigm which she did so much to foreground. William W. Stowe, in his essay "From Semiotics to Hermeneutics," denounces Christie's paradigm as imprisoned by Cartesian methodological certainties, and, as has been done many times, opposes it to the more "open" and "undecidable" realm of the hard-boiled story. This opposition has been characteristic of much criticism of the detective story, yet its overarching assumptions have all too infrequently been scrutinized. The casualness with which Christie is dismissed as "formulaic" whereas the hard-boiled writers are praised for giving us full unhindered access to our primal selves is untenable in the face of contemporary discussions about the constructed nature of all fictional representation.

It is for example questionable whether the full reverberations of developments in literary theory up to and including the work of Jacques Derrida have yet been accommodated in these interpretations. Derrida's work comes out of a Heideggerean background similar to that of the Geneva critics who so influence Grossvogel, but unlike them he does not endow "being" with a particular metaphysical puissance. Derridean deconstruction vigorously resists the sorts of existentially based oppositions found in approaches such as those of Stowe and Grossvogel, with their privileging of an authentic, inner kernel of expressive meaning against an outer world composed "merely" of codes and paradigms. Derrida would no doubt see the hunger for authenticity in mystery-stories as similarly misbegotten (and, given the nature of form, not nearly as inevitable) as the hunger for authenticity and unimpeachable verbal authority in Western metaphysics which he terms "logocentrism." A Derridean analysis of the detective form would not simply be a rhetorical shifting of evaluative terms such as "formulaic" and "authentic" whereby "formulaic" would become "logocentric" and "authentic" would become "deconstructive"; this would retain the metaphysical urge latent in the distinction originally, instead of seeing the detective story, like all modes of linguistic expression, as inevitably problematic and constructed, not ontologically inherent.

Another critical method which problematizes the aforementioned denunciations of the mystery form is psychoanalysis as practiced by Jacques Lacan. While accepting and re-employing Freudian methodology, Lacanian psychoanalysis distrusts any proclamation of a core personality, an essential ego. Thus the phenomenological brio sought in the mystery form by a critic such as Grossvogel would for Lacan inevitably be occluded by the nature of the self, which is not a pre-existent organism but rather arises out of the very loss of wholeness that occurs in the process of the individual's shift into the symbolic order comprised by language and culture. The self in the Lacanian model cannot have it both ways as Christie's existential denigrators seem to want it to: it cannot be both unpredictable and whole, both expressive and ontologically unhinged—it is inevitably both partial and dependent on entities outside it.

A third theoretical prolegomenon for reading Christie more insightfully would be a method less renowned on this side of the Atlantic than those of Derrida and Lacan, namely the semiotic theories of the French linguist A. J. Greimas. "Semiotics" here is hardly the simple decoding and puzzle-solving that Stowe means when he uses the term in the title of his article, or even the determinate polysemy, borrowing heavily from the techniques of medieval allegory, made familiar to readers of the detective story through Umberto Eco's *The Name of the Rose* (1980). Greimassian semiotics is a pluralistic, multivocal process that seeks to situate the terms of discourse in dynamic collaboration with one another, not in any external universe or existential plenum but within the signifying textures of language itself, most often figured emblematically in terms of his "semiotic square." Greimas is probably of the greatest practical relevance with respect to Christie, because he demonstrates how a literary text can be at once manipulative and meaningful, composed totally of the interrelations among language yet managing to resonate and affect readers even without offering them access to any realm of ontological purity or freedom. With these three theoretical guides in tow, it can be seen that Christie's "formulas," whether or not less correspondent to human "reality" than Raymond Chandler's, are no more or less formulas than his, or any other writer's. Christie should not be criticized for doing what all successful fiction does—make the reader partially aware of how and why it is made.

It is in a way a happy coincidence that Grossvogel chose to focus only on Christie's first mystery, because, although her achievement went far beyond this beginner's work, Christie's canon is truly a mysterious affair of styles. Christie's stylistic aptitude is strengthened, not vitiated, by what critics have chastised as her shallow or "flat" characterization. The irony of this complaint is that the flatness of her characters is one of the constitutive features of a Christie novel. Difficult as it may be for those used to the idea of character as formulated in the nineteenth-century mimetic novel, Christie's use of the social mask, her employment of the type, of the generic rather than the specific character is not only an essential aspect of her stories of crime and detection, but constitutes a vision of society, text, and discourse that transcends any specific mystery formula. Christie's use of the mask in her fiction has its roots in the nature of mystery novels, which depend on their highlighting a doubleness, a dichotomy between appearance and reality, a dichotomy which the detective in his investigations enacts rhetorically but only provisionally solves.

From *The Moonstone* (1868) to *The Mystery of Edwin Drood* (1870) to *Dr. Jekyll and Mr. Hyde* (1886) to the present day, the theme of doubleness or duplicity is central to the form. As Betteredge puts it in Wilkie Collins' *The Moonstone*, we are "all . . . listening to surprise each other's secrets" (83), hidden underneath the surface of the human situation. In detective fiction, the world is to some degree a stage, and the people in it merely players, deceiving those around them and sometimes even themselves as to their true motives and actual deeds. It is the task of the mystery novel to "see through" the staged reality, a false good which has been rendered false as a result of the malice, greed, envy, and sundry other deadly sins the discovery of crime reveals. Christie has received this form and given it another turn of the screw, as it were, by approaching characters as a theatrical company, a familiar dramatis personae of social types, none of whom are as they seem. In fact, many of her novels are prefaced by a "Cast of Characters," namely the possible suspects in the ensuing mystery, and the metaphor of performance pervades her work.

The pretense, disguise, play-acting, and outward show that are essential to the mystery genre are given a special intensity in Christie's work by her constant emphasis on and reference to the "theatricality" of her characters' actions. A well-known example is **Murder on the Orient Express** (1934), in which Hercule Poirot comes to realize that he has been an audience of one for a careful series of performances. In this book, Christie is at the furthest extreme from the romanticization of the criminal as a solitary outlaw; Christie's criminal is far less often a rogue psychotic (her few attempts at this sort of portrait, as in **Endless Night** [1967], are, though not uninteresting, uncharacteristic) than somebody who is manipulating the known and tolerable conventions of English society to his or her own advantage. Aboard the

Orient Express, the solution to the crime, that "they were all doing it," foregrounds a persistent feature of Christie's characterization: she is less probing the souls of her characters than seeing how their enactment of roles implicates them in carceral circumstances that are sometimes apprehended as "criminal," sometimes not.

Such impersonations and performances are numerous in Christie's texts. Many, if not all, of the characters in a Christie novel are playing roles, so that although it is the murderer who is revealed to be the most hypocritically estranged from his or her performed self, Christie suggests a general doubleness in the human character. This allows her to cast suspicion on all of her characters, giving her a satisfying list of possible villains. But it also creates a vision of life in which the self is "presented" in what sociologist Erving Goffman has described as the staged reality we call "everyday life." Similarly, at the conclusion of *Mrs. McGinty's Dead* (1952), Poirot suggests that the murderer has planned "the whole *mise en scene* . . . the whole thing was a theatrical scene setting with prepared props." Of the murderer in *Towards Zero* (1944) Superintendent Battle comments:

> "He played the part of the good sportsman, you know. That's why he could keep his temper so well at tennis. His role as a good sportsman was more important to him than winning matches. But it put a strain on him, of course, playing a part always does. He got worse underneath."

Nevile Strange is the paragon of the British sportsman, but this does not prevent him from being a cold-blooded killer; in fact, it aids him. The methodical manner in which he plans, in a detailed, outlined way, the murder of his former wife, is not full of manic frenzy, but of the same restraint and concern for "good form" that has made him so successful as a sportsman. The psychotic temperament may be lurking underneath, but, as elsewhere in Christie's universe, criminality is manifested in and through many of the forms, the self-assumed roles, that people play in ordinary civilized life. Rather than being simply flat, the shallow personae in Christie's dramas are endowed with a tantalizing, mysterious, and very deliberate artificiality. This is why, in a Christie mystery, we are immediately aware that any of her characters may prove personally malevolent, since all of them seem to be masking some troublesome aspect of their identity. The highly limited, rigidly defined social images of dubious authenticity that populate Christie's country houses, Calais coaches, vicarages, and seaside resorts beg us to wait, expectantly, for the inevitable hidden "Mr. Hyde" side of the human animal to surface. It is important to the experience of Christie's fiction to appreciate the duplicity inherent in her conventionally masked men and women, since this staging is, in fact, what makes her novels mysterious.

With this emphasis on the "staged" quality of reality, Christie is clearly participating in one of the major literary tendencies of her day, the modernist turn against the Romantic stress on the priority of an unhindered, expressive self. This can be seen in the terrain of the theater itself; Christie's theatrical procedures are less like those of the Romantics, with their emphasis on character, than those of such modernist dramatists at Yeats, with his interest in "masks," or Brecht, who sees character as above all a way of highlighting social convention, radically foregrounding the characteristics of a given scene. In preferring spliced, abbreviated samples to fully unfolded interiorities, Christie is linked to her near-contemporaries, T. E. Hulme and Wyndham Lewis, as well as thinkers such as Wilhelm Wörringer who looked back to medieval stylization and symbolism as a way to outflank Romantic individualism in the modern era.

Reclaiming Christie as modernist does not entail upholding the reverent view of modernism as the pinnacle of Western literary achievement that reigned in the academy until quite recently. Modernism, whatever its "international" pretensions, is a local phenomenon that arose at certain places and times and constituted itself in certain discursive frames. Modernism was full of ideological mystification. In this respect, Christie's political conservatism and generally approving view of tradition link her to such eminent modernists as Pound and Eliot, and her penchant for occasional anti-Semitic remarks recalls these two as well as Céline. But it is difficult to single out Christie for her references to scheming Jewesses and oily Semites when the major poet writing in England was the author of "Bleistein with a Bacdeker, Burbank with a Cigar." Modernism had its darknesses as well as its triumphs, and Christie partook equally of both. But even though Christie shared the prejudices of some modernists, she also, like all the above, participated in promulgating new forms which claimed, if they did not always manifest, a radical discontinuity with those of the past. This is more difficult to see at first hand than the previous assertions; where are the Christian equivalents of modernist fragmentation, rupture, chaos? The approach of the Russian Formalists, with their stress on how extraordinary works of literature gain their power from affirming and radically extending the genre to which they belong, may point toward where to look in Christie for this aspect of modernism. Christie is in precisely this position with respect to the classical detective story: it is her triumph, not her liability, that she made what had been an inchoately defined genre into a formulaic one whose characteristics could be enumerated with almost Aristotelian rigor.

Moreover, the very idea of "genre fiction" is a peculiarly modern one. The novel had always been the quintessentially mixed genre, melding aspects of epic, journalism, anecdote, *conte,* into an overall whole. It is with the twentieth-century breakdown of the conventional perimeters of the novel, the breakdown decried by Lukacs and other Marxist humanist critics, that all the major "genres"—for example, the thriller, the detective story, science fiction, although all ultimately Romantic in origin—achieved a formal consistency and a generic autonomy. Thus the kind of criticism which seeks only to "expose" the generic conventions of mystery or science fiction, ridiculing their procedures from the perspective of the psychological-naturalist novel circa 1910, is indulging in a chimerical enterprise. It is puzzling to see an approach such as this, so inconsistent with the general critical approach to twentieth-century fiction, predominate in many intellectual responses to the detective genre. Thus Christie's novels are often dismissed as "trash," whereas those of P. D. James are praised as penetrating expeditions into human nature. Even though the rest of the literary world has gotten beyond seeing the psychological-naturalist novel circa 1910 as the norm, Christie is still being judged by the fictional procedures of others rather than her own. A part of this tendency is a kind of intellectual status panic, an anxiety that reading Christie is reading "trash," that even in our leisure time we should not be reading books we would be embarrassed if our students caught us reading. Surely the line between "trash" and "non-trash" is now irretrievably permeable, and Christie's work should be assessed by the degree to which it executes and experiments with its generic characteristics and displays an awareness of its own nature as fiction.

An objection as strong as the aesthetic demurral against Christie has been the social one. Her work is routinely seen as uncritically pandering to a nostalgic projection of the English class system, as straightjacketing and undermining any idea of radical social dissent or change. While recent events in Eastern Europe have shown that people may not want precisely the sort of radical social change desired by some midcentury Western intellectuals, the objection, on first look, has some force. Many of Christie's plots seem to be designed to eliminate the outsider and reinforce a sort of hegemony of the settled and pawky, an ersatz harkening-back to an imperial and class-stratified past whose irrecuperable disappearance is memorialized by poets such as Philip Larkin. That the social formulas in Christie's novels can reverberate along an ideological axis can be seen in the 1950's debate over the merits of the classical detective story between W.H. Auden, the poet and Christian convert, and Edmund Wilson, the Princeton Marxist. Auden, struggling to uphold decorum in a spiritual universe stained and compromised by original sin, found the classical detective story, with its acknowledgment of guilt and its determination to resolve that guilt within an ordered structure, congenial to his state of mind. Wilson, on the other hand, found the form socially regressive and lacking in the literary merit and emotional pathos (or, perhaps, bathos) of Dostoevsky. While revealing strikingly the differences between the two critics (who were to have a similar debate some years later concerning

Tolkein's *The Lord of the Rings*), the Auden-Wilson argument tends to miss some of the ways in which Christie was socio-politically cannier than she may seem at first.

A good example of this is the late work, *At Bertram's Hotel* (1965). Here, we find Miss Marple coming to a similar conclusion about her mystery:

> It was all too good to be true—if you know what I mean. What they call in theatrical circles a beautiful performance. But it was a performance—not real.

In *At Bertram's Hotel,* Miss Marple discovers that what appeared to be the incarnation of a good, old-fashioned British hotel was in fact an elaborate stage set for a group of actors hired to perform characters and values that had, in reality, been rendered highly problematic by the war, Labor, Suez, the Beatles. The "hollowness" of Christie's people may be, in fact, what differentiates her work from the nineteenth-century novel with its fully realized selves, and its expectation of a deeply internalized moral sense. The curious emptiness of her people is rather a testimony to Christie's perception of modern deracination than a failure of creative power. This is demonstrated by Christie's gradual exposure of the civilized English masks her characters assume. Redolent of Rupert Brooke's "Stands the Church clock at ten to three?/And is there honey still for tea?", this idea of English society is invariably contradicted and destabilized by a society that is not so "English," that is, not so paradisally Edwardian, as it used to be.

The changing face of English civilization in the twentieth century, in which received conventions compete with new "unconventional" ways of being, is in fact far from neglected in Christie's oeuvre. Beginning with her mysteries after World War I, her stories reflect a nostalgia for an earlier, arcadian time as well as a realization that this society is now, at best, a form of play-acting or pretense, at worst a tragic deception. Her dowagers, matrons, majors, colonels, good doctors, her well-bred gentlemen and ladies are now grown unauthentic, become a species of fakery covering a far more alarming reality. The world of friends, neighbors, and relatives has in Christie's novels become a world of strangers, creatures of selfish, aggressive drives at variance with the brittle, flat, and unconvincing postures of gentility they perpetuate publicly. Bertram's Hotel thus employs decayed aristocrats and impoverished members of the old county families to recreate the look of Edwardian England. But Christie's policeman, Fred "Father" Davy (the sobriquet probably no accident, as the novel is preoccupied with the passing of generations), views the hotel's five o'clock tea with the eye of a detective:

> From the staircase, Father cast a jaundiced eye over

the occupants of the lounge, and wondered whether anyone was what they seemed to be. He had got to that stage! Elderly people, middle-aged people (nobody very young), nice old-fashioned people, lawyers, clergymen, American husband and wife near the door, a French family near the fireplace. Nobody flashy, nobody out of place, most of them enjoying an old-fashioned English afternoon tea. Could there really be anything seriously wrong with a place that served old-fashioned afternoon teas?

In reality, the hotel is run by a new, more ruthless society that cynically exploits the old traditions without really believing in them. Often in Christie's work, the seemingly cozy, stable image of England is in fact a copy of something that has largely disappeared; it is a deficient or false England masquerading as the real thing. The detective (and, therefore, the reader) is lured by the specter of a gratifying regression, an atavistic nostalgia for the Great Good Place where Things Were Better, where sensibilities were undissociated. But, with the revelation that the cozy, traditional Bertram's is in fact a front for an international drug-running scheme, the reader's expectations are foiled and trumped. We, who had been caught by Christie thinking, "Ah yes, we may have a more egalitarian society now but truly, we do not know how to live as we did then," are awakened into a realization of the impossibility of this sort of nostalgia. The characters in the novel, who are not as they would have us (and we expect to) see them, also prevent us from lapsing into a false nostalgia. We, like Miss Marple, are meant to disapprove of the modern loose-living wild woman, Lady Bess Sedgwick, but in the end Lady Bess behaves well, sheltering the daughter whom she had failed. And her daughter Elvira's depravity frustrates our wish for an old-fashioned innocent ingenue. In *At Bertram's Hotel* we are prohibited from shrugging off our own modernity.

A similar resistance to nostalgia is evinced in *The Hollow* (1946), which, true to form, presents a staged murder that directs us away from the person who seems to be the most-likely-suspect. The murderer, Gerda Christow, hides behind a facade of stupidity—we learn that she has been "playing dumb." Underneath the blankness is a calculating mind. Christie writes of Gerda:

> . . . she had been able, behind her blank expression, to hug herself a little in her secret knowledge. . . . For she wasn't quite as stupid as they thought. . . . Often, when she pretended not to understand, she did understand. And often, deliberately, she slowed down in the task of whatever it was, smiling to herself when someone's impatient fingers snatched it away from her.

The literal hollow in *The Hollow* refers to the name of the estate where the novel takes place, but hollowness is also an abstract theme in this novel, and it is a reality to be found in all of Christie's work. There is a certain hollowness of heart in her characters, a sense of emotional isolation that is characteristic of other characters besides her murderers. Lucy Angkatell, in *The Hollow,* for instance, while an innocent bystander, is in her own way as heartless as Gerda. She says of the murder victim, John Christow:

> "I found him amusing, and he had charm. But I never think one ought to attach too much importance to *anybody.*"

And gently, with a smiling face, Lady Angkatell clipped remorselessly at a vine.

This "hollow" quality of the characters reverberates back onto the estate, which is a hollow not only in name, but in fact: "The Hollow" is doomed to take perpetual second place in the hearts of the Angkatell family to Ainswick, the immemorial family estate which had belonged to Lucy's father but, because of ironbound primogeniture, has evaded the grasp of Lucy. Though her determination would make her a very able estate-head, the estate has instead fallen to the next male in line, the phlegmatic Edward. All the characters except the Christows, who are outsiders, are in a perpetual funk about the loss of Ainswick; the Hollow is a hollow of Ainswick, existing only as its trace, its privation. The novel's resolution deftly negotiates the Angkatells away from this fixation. Edward's lifelong crush on the artist Henrietta, who had been having an affair with the slain Christow, is gradually revealed to have been only an obligatory accompaniment of his status as estate-head, a sort of emotional analogue to the aspiration to redeem the past that strikes at the core of the Angkatell clan. When Edward renounces this aspiration and settles down with the more middle-class Midge, he definitively puts behind him any hope of reconstituting a privileged, aristocratic past, and thus frees the Hollow from the specter of Ainswick and Ainswick from its own hollowness.

An even more graphic display of Christie's socio-political complexity is the wartime novel *An Overdose of Death* (1940). In this work, Poirot originally suspects Mr. Raikes, one of Christie's stereotypical, frenetic Marxist agitators who is the fiancé of Jane, the niece of the wealthy corporate magnate Alistair Blunt. We are initially led to believe that Blunt is the intended victim of the various murders already perpetrated in the book, and Mr. Raikes's social convictions render him a likely suspect to the side of Christie all too ready to dismiss any threat to the established order. But at the end, the tables are turned: Poirot discovers that Blunt is in fact the murderer. Blunt pleads with Poirot for mercy, stating that his ability to coordinate the English military-industrial complex makes him invaluable to the war effort. Poirot, though, refuses to put the logic which later led to such entities as multinational corporations and superpowers ahead of his responsibility to the individual, particularly the innocent victims of Blunt's crimes. Refusing to submit to Blunt's rhetoric of "expertise" and "professionalism," Poirot exposes his criminality, leaving the way for Jane and the now-exonerated Raikes to marry. Here, far from being expelled or eliminated at the end of the social renovation accompanying the solution of the mystery, the Marxist outsider is integrated into the ongoing order, whereas the corporate magnate is expelled. There may be some residual quietism, some co-optation, in the vista of the revolutionary being integrated so eagerly into the domestic life, but Poirot's words at the end, "In your new world, my children, let there be freedom and let there be pity," indicate a real willingness on the part of the detective, and the authorial function he replicates in the novel, not to rule out any promise to be gained from social change and reform. In fact, it is the very qualifier Christie puts on the ending by the stock device of marriage that makes the conclusion as interesting and tentative as it is. By guiding her books to such a comic close, Christie highlights their fictiveness, and makes clear that these endings can only be partial, that we are not to take them conclusively, but rather as provisional ways to give shape to a book, a plot, a life.

Christie's detectives operate crucially in orchestrating these plots. Miss Marple and Hercule Poirot delight in assuming ridiculous, caricature like disguises only to reveal a surprising potency as the books move on. They depend on an innocuous facade not only to lull those about them into a false sense of security but also to surprise the reader with their almost ruthless perspicacity. Because disguised as a harmless old English tabby, or as a humorously Belgian rather than dangerously French elf, Christie's detectives astonish the reader and the other characters with their mental and imaginative powers. The grotesque exaggeration involved in the characterization of, say, Poirot (for one thing, it is very unlikely that a Belgian emigré could ever become the leading practitioner of a method of critical investigation conducted in the English language) means that his character is more or less fixed. This does lead us to invidious comparisons with the detectives of hard-boiled writers such as Raymond Chandler, whose detective is altered by what he investigates and renounces his own assumptions of epistemological supremacy, an aspect that has been interestingly developed by several practitioners of the metaphysical detective story. But rather than make the "depth" of these detectives a master term, it might be more profitable to simply grant the hard-boiled model its ontological complexity, the classical model its tropological density, that is to say its multiplicity of rhetorical moves, and let them coexist. The tropological density, in its foregrounding of the constructed, linguistic nature of the text, indeed does not allow the classical model's characters to be as "deep" as those of the hard-

boiled model. Again, this need not be counted as a defect. For indeed, Miss Marple and Hercule Poirot are not just empty containers, but central plot-functions operating in a legitimate and interesting mode of discourse. Both detectives take as their characteristic mode acting a part that protects and serves the detecting self hidden "inside," a subterfuge which persuades the criminal as well as the reader into believing that the detective will present no significant challenge, has no convincing authority—an illusion always pierced by book's end, when the authority of the detective is subtly, but thoroughly affirmed. Both of Christie's major detectives become, as their careers unfold, more stylized, more purely plot functions; unlike many later detectives, their lives do not particularly change from story to story.

Christie found the masked quality of her detectives' selves somehow fascinating, this intriguing quality having less to do with the souls of the detectives than with their minds. The classical model is, preeminently, a cerebral, ratiocinative one. Most critics have denounced this cerebrality as being in some way oppressive and limited. But Christie, instead of focusing on the cerebral or rational as structures of normative containment, as they are portrayed by the advocates of the Romantic celebration of the expressive will, calls attention to precisely the way in which the cerebral and the ratiocinative are unusual, weird, preternatural. In doing this, she is only following the tradition of Poe, the explorer of the turbid underside of the psyche who was also lured by the strangely similar obverse presented by the intellect in the shining excess of its power. Possessed of a cerebrality that is as out-of-the-ordinary as any criminal impulse, Christie's detectives function not only to discover crime, but to possess a peculiar empathy with the criminal sensibility.

The emotional undercurrent of this central revelation in Christie's work always suggests an element of the uncanny. Like Christie's detectives, Christie's villains employ the "typical" selves they present to others in order to conceal what they prize as their true nature, relying on what Goffman has called "normal appearances" to allay suspicion. Christie's villains are shown to hide an incivility, an "imperfect socialization" that amounts to a truncated humanity and indicates a dangerous fragility in the social nexus that had heretofore been an important ingredient in creating the fully human self. The "surprise ending" of a Christie mystery turns not only on the discrepancy between role and "real self," but on our trust (always misplaced) that people are fully identical with the repertoire of roles which constitute their participation in society. On the contrary, people who appear to be generic figures, such as the Sweet Little Old Lady, the Fetching Young Mother, the Helpful Policeman, the Adorable Child, the Good Doctor, not to mention the Great Detective himself, are exposed in Christie's fiction as deliberately flattened by roles that trick us into discounting them as murder suspects. A characteristic Christie embodiment of this surprise is the plot device called "the double bluff," in which a character is initially suspected of the murder, exonerated, and then turns out in the end to have committed the crime, or, alternately, where a character who has been seen by the reader exclusively as a potential victim of a crime, is in fact the perpetrator.

Christie did this many times, but never more skillfully, as Robert Barnard (Christie's finest successor in the classical mode) and others have noted, than in *Peril at End House* (1932). Nick Buckley, an attractive young woman, appears to be the victim of a crime that has "mistakenly" been perpetrated on a relative with a similar name. Poirot makes an exhaustive (almost, we might say, Nevile Strange-like) outline of possible suspects, even allowing for an unknown, but does not include Nick at all. Nick, in being exempted from the list of suspects, becomes an authorial surrogate with whom both reader and, seemingly, author identify. We are led to believe that it is as unlikely for Nick to have been the murderer as it is for Poirot, or for that matter, Agatha Christie, to have committed the crime. But in the end, Nick indeed turns out to be the criminal. By carefully arranging for herself to seem the victim, she has allied herself with the detective, with the forces of authority, hoping thus to evade the otherwise incriminating circumstances. The winning aspect of this trick is its exploration of the ideas of sameness and difference—we expect the murderer to be someone different from the bluffing figure, when it turns out it has been the bluffer all the while. Thus the bluffer is at once a different person from the one whom we saw as the murderer, but the same person as "the murderer" really is. Although Nick asserts her own difference from herself, this is a mask that is ultimately exposed by Poirot.

But where, we might ask, does this leave Poirot? Poirot, and, with him, Christie, has bluffed his way through the case much as has Nick. Just as Nick turns out to have *really* been the murderer all the while, so has Poirot turned out to have *really* known she was the murderer for at least a significant amount of time. Poirot shares the same delight in saying "I know something you don't know," the love of pulling rabbits out of a hat when the reader least expects it, as does the criminal. Both of them operate on a perceived confusion between mask and reality, a confusion which they think they can solve, but which others cannot. Finally, the most important difference between them is that Poirot's solution wins out (i.e., is fictionally successful) and Nick's does not.

Yet Christie's detectives do not always operate with this degree of cynicism and false self-presentation. One of Christie's most deft triumphs is the way she gives her detectives a positive social and psychological function, in a way despite themselves, although Miss Marple is far more socially assimilated than the always-bizarre Poirot. The role

of the detective adumbrates a kind of benign association of self and society in which the self operates within social structures, but avails itself of those very structures in order to guarantee its own privacy. It is in this respect that Christie's modernism is not only that of the classical, ironic Hulme, Lewis, or Eliot, but also partakes of the humanistic modernism associated with the Bloomsbury group, with its emphasis on the interweave between self and society. In this tradition, established by Virginia Woolf and E.M. Forster and in many respects continued by postwar work in British psychoanalysis such as the "object-relations" theories of D.W. Winnicott, the self is neither whole nor splintered. It is a constructed personality that, although it is not "natural," is the product of cultivation and invention, is yet capable of affirming its own condition. The self in this model is not self-engendered, but can build outward from the foundations provided for it. This view of the self is compatible with Christie's tendency to elucidate other "selves" besides the Self celebrated by existentialism, which inherited Romantic views of the stark, isolate ego confronting the abyss.

Christie is interested in selves who are less than "whole" selves, who are on the margins not only of society but also of selfhood. Thus her extraordinary interest in (and depiction of) old people and children, two categories that are hardly capable of pretending to operate outside a social nexus, yet within that nexus add perceptions and states of being that by their idiosyncrasy make all selves more aware of the nature of their selfhood. It is therefore no accident that Lewis Carroll is the most often quoted author in Christie's stories, not merely as a result of a shared interest in games and puzzles, but a shared sense that ordinary life is only to be found on the obvious, transparent side of the looking glass, and that a more unpredictable and unconventional reality is lurking under the surface of things. As with Lewis Carroll, noted for an interest in young children that in many minds went past affection into a subversive identification, Christie's children, as well as her old people, are not merely cute and innocent, but threateningly raw and inchoate. The image of the child, especially in the light of the child-murderers in books like *Crooked House* (1949), *Hallowe'en Party* (1969), and *At Bertram's Hotel,* is not idyllic, but exposes the "pre-rational" condition of children as a threat to the stability and order of the soi-disant adult world. This is yet another image of the self that hardly conforms to the heroic autonomous agent so prized in the post-Romantic tradition, a tradition continued by hard-boiled detectives such as Chandler's Philip Marlowe, whose cynicism and despair only serve to underline his existential prowess.

Christie's interest in new aspects of the self attends not only to the substance of the self but to the means of its representation. Christie, rather like Virginia Woolf, often experiments with points of view, and her frequent use of third-person indirect speech to represent the thoughts of a character often verges on interior monologue. *Ten Little Indians* (1939), among other books, offers many examples in which the conscious self's representation is whittled away to its fragmentary components as relentlessly as the "inexorable diminishment" (to use the wording of Justice Wargrave himself) that overtakes the characters isolated on Indian Island. But this access to inner speech does not lead to full existential interiority. It is just one of a number of modes of representation, not privileged as a wellspring of "real" emotion. The insight Christie has shown into the self's constructed, masked nature thus gains a complex reciprocity. It can reveal the self's hidden strengths and aspirations as much as it can expose its pretensions and self-delusions. This process is troped by the detective figure in Christie's fiction, who often operates as a paratherapist, someone whose function is not only to solve a crime but to construct a viable personal solution out of the aftermath of that crime.

Christie's formalism, what her critics have called her "formulaic" qualities, ties her closely to the modernist movement. Her innovative, complicated, and humanistic view of the self is, far more than has been suspected, a surprisingly modern one, restraining and yet enriching the view of the self that had prevailed throughout the great European centuries that preceded Christie's own.
—*Nicholas Birns and Margaret Boe Birns*

A paradigmatic instance of this dual process is found in the underrated late novel *Third Girl* (1966). In this book, Norma Restarick, ostensibly the "third girl" of the title, is deceived by a man claiming to be her father into believing that she has committed a crime which she is not, psychologically or logistically, capable of committing. As it turns out, not only is the man who claims to be her father truly responsible, he has done it with the aid of his wife, who has assumed the disguise of one of Norma's two roommates. Norma had previously seen herself as the "third girl," the extra wheel, the person who did not fully understand herself or know her own identity. But as the result of Poirot's investigations, the ersatz roommate is revealed to be the "third girl"—it was she who had always been the enigma, the unknown quantity. Norma is ostensibly at the end of the book her own "first girl"; she has finally come to an appropriate centering of her own private identity. But it is important to say "private" rather than "personal" because Norma does not come to this solution wholly through her own efforts, but with the aid of others—thus "private," with its secondary connotation of "privation," in the sense of a selfhood needing others in order to be fully complete.

The term "Third Girl" has an intriguing resemblance to the Lacanian idea of the "Third Term," the agent of language and the symbolic that disrupts the narcissistic stability of the child-mother dyad. At the beginning of the book Norma is embroiled in a welter of emotional confusion that is a residue of her parents' early divorce and her marred girlhood. By the end, Norma is delivered from this nightmarish crypt, but it is the price of this delivery that her comfortable idealizations of her parents and her past are shattered, and that she is ushered into her future not only emancipated from her past but barred from its shelter. Thus there is even at the end a bit of "thirdness," a psychological position in which the autonomous, self-sustaining ego is prohibited from a fully clear intuitive self-knowledge and subject to the compromises of discourse, culture, and other "selves," even in the midst of Norma's recovered "firstness." In bringing about this conclusion, Poirot, as the representative of the symbolic order, acts as the Lacanian "Name of the Father." This is a principle that simultaneously privileges the phallic potency of the dominant male order yet reveals it as ontologically empty, of an only procedural rather than substantial nature. Poirot's combination of absolute authority and lack of any "deep" personality makes him the ideal vehicle for this phallic disruption-and-reconstitution.

One of the chief helpers in this recuperative process in *Third Girl* is Dr. John Stillingfleet, a friend of Poirot's whom the detective asks to help him on the case, and who at the conclusion of the book marries Norma and goes with her to Australia. It is revealed at the end that this was no accident; Poirot has manipulated the meeting of Norma and Stillingfleet as much as he has manipulated the solution of the plot. Operating like a Euripidean *deus ex machina,* Poirot at once ministers to the psychological needs of those involved in his investigation, yet braids and threads them into his solution as tidily as he does the criminals themselves. Christie movingly and humanistically represents emotional pathos, yet is confident that these emotions can be assimilated into the discursive framework of society, although not in a way that would conclusively solve the dilemmas they pose. This is vouchsafed by her portrayal of Dr. Stillingfleet. Unlike Woolf's *Mrs. Dalloway,* where the psychologist who treats the war veteran Septimus Smith, Dr. Bradshaw, is an insensitive lout whose only interest is in maintaining, in a manner that would not have surprised Michel Foucault, the order and technique of his discipline, Stillingfleet is interested in his patient on a human level, not merely as a specimen for "scientific" practice. This reflects advances in therapeutic technique from the 1920s to the 1960s, advances which Woolf would not only have understood but in a way helped bring about. Yet it also demonstrates that Christie, who, like Woolf, had times in her own life of considerable emotional turbulence, was capable of embodying that turbulence in fiction. Christie's linguistic devices give access to a serious psychological introspection, without for a moment hailing this introspection as a "truer" or more authentically expressive mode of writing than near-arbitrary plot puzzles. In the use of the detective as therapist and the therapist as agent of the detective in *Third Girl,* Christie demonstrates her sophistication by making sure that the emotional depths she illumines are framed reflexively in the formal dynamics of her narrative.

As we have seen, Christie's formalism, what her critics have called her "formulaic" qualities, ties her closely to the modernist movement. Her innovative, complicated, and humanistic view of the self is, far more than has been suspected, a surprisingly modern one, restraining and yet enriching the view of the self that had prevailed throughout the great European centuries that preceded Christie's own. That Christie is implicated in the modernist epistemological field to a far greater extent than has been supposed does not mean that her work represents assumptions which our present postmodern age can unquestioningly support. Now that modernism is a fully historicized phenomenon, though, we can appreciate the extent to which its assumptions and practices were reflected even in writers who are not commonly associated with the avant-garde or the abyss. And Christie's work does not demonstrate these practices mechanically or reductively. However deft her formulas are as tropes, she often, as in *Third Girl* and many other places, evades them by manifesting an illative thrust, a going-inside that is underwritten by the maneuverability provided by her formulas' rich narrative strategies. As in Greimas' semiotics of action, the fact that her characters are less inner voices than rhetorical actors bestows upon rhetorical action a semantic complexity that enables it to express the various aspects of human action that are likely to occur in a narrative plot. Christie exemplifies this process in a flexible way that allows us momentary empathy with the actions of her plots without ever permitting us to forget that these actions are embedded in a linguistic field. This flexible going-inside is exhibited in a context not explicitly mentioning Christie at all, namely one of the classic postmodern explorations of the detective story, Frank Kermode's essay "Novel and Narrative," first published in 1974, in which an analysis of E. C. Bentley's *Trent's Last Case* (1912) plays a prominent role. Kermode uses this novel, one of Christie's most important precursors in the classical detective paradigm, as a test case for the kinds of narrative criticism pioneered by structuralism; already sensing, in his own way, the poststructuralist tide, Kermode gently stresses that even in so code and "formula" dominated a novel as this one, there is still maneuvering room. The formulas used by Bentley do not constrict, yet lead to significance and exchange of meaning. Kermode has his mind very much on issues of literary theory here, and his respectful diminution of the heuristic potential of structuralism, which in the light of its historical replacement tends increasingly to be parodied and underread, may need to be revised. Yet his treatment of Bentley is exemplary for the

kind of sophisticated, unbegrudging approach to the detective form needed in the coming years.

At the beginning of his discussion of Bentley, Kermode quotes the famous first sentence of the book, "Between what matters and what seems to matter, how shall the world we know judge wisely?" The interpretive effort required of the "world" of the detective story, that is the detective, the author who writes the detective, and the reader who reads the writing, is not a matter of mere differentiation, of telling the good from the bad, the orderly from the disorderly, as Christie's denigrators have so often implied. Rather, we are asked not only to judge, but to judge wisely. Christie's formal subtleties, her fractured yet resonant selves, and her often-brilliant modernism demand the kind of treatment that their complexity solicits. Christie asks that her readers judge her wisely.

Gary Day (essay date 1990)

SOURCE: "Ordeal by Analysis: Agatha Christie's *The Thirteen Problems,*" in *Twentieth-Century Suspense: The Thriller Comes of Age,* Macmillan, 1990, pp. 80-95.

[*In the following essay, Day discusses the structure of* The Thirteen Problems, *refuting many commonly held beliefs about the simplicity of the formulaic mystery novel.*]

Critics of the detective story have commented that its appeal lies less in characterization than in the solution of a problem. Jacques Barzun writes that 'detection rightly keeps character subordinate' while George Grella comments 'that the central puzzle provides the form's chief appeal'. Generally, characters are types who perform specific functions and only the detective is allowed to be interesting.

This description derives from a certain view of the detective story as formula, and considering it on that basis it is fairly sound. However, it does beg certain questions, the most obvious being whether the majority of readers are really motivated by the intellectual pleasures attendant on successfully discovering who did it. Do they really read so attentively as to register every clue and check every alibi or is it more a case of simply wanting to know? And is this desire for knowledge, roused by the detective story, satisfied by the detective story?

There is less quarrel with the view that there is little characterization in the detective story but this does not mean that elements of characterization do not have a part to play in it. In Agatha Christie's *The Thirteen Problems*—which is the text on which this essay will focus—Miss Marple's combination of fluster and flair, of strength and vulnerability, together with her respectability all serve to legitimate the reader's interest in murder. Miss Marple's presence and her unerring ability to solve what has perplexed everyone else somehow removes those qualities from murder which excite the reader's forbidden desires, sublimating them instead into acceptable curiosity.

Characterization can thus work like the censor in dreams, which ensures that repressed material only gains access to consciousness in a distorted form. The village where Miss Marple lives may be of significance in this context, since its name, Saint Mary Mead, suggests mediation, compromise between two opposing forces. To see Miss Marple in this light, however, is somewhat ironic since it implies that she enables the expression of anti-social desires to which her bringing criminals to justice would suggest she was opposed.

It is only through its relation to crime that Miss Marple's character is important, for with her sense of duty and respect for hierarchy she evokes a bygone age of contentment and tranquillity. The stories in *The Thirteen Problems* reassure the reader that life, despite its chaos and uncertainty, is really a very ordered affair. This reassurance stems not only from Miss Marple and the world she inhabits but also from the structure of the stories. Another word for this structure is formula, and however critics may disagree over what constitutes this formula they are in little doubt that the detective story follows one of some kind.

One of the most clearly identifiable formulae is to be found in the 1920s and 1930s, the so-called Golden Age of detective fiction, which was when *The Thirteen Problems* was published. George Grella has listed the main characteristics of the detective short story in this period. He says that it involves 'a group of people assembled at an isolated place—usually an English country house—who discover that one of their number has been murdered'. The situation is complicated, Grella continues, by there being either no clues, or too many, and by the fact that 'everyone or no one has had the means, motive and opportunity to commit the crime, and nobody seems to be telling the truth'. Eventually, the problem is resolved by the superior reasoning powers of the amateur detective, and this sequence, claims Grella 'describes almost every formal detective novel'. It is certainly an adequate, if not entirely accurate, description of the stories in *The Thirteen Problems.*

Behind Grella's taxonomy is a concern with what constitutes the aesthetic of the detective story, and implicit in a great deal of critical writing on the detective story is the assumption that its formula is in some sense its aesthetic. Discussion thus takes the form of asking whether it is plausible, whether it deploys the right conventions and whether the author plays fair with the reader.

This is particularly likely to happen in discussions of texts written in the Golden Age, but critics can hardly be blamed for this when the Detection Club, founded in 1928, at first for writers but then also for readers, made adherence to its rules of how to write a detective story a matter of principle. Debates about rules and aesthetic categories, however, run the risk of ignoring how detective stories articulate the times in which they are written. Exactly how they do this is something of a problem. Do they simply reflect history or do they have a more dynamic relationship with it?

> **In Agatha Christie's *The Thirteen Problems* . . . Marple's combination of fluster and flair, of strength and vulnerability, together with her respectability all serve to legitimate the reader's interest in murder. Miss Marple's presence and her unerring ability to solve what has perplexed everyone else somehow removes those qualities from murder which excite the reader's forbidden desires, sublimating them instead into acceptable curiosity.**
> **—Gary Day**

The Thirteen Problems gives information about the period in which it was written concerning furniture, household organization, eating and leisure habits, class and the position of women. The passive presentation of those details underlines the tranquillity of the world of which they are a part. However, that tranquillity is disturbed elsewhere in the text by a troubled awareness of the difference between the past and the present. For example, Colonel Bantry remarks that it's the done thing 'nowadays—to be brutal and outspoken; but I never get used to it' (**'The Blue Geranium'**). This sort of awareness means that the village and its inhabitants cannot always function as a symbol of contentment. Indeed that quality is predicated on its being 'untouched by civilization' (**'The Four Suspects'**). But this remark has little meaning given that Miss Marple finds a village parallel for every incident that happens outside of it. Through this process the village may come to represent that dark criminality to which it is intended as a contrast. The text seems less aware of this problem than it does of the gap between past and present. It deals. with this troubling perception of historical change, which it is trying to exclude, by parodying the character who comments on it—hence Colonel Bantry is bluff and avuncular but also slow witted.

The pressure of history can be felt in what a text excludes as well as in what it includes. What *The Thirteen Problems* excludes is the social and economic context of the crimes which are the subject of the stories the characters tell one another. Crime is seen to be the result of 'weak moral fibre'

('**The Tuesday Night Club**'). The general assumption of *The Thirteen Problems* is that human beings are responsible for their actions and so if they break the law they should be punished. Thus Miss Marple thinks that it is 'a good job' that Sanders was hanged for murdering his wife and she adds 'I have never regretted my part in bringing that man to justice. I've no patience with modern humanitarian scruples about capital punishment' ('**A Christmas Tragedy**').

Where social and economic considerations do enter a story it is only as background and the reader is discouraged from making any causal connections. Hence, although Amy Durrant was 'wretchedly poor' and money 'was wanted desperately' she is nevertheless regarded as a 'woman, completely lacking . . . in some moral sense' ('**The Companion**'). Her desire to relieve her own and her family's poverty and the offhandedness of her rich relation are regarded as irrelevant factors when it comes to understanding why she murdered the relation. The curious thing here is that though the social and economic context is juxtaposed with the crime it is not offered as a way of understanding the crime. Despite the clear part it plays in the crime it is there only to be rejected as something which might have had a possible influence upon it. In this respect the text is at odds with itself for it denies what it so clearly shows.

This disregard for other factors in the determination of behaviour, apart from choice, separates *The Thirteen Problems* and other detective stories from the kind of thinking about society which can be found, for example, in the works of John Galsworthy. Such thinking accepted that environment could affect behaviour and it was more characteristic of the late 1920s than the assumptions of detective stories written in the same period.

This failure to take cognisance of the social and economic context of actions flouts Miss Marple's guiding rule that one should always 'face facts' ('**A Christmas Tragedy**'). Miss Marple scrutinizes the facts in conjunction with her knowledge of, among other things, clothes, flowers, poisons and 'the habits of gardeners'. Hers is thus an empirical approach, yet it bears little relation to her beliefs about human nature, which are what she ultimately relies on when it comes to solving a crime. The text asks us to accept that Miss Marple's beliefs have a foundation in fact, but this is obviously not the case since she denies that social and economic factors can influence action, even though this was known to be true at the time this collection was published. *The Thirteen Problems* offers a false relationship as true and a true relationship as false, and it is in this confused thinking that it shows its relationship to the times in which it was written. Miss Marple's beliefs are not rooted in fact, and this inconsistency undermines the premise of all detective fiction—to go by the evidence. In not going by the evidence

the stories in this collection tacitly announce themselves as fiction, a point to which I shall return.

The ambiguous attitude to facts in *The Thirteen Problems* represents a change in the detective story which arose as a response to a new perception of the city as a place of darkness and poverty, in addition it was felt to be undifferentiated and inhabited by swarming masses. Raymond Williams argues that this society produced a new way of seeing, as exemplified in the writing of Charles Booth. This 'deliberate impersonality' and 'systematic tabulation' were typical of the empirical vision which brought some order to the otherwise confused sense of 'a civilization of this scale and complexity'. This was expressed in a number of ways in fiction, one of them being the detective story with its emphasis on observation and facts.

From this it can be seen that *The Thirteen Problems* not only excludes its contemporary history but also its own literary history, and this seems doubly ironic for a form which is so committed to reconstructing the past as it was since that it is the only way to solve a crime successfully. *The Thirteen Problems* represents a move away from the tradition Williams describes, firstly by being set in a village, secondly by its conflicting treatment of facts and thirdly by the loss of distance and impersonality. In this connection Miss Marple notes that living in a village gives her 'opportunities and leisure for seeing [human nature] at *closer* quarters' ('**The Companion**').

Despite the lip service paid to the primacy of facts, they are often shown to be of secondary importance. This had to do with a distinction Miss Marple makes between 'knowing' and 'knowledge'. She says, for example, that she knows who murdered Rose Emmott though she admits she hasn't 'got any—what you might call *knowledge*' ('**Death by Drowning**'), where knowledge is to be understood as facts; 'I have no facts' she remarks in the same story. The facts she lacks both in this story and in '**A Christmas Tragedy**'—'I knew' she says, 'but there was no proof'—eventually appear to support what she already knows. Miss Marple does not build up an interpretation from the facts, she uses the facts to confirm the interpretation. The facts are shown to be an effect of her knowing which is the cause. It is clear from this that facts never extend knowledge in the stories, they only endorse it.

This conservative use of facts is perfectly consistent with Miss Marple's belief that 'one thing [is] very like another in this world' ('**The Bloodstained Pavement**'). She solves each problem by reference to some incident in her village. Thus she is able to solve the problem of how Mrs Jones was murdered because it reminds her of 'old Mr Hargreaves' ('**The Tuesday Night Club**'). 'This story,' she remarks 'made me think of him at once'. One effect of this outlook is that it closes the gap between past and present which occasionally troubles the text, for it demonstrates that nothing has happened which has not, in some sense, happened already. The reassurance that these stories give about the ultimate order of life is based on repetition; without that repetition there would be no reassurance, and yet what is repeated is crime. Perversely, crime comes to reassure perhaps because crime allows things to be known and without crime nothing can be known. The crime reveals the criminal and in doing so promises a world that can be known but somehow always escapes knowledge, chiefly because of the contradictions implicit in the process of discovering the criminal. Besides, it is very difficult to acquire knowledge when it is assumed that the body of knowledge is complete; an assumption inherent in Miss Marple's claim that 'human nature is . . . the same in a village as anywhere else' (**'The Companion'**). Such a statement generates a picture of a world that can never be disrupted because nothing new or different can ever happen in it.

In addition to her beliefs about human nature and the importance of facts, another aspect of Miss Marple's approach to a problem is her idea that everything should fit together. When it does, that is a guarantee that she has found the correct solution. 'I was absolutely sure [that this solution] was the correct one because all the pieces fitted in logically' (**'The Thumb Mark of Saint Peter'**). However, it is not a matter of the facts generating their own pattern, rather it is that they fit into the pre-existent one of village life. Thus logic reveals itself as analogy and something that appears to be one thing is really another. This is a fundamental feature of all these stories and it suggests that perhaps the real movement of the detective story consists in this slippage of meaning and not in the disclosure of who did it.

Through being compared to incidents in the village, crime is eventually displaced from the centre of these stories. Instead it becomes an illustration of village life. In this way, crime loses its primordial purity as a thing in itself and comes to represent other things; it becomes, in a sense, the story of other things. Crime has moved from being the signified in the stories to being a signifier, and nothing has replaced it in its former capacity. The representation of the village by crime and vice versa show that the village is so identified with criminality that it can hardly function as an image of repose. Miss Marple does not solve a crime so much as displace it to the village; her method-if it can be called that-does not cast crime out of her world but situates it in the centre of it.

Miss Marple's outlook on life is nourished by her religious beliefs: 'when I am in really bad trouble', she remarks, 'I always say a little prayer to myself. . . . And I always get an answer' (**'The Thumb Mark of Saint Peter'**). She also believes that 'The hand of God is everywhere' (ibid.). Since

this is the case then the plot of each story fits into the divine pattern in the same way that crime fitted into the pattern of village life. Like the village analogy, the divine provides a common reference point so that apparently different experiences can be shown to be the same. The divine narrative authorizes and guarantees the village narrative; it also ensures that if the law fails, justice does not. 'You say crime goes unpunished; but does it? Unpunished by the law perhaps; but cause and effect work outside the law . . . every crime brings its own punishment' (**'The Four Suspects'**). Nothing, it seems, can exist outside these interlocking narratives.

The contradictions in Miss Marple's approach to crime reveal that what is happening in the stories is that the language of science is being used as the language of religion; fact comes to mean faith and logical order comes to mean providential order. *The Thirteen Problems* uses the language of science to validate religious truths in the same moment that it rejects purely religious terminology and the body of science. *The Thirteen Problems* dismisses a scientific approach to problems yet uses the language of science to support its own views of those problems, and thus it legitimates what it tries to repress. It is possible to see in this conflict *The Thirteen Problems* thinking through an issue that was current in the time it was written: are social problems the result of environment or individual will? The stories subscribe to the latter view but, at times, the language they use is more consistent with the former.

There are other contradictions in **The Thirteen Problems,** all of which act to destabilize the meanings of the text producing, on the one hand, indeterminacy and, on the other, the text's consciousness of itself as fiction. One of these contradictions concerns rumor or gossip which is seen as 'idle' (**'The Tuesday Night Club'**). Rumor is viewed as pernicious talk without foundation or substance and it is therefore to be distinguished from the thoughtful, fact based discussions of the main characters as they try to solve the various crimes with which they are confronted. In direct contrast to this view of rumor, however, Miss Marple declares that 'tittle tattle' is often 'true' (**'A Christmas Tragedy'**). This kind of contradiction where rumor is both true and false means that it loses its meaning and becomes indeterminate along with other words like 'knowing', which is simultaneously dependent and independent of facts—another word whose meaning is in doubt.

Another contradiction in the stories concerns atmosphere. In trying to solve the problem of how Raymond Elliot was killed, Miss Marple observes that one should 'look . . . at the facts and disregard . . . all that atmosphere of heathen goddesses' (**'The Idol House of Astarte'**) and yet it turns out that it was precisely the atmosphere of the place which caused the murderer to kill Raymond Elliot: what is rejected as irrelevant turns out to be vital—and perhaps this may have some bearing on the problem of the effect of the social and economic context mentioned earlier.

If atmosphere is both necessary and unnecessary in respect of solving a problem it is an essential requirement of most of the stories. According to Colonel Bantry, a proper story has two characteristics; embroidery and facts (**'The Herb of Death'**) and Miss Marple has a similar dualistic view of stories as mysteries and solutions (**'Death by Drowning'**). Miss Marple's description of stories brings out a dimension which is missing from Colonel Bantry's, namely that they are problems to be solved and in that sense they both necessitate and engage an audience. Nevertheless, Miss Marple's idea of a story is roughly equivalent to his; and mystery and embroidery can both approximate to atmosphere. The dualistic view of the story contains a paradox, for without atmosphere the story would not be possible and yet the whole aim of the story is to brush aside the atmosphere and penetrate the mystery. Atmosphere and mystery provide setting and red herrings which create the possibility of misinterpretation, adding suspense and excitement before the real criminal is unmasked. At the same time, atmosphere and mystery may be regarded as embroidery, in that they interfere with a true picture of events, yet without that embroidery, without the delay it introduces, there would be no opportunity for Miss Marple to exercise her skills as a sleuth. It can be seen from this that the dualism on which the stories are based is a complex one. Atmosphere can be both fact and embroidery: the terms of the dualism thus bestride the dualism. It would be interesting to develop this idea in relation to embroidery. How, for example, does it relate to Miss Marple's habit of knitting? We rarely learn what she knits, which suggests that it is something inessential. Yet, at the same time, it serves to focus her mind on a problem. Miss Marple, who always looks for the facts is, through knitting, associated with embroidery, which is at once both inessential and yet seen as essential because it sharpens her powers of concentration.

The contradictions surrounding atmosphere and gossip as well as other terms in the book result in *The Thirteen Problems* becoming conscious of itself as a work of fiction. This is shown by various references to detective stories throughout the text. 'One would know better nowadays' comments Dr Pender 'owing to the prevalence of detective fiction' (**'The Idol House of Astarte'**) and Miss Marple herself, who is referred to as the 'typical old maid of fiction' (**'The Blue Geranium'**) remarks that it 'turned out to be the most unlikely person—just like in the detective stories' (**'The Four Suspects'**). These references play with the idea of real and not real in comparison to the detective stories to which they refer. Indeed the whole structure of the book, whereby characters present each other with problems to solve in the form of stories, is described by Miss Marple as 'a pleasant

kind of game' (**'Death by Drowning'**). This sense of play and game may undermine the text's claim to pronounce on serious subjects such as human wickedness, but it does legitimize the merry-go-round of meaning which has been set in motion by the text's failure to cope with the requirements it has set itself. The game, however, does draw the reader in and encourage him or her to think, as the text would like to think, in terms of simple cause and effect; that is, who did what and why? In other words, the game suppresses what is most characteristic of the detective story, namely that everything has meaning and everything is connected. It does this because if the reader were to consider how everything is related in the stories, then they would be revealed, like the criminal, to be other than what they pretended to be. Thus the game may appear to celebrate the free play of meaning, but only so that it compels the reader to adhere more closely to the rule of one cause for one effect.

The game is the text's defence against redundancy, for if it is shown that it can never be anything other than fiction then, on its own terms, it has to be disregarded in the same way that Miss Marple disregards the storylike speculations of others as they struggle to make sense of a case. The dynamics of the game can never quite negate the playful references to detective stories: despite their common ancestry game and play in *The Thirteen Problems* ultimately seem to be in an antagonistic relationship. The failure to neutralize these references causes the text to signal, unmistakably, its fictional status and so its claim to be a discourse of truth and knowledge turns out to be a red herring. Indeed there seem to be only red herrings, and with this revelation the text exposes the emptiness of its attempt to deal with the historical problems, symbolized as murder, of character versus environment. It breaks up under the unbearable pressure of flying in the face of the evidence while insisting on the importance of it.

It has already been mentioned that the structure of *The Thirteen Problems* is that characters narrate problems in the form of stories which the audience have to solve. The bare structure of a group of people telling each other stories also applies to Boccaccio's *The Decameron*. Storytelling in *The Decameron* is a response to a crisis, the plague, which hit Florence in 1348. The narrators of the stories, seven women and three men, flee the city for neighboring villas where they remain for the next ten days to tell their tales. It is possible to see *The Thirteen Problems* as a response to a crisis too, for the late 1920s saw the intensification of problems of poverty and unemployment which would last right up to the outbreak of the Second World War. These problems aggravated consciousness of divisions in society and led to talk, as well as fears, of social upheaval. A further parallel is that just as the narrators of *The Decameron* flee to a rural idyll so the narrators in *The Thirteen Problems* tell their tales in a countrified setting. While the response of both *The Decameron* and *The Thirteen Problems* to their respective historical periods seems to be an escape into storytelling, we have seen how, at least in the latter, the problems of history are not left behind so easily but rise like a spectre to haunt and even determine the text.

Another insight into the structure of these stories can be gained from examining the significance of the references to Scheherazade, which occur in both **'A Christmas Tragedy'** and **'The Herb of Death'**. Scheherazade escaped the death that was the usual fate of King Shahriyar's wives by telling him tales and interrupting each one at a dramatic point so that it could be continued the next evening. Here too storytelling is seen as a response to a crisis which gives the narrator a sense of urgency. *The Thirteen Problems* can certainly be seen as *some* kind of response to a crisis but whether or not there is an urgency about the narration remains, for the moment, an open question.

The first point to be made in moving from the structure of the book to a more detailed consideration of its narrative again concerns the instability of meaning; how distinctions dissolve and everything starts to merge so that criminal and detective become one. This process is similar to what Peter Brooks has to say about narrative generally, that it 'operates as a metaphor in its affirmation of resemblance . . . [and metaphor] is in this sense totalizing'. What seems to be happening in *The Thirteen Problems* is that narrative logic is overwhelmed by narrative movement; the former requires that everything remain distinct while the latter draws everything together, as Miss Marple does with her analogies—and perhaps also with her knitting which possibly 'knits up the ravell'd sleave of care' as well as the social fabric.

Miss Marple's habit of seeing events in terms of village incidents is not dissimilar to the totalizing power of metaphor which Brooks sees at work in narrative. To put it another way, Miss Marple's method is a mode of narrative, indeed is narrative or at least one part of it. It is not therefore something which she controls but something which controls her, along with all the other characters. Its attempts at totalization are manifested in the way that characters become more and more like one another as the stories progress. Miss Marple and Miss Helier are a case in point. They are different from one another in a number of ways, the most important being age, and yet they are similar in many respects. They both, for example, find it difficult to express themselves 'One wanders from the point' says Miss Marple (**'A Christmas Tragedy'**), a sentiment echoed by Miss Helier who remarks that 'One gets things mixed up' (**'The Affair at the Bungalow'**). Incidentally this similarity cuts across class boundaries for Gladys Linch, a servant, also finds it hard 'to keep to the point' (**'The Tuesday Night Club'**). The resemblance between Miss Marple and Miss Helier is strengthened by their both having the same christian name, Jane, as well as by their

both being marginalized and humored by the company. In the end they appear more like than unlike.

Miss Marple's analogies, then, are similar to Brooks's description of how narrative operates as metaphor. However, narrative also needs metonymy without which it would lack movement. Metonymy is 'the figure of contiguity and combination, the figure of syntagmatic relations'. As such it resembles Joseph Wood Krutch's description of the detective story as a 'perfectly concatenated series of events'. Brooks, following Lacan, equates metonymy and desire and claims that 'desire must be considered the very motive of narrative, its dynamic principle'. This desire, says Brooks is a desire for the end—of a novel, a poem or a play—for the end 'eventually has to do with a human end, with death'. Here Brooks refers to Walter Benjamin's idea that what we seek in fictions is the knowledge of death which is denied us in our own lives. Perhaps this might explain the appeal of detective fiction, which gives a knowledge of death in the form of the murderer's identity; knowledge of death, in other words, is displaced to become a knowledge of the killer, whose unmasking usually ends the story.

Desire, according to Brooks, is what initiates narrative and propels it forward. That desire seeks discharge but, adds Brooks, it must be the right discharge for 'improper end[s] . . . lurk . . . throughout narrative . . . as the wrong choice'. What ensures the correct discharge is repetition. This binds textual energy, defined as 'all that is aroused into expectancy and possibility in a text', in order to make its final discharge the more effective. These bindings, Brooks explains, 'are a system of repetitions which are returns to and returns of, confounding the movement forward to the end with a movement back to origins . . . offering the possibility (or the illusion) of "meaning" wrested from "life"'.

The desire that keeps narrative moving 'can never quite speak its name', hence narrative is condemned 'to *saying* other than what it *would mean*'. This idea of narrative being compelled to say something other than what it would mean can be applied, in a limited way, to *The Thirteen Problems*. At the very simple level the idea of desire not being able to speak its name finds its parallel in those stories where the narrator is unable to explain what has happened, 'I can't give you [the] solution' says Raymond West (**'Ingots of Gold'**). It is precisely this desire for an end that begins his story but he does not recognise this claiming instead that his desire is for the 'curious' and 'interesting' (ibid.). More importantly, however, nearly all the narrators experience difficulty in telling their stories for if they manage to keep to the point they may suffer interruptions from others which might cause them to digress. In **'The Blue Geranium'** Mrs Bantry cuts in on her husband as he is about to describe Mrs Pritchard's room '"You'd better let me do that", interrupted Mrs Bantry'. This leads to a digression on flowers and it is some moments before Colonel Bantry can resume his tale. By contrast Dr Lloyd finds it so difficult to keep to the point that his audience mistake the subject of his story: '"Go on", said Mrs Bantry . . . "I love stories about sinuous Spanish dancers" . . . "I'm sorry", said Dr Lloyd . . . "this story isn't about the Spanish woman"' (**'The Companion'**). Even Miss Marple admits that she is 'very inclined to become rambling' (**'A Christmas Tragedy'**). The interruptions, digressions, irrelevancies and ramblings all suggest that *the text* is trying to say something other, something different to the clear statement of who committed the crime and why, which is what it actually says.

It might be argued that these various meanderings represent the wrong choices or the improper ends of desire's discharge and it will be remembered that Brooks claims these wrong choices are avoided by repetition. In this case, however, these improper ends occur so often that they take on the nature of repetition, which as well as binding also signifies a desire for the end, a desire, comments Brooks 'to be heard, recognized, understood, which, never wholly satisfied or indeed satisfiable, continues to generate the desire to tell, the effort to enunciate a significant version of the life story in order to captivate a possible listener'. It is this desire that seems to motivate the narrators of the stories which make up *The Thirteen Problems.*

These stories are less about the problems than about the characters who tell them. Each story seems to reflect its narrator in some way, direct or indirect. Dr Lloyd, for example, who appears a somewhat isolated figure fittingly tells a story called **'The Companion',** while Joyce Lenpriere, the artist, tells a story which shows how, as an artist, she is more sensitive than other people and hence is able to see the bloodstains on the pavement which her companion does not: 'I *knew*—I *knew* that he wouldn't see what I was seeing' (**'The Bloodstained Pavement'**). Although the stories seem to be an extension of the characters—and therefore autobiographical—the characters are only, for the most part, indirectly involved in the actions they describe. This suggests their alienation from the desire which tries to use them to name itself as they try to use it to name themselves. The failure of desire to name or be named condemns it to repetition.

Failure to name or be named by desire means that the narrators look to their audience to be recognized and understood. The accounts they give themselves, which are vague and rambling and seem to be about something else, evoke the analytic situation, where the patient gives an equally elliptical account of his or her experience in the hope that the analyst will be able to understand it, and give it a new significance which will free the patient from the compulsion to repeat it. To put it another way, the narrators recount a problem for others to solve in the same way that the patient

recounts a problem for the analyst to solve. The solution of the problem will confer recognition and understanding and bring an end to the repetition of desire. What is required to solve the problem is a discourse which is free of the problems that entangle the very conditions of story. However, the only discourse on offer is Miss Marple's, which is simply another story (since her solutions are only village anecdotes).

While some narrators like Raymond West do not know the solution of the puzzle they give their audience, others do. However this solution is only a solution to a displaced problem and is therefore not a real solution. What these narrators seem to require is that they be confirmed in what they already know but as everything in *The Thirteen Problems* is known in terms of something else nothing can be known for what it is; for example, Sir Ambrose and his ward are 'like Mr Badger and his young housekeeper' (**'The Herb of Death'**). What the analogous discourse of Miss Marple confirms therefore is the analogous discourse of the speaker: desire is confirmed in its displacement but it is precisely because it is displaced that it continues to solicit recognition, proving that the solutions in these stories are really no solutions at all. In contrast to the displacements of the various narrators' stories are the confessions of the criminals which are referred to in a number of stories. These are straight statements of identity, declarations of self, which the narrators never achieve in their stories. Thus the former are recognized and understood for what they are in a way that the latter are not. It is almost as though crime gives an opportunity to declare one's identity—an opportunity denied to the narrators themselves. The desire for recognition is most clearly fulfilled in the figure of the criminal who is known for what he or she is, either through discovery or confession. And perhaps it is for this reason that the criminal is cast out, because he or she is a reminder of the fulfillment the narrative cannot have.

One story which seems to bring together, though not in a very coherent way, the problems inherent in the narrator's discourse with the spontaneous confession of the criminal is **'The Affair at the Bungalow'**. It is narrated by Jane Helier who, as has been mentioned, has the same Christian name as Miss Marple and her identity blurs even more when it is realised that she is an actress. Thus far she is partially obscured like the other narrators. However, she differs from them in a number of ways. To begin with, despite being an actress she cannot disguise the fact that she is the person referred to in her story. But this failure actually serves to mask her more completely for no one, except Miss Marple, and then only with difficulty, recognizes her in the story as the parlourmaid, just as no one recognizes any of the other narrators in their stories. The difference here, however, is that her relation to her story has been made an issue whereas with the other narrators it has not. To complicate matters even more she is going to expose another woman, to show her as *she* really is but she can only do this by performing a criminal act of stealing some jewels. The final twist in the tale is that none of this has happened yet. This allows her to confess like a criminal without actually being one.

This story dramatizes the play between concealment and revelation, desire and recognition, without bringing the issues to any conclusion. In that sense it is the 'truest' story in the collection, for it highlights what the spurious solutions of the others disguise—the unquenchable possibility of meaning. The repetitions within and across the stories bind the sort of energy that animates **'The Affair at the Bungalow'** in order that desire can be discharged *correctly,* to use Brooks's terminology. That desire is discharged in the moment the criminal's identity is made known, a revelation which confers meaning and therefore order on the preceding narrative with its false clues and red herrings. However, this end cannot quite contain those other possibilities which seem to want to say something other than become another repetition demanding a different kind of recognition. Thus as the stories end they are renewed; the necessity for telling stories knows no cessation, it compels narrators in the same way that it compelled Scheherazade. She and they confront death either *in situ* or in story the better to be rooted in life, which is simply another way of saying *the better* to be hard, recognized and understood.

Perhaps the final thoughts should come from Miss Marple:

> 'Has it every occurred to you', the old lady went on, 'how much we go by what is called, I believe, the context? There is a place on Dartmoor called Grey Wethers. If you were talking to a farmer there and mentioned Grey Wethers he would probably conclude that you were speaking of these stone circles yet it is possible that you might be speaking of the atmosphere; and in the same way, if you were meaning the stone circles, an outsider . . . might think you meant the weather. So when we repeat conversation, we don't, as a rule, repeat the actual words; we put in some other words that seem to us to mean exactly the same thing.' (**'The Thumb Mark of Saint Peter'**)

The assumption exposed here that subjectivity is an inevitable part of discourse pre-empts any attempt to gain objective knowledge of the text in which it appears. At the same time, this rebounds back on the text necessarily revealing its subjective character, thereby undermining its privileged relation to truth. In this movement the text is freed from the single, unified meaning it tries to present and becomes, like Jane Helier's future, an open possibility. Incidentally, this view of Miss Marple's also shows the importance of context which elsewhere she denies.

This essay began with a brief consideration of the limitations of the formula approach to detective fiction before moving on to look specifically at *The Thirteen Problems* in terms of its structure, narrative and relation to history. This revealed that the apparently simple form of the detective short story can have both depth and complexity, unless of course Miss Marple is correct, which would mean that all the foregoing is just a creation of criticism and not a true picture of the thing itself. To sort that one out it is going to need a mind at least as astute as hers. It would certainly be one of the most difficult problems she has had to solve, and that is in no small part due to its being of her own making.

John Wren-Lewis (essay date May 1993)

SOURCE: "Adam, Eve, and Agatha Christie," in *The Chesterton Review,* Vol. 19, No. 2, May, 1993, pp. 193-99.

[*In the following essay, Wren-Lewis analyzes what the success of Christie's* The Mousetrap *reveals about changes in popular perceptions of sin and evil.*]

The longest-running play in human history is now well into its forty-first year on the London stage. Agatha Christie's detective-thriller *The Mousetrap,* which celebrated the fortieth anniversary of its opening on November 25th last year, has now become almost a British National Monument. When I went to its opening night, to see the young Richard Attenborough playing the detective, we were still only just emerging from the shadows of World War Two. The possibility that forty years on I'd be in Australia wasn't in my mind then, but even more remote was any thought that the play could still be going near the end of the century. And I don't think the idea crossed anyone else's mind either; Agatha Christie herself, interviewed on the then-phenomenal occasion of the play's tenth anniversary, said she had expected a run of no more than three months and was greatly buoyed by the assurance of impressario Peter (now Sir Peter) Saunders that it was good for at least a year!

> **Agatha Christie's detective-thriller *The Mousetrap,* which celebrated the fortieth anniversary of its opening on November 25th last year, has now become almost a British National Monument.**
> **—*John Wren-Lewis***

In fact the extraordinary success of this rather ordinary well-made play is itself something of a mystery, and the detective in me has been stimulated to investigate the reasons. In doing so, I've been led into some very deep waters of the human psyche, regions where psychology overlaps with anthropology and even theology, and to some insights about the underlying forces that make detective stories so fascinating, particularly, it seems, to people with religious interests. For it's not only English vicars who are notoriously "whodunnit" fans: Jiddu Krishnamurti, who read practically nothing else, delighted in them, and so did Carl Jung, who read almost everything else. Religious thinkers have also been prominent amongst the producers of the genre: G. K. Chesterton, Dorothy L. Sayers and Father Ronald Knox were co-founders, along with Agatha Christie, of London's famous Detection Club in the 1930s. And after Sherlock Holmes and Hercule Poirot, probably the most famous of all fictional detectives is a priest—Chesterton's Father Brown, who latterly has been joined on the shelves by several other persons of the cloth, such as Harry Kemmelman's Rabbi Small and Brother William of Baskerville in Umberto Eco's *Name of the Rose.*

Reflecting on these latter points, I began to scent something more than coincidence in the fact that the "whodunnit" is a fairly new literary phenomenon. Tales of good defeating evil after a struggle are probably as old as humanity, but until the second half of the nineteenth century, the age of Poe, Wilkie Collins and Conan Doyle, there were hardly any stories in which the struggle took the form of a mystery, with the unmasking of a *hidden* villain as the climax. The ascendancy of detective fiction as we know it coincides with the post-Darwinian period when, for the first time in human history, religious belief was declining sharply amongst the literate Western public. The detective emerged as a savior-image as people began to lose faith in those more traditional saviours, the holy man, the righteous ruler, and the knight in shining armor. And stories about evil as a mystery became popular as ancient myths about the so-called "problem of evil" began to seem discredited.

While public debate on "science versus religion" revolved around issues such as the conflict between new discoveries and the literal truth of bible-stories, the real cause, we now know, went deeper. Few serious thinkers in the Judao-Christian-Muslim tradition have ever been over-much concerned with the literal truth of the Adam and Eve story or the six-day timetable for creation, and the same holds for myths of origin in other religious traditions. The primary reference of such ideas has always been to the felt existential human situation, and that was what science in general and Darwinian science in particular seemed to have changed in a radical way, by undermining the notion of harmony as the basic characteristic of reality, for which metaphors such as *Tao* or Divine Purpose could be appropriate expressions, and replacing it with the principle of "nature red in tooth and claw." Human destructiveness needs no explanation if we are simply children of a universal struggle for survival: the only problem of evil in that case is the practical one of preventing the struggle from making life intolerable, and the best hope for doing that seemed to lie in developing the faculty of intellect, which was apparently where the wish for something better had entered the picture in the first place.

But evidently the feeling of evil as something out of tune with the general nature of things and requiring explanation wouldn't go away, for there grew up in the West this new addiction for stories in which an act of violence shatters a previously harmonious scene, causing waves of conflict and suspicion to spread everywhere until the new-style savior-figure, the detective, brings to bear a special kind of intelligence in ferreting out where the violence came from. Is this just a case of an outdated habit of thought lingering on in the form of popular entertainment, such as the myth of the Evil Demiurge surviving as the Demon King of pantomime? I think there's much more to it than that, for three reasons. In the first place, science itself has now shown from the study of dreams, that while the expression of thoughts and feelings in dramatic from may be an older from of mention than rational analysis, it is in no way outdated; on the contrary, it is the basic mode of all mental activity, underlying rational analysis itself. Thus we are well advised to pay serious attention to its collective manifestations. Secondly, evidence had emerged from biological science during recent decades to indicate that the popular perception of nature as *essentially* red in tooth and claw was a gross over-reaction to Darwin's discoveries, a failure to see the wood for the trees. And thirdly, there are good philosophical grounds for believing this to have been the case, for if there's no problem about how evil originates, then the human mind's desire for something better than constant struggle-for-survival itself becomes a problem; where does it come from, if tooth and claw are nature's basic reality?

Darwin was not, after all, the first to observe the ubiquity of conflict and violence in the organic world—it was every bit as obvious to anyone with half an eye in earlier cultures as it is to us today, and probably more so, since urban life has never been really sheltered from nature until quite recently. When earlier cultures assumed that there was a harmony underlying the conflict, and expressed that assumption in various kinds of theistic image, it was because elementary logic dictates that unless something like this were the case, nothing would ever survive at all—and Darwin as a naturalist took this as much for granted as any theologian, even if he was a little more tentative about the use of theistic imagery. In fact it would be fair to say that biological science has provided massive confirmation for what was earlier just a common sense assumption, by using microscopes and, in more recent times, cine-cameras and a plethora of other instruments, to uncover in minute detail the astonishing built-in mechanisms which *limit* the expression of competitive and destructive urges throughout the sub-human biosphere, curbing them so that they are always ultimately contained by harmony. And the specific contribution of evolutionary theory, of which Darwin is the archetypical representative, has actually been to extend our understanding of this principle into the time-dimension, by showing how conflict and competition serve development by selecting the strongest and most flexible strains for breeding. In the years since World War II biologists themselves in growing numbers have begun to articulate this thought, a notable example being the work here in Australia of Professor Charles Birch, which recently won him the prestigious Templeton Prize and is very clearly set out in his excellent book *On Purpose.*

Now this means there's something very odd, almost *un*-natural, about our human species, where aggression and competitive greed continually shatter harmony, between individuals, between tribes and nations, and between us and the rest of the biosphere. Something has been going wrong throughout recorded history, so that the best efforts of holy men, of well-meaning rulers and of knights in shining armor to contain the destructive urges always come unstuck. To paraphrase a famous declaration of St. Paul, the human mind dreams of harmonies more wonderful—more gentle and loving—than the rough but powerful balances of the animal kingdom; yet, in practice, human intelligence again and again finds itself side-tracked into the service of greed, of aggression and even of cruelty, such as would shame any animal. And here too, science has served to make explicit something which formerly could only be intuited in a general way; the "unnaturalness" of human nature, which was formerly expressed in stories about a primordial Fall, has today become inescapable, as the cumulative results of our intelligence threaten to destroy our species altogether, and maybe even the whole planet.

When I was young, and the nuclear arms race was just beginning to make these dangers apparent, most scientists and most religious folk alike thought in terms of humanity's "higher ideals" battling against "lower animal instincts"; but we know now that if our instincts were *really* animal, the drives towards harmony would always contain the destructive ones. It is at the level of mind or of spirit itself that something goes wrong, and I believe that it's a gut realization of this fact that finds expression in the popularity of detective fiction, where in all the best stories the harmony-shattering act of violence is tracked down to a source quite unsuspected by the society concerned; the hidden villain turns out to be someone who, until the denouement, is considered beyond suspicion. True, in the very early days of the genre, this feature was by no means universal: in fact one famous classic, Poe's *Murders in the Rue Morgue,* is a perfect expression of the belief that our troubles spring from animal instincts getting out of rational control—the murders are eventually traced to an escaped savage ape! But as the art-form developed, the main focus came to be on the author's skill in finding ingenious ways to keep the

villain above suspicion until the end, and the Detection Club even drew up rules about it. On the hypothesis I have been developing here, this can be seen as something more than a need to tickle the reader's crossword-solving faculty: it was also the refinement of a new mythological form relevant to our modern understanding of humanity's great existential problem.

And against this background, the extraordinary success of *The Mousetrap* would imply that it contains some particularly acute, nerve-touching insight about the origin of evil in the human psyche, and I believe this to be indeed the case. For the play gives a very special twist to the "least likely suspect" theme, a twist anticipated occasionally in earlier stories (for example, in more than one by G. K. Chesterton), but never (to my knowledge) before put into drama-form, the mode which appeals most directly to the mythopoetic imagination. After all these years of exposure on the London stage, I don't think I shall be giving away any secret by mentioning what that twist is (and anyway, the characteristic of a really significant mythic theme, as I believe this to be, is that it retains its appeal even when the "plot" is common knowledge.) At the end of *The Mousetrap,* the detective himself, the young policeman who appears as the protector of the innocent and as the guardian of law and order, turns out to be the murderer. And here I find a clear echo of a theme expressed in different ways in many of the world's ancient stories about the Fall, but most clearly in the one which, more than any other, has exercised emotional appeal across many different cultures, the biblical story in which the Loss of Eden comes about because of a "snaky" temptation to assume a divine role of moral guardianship, "knowing good and evil."

I would translate this idea as a diagnosis that the responsibility for humanity's unnatural destructiveness lies with the very element in the psyche that purports to aim at harmony, the moral impulse—not that it is too weak, as conventional social wisdom assumes, but that it usurps power and tries to control all other impulses by judging and repressing. It was an insight central to William Blake's attempts to uncover the true essence of Christianity in his mythic epics: "The punisher alone is the criminal of Providence." And this too is surely something we are in a better position to understand today than any earlier generation, thanks to the detailed investigations of psychologists and sociologists. There is now ample evidence that behind all really violent and destructive human behaviour, whether it be the ridiculously excessive ambitions of the military conqueror or the empire-building of the capitalist, or the sadism of tyrants great or small, or the insatiable violence of the rapist, or the blind destructiveness of the hoodlum or child-batterer, there lies a screaming protest on the part of some much more limited desire that has been repressed by an overweening morality, in society, in the family, or in the individual psyche itself. And on the other, outer side of the coin, egoistic and aggressive urges become really dangerous and outrageous precisely when they are moralized and amplified by righteous indignation. The Inquisition really did think that they were saving souls, and while mere greed or ambition would never lead any sane person to plunge the world into nuclear winter, a holy war might easily do so, on the judgment that it is better to be dead than red or, in more topical terms, better to have a nuclear holocaust than to submit to the Great Satan of American Capitalism.

"Better to rule in Hell than serve in Heaven" were words which Milton put into the mouth of Satan himself. His poem followed much Christian tradition in linking the Biblical story of Paradise Lost with another ancient tale, giving it, in the process, a definite "whodunnit" flavor of its own, by suggesting than the serpent was just a disguise for the cosmic Mr. Big—Lucifer, the Archangel of Light, who subverts humanity in the course of trying to usurp the role of God. The moral impulse, or "conscience," could indeed be described as the angel (the messenger) of light in the human psyche, and this story unmasks its constant tendency to get above itself and rule the roost instead of simply serving life. Thus a vicious circle is created, because repression and moralization exaggerate the very impulses they claim to control, and thereby give "conscience" the excuse for attempting still more repressive measures and expressing still more moral outrage against others. This was why Blake went beyond Milton's interpretation of the story and represented Satan as having to all intents and purposes already taken over the place of God in most religions by making them agents of repressive moralizing, rather than of salvation. That, he argued, was why Jesus of Nazareth "died as a reprobate . . . punished as a transgressor"—because he had seen what was going on in the world and tried to reverse the process by urging "mutual forgiveness of each vice," only to have his name and image taken over in turn in the service of repression and indignation.

The Mousetrap doesn't attempt to pursue the story into those depths: its villain simply gets killed at the end, much as in most other "whodunits." But Chesterton did try to take that extra step: Father Brown never sought punishment or death for his villains, but unmasked them only as a first step in trying to redeem them. And for Blake that was the ultimate goal both in society and in the psyche itself, to "have pity on the Punisher" and restore the moral sense to its proper role as servant of life, by subordinating its judgments to forgiveness. He had the mystic vision that while no individual can hope to make more than a small impact on the destructive patterns of society by pursuing this goal, determined exposure of satanic judgementalism within the psyche will open up direct experience of eternity even in the midst of the world's still-unresolved conflicts. He identified this as "the Everlasting Gospel of Jesus"; yet he also insisted that

"All Religions are One" prior to satanic perversion—and in our own day his insight, expressed in different terms, has been the core "gospel" of Krishnamurti, who stood apart from all formal religion: he urged the regular practice of "non-judgmental choiceless awareness" as the way of opening to the eternal. Maybe he wasn't a detective-story buff for nothing.

The ending of any detective-story after the unmasking of the villain is inevitably something of an anticlimax (a post-climax, perhaps?), and in my view one of Blake's most profound insights was that the unmasking of the Great Originator of Sin in human life brings something of the same feeling. Like the Wizard of Oz, pretension is the essence of Lucifer's power in the world and in the psyche: unmasked, he becomes something of a joke:

> Truly, My Satan, thou art but a Dunce,
> And dost not know the Garment from the man.

Perhaps that was what Chesterton was getting at, in a different idiom, when he said that if humanity were to be suddenly struck with a sense of humor, we would find ourselves automatically fulfilling the Sermon on the Mount. And perhaps, too, this is why the motivation of the crime in *The Name of the Rose* is the suppression of humor. So do join me as a detection buff, for the sheer fun of it, and go and see *The Mousetrap* if you're in London—it's fun even if you do know the ending.

FURTHER READING

Criticism

Corrigan, Maureen. "Melodrama and More." *Washington Post Book World* XXVII, No. 16 (20 March 1997): 8.
    Argues that the stories collected in *The Harlequin Tea Set* lack merit.

DeMarr, Mary Jean. "The Comic Village." In *Comic Crime,* edited by Earl F. Bargainnier, 75-91. Bowling Green, OH: Bowling Green State University Popular Press, 1987.
    Considers Christie's use of the village setting and its contribution to the mystery genre.

Hoffman, Nancy Y. "Mistresses of Malfeasance." In *Dimensions of Detective Fiction,* edited by Larry N. Landrum, Pat Browne, and Ray B. Browne, 97-101. Popular Press, 1976.
    Places Christie in the historical context of women crime writers.

Johnson, Pam. Review of *The Harlequin Tea Set and Other*

Stories, by Agatha Christie. *School Library Journal* 43, No. 11 (November 1997): 146.

Argues that while the stories in *The Harlequin Tea Set* are predictable, they testify to Christie's skill as a writer.

Keating, H. R. F., ed. *Agatha Christie: First Lady of Crime.* New York: Holt, Rinehart and Winston, 1977, 224 p.

Collection of essays examining various aspects of Christie's life and works, including essays on Miss Marple and Hercule Poirot.

Rifelj, Carol DeDobay. "Time in Agatha Christie Novels." *Language and Style* XII, No. 4 (Fall 1979): 213-27.

In the following essay, Rifelj applies Gerard Genette's theories of time structure to Christie's novels.

Additional coverage of Christie's life and career is contained in the following sources published by Gale: *Authors and Artists for Young Adults,* **Vol. 9;** *Authors in the News,* **Vols. 1 and 2;** *Contemporary Authors,* **Vols. 17-20R and 61-64;** *Contemporary Authors New Revision Series,* **Vols. 10 and 37;** *Concise Dictionary of British Literary Biography 1914-1945; DISCovering Authors: British; DISCovering Authors: Canadian; DISCovering Authors Modules: Novelists; Dictionary of Literary Biography,* **Vols. 13 and 77;** *Major 20th-Century Writers;* **and** *Something about the Author,* **Vol. 36.**

Barbara Ehrenreich
1941-

American lecturer, journalist, novelist, and critic.

The following entry presents an overview of Ehrenreich's career through 1997.

INTRODUCTION

A lifelong member of the Democratic Socialist Party, Barbara Ehrenreich has never been circumspect about her politics. Even critics at the opposite end of the political spectrum have found this directness refreshing: Writing for *The American Spectator,* Andrew Ferguson said of her frequent essays on the back page of *Time* magazine, "her unabashedly left-wing views make a pleasant contrast to the abashedly left-wing views found in the pages preceding it." Ehrenreich, sometimes with co-authors, has written about the world-wide student movement, health care, poverty, politics, feminism, and most of the other social and political issues of the second half of the twentieth century.

Biographical Information

Ehrenreich was born August 26, 1941, in Butte, Montana. Her first marriage, to John Ehrenreich in 1966, and produced two children, Rosa and Benjamin, and ended in divorce. She married Gary Stevenson in 1983. Raised in a working-class atheist family that had a longstanding ethic of independent thinking, Ehrenreich became a left-wing political activist, although her college career prepared her for the hard sciences. She received a B.A. in chemical physics from Reed College in Portland, Oregon in 1964. In 1968 she completed a Ph.D. in cell biology at Rockefeller University in New York City. While at Rockefeller, Ehrenreich became involved in the Vietnam War protests and the civil rights movement.

Major Works

In *Long March, Short Spring: The Student Uprising at Home and Abroad* (1969), written with her husband John, Ehrenreich reported on the student movements in the United States and Europe. Ehrenreich's identity as a socialist and feminist was reinforced by the poor quality of care she received during the birth of her daughter in 1970. This experience with health care was the impetus for the next book co-authored with her husband, *The American Health Empire: Power, Profits, and Politics, a Report from the Health Policy Advisory Center* (1970). Ehrenreich continued her exploration of women's health-care issues with two books co-authored with Deirdre English, *Witches, Midwives, and*

Nurses: A History of Women Healers (1972) and *Complaints and Disorders: The Sexual Politics of Sickness* (1973). Her next book with English, *For Her Own Good: One Hundred Fifty Years of the Experts' Advice to Women* (1978), examined the sexual politics of the advice literature genre. In the book, the authors argued that much of the writing ostensibly intended to make women's lives better was in fact intended to keep them in positions of subservience to the male-dominated hierarchy. In *The Hearts of Men: American Dreams and the Flight from Commitment* (1983), Ehrenreich argued that both men and women were beginning to break away from the traditional roles of breadwinner and housewife. In *Re-making Love: The Feminization of Sex* (1986), co-authored with Elizabeth Hess and Gloria Jacobs, Ehrenreich voiced her concern that the women's sexual revolution had become separated from the general thrust of the feminist movement. In *Fear of Falling: The Inner Life of the Middle Class* (1989), Ehrenreich examined the drift of the Middle Class to conservatism, describing it as a defensive reflex arising from uneasiness caused by uncertainty in the economy and massive corporate layoffs. The author addressed themes such as increased selfishness and the loss of generosity in *The Worst Years of Our Lives: Irreverent Notes from a Decade of Greed* (1990), a collection of essays previously published in several periodicals. In *Kipper's Game* (1994), a science fiction novel and Ehrenreich's first work of fiction, she examined many of the issues previously considered in her essays. ehrenreich offered another collection of previously-published essays with *The Snarling Citizen* (1995). *Blood Rites: Origins and History of the Passions of War* (1997) is an alternative theory to the origins of war. Contrary to the common belief that man is aggressive by nature, Ehrenreich argues that the nature of this behavior is a codification of the relatively recent progression of mankind from prey to predator.

Critical Reception

Ehrenreich's work has received mixed critical response. The author has been faulted for her oversimplification of complex issues and her reliance on pop culture sources and television to support her arguments, however, reviewers acknowledge her writing skill and perceptiveness. While critical of the theories presented in *Fear of Falling*, Joshua Henkin asserted, "the book is elegantly written, and the insight and wit that characterize her journalism are also abundant here. . . . Throughout, she has a keen eye for the contradictions of our culture." Despite her keen insight, critics focus on Ehrenreich's tendency to overgeneralize from a limited number of sources. In a critique of *Re-Making Love*, Julie Abraham stated, "[The authors] have not talked to enough people, or considered the complex interactions between sexual and social change that even their own writing illustrates." Reviewers have praised Ehrenreich's ability to entertain and to "provide aphoristic observations on modern life." Wilfred M. McClay wrote, "she is a graceful and often witty essayist, usually at her best in writing of everyday, commonplace things—food, dieting, fashion, leisure, "relationships," and pop culture—from a mildly heterodox feminist position."

PRINCIPAL WORKS

Long March, Short Spring: The Student Uprising at Home and Abroad [with John Ehrenreich] (journalism) 1969

The American Health Empire: Power, Profits, and Politics, a Report from the Health Policy Advisory Center [with J. Ehrenreich] (essays) 1970

Witches, Midwives, and Nurses: A History of Women Healers [with Deirdre English] (essays) 1972

Complaints and Disorders: The Sexual Politics of Sickness [with English] (essays) 1973

For Her Own Good: One Hundred Fifty Years of the Experts' Advice to Women [with English] (essays) 1978

The Hearts of Men: American Dreams and the Flight from Commitment (essays) 1983

Re-making Love: The Feminization of Sex [with Elizabeth Hess and Gloria Jacobs] (essays) 1986

The Mean Season: An Attack on the Welfare State [with Fred Block, Richard Cloward, and Frances Fox Piven] (essays) 1987

Fear of Falling: The Inner Life of the Middle Class (essays) 1989

The Worst Years of Our Lives: Irreverent Notes from a Decade of Greed (essays) 1990

Kipper's Game (novel) 1994

The Snarling Citizen (essays) 1995

Blood Rites: Origins and History of the Passions of War (nonfiction) 1997

CRITICISM

Edward Edelson (review date 24 January 1971)

SOURCE: "In Sickness and in Wealth," in *The Washington Post*, Vol.V, No. 4, January 24, 1971, pp. 1, 3.

[*In the following review, Edelson praises* The American Health Empire *as an innovative look at the problems with health care in America, although he finds some flaws in the authors' presentation.*]

The American Health Empire is yet another book about the sad state of American medicine—but don't stop reading there. This one is different. It is galvanizing, irritating, flawed and fascinating, and it presents an argument that has never been touched in what can be called the standard book on the health care crisis.

The standard book has been written under a score of titles by a score of authors. The standard book's villains and heroes are unvarying. On one side, in the black hats, are the old-line doctors, whose spokesman is the American Medical Association and whose aim is to keep American medicine disorganized in the interests of personal profit. The men in the white hats are the medical liberals, working out of modern hospitals and university-based medical centers, eager to press medical research, hopeful about drastically different methods of financing medical care (such as national health insurance) and anxious to use computers and the other tools of technology to end the present "nonsystem" of medical care for the benefit of the health consumer. If we can just help the liberals beat the AMA, says the standard book, our health care problems will be over.

It is at this point, where the standard book ends, that *The American Health Empire* begins. Its authors are members of a group of young activists working out of a self-created think-tank called the Health Policy Advisory Center. They present the reader with an entirely new villain—the very medical liberal whom most authors present as the last great hope of American medicine.

Health-PAC dismisses the AMA briefly as a declining organization whose prestige and power are falling rapidly, chiefly interested in fighting a forlorn rear guard action against the twentieth century. (Just last year, for the first time, the AMA's membership fell below 50 per cent of the nation's physician population. The AMA is now a minority group.)

With the AMA out of the way, Health-PAC follows the first rule of investigatory reporting: Look where the money goes. It finds that the money is going chiefly to the large university-based "medical empires" that are run by medical liberals. These centers carry on most medical research, use most of the new medical technology, sponsor most of the community action medical programs.

Between 1960 and 1969, Health-PAC says, the amount of money spent on medical care in the United States doubled, but the quality of medical care for most Americans held even at best, while costs are rocketing beyond the reach of even the respectable middle class. The standard book explains the paradox of rising costs and lowered standards by the greed of individual doctors. Health-PAC blames it on institutionalized greed—the greed of the "medical empires."

Those empires Health-PAC argues are not dedicated to medical care. Rather, they are dedicated to three goals: increasing institutional profits and individual salaries, feeding medical research that often has only a tenuous relationship to any real medical needs, and insuring its own perpetuation by controlling medical education. In short, the medical empire described by Health-PAC is essentially similar to any other unit of the technocracy described by John Kenneth Galbraith.

Health-PAC goes on to set forth what can only be called an institutionalized plot against good health care. Most of the money that pays for health care comes from Blue Cross, Blue Shield, Medicare and Medicaid, the book says. But the hospitals that get this money control the organizations that give the money, through a system of interlocking directorates. So "the Blues" never question the size of hospital bills—which means that the hospitals can raise prices as much as they please while the hospitals, in turn, are always ready to support requests for higher medical insurance rates. The medical instrument and drug companies, sensing profit opportunities, are in the conspiracy too.

Given this comprehensive plot, there is little hope for reform within the present system, says Health-PAC. National health insurance, the current bright hope of the medical liberals, is described as merely more of the same pouring larger amounts of money into the same leaky jug, with the same end results of higher-costs without any basic improvements. The only real hope, says Health-PAC, is community control and a thorough overhaul that will take medical care out of the hands of the monopolists and put it in the hands of the people.

The whole argument is stunning in its sweeping denunciation of every standard hope for better medical care. It is, in fact, just crazy enough to be true. Unfortunately, *The American Health Empire* has such serious flaws that its basic argument is imperiled.

To start with, the volume is full of statistics, anecdotes and quotations supporting its case. Yet it lacks supporting references for any of these. Presumably, documentation does exist for the highly personal and potentially damaging charges against respected individuals and institutions. These charges will be hotly contested. It is inexcusable to omit the documentation that would permit an objective evaluation by the reader.

Secondly, *The American Health Empire* is not really a book about the United States.

It is a book about New York City. All of its detailed case histories are from New York, a situation justified by the authors on the grounds that New York traditionally is a step ahead of the rest of the nation in the field of medicine. It can just as well be said that New York is so different that it cannot be compared to the rest of the nation.

Third, the Health-PAC activists are so eager to make their case that they often forget common sense and internal consistency. Firing wildly in all directions may be great for the soul, but it is not good journalism.

Finally, some functional failures. The volume is the outgrowth of a series of articles in a newsletter. Little care was taken in editing those articles, so the book is irritatingly repetitive. And it has no index; I only hope that the person responsible for that decision one day has to look up a subject in the book.

But after all the faults are ticked off, the basic value of *The American Health Empire* remains. Even if only half of its shots are on target—and that seems a reasonable estimate—it seems to come closer to the core of the health crisis than any other book yet published. Unreasonable and partisan as it is, it is required reading for anyone concerned with better health care.

Tod Gitlin (review date 28 May 1983)

SOURCE: "Where the Boys Aren't," in *The Nation,* Vol. 236, No. 21, May 28, 1983, pp. 663-65.

[*In the following review, Gitlin praises the insights and synthesis of divergent cultural icons in* The Hearts of Men: American Dreams and the Flight from Commitment.]

If the specter that haunts the American home is that of the woman walking out the door, Barbara Ehrenreich tells us in her stunningly subversive new book, our culture is once again deceiving us. Backlash panic has inverted the truth of the sexual war, which is that the family is threatened not because women want to get out but because men do.

Ehrenreich argues that men have been plotting their escape for thirty years because they resent having to support dependent wives and children. In earlier days, men succeeded in organizing the wage system around their breadwinner status, thereby justifying their higher pay. There was a hard economic reason why women needed to catch men and why men, having something to lose, wriggled on the hook. American popular culture has acknowledged this state of affairs in countless images: the elusive hero of westerns who rode into town only to ride out again; the grimacing Thurber husbands squeezed by grasping, all-devouring wives; Superman and Philip Marlowe and Jack Kerouac's wandering heroes.

But the breadwinner ethic has been collapsing since the 1950s, Ehrenreich maintains, and the hearts of men have been breaking away: before there were liberated women there was male flight and the threat and dream of it. This elegantly simple idea enables Ehrenreich to grasp a remarkable amount of recent cultural history. What could seem to have less in common than the *Playboy* philosophy and the Beat Generation? With iconoclastic glee, Ehrenreich links them not only with each other but with the cardiological hue and cry about the dangers of Type A behavior, the counterculture, the human potential movement, men's groups, the fitness cult and even feminism itself. In a brisk, witty and compact—if at times breathless—fashion, she interprets Hugh Hefner, Jack Kerouac, Timothy Leary, Abraham Maslow and Charles Reich as a choir chanting in unison to men: Don't let the wife and kids drag you down. Since she focuses on packaged images of mass culture, her evidence is sometimes stretched: her picture of the counterculture draws far too heavily on the *Time, Newsweek, Look,* and *Life* versions; and as she briefly acknowledges, not all men's groups conspire to leave women in the alimonyless lurch. Still, the force of an insight isn't damaged by some exaggeration. All in all, I can't think of a more compelling and ingenious assault on recent hip culture.

Ehrenreich's case is also timely, for it addresses the failure of the Equal Rights Amendment. As she correctly notes, the campaign against the E.R.A. was largely a women's movement, capitalizing on women's fear of losing the economic support of men. "In the ideology of American antifeminism," she writes, "it is almost impossible to separate the distrust of men from the hatred of feminists, or to determine with certainty which is the prior impulse." She cites a 1980 speech "in defense of the Christian family" by antiabortion leader Mrs. Randy Engel, who said: "Men desire sex without responsibility. They become unmanly and frightened by the thought of having to assume economic responsibility for a family: They instinctively try to escape." Feminism, says Ehrenreich, has failed to fathom the depths of women's structural dependence; in a way, feminists have failed to reckon with the force of their own analysis of the economy's bias against women: "While the feminist analysis spoke to the housewife's anger and frustration, the anti-feminist analysis spoke to her fear—fear that she might, after all, be a parasite whose support rested on neither love nor accomplishment, but only 'obligation.' At bottom the antifeminists accepted the most cynical masculine assessment of the heterosexual bond: that men are at best half-hearted participants in marriage and women are lucky to get them."

Mainstream feminism's embrace of the goal of female financial independence has "proved to be too radical for an influential minority of women. . . . It is as if, facing the age-old insecurity of the family wage system, women chose opposite strategies: either to get out (figuratively speaking) and fight for equality of income and opportunity, or to stay home and attempt to bind men more tightly to them." Feminists have noted that men pay precious little alimony and child support, but (no fault of their own) haven't been able to come up with a solution, while antifeminists have "offered a way to hold on to a man." (Ehrenreich might have mentioned Marabel Morgan's Total Woman as the answer to the Vanishing Man.) Meanwhile, to use the sociologist Diana Pearce's term, poverty is being "feminized": more than two out of three adults below the official poverty line are women, many of them refugees from the middle class whom divorce sent plummeting down the class scale.

The pivot is economics, in Ehrenreich's view, and if her book has a sizable shortcoming, it's the other side of her insistence that men's hearts are out the door because their minds are on the bottom line. Admittedly, this is an important truth. There's evidence that the poorer a married man, the more likely he is to leave his wife; high salaries make for longer marriages, which is consistent with Ehrenreich's view that—most? many?—men are calculating machines doing cost-benefit analyses.

But economics is only part of the story. It does not explain why men get married—in numbers, as she wittily points out, equal to women. Men do not live by the hope of cheap domestic labor alone. Ehrenreich's scorn for pop psychology extends too far, toward a dismissal of emotional dependencies—and ambivalences—altogether. She briefly acknowledges that men, like women, marry for love and security, but doesn't incorporate this fact into her scheme of things. Likewise, men break away partly because of the psychic terrors of dependency, the ways in which long-term commitment rekindles the unnameable needs and rages of infancy. Attention to the psychology of male dependency—as in Dorothy Dinnerstein's *The Mermaid and the Minotaur* and Lillian B. Rubin's new *Intimate Strangers*—would actually have strengthened Ehrenreich's formidable analysis of the ways culture is arrayed against love.

But this is little more than a quibble in the face of a provocative and original argument. Ehrenreich can be acerbic when her scorn is aroused, but she ends with a moving vision of "some renewal of loyalty and trust between adult men and women" on equal terms. The Me Generation has to yield to a We Generation, else we will inhabit a world in which we are left to size one another up as singles-bar consumables. Ehrenreich hopes "we might meet as rebels together—not against each other but against a social order that condemns so many of us to meaningless or degrading work in return for a glimpse of commodified pleasures, and condemns all of us to the prospect of mass annihilation." Surely that is the core of a feminist vision for the rest of the millennium—and beyond.

Carol Tavris (review date 5 June 1983)

SOURCE: "Who Started This?," in *The New York Times Book Review,* June 5, 1983, pp. 12, 31, 32.

[*In the following review of* The Hearts of Men, *Tavris finds Ehrenreich's analysis of male/female role dynamics insightful, but criticizes her conclusions about cause and effect.*]

Over the past two decades we've heard many criticisms of the housewife's lot, mostly from women, and counterattacking complaints about the breadwinner trap, mostly from men. Now Barbara Ehrenreich offers a provocative new argument: Male complaints about their restrictions and responsibilities, and their grievances about women, did not follow the women's movement; they preceded it. Indeed, Miss Ehrenreich says, men's weakening commitment to their wives and children gave rise to both feminism and antifeminism. Women, faced with the unpredictability of male commitment and the insecurity of the family wage system—which pays more to men than to women on the crumbling assumption that men support their families—had two choices. They could struggle for economic self-suffi-

ciency (the direction of feminism), or they could try to bind men more tightly to them (the direction of anti-feminism).

Miss Ehrenreich draws these conclusions from her study of "the ideology that shaped the breadwinner ethic" and the collapse of that ideology in the last 30 years. In the 1950's, she shows, the same ideology that was directing women to become steady wage spenders, docile wives and willing mothers was directing men to become steady wage earners, docile husbands and willing providers. According to the dominant ideology, men who resisted were not being "mature," responsible or heterosexual; they were failures as men and red-blooded Americans.

> By the 60's, Miss Ehrenreich says [in *The Hearts of Men*], the male revolt had begun to pick up support from physicians who maintained that the male role was unhealthy and from psychologists who maintained that it made men rigid, uptight and cranky.
>
> —*Carol Travis*

Over the years, as Miss Ehrenreich wittily demonstrates, the culture shifted to an ideology that celebrates "irresponsibility, self-indulgence, and an isolationist detachment from the claims of others"—in the name, of course, of independence, personal growth, physical health and emotional liberation. Our medical and psychological experts provided a scientific rationale for the new ideology with dizzying speed. The advicemongers of the 50's are easy targets of ridicule, but Miss Ehrenreich reminds us that today's experts are no less biased, even when their judgments are "buried under the weary rubric of 'changing sex rules.'"

Miss Ehrenreich does not consider the cultural shift a phenomenon to which men succumbed passively but the product of an active protest, a "male revolt" against maturity and responsibility in general and against women in particular. If the rebels were not always organized and conscious of their goals, she maintains, they were united in their rejection of the breadwinner philosophy.

The author begins her argument with a discussion of some "early rebels": the Gray Flannel Dissidents of the 50's, for whom "conformity" was a code word for male discontent with the demands of careers; the purveyors of *Playboy* magazine, for whom "sexual freedom" was code for discontent with the demands of marriage; and the Beats, who resented the demands of both work and marriage. Miss Ehrenreich is at her best here. *Playboy* (whose very name, she observes, "defied the convention of hard-won maturity") was not the voice of the sexual revolution, which accelerated in the 60's;

it was the voice of the male rebellion, which had begun in the 50's. "The magazine's real message was not eroticism, but escape . . . from the bondage of breadwinning. Sex—or Hefner's Pepsi-clean version of it—was there to legitimize what was truly subversive about *Playboy*. In every issue, every month, there was a Playmate to prove that a playboy didn't have to be a husband to be a man."

By the 60's, Miss Ehrenreich says, the male revolt had begun to pick up support from physicians who maintained that the male role was unhealthy and from psychologists who maintained that it made men rigid, up-tight and cranky. By the 70's the men's liberation movement—which Miss Ehrenreich by and large considers "the old male revolt in new disguise"—transformed male self-interest into a spiritually and politically correct way to behave.

Miss Ehrenreich concludes that men have won their revolt—and won it at the expense of women. Men have abandoned the breadwinner role while retaining their misogyny; they want women to remain submissive and nurturing while also becoming financially self-supporting. "The responsibilities that men gave up," Miss Ehrenreich says, "have come increasingly to rest with us." Feminism and antifeminism among women represent efforts to assume, or hand back, those responsibilities.

The Hearts of Men is a pleasure to read, entertaining and imaginative. It reminds us that sex roles do not apply to one sex only; that women have not been the only sex to chafe under the narrow restrictions of their "proper" place; that many men and women have been locked in a sad little dance in which each partner is doing different steps. For every wife who accuses her husband of wielding patriarchal power there is a husband who accuses his wife of parasitic pushiness. To listen to the grievances of one sex and not the complementary grievances of the other is to hear the sound of one hand slapping.

But Miss Ehrenreich's analysis falters in its confusion of causes and effects. She continually implies a sequence (first came concerted pressures upon men to conform, then male protest, then scientific legitimation of male protest) when her own evidence shows simultaneity. In the same decade that psychiatrists were lauding maturity and responsibility, there appeared *Playboy, The Lonely Crowd* (David Riesman's textbook for the gray flannel set), the Gestalt guru Fritz Peris and public worries about the male mortality rate. Conversely, as late as 1975, textbooks were still describing the "pathology" of men who couldn't or wouldn't choose a job and a mate. And the media she cites as pressuring men to conform in the 50's were simultaneously scaring them with the idea that too much conformity kills.

Further, to suggest that feminism came after the male revolt

is to mix what people say with what they do. If rebellion is defined as what people do, then keep in mind that in 1953, the year *Playboy* began, 26 percent of all married women were working—far more, I suspect, than the number of men who, regardless of what they were reading, quit their jobs or remained bachelors.

In arguing that male protest preceded female protest, Miss Ehrenreich succumbs to an unhelpful, unanswerable "Who started this?" spiral. She is hampered by her decision to concentrate on only the last 30 years—an extremely lively 30 years, to be sure. But she has described one inch of a 10-foot trajectory, thereby losing sight of the antecedents of the breadwinner role, the housewife role and the disintegration of both. As the sociologist Jessie Bernard observed, the male role of "good provider" emerged about 150 years ago and ended in 1980, when the Census Bureau stopped assuming that a man was "head of household."

> **In arguing that male protest preceded female protest, Miss Ehrenreich succumbs to an unhelpful, unanswerable "Who started this?" spiral. She is hampered by her decision to concentrate on only the last 30 years—an extremely lively 30 years, to be sure. But she has described one inch of a 10-foot trajectory, thereby losing sight of the antecedents of the breadwinner role, the housewife role and the disintegration of both.**
>
> **—*Carol Travis***

In addition, by looking into the hearts of men and not into their social worlds, Miss Ehrenreich cannot account for the change in male ideology (except in terms of "male self-interest"). One profound reason for the change, as obvious and as invisible as the purloined letter, has been identified in a recent book by the social psychologists Marcia Guttentag and Paul F. Secord: the greater ratio of marriageable women to marriageable men in virtually all age brackets since World War II. This imbalance alone has given men a leverage in mate selection and shifted the emotional power in relationships to men (they can always get another wife, while wives must compromise or lose), and, as Miss Guttentag and Mr. Secord document, the divorce rate and male "irresponsibility" increase in most cultures in which such imbalance exists. Conversely, when women are scarce, men tend to value romance, marriage and commitment.

Because Miss Ehrenreich doesn't have an explanation for the changes she documents so well, her point of view and conclusions shift. She pokes as much fun at the psychiatric model of maturity and responsibility of the 50's as she does at the human potential movement of the 70's, but later she laments the abandonment of the ethic of responsibility; she does not discuss how her notions of responsibility differ from the psychiatrists' (if they do). She lampoons the unverified assertion that working women are dying of heart attacks in unprecedented numbers (they aren't), but she is ambivalent about whether some aspects of the male role are hazardous to men's health or whether men simply use medical worries as an excuse for selfishness.

As she herself says, she is not sure whether the male revolt is a childish flight from responsibility, an accommodation to consumer culture or a libertarian movement for social change; in any case, she correctly adds, the consequences for women have been the same. But the book would have benefited from an effort to disentangle these three elements. More than that, it would have moved us from description to diagnosis.

Diagnosis matters if men and women are to travel beyond blaming. As it is, Miss Ehrenreich shrinks from the gloomy conclusions of her own account—that men will continue to pursue their own economic and psychological self-interest and women will have to fend for themselves and their children. Perhaps, she suggests wistfully, "the male revolt can be seen as a blow against a system of social control which operates to make men unquestioning and obedient employees. If men are not strapped into the role of breadwinners, perhaps they will be less compliant as assemblers of nuclear weapons, producers of toxic wastes, or as white-collar operatives of the remote and unaccountable corporations."

This sounds like the early feminist vision of women entering the worlds of government and business and transforming them into arenas of warmth and nurturance. Still, this lively book will do much to get men back into the conversation.

Benjamin R. Barber (review date 11 July 1983)

SOURCE: "Beyond the Feminist Mystique," in *New Republic,* Vol. 189, No. 3, July 11, 1983, pp. 26-32.

[*In the following excerpt, Barber summarizes developments in the Feminist Movement that he describes as anti-women and then discusses Ehrenreich's* The Hearts of Men *as a fresh perspective on the dynamics of male/female relationships, but oversimplified and flawed.*]

This is more than the internecine bickering of ideological purists. It issues out of a basic disenchantment—a revisionism that is ready to rewrite the history of the past without yet being ready to revise its blueprint for the future. Bar-

bara Ehrenreich, who is a loyal and unswerving feminist in the face of Elshtain's revisionism, nonetheless perpetrates an even more startling revisionism of her own in her new book, *The Hearts of Men: American Dreams and the Flight From Commitment.* In her fresh if highly selective rewriting of American social history since World War II, Ehrenreich argues that well before the feminist revolt, men were being led into rebellion against their traditional male roles as breadwinners and mortgage-holders by a most unlikely configuration of social movements. These included Hugh Hefner's *Playboy* philosophy (the magazine made its debut in 1953), which urged men to prefer an irresponsible bachelorhood where women figured only as particularly delectable consumables, to the responsibilities of marriage and the family; the medical discovery of stress as a major factor in heart disease for the hard-working overachievers who, it now turned out, were literally risking their lives to keep "spoiled" wives and children in the suburban comfort to which they had become accustomed; and finally the Beat Generation, which in its apotheosizing of irresponsibility, sexual promiscuity, male bonding, and "on the road" mobility, had redefined marriage as bondage and achievers as squares.

These three strains of postwar irresponsibility, Ehrenreich argues, infected the newly fashioned suburban family and undermined its foundations in the social culture well before Friedan got around to calling it a comfortable concentration camp.

> The promise of feminism—that there might be a future in which no adult person was either a "dependent creature" or an overburdened breadwinner—came at a time when the ideological supports for male conformity were already crumbling. Physicians had found men the weaker sex; psychologists were finding them perilously "rigid." The War [in Vietnam] reinforced the medical dictum that male aggressiveness was a lethal force; and the counterculture reinforced the promise, from the new psychology, of a richer life for those who could overcome their masculine hang-ups.

This is fascinating if debatable social history. Skeptics will point out that Ehrenreich picks and chooses among a plethora of possible sources, and that her actual themes come from the fringe rather than the heart of the 1950's social environment. A quite different moral emerges if one looks not at *Playboy,* cardiological stress, and the Beats (lesson: men were being tempted to abandon the family long before women were being tempted by feminism to imitate them), but at *The Saturday Evening Post,* Salk's polio vaccine, and the growth of television (lesson: marriage was great, kids were getting healthier, and everyone was staying home more—i.e., the family was flourishing as never before), or at *The Bulletin of Atomic Scientists,* the elevation of cancer into a number-one killer, and serial music (lesson: anxiety and alienation were undermining individuals and families).

There are as many lessons to be drawn from social history as there are permutations and combinations of social movements, subgroups, trends, fashions, novelties, and revolutions. To be sure, men were anxious about stress, but they also worried about communism *and* McCarthy, cancer and the Bomb, and on the whole they mostly stayed on the corporate ladder and limited their rebellion to Sunday football on television or chronic insomnia. Men were doubtless resentful of the pressures associated with playing breadwinner, but they did not dream of permitting their wives to work or otherwise share their "man-size" burdens. They were fascinated by the Beats and titillated by the *Playboy* life style, but wore button-down shirts and chinos and restricted their yen for bunnies to Easter with the kids.

Nonetheless, for the purposes of this discussion, what is interesting is not Ehrenreich's selective reading of social history but the conclusions she draws from it—or, rather, fails to draw from it. Are her 1950's dropouts heroes to be welcomed as allies in the feminist struggle against the constraints of the bourgeois family? Or cowards and narcissists to be despised for their immaturity, their materialism and their mistrust of women? Does portraying Hugh Hefner as a weird predecessor of Betty Friedan exonerate him of sexism or indict her of narcissism? If Jack Kerouac is a harbinger of liberation, then are not feminists so many latter-day hippies in search of missing selves and in flight from the responsibilities of maturity? Ehrenreich does not and apparently cannot answer these questions. She notes that the male revolt of the 1950's was "a blow against the system of social control," which flatters her socialist instincts, but she also recognizes that it was self-indulgent, materialistic, and woman-hating, which offends her feminist instincts.

> **In the end, Ehrenreich can neither avoid nor resolve the central dilemma of feminism: how to be free without mimicking men—how to nurture femininity without relinquishing equality.**
> **—*Benjamin R. Barber***

In the end, Ehrenreich can neither avoid nor resolve the central dilemma of feminism: how to be free without mimicking men—how to nurture femininity without relinquishing equality. Those like Elshtain and Friedan who remind women of the joys and responsibilities of loving and generativity (the new acceptable term for "reproductivity"), end up being viewed as traitors using liberal credentials to make arguments no less reactionary than those of a Midge Decter or a

Rita Kramer. (Kramer's new book *In Defense of the Family,* [see "What Are Families Really For?" by Peter Steinfels and Margaret O'Brien Steinfels, TNR, May 16], is a neoconservative attack on feminism that does simply celebrate the traditional woman and the traditional family.)

From the point of view of practical politics, feminism's second stage is thus an unmitigated disaster. Its honorable ambivalence, if it does not actually encourage backlash, can produce political paralysis. Its welcome confusions yield factionalism, recantation, and apostasy. Dilemmas and conundrums may occasion great literature and subtle theory, but they do little to rid the world of gender discrimination and sexual inequality.

Phyllis Rose (review date September 1986)

SOURCE: "Sex in Our Time," in *The Atlantic,* Vol. 258, No. 3, September, 1986, pp. 100-103.

[*In the following review, Rose compares the opposite philosophies expressed in the books* Re-Making Love *and Willard Gayling's* Rediscovering Love.]

"Higgimus, hoggimus, men are monogamous. Hoggimus, higgimus, women polygamous." My friends tell me I have got this wrong. It should be "Hoggimus, higgimus, men are polygamous. Higgimus, hoggimus, women monogamous." But I prefer my version, because it expresses a partial truth less often heard: many women have an instinct for sexual adventure, most often stifled, and many men, even promiscuous men, are at heart romantics, sexual conservatives.

These two books, with such similar titles, both addressing themselves to the unendingly interesting subject of sex in our time, could hardly be more different in outlook and intent. Moreover, they bear me out. Gaylin, a psychiatrist, is a self-confessed romantic who fell in love at sixteen, married his childhood sweet-heart at twenty-one, and has lived with her for over thirty-five years. He gives this news in the preface and refers so frequently throughout the text to the pleasures of family life that, frankly, were Gaylin not a man and a psychiatrist, one might think him defensive, or sentimental. His book's message (at one point he refers to it as a "here-and-now gospel") is that "we" need to shift our emphasis from the narcissistic pleasure of receiving love to the more mature and deeply satisfying pleasure of giving love; that in order to overcome our "mounting sense of isolation, purposelessness, and ennui," we must rediscover long-term, committed, monogamous, preferably married, and (but this goes without saying) heterosexual love.

Whereas Gaylin writes in the hortatory mode of psychoanalytic-wisdom literature and adopts unabashedly the priestly role of spiritual adviser, the authors of **Re-making Love,** Barbara Ehrenreich, Elizabeth Hess, and Gloria Jacobs, more modestly offer an account of the sexual revolution which shows its hidden feminist content. Their thesis is that the sexual revolution beginning in the 1960s had more of an impact on women than on men. They trace the evolution of the culturally encoded "meaning" of sex from the 1950s, when male dominance and female submission were the norm in bed as in the work-place, to the present, when in various ways power is still at the heart of sexual activity but the roles of dominance and submission are not so unvaryingly assigned by gender. They believe that all revolutions in meaning present themselves initially as nihilism, an absence of meaning. They feel strongly that sex has had too much meaning in the past, always reinforcing male power, and that now, when it seems we are stripping all meaning from sex, we are merely in the process of giving it a new meaning. Students of culture, they assume that love is something we reconstruct in every age, not something we rediscover, like the lost city of the Incas.

Their materials are the materials of popular culture: *Life, People,* Beatlemania, *Valley of the Dolls, The Hite Report, The Total Woman.* In fact, this history of the sexual revolution is written cleverly in terms of key texts, so that the authors don't have to make any rash statements about what people do but can merely report on what they can conceive of doing. *Sex and the Single Girl; The Feminine Mystique; Our Bodies, Ourselves;* Masters and Johnson; *The Sensuous Woman; How to Make Love to a Man*—what a parade! Remember those sex manuals of the 1950s, which told you nothing you wanted to know about sex? How did we get from Theodoor van de Velde's *Ideal Marriage* and other books popular in the 1950s, which told us that women's role in sex was even easier than falling off a log, because it was *being* the log, to the hairy and energetic lovers illustrated in *The Joy of Sex?* We can't help being struck by the eerie inexorability of cultural change as we watch the ideal of female passivity in sex (can it be said?) go down.

It all began with the Kinsey report's methodology. Its literalist, quantitative counting of orgasms changed the way Americans thought about sex even more than did its shocking revelations about the amount of premarital and extramarital sex people were in fact having. The methodology implied that anything that produces an orgasm is as good as anything else, and that one orgasm is as good as another. Female pleasure began to be as important as male pleasure. Soon Helen Gurley Brown, more radical in some ways than Betty Friedan, told women they could do without marriage. The medical profession lost its monopoly on sex books. The bedroom became a place of "negotiation." The new emphasis, codified in books like *The Joy of Sex,* was on sexual "options." With the growing visibility of homosexuals and the

divorce of sex from reproduction, heterosexuality—that is, the traditional "micro-drama of male dominance and female passivity"—seemed more and more an institution, a cult. *Re-making Love* brilliantly suggests why sadomasochism inevitably became the cutting edge of sex: because it plays with dominance and submission but doesn't assume that the choice of who plays which role is predetermined by gender. "For some women, S/M may have been an improvement on the old, unconscious variety of sadomasochism promoted by the marriage manuals of the fifties." *Re-making Love* argues that even in the Christian right, women are assuming more-active sexual roles, seducing their husbands to the heterosexual micro-drama, as Marabel Morgan suggested they should in *The Total Woman.* It ends by documenting a growing sexual conservatism, which began before the AIDS epidemic but was certainly reinforced by it.

While the authors of *Re-making Love* talk about orgasms and sexual politics, Gaylin talks about commitment. While they sponsor realism, he encourages idealism. He takes the high road and they take the low. I imagine he would see them as signs of "our" malaise. They would surely see him as a predictable mouthpiece for the current backlash—reactionary, revisionist, trying to lure women back to traditional sexual roles through that age-old instrument romantic rhetoric. I confess I'm on their side.

It's not that I don't believe in love, and it's not that I don't value it. But let me not talk about me. I will talk about "the people I know," who are very different from the people Gaylin posits. The people I know—admittedly, flaky bohemians and deviant intellectuals—still occasionally manage to stay married. Sometimes they settle for casual sex, because that's the best they can get, but they generally prefer a daily kind of love, for all its occasional tedium and its inevitable troubles. They sometimes turn to promiscuity, often to prove something to themselves about their own attractiveness or power, but it is rarely a lifetime habit. Their impulse toward monogamy may hook them up for too long with people who are less than satisfactory to them. So they go from one five-year or ten-year relationship to the next. Is this a failure of commitment or an exercise in commitment? The people I know do not fly out of their marriages as though from one cocktail party to the next but leave them, if at all, with deep reluctance, difficulty, and guilt. The last thing the people I know need to be told is to reverence love more, because they already reverence it too much and suffer from its absence too deeply. Where are these shallow narcissists on whom Gaylin's gospel is predicated? He himself is not one. Why does he imagine he's the only boy on the bus who believes in Santa Claus?

His battle is not really with us debased narcissists, frantically pursuing sexual pleasure, but with debased Freudian thought, which imagines people as motivated exclusively by the pursuit of sexual pleasure. Gaylin believes that by enshrining the sex drive as the primary factor in human activity, Freudian theory vulgarized love and trivialized sex. Freud's works contain no discussion of what Gaylin would call love, and he complains that psychoanalysts are encouraged to talk not about it but about "cathexes," "object relationships," and "attachments."

"Psychoanalytic theory created a loveless world," Gaylin writes, missing the entire point of Freud's effort to unmask love as a genteel cover for instinctual desire. To rehabilitate love and free us all from our delusion that sex is the central activity of life, Gaylin sets out to develop a notion of pleasure more sophisticated than the one he assumes we have—that pleasure is the release of tension. Pleasure results from "an enhanced sense of self," so mastery, concentration, and giving can all produce pleasure. He proves a great many things one would think didn't need proving. Human love, he tells us, is different from and higher than that of the animals. Sex is more than instinctual. It is a highly nuanced cultural activity. (This is where Ehrenreich et al. begin.)

Gaylin offers an intriguing neo-Freudian explanation for why we risk humor, pride, and sanity, spend money and time, in order to find someone to go through life with. It's more than libido. Paired, he suggests, is the natural state of humanity. We begin life as part of a pair—us and Mom, self and other—and we never feel really comfortable until we get back to that situation. To support his hypothesis, he invokes Aristophanes' myth (as recounted in Plato's *Symposium*) of the dual nature of man. It's a lovely story. Originally, man was a circular, two-headed, four-legged, and four-armed creature. Zeus punished man by splitting him in two, and ever after, each half was doomed to seek its original mate and to feel incomplete without it. When the two halves meet—which is rare—they feel the excitement of reunion that we call falling in love. This myth has always appealed to people, perhaps, as Gaylin suggests, because it is in some sense true. He argues that "fusion," the return to an earlier state of oneness with another, is the "central phenomenon of loving." In real love two identities merge to create something new, a third thing, a third identity, with the boundaries between self and other blurred.

The tactic of making the love between parent and child the essential experience of love in life is attractive for many reasons. It does away with what Gaylin rightly calls the trivial notion that sexual gratification impels us to love. It suggests a model for loving which is based on nurturing and giving as well as getting. Parental love may well be the most satisfying of all forms of love, and an element of maternal or paternal love within the shifting play of erotic love may be a good thing indeed. But there is danger in making the relationship between parent and child the model for the relationship between adult lovers, even if that model is modified so that the roles of responsibility and dependence can be traded off, so that each member can be the child or the parent at various times. The relationship between adults is consensual, and that between adult and child is not; therefore the parent has an unending and unbreakable responsibility for the child he has brought into life, whereas the adult has no such responsibility for his or her mate. The model is a covert argument for the indissolubility of marriage. "When presented by a quandary as to how to handle a difficult five-year-old," Gaylin writes, "we do not consider as one alternative, abandonment of the child. We are committed to her care, and we do not conceive of 'divorce' as an alternative to this commitment."

The merging of selves to form a new identity in love is another beautiful but dangerous idea. Traditional marriage has been based on this very notion, and in practice it produces dependent women with no identities, or with identities so contingent upon their husbands' that they are devastated if their husbands leave them for other "fusions." A woman these days would be a fool to let herself "merge" her identity unreservedly. Yet nothing seems more lovely to me than the notion of such a merger. I hope it will not seem bitter if I say that a certain kind of idealism about marriage and love comes easier to men than to women. Which brings us back to "Higgimus, hoggimus."

Judith Viorst (review date 14 September 1986)

SOURCE: "Rolling Back the Lust Frontier," in *New York Times Book Review,* September 14, 1986, p. 9.

[*In the following review, Viorst praises* Re-Making Love.]

It was women—it wasn't men—whose sexual attitudes and behavior drastically changed within the past two decades. The sexual revolution, Barbara Ehrenreich, Elizabeth Hess and Gloria Jacobs compellingly argue, is actually women's sexual revolution. Thus the counterrevolution, the sexual backlash that emerged in the early 1980's, is primarily directed against women and is a threat to women's achievements in "the remaking and reinterpretation of sex."

Much of *Re-making Love* is devoted to tracing these achievements over the past 20 years. The high value placed on virginity, the primacy of the vaginal orgasm, the linking of femininity to passivity, the condemnation of sexual fantasy and variety were accepted mainstream doctrine until the 60's. And although there is not much new in the parts of the book describing how we got from there to here, this intelligent, thought-provoking social history makes very lively reading.

The authors begin with Beatlemania, arguing that this shriek-ing, sobbing, moaning outburst of mass hysteria, this total abandonment of control, was "the first and most dramatic uprising of *women*'s sexual revolution. "True, we had seen such carryings-on before—in the swooning over Frankie, the screaming for Elvis. But Beatlemania far surpassed these earlier teen-age frenzies, blowing the lid off a lusty sexual-ity that nice young girls were not supposed to possess.

The 60's were also a time, note the authors, of a rapidly emerging singles culture, as thousands of women—explor-ing new vistas between graduation and Mr. Right—flocked to cities. The message was growing louder that nice girls not only wanted to do it but were actually doing it. The birth control pill, commercially available in 1960, was helping them do it without getting pregnant. And the validation of clitoral sexuality was helping them do it with more pleasure.

Soon mainstream women, inside and outside marriage, were pursuing not only more but better sex, instructed by guides, available at every local bookstore, to the wilder shores of sexual rapture. As women became consumers of sexual plea-sure, the marketplace offered ever more daring sex gear—vibrators, fruit-flavored lotions, ankle restraints—sometimes sold in middle-class homes at women's Tupperware-style get-togethers. Indeed, the authors say, the commercialization of sex and the search for new commodities continue to ex-pand "the lust frontier" to the point (and I find this asser-tion surprising) where sadomasochism has been brought into the mainstream.

The sexual revolution has been broad enough to include radi-cal feminist lesbians as well as Christian fundamentalist women. In her popular book *The Total Woman,* the funda-mentalist Marabel Morgan urged wives to transform them-selves into one-woman harems. Her piquant mix of sex and evangelism inspired a flood of zesty Christian sex manuals. But female fundamentalist sexual pleasure, the authors point out, is restricted to marriage, which still insists upon the sub-mission of women.

It is clear that women's sexual transformation is not always linked to the liberation of women. Indeed, the feminist move-ment, which had initially embraced the women's sex revo-lution, is now separated from and to some extent at odds with it. Why? Because most feminists, say the authors, consider sexual issues peripheral to women's political and economic goals and because some feminists regard heterosexual sex per se as female subordination.

In the last chapters the authors move into a fascinating, dis-turbing discussion of women's reactions to their own revo-lution. They note that women have for the most part failed to claim their victory the transformation of physical sex from phallocentric intercourse to a variety of erotic possibilities,

from an act burdened with meanings like love and surren-der to one that might be engaged in simply for pleasure. They find that while women enjoy their expanded sexual opportunities, they are also afraid of sexual liberation. For if sex is not to be bartered for a relationship, more women may wind up going it alone. More often than men, they will face the prospect of economic hard times, of depreciation of their sexual value in the marketplace as they age and of life without sex.

The sexual backlash—urging less promiscuity, more re-straint—has been able to feed on these real anxieties. The authors, giving too little weight to both sexes' fears of herpes and AIDS, take the view that this counterrevolution is "a campaign against women and their sex lives. "They conclude with an eloquent plea to feminism to involve itself with sexual liberation, to acknowledge the great victory that women have achieved, to protect it from being trivialized or rescinded, to assert that pleasure for women—sexual plea-sure unburdened by meaning—is a legitimate social goal.

The authors, all of whom have written widely on feminist topics, present their views with clarity and forcefulness. They ask us "to set aside, at least temporarily, both feminist and conservative dogmas about what is good and bad or right and wrong when it comes to sex." If anyone needs remind-ing of the distance women have come, this is the book to read—and then to wrestle with. For ***Re-making Love*** re-quires us all to think about the meaning of sex in our lives.

I find the authors persuasive when they claim that a broader view of the physical sex act is sexual progress. But I find myself resisting their wish to free sexual pleasure from larger meanings—not because such divestiture is immoral but because it is a gyp.

—Judith Viorst

I find the authors persuasive when they claim that a broader view of the physical sex act is sexual progress. But I find myself resisting their wish to free sexual pleasure from larger meanings—not because such divestiture is immoral but be-cause it is a gyp. There are plenty of pleasures around that can be savored with little emotional investment. I think ev-eryone gains if we—men and women—regard sex both as a pleasure and a big deal. Barbara Ehrenreich, in a brilliant earlier book, ***The Hearts of Men,*** called for "some renewal of loyalty and trust between adult men and women." Can ca-sual sex be the answer to that call? The old male styles of careless love need not remain the model for female—for hu-man—sexual liberation. Linking erotic pleasure to genuine concern for one's sexual partner may be a better way of re-making love.

Julie Abraham (review date 28 February 1987)

SOURCE: "Not My Revolution," in *The Nation,* Vol. 244, No. 8, February 28, 1987, pp. 266-67.

[*In the following review, Abraham finds the source material in* Re-Making Love *too superficial, and the resultant conclusions over-generalized.*]

Singles in the cities, paraphilias in the suburbs and sex aids in Ohio: according to **Re-making Love,** these are all manifestations of a women's sexual revolution that far outweighs the male-dominated phenomenon known as *the* sexual revolution. The latter, as Barbara Ehrenreich, Elizabeth Hess and Gloria Jacobs describe it—"what Gay Talese found when he set out on his quest to see what middle-aged, middle-class men had been missing all these years"—was no revolution at all. The revolution that did occur, and that they follow from Beatlemania to the G-spot, was marked by dramatic changes in women's sexual expectations and experience.

Much of their evidence for this transformation is familiar: the appearance of clubs featuring male strippers for female audiences; Marabel Morgan's *Total Woman;* "home parties" where sexual paraphernalia rather than tupperware are sold; the results of surveys done by magazines like *Redbook, Playboy* and *Family Circle.* But, they argue, the sweeping change in women's sexual behavior that this evidence represents has not been acknowledged. Once again, "men have evaded a feminine innovation they found vaguely troubling—or perhaps even overtly disturbing."

The purpose of **Re-making Love** is overtly political: to help women to claim and build on the gains that have been made, especially in the face of the 1980s backlash against sexual freedom. Ehrenreich, Hess and Jacobs argue that the development of the women's liberation movement in the late 1960s was closely connected to the women's sexual revolution and insist (contrary to activists' fears at the time) that feminism's acceptance and promotion of sexual liberation was crucial to its course:

Instead of narrowing the movement to a subculture of politicized, urban women, sexual liberation contributed to the populist outreach that eventually brought the movement itself into the mainstream of American culture and politics.

The authors' goal is a reunion of sexual liberation and women's liberation, for the renewed benefit of each. Sex will save feminism as feminism saves sex, and **Re-making Love**

will have served both as contemporary history and as organizing tool.

Unfortunately, the book's version of story is based on flimsy anecdote her than solid evidence. Ehrenreich, Hess, and Jacobs begin in the early 60s, with glances back to such post-war gems of advice as this, from Ferdinand Lundberg and Maryina Farnham's 1947 *Modern Woman: The Lost Sex:*

> For the male, sex involves an objective act of his doing but for the female it does not . . . her role is passive. It is not as easy as rolling off a log for her. It is easier. It is as easy as being the log itself.

After that, any acknowledgment of women's sexuality can be made to seem revolutionary, from *The Joy of Sex* to pornographic videos marketed for female audiences. The authors' eagerness to claim every possible victory for women leads them to some unduly positive readings. It might be original to include *Total Woman* as a contribution to the women's sexual revolution, but as anything but a worst-case scenario, it is not convincing.

Re-making Love is a self-consciously popular product of the debate about sexuality that has been going on in the feminist community for the past five years. Ehrenreich, Hess and Jacobs address that debate briefly, but the effect of their book is to gloss over it by distorting its history and origins. Early feminist critiques of the male "sexual revolution" co-existed with an equally important insistence on women's right to sexual pleasure. Those two strains are still evident in recent disagreements over much matters as pornography and lesbian sado-masochism. By dismissing the male sexual revolution as a non-event, the authors have pulled the rug out from under the antipornography position in contemporary feminism—a rhetorical if not an analytical coup.

Re-making Love also glosses over other differences between women. The text is interspersed with brief fictionalized character sketches and the statements of nameless informants: Jane Cooper, a Washington housewife; Ellen, who works for the telephone company; a Beatlemaniac who grew up to direct a public-policy interest group. The authors' willingness to generalize on the basis of these voices is breathtaking. They seem not to have noticed that speaking for women as a group has become a questionable practice over the past fifteen years.

Ehrenreich, Hess and Jacobs state explicitly that their interest is in the "mainstream," and their representative woman is white, middle-class and heterosexual. They quote lesbian writers, refer to lesbian sado-masochism and admonish their readers that gays and lesbians should be honored as the sexual vanguard. But while there are, for example, extended discussions of heterosexual sado-masochism and the sexual plight of fundamentalist wives, lesbians are not seen as women who might have been part of this women's revolution. They are merely invoked from time to time to signify sexual radicalism in a book about options for ordinary people.

By the time the reader gets to the feminist call to arms in the book's conclusion, the authors' vision of "the public" has seriously undermined their purpose. The questions they raise about contemporary sexual experience are particularly urgent in the face of a conservative onslaught that has found a new excuse in AIDS. But they have not talked to enough people, or considered the complex interactions between sexual and social change that even their own writing illustrates. Ehrenreich, Hess and Jacobs themselves don't seem to believe in the revolution they claim.

Leslie Dick (review date 9 October 1987)

SOURCE: "Why Don't We Do It in the Road?" in *New Statesman,* Vol. 114, No. 2950, October 9, 1987, pp. 25-26.

[*Below, Dick gives a negative review of* Re-Making Love.]

In 1964, when we were nine, my best friend and I played a secret game, enacting elaborate adventures in which we would take turns to be Paul McCartney or John Lennon. The story always ended with us "falling in love": we would roll around on the floor, kissing passionately.

In **Re-making Love,** the roots of the Women's Liberation Movement are found in the rebellion against the female sexual predicament of the early 1960s, as evidenced by *Sex and the Single Girl*-ism (nice girls in big cities having affairs) and Beatlemania (which the authors see as a proto-feminist outburst against rigid gender roles and teenage sexual repression). Later, *Cosmopolitan* magazine and manuals like *The Joy of Sex,* with their "reassuring" injunctions to experiment, to seek out the ideal orgasm and assert your "right" to sexual pleasure, apparently brought non-feminist women into contact with euphoric feelings of self-determination and control. Indeed the authors claim it was at least party due to the "sexual revolution" that feminism was not limited to a "subculture of politicized, urban women", but moved into the mainstream of American culture and politics.

The book is only concerned with mainstream America—and one quickly longs for an interrogation of the whole idea of the "mainstream", with its connotations of the Normal and the Average. The "housewife in Ohio" reappears often, as does her counterpart, the "professional" single in the city— it goes without saying they are both white, middle-class and heterosexual. In a sense the book is both *about* these women and addressed *to* them, despite their status as convenient sociological fictions. The authors state they will not tackle the thorny issues around homosexual and lesbian love, except as a "sense of possibility", or source of sexual fantasy for the (normal) heterosexual woman.

That silent "(normal)" is present throughout the book, obscured by overt denunciations of 1950s sex manuals and their insistence on female sexual passivity. But the fundamental implication of *all* sex manuals is that sex can be (must be?) defined, "fixed" and quantified, that there are achievable goals, definable expectations, alphabets and menus of sex: "Twenty years ago the woman dissatisfied with sex was made to believe she was lacking something . . . Today . . . it is the woman who does not know how to negotiate or find her own way to pleasure who wonders if she is different, abnormal." We call *this* liberation?

A grim picture emerges of the dutiful pursuit of sexual pleasure, as all over America "equal partners" enter into bedroom negotiations over the exchange of labor necessary to produce this elusive thing, this final goal, the female orgasm. (Of course *male* sexual pleasure is supposed to be as simple as abc, but that's another story . . .) In the 1970s, one expert suggested that each couple acquire two copies of *The Joy of Sex,* his "n" hers, and work their way through all the positions, scoring each with marks out of ten, and then exchange books. In this scenario, it's impossible even to say "gee, I like that", as the sex manual becomes both the source of sex and the means of communicating a response.

Which is not to imply there's some *natural* sexuality somewhere that doesn't "need" all these instructions; the hard information produced by the Kinsey Reports of 1948 and 1953, and the Hite Report of 1976, backed up by the purely physiological researches of Masters and Johnson (1966), was extremely useful to women long oppressed by myths of the vaginal orgasm, female sexual passivity, etc. One problem is that if you're going to be scientific about sex, you have to have something to count, something to measure: orgasms. Who dares say pleasure is not equivalent to orgasm? Stephen Health's book *The Sexual Fix* (1982) shows how the official approval of experimentation in pursuit of the orgasm ("just so long as nobody gets hurt!") both functions as a definition of sexual expectation and overlooks the fact that psychic pain, like pleasure, isn't measured by electrodes and dials.

Nevertheless, **Re-making Love** presents an entertaining survey of sexology, from the 1948 book that describes sex for women as easier than falling off a log ("it is as easy as being the log itself"), to the 1982 "G-spot" and its resurrection of penetration as the way to ultimate female orgasm. The authors analyze the 1970s movement of S/M style and paraphernalia from the cities into the suburbs. Once everyone had bought their vibrators, S/M allowed a whole new range of sexual commodities to be marketed and consumed: "From a strictly capitalist viewpoint, it is the ideal sexual practice." Equally fascinating is the chapter on sex manuals for born-again Christians, which encourage the devout wife to dress up in costumes (thus sustaining her husband's interests and preserving monogamy) and to imagine herself as a "love-slave to Christ", delighting in sexual submission.

Tragically, *Re-making Love* appears at a historical moment when the repercussions of the AIDS epidemic are changing the parameters of this debate. Biology wreaks havoc with ideology. . . .
—Leslie Dick

Tragically, ***Re-making Love*** appears at a historical moment when the repercussions of the AIDS epidemic are changing the parameters of this debate. Biology wreaks havoc with ideology; as feminists we must continue to celebrate sexual pleasure, without ceasing to question the terms of our "sexual liberation".

Jefferson Morley (review date 6 August 1989)

SOURCE: "The Discreet Anxiety of the Bourgeoisie," in *New York Times Book Review,* August 6, 1989, pp. 12-13.

[*In the following review, Morley praises the insights in* Fear of Falling.]

I was a teen-age neoconservative, I came of age politically in the 1970's with a low tolerance for the foibles of my parents and an all-too-cool critique of the 1960's, especially of the decade's "permissiveness." The cultural contradictions of capitalism seemed less disturbing (and more fun) to me than the cultural contradictions of Communism, and I imagined I was rejecting middle-class culture. But in fact, as Barbara Ehrenreich's *Fear of Falling* makes clear, it defined my every thought.

For me, not the least of this book's achievements is its explication of my peculiar coming of age. But any citizen of the educated middle class will find something even more useful here: a persuasive account of an intellectual dispute that has been simmering in the superego of the American professional-managerial class for the last 30 years or so. This dispute has helped shape American politics.

Ms. Ehrenreich, an intellectual journalist with a gift for apho-

rism and the author of several books, picks up her story of middle-class anxiety in the late 1950's. At the time, it was claimed there was no need for a major political restructuring of society, although divisions of class and race remained powerful elements in American life. Frequently, conflicts were dealt with euphemistically. Affluence, Ms. Ehrenreich notes, became "a way of talking about, wealth without talking about class."

A larger problem was "discovered" in the early 1960's: poverty. After millions of Americans were revealed to be impoverished, a number of leading sociologists, together with a spate of cover stories in the news weeklies, blamed the conditions not on class but on a lack of character, deficient morals among the poor. This explanation, Ms. Ehrenreich observes, served as a kind of psychological projection. The poor represented "what the middle class feared most in itself," she says—a "softening of character, a lack of firm internal values."

The emergence of the counterculture in the mid-1960's, however, mocked the pretensions of the American middle class. There was no longer any need for it to project its anxieties onto the poor. Its own children were softening up the sturdy internal middle-class values with large dosages of drugs, sex and rock music.

The latter, Ms. Ehrenreich says, was especially important. "If theories of the 'culture of poverty' were the middle-class critique of the poor, rock was a critique of the middle class, bubbling up from America's invisible 'others.'" Rock, she notes, was the music of the underclass, and by the late 1960's its influence extended literally everywhere in America.

As a result of this youthful upheaval, several leading writers of the intellectual middle classes took up the theme of "permissiveness," and this, according to Ms. Ehrenreich, has been the central insight of American conservatism since the 1960's Ivy League professors, intellectuals of the Old Right, astute bureaucrats in corporate public relations and all manner of aspiring Washington policy makers built a school of political thought around the permissiveness problem.

Concurrent with the emergence of permissiveness in mid-70's intellectual discourse was the discovery of the working class, especially in its "silent majority" incarnation. This group was said to be imbued with traditional values, scornful of countercultural foolishness and confident of American purpose abroad. Increasingly. It was argued that the intellectuals of the educated middle class would do well to emulate these folk. I can personally attest to the appeal of this argument, at least to the adolescent mind.

Ms. Ehrenreich is again on firm ground in diagnosing projection. The anxious middle class was once more seeing what it wanted to see. Yes, there was an emerging Republican majority, at least in Presidential elections, but the working class in the late 1960's and early 1970's could not be neatly encapsulated, particularly when it came to the war in Vietnam. As Ms. Ehrenreich points out, the American working class was more, not less, opposed to the war than was the population as a whole, and more, not less, inclined to regard the conflict as a criminal enterprise and not an exercise in mistaken idealism.

But middle-class scholars and analysts, Ms. Ehrenreich insists, were not eager to perceive rebelliousness in the working class. "Its activism—the upsurge of strikes and militant job actions in the late sixties—was scantily covered relative to the movements of students or minorities, and was never framed as a 'crisis,' a challenging new phenomenon with its own media heroes and personalities."

Instead, the conservatives among middle-class intellectuals, with an impressive sense of self-importance, blamed intellectuals in general for society's permissiveness, employing a rather simplified version of Milovan Djilas's notion of the New Class. Mr. Djilas, a Yugoslav dissident, noted that under Communism a new class, whose authority was based on its command of ideas, had come to power in Eastern Europe. In the United States, neoconservatives argued, a permissive New Class was dismantling the traditional American value system and substituting its own secular and countercultural, if not socialistic, values.

By making this argument, Ms. Ehrenreich declares, the conservative intellectuals were defending their own professional interests. Black nationalism, rock music and other cultural innovations were entirely in the American grain. But they called into question the relevance of the work of middle-class intellectuals, who were afraid of falling out of positions of authority.

Even in the late 1970's, the inadequacy of the neoconservatives' diagnosis was plain. The kind of mindless hedonism that could ruin character did not originate solely in the 1960's counterculture, as any student of disco and cocaine could see. In American society, the tensions between modernism and tradition, consumerism and self-discipline were being played out not among the isolated left-wing intelligentsia, but in the marketplace. The multi billion-dollar cocaine industry, to cite but one example, is hardly the work of permissive Ivy League intellectuals. It is the creation of profit-seeking entrepreneurs—many of whom have impeccable right-wing credentials.

The American working class, as the object of the conservative intellectual's affections, fared pretty badly once the conservative agenda was enacted under President Ronald Reagan. Ms. Ehrenreich explains that capital was shifted from manufacturing to speculation; that the maldistribution of income grew worse; that the possibility of buying a house receded, and that well-paying jobs grew scarcer. There were, however, plenty of job openings for New Class conservatives in Washington. And the problems of permissiveness had spread to Wall Street, to the savings and loan industry, to the Department of Housing and Urban Development.

Ms. Ehrenreich blames the conservative intellectuals for discrediting the idea that the educated middle class has any duty or ability to contribute to public life. She insists it does—if it puts aside status anxieties and the sometimes strange language of current political debate. At present, American society seems divided between its allegiance to the speculative free market and its yearning for productive work. The intellectual can make a contribution to the debate over the market place, she says, simply by asserting the value of pleasurable work. "The pleasure of work is the middle class's tacit rebuttal to capitalism," she says, "a pleasure that cannot be commodified or marketed, that need not obsolesce or wane with time." It is a modest, humane and (I'm tempted to say) neoconservative suggestion.

Mary Warner Marien (review date 11 September 1989)

SOURCE: A review of *Fear of Falling: The Inner Life of the Middle Class,* in *Christian Science Monitor,* Vol. 81, September 11, 1989, p. 13.

[*In the following essay, Marien praises Ehrenreich's perception and compassion in* Fear of Falling.]

The recent death of Michael Harrington was taken by many to symbolize the end of socialist influence in American political thought. Through his many books, including *The Other America* (1982), the work said to have sparked the War on Poverty, Harrington served as the conscience of the left. "I see Michael Harrington as delivering the Sermon on the Mount to America," Senator Edward M. Kennedy once said.

There may never again be a voice like Harrington's, one that could make claims on the heart without hectoring. But those who think that socialist idealism has passed from the American landscape should consider Barbara Ehrenreich.

As she did in her controversial book on gender and family life, ***The Hearts of Men*** (1983), Ehrenreich uses her current text to trace a psycho-history of the professional-managerial middle class. The result is an alternative anthropology of American social relations from the 1950s through the 1980s.

Ehrenreich's reliance on the notion of class is a socialist legacy, but in the broader sense it also owes to 19th-century authors, like Balzac and Zola, who struggled to lay open the mental life of a class in order to expose the defining experiences of a nation. Her thesis, that middle-class life in our culture is taken as a social norm, has formed the basis of some of America's most influential books. Both David Riesman's *The Lonely Crowd* (1951) and Charles Reich's *The Greening of America* (1970) rest on the assumption that middle-class behavior is the mirror of society. More recently, Robert N. Bellah and his colleagues portrayed contemporary moral values through a surprisingly popular study of the middle-class mores entitled, *Habits of the Heart: Individualism and Commitment in American Life* (1985).

Ehrenreich's chronicle begins in the late 1950s, before poverty was "discovered," at the point where the perceived boon of American affluence was beginning to feel like a burden. She recounts that leading intellectuals, like David Riesman and Daniel Bell, were beginning to suggest that problemlessness was itself a problem. In the postwar period, the middle class worried that it might lose its creative energies and suffocate in a sea of consumer goods.

> As she did in her controversial book on gender and family life, *The Hearts of Men* (1983), Ehrenreich uses her current text [*Fear of Falling*] to trace a psycho-history of the professional-managerial middle class. The result is an alternative anthropology of American social relations from the 1950s through the 1980s.
> —*Mary Warner Marien*

The War on Poverty provided the middle class the challenge it needed to rouse itself from malaise and a generalized fear of decadence. Ehrenreich notes that the rhetoric of renewal grew so fiercely uplifting, so focused on stirring the middle class, that it frequently lost sight of the objective fact of poverty.

It was, Ehrenreich suggests, a misfortune for the poor to be discovered by a middle class tormented by the forebodings of its own decline. Fear of falling grew more intense during the student movement of the late 1960s, when America's children of privilege seemed to be rejecting middle-class values. Ehrenreich sees the student movement as a pivotal time, a period in which the middle class became more defensive and a lot less liberal. It was also the moment when the middle class made another discovery, or one should say, created another temporarily soothing symbol. This time it was the working class who suffered the anxieties of middle-class insecurities.

Working-class stereotypes came to stand for traditional American values, like hard work, independence, and self-discipline, which the middle class felt were slipping away. At the same time, the liberal elite, disparagingly called the "New Class" by neoconservatives, came to be seen as less American, that is, as selfish, slothful, and ineffectual. To neoconservatives and their growing number of supporters, cutting social programs was a way to reduce the bloated roster of New Class bureaucrats. To the New Right, the New Class had generated poverty by inducing dependency on federal programs. To end poverty, then, one had to reduce social spending.

The yuppie phenomenon-hard work, hard spending, and high seriousness-drew on neoconservative values. Ironically, in Ehrenreich's view, the yuppies have brought the saga of the middle class almost full circle. She characterizes the present moment as one of anxious affluence and pent-up idealism.

What will be the next great shift for America's definitive class? Ehrenreich hopes that contemporary middle-class anxiety over consumption will spur greater class consciousness, and ultimately lead to revisioning the middle class not as an elite, but as a class bearing strong affinities with the poor. Just as the middle class in the past discovered poverty and the working class, she hopes that it will discover the rich in the 1990s.

Overall, Ehrenreich's analysis of the psychic tides of middle-class life is on-target. Her writing, spiked with aphoristic observations of modern life, is always entertaining. When, in her conclusions, she recommends that the middle class undergo an implausibly abrupt change of heart, one still admires her moral purpose, and the principles of equality and social justice that give the book its bearings.

Joshua Henkin (review date 20 November 1989)

SOURCE: "A Touch of Class," in *The Nation,* Vol. 249, No. 17, November 20, 1989, pp. 607-09.

[*Although critical of several of Ehrenreich's conclusions, in the following review, Henkin finds much to like in* Fear of Falling.]

Most books that make sweeping assertions about American culture, Barbara Ehrenreich argues, are really only about the middle class. When authors tell us that "Americans" are becoming "more self-involved, materialistic, spineless, or whatever," they are really referring to the relatively small "professional . . . middle class . . . from which every other group or class is ultimately [considered] a kind of deviation." In *Fear of Falling: The Inner Life of the Middle Class,*

Ehrenreich claims to do consciously what others have done unwittingly.

Fear of Falling is an attempt to demythologize the professional middle class, to portray it as it is: one class among several, with its own interests, fears and obsessions. But the book is not simply an exercise in cultural anthropology. The professional middle class, Ehrenreich notes, "plays an overweening role in defining 'America': its moods, political direction, and moral tone." By tracing the attitudes of the middle class from the late 1950s through the late 1980s, Ehrenreich hopes to understand America's move to the right.

According to Ehrenreich, the middle class is preoccupied with the fear of growing soft, of losing discipline, of submitting to "the imperatives of consumption, the tyranny of affluence." This is so because the middle class must rely on hard work and deferred gratification in order to retain its privileged position. The rich can almost always expect to maintain their status for life. The same, unfortunately, is true for the poor. Only the middle class depends, in Margaret Mead's words, "not upon birth and status, not upon breeding or beauty, but upon effort."

This struggle to maintain discipline is, according to Ehrenreich, particularly difficult under modern capitalism, whose success depends on self-indulgence. Barraged by advertisers, afflicted with consumption overload, the middle class both craves and distrusts affluence—hence its almost schizophrenic relationship with material goods and its enduring fear of falling. In Ehrenreich's opinion, this fear is the principal force guiding middle-class life. It helps explain the way members of the middle class think, the goods they buy, the people they vote for, the relationships they seek out.

But why so profound a fear? And why the last three decades, in particular? Here Ehrenreich turns to the 1960s, which proved to be a watershed in middle-class consciousness. The student protest movement shook middle-class foundations. A radically egalitarian future would have meant that "education and intellect would be valued no more than, say, the skills of a mechanic or the insights of the downtrodden." The university, the bastion of middle-class power, was under attack and the middle class began to see itself not as an amorphous, all-inclusive body but as an elite with interests to protect. More important, most of the student radicals came from the middle class and were supposed to grow up and assume their parents' positions of power. When it turned out that these kids had other things in mind, their parents grew introspective—and self-critical.

The most frequent (and flawed) explanation for student radicalism was that middle-class parents had been too permissive. Childrearing techniques underwent massive scrutiny. "Is It All Dr. Spock's Fault?" read one *New York Times Magazine* headline. Neoconservative journalist Midge Decter said that the younger generation had no "capacity for deferred gratification." Permissiveness led to hedonism, which led to trouble. It also became an all-purpose charge against liberalism, an epithet that helped cement the strange relationship between the neoconservatives and the New Right.

By the late 1970s conservative intellectuals were defining and excoriating the so-called New Class—middle-class professionals working in the media, in universities, in think tanks, in the upper echelons of government bureaucracies. The New Class, in the eyes of its detractors, was liberal and elitist. Although the New Right distrusted the neoconservatives, suspecting, correctly, that they were themselves thinly disguised members of the New Class, it didn't hesitate to crib neoconservative theories. But it added a twist. While the neoconservatives had described the New Class as power hungry, the New Right portrayed it as immoral and hedonistic, too. The problem, again, was permissiveness. With the New Class playing the role of enemy, the ultimate miracle took place in 1988: a millionaire Republican, straight from Skull and Bones, winning the Presidency by portraying his middle-class rival as an elitist.

How did it happen? Again, Ehrenreich points to the middle class's fear of falling. Middle-class liberals failed to respond to right-wing attacks because these attacks struck chords of middle-class self-doubt. The charge of permissiveness was inaccurate, but it "rang true because it touched on that perennial fear within the professional middle class of growing soft, of failing to strive, of falling into the snares of affluence."

Ehrenreich admits that her overall argument is "rashly speculative." That, in itself, need not be a problem. But speculation calls for more qualification, more caution than she usually displays.

Ehrenreich's definition of the professional middle class covers "all those people whose economic status is based on education, rather than on the ownership of capital or property." Included, among others, are "schoolteachers, anchorpersons, engineers, professors, government bureaucrats, corporate executives (at least up through the middle levels of management), scientists, advertising people, therapists, financial managers," and Ehrenreich herself. Wow. This is a very diverse bunch, particularly when it comes to Ehrenreich's principal concern: attitudes toward consumption. It is unlikely that people whose tastes run from Beethoven to Bon Jovi, Fiorucci's to Filene's basement, Windows on the World to Wendy's, are all going to have more or less the same perspective on hedonism. It is hard to believe, in other words, that for all these people the fear of consumption is all-consuming.

Much of what Ehrenreich says has a grain—often many grains—of truth. But she tries to turn her theory into the whole truth, and in so doing she is on shaky ground. Her monolithically psychological approach comes close to reducing conservatism to a neurosis. Tempting but insufficient.

Much of what Ehrenreich says has a grain—often many grains—of truth. But she tries to turn her theory into the whole truth, and in so doing she is on shaky ground.
                                        —*Joshua Henkin*

The specifics of Ehrenreich's theory are equally troubling. Does the middle class hold stereotyped conceptions of the poor simply, as Ehrenreich claims, because the poor have "come to represent what the middle class fear[s] most in itself: softening of character, a lack of firm . . . values"? Or might there be other reasons, such as fear of crime or plain ignorance? Has "yuppiehood" fallen into disrepute because "the upwardly mobile middle class began to lose its own fragile sense of identity"? Or might it be simpler: that middle-class people, like others before them, found excessive materialism unfulfilling? Is the fear of falling the only, even the principal, cause of internal conflict between indulgence and self-restraint, between spending and saving, between the present and the future? What about divorce, loss of community, political unrest, the threat of nuclear war? All these shake our sense of stability and may send us reeling from cautious preparation for tomorrow to extreme focus on today—and back again.

Moreover, to the extent that a fear of falling does play a role in the inner life of Americans, it is not clear that the middle class has a monopoly on it. The working class and poor, it might be argued, are even better candidates for this fear. Although the precipice on which the middle class stands is higher, the pit into which the lower class falls is deeper. Family and friends can almost always insure that a middle-class person in trouble does not go homeless, does not starve. Not so for a member of the lower class.

Finally, Ehrenreich's understanding of George Bush's campaign success, and her explanation of the right's ability to paint liberals as elitists, is unconvincing. It is true that some liberals, to their detriment, failed to respond to right-wing smears. But the relevant question is how the charge of elitism became credible in the first place.

Ehrenreich seems intent, for the most part, on avoiding this question, perhaps because she realizes that, when the charge comes from Norman Podhoretz and George Bush, the pot is calling the kettle black. But it is not sufficient to argue that the right is more elitist than the left.

In fairness to Ehrenreich, she does, at one point, admit that there is a "grain of . . . disturbing truth" in the right's attack on the liberal elite: "Middle-class-led reform movements, from the Progressive Era to the War on Poverty, have been marred by an elitist distance from the would-be beneficiaries of reform." But this is a departure from an argument that focuses almost exclusively on the middle class's internalization of the charge of elitism, not on the substance of the charge itself.

The charge's effectiveness comes from the fact that the university, which has long been associated with snobbery and elitism, with lofty theories untested by real-world problems, is also associated with liberalism. To a great extent, this is a consequence of the 1960s. But even today, many universities are liberal strongholds. Conservative intellectuals, despite their prominence, are a relatively strange sight. And although, as Ehrenreich notes, students in general are now as conservative as the rest of the population, in the more elite universities, the universities that produce many of the most prominent members of the professional middle class, the student body remains predominantly liberal. Polls of Ivy League students in 1988, for example, showed disproportionate student support for Dukakis.

The attitude of some middle-class liberals has helped strengthen the charge of elitism, and Ehrenreich's theory about the middle class may help us understand why. Ehrenreich notes that knowledge and expertise are the "capital" of the middle class. Without them, middle-class members would indeed fall. But this argument suggests something deeper. The professional middle class, which is constantly reminded that it lacks the influence of the truly powerful, can console itself by flaunting its "intelligence," its superior knowledge. And in doing so, it reinforces the charge of ivory-tower elitism.

Take, for example, Ehrenreich's response to a Nixon diary entry that lambastes the New Class and praises "middle America" for its guts and character and patriotism. She writes: "There, in ungrammatical outline, was the germ of the New Right's eventual strategy."

Now, Ehrenreich can surely be forgiven for taking a jab at Nixon's syntax. Still, she inadvertently explains his attitude. What Nixon likes about middle Americans is that they don't care about his grammar. The people who do care are, in George Wallace's words, "the over-educated ivory-tower folks with pointed heads looking down their noses at us." In the public mind (and often in reality), these pointy-heads are liberals.

Despite these problems with Ehrenreich's central argument, there is a good deal to recommend in *Fear of Falling*. The book is elegantly written, and the insight and wit that characterize her journalism are also abundant here. Ehrenreich's chapter on the New Class is particularly good, as she dissects neo-conservative dishonesty and hypocrisy. She is equally incisive when attacking the permissiveness theory, noting that capitalism, the main source of permissiveness, is never a right-wing target. Throughout, she has a keen eye for the contradictions of our culture. Her book, its faults notwithstanding, is worth a careful read.

Wilfred M. McClay (review date January 1990)

SOURCE: "High Anxiety," in *Commentary,* Vol. 89, No. 1, January, 1990, pp. 64-7.

[*While praising Ehrenreich's writing, in the following review, McClay finds many flaws in the thesis of* Fear of Falling.]

The debacle of the 1988 presidential election not only left the very word "liberalism" badly battered, but may have administered the *coup de grâce* to the only opposition movement with a shred of intellectual and political vitality: the so-called "neoliberals." Hence, in 1992, the Democratic party will find that it once again has to face the relentless demands of its Left; and that Left, if it is feeling any vestigial desire to win elections, will have to come up with a plausible strategy for attracting middle-class voters, rather than continuing to invoke the *deus ex machina* of the unregistered and nonvoting masses—a strategy that might better be called "waiting for Godot."

Such is the very problem that *Fear of Falling* is designed to address. Stitching together an elaborate account of the changing structure of classes and class perceptions in postwar America. Barbara Ehrenreich hopes to provide arguments that will persuade the middle class, particularly that part of it she calls "the professional middle class." to make common cause with the working and "lower" classes, and thereby reinvigorate the Left's prospects in contemporary American politics.

The principal obstacles standing in the way of such solidarity, she believes, are the persistent misunderstandings and phantasms infesting the mind of the middle class. She intends to dispel these elements of false consciousness, in particular by persuading the middle class of two things: first, that its persistent fears, since the end of World War II, of "going soft" or "losing ground," and thus "falling" into the lower classes, have been selfish and harmful delusions; and second, that its position in the structure of the U.S. economy is infinitely more insecure than it appears to realize. It is hard to see how both these propositions can be true.

One would be justified in hoping for a more compelling thesis from Barbara Ehrenreich. She is a graceful and often witty essayist, usually at her best in writing of everyday, commonplace things—food, dieting, fashion, leisure, "relationships," and pop culture—from a mildly heterodox feminist position. As a prominent figure in the "communication" Left, she seems to have a genuine, if somewhat abstract and overly economic, appreciation of the forces that hold a community together. Beneath her rather conventional attacks on "consumer culture" lies a grudging admiration (an admiration one sees more clearly in a cultural critic like Christopher Lasch) for the old-fashioned Victorian virtues, especially work, family, thrift, and self-restraint.

But it is a grudging respect at best, deriving more from hatred of contemporary consumerism than from genuine regard for bourgeois values. Indeed, she finds consumption all-consuming, and attributes enormous coercive and hegemonic power to the "consumer culture." One never knows quite what to make of this fashionable term, which seems to designate what Poles, Russians, Chinese, and much of the rest of the world so ardently desire. But its use seems especially peculiar in a writer whose prose and thinking show so conspicuously the marks of the slick "lifestyle" journalist.

In the 50's, Miss Ehrenreich begins, all middle-class Americans believed themselves to be living in an affluent, classless society. A comfortable middle-class suburban existence was thought to be the American norm. But despite their well-being, members of the middle class were nagged by a persistent "fear of falling" out of their station (an understandable feeling, one would have thought, for those who could remember the Depression and the war).

Such anxieties, the account goes on, found a diverting outlet in the obsession with juvenile delinquency, which "gripped the public imagination in the 50's," and at the same time served as a "comforting distraction" from the "issue of class." Then, with the burgeoning civil-rights movement, and Michael Harrington's *The Other America* (1962), the middle class was induced to "discover" the existence of poverty. But instead of extending the range of its sympathies, the middle class merely projected its fears of downward mobility onto the poor, whom sociologists had conveniently taught Americans to think of stereotypically as "infantilized" products of a "culture of poverty."

According to Miss Ehrenreich, these condescending misperceptions of the "lower" classes were but the first in a parade of similarly self-protective illusions. Next came the charge of "permissiveness," directed especially against the "class traitors" who populated the student movement of the

1960's—traitors because they challenged the "class fortress" of the professions by their disdain for authority and expertise, and because they adopted rock and roll, the subversive "invention of the poor," as their own. Now the middle class was projecting its intense "fears of falling" onto its very own unruly youth.

But there arose an unexpected source of self-exculpating relief. Thanks to the well-publicized anti-antiwar militancy of the "hard-hats," and the presidential candidacy of George Wallace, the middle class suddenly "discovered" the existence of the working class, and promptly projected onto *it* all manner of contradictory urges: on the one hand, the working class could be a reservoir of traditional values in a time of cultural upheaval; on the other hand, it was a cesspool of authoritarian personality traits, bigotry, and hopelessly bad taste.

The working class could thus be seen as a bulwark of "middle-American" values, at a moment when middle-class kids were deserting those values; and simultaneously the Archie Bunkers of the world could still be regarded with a comfortable sense of superiority.

The middle class also found that it could project onto the "liberal elite" or "New Class"—media elites, university professors, Washington intellectuals, foundation bureaucrats, etc.—all the "permissive" qualities that it most feared in itself. For the neoconservatives and the New Right, in particular, the concept of an ambitious and arrogant New Class became a "bludgeon" with which to beat opponents into submission—and self-contradictorily so, for what were the neoconservatives themselves but denizens of the New Class?

Finally, inevitably, came the yuppie. Emboldened by the intellectual Right's discrediting of anti-business attitudes, and freed from the sense of moral responsibility which professional status once entailed, the yuppie simply threw in his lot with the corporate elite, displaying the seasoned cynicism of the well-paid courtesan. He accepted the fact that his class was a privileged one, and intended to make the most of those privileges, gorging himself at the cornucopia of consumerism while also working excessively hard at his job and exercising compulsively at the health club—all to prevent "going soft," to allay the "fear of falling."

Fortunately, however, the reign of the yuppie was brief, punctuated by the stock-market crash of 1987. His extreme self-centeredness was just too much for the middle class to take as a plausible image of itself; and the yuppie has crawled back into the mahogany wood-work. But the "fear of falling" remains, reassuming much the same form it took in the 1950's.

This, then, is Barbara Ehrenreich's walk through recent American history. It is like a stroll through a hall of funhouse mirrors; one finds oneself surrounded by a crowd of grotesque images whose apparent agitation and movement exist only in the eye of the beholder. We learn little about the lives of real Americans except that we do not know what we thought we knew about them. We learn little about the inner life of the middle class, other than a glimpse of its alleged fears, obsessions, and delusions. Readers who doubt whether the terms of individual psychology are so fully applicable to groups will have to suspend disbelief and enjoy the show; for this is one of those books that must be believed to be read.

Of course: middle-class people seem to have certain characteristic anxieties. But that is not exactly a new discovery. The "fear of falling" has always been a defining characteristic of modern middle-class life, as Tocqueville recognized a century and a half ago, long before the "consumer culture" or the solipsism of the suburbs.

Nor is there much that is persuasive in Miss Ehrenreich's oddly conflicted view of the professions. For the most part she accepts the standard radical critique: with their high educational demands, long periods of apprenticeship, and absolute control over accreditation and access, the professions are artificial barriers thrown up by ambitious middle-class "experts" for the purpose of monopolizing cultural authority and keeping out intruders and poachers, particularly those of the "lower" classes. There is an element of truth in this view, but like Miss Ehrenreich's favorite notion of "projection," according to which ideas of reality are only so much evidence of psychic delusion, it is rendered false and pernicious if carried too far.

For one thing, the radical critique ignores the degree to which the internal discipline and cultural authority of the professions contribute to, and in turn derive from, the genuine pursuit of real knowledge. Ehrenreich prefers to think the middle class erected steep barriers to the professions solely to make and protect a fortress. Yet she also argues that a major source of anxiety for the perpetually anxious middle class lies precisely in its fear that its own children will be unable to mount those very walls; hence its "obsession" with "permissiveness" and with "going soft." A less tendentious writer might have conceded that the professions deserve high marks for attempting to impose rigorous and impartial standards for admission to their "fortress"; in Miss Ehrenreich's account, it looks more like the story of the class that couldn't shoot straight.

What is most disappointing about this book, however, is its total unwillingness to take its opposition seriously. One would never guess from Miss Ehrenreich's account that a lively and wide-ranging debate over the means and ends of the welfare state has been taking place in this country over the last two decades. In her rendering, writers like Charles Murray have not been engaged in a reconsideration of public policy; they have merely been—guess what?—projecting onto the poor (and the fictive New Class liberals) "the anxieties of their class." And as for the liberals who ought to have been countering them, well, these "tortured" souls have suffered a failure of nerve and need to "regain the use of their backbones." This is bizarre, ostrich-like way of reading recent American history.

But enough of the sordid past. What lies ahead for the feckless middle class, which this book means to woo as well as to indict? Perhaps, Miss Ehrenreich opines, echoing the cyclical sentiments of Arthur Schlesinger, Jr., a release of its "pent-up idealism"—but first it must clearly understand where its interests lie. That understanding will begin with one central fact: "the discovery of the rich" as the main enemy. So long as the middle class does not recognize the degree to which it, too, like the working and lower classes, is putty in the hands of capital, so long will the middle class remain separate from its "natural" allies.

Now we can see where all this has been leading. By cultivating a loathing for the Trumps, Forbeses, Iacoccas, and Helmsleys who run the world, the middle class will shake free of the insubstantial projections flitting across the walls of its Platonic cave. In alliance with the classes below, it will walk in the sunshine at last, and no longer fear falling. For all the conditions engendering that fear will have withered away. Nor, in a truly egalitarian society, will the professional middle class disappear—far from it; it will expand and expand, "until there remains no other class." Huey Long's slogan, "Every Man a King," will be updated for the 90's: "Every Person a Professional." And all the children, presumably, will be above average.

Idealism is generally to be preferred to cynicism; and there is nothing cynical or insincere about this earnest effort to reunite the appeals of democratization and expertise, populism and progressivism. Whether it is any more realistic than the other phantasms haunting this book, however, is another matter. If, for example, the structure of the professions is a specific cultural formation which reflects and aids the ascendancy of a particular class, then why would that class willingly open its "fortress" to the classes below? What would make it willing, Barbara Ehrenreich answers, is a more richly informed and visceral hatred of the rich. But it is hard to understand why she is so sure the middle class has nothing to fear from such blatant appeals to class-conscious resentment. As the example of Weimar Germany suggests, hatred, once released, can be exceedingly difficult to contain or direct.

It is more than a little discouraging to see the argument finally descend to this level. Henry Adams—who *was* some-

thing of a cynic, albeit a less than sincere one—asserted near the end of his life that politics is "the systematic organization of hatreds." But that formulation, like much about Henry Adams, was more clever than wise. What has been valuable about the communication Left today has been its willingness to question some of the Left's longstanding assumptions, in the pursuit of a more elevated definition of politics and the public realm. A book like this one raises doubts about how deep that willingness runs.

James Fallows (review date 1 March 1990)

SOURCE: "Wake Up, America," in *New York Review of Books,* Vol. 137, No. 3, March 1, 1990, pp. 14-15.

[*In the following excerpt, Fallows examines the correlation among culture, prosperity, and security and their place in* Fear of Falling.]

Economists don't like to talk about the effects of culture or of ethics on economic development, since these are such subjective and imprecise matters. But most people, including economists off-duty, assume that there is a connection between the kinds of everyday behavior a society encourages and its stability and prosperity.

In nearly every discussion about Europe's future, for instance, all sides take it for granted that a reunited Germany would be truly powerful. This has to do only partly with measurable factors like investment rates or manufacturing productivity. It also reflects widespread awe, or dread, of Germany's record of organizing human energy. For a variety of reasons having to do with national history and personal status, jobs in the government bureaucracy are among the most desirable in Korea, Japan, Singapore, and other East Asian societies with Confucian influence. Ambitious young graduates compete for positions with the Japanese Ministry of Finance or the Korean Economic Planning Board the way ambitious young Americans compete for jobs at what we drolly call "investment" banks. (This spring, 36,000 American graduating college students applied for eight positions at Wasserstein and Perella, the mergers-and-acquisition house that was spun off from First Boston. The obituaries for the Eighties may be a bit premature.)

The ability to attract talent gives these Asian governments more legitimacy—and more competence—in dealing with businesses than the US government can bring to hear, and it has helped to build more successful economies than those in the Philippines or Latin America, where government power has largely been a route to personal wealth. In a forthcoming book called *Tropical Gangsters,* the economist Robert Klitgaard wryly describes his two years of work as an adviser to the government of Equatorial Guinea, a tiny enclave on the west coast of Africa that has become one of the most hopeless economies on earth. Taken one by one, many of the ministers he dealt with were both honest and competent, Klitgaard says; but their country's history, and their degrading relationships with international aid organizations tempted nearly all of them to act in their own interests first. In Japan, those who have sacrificed their own interests for the nation's welfare have been seen as cultural heroes; whereas in the Philippines they have been easy prey for the likes of the Marcoses.

It's easy to make too much of cultural influences on economics—and whatever group is on top at a given moment tends to make too much of them, by moralizing about the reasons for its own success. Until the last decade or two, Westerners observing Asia have usually concluded that its culture could never be adapted to modern industrial capitalism. Confucianism, the Japanese willingness to sublimate individual interests to the group, and other traits that are now cited in the West to explain East Asia's boom were used earlier in this century to prove that Asia would never catch up. ("My impression as to your cheap labor was soon disillusioned when I saw your people at work." an Australian expert reported to the Japanese government before World War I. "To see your men at work made me feel that you are a very satisfied easy-going race who reckon time is no object.")

Still, there are two cultural traits that most successful capitalist economies have shared, however much the societies may differ in other ways. One is an emphasis on deferred gratification. Capitalism requires people to consume, but it also requires society to set aside some share of its income for further investment. The other is some recognized link between individual and collective well-being. Anyone who has lived in the third world recognizes what happens when this link does not exist. No one can afford not to press his own advantage as far as possible, since everyone else will be doing the same: if a bureaucrat does not take bribes, he's merely robbing his family. The most impressive postwar recoveries, those in Germany, Korea, and Japan, have been propelled largely by the belief that improvements in the nation's welfare will pull everyone up together.

When American commentators have examined their society, they have usually concluded that its values served capitalism very well. Apart from the worry that capitalism would eventually make people too rich, spoiled, and hedonistic to be good, forward-looking capitalists (a fear classically expressed by Daniel Bell's *The Cultural Contradictions of Capitalism,* published in 1976), the main cultural problem with American capitalism has seemed to be its exceptions— the pockets of people who haven't decided to pitch in and get ahead. In the mid-nineteenth century, Irish immigrants were thought to be the problem; since the 1950s, we've heard repeatedly about the "culture of poverty" affecting rural Appalachian whites, Mexican and Puerto Rican immigrants, and now of course the urban black underclass. The pattern of behavior in this culture has been described with sympathy by Oscar Lewis and Michael Harrington and with scorn or alarm by Edward Banfield and Charles Murray. But their descriptions all boil down to the opposite of what it takes to succeed as a capitalist: short-term gratification rather than stolid investment and planning, fatalism and resentment rather than a Benjamin Franklinesque belief that God helps him who helps himself.

Arguments about the "culture of poverty" are old and familiar ones in America. They are now taking on an intriguing twist. In much of the rest of the world, especially Asia, they are being applied not to defeated enclaves within America but to *American society as a whole.*

For instance, instead of listening meekly as American negotiators criticize them for keeping out imports from the US, Japanese officials have recently taken the offensive and said that America's culture is America's main trade problem. Late last year, the United States and Japan began a bizarre series of negotiations known as the "Structural Impediments Initiative." The original idea, on the American side, was to concentrate attention on the structural factors, such as a prohibition on discount stores, that made it hard for outsiders to penetrate the Japanese market. The Japanese government deftly switched the focus of the meetings to the structural problems that made American exporters ineffective, and began speaking to the United States much as middle-class whites typically talk to the shiftless poor. It's time to work harder, study more, hit the books, and think of the future for a change, the Japanese government now says. The secret of success is to pull yourself up by your own boot-straps; no one ever got rich by blaming other people for his failures.

Akio Morita's speeches about America's business failures, summarized in the notorious *"No" to Ieru Nippon,* or A *Japan That Can Say No,* follow quite similar "culture of poverty" lines:

> As I told the Americans, we are focusing on business ten years in advance, while you seem to be concerned only with profits ten minutes from now. At that rate, you may well never be able to compete with us.

Japan is telling America: "Stop loafing, get a job!"

Even the things the rest of the world admires about America increasingly fit the same pattern:

> Living in the present [one] may develop a capacity
> for spontaneity, for the enjoyment of the sensual,
> which is often blunted in middle-class, future ori-
> ented man.

In one way, and no doubt to their mutual consternation, Barbara Ehrenreich is on the same side as [George] Gilder. The
resemblance is peculiar, because in so many other respects
these books (and their authors) are each other's opposite.
Ehrenreich is as established a figure of the left as Gilder is
on the right. While the strength of Gilder's book [*Microcosm*] is its reporting and anecdotes, [Ehrenreich's] *Fear of
Falling* contains very little original research and is strongest when Ehrenreich analyzes familiar cultural patterns expressed in movies, books, and TV. Gilder keeps leaping for
the cosmic; Ehrenreich's tone is consistent, understated,
dryly amused.

The point of convergence is the idea that the stolid corporate men in Brooks Brothers suits are ruining America. For
Gilder, they reflect the dead weight of bureaucratic caution
and staleness. For Ehrenreich, they are a distinct, relatively
small class, whose interests are at odds with those of the
great majority beneath them, and whose self-absorption has
warped the class politics of the postwar era.

Ehrenreich's argument turns on the strangely insecure position of the American middle class. The term "middle class"
itself illustrates the problem; it suggests a condition typical
for Americans, but Ehrenreich says it has been appropriated
by a smaller group that should more accurately be called the
"professional class." These are people whose position in society fundamentally depends on their education. She never
makes clear exactly how many people she is talking about,
but says they are an assortment including

> such diverse types as schoolteachers, anchorpersons,
> engineers, professors, government bureaucrats, cor-
> porate executives (at least up through the middle
> levels of management), scientists, advertising
> people, therapists, financial managers, architects,
> and, I should add, myself.

People in such jobs can tell themselves that their privileges
are based on the American ideal of reward for effort. They
studied, stayed in college, got degrees. Ehrenreich is of
course aware that professional privilege is not fully "earned"
in a moral sense, since children of professional-class parents have a head start toward the schooling that will keep
them in that class. But the fact that it's only a head start,
not a guaranteed inheritance (as it would be for the truly rich,
or in a more deeply class-bound society), creates a destructive mixture of smugness and insecurity in the professional
class. His belief that he has earned his status limits the
professional's sympathy for those who haven't made it,

Ehrenreich says, but also increases his fear that he or his children will fail to keep earning their place. Because this class
dominates discussion of the American condition. Ehrenreich
says, its increasing nervousness has intensified the crabbed,
ungenerous tone of political and cultural debate.

The class anxiety Ehrenreich is describing was probably
most vivid in the mid-nineteenth century, when today's professional class was just beginning to form. In those days,
doctors, lawyers, accountants, and professors were just variants of tradesmen, without professional guilds to protect
them or educational requirements to keep newcomers out.
In his classic book on the subject, *The Search for Order*
(1966), the historian Robert Wiebe said that a century ago,

> The concept of the middle class crumbled at the
> touch. . . . The so-called professions meant little as
> long as anyone with a bag of pills and a bottle of
> syrup could pass for a doctor, a few books and a
> corrupt judge made a man a lawyer, and an unem-
> ployed illiterate qualified as a teacher.

In the century since, the professional class made the American school system into a vehicle for greater fairness and
greater rigidity at the same time. Schools were in principle
opened to all, and virtually anyone who stayed in school long
enough could eventually enter the professional class. But
with the rise of formal professions, those who didn't stay in
school were more trapped than before. Thomas Edison, who
dropped out of elementary school, could conceivably still
find a place in the oddball world George Gilder describes,
but not within the respectable, meritocratic, professional
class.

"The professional and managerial occupations have a
guildlike quality," Ehrenreich says, following Wiebe.

> They are open, for the most part, only to people who
> have completed a lengthy education and attained
> certain credentials. The period of study and appren-
> ticeship—which may extend nearly to mid-life—is
> essential to the social cohesion of the middle class.

One of the few parts of American life that is becoming less
tied to credentials is public school teaching. During the
1980s, half a dozen states decided to permit the hiring of
teachers who didn't have degrees from education colleges
but who knew about French, math, science, or whatever subject they were supposed to teach. But the larger trend is the
other way. Because of the reliance on education and credentials. Ehrenreich concludes, the professional-class system is
rigged enough to keep most members of the working class
out—but not rigged enough to make its members feel secure.

Ehrenreich devotes most of her book to an examination of

how this mixture of complacency and anxiety affects the behavior of the professional class. The complacency shows up in the repeated "surprise" revelations that not all of American society is made of people with white-collar careers and orthodontists for the kids. In the 1930s, she says, people who still had jobs knew many others who didn't: the poverty of the Great Depression was not merely a theoretical concern to the opinion-making classes. By the 1960s, she says, professional-class life had become insulated enough that people could be astonished by Michael Harrington's "discovery" that some forty million Americans lived in poverty. A decade later the big surprise was that the white working class was angry—angry because its children were dying in Vietnam while privileged children were protesting in college; because judges who lived in the suburbs were handing down bussing orders for working-class schools; because managers of big companies seemed to view workers as disposable parts of the industrial machine. Since then, of course, American life has seemed designed to spare members of one class routine contact with members of another. The two great institutions of postwar class mixing, the public schools and the pre-Vietnam drafted military, no longer function that way, and many other institutions keep people apart.

The most powerful parts of Ehrenreich's book, I think, demonstrate how this continuing class tension has spread, showing it as reflected in books, movies, and the news organizations. "The pundits who dominate the talk shows are, to a man and an occasional woman, all members of this relatively privileged group," she says.

> When we see a man in work clothes on the screen, we anticipate some grievance or, at best, information of a highly local or anecdotal nature. On matters of general interest or national importance, waitresses, forklift operators, steamfitters—that is, most "ordinary" Americans are not invited to opine.

Ehrenreich says that in movies and TV shows it has become unacceptable to use stereotypes in portraying blacks, gays, or other minority groups, but not the working class as a whole. The overall message of movies such as *Joe, Taxi Driver, Looking for Mr. Goodbar,* and *The Deer Hunter,* she says, was that working class whites had ended up in the station of life that they deserved.

> To middle-class men, the blue-collar stereotype could never be such a distant "other" as the poor, especially the black poor. Here were blood brothers, personified, in personal memory, by the high-school teammate left behind in one's hometown pumping gas. . . . Yet the blood between the classes, as anyone could see through the lens of the media discovery, was mostly bad.

The discovery that it was unloved, Ehrenreich concludes, made the professional class even more narrowly self-protective more intent on insulating its children from the public schools, more determined to show its sophistication by not buying products that the ordinary Joe might use. Ehrenreich nicely describes the way almost every consumer product cars, beer, cereal—not to mention entire store chains have split into an upscale and downscale version, further weakening the sense that Americans of different classes might have anything in common. She quotes a market analyst on redundant buying patterns among the professional class:

> When they have friends over, these people do not want those friends to see names like Sears or Kenmore. They want people to see names like Sony or Kitchen Aid.

She emphasizes that even the women's movement, while making life somewhat fairer between men and women, has pushed the working and professional classes farther apart. In the old days, a male doctor might marry a female nurse; now, she says, two doctors are likely to marry each other. In 1987 the median income for men with at least one year of graduate-school education was $34,731, and for women with the same education, $26,399—$61,130 for the median professional-class couple. The median for a working couple with high-school education was only $36,888.

Ehrenreich's book is more valuable for its incidental perceptions than as a sustained thesis. (To put it another way, this book seems to have been a convenient vehicle for a number of class-related subjects Ehrenreich wanted to discuss, even though some subjects aren't clearly connected to the others.) Her main political conclusion is that the professional class should overcome its sense of precarious isolation and make common cause with the workers against their mutual enemy, the truly rich.

In a symbolic sense, this is certainly right: people like the Helmsleys and Michael Milken greatly damage the idea that American society is in any way fair. But, as economists have pointed out for years, there is not as much money in the hands of the truly rich as the rest of us would like to think: most tax money must come from professional and middle classes largely because that's where so many people are.

Ehrenreich's other large ideal is a society that has outgrown consumerism, and that offers everyone a professional-style job, one that can be enjoyed rather than endured. There are a few missing pieces to this argument, of course. The societies that have the most professional jobs are usually those with the most productive industries, and with strong consumer cultures too. Ehrenreich is so reluctant to say anything positive about business, industry, or productivity that it's hard to know exactly what economic base her new society would stand on: she gives only a hazy idea of the jobs most people would have, the products they would make.

Still, her book is insightful and sensible, and—to come back to the original question—it establishes two central points about America's productive culture. One is that people are devoting more and more energy to defending what privileges they have and to protecting their status within the class system, instead of creating new opportunities or strengthening the US economic system as a whole. The fundamental source of anxiety is the widespread sense that today's young adults—those born in 1960 or later—may never live as well as their parents did. In 1950, a median-price house cost the average wage earner 14 percent of his gross monthly wage; in the mid-1980s, it cost 44 percent. On the whole, today's houses are bigger and better-equipped, but despite the recent softening of prices they are not automatically available, as they seemed to be for two decades after World War II. It is hard for a family to do anything about housing costs, and so the struggle to avoid decline has concentrated instead on the schools, and in a peculiar way.

The one "school crisis" that affects the professional class directly is the competition for places in the right elementary (or even nursery) schools, which feed into the right prep schools and in turn the right universities. Many readers of this journal will know how much time, money, and emotion go into this competition—yet from the larger perspective, it's a meaningless exercise. The proliferation of prep schools and SAT cram courses is the moral equivalent of bond trading, an activity that shuffles temporary advantages while adding nothing to the common wealth.

Only about fifty of the nation's nearly two thousand colleges have serious competition for admissions. In the United States, unlike Japan, it is still possible for people who don't go to those three dozen colleges to rise to the top in business and politics. Between our last two Ivy League presidents. John Kennedy and George Bush, our presidents have come from Southwest Texas State. Whittier College, the University of Michigan, the Naval Academy, and Eureka College. In contrast, nearly all of Japan's postwar prime ministers have been graduates of the University of Tokyo.

The academic standards in the best American colleges, and the schools that feed them, are already above those of their Japanese, Korean, or Singaporean counterparts which suggests that raising the standards and increasing the pressure in these schools probably won't do much for America's overall strength. Most scholars of Japanese education, including Thomas Rohlen and Merry White, emphasize that the Japanese elementary and high schools succeed precisely because the *worst* graduates are so well educated. But applying that lesson to America, with a crusade to improve ghetto schools,

is not seen as an urgent task by the American professional class, Ehrenreich rightly suggests that it should be.

Ehrenreich's other fundamental point is that as professional-class consciousness has risen, the sense of the public good has declined. A few days after I moved back to the United States from Japan last fall. I tried to use a pay phone in midtown Manhattan. The first one I tried was full of gum: with the next the booth smelled of urine: in the next the handset was ripped off its cord: the next would not take coins. Meanwhile, people were driving by happily talking on their cellular car phones. It was a depressingly neat symbol of the shift from public to private well-being: as the public facility was left to crumble, people with money tried to recreate it on their own.

In larger ways, Ehrenreich shows, the professional class has followed the rich in insulating itself from public institutions. The public schools may be bad, but you can keep your children out of them. The parks may be run-down and dangerous, but you can join a private health club. Powerful Americans learn to prosper even if the whole society is weakening. Without belaboring the obvious this is not a sign of social health.

Michiko Kakutani (review date 13 July 1993)

SOURCE: "A Plague of Gray Caterpillars and a Preacher," in *The New York Times*, July 13, 1993, p. C18.

[*In the following essay, Kakutani negatively reviews* Kipper's Game.]

It's no surprise that science-fiction and futuristic novels are a favorite forum for social critics: after all, they provide an easy means of extrapolating and satirizing the problems of the contemporary world. Certainly, this is what the author and magazine columnist Barbara Ehrenreich seems to be up to in her first novel. "Kipper's Game," a dark, convoluted piece of apocalyptic fiction that enables her to combine her scientific training (she holds a Ph.D. in biology from Rockefeller University and a B.A. in chemistry and physics from Reed College) with the moral outrage she has cultivated as an essayist and observer of the American scene.

Set in a faintly futuristic world that bears a decided resemblance to the present-day United States, *Kipper's Game* begins with a series of unsettling portents: the trees in Ms. Ehrenreich's unnamed city have been devoured by a plague of bizarre, gray caterpillars; a faintly sinister preacher known as Sister Bertha has begun to haunt the airwaves on a pirate frequency, and hazardous wastes have begun to leak from the local Human Ecology Complex.

Both Ms. Ehrenreich's main characters work at the Human Ecology Complex, otherwise known as HEC, or, as its disgruntled employees refer to it, as "hell." Della Markson, who has had to get a job after her recent separation from her husband, works as a low-level clerk in the office of Dr. Hershey, a medical researcher on the trail of a mysterious and deadly new virus. Alex MacBride, Della's former professor, works there as a sort of all purpose gofer for Dr. Leitbetter, the head of HEC and a well-known television personality.

Dr. Leitbetter, we soon learn, purveys an eccentric, New Age view of science and religion. He believes or says he believes that knowledge yields pleasure, that human beings have an innate drive toward knowledge and that knowledge must be assembled and distilled in preparation for the arrival of a visitor from outer space, a superior being who will one day redeem the fallen creatures of earth.

Dr. Leitbetter's latest assignment for Alex is to research the life and work of an obscure physiologist from New Jersey, Henry Relnik, who may or may not have had Nazi connections in World War II. Much to his dismay, Alex soon discovers that mysterious others are also in pursuit of Relnik's missing papers: not only is his apartment ransacked, but he also receives death threats from gangsters, apparently working for an enormously powerful computer and information-gathering organization.

Della, meanwhile, has been preoccupied with a search of her own: her college-age son, Kipper, has been out of touch for a year, and when two of his computer-hacker friends turn up dead, she starts worrying that something terrible has happened to him, too. Her search for Kipper, strangely enough, begins to overlap with Alex's search for Henry Relnik's papers; both Kipper and Relnik, it seems, have been drawn into a utopian but diabolical quest that could save or redeem humanity.

Although Ms. Ehrenreich's narrative method of manically cutting back and forth between several story lines seems intended to build suspense, it has the effect of making the reader feel manipulated. We suspect that information is being deliberately withheld from us to tease our curiosity and that other events have been concocted for the simple purpose of raising further questions. Indeed our suspicions are confirmed by the novel's contrived and overly melodramatic conclusion, an ending that lacks the organic sense of completion possessed by successful novels of suspense.

Both the plot and conclusion of *Kipper's Game* are meant to underscore a few simplistic themes; that science can be used for good or ill, that the pursuit of knowledge can be turned into a Faustian bargain with nature, that madmen and philistines alike can exploit the interface between science and metaphysics.

Unfortunately, little of the irreverent wit that animates Ms. Ehrenreich's essays is in evidence in these pages: instead of beguiling and provoking the reader, she makes her points with the solemnly and portentousness of a third-rate preacher. The novel is filled with lugubrious disquisitions on computers and information-retrieval systems, ponderous speeches about the coming millennium and ridiculous discussions about extraterrestrials.

Where *Kipper's Game* does display flashes of Ms. Ehrenreich's usual verbal agility is in its all too rare descriptions of ordinary life: the liberating but frightening experience of driving along a highway late a night when none of the usual rules seem to hold; the oddly soothing, if numbing, experience of going to a shopping mall to have a solitary meal; the Kafkaesque experience of working in a huge modern building filed with dozens of identical, dimly lighted corridors and hallways.

It is with such descriptions of the everyday that Ms. Ehrenreich is able to display her generous gifts as an observer. One hopes her next novel does more justice to these talents.

Barbara Ehrenreich with Wendy Smith (interview date 26 July 1993)

SOURCE: An interview in *Publisher's Weekly,* Vol. 270, No. 30, July 26, 1993, pp. 46-47.

[*In the following interview, Ehrenreich discusses the writing of her first fiction book.*]

"I feel like a criminal," says Barbara Ehrenreich. "I didn't mean to do it!" She's not referring to an act of civil disobedience from her anti-war past (about which she'd be unlikely to repent); she's talking about the reckless act of writing a novel. *Kipper's Game* (Farrar, Straus & Giroux, Fiction Forecasts, Apr. 26), an adventurous tale involving a computer game, Nazi scientists and a mysterious illness that causes uncontrollable bleeding, is indeed not the book you'd necessarily expect from a 51-year-old writer best known for her journalism and such works of social and cultural analysis as *The Hearts of Men: American Dreams and the Flight from Commitment* and *Fear of Falling: The Inner Life of the Middle Class,* all written from a bracingly left-wing point of view.

That was the idea, she says. "It was escapism. I started the novel when we'd had two terms of Reagan, Bush had just been elected, and I was constantly grinding out columns and articles trying to make my good little moral points: don't fight, share things, all that stuff." (You can tell she's a mother, although Rosa, 22, and Benjamin, 20, presumably no longer need to be told to share.) "I just felt that I had to go into another dimension for part of the time."

The decaying suburb of the near-future in which *Kipper's Game* is set may not strike everyone as the perfect place to flee to. Its trees have been stripped bare by a plague of caterpillars, brownouts are frequent, escaped laboratory animals roam the halls of the decrepit scientific complex where the heroine works and radio evangelists warn of the coming apocalypse. Even when she's getting away from it all, Ehrenreich can't abandon habits of social observation she's honed over three decades: her unnamed locale is based on some of the grimmer sections of Long Island, where she lives and her protagonist, whose husband leaves in the novel's first scene, "is a character I had been thinking about for quite a while, because I had written a few articles about middle-class women who are suddenly divorced and completely unprepared to enter the world."

"I'm not grinding an axe; there's not a feminist point or a humanist point—that I know of," the author comments. "But it wasn't going to work as escapism for me unless it was a very challengingly complex sort of plot, with too many subplots and lots of mysteries I wasn't sure they were all going to come together at the end; there were many points when I really thought it wasn't going to work."

Fiction, she discovered, "is completely different; it didn't seem like anything I'd learned writing nonfiction particularly applied. Fortunately, I've read a lot of novels, so I started studying whomever I was reading to see how they did it I would say, 'Hey, wait a minute: how did this author get the characters from place A to place B?'"

Crowded with intellectual characters who consider issues like the nature of truth, the role of religion and the possibility of extraterrestrial visitors, *Kipper's Game* is an ambitious project for a first-time novelist. "There are certain books I've admired enormously that gave me permission to do this. I don't like family dramas; I like books that have insanely complicated plots and deal with major philosophical themes: *Riddley Walker* by Russell Hoban, which I'm going to have to read again to understand; *Unassigned Territory* by Kem Nunn, borderline SF with a very paranoid plot; Don DeLillo's *Ratner's Star*—that's a really loony book; it's wonderful A lot of the ideas my characters explore are real thoughts I've had that could potentially have been expressed in a nonfiction way, if I could have figured out what *that* would have been. We don't have a big market for metaphysical speculation, so you're almost forced to put it in another form."

The novel's scientific material was no problem for Ehrenreich, who graduated from Reed College in 1963 with a B.A. in chemical physics and received her Ph.D. in biology at Rockefeller University in 1968. How did she get derailed from her training "to be a seven-day-a-week, 14-hours-a-day scientist? I got swept up in the anti-war movement, as so many people did. I went into college as someone who loved the existentialists, had a soft spot in my heart for Ayn Rand, had no social or political views of any kind. Then I saw a little more of the world, read some newspapers—the war in Vietnam, the civil rights movement, those got me involved.

"I was more of a science appreciator than a scientist, and I knew as I got more involved in the movements of the time that I didn't want to be a professional scientist, that whole macho ethos of being at the bench all the time. So I started with little journalistic things, but I didn't really think of myself as a writer until the late '70s, when I noticed that's how I was earning my living—not much of a living!" she adds with a laugh.

In the late '60s, Ehrenreich and her first husband were asked to write a book about the international student movement ("the publisher paid our way to Europe and would have made bail if necessary"), and in 1970 they co-authored a scathing critique, *The American Health Empire.* Medical issues remained her focus in two pamphlets she wrote for the Feminist Press with fellow activist Deirdre English, who also collaborated with Ehrenreich on *For Her Own Good: One Hundred Fifty Years of Experts' Advice to Women* (Doubleday, 1978).

"I was making the transition to being 'socially relevant,' as we called it in the '60s, and the obvious thing to write about was medical and public health issues. My background in biology meant I wasn't intimidated by doctors or their pronouncements about how the medical system should work, because research biologists look down on doctors!" She continues to keep up to date in the field and recently completed an essay about the current debate over health insurance; after reading voluminous material by the proponents of "managed competition," she professes herself "appalled: it's like turning everything over to Empire Blue Cross."

Ehrenreich was past 40 when she wrote her first book solo. "I guess I'm a real slut when it comes to collaborating," she comments jokingly. "I've been promiscuous in doing it all my life! I got a lot out of it, but now that I have my own style I probably won't be collaborating much anymore. It wasn't that I had to shake anybody off for *The Hearts of Men;* I just had this idea and knew exactly what I wanted to do with it." Published by Doubleday in 1983, the book argued cogently—and controversially—that men's abdication of the breadwinner role was at least as responsible as the revived feminist movement for the break-down of the American family. "People thought that I said this male revolt *caused* feminism, but I just pointed out that it came earlier."

Although she had an amicable relationship with Loretta Barrett, who edited *For Her Own Good* and *The Hearts of Men,* Ehrenreich found herself less comfortable at Doubleday after it was purchased by Bertelsmann. The publication of *Re-Making Love: The Feminization of Sex,* a return to collaborative writing with Elizabeth Hess and Gloria Jacobs that appeared in 1986, led to a break. "It got completely lost in the corporate shuffle. I don't blame Loretta; it just seemed better to go to a smaller place where they watched each project carefully."

That smaller place, ironically, was Pantheon, which in early 1990 caused an enormous uproar over corporate interference in publishing matters. Ehrenreich, along with fellow Pantheon author Todd Gitlin, spearheaded the determined protest against the forced departure of managing director André Schiffrin, which prompted fears in the literary community that profitability had become such an overriding goal at the major houses that it might preclude the publication of the kind of provocative, socially conscious books for which Pantheon was known.

"Todd and I got on the phone to lots of people; we had a demonstration—it was the first time a major publishing house had been picketed by authors—and we published a letter signed by hundreds of famous writers. I had done a lot of organizing, but never of hot-shot intellectuals; we were very proud of all the big names we were able to get on the letter. Along with the support for Salman Rushdie a year earlier, it showed that the intellectual community could come together, which was good, because by and large the New York literary world is pretty stuffy and conservative; it's not a lively or politically active bunch.

"I didn't have any illusions that we were going to get Random House to change its mind about Pantheon, but I did think it would be good to create some cost. Writers are so powerless compared to these guys who run the mega-corporations that control so much of publishing that all we can do is now and then bring a faint blush to the pinched cheeks of these Scrooge-like fellows!" She gives a short laugh, acknowledging the hyperbolic tone of her comments, but standing by their substance. With her blonde hair pulled loosely back by a barrette, wire rimmed glasses framing a makeup-free face, clad in jeans, a royal blue shirt and sneakers, Ehrenreich has abandoned neither the look nor the political attitudes of her student days.

The author followed Sara Bershtel, who had edited *Fear of Falling* and a collection of Ehrenreich's articles entitled *The Worst Years of Our Lives,* from Pantheon to FSG. "Sara's a very involved editor, maybe the hardest working editor on

earth, and I think she improved *Kipper's Game* a lot. There were about 20 more subplots until she took a look at it, and she made Kipper appear at the end—he wasn't going to, there was another ending, but she felt that he should. I actually enjoyed the revisions, because I didn't want to leave the book; I probably could have gone on forever."

Peter Biskind, executive editor of *Premiere* magazine and an old friend, also commented on the first draft, and Ehrenreich discussed nearly every chapter with her son, now a religious studies major at Brown. "Benjamin was a big supporter of my writing a novel; I kept losing confidence, but he would read things almost as I was writing them, we would discuss it and that kept me going." Her daughter is also an author; Rosa's book about her experience as a female student at Oxford will be published in England next year. Ehrenreich's husband of 10 years, Gary Stevenson, "is just reading the novel now. He's a union organizer, which is like being an elevator operator: up and down." Thrown out of the Teamsters by its previous corrupt administration, Stevenson came back with the current, reforming leadership and now serves as Eastern regional director of organizing. *Fear of Falling* was dedicated "To Gary—and the old-fashioned struggle against class injustice that he so ably serves."

> **People have sometimes thought [I] was a sociologist or a historian, but since I have no formal education in any of these things, I'm not tied to a discipline, so I can rampage through any kind of material I want."**
> —*Barbara Ehrenreich*

Ehrenreich's current project is, typically, a radical change of pace. "It's about theories of war, and it's serious: I'm reading 18th-century treaties and learning about cross-bows! You have to know the details, and there's a tremendous amount to learn. All my previous history work was social history, women's things, so now I'm finding out what men have been doing all this time. I like to learn a completely new area; I don't think that constitutionally I could specialize in an academic way. People have sometimes thought was a sociologist or a historian, but since I have no formal education in any of these things, I'm not tied to a discipline, so I can rampage through any kind of material I want."

Ehrenreich continues to produce a monthly column for *Time* magazine and whatever other journalism strikes her as necessary. "I like to do both. They're completely different ways of thinking and living for me: journalism is a more frenetic lifestyle—I'm switching on CNN all the time and maybe going on television myself to argue with somebody—and writing books is more solitary, contemplative, reclusive and obsessional." She also remains active in the Democratic Socialists of America, formed in 1983 out of the union of two earlier left-wing groups ("an anti-corporate merger, as it were"), which like all political organizations requires time-consuming meetings and discussions. "Too bad there aren't 48 hours in the day!" she comments wryly.

Somehow, you get the feeling that Barbara Ehrenreich will always manage to squeeze it all in.

Steven J. Kellman (review date Spring 1994)

SOURCE: "Ehrenreich's Game," in *Michigan Quarterly,* Vol. XXXIII, No. 2, Spring, 1994, pp. 375-84.

[*Below, Kellman offers a mixed review of* Kipper's Game.]

"When a scholar of John Kenneth Galbraith's immense sagacity has a tale to tell, it is time to put away our toys, sit quietly and attend with great care," wrote Barbara Ehrenreich in *The New York Times Book Review* of February 11, 1990. It is the opening sentence to the enthusiastic account she gave of *A Tenured Professor.* The book was Galbraith's third published novel, but he is much better known for his nonfiction, including *The Affluent Society, The Liberal Hour,* and *The New Industrial State.* Although he has been a tenured professor, at Harvard, for many decades, Galbraith's authority derives from his ability and propensity to address public issues in a manner that has engaged educated non-specialists. When an intellectual of Galbraith's immense accomplishment turns to fiction, it is time to wonder why and how, questions not directly addressed in Ehrenreich's discussion of his novel.

Six months later, Farrar, Straus & Giroux announced the signing of a two-book contract with Ehrenreich. The first would be a novel, the author's first, while the second would be the ninth volume of nonfiction that Ehrenreich has published alone or in collaboration. The novel, *Kipper's Game,* was published in 1993, while the nonfiction book, on theories of war, is still in preparation. Like the octogenarian Galbraith, Ehrenreich, who was born in 1941, belongs to the endangered species of public intellectual: an essayist who may or may not be affiliated with a university but whose constituency is the general reader and whose matter is the commonweal.

Edmund Wilson is the prototype of the American intellectual. "A professor without a university, a critic without a 'field,' a historian without a 'period,' he became the exemplary intellectual of his generation," wrote biographer David Castronovo. Wilson did publish a novel, *I Think of Daisy*

(1929), but few think of that book—or his volumes of poetry, short fiction, and drama—when they ponder Wilson's vigorous contributions to the national dialogue. Though she left her last tenure-track position, assistant professor of health sciences at the State University of New York at Old Westbury, in 1974, Ehrenreich has become one of the most prominent intellectuals in the United States, heir to the mantle of Wilson, H. L. Mencken, Lionel Trilling, Mary McCarthy, Michael Harrington, and Irving Howe. If she—or Noam Chomsky, Garry Wills, Irving Kristol, Christopher Lasch, Stephen Jay Gould, Daniel Bell, or Cornel West—abandons polemical discourse for literary invention, Samuel Johnson's abusive analogy between a woman preaching and a dog walking on its hind legs applies: You marvel not so much at how well it is done but that it is done at all.

"I feel like a criminal. I didn't mean to do it," replied Ehrenreich when an interviewer for *Publishers Weekly* questioned why the essayist had just committed fiction. In 1973, Tom Wolfe announced the triumph of the New Journalism, boasting that the nonfiction of Gay Talese, Norman Mailer, Truman Capote, Joan Didion, George Plimpton, Michael Herr, Wolfe himself, and others had succeeded in "dethroning the novel as the number one literary genre." But Wolfe's own reversion to the antique form, with *The Bonfire of the Vanities* (1987), demonstrated that the monarchy of the novel was never truly overthrown. Fiction is the tribute that sober thinkers pay to the glamour of imagination. Interring the novel has been a familiar ritual since Cervantes closed the coffin on the preposterous *Amadis de Gaula,* yet, even in 1994, no literary career seems complete without one in the corpus. Though William F. Buckley, Jr. and Susan Sontag are best remembered for their essays, they also indulge in the atavistic narrative. With *Kipper's Game,* so, too, does Ehrenreich.

Like a veteran jurist nominated to the Supreme Court, an intellectual who writes a novel leaves behind a paper trail. In the prolific case of Ehrenreich, contributing editor to *Ms.* and *Mother* Jones, columnist for *Time,* and occasional contributor to *The Nation, The New York Times, The New Republic,* and other prominent publications, the trail is a veritable highway. The trendy trinity of race, class, and gender are her cardinal themes, but the greatest of these, for her, is class. The white-collar descendant of a clan of "small farmers, railroad workers, miners, shopkeepers, and migrant farm workers," Ehrenreich retains inherited class suspicions of affluence; she recalls learning from her blue-collar parents that "wealth always carried a presumption of malfeasance." She is a copper-miner's daughter, and proud of it. *Fear of Falling,* Ehrenreich's most considerable work, is a study of the beleaguered American bourgeoisie. Co-chairperson of the Democratic Socialists of America, she defines herself as "socialist and feminist" and contends that: "Dissent, rebellion, and all-around hell-raising remain the true duty of patriots."

Her patriotic prose is leavened with personal references, to her two husbands, two children, and two abortions. Though she now lives in Syosset, Long Island, she was born in Butte, Montana, where her father Ben Howes mined copper and worked for the Union Pacific Railroad. Ehrenreich received a B.A., in chemical physics, from Reed College in 1963 and a Ph.D., in biology, from Rockefeller University in 1968. Long after her 1966 marriage to John Ehrenreich came to an end, she was still, in the 1989 *Fear of Falling,* acknowledging that: "Some of his ideas persist here, and, I hope, some trace of his clear and logical approach to things." But the book is dedicated to Gary Stevens, the Teamster organizer she married in 1983: "To Gary—and the old-fashioned struggle against class injustice that he so ably serves." Ehrenreich comes from an upwardly mobile mongrel family "of blue-eyed, Scotch-Irish Democrats" and other strains and, dissenting from the ethnic chauvinism now rampant on the left, celebrates skepticism toward jealous tribal deities. An avowed atheist, she venerates democratic socialism as "an evangelical, visionary cause, and the only one ultimately capable of reclaiming the lost language of human solidarity."

Ehrenreich's most pungent use of language is displayed in *The Worst Years of Our Lives,* a screed against the "decade of greed" for which she portrays the Reagan presidency as cause, symptom, and syneedoche. A collection of essays previously published in magazines and newspapers, the book employs Swiftian hyperbole to lampoon and lambaste the mores and amorality of recent American culture. Surveying the contemporary scene, she is inspired to witty indignation by consumer self-indulgence and political self-righteousness. Observing "traditional values" exploited by partisan opportunists to discredit their opponents and advance their own careers, Ehrenreich thunders: "From the vantage point of the continent's original residents, or, for example, the captive African laborers who made America a great agricultural power, our 'traditional values' have always been bigotry, greed, and belligerence, buttressed by wanton appeals to a God of love." Always be wary of pronouncements with "always." The nascent novelist demonstrates a creative flexibility toward precision in her proclamation that "there can be no more ancient and traditional American value than ignorance." In the May 24, 1993 issue of *The Nation,* Ehrenreich dramatized the dangers of military intervention in Bosnia by concocting a caricature: "A uniformed American with firepower is much like a three-year-old with a garden hose; someone in whose presence no one can expect to remain dry and composed for long."

Whether mocking yuppie food fads or rupturing the myth of a dearth of marriageable men, Ehrenreich's prose is neither dry nor composed. Proudly *engagé,* a moralist whose prose is fecundated by conjugating the verb *ought,* she has developed a style of discourse that is both passionate and playful. *Fear of Falling,* her previous book of nonfiction, even adopts the coloration of a novel. If *The Worst Years of Our Lives* (1990) is—like Raymond Carver's *Where I'm Calling From* (1988), also an exposé of desolation during the chipper interregnum of the Gipper—a compendium of short stories, *Fear of Falling,* a book length work of sustained argument, is novelistic in ambition. Its title echoes Erica Jong's randy 1973 novel, and its subtitle promises, like *Middlemarch, The Awakening,* and *To the Lighthouse,* to reveal *The Inner Life of the Middle Class.* Ehrenreich explicitly presents her thesis—that, contrary to its self-deceptions, the American middle class is embattled, puritanical, intolerant, and elitist—as if it were a narrative, "a more or less coherent story."

But before chronicling how, during the past three decades, the middle class became conscious of itself as a class, Ehrenreich pauses to introduce the protagonist of her plot: "Before this story can be told, I must first introduce its central character, the professional middle class." After specifying the occupations, defining experiences, income levels, and "lifestyle and tastes" of her collective anti-hero, Ehrenreich proceeds to trace its development, "from the naive solipsism of the middle class in the fifties to the thoroughly pessimistic self-assessment that accompanied the conservative mood of the eighties." Much of that story is understood in terms of inadequate or inaccurate fictions—that the middle class in permissive, that the proletariat is reactionary, that yuppies are hedonists. Ehrenreich's larger story absorbs and supersedes these, as if she were constructing an elaborate frame narrative. When, at last, her protagonist begins to repudiate its ethic of avarice and revert to the idealism it abandoned earlier, Ehrenreich can conclude: "So, in some sense, our story has come full circle."

Ehrenreich deplores the middle-class tendency to obscure social realities through abstract, impersonal rhetoric. She berates professional jargon for being disingenuous and, by privileging the general over the individual, undemocratic.
—*Steven J. Kellman*

Ehrenreich deplores the middle-class tendency to obscure social realities through abstract, impersonal rhetoric. She berates professional jargon for being disingenuous and, by privileging the general over the individual, undemocratic. "Is there a way to 're-embody' the middle class's impersonal mode of discourse, so that it no longer serves to conceal the individual and variable speaker?" she asks, "For we may need to find *ourselves* in the language of abstraction, if we are ever to find the 'others' in the language of daily life."

Academic sociology rarely speaks that lucid, supple language, but Ehrenreich has, through eight books of social observation and admonition, evolved an idiom that is accessible to the general reader and responsive to the individual instance. Even without inspiration from the versatile intellectual whom, in a 1988 essay in *Mother Jones,* she called "the perennially clever John Kenneth Galbraith," Ehrenreich was ripe to write a novel, the form with enough residual prestige to remain the number one literary genre. When a tycoon's jilted wife or a president's disgraced aide writes a novel, the result is likely to be a *roman à clef* whose key is in the events of the author's public frustration. When an intellectual indulges in fiction, we expect a *roman à thèse,* in which the novel becomes the conflict of ideas through other means. In that, *Kipper's Game* does not disappoint.

At the outset of *Fear of Falling,* Ehrenreich, decrying the myopia of current culture, includes recent novels in her censure. "Much, though certainly not all, contemporary fiction shows a similar narrowness of focus," she complains. "A typical 'quality' novel of recent vintage will explore the relationships and reveries of people who live in large houses and employ at least one servant to manage all those details of daily living that are extraneous to the plot." It is hard to credit Ehrenreich as a literary critic, or even to determine just which "quality" novels she has in mind, unless they be by Judith Krantz, Sidney Sheldon. Danielle Steel, or other popular fantasists of material gratification. It is hard to think of a recent "quality" novel whose main characters lead privileged lives insulated from the material needs of others. The description certainly does not apply at all to the works of William Kennedy. Toni Morrison, Cormac McCarthy, Jane Smiley, Louise Erdrich, or Oscar Hijuelos, and only rarely to those of Saul Bellow, John Barth, John Updike, E. L. Doctorow, Philip Roth, or Joyce Carol Oates. *Fear of Falling* offers itself as an alternative vision to the otiose fiction that Ehrenreich imagines, in order to denounce. So does *Kipper's Game.*

It begins in a drear suburban landscape that is the physical correlative of the moral devastation diagnosed in *Fear of Falling,* where, at the outset of the nonfiction story, the 1950s middle class is seen as suffering from malaise, some indeterminate dread. In the opening pages of *Kipper's [Game]*, set in an undefined near future in an unnamed American locale, the sky is permanently dimmed by haze, the vegetation has been devoured by a plague of grayish caterpillars, and electrical brown-outs are commonplace. Anthropologists at the local university have devised an Index of Mass Anxiety, and the signs are not salutary. Even the shopping mall has "reached a steady state of disrepair and abandoned promises. Huge drapes of plastic sheeting hung from the see-through plastic ceiling, which let in rain now, and starlings. Paper cups and Styrofoam containers drifted along on the floor, piling up against the benches made de-

liberately uncomfortable to discourage teenagers and vagrants. From the aggressive interiors of the clothing shops, clerks looked out on the fake outdoors of the mall interior—a part of the world that had died, somehow, in captivity." Della Markson's twenty-year marriage dies, as well, when she picks up an extension phone and accidentally overhears her husband Leo in passionate conversation with another woman.

Assisted by their black maid Maisy, the Marksons might, before the start of Ehrenreich's novel, have been precisely what the author deplored in current fiction—"people who live in large houses and employ at least one servant to manage all those details of daily living that are extraneous to the plot." But Della immediately moves out and into a modest apartment of her own, in a subdivided former private house. She obtains a low-paying job at the Human Ecology Complex (HEC), a vast, dilapidated research empire oozing with toxic waste, on the campus of a nearby university. Della serves as an assistant in a laboratory where scientists are closing in on the virus that causes a mysterious and fatal new disease. The entire HEC is run by Richard Leitbetter, an academic celebrity adept at raising funds and enhancing his own reputation by appropriating the work of others. Through an insidious system of internal espionage, Leitbetter keeps tabs on the work in Della's laboratory and ends up claiming personal credit for its discoveries.

Meanwhile, Della is intent on tracking down her missing son Steve, a twenty-one-year-old computer genius who used to work for Leitbetter and who walked out on his parents a year ago. Within the underworld of hackers, Steve goes by the code name Kipper and is said to have been developing the consummate cybernetic game. Her search parallels and intersects with one conducted by Alex MacBride, a bibulous academic hack who is described as being "suspended between whiskey and science." Deprived of grants and any prospect of scientific accomplishment, Alex has become Leitbetter's factotum. Leitbetter, who plans to survive the story through cryonic technology, dispatches Alex to track down the papers of Henry Relnik, a brilliant scientist who died in the fifties and was involved with Nazi experiments conducted on involuntary Jewish subjects. The ultimate goal of both Relnik and Kipper is both inclusiveness and concision—to condense the entirely of human knowledge into the most compact portable form, in order to pass it all on to an alien visitor.

This is no ordinary potboiler. For the plot of her first novel, Ehrenreich has cooked up a bizarre bouillabaisse, but, concludes the psychiatrist in the hospital where a distraught Della is finally confined, "when you mix together Nazis and extraterrestrials and mind-altering computer technologies, you are traveling down one of the main thoroughfares of the contemporary mind." That is a thoroughfare that Ehrenreich has been attempting to navigate throughout her career as a writer. Is fiction her most efficient vehicle?

"The chief defect of a novel of ideas," observes Philip Quarles, the intellectual protagonist of Aldous Huxley's 1928 novel of ideas *Point Counter Point,* "is that you must write about people who have ideas to express—which excludes all but about .01 percent of the human race." Such exclusiveness would seem at odds with Ehrenreich's populist sympathies, her mistrust of fiction that centers on an affluent minority whose exploitation of others labor allows them to indulge in cogitation. But Ehrenreich clearly has ideas to express, and she has constructed *Kipper's Game* as a medium to express them. Despite the dishwashers, charwomen, and bartenders who lurk at its peripheries, this is an academic novel whose erudite and articulate characters obsess over difficult ideas. This is intellectual debate by other means, though it is unlikely that the book will reach the wide readership that Ehrenreich commands in *Time.*

In the May 20, 1991 issue of that weekly newsmagazine, Ehrenreich published a column, **"Science, Lies, and the Ultimate Truth,"** that addresses the ethical issues raised by the David Baltimore scandal. A Nobel laureate and president of Ehrenreich's alma mater, Rockefeller University, Baltimore published the defective results of a research project in which a zealous subordinate had altered the data to fit what they were seeking. Occupied with a wide range of activities, Baltimore claimed to be unaware of what had been done in his name, but he did attempt to intimidate and stifle the whistleblower who first challenged the validity of the published study. "If a Nobel laureate in science could sink to the moral level of Milli Vanilli or a White House spin doctor," raged Ehrenreich, "then maybe the deconstructionists are right and there is no truth anywhere, only self-interest masked as objective fact." As if to test that hypothesis, Ehrenreich inserts a deconstructionists into her novel, a trendy interdisciplinary scholar named Caragiola who gives a televised guest lecture at the HEC on the analogies between science and literature. Deconstructing both, she notes that the prevailing criterion for scientific truth is an aesthetic one: the elegance and economy of a proof. The rest of the novel unmasks the self-interest that motivates the scientists at the institute that Dr. Caragiola visits.

The megalomaniacal charlatan Leitbetter, who even describes himself as "a narcissist, a martinet, a vain and callow bully," is Ehrenreich's cautionary caricature of Big Science run amok, a way to extend her indictment of David Baltimore without courting libel. He is an empirebuilder as ambitious as Robert Gallo, the powerful AIDS researcher reportedly more intent on humbling a rival French laboratory than curing the disease. But Leitbetter, the host of a TV series called *The Limits of Knowledge* and a frequent guest on a news program called *Nightzone,* is a flamboyant showman and in that resembles the more benign Carl Sagan. Like Sagan, a champion of the SETI (Search For Extra-Terrestrial Intelligence) program, Leitbetter is obsessed with making contact with a being from beyond the earth.

"Through research," wrote Ehrenreich in her Baltimore column, "we seek to know that ultimate Other, which could be called Nature if the term didn't sound so tame and beaten, or God if the word weren't loaded with so much human hope and superstition." Through *Kipper's Game,* Ehrenreich seeks to illustrate the ways in which the scientific spirit, even when corrupted and distorted, approaches the ultimate Other. Kipper's search for artificial intelligence becomes a search for extraterrestrial intelligence, for a celestial visitor who patrols the cosmos collecting information about each world. The project on which Relnik was working, like the program Kipper is developing, would provide a transistorized rendition of all earthly information for the benefit of a foreign intelligence. "The whole point of the Human Ecology Complex," according to Leitbetter, "is to put together all knowledge of human life. In case we should be asked."

To be both complete and concise. It is the ancient dream of poets and of scientists, and nothing perhaps fulfills it as well as the microscopic threads that write the genetic code. Like everything else, even the strange new virus isolated in the HEC aspires to the principle of condensation: invading the brain, it forces linkages and mergers among all nerve cells. In 1937, in a nonfiction book he called *World Brain,* H.G. Wells declared: "There is no practical obstacle whatever now to the creation of an efficient index to all human knowledge, ideas and achievements, to the creation, that is, of a complete planetary memory for all mankind. And not simply an index; the direct reproduction of the thing itself can be summoned to any properly prepared spot." Wells was reformulating the encyclopedic quest of epic bards and lexicographers, even as he was anticipating current work by computer scientists, geneticists, cosmologists, and even conceptual artist On Kawara, whose *One Million Years* (1970) is a ten-volume list of all the years that humans have inhabited the earth. Ehrenreich makes no reference to Wells, but her contribution to the theme is to join pleasure to comprehensiveness, to suggest that gratification is the basis of both our urge to know it all and what we want to know. The joy of science, "the unbridled hedonism that impels the search for truth" according to Relnik, has its echo in the fact that, as a relative of his puts it, "the universe *desires* to be known." If only they can find and activate the brain's pleasure center, the men in charge of the HEC hope to consolidate all knowledge into a form appropriate to the advent of the Visitor.

For all her militant skepticism, Ehrenreich is flirting with messianic mysticism. She is not entirely contemptuous of Claire, the stridently Christian lab assistant who loudly denounces her bosses as infidels. A radio preacher named Sister Bertha pronounces oracular gibberish, and the author seems to take her almost as seriously as do Kipper and Della, who are willing to follow Bertha's babble anywhere. They manage to track her down with merely a portable radio and the confidence that the clearer the transmission the closer they are to its source. The FCC could save considerable time, energy, and money if technology so primitive sufficed to pinpoint pirate broadcasters.

Ehrenreich peppers her plot with abductions, murders, and enough conspiracies to earn her a fellowship to the Academy of Fiction as Cosmic System run by Thomas Pynchon, Don DeLillo, William Gaddis, and Joseph McElroy. "In many ways," maintains Dr. Hershey, determined to isolate a lethal new virus, "science was a test, perhaps the highest test, of man's mettle and will to survive—a game, the ultimate game perhaps." Often, however, Della Markson's amateur sleuthing about the fate of Kipper and the truth behind the HEC resembles a Nancy Drew caper. Ehrenreich's game can sometimes seem metallic, like a test of the reader's will to persist.

Devastated to find herself suddenly *déclassée* and *divorcée,* Della is a figure familiar to readers of Ehrenreich's social commentary. She is another reminder of the fragility of middle-class security and the frailty of feminine power. The author described Della to *Publishers Weekly* as "a character I had been thinking about for quite a while, because I had written a few articles about middle-class women who are suddenly divorced and completely unprepared to enter the world." She has also written articles about ethics in science, environmental degradation, spiritual hunger, academic fraud, and other contemporary issues now kippered together to produce her first novel. "Maybe this is all crap, invented by someone who thought I was running out of conversational topics," suggests Alex about the outlandish story he has assembled linking Holocaust experiments with artificial intelligence, epidemiology, spiritualism, commercialism, and the search for life on this and other worlds. A reader is likely to run out of patience before the clever **Kipper's Game** runs out of topics. "Trouble with you," says the bartender Chris to his devoted patron Alex MacBride, "professors and so on, think everything comes from ideas." In Ehrenreich's compelling prose, everything does indeed come from ideas. Because the essay form has offered her the best forum for her ideas, an opportunity to exercise her wit, acumen, and moral indignation, Ehrenreich might be more temperamentally suited to the short story than the novel. She has yet to master the mystery of completeness and concision.

Vicky Hutchings (review date 20 May 1994)

SOURCE: "Lamb Stakes," in *New Statesman & Society,* Vol. 7, No. 303, May 20, 1994, pp. 37-8.

[*In the following review, Hutchings provides a summary of the plot elements in* Kipper's Game.]

Like the famous trick with mirrors, this book endlessly repeats itself in different sizes. The *leitmotif* is the search for understanding. It starts with an addictive computer game condensed on to three disks: you have to get the scrolls to the wise woman, past the black knights, past all the obstacles in the way. The game is also a pedagogical tool, a summary of all that we are capable of and all we have learned. Hey, these disks can lead to "Enlightenment, the mystic goal of mankind".

The novel follows the same path: Steve, or Kipper as he calls himself, happy hacker and the game's creator, tries to keep the disks out of the clutches of his former employers, the drug-dealing, New Ageish Harvest Enterprises, scientist-descendants of the Nazi *Erntegruppe* who once experimented on Jews. His dream is to give them to Sister Bertha, the pirate-radio preacher, who says that "everything we have is worth giving away". Could Sister Bertha, perhaps, be the Visitor Harvest is expecting: one of the extra-terrestrial Others who "programmed us, through the wiring of our brains", come back for the pay-off?

When you play the game, "everything is a clue". Just like the book. And so we come full circle. This is *Foucault's Pendulum* territory without the laundry list, but now it's the reader who is searching for enlightenment.

Here are a few pointers: Claire predicts that "The Lamb shall rise up and slay the lion"; Harvest designs a deadly virus in its labs, whose symptoms unaccountably are the stigmata; the fish is a Christian symbol; Stephen was the first Christian martyr. After Kipper kills his father Leo, in cahoots with Harvest, he later dies, blood oozing from his palms.

Now let's turn to some of the characters associated with Harvest: Kentwell Brabant, has a "pink glow" in his eyes; Doctor Leitbetter, in its pay, smells of something "rare and stratospheric like ozone"; the Human Ecology Complex he heads is nicknamed Hell. Have you had enough clues yet?

"There are two times only that He comes for us," says Sister Bertha. "The first time was the sowing, the planting of His flesh. The next time is the reaping, and the next time is the last." And the next time, it seems, She is a woman.

By the end, Kipper's mother Della is in therapy, coming to terms with the death of her husband and son, and her encounter "with the Visitor . . . with God, if we're to call it God." The psychiatrist is rather underwhelmed by Della's story: "When you mix together Nazis and extra-terrestrials and mind-altering computer technologies, you are traveling down one of the main thoroughfares of the contemporary mind. A well-worn path, not to say trite. Oh yes, the second coming too: that's fine, that's usually in there. Some people think reality is boring and oppressive. They should have to sit in [my] chair and hear the same fantasy ingredients . . . again and again." Most people will know Barbara Ehrenreich from her column in the *Guardian.* This is her first novel. A lot of readers may not like these fantasy ingredients. But *Kipper's Game* is also sharp and funny, in a dry sort of way.

Sometimes the observations make your hair stand on end. The scene when Della accidentally picks up the phone and overhears two voices "which seemed to know each other far better than she knew anyone, including her husband, who was one of the voices" is one of the finest depictions of the end of a marriage I have ever read. The bastard deserved all he got. This is Virago at its best.

Penelope Mesic (review date 28 May 1995)

SOURCE: "The Heat and the Intimacy," in *Chicago Tribune,* May 28, 1995, sec. 14, p. 3.

[*In the following review, Mesic compares the essay styles of Ehrenreich and Joseph Epstein.*]

Other than a review, these two collections of essays by Joseph Epstein and Barbara Ehrenreich deserve something more closely resembling a National Geographic Special. For no team of Sherpaled climbers or divers finning through the crannies of a coral reef, ever discovered more diverse or improbable life forms thriving in a single culture. Well-adapted to the hot, volcanic slopes of national politics we find the highly colored clusters of barbed remarks known as *commentarius Ehrenreichii.* At a more rarefied elevation, flowering profusely in a sheltered nook, are the exquisite blooms of Epstein's *mots,* called anglophile's necktie.

Ehrenreich is passionate, public and politically engaged, with a style as subtle as a hand grenade. Epstein is intensely private, and succeeds when he has, with the smallest pressure, extracted the essence of the quietest moment of ordinary life. Their very virtues are at war with one another. Thus the same sense of wonder that comes to the naturalist confronted with life's variety, is aroused in the reader. We marvel that our much maligned American society, supposedly homogenized by the mass media, can sustain two such fiercely distinct personalities.

Most of the essays in Ehrenreich's *The Snarling Citizen* first appeared in *Time* or the *English Guardian.* They startle and invigorate because those who espouse liberal causes feminism, day care and a strong labor movement—all too often write a granola of prose: a mild, beige substance that is, in a dull way, good for us. Ehrenreich is peppery and salacious, bitter with scorn, hotly lucid. She can find something shocking to say about cleaning house, exulting in the fact that working women, after "decades of unappreciated drudgery" are no longer measuring their worth by keeping their homes "cleaner than a motel room." Moving to a bigger, dirtier House—of Representatives—she cheerfully lambastes it as a "half-way house for long-term miscreants and un-indicted felons."

In **"S & M as Public Policy"** she blisters those eager to build punitive measures into the welfare system, writing, "For poor males we have prison; for poor females, welfare—and there's no reason why one sex's punishment should be any less onerous than the other's." Her further, Swiftian recommendation is flogging indigent mothers—"it will make the hawks and wonks feel much better without starving a single child."

> **Ehrenreich is passionate, public and politically engaged, with a style as subtle as a hand grenade.**
> **—Penelope Mesic**

More gently mocking the "celebrants of Purim and Kwanzaa and Solstice" who overstress their ancestral traditions, she remarks that when asked to fill in a blank for ethnic background, she always writes "none," and dryly notes, "Skepticism, curiosity, and wide-eyed ecumenical tolerance are also part of the human tradition."

Show Ehrenreich a sacred cow and she will tie its tail in a knot. Writing of Salmon Rushdie, she feigns envy: "for what writer has not dreamed of enjoying global fame while his publishers are picked off one by one?"

Occasionally, Ehrenreich relents, admires and bestows sober praise. This is most apparent when she writes about the separation of church and state, pointing out that "not all the founding fathers believed in the same God, or in any God at all." She goes on to remind us that the real issue is not that of giving the church too much power, but of giving the state too much power. To associate government intimately with religion, is to endow it with more than earthly legitimacy: "By stripping government of supernatural authority, the Founding Fathers created a zone of freedom around each individual human conscience . . . They demystified government, and reduced it to something within reach of human comprehension, protest, and change."

These moments, when Ehrenreich lays mockery aside, are

rare. In general her essays are slash and dazzle, outrageous generalization with an underpinning of scrupulously accurate fact—designed to fix our attention and hold it by force. These pieces are indeed wonderful, but they were designed to be read in the public press, against a background of border wars and plane crashes. This is a voice lifted to carry to the back of a crowd.

A voice in every way more intimate is Joseph Epstein's. As the Godfather Don Corleone once said, "Everything is personal," and reading these essays we feel Epstein would say much the same thing but with a more benign inflection. Like the first essayist Montaigne, Epstein tells us a good deal about himself. He is something of a dandy, at least in his choice of neckties. He abhors the notion of carrying other people's business slogans and logos on one's person and can't see a poor fish in clothes emblazoned "Ralph Lauren," without thinking of Art Carney on the old Honeymooners show exclaiming. "Yo, ho, ho, Ralphie boy!" He loves colored paper clips, fine-leaded mechanical pencils and is in general, as many authors are, "quite nuts about office supplies." In the course of two pages he can, and does, quote Evelyn Waugh, Gertrude Stein, Samuel Goldwyn, Gustav Mahler, Arnaldo Momigliano, the economic historian Alexander Gerschenkron, Clifton Fadiman and his own mother, thus giving the impression that his solitude is like most people's cocktail parties.

But the point of Epstein's kind of essay is neither to press quotations into a sort of bouillon cube of experience nor to make a collage of one's foibles. It is to capture ordinary life and thought and render it significant without robbing it of its freshness—in other words, an impossible task. The great danger in the enterprise is creating the same triviality life itself is often guilty of, producing well-turned phrases on a so-what theme. To this danger Epstein occasionally succumbs.

But more often he uses his elegance and beauty of cadence humbly, in the service of his affections. In the essay "Here for Mink" he writes of his mother, a "woman without sentimentality or nostalgia," who "granted [him] enormous freedom," and of whom Epstein says: "We were beyond intimacy. We were at that stage of affection where we understood each other without having to explain much, where we knew we could rely on each other without any qualification, where we loved each other so much that we didn't have to display our love in outward endearments. I miss her, like mad."

By offering us this vision of a reciprocal and uncomplicated love, he is following his own advice: "If everyone seems to be rushing to blow out the trembling match of culture and leave us in darkness . . . then those who love life are under the obligation not to desert it not yet anyway. Best not to

concentrate altogether on the sycophancy, cowardice, and fraudulence of a society that feels as if it's in decomposition . . . Better to think instead of large-hearted men and women who refused to be daunted in much darker times than ours."

For all their differences Epstein and Ehrenreich have this much in common: they scorn the generality of human conduct, its veniality, its spite and dumbness, precisely because they have worked to keep before them an image of what is better.

Andrew Ferguson (review date August 1995)

SOURCE: A review of *The Snarling Citizen,* in *The American Spectator,* Vol. 28, No. 8, August, 1995, pp. 66-7.

[*In the following review, Ferguson suggests that Ehrenreich's writing is rife with factoids and faulty syllogisms.*]

Barbara Ehrenreich's career as a journalist has followed an interesting trajectory. She is a witty, graceful stylist who first came to prominence in the *Nation, Ms.,* and *Mother Jones.* Unlike Molly Ivins, she's a mom—a working mom!—and unlike Anna Quindlen, she never whimpers. The fat cats of "main-stream" journalism do not allow writers with Ehrenreich's attributes to languish on the leftward fringe, and so for the past several years she has been a featured essayist on the back page of *Time* magazine, where her unabashedly left-wing views make a pleasant contrast to the abashedly left-wing views found in the pages preceding it. She is now so certifiably mainstream that mainstream publishers are happy to get out collections of even her most quotidian pieces. Hence **The Snarling Citizen,** a loosely packed duffel of Ehrenreichiana previously published in *Time,* the *Nation,* the *Guardian,* and elsewhere.

The essays here are brief without exception; the longest couldn't be longer than 1700 words. To impose coherence she has grouped them under chapter headings: "Trampling on the Down-and-Out," "Sex Skirmishes and the Gender Wars," and so on. The collection begins with "Life in the Postmodern Family," raising the question, right at the start, of what a postmodern family might be. I don't know, and neither, I suspect, does Ehrenreich, but "postmodern" is one of her favorite words, recurring even more often than such phrases as "apocalyptic frisson," "post-Judeo-Christian generation," "posttrend era," "post-feminist era," and "advanced capitalism"—the big, blowy tropes that dazzle editors while allowing a writer to elide from the concrete to the dubious, and from the self-evident to the debatable, without debate.

This stylistic trick is essential to her appeal as an essayist, for when Ehrenreich does offer a straightforward observation or assertion of fact, she tends to wobble. Her facts, for example, aren't really facts. She opens her first essay on the family with the statement: "The U.S. divorce rate remains stuck near 50 percent." This is a chestnut of newsmagazine chin-waggers, but in fact the divorce rate is 4.8 percent per 1,000 Americans. "According to surveys [block that phrase!], somewhere between 26 percent and 41 percent of married women are unfaithful." The most recent and exhaustive survey, *Sex in America,* puts the figure at less than 15 percent. She writes: "Studies show [ditto!] that teachers tend to favor boys by calling on them more often, making eye contact with them more frequently, and pushing them harder to perform." Actually, "studies show" that teachers don't "call on" boys more often, they call them out more often—reasonable enough, since schoolboys make more trouble than schoolgirls, requiring more frequent eye contact and more pushing to perform.

Ehrenreich's journalism is filled with such casual misstatements—little wisps of faulty data upon which she builds whole cathedrals of commentary. The errors of fact don't make much difference to the quality of her arguments, for Ehrenreich, as an ideologue, is impervious to any data that don't serve the larger points she wishes to make. And her points are larger than you can imagine. When she deals with "the family," as she often does, she can be funny but uncomfortably bitter—imagine Erma Bombeck, if Erma Bombeck's husband ran off with a call girl and her son decapitated the family cat. Erma's treatment of the family, jaundiced as it was, was at bottom affectionate, confined to small but endearing frustrations: Ehrenreich's balloons into a genuine, ill-disguised hostility toward civilization itself. When she makes an argument she tends to jump around.

> Americans act out their ambivalence about the family without ever owning up to it. Millions adhere to creeds—religious and political—that are militantly "pro-family." But at the same time, millions flock to therapists and self-help groups that offer to heal the "inner child" from damage inflicted by family life. Legions of women band together to revive the self-esteem they lost in supposedly loving relationships and to learn to love a little less. We are all, it is often said, in recovery. And from what? Our families, in most cases.

It would be difficult to write a paragraph with more confusions than this one. "Act out" is a cant phrase, coined by counselors and facilitators. The two sentences about millions being religiously pro-family and millions flocking to self-help groups are logically unrelated, but the juxtaposition is meant to imply that the second sentence discredits the first. And what's an "inner child"? How do you "learn to love a little less"? It is indeed often said that "we are all in recovery," but that doesn't mean it's true, or that the phrase has any content at all. This is Oprahspeak, unbecoming a writer who fancies herself a skeptic.

But here in postmodern, postfeminist America, Oprahspeak seems all that's left to the left. "There is a long and honorable tradition of what might be called 'anti-family' though," she writes, invoking authority to buttress her case. But the line of authority trails off. Ehrenreich traces the tradition to the Rousseauian philosopher Charles Fourier, through unnamed "early feminists" and "radical psychiatrists," to the renowned British crank Edmund Leach. As an intellectual genealogy it's not quite Aristotle-to-Aquinas-to-Kant, but it will have to do. We live in a post-traditionalist age.

So where is a left-wing polemicist to turn—when facts fail you, when the "surveys" don't "show" what you want them to, when your intellectual tradition is neither long nor particularly honorable? There will always be straw men, and the book is overstuffed with them. One essay—to choose a typical instance—attacks the "dangerous" idea that "history repeats itself." She writes: "Everything that happens, we are led to believe, is a historical reenactment," and the belief makes us putty for the forces of reaction. Ehrenreich herself is undeluded. She argues against the notion with great force and indignation, mustering facts and examples, moving elegantly from the specific to the general, from the personal to the universal and back again, without once stopping to consider that nobody in his right mind takes the idea literally. It's like watching Fred Astaire dance with a mop.

She has her gifts. She's good with a joke—about that most public recluse, Salman Rushdie, she writes: "What is it with these fatwa guys—can't they get a copy of Rushdie's schedule from his publicist, like everybody else?" And you can't completely write off a woman who has the taste to call Jack Valenti an "ancient lounge lizard." (Query to *Time* editors: Ageist? Offensive to the amphibian community?) She knows that caricature can be a verbal art, with the capacity to expose an essence more quickly than a dozen arguments, but too often her fondness for exaggeration and hyperbole drags her into mere buffoonery. Why do we watch the Academy Awards? "We watch for what might be called political reasons: because everyone knows that the movie-star class now rules the earth." How clever, how unconventional, how not even remotely true!

Even so, I agree with the many blurbsters on the dust jacket—Susan Faludi, John Kenneth Galbraith, and Ellen Goodman among them—who suggest that Barbara Ehrenreich may be the best polemicist the left-wing can produce nowadays. This alone makes her stuff worth reading. For liberals she distills contemporary liberalism down to its essence, which by now is nothing more than a series of attitudes and poses and sneers. For conservatives she is cause for rejoicing, a knowledgeable, highly credentialed, top-of-the-line tour guide to the Potemkin Village they hope to over-run.

Kirkus Reviews (review date 15 March 1997)

SOURCE: A review of *Blood Rites: Origins and History of the Passions of War,* in *Kirkus Reviews,* Vol. LXV, No. 6, March 15, 1997, pp. 432-33.

[*Below, the reviewer describes* Blood Rites *as an iconoclastic study in which social commentator and* Time *essayist Ehrenreich challenges accepted notions of why human beings wage war.*]

In her tenth book Ehrenreich (***The Worst Years of Our Lives,*** 1990, etc.) takes a multidisciplinary approach in her investigation of "the feelings people invest in war and often express as their motivations for fighting." She makes a thorough examination of a wide range of historical, psychological, sociological, biological, and anthropological literature to come up with her unique theory: that the accepted view that human beings engage in wars because of an innate aggressive, warlike instinct—especially in men—is untrue. Instead, Ehrenreich persuasively argues that the "roots of the human attachment to war" can be found in feelings and emotions that are imprinted on all of us due to events that took place many millennia ago, when our earliest ancestors spent most of their waking hours in fear of being devoured by predators. What Ehrenreich calls humankind's "sacralization of war" (the tendency to invest the emotional trappings of religious fervor in war) stems from the evolu-

tion of humans from prey into predators, the feelings engendered in "a creature which has learned only 'recently,' in the last thousand or so generations, not to cower at every sound in the night." The human predilection for war, as Ehrenreich puts it, can be viewed "as a way of reenacting the primal transformation from prey to predator." Also key was "a global decline in the number of large animals, both 'game' and predators, for humans to fight against." In making these original arguments, Ehrenreich challenges long-held theories of evolution and psychology promulgated by Darwin, Freud, and other scholars.

Ehrenreich's work is convincing, at least to the general reader. Her ideas likely will be challenged by those whose theories she seeks to discredit.

FURTHER READING

Criticism

"The Coming Medical War." *New York Review* (1 July 1971): 33-38.
> Examines several books on the issue of health care, including the Ehrenreichs' *The American Health Empire: Power, Profit, and Politics.*

Ross, Leonard. Review of *The American Health Empire: Power, Profit, and Politics,* by John and Barbara Ehrenreich, and *In Failing Health,* by Ed Cray. *New York Times Book Review* (7 March 1971): 3, 50.
> Provides a summary of the two books and an argument in favor of national health care.

Additional coverage of Ehrenreich's life and career is contained in the following sources published by Gale: *Contemporary Authors,* Vols. 73-76; *Contemporary Authors New Revision Series,* Vols. 16 and 37; *Bestsellers,* 90:4; and *Major 20th-Century Writers.*

Oriana Fallaci
1930-

Italian journalist and novelist.

The following entry provides an overview of Fallaci's career through 1998. For further information on her life and works, see *CLC*, Volume 11.

INTRODUCTION

Best known as a hard-nosed interviewer to whom, as Elizabeth Mehren of the *Los Angeles Times* said, "virtually no world figure would say no," Oriana Fallaci is a writer who combines the methods of fiction with the reporting of facts. She is a valuable contributor to a genre of writing known as new journalism, or creative non-fiction, which includes writers such as Tom Wolfe, Norman Mailer, and Gay Talese. Fallaci's personality plays a strong role in her writing. As she states in her book *Intervista con la storia* (1974; *Interview with History*): "On every professional experience I leave shreds of my heart and soul; and I participate in what I see or hear as though the matter concerned me personally and were one on which I ought to take a stand." Fallaci eschews objectivity to get at the truth, a controversial approach that has gained her notoriety, but which illustrates her belief that she is not simply a journalist, but also a chronicler of her time.

Biographical Information

Oriana Fallaci was born on June 29, 1930 in Florence, Italy, the daughter of Edoardo and Tosca Fallaci. Edoardo, a cabinet maker and politician, was a leader of the Resistance in Italy during World War II. Fallaci began writing what she called "short naive stories" at age nine and was involved in the Resistance as a teenager. To pursue her writing ambitions, at sixteen she became a reporter in Florence for *Il Mattino*. She later became special correspondent for the journals *Epoca* and *L'Europeo*, and eventually contributed articles to *Corriere della sera, Le Nouvelle Observateur, The New York Times, Life, New Republic, Washington Post*, and *Der Stern*. Initially she interviewed show-business personalities like Dean Martin and Michael Caine, but she soon found her true calling: interviewing political figures such as Henry Kissinger, Yasir Arafat, Golda Meir, Nguyen Cao Ky, The Shah of Iran, the Ayatollah Khomeini, and Mu'ammar Muhammad al-Gaddafi. "I do these interviews to understand the person, to study how power takes place," said Fallaci. She has won several awards for journalism in Italy and North America and has been a university lecturer at Yale, Harvard, Chicago and Columbia. She is a two-time winner of the St.

Vincent prize for Journalism and was awarded the Bancarella prize in 1971 for *Niente e cosi sia* (1969; *Nothing, and So Be It*), her account of the Vietnam war. She received an Honorary Doctorate in Letters from Columbia College (Chicago) and earned the Viaggio Prize for *Un uomo* (1979; *A Man*), a novelistic account of Fallaci's experiences with Alexandros Panagoulis, a Greek political activist who was killed on May 1, 1976. Fallaci met Panagoulis for an interview two days after he was released from a five-year prison term served for an assassination attempt on Greek dictator Georgios Papadopoulos. Fallaci and Panagoulis became lovers and were together until his death. Fallaci claims to never have written for money. Her motivation, she relates, has been "a great emotion, both a psychological or political and . . . intellectual emotion." The influence of Fallaci's interviews is legendary; for example, a 1972 peace treaty between India and Pakistan was jeopardized because of comments elicited from Prime Minister Zulfikar Ali Bhutto during an interview with Fallaci. Her approach is unconventional, but effective. As she told journalist Mike Wallace on CBS's *60 Minutes:* "I hate objectivity. . . . I do not believe in objectivity, I believe in what I see, what I hear, and what I feel."

Major Works

Fallaci's work has been translated from the original Italian into many languages, including English, French, Spanish, German, Swedish, Dutch, Croatian, and Greek. She is drawn to issues of power, although she has developed other themes. An early book, *Il sesso inutile* (1961; *The Useless Sex*), covered the status of women around the world at that time. Fallaci has observed that "when you are a woman, you have to fight more. Consequently, to see more and to think more and to be more creative." Gender is also an important issue in *A Man* which Fallaci considers her most important work. In it she explores the male heroic ideal exemplified by Greek freedom fighter Alexandros Panagoulis. War is a central focus in several of her works, most notably in *Nothing, and So Be It*, a reportage on the Vietnam war that placed Fallaci among the critics of American involvement. She returned to the subject of war in *Inshallah* (1990), where she covers the Lebanon conflict from the Italian camp. In *Se il sole muore* (1965; *If the Sun Dies*), Fallaci reported on the American space program and in *Lettera a un bambino mai nato* (1975; *Letter to a Child never Born*), written after the miscarriage of her child, she deals with abortion, motherhood, and death. Commonly regarded as Fallaci's most significant work is *Interview with History,* a collection of interviews with commentary by the author. In the book, prominent political figures of her time are confronted in the provocative manner that is Fallaci's trademark. She confronts her subjects with probing skepticism and a consuming desire to have her questions answered. "I went with a thousand feelings of rage, a thousand questions that before assailing them were assailing me," Fallaci explained. She observed that "those who determine our destiny are not really better than ourselves; they are neither more intelligent nor stronger nor more enlightened than ourselves."

Critical Reception

Fallaci's writing and interviewing methods have met with mixed appraisal. By some she is seen as a fresh voice in a new genre, while others see in her work a violation of fundamental tenets of journalism. The latter opinion is voiced, for example, by Vivian Gornik in *The New York Times Book Review* who, in discussing *A Man*, complains of a "passionate enslavement" to a "poetic ideal," and finds that when the techniques of fiction are applied to reportage the writing is particularly troublesome, due to a lack of self-control. Jeffrey Burke also noted a tendency for poetic excess and for polemic. However, many critics applaud Fallaci's approach. John C. Kendrew, reviewing *If the Sun Dies,* saw it as "one of very few pioneer works in a new genre: the criticism of science and technology as ways of life, as sets of values" and praised her method, which although imperfect, he saw as "breathing with life." Many reviewers have found in Fallaci's direct confrontation of her subjects an engaging

application of the journalistic method. They maintain that Fallaci gets extraordinary results due not only to the degree of preparation she brings, but also to the knowledge and intelligence she applies to her trade. David Sanford uses the term "surgical journalism" to explain how Fallaci dissects an interview subject until she gets to the truth. Furthermore, Santo L. Arico remarks that Fallaci's methods are akin to those of *cinéma vérité* and direct cinema in that her comprehensive study of and involvement with her subjects stimulates disclosures that a more objective, detached approach would not. Another similarity to these kinds of documentary film techniques is Fallaci's habit of commenting on the unfolding story, the whole resulting in a kind of "psychodrama," not simply an interview. Arico concludes that "Fallaci's virtue as a writer lies precisely in showing the possibility of something strikingly different in journalism and in furthering efforts to replace earlier types of fiction with a new brand of literature."

PRINCIPAL WORKS

Il sesso inutile [*The Useless Sex*] (journalism) 1961
Penelope alla guerra [*Penelope at War*] (novel) 1962
Se il sole muore [*If the Sun Dies*] (journalism) 1965
Niente e cosi sia [*Nothing, and So Be It*] (journalism) 1969
Intervista con la storia [*Interview with History*] (journalism) 1974
Lettera a un bambino mai nato [*Letter to a Child never Born*] (novel) 1975
Un uomo [*A Man*] (novel) 1979
Inshallah (novel) 1990

CRITICISM

The Economist (review date 14 November 1964)

SOURCE: "Report—Italian Style," in *The Economist,* Vol. 213, November 4, 1964, p. 715.

[*In the following review, the critic considers Fallaci's descriptions of women's liberation around the world in* The Useless Sex.]

The motive behind this book [*The Useless Sex*] is "a reportage on the status of women." The author departs via Ankara for points east to inquire into the conditions of the female species, accompanied by a Roman photographer who grows more and more disillusioned about his chances of amorous escapades as the trip proceeds.

The result is totally subjective, not very profound, but interesting and often amusing. The theme is a natural for an illustrated weekly like *L'Europeo,* parcelled into installments with illustrations: it does not adapt so well to book form. One keeps reading about Duilio taking photographs and feels frustrated at not seeing any. To compensate, Signorina Fallaci has a true Italian eye for colour, costume and decor, combined with professional skill in reporting the various interviews en route, and she greets new people and places with a receptive mind.

There are excellent descriptions of the oppressive isolation of Moslem women, shrouded in purdah, who cannot conceive the meaning of love matches, and are still married, in tears, at fourteen. In India the author is shocked at the drastic use of sterilization as one solution to population problems, and the Indian women themselves are confused by the ethics involved: "We have all changed so quickly. We're all a bit bewildered," says one intelligent, educated woman. A good section pinpoints the difference between the women of Hong Kong and those of communist China, the former the most attractive in Asia," the latter wearing plaits, shapeless garments and no makeup. But on both sides of the border they have escaped literally from bondage, epitomized most cruelly by the barbaric custom of binding girls' feet until the bones broke, to achieve the requisite minuteness for finding a husband. As in India, emancipation is a mixed blessing: "People who haven't lived through our metamorphoses cannot understand our bewilderment, our relief and our fears."

In Japan too women seem somewhat disoriented by their new freedom. Here, unlike India, they abandon traditional costume, dye their hair, achieve Western eyes in a fifty minute operation and bolster their bosoms with injections, thus achieving only ugliness in Signorina Fallaci's eyes. So is one to look for the true Japanese woman among the geisha girls? The author and her companions find this approach even more disillusioning, not to say expensive, but the whole Japanese episode is treated vividly both in character and landscape sketches. Perhaps the journey should have ended there: the final passages on Hawaii and especially America are perfunctory and bored in tone. The attitude to American women is too "anti" to have much meaning, in contrast to the open mind displayed elsewhere. It might have been more profitable to carry the inquiries on to home ground. A report on the conditions of Italian women would reveal a lot.

Peter J. Henniker-Heaton (review date 17 November 1966)

SOURCE: "Diary of an Infatuation with the Future," in *Christian Science Monitor,* November 17, 1966, p. 14.

[*In the following review, Henniker-Heaton relates the style and substance of Fallaci's* If the Sun Dies, *which she describes as a "diary of a year in my life."*]

"This book," writes Oriana Fallaci in her first chapter [of *If the Sun Dies*], "is the diary of a year in my life." After serving with the Italian underground against the Nazis, she received at age 14 her honorable discharge and $23.50. A diary of any year in her life could be interesting.

But Miss Fallaci, as she carefully makes plain, doesn't go for religion or prayers or an afterlife; else she might have been cautious and recalled that old saying about man proposing and God disposing. Her book begins as a personal diary; but in no time its theme takes over.

Its theme is the future. Sometimes this future looks like the moon, sometimes like Mars, or a rocket at lift-off, or that state of mind called America. Always, underneath, it is the five billion years left before the sun dies. Five billion years of furious living. Five billion years of grace in which humanity has to find itself new homes in new planetary systems with younger or longer lived suns.

A Chinese courtship

Swiftly the diary becomes the chronicle of a passionate wooing. Many handwritings contribute. It is a wooing of Florence by New York, or possibly of New York by Florence. The intermediaries are several: Houston, Texas, and Cocoa Beach, Florida, Huntsville and White Sands and Las Cruces.

In spite of its intensity the wooing unfolds with the slow complex inexorability of a traditional Chinese courtship. Here on hand are the groom's supporters, the Magnificent Seven, the original astronauts, alive in three dimensions, perhaps four. Here are the lesser astronauts of the second and third batches. The nurse and doctor of the astronauts. Their wives and their children. None of them doodled or squeezed into the margin; each perceptively drawn squarely on the page in full color.

Here, too, are the marriage brokers, acting for the future; Willy Ley, the rocket expert who fled before the Nazis in 1935. Wernher von Braun, the rocket expert who made his smooth get-away from Peenemünde in 1945, Ernst Stuhlinger, the rocket expert who broke it to Oriana that the moon's surface is black, not gold. And the Master of Ceremonies who decides which astronaut shall interview whom, and the great Chief who decides which astronaut shall go up on which mission; and all the minor functionaries and officials, endlessly intertwined like a Maurits Escher drawing. And somewhere, hidden away in the innermost throne room, controlling the strings of power, is NASA itself.

Astronauts and Florence

Back in Florence is the lady's family. Particularly her father, devoted to the old ways, devoted to the earth, certain that no good can come from rockets and star travel and the whole five billion years ahead. In vain his daughter tells him of the plan hatched by her and the astronauts to steal the cheese with holes in it, of which the moon is made; or to set up a chain of drive-in restaurants on the planets. And he remains unimpressed by her story of the astronauts all standing round a swimming pool in their trunks exchanging quotes from Shakespeare's "Julius Caesar." All right, metalaw is the law of the galaxies. Then let his daughter discuss it face to face with the science-fiction writer Ray Bradbury. For himself he will have none of it. So she marries the future without her father's consent, but with all the proprieties of metalaw; and she settles down in New York.

With mighty NASA itself, Miss Fallaci never even asks for an interview. Throughout her chronicle Oriana is something of a Model 1966 Alice. Perhaps she is afraid. Perhaps, if she penetrates to the final throne room, she will find no one, nothing, there. Then the astronauts and all the other strange unbelievable characters who throng her pages will come tumbling about her head like Alice's pack of cards.

Willy Ley (review date 5 February 1967)

SOURCE: "Out of Orbit," in *New York Times Book Review,* February 5, 1967, p. 49.

[*In the following review, Ley comments on Fallaci's reactions to the American space program in* If the Sun Dies.]

Oriana Fallaci is an Italian journalist who came to the United States a few years ago to have a personal look at the space program and related activities. She came to this task armed with nothing more than the knowledge of a few American science-fiction stories, and she found the impact of advanced science and technology quite disturbing. She interviewed engineers, medical doctors, public relations men and astronauts. Throughout, she had a pronounced tendency to veer off the theme and to ask irrelevant questions.

In fact, she reminds me of a long-dead aunt of mine—whom I am dragging in at this point because one such question is the only thing I really remember about her. I was roughly 8 years old then, and I had saved the lead foil from wine bottles and cast them into a mold that looked like a ship's hull. When said aunt came for a *Kaffeeklatsch* I proudly showed her my lead boat and told her how I had made it. "But," she said, "what will you do when it explodes?"

Miss Fallaci (though indubitably far more intelligent than my aunt) has a penchant for making queries of this kind at precisely the wrong moment. While being driven to Merritt Island, the site of the Apollo Launch Complex in Florida, she wanted to know what would be done if an astronaut died during the mission. When taking a preliminary psychological test for astronauts (she had the idea of taking *all* the astronaut's tests, but gave up soon) she was asked the question: "What do you do if you find an addressed and stamped letter in the street?" Her answer: "I'd put it in my handbag" "And then?" the psychologist asked. "Then it will stay there, along with all my own letters."

Her surprise at receiving an indignant reaction is in itself surprising, to put it mildly. Doesn't she know yet that psychologists, with the exception of Dr. Theodore Reik, have no sense of humor? In a similar vein, she pestered astronauts, who would have preferred to do just nothing for half an hour, with questions about "fear" and "courage"—and, again, was wild-eyed with surprise that most of them felt disinclined to engage in philosophical discussions.

The result of all this is a fairly long book. It is not, as she herself stresses, reportage. (No, it isn't; reportage should not contain so many errors of fact.) It is a long diary about her personal reactions to rockets and space and research engineers; it reminds me of a series of waterfalls near Colorado Springs, where one cascade only ceases when it gives birth to another. The whole is addressed to her father, a justification for having taken an interest in the "new things."

I don't know how the book was received in Italy, though I can imagine Italians might have been greatly interested in the impressions made by Americans on their compatriot. But even Italian readers (who, I suppose, are less well informed about the details of the space program than their American counter-parts) must have felt that all these impressions should have been interspersed with a few explanations and factual statements. How *If the Sun Dies* will affect readers in the United States is something I dare not prophesy. I don't know myself whether I should be amused or not.

One thing that Oriana Fallaci has done to me is to weaken a cherished belief I have held for over 30 years—i.e., that (discounting some kinds of fiction) the idea of books "for men," or "for women," is nonsense. Here, I find I would advise Mr. Reader to look for something more concise and informative, while I would tell Mrs. Reader or Miss Reader to find out for herself.

John C. Kendrew (review date March 1967)

SOURCE: A review of *If the Sun Dies,* in *Scientific American,* Vol. 216, No. 3, March 1967, pp. 144-45.

[*In the following review, Kendrew praises Fallaci's* If the Sun Dies *as "one of very few pioneer works in a new genre."*]

The knowing publishers have placed on the dust jacket of this book [*If the Sun Dies*] a full-page photograph of its young Florentine author, curled barefoot in a chair with her long blonde hair loosened. This is the lady who visits NASA, in Houston and Los Angeles and Cape Kennedy and Huntsville and White Sands, who confronts astronauts and Ray Bradbury, public-relations men and motel keepers with her memories of vineyard and basilica, her literary values and her human charm. She asks these people "Why?" and "Who are you?" She tells the story with hot candor and a sharp eye, out of a remarkable experience of life.

The book, in rushing and poetic prose, turned into flowing colloquial English by Pamela Swinglehurst, takes the form of long reflective letters to a distant father—off there in a villa in Chianti, a Tuscan country gentleman who was something of a hero in the Resistance. The war and the Nazi terror are strong in the book. Wernher von Braun (*Doctor* von Braun, the public-relations man insists weakly throughout the colloquy) is portrayed: likable, forceful, versatile, extraordinary, dominant. But over the whole of this expansive interview the scent of lemon hangs like the memories of Proust's childhood. Then she recalls. The German soldiers with the tommy guns who broke the door down to find and deport the two partisans she had just hidden in the well carried the same scent: German soap. "'The future is always interesting,' said von Braun. 'More than the past,' said I."

She met a dozen or two of the astronauts. They come off not badly. To be sure, she finds most of them venerable, dull, bored, bald, mechanical. A few—she was fortunate—are different. She found a poet and a philosopher, and a few others who knew what wit and doubt and fancy mean. One day while driving with the astronauts' physician she invented a Project Cheese, which proposed to subvert Apollo to mine the moon, to sell the cheese here at great profit, working all the while on the other side of the moon to evade discovery. The rumor spread to all the astronauts, and a few of them understood.

And so this woman, a partisan at 14, an incredulous European witness of the vulgarity of Highway 66, of our motels and our extortionate economy, comes in the end not to bury Apollo but somehow to praise it. "And if the Earth dies, and if the Sun dies, we shall live up there, Father. Cost what it may: a tree, a billion trees, all the trees that life has given us."

No capsule review can exhaust the manysidedness and perceptivity and eccentricities of this book. It is one of very few pioneer works in a new genre: the criticism of science and technology as ways of life, as sets of values. It is not exposition of events or good reporting or philosophical analysis. It is quick and imperfect, but it is breathing with life.

Margaret Parton (review date 18 March 1972)

SOURCE: A review of *Nothing, and So Be It*, in *Saturday Review*, Vol. IV, No. 10, March 18, 1972, pp. 75-76.

[*In the following review, Parton considers the Vietnam experiences that are the basis of Fallaci's* Nothing, and So Be It.]

"Life, what is it?" asked Oriana Fallaci's small sister the night before the well-known Italian journalist was to leave for Vietnam. "Life is the time that passes from the moment we're born to the moment we die . . . that's all" the older sister replied. *Nothing, and So Be It* is the harrowing account of Miss Fallaci's search, in the midst of man's utmost bestialities, for a better answer to that question.

The diary of her three trips to Vietnam in 1967 and 1968, which comprises the bulk of the book, reveals Miss Fallaci as a woman who is not only courageous but passionately honest as well. She admits to being terrified at Dak To, an American airstrip under constant fire by the North Vietnamese, but she unflinchingly faces mutilated corpses or the stray, detached hand—"yellow, stiff-fingered . . . Leftover from three days ago." The blood of dead Americans, South Vietnamese, and Viet Cong stains her pages, and Miss Fallaci tells us exactly how these people died. The screams of a three-year-old burned by napalm, a pregnant woman with her abdomen ripped open, a man undergoing the torture of electric shocks in the genitals are heard throughout this book. So be warned.

> The diary of her three trips to Vietnam in 1967 and 1968, which comprises the bulk of [*Nothing, and So Be It*], reveals Miss Fallaci as a woman who is not only courageous but passionately honest as well.
> —*Margaret Parton*

"I'm here to prove something I believe," she wrote in her diary near the beginning of the first trip: "that war is useless and stupid, bestial proof of the idiocy of the human race. I'm here to explain how hypocritical it is for the world to rejoice when a surgeon substitutes one heart for another but accepts the fact that thousands of strong people with healthy hearts are slaughtered like cattle for the sake of a flag." During her initial forty-day stay in South Vietnam her exploration of this thesis led Miss Fallaci not only to battle fronts but to a study of the futility of the Buddhist immolations and to an examination of the twisted mind of General Nguyen Ngoc Loan, the brutal head of the National Police and the man who, in a famous photograph, was shown firing into the head of a prisoner whose hands were tied. "I adore roses . . . with a pearl of dew in each," he told her.

In the United States Miss Fallaci experienced what the late Christopher Rand, another fine journalist, called "the law of diminishing reality." But when the Tet offensive exploded in February of 1968, she could not bear to be away. Returning to a hard-hit and badly shaken Saigon, she resumed her "terrible effort to understand what death was, what life was, and what it meant to be a man." It was on this trip that Miss Fallaci was given two diaries (which she here reproduces) by dead Viet Cong, full of love for the beauty of their country and longing for their young wives. In Hue, she nearly reached the end of her emotional resources, for there she saw children playing with corpses as if with toys, and the thought of belonging to the human race made her ashamed. Like other women correspondents who have seen more horror than they can bear, Miss Fallaci reached out for fresh life in a vain effort to adopt a Vietnamese child.

The Italian reporter had two interviews with then Vice President Nguyen Cao Ky before leaving once again for the United States. During the second of these, Miss Fallaci writes, she began to realize "something very simple" about the Vietnamese people:

> These people don't hate each other, although they go on killing each other. It's we they hate. Because we are the ones who force them to kill each other in the name of a civilization that thinks it's superior because of its bigger bombs. We are the ones who invaded their rice fields; corrupted their conscience, destroyed their towns, and finally cut them into two: the North for you, the South for me. Not realizing that the same wind blows over the North as over the South, and the same dreams.

On her third visit, a few months later, she was shocked because the Viet Cong murdered several correspondents in cold blood. "Western journalists have always been generous to the Viet Cong," she writes, ". . . for years they've defended, and even praised them . . . I feel very disillusioned. I feel like crying." By the time she left Vietnam for the last time Miss Fallaci's bitterness toward mankind was profound, and she composed a prayer to express her discouragement:

> Our Father who art in heaven, give us this day our daily massacre, deliver us from pity, love, and the teachings your Son gave us. As it has been good

for nothing, it is good for nothing. Nothing and amen.

Only after witnessing an appalling massacre of the innocents in another part of the world—in Mexico City where, in the fall of 1968, "more than three hundred . . . boys, pregnant women, children" were killed by the police—did she discover the falsity of her prayer and find an answer to the question with which she had begun her search.

American readers of this moving book will have no cause to feel proud, for at the worst we emerge as savages and at the best as well-meaning, clumsy innocents. But Miss Fallaci is as critical of Russian guns in Prague as she is of American artillery in Vietnam, for she has learned that man's inhumanity to the poor and defenseless is the ultimate obscenity regardless of who displays it.

Thomas H. Stahel (review date 26 March 1977)

SOURCE: A review of *Letter to a Child Never Born,* in *America,* Vol. 136, No. 12, March 26, 1977, p. 279.

[*In the following review, Stahel discusses the plot outline and the ideas raised in Fallaci's novel* Letter to a Child Never Born.]

Imagine the embarrassment of an Italian journalist, Oriana Fallaci, who, because she has written a novel that certain Catholics approve, now finds that her liberal credentials have grown suspect. In one effort to rehabilitate herself (and to sell her book), she appeared on the "Today" show recently and assured Tom Brokaw that she, like other "civilized people," was politically for abortion. When Mr. Brokaw assayed the touchy question as to whether this short novel were autobiographical, Miss Fallaci, who is unmarried, answered: I am a woman, with a womb, who was pregnant, who lost her child; but the novel is a construction. It uses the author's experiences and ideas, but it is not the author's history.

Fair enough.

The protagonist of this quasi-autobiographical novel explicitly rejects belief in God, family and the Catholic Church. Yet she resolutely decides not to have the abortion that lover, friend and employer urge, and she even hangs near her bed pictures of a developing fetus—at four weeks, eight weeks and so on—the kind certain pro-lifers distribute so aggressively and pro-abortionists ignore so determinedly. In the end, this incipient life (the child never becomes more than a tiny fish-like fetus) dies within her, and she has to have it removed, though she resists this so long that she almost dies of blood poisoning.

As its title implies, a large part of the novel is addressed to the new human life that the protagonist carries within her. But other people are given voices, too, including, at the end, the fetus itself, who speaks in the voice of the adult male he would have been.

That may sound sentimental, but, like its author, the novel is both tougher and more real than that.

It is full of ideas, for instance: the philosophical inspection of arguments for and against abortion; existentialist questions about the quality of human life and freedom; a worldly-wise, 20th-century skepticism that favors political and personal commitment, but scorns religion and other superstition. It also has set pieces: three parables told the fetus by its mother to teach him that "good" and "bad" don't count, that there is no equality in this life and that the world never changes; also, a "trial" to determine the guilt or innocence of the ambivalent mother when the fetus dies.

Despite universal doubt, a pervasively mocking tone and numberless arguments overturned, the tough journalist of the novel decides to have the baby, because, after all, life is better than nothingness and the little blob in her gut deserves a chance at joy and love. She refuses to simplify things for herself, to sacrifice the life of her child for the sake of her freedom. She is more likable than all her intellectual agonizing in the way that Italian people are more likable than French ideas. If she—Oriana Fallaci, I mean—heard that from me, a Catholic priest, she might laugh a hard metallic laugh and blow smoke in my face. I would like her anyway.

Jeffrey Burke (review date November 1980)

SOURCE: "Fallaci Records: Unanswered Questions," in *Harper's*, Vol. 261, No. 1566, November 1980, pp. 98-99.

[*In the following review, Burke considers Fallaci's devices in genres such as interviews, non-fiction works, and the novel.*]

> *Oh, come now, there's no need to be Herodotus; for better or worse you'll contribute a little stone to help compose the mosaic; you'll provide information to help make people think. And if you make a mistake, never mind.*
>
> —from the introduction to *Interview with History*

Oriana Fallaci has done rather well for herself by asking famous people questions. In the beginning of her career she interviewed entertainment celebrities, like Dean Martin and Michael Caine. Then she hit her stride with political figures, like Henry Kissinger, Yasir Arafat, and Willy Brandt. *Rolling Stone* is credited with a blurb on the paperback cover of *Interview with History* (1976), her collection of fourteen political *tête-à-têtes*: "the greatest political interviewer of modern times." I suppose one might consider Socrates a great interviewer of ancient times. Question-and-answer journalism as a self-sufficient genre, however, is a fairly recent phenomenon and one that has certified as celebrities Fallaci in print and Barbara Walters, among others, on television. In fact, to Fallaci the spotlight seems about equally split between her and her subject. If that sounds excessive, consider Fallaci versus Zulfikar Ali Bhutto. Interviewing him in April 1972, she extracted such insults of Indira Gandhi that a peace agreement between India and Pakistan nearly went unsigned. She relates the denouement in an introduction to the interview as it appeared in *Interview with History:*

> Bhutto lost his head and, not knowing where on earth to turn, turned to me. . . . Wherever I went I was pursued by an important Pakistani who begged me to disavow the interview, then reminded me that the lives of six hundred million people were in my hands. Vainly I replied that my hands were too small to contain six hundred million human beings, vainly I shouted that their demand was absurd and insulting. The nightmare ended only when Indira magnanimously decided to act as though Bhutto's error had never happened. And the two of them met to sign the peace accord.

Immodesty unbecoming to a journalist? But then, "what other profession allows you to write history at the very moment it happens and also to be its direct witness?" she asks in the introduction to *Interview with History*. And her professional attitude is reinforced by personal reflection. In an article entitled "Why I Never Married" (*Ms., December 1974*), she writes: "Though celebrated, at times, and respected, the men I knew weren't very worthy, and the day always came when I proved to have more balls than they."

Ironically, Fallaci may have so eclipsed her past subjects that her future interviewing is questionable. Besides, there are only so many world leaders, and she has covered most of the ones worth covering. Perhaps that explains why she has turned to fiction in a recent book and in her new one—a kind of fiction that begs the genre itself but that is most agreeable to her talents as a journalist.

A woman who had suffered three miscarriages, Fallaci brought to the writing of *Letter to a Child Never Born* the physical and emotional wherewithal for a poignant novel about a woman who suffers one. Unfortunately she chose to emphasize the woman's struggle against the stigma of being an unwed mother (as Fallaci was), a choice that mires the novel in a feminist tract of various, but mainly strident, pitches. All the while, the woman is talking to the unborn child, advising it about women and men and life and death, addressing it in the second person: "One day you and I will have to have a little talk about this business called love. I still don't understand what it's all about." The second-person technique can be tender and honest in the context, and it can be absurd unless you make allowance for the woman talking to herself.

It can also remind you that you have heard that *you* somewhere before in Fallaci's writing. Sure enough, it's the *you* implied or stated in every interviewer's direct question: "Let's talk about war, Dr. Kissinger. You're not a pacifist, are you?" Through miles of recording tape, that *you* has been Fallaci's creative peg, her link to history and its representatives, her bread and butter, and her stylistic constant. Although **Letter to a Child Never Born** might have been far more powerful as a straight essay on the politics of pregnancy, I can see why Fallaci would feel more comfortable with a tried and true device.

(With the sanction of a little dime store psychology, I would also speculate that Fallaci, in confronting one prestigious *you* after another, sensed a cumulative growth in the *I,* the ego that was the one constant in every interview.)

Certainly she felt comfortable enough to exploit the device again, this time playing off an actual interview. *A Man* is a novel about Alexandros Panagoulis, the leader of the Greek Resistance in the Sixties and Seventies, whom Fallaci interviewed two days after he was released from prison in September 1973. Their conversation, including twelve pages of introduction, makes up the last forty-four pages of **Interview with History.**

In that brief space, Panagoulis is revealed as a true hero, an extraordinary individual. He had tried in 1967 to assassinate Papadopoulos, had failed, and was captured. In the interview he describes the subsequent months of torture, during which he was frequently subjected to the phalange, which involves beating the soles of the feet with a metal bar until the pain shoots to the victim's brain and he passes out, only to be revived with forced walking or more blows; he was hung by his wrists from the ceiling until his arms and shoulders were paralyzed and his breathing cut off; while one torturer pointed a gun at his head, another tore his chest open with a jagged letter-opener; a wire was inserted in his urethra and heated with a cigarette lighter; a nearly severed finger was stitched without anesthetic; and—Panagoulis's worst fear— he was often threatened with near suffocation. He revealed nothing, never broke. The torturers finally gave up, and eventually they imprisoned him in a specially designed isolation cell that resembled a tomb and permitted him three paces

of movement in the one place in the cell where he could stand up straight.

That is a summary sketch of the horrors, neglecting all the psychological torture and deprivation. Throughout he constantly rebelled, incurring more beatings, or went on hunger strikes to gain small privileges. The authorities did not want him to die, because he had become an international hero whose martyrdom would have been at least embarrassing, if not dangerous. He was pardoned in 1973 for political reasons.

Fallaci's function in the interview is, for the most part, to listen, awestruck, until the *you* and *I* change places during the last question and Panagoulis asks, "And for you, what is a man?" to which she replies: "I'd say that a man is what you are, Alekos."

That Panagoulis was the only man with whom she could make that exchange on equal terms is acknowledged in *A Man,* which recounts the torture and imprisonment as a lead-in to their becoming lovers a week after the interview took place. They lived together for long stretches, broken by Fallaci's going out on assignment. Panagoulis was often harassed, under constant surveillance, yet still was working to organize the Resistance. When that method failed to draw support, he entered politics, determined to find the documents that would provide a political anatomy of the military junta and its civilian successor. He succeeded, but allegedly was murdered before enjoying any sort of triumph.

Panagoulis had entrusted copies of the documents to Fallaci and had made her promise to tell his story. *A Man* is the promise fulfilled. It is a true story. Why then has she insisted on calling it a novel? I put that question to her editor at Simon and Schuster and was told that because Fallaci had recreated scenes between Panagoulis and his jailers that she could not possibly have known accurately, the journalist in her felt the book had to be called a novel. I still had my doubts. Was it just the jail sentences, and if so, why not italicize the re-created sections and call the whole thing a "narrative and documentary" or something less cumbersome but equally qualified?

I asked an Italian friend of mine named Gennaro Chierchia, who was in Italy when the book came out there, what sort of reception it got. Of course, it was a best-seller. And there was some political furor because Fallaci had reproduced or described the most important documents, some of which indicated collusion between Italy and Greece. In addition, Fallaci had not made Panagoulis's family very happy. She had characterized their son and hero as a melancholic, obsessive man given to bouts of drunkenness and lechery; and she had denied the official explanation, which they were willing to accept, that his death had been an accident.

Curiouser and curiouser. Panagoulis was not always a pleasant man to live with, by Fallaci's account. He even caused one of her miscarriages. But in her way she seems to have loved him, even if it was during their time together that she made the statement in *Ms.* about her anatomical superiority to the men she knew. Is it possible that she could not bear the idea that Panagoulis had more balls than she, and so she reduced him in fiction to preserve her high self-esteem?

I don't think so, but alas I will never know. *A Man,* however much matter of record it contains, calls itself a novel, and even to that claim it is a dismal pretender. Fallaci is a journalist who handles facts well, possesses a sense of history, and analyzes the contemporary scene—granting her radical point of view—perceptively. She also owns a few too many bottles of purple ink, delights in repetition to little effect, lurches suddenly and frequently into polemic, and displays a heavy hand with such basic tools as metaphor, motif, and foreshadowing. Needless to say, her use of the second person is bludgeoning at this length.

I reminisced recently with a friend of mine, Roger Fox, on the several days we spent in Athens in the spring of 1972. We were blithe, truant college students traveling through Europe on as few dollars a day as our health and seeing the sights would allow. Panagoulis was in prison. Fallaci was talking to Bhutto. We knew vaguely, naively of the political tension in Greece, a suspicion confirmed when we were hushed to silence on busy street corners for asking about the government or how people liked Papadopoulos. We stopped asking after Easter eve. On that night, hundreds of soldiers with machine guns lined a broad avenue, facing the mutely expectant crowd. A procession of government limousines drove from the palace to a nearby church and back. The name *Papadopoulos* passed in whispers along the avenue as people strained to see which car bore the leader on his ceremonial visitation. Roger and I offered our shoulders to a couple of children so that they wouldn't miss the Easter parade.

Now I would like to offer those children copies of *A Man,* with the inscription: "She made mistakes, but never mind."

Vivian Gornick (review date 23 November 1980)

SOURCE: "A Journalist in Love," in *New York Times Book Review,* November 23, 1980, pp. 14, 35.

[*In the following review of* A Man, *Gornik assesses the strengths and failings of Fallaci's method and style.*]

It becomes more and more common that a book feels like a memoir, essay or reportage but is called fiction, and at book's end one finds oneself protesting: "*That's* not a novel." The source of the protest is not, I think, either devotion to literary orthodoxy or a concern that a spade be called a spade. It is just that most often when journalism is called fiction, the authority of honest reportage is mysteriously lost without the command of imaginative transformation having been gained, and sometimes atrocities of language clearly related to the ambition released by the words "a novel" are committed as well. The book under review is a case in point.

Oriana Fallaci is an Italian journalist famous the world over for her political interviews. Indignantly democratic and possessed of a vigorous hatred of dictatorship, Miss Fallaci's work is characterized by a pugnacious insistence, somewhat like that of an aroused child stamping her feet and demanding to be told the truth. From her inviolate position behind the microphone she points, probes, insinuates and mocks, provoking her subjects—mainly men of great power—into regretted revelation. The results are almost always scandalous, distasteful and remarkably effective. Miss Fallaci the journalist is master of her trade.

> **Oriana Fallaci is an Italian journalist famous the world over for her political interviews. Indignantly democratic and possessed of a vigorous hatred of dictatorship, Miss Fallaci's work is characterized by a pugnacious insistence, somewhat like that of an aroused child stamping her feet and demanding to be told the truth.**
>
> **—*Vivian Gornick***

In August 1973 Miss Fallaci flew to Athens to interview Alexander Panagoulis, a Greek political dissident who had spent five years in prison for an attempted assassination of the dictator George Papadopoulis, and who had just been freed by a general amnesty. These two took one look at each other and both knew instantly that destiny had been achieved. Especially Miss Fallaci. She really knew. When Panagoulis asked her why they hadn't met before, where had she been when he'd been caught, tortured and imprisoned, she had to answer: "Saigon . . . Hanoi . . . Sao Paulo . . . Amman . . . Calcutta." But she hastened to assure him that they *had* met before—many times in fact: "You were to have many faces, many names, in those years. In Vietnam you were a Viet Cong girl with cheeks and chin and forehead defaced by scars. . . . In Bolivia you were the last of the Peredo brothers, the first [of whom] had died with Che Guevara. . . . And then you were a Dominican monk whose face and age I didn't even know." Only in order to accomplish their fate, it had been necessary to wait until this moment for them actually to come together.

A Man is a 463-page account of the three-year-long affair between Miss Fallaci and Panagoulis, begun at their meeting, conducted through a nonstop disheveled flinging about between Athens and Rome, and brought to a distraught end in May 1976 when Panagoulis was ambushed and killed in Athens. Written in the form of an elegiac address to the dead man, it is in effect a journalist's recital of the events of those years, masquerading as a historical romance of the kind that can only be called torrid-mythic. Panagoulis is for Miss Fallaci openly and unashamedly a figure of fantasy—a hero of legendary proportions, not an actual man at all but an incarnation of spiritual resistance (political resistance is here clearly a metaphor). As such, he—his life, his person, his immediate history—is described in language that would draw from D'Annunzio an admiring "So *that's* how you do it these days."

The words "destiny" and "fate" are used repeatedly in this book, along with a steady, rhythmic variation on the phrase "This is the tragedy of a man condemned to be a poet, a hero, and thus to be crucified." These words and phrases, surrounded by whole paragraphs of a suffocating thickness, are like bits of lard studded throughout an old-fashioned dish of hearty melodrama being offered as though it were the cuisine of tragedy.

There is a certain sense in which *A Man* is not only ludicrous, but offensive as well. In a time of unimaginable cruelty, when we are surfeited by accounts without number of daily atrocity, the only way to convey the pain and dread of an honest rebel's life in some police-state part of the world is through the sparest of prose, the leanest of eloquence. What one feels here is not only Miss Fallaci's inability to trust in the emergence of the inherent power in Panagoulis's life by writing quietly about it, but her unwillingness as well. The syntax must be inflated to include a self-portrait of Oriana running about Greece and Italy with her freedom fighter, he acting out the anti-social behavior his existential tragedy has entitled him to in her eyes, she all self-important nerve endings, registering herself hourly as an intimate of history.

In a rather astonishing passage toward the end of the book, Miss Fallaci—writing as though she's now going to set the record straight with an "honest" admission—announces that she never did love Alekos. He was sexually repellent to her (not to mention compulsively unfaithful), had the character of a primitive and a mind in a state of permanent intellectual arrest. In those pages we suddenly see Panagoulis for what he is: A caricature of smoldering force (shoulders braced, eyes narrowed, one foot pawing the ground) being made flagrant use of by a writer whose sense of things is foolish and self-deceived. The other side of Miss Fallaci's foot-stamping righteousness in the presence of dictatorship is the eager plunge into "passionate enslavement" to the po-

etic ideal: two parts of an adolescent's rebelliousness, neither one having much to do with independence of mind or spirit.

What makes Miss Fallaci's journalism useful is her mythic sense of political evil. What makes her "fiction" trashy is her mythic sense of the hero. In the first instance, since it is in her psychic interest to distance herself, her intelligence and temperament serve her well. Since it is also in her psychic interest to merge herself in the second instance, she comes to disaster. It is conceivable that *A Man* might have had power and integrity if Miss Fallaci had had the wisdom and self-control to write an honest piece of reportage.

Santo L. Arico (essay date 1986)

SOURCE: "Oriana Fallaci's Discovery of Truth in *Niente E Cosi Sia,*" in *European Studies Journal,* Volume III, No. 2, 1986, pp. 11-23.

[*In the following essay, Arico compares Fallaci's style and techniques with those of the documentary film genres cinéma vérité and direct cinema.*]

Although Oriana Fallaci is best known as a political interviewer, she is also recognized as an accomplished author of three novels and five works of non-fiction. *Niente E Cosi Sia,* [*Nothing and So Be It*] the writer's novelistic report of the most unpopular war in American history, earned Italy's *Premio Bancarella* and placed her in the ranks of the most severe critics of United States foreign policy during the Vietnam War. Fallaci went to Vietnam in November 1967 with definite pro-Vietcong convictions. The reasons for her political stance are clearly developed in *Niente E Cosi Sia* and are characteristic of many thinkers who were critical of American involvement. Nevertheless, the author's political view evolves: her personal opinions change drastically. After a bitter inward struggle, what was apparent truth becomes less clearly defined and takes on a new complexion. The odyssey toward a final and different level of veracity constitutes one of the outstanding features of the work and helps to elevate what could have been just a journalist's diary to the category of good literature. What is equally important, however, is how and why a new attitude comes to the surface. Fallaci accumulated the raw materials for her book with journalistic methods that are analogous to cinematic documentary techniques. These professional strategies unexpectedly forced her to conform to a new reality that becomes irrefutable and bitter. Although personal bias is often reflected in the writer's selectivity of content, her style produces evidence that acts as a catalyst for change and becomes as important as the discovery itself.

In *Documentary: A History of the Non-Fiction Film,* Erik Barnouw proposes that the basic drive behind all documentary film inventions is a compelling need to document some phenomenon or action. The same critic also states that the two main patterns for documenting—*cinéma vérité* and direct cinema—capture reality in a different manner. Adherents of *cinéma vérité* embark on an anthropological study of human beings involved in a particular set of events. These documentarists are not content to remain mechanical bystanders but actually instigate moments of revelation and provoke action. At a certain point in time, they become on-camera participants in a venture, evolving procedures that act as psychological stimulants; they enable people to talk about things that had been previously concealed. Film participants are eventually invited to see the footage in a screening room and to discuss it. The discussion is then filmed and becomes part of the motion picture. The entire procedure has aspects of psychodrama.

According to Erik Barnouw, direct cinema is the procedure of the observer-documentarist who transmits objective productions. The director refrains from participating in the scene and limits his activity to capturing factual information. What transpires may exert an influence on emotional sensitivity but happens without a helping hand. Film makers who accept this process are intent on listening and watching rather than promoting a point of view or soliciting personal disclosures. The tape recorder and camera open a new world to readers, fascinating them by its sounds, speech, rhythm, and scenes. Producers often venture into new places that society is inclined to ignore or keep hidden: they keep their eye on people in action or involved in spontaneous talking. This type of presentation opens a new world from which viewers could draw disturbing inferences and free conclusions. The genre's special quality of unpredictability and ambiguity prove exhilarating to some film-goers and infuriating to others.

Although both approaches have stylistic similarities, they are actually a world away from each other. The documentarian of direct cinema takes his camera to a situation of tension and films a crisis that is in process or waits for one to happen; the artist of *cinéma vérité* tries personally to precipitate significant transformation. The former aspires to invisibility and plays the role of an impassive recorder of data, while his counterpart is often an important protagonist and espouses the role of prompter. Direct cinema finds its truth in events available to a movie projector, whereas the other is committed to the paradox that artificial circumstances can bring hidden reality to the surface. The main difference between the two is the prestigious status that *cinéma vérité* gives to the interview technique, a device that had been shunned by most directors in the earlier development of the documentary.

In **Niente E Cosi Sia,** the interview is one of Fallaci's most used mechanisms for obtaining data and is the basis of an analogy with *cinéma vérité*. The cassette player, records, documentation, photographs, or personal observation constitute the groundwork of a comparison with direct cinema. Both systems make abundant use of commentaries. In the former, she includes narrative annotations on what she and her subject say to each other; this procedure resembles that of film producers who talk about a product and then include their statements as part of the end result. In the latter, personal comments differ from those dealing with exchanges between the author and her subjects. The technique of direct cinema can lead to unexpected results in a person; after witnessing a powerful scenario, individual sensitivity hardly ever remains unmoved. Thus, the writer explains how the emotions respond. In the first instance, her remarks relate to a state that she creates; in the second, they focus primarily on internal change, occurring as the effect of conditions that Fallaci herself does not inspire. On the one hand, the author comments on her own interview, which is a professionally fostered situation; on the other, she objectively captures fact, experiences a repercussion and then elaborates on the effect that this particular incident produces in her.

During her Vietnam experience, the journalist initiates dialogues with scores of important figures and uses these conversations to construct a meaningful story. Her discussions with fighting soldiers and officers directing the action or with key personalities behind the scene aim at throwing light on a subject that is of great importance—war's terrible destruction of human dignity. "Perché quasi niente quanto la guerra, e niente quanto una guerra ingiusta, frantuma la dignità dell'uomo" (XVII). Thus, the writer begins moments of revelation by getting highly involved in the scenario; she does not simply record or photograph; she uses questions as a tool to probe into the minds and hearts of people, enabling them to express their passions candidly.

On November 21, 1967, Fallaci visits Hill 1383, where a vicious battle rages. She successfully converses with two artillery men, actively engaged in combat. The first individual is Larry who directs mortar fire against enemy Hill 1875. He views his enlistment in the army as an act of stupidity. The journalist logically questions his reasoning. "E perché sei andato volontario?" His response then provides insight into his monetary motives and into his regret at having made such a decision. "Alla fine mi dissi: meglio andar volontario, o la va o la spacca, se torno mi becco un congedo di centocinquanta dollari al mese. I miei genitori si arrabbiarono molto [. . .] Anche per questo mi pentii subito di quello che avevo fatto." Fallaci quickly takes her cues from the soldier's concluding thought: "Quando I'hai fatto, Larry?" She, therefore, helps him to disclose additional private information. "Oh, mi sembra un secolo. E fu solo tre mesi fa. Ho ancora nove mesi da passare qui. Credi che torneró a casa?" Fallaci's brief statement "Certo, Larry" is an attempt to assuage Larry's fear of dying in combat but also creates the climate for an additional emotional reaction. "A volte ho paura di no. E prego, sai non of che pregare. Prego anche quando non ho tempo. Per esempio quando vo all'assalto. Dico alla svelta: Dio, non farmi morire."

Fallaci's second exchange on Hill 1383 is with Larry's fellow gunner George, an Italian American who had recently married. She begins by asking what he is thinking and thus makes it easy for him to start. "Ad uccidere. A non essere uccisi. A non aver troppa paura, lo, quando andai all'attacco, avevo tanta paura. Era la prima volta che andavo all'attacco, capisci, e mia moglie aveva scritto d'essere incinta, ed io avevo tanta paura." After George asks whether he can reveal something that troubles him, her reply is simply: "Dilla a me." The young man then painstakingly explains how he saved himself during a rocket attack but failed to pull his closest friend Bob down to shelter on the ground. "Non pensavo che a me. E mentre non pensavo che a me vidi Bob scoppiare. Proprio scoppiare, centratato nel petto. E mori [. . .] Gridai: Bob! Ma lui era gia morto." When George still feels the need to communicate another torturous thought, the writer uses the same laconic structure: "Dilla a me, George." The soldier proceeds to admit shamefully that he is happy his friend died rather than himself. "Te la dico sennó divento pazzo. E poi, ecco, poi fui cosi felice che il razzo avesse preso lui anziché me. Ci credi?" Fallaci's one word "Si" facilitates an additional confession. "E ti dico di più, lo sai che ti dico? Se in questo momento arriva un altro razzo, io spero che prenda te anzichè me."

During her interview with the artillery gunner's superior, Fallaci's lead question concerns the horrible effect that the war has on George. "Quel soldato . . . George. E ancora sconvolto. Dev'essere stato tremendo. Vero, tenente?" Although the writer poses only one question to the officer, it acts as a catalyst that releases a torrent of emotions. The Lieutenant loses no time telling about the anguish of the war. "Tremendo. Io la guerra l'avevo vista al cinematografo e basta, non credevo che fosse cosi." He admits counseling his eighteen year old brother to avoid coming to Vietnam at all costs. "Gli ho scritto: non voglio che tu veda quello che ho visto io, non farti fregare con il Vietnam. Vai volotario in Marina, cosi sfuggi al Vietnam." He follows with a sketch of the battle in which George actually kills for the first time. "Le pallottole ti passavano sopra la testa, e colpivano l'albero. Allora volevi cosi bene all'albero che l'avresti abbracciato: per non lasciarlo mai piu." During their assault, it is always instinctive to protect one's head. "Forse perché il primo che avevi visto morire aveva perso la testa, gli era volata via come unpallone.' The Lieutenant's final thoughts first state again his desire to spare his younger brother the agony that he experiences and also to prevent the possibil-

ity of two casualties in the same family. "Non voglio che mio fratello veda queste cose, non voglio che muoia. Se l'America pretende ch'io muoia qui, pazienza. Peró mio fratello no." In conclusion, he summarizes the American soldier's dilemma—the tension between loyalty to the United States and an honest aversion toward a military presence in Vietnam. "E malgrado sia un cittadino ubbidiente, malgrado sia abbastanza d'accordo sulla nostra presenza in Vietnam, chi vuol essere qui? Chi ne è fiero?"

Fallaci next meets with the American Captain Scher, who courageously led his troops in the assaults against enemy positions around Hill 1383. Her questions are again direct and motivate moving responses: Fallaci: "Capitano, quante vite e costata questa collina?"; Scher: "Tante, Troppe, Centocinquanta, duecento [. . .]"; Fallaci: "Capitano, e i prigionieri?"; Scher: "Non si fanno prigionieri in Vietnam." Other queries take their cues from the Captain's statements. After he laments—"Dio che cosa schifosa é la guerra"—she formulates a comeback: "Allora perche la fa, capitano? Perché l'ha scelta come mestiere?" Her examination is also emotional in nature. While pointing to the Vietcong soldier that he killed, she asks: "Cosa senti, capitano, quando lo ammazzò?" Occasionally, her interrogation will be brief but a stimulant to further self-revelation. When the American states that he felt fear upon shooting the enemy soldier, she simply adds: "Lei, paura?"

Fallaci's approach to writing is also like that of the *cinéma vérité* documentarist when she includes a commentary in the narration on what she and her subject say to each other, thereby increasing the aspects of melodrama in an already tense situation. Her commentary will either follow the interview, precede it or appear between the fragments of the dialogue. Her comments add interest to what could have been a mere repetition of a tape recording. During her exchange with Captain Scher on Hill 1383, she reacts to his belief in the positive effects of the American presence in the country after the interview is actually completed and has taken time to reflect on his point: "Malgrado la sua umanità egli è convinto d'esser nel giusto a trovarsi su questa collina che non gli appartiene, come le altre colline e le pianure ed i fumi, è convinto d'avere ucciso in nome della giustizia, della libertá, mi guarderebbe con stupore innocente se gli dicessi: quale giustizia, quale libertà?" The Vietnamese soldier, whom the Captain sprays with bullets, first killed three Americans. In her commentary, the writer prefers to direct her sorrow at the former, as well as his cause. "Dal giorno in cui era nato, forse diciotto, forse diciannove anni fa, egli non aveva visto che guerra. La guerra ai francesi, la guerra agli americani, la guerra a qualcuno che non doveva esserci [. . .] perché al diavolo il comunismo e il noncomunismo, questa collina apparteneva a lui, come le altre colline, e le pianure ed i fiumi, e i tre ragazzi bianchi erano li per rubargliela."

When Fallaci meets with Barry Zorthian from the American embassy in Saigon, the same interview-commentary technique structures the narration. Zorthian believes in the American obligation to bring civilization to the Vietnamese and predicts that they will become as rich as the Japanese, after they are taught how to exploit their natural resources. "Ovunque sorgeranno fabbriche, grattacieli, autostrade, e il Delta del Mekong gareggerà con la Florida." In her commentary, the journalist sarcastically states that the Vietnamese have no desire to compete with Florida, "che vogliano solo vivere in pace, col loro riso piantato a mano, raccolto a mano, mangiato coi bastoncini." She also blasts Zorthian's paternalism by pointing out the prices being paid for creation of this paradise: "Il particolare che l'ipotetico paradiso essi lo stiano pagando con la distruzione del loro paese, il massacro dei loro figli, la fame, è un particolare cui non pensa." Zorthian explains the necessity of an official defoliation policy as a needed weapon against guerrilla fighters who hide in the jungle. Fallaci's reflections attack this strategy: "Ma dimenticava di dirci che gli alberi arsi cosi non rinascono per almeno vent'anni, che l'anidride arseniosa, l'arseniuro di sodio, gli arseniati di piombo e di manganese, la calciocianamide eccetera, uccidono anche le vacche ed i bufali, e all'uomo producono ustionmi, diarrea emorrragica, cecita, magari la morte."

After an American lieutenant saves [Fallaci] from a Vietnamese sniper, a conversation ensues in which the soldier labels her a liberal journalist who unfairly and conveniently disparages Americans in favor of enemy forces. He points out that he, an American, has killed to save her life, whether or not she likes it, and that she is free to leave with a clear conscience. He however, lives with the knowledge that he has taken someone's life and must remain to do more of the same.
—*Santo L. Arico*

Fallaci's *cinéma vérité* technique is particularly useful for expressing a biased opinion. In her interview with Nguyen Van San, the terrorist who had blown up the My Canh restaurant in Saigon, Fallaci's commentary precedes the conversation and immediately expresses an impression that favors him. "E gli ho voluto subito bene malgrado avesse ammazzato cinquantotto persone in ventinove attentati." Her initial line of questioning bypasses the suffering that he inflicts on a civilian population but stresses both his humaneness and heroism as he suffers brutal torture at the hands of the South Vietnamese police. When she finally addresses his killing of so many people, she reinforces her partisan attitude by failing to challenge the fact that he shifts the em-

phasis of guilt to the American side. "Mi sentii, ecco, mi sentii come penso si debba sentire un pilota americano dopo avere sganciato le bombe su un villaggio inerme. La differenza è che lui vola via e non vede quello che ha fatto, lo Io vidi."

A commentary similarly structures the introduction to the dialogue of the writer's second interview with Barry Zorthian. According to Fallaci, the embassy official's invitation to breakfast provides him the opportunity to express delicately his displeasure toward her writings. She points out that his initial cordiality, as well as the idyllic setting of his bedroom terrace, suggests the romantic behavior of a man in love. His first question relieves her anxiety concerning any amorous intentions and also contrasts sharply with the lace tablecloth, crystal glasses and silverware of a refined table setting. "Darling, sei communista?" She then bluntly reveals her anti-American feelings. Fallaci: "No Barry."; Zorthian: "Molti dicono di no e invece lo sono."; Fallaci: "La solita storia, vero Barry? Chi non è con voi è contro di voi. E chi non è con voi è iscritto al Partito."; Zorthian: "Sei con noi o no?"; Fallaci: "No, Barry. Non sono con voi. Lo ero, molti anni fa, quando vi amavo. Ora non vi amo piu."

Although Fallaci's views clearly favor the Viet Cong, her *cinéma vérité* methods also yield results that are antithetical to her personal bias. The unforeseen turn of an interview often overpowers individual prejudice and produces unexpected outcomes that are free of partiality. In February 1968, Fallaci visited the city of Hue, where a savage battle was taking a terrible toll of human life. After an American lieutenant saves her from a Vietnamese sniper, a conversation ensues in which the soldier labels her a liberal journalist who unfairly and conveniently disparages Americans in favor of enemy forces. He points out that he, an American, has killed to save her life, whether or not she likes it, and that she is free to leave with a clear conscience. He however, lives with the knowledge that he has taken someone's life and must remain to do more of the same. Fallaci appreciates his point and questions her own objectivity in analyzing good and evil: "Dio, come è difficile giudicare, capire dove sta il bene e dove sta il male. Sbagliavo dunque scegliendo di piangere solo su Le Vanh Minh e Tuyet Lan? Mi sembra d'essermi cacciata in un vicolo cieco, a venire quaggiù." The uniqueness of the writer's conversation with this soldier is that the interview-commentary obtains a different type of effect. For the first time, Fallaci begins to doubt her absolute views on what is right or wrong. After her experience in Hue, her reflections tend to become more universal than particular and to express her shame as a member of the human race. "All improvviso mi ha colto una paura che non è paura di morire. E paura di vivere."

In contrast to interviews and commentaries on the conversations, direct cinema finds its analogy in Fallaci's consuming drive to be where the action is, to expose it and to open her reader's eyes to a new dimension of truth. Immediately after her arrival in Vietnam, Fallaci made arrangements to go to Dak To, where the bloodiest fighting was taking place. On route, she uses her cassette player to record a conversation in a military cargo plane that was transporting troops. A sergeant cynically explains to his soldiers how a flight similar to theirs crashed the day before, killing all on board. Sergeant: "Ragazzi, sapete che ieri un C130 è precipitato fra Pleiku e Saigon?": Soldier #1: "Chiudi il becco.": Soldier #2: "E perché?": Soldier #3: "Già, perché?": Sergeant: "Un sabotaggio forse, o una cannonata. Nessuno ha fatto in tempo ad usare il paracadute, del resto il paracadute a che serve, mettiamo che ora succeda lo stesso, mentre cali a terra li sparano.": Soldier #4: "E chiudi il becco!" The writer's impassive presentation of the dialogue projects a new insight into interpersonal relationships between an officer and his subordinates.

During her first night in Dak To, a mortar attack forced Fallaci to seek safety in one of the bunkers on Hill 1383. Although it was light bombardment that lasted one hour, she had time to record a group of soldiers conversing about draft dodging. Soldier #1: "Capisci, con la storia della mamma a carico, lui è rimasto a Los Angeles e s'è fatto la piscina"; Soldier #2: "Be, Jack e stato ancora più furbo"; Soldier #1: "Che ha fatto?"; Soldier #2: "Si mise a here, a here, finche gli venne l'ulcera e lo riformarono per via dell'ulcera"; Soldier #1: "Mi venisse un'ulcera!" According to one of the men, his friend Howard was the most skillful at obtaining a deferment. Soldier #3: "Quando gli hanno chiesto se gli piacevan le donne, ha risposto: oddio, no, lo sanno tutti che vo coi ragazzi"; Soldier #4: "Ci va?!?"; Soldier #3: "No certo, sei pazzo? Ma se dici d'essere frocio, ti riformano immediatamente: non lo sapevi?"; Soldier #4: "Maledizione, no! E se lo dicessi ora?"; Soldier #3: "Troppo tardi, mio caro. Dovevi pensarci prima. E io con te." The journalist's restatement of this conversation casts a new light on the real attitude of many soldiers toward the war.

Fallaci also uses commentaries as part of her direct cinema technique. However, this aspect of the method does not make the procedure less objective or neutral. Instead of reacting to an interview, she responds to what is seen or heard and, thereby, reveals what effect the event produces on her personal life. In contrast to *cinéma vérité*, her remarks now relate to a scene that she herself does not help to create. The objective documentary does not imply that the bystander is immune to feeling; it simply exposes data in the act of unfolding and that needs simply to be filmed rather than incited. In this system, producers witness action that would have occurred even if the individual had been absent. The fact that Fallaci has emotional sensations and then states them makes her approach no less impartial. Objectivity results from her attempt to seize an historical moment that is

in the making and not from stifling human sensitivity.

On the way from Pleiku to Dak To, the writer had to take a helicopter, explaining that there was enough room for only four passengers, in addition to the two pilots and two machine gunners.

Objective Description: "Uno dei quattro era un telecronista appena giunto da New York. In preda a un tremito convulso, il viso colore del gesso, si agitava, si mordeva le mani, gemeva: a un certo punto s'è perfino alzato per scongiurare il pilota di tornare indietro, e il pilota non gli ha neanche risposto." Her reaction illustrates that the television reporter's fear helped to cure her own state of anxiety.

Commentary: "Ecco, ho provato una tale vergogna che subito son diventata un'altra persona: tranquilla, lucida, attenta. Mentre lui gemeva potevo addirittura sporgermi fuori dell'elicottero, osservar freddamente le colline a sinistra da cui si alzavano fumate nere, il napalm che i caccia americani sganciavano sui nordvietnamiti [. . .] non mi preoccupava nemmeno che ci stessimo volando nel mezzo."

In her book the writer makes use of priceless records that then become an integral part of the account. However, the truth is selective here and an expression of her anti-American attitude. The technique is objective since the materials were available and already in existence; the writer does not actively participate in generating them. Her individual prejudice is a separate issue that influences what part of the documentation she finally selects. The preface of her work consists mainly of statements made by soldiers of Charlie Company who had participated in the My Lai massacre. The reader senses her exasperation as she quotes from testimony like that of Corporal Jay Roberts: "Fuori del villaggio c'era questa pila di cadaveri. E c'era questo bambino minuscolo che aveva addosso una camicina e basta. E questo bambino avanzò a piccoli passi verso la pila dei cadaveri e sollevò la mano di una morta. Allora uno dei GI dietro a me si inginocchiò in posizione di sparo, a trenta metri da questo bambino, e lo ammazzò con un colpo solo" (XI). Other testimony offered by witnesses, like the farmer Do Thi Chuc, to *Time, Look* and *Europa* reinforces the shock aroused by the slaughter of innocent victims. "Non ricordo altro che la gente ammazzata. C'era sangue dappertutto. Sia gli americani bianchi che gli americani neri ammazzavano. Spaccavano le teste in due e molti americani avevano addosso pezzi di carne. A me ammazzarono una figlia di ventiquattro anni e un nipotino di quattro anni" (XIII).

Fallaci's bias is just as poignant when she publishes selected passages of Vietcong diaries that American intelligence had obtained. Her carefully chosen selections romanticize the Vietcong writers as heroic freedom fighters. One unknown author explains how he was obliged to leave his new wife in order to combat the ugly American invaders: "E le lacrime cascano. Addio, mia adorata. Quante cose restano da fare [. . .] Ma un giorno non ci sarà piu un diavolo americano in questo paese. Se non fosse per gli americani io e te non ci daremmo baci d'addio." In a second diary, a soldier, identified as Le Vanh Minh, poetically describes his feelings as the war inflicts hardships on himself and the ones he loves. He addresses his wife as "Tuyet Lan, mia adorata" and dolefully requests a sparrow, flying in the direction of his village, to carry a message to his beloved: "Le ho chiesto di portarti il mio amore e chiederti di aspettarmi pazientemente." These selections depict the guerrilla fighters as noble and utopian heroes, who possess sensitive minds and hearts. The journalist's sympathy for the Vietcong and distaste for Americans seem to have reached their apex, as she chooses personal writings from the diaries of these dead Vietcong soldiers. When François Pelou, director of the *Agence France Presse* in Vietnam, expresses his solidarity with all people on this earth, Fallaci refuses to identify with every human being but prefers to choose carefully those to whom she will extend support. "E dacché ho in mano questi fogli io piango assai meno sui Larry e sui Johnny giunti qui con le loro vitamine, le loro razioni e il loro superequipaggiamento, le loro buone intenzioni. Le Vanh Minh mi piace di piu."

As a journalist permitted to cover the battle of Hue, Fallaci becomes overwhelmed by the extraordinarily high number of civilian casualties. Both Americans and Vietcong bear the responsibility for causing so many deaths. However, the salient feature of the commentary is an indictment of the Vietcong. For the first time, her comments toward them are directly critical and negative. "Da ringraziarci insieme americani e Vietcong. Infatti sarebbe difficile stabilire se hanno causato piu vittime gli americani con le cannonate, i mitragliamenti, il napalm, oppure i Vietcong con le esecuzioni in massa." The Vietcong had summarily executed masses of people, killing anyone who refused to shoot at an American helicopter or who had refused cooperation in any manner. Speaking of the massacres, she expresses her dismay: "Sembra di riguardare Mathausen, Dachau, le Fosse Ardeatine: il mondo non cambia [. . .] né gli uomini. Qualunque sia il colore della loro pelle, della loro bandiera."

During the second battle of Saigon in February 1968, the Vietcong begin to execute captured journalists. When Fallaci sees photographs of these slayings and visits the execution sights, her outrage against this group becomes even stronger. News correspondents had been under the general impression that they were immune from Vietcong killings. "Non era mai successo che i vietcong fucilassero dei giornalisti. Mai dall'inizio della guerra in Vietnam. Chiunque sia stato catturato n'è uscito indenne." However, the Vietcong's execution of four journalists—Ronald Laremy, Michael Bird, John Cantwell, Bruce Pigott—offers no possible justifica-

tion and is seen as an act of pure barbarism. The subsequent extermination of Ignacio Ezcurra, the young South American journalist whom Fallaci had befriended, completes the deromanticization process and shatters her idealistic vision of the Viet Cong. The realization that even they behave in animalistic fashion summarizes her response to the situation. "E difficile, sempre piu difficile, accettare il fatto che i vietcong commettano tali vigliaccate. Insomma che neanche loro siano i cavalieri di giustizia e liberta che abbiamo finoggi dipinto. E doloroso, sempre piu doloroso, ammettere che valgono gli altri, sono hestie come gli altri."

Fallaci's observations of the casualties in Hue and of the photographs of slain colleagues form part of the technique of direct cinema. She herself sees the mass graves filled with Vietcong victims; she herself views the pictures of their barbarous killing of reporters. The realization that a photographer's snapshots do not always capture their atrocities, whereas there always seems to be a picture of a brutality committed against them by an American or South Vietnamese, places her vision in a more objective perspective. The writer's commentary summarizes the evolution of her frame of mind. "Quanti altri delitti hanno commesso i vietcong senza che un fotografo li immortalasse? C'è sempre un fotografo per l'esecuzione di un vietcong, per la testa tagliata di un vietcong, ma non c'è mai un fotografo per l'esecuzione di un americano, per la testa tagliata di un sudvietnamita."

Perhaps the death of Eczurra and the other journalists was the deciding factor in Fallaci's change of attitude. In reality, their death was no different from the brutal killings of so many other innocent people and intellectually should have been viewed in the same objective context. However, seeing photographs of Ezcurra with his hands bound and with a bullet wound in the back of his head to ascertain successful completion of the execution was too much for the writer simply to accept intellectually. "Nel segreto di me stessa, quei cinque cadaveri m'avevan sconvolto quanto il cadavere di Martin Luther King aveva sconvotto i negri di Washington: invece dei negozi lungo la 14a strada, insomma, io avevo bruciato la mia simpatia pei vietcong, la mia ammirazione per loro." Fallaci seems overpowered by the evidence before her. The writer openly acknowledges that she has great confidence in her feelings. "I believe in what I see, what I hear and what I feel." Thus, it may have been necessary for her to experience directly the savage murder of colleagues, as well as the senseless execution of thousands of civilians, before she could have actually deflated her vision of the heroic Vietcong.

Shortly after Ignacio Ezcurra's death, Fallaci receives a copy of Pascal's *Pensées* as a gift from her close friend François Pelou. The writings of the French philosopher offer some insights into the more mature realization that truth is not always clearcut and perhaps communicate to her the most satisfactory explanation for the chaotic state of affairs in the world, as well as for man's inhumanity to man. According to Pascal, heroes may frequently delude us, while objects of scorn may suddenly become attractive. The knowledge and understanding that truth and falseness blend into a given set of ideals change the author's absolute views on right and wrong: "Qualsiasi cosa é vera solo in parte, falsa solo in parte, e il giusto e l'inguisto si mischiano, e coloro che rispetti possono deluderti, coloro che disprezzi posson commuoverti." Pascal's belief that each man contains both the angel and the beast within himself goes right to the heart of the matter and succeeds in facilitating the final stage of the writer's transformation. "Aveva mitigato il mio assolutismo, Pascal, le mie cecita." The bitterness of truth has brought about a new vision of the world in Fallaci the journalist, writer and thinker.

Fallaci's methods make possible her arrival at a more mature stage of thought. Both the interview and direct observation produce unforeseen results that help shape her outlook. The talk in Hue with the soldier who saves her life makes it clear that criticism of military actions comes more easily when a person stays removed from conflict conditions. Her commentary indicates that a negative attitude toward Americans represents an overly harsh and simplistic stance. Contemplating Vietcong atrocities, whether they be on a film or with the naked eye, also justifies the impassioned repercussion that she did not expect. The author's commentaries reveal that barbarism exists on the other side, too, and that their savagery senselessly eliminates innocent colleagues, as well as a significant part of the civilian population. The writer's remarks about her feelings permit the reader to follow the changes that occur in her attitudes.

As Erik Barnouw summarizes, documentarists capture fragments of actuality and then combine them meaningfully. Such an endeavor stresses two main functions: 1) recording (of images and sounds): 2) interpretation. Fallaci's journalistic procedures parallel this role. Her use of the interview corresponds to the art of *cinema vérité*. When she reprints significant documents or visually observes events. She resembles the technician of direct cinema. The commentary constitutes a significant feature of both methods and allows her state of soul to become transparent. Adhering to this craft. Fallaci clearly projects a slanted point of view and then expresses an opinion on it accordingly. However, her tactic is also conducive to witnessing and to comprehending hardcore reality that subsequently shapes her outlook into a more significant degree of thought. Evidence imposes its own force on the viewer and then overpowers any preestablished judgments. The mature truth that she finally discovers is powerful but no more so than the becoming which her technique fosters. The process of change not only causes her personal, ideological and political perspectives to evolve but

also transforms *Niente E Cosi Sia* from a professional and editorial account of the Vietnam conflict into a soul-searching and literary achievement of merit.

Santo L. Arico (essay date Autumn 1986)

SOURCE: "Breaking the Ice: An In-Depth Look at Oriana Fallaci's Interview Techniques," in *Journalism Quarterly*, Vol. 63, No. 3, Autumn 1986, pp. 587-93.

[*In the following essay, Arico examines the techniques that he believes make Fallaci an effective and engaging interviewer.*]

Although Oriana Fallaci is recognized as an accomplished author of three novels and five works of nonfiction, she is best known today as a political interviewer. Using her skills, she has not only exposed some of the world's most powerful and intransigent political leaders but has also made history with them. She confronts her interviewees with no inhibitions but as their intellectual peer and social equal. She boldly interrogated Lieutenant General Nguyen Van Thieu about the corruption in South Vietnam's regime during the Vietnam war and lured former Secretary of State Kissinger into describing himself as a lone gunslinger on a horse as he traveled around the world on diplomatic missions. After Fallaci printed her interview with Ali Bhutto, the Pakistani Prime Minister had so many adverse political repercussions that he begged her several times to retract her statements and to proclaim publically that she had fabricated the story. When Alvaro Cunhal openly admitted that his Portuguese Communist Party viewed national elections as a game, he severely set back the efforts of European Communism to prove its faith in the democratic process and to assume a shield of respectability. Her emotion laden questions to Haile Selassie on the poverty of his people caused him to recall angrily his Ethiopian ambassador from Italy.

Although Fallaci's interviews have made her both respected and feared, her methods are not unique and innovative; they are traditional procedures that most professionals utilize. What makes her approach different is the degree of commitment and passion that she brings to journalism. Her work is not only the reflection of an acquired craft but also the expression of a personality. This unusual woman becomes her interview; the technique becomes a verbal projection of the person herself. The intensity of her line of questioning impregnates the colloquies with a dynamism that places them in a class of their own. Fallaci's stock in trade techniques, as well as her originality, have been the study of several short articles. However, none of them has done justice to isolating her skills or emphasizing her uniqueness as an interviewer. Instead, they accentuate one aspect of a narrow segment of her discourses. The present analysis attempts to rectify this deficit and to discover the hidden force that motivates the interviewer.

> **Although Fallaci's interviews have made her both respected and feared, her methods are not unique and innovative; they are traditional procedures that most professionals utilize. What makes her approach different is the degree of commitment and passion that she brings to journalism.**
> —*Santo L. Arico*

Fallaci's repertoire of techniques seems endless and always reflects a fervent desire to discover the hidden truth in each figure that she encounters. Before every confrontation, she guesses where the person is most vulnerable and calculates her questions accordingly. Her flattering queries to Kissinger reflect her belief that his particular weakness is his vain and massive ego. "Dr. Kissinger, how do you explain the incredible movie-star status you enjoy; how do you explain the fact that you're almost more famous and popular than a president? Have you a theory on this matter?" At this point, Kissinger made his disastrous cowboy statement, which became prime subject matter in the American press for months afterwards.

Another of her strong points is the thoroughness of her preparation before each of her interviews. Her preparedness sometimes catches her subject off guard and enables her to assume an advantageous stance. During her meeting with Kissinger, she brought out speeches and clippings in which President Thieu of South Vietnam challenged the American Secretary of State to tell the real reasons for their disagreeing on a peace treaty with North Vietnam. Kissinger's response reflected his awkwardness: "Let me see it . . . Ah! No, I won't answer him. I won't pay any attention to this invitation." Fallaci is also master of the old rope trick, giving people just enough line to hang themselves. To Ali Bhutto, she simply alluded to the antagonism that existed between him and Indira Ghandi. "You two really can't stand each other, can you?" Bhutto then imprudently allowed his hatred to arouse a string of insulting remarks toward Ghandi and subsequently suffered humiliation when India retaliated by retracting the agreement to sign a peace treaty with his country.

In many of her exchanges Fallaci formulates inductive conclusions after listening to a speaker's statements. According to former CIA Director William Colby, influential Italians taking bribes from his organization were regarded as good clients rather than corrupt officials. Fallaci then bit-

terly sums up the idea. "So you consider yourself the lawyer for Christian Democrats and Social Democrats in Italy." In the same exchange, Colby admits that the FBI would arrest Fallaci if she were to finance American politicians in order to protect her interests in the U.S.A. She then states her own ending: 'Fine. So I ought to report you, your ambassador, and your agents to the Italian police and have you arrested." Occasionally, the writer's summary statement also acts as a stimulus for further conversation. When Thieu expressed feelings of betrayal by American politicians, she both summarized and instigated: "In other words, Mr. President, you expected just what has happened." Then, after Thieu completed his hypothesis, she again used the same technique and provoked a response that supplied additional information. "In other words, Mr. President, you think that Kissinger was about to sell Vietnam in the name of his world strategy." After Thieu openly accused Nixon and Kissinger of bad judgment in dealing with North Vietnam, she varied the basic strategy by adding a simple question to her conclusion. "So, in your opinion, Nixon and Kissinger made a mistake. Mr. President, how do you explain the fact that they made a mistake?" When Golda Meir made it clear that Israel would not return captured Arab territory, Fallaci accurately grasped the heart of the question. "And so it's obvious that you'll never go back to your old borders." When Kissinger compared himself to an adventurous cowboy leading a caravan into an isolated town, she again hit the nail tight on the head. "I see. You see yourself as a kind of Henry Fonda, unarmed and ready to fight with his fists for honest ideals. Alone, courageous . . .'"

Techniques Vary

Fallaci's techniques vary and change according to the particular set of circumstances. In the Kissinger talk, one tactic was to go from the general to the particular. First, she asked in broad terms what he would do after his term of office expired. Not receiving a satisfactory answer, she changed to a specific possibility. "Would you go back to teaching at Harvard?" During her Cunhal interview, she posed a sly question, acting as though she had inside information regarding his forthcoming dismissal as secretary of the Portuguese Communist Party. After he became emotionally involved in the game, he asked if it was due to his old age. Fallaci then continued to push the tactic to the limit, "No, no, because you are too arrogant. Too Stalinist. Because you cause Socialist newspapers to be shut down and organize lots of troubles for Communists in other countries." Then, when she finally discloses the prank, her retort was one of bantering: "You really got scared, didn't you?" At other times, she leads her victims on what seems to be a safari of irrelevant questions and then, when they least expect it, succeeds in obtaining the desired information. This method was particularly useful during her interview with Haile Selassi who had refused to discuss the coup that his two trusted advisors, Menghistu and Giramané Neway, had initiated. Both men died before Selassie could have had the pleasure of seeing them executed. After an attempted escape became impossible, Giramané shot his brother to prevent capture, then, he took his own life in prison before his scheduled day of execution. Selassie vengefully ordered their bodies to remain hanging from the gallows for eight days. In order to discuss this untouchable topic, Fallaci posed an apparently unrelated question: "Your majesty, if you don't wish to speak about certain things, speak to me still about yourself. It is said that you love animals and babies very much. May I ask you if you love men as much?" He responded that he only respected men who were courageous and dignified. Then, she made her key statement. "The two protagonists in that *coup d'etat* had dignity your majesty. They had courage." Selassie realized that he had been intellectually cornered and gave vent to his annoyance by angrily commanding her to refrain from her line of questioning. "That's enough, that's enough! Enough of it!" During the course of her exchange with the Ethiopian monarch, Selassie vehemently ordered her to change the subject at least six different times.

Part of Fallaci's talent is an instinctive ability to adapt quickly to each situation and to perceive an advantageous direction after an unexpected and indiscreet disclosure. During her talk with the Shah of Iran, he revealed that he had not only had visions of the saints and prophets but had actually spoken to them, Fallaci profited from this revelation by making fun of him: "You mean you could shake hands with them?" After an affirmative response, she continued her sarcasm: "If I am there with you, can I seem them?" In the same interview, she noticed that the Shah's profile communicated an expression of forlornness and thus composed an appropriate question: "Why are you so sad, Majesty? I may be wrong, but you always have such a sad and worried look." Right before she met with Quadaffi, the Libyan dictator began to yell hysterically like a broken record for ten minutes straight that he was the Gospel and naturally intimidated the entire entourage. At a certain point, Fallaci, who almost never interrupts, boldly cut him off and put forth the appropriate punch line: "Stop! Stop! Do you believe in God?" Quadaffi: "Of course, why do you ask?" Fallaci: "Because I thought you were God." During the course of their conversation, Quadaffi asserted that he was much loved by his people. Her response was appropriately provocative as she gestured to his battalion of bodyguards: "Colonel, if the masses love you so much, then why do you need so much protection?"

Fallaci skillfully uses all the techniques mentioned but is certainly not alone in that regard. Any good interviewer prepares well, adapts to different statements, summarizes the main idea in a concise conclusion, and tries to understand the personality of the subject before the actual confronta-

tion. Fallaci's originality is the emotional entanglement that takes place when she meets the other person. Her degree of involvement makes most exchanges seen on American television look tepid. Journalists in the United States appear far too objective and composed to rate a valid comparison. On CBS's *60 Minutes*, Fallaci, who has never understood the American insistence that all reporters remain impartial, said to Mike Wallace: "I hate objectivity, you know, I have told it many times, I do not believe in objectivity, I believe in what I see, what I hear and what I feel which is a kind of blasphemy . . . . especially for the American press." When Wallace accused her of emotionalism and subjectivity, she did not deny it; indeed, she elaborated on what he perceived as peculiarities, "I don't only put my opinion but my sentiment in it." Consequently, every time the writer meets someone, she throws her entire being into the experience and takes a moral stance on every issue. When she met Golda Meir in Israel, she knew exactly where she stood on the Palestinian issue and immediately proposed that Arab terrorism would exist as long as there were Palestinian refugees. When the prime minister tried to assuage her concern, comparing this problem to the case of German and Czech refugees, who were homeless after World War II, Fallaci resisted and countered: "But the case of the Palestinian is different, Mrs. Meir . . . ." She suggested that Israel should allow them to return to their homeland or to create their own nation on the West Bank. When Meir explained that Jordan should welcome them into its territory, Fallaci found this idea unacceptable, "because they say they are Palestinians and that their home is in Palestine, not Jordan." There is no interview in which she remains detached and objective; each one seems like a moral debate.

According to her admission to Robert Scheer, Fallaci meets with important people in order to understand the logistics of world decisions. "I do these interviews to understand the person, to study how power takes place." This desire to perceive how leaders determine the destiny of all mankind turns her appointments into stalking sessions in which she holds her subjects accountable for all deeds and actions. Before seeing Alvaro Cunhal, she knew that the Communist Party had seized control in March 1975 of *Republica*, Portugal's last free newspaper, and ignored the country's mandate in favor of the Socialists. Therefore, she immediately brought him to task: "You can say whatever you wish, think whatever you wish: it is not licit to neutralize and to ignore a party that represents the greater majority of the people, that has won the elections." When the ex-CIA Director William Colby agreed to receive her, there were no holds barred on the various activities of the agency. She condemned its desires to control other nations for selfish interests and denounced the harm done to genuine freedom in the process. "From Franco to Caetano, from Diem to Thieu, from Papadopulos to Pinochet. Without counting all the Fascist dictators in Latin America. Tortured Brazilians, for example.

In this way, in the name of freedom, you became the supporters of all those who kill liberty from the other side."

Takes Personal Stand

Fallaci takes such a strong stand on issues that she frequently expresses her sense of outrage by actually insulting or injecting elements of melodrama into the exchange. Her debate with Colby became so heated that she refrained from direct bombast only with difficulty and referred to him as a corruptor. "There is only one type more disgusting than the corrupt: the corruptor." Then, she accused him of plotting to overthrow governments throughout the world: "And under Johnson what knavery did you organize? Ah, yes: the overthrow of Papadopulos." Finally, she bitterly equated him to a hard-line Stalinist: "If you had been born on the other side of the barricade, you would be a perfect Stalinist." To the Ayatollah Khomeini, she hurled a pointed challenge: "Are you a fanatic?" When the Iranian leader smugly insulted her, stating that the chador was appropriate attire for proper young women and that, therefore, she had no need to wear it, she retaliated angrily by tearing the veil off, throwing it to the ground and shouting: "This is what I do with your stupid medieval rag!" He, in turn, stormed out of the room, only to hear her insultingly call after him: "Where do you go? Do you go to make pee-pee?" Fallaci's tactic was next a lengthy sit-in demonstration until he swore on the Koran that he would again meet with her on the next day. Her use of dramatics was also evident during the time spent with Kissinger, when she used a pistol-to-the-headtype question. "Dr. Kissinger, if I were to put a pistol to your head and ask you to choose between having dinner with Thieu and having dinner with LeDue I ho . . . whom would you choose?" During the Colby interview, Fallaci repeatedly alluded to his readiness to overthrow any possible Communist regime in Italy, just like the Allende-Pinochet experience in Chile and dramatized her statements by sarcastically challenging the notion that her country was his personal banana republic: "Mr. Colby, I am trying to get you to admit that Italy is an independent state, not a banana republic, not your colony!"

In his analysis of Fallaci's techniques, Thomas Griffith spoke of trials of strength in which the writer stress tested her subjects. Right from the start, she placed continued pressure on the person and mercilessly persisted in her taxing pressure, until the point had been exhausted. In Portugal, the Communists could have managed to control the government after their loss in the 1975 elections, only if the military had given their support to this paradoxical condition. Thus, Fallaci asked Cunhal the loaded question whether his party had accomplished the manoeuvre alone or with the help of the military. "The Communists and no one else, or the Communists together with the military?" When Cunhal tried to dodge the question, she emphatically repeated it four more times until he answered. She continued to bombard Kissinger with questions on Vietnam and the impending peace agreement with the North to the point that he practically had to implore her to stop pursuing the topic: 1) "No, I don't intend to argue about this"; 2) "That's enough, I don't want to talk anymore about Vietnam, I can't allow myself to, at this time. Every word I say becomes news. At the end of November perhaps . . . Listen, why don't we meet again at the end of November?"; 3) "I cannot answer that question."; 4) "I cannot, I cannot . . . I do not wish to answer that question"; 5) "And don't make me talk about Vietnam anymore, please"; 6) "But are we still talking about Vietnam?" Fallaci made use of this same persistence technique with William Colby, when he avoided revealing his plans in the event that the Communist Party were to win a majority in an Italian national election. 1) "Mr. Colby, what would you do, you Americans, if the Communists were to win the elections in Italy?" 2) "Mr. Colby, would you have a *coup d'etat* like in Chile?"; 3) "Answer me, Mr. Colby; another Chile?"; 4) "But I insist on the question which you don't want to answer: what would the Americans do if the Communists were to win control of the government in Italy?"; 5) "Courage, Mr. Colby. Do you believe it would be legitimate for the United States to intervene in Italy with a Pinochet if the Communists were to gain control of the government?"

In her discussion with David Sanford, Fallaci was very clear about her efforts to badger and intimidate her subjects. "I know that I make psychological violence on them." Thus, the questions she poses are intensely direct, personal and frequently provocative. To General Thieu, she offered a series of four consecutive brutal inquiries that took their toll on his emotional equilibrium: 1) "Here's the first: What have you to say about the fact that you're called an "American puppet" or the "man of the Americans"?; 2) "Question number two. What do you have to say to those who accuse you of being corrupt, the most corrupt man in Vietnam?"; 3) "And is it true that today you're immensely rich, with bank accounts and houses in Switzerland, London, Paris, and Australia?"; 4) "Question number four. Aren't you afraid of being killed? For instance, assassinated like President Diem?" Fallaci's directness in no way resembles the Barbara Walters whammy number, made famous when she cunningly obliged Jimmy Carter to discuss whether he and Rosalyn slept in a single or double bed in the White House. No, Fallaci asked Golda Meir if she would ever give up Jerusalem, whether she would return the West Bank to Jordan and Gaza to Egypt, whether the Golan Heights would be permanently annexed, and whether the Sinai would become part of Israel. Fallaci's technique has no place for the banal type of question that Barbara Walters asked Anwar Sadat: "What is your biggest thrill?"

She prefers to get right to the point, asking the Shah of Iran about attempts on his life: "Majesty, how many times have they tried to kill you?" She commented on the fear of his Iranian people toward him—"When I try to talk about you, here in Teheran, people lock themselves in a fearful silence. They don't even dare pronounce your name, Majesty. Why is that?"

In Fallaci's last question to Haile Selassie, she asked how he felt about death and his personal mortality. The query was particularly provocative, since the monarch disliked the word death and was petrified of dying. The emperor's anger and frustration hysterically burst forth, as he ordered Fallaci to leave his presence at once and demanded to know who this woman was. "Death? death? Who is this woman? Where does she come from? What does she want from me?!? Away, enough, that's it! That's it!" Like Selassie, many people have wondered about Fallaci. Gloria Emerson refers to her as a "divine troublemaker." Elizabeth Peer writes that she bullies, baits, charms "and harvests disclosures of stupefying indiscretion from statesmen who ought to know better." David Sanford uses the term "surgical journalism" to explain how she dissects a person's mind until she gets to the truth. In the Introduction to *Interview with History,* the writer herself tries to explain who she is. All of her motivation derives from her desire to understand the powerful and how they control our lives. She does every interview "with the hope of understanding in what way, by being in power or opposing it, those people determine our destiny." She painstakingly inflicts a torturous preparation on herself before doing the same to the other person. "I went with a thousand feelings of rage, a thousand questions that before assailing them were assailing me." Fallaci believes that our existence is controlled by a handful of individuals and calls this condition an "atrocious hypothesis." According to the writer, world leaders are capable of changing the course of events by means of an idea, a discovery, a revolution, an assassination or even a simple gesture. In view of this overwhelming belief, she acts as the official representative of the cheated, the abused, the suspecting, the defiant, the insanely brave—all the people who say no to those who attempt to decide our destiny.

Fallaci refuses to become a mechanical repeater of what has been seen or heard; she refuses to define herself as a journalistic doctor of anatomy or an impassive recorder of events. Each encounter becomes not only a power study but also a portrait of herself.
—*Santo L. Arico*

Once she succeeds in obtaining an appointment, Fallaci then becomes involved in the game of getting at the truth. "Once there, however, it became a game to reach the truth." The

truth that she has discovered in her interviews is both harsh and revolutionary. According to the writer, all the selective criteria possible do not justify power. "Not even a selective criterion justified their power. Those who determine our destiny are not really better than ourselves; they are neither more intelligent nor stronger nor more enlightened than ourselves." In order to discover the intricacies that actually produce decisions, Fallaci uses every professional interview skill possible. What makes her original, however, is the degree of conviction she injects into her work. "On every professional experience I leave shreds of my heart and soul." Her passionate involvement renders each interview more than a document "for students of power and antipower." Fallaci refuses to become a mechanical repeater of what has been seen or heard; she refuses to define herself as a journalistic doctor of anatomy or an impassive recorder of events. Each encounter becomes not only a power study but also a portrait of herself. "They are a strange mixture of my ideas, my temperament, my patience, all of these driving the questions." This journalist certainly knows how to pose the questions. In addition, she adds something extra that provokes her subjects to openness and emotion. It is as though this woman has fallen in love with the interview process even though she might hate the person in front of her. She seems to experience a sexual excitement as she succeeds in getting Kissinger on the record, in making a fool of the Shah of Iran, or in arousing the rage of the Lion of Judah Haile Selassie. In her own words, Fallaci says it all: "An interview is a love story for me. It's a fight. It's a coitus."

Robin Pickering-Iazzi (essay date 1989)

SOURCE: "Designing Mothers: Images of Motherhood in Novels by Aleramo, Morante, Maraini, and Fallaci," in *Annali d'Italianistica,* Vol. 7, 1989, pp. 325-40.

[*In the following excerpt, Pickering-Iazzi compares the treatment of women and motherhood in novels by Fallaci and three other Italian writers.*]

For its poetical suggestiveness and socio-cultural significance, motherhood has been a central interpretative image for twentieth-century women writers, designed to express female existence in its personal and social dimensions. The content and configurations of the maternal images in *Una donna, La storia, Donna in guerra,* and ***Lettera a un bambino mai nato*** [***Letter to a Child Never Born***] explain ways in which women writers conceptualize maternity, delineating the essential designs of motherhood as social institution and as personal experience. Aleramo, seeking to create an authentic rendering of female existence, articulates the protagonist's intimate drama of entrapment within the socially imposed maternal role and her escape for purposeful identity as woman, mother, and writer, thereby illustrating the disparity between institutionalized motherhood and the realities of mothering. Morante's depiction of Ida explicates the male-authored metaphor of motherhood, subverting the institution's ideological and historical designs as a means for an authentic relationship to self and being. The novels by Maraini and Fallaci interpret a period of disrupture between the traditional attitudes and values of institutionalized motherhood and alternative notions that reflect women's knowledge and experience. Though both writers refute the ideology of motherhood as women's biological destiny and primary source of identity, Fallaci posits a regenerative notion of maternity, charging that when motherhood is a conscious choice the mother/child relationship has the potential to transform the nature of society and culture. While taking into consideration the recurring and divergent components within these feminist and women's discourses, this study examines the designs of motherhood, the architecture and aesthetic purpose of its imagery, and the meanings enclosed in and suggested by the maternal images.

. . . . .

In *Donna in guerra* and **Lettera a un bambino mai nato,** the writers forge alternatives to women's silence, fashioning a new contextual framework for female identify that expands women's designs, as content, form, and intent. Each novel reflects key positions within the broad spectrum of women's ideas and attitudes concerning motherhood that were articulated in the 1970s. Interpreting the variety of views women hold with regard to maternity, Maraini states: "la posizione è ambivalente tra le donne, da una parte c'è il rifiuto dell'identificazione della personalità della donna con la riproduzione, col ruolo materno, dall'altra c'è la rivalutazione della maternità come forza e privilegio della donna: in origine la donna ha avuto questa forza, che era il suo potere sociale, insomma la creatività della donna, la capacità di formare un altro essere umano era una cosa straordinaria, unica." Fallaci's vision of the mother/child relationship reveals the power of women's mothering to transform life and society, whereas Maraini explores promising courses, exclusive of motherhood, for women's individuation and self-originated social action, and therefore, fulfillment.

. . . . .

From the multi-voiced narrative in **Lettera a un bambino mai nato** emerge two essential images of motherhood; one clarifies the designs of the institution as social imperative, the other expands the meanings of motherhood in its personal and social dimensions. This latter aspect of Fallaci's novel, as well as her scathing indictment of societal institutions and systems of belief have been much overlooked by critical commentary. However, with the initial question posed by the protagonist, concerning possible reasons for bringing a child into the world, Fallaci provides the essential framework for a close examination of contemporary life and society, as well as the attendant attitudes, beliefs, and values that bear upon the nature and realities of motherhood.

> **From the multi-voiced narrative in *Lettera a un bambino mai nato* emerge two essential images of motherhood; one clarifies the designs of the institution as social imperative, the other expands the meanings of motherhood in its personal and social dimensions.**
> —*Robin Pickering-Iazzi*

The voices of the unborn child's father, the male obstetrician, and the protagonist's employer form a composite of motherhood that reflects dominant ideas and attitudes in a world "fabbricato dagli uomini per gli uomini," recalling the images of institutionalized motherhood in *Una donna* and *La storia*. This notion of motherhood values maternity only in the traditional family nucleus, and considers mothers and their offspring to be possessions of the State. Furthermore, since this concept of maternity is designed upon the social imperative of women's self-sacrifice, it restricts female identity to the maternal function, thereby denying individual faculties and aptitudes, and their complementary range of expression in society. The protagonist's modes of existence and mothering undermine these conscious and unverbalized beliefs, upsetting the social order, which is a function of the writer's regenerative notion of motherhood.

The mother-to-be, her close friend, the woman obstetrician, and the unborn child express different dimensions of an alternative vision of maternity that reconceives the terms, content, and configurations of the potential relationships between mothers and daughters, and mothers and sons. Central to Fallaci's reconceptualization of motherhood is the right of choice, a premise she has in common with Maraini. To be a mother, the writer maintains, is not a vocation, a duty, or women's biological destiny. Rather, it is a right, which should be exercised solely on the basis of women's individual choices. Although the character does not give birth to a living child, she begins to mother when she makes the conscious decision to have the child.

Like Aleramo's fictionalized memoirs, the letters written by the protagonist to the child she is carrying evoke with reflective frankness and sensibility the enigmatic muddle of feelings—encompassing the spectrum between joy and despair—that she experiences. Fallaci's discourse, which includes introspective narrative, dreams, fairy tales, and stories, articulates her insights about the complex relationship between the conscious and unconscious content of maternity, and the highly variable realities of motherhood. For example, the protagonist endeavors to refashion the terms of the maternal relationship with such ideals as autonomy, self-respect, and reciprocity, all of which are frustrated by unforeseeable complications in her pregnancy requiring bed rest and hospitalization. The consequent loss of freedom, evoked in powerful images of literal and figurative entrapment, threatens the woman's identity. Nonetheless, the values inherent in the character's manner of coping break the conventions of motherhood, revealing women's aspirations and concerns, as well as the potential of the mother/child relationship to transform life and culture.

The recurrent references to teaching in Fallaci's novel, conveyed by her discourse and the repetition of such words as *lezione, spiegare, insegnare, insegnamento, imparare,* and *apprendere,* underscore the formative role mothering may play in reshaping ideas, values, and culture. Subverting the traditional scope of the maternal vocation—to transmit dominant societal systems of meaning—the mother undermines such patriarchal institutions, ideals, and myths as the State, the Church, patriarchy, the family, and gender roles. The writer posits new determinants of human conduct, irrespective of gender, embodying individual desire and thought. Whether her child is a girl or a boy, she will be equally pleased:

> essere donna è così affascinante. E' un'avventura che richiede un tale coraggio, una sfida che non annoia mai. Avrai tante cose da intraprendere se nascerai donna. Per incominciare, avrai da batterti per sostenere che se Dio esistesse potrebbe anche essere una vecchia coi capelli bianchi o una bella ragazza. Poi avrai da batterti per spiegare che il peccato non nacque il giorno in cui Eva colse una mela: quel giorno nacque una splendida virtù chiamata disubbidienza. Infine avrai da batterti per dimostrare che dentro il tuo corpo liscio e rotondo c'è un'intelligenza che urla d'essere ascoltata.

If born a male, the child will be free from certain humiliations, but his mission will be no less demanding. He will have to fight against the same patriarchal institutions, ideologies, and injustices, as well as others, dependent upon gender assumptions, which limit the range of human experience. The vision the mother projects of the values she wishes to instill in her potential son designs alternative forms for male self-expression reflective of women's experience and ideas:

> se nascerai uomo, spero che sarai un uomo come io l'ho sempre sognato: dolce coi deboli, feroce coi prepotenti, generoso con chi ti vuol bene, spietato con chi ti comanda. Infine, nemico di chiunque

racconti che i Gesù sono figli del Padre e dello Spirito Santo: non della donna che li partorì.

Most importantly, the behavior of the child, whether male or female, must manifest kindness and intelligence.

In the course of teaching her child-to-be to question and, moreover, to resist the established beliefs and forms of society, the protagonist elucidates perhaps the most significant means for transforming life and culture. Fallaci's pluralistic vision, operating upon the values of individuality, human dignity, and relationship, expands the designs of women's and men's experience. As portrayed by the dream sequence of the trial, and the words of the mother and child, there exist many realities, many truths, and many kinds of consciousness, dependent upon experience and contextuality. By incorporating their own beliefs and aspirations in the content of mothering, women may generate further meanings and forms for society. Although the protagonist miscarries and may die, the concluding images of the woman express a life-affirming vision; the daily struggle, to question, to meet and create opportunities, produces a life of committed belief and purposeful action.

Fallaci posits a regenerative notion of motherhood, whose primary tenets are choice, the affirmation of self-identity, and social transformation. Her conceptualization endeavors to reconcile the disjuncture between the domestic and social spheres described in *Una donna, La Storia,* and *Donna in guerra.* Each of these artistic visions expands the readers' consciousness of the meanings and designs of motherhood, creating new metaphors for women's experience, thought, action, and desire.

Santo L. Arico (essay date 1990)

SOURCE: "Oriana Fallaci's Journalistic Novel: *Niente e così sia,*" in *Contemporary Women Writers in Italy,* edited by Santo L. Arico, The University of Massachusetts Press, 1990, pp. 171-82.

[*In the following essay, Arico examines the meeting of journalistic and novelistic techniques in Fallaci's* Niente e così sia.]

Although Oriana Fallaci is best known as a political interviewer, she is also recognized as an ardent practitioner of New Journalism. According to the critic James C. Murphy, this innovative approach allows the journalist's opinions, ideas, and commitments to permeate the story. Correspondents become so intensely involved that they attack their assignments with missionary zeal. Murphy refers to this subjectivity as activism in news reporting. Fallaci's effort to write **Niente e così sia** (*Nothing and Amen*), her report of the war in Vietnam, is a classic example of such activism. The personal nature of her account runs counter to more conventional journalistic objectivity, and her bias colors the narration. Her anti-American and pro-Vietcong feelings are a matter of public record, but during her stay in wartorn Vietnam, Fallaci's perceptions undergo a noticeable transition and this change develops into one of the most interesting aspects of her book. The zeal with which she embraces her assignment is obvious. She spends nearly a year on location, compulsively covering dangerous situations, interviewing fighting men at the bloody conflict in Dak To, flying on a bombing mission in order to experience a pilot's emotions during combat, and almost losing her life during the battle of Hue. Indeed, Fallaci's absorption in her professional pursuits consumes her so completely that any comparison with traditional reporting appears misleading.

Departing from customary methods of gathering data, Oriana Fallaci practices a distinct type of writing. Murphy points out that some scholars consider New Journalism to be a literary genre. Such an interpretation sees the writer's exposé as more than just a forum for viewing and experiencing incidents through the medium of her own individuality; it is also nonfictional prose that uses the resources of fiction. Her work stands as a classic example of what Seymour Krim labels "journalit" and classifies as the de facto literature of our times. In his article "The New Confusion," William L. Rivers proposes that writings in this modernistic style add "a flavor and a humanity to journalistic writing that push it into the realm of art." Fallaci's virtue as a writer lies precisely in showing the possibility of something strikingly different in journalism and in furthering efforts to replace earlier types of fiction with a new brand of literature. Her total immersion in the Vietnamese conflict explains a large part of the popularity that her book attracted. Her writing exerts, however, an even greater impact when she elevates factual statements to artistic invention, demonstrating that it is possible to write accurate nonfiction while using literary devices such as traditional dialogues and stream-of-consciousness.

In 1972, Tom Wolfe hailed New Journalism's replacement of the novel as literature's main event and detailed the historical development of this movement. According to Wolfe, authors like Truman Capote (*In Cold Blood*), Gay Talese (*Honor Thy Father*), Norman Mailer (*Armies of the Night*), and John Sack (*M*) write journalistic novels, using the same techniques that gave the literature of social realism its impact. Discovering the joys and power of faithful portrayal, these writers applied their new knowledge to the richest terrain of the novel—the manners and customs of society. Wolfe points out that in the 1960s journalists began employing the techniques of realism—particularly those of Fielding, Smollett, Gogol, Balzac, and Dickens. "By trial and error, by 'instinct' rather than theory, journalists began to discover the devices that gave the realistic novel its unique power, variously known as its 'immediacy,' its 'concrete reality,' its 'emotional involvement,' its 'gripping' or 'absorbing quality.'" Wolfe proposes that this extraordinary dynamism derives its force from just four devices: scene-by-scene construction, full record of dialogue, third-person point of view, and the portrayal of everyday details in the lives of people to round out character development.

Although Fallaci makes use of the literary conventions of mood development, interviews, character portrayal, satire, and humor, she mainly relies on the four techniques of realism that Wolfe summarizes. By doing so, she changes what would have been an objective record of an armed conflict into a fresh form of art. According to Wolfe, the first characteristic that sets dramatic fiction apart from documentaries is scene-by-scene construction. The writer relates a series of events by moving from one situation to another, resorting as little as possible to sheer historical narrative. Although novelists have relied heavily on this method, its role in classical journalism has been minor. In the new style, however, background building is paramount to storytelling: it eliminates any similarity to detailed documents; it explains, too, why journalists undertake extraordinary feats in order to obtain the information needed to construct a scenario.

The first scene that Fallaci describes is one that takes place after her arrival in Saigon on 18 November 1967. She uses the classical approach of juxtaposing sights that catch her attention en route from the airport to her hotel. At the Than Son Nhut terminal, she indicates the setting's main features: "Jet fighters, helicopters with heavy machine guns, trailers loaded with napalm bombs, stood in line with unhappy-looking American soldiers." She notes salient aspects of the countryside on the way to Saigon: "Guarding the road leading into town were sandbag fortifications surrounded by barbed-wire fences and ending in turrets with rifles sticking out." The author next concentrates on the vital signs of life in the city itself and highlights jeeps full of American soldiers, trucks with cannons leveled, convoys carrying ammunition boxes, rickshaws plunging into traffic and swiftly pedaling on, water sellers scurrying about, their merchandise swinging from bamboo sticks across their shoulders, minute women in long dresses, their loose hair waving beyond their shoulders like black veils, bicycles, motorcycles, shoe-shine boys, and filthy, reckless taxicabs.

Fallaci reveals surprise at not immediately seeing the full impact of the war, and her commentary reinforces her technique of accumulation. "There was a chaos almost gay in this Saigon in November of 1967. . . . It seemed more like a postwar period: the markets filled with food, the jewelry shops stocked with gold, the restaurants open and all that sunshine." The tranquil atmosphere at the hotel creates the impression of a relaxed city that is oblivious to its country's agony: "Even the elevator, the telephone, the fan on the ceiling were working, and the Vietnamese waiter was ready to respond to any gesture you might make, and on the table there was always a bowl of fresh pineapple and mangoes." One final observation summarizes her overall impression: "Dying didn't occur to you."

Fallaci uses the same procedure as she constructs the scene at Battery 25 when she visits an army chaplain, Father Bill. The besieged outpost occupies a barren plateau surrounded by North Vietnamese positions and receives a steady barrage from enemy artillery. "On the bare earth, all you could see were artillery posts, five or six trenches and a hundred dirty soldiers who needed a shave." Father Bill, who regularly enters the encircled area by helicopter in order to minister to the men's spiritual needs, explains that the North Vietnamese, who occupy all the surrounding hills, bombard the American position with mortars twice a day and attack it once a week. The priest quickly prepares an altar by placing a cardboard box on two empty howitzer shells. The recruits assemble in the open space and Mass begins, lasting for about twenty minutes. During that time, two Phantoms drop napalm ten kilometers to the southeast, causing black clouds to darken the blue sky. Farther away to the northeast, cannons thunder. There is, however, absolute quiet at Battery 25, where Father Bill raises his cardboard beaker, calling on the Lord and leading the men in prayer. "All this took place in the most complete serenity, the most absolute silence. In the same silence the boys got up, stood in line, and Father Bill gave them communion: laying little hosts like peppermints on their tongues."

In her personal reflections, Fallaci wonders incredulously why the North Vietnamese did not fire during the service. Since they are able to see clearly the American position with or without field glasses, the writer concludes that enemy gunners chose not to initiate action until the men had finished their prayers. "It seems absurd, I know, but I think they really did want that, because as soon as Mass was over, when Father Bill had hardly put away his crucifix and his jars, the first mortar fire fell. Right into the camp."

The re-creation of scenery and atmosphere is central to Fallaci's technique. Her mimetic ability and talent for acute description enable her readers to receive as full an experience of the war as possible, short of actual, physical presence. The portrayals of Than Son Nhut Airport, Saigon, Dak To, Battery 25, and many other locations bring people and situations alive in a way that makes conventional journalism seem bloodless. Fallaci differs from traditional reporters, who have also been writing anecdotes for years, by her literary technique of building scenes, which she does throughout the book.

The second technique of realism that Wolfe identifies as part of journalistic literature is fully recounting a dialogue. The skilled novelist allows characters to develop action, plot, and personalities in free colloquial exchanges rather than in descriptions or explanations. This device also defines each protagonist quickly, efficiently catches the reader's attention, and creates a sense of proximity to what occurs in the story. Fallaci capitalizes on this tactic by having her subjects' words carry great portions of the story and by developing their uniqueness through these conversations or simple monologues.

Immediately after her arrival in Vietnam, Fallaci made arrangements to go to Dak To. During her first night there, a mortar attack forced her to seek safety in one of the bunkers on Hill 1383. Although it was a light bombardment that lasted an hour, she had time to listen to a group of soldiers conversing about draft dodging. The journalist's restatement of this conversation casts a new light on the character of many soldiers, as well as their real attitude toward the conflict:

> "You see, he told me he had to take care of his mother and so he managed to stay in Los Angeles and built himself a swimming pool."
>
> "Well, Jack was even smarter."
>
> "What did he do?"
>
> "He started drinking and drank himself into an ulcer, so they turned him down because of the ulcer."
>
> "Roll on the ulcers!"

According to one of the men, his friend Howard was the most skillful at obtaining a deferment:

> "When they asked him if he liked girls he said: 'Goodness no, everyone knows I go for boys.'"
>
> "Is he a queer?"
>
> "Of course not. You crazy? But if you say you're queer, they turn you down flat, didn't you know?"
>
> "No, dammit. Suppose I said it now?"
>
> "Too late, buster. You should have thought of it sooner. I should've, too."

During the battle of Dak To, the North Vietnamese controlled most areas around the American positions and shelled them day and night. Most of the firing came from Hill 875, which seemed impregnable. Any attempts to overrun the enemy emplacement resulted in failure and major casualties.

FALLACI   *CONTEMPORARY LITERARY CRITICISM, Vol. 110*

American soldiers whom the North Vietnamese had pinned down there were accidentally bombed by their own aircraft trying to dislodge the opposition. When help finally arrived, the full impact of losses became evident. Fallaci's recordings catch the anguish and depression of the wounded as they are prepared for evacuation. One of them grabs her, laughing hysterically: "The order was to take the hill. Take the damned hill! But we couldn't, you see, we couldn't!" Another, half naked, shakes and stomps around, slapping his forehead, sobbing: "I hate them! I hate you! You bastards! You pigs!" Others try to calm him and lead him off to sick bay, but they cannot. A black man sits quietly eating a bowl of soup and weeping as he recalls the heaps of dead after that bomb: "You didn't know where to go, you didn't know where to hide. You slept with the corpses. I slept under Joe. He was dead, but he kept me warm. Give me a cigarette. Have you ever slept under a corpse that kept you warm?."

The soldiers in camp 1383 had received the brunt of the attack and, in many cases, fell victim to depression in these trying circumstances. Fallaci captures the men's intense agony and frustration by simply restating their words. A young Puerto Rican from New York vents his despair. He neither knows what communism is nor understands why he should fight for the benefit of a distant nation in southeast Asia. "I don't know what the hell this communism is and I don't give a damn and I don't give a damn about these fucking Vietnamese. Let them fight communism themselves. There's not a single South Vietnamese here." When a corporal tries to silence him, the soldier not only angrily refuses to be still but also heatedly recalls his father's anger after he had volunteered. "And he was right! He said: 'You're a fool; let the rich boys go.' They never do, you know. My father's a workman and let me tell you something: it's always the sons of the working people that die in wars. Never the rich boys, never!"

> **Rather than describe each fighting man in concrete terms, Fallaci gives glimpses of their inner selves by relating their free and spontaneous statements.**
> —*Santo L. Arico*

Rather than describe each fighting man in concrete terms, Fallaci gives glimpses of their inner selves by relating their free and spontaneous statements. The writer is able to communicate a frame of mind by reporting revelations of their fullest and most intimate sort. This gives the narration its atmosphere of accessibility and nearness; it, together with scene construction, separates the writer's work from traditional journalism and makes it technically more like a novel.

According to Wolfe, seeing the world through someone else's eyes is the third characteristic of journalistic literature. Eye-witness accounts permit both Fallaci and the reader to experience sights from the vantage point of an observer. This slant avoids the limits of exclusivity invoked with a first-person perspective, and also generates a climate of intimacy through its full exposure of a character's mind and emotional life. Wolfe's term was "chameleon," i.e., taking on the coloration of whomever or whatever was being written about.

Most instances of this technique occur when François Pelou, director of *France Presse,* describes for Fallaci major events that she had not witnessed herself. During a conversation with him about Buddhist self-immolation, Fallaci expresses a desire to witness one. Her colleague reacts negatively to the request but then proceeds to describe a burning that took place in Saigon in July 1966, which he witnessed while he was on his way to a press conference. After hearing the noise of an explosion and seeing flames rising up, Pelou approached the fire and recognized a young monk in the flames, sitting with his legs crossed in the lotus position. "Around him there are kids playing, women crying, and two nuns who stare emotionless. Though everybody seems to respect his decision, the traffic is hardly disturbed by the show."

Pelou attempts to save the burning victim who begins to move and twist with pain; fellow monks, however, block his efforts to aid the victim. Except for the covering of his shoulder, the victim's skin slips away from his arm and hand. After a nun places burning material back on the suffering person, Pelou quickly removes it once more, only to have it thrown back by the religious. "The whole thing is grotesque, this coming and going of burning clothes, while it's obvious that the poor monk has lost any will to die. Now he waves his hands, all his body clearly asking for help." Pelou and other newsmen eventually succeed in extinguishing the flames and getting the monk to a hospital, where he finally dies. This third-person point of view exposes the horrible suffering endured by the victim and also suggests the influence of chemical drugs and brainwashing to keep the individual resolved during burning. Pelou believes that no willpower on earth can keep a person standing still during such agony. "Not to mention another kind of drug—the one we call brainwashing. Get it into the head of a monk of seventy or a nun of seventeen that the destiny of Vietnam depends on his sacrifice and he'll agree to be roasted straight away."

In another conversation, Pelou expresses his thoughts on the insanity of dying in combat and his belief that incidentals frequently distract from an actual slaughter. He illustrates this with two anecdotes that deal with his experience as a Korean War correspondent. The first story deals with a heated engagement between a French battalion and North Korean units. Action began early in the morning and lasted until six in the evening. During the subsequent period of calm, Pelou interviewed a group of men. At a certain point, however, an artillery shell landed amidst these very soldiers. "It fell on them and the bodies shot out in pieces. A head in one place, a foot in another." Rather than experiencing grief at the sight of severed members, the journalist explains that his attention was caught by a helmet flying much higher than the heads or feet and completely absorbed him: "Up, up, up till it was nearly still and turned a somersault and came down in a spiral, down, down, till it hit the ground with a resounding thud."

The second incident occurred during the same period. After one particular battle, many of the dead remained exposed to the elements in subzero weather. Only after a few days could military personnel begin the grizzly task of retrieving frozen bodies. It was unbearably cold and the corpses were statues of ice, crystallized into absurd positions. Their awkward postures made it impossible to align them horizontally in containers. "You couldn't lay them out in a normal position, before putting them into the plastic bags. And so you were forced to bend the arms and legs till they broke like a glass—crack—and then you had to jump on the body and crush it well." Pelou explains how workers begin to perspire and how the sweat froze into snow on their faces. An unexpected detail again detracts from the morbid scene. One particular soldier appears relaxed and unruffled by his labor. "He wasn't working hard. In fact he didn't even try to stretch out their arms and legs; he just gave them a whack with a stick and that laid them out. And as he hit them, he sang: 'Mona Lisa . . . when you smile, Mona Lisa . . . I love you!'"

Third-person point of view considers reality through someone else's perceptions and exposes a person's intimate feelings. In the description of a Buddhist self-immolation, the reader is presented with Pelou's frantic attempts to save a human life and his frustration as all rescue attempts fail. Pelou's earlier experience permits him to formulate a personal philosophy of death. Nonetheless, the incidental details in his two Korean stories—a spiraling helmet, a soldier's failure to perspire like everyone else, and his irreverent song as he performs his horrible duty—distract from the actual fact of death, while simultaneously creating a surrealistic atmosphere of the macabre and absurd.

Wolfe refers to social autopsy as the fourth technique that distinguishes journalistic literature. The writer pays close attention to the minute manners and other trappings of a subject's life and, consequently, presents a comprehensive picture that communicates insight into personalities and situations. Symbolic details represent entire patterns of behavior and positions in the world. Recording of such incidentals is not embroidery; it contributes as much to the power of realism as any other literary device. It resembles third-person point of view because it also casts unexpected clarity on a character.

Fallaci's use of social autopsy takes various forms—brief informative details, humor, mood, portraits. She best utilizes this approach, however, when she paints a word picture of particular people whom she encounters. In each case, her sketch places emphasis on what she perceives as the character's principal trait. Physical features reinforce her observations, correspond directly to each person's inner spirit, and satirize obvious weaknesses.

The press officer at Dak To with limited intellectual vision: "He has a small ridiculous mustache on his dumb mouselike face and looks as if he'd been born in his helmet. Probably he sleeps in it." In his pants pocket, he keeps a box of color slides that he shows everyone: his girl in a nightgown and without it, naked, photographed while he was on leave in Honolulu. "Showing us the slides he scratches himself. How depressing to think that we shall have him around for most of the time."

The mysterious silence of François Pelou's accountant, Than Van Lang: "When you happen to look his way and see him, he comes as a surprise; he seems to have materialized that very moment." He never gets up, never speaks; he only writes with long, slim fingers and an old-fashioned pen that he dips in an inkwell. "The movement carrying the pen to the mouth of the inkwell is so strangely slow that it seems as if it weren't happening at all." Nothing upsets or bothers him; he shows no emotion, even in the face of death. "An invisible wall round his desk isolates him from us, and beyond that wall his eyes move only to look at François. Secretly, though, while the face remains impenetrable. A thin, yellow, ageless face."

General Loan, who has the reputation of being the cruelest individual in Vietnam: "The ugliest little man I had ever seen, with a tiny twisted head screwed on to his meager shoulders. The only thing you noticed about the face was the mouth—so large and so out of proportion." According to Fallaci, one looked directly down to the neck from the mouth because the chin fell away so fast that one wondered if it had existed. His eyes were not really eyes; they were eyelids that were scarcely visible through the slit. "The nose, on the other hand, was a nose but so flat it was lost in the cheeks, which were also flat. I looked at him and felt a kind of uneasiness."

The gross policeman dressed only in underwear who receives Fallaci and another journalist at central headquarters: "Fat, barefoot, sweating. He looked at us as if we were a couple of criminals, pulled up his pants and spat on the floor. Then he stood admiring the spittle, scratched himself down to his genitals and pushed us toward a desk."

Catherine, the French journalist whose false timidity camouflages an aggressive nature: "Catherine, with that little each-man-for-himself face of hers. I shall never understand that girl. You look at her and feel, immediately, that you want to protect her: so blonde, so worn, so tiny." A second glance, however, quickly changes the initial reaction. "You feel that you want to protect yourself—from her. Perhaps it's her eyes—pitiless, cold. Perhaps it's her fingers—large, knotty, always held forward like the claws of an eagle."

The impractical and mistaken patriotism of Barry Zorthian, director of the Joint United States Public Affairs Office of Vietnam and considered one of the most important men in Saigon: "Mr. Zorthian . . . has a large nose, a large belly, a large faith in this war, and an unshakable conviction that the United States must teach civilization to poor people who have never heard of democracy and technological progress."

The superficial and convenient Catholicism of the adoption agent Tran Ti Au, who takes Fallaci to an orphanage: "She has a pretty face of old ivory and owns a factory that makes chemical products, a house full of china and servants. She deals with adoptions and she looks like the charity ladies who think they'll get to heaven on bazaars and good works." Fallaci had gone to see her about adopting a child. When she informs her that she is neither a good Catholic nor a bad one, the lady seems irritated. When she hears that the writer has a chapel in her country home, however, she appears satisfied "as if someone with a chapel was automatically on the right side of the angels."

The highly intelligent American lieutenant Teaneck from Oklahoma who saved Fallaci's life at the Battle of Hue: "He has a wide, red, Indian face mixed with some other race—high cheekbones, thin nose, Asian cheeks." He does not fit the stereotype of the unthinking, ignorant foot soldier, who simply obeys without thinking. On the contrary, he labels Fallaci a liberal who has unfairly disparaged American soldiers in favor of the Vietcong. "It's one thing to take risks with a return ticket and another to take risks with a one-way ticket. Like me." He questions her fairness and justice, objecting to the journalist's partiality. "The fact of being in the war doesn't authorize you to despise us and respect them. Because when you escape, as you did today, you owe it to us mediocre men. To us Ugly Americans. To us who fire for your sake, to save your life and your conscience."

The coldness and impenetrability of Vietnam's president Cao Ky: "He's a Vietnamese like plenty of others, neither tall nor short, neither strong nor frail, and physically distinguished from the others only by a black mustache that stands out on his dark amber face." Fallaci sees his profile as unattractive and closed in by a sad, arrogant expression; his glance is direct but at the same time somber and melancholic. What he says, however, is greatly interesting to her and makes a profound impression. Ky is the only one on his side of the barricade "who dares admit he belongs to a powerless, inefficient, corrupt regime. I'm the only one who says the Americans are here not to defend us but to defend their own interests and set up a new colonialism."

Before her subjects even speak, Fallaci points out physical features that often indicate their personalities and provide a key to their emotional constitution. Scarcely a detail does not illuminate some point of their temperament. These clues, in combination with the writer's evaluations and comments, constitute the very essence of her literary portraits. The relentless and meticulous accumulation of these character profiles not only reveals Fallaci's private interpretations of each protagonist but also projects a comprehensive panorama of Vietnamese society during the war.

According to Seymour Krim, journalists enjoy a definite advantage in their attempts to re-create reality if they use every conceivable literary avenue open to them. Oriana Fallaci does so and particularly profits from the techniques of realism that Wolfe outlines. By observing the facts of a ruthless conflict and selecting them with an artist's touch, she captures the deeper half of reality, which old-time journalism excluded, and structures a narrative with skills that had always been associated with novels. If for some reason Fallaci had written a fictional sketch, changing names and location, she would have disgraced the reality of what she had seen. She ascertains, however, the veracity of all her data while simultaneously structuring her information in the manner of narrative prose writers. The result is a form that looks like fiction but unquestionably remains reportage. The impact of *Niente e così sia* lies in its portrayal of reality and the realization that its subject matter has not been imagined.

Oriana Fallaci combines her talent as a reporter and interviewer with a proven ability to write novels. The end result of her efforts, however, is not "fictional" literature. Such a label would suggest that the author has made up her story. It is true that *Niente e così sia* is indeed "imaginative," but that is not because Fallaci has distorted data but because she has presented them in a full manner instead of in the style of cold, clipped, factual newspaper journalism. She has brought out the sights, sounds, and feelings surrounding the raw material of her report, connecting them in an artistic manner that does not diminish but gives greater depth and dimension to the information.

Krim proposes that writers like Hemingway, Fitzgerald, Wolfe, and Faulkner were "in the most radical sense *reporters* whose subject matter and vision were too hot or subtle or complicated or violent or lyrical or intractable or challenging for the mass media of their period." He proposes that twenty or thirty years ago writers of talent necessarily expressed themselves in fiction because only this form was able to bypass the narrow framework of journalism and provide a channel through which invented characters with made-up names in imagined situations could express their creators' world. Fallaci, however, takes part in a movement that reverses this trend. Her success lies precisely in the ability to communicate directly an investigation of the war in Vietnam as if she were writing a novel.

Fallaci accepts the ideal that art remains at all times the highest condition to which a person can aspire. In fact, she speaks openly of her burning desire to write novels after having dedicated so much of her life to the professional aspects of journalism. She projects the full weight of this desire and belief on the war in Vietnam, creating in the process an imaginative nonfiction that profits from acceptable literary techniques, especially those of social realism. In 1972, Tom Wolfe wrote: "I think there is a tremendous future for a sort of novel that will be called the journalistic novel or perhaps documentary novel, novels of intense social realism based upon the same painstaking reporting that goes into the New Journalism." Fallaci's *Niente e così sia* stands as a classic example of this imaginative truth writing—a genre as creative as fiction used to be, which uses the staples of the older art, in particular the four techniques outlined by Wolfe, when it needs or wants to, but expands them into deeper and more authentic worlds of contemporary reality.

Thomas Keneally (review date 27 December 1992)

SOURCE: "Waiting for the Suicide Truck," in *The New York Times Book Review,* December 27, 1992, p. 8.

[*In the following review, Keneally discusses Fallaci's reportage of the Beirut conflict.*]

"Inshallah" is a phrase one hears everywhere in the Arab world. It is an utterance of Arab stoicism, meaning "God willing." But God's will is savage indeed in the Beirut that Oriana Fallaci so palpably renders for us.

With the large-scale vigor that is typical of Ms. Fallaci's work, *Inshallah* begins on the night in October 1983 when two members of a Khomeinist sect, the Sons of God, crash suicide trucks, one into the American Marine compound, the other into the French compound. Nearly 300 young American marines and French troops are destroyed in an instant.

The third large peace-keeping force in the city is the Italians, and Ms. Fallaci's novel is concerned with the Italian officers and men during the three winter months following the explosion as they wait for the "third truck" to strike.

On the edge of the mass graves of the Shatilah Palestinian refugee camp, the Italians try to keep peace between the Palestinian Amal militia and the Lebanese Government forces of President Amin Gemayel, and dodge suicide attacks by the Sons of God and stray shells from the artillery fire of the Druze.

The main onus of preventing the "third truck" from tearing to pieces the Italian marines, alpine troops and carabinieri (Italian police units) falls on Charlie, an extremely civilized and sentimental intelligence officer, who is excessively tender toward his men, going around the outposts in the dark to make sure they are cautious enough and have their winter wear on. To forfend the Armageddon truck, Charlie has to trade in plasma and anything else he can think of with a serpentine power structure that includes the local militia leader, Bilal, a dwarf street-sweeper, and the Imam of the Lebanese Shiites, Ayatollah Zandra Sadr, who has the power to make the muezzins in their towers utter instructions favorable to the Italians.

Ms. Fallaci is not the first journalist to find that truth escapes the net of reportage but belongs to those who make appropriate myths out of the chaos. In *Inshallah* she manages to make the confused universe of Beirut factions and political goals internally coherent and weirdly rational. As always, she is not timid about writing about men, their sensibilities, brashness and occasional fated courage. If there is any shallowness of characterization, she compensates by giving us a generous range of men and officers.

Besides Charlie, we encounter an austere, old-fashioned soldier, Condor, who feels debased by all Charlie's deal making and by the tortuous way modern peace-keeping has to be conducted. There's Crazy Horse, a lover of antiques and of the classics, who is likely to speak in moments of crisis in maxims by Cicero or Seneca. A young failed mathematician, Angelo, is—like half the Italian peace-keeping force—in love with an Arab woman.

Ms. Fallaci writes with a muscular eloquence when giving us the squalor, yearning and shadowboxing of the soldiers' existence. And what works especially well for her is the fact that they are Italian, with a European heritage and therefore a different world-view from that of the Americans. From the peculiarly Roman Catholic consciousness of these Italian soldiers arises a sense that their occupation of Beirut is simply one item in a string of historic follies involving Europe and the Arab world. Like a medieval crusader, one officer, Pistoia, thinks that the real war has always been "between those who eat pig meat and those who don't, those who drink wine and those who don't, those who mumble the Pater Noster and those who whimper Allah rassullillah!" Both sides uttered the same basic prayer. "Our Father and Our Allah who art in Heaven, supply us our daily 7.62's and

5.56's and rockets and bombs, lead us not into the temptation of making peace."

Ms. Fallaci's hashish-dazed soldiers are aware that in falling for Arab women they are facing the same divide as susceptible crusaders. A sense of history being repeated explains to them such mysteries as a Norman-featured, flaxen-haired, teen-age Amal militiaman called Passepartout, the lover of a guerrilla leader, who comes up to the Italian outposts gesturing with grenades and yelling insults.

And the divide has its own comedy. One Italian soldier, in love with a Muslim woman and saving up to pay her father her bride-price, runs up against the problem that she has now read the Gospels and been deeply impressed by Jesus Christ, "particularly by the fact that He befriended a streetwalker named Mary Magdalene and prevented the Pharisees from stoning the adulteresses."

Ungovernable Beirut, as rendered by Oriana Fallaci, will stay with the reader. It is just as well, because in company with her vigorous narrative comes dialogue that creaks and overreaches for effect in her translation, done from a first translation by James Marcus. And on top of that there seem to be too many huge, banal swaths of musing on destiny and chaos.

A characteristic unnecessary sentence runs, "When something big happens, something that changes the status quo or even provokes a tragedy, we don't wonder which weft of marginal and apparently trivial episodes has eased or determined its realization." Such observations occur again and again, and are often backed up in Angelo's thoughts by the frequently repeated formula for chaos devised by the physicist Boltzmann. American readers will find some of the book's expletives similarly stretched. "By Christopher Columbus and his mother's dirty underpants!"

I heard an author as full-blooded as Oriana Fallaci recently boast at a reading that at least his book was not about someone's second divorce. Ms. Fallaci can make a similar assertion. She is profligate with plot and detail, and her openhandedness and the inherent tensions of her large story should insure that most readers will overlook her equally spacious faults, including the banality of her asides.

Ronan Bennett (review date 11 February 1993)

SOURCE: "Dogs," in *London Review of Books,* Vol. 15, No. 3, February 11, 1993, p. 19.

[*In the following review of* Inshallah, *Bennett assesses the strengths and weaknesses of Fallaci's portrayal of war-torn Beirut.*]

Set in Beirut in the early Eighties, Oriana Fallaci's novel [*Inshallah*] opens at the moment when, on the morning of 23 October 1983, an Islamic Jihad militant drove a truck laden with explosives into the headquarters of the US contingent of the Multinational Force (MNF). A second suicide bomber attacked the French military base at the same time. Altogether more than three hundred servicemen were killed.

The Americans and French had returned to the city the previous year, along with a body of Italian troops, after the catastrophic Israeli invasion of the Lebanon. The MNF's presence was highly controversial and subject to conflicting interpretations. Its self-proclaimed goal was vague and, with hindsight, absurdly optimistic: to protect the innocent from slaughter and oversee a return to some kind of normality. Others, perhaps casting their minds back to 1958 when US Marines landed at Beirut to fight off 'international communism', saw the MNF's presence as yet another show of force on the part of a Western bloc determined to impose its will on a vulnerable part of the Arab world. Fallaci takes the generous view of the MNF's role, and the book's heroes are the soldiers of the Italian contingent. In the aftermath of the bombings, they ready themselves to face a similar attack. But there is no third truck, no third suicide bomber.

Having been spared annihilation, the Italians are condemned to a living hell in which violent death is part of everyday life, cruelty the norm. They live under constant threat of being targeted. Negotiating the tricky currents of Beirut's political underworld, they do what they can to guard their lives; but this is straightforward compared with the difficulty of preserving their sanity and moral perspective. Will they survive their time in Beirut? Will they get home body and psyche intact?

Beyond this, *Inshallah* has little in the way of narrative. The novel is a shapeless, sprawling mess, a densely crowded, confusing and episodic collage in which incident, portentous speculation and opposing galleries of goodies and baddies take the place of plot, theme and characterization. There are more than a hundred characters: few are sufficiently differentiated for the reader to recognize them on second meeting. The Italians have names like Condor, Eagle and Onion. If Fallaci, in giving her characters such names, was striving to enhance the surrealism of the nightmare the soldiers inhabit, the effect is immediately undercut by a naive literalism. Onion, we discover, is so called 'because his face was shaped like an onion'. Sugar, the bomb disposal expert, is so called because 'his gentle face emanated an almost sugary sweetness.' Then there is String, who is nicknamed String 'because, besides being very tall, he was as thin as a string.' Fallaci makes an extra effort with his characterization: 'like a string he could squeeze nay strangle you each time he opened his mouth.' The picture conjured up by this line can hardly have been the intended one, and Fallaci makes it worse by forgetting to give String any good lines.

Fallaci's treatment of the Arabs makes her handling of the Italian soldiers look subtle. They are, without exception, villainous; many are psychopathic, some are out of their heads on drugs. Zandra Sadr, a Shiite Imam, is a cunning, fork-tongued politician who plays a double game with the Italians. Hezbollah militants are crazed fanatics. An adolescent thug murders the girlfriend of Angelo, one of the Italian soldiers and the nearest the book comes to having a central character. The Arabs are men who, when they are not raping and murdering nuns, will disguise a bomb as a doll in the hope of maiming the man who stoops to pick it up. In Beirut people drag around guns the way 'normal people' drag around umbrellas on a rainy day. A child can strip and clean a rifle the way 'normal children' fiddle with toys.

The book was published in Italy in 1990 and later appeared in translation in the US. This accounts for the American cast of speech—'Buttfuckers','Don't bust my balls,' and so on— but does not help the strained and artificial dialogue. This effect is heightened by the disjointed and deliberately impressionistic use of language. It is a device from *Catch 22:* to capture the insanity of war by adopting, in the writing, something of war's surrealism. This is fine when it is done well. When it fails, as it frequently does in *Inshallah,* it fails badly. Some of the language is surreal in other ways; no matter how some sentences are read, they fail to make sense. The book is really only partly fiction. Oriana Fallaci made her name as a reporter and interviewer. Her work—in books and in articles—has always been passionate and opinionated. She has never been shy about setting out her position; and *Inshallah* is no different. Here is her version of the Lebanon before the civil war:

> Beirut had been one of the most agreeable spots on this planet: an extremely comfortable place to live and die of old age or illness. Whether you were rich and corrupt or poor and honest, there you found the best a city can offer: a mild climate in the summer and winter, blue sea and green hills, work, food. . . . A more or less democratic regime existed, civil liberties were respected. . . . War didn't exist. . . . It was called the Switzerland of the Middle East.

But then 'one ugly day the Palestinians had arrived. With their anger, their pain, their money.' These violent sectarians destroyed the splendid villas, the 'immaculate gardens and verandas paved with superb Alexandrian mosaics', the 'stunning' residences and 'exquisite' art deco houses, the 'magnificent' racetrack, and the 'sumptuous' hotels.

It is not clear what day Fallaci is referring to, but one assumes she is thinking of September 1970, when the PLO was driven out of Jordan. However, there had been Palestinians in the Lebanon for almost a quarter of a century before the PLO set up its new headquarters in Beirut, and their lives had been anything but pleasant. It is hard to recognize the 'Switzerland of the Middle East' in *The Disinherited,* Fawaz Turki's account of his family's flight from Haifa to Sidon and on to Beirut in 1948. His experience, shared by thousands of Palestinian refugees in Lebanon, was one of poverty, deprivation, surveillance and discrimination. Nor could the Shia of South Lebanon—among the poorest people in the country—have had many opportunities to enjoy a day at the races and a night at a sumptuous hotel in the capital.

The truth is that Lebanon before September 1970 was a great place to be if you happened to be one of the rich Muslims or rich Christians who had divided up the country and its spoils. For these people, there were few if any irksome regulations in the way of turning a dishonest dollar. If you made your money out of smuggling guns or drugs, that was no one's business but your own. If you sold your ministerial vote, only the most churlish would criticize you. And there was always plenty to distract you from the pressures of high finance and politics. In Fallaci's disingenuous phrase there was 'a thoughtlessness that put up for sale any kind of pleasure'. For the rich whose interests ran in that direction there was unrestricted access to prostituted women and children, and drugs of every variety. Lebanon before 1970 was as much a paradise as Havana before 1959. The disparities of wealth and the polarization of politics—the Christian fascists, the Phalange, had been around long before 1948— meant that Lebanese society was unstable in a way Swiss society never was. Lebanon was, moreover, a 'fake' state, the result of post-colonial realignment, a hodge-podge detached from Syria after the imperialist misadventures of the French. The arrival of the PLO in 1970 merely provided the trigger for a civil war that had been brewing for years.

How important is this for *Inshallah,* which is, after all, fiction spiced with polemic rather than polemic with fiction thrown in? It seems to me to go to the core of the book's weakness. What it demonstrates is the imaginative shortcomings of an intellectual from a modern agnostic culture faced with strong, anti-liberal belief in another. The civil war in the Lebanon is just one of the many 'ethnic' conflicts that seem to defy all reason. The novelist wanders, weary and outraged, around the hell that has been created. And the book the novelist writes from the inferno is the equivalent of the white flag of reason and peace, of compassion and humane wisdom, a flag all the more poignant because it is spotted with the blood of the innocent. This is the understandable reaction, the instinctive response to slaughter on such a horrific scale. But if the reaction goes no further than this, the writing will be all too predictable. And indeed, *Inshallah* deploys a familiar metaphor on its first page: 'At night the stray dogs invaded the city . . . Like men they divided into bands consumed by hate, like men they wanted only to tear each other to pieces, and the monotonous rite always took place under the same pretext: the conquest of a sidewalk made precious by food scraps and scum.'

The book closes with the same image. The dogs are still there, still tearing each other apart: 'Filthy, bloody, covered with sores, encrusted with tinea, some with only one eye, one ear, three paws.' The madness goes on. And the dogs, far from being reduced by their mutual slaughter, are strengthened by it: they kill each other without mercy, but they seem possessed of such energy and life. And while the dogs thrive on violence, the innocent suffer. Angelo arrives at the bombed US barracks: 'Every step, a stab of rage and horror. Here a finger, there a foot, or a hand, a forearm, an ear that improvised sextons picked up and threw in plastic bags like the garbage of a butcher shop: most of the bodies had been in fact dismembered into dozens of pieces.' Angelo finds a Marine cradling a helmet in his arms 'with the obstinacy of a child who refuses to give up an object very precious to him'. The Marine's histrionics irritate Angelo until he realizes that the helmet contains the decapitated head of the Marine's buddy.

Fallaci's simplistic and apolitical take on the situation has not helped her. Her sensitivity to the suffering and the slaughter is evident, but what comes across most strongly is her naivety and the sense of our having heard and seen it all before. Every step of the territory Fallaci traverses is familiar; it carries echoes from Hemingway, Joseph Heller and Michael Herr without possessing a fraction of their power: the descriptions of the war-torn city, the psychotic gunmen, the well-intentioned if ineffectual soldiers doing their best to 'hold the ring', the brutalized population, the dead children, the doomed love—the novel's treatment of these people and things has suffered because the author is transfixed by the corpses and the rubble and does not know where

else to look. Most of all, what is tellingly absent is a convincing psychological portrait of someone from the other side, the anti-Western, anti-liberal side, the side engaged in the fighting. What Fallaci serves up here, unintentionally is further proof of how difficult modern novelists—with exceptions, like Timothy Mo and Amos Oz—find it to write about sectarian conflict.

FURTHER READING

Criticism

Brunette, Peter. Review of *A Man,* by Oriana Fallaci. *New Republic* (22 November 1980): 37-38.
    A brief review of Fallaci's book, *A Man.*

Kapp, Isa. "Oriana Fallaci and the Facts of Life," in *Washington Post Book World* (13 February 1977): G7, G10.
    A short review of Fallaci's book *Letter to a Child never Born.* Kapp comments briefly on how the subject of abortion has had "relatively little place in literature until recently," and on Fallaci's advanced style and technique in the semi-autobiographical novel.

Interview

Cott, Jonathan. "How to Unclothe an Emperor: The *Rolling Stone* Interview with Oriana Fallaci, The Greatest Political Interviewer of Modern Times," in *Rolling Stone* No. 215 (17 June 1976): 44-47, 66, 68, 71.
    An in-depth interview in which Cott reveals Fallaci's methods for preparing for interviews, and discusees several of the high points of her interviewing career, including excerpts from talks with Henry Kissinger, Yasir Arafat, South Vietnamese President Nguyen Van Thieu, and Indira Ghandi.

Additional coverage of Fallaci's life and career is contained in the following sources published by Gale: *Contemporary Authors,* Vols. 77-80; *Contemporary Authors New Revision Series,* Vol. 15; and *Major 20th Century Writers.*

Kazuo Ishiguro
1954-

Japanese-born English novelist, short story writer, and scriptwriter.

The following entry presents an overview of Ishiguro's career through 1995. For further information on his life and works, see *CLC,* Volumes 27, 56, and 59.

INTRODUCTION

Considered one of the preeminent novelists of his generation, Ishiguro garnered international acclaim with his first two novels, solidifying his reputatuion with the Booker Prize-winning *The Remains of the Day* (1995). Praised for the precision of his narratives, Ishiguro typically deals with themes of self-deception and self-delusion. The recipient of numerous literary awards, Ishiguro is often credited with infusing the British literary scene with new life.

Biographical Information

Ishiguro was born in Nagasaki, Japan on November 8, 1954 to Shizuo, an oceanographer, and Shizuko Michida Ishiguro. In 1960, Ishiguro's father was temporarily assigned to help explore and develop oil deposits in the North Sea and the family, including two sisters, moved to England. By 1970 the family decided to remain in England; Ishiguro would not return to Japan again until 1989. He lived in an affluent London suburb and received a typical English up-bringing; however, he also spoke Japanese at home and was immersed in Japanese culture. After a period of indecision and travel, Ishiguro attended the University of Kent where he received a B.A. with honors in philosophy and literature in 1978. While working as a social worker in London, he met social worker Lorna Anne MacDougall whom he married on May 9, 1986. In 1980 he received a M.A. in creative writing from the University of East Anglia. While earning his degree he had three stories published in a new writers anthology and received a contract for his first novel, *A Pale View of Hills* (1982). He received the Winifred Holtby Award from the Royal Society of Literature in 1983 for his first book and the Whitbread Book of the Year Award in 1986 for his second novel, *An Artist of the Floating World* (1986). In 1989 he won the coveted Booker award for his bestseller *The Remains of the Day.* Ishiguro was named to the Order of the British Empire for his literary work in 1995. He continues to write and live in London.

Major Works

Ishiguro's novels share similar stylistic elements and subject matter. In *A Pale View of Hills* and *An Artist of the Floating World,* he examines Japanese culture from a Western perspective. In *The Remains of the Day* he shifts his focus to post-World War I England and in *The Unconsoled* he retains an English character but moves the setting to a surreal city in Central Europe. However, through all of these novels, he remains committed to telling the story of isolated characters who are self-delusional—consumed with appearances, honor, and duty. Through a unique, finely crafted first person narration, the reader uncovers the reality of the central characters' lives. Ishiguro does not present characters as much as he slowly reveals them through the stories they tell of their lives. *A Pale View of Hills* centers on Etsuko, a former Japanese housewife who resettled to England to live with her English husband and their daughter Niki. As Etsuko recounts the events of her life in Japan, a portrait of her develops as a submissive woman who has been unhappy with her life choices but has been consumed with maintaining appearances. *An Artist of the Floating World* takes place in a provincial Japanese town between 1948 and 1950 as the protagonist, Masuji Ono, attempts to reorder his life and his country in the wake of World War II. However, despite his efforts to move his thinking forward, Masuji is unable to comprehend how his family perceives him. *The Remains of the Day* is narrated by an elderly butler named Stevens who has spent his entire life in unquestioning service to an English Nazi sympathizer. In the name of duty he has fired Jewish maids, neglected his father, and failed to realize a relationship with Miss Kenton, the housekeeper. Stevens slowly realizes that his life has been overwhelmed by illusions and self-deception. *The Unconsoled* centers on a concert pianist named Ryder who has arrived in a Central European city to perform. However, Ryder seems to be disconnected, as if his life has turned into a Kafkaesque nightmare in which he moves from one disaster to another. Despite its greater length and its unrealistic tone, the novel still centers on the concept of self awareness and choices.

Critical Reception

Critics have focused heavily on the influence of Japanese philosophy and culture in Ishiguro's work, sometimes to the dismay of the author, who insists that his novels are firmly grounded in the British literary tradition. Beyond commenting on the obvious subject of Japanese characters and setting in Ishiguro's first two novels, critics have credited the author's taciturnity, fine sense of timing, and quiet tone to his Japanese heritage. Scholars and other writers have been almost universally impressed with Ishiguro's novels, as testified by the number of awards he has won at a relatively young age. Malcom Bradbury has credited him with saving the English novel by infusing it with new style. Ishiguro is often named with other writers such as Salman Rushdie for adding new dimensions to the British literary scene. However, critics are divided over *The Unconsoled*. While many praise Ishiguro for his ambition, some claim that the work is too long and fails to engage the reader. Others, such as Charlotte Innes, believe that *The Unconsoled* is exciting and humourous as well as poignant.

PRINCIPAL WORKS

A Pale View of Hills (novel) 1982
An Artist of the Floating World (novel) 1986
The Remains of the Day (novel) 1989
The Unconsoled (novel) 1995

CRITICISM

Kazuo Ishiguro with Gregory Mason (interview date 8 December 1986)

SOURCE: "An Interview with Kazuo Ishiguro," in *Contemporary Literature*, Vol. 30, No. 3, Fall, 1989, pp. 335-47.

[*In the interview below, which was conducted on December 8, 1986, Ishiguro discusses Japanese and Western influences on his writing, his characters, and the writing process in his first two novels.*]

In January 1987, Kazuo Ishiguro confirmed his position as Britain's leading young novelist. He was awarded the Whitbread Book of the Year Prize, the largest such cash prize in Britain, for his second novel, *An Artist of the Floating World*. Born in Nagasaki in 1954, Ishiguro left Japan at the age of five and has not returned since. In most respects he has become thoroughly English, but as a writer he still draws considerably on his early childhood memories of Japan, his family upbringing, and the great Japanese films of the fifties.

Soon after publishing a few short stories, Ishiguro jumped to prominence in 1982 with his first novel, *A Pale View of Hills. A Pale View of Hills* was awarded the Royal Society of Literature's Winifred Holtby Prize and has since been translated into eleven languages. With great subtlety, Ishiguro presents a first-person narrator, Etsuko, a middle-aged Japanese woman, now exiled in England some thirty years after World War II. Traumatized by the recent suicide of her elder daughter, she tells her own story and that of a wayward friend in postwar Nagasaki before she left. Her enigmatic recall, tantalizingly hamstrung by gaps and internal inconsistencies, works toward a dis-quieting and haunting revelation, masterfully embedded in the point of view itself.

Ishiguro's second novel, *An Artist of the Floating World,* is set in the Japan of the late forties. Ono, an aging painter, gropes in his diary entries toward a realization of the ironies of Japan's recent history, in which his own earlier, sincere convictions have enmeshed him. The gently ironic conclusion leaves Ono both humiliated and dignified, a kind of comic Everyman figure, wistfully trapped within his own horizons. Once more, the first-person perspective allows Ishiguro to finesse the confines of a linear plot, and again the author evinces an extraordinary control of voice, an uncannily Japanese quality emanating from his perfectly pitched English prose.

This interview took place on December 8, 1986, in Mr. Ishiguro's South London home. Throughout the course of his remarks, Ishiguro emerges as his own most discriminating interpreter and sternest critic. His meticulous interest in the craft of fiction and lucid grasp of his own aims and methods make this conversation an unusually valuable introduction and companion to the author's works.

[Mason]: *How did your family's move in 1960 from Japan to England affect your upbringing and education?*

[Ishiguro]: My parents have remained fairly Japanese in the way they go about things, and being brought up in a family you tend to operate the way that family operates. I still speak to my parents in Japanese. I'll switch back into Japanese as soon as I walk through the door. But my Japanese isn't very good. It's like a five-year-old's Japanese, mixed in with English vocabulary, and I use all the wrong forms. Apart from that, I've had a typical English education. I grew up in the south of England and went to a typical British school. At Kent University, I studied philosophy and English, and at East Anglia I did an M.A. in creative writing.

Do you feel you're writing in any particular tradition?

I feel that I'm very much of the Western tradition. And I'm quite often amused when reviewers make a lot of my being Japanese and try to mention the two or three authors they've vaguely heard of, comparing me to Mishima or something. It seems highly inappropriate. I've grown up reading Western fiction: Dostoevsky, Chekhov, Charlotte Brontë, Dickens.

Are there any influences from the Japanese side as well?

Tanizaki, Kawabata, Ibuse, and a little Soseki, perhaps. But I'm probably more influenced by Japanese movies. I see a lot of Japanese films. The visual images of Japan have a great poignancy for me, particularly in domestic films like those of Ozu and Naruse, set in the postwar era, the Japan I actually remember.

Your first novel, **A Pale View of Hills,** *also deals with memories of Japan, but they are repressed memories with ellipses that the reader has to work to fill in.*

Yes. In that book, I was trying something rather odd with the narrative. The main strategy was to leave a big gap. It's about a Japanese woman, Etsuko, who is exiled in Britain in middle age, and there's a certain area of her life that's very painful to her. It has something to do with her coming over to the West and the effect it has on her daughter, who subsequently commits suicide. She talks all around it, but she leaves that as a gap. Instead, she tells another story altogether, going back years and talking about somebody she once knew. So the whole narrative strategy of the book was about how someone ends up talking about things they cannot face directly through other people's stories. I was trying to explore that type of language, how people use the language of self-deception and self-protection.

There are certain things, a bit like in Henry James's The Turn of the Screw, *that are just unresolved. For instance, in the pivotal scene on the bridge when Etsuko is talking to her friend Sachiko's daughter Mariko, she switches without warning to addressing the child as if she herself were actually the child's mother. At the most extreme, that leads the reader to ponder whether the two women were not one and the same person.*

What I intended was this: because it's really Etsuko talking about herself, and possibly that somebody else, Sachiko, existed or did not exist, the meanings that Etsuko imputes to the life of Sachiko are obviously the meanings that are relevant to her (Etsuko's) own life. Whatever the facts were about what happened to Sachiko and her daughter, they are of interest to Etsuko now because she can use them to talk about herself. So you have this highly Etsuko-ed version of this other person's story; and at the most intense point, I wanted to suggest that Etsuko had dropped this cover. It just slips out: she's now talking about herself. She's no longer bothering to put it in the third person.

I thought that the effect of this scene was quite stunning.

Yes, that scene itself works all right, if the rest of the book had built up to that kind of ambiguity. But the trouble is that the flashbacks are too clear, in a way. They seem to be related with the authority of some kind of realistic fiction. It doesn't have the same murkiness of someone trying to wade through their memories, trying to manipulate memories, as I would have wanted. The mode is wrong in those scenes of the past. They don't have the texture of memory. And for that reason the ending doesn't quite come off. It's just too sudden. I intended with that scene for the reader finally to realize, with a sense of inevitability, "Of course, yes, she's finally said it." Instead, it's a shock. I didn't quite have the technical sophistication to pull it off, and the result is that it's a bit baffling. Fortunately, a lot of people quite enjoy being baffled. As you say, you're knocked over sideways. You feel you have to read the book again, which is a different sort of effect.

There is a dissonance between the picture that Etsuko paints of herself when back in Japan as a very timid, conventional person and the rather bold, unconventional things she emerges as actually having done: leaving her husband, leaving her homeland, and so on. That's another gap the reader has to wrestle with.

Yes, that's the gap in *A Pale View of Hills.* We can assume that the real Etsuko of the past is somewhat nearer the mousy Etsuko she talks about in the forties than she is to the Sachiko figure. After all, that is her account, the emotional story of how she came to leave Japan, although that doesn't tell you the actual facts. But I'm not interested in the solid facts. The focus of the book is elsewhere, in the emotional upheaval.

In some ways, especially in the dream sections, it seems as if Etsuko is trying to punish herself. She lashes herself with grief and guilt at the suicide of her daughter Keiko. Yet in other ways, it seems as if she's trying to rearrange the past so that she doesn't come out of it too badly. Am I right in seeing these two things?

Yes, the book is largely based around her guilt. She feels a great guilt, that out of her own emotional longings for a different sort of life, she sacrificed her first daughter's happiness. There is that side to her that feels resistant to her younger daughter Nikki, who tells her, "You've got nothing to worry about," and that she did exactly the right thing. She feels that this isn't quite a true account. But on the other hand, she does need to arrange her memories in a way that allows her to salvage some dignity.

There were some partly developed comic themes in **A Pale View of Hills,** *but they didn't quite take hold.*

If you really want to write something, you shouldn't bring things into your book lightly. It's a bit like taking in lodgers. They're going to be with you a long time.
—Kasuo Ishiguro

Yes, whatever echoes I wanted to start between Etsuko and Ogata, the father-in-law, very much faded away. Let's say I was a less experienced writer at that point, and I think that one of the things that happens to less experienced writers is that you cannot control the book, as more experienced writers can. You bring in an element without realizing what the implication of this is on the rest of the book. A lot of the things I was initially most interested in got completely upstaged by things I almost inadvertently set in motion. But you get very excited when you're writing your first novel. And once having figured out these clever little narrative strategies, then you bring in this and you bring in that, and suddenly you find that two-thirds of the book is concerned with something else altogether. The Etusko-Sachiko story about exile and parental responsibility was essentially something which I waylaid myself into. I often would bring in things simply because they worked rather nicely on that particular page in that particular chapter. And suddenly, I'd find myself with a daughter who'd hung herself, or whatever, on my hands and I'd have to figure out how to deal with that. If you really want to write something, you shouldn't bring things into your book lightly. It's a bit like taking in lodgers. They're going to be with you a long time. I think the most important thing I learned between writing the first and second novels is the element of thematic discipline.

What drew you to your subject and to the theme of the older

artist in your second novel, **An Artist of the Floating World***? Were you thinking of anyone in particular, or of any groups?*

Not really, no. I suppose I was thinking of myself and my peers, the generation that came to university in the sixties and the seventies. I write out of a kind of projected fear of reaching a certain age and looking back. I am interested in that particular form of wasting one's talents, not because you spent your whole life lying on your back, not doing anything. I'm interested in people who, in all sincerity, work very hard and perhaps courageously in their lifetimes toward something, fully believing that they're contributing to something good, only to find that the social climate has done a topsy-turvy on them by the time they've reached the ends of their lives. The very things they thought they could be proud of have now become things they have to be ashamed of. I'm drawn to that period in Japanese history because that's what happened to a whole generation of people. They lived in a moral climate that right up until the end of the war said that the most praise-worthy thing they could do was to use their talents to further the nationalist cause in Japan, only to find after the war that this had been a terrible mistake. *An Artist of the Floating World* is an exploration of somebody trying to come to terms with the fact that he has somehow misused his talents unknowingly, simply because he didn't have any extraordinary power of insight into the world he lived in.

Where is **An Artist of the Floating World** *set?*

It's just an imaginary city, for various reasons. Once I set it in an actual city, then the obligation to actually check up would become boringly relevant, and there seemed to be no point. It was of no value to me if I could claim that it's authentically set in Tokyo or not. In fact, in many ways it would play into the hands of a certain kind of misreader, who wished the book to be simply some kind of realist text telling you what Tokyo was like after the war. By setting it in an unspecified venue, I could suggest that I'm offering this as a novel about people and their lives, and that this isn't some piece of documentary writing about a real city. And it just gave me a lot more freedom. If I wanted a pavilion with lanterns around its eaves, I could just invent one. I could invent as many districts as I could think of names. All these things would have been technically rather irksome, if I had had to keep referring to a map, and to the actual history of Tokyo.

The other temptation was to set it in Nagasaki, the only Japanese city I have some familiarity with, and which I could have got some people to tell me about. But of course, overwhelmingly for Western readers, when you bring in Nagasaki they think of the atomic bomb, and I had no place for the atomic bomb in this novel. And so, although possibly I might have been able to refer more or less authentically to Nagasaki landmarks and districts, I didn't want to do it simply because it would have been another bomb book.

Was there any particular reason why you had your central character be a painter, rather than a writer, or even an actor?

No great reason, no. I was not intrinsically interested in painting or painters. It just seemed to me that a painter served my purposes better than some of the other careers. I think it's always dangerous to have a writer in a novel. That leads you into all kinds of areas, unless you're specifically interested in talking about the nature of fiction. But I try to avoid that very postmodern element in my books.

Did you do any research into how painters' groups at the time behaved? What props did you have in imagining these scenes?

I did very little research, primarily because research is only of any interest to me in order to check up after I've done something, to make sure I'm not getting anything wildly wrong. I need certain things to be the way they are in my books for the purposes of my themes. In *An Artist of the Floating World,* I needed to portray this world where a leader figure held this incredible psychological sway over his subordinates. And for subordinates to break free, they had to display a remarkable amount of determination. That's what I needed, and as far as I was concerned, things in my Japan were going to operate like that. I am not essentially concerned with a realist purpose in writing. I just invent a Japan which serves my needs. And I put that Japan together out of little scraps, out of memories, out of speculation, out of imagination.

*In some respects, you have a narrative setup in **An Artist of the Floating World** similar to that in **A Pale View of Hills.** The whole narrative is recounted by a person who is somewhat unreliable, so the reader has to attend to other things to gauge the extent of the unreliability. Ono, the narrator, addresses the reader directly with the book's opening sentence: "If on a sunny day you climb the steep path. . . ." This strikes an almost intimate tone, as if he is talking to a friend or acquaintance. Elsewhere, his account sounds more like an apologia, a public explanation for what he did. Who is the "reader" here, and what exactly is the narrative situation?*

The reader that I intended obviously isn't the "you" that Ono refers to. Ono in his narrative assumes that anybody reading it must live in the city and must be aware of its landmarks. I used that device mainly to create a world. I thought it helped strengthen this mental landscape mapped out entirely by what Ono was conscious of, and nothing else. And

whether the reader registers it consciously or not, it cannot help but create the effect of actually eavesdropping on Ono being intimate with somebody in his own town. To a large extent, the reason for Ono's downfall was that he lacked a perspective to see beyond his own environment and to stand outside the actual values of his time. So the question of this parochial perspective was quite central to the book, and I tried to build that into the whole narrative. At the same time, I'm suggesting that Ono is fairly normal; most of us have similar parochial visions. So the book is largely about the inability of normal human beings to see beyond their immediate surroundings, and because of this, one is at the mercy of what this world immediately around one proclaims itself to be.

With the somewhat doddery narrator's constant digressions, the plot line keeps fanning out all the time. Does this suggest that you're trying to escape from the tyranny of a linear plot?

Yes, yes it does! I don't like the idea that A has to come before B and that B has to come before C because the plot dictates it. I want certain things to happen in a certain order, according to how I feel the thing should be arranged tonally or whatever. I can have Ono in a certain kind of emotional mood or emotional way of talking about things when I want him to be, and it looks like he's just drifted, but from my point of view, it's quite contrived. I've figured out little transitory connecting paragraphs whereby he appears to drift from one section to the next. This might give the sense of his being old and vulnerable, but people to tend to talk like this anyway. And more crucially, people tend to think like this. So I'm not dictated to by the chronology of events, and I can reveal things just when I want to.

And again, there are unresolved points of fact in the narrative, open to varying constructions by the reader.

Yes, As usual, I'm not overwhelmingly interested in what really did happen. What's important is the emotional aspect, the actual positions the characters take up at different points in the story, and why they need to take up these positions.

At the same time, you draw a very explicit thematic parallel between the way Ono's mentor treated him, confiscating his pictures and expelling him from his villa, and the way that Ono subsequently treats his own pupil, Kuroda.

I'm pointing to the master-pupil thing recurring over and over again in the world. In a way, I'm using Japan as a sort of metaphor. I'm trying to suggest that this isn't something peculiar to Japan, the need to follow leaders and the need to exercise power over subordinates, as a sort of motor by which society operates. I'm inviting Western readers to look at this not as a Japanese phenomenon but as a human phenomenon.

In the floating world of urban Tokugawa Japan, with its pleasure quarters and puppet plays, or at least in the art that came out of the floating world, irreconcilable conflicts are often resolved by melodramatic suicides. The title of your book, An Artist of the Floating World, necessarily conjures resonances of this whole tradition. Yet you offer a gently ironic, comic solution to your tale, somewhat at variance with the more melodramatic, conventional expectations of the genre. Life-affirming values prevail, rather than everything descending into a welter of despair or the cliché of suicide. The narrative does hint, at certain points, that Ono's family are worried about such a possibility. Instead, Ono owns up to his errors, makes his accommodation with the changing times, and still manages to cling to a measure of self-vindication. Were you in any sense offering an untraditional or even un-Japanese resolution to his conflict?

Well, you see, I don't feel that it is un-Japanese. A while ago, I published a short story entitled **"A Family Supper."** The story was basically just a big trick, playing on Western readers' expectations about Japanese people who kill themselves. It's never stated, but Western readers are supposed to think that these people are going to commit mass suicide, and of course they do nothing of the sort.

This business about committing *seppuku* or whatever. It's as alien to me as it is to you. And it's as alien to most modern Japanese as it is to Western people. The Japanese are in love with these melodramatic stories where heroes commit suicide, but people in Japan don't go around killing themselves as easily as people in the West assume. And so my book may not have a traditional Japanese story ending in that sense, but a lot of the great Japanese movies of the fifties would not dream of having an ending like that. And if I borrow from any tradition, it's probably from that tradition that tries to avoid anything that is overtly melodramatic or plotty, that tries basically to remain within the realms of everyday experience.

I'm very keen that whenever I portray books that are set in Japan, even if it's not very accurately Japan, that people are seen to be just people. I ask myself the same questions about my Japanese characters that I would about English characters, when I'm asking the big questions, what's really important to them. My experience of Japanese people in this realm is that they're like everybody else. They're like me, my parents. I don't see them as people who go around slashing their stomachs.

What sort of mood did you wish to portray in the narrator, Ono, by the end of the book?

I wanted that slightly painful and bittersweet feeling of him thinking: "Japan made a mess of it, but how marvelous that in a few years it's all set to have a completely fresh go. But a man's life isn't like that. In a man's life, there's only room for this one go." And Ono's done it, he made a go of it, and it didn't turn out well. His world is over, and all he can do is wish the younger generation well, but he is no part of that world. And I was interested in the various strategies somebody would employ to try to salvage some sort of dignity, to get into a position where he could say, "Well, at least X, Y, and Z." In a way, Ono is continually being cornered. He keeps having to admit this and admit that, and in the end he even accepts his own smallness in the world. I suppose I wanted to suggest that a person's dignity isn't necessarily dependent on what he achieves in his life or in his career that there is something dignified about Ono in the end that arises simply out of his being human.

And through the course of his narrative, the reader can see Ono, to preserve his self-esteem, gradually making concessions and accommodations that he himself cannot see?

Yes, that certainly was the intention. It uses very much the diary method. Technically, the advantage of the diary narrative is that each entry can be written from a different emotional position. What he writes in October 1948 is actually written out of a different set of assumptions than the pieces that are written later on. That really was the sole reason for dividing the book up into four chunks, each ostensibly written in a sitting or whatever at the point when the date is given; just so we can actually watch his progress, and so that the language itself changes slightly.

And this in turn underscores the larger theme of the ironies and vicissitudes of the floating world. Having rejected the demimonde "floating world" subjects of his mentor, Ono received the patriotic award for his propagandist poster art and experienced a short moment of triumph. But this too was fleeting.

Yes, that's why he is the artist of the floating world, just as the floating world celebrated transitory pleasures. Even if they were gone by the morning, and they were built on nothing, at least you enjoyed them at the time. The idea is that there are no solid things. And the irony is that Ono had rejected that whole approach to life. But in the end, he too is left celebrating those pleasures that evaporated when the morning light dawned. So the floating world comes to refer, in the larger metaphorical sense, to the fact that the values of society are always in flux.

Your first-person narrators, a late middle-aged woman in A Pale View of Hills and an older man in An Artist of the Floating World, are far removed from you in your personal situation. How did you manage to inhabit these people? Through some kind of imaginative migration?

It never occurred to me that it would be a technical difficulty. It's rather like the question about realism and Japanese details. I didn't start from the point of view of saying, "What does a middle-aged woman think like?" That way you can get very intimidated by the whole project. I needed a certain consciousness, a certain state of mind, and it just naturally followed that this would be a middle-aged woman or an older man. Ono couldn't be anything else.

It is remarkable, for someone writing in English, how much of a Japanese texture your writing achieves. How, for instance, did you set about the problem of projecting differentiated Japanese voices through the medium of the English language?

There are two things. Because I am writing in the first person, even the prose has to conform to the characterization of the narrator. Etusko, in **A Pale View of Hills,** speaks in a kind of Japanese way because she's a Japanese woman. When she sometimes speaks about Japanese things, explaining what a kujibiki stand is, for instance, it becomes clear that she's speaking English and that it's a second language for her. So it has to have that kind of carefulness, and, particularly when she's reproducing Japanese dialogue in English, it has to have a certain foreignness about it.

The thing about Ono in **An Artist of the Floating World** is that he's supposed to be narrating in Japanese; it's just that the reader is getting it in English. In a way the language has to be almost like a pseudotranslation, which means that I can't be too fluent and I can't use too many Western colloquialisms. It has to be almost like subtitles, to suggest that behind the English language there's a foreign language going on. I'm quite conscious of actually figuring these things out when I'm writing, using a certain kind of translationese. Sometimes my ear will say: "That doesn't quite ring true, that kind of language. Fine if this were just English people, but not here."

When you write, do you have anyone who helps you to revise?

I tend to work entirely alone. I have an editor at Faber, Robert McCrumb, who often sees the penultimate draft. In both novels, he made suggestions that were very helpful, but they tend to be pretty minor. Normally he'll point to that part of the book that seems to be weak and ask me to look at it again. But I'll only show him my manuscript when I think it's more or less finished. And I certainly don't do this business of going through the prose with somebody else, page by page.

Do you feel any pressure to experiment formally?

I did at a certain time. When literary people talk about "young writers," they almost imply that this is synonymous with writers who are experimenting. You often read phrases like, "They're smashing up this, or subverting that." So I think that it's very natural to feel that the older generation has somehow already done that, and that now you've got to. But I try not to let it become too central to what I'm writing. The kind of book I find very tedious is the kind of book whose *raison d'être* is to say something about literary form. I'm only interested in literary experiment insofar as it serves a purpose of exploring certain themes with an emotional dimension. I always try to disguise those elements of my writing that I feel perhaps are experimental.

What are you working on now?

I'm writing another novel. This one is set in England. It's about a butler who wants to get close to a great man, close to the center of history. I also write television films. I've written two of these and we're trying to get a third off the ground, this time a cinema film. So I've always got at least two things going, a screenplay and a novel. Filmmaking is very, very different from writing. You shoot to a set schedule, and the crew knocks off at a certain time; otherwise you pay a fortune in overtime. You just haven't got the opportunity to keep doing scenes over and over till they're perfect. It's almost like a concert performance or something, where you've got to get it right, then and there. It's somewhere between a performance art and the more meditative, deliberate production that writing is. In writing, you can rewrite and rewrite and rewrite at no cost, other than what it costs for the paper, and you can spend a long, long time.

How do you see your work developing, and what do you see as your abiding preoccupations?

Well, it's very difficult to say if I'll have the same preoccupations in ten years' time that I have today. There are certain things in my books that I'm not particularly interested in, although they have taken up a fairly important chunk of my writing. I'm not particularly interested in themes about parental responsibility, or even about exile, although these seem to be very much to the fore in the first book. I'm not at all interested in the question of suicide, although I'm aware that that has been in both books in some form or another. But things like memory, how one uses memory for one's own purposes, one's own ends, those things interest me more deeply. And so, for the time being, I'm going to stick with the first person, and develop the whole business about following somebody's thoughts around, as they try to trip themselves up or to hide from themselves.

Merle Rubin (review date 30 November 1989)

SOURCE: A Review of *The Remains of the Day*, in *Christian Science Monitor*, November 30, 1989, p. 13.

[*In the following review of* The Remains of the Day, *Rubin praises Ishiguro's ability to get inside his characters and portray all their complexities.*]

Stevens, the hero of Kazuo Ishiguro's third novel, is the perfect butler. All his life he has sought to embody the ideals of his profession: service, composure, dignity, and discretion. Having reached an age when, although still fully employed, he is starting to think about the shape of the rest of his life—"the remains of the day"—Stevens has set out (with his employer's blessing, to be sure) on a highly unaccustomed (for him) motoring trip. His general aim is to see something of the countryside (where he's lived all his life but never really visited). More specifically, he hopes to persuade Miss Kenton (now Mrs. Benn), a former housekeeper, to return to Darlington Hall, which he hopes will run more smoothly again with her to help him.

Stevens is the narrator of his own story, and his perfect, perfectly parodied, butler's style of speaking can be contagious! That a writer born in Nagasaki in 1954 should have written a novel that so brilliantly captures the voice of a middle-aged English butler in the summer of 1956 reflecting on times past is remarkable, but not really another instance of the current "the Japanese do us better than we do ourselves" syndrome. Ishiguro has, in fact, lived in England since 1960, which makes him almost as English as Stevens, because Stevens (by his own unwitting admission) has tailored his life to produce a complete facade. What makes his narrative so poignant as well as funny, its pathos and satire evenly matched, is the sincerity with which the facade has been cultivated.

As he travels westward, taking in the scenery, Stevens's mind is more on the past than on the landscape. Yet, because he is hardly the sort of person who would launch into any activity as personal—and hence, improper—as recounting his own history, his story begins as a meditation on the "greatness" of the British landscape, which, in his view, consists in its quiet, self-confident lack of conspicuous greatness. This leads him on to consider the "greatness" of Great Britain and greatness in general—which leads, in turn, to the burning question, what constitutes a great butler?

For Stevens, the answer is contained in the word "dignity," a concept that means something different to him than it does to most other people:

> "'Dignity,'" explains Stevens, "has to do . . . with a butler's ability not to abandon the professional being he inhabits. Lesser butlers will abandon their professional being for the private one at the least provocation . . . The great butlers are great by virtue of their ability to inhabit their professional role . . . to the utmost; they will not be shaken out by external events, however surprising, alarming, or vexing. They wear their professionalism as a decent gentleman will wear his suit: he will not let ruffians or circumstances tear it off him in the public gaze . . . "

As the narrative unfolds to reveal those occasions on which Stevens has displayed such dignity, the painful truth becomes ever more evident—to us, if not to him. Dignity for Stevens has consisted in remaining downstairs to serve at an important reception while upstairs his own father is on his deathbed. Dignity has meant voicing no objection, or even regret, when his employer, Lord Darlington, dismisses two servant girls because they are Jewish. In sum, Stevens's dignity has been based upon eviscerating himself both as a private and public person—as a man and as a citizen. He has mistaken the amorality of his professional code for a species of moral idealism: He believes that he has served humanity by having served a great gentleman in a great house.

Lord Darlington, the great gentleman in question, is now deceased. Stevens's current employer—the one who has so kindly encouraged him to take this brief vacation—is an American. Stevens respects him well enough, but his fondness for informality and banter puts Stevens at an uncharacteristic loss.

It's his time with Lord Darlington that Stevens considers the apex of his career in service. Stevens is proud of the contribution he made, but as we gradually discover the nature of what he was contributing to, we—and even Stevens himself—must drastically reevaluate his life's work.

In those years between the two world wars that Stevens served him, Lord Darlington did his best to foster ties between Great Britain and Germany. His gentlemanly, behind-the-scenes diplomacy began as a well-intentioned effort to temper the harsh terms of the Versailles Treaty. But it soon gave way to muddle-headed, but far less innocent, maneuverings on behalf of the Nazi regime. Ignorance, complacency, and upper-class smugness have combined to lead Darlington into a position that eventually tarnishes his name: His attitude and actions have run a course parallel to his butler's folly.

Interestingly enough, Ishiguro's previous novel, ***An Artist of the Floating World,*** explored the soul of a Japanese artist whose sense of mission led him to become involved in the imperialist movement that propelled Japan into World War II. Ishiguro's subtle understanding of both these mentalities—the British butler and the Japanese artist—enables him to portray them from within. ***The Remains of the Day,*** however, relies even more heavily on the narrative of a single character to reveal the blindness of his own sensibility.

Not surprisingly, Ishiguro's use of a narrative voice turned against itself has earned him comparison with Ford Madox Ford. Like *The Good Soldier,* ***The Remains of the Day*** exposes assumptions about class, correct behavior, and the "right kind of people," and exposes them from within, where we can see the damage done to those who presume as well as those who are presumed against.

Delicate, devastating, thoroughly ironic, yet never harsh, this is a novel whose technical achievements are matched by its insightfulness.

Gabriele Annan (review date 7 December 1989)

SOURCE: Gabriele Annan, "On the High Wire," in *New York Review of Books,* December 7, 1989, pp. 3-4.

[In the review below, Annan argues that in Ishiguro's first three novels he has brilliantly portrayed characters who are unable to see their own faults, evoking condemnation and pity.]

Kazuo Ishiguro was born in Japan thirty-five years ago. He came to England when he was six, and has lived there ever since. This is a stranger experience than being Japanese in the United States, where the landscape is dotted with second and third generation Japanese. Even twenty years ago, few Japanese lived in England, and a Japanese child, except in a group of tourists, was a rare sight indeed.

Ishiguro writes in English. His English is perfect, and not just in the obvious sense it is accurate, unhurried, fastidious, and noiseless. A hush seems to lie over it, compounded of mystery and discretion. The elegant bareness inevitably reminds one of Japanese painting. But at the very start of the first novel, ***A Pale View of Hills,*** he warns against such a cliché response. A Japanese girl has committed suicide in England:

> Keiko . . . was pure Japanese, and more than one newspaper was quick to pick up on this fact. The English are fond of their idea that our race has an instinct for suicide, as if further explanations are unnecessary.

In a sense, all three of Ishiguro's novels are explanations, even indictments, of Japanese-ness, and that applies equally to the third novel, ***The Remains of the Day,*** in which no Japanese character appears. He writes about guilt and shame

incurred in the service of duty, loyalty, and tradition. Characters who place too high—too Japanese—a price on these values are punished for it.

In a sense, all three of Ishiguro's novels are explanations, even indictments, of Japanese-ness, and that applies equally to the third novel, *The Remains of the Day,* in which no Japanese character appears.
—*Gabriele Annan*

A Pale View of Hills is eery and tenebrous. It is a ghost story, but the narrator, Etsuko, does not realize that. She is the widow of an Englishman, and lives alone and rather desolate in an English country house. Her elder daughter, Keiko, the child of her Japanese first husband, killed herself some years before. The novel opens during a visit from her younger daughter, Niki, the child of her English second husband. Etsuko recalls her past, but Niki, a brusque, emancipated Western girl, is not very sympathetic. Her visit is uncomfortable and uncomforting, and she cuts it short: not only because of the lack of rapport with her mother, but because she can't sleep. Keiko's unseen ghost keeps her awake.

Etsuko's reminiscences go back to the days just after the war. She is newly married to a boorish company man, and expecting his child. They live in one of the first blocks to be built in the ruins of Nagasaki. Etsuko is lonely and strikes up an acquaintance with an older woman, an embittered post-1945 Madam Butterfly. Sachiko lives in a derelict cottage among the rubble, and receives visits from an American who is always promising to take her to the States, but never does. She has lost everything in the war except her ten-year-old daughter, Mariko. The child is hostile to people but deeply attached to her cat and kittens; her mother leaves her alone for long periods while she goes into Nagasaki about her dubious business. Mariko speaks of visits by a strange, silent woman during her mother's absence. Sachiko explains that this is all imagination, the result of an experience Mariko had in the last days of the war: she saw a woman drown her baby. The woman later killed herself.

Etsuko tries to befriend the disturbed and neglected child, but is rebuffed. Eventually the American lover really seems on the point of taking Sachiko and Mariko away. The kittens are to be left behind. Mariko pleads for them, but her mother drowns them before the child's eyes. Mariko runs away—she has done it before and always come back. Nevertheless, Etsuko insists on going to look for her. It is dark when she finds her by the river. Mariko seems frightened and asks Etsuko why she is trailing a rope. Etsuko replies that it got caught on her foot. Mariko runs from her in terror. The scene is a replay of a earlier occasion when Etsuko also went to retrieve the child, who noticed the rope and fled.

Mariko disappears from the story. Her suicide—actual or just probable—is the second of three, beginning with the woman who drowns her baby and ending with Keiko. They overlay one another like shadows—which they are—on a trebly exposed negative. The fourth shadow is Etsuko herself, though the hint that she too may take her own life is so faint that it may not be there at all. Ishiguro leaves a lot of room for reflection and conjecture, and after one puts down his novels insights go on plopping into one's mind like drops from a tap that is supposed to be turned off.

Etusko feels guilty about having up-rooted Keiko and taken her to England when she remarried. She knew the child would be unhappy in an English environment, though one can be sure she did not force her to leave Japan with the brutality displayed by Sachiko toward her own daughter. Brutality is not part of Etsuko's docile, self-effacing, well-behaved persona—the traditional persona for a Japanese woman of her generation. Even when she was young it was already so much a part of her that she was unable to see how unhappy she was in her role of Japanese wife, or why she could not get through to Mariko. She wanted very much to help the child, but only to become a well-behaved little Japanese girl; and the only method she could think of was to offer her trivial distractions from her obsessions and her misery.

Ishiguro puts across Etsuko's inadequacy behind her back, as it were, even though he does it in her own quiet, resigned, but very faintly smug voice. Her mask never slips: it faces inward as well as outward, blinding her with self-deception. Masks are what Ishiguro's novels are about, and he himself always chooses the mask of a first-person narrator. All the narrators are sedate and formal people so he never needs to drop into any kind of vulgar slang or colloquialism, and hardly to change gear when he allows them to call up a landscape or an atmosphere. Descriptions are as factual and plain as a Morandi still life, but they exude powerful moods and mostly sad ones: nostalgia, regret, resignation.

Just as Etsuko's disapproval of Sachiko in the past and Niki in the present seeps out from under her mask, so does Ishiguro's disapproval of Etsuko herself. The tension of the novel depends on the gradual revelation, clue by clue, of how misguided her behavior has been throughout her life. Ishiguro uses this detective-fiction format in all his novels and with cunning. The narrator is always blind, a well-intentioned person in good standing with him—or herself—when the story begins. The degree of insight and disillusion they attain, the shame and remorse they suffer varies from novel to novel. They never go unpunished, though. Ishiguro is severe, vindictive sometimes; but then he is also very good

at compelling the reader's pity, sometimes with positively Dickensian pressure.

A Pale View of Hills is about private guilt, but it has a small subplot about public guilt as well. Etsuko's first father-in-law is a retired teacher, proud of his old pupils and what he did for them. What he did for them was to imbue them with imperialist values and spur them on to die in a patriotic war. In postwar Nagasaki these ideas are discredited. The old man is attacked in print by one of his former pupils, and treated with contempt by his son, and even by Etsuko.

In the second novel, *An Artist of the Floating World,* the teacher of discredited values is the narrator and main character. Mr. Ono is a retired painter and art master, and as in *A Pale View of Hills,* the story bobs about between reminiscences of different periods of the hero's life. Not that Mr. Ono is a hero: in fact, he is the least admirable and sympathetic of Ishiguro's chief characters, an opportunist and timeserver, adapting his views and even his artistic style to the party in power. So it comes that in the Thirties he deserts his first, westernizing master of painting for the strict, old-fashioned style and patriotic content of the imperialist, propaganda art.

An Artist of the Floating World shows the traditional Japanese atelier system of art training in operation. The pupils all work in the master's studio; in this case they even live together in his villa. The arrangement is charming and convivial up to a point: but there is a lot of unkind teasing, ostracizing, and jockeying for position. Still, the students develop a mutual sense of loyalty, especially toward the master, far more intense than loyalties bred on a Western campus. So Ono's breakaway is seen as a betrayal, and causes much pain.

Worse still, he denounces a dissident colleague to the police, but he remains able to persuade himself that all his apparent disloyalties spring from the best of motives—in this case concern for the future of Japan. His own favorite creation is a painting of boys arming for war while politicians debate; he calls it *Complacency.* The title would fit the novel itself: It is a wry and funny novel, with the comedy springing from Ono's impregnable self-regard in the face of every kind of humiliation.

The plot hinges on the difficulty of getting Ono's younger daughter married. One match has already fallen through, and delicate negotiations are in progress to arrange another. Ono's daughters persuaded him that the first attempt failed because of his political past. So during the traditional miai—a dinner arranged by the marriage broker to bring the families together—Ono takes it upon himself to confess that he made political mistakes. Everyone is terribly embarrassed, except for Ono, who manages to extend his complacency to being proud of his courageous admission. The marriage takes place, but the irony is that it does not depend on Ono's admission at all. The bridegroom's family, and Ono's family too, consider him much too unimportant for his political record to be of any consequence. But even when his eight-year-old grandson begins to patronize him, his smugness is unshaken, his optimism undiminished. The little macho grandson is a beguiling comic portrait, and the novel as a whole is highly enjoyable, especially for the author's delicate duplicity toward his hero.

It could be called a comedy—just. Ishiguro's third book, ***The Remains of the Day,*** is a tragedy in comedy form, both played to the hilt: it is more harrowing than the first book, more broadly funny than the second, but in spite of having recently won the Booker Prize in London, it has more flaws than the others and seems more naive. This time Ishiguro impersonates an aging English butler—one can't help seeing the work as a performance, an act put on with dazzling daring and aplomb. The chronological template is the same as before: from a Fifties present Mr. Stevens recalls the Twenties and Thirties, when he worked for Lord Darlington.

Ishiguro gives a virtuoso performance, telling the story in the old man's pompous, deferential voice. A Japanese soul (or at any rate Ishiguro's critical version of the Japanese soul) could not have chosen a better body to transmigrate into than Stevens's: the butler runs on loyalty, devotion, propriety, and pride in his profession, and after much rumination he decides that the most important quality for a great butler—which his father was and he aspires to be—is dignity. He arrives at this conclusion during a meeting of the Hayes Society, a group of upper-echelon butlers who meet to discuss the finer points of their "profession" with other "professionals."

Sometimes the ghost of P.G. Wodehouse gets into the works. It causes havoc when Stevens tries to carry out instructions to explain the facts of life to Lord Darlington's godson, a young man who has just become engaged to be married. Stevens never gets very far because he keeps being interrupted by the demands of the French foreign secretary, who is staying in the house and wants him to attend to the blisters he got from too much sightseeing. The episode is about as convincing as a country house charade.

While it is going on, Steven's old father lies dying upstairs. Too frail to go on as head butler in his old post, he has joined Lord Darlington's household as second butler, serving under his own son. Their relations are strictly "professional," without intimacy or warmth. One day the old man falls with a trayful of tea things: he has had his first stroke. His duties are curtailed until all he is allowed to do is push a trolley. The second and final stroke comes on during an important house party: Stevens is too busy with the guests to be with his father when he dies. He just carries on:

> If you consider the pressures contingent on me that night, you may not think I delude myself unduly if I go so far as to suggest that I did perhaps display, in the face of everything, at least in some modest degree a "dignity" worthy of someone like Mr. Marshall [a model "great" butler]—or come to that, my father.

Ishiguro specializes in the humiliations and sorrows of old age, and I found old Stevens's end as afflicting as Dickens's readers found the deathbed scene of Jo the crossing-sweeper boy.

Stevens sacrifices to his profession not only filial affection, but his own prospect of happiness. Miss Kenton joins the household as housekeeper. She is almost impeccable, and we watch Stevens becoming obsessed with her. Their relationship is prickly: if porcupines had a mating dance it would be like this. Still, the edgy repartee is the nearest thing to a love scene in any of Ishiguro's novels, and there has been no sex at all so far—Miss Kenton makes overtures, Stevens pretends not to notice, and when he hears her sobbing in her room, he pretends he may have been mistaken. "Why, Mr. Stevens, why, why, why do you always have to *pretend?*" she says, and makes a loveless match with another man.

Lord Darlington, in Stevens's eyes, is the truly distinguished employer a butler has to have in order to be a truly distinguished butler. He is an *eminence grise* in British politics: his house parties are arranged to further certain causes, and Stevens is convinced that by helping to make the arrangements perfect he is serving not only a great man but his country as well. There is a problem about Lord Darlington though: we watch him develop from a chivalrous critic of the Versailles Treaty into a Nazi sympathizer. Admirers of Hitler gather at Darlington Hall: Her von Ribbentrop is among the guests: an Anglo-German alliance is being plotted.

After the war Lord Darlington dies, discredited and broken, but Stevens's loyalty to his memory is unshaken. Darlington Hall has been taken over by an American, and Stevens with it, an authentic English butler to go with the authentic Chippendale. Mr. Farraday's genial style is very different from Lord Darlington's hauteur, and the novel opens with Stevens resolving to learn how to banter, since Mr. Farraday's seems to expect bantering from him. It is a move in the direction of democracy, and Stevens is proud of his own progressive attitude in making it. When Mr. Farraday takes a holiday he encourages Stevens to do the same. It will be Stevens's first, and Mr. Farraday lends him a car.

Stevens motors sedately towards Cornwall, where the former Miss Kenton has settled. A letter telling him that she has left her husband has given him an inspiration: she might consider returning to Darlington Hall, where an extra pair of capable hands would not come amiss. Stevens manages to have trouble with his engine, run out of petrol, lose his way. These mishaps may symbolize his incompetence in the face of real life, but they themselves are much less competently handled than the rest of the book. Stevens encounters specimens of ordinary, warm-hearted, decent humanity; each one is an argument for spontaneity, openness, and democracy, and against Japaneseness. They are wooden and implausible, but not as implausible as the sacked maids we read about earlier on: Ishiguro wants us to believe that in the early Thirties there were two Jewish maids on the Darlington Hall staff, and that Lord Darlington instructed Stevens to sack them (he did, of course). I would be prepared to bet that before the arrival of the first German refugees no Jewish maid had ever been seen in an English country house: not for anti-Semitic reasons, but because Jews didn't go in for domestic service. Still, this is Ishiguro's only gross sociological error.

When Stevens finally has his rendezvous with the former Miss Kenton over tea in his hotel, it turns out that she has made it up with her husband.

> It took me a moment or two to fully digest these words of Miss Kenton. Moreover, as you might appreciate, their implications were such as to provoke a certain degree of sorrow within me. Indeed—why should I not admit it?—at that moment, my heart was breaking.

On the homeward journey Stevens breaks down and bursts into tears while defending Lord Darlington to yet another person he happens to meet:

> He chose a certain path in life, it proved to be a misguided one, but there, he chose it, he can say that at least. As for myself, I cannot even claim that. You see, I *trusted.* I trusted in his lordship's wisdom. All those years I served him, I trusted I was doing something worthwhile. I can't even say I made my own mistakes. Really—one has to ask oneself—what dignity is there in that?

Still, he pulls himself together and returns to the pursuit of perfect butlering.

> It occurs to me, furthermore, that bantering is hardly an unreasonable duty for an employer to expect a professional to perform. I have of course already devoted much time to developing my bantering skills, but it is possible I have never previously ap-

proached the task with the commitment I might have done.

Compared to his astounding narrative sophistication, Ishiguro's message seems quite banal: Be less Japanese, less bent on dignity, less false to yourself and others, less restrained and controlled. The irony is that it is precisely Ishiguro's beautiful restraint and control that one admires. . . .
—Gabriele Annan

The end is touching, but all the same, *The Remains of the Day* is too much a *roman à thèse,* and a judgmental one besides. Compared to his astounding narrative sophistication, Ishiguro's message seems quite banal: Be less Japanese, less bent on dignity, less false to yourself and others, less restrained and controlled. The irony is that it is precisely Ishiguro's beautiful restraint and control that one admires, and, in the case of the last novel, his nerve in setting up such a high-wire act for himself.

Hermione Lee (review date 22 January 1990)

SOURCE: Hermione Lee, "Quiet Desolation," in *New Republic*, January 22, 1990, pp. 36-9.

[*In the review below, Lee discusses the relative influence of Japanese and English culture on Ishiguro's first three novels.*]

On the strength of three dazzling short novels, Kazuo Ishiguro is now, at 35, a famous prize-winning writer in Britain. (Hardly anyone in America had heard of him until this year, but that's changing.) Still, I notice that people are always getting the titles of his books slightly wrong. Is it *A Pale View of the Hills? The Artist of the Floating World,* or *Artist of the Floating World,* or *The Artist of a Floating World?* *The Remains of the Day* sometimes loses its first definite article. Like all slight but persistent mistakes— Ishiguro's characters are much given to them—these are symptomatic slips.

For Ishiguro's titles do indeed contain evasive articles. "An" artist (unlike Joyce's definitive portrait of "the" artist) is open to amendment and uncertainty, and the floating world he portrays, and betrays, is "transient, illusory." It's not "the hills," but "hills"—some, where?—and it's not they that are pale, but the view of them, as if paleness were a quality of the haunted, ghostly viewer, who describes herself as having "spent many moments—as I was to do throughout succeeding years—gazing emptily at the view from my apartment window . . . a pale outline of hills . . . not an unpleasant view." The "remains" are ambiguous, too: Are they waste, ruins, leftovers, or are they what is salvaged? Is this a metaphorical day, as in "our day is done," or is it "a day in the life"?

The titles hover on the borders of allegory. The openings of the three novels give off a similarly puzzling and contingent air:

> Niki, the name we finally gave my younger—daughter, is not an abbreviation; it was a compromise I reached with her father. For paradoxically it was he who wanted to give her a Japanese name, and I—perhaps out of some selfish desire not to be reminded of the past—insisted on an English one. He finally agreed to Niki, thinking it had some vague echo of the East about it.
>
> [*A Pale View of Hills*]

> If on a sunny day you climb the steep path leading up from the little wooden bridge still referred to around here as "the Bridge of Hesitation," you will not have to walk far before the roof of my house becomes visible between the tops of two gingko trees. Even if it did not occupy such a commanding position on the hill, the house would still stand out from all others nearby, so that as you come up the path, you may find yourself wondering what sort of wealthy man owns it.
>
> But then I am not, nor have I ever been, a wealthy man.
>
> [*An Artist of the Floating World*]

> It seems increasingly likely that I really will undertake the expedition that has been preoccupying my imagination now for some days.
>
> [*The Remains of the Day*]

All three speakers introduce themselves by way of fine distinctions between appearances and actuality, intentions and achievements. The effect is punctilious but cryptic. All three demur from the positive: the apparent nickname, the commanding house, the preoccupying journey are not straightforwardly arrived at. Something is being denied or held off. The artist's invitation into his floating world is itself a "bridge of hesitation," picking its way through hypotheses, negatives, qualifiers, so that "you may find yourself wondering" about the status, the emotions, and the reliability of the narrator. The opening of *A Pale View of Hills* names "compromise" and "paradox" as its subjects, and tells us that a short name—like a short novel—need not be an "abbreviation" of these subjects, a lightweight version of something

larger, but may be a very exact expression of them. And the "confession" of the third narrator immediately induces uncertainty ("seems"? "likely"? "really will"? What is the problem, what is he not telling us yet?), not least because of its peculiar formality, its air of being written in translation.

Part of Ishiguro's appeal is the novelty he seems to provide of a "translation," a little bridge, between Japanese culture and English writing. But the abbreviation at the start of the first novel sets up the paradoxes here. The Japanese-looking name is actually a mixed product of the narrator's desire to get away from Japan to England, and of her husband's romantic attraction (like the attraction some of Ishiguro's Western readers feel?) to "an echo of the East." What looks to a Western reader like a Japanese text may have a Western content for an Oriental reader. Ishiguro was born of Japanese parents in Nagasaki in 1954, but they came to England when he was only six, and he has only once gone back. So far he has made three variants of his translated identity. *A Pale View of Hills* poises itself between England and Japan, *An Artist of the Floating World* is set entirely in Japan, *The Remains of the Day* entirely in England.

A Pale View of Hills is told by Etsuko, a Japanese widow living alone in an English village, haunted by two layers of memory, which are hesitantly and evasively broached. The more recent retrospect is on the visit of her younger daughter, Niki, the entirely Westernized daughter of an English father. The visit follows the suicide of Etsuko's older daughter, Keiko, Niki's half-sister, who had left home some years before in a state of very serious depression, and was found hanging in her rented room. After leaving her first husband, a conventional Japanese businessman, Etsuko brought Keiko to England when she was seven. She approaches her unacknowledged guilt about what she may have done to her older daughter indirectly, by way of her more distant memories of a hot post-war summer in Nagasaki, when she was pregnant with Keiko.

In a surreal landscape of new apartments built over a wasteland of destruction, Etsuko remembers that summer's friendship with a single woman—a rather dubious, louche character—and her daughter. The woman, Sachiko, is waiting to be taken away from Japan by her American lover; her daughter, Mariko, a disturbed little girl, resents the lover, fastens all her affection on her cats, and is haunted by the sight of a woman drowning her child in the nightmare of wartime Tokyo. Child-murders and suicides push into the edges of the narrative. Sachiko drowns the cats; Mariko—possibly—kills herself. These images of despair are crosscut against older figures who are surviving out of total loss and destruction: the woman who runs a noodle shop and whose children were killed by the bomb; Etsuko's father-in-law, a well-intentioned retired teacher, who laments the lost spirit of Japan and is discredited by the next generation for doing what he thought was right.

In *An Artist of the Floating World,* that figure of the discredited old teacher becomes central. Masuji Ono, a "retired" painter whose life encapsulates, though he doesn't quite realize it, the history of 20th-century Japan, narrates his story piecemeal, with Ishiguro's characteristic strategies of pauses, repetitions, and slow accumulations of a half-admitted past. The "action"—it takes place in 1948 and 1949, in an unnamed but eloquently rendered Tokyo—is (as in all these novels) of a visit. Ono's married daughter comes with her little boy, Ichiro, to discuss wedding plans for her sister, whose previous attempts at marriage have been sabotaged, it seems, by Ono's postwar reputation.

As the difficult old man and the belligerent little boy establish a tender and funny relationship (Ishiguro writes extremely well about children), we begin to gather the salient facts: that his son and his wife have been killed in the war, that an old friend and mentor, Matsuda, is dying, that his patriotic work for the Empire ("artist and member of the Cultural Committee of the Interior Department") is now dismissed as a negligible ingredient in the dishonored past. As his grandson puts it, brutally: "Father said you had to finish. Because Japan lost the war."

Gradually, reluctantly, the old man's memory tracks back through an unsettling mist of self-deception. The story is of a series of bold moves for advancement. As a young man he defied a traditional, authoritarian father to become a painter, going to the big city in 1913 to work for a commercial artist's studio, where they turned out "Japanese"-looking geishas and cherry trees for foreign consumption. He left this trade for the studio of a distinguished painter, Moriyama, described as a kind of Japanese Degas, his subject the "floating world" of erotic beauty, the courtesans and pavilions and parties of a way of life that, like the old "pleasure districts" of the city, have been wiped out by the war.

Ono betrays his master, moving with the times (under the influence of the pragmatic Matsuda) from "escapist" romantic art to relevant social realism, and then, in the 1930s, to imperialist propaganda. (This is nicely illustrated by his reworking of a satirical painting of Japanese society, *Complacency,* which he turns into an advertisement for militant nationalism and retitles *Eyes to the Horizon,* with the caption "Japan must go forward.") Ono's opportunism (like the actor-manager in *Mephisto*) involves the betrayal of a friend and pupil for decadence and lack of patriotic spirit. It is a betrayal that haunts him. We are made to see, though—and it's the novel's most painful and delicate operation, as well as a form of comedy—that he has not been an evil or a dangerous man, only inadequate. As the dying Matsuda says to him:

There's no need to blame ourselves unduly. . . . We at least acted on what we believed and did our utmost. It's just that in the end we turned out to be ordinary men. Ordinary men with no special gifts of insight. It was simply our misfortune to have been ordinary men during such times.

Still, Ono does blame himself unduly. Like the writers of patriotic songs and the political leaders who are making their public apologies after the war by killing themselves (and this may be what Ono is about to do), he has internalized the country's shame, and is "floating" without the ballast of his self-esteem. What sounds at first like a carefully controlled voice turns out to be a man desperately trying to hold together his sense of himself.

Like all true novelists, Ishiguro is obsessional; and *The Remains of the Day* reworks his obsession with false control and self-deception. The novel is an extraordinary act of mimicry, an impeccably professional miming of the thoughts of an impeccable professional. There are close similarities with *An Artist of the Floating World.* Like Ono, the English butler Stevens has committed his life to an ideal of service, an ideal that is repeatedly analyzed in the course of his narrative. One of the pleasures of the book is that his profession is such an unlikely subject for a novel. Butlers in British fiction are a joke, associated with *The Importance of Being Earnest,* Jeeves, country-house thrillers, and "What the Butler Saw." Ishiguro's cunning is to invoke these associations—Stevens, after all, is a comic figure, pompous, funny, antiquated, and obtuse—and turn them to serious ends.

Stevens's burning question—we are asked to imagine it debated in the servants' halls in rather the way Japanese art students discuss the future of Japanese art—is, What makes a great butler? It seems a ludicrously quaint question to put at the center of a contemporary novel. But the debate, characteristically hovering on the edge of allegory, comes to be read, in part, as an analysis of "ordinary" people's political responsibilities.

Our butler has inherited from his father a belief that "greatness" in his profession consists not just of unflawed professional excellence, but of three deeper qualities: "dignity," either innate or acquired through "years of self-training and the careful absorbing of experience"; a life of service dedicated to "a great gentlemen" and through him to "humanity"; and, above all, the total "inhabiting" of the role, a professional being to be worn like a suit of clothes, not a "façade" or a "pantomime."

Like Ono's artistic creation, the butler's ideal of service is defined as a form of patriotism. No country but England has great butlers. And, like Ono's, his patriotism is entirely discredited by the end. Steven's "great gentleman," Lord

Darlington, proves to have been a well-meaning but disastrous meddler in Anglo-German relations between the wars, a critic of the Versailles Treaty who became a dupe of the Nazis. Their ruthless "professionalism" gives another meaning to the word, and exposes it as a dangerous and dubious standard for living. Stevens's lifetime of commitment to Darlington (whose name has been as disgraced as the prewar Japanese leaders, as disgraced as Mosley) has involved getting rid of Jewish housemaids, waiting on von Ribbentrop, listening in on debates over the futility of democracy.

Now, in July 1956, the summer of the Suez crisis (like the bombing of Nagasaki in the earlier novel, it is not directly mentioned), Darlington Hall has been bought by a rich American. (Like England? Like Japan?) Stevens is a part of his new master's investment in a piece of authentic old England. He has been allowed out for a motoring trip, which is also a quest journey, through southwest England. On his quest, he encounters some rather artificial-sounding villagers, who discuss, inconclusively, the rights of ordinary British citizens.

Set at the terminal point of British imperialism, and, perhaps, of ordinary English people's faith in their leaders, *The Remains of the Day* reveals the vulnerability of societies based on traditional hierarchies and habits of trust. Stevens's bewildered, pathetic argument for the innocence of loyalty could apply to all who assume that those in authority are to be relied on:

> One is simply accepting an inescapable truth: that the likes of you and I will never be in a position to comprehend the great affairs of today's world, and our best course will always be to put our trust in an employer we judge to be wise and honorable, and to devote our energies to the task of serving him to the best of our ability.... It is hardly my fault if his lordship's life and work have turned out today to look, at best, a sad waste—and it is quite illogical that I should feel any regret or shame on my own account.

Thus far, *The Remains of the Day* replays the themes of *An Artist of the Floating World,* with less complexity and less historical inwardness. There could be grounds for saying that, like an inferior butler whose role keeps slipping, it is only "pretending" to be an English novel. Really it's a Japanese one in disguise, and our formal, archaic butler is standing in for the classic Japanese figure of the *ronin,* the faithful servant left without a master. Certainly Ishiguro does invoke such Japanese items: Sachiko is a version of Madame Butterfly, and Ono speaks of gathering his men like an old warlord. In all three novels there is an un-English insistence on the link between paternal inheritance and honor. Ono's encouragement of his grandson's juvenile machismo is echoed

in *The Remains of the Day.* Stevens's best example of "greatness" is his own father, flawlessly attentive to a general whose incompetence in the Boer War was directly responsible for the futile death of his older son, Stevens's lost brother. (He is one of several lost siblings who haunt Ishiguro's novels.) And Stevens is extremely proud of having been so committed to Lord Darlington's service that he was unable to be present at his own father's death.

The appalling paternal legacy of repression and stultification suggests not a "Japanese" novel dressed in transparent English clothes, but a novel whose crucial subject is something other—something more—than a political inquiry into habits of service. *The Remains of the Day,* unlike Ishiguro's other novels, is a love story. Stevens's country drive is in quest of the ex-housekeeper, Miss Kenton, who left the Hall some years before to get married, but whose letters have suggested that she may be unhappy. Stevens, as his father once did, is beginning to make mistakes in his work; he has too much to look after. Perhaps Miss Kenton—no, Mrs. Benn—might be persuaded to return? Through the refusals of feeling in Stevens's voice, we understand that she once tried to penetrate the "pretence" he "inhabits," to get through to the private self he is so committed to concealing. After their reunion, as his day closes, Stevens at last realizes what he has refused: his life itself, his only chance.

Since what has been suppressed is the true story, the cauterized narrative voice through which we read the suppressions is constantly stopping, going around, repeating itself, picking its way through a landscape of lost opportunities and stifled emotions:

> But what is the sense in forever speculating what might have happened had such and such a moment turned out differently? One could presumably drive oneself to distraction in this way. In any case, while it is all very well to talk of "turning points," one can surely only recognize such moments in retrospect. Naturally, when one looks back to such instances today, they may indeed take the appearance of being crucial, precious moments in one's life; but of course, at the time, this was not the impression one had. Rather, it was as though one had available a never-ending number of days, months, years in which to sort out the vagaries of one's relationship with Miss Kenton: an infinite number of further opportunities in which to remedy the effect of this or that misunderstanding. There was surely nothing to indicate at the time that such evidently small incidents would render whole dreams forever irredeemable.

"Such evidently small incidents" are rendered with heartbreaking quietness. In one of these, Stevens and Miss Kenton look out the twilit gardens of the Hall, to see Stevens's old father, who has just humiliatingly tripped (with a full tea-tray) on the steps up to the summer-house, going up and down them in the dusk, trying to memorize them. Ishiguro can make such small incidents seem catastrophic. They take place in a dark landscape, often foggy or dusky, vaguely invoking regret and remorse. So, at the end of the novel, Stevens sits on Weymouth Pier, watching the lights come on and the crowds go by, weeping in the dark on his "bench of desolation."

Ishiguro often reminds me, as there, of Henry James, especially of Lambert Strether, urging others to take the second chance he never had: "Live all you can. . . . It's a mistake not to." To accuse Ishiguro of costive, elegant minimalism is to miss the deep sadness, the boundless melancholy that opens out, like the "deserts of vast eternity" his characters are reluctantly contemplating, under the immaculate surface.

Kazuo Ishiguro with Allan Vorda and Kim Herzinger (interview date 2 April 1990)

SOURCE: "Stuck on the Margins: An Interview with Kazuo Ishiguro," in *Face to Face: Interviews with Contemporary Novelists,* edited by Allan Vorda, Rice University Press, 1993, pp. 1-35.

[*In the following interview, which was conducted on April 2, 1990, Ishiguro discusses Japanese and British culture, perceptions of himself in each country, and how these perceptions have helped and hindered his career as a writer. Questions are posed by Vorda unless otherwise noted.*]

Kazuo Ishiguro was born in Nagasaki, Japan, in 1954, and emigrated to Britain in 1960. He attended the University of Kent at Canterbury and received an M.A. in creative writing from the University of East Anglia. In 1982 he was included in the original "Best of Young British Novelists" after having become a British citizen earlier that year. He is the author of three novels, and each has received a literary award: *A Pale View of Hills* was awarded the Winifred Holtby Prize by the Royal Society of Literature in 1982; *An Artist of the Floating World* won the 1986 Whitbread Book of the Year Award; and *The Remains of the Day* won the Booker Prize in 1989, Britain's top literary award. He currently lives in London with his wife, Lorna MacDougall, and their daughter.

The interview with Kazuo Ishiguro occurred on April 2, 1990, in Houston, where the author was a guest of the Houston International Festival. (Additional questions were provided by Kim Herzinger of the *Mississippi Review.*) Originally, we were to conduct the interview in his hotel downtown, but when I arrived Ishiguro seemed restless. Courteously, he asked if the interview could be conducted somewhere else, since he had been cooped up in his hotel for three days. We drove to my house in Sugarland, a sprawling suburb southwest of Houston, and conducted the interview in the kitchen, with Ishiguro talking and sipping ice water. As we talked, I studied his face with its broad Oriental planes and features and listened to his very clipped British accent, a startling juxtaposition—at first. During the course of the interview, I came to realize that this was an extraordinary young writer with a tremendous understanding of his craft. At the end of the interview, Ishiguro asked if we could have a late lunch of Mexican food since he never could find it in England.

[*Herzinger*]: *Last year, just before you went back to Japan for the first time since you left at the age of six, you were somewhat worried that the Japanese would expect you to know a great deal more about the culture and the country than you actually did. Were your fears realized?*

[Ishiguro]: Not really. It's partly because they knew I was coming. I had a very kind of closeted journey to Japan. I was invited by the Japan Foundation, which is part of the government, so there was always an escort hanging around. In fact, there was far more media interest in me than I had anticipated. I caused a great stir in the press—not because they were particularly interested in me as a literary figure—but because I touched a *strange nerve* from the social aspect. Japan is, at the moment and perhaps for the first time, facing the idea that they cannot remain a homogeneous society.

This question about immigrants from Southeast Asia as well as a greater number of Western people living in Japan has started up a process. They now have to start thinking about what it means to be Japanese and what sort of country Japan might be. This has suddenly become a live-wire issue. This idea that somebody who is racially Japanese and looks very Japanese could go to England and have lost his Japaneseness in some ways is at the same time fascinating and I think rather threatening. So there was all this interest in what kind of person I was and what messages I could bring and what the West thought about Japan. They somehow thought that I was somebody they could actually ask. So I found myself put in that sort of false territory there.

I was on TV and I did a lot of interviews and things—but very rarely about literature. There were always these questions about what do people think of Japan and what did I think of Japan.

[*Vorda*]: *Did you respond in Japanese?*

No, I spoke English all the time and I was advised to do so.

Really just to avoid this confusion—that was my way of saying I'm not a regular Japanese guy. My Japanese isn't good enough anyway to speak correctly. I could make myself understood, but in Japan that is not enough. There are about seven or eight different ways to say the same thing depending on how you perceive the status of the person you are speaking to, vis-à-vis yourself. To get this kind of thing even slightly wrong produces tremendous offense. It's terribly hierarchy-conscious society, although, in a curious way, it is a classless society. It means people aren't worrying about whether they are upper class or middle class or working class. They are worrying about what number they are on the ladder.

Did the people there like the answers you gave them, or did your answers increase their xenophobia?

I avoided giving any clear-cut answers, but I think just my very being is a kind of embodiment of the whole issue.

A lot of Japanese are starting to properly travel for the first time, and by this I don't mean just as tourists. Business and international trade means that they are spending more time abroad. Of course, they have children who are growing up abroad. This is something that some people say is good and others say is horrifying because their Japaneseness is going to become dissipated. The fear is that these people and their children will come back to Japan having lost something, such as eating with chopsticks, which is part of the cultural tradition.

A lot of the younger Japanese, particularly in Tokyo, know very little about things that people in the West consider to be traditionally Japanese. They don't even know how to put on the kimono. (I suppose I would be a good example since I don't know.) If you do it the wrong way around—the left on the inside or the right on the outside or whichever way it is—it's a terrible blunder because one way you only do to a corpse; living people have it the other way, and I never can remember which way it is. But what was interesting is a lot of the young Japanese don't know because they don't wear kimonos and they don't know a lot of the basic things. The younger kids, particularly in Tokyo, are kind of like Western kids in that sense. It is a kind of baffling, weird thing from a bygone era.

They also eat meat all the time. I was shocked at how tall they were as well. Anyone under thirty is six or seven inches taller on average than anyone over thirty. This is partly due to eating American junk food, so, of course, they may not live as long.

The older Japanese are small, but they live a long time. I think they still have the longest life expectancy in the indus-

trialized world, although sometimes the Scandinavian countries compete in this area.

Thus, the whole trip was interesting and I think it's the way the world is going now since we're becoming much more international. America has always had this melting pot reputation, and now Britain has to face up to the question of multiculturalism. The Japanese are beginning to realize it's going to be their turn since Japan is the last large industrialized country that hasn't yet faced this problem.

You stated in the New York Times Book Review *that, "Publicity for me has to a large extent been fighting the urge to be stereotyped by people." Do you think the stereotyping is due to your ethnicity and to the fact that your first two novels were set in Japan?*

There is a kind of paradox about my books being set in Japan and whether this stereotypes me or not. In Britain, around the time when I published my first novel, the climate had actually turned toward a great deal of interest in writers who wrote books set in that particular setting. I think there was a very peculiar thing going on in Great Britain at that time. I tend to think if I didn't have a Japanese name and if I hadn't written books at that stage set in Japan, it would have taken me years longer to get the kind of attention and sales that I got in England with my first two books. What happened in Britain, certainly during the time when I was at university, contemporary fiction was, I won't say dead, but it seemed to be the preserve of a very small strata of a very small British society. We all had this image of contemporary British novels being written by middle-aged women for middle-aged middle-class women.

Some of them are good and some of them are appalling, but that wasn't one of the exciting things that was happening when I was growing up. Anyone interested in the creative arts was interested in theater. There was a whole explosion with a kind of radical theater. Rock music, cinema, and even television—because we have quite serious arts television in Great Britain—were the kind of things that everyone was talking about while the novel had a kind of sleepy, provincial, cozy, inward-looking kind of image and no one was interested in it.

Around 1979 and 1980 things changed very rapidly. There was a whole new generation of publishers and a whole new generation of journalists who came of age at that time, and they desperately wanted to find a new generation of writers to rediscover the British novel. I think there was something wider going on in English society at that time, too. There was an awareness that Britain was a more international place, a more cosmopolitan place, but it wasn't the center of the world. It was kind of a slightly peripheral, albeit still quite wealthy, country. It started to be aware of its place within the context of the whole international scene. In the early 1980s there was an explosion of tremendous interest in literature that suddenly appeared almost overnight. This occurred in foreign-language literature with people like García Márquez, Milan Kundera, and Mario Vargas Llosa, who became very trendy people. At the same time, there was a whole generation of younger British writers who often had racial backgrounds that were not the typical white Anglo-Saxon. Even some of the "straight" English writers were also using settings or themes that tend to be international or historical. So there definitely was this atmosphere where people were looking for this young, exotic—although exotic may be somewhat of an unkind word—writer with an international flavor. I was very fortunate to have come along at exactly the right time. It was one of the few times in the recent history of British arts in which it was an actual plus to have a funny foreign name and to be writing about funny foreign places. The British were suddenly congratulating themselves for having lost their provincialism at last.

The big milestone was the Booker Prize going to Salman Rushdie in 1981 for *Midnight's Children.* He previously had been a completely unknown writer. That was a real symbolic moment, and then everyone was suddenly looking for other Rushdies. It so happened that around this time I brought out **A Pale View of Hills.** Usually first novels disappear, as you know, without a trace. Yet I received a lot of attention, got lots of coverage, and did a lot of interviews. I know why this was. It was because I had this Japanese face and this Japanese name and it was what was being covered at the time.

I tend to think I got a very easy ride from the critics. I subsequently have won literary prizes with each book, which is very important in Britain, career-wise. It's one of the things that help you climb the ladder. All these things sort of happened to me, and I think it greatly helped that I was identified as this kind of person.

Yet, after a while, this became very restricting, and the very things that helped me in the first place started to frustrate me as an artist and as a serious writer. I don't want to be confined by these things even though they were quite helpful publicity-wise.

[*Herzinger*]: *In Britain there is a rather large community of extremely important and active writers who come from, or often write about, cultures quite different from the English, Irish, Scottish, and Welsh. I'm thinking of V. S. Naipaul, Salman Rushdie, William Body, Lisa St. Aubin de Teran, Doris Lessing, Ruth Prawer Jhabvala, and even Americans like Paul Theroux, David Plante, and Russell Hoban. Do you find yourself grouped with them often? Do you mind it? Do you resist it? Do you think such a grouping is of any use in coming to grips with your work?*

Like any writer, I resist being put in a group. The group you mentioned there is quite an eclectic one. I'm usually put in a much more narrow group—usually with Rushdie and a writer called Timothy Mo, who probably isn't that well known in America.

He's a Chinese-British writer who is quite prominent in Britain and has been nominated for the Booker Prize twice. He hasn't won it yet.

I write so differently than someone like Rushdie. My style is almost the antithesis of Rushdie's or Mo's. Their writing tends to have these quirks where it explodes in all kinds of directions. Rushdie's language always seems to be reaching out—to express meaning that can't usually be expressed through normal language. Just structurally his books have this terrific energy. They just grow in every direction at once, and he doesn't particularly care if the branches lead nowhere. He'll let it grow anyway and leave it there, and that's the way he writes. I think he is a powerful and considerable writer.

I respect Rushdie's writing enormously, but as a writer I think I'm almost the antithesis. The language I use tends to be the sort that actually suppresses meaning and tries to hide away meaning rather than chase after something just beyond the reach of words. I'm interested in the way words hide meaning. I suppose I like to have a spare, tight structure because I don't like to have this improvised feeling remain in my work. From a literary point of view, I can't see anything that links me with someone like Salman Rushdie or Timothy Mo.

If we can generalize at all about these writers, I think there is something that unites most of the writers that you have mentioned, especially the younger writers of Britain at the moment. There is something different about them, if you compare that group with the older generation of writers of Britain. The one possible, valid thing that unites the younger group is the consciousness that Britain is not the center of the universe. There was a time when Britain thought it had this dominant role in the world for a long time, that Britain thought it was the head of this huge empire. I think for a long time it was supposed you could just write about British issues and about British life and it would automatically be of global significance, since people all around the world would be interested. British writers didn't have to consciously start thinking about the interests of people outside Britain, because whatever concerned them was, by definition, of international interest.

I think there was this gray period—because literary habits take a long time to die—before the British finally, both intellectually and consciously, had accepted that the empire had gone. No longer did they have this dominant, central place in the world to go to anymore. I think perhaps the styles of writing and the assumptions of writing took a while to catch up with that, and I think this was rather a dull period in English writing. The writers were writing things in which nobody was interested, since it meant nothing to anyone outside of Britain; yet, they carried on with the assumption that Britain was the center of the world. In fact, it was this that turned it into this provincial little country.

I think the younger generation of writers not only realized that, but are now suffering from a kind of inferiority complex. There's great sense that the front line where the great clashes of ideologies were happening was elsewhere. So whether you are looking at communism and capitalism clashing or the Third World and the industrialized world clashing or whatever it is—people have this idea if you're actually based in Britain and British life is what you know—then you have to make some sort of leap. Either you go out there physically and start searching around as V.S. Naipaul and Paul Theroux did, or you have to use your imagination. It's much more normal for the younger generation of British writers, and, apart from the people you mentioned, I would also include Julian Barnes and Ian McEwan, that they will very often not write books in the contemporary British setting they live in. They will search far and wide in their imaginations for mythical settings or historical settings. For example, McEwan's novel *The Innocent* is set in the Cold War period of Berlin. This is not atypical of the differences that separate the younger generation from the older generation of writers.

[*Herzinger*]: *Americans like to believe that English language literature somehow became theirs after World War II. We pay some lip service to Greene, Golding, Lessing, Amis, Fowles, Larkin, Heaney, Hughes, Powell, Murdoch, and the rest, but not much. In fact, I would say that Americans half feel that English literature never quite recovered from the deaths of Joyce and Woolf and the war itself. How do you see yourself, and other young contemporary British writers, in terms of the twentieth-century tradition of British writing?*

What I just said previously raises questions about style and technique as well as setting and theme. If you happen to actually live in a country that you think won't actually provide a broad enough setting to address what you see as the really crucial issues of the age, that inevitably means you start moving away from straight realism.

If you happen to be, let's say, living in East Germany at the moment, perhaps there's no overwhelming reason to not write realism. I think there's a natural instinct to write realism. It takes much more to start thinking of other ways to write. It's when you are actually *stuck on the margins*. Then you start to become conscious that you are stuck on the margins and the things that you know intimately on that con-

crete, documentary level just won't do. Yet, on the other hand, you realize you won't have the same authority as someone who lives in Eastern Europe, or someone who lives in Africa, or the Soviet Union, or America to write about the places that you think are rather central to the things you would like to talk about. What can you do? You know about English life and the texture of English society, but it's something you feel you can't use that well. So you start to actually move away from realism. You have to start looking for other ways in which do work. I think here you start to move, not so much into out-and-out fantasy, but you start to create a slightly more fabulous world. You start to use the landscape that you do know in a metaphorical way. Or you start to create out-and-out fantastic landscapes. Perhaps Doris Lessing got caught up in that when she went off on her science fiction venture.

It may well be that Americans are going through some of the stages that British writers once went through because American society is today so central to the world community. What are the international themes that are of interest to everybody? In America there is no need to ask this question consciously. Americans are almost exempt from having to ask that question. Perhaps they shouldn't be. In any case, at this moment, I think people can write about American society and American life and it will be of interest to people in Kuala Lumpur or the Philippines because American culture has a broad appeal. It has gotten to the point that some people say American culture is invading or taking over everywhere you go in the world. Thus, a lot of people are trying to stop it, but a lot of people are bringing it in. It's very difficult to think of any point on the globe—or any society in the world today—where people shouldn't have a valued interest in American culture.

For the time being, just because of the way things are, I think American writers find themselves in this position—that they can write in a way that at other times might seem very inward-looking and parochial. Just by virtue of America's cultural position in the context of international culture, American writers are going to be relevant. So writers who haven't tried to be of great interest to people all over the world end up being so, sometimes precisely because they're so inward-looking and unconscious of the world beyond, and they reveal so much about where a lot of these influences are coming from. I think there was a time when British writers were in this position. Perhaps American writers need to be aware of a time when it will no longer be the case for them.

[*Vorda*]: *Do you see your prose as participating in the more traditional, twentieth-century style of such writers as W. Somerset Maugham, E.M. Forster, Evelyn Waugh, and Joyce Cary?*

Not really. Most of them I haven't even read. With **The Remains of the Day** it's like a pastiche where I've tried to create a mythical England. Sometimes it looks like or has the tone of a very English book, but actually I'm using that as a kind of shock tactic: this relatively young person with a Japanese name and a Japanese face who produces this extra-English novel or, perhaps I should say, a super-English novel. *It's more English than English.* Yet I think there's a big difference from the tones of the world in **The Remains of the Day** and the worlds created by those writers you mentioned because in my case there is an ironic distance.

Maybe I misread you somewhat. Are you saying that readers have to get past the realism in order to reach—as Barth or Borges or García Márquez have termed it—the irrealistic or fabulist world? This is more of your intent with **The Remains of the Day** *than just writing a traditional British novel?*

Absolutely. I think it's almost impossible now to write a kind of traditional British novel without being aware of the various ironies. The kind of England that I create in **The Remains of the Day** is not an England that I believe ever existed. I've not attempted to reproduce, in a historically accurate way, some past period. What I'm trying to do there, and I think this is perhaps much easier for British people to understand than perhaps people abroad, is to actually rework a particular myth about a certain kind of England. I think there is this very strong idea that exists in England at the moment, about an England where people lived in the not-so-distant past, that conformed to various stereotypical images. That is to say, an England with sleepy, beautiful villages with very polite people and butlers and people taking tea on the lawn.

Now, at the moment, particularly in Britain, there is an enormous nostalgia industry going on with coffee table books, television programs, and even some tour agencies who are trying to recapture this kind of old England. The mythical landscape of this sort of England, to a large degree, is harmless nostalgia for a time that didn't exist. The other side of this, however, is that it is used as a political tool—much as the American Western myth is used here. It's used as a way of bashing anybody who tries to spoil this Garden of Eden. This can be brought out by the left or right, but usually it is the political right who say England was this beautiful place before the trade unions tried to make it more egalitarian or before the immigrants started to come or before the promiscuous age of the '60s came and ruined everything. I actually think it is one of the important jobs of the novelist to actually tackle and rework myths. I think it's a very valid ground on which a novelist should do his work. I've deliberately created a world which at first resembles that of those writers such as P.G. Wodehouse. I then start to undermine this myth and use it in a slightly twisted and different way.

I was asking you earlier on, and this is a question I ask a lot of American people who know American literature, about the genre of the Western myth. It's always puzzled me that serious writers have not to a greater extent tried to rework that myth because it seems to me a nation's myth is the way a country dreams. It is part of the country's fabulized memory, and it seems to me to be a very valid task for the artist to try to figure out what that myth is and if they should actually rework or undermine that myth. It has happened in the cinema as far as the Western is concerned, but when I ask this question people don't seem to be able to offer many serious literary works that go into that area.

To a certain extent, I suppose I was trying to do a similar thing with the English myth. I'd have to say that my overall aim wasn't confined to British lessons for British people because it's a mythical landscape which is supposed to work at a metaphorical level. **The Remains of the Day** is a kind of parable. Yet this is a problem I've always had as a writer throughout my three books. I think if there is something I really struggle with as a writer, whenever I try to think of a new book, it is this whole question about how to make a particular setting actually take off into the realm of metaphor so that people don't think it is just about Japan or Britain. Because ultimately I'm not that interested in saying things about specific societies; and, if I were, I think I'd prefer to do it through nonfiction and follow all the proper disciplines such as to actually produce evidence and argument. I wouldn't do it by emotional manipulation.

Perhaps it is less interesting to do it through nonfiction because it is less imaginative. I guess that is one of the joys of writing fiction.

I think one of the joys of fiction is that you are actually saying things that are universal and not just about Great Britain or America or whatever. It can be about America or Britain, but I think when fiction really takes off it is because you can actually start to see how it is relevant to all other kinds of contexts and how there is a universal streak to these things. I always have this real problem because, on the one hand, you have to create the setting in your novel that feels firm enough, concrete enough, for people to be able to find their way around it. On the other hand, if you make it too concrete and too tied down to something that might exist in reality, that fictional work doesn't take off at that metaphorical level and people start saying, "Oh, that's what it was like in Japan at a certain time," or, "He's saying something about Britain in the 1930s." So, for me, it is something that I feel I haven't quite come to terms with yet, but I'm trying to find some territory, somewhere between straight realism and that kind of out-and-out fabulism, where I can create a world that isn't going to alienate or baffle readers in a way that a completely fantastic world would—but a world which, at the same time, can actually prompt readers to say that this isn't documentary or this isn't history or this isn't journalism. I'm asking you to look at this world that I've created as a reflection of a world that all kinds of people live in. It's the movement away from straight realism that is actually the real challenge. You get that wrong and you could lose everything, whereby no one identifies with your characters or they don't care what happens in this funny, weird, bizarre world. I just wanted to somehow move it away so it's just a couple of stages from straight realism in order to let it take off with that metaphorical level. I think I've come closer to doing that in *The Remains of the Day* than I did with the two Japanese novels, but I still feel this is a challenge I have to meet.

Your prose is a joy to read. For example, on page twenty-seven of **The Remains of the Day** *you write: "I was then brought up to this room, in which, at that point of the day, the sun was lighting up the floral pattern of the wallpaper quite agreeably." And shortly thereafter, the butler Stevens thinks that the "greatness" of Britain paradoxically comes from "the lack of obvious drama or spectacle that sets the beauty of our land apart." Can the same analogy be made to your writing style?*

When Stevens says that about the British landscape he is also saying something about himself. He thinks beauty and greatness lie in being able to be this kind of cold, frozen butler who isn't demonstrative and who hides emotions in much the way he's saying that the British landscape does with its surface calm: the ability to actually keep down turmoil and emotion. He thinks this is what gives both butlers and the British landscape beauty and dignity. And, of course, that viewpoint is the one that actually crumbles during the course of Stevens' journey.

To a large extent, when I wrote **The Remains of the Day,** that was the first time I started to become very conscious of my own style. And, of course, quite rightly, these references that Stevens makes are also a reference to my own style. I think what happened was this. My first two novels I just wrote these sentences without really thinking about style. I was just writing in what I thought was the clearest way possible. Then I started to read review after review which talked about my understated or clipped style. It was the reviewers and the critics who actually pointed this out to me—where my style seemed to be unusually calm with all this kind of strange turmoil expressed underneath the calm. I actually started to ask myself, "Where does this style come from then?" It's not something I consciously manufactured. I had to face the possibility that this was actually indeed something to do with me. It's my natural voice. In **The Remains of the Day,** for the first time, I started to question to what extent that was a good or bad thing from the human point of view regarding this whole business about the suppression of emotion.

Perhaps this was actually revealed by this style, by this inner voice, that I produced in my first two books. To a certain extent, **The Remains of the Day** actually tackles on a thematic level the implications of that kind of style. Of course, Stevens' first-person narrative is written in that style, but of course his whole life is led in that style. And in the book I try to explore to what extent it is indeed dignified and to what extent it is a form of cowardice—a way of actually hiding from what is perhaps the scariest arena in life, which is the emotional arena. It is the first book I've written in which I was actually conscious of my own style and to a certain extent tried to figure out what it is and why it's like that and where it's coming from.

[*Herzinger*]: *Despite a comparatively paltry audience in the United States, there is a feeling that you, along with Ian McEwan, William Body, Martin Amis, Salman Rushdie, Julian Barnes, Graham Swift, and a few others—plus the international success of* Granta—*are leading an energetic new wave in English fiction. How does it seem to you?*

It is very hard for me to assess what is going on in America because I have just visited, but it does surprise me the extent to which the Atlantic does seem to be this huge gap between the two literary cultures. There are household names here that aren't even available on the bookshelves in Britain and vice versa.

When I came over here to do my tour with Knopf in November, I discovered that there were these people who are literary giants here. For instance, consider Ann Beattie, who I don't think is readily available on the bookshelves in England. You might be able to track down a copy of an Ann Beattie book, but you could talk to a lot of literary journalists in London and they would not have heard of her. Quite likely they would not have heard of Russell Banks. On the other hand, Raymond Carver has become very well respected in England, as has Richard Ford. I would say these two writers have broken through to significant respect and readership in Britain.

All the time I'm coming across books here that I realize are very well known over here, but quite often these names mean very little to me. I've been given a book by Pete Dexter called *Paris Trout,* which I think is quite a well-known book here and I've noticed he's won the National Book Award. Personally, I had a hell of a time breaking through here. I don't know why there should be this huge gap, but I think it just points to the fact that—even though we share the same language—the literary cultures are so different.

The other factor has to do with the actual publishing industries, because so much of publishing has to do with contacts and literary politics. I think one of the real weaknesses of the system as it operates at the moment is that there is a tendency toward insularity. If you start operating any contact games then the mediocre domestic talent is always going to get promoted over more interesting stuff from abroad.

[*Herzinger*]: *Since you studied American literature at university, were there any American writers who influenced your work? I hear that you think Hemingway, for instance, wrote great titles, but that perhaps the books that followed were a bit of a letdown.*

I think Hemingway did write marvelous titles. I like Hemingway's early work, but I find some of his later stuff pretty mediocre, almost embarrassingly so, but his standard of title writing remained high right to the end. I think *Across the River and Into the Trees* is a marvelous title, but the discrepancy between the quality of the title and the book is one of the greatest discrepancies I've come across in world literature. It is staggering someone who could write a title like that could write such an appalling book, but he did write some fine stuff early on.

With American writers I tend to like the older guys from the nineteenth century, such as Mark Twain. I think *Huckleberry Finn* is a very beautiful book with a real liveliness to the language and the vernacular is very exciting. *Moby Dick* is a crazy book, yet very interesting. I like Edgar Allan Poe, who raises some very interesting questions about literature as a whole.

What about contemporary American writers such as Pynchon, Gass, and Barth?

These are all people that I should say that we don't really read in England. Pynchon is read . . . well, I don't know . . . he is bought. Usually the only book of his that anyone has read is *The Crying of Lot* 49, because it's short. A lot of people possess *Gravity's Rainbow* and *V.,* but I know very few people who have gotten over one-third of the way through. It remains to be seen if people will finish *Vineland* in England, but people are buying him. Pynchon may very well be a very important writer, but I've only read *The Crying of Lot* 49, so I'm not in a position to say. From what I've read, it is a little too over-intellectualized for me. I suppose one of these days I should tackle his big novels.

I can't think of one writer in America who gets more critical attention than Pynchon.

Perhaps he is a great writer, or it could be because there will always be a certain kind of writer who is good for academics.

Can you name one thing that separates American literature from British literature?

One feature of your literary scene here that we don't have in Britain and generally in Europe is the creative writing industry. I think that is one of the enormous differences in the two literary cultures. It's probably true to say, and I've heard it often said, that you can't find a single American writer today of any significance who hasn't in some way been directly touched by the creative writing world, either as teacher or student. Even someone who kept away from it is going to be affected by it indirectly, because so much of the criticism and so much of the opinions of his fellow writers are going to be touched by it. I think this is something that would certainly make me nervous if I were living in a literary culture where the role of the universities and faculties who taught creative writing began to have that sort of dominant influence.

I'm not actually suggesting that the Thomas Pynchon phenomenon is something closely related to this, because I'm not in a position to comment on him. All I would say is that I would want to assess quite carefully what the role of the creative writing faculties actually is within the whole literary culture because, whether you like it or not, American literature is going a certain direction because of this and I would want to determine if the influence were benign or whether it was actually leading us up a garden path.

[*Herzinger*]: *Lately in this country there has been some debate over the virtues of fictional "minimalism" (*Granta *called it "dirty realism")—Raymond Carver, Ann Beattie, Frederick Barthelme, Max Apple, Mary Robison, Richard Ford, Tobias Wolffe, and a number of others have been called "minimalists." Readers seem to like the work, but it has sent critics into spasms of concern over the death of the novel, the end of American fiction, and so on. Do you have any thoughts on the subject? Is there anything like minimalism and the subsequent outcry from the critics in contemporary British writing?*

No. There isn't a compatible movement or phenomenon in British writing at all. Minimalism isn't a word that you hear very often in British literary debate. I should say in relation to the previous question that Richard Ford and Raymond Carver are two American writers that I admire enormously. Raymond Carver is a profoundly moving writer while Richard Ford has written two or three short stories that are amongst the finest short stories I've ever read. Perhaps it is the influence of the creative writing industry that somehow led to that sort of style, but if that's the case, then that is an aspect that I'll be quite well disposed toward because I think those two writers write with great emotional honesty about things that strike me as being genuinely deep at the human level.

The thing I fear from the creative writing industry and universities in general is that people elevate priorities that I would not consider to be terrifically important. They'll elevate to some special status issues like the nature of fiction or some rather cerebral intellectual ideas. Such issues become esteemed in that kind of environment because, after all, that is what that kind of environment celebrates. But, for me, while the nature of fiction or fictionality are things that writers might need to be concerned with to get on with their work, I don't believe that the nature of fiction is one of the burning issues of the late twentieth century. It's not one of the things I want to turn to novels and art to find out about. I think reading Ford and Carver for me is a kind of an antidote really to those over-intellectualized or self-conscious literary creations that almost seem to be created for the professor down the corridor to decipher. Carver and Ford seem to write about life in a way that is profound. Also, at the technical level, I think they are in a different league from a lot of these people who are just trying to show off or make comments about their literary techniques. The technique applied by Ford or Carver is one at the highest level and to the point that perhaps it's not that obvious. I think they say great things about the emotional experience of life.

Minimalism is not something that is discussed very much in Britain. Short stories haven't really caught on in Britain recently. You can bring out a volume of short stories and you know that only about one-third of the people read it, as opposed to the number of people who read a novel that you have written. For some reason the British don't get into short stories.

[*Heringer*]: *To what extent has Japanese fiction influenced your work? If we look around for writers who sound a bit like Ishiguro, it would seem that Tanizaki—especially his cool precision and delicate touch—is closer to you than anybody else.*

Tanizaki wrote in various different styles, and a lot of his books I wouldn't describe as cool or delicate. I think the book that is best known in the West is one called *The Makioka Sisters.* It is really like a Western family saga. It is one of those stately, long books like Henry James, Edith Wharton, Theodore Dreiser, or George Eliot would have written. It's about this rich merchant family where nothing terribly dramatic ever happens, but it follows the different family members through a period of social change. I think a lot of people think that Tanizaki always writes like that, but he also writes kind of weird, kinky, perverted stuff.

[*Herzinger*]: *What book would you be referring to?*

The Secret History of the Lord of Musashi, which is about a medieval lord who, the first time he gets sexually turned on, is wandering around a battlefield shortly after a battle and he sees these severed heads. I think that night he peeks through a hole and sees some women dressing the severed heads of fallen clan members and he starts to get sexually turned on.

I'm sure Freud would have had a good time with this.

It gets even weirder because the thing that really turns him on is a particular head that has a nose missing. So when he becomes a powerful lord later on, he has a real sexual craving for severed heads with missing noses. It gets really funny because there is a particular guy that he takes a liking to and he really wants to see this guy without a nose and so he keeps trying to arrange it so that his nose will get cut off, but it never quite works. This poor guy doesn't know what the hell is going on. Every few weeks he loses an ear or something happens to him, or somebody is after him, but he doesn't know why. There is this weird scene where the lord gets his servant to impersonate a severed head without a nose while he is making love to one of his concubines.

I mean, this is real Tanizaki territory, and this is where Tanizaki is really interesting. And there are a few other books like that. This is, by way of saying, that there is this tendency, just because I have a Japanese name, to pull out one or two other Japanese writers somebody else has heard of and say there is a similarity to my writing. Yet the critic perhaps is basing this comparison to a Japanese writer whose book is not typical of others he has written. For example, Tanizaki wrote in a lot of different styles and he wrote for a long, long time. Tanizaki actually went into his eighties, and he produced an enormous amount of books as he went through lots of different stages. I can't really see that anybody would particularly compare me to any Japanese writer if it weren't for the fact that I have this Japanese name. Now if I wrote under a pseudonym and got somebody else to pose for my jacket photographs, I'm sure nobody would think of saying, "This guy reminds me of that Japanese writer." I often have to battle and to speak up for my own individual territory against this kind of stereotyping. I wouldn't say it's wildly unfair, but then I can think of a dozen other writers with whom I could just as easily be compared. I would say I am not wildly dissimilar to the Tanizaki of *The Makioka Sisters,* but then someone could equally say that for anybody almost—whether it was George Eliot or Henry James or the Brontë sisters.

[*Herzinger*]: *How about Chekhov? He would seem to be the one overwhelming influence on American writing over the past ten to fifteen years.*

Chekhov is a writer that I always acknowledge as one of my influences. When people ask me about the writers I really like, I always say Chekhov and Dostoyevsky.

To backtrack just slightly on my refuting any affiliation with Japanese literature, there are some things I have learned from the Japanese tradition, if you like, but perhaps more from the Japanese movies. I think it is the same thing that perhaps I've taken from Chekhov, and that's from reading these people and seeing movies by film makers like Ozu and watching the plays of Chekhov and reading Chekhov's short stories. I think it's given me the courage and conviction to have a very slow pace and not worry if there isn't a strong plot. I think there is an overwhelmingly strong tradition in Western literature—at least I should say British literature and American literature since I think the French have a slightly different thing going—in which plot is pretty important. By fiction I also mean movies and the way television stories are told and so on. It is almost assumed that plot has to be the central spine around which the story is fleshed, and that is almost the definition these days. When you actually think about Chekhov, it is really rather hard to actually see his pieces as plots with flesh on it. What is interesting is in Japan, until very recently, this kind of plot-with-flesh model just didn't exist in Japanese fiction.

There are writers like Kawabata, whom I find quite baffling and alienating, because he's from such a different tradition, but at the same time fascinating because he writes kind of long short stories. I believe he is the only Japanese Nobel Prize winner for literature. Kawabata's stories are often completely plotless. They are not only plotless, but the pace goes so slowly sometimes it almost stops. These things seem to break all the rules people teach about how to write screenplays for Hollywood.

This business about pace, you read these books on how to write a screenplay or books on how to keep the narrative drive going, yet reading Chekhov or some of these Japanese writers has indicated that you don't have to worry about that very much. I've really started to get into this idea of slowness with things almost stopping.

[*Vorda*]: *This seems evident in* **The Remains of the Day** *where the plot is loosely based; yet, you are able to piece things together. For example, Miss Kenton disappears for much of the novel, but she is always there when you need her to pull things together. The use of Miss Kenton's character seems to allow you to intermingle different elements.*

I don't structure my books around plots, and I find it a great liberation. If you have to worry about making a plot work, you often have to sacrifice other priorities to the mechanical workings of the plot, and you start to distort characters and all kinds of psychological insights. I find a great deal of freedom in not having plot, but that does actually mean you have to face lots of new challenges about not boring the reader and how to structure your work. These are some of the things in Chekhov which I find a continual revelation. How does he keep you absorbed when all the people are doing is just sitting around a field and asking whether or not

they are going back to Moscow? He should be crushingly boring. In fact, one or two of those great plays *are* boring, but some of his short stories are masterpieces.

Which ones in particular?

It's probably not that well known, but I like "Ionych." Other stories that come to mind are "A Boring Story," "Lady with Lapdog," and "The Kiss."

You stated after you wrote **A Pale View of Hills** *that, "If you really want to write something, you shouldn't bring things into your book lightly. It's a bit like taking in lodgers. They're going to be with you a long time. I think the most important thing I learned between writing the first and second novels is the element of thematic discipline." Do you now feel you have control of your thematic discipline after having written* **The Remains of the Day***?*

I'll never say I've got control, but I think I've gotten more and more control with each book. When I read reviews, I've always read the opening and closing paragraphs to see if they're saying this is good or not so good, but then after that the next thing that concerns me is the summary. Have they actually summarized the book in the way that I wanted the book to come over? For a long time, at the beginning of my career, I would actually get favorable reviews that praised me for a book that I didn't wish to write. They were emphasizing all the wrong things and praising me for things I didn't intend to do. So I could keep quiet about it and accept unwarranted praise. Of course, this isn't very satisfying, and the question of thematic discipline comes in here. There is a real satisfaction to be gotten from being praised for exactly the right things you wanted to be praised for and not for some accidental effect you created. Because that is what you're trying to do. You're not just trying to get people to like your book—you're trying to communicate a vision. This is why thematic discipline is so important to me. I used to read all these reviews recommending that people should read my first book for the weirdest reasons, but it had nothing to do with what I was wanting to do. I was pleased because they were favorable reviews, but that was a very frustrating experience for me.

The one point I still feel an element of frustration about, and I mentioned this before, is that people have a tendency to say that **The Remains of the Day** is a book about a certain historical period in England or that it is about the fall of the British empire or something like that. They don't quite read it as a parable or see it take off into a metaphorical role. Now, a lot of reviewers have understood my intent and said this is not just a book about a butler living in the 1930s. It is interesting that reviews vary from country to country. It tells you something about that country, but it also reminds you that as a writer you're going to be read by lots of different people in lots of different social contexts coming at the book from lots of different directions. I think it's always a healthy thing to remind oneself that you shouldn't assume every reader's assumption is going to be the same as a British reader's assumption. There are going to be very obvious reasons why some people see it in a completely different way. And usually the further I get from Britain the happier I am with the readings, because the people are less obsessed with the idea of it just being about Britain. In Britain, I suppose I'm still slightly locked into this realist reader and I recognize that a part of that is my own responsibility. I hate to use the word "fantastic," but the book is still too realistic for the metaphorical intentions to be obvious if the people actually come from the society which the book superficially resembles.

I've been very happy about the way the American reviewers, on the whole, have read *The Remains of the Day.* One or two have thought it was specifically about British history, but, by and large, most people read it the way that I intended them to. As I say, I think I had more trouble in Britain, where some people thought it was about the Suez Crisis or it was about British appeasement of Nazi Germany.

[*Herzinger*]: **The Remains of the Day** *and* **An Artist of a Floating World** *both seem to be about men who have an extraordinary capacity to lie to themselves while presenting themselves as very precise and cautious truthtellers. Should we imagine that this is going to be the central obsession in your work? So far, the central notions in your work would seem to demand first-person narration. Are you planning to work in any other forms?*

I think this is always a difficult question about how you're going to develop as a writer. I find it rather difficult to plan more than one book at a time, and I can't really say now which other themes I'm going to be obsessed about in two or three books from now. I think, certainly, what happened with my first three books is that I was actually trying to refine what I did over and over again, and, with *The Remains of the Day,* I feel that I came to the end of that process. That is why the three books seem to have a kind of similarity. It's not a similarity for which I can apologize; I have no other way of working.

I don't actually think of my writing as being an attempt to cover this territory and finish it and then move over to a different territory altogether and have a go at that. I don't see it like that. I feel like I'm *closing in on some strange, weird territory* that for some reason obsesses me, and I'm not sure what the nature of that territory is, but with every book I'm kind of closing in on this strange territory. And that's the way I see my development as a writer. Quite often I will have an idea for a story which is intrinsically quite interesting, but I know immediately that I can't use it because I know

it's not going to help me close in on this territory. It has gotten to the point now that I recognize this. I know the things that apply to this territory which will be relevant or might be relevant from the ones that are quite diverting and therefore irrelevant. If I'm reading a newspaper and I come across an item, occasionally something will hit me, something that is perhaps quite banal, but it rings some kind of strange bell. The item doesn't necessarily have to be some kind of weird human interest story, because quite often some ordinary situation will just spring out from the page at me and I'll think that's something I could use.

I don't intend to write about old men looking back over their lives all the time because I think I've come to the end of that, but I think the real challenge that always faces writers is what to keep and what to cast off from their previous concerns and previous books. I think it is important to try to identify those things that still mean something to you, that still feel unfathomed in some way, and that is the way that you close in further and further on this territory. I think most writers do write out of some part of themselves—that is, I wouldn't say "unbalanced," but where there is a kind of lack of equilibrium. I'm not suggesting that writers are usually unbalanced people. I know many, many writers, and I would say that most of them are *more than averagely sane* and responsible people, but I think a lot of them do write out of something that is unresolved somewhere deep down and, in fact, it's probably too late ever to resolve it. Writing is kind of a consolation or a therapy. Quite often, bad writing comes out of this kind of therapy. The best writing comes out of a situation where I think the artist or writer has to some extent come to terms with the fact that it is too late. The wound has come, and it hasn't healed, but it's not going to get any worse; yet, the wound is there. It's a kind of consolation that the world isn't quite the way you wanted it but you can somehow reorder it or try and come to terms with it by actually creating your own world and own version of it. Otherwise, I can't see any other explanation for why people should actually do this time-consuming, antisocial activity of locking themselves away and obsessively writing. I think serious writers have to try, in some way or the other, to keep moving in a direction that moves them toward this area of irresolution and lack of balance. I think that's where the really interesting, deep writing comes from. This is partly why I'm very wary of the creative writing industry. I think it could actually deflect potentially very profound individual voices away from what their muses are trying to tell them.

[*Herzinger*]: *Please comment on such characters as Etsuko, Ono, Miss Kenton, and Stevens, who have misused their talents or have not led lives of fulfillment because of a lack of insight. And also, conversely, would their lives be better off if they had insight and no talent?*

I wrote about these people not actually to pass judgment on

them, because I am interested in people who do have a certain amount of talent—not just talent—but who have a certain passion, a certain real urge, to do a little bit more than the average person. They've got this urge to contribute to something larger.

I can see where this applies to Ono in **An Artist of the Floating World,** *but do you think it applies to Stevens?*

Yes, definitely. Stevens is somebody who desperately wants to contribute to something larger, but he thinks he is just a butler and the only way he can do this is to work for a great man. He gets a lot of his sense of self-respect from an idea that he is serving a great man. If he were someone who didn't care at all about how his contribution was being used, then he wouldn't end up a broken man at the end. He is driven by this urge to do things perfectly, and not only do things perfectly, but that perfect contribution should be, no matter however small a contribution it is, to improving humanity. That is Stevens' position. He's not content to say, "I'll just get by and earn money so that I can feed myself."

But then again, it doesn't seem that Stevens has any great insight as to why he does things. Nor does he seem to have a great understanding of the world.

That's true, Stevens doesn't have a great understanding. I think this is where my characters go wrong. Their lives are spoiled because they don't have any extraordinary insight into life. They're not necessarily stupid; they're just ordinary. (I write out of this fear that I, myself, will waste my talent—not only waste my talents, but, indeed, end up backing some cause that I actually disapprove of or one that could be disastrous.) Yet, these ordinary characters often are going to get involved in a kind of political arena even if it's in a very small way. The reason I chose a butler as a starting point was that I wanted a metaphor for this vehicle. Most of us are like butlers because we have these small, little tasks that we learn to do, but most of us don't attempt to run the world. We just learn a job and try to do it to the best of our ability. We get our pride from that, and then we offer up a little contribution to somebody up there, to an organization, or a cause, or a country. We would like to tell ourselves that this larger thing that we're contributing toward is something good and not something bad, and that's how we draw a lot of our dignity. Often we just don't know enough about what's going on out there, and I felt that's what we're like. We're like butlers.

You also briefly present the lives of Lisa and the footman with whom she elopes. This seems to be a microcosm of what could have been a more fulfilling or happier life if Stevens had allowed himself to fall in love with Miss Kenton instead of denying his feelings.

I had this story of Lisa and the footman because I just wanted a scene where they were confronted with just such a situation and how they (Stevens and Miss Kenton) would actually talk about it and discuss it. It refers to something they're both painfully concerned with, and, yet, they have to discuss it as a kind of professional incident or setback. When Stevens is thinking back over his life, this is one of the things that comes back to him, which is the closest they ever got to discussing their romantic possibilities. So even when Stevens and Miss Kenton are discussing their unfulfilled romance, they do it indirectly by discussing Lisa and the footman.

Stevens' vision is very myopic in that he never seems to give a thought to anything, nor is sex an issue. Do you agree that he is a pathetically tragic figure that is almost nonhuman in his thoughts and feelings?

I wouldn't want to say nonhuman.

Maybe if I could digress just one second. You had that interesting metaphor in **The Remains of the Day** *where Mr. Cardinal suggests to Stevens that it might be better if people were created as plants, "firmly embedded in the soil," then there wouldn't be any disagreements about "wars and boundaries." Then Mr. Cardinal adds, "But we could still have chaps like you taking messages back and forth, bringing tea, that sort of thing. Otherwise, how would we ever get anything done?"*

I think he's in danger of turning himself into something less than human partly because he's got this sense of perfectionism. It's this kind of terribly misguided sense of perfectionism, which, if he actually achieves it, would actually mean turning himself into something less than human. But it's not just perfectionism. It's a kind of a cowardice. That is what I'm trying to suggest and, hence, the juxtaposition of his ambition to be a great butler with his avoidance of a romantic life with Miss Kenton. I suppose I'm suggesting that often that kind of drive to that kind of professional perfectionism is rooted in some kind of cowardice about the emotional arena. It's not just a determination to be the best. Once again, I was drawn to use a butler in this kind of metaphorical way because that seemed to be a profession in which at least a stereotypical view of the professional butler is that you have to kind of erase the obviously human from yourself. This was probably a social requirement because people wanted privacy at the same time as wanting to be served. So the butler was obliged to be a kind of robot-like figure.

Nevertheless, it seems as if Stevens is devoid of any feelings. For example, his proudest moment as a butler is during Lord Darlington's political conference when his father is dying upstairs. He ignores being with his father since his duty lies elsewhere—primarily trying to get bandages for the sore feet of the snotty Dupont. Even after his father dies, Stevens does not go to attend to the corpse, whereupon Miss Kenton sarcastically says, "In that case, Mr. Stevens, will you permit me to close his eyes?" It's as though Stevens is made of cardboard, without any identity or feelings.

The role of the butler is to serve inconspicuously while creating the illusion of absence and at the same time being physically on hand to do these things. It seemed to me appropriate to have somebody who wants to be this perfect butler because that seems to be a powerful metaphor for someone who is trying to actually erase the emotional part of him that may be dangerous and that could really hurt him. Yet, he doesn't succeed because these kinds of human needs, the longings for warmth and love and friendship, are things that just don't go away. This is what Stevens probably realizes at the end of the novel when he starts to get the inkling about this question of bantering. He starts to read more and more into why he can't banter, and this is an indication of the fact that he's somehow cut off from other people. He can't even make the first steps in forming relationships with other people.

In the New York Times Book Review, you say your next book will not be repetitive stylistically and that you might "like to write a messy, jagged, loud kind of book." What kind of book can your readers expect next?

It is very difficult to say. I write very slowly, and most of my writing time I'm not actually writing prose. **The Remains of the Day** took me three years and during that time I did nothing else. I don't have any other job, and I turn down any offers to do journalism. I was full-time working on that book, but I realized afterwards, looking through my diary, that I actually spent only twelve months writing the words that ended up in that book. It horrifies me to think that I spent two years just working up to it, but I find that I have to have a very close map of where I'm going to go before I actually start to write the words. I have to have it almost all in place in my head first. This is once again quite unusual, because I know plenty of writers who write brilliantly, although they know very little of where they're going when they start the first draft. I have to have all these things worked out and researched. Now things may change, obviously, in the execution, when I'm actually writing the words, but I usually have to know fairly precisely what I'm trying to achieve with every paragraph. So it takes me a long time to get to that situation. I fill folders and folders up with notes and ideas which look like excerpts from a longer work. I may experiment with a particular tone or a character during the very early stages when it's very difficult to say even where the book is going to be set. All I know are the themes.

Cynthia F. Wong (essay date Winter 1995)

SOURCE: Cynthia F. Wong, "The Shame of Memory: Blanchot's Self-Dispossession in Ishiguro's *A Pale View of Hills*," in *Clio*, Vol. 24, No. 2, Winter, 1995, pp. 127-45.

[*In the following essay, Wong employs literary theorist Maurice Blanchot's theories on first person narration to analyze Ishiguro's* A Pale View of Hills.]

" . . . the necessary condition for the solitude of a madman is the presence of a lucid witness."

—Blanchot

The first novels of the Japanese-born and British-educated contemporary writer, Kazuo Ishiguro, employ a deceptively simple narrative strategy to develop the remembrances of protagonists reflecting upon and finding a meaning for their personal lives. Speaking in the period after turbulent historical times, the first-person narrators set private experience into a public realm; they seek to induct a reader, a witness, into their stories. They make an admission that their seemingly ordinary tales will be insufficient given the limitations of memory but, in establishing the fact of forgetfulness and the gaps in retelling, they also critique significant world events from their uniquely estranged perspectives.

In acknowledging the limits of their telling, however, the narrators reveal what literary theorist Maurice Blanchot calls their "torment of language," their search for a way to divest themselves of the prior period within the very act of retelling:

> It is narrative (independently of its content) that is a forgetting, so that to tell a story is to put oneself through the ordeal of this first forgetting that precedes, founds, and ruins all memory. Recounting, in this sense, is the torment of language, the incessant search for its infinity. And narrative would be nothing other than an allusion to the initial detour that is borne by writing and that carries it away, causing us, as we write, to yield to a sort of perpetual turning away.

The narrators at first seek order and a means to revise the personal past. The narrators' initial gesture toward self-understanding soon gives way to what Blanchot calls the effect of their narrative's "deflected relation" to life, a tension the reader acknowledges in the narrators' effort to locate memory in order to master it. For the narrators, self-knowledge from retrieval and telling evolves not merely as a form of self-mastery but also self-dispossession, "unworking" the memories and "turning away" from one's past. In other words, they remember in order to forget; they reconstruct the past in an effort to obliterate it. Blanchot's concerns with speech and speechlessness are important in depicting how narrators apprehend "disastrous" personal and world events, and his critical theory may amplify the strategies important to Ishiguro's work.

Ishiguro's first published novel, *A Pale View of Hills* (1982), sets forward the estrangement effect described by Blanchot through a narrative technique that also characterizes his two later works. I will analyze this novel primarily to highlight the implications of Blanchot's narrative theory for Ishiguro's novels. In *A Pale View of Hills,* Ishiguro presents an unusually "quiet" and oddly tranquil narrative told by an elderly Japanese woman living in England in the story's present moment; the occasion for the tale told by Etsuko is the recent suicide of her oldest daughter Keiko, an event which is painfully heightened by a visit from her second daughter Niki (Keiko's half-sister), but which is curiously subdued in Etsuko's remembrances. Most of Etsuko's tale is recounted in solitude; Niki's visit only emphasizes Etsuko's privacy, especially when the narrative moves into past events. In working through the meaning of her dead daughter's life, Etsuko situates her tale in Nagasaki and focuses on a strange and enigmatic friendship with another woman named Sachiko, whose own daughter's actions seem to foretell the suicide of Etsuko's daughter years later.

In all his novels, Ishiguro's narrators join two realms—personal experience and historical event—to produce an unusual narrative tension, or what Blanchot calls the narrator's struggle to "maintain the primacy of an individual consciousness" in order "to cover up by revealing." Years later, in recounting private experiences, the narrators establish the context of those individual moments against history; the narrators' consciousness of historical circumstances prompts their reassessment of the private past, but their determination to maintain the primacy of self is tied to producing a false disclosure. Significantly, they each express doubts about the veracity and clarity of memory, as if such admission of their uneasiness would also undo the pain associated with the past.

Specifically, in Etsuko's narrative, the two events found in past and present are tied to her subsequent dissociation of pain itself. Remembering Nagasaki, Etsuko is able to forget the premonition of death she connects with that period. Remembering the pain of the past, she is able to forget, momentarily, the horror of her daughter's demise. However, as Etsuko reconstructs the past period, she also reveals her reluctance to either *fully* remember or reveal, a technique Ishiguro uses in other novels. Like Etsuko, Stevens, the narrator of *The Remains of the Day* (1989), for instance, also critically assesses the function of his memory with the idea that "when with the benefit of hindsight one begins to search one's past for . . . 'turning points,' one is apt to start seeing

them everywhere," and he implies that such articulation of a consciousness may reveal truth's elusiveness. Similarly, the narrator Masuji Ono of *An Artist of the Floating World* (1986) punctuates his story with remarks that any reconstructed narrative may be flawed representation, "may not have been the precise words I used that afternoon." His narrative, in this continued fabrication, becomes a self-acknowledged tale comprised as much from forgetfulness as remembrance. And Etsuko herself observes how memory "can be an unreliable thing" as she struggles for correspondence in recalling what she might have felt or experienced in the tumultuous period with what actual memory produces.

All of Ishiguro's novels deal with a great divide, whether between individuals or nations. By endowing his characters with knowledge of their flawed memories, Ishiguro tests the limits of their telling against their struggle both to reveal and to veil meaning. How does the dual desire to remember and reveal correspond with the compulsion to "unwork" and dissociate oneself from the memories of the past? Moreover, what does the uneasy conjunction of private experiences and public contexts mean in the relationship between the individual and history?

All of Ishiguro's narrators structure their tales according to discernible historical events and, in the unfolding of their texts, the narrators appear to arrive closer at uncovering some missing version of truth about that period. The narratives' evasive movement toward the respective disclosures indicates some secret to be revealed about the narrators' past guilt, embarrassment, or disgrace. For instance, Stevens' motor trip toward Mrs. Benn is also an internal journey reflecting on his repressed love for Miss Kenton (prior to becoming Mrs. Benn) which had resulted from his loyalty to Lord Darlington at a crucial period in world history—the moment between world wars concerning the future of Germany and Great Britain. Masuji Ono's hopeful anticipation of the lives of his two daughters is a retrospective examination of his role in Japanese imperialism, which led to postwar denunciations of artists like himself. Etsuko's mourning for a recently deceased daughter is transformed into a remembrance of the period following the nuclear devastation of Nagasaki, particularly to events which might help explain her daughter's suicide. For all three narrators, the return to the past is prompted by an intense and personal emotion in the present moment of narration; each foretells in the opening of the respective texts of a futile, but necessary, effort to reconfigure the events owing to a subsequent emotion which the reader will identify as their shame about the past. Each returns to a past which might atone for the present. Even a failed memory might allow each to reexamine significance in the new context and to account for the solitude of that past. Therefore, each does not undertake a "revision" in the usual sense of simply re-seeing the events again. Rather, the narrators reposition themselves in the new contexts and assess their own roles in contributing to both private and historical events. In light of the new knowledge, they reveal two important inversions: one between private and public and the other between narrative past and future. The act of remembering is tied to their unworking—or inverting—the shame of an irrevocable past. Importantly, their eventual remembrances become emblems of their self-dispossession from the past period, and it is this redoubling that I will examine.

In the second part of this essay, I will concentrate on the first-person narrative strategy of Ishiguro's first novel, *A Pale View of Hills,* and indicate later how Ishiguro's next two novels also develop a similar concern for the protagonists' limits of memory, as well as their simultaneous desire for and dread of disclosure. Because the return to the past is charged by Etsuko's desire to master the substance of memory, I will begin with Genette's structural analysis of temporal development in order to suggest that the manner of Etsuko's telling is thematically linked to the way memory is shaped by a will to dissociate herself from this period. Such a formal examination of the narrative reveals the tension between individual consciousness and historical circumstances; it also extends Blanchot's discussion of the narrator's strained tale that results from such a form. I then will indicate how the content of Etsuko's tale, which seems to derive at first from the act of remembrance, is indeed an inversion of memory itself—the reappearances from the dreaded past arrive in the form of her desire to forget the shame associated with the events. From the mutual interdependence of the two constructions—of self and history—I will indicate how this novel might reestablish the role of fiction in the interpretation of human events according to Blanchot's claim that literature is bound to language in a special way which renders it both "reassuring and disquieting at the same time." More specifically, through analysis of this first novel, I will suggest that the narrators of Ishiguro's next two novels also develop a growing awareness of missed opportunity and obligation in the past which propels them to reconfigure, perhaps even fictionalize, that prior period. For these narrators, the construction of a narrative in the "present" moment evolves into an assertion of the shame that both indicts and forgives them.

> "No one likes to recognize himself as a stranger in a mirror where what he sees is not his own double but someone whom he would have liked to have been."

As narrator of Ishiguro's first novel, *A Pale View of Hills,* Etsuko tells the tragic tale of her daughter's suicide. The "madness" of Keiko's act is subtly linked to Etsuko's memory of her own self. In one brief scene with her father-in-law, Etsuko Ogata refers to herself as once being "a mad girl" and asks Ogata-San, "'What was I like in those days,

Father? Was I like a mad person?'" Father's response, "'We were all shocked, those of us who were left,'" alludes to the historical moment which would have produced Etsuko's "madness" in a way that not only validates Etsuko's memory of herself but which also attributes a similar pain to others who remain. Ogata-San's words are both consoling and disrupting: his assessment establishes a relationship between Etsuko's past and present.

Etsuko constructs her personal story using three distinct temporal orders, what Genette terms prolepsis (anticipation), analepsis (flash-back), and anachrony or discordance between the *récit* (telling) and *histoire* (tale). Against the backdrop of Nagasaki's reconstruction in the late forties, Etsuko in England in the early eighties returns to two pasts—her own during the reconstruction and an earlier past remembered by others in this same period—in order to clarify the meaning of two futures: the "present" when she undertakes the narrative task and time beyond. However, if Etsuko's first-person account is dubious given her own awareness of being mad immediately following the bombing, it also is filled with lucid observation of the way historical circumstances produced one's sense of self in those times. This anachronic feature in the narrative extends the personal story and urges the reader to examine the sociohistorical aspects which inform it. A preliminary structural analysis of the narrative reveals the deeper implications of the discordance, that the attempt to produce a coherent narrative is tied to a desire to forget those very events.

Etsuko's own admission of madness attests to an understanding of self that requires another person to either validate or challenge; she seeks a lucid witness. Ogata-San's assessment propels Etsuko toward this understanding. His perspective, like those of other principal characters in her past, serves to either mirror or deflect what she herself attempts to recollect. In telling what she recalls, then, she is aware of her limitations: she says, "Memory, I realize, can be an unreliable thing; often it is heavily coloured by the circumstances in which one remembers, and no doubt this applies to certain of the recollections I have gathered here.'" Etsuko expresses an important condition of analepsis or flashback; moreover, she approximates an important truth about the temporal limits of narrative and marks what Blanchot calls its principle of incompleteness in her telling:

> A [human] being, insufficient as it is, does not attempt to associate itself with another being to make up a substance of integrity. The awareness of the insufficiency arises from the fact that it puts itself in question, which question needs the other or another to be enacted. Left on its own, a being closes itself, falls asleep and calms down. A being is either alone or knows itself to be alone only when it is not.

Etsuko reconstructs her self from the mirrors of the past and from her interactions with other people, although what is reflected back to her may or may not coincide with her eventual understanding of that past. Blanchot's enigmatic assessment above expresses Etsuko's solitary condition when she first undertakes the narrative task: her self-absorbed memory alone is insufficient to convey the fullness of any event. Etsuko seems to understand intuitively this incompleteness when she searches for remembrance of the relationships she had with others. Whether these interactions were self-flattering or complementary to her own desire for eventual self-understanding Etsuko leaves ambiguous. The memory of other people in this period allows her to locate and place into perspective the different pieces of the past. While the personal story serves as the platform for the telling of other stories, it also reconsiders the past from new vantage points, thus reestablishing Etsuko's interpretation of events each time a new piece is added to memory.

The circumstances of Etsuko's emigration from Japan to England about a decade after the end of the Pacific War are revealed through a retrospective narrative which is instigated by a family tragedy, with each backward look revealing some historical development. She recalls three primary episodes from the past, a period which is characterized by its transient and impermanent state. Each aspect develops a distinct level of meaning pertinent to Etsuko's recollection as a whole. The first involves the developing but abruptly terminated friendship with a woman (Sachiko) and her young daughter (Mariko) who appear in Etsuko's neighborhood soon after early efforts to rebuild Nagasaki are underway; the second concerns the strained relationships with her first husband (Jiro) and her father-in-law (Ogata-San) and signifies the decline of traditional kinship ties; and the third is an enigmatic and non-chronological sequence which appears mostly as a remembrance of her dead daughter (Keiko) through disjointed images that merge past and present, but which do not develop the daughter's character given their fleeting recall. The framing device for these past reflections stems from the five-day visit of Etsuko's second daughter (Niki) from her dead second husband, an English journalist (Sheringham) who had written articles about Japan. Niki's early spring visit reminds Etsuko of the particular summer in the past, and it also prompts the narrator to consider her daughter's future in the context of past errors and omissions.

The analepsis of the narrative is triggered by images which visit Etsuko during Niki's stay, while the moments of anticipation from the past slowly evolve into meaning for Etsuko years later in England, a completely different space. Specifically, conversations with Niki concerning motherhood oblige Etusko's return to the period of her first pregnancy which is marked by the unusual friendship with Sachiko and mysterious encounters with the daughter Mariko. In one scene, Etsuko assesses the meaning of such an encounter, that it had

been "capable of arousing in me every kind of misgiving about motherhood."

Etsuko's own calculated examination of such past moments suggests their key role in perhaps "explaining" the later events. What remains unspoken in the mother's narrative is the pain of death, including the destruction of Nagasaki and her daughter's own suicide years later in Manchester, England. Like the nuclear destruction which fragmented Japan, the imminent loss of Etsuko's daughter in the anterior future of the narrative is shown from the perspective of the past which contains Sachiko and Mariko, with these scenes serving to fill in the missing pieces of Etsuko's own life between Nagasaki and England, the time of Keiko's upbringing. The parallels between the two grown women in the past reflect, structure, and then compound the mysteries hinted at in the text; they also create an important link between the young girl in the past (Mariko) who might help explain another dead girl's lifetime later in the narrative.

In other words, analepsis and prolepsis clarify episodes concerning Mariko in this particular past and foretell the future which contains Keiko who is, at that time, still in her mother's womb. The figurative rebirth of the dead girl through another girl from Etsuko's past structures the narrative and charts the fateful outcome. The meaning of the past and its eventual "future" culminate in the final scene of Niki's departure from Etsuko's English home, with the mother bidding her second daughter a farewell that nevertheless suggests future meetings between them. Departure, with the extreme condition entailing death in the cases of the war casualties and Keiko, serves as formal limits in the narrative.

Etsuko recounts that prior period in order to understand how the events might have determined the outcome of the present. The gesture is also an effort to look onward to an uncertain but promising future for a living daughter who remains. The overlapping temporal structures thus anticipate the theme of optimism in the novel reiterated by Mrs. Fujiwara, who had lost practically everything in the war. She says to Etsuko during her pregnancy, "'You must keep your mind on happy things now. Your child. And the future.'" In remembering this utterance Etsuko considers how it applies to a "future" that is now past; the futility of meaning behind Mrs. Fujiwara's words, no matter how hopeful, nevertheless points toward the shame associated with Etsuko's memory of this period.

If the processes of looking backward and moving forward are discernible in the narrator's shuttling of key events, the anachronistic aspect of the text is conveyed by discordance between what Etsuko reveals of the past in relation to the reader's perception of meaning in the present. If Etsuko's own perceived "madness" is contested by Ogata-San's assessment of her "shock," that same self-perception has the effect of dismantling some of her narrative authority. Etsuko's ability to present a fair assessment of the historical past in the personal narrative produces another possible reading of *A Pale View of Hills* as the self-revelation of one woman's madness. Such a reading might clarify the mysterious relationship of Sachiko and Mariko to Etsuko, Keiko, and Niki; it also might be the key to uncovering a secret about Nagasaki, what Etsuko characterizes, but initially fails to elaborate, as "the tragedies and nightmares of wartime." Etsuko's augmenting knowledge of the past provokes the reader toward a gradual move toward disclosure, what Blanchot calls a "desoeuvrement" or unworking, of the wartime past remembered by Etsuko.

Such a reading might reveal discord in the narrator's remembered past, but it would do so by "conferring on the second narrative an *explanatory* function." Despite Etsuko's otherwise lucid recounting of the past, the reader grows increasingly uneasy as the events unfold because what Etsuko remembers seems as if it ought to interpret what she in the present moment leaves unspoken—but in fact it does not. Memory here serves not to explain the past as much to set it in the perspective of the present, with the reader's emerging realization that a comprehensible past is finally impossible. In other words, Etsuko's narrative is incomplete; what Blanchot above defined as an insufficiency that permeates the tale collides with the reader's expectation of a full and coherent disclosure. The reader cannot truly validate the incompatible details of Etsuko's past and future without undermining conventional aspects of the narrative itself; only by casting doubt on Etsuko's veracity can the reader probe the veiled truth in a manner set forth by the narrative itself.

Etsuko's narrative provokes instead a reading which allows for complexities without eradicating narrative authority. To indicate that Sachiko is Etusko's alter-ego is to diminish the horrible fact that only Etusko might have been affected by the aftermath of war. Rather than regard Etsuko as an unreliable narrator, it may be more fruitful to see how her "madness" is a testament to the fatal outcomes of nuclear ruin. Her memory of the devastation reveals the perverse democratization of the destruction: everyone suffered the pain and the ruin in ways markedly similar. To compress all the events of Etsuko's narrative past into one woman's confused ranting about that time is to diminish one meaning of Nagasaki's legacy, that its aftermath had tentacles reaching far beyond the moment. More precisely, to fuse the identities of Sachiko with Etsuko in the schizophrenic interpretation amounts to a reader's refusal to see that Etsuko was among many women affected by the bombing of Nagasaki. That Sachiko "really" existed may not be the point worth quibbling about. Instead, it is more important that Etsuko remembered Sachiko at all, especially given the turbulence of those times.

In truth, any narrative of a historical event can be told only from a select perspective, with attention to the limits of that telling. To regard *A Pale View of Hills* as solely one woman's experiences—and a neurotic one at that—is to demolish the painful truth of human destruction, that it is often unspeakable, except through the private events and tragedies which reflect a larger social situation. While Etsuko's narrative appears at times to withhold important information, the reluctant disclosure is consistent with her narrative task to show the effects of the war, rather than to make manifest polemical assertions. The diminishing of personal facts corresponds with the narrative task of telling world, not merely personal, history. Etsuko's effacement is therefore necessary to this construction if it is to emulate the pain of destruction.

If the past appears no less explanatory in the present, even with the benefit of time for possible reflection, the narrative's seemingly evasive strategy reinforces how, in death and destruction, so much remains unspeakable and incomprehensible. More poignant in Etsuko's withholding or refusal to disclose is the silent fact that many civilians of Nagasaki already had died or were dying from nuclear radiation during the time recounted in Etsuko's reexamination. Most, like Mrs. Fujiwara, were literally picking up small pieces from the pain and sorrow to reconstruct an existence of some dignity. When Sachiko scoffs at Mrs. Fujiwara's humble noodle shop operation, the reader—through Etsuko's sympathies—understands the magnitude of human loss in the face of another person's refusal to valorize the efforts of reconstruction. Silence, therefore, serves as affirmation of destruction's aftermath; verbal consolation could only exist at the margins of the pain of truth and loss, beyond its possibility as narrative.

Etsuko's retelling of Nagasaki's efforts to rebuild might serve as personal solace for her own present circumstances, but the quiet tone which permeates the telling hints at the story's implication for assessing historical facts. What Genette terms the "narrative mood," or the spatial distance and temporal dislocation contributing to a narrative's tone, shows how Etsuko chooses "to regulate the information [her narrative] delivers, not with a sort of even screening, but according to the capacities of knowledge of one or another participant in the story." That Sachiko might be the other "participant" in Etsuko's story becomes evident as the story centers on a woman's efforts to leave Japan. Sachiko's desire to leave Nagasaki in the period of reconstruction mirrors Etsuko's own unknowing desire to reconstruct a tale which would come years later. The conjunction of the two women's stories also culminates in Etsuko's effort to refashion an image of herself through Ogata-San's recollection.

Importantly, if Sachiko's attempts to escape from Nagasaki are manifested through the later, though unfinished, portrait of Etsuko's own departure to England, Mariko's response to her mother's desires seem to foretell Keiko's fate. During Niki's visit, the household is filled with tension about Keiko, and it is Etsuko's constant remembrance of the past which deflects an extended discussion of death in the "present." Etsuko's return to the past serves to recapitulate history in a moment filled with personal pain, but it is a thwarted effort to merge the private with the social, or what Blanchot calls "the sharing of the secret" between mother and daughter in the present moment of narrative. In other words, Etsuko slowly turns toward what had been kept guarded or hidden and begins the process of unworking the pain in the very silence between herself and Niki. Blanchot calls this condition of "sharing" the first step toward breaking the limits of the repressed past:

> It is also in this sense that what was most personal could not be kept as the secret of one person alone, as it broke the boundaries of the person and demanded to be shared, better, to affirm itself as the very act of sharing.

Etsuko's account of her present life in England and of the past, comprised mostly of family and a limited social life in postwar Nagasaki, has no more subversive intent than to reveal the pain suffered by common people during a turbulent historical period. In other words, the narrative act itself becomes the possible sharing of grief among people. By referring to the past community in Nagasaki and speaking about the present state of affairs, Etsuko gives in to the inevitability of the past as it will determine the outcome in the future, which has already occurred by the time the narrative begins; she does so by producing a private story which is the mirror of other stories still untold. Ishiguro examines the wounds of nuclear destruction in the psyches of a few individuals as seen through Etsuko and, in this way, achieves a fuller portrait than what factual records such as a body count, for instance, might reveal.

What propels the narrative forward, then, has less to do with exposing political depths or revealing family secrets than exploring the peculiar atmosphere of a society reconstructing itself from the remains of nuclear destruction, a fact of the community that is revealed in public records. Everyone in Nagasaki was profoundly affected by devastation, not just a few select individuals singled out for private pain. Foucault's "common odyssey" of people suffering destruction required a maintenance of human dignity in the face of adverse social conditions. This odyssey establishes what Blanchot above called the affirmation of self and others within the community. By remembering the details of existence, one procures—even if years later—the anticipated, but persistently deferred, meaning of those particular episodes. Because the only precedent to such a cataclysm occurred but one day earlier in Hiroshima, the people of Japan were faced

with the monumental task of preserving what vestiges remained of their material lives before rebuilding their emotional and psychological ones as well. Thus enveloped in death and knowledge of destruction, most acted out of instinct and a will to survive the aftermath of horror. No wonder, as in Etsuko's case, that so much time passed before a private horror prompted her to revisit her experiences in Nagasaki and, in so doing, examine the meaning of the personal against history.

In their efforts to rebuild a future for themselves and therefore reconstruct a strong society, the Japanese of *A Pale View of Hills* find a dependable structure in the institution of the family, although in Etsuko's case, this familiar structure eventually collapses. In emulating their symbolic head of state, their emperor, the characters in the novel stress the importance of solidifying their familial relationships. Their interactions are rooted in a discourse of family: loyalty, allegiance, and guidance are important traits of this strengthening. Those who fail to fulfill the terms of these expectations are held in shameful regard while those who put aside personal gain for the benefit of making the family unit cohesive are viewed more positively. This perspective is best reflected in the words of Ogata-San, who speaks for his pre-war generation when he says, "'Discipline, loyalty, such things held Japan together once. That may sound fanciful, but it's true. People were bound by a sense of duty. Toward one's family, towards superiors, towards the country.'" Stated in a rhetoric inflammatory to American democracy, Ogata-San's perspective contests the views of the young, such as those embodied by his son's contemporary, Shigeo Matsuda, who was once Ogata-San's pupil and who, after the war, had written an offensive article against the previous generation. Matsuda tells Ogata-San during a confrontation of wills: "'In your day, children in Japan were taught terrible things. They were taught lies of the most damaging kind. Worst of all, they were taught not to see, not to question. And that's why the country was plunged into the most evil disaster in her entire history.'" Etsuko's representation of these two opposing views shows the impact of individual action upon the collective. During the period of reconstruction, the important terms of the family were thus destabilized: especially for the young, loyalty to the family and state was less effective than a thorough critique of the institutional apparatus. Destruction in Nagasaki was more than physical ruin; it also dismantled values long held sacred in the secular foundation of Japanese society, and it split the Japanese into generational factions.

Not surprisingly, then, in the period Etsuko recounts, the people of Nagasaki are undergoing massive transitions, and the simple dichotomies of right and wrong behavior seem permanently contestable. Following a lull from the worst of the devastation, Etsuko expresses the dubious atmosphere still lingering, that "on the whole the feeling among the occupants seemed one of satisfaction. And yet I remember an unmistakable air of transience there, as if we were all of us waiting for the day we could move to something better." In maintaining strong relationships among family members and friends, people sought to establish the terms for their uncertain future. However, the nuclear destruction sufficiently guaranteed that families would be rent apart in irrevocable ways. The older generation lost faith in the younger, while the latter held the former responsible for unspeakable acts. On the one hand, those who survived the bombing suffered privately; on the other, it is also true that the privacy of the pain was generalized to the society at large. If at times it appeared that Sachiko and Etsuko were the same person, it is also true that many people experienced similar forms of devastation. While the generalities do not diminish the personal suffering, neither do they disperse, and in effect lessen, their intensity among the collective.

To examine this manifestation of the private onto the public during the time of Nagasaki's rebuilding, Etsuko herself reports that the city is intermittently struck by child murders; the news brings report of the tragedies which occur with no discernible pattern. The murders are a double wound on the society, because the young are regarded symbolically as the purveyors of their parents' legacy and thus hold the promise of a new future; in this way, children of the reconstruction period—those who survived the bombing and those waiting to be born—became the salve for those who died in war, even while their parents were denouncing the grandparents. The senselessness and arbitrariness of the violence are reflected in the way the child murders also metaphorically pronounce a death of the future, a message that is embedded in several incidents in Etsuko's narrative. When she speaks of the "misgivings" of motherhood, for instance, she herself embodies the fears and uncertainly of, literally, letting out the next generation.

> "There is nothing that the madness of men invents which is not either nature made manifest or nature restored."

> "Moreover, the power of destructive forces, both outside and within the individual and society, has never appeared as incontestable and irrevocable as it does today."

What begins for Etsuko as a personal postmortem, inquiring into her daughter's death, evolves into a tale about Nagasaki after the bombing. Inquiry into the past serves as the platform for Etsuko's historical consciousness. From the personal tragedy to the fact of Nagasaki, the narrative's unfolding resembles what Blanchot earlier called the sharing of a secret between Etsuko and the reader: there are some events in life rendered forever unspeakable, but it is in the effort to find expression that one deflects the torment of life

onto language. Keiko's death, devastating for the mother who could not guarantee her daughter's happiness and salvation in a foreign land, parallels the meaninglessness of the many lives lost to the atomic bomb. Just as horrific in the tale are the shattered lives being salvaged amidst the wreckage. Etsuko imagines the many days her daughter hung dead and undiscovered in a city of strangers:

> I have found myself continually bringing to mind that picture—of my daughter hanging in her room for days on end. The horror of that image has never diminished, but it has long ceased to be a morbid matter; as with a wound on one's own body, it is possible to develop an intimacy with the most disturbing of things.

The indelible image becomes, paradoxically, the inverse process of destruction; rather than seeing it as an alienated image, the viewer allows it to inhabit her own self so that, in refusing to diminish the power of the image, Etsuko here allows instead for a macabre intimacy, a kind of emotional scab for possible healing.

In thus speaking Nagasaki's story through her daughter's anomalous death, Etsuko manages to infuse the narrative with its strange effect, its seemingly straightforward narration compounded by the subtle suggestions of much deeper implications. As Etsuko leaps back into the past, the reader begins to understand that what remains below the surface of her speech and admission of pain struggles not for expression but silence. Etsuko's mysterious compilation of details concerning Sachiko's life, for instance, evolves less as an effort to speak fully that tale than to represent the grief enveloping her own life—and by extension, the lives of those remaining after Nagasaki—as a silent and ineffable tale. Of this inexplicable state of affairs between self and history, between private experiences and their public contexts, Blanchot writes about the personal and the communal efforts to merge the two realms:

> It does not follow, however, that the community is the simple putting in common, inside the limits it would propose for itself, of a shared will to be several, albeit to do nothing, that is to say, to do nothing else than maintain the sharing of "something" which, precisely, seems always already to have eluded the possibility of being considered as part of a sharing: speech, silence.

Impossible to present the story even to herself, Etsuko can deliver the tale only as the "torment of language" that seeks a beginning and an end to infinite pain of memory and its associated images. Ishiguro's deceptively simple manner of presenting Etsuko's retrospective narrative is complicated by the determination to let silence itself speak. In turning toward the dreaded past, Etsuko conveys a tale that is the disclosure not of a tangible secret, but of a private shame associated with the memories now on the verge of becoming public.

Still, in order to understand how the historical conditions compel either silence or speech, it is necessary to consider how Etsuko's personal case elucidates the political circumstances of postwar Japan. Through Etsuko, Ishiguro seems to ask who or what is, in the end, responsible for the destruction experienced by the common people? What might a postmortem on the political facts reveal to these civilians? The policy of silence which Niki and Etsuko maintain about Keiko's suicide corresponds to the civilians' silence concerning the role of the Emperor in the war. In the novel, Etsuko's husband Jiro covertly establishes a rift against his father, Ogata-San, and shows how young Japanese will use innuendo rather than speak directly in order to convey their hostile sentiments. Jiro most piercingly displays his anger during the chess game with his father. Furthermore, Jiro refuses to speak with his former classmate (Matsuda) about the article written explicitly against the policies of his father's generation. Ogata-San, in keeping with the Japanese tradition of biting back his tongue on any confrontation, is reduced to the shame of having to approach Matsuda himself. What might have remained a family matter turns into a public forum for confrontation. However, as seen in Etsuko's efforts to speak about her own family, the public realm often makes the concealed and the personal more evident, therefore calling attention to the very facts which one sought to conceal.

The themes of individual responsibility and action reappear in Ishiguro's next two novels. The attendant concerns of memory and shame recur as narrative strategies and produce the tension associated with disclosure and concealment. Masuji Ono's tale is less a reflection of his glory days as an artist in Imperial Japan than a rationalizing account of his own participation in world affairs. The narrator Ono notes at the end of the novel that those like him, "have the satisfaction of knowing that whatever we did, we did at the time in the best of faith . . . When one holds convictions deeply enough, there comes a point when it is despicable to prevaricate further." The consolatory tone that characterized Etsuko's farewell to her two daughters—one dead, another alive—reappears in Ono's rationalization, moreover, the tone betrays the very prevarication that arose from the limits of his remembrances. Ono's tale, like Etsuko's, is wrought from the pain of the unspeakable; the efforts to tell the stories of the past are wound into the narrator's growing awareness that the tale is finally unaccountable and inexplicable. In *The Remains of the Day,* Stevens' tale, evolving at the outset as the mission to restore housekeeping help, becomes a confrontation with his allegiance to Lord Darlington, a Nazi sympathizer. To the very end he maintains the onerous lie of his lordship's indirect encouragement of genocide. Stevens' evasion of Darlington's guilt coincides with his silence about love for Miss Kenton/Mrs. Benn, with the two relationships establishing private "enlightenment" and public shame in that narrative.

All three novels appear to end with the narrator's renewed understanding about the past, although their dissimulation remains just below the surface of their overt telling. Even though each confesses to a flawed memory, each also structures the telling to reveal less the substance of an emerging secret than their desires to dispossess or unburden themselves of this past. They are in effect tormented by the confrontation with the past; they seek the compassionate ear of a reader and eye of the witness to ascertain for themselves the necessity of reconstructing an acceptable past. In so doing, however, they attempt to conceal the overbearing shame associated with this past. Their telling emerges as the effort to eradicate shame in the very engagement with language.

At the heart of Ishiguro's fiction lies the mortal's confrontation with empirical realities which preclude the possibility of expression.
—*Cynthia F. Wong*

Conversely, the narrator's evasions are tied to the pain of lurid history itself. In Etsuko's case, if the nuclear arsenal once, literally, dazzled those from afar, that same power casts unspeakable destruction so that even those who survived never recover a language to speak fully that explosion. At the heart of Ishiguro's fiction lies the mortal's confrontation with empirical realities which preclude the possibility of expression. Ishiguro's narrators disarm the reader who searches for the recognizable stutters characteristic of so much contemporary literature. Rather, the narrators speak easily and calmly at first, with the difficulties of telling everything veiled by the very eloquence which masks their pain. Rather than actually deflect this pain, however, their efforts to locate and name the source and site of their experiences thrust them into the torment that both challenges and validates their silence. Only by first acknowledging the catastrophes of their past are they able to begin a critique of their significance. The preliminary gestures of naming and resisting the silence place them on the threshold of admitting to the shame which had structured their memories of that period. Subsequently, they move toward self absolution in language which also contests this possibility.

Bert Cardullo (essay date Winter 1995)

SOURCE: Bert Cardullo, "The Servant," in *The Hudson Review,* Vol. XLVII, No. 4, Winter, 1995, pp. 616-22.

[In the following essay Cardullo compares the movie version of The Remains of the Day *with the novel.]*

Milan Kundera once made a helpful distinction between two sorts of novels set in the past. There is, on the one hand, "the novel that is the illustration of a historical situation . . . popularizations that translate non-novelistic knowledge into the language of the novel," and on the other hand the novel that examines "the historical dimension of human existence." In the first case, cardboard cutouts are wheeled out to represent "the bourgeoisie" or "the last throes of imperialism"— in other words, important social tendencies in the historical scheme of things rather than individualized or self-determined human beings. Here, the background effectively replaces the foreground. In the second case, history is only one part of a multifaceted portrayal of characters whose lives are inevitably and decisively, but not reductively, shaped by larger public events. In this sort of novel, that is, social institutions are presented in the form of complex human relationships; complex human relationships are not reduced to mere social symbols or signposts. Here, the background and the foreground bleed into each other at the same time that each retains its separate identity.

What Kundera says about the novel is transferable to its visual equivalent or rendition, the cinema, and all the more so in the case of a movie that has been adapted from fiction, like **The Remains of the Day.** This film, set in the past and dealing with issues of war, politics, class, and sexuality, has inspired diametrically opposed interpretations following Kundera's scheme. On the one hand, there are those who believe that **The Remains of the Day** states its political themes rather bumptiously, at the expense of character. On the other hand, there are those who consider James Ivory's latest film to be a poignant-pregnant portrait of the English class system up to World War II, of English hierarchies, rigidities, and blindnesses and their human perpetrators as well as victims; a portrait that has far more time to spend on the intimate portrayal of character from which metaphor can be inferred because it need only suggest the history of Hitler's rise and fall, with which its audience is intimately familiar. I propose to sort out these conflicting views, which are to some extent my own, in what follows.

I have not been a big fan of James Ivory's work in the past. It has suffered from a combination of Anglophilia, over-design, and under-emotion. Such films as *Howards End* (1992), *Heat and Dust* (1983), and *The Europeans* (1979) are in the grand British-museum tradition of Alexander Korda, except that Korda's museum for the display of the aristocracy looks now like nothing more than its mausoleum. But that hasn't stopped Ivory, along with his regular producer, Ismail Merchant, and his usual screenwriter, Ruth Prawer Jhabvala, from adding to the list of the dead and embalmed. These movies have nothing to do with contemporary British life; they don't use the past as a combined distancing-telescoping mechanism on the present; and they don't even have much to say about the past *as past.* **The Remains of the Day** marks a break from this tradition for Ivory and company, partly because of the very nature of its subject: the life of an emotionally and sexually repressed *butler* as it dovetails with that of his employer, a well-meaning but wrong-headed aristo-twit who, in the mid-1930s, secretly works to appease Hitler, avoid war, and preserve England's rigid social hierarchy.

The novel was written by Kazuo Ishiguro, who was born Japanese but bred English; it was supposed to have been adapted to the screen by Harold Pinter, but James Ivory discarded his script in favor of Jhabvala's. This is unfortunate because Pinter has proved himself adept at adapting novels with first-person narrators (e.g., *The Go-Between* [1970], *The Proust Screenplay* [1977], *The Heat of the Day* [1989]), something that is made difficult by the natural omniscience of the camera eye. The solution is obviously not to use a first-person camera throughout, to show only what the narrator can see and never the narrator himself, nor to employ large chunks of first-person voiceover narration; what the camera eye must do as much as possible is *see as the narrator in the book does,* see as if it were using the narrator's eyes. This is a neat trick, a kind of imaginative leap, and it can be made only by a screenwriter who is genuinely creative in her own right yet spiritually faithful to her source. Ruth Prawer Jhabvala, alas, is not such a scenarist, though she isn't without a certain skill.

The story begins in 1958, shortly after Lord Darlington's death and the sale of his palatial manor, Darlington Hall, to a solitary, rich American. Stevens, the butler, is staying on to work for the new owner, Mr. Lewis, but with a staff reduced from twenty-eight at the climax of the British Empire to four during its present decline. Stevens is thinking of adding to that staff one Miss Kenton, the former (superbly efficient) housekeeper of Darlington Hall, who has recently sent him a letter (parts of which she reads in voiceover, and to which Stevens responds with his own letter read in voiceover) implying that she would like to return to her old position. So, having been given a week's vacation by his new employer, together with the use of the American's car, he sets out from Oxfordshire on a journey to the West Country to meet Miss Kenton. She's been Mrs. Benn for the past twenty years, during which time Stevens has not seen her, and by now has a grown daughter, but her marriage is in trouble. Miss Kenton seems to be searching for something, then, to be reaching out, and so does Stevens. As he rides through the countryside to his appointment with her, he flashes back to their relationship—or nonrelationship—in the past, as well as to his role as master servant in a house once brimful of statesmen and ambassadors.

It was Stevens' role as servant, as server of Lord Darlington rather than fulfiller of himself, that got in the way of any personal relationship he might have had with Miss Kenton. A love seemed to evolve between these two household workers who never so much as call each other by their first names, but it remained unacknowledged and unexpressed—at least on Stevens' part. There is no real acknowledgement of its existence by Miss Kenton either, but there is some expression of feeling, which unexpectedly gets underscored in the film. Indeed, even Stevens' feeling gets expressed in the movie version, which recasts Ishiguro's exquisitely balanced tale more as doomed romance than as political allegory. This is a direction Pinter, with his latter-day political engagement, may have reversed, and a direction the normally reticent Ivory has apparently chosen to take in the condescending belief that the lower orders of society are more given to venting their emotions. For example, during one of their nightly meetings to discuss the management of the house, Miss Kenton responds to Stevens' question "Are you with me?" with the excuse that she is very tired. She is tired, of course—tired of meeting with him under these circumstances, solely to discuss work—but this meaning of "tired" remains subtextual in the novel. In the film, Miss Kenton directly express the sentiment that she wants to *be* with Stevens, not merely to talk with him about the discharge of their servants' duties.

The next day, her day off, she has a date in a pub with Tom Benn, a former butler who wants to marry her and open his own seaside boarding house at Clevedon. There is no such scene in the book; it fractures the first-person perspective of Stevens; and it's almost immediately followed by another insertion, Miss Kenton's desperate revelation to him of her impending engagement, to which he reacts by hastily leaving the room. Later, after she becomes formally engaged, Stevens impatiently offers her his "warmest congratulations," for "there are matters of global significance taking place upstairs and [he] must return to [his] post." Then, in the process of fetching drinks for Lord Darlington's guests, he drops a fine bottle of port—one more "emotional" event that does not occur in Ishiguro's novel—peremptorily replaces it with another, and proceeds to deliver it. But he must pass Miss Kenton's room in order to do so, and here again the film tellingly diverges from its source. This is what the author understatedly writes:

> As I approached Miss Kenton's door, I saw from the light seeping around its edges that she was still within. And . . . that moment as I paused in the dimness of the corridor, the tray in my hands, an ever-growing conviction [mounted] within me that just a few yards away, on the other side of that door.

Miss Kenton was at that moment crying. As I recall, there was no real evidence to account for this conviction—I had certainly not heard any sounds of crying—and yet I remember being quite certain that were I to knock and enter, I would discover her in tears.

In Ivory's film, as you might guess, the door does get opened and Stevens discovers Miss Kenton in tears, only to advise her that some household article wants dusting! Further, after the butler departs, the camera remains on Miss Kenton, regarding her heartbroken face in a way that Stevens could never bring himself to do.

The camera does this once more near the end of *The Remains of the Day.* Stevens and Miss Kenton have had their meeting and character-history has proved to be human destiny: the aging butler will return to his butlering without ever having brought up the subject of their dormant love, and the now matronly housekeeper will go back to her marriage and the promise of a grandchild from her expectant daughter. As he puts Miss Kenton on a bus in the novel, Stevens notices that she is crying and comforts her with some pleasantries—nothing more. As he puts her on that same bus in the film, Miss Kenton is not yet in tears. For heightened effect, we see her crying through the window of the departing bus as Stevens does; then, after he leaves the frame, we get another shot of her face receding in tears. From whose point of view? The omniscient camera-as-narrator, or Ivory-cum-Jhabvala as *nouveau* italicizers of emotion. This team even manages to inject heat into the novel's politics, or to put its heart where Ishiguro's head has prevailed. For instance, in the novel Lord Darlington, after "doing a great deal of thinking," tells Stevens to dismiss two Jewish housemaids, which he summarily does despite the strenuous objections of Miss Kenton. We never learn from Ishiguro what becomes of them, because in the book the girls are *English* Jews and therefore would not have been in danger of deportation. But in the movie the two maids are *German*-Jewish; Darlington decides they must be let go as he reads *Mein Kampf* (!); and, without work, the two young women are soon sent back to Germany, whence they are dispatched to concentration camps.

Ivory and Jhabvala readily seize on other opportunities to show the audience that their political heart is in the right place. Before departing for the West Country, Stevens is sent by them on business to the local general store, where he denies ever having known Lord Darlington, whom the clerk has decried as a Nazi sympathizer. No such scene occurs in the novel, and its effect is to change Stevens from an obtusely loyal, blindly trustful servant to a shifty timeserver masquerading as a man of conscience. En route to Clevedon, Stevens has a similar encounter—embellished by the filmmakers—with a doctor at an inn, where customers mistake the butler for a gentleman on account of his proper diction and dignified bearing. The high-born doctor senses Stevens' working-class origins and gets him to admit, in the film, that he is "in service" at a great house in Oxfordshire. Inevitably, their cinematic conversation comes around to Lord Darlington of Oxfordshire, whom the doctor pillories for his virtual collaboration with the Nazis, and with whom Stevens once again disavows any acquaintance. Then he relents and tells the truth: he was proud to have served Lord Darlington but his job was just that, *to serve,* not to agree or disagree with his employer's political views. He goes on to say that, in attempting to accommodate Hitler, Darlington made a mistake for which he later sincerely repented; whereas he, Stevens, once made a mistake too—but one that he can correct rather than lament. The teasing implication, of course, is that his mistake was a matter of the heart rather than politics: to have repressed his love for Miss Kenton, which he will shortly *express* to her in Clevedon.

Stevens' words here are a complete reversal of what he says in the novel, *two days after* Miss Kenton's departure by bus, to a man sitting next to him on a pier in Weymouth:

> Lord Darlington wasn't bad man. He wasn't a bad man at all. And at least he had the privilege of being able to say at the end of his life that he made his own mistakes. His lordship was a courageous man. He chose a certain path in life, it proved to be a misguided one, but there, he chose it, he can say that at least. As for myself, I cannot even claim that. You see, I *trusted.* I trusted in his lordship's wisdom. All those years I served him, I trusted I was doing something worthwhile. I can't even say I made my own mistakes. Really—one has to ask oneself—what dignity is there in that?

Stevens appears less politically correct in this speech, since he calls Darlington courageous if misguided; but he also appears more emotionally honest because he speaks of his mistakes as irremediable in addition to undignifying, as inherent in his character as the narrative has established it. And they are *mistakes,* not one mistake, the use of the plural serving to conflate Stevens' relationship to Lord Darlington with his relationship to Miss Kenton. For the two relationships, and the butler's mistakes in them, are indeed related, as is Stevens' first-person perspective to the novel's thematic intent.

Ironically, Stevens gets to speak for himself in Ishiguro's tale, whereas in the past he had always allowed Lord Darlington to speak for him or at least to speak in his place. But in speaking for himself, he only reveals the tragicomic extent of his political capitulation and emotional barrenness, his substitution of a life of peripheral protocol for one of direct involvement. Being a butler, for Stevens, has been an act of

selfless fealty toward a lord, not a mere profession or business—moreover, toward a lord engaged in great undertakings designed to secure England's future. He has allowed nothing to come between him and his duty to Darlington, not even the love of Miss Kenton, so satisfactory has his relationship with his master been. And Lord Darlington, for his part, has allowed nothing to come between him and his duty to his country, not even the love of a wife, so satisfactory has his life of (behind-the-scenes) public service been. As a member of the household staff at Darlington Hall, Miss Kenton serves Stevens even as he serves his lord and his lord serves the state. The problem with this hierarchy of faithful service, however, is that it permits no room for second-guessing, and second-guessing is what the action of both master and butler so desperately require. When Miss Kenton tries to question the actions of her "betters"—particularly in the dismissal of the Jewish maids—she is rebuffed. No one questions the fact that the happy "partnership" of Stevens and Lord Darlington seems to rule out the need for female companionship, though I hasten to add that there is nothing overtly or even covertly sexual about their relationship.

Ishiguro means, I think, to make Stevens' blindness—both to Darlington's political naïveté and Miss Kenton's emotional warmth—stand as a metaphor for England's blindness to its own national character and destiny. Just as Stevens trusted in Lord Darlington, Darlington trusted in his, and his country's ability to broker a lasting peace with the Germans where no one else had been able to. That is, he and his associates—who recall the members of the notorious if somewhat mythologized "Cliveden set"—placed their trust in the cachet of British empire and aristocracy, as did Prime Minister Neville Chamberlain after them. They were mistaken to do so because, as Hitler clearly saw, the empire and its royalty were headed for extinction. Stevens thought he was serving the empire by denying himself, but all that he really did was deny himself, deny the love that could have given his life some dimension. He unquestioningly accepted the class system and his insulated place in it, and his reward, like that of many of his countrymen high and low, was a life of lovelessness if not brutality, of coldness if not desolation, of constriction if not misery. Stevens' singular detachment or self-enclosure is well conveyed by the novel's first-person perspective, which naturally permits no other points of view to interject themselves and which furthermore allows Stevens to create his character, as well as its social significance, by indirection, without resort to psychologizing on the one hand or historicizing on the other. One of the problems with Ivory's film, as I've indicated, is that the omniscient camera *does* intervene and perhaps had no choice but to intervene. In doing so, however, it sacrifices Stevens' integral tunnel vision without providing any compensatory light.

The title of Ishiguro's novel refers both to the remains of

Stevens' own day—to the quiet evenings following his daily yeoman's service as well as to the lonely retirement that awaits him—and to the twilight of British imperialism. That twilight tends to get moved back to its heyday or sunshine in Ivory's film, partly because of Tony Pierce-Roberts' cinematography, which appears celebratory instead of elegiac, lush rather than weathered; partly because of the movie's ending, which instead of finding Stevens sitting alone on a seaside bench in the evening (as the novel does), shows him back at Darlington Hall the next morning going about his duties, which happen to include—oh, cliché of cinematic clichés!—releasing a trapped pigeon into the verdant beauty of the surrounding countryside; and partly because of the documentary-like sequences showing, even glorying in, how a great manor is run, from the butler's ironing of the morning paper page by page to the scullery maid's cleaning of the cutlery, from the elaborate preparation of meals to the equally elaborate accommodation of numerous important guests. The camera remains somewhat removed through all of this, yet one can't help thinking that the preoccupied Stevens would never take the time to scan the place and process of his work in such loving detail. Nor, as I've already pointed out, would he regard Miss Kenton in the way the camera does: lingeringly and lovingly. In the novel, she's a figure of imagination, created by words, a player in Stevens' internal dramas whose face we never see. In the film, Miss Kenton takes on a life of her own—especially as acted by the estimable, I dare say enchanting, Emma Thompson. And that life with its drama detracts a bit from Stevens' own. Anthony Hopkins doesn't play the butler, he *inhabits* him as he knew he must if he were going to capture the inner life of a man who very nearly has no outer life, and whose appeal to any woman has to come from deep inside his self-imposed carapace. Hopkins creates a similar character in a film released almost at the same time as *The Remains of the Day:* Richard Attenborough's *Shadowlands,* the love story of C. S. Lewis and the American poet (as well as film critic) Joy Davidman. But there he is burdened by a script and direction far more sentimental than what Ivory and Jhabvala give him.

I obviously have my problems with their *Remains of the Day,* but I'll take it rather than no film version at all. And not least because of the generally fine supporting cast, among whose members two stand out: Hugh Grant, as Lord Darlington's presciently critical, refreshingly playful godson, and Peter Vaughan, as Stevens' aged underbutler of a father whose death inspires little filial emotion in his son. Even here, however, a mistake was made in (1) conflating the parts of the postwar American millionaire who buys Darlington Hall and an American Congressman who attends a prewar Darlington conference to speak against the appeasement of the Nazis; and (2) casting the eager but wooden Christopher Reeve in the "collapsed" role. The man whose denunciation of Hitler at the Hall fell on deaf ears would most likely not revisit such a painful and frustrating memory in his retirement, nor would he then dimly declare—in Jhabvala's screenplay—that he couldn't recall what he said that evening in Oxfordshire more than twenty years ago. This puts his character on an intellectual level with Lord Darlington himself, and even Christopher Reeve is not *that* stupid. Neither, finally, is the film of which he is a part.

Roz Kaveney (review date 12 May 1995)

SOURCE: Roz Kaveney, "Tossed and Turned," in *New Statesman and Society,* Vol. 8, No. 352, May 12, 1995, p. 39.

[*In the following negative review, Kaveney calls* The Unconsoled *a "talented mess of a novel."*]

Dreams are the most personal of universal experiences. Writers who deal in them may get credit for what is recognised or for what forces its way into the shared grammar of dreaming, but will be told there is no art in telling what everyone knows. They will be blamed for anything that seems too personal or feels like mere invention. Ishiguro's tortuous tale of missed appointments suffers, and occasionally succeeds, under all these rubrics.

Freud claimed all dreams for literary criticism, to be decoded as a poem full of hermetic symbolism. Jung added historicist New Criticism: your dreams are not your own, but merely inheritors of rules. They imposed a loss of innocence on the telling of dreams that is responsible for the sheer guarded mundanity of this novel. Ishiguro's discreet refusal of florid invention evades potentially embarrassing tropes at the cost of a deep dullness.

Ryder, an international virtuoso, arrives in a small town to play in a concert. The town combines an old quarter full of quaint bars where folksy Germanic porters engage in trials of strength with housing estates full of people Ryder knew in his suburban teens; its dignitaries and eccentrics are Mittel-European or middle-class English. He wanders around trying to honour commitments from which he is deflected, sometimes in the company of Sophie and her son, Boris, who may or may not be his wife and child.

Sometimes a gear shifts and he shares the consciousness of the underrated pianist son of the local hotelier, or the rehabilitated drunk conductor Brodsky. They perform, and are humiliated; Ryder never plays, practises, eats or sleeps, but wanders down irrelevant corridors or onto trams without destinations.

What is wrong with all this? Part of the trouble is what looks like awful literary knowingness. Ryder shares a surname with the narrator of *Brideshead Revisited,* another novel of going back and not doing that which you ought to have done. His name is also cognate with Ritter, the German knight: the chess piece that sets off in one direction and then turns in another. It is hard to be certain whether the S and B pairing of Sophie and Boris is intended to echo Carroll's *Sylvie and Bruno,* or whether this is simply the sort of book that plays so many irritating precious gambits that the attentive reader moves from closer reading to paranoia.

In *The Remains of the Day,* the butler protagonist spoke in a pompous idiolect that revealed him as an unreliable narrator. Hardly has Ryder arrived when he is subjected to a lecture from Gustav, the hotel porter and Sophie's father, on the duties of porters, delivered in a similar idiolect. The dignitaries fall into yet another one. It makes reading the novel rather like having Anthony Hopkins loom out at you from dark corners in a variety of thin disguises.

My own impression of high culture in dreams is that it mingles the imaginary and the well-known with things one knows exist, and can guesstimate the experience of Ryder and his colleagues only ever play or discuss non-existent music, which all sounds as if it is written by Michael Nyman. This is not credible: even in dreams, musicians have to play the *Moonlight Sonata* or the *Maple Leaf Rag.*

Ishiguro is representing as a realm a place that is actually a border post. He writes as if the rules of dream were constituted by the unconscious, rather than by the protocols of trade between the waking and sleeping self. This intermittently evokes how it feels to have an anxiety dream, but in 500 pages we expect more. Joyce alluded to the whole of western culture in the dream of *Finnegans Wake.*

The novel's various closures—the death of Gustav, the humiliation of Brodsky, the departure of Sophie and Boris—feel artificial. The only proper closure of a dream is to wake up, usually with nothing settled. Ishiguro has produced a talented mess of a novel that leaves one with the ill temper and headache produced by lying for too long in the wrong position.

Merle Rubin (review date 4 October 1995)

SOURCE: "Probing the Plight of Lives 'Trapped' in Others' Expectations," in *Christian Science Monitor,* Vol. 87, October 4, 1995, p. 14.

[*In the following review of* The Unconsoled, *Rubin argues that while the book may seem labyrinthine and nearly boring, it is also fascinating and skillfully written.*]

Kazuo Ishiguro*'s* first novel, *A Pale View of Hills* (1981), portrays his native city, Nagasaki, in the wake of the bombing that devastated it nine years before his birth. His second novel *An Artist of the Floating World* (1986), unfolded in the alien milieu of prewar, imperialist Japan. In his third novel, the Booker Prize-winning *Remains of the Day* (1990), Ishiguro imagined the world seen through the eyes of a stuffy, repressed English butler on the verge of retirement.

Now, in his fourth novel, *The Unconsoled,* this gifted and versatile writer, raised and educated in England, takes on a theme of Kafkaesque complexity that is played out in an ambience as overwhelmingly Central European as a vat of steaming goulash with dumplings.

The story is narrated by Ryder, a world-famous pianist who arrives in an unidentified European city to give a concert. From the instant of his arrival, Ryder is politely but relentlessly besieged by people wanting him to do small favors that will only take a "moment" out of his busy schedule but which will supposedly change their lives immeasurably. From the hotel manager who begs him to take a few minutes to look at the collection of press cuttings his music-loving wife has assembled about his career, to an old friend who pleads with Ryder to stop by her women's cultural group to prove that she really knows him, everyone wants to make use of the visiting celebrity.

As if this were not daunting enough, Ryder is already at a distinct disadvantage from the moment he sets foot in town: For some reason, he can't remember where he is or what he is expected to do.

He is supposed to be following a schedule of lectures, meetings, and social events leading up to his concert. But he has no copy of this schedule, and —-what is stranger still— doesn't tell his host. If Ryder is a man who has stumbled into a situation that makes very little sense, he is also one who doesn't try very hard to make sense of it.

As in his previous novel, Ishiguro is concerned here with the ways in which role-playing, the fabrication of a public facade, can eviscerate the private self. It's not surprising that in attempting to describe this strange and elusive novel, its publishers should characterize its protagonist as "a man whose public self has taken on a life of its own." Certainly, Ryder is portrayed as having been too busy with his career to spend enough time with his family and as someone who allows his daily activities, sometimes his very thoughts, to be shaped by the demands of his so-called public.

But this is just the beginning. Not only Ryder, but everyone else in town seems caught in a trap of his or her own making. And in each case, this "trap," this inability to act, is based upon that person's misconception of how others see him. There's the kindly old hotel porter who stopped talking to his daughter for the most trivial of reasons years ago when she was a child, and still cannot bring himself to address her now, except by communicating his comments via her little boy. There's the man who married a music-loving woman who mistook him for an aspiring composer: Nearly two decades later, never having actually discussed this with her, he keeps wondering if she knows the truth and will leave him.

Ryder himself is obsessed with the fact that his parents are expected to come to town for the upcoming concert: He still sees them as the ultimate arbiters of his success.

Ishiguro brilliantly conveys the claustrophobic atmosphere of this status-conscious city that prides itself on its reverence for culture and suffers from a mild inferiority complex vis-a-vis larger places, such as Vienna or Stuttgart. The citizens are exaggeratedly deferential, indeed, obsequious, toward their distinguished guest, yet underlyingly demanding and bossy.

"If you find time to sit down at the Hungarian Cafe . . . ," advises the helpful porter, "I feel certain you won't regret it. I would suggest you order a pot of coffee and a piece of apple strudel. Incidentally, sir, I did just wonder . . . if I might ask a small favor. . . . You see, I just know my daughter will be at the Hungarian Cafe. She'll have little Boris with her, she's a very pleasant young woman, sir, I'm sure you'd feel very sympathetic towards her. . . ."

And on he rambles for another few pages, pressuring Ryder to meet his daughter. Everyone else in town seems afflicted with the same logorrhea, launching at a moment's notice into interminable dialogues, trying to draw him into their obsessions.

The physical layout of the city reinforces this sense of entrapment: Hallways lead into rooms in distant buildings, brick walls loom suddenly between pedestrians and their goals, and the harried Ryder often gets lost in a labyrinth or finds himself going in circles. The distinguished visitor is often overwhelmed by a sensation of powerlessness. Worse yet, he begins to find himself behaving quite as irrationally as his hosts.

Needless to say, the cumulative effect of some 500 pages of frustration and anxiety is something akin to boredom. Yet this boredom—though scarcely "exquisite" in the manner of Proust—is oddly fascinating. Occasionally, when some small breakthrough occurs and someone manages to express a true feeling, there is a poignant glimmer of hope.

Wending one's way through the labyrinth of atrophied emo-

tion and blocked expression, one may chafe at the longueurs, but still appreciate the imagination and artistry with which they have been rendered.

Richard Eder (review date 8 October 1995)

SOURCE: Richard Eder, "Meandering in a Dreamscape," in *Los Angeles Time Book Review,* October 8, 1995, pp. 3, 7.

[*In the following review, Eder claims that* The Unconsoled *is a complex and ambitious novel which becomes wearisome but is also rewarding.*]

Awake, we choose our life or our life chooses us, and we spend our days living out the consequences of the choice. Asleep and dreaming, we are haunted by all the choices we didn't make and their exfoliating consequences. A kind of vital mainspring usually lets us give priority to our daytime acts and keep at bay the infinite alternatives, which, if admitted, would bring us to a clogged halt.

Any choice or action, however virtuous or prudent, will cause some pain, loss or dilapidation somewhere, even if it is only for what is not chosen or done. Daytime's mainspring lets us lock down the possible guilt and regret for these things. At night the guilts, the insufficiencies, the terrors have nothing to check them but the twin facts that they are bodiless and that we are going to wake up.

Kazuo Ishiguro, in whose tersely sculpted novels of moral complexity and regret the night world looms faintly through the daylight (*The Remains of the Day, An Artist of the Floating World*), has now published a full-fledged nocturnal sprawl. It is not, of course, as huge and unrestrained as the most famous of dream novels: H.C. Earwicker's 678-page sleep in *Finnegans Wake.* It lacks the vast web of conscious and unconscious digression, the portmanteau inclusiveness of just about everything its author knew, its quadrilingual puns, its global myth and its fearful difficulty.

For all that, *The Unconsoled* is complex and ambitious, and undeniably difficult. If not a literary Everest—oxygen! Sherpas! can we please go home!—it is at any rate a Mt. Washington, and formidable enough. It offers some remarkable views, and flowers that grow only in the thin air of heights. Whether they are worth the climb is beyond even the subjectivity of a review. At any rate, it is a book that is not given but has to be earned.

The Unconsoled is the life of a public man seen by the infrared light of his dreaming vulnerabilities. Ryder is a famous pianist but he could be any celebrated artist. The night doubts and demons that declare the unreality of his achievements presumably reflect something of what goes on between the much-honored Ishiguro and his own pillow.

Ryder finds himself the honored guest of a nameless European city, German or Swiss in feeling, and plunged into a profound moral and spiritual crisis. In this allegorical place such a crisis is declared in terms of music. The city's tutelary composer, Christoff, an abstract modernist, is in disgrace; a movement is afoot to replace him with his predecessor, Brodsky, a once-revered romantic destroyed by his own debauchery and the winds of fashion.

A cabal made up of local politicians, a countess who is a leading art patron and the manager of the finest hotel is working to rehabilitate him. It is no mere musical matter; it means restoring the god to the abandoned civic temple. Either we succeed, one Brodsky supporter says, "or resign ourselves to being just another cold, lonely city."

Thus Ryder's effusive welcome. He is to play and speak in a few days' time at a concert at which Brodsky is to demonstrate his regained mastery as a conductor. Ryder's international prestige will put the seal on the enshrinement.

From the moment he checks into his hotel, everything goes askew, not as in life but as in a nightmare. He is told that he has a crowded schedule of vital meetings and events but never learns what it is. Everyone makes a claim on him he can't refuse. The hotel manager wants him to spare a moment to examine a book of clippings collected by his wife, ostensibly a Ryder fan; her sanity, he implies, depends on it. The manager's son, Stephen, a failed pianist who has taken up the instrument again, wants him to listen to a fearsomely difficult piece he will play at the Brodsky concert.

A hotel porter, Gustav, asks him to attend a meeting of the city's hotel porters and work a reference to their devoted work into his concert talk. He also asks him to talk to Sophia, his daughter, who is in a deep depression. Sophia, it turns out—everything displaces and reassembles—is Ryder's estranged wife. She wants him to abandon his peripatetic celebrity and make a home with her and their mournful little son, Boris. Boris wants Ryder to take him to their old apartment and reclaim a favorite toy.

The interruptions and demands escalate. Each time he sets out to fulfill one, he is waylaid by a new one. They become more and more insistent, and each is connected obscurely to a primal failure of his own. An old English schoolmate turns up indignant because he has not come to tea. An old English girlfriend accosts him on the tram where she is a ticket-taker and demands to know why he hasn't turned up at a Ryder fan circle she has organized. He churns in all directions, never manages to get where he is going—typical of a nightmare—and all the while time is running out for him

to practice for the concert. It is another typical nightmare, the performer's, at finding himself onstage unprepared.

Not only do the claims, and Ryder's sense of failure, multiply, but each proliferates in its own complexity and intensity. Different town factions make use of him. Everywhere he goes he is effusively welcomed, yet before long each welcome turns into recrimination or, still worse, invisibility. At the receptions in his honor nobody pays attention to him unless it is to allude to some past failure or present omission. When he finally gets to the meeting of his fan club, the women ignore him while talking excitedly about how they almost met him at one of his public appearances.

The succession of inexplicable claims, frustrations and cordialities that turn into recriminations, the frequent refusal of places to stay put, and a tendency for destinations to recede as Ryder approaches them—there is more than a suggestion of "Alice in Wonderland"—go on and on. Amid the dreamlike figures, some—Sophia, the forlorn Boris, the maddened Brodsky—acquire a sharp and vivid poignancy. The absurdities become even more spectacular.

Ishiguro writes them with his characteristic grace and offbeat pungency. But for much of the book he strings them together, link by link, in a chain that seems to exist for itself, without binding anything up. It is a long meander whose picturesque curves grow wearisome after a while, for lack of a sense of a sea beyond. There is indeed such a sea. Ryder's long nightmare operates a change in him; he has a ruefully chastened awakening at the end. It is an unexpectedly satisfying end but it needed to come sooner. The recounting of a dream is as quick to fade as the dream itself.

Brooke Allen (review date 11 October 1995)

SOURCE: Brooke Allen, "Leaving Behind Daydreams for Nightmares," in *The Wall Street Journal,* October 11, 1995, p. 12.

[*In the following review of* The Unconsoled, *Allen argues that while Ishiguro has chosen a new writing style, his subject matter remains the same.*]

Six years ago, at the age of 35, Kazuo Ishiguro came to international attention as the author of *The Remains of the Day,* an elegant novel that won the 1989 Booker Prize and was made into a film by Merchant and Ivory. In *The Remains of the Day* Mr. Ishiguro trod territory that he had already explored in his first two novels. *A Pale View of Hills* (1982) and *An Artist of the Floating World* (1986). The narrator was once again an elderly person—in this case an English butler—looking back upon a life of meaningless ritual, missed opportunities, failed love. It established Mr. Ishiguro as a realistic artist, who wrote traditional stories in a formal, rather anachronistic style. Some even compared him to Henry James.

Mr. Ishiguro later admitted that he wanted to write something less realistic in form. The result is *The Unconsoled,* a departure for Mr. Ishiguro and an unusual, striking piece of work.

Imagine an alternate world in which life is not a dream but in which the dream is your life—in other words, where you must live your life by the inexplicable logic and ever changing rules imposed by the dream itself. This is the fate of Ryder, the dreamer and the novel's narrator.

The middle-aged Ryder, an English-man, is a world-famous pianist. He finds himself at a hotel in a small and obscure city somewhere in Central Europe and is greeted by the manager, Mr. Hoffman; on Thursday night, it transpires, Ryder will be giving an important concert, and in the two intervening days he has numerous engagements and duties to fulfill. Ryder has no idea what these duties are, nor does he know what pieces he is supposed to play in the concert. With misplaced diffidence, however, he refrains from asking his hosts to elucidate matters.

Thus he sets out on a lengthy misadventure in an aura, peculiar to anxiety dreams of extreme disorientation. Ryder is always lost, always desperately trying to get from one location to some vital appointment for which he is horribly late. And as he struggles to meet his myriad obligations, he finds himself constantly impeded by people in desperate need of succor that only he can give.

All the frustrations so characteristic of anxiety dreams are placed in Ryder's path. He addresses a formal gathering with his genitalia exposed, trying to identify himself, he is unable to articulate his own name and can only strain and grunt; an unbreachable brick wall separates him, just before curtain time, from the concert hall; he is borne away on a tram by bossy journalists, having left a small child alone in a cafe.

Mr. Ishiguro is skillful at evoking the claustrophobia and chaos of a dream; more important, he puts across, with great force, the very real emotional urgency that infuses such dreams. The comic potential in Ryder's travails is always there, but it is overshadowed by his obvious fear, his sense of personal inadequacy in the face of overwhelming responsibilities, his foolish attention to minor duties at the expense of the people who should be most important to him.

For as the tale progresses Mr. Ishiguro artfully points to the fact that alongside the dream-story of Ryder's European sojourn exists another story, Ryder's real story. While Ryder grapples with the complications of his schedule, Sophie and Boris, incidental characters—the daughter and grandson of the hotel porter—impinge on Ryder's attention until it slowly be comes evident that they are not wholly un familiar to him, that they are, in fact, his wife and child. Various friends from Ryder's English childhood appear in odd places, recalling seminal emotional episodes of his early life. A gifted young pianist who is crushed by his egotistical parents might just be a version of Ryder as a youth. And as Ryder takes out his rage toward his parents on Sophie and little Boris, he repeats the cycle of familial sickness that has blighted his own life.

It would seem, then, that Ryder is not so very different from Stevens the butler, another antihero whose obsession with petty duties has kept him from attending to his major one, his duty toward his own heart. Yet *The Unconsoled,* while unlikely to be such a crowd-pleaser as *The Remains of the Day,* is the better novel. *The Remains of the Day* was a meticulous piece of work, but in it Mr. Ishiguro told us nothing that had not been told better by predecessors like E.M. Forster and Christopher Isherwood. The Briton's familiar catalogue of faults—his fear of emotion, his slavish love of form and tradition—were faithfully rehearsed.

The Unconsoled is more universal. Its melding of conscious and subconscious is effective, and the novel is entirely fresh, with no old-fashioned surrealism or Freudian cliché. No doubt some readers will liken it to Kafka, or to Lewis Carroll, but it is not a derivative book. Nor is it heavily stylized. "The kind of book I find very tedious is the kind of book whose raison d'être is to say something about literary form," Mr. Ishiguro has stated. While *The Unconsoled* might seem more "experimental" than his earlier works, Mr. Ishiguro's subject continues to be, as it has always been, character and emotion.

Charlotte Innes (review date 6 November 1995)

SOURCE: Charlotte Innes, "Dr. Faustus Faces the Music," in *The Nation,* Vol. 261, No. 15, November 6, 1995, pp. 546-48.

[*In the following review of* The Unconsoled, *Innes praises Ishiguro for creating an exciting, well written, and humourous novel.*]

How hard it is to be true to yourself when people expect you to be something else. Kazuo Ishiguro, the Japanese-born English writer, known to millions for the movie version of his Booker Prize-winning novel *The Remains of the Day,* has wrestled for his identity more than most, first as an immigrant writer struggling to throw off the noose of stereotype and now as a postmodern novelist who jolted British critical preconceptions earlier this year with his fourth novel, *The Unconsoled.*

A discordant, plot-entangled, sometimes farcical nightmare of a book, nearly three times longer than his earlier works, filled with literary echoes and characters who won't shut up, Ishiguro's latest work has prompted reactions like "a stinker," "boring" and "chaotic."

Early American reviews sound puzzled. Like other writers who switch styles, Ishiguro will surely spark passions of every hue. For me, this is the first Ishiguro novel to arouse not only admiration but visceral excitement. As I read, it was as if Ishiguro were speaking directly to my concerns—how to juggle family, community, political activism and art. His nightmarish dreamscape doesn't entirely work. But he more than makes up for it. Here is a great writer spreading his wings and soaring high.

If controversy is new for Ishiguro, who has long been admired for his easy narrative style, he certainly knows what it's like to be misunderstood. His first two novels, *A Pale View of the Hills* and *An Artist of the Floating World,* which were set largely in post-World War II Japan, drew praise for their delicate "Japanese style"—even for the quality of the "translation"—though Ishiguro hasn't seen his birthplace since he was 5 and can only speak, not write, Japanese. Likewise, *The Remains of the Day,* which focused on the changing life of a butler called Stevens, drew puzzled admiration for his intimate knowledge of the day-to-day running of British aristocratic households.

In *The Unconsoled,* it's almost as if Ishiguro took reviewers' misconceptions to heart and cast a fog of vagueness over characters, setting and action to avoid stereotyping. An internationally renowned pianist named only Mr. Ryder arrives in an unnamed, seemingly Middle European city of flawlessly polite citizens to give a recital. Almost immediately, he finds he's also expected to solve a civic crisis that's never clearly explained. The symptoms are hinted at: "dozens of sad cases. . . . Of lives blighted by loneliness. Of families despairing of ever rediscovering the happiness they'd once taken for granted."

But the problem is not political or economic but musical. Citizens feel their hometown music is technically brilliant but lacks soul. The proposed solution is to dethrone the current musical leader, a cellist named Henri Christoff who is an advocate of stylistic restraint, and replace him with someone who has more verve and passion—or what one city father sinisterly describes as "true music" that shares "our values." They have chosen Leo Brodsky, an alcoholic who, it has been discovered, once had a remarkable career as an orchestra conductor.

Mr. Ryder is too polite or too afraid to ask some basic questions about this strange musical crisis, yet he feels compelled to help these people in the spirit of solving the city's problems with a sense of empathy so marked it sometimes becomes an uncanny ability to see into people's minds. He also suppresses any will of his own. A strange woman called Sophie asserts that he is her husband and the father of her little boy, Boris, and Mr. Ryder takes even this for granted, half-remembering a past with them.

Gradually, people's needs inflate Mr. Ryder's sense of mission. But as he struggles to be all things to all people—brilliant musician, devoted family man, consummate politician and social therapist—his life turns into a mess of tortuous car rides, missed appointments and barely kept tempers, culminating in the recital, a disaster that only confirms his outsider status.

Mr. Ryder sits alone on a tram with a sense of solitude so painful he breaks down and sobs. A friendly stranger offers comfort—echoing the end of *The Remains of the Day*—an act of spontaneous kindness that allows Mr. Ryder, like Stevens, to bury his anguish and don his rose-colored spectacles.

Clearly, *The Unconsoled* is tackling some old obsessions from a new angle.

In not naming the city, yet giving it a Germanic flavor and inhabitants who are unfailingly polite even under great stress, Ishiguro offers his usual cast of repressed and self-deceiving characters but in a different guise. Mr. Ryder is as misguided (and as easily swayed) in his attempts to help the city as Masuji Ono, the artist in *An Artist of the Floating World* who compromises his art to serve imperialist Japan. He's also like Stevens, who believes that with his unquestioning service as a butler he is making a better world.

> **Like Schönberg's dissonant, atonal music, *The Unconsoled* whacks us again and again with its unharmonious message about failed communication.**
> **—*Charlotte Innes***

Ishiguro's choice of music to represent a Germanic city's crisis is also significant. It suggests Thomas Mann's *Dr. Faustus,* in which a great composer, Adrian Leverkühn (modeled on the inventor of atonal music, Arnold Schönberg), struggles to write a new kind of music: a dark tone poem, based on the legend of Faust's pact with the devil, to reflect the growth of German fascism, which famously bent the public will to its own ends with the aid of a charismatic leader. (In Ishiguro's punning dream language,

Christoff suggests both Christ and Mephistopheles, and Brodsky too is a crucified savior in permanent pain from an old "wound.")

Like Schönberg's dissonant, atonal music, *The Unconsoled* whacks us again and again with its unharmonious message about failed communication. Worse, all this division and self-absorption is passed from one generation to the next. Mr. Ryder's unhappy childhood memories are reflected in his fraught relationship with Boris—who desperately and touchingly tries to get Mr. Ryder's attention by studying a tiling manual—and in his dealings with Stephen, a would-be pianist whose cruelly perfectionist parents remind Mr. Ryder of his own.

In Ishiguro's work, as in Mann's, people cannot handle complexity. They prefer to sweeten and deny, as Mr. Ryder does on the tram and as the citizenry does in rejecting Brodsky's debut conducting session. Like Mann's burghers who are repulsed by the torment of the mad composer and a Faust who is allowed "no consolation, appeasement, transfiguration," Ishiguro's community is shocked by the anguish Brodsky evokes in the music. (Thus in shuttered minds, the seeds of fascism grow.)

Far from being "chaotic," *The Unconsoled* is as tightly plotted as anything Ishiguro has written, with many interwoven narrative threads. As in his other novels, none of these threads are happily tied by story's end. With so many unresolved problems, the sadness is all the more overwhelming. Yet thanks to Ishiguro's impeccable timing, his ability to deploy the techniques of suspense thrillers and his hectic humor, what could have been a gloomy tale is a positive joy to read. Hilarious, satirical potshots are lobbed at exploitative journalists, cynical local officials, snobby intellectuals, political opportunists, smug volunteers, even a surgeon who wields a hacksaw to chop off a leg.

Still, it's no wonder critics got upset. Though the story is told in Mr. Ryder's steady and rational-seeming tone (shades of Stevens and Masuji Ono), this book feels like a nervous breakdown waiting to happen. It's every awful scenario you've ever dreamed of—from drifting down interminable corridors to dressing inappropriately. It's also a deeply personal Conradian voyage into Mr. Ryder's subconscious where he battles, mid-life crisis-style, with painful memories of which we catch only glimpses.

The Unconsoled conveys the same bleak messages as the rest of Ishiguro's much-praised work. Our self-deceptions are intolerable. Denial is a hedge against madness. Life is one long search for consolation and the ability to compromise humanity's dubious achievement. But his emphasis on the tremendous relief to be drawn from the complementary comforts of kindness and art suggest something more ambiva-

lent here. Just as true kindness has no motive, Ishiguro says, great art, with its blend of intellectual control and instinctive sensual passion, is beautiful for an inner integrity that can't be compromised by arbitrary pressure. Music carries no moral force. But the feeling it projects, like the life-giving exuberance of Ishiguro's prose, is unmistakable.

Stanley Kauffmann (review date 6 November 1995)

SOURCE: Stanley Kauffmann, "The Floating World," in *The New Republic*, Vol. 213, No. 19, November 6, 1995, pp. 42-5.

[*In the review below, Kauffmann suggests that* The Unconsoled *builds on Ishiguro's first three novels and should be interpreted in terms of the earlier works.*]

Those who were lucky enough, or smart enough, to read Kazuo Ishiguro's first three novels in order of publication came to the third one, *The Remains of the Day,* with an advantage over the rest of us. Ishiguro was born in Japan and he has lived in England since he was five. (He is now 41.) To those who began with the third book, including myself, Ishiguro's huge cultural shift made that very English novel remarkable for what I would now call misconstrued reasons: we thought it an extraordinary feat of osmosis. But viewed through the perspective of his first two books, *The Remains of the Day,* wonderful anyway, seems even better.

Ishiguro's first novel, *A Pale View of the Hills* (1982), focuses on a Japanese woman now living in England, one of whose daughters has recently committed suicide and whose other daughter is in difficulties. The story interweaves the woman's past life in post-war Nagasaki with her subsequent English life and brings the braiding up to the present. The book concludes with a sudden, startling enigma. (That puzzle, though presumably this was not in Ishiguro's mind at the time, prefigures his latest, fourth novel.)

In his second novel, *An Artist of the Floating World* (1986), that world is the pre-war "night-time world of pleasure, entertainment and drink" in a Japanese city. This world was the chief background for the youthful paintings of the now-elderly painter who is the protagonist. But the phrase has taken on another resonance. Like the first book, the "present" of the novel is post-war, the protagonist and his artist-contemporaries feel some guilt about their work before the war that may have inflamed jingoistic feelings. One of the painters commits suicide in remorse. The "floating world," particularly as dangled before us by the title, comes to reflect other glints, other kinds of delusory gratification.

Ishiguro's first two books are masterly, in several ways. In each, the control is flawless without seeming arbitrary: every incident, every comma, appears to fit. Balance and rhythm are just, and in a gentle, oblique way, the story amplifies in texture. Remarks, observations, small incidents heighten our interest without the use of anything as crass as overt suspense. Yet the salient quality of these books is their method of characterization. Ishiguro doesn't use much physical description or interior delving. These people become familiar by the shapes of their lives—the way they choose and care, their daily routines, their harboring or shedding of grievances, even their liking of particular foods and their skill in cooking.

With many novelists, including some great ones, we sense that the author is carefully presenting his characters; at its crudest, it's the puppetmaster putting on a play. With Ishiguro, it's quite different. In these two books, he doesn't present his characters, he nestles among them. He watches them, respects them, obeys them, and conveys to us quietly what they tell him. He seems almost to chat with them from time to time "off-stage."

The quietness is the key. The children in these two books make some noise, but only the children. Ishiguro treats them with cunning, as citizens of a tangential world distinct from that of their parents and elders. Sometimes they permit their elders to enter, sometimes not; and often they are rackety. Except for their racket, the air of these two books is quiet. One of Ishiguro's triumphs is that their considerable range of emotion is brought close without a lot of fuss.

To arrive at *The Remains of the Day* (1989) through the avenue of the first two books is, peculiarly, to be both unsurprised and newly impressed. The "Japanese" qualities of the first two books—the taciturnity, the subtle brush strokes, the aim to evoke form rather than create it—persist. We cannot be quite so acutely aware of these qualities without knowledge of the earlier books; in this aspect the third novel grows directly from the first two. Yet, along with those persisting qualities from the past, Ishiguro is a secret member of a household in an utterly different culture. His Japanese past helped him to get there.

Darlington Hall, his main venue, has its own intricate grid of protocols. They have some analogies with Japanese social behavior, but it would be gross to call the two sets similar. Still, the third book has no whiff of exploration or discovery: Stevens, the butler, is as intimate to Ishiguro as any character he has written. This conviction is continually certified throughout the book because we see and hear everything through Stevens. Without tremor or cleverness, the book exists through the existence of Stevens. This fact becomes all the more telling, more moving, when we realize that through his eyes and ears we are seeing and hearing more than he ever comprehends.

About *The Remains of the Day* it is possible to risk the word "perfect." The book's special beauty is that it is a political allegory, bitter and sad, without losing any ground as a full-bodied novel. It has been compared favorably with Henry James; I would add Evelyn Waugh, Henry Green, Ivy Compton-Burnett and Anthony Powell. Ishiguro's book belongs with the best of English fiction that treats the English class system with combined satire and relish, with perception of both its cruelty and its rigorous ethos, as a distillation of English history.

Passage through the first two Ishiguro novels is a fruitful way to reach the third. Passage through all three of those novels is helpful, though in a quite different way, for the fourth. To begin with a blunt fact: we know, when we pick it up, that *The Unconsoled* is a departure for its author because of its size, 535 pages. His longest previous book was 245 pages. Familiarity with his previous style—laconic loveliness, space compacted for intensity—makes us immediately curious about the differences we will discover.

They start to appear at once. The setting is Europe. On the first page a man named Ryder, whose first-person narrative this is, arrives at a hotel in an unspecified city. (It remains so.) The magazines in the lobby rack are in several languages, and the names we begin to hear are German. After Ryder has registered, he is taken up in the elevator by an old porter, Gustav, who carries his bags and doesn't set them down as they ascend. His face is growing red with the strain: Ryder urges him to set down the bags. "I'm glad you mention it, sir," says Gustav, then launches into a four-page explanation of the portering principles involved and the resolution of the porters in this city to abide by them. He even mentions the café where the porters meet to discuss these things. He concludes: "I'm sure Miss Hilde will vouch for what I'm saying." Then Ryder notices a young woman behind him. She, too, then speaks at length—about the attractions of the city and about the preparation of Ryder's schedule, though we don't yet quite know why there is a schedule.

Sensors flash in us. We have recognized already that the style has changed: the loquacity of those monologues is in stark contrast to the honed dialogue in the previous books. But more basically, the criteria of realism have shifted. Gustav's and Miss Hilde's comments are so lengthy that the elevators would have had to climb to the top of the World Trade Center, slowly, for those two to have time to speak them. Miss Hilde's could not possibly have been unnoticed by Ryder when he entered the elevator. Ishiguro patently wants these factual distortions to strike us: traditional realism is not to be this book's habitat. Yet the details are veristic.

This contradiction, plus the first tremblings of mystery around the seemingly commonplace, plus the scent of

Middle Europe in the atmosphere, make our literary radar signal: Kafka. But this perception doesn't take much subtlety on our part. Ishiguro wants us to know that he has taken a master for this book. (Later he calls one of the streets in this city Walserstrasse. Robert Walser, the Swiss author who began publishing a few years before Kafka, was often compared to his junior; when Kafka's work first appeared, some readers thought that Franz Kafka was a pseudonym for Robert Walser.)

Before the first chapter is ended, Ishiguro has fixed his book in the realm of paradox that uses veristic minutiae to tack down the edges of billowing non-realism. Erich Heller says: "Kafka's style—simple, lucid, and 'real' in the sense of never leaving any doubt concerning the reality of that which is narrated, described, or meditated—does yet narrate, describe or mediate the shockingly unbelievable." This might have been Ishiguro's motto for his book. We learn that Ryder, whose first name is never mentioned, is an English pianist; he is to appear in a few days in a concert over which the city is making a to-do. A great deal happens in those few days, all of it couched in that ballooning/contracting sense of time, that melting/solidifying sense of place that quickly become integral in the book.

Another surreal element is soon added. The day of his arrival, when Ryder wanders into the square where the porters' café is located, he sees a woman around 40 and her small son seated there. Gustav had told Ryder that they might be there, his daughter and grandson, Sophie and Boris. She waves at Ryder, which surprises him, and when he goes over, she addresses him by name. In a moment Sophie asks Boris to go off for a bit; then she talks to Ryder about a house she is buying for him and her and Boris. Instead of asking what in the world she means, Ryder slips, slides, into acceptance of this new circumstance in his life:

> She began to give me more details about the house. I remained silent, but only because of my uncertainty as to how I should respond. For the fact was, as we had been sitting together, Sophie's face had come to seem steadily more familiar to me, until now I thought I could even remember vaguely some earlier discussions about buying just such a house in the woods.

Other instances of Ryder's malleable consciousness soon occur, not as if he were being dragooned into accepting something but as if he were vaporously recalling it. This phenomenon strongly suggests another influence on Ishiguro: Pinter, especially *Old Times*. In Pinter's play, states of being, consistent in themselves, overlap other, contradictory states of being and memory in the same person—a kind of interior cubism. After these overlappings have gone on for a bit in the play, a woman says:

> There are some things one remembers even though they may never have happened. There are things I remember that may never have happened, but as I recall them so they take place.

This is one of the insistent modes of Ishiguro's novel. (It's worth noting, not as proof but as linkage, that Pinter was for a time involved in the screen adaptation of *The Remains of the Day*.)

The café encounter is the merest corner of the long, complexly layered journey-saga that Ryder undergoes before the evening of the concert, and it doesn't end there. The hotel manager, Hoffman, his wife, and their pianist son Stephan; the conductor Brodsky and his estranged wife; some boyhood chums, now grown, from his English school-days—these and many, many more wander in and out. Almost everyone whom Ryder meets wants something from him: Hoffman wants him to look at his wife's albums of clippings about Ryder's career, Stephen wants Ryder to listen to his playing, Gustav wants Ryder to say something in public at the concert about the conditions of the porters; and more.

In the course of the book Ryder travels about on foot, by car, by tram, and he moves, suddenly and almost every time, from crowded streets to lonely country-side, from busy rooms into straitened corridors, all these transitions melding into a vivid but intentionally unreliable continuum of place. Added to this kaleidoscopic geography are multiple points of view—in a first-person narrative. A man who is driving Ryder somewhere parks in front of a house and asks to be excused for a minute while he goes inside. Ryder, sitting in the car, then sees and hears the conversation deep within the house.

These dissolvings of one place into another, this super-vision, suggest film. (The English paperbound editions of Ishiguro's work mention his "keen interest in the cinema.") The book has other filmic touches, of Bergman particularly. When the child Boris wanders in the hotel corridors, we think of *The Silence*; with the quasi-phantom classroom, *Wild Strawberries*. Several film references are frank. In Ishiguro's city there is Sternberg Garden; the city's "most senior" actor is named Jannings; a modern composer is named Kazan. Valentino and Groucho Marx are used as points of reference. *2001: A Space Odyssey* is mentioned a few times. (With the wrong cast. This is deliberate, I'm sure, but no reason for this "mistake" is apparent.)

Like Kafka before him, Ishiguro conveys the immanence of a kind of spectral humor throughout, and sometimes that humor bulges into the foreground. (Just before the concert, Brodsky, the conductor, is in a car accident, pinned by his leg. The doctors have to amputate the leg to free him, but the leg they cut off is wooden. He appears on stage at the concert using an ironing board as an improvised crutch.) Unlike Kafka, however, Ishiguro, no hunger artist, frequently uses food for homely sensuality, even more than in his first two books. From the mention of strudel in the first chapter to the closing scene on a tram where a lavish buffet breakfast is being served, food figures.

The incongruence of that setting for a buffet is part of another technique in the book: disproportion. Of the numerous instances, here are two. It's disproportionate that, on the very evening of the recital, just before Ryder is to play, Hoffman insists on showing him his wife's albums; or that, for other reasons, Ryder gets lengthily sidetracked before he is to go on. And after all the disproportions, after all the frustrations and divagations, the story winds its way to the concert itself. Which, unsurprisingly, does not proceed as planned. The book leaves us with Ryder presumably en route to his next engagement in Helsinki.

It also leaves us with an ache of disappointment that has been growing in us as we read. Very early we realize that, as against earlier Ishiguro, we are not to savor character development. The author cannot nestle among his characters here, because there are none: there are only supposedly signifying figures. Neither are we to be absorbed in deepening narrative; one episode follows another with no cause except the author's mandate. We read along because we expect that all these teasings and suggestings, in the hands of a fine writer, will lead to thematic, aesthetic completion. But Ryder simply passes through it all on his way to Helsinki. None of it, not Sophie or Boris or anything else, affects him lastingly. Central though he is, Ryder is only one more of the book's charade figures.

But what is the charade about? Erich Heller observed that "there is only one way to save oneself the trouble of interpreting *The Trial:* not to read it." Ishiguro lays the same exigency on us, but without much reward. This is not to belabor him with the need to equal Kafka: it is to point out that, for all his skill, he has followed his model incompletely.

Finally, desperately, we ask: Is this whole book a dream? That facile *raison d'être* must be considered, especially since the book is laced with sleep. Chapter Two begins: "When I was roused by the bedside telephone, I had the impression that it had been ringing for some time." Chapter Ten, too, begins with the telephone waking him. Parts Two and Three and Four begin with nearly identical sentences about waking with the fear of having slept too long. But, among other questions about such an interpretation, did Ryder dream all those extensive monologues that other people deliver? (He never speaks one himself.) After a while they seem less like instruments of prose than like elements in graphic design, as a designer might use blocks of black, except that in this case we must traverse them, inch by inch. They crush the suggestion of dream with their sheer black weight.

Anyway, to tag this book a dream is not to justify it, only to alter its unfulfilled debt. We may indeed be such stuff as dreams are made on, but before our little lives are rounded with a sleep, those dreams affect us with agony and exultation. Ishiguro's book does not. It parades its episodes before us. We feel little.

And the title doesn't help. *The Unconsoled* explains nothing. The word "consolation" occurs only a few times, in connection with Brodsky, his music, his lady love, and a wound of his that will not heal. (Hinting at Amfortas in *Parsifal*? . . . But enough puzzle-solving.) The people in this book are no more stringently unconsoled in any sense than many of us.

The book's most plausible meaning is its very existence. To put it otherwise, it opens a new territory in Ishiguro's interests, even if it doesn't prevail in that territory. If Ishiguro's two "Japanese" novels help us to appreciate *The Remains of the Day,* then all three of his preceding novels, taken together, are the best available justification of the fourth. He has moved from the taciturn beauty of the earlier books to a larger scope, a much more explicitly intricate structure— a move from Japan and Britain to the heart of Middle Europe. Previously, he dealt with the psychological and spiritual aftermath of World War II in Japan, then with English confusions and self-betrayals in that war. Now he moves to the continent, to the involuted psyche and spirit that was the root of much of that war, that bred most of our culture and also of our horror.

Ryder, the English artist, enters a shadowy European city. Ishiguro, another English artist, enters the morass of the European novel. We may wonder what will happen to the rest of Ryder's career. With a great deal more hope, we may ask the same question about the extraordinary Ishiguro.

FURTHER READING

Criticism

Wilhelmus, Tom. "Between Cultures." *The Hudson Review* XLIX, No. 2 (Summer 1996): 321-22.
    Argues that *The Unconsoled* comments on the difficulties of being caught between cultures.

Additional coverage of Ishiguro's life and career is contained in the following sources published by Gale: *Bestsellers 1990,* No. 2; *Contemporary Authors,* Vol. 120; *Contemporary Authors New Revision Series,* Vol. 49; *DISCovering Authors Modules*; and *Major 20th-Century Writers.*

Neil Jordan
1950-

(Full name Neil Patrick Jordan) Irish screenwriter, director, dramatist, novelist, and short story writer.

The following entry presents an overview of Jordan's career through 1997.

INTRODUCTION

Neil Jordan has been hailed as "one of Ireland's preeminent fiction writers," by Alex Raksin and others, but he is better known as a screenwriter and director of such acclaimed films as *Mona Lisa* (1986) and *The Crying Game* (1992). His work reflects his Irish heritage as he explores his country's politics and culture. His unique style combines lyricism and surrealistic images to subvert common notions about such topics as violence, gender, sex, and race.

Biographical Information

Jordan was born in 1950 in Sligo, Ireland, but grew up in Dublin. He studied English literature and history at University College in Dublin. He began writing at an early age and published his first short story collection, *Night in Tunisia and Other Stories* in 1976 while working in theater. The collection won the 1979 *Guardian* Fiction Prize. Subsequently Jordan wrote for Irish television and the British Broadcasting Corporation. In addition he worked for director John Boorman, helping him on the final draft of *Excalibur*. Jordan then decided to tackle the film medium himself, writing the screenplay for and directing the film *Angel* (1982). He continued writing screenplays in addition to writing several novels, and went on to direct several of his own movies. His first critical success came with *Mona Lisa,* and in 1990 he directed *We're No Angels,* his first big-budget Hollywood movie. He enjoyed both commercial and critical success with *The Crying Game,* which won an Academy Award for best screenplay. Jordan has gone on to direct several other successful Hollywood features.

Major Works

Jordan's work often focuses on people who have gone astray. *Angel* deals with the political violence in Ireland. The film is set in Northern Ireland and tells the story of Danny, a saxophone player. After playing at a wedding reception, Danny takes a deaf-mute teenager, Annie, outside and makes love to her. While outside, the pair witness four men murder the manager of the band, whom they suspect has paid protection money to a rival paramilitary group. The men also kill

Annie and blow up the ballroom. Danny seeks revenge and trades in his saxophone for a gun. He slowly descends into madness and violence as he tracks down the four murderers. Jordan never makes clear the political affiliations in the film; instead he shows how violence of any source causes men to lose their individual identity. Jordan's novel *The Dream of a Beast* (1983) is filled with imagery and follows a man as he travels through his dreams. The man and his community slowly transform, and the man finds himself identifying more with nature than with society. As he transforms into this "beast" he reverts back to a childlike consciousness. In the process he finds himself closer to his wife and daughter. Jordan's screenplay *The Company of Wolves* (1984) is based on Angela Carter's short story of the same name. The film is a version of the Little Red Riding Hood tale, which takes the form of a young girl's dreams. The girl visits her grandmother who warns her that all men are wolves in disguise. The girl meets a handsome prince in the forest who turns out to be the wolf of the fairy tale. The film concludes with the girl herself turning into a wolf. The tale is a metaphor for the young girl's awakening sexuality as she encounters the predatory nature of male sexuality. *We're No*

Angels is a film about two convicts serving life sentences in a hard-labor prison. They escape and pretend to be priests while on the run. *The Miracle* (1991) is a four-person character study of an Oedipal relationship between a mother and the son she gave up for adoption twenty years earlier. *The Crying Game* has been Jordan's most talked about and controversial film. It follows an ex-IRA soldier, Fergus, as he struggles to atone for the death of a British prisoner. He becomes involved in a relationship with the dead prisoner's girlfriend, who eventually reveals herself to be a man in the conclusion of the film. The film analyzes otherness and overturns common preconceptions about sex, gender, and race. *Michael Collins* (1996) tells the story of Irish Republican Army founder Michael Collins, and is based on the history and myth surrounding the real man.

Critical Reception

Reviewers often discuss the imagery and lyricism in Jordan's work. They also point out the multiple layers and symbolism common to Jordan's fiction and films. Marlaine Glicksman states that "Both his literature and films are like Chinese boxes: stories within a story, films within a film, dreams within a dream." Critics also discuss the place of myth in Jordan's work. In his analysis of *Angel*, Richard Kearney asserts: "While Jordan would seem to subscribe to the conviction that myths contain what is important about a race, he does not approach the mythical in terms of ancient legend or folklore, but in terms of contemporary lived experience." Jordan is well known for upsetting traditional conceptions about identity, especially in *The Crying Game*. The film sparked critical discussions surrounding the sexual and racial politics of the film. Some critics argued that the film failed to escape traditional conservative representations. Frann Michel states: "Where its disruptions are insufficient or excessive, the film [*The Crying Game*] implies a conservative politics at odds with the screenplay's apparent intentions." Most critics, however, praised Jordan for his attempt, and even Michel goes on to say "*The Crying Game* is visually, intellectually, and emotionally engaging. If the film falls short of the radical innovations it sometimes promises, it nonetheless offers profound dislocations of vision: the chance to try to see anew." David Lugowski agrees, stating: "What is original and special about *The Crying Game* is its execution, the mileage Jordan gets from the conventions he respects and those he upsets, and the complexity of its discourse on racial and gender issues."

PRINCIPAL WORKS

Night in Tunisia and Other Stories (short stories) 1976
The Past (novel) 1980

Angel [writer and director] (screenplay) 1982; released as *Danny Boy,* 1984
The Dream of a Beast (novel) 1983
The Company of Wolves [with Angela Carter; writer and director] (screenplay) 1984
Mona Lisa [with David Leland; writer and director] (screenplay) 1986
High Spirits [writer and director] (screenplay) 1988
Angel (play) 1989
High Spirits (play) 1989
We're No Angels [director] (film) 1990
The Miracle [writer and director] (screenplay) 1991
The Crying Game [writer and director] (screenplay) 1992
Interview with a Vampire [director] (film) 1994
Sunrise with Sea Monster (novel) 1994
Michael Collins [writer and director] (film) 1996
The Butcher Boy (film) 1998

CRITICISM

Richard Kearney (essay date Autumn 1982)

SOURCE: "Avenging Angel: An Analysis of Neil Jordan's First Irish Feature Film," in *Studies,* Vol. LXXI, No. 283, Autumn, 1982, pp. 296-303.

[*In the following essay, Kearney praises Jordan's* Angel *and asserts that "the credit must surely go to Neil Jordan himself whose inspired scripting and directing prove him to be one of the most talented imaginations working in Ireland today."*]

Angel, directed by Neil Jordan, is ostensibly a film which deals with political violence in Ireland. I believe it does so in a highly original and perceptive manner. But before analysing and assessing **Angel** in detail, I think it may be useful to give a brief account of other Irish films to have tackled such a theme.

In 1934, Frank O'Connor's *Guests of the Nation,* treating of the I.R.A.'s reluctant execution of two British soldiers in 1921, was made into a silent movie. O'Connor was so impressed by the merits of the film, directed in theatrical fashion by Denis Johnston, that he wrote:

> The government would be well advised to provide the necessary money to have the picture refilmed. It would add to the prestige of the Irish abroad, as showing the great spirit of the War of Independence and the spirit of comradeship that existed between the opposing forces, as well as the devotion to duty of the men who fought.

Needless to say, O'Connor's appeal for government financing fell on deaf ears. Perhaps one of the reasons being that no one—besides O'Connor and a few well-wishers—really believed that a 'spirit of comradeship' did exist between the I.R.A. and the British Army during that internecine war.

In 1935, *Dawn,* produced and directed in Ireland by Dan Cooper, was released. This film also dealt with the War of Independence, but in a far less sanguine spirit. *Dawn* portrayed the brutal atrocities of the Black and Tan Brigades and celebrated the heroic resistance of one Brian Malone, who deserted from the Royal Irish Constabulary to join the I.R.A. It concluded with a dawn funeral procession by the I.R.A. and a call for 'the struggle to continue'.

Two other, more recent Irish films featuring the political violence of the national struggle are *Lament for Art O'Leary* and *Maeve.* The former, directed by Bob Quinn, is based on the murder of O'Leary, a dispossessed Gaelic aristocrat, by English soldiers in 1773 because he had refused to pay his 'squireen' landlord five pounds for the possession of his horse (one of the colonial Penal Laws against Irish Catholics). *Maeve,* directed by Pat Murphy, charts the course of a young Catholic girl from Belfast who transcends the ghetto-nationalism of her environment and her Republican boyfriend, in the name of a supra-national feminist solidarity: the real struggle is not that between Catholic and Protestant, republican and loyalist, provo or Brit, but between male and female.

All of these four films interpret violence according to the yardstick of a particular political ideology. *Guests of the Nation* could be said to illustrate the Free State notion of a *frères-enemies* comradeship in war; *Dawn* promotes the Republic ideal of uncompromising, armed resistance to the alien oppressor; *Lament for Art O'Leary* endorses the Official I.R.A. program of passive, 'social' resistance to colonial and class imperialism (the film was financed by *Official Sinn Fein/The Workers Party*); while *Maeve,* arguably the most subtle of these films, is a thinly disguised pedagogy of feminist liberation.

I mention these four ideological interpretations of national violence by Irish film-makers, not to adjudicate between them, but to contrast them with Jordan's unusual and indeed unprecedented treatment of Irish political violence in *Angel.* This film does not sponsor any specific ideology; it concentrates on the *mentality* which produces violence—regardless of whether it is inflicted by Republican, Loyalist or British law-and-order agents; or by somebody totally non-political. And this concentration on the psychic roots of violence permits Jordan to penetrate to the common core of metaphysical nothingness (what he calls, borrowing from Blake, the 'nobodaddy') from which acts of violence ultimately derive. He thereby uses cinema to cut

through all *conscious* forms of socio-political ideology to a *metaphysics of the unconscious.* Perhaps the term 'mythology' of the unconscious could also serve here; for Jordan employs the visual image to burrow beneath the upper layers of verbal rationalization to the pre-conceptual subworlds of imaginative obsession. He is delving into the dark, hidden atavisms of the psyche which is the ambivalent source of *both* poetic mystery *and* violent mystification.

Someone, I think it was T. S. Eliot, defined the genuine artist as someone with an educated nervous system. According to this definition, *Angel* is an eminent instance of genuine art, functioning as it does to educate the viewer's nervous sensibility, to enable us aesthetically to experience the unconscious drives which determine our everyday actions and perceptions. As Jordan himself explains: 'What I get the greatest pleasure out of is trying to make manifest how . . . a perceiving eye can see and feel the world. I suppose really that fiction or any art is like sensual thinking. It's like thinking through one's senses . . . [which] is deeper, more valuable than abstract thinking.'

Jordan would seem to have learned much from his mentor, John Boorman, with whom he has worked on several projects, serving as creative consultant for *Excalibur,* directing an excellent documentary on the making of this same film, and co-scripting Boorman's forthcoming feature, *Broken Dreams.* Jordan shares Boorman's preoccupation with the prerational powers of mythic experience, those elemental obsessions of the collective, national or personal psyche which condition our existence quite as much, if not more so, than socio-political forces. This pre-occupation was already evidenced in Jordan's sensitive exploration of the preconscious, shaping voices of memory in his first novel, *The Past.* But Jordan's apprenticeship with Boorman (who has been so devoted to Irish film-making over the years) has surely facilitated his transition from prose to the screen. A difficult and hazardous transition at the best of times. Boorman has eloquently expressed his own feelings about cinema as the exploration of an unknown, subconscious language as follows:

> Each movie is an exploration, a quest. If I know what a film is about before I start, I never do it. It's only when I'm grappling with something I don't understand that I'm excited enough to move forward through all the stages—writing, casting, shooting, editing—at each stage discovering more about it, always struggling towards revelation . . . Cinema is an extremely easy language to understand, but it's very difficult to speak, and we're spastics in it. I've been working at it all my life (but) still I feel that I'm struggling with an unknown language.

(It is interesting to note that Boorman and Jordan have both written and directed their own films thereby providing their work with a unifying vision or intelligence which many contemporary films lack).

I suspect that Boorman is not just describing the *technique* of his art here, but also the particular *type* of cinematic content which most fascinates him: human existence as a quest for mythic or metaphysical significance. The mythic quest has been strong in all of Boorman's films but never so explicitly as in *Excalibur* (on which Jordan also worked) where he engages the Arthurian legend of the Holy Grail. Boorman has defined his aesthetic fascination for myth in Jungian terms:

> I read Jung and began to feel, as Jung did, the importance of keeping them alive, and renewing and refreshing them, and that the myths contained all that was important about a race, not only about its past, but also intimations of its future.

While Jordan would seem to subscribe to the conviction that myths contain what is important about a race, he does not approach the mythical in terms of ancient legend or folklore, but in terms of contemporary lived experience. As in *The Past,* Jordan begins with a personal and particular situation and moves gradually towards a disclosure of its universal or archetypal meaning. Furthermore, he seems to bring ethical scruples to bear on his consideration of the mythic obsessions of the unconscious, acknowledging them to be as conducive to destructive fanaticism as to creative renewal.

While Jordan would seem to subscribe to the conviction that myths contain what is important about a race, he does not approach the mythical in terms of ancient legend or folklore, but in terms of contemporary lived experience.
—*Richard Kearney*

Angel tells the story of a saxophone player, Danny (Stephen Rea), who encounters the evil of violence and eventually becomes seduced by its allure. It is set, significantly, in Northern Ireland and opens with a dance band playing in a garish, rural ballroom. The opening sequence introduces three women into Danny's orbit of performance: Deirdre or D (Honor Heffernan), the beautiful lead singer in the band; a deaf-mute teenager named Annie (Veronica Quilligan); and a young bride in white (Lise-Ann McLaughlin) who asks Danny to dance but is snatched away by her jealous, overbearing husband. Danny is drawn to each in turn. But it is with the mute Annie that he makes love after the gig in a shelter outside the ballroom. Though their encounter is casual, almost accidental, it is far from being crude or manipu-

lative. Instead of destroying Annie's innocence, as might have been expected, Danny discovers in Annie the very incarnation of this virtue in all its prelapsarian simplicity. In an edenesque love scene of unusual delicacy, heightened by the high angelic pitch of Verdi's requiem, and shrouded in an aura of fairylamps suspended from a nearby wishing-tree, the spectator glimpses a tale of innocence.

The tale of experience unfolds fast upon its heels. From their shelter, Annie and Danny see a car drive up to the ballroom. Four masked men exit and proceed to murder the manager of the showband because they believe he has paid protection money to a rival paramilitary group (which remains unidentified). When the horrified but unsuspecting Annie leaves the shelter to approach the killers they shoot her also. The gang escapes just before the ballroom, which they have mined with explosives, erupts into an inferno of flame. Thus begins Danny's first encounter with the horror which will lead him to the heart of darkness.

This episode of violence is shot with an arresting rapidity, each image of mounting brutality cutting in upon the next. But amidst this traumatic sequence of terror—reminiscent of the nightmare blood-spilling of *Taxi Driver, Apocalypse Now* or *Midnight Express*—Danny fastens upon the stark image of a raised orthopaedic shoe like a cloven hoof, worn by one of the killers. This frame is to become an indelible memory for Danny, successively repeated in instantaneous flashbacks, as he plummets towards an ever-deepening obsession with revenge. (This repetitious crosscutting or reverse montage technique has also been used by Boorman to good effect in such films as *Point Blank* and the *Exorcist*).

Recovering from shock in a Belfast hospital, Danny is visited by two police detectives, presumably R.U.C. or the Anti-Terrorist Squad, called Bloom (Ray McAnally) and Bonner (Donal McCann). He tells them less than he knows and says nothing of the central clue—the orthopaedic shoe. The violence has become so internalized and so personalized for Danny that he is determined to investigate it for himself and by himself. (Little does he realize that his personal quest will become an impersonal madness). Danny chooses to explore evil at a metaphysical level beneath or beyond the legal competency of politics and police. His refusal to co-operate with the forces of Law and Order is portrayed as a preliminary complicity with the criminal act itself. Danny is slowly becoming entranced by the malignity he seeks to destroy.

And so begins Danny's gradual substitution of violence for art. This transition from an 'angelic' to a 'demonic' *persona,* is epitomized by Danny's departure from the band and his musical/love partner, Deirdre, as he removes his saxophone from its case and replaces it with an armalite. This exchange of the musical instrument and the gun is one of the pivotal scenes in the film. It occurs in Danny's childhood bedroom at his Aunty Mae's house (an apt enough place for a psychic turn-about!). Employing sombre, dreamlike images, Jordan shows Danny undergoing here what psychoanalysis has rather clinically described as a 'transfer of unconscious desires', as he switches from one 'transitional object' (the sax) to another (the machine gun). The transfer is patently a regressive one. This painstakingly detailed and almost trance-like sequence, without using words or succumbing to the temptation of abstract theorizing, conveys the crucial turn of the psychic screw.

Jordan offered the following significant account of this transition from artistic creativity to violent destruction in an interview shortly after the release of the film:

> When you begin to work artistically you throw yourself to a certain extent into chaos, into the area of your mind and experiences which is very volatile, even in some cases dangerous. The attraction of art, and perhaps the beauty of it, is that it can encapsulate all the beauty of sensual experience and at the same time allow you to meet this chaos and the darker side of your personality in, perhaps, the most meaningful way. Now violence to me—the attraction of violence—is the polar opposite to that. It does throw one into contact with chaos, with the darker side of human experience, with evil, and it does so, obviously, in the most brutal way imaginable.

But while stressing the difference between art and violence as two ways of responding to the 'dark side' of the psyche, Jordan is equally aware, as is clear in *Angel,* of the uncanny similarities they possess:

> I think the lure of art for people is that very often it will give their lives a pitch of intensity they don't normally have. The lure of violence is quite similar, because it gives them this pitch of excitement, this visceral drive, and results in the decay of the human person . . . In Danny, I wanted to posit a very innocent character who plays the saxophone and is obsessed with his instrument the way any musician is. It's interesting, by the way, that a lot of musicians call their instruments their axe. It's a strangely violent image. But there's a mechanic-of-the-arts thing about him; he's at home with his instrument, he knows how the key works, he could mend it himself even, and the first time he sees the gun, the appalling paradox of it is that on that basic mechanical level—a child's fascination with how the thing works—it has the same draw for him as the saxophone.

One of the most salient strengths of *Angel* is its precise abil-

ity to focus on this 'basic mechanical level' of reflex attraction and recoil, symptomatic of the covert workings of the subconscious. In this way Jordan investigates that fundamental nexus between aesthetic creativity and violence which has become one of the most frequented stamping grounds of contemporary art. One thinks of Yeats's *Ben Bulben,* Heaney's *North*—to mention just one of the Ulster poets preoccupied with this theme—D. M. Thomas's *White Hotel,* Visconti's *The Damned,* Klaus Mann's *Mephisto* and perhaps most significant of all: Thomas Mann's *Dr. Faustus.* This last work brilliantly examines the subterranean relationship between musical invention (the atonal symphonies of Schoenberg) and political barbarism (Nazism), concluding with an impassioned plea for the recognition of the artist's immense responsibility: 'One does wrong to see in aesthetics a separate and narrow field of the human. It is more than that, it is at bottom everything; it is what attracts and repels . . . Aesthetic release or the lack of it is a matter of one's fate, dealing out happiness and unhappiness, companionship or helpless if proud isolation on earth.'

Mann's conclusion would serve equally well as an epilogue to *Angel.* Unable to find aesthetic release through his music, due to his psychic paralysis after Annie's murder, Danny resorts to the alternative 'play' of destruction (i.e. that which, ironically, occasioned his paralysis in the first place). Though initially motivated, it seems, by the moral sentiment of avenging his lover, he soon finds himself enthralled in an inexorable spiral of blood-letting.

After he leaves hospital, Danny succeeds in tracking down one of the killers, thanks to the cleft-foot clue and a chance encounter (as 'chance' indeed as the original encounter with the angelic Annie). He executes the 'terrorist' with the same mechanical ease with which he formerly played his instrument; and from then on it's simply a question of tracking down the other three members of the gang. As Danny progresses in his new vocation of avenging angel (and in avenging his angel—Annie—he himself becomes an avenging 'fallen' angel), he discovers that the assassins he has pledged to assassinate have private lives just like himself. This theme of the 'double' or *Doppelgänger,* reminiscent at times of a Dostoyevskean psychodrama, is heightened by the fact that each revenge-shooting is preceded by a scene where Danny confronts his paramilitary opponent in the intimacy of his domestic existence. The first two assassins (the assistant and George) are confronted by Danny in the secluded privacy of their homes, the third (the 'bride's' husband) in his sequestered forest love-nest. And the fourth gang-leader—who in a surprise denouement turns out to be the police inspector, Bonner—is confronted in his birthplace: Bonner dies, gripping Danny in a desperate love/hate embrace, with the words—'Stay with me. I grew up around here'. It is interesting that this same phrase, 'stay with me', was also uttered by George after he had been shot by Danny, thereby functioning as a refrain to reinforce the sinister collusion between Danny and the killers. Thus Danny mimetically emulates the horror that first repelled him, convinced, like James in *The Past,* that 'everything turns into everything else'.

On each occasion, Danny feels compelled to enter the inner circle of the assassin's life, to find out his name, to understand his secret loves and hates. 'I want to know everything he ever did', Danny says of one of the killers. I think it is this subtle mode of interplay between the public outerworld of the thriller plot and the private innerworld of psychic motivation which hallmarks *Angel* as an original exploration of Irish (and non-Irish) violence.

Jordan masterfully juxtaposes the *surface-structure* of the 'detective' narrative, full of fast-moving suspense, with a *deep-structure* of metaphysical probing. This latter structure penetrates to the psychic underworld of archetypally recurrent and almost timeless emotions which precondition the narrative action of the surface 'political' plot (i.e. the gang's assassination of Annie, Danny's assassination of the gang, and the police hunt for both the gang and Danny, and so forth). The psychic deep-structure of the film lies beneath the 'police story'—as the detective, Bloom, says to Danny: 'You can go places where I can't go'—and operates according to a radically different temporality. While the deep-structure unfolds synchronically by the repetition of key visual and sound motifs, which I call *archetypal;* the surface-structure progresses diachronically according to the standard conventions of a sequential plot.

> 'Given that the film is a thriller', says Jordan, 'and given that I wanted to speak about morality and questions of good and evil and the soul, I didn't want to make it with the speed, and the glitter, and the *distractions* with which action films are normally made. I wanted to do precisely the opposite of that. When someone is holding a gun on somebody else I wanted him to be actually asking the question of what they're like. I wanted all the time to polarise and contrast the act of violence with the actual poetic dimensions of people's lives.

Having traced the broad outlines of the surface plot, I will not attempt to isolate some of the archetypal motifs of the deep-structure. These can be grouped into two central categories: (i) the *feminine* motifs; and (ii) the *framing* motifs.

The portrayal of women in this film tends to conform to what might be termed the 'angelic' order of epiphany; they are the bearers of illumination, love, dance and music. The men, by contrast, gravitate towards the 'demonic' order of political intrigue and violence. Most of the women—in particular Annie, Deirdre, the bride and Mary (the widowed farm girl, played by Sorcha Cusack)—are all innocent, and often sacrificial, sufferers of male brutality. This by no means amounts to an inverted sexist dualism. For the film shows us that men too, Danny being the paramount example, possess a 'feminine' or 'angelic' sensitivity which draws them towards the healing powers of art and tenderness. Men ignore this creative side of themselves at their own peril, that is, at the risk of becoming mindless demons. As the bride says to Danny, referring to her hapless marriage, when their paths accidentally reconverge later in the film: 'Men start out as angels but end up as brutes'. In short, the term angel in this film seems to denote not some spineless, incorporeal effeminacy but a metaphysical principle of creative salvation. Rilke used the term in a similar sense in *The Duino Elegies,* when he declared: 'Who, if I cried, would hear me from the order of Angels?' or affirmed that only the gaze of the angel can 'redeem' us from the 'dark turn of the world', from 'the guilty river god of the blood'.

The feminine motif comprises the following archetypal scenes in which Danny experiences the angelic order: the dancehall and love scene with Annie; the recurrent band sequences with Deirdre; the love scenes with Deirdre (in the dressing room, the hospital ward, the hotel bedroom, the asylum woods, and the car—where a cross-cutting from deep to surface structures is cleverly achieved as Danny listens to Deirdre reciting a Shakespearean love sonnet while he simultaneously watches one of the assassin's houses through his rear mirror); the dance sequence with Deirdre in the night-club; the dance and card scenes with Aunty Mae; the dance and bakery encounters with the bride (whose jealous and unfaithful husband turns out to have been one of the killers); the haircutting and suicide episodes with the widowed Mary, in whose farm Danny seeks refuge from the police.

The archetypal moments of insight occur during these 'feminine' scenes of the film's deep-structure. Danny learns from Annie the real meaning of sexual love and innocence. From his Aunty Mae he learns not only how to dance and love music as a young parentless boy (perhaps another factor in Danny's quest for identity?), but also that he is threatened by the malevolent forces of the faceless 'nobodaddy'—she has been turning up hundreds of the ace of spades in her fortune-telling cards. The madonna-like Mary reminds Danny of the simple truth that 'hating is wrong'; she ritually cuts his hair before a picture of the Sacred Heart, tends his wounds and clothes him with her dead husband's shirt, before taking her own life and reclining *pietà*-like in his arms. It is also in this sacramental rite with Mary that Danny makes his significant confession that he has been taught to hate and kill by 'those I am after'. Lastly, it is from Deirdre, the most significant female character in the film, that Danny learns that he is 'charmed' by a 'dream' of violence. Deirdre is *the belle dame de merci* who makes relentless efforts to retrieve Danny from the engulfing void of evil. But she fails to convince him to resubstitute the armalite for the saxophone; and in their final encounter in the magic-lantern marquee she ultimately recoils from his contaminated nothingness. 'You're dead', she cries, 'you make me feel unclean'. It is at this point that Deirdre explicitly affirms one of the major themes of the film—that the impersonalizing spell of violence makes all men, whatever their political persuasion, the *same*—when she announces that detective Bonner is hunting for Danny: 'They're looking for you, them like you only they have uniforms on.'

Angel shows us how violence deprives men of their individual identity and makes them into 'nobodaddies' of death. 'I am nobody', admits one of the killers to Danny, thereby announcing their common identity (the same phrase is casually repeated by Danny later in the film). Or as the police inspector, Bloom, puts it: 'It's deep, it's everywhere, it's nowhere . . . Nothing can get hold of you . . . Nowadays, here, everybody's guilty'. It is surely significant that for most of the film Jordan leaves the spectator in doubt with regard to the political identity of the various agents of violence. As the plot unfolds, there are some hints that the protection-racket gang are Republican/Catholic and that the four assassins (including the police agent, Bonner) are Loyalist/Protestant. But Jordan really seems to be saying that the particular ideology of bloodshed is irrelevant; violence is equally pernicious whatever its source.

The various archetypal scenes of humanizing womanhood, listed above, are interwoven by a skillful technique of cross-reference. Firstly, there is the dance motif: Annie, the bride, Deirdre and Aunty Mae all invite Danny to dance with them at different points in the film. Secondly, there is the music motif: Danny's most intimate moments of communion are signalled by music or song—D's singing of *Danny Boy,* Aunt Mae's improvisation of a music-hall ditty, the Verdi chant which accompanies the love scene with Annie (and recurs at key junctures throughout the film), and the unforgettable musical performance in the asylum where the inmates waltz in a ghost-like trance. Another telling piece of music in the film is 'Strange Fruit', Billie Holiday's celebrated anti-violence song of the thirties. 'You could almost transpose the whole lyrics over to Ireland', comments Jordan, 'there you're speaking about a situation where human beings killed people they didn't know for reasons which had nothing to do with any kind of human emotion whatever. It was just to do with racial differences; and it's a similar kind of situation that I was talking about in the film. In short, the women in *Angel* are the harbingers of music and dance, the civilizing agencies of mankind.

A third paradigm of cross-reference is the *laying on of hands;* this healing 'angelic' act recurs throughout the film, as Danny is touched or embraced by Annie, Deirdre, Aunty Mae and Mary. The accumulative significance of the act is crowned when the child faithhealer lays his hands on Danny's bleeding hand in the closing sequence of the film. Danny's *navigatio* has come full circle. He meets the faithhealer in a caravan shrine constructed on the very site where he had originally been embraced by Annie outside the country dance hall. Surrounded by burning candles, which recall the fairy lights of the opening sequence, Danny kneels to receive the purgative touch of another angel-child: a second liturgy of innocence. Unlike his prototype, Macbeth, Danny is thus redeemed from the infernal circle of hate by the 'healing powers of benediction'. He goes forth from the caravan to encounter the fourth killer, Bonner, in the burnt-out dance hall. But he miraculously escapes death when Bloom arrives on the scene to shoot Bonner. The film ends with an apocalyptic, cleansing wind sweeping through the gutted ballroom.

The second major motif of archetypal scenes in the film constitutes what I called 'framing' episodes. These episodes introduce a mood of meditative stillness (*stasis*) which cuts across or frames the high speed action (*kinesis*) of the surface-plot. Some conspicuous examples of such framing scenes are: the haunting, but strangely unreal montage of the asylum sequence which prefaces the second execution, brilliantly counterpointing the rival worlds of sanity and madness; the elegiac scene with the Salvation Army band on the waterfront which follows the second assassination; the mountain landscape of pastoral silence which terminates the frenetic execution of the third killer in his car; the final faithhealing rite which precedes the execution of Bonner.

These four framing episodes are *archetypal* to the extent that their stylized intensity and texture interrupt the linear tempo of the thriller narrative, turning our attention to a deeper psychic timelessness; they enable us to shift from the rhythms of *melodrama* to the more poetic rhythms of *myth.*

> **These four framing episodes [in *Angel*] are *archetypal* to the extent that their stylized intensity and texture interrupt the linear tempo of the thriller narrative, turning our attention to a deeper psychic timelessness; they enable us to shift from the rhythms of *melodrama* to the more poetic rhythms of *myth*.**
>
> **—*Richard Kearney***

Angel's greatest originality lies, I believe, in its ability to cut beneath the ideological clichés of political violence to its hidden psychic roots. In this respect, Jordan's exploration of the metaphysical subworld of contemporary Ulster bloodshed (one thinks in particular of the murder of the Miami Showband by Loyalist paramilitaries) might be compared to similar approaches used by Dostoyevsky in *The Possessed* or by Conrad in *The Secret Agent,* to portray the psychological and metaphysical obsessions behind 'terrorist' violence: in the case of the former, the anarchist assassinations in Czarist Russia, in the latter, the anarchist bombing attempt in London in 1894.

As the first Irish film of such an ambitious and original nature, working with the modest budget of £500,000, *Angel* inevitably has certain shortcomings. The interplay between surface and depth structures is, on occasion, too abrupt and simplistic; the dialogue is frequently wooden and contrived; and the political inferences, where they exist, sometimes border on the banal—smacking of Thatcher's 'murder is murder is murder'. But to dwell on such minor infelicities would be ungracious. We have in *Angel* not only the first Irish feature film of its kind, but also the most accomplished piece of work to have emerged in this country under the auspices of the National Film Board. The singular achievement of *Angel* is due to several factors—not least the moving performances of Honor Heffernan, Stephen Rea, Marie Kean, Donal McCann and Ray McAnally; the ingenious musical score; and the impressive camerawork of Chris Menges. But above all, the credit must surely go to Neil Jordan himself whose inspired scripting and directing prove him to be one of the most talented imaginations working in Ireland today.

D. A. N. Jones (review date 20 October-2 November 1983)

SOURCE: "Saint Jane," in *London Review of Books,* Vol. 5, No. 19, October 20-November 2, 1983, pp. 17-18.

[*In the following excerpt, Jones discusses Jordan's* The Dream of a Beast *and concludes, "To dismiss this well-tuned story as self-indulgent nonsense would be easy—but very unmusical."*]

. . . Another way to offer experience of a derangement of the senses, especially the exultant, ecstatic sort of derangement, is to make use of our shared knowledge of dreams. Telling other people our dreams often bores them. But anyone who has been taken by the writing of Traherne, or Rimbaud, may turn to Neil Jordan's novel, *The Dream of a Beast,* without fear of tedium. What happens to the narrator is pleasingly tangible and sensuous, stimulating excitement without fear. The dreamer takes it for granted that the world has changed suddenly—the heat, the pavements cracking, strange plants sprouting thick, oily, unrecognisable leaves over plate-glass windows; he walks to work along the buckled tracts of the railway line, stopping to take advantage of the rare trains but not expecting them. He notices young soldiers getting

younger as they prowl efficiently, keeping guard, perhaps obeying some master plan to control the heat.

The narrator is becoming a beast. His skin and his hair are changing. Do the women, the beauties, like this beast? The dreamer seems unable to see himself: he can only guess about his looks, from the women's advances and revulsions. He covers himself with bandages—not in self-disgust, like Mr Samsa in Kafka's tale, ashamed that he has become a beetle—but rather as a useful, interesting disguise. He climbs buildings as if he were flying, his bandages unfurl and roll down to earth, caught by an admiring boy who returns them—'I brought your things, sir!'—and fetches green corn-tips for the beast to eat. Sprinklers are hissing over the lawns and a fish is walking by the mareotic lake and a tree has shed its covering of scales. The last thing the dreamer tells us is that he is looking into the globes of a girl's eyes and seeing in his face reflected there 'something as human as surprise'. Perhaps he is waking from his dream, for better or worse. To dismiss this well-tuned story as self-indulgent nonsense would be easy—but very unmusical. . . .

Alex Raksin (review date 5 February 1989)

SOURCE: A review of *The Dream of a Beast,* in *The Los Angeles Times Book Review,* February 5, 1989, p. 4.

[*In the following excerpt, Raksin asserts that "Ultimately, then,* The Dream of a Beast *is an eloquent testament to the value of listening to the poetry of everyday life. . . ."*]

Like *Blue Velvet* and *Parents,* two recent films about the domestic 1950s, this inspired, surrealistic novel reveals the emotional currents swirling beneath the calm surface of suburban life. But rather than depicting these feelings as a dark, dangerous underworld best suppressed with a smile, as the films have done, Jordan, director of the 1986 film *Mona Lisa* and one of Ireland's pre-eminent fiction writers, presents them as sources of great energy and creativity. By relating to our environment more viscerally, Jordan suggests, we can overcome the alienation that arises from stultifying routine.

The novel begins with portents of change and decay hanging in the air. A heat wave envelopes the narrator's community and strange blooms begin to grow from cracks in the pavements, easing their way along the shop fronts and covering plate-glass windows with "thick, oily, unrecognizable leaves." The mysterious "changes" begin to transform the narrator as well, who becomes acutely sensitive to his neighborhood for the first time, noticing "the extraordinary scent" of its gardens, "moist and heavy, like a thousand autumns, acres of hay longing to be cut. . . . All the gardens seemed to sing at once, a symmetrical hum of praise to (the) afternoon." As his sensitivity to the natural world grows, however, his connection with human society becomes more tenuous; soon, he loses hold of even language's tether, hearing only the underlying patterns in cocktail party chatter, from the "soft, conch-like" voice of his wife, "falling like a wave, as if to protect me," to the hum of a timid friend, like "an insect beating its wings fiercely, to escape."

The narrator then undergoes a symbolic journey, brilliantly portrayed with vivid, thoughtful imagery, which ultimately brings him closer to his wife and daughter than he had been when the "changes" began. His odyssey might be called a dream, but it is actually more reminiscent of a journey back to childlike consciousness, where colors, textures and sounds surprise and evoke intense feelings. The narrator's journey suggests that this state of consciousness can be far more revelatory than adulthood, an abstract state of mind based on *not* being surprised (and thus endangered) by the environment.

Ultimately, then, *The Dream of a Beast* is an eloquent testament to the value of listening to the poetry of everyday life, something the narrator appreciates one night as his daughter sleeps in a nearby room: "The house was silent now but for a rustling of bedclothes somewhere and the tiny hum of Matilde's breath. I stood on the landing, listening to the new quality of this silence. Slowly it came to me that silence was not what for years I had supposed it to be, the absence of sound. It was the absence, I knew now, of the foreground sounds so the background sounds could be heard. These sounds were like breath—like the breath of this house, of the movement of the air inside it, of the creatures who lived in it."

Neil Jordan with Marlaine Glicksman (interview date January-February 1990)

SOURCE: "Irish Eyes," in *Film Comment,* Vol. 26, No. 1, January-February, 1990, pp. 9-11, 68-71.

[*In the following interview, Jordan discusses different influences on his work and how he approaches filmmaking.*]

Neil Jordan lives in Bray, near Dublin and even nearer to the Irish Sea, just next door to the house where James Joyce lived and wrote. The setting couldn't be more perfectly suited had he been a character in one of his own stories or films: quintessentially and romantically Irish, yet also one step beyond, off the beaten path. Jordan's "Irishness" comes through most clearly in his literary finesse—including his

film scripts—as well as his subterranean Stephen Dedalus-like view of love and sexuality.

The author of a collection of short stories, *Night in Tunisia,* and the novels *The Past* and *Dream of a Beast,* Jordan has written and directed several feature films: *Angel,* released in the U.S. as *Danny Boy, The Company of Wolves, Mona Lisa* (co-written with David Leland), *High Spirits* and, most recently, *We're No Angels,* penned by David Mamet and starring Robert De Niro and Sean Penn.

Jordan was born in 1950 in Sligo, Ireland, and grew up in Dublin, where he also attended university. Though he had written, since an early age, he studied English literature and history. "You can't study writing here for some strange reason," Jordan explains. "It's odd—it's a country where everybody writes." He wrote *Night in Tunisia* while working in fringe theater, began to write for Irish TV and the BBC and did uncredited work with director John Boorman on his last draft of *Excalibur.*

Jordan's work typically deals with people gone astray, from the prostitute (Cathy Tyson) and lovable thug (Bob Hoskins) in *Mona Lisa,* to the priests in *We're No Angels.* Jordan's women are commonly redemptive-but-distant Madonnas or "Mona Lisas" and sometime whores; his men are beasts. Together, inevitably—or inevitably together—the two conflict. Both his literature and films are like Chinese boxes: stories within a story, films within a film, dreams within a dream. Nowhere is this more evident than his adaptation of Angela Carter's *Company of Wolves,* a fairy-tale-like piece that deals with a young girl's coming-of-sexual-age.

We're No Angels marks Jordan's Hollywood debut. De Niro and Penn play two petty cons serving life in the bowels of a hard-labor prison who escape and turn priests on the lam. The project was brought to Jordan via producer Art Linson (*The Untouchables*) and the Irish post. Why an Irish director was chosen for this all-American, Cagney-style movie wasn't quite clear: "Somebody thought I was appropriate to make the film." He read the script and couldn't deem himself a more perfect match with this story set in northern New England and shot in Canada.

The director made his first three films independently, with backing from Britain's Channel Four, in addition to finance from Palace Productions (*Wolves, Mona Lisa*) and Handmade Films (*Mona Lisa*), and was used to virtual free rein. This was not the case with *High Spirits,* however. "The people I worked with were at the grosser end of Hollywood and the independents," recounts Jordan. "They wanted something totally different than I did and the thing got mangled in-between. After *High Spirits,* I was almost gonna retire." He approached *We're No Angels* and Paramount with trepidation.

"I thought it was going to be really tough, that the higher up, the more complicated politics get and the more your work is interfered with. But the support that I got from the studio surprised me and I found within certain limits, it was almost the same as the films I made in England. I definitely was dealing with a big budget movie, but I didn't feel that I was encountering a 'system.'"

I met Jordan at his home in Bray. The man I spoke to was comfortably disheveled and soft-spoken, not necessarily the type you'd expect to create such sexually-charged work. Obviously, like his films and stories, much lurks beneath the surface.

[*Glicksman:*] *You were a writer. What led you to film?*

[Jordan:] I used to see a lot of films when I was young. But I never took them seriously. It was when I had been to see a few "masterpieces" that I knew there was much more to this than I thought.

I had always envied movies. The novel, as a form, seemed to me overloaded with history. Narratively, there were more interesting things you could do in the cinema. And I also found that I was writing myself into a corner because my prose and fiction were so visual, they were almost like blueprints for movies.

I began to write for TV—Irish TV, the BBC and stuff. And I got more interested in filmmaking. But there haven't been any features made in Ireland for years. There are studios up the way [Bray Studios], but they did general services for international production.

I wrote a feature film about this place and the social realities I knew. I forget what it was called now. It was an independent film for TV and wasn't financed, nor was it made as I had envisioned it. John [Boorman] read my work and asked me to write a script with him that was never made. Then he asked me to work on his last draft of *Excalibur* and to be around when he made the film and to make a documentary. It was like a training ground for me, because I had never made any films before. Then I wrote *Angel* in 1981 and decided to direct it myself.

The original **We're No Angels** *was made in the Fifties. Does this version hold particular relevance now, for the Nineties?*

The film that David wrote has nothing to do with the original except for the title. Basically, David's written a comedy about mistaken identities. I don't think it has any particular relevance to the Eighties or the Nineties. It's a kind of little play really.

You called it a comedy.

We're No Angels? Oh yeah, I think so. It's a little fairy tale with a very ironic twist to it. You know, everybody hopes that miracles will happen. And to these two strange, unfortunate guys, they do.

But fairy tales are also always harsh. The forests are always terrifying, and there are always monsters that will gobble you up. They are quite brutal affairs, really. The only reason they are called "fairy" tales is because they have happy endings.

We're No Angels belongs in that realm of things. Things happen that we all know don't happen in real life. But they happen with a logic and beauty to them, the way we want them to happen.

This was the first time that you hadn't either written or co-written the script. How was that?

It was very strange. I never considered myself a film director. I don't know what I thought of myself as really. I had always conceived the film and been involved in the financing, putting the whole thing together. I had to, because there are no studios here and films are generally put together independently. It was fascinating to work out what exactly is a film director.

What is it?

The person who rushes to make the decisions before anyone else.

The reason I wanted to do the script was because it had a certain kind of imagery that was very close to me and what I had done in the past. That's what amazed me when I read it.

Did you work on the script with Mamet?

I worked as a director would work in terms of shaping it. We had several meetings, and David came up with another draft. I worked on the orchestration of the narrative, but I never attempted to handle the dialogue, because his is impossible to emulate.

That's what I found most difficult in directing the movie. I had been used to changing the dialogue at will during a scene if it doesn't suit or if the actors found it awkward. I would just rewrite it very quickly. But because David's stuff is so particular to him, it was very difficult to change a line.

Your previous films, like **Mona Lisa** *and* **Wolves,** *dealt heavily with female sexuality. Yet* **We're No Angels** *was very male.*

I wasn't aware of that actually. But it is about a Madonna,

isn't it? At the center there is a woman—who happens to be a statue [laughs].

It's an extended joke on the irony of religious belief and rituals. You know, the country I come from—even the dogs bless themselves. It's a very religious place.

It's a very American film. Did that present difficulties?

We built the entire town in Canada. So if there was an America that we related to in the film, it wasn't a real one—it was the America that comes out of old films. We constructed the town using a lot of visual references and built a tiny world that was emblematic rather than real. I had no problem relating to that world, because I made a lot of the choices that lead to it: what the buildings, monastery, and shapes looked like—the emotional associations that one gets from the visual look of the place.

Thematically, I didn't find it a departure from anything I had done before. Which was odd to me, because it was a film that was shot in a language and culture I didn't know. But somehow, everything about it was familiar. Maybe because there was a kind of universal chord in what David had written.

The acting was stylized, reminiscent of Cagney. How did you arrive at that choice?

That was implicit in David's dialogue. Generally, I tend to be impatient with realism. And in the way I approach the acting, I tend to want the actors to go on to a level that is removed from straight naturalism. Those are my instincts, anyway. And David's dialogue was hard Thirties, tough-guy speech. Together, they properly met to what we have.

I was very pleased with the way Bob and Sean approached that aspect of things. What I associate with Bob is this kind of magnificent realism, but in this film, both he and Sean really stretched themselves to that level of farce.

How did you work with them to get there?

These things are implicit in the script. We would discuss ideas about the characters, the kinds of associations we wanted. We rehearsed a lot on camera to find the specific style that was appropriate to each scene.

You've often worked with American actors. Do you find a difference?

I find with American actors, the whole reality of the character is far more important to them than it is to British actors. They come out of an entirely different tradition. To say

it has to do with the Method is to demean it in some way. They come at acting with a tradition that has a direct relationship to the camera and to cinema.

It's also a matter of knowing the realism with which you play or the emotional resonance that you hold in yourself. When you are shooting or performing, there has to be a very strong truth in you, not a false thing. Whereas a lot of British actors come from a more theatrical tradition and are more in love with the idea of acting. They say, "Well you know, my dear boy, if you can't just act it, pretend it." Whereas American actors are unwilling to fake it.

With actors the stature of Bob and Sean, you start with that level of emotional integrity. However else you build on that, you'll never have less. Which is a great foundation for a character or performance. American actors also tend to assume that they will build the characters themselves. Which threw me a bit at the start. . . .

As opposed to having your input as a director?

I didn't know whether American directors stay further from the actors. I just want to get my hands in it. It did take a lot of time, but it was a wonderful experience.

If there was any difficulty, it was in orchestrating the set pieces and large crowds, with stunt events happening behind the principals. And to get that level of acting integrity, the backgrounds correct and the very complicated camera movements. . . . That's what I suppose a director is.

Your work often deals with sexual myths. Sometimes it humors them, other times it challenges. Why does that interest you?

I don't know. Maybe because I'm Irish.

For one thing, for a male director or writer, to imagine female characters is sometimes more rewarding than imagining male characters. It's a total challenge. You get yourself into territory that is quite unknown, so it's an imaginative stimulus. But it's hard to answer that question. I suppose there are two themes: there's sex and dying and between the two very little. . . .

So Freud influenced your work?

I wouldn't say that. It's just my cast of mind.

Is that particularly Irish?

No. If you're Irish, you'd say there is religion and dying. You wouldn't say that sex has anything to do with it.

You also confront the "bestiality" of man in your work. The prison scene in **We're No Angels** *dealt with that.*

I do have a very black-and-white vision of the world. That was what I wanted to construct in **We're No Angels.** The characters go from hell into a kind of purgatory, and they end up in some kind of heaven—which is Canada, strange place. It's freedom, basically. Because the movie was a religious joke, to impose that kind of a scheme on it seemed appropriate. That was the main work I did on the script. Maybe it comes from my lost Catholic background.

The sense of bestiality? It reminded me of Joyce's Stephen Dedalus.

Yeah. You have a sense that one's nature, if unrestrained, would be very destructive or terrifying. One does feel that human beings are poised between chaos and order in some way.

If man is a beast, then what is woman?

Oh, a beast too. These are difficult questions for me to answer.

There's that image of women as both Madonna and the one who also leads you astray.

That's a traditional thing that the Catholic Church teaches and leaves you with. It's beaten into you unconsciously.

In Ireland, women are very strong. There's a tolerated oppression—the divorce and abortion laws—all those things are quite medieval. Maybe it's because of this that you find extraordinarily resourceful, independent women here—who have six children and hold down two jobs while their husbands do nothing. So you do get that kind of image.

Are there other myths that you would like to challenge?

I'm not aware of actually challenging myths. **Wolves** was based on Angela Carter's stories. Angela had written this wonderfully wicked treatment of a series of fairy tales. And it had a kind of mythological sweep to it that I loved. That's why I did that film.

I wrote **Mona Lisa** with David Leland: I wrote the story, David wrote the first draft, then I wrote the others. If I have a point of view, it probably emerges more in that film than in anything else I have done.

Dream of the Beast *reminded me of Robbe-Grillet; it plays with literary form. While your screenwriting is more mythical in style and scope.*

Well, yeah. That was one of the reasons I actually wanted to make films. Because for some reason they allowed me to tell stories and operate with more operatic sweep than I could do in fiction. I think it's very difficult to write like Dickens now or a book like *Les Miserables.* In movies, there are far more choices available to you with regard to the kind of emotions and stories that you deal with. They gave me more freedom to explore things that I probably would never have done in fiction.

You mention films being operatic. Music often comes up in your writing.

I would have loved to have been a proficient musician. When I was a kid, I used to play classical guitar, and when I was about 24, 25, I used to play various things—piano, saxophone. And I fell in love with Charlie Parker.

Music seemed to me like a very appropriate metaphor for the kind of stories that I was writing. It's the most abstract of the arts and, in many ways, the most pure. A lot of those stories in **Night in Tunisia** were about kids at that age of adolescence where they want the inexpressible, and I use music as a way of talking about the inexpressible things they want.

Weren't you a working musician at one time?

I was just trying to make money. I used to just play in dance bands, and I was touring up and down the North of Ireland. And at the time, there was a lot of conflict going on up there. Musicians were traditionally immune to whatever fighting was going on in the North. But a bunch of musicians. [The Miami Showband] were taken out one day and machine-gunned.

That's what my first film came out of. It was a world that I knew, that world of dance halls and of traveling from little parish to parish playing for adolescents and old-timers. Around the same time, I was writing **Night in Tunisia,** and [music] enabled me to get out, travel around and play for a roomful of 600 people. It was a good release.

You never wanted to make a musical?

Yeah. Oh, I'd love to make a musical—desperately. Particularly a backstage musical. But it's very difficult. It's like Westerns—people just don't make them anymore.

Your characters have often "strayed from the path." In **We're No Angels,** *it's clear what these two men have done.*

Absolutely. **Angel** was the most appalling stray from path, about a saxophone player who became involved in sectarian killings in Northern Ireland and who, instead of keeping a saxophone in his case, kept a gun.

I know what you mean. It's about those moments when you're in an ordinary, realistic situation—in the drab ordinariness of everyday life. And you go off the road a little bit, and suddenly you find something really wonderful and terrifying—something that doesn't belong to the real world.

The stories that I tell start from realistic beginnings and proceed to very unrealistic, mythological territories. I like to choose characters who are surrounded by a life that seems understandable and who slowly find themselves in situations where everything has changed, where no rules exist and where emotions and realities are brought into play that they are not prepared for.

"Straying from the path" also seems very Catholic.

So it's a Catholic thing again, is it? No, it's the idea, actually, of the experiences that you put yourself through that change you. The experiences that are dangerous, frightening, terrifying and maybe, in some ways, unsavory are often the ones that broaden your emotional resonance, your understanding of things.

Your work is very apolitical, and that has given rise to criticism among your Irish peers.

It's a certain dissatisfaction with politics, with political explanations of human behavior, that's reflected in it, because I don't think they tell the whole story. I did write a novel about Irish politics called **The Past,** but it was a most convoluted one. When I made **Angel,** there was a big outcry here because people felt that on an issue like that you should take a stand—on the Republic, or whatever side. I just wanted to make a film about the barest facts of the matter: that individuals kill people they don't know. What happens in the North of Ireland does happen continuously; people kill people that in other circumstances they could have tea or a drink with. So I wanted to make a film about this guy who, before he killed anyone, wanted to know their name, to tell a story that didn't require any explanations—social, political, religious or even metaphorical. I didn't want to comment in any way at all.

Your films could be set almost anywhere. Whereas a lot of English films, particularly now, need to be set specifically.

The funny thing is, because I'm Irish, I've got a different attitude toward that. There are two strands of British cinema: costume drama and realism. In many ways, the whole of the last ten years of British cinema have been about the Thatcher years.

I come from a country where people make political statements and die for them at the same time. A lot of people that I knew are not around anymore because they involved themselves in politics.

But it's a thing I try consciously to do: to broaden the frame of reference beyond the place it's happening. A lot of things I've done were in studios. Again, it's impatience with basic realism.

Would you say your work is particularly Irish or particularly individual?

I would say that it's particularly Irish in its impatience with reality. Because that's the one thing that unites this entire place: one's sense of reality is at its thinnest in this country.

It's probably because of its political history. It's a strange little country, because it's terribly different from Britain but it has been ruled by them for years and its politics are still dominated by them. And Britain is bourgeois—I don't want to insult that country, but it's a very sedate and prosaic place in many ways. This country may be many things, but it is neither sedate nor prosaic.

John Collick (essay date 1991)

SOURCE: "Wolves through the Window: Writing Dreams / Dreaming Films / Filming Dreams," in *Critical Survey,* Vol. 3, No. 3, 1991, pp. 283-89.

[*In the following excerpt, Collick discusses the role of dreams in Jordan's* The Company of Wolves *and asserts that "What is being offered appears to be a parody of the Freudian dream work in which the dream symbols, instead of being scrambled images or 'puzzles' that represent unconscious wishes, turn out to be familiar literary images."*]

In this essay I'm going to discuss films of texts which have dreams or dreaming as their central theme. Movies and dreams have always been closely linked. Cinema history is filled with examples of movies that try to imitate the imagery and structure of the dream world, either by making the entire film appear like a dream or by including dreams in the narrative. Luis Buñuel's *Un Chien Andalou* presents the audience with images that possess the disruptive logic and absurdity of a nightmare. In Alfred Hitchcock's *Spellbound,* the solution to a murder is discovered by analysing the dream of an amnesiac who witnessed it and a dream sequence, based on Salvador Dali's paintings, is included in the film. Movies which are not adaptations of texts, like *Un Chien Andalou* or Jean Cocteau's *Testament d'Orphée* are often radical because they interrogate the audience's notions of film realism and narrative. Can films of dreams that are based on texts be equally challenging? The question is complicated by the fact that the relationship between these films and the texts, and between the audience and the films, is often constructed in such a way as to mimic the relationship between a psychoanalyst and a patient. This tends to endorse the position of both the audience and the objective scientist/analyst as the source of understanding. In other words, to take a text and, in the process of filming it, transform it into a dream is to render it problematic by confronting viewers with unfamiliar images and techniques, and then to make it safe by rendering its arbitrary shifts of logic explainable. Orson Welles's film of Franz Kafka's *The Trial* is a good example of this.

In his biography of Franz Kafka, Max Brod describes his friend's familiarity with the theories of Sigmund Freud. Kafka thought Freudian psychoanalysis too crude: 'a rough and ready explanation which didn't do justice to detail'. Despite this, his stories and short pieces often appear to echo Freudian ideas and imagery; especially in the works that relate to his unsettled relationship with his father: *The Judgement* and *Metamorphosis*. For this reason Freud has often been used to read and interpret Kafka, often from an almost clinical point of view. In other words, it is presumed that the 'meaning' of the text can be traced to some psychological problem or condition in the mind of Kafka. Shoshana Felman characterises this approach as one of 'applied psychoanalysis' since the concept of 'application' implies a relation of exteriority between the applied science and the field which it is supposed, unilaterally, to inform'. From a position of objective science the analyst unravels the mystery of the text or dream, locating its source in the unconscious. In the case of Kafka, many of his stories are read as dream narratives in which images of alienation, illogical worlds and shifts of focus are symptoms of a hidden, fundamental sickness. Mark Spilka, for example, has suggested that Kafka's writing stems from the author's 'arrested childhood consciousness'; in other words he was unable to break free from his perception of himself as a victimised child in an arbitrary adult world and this led him to write grotesque, nightmarish stories.

At the beginning of Orson Welles's film of Kafka's *The Trial*, the director reads the short tale 'Before the Law' which Kafka both included in his novel and published separately in 1919. 'Before the Law' is an unsettling piece of writing about a man who wishes to pass through the door that leads to the Law. A doorkeeper tells him he must wait, so the man waits until he finally dies of old age. Just before his death he is told that the door was meant specially for him, and that the doorkeeper will now close it. Offered as a parable in *The Trial,* 'Before the Law' tacitly claims to explain the relationship between the hero, Joseph K., and the Law which has found him guilty of an unspecified crime. In fact, it explains nothing. In his film Welles concludes his reading of the short extract by stating that 'It has been said that the logic of this story [*The Trial*] is the logic of a dream, a nightmare.'

By linking Kafka's *The Trial* with the dream world, the movie interprets the novel in a specific way, suggesting two things. Firstly it underscores the unsettling, arbitrary nature of the world that Joseph K. inhabits where rules of space, dimension and rationality are perpetually disrupted. Secondly, it offers the story to the viewer as an object for analysis, a dream which can supposedly be unravelled, analysed and understood by the viewer who is placed in the vicarious position of the psychoanalyst. So at the same time that the audience is intimidated by the breakdown in conventions of narrative cinema (i.e. in one shot K. closes a normal size door, in the next he is shown dwarfed by the same door which has suddenly grown massive), they are also coaxed into believing that they are watching a symbolic manifestation of hidden meaning, one which they as viewers/analysts can unravel. Welles plays on this by including symbols that are easily recognisable as references to Nazism, the McCarthy era and the atomic bomb. Thus, by recreating Kafka's novel in the form of a dream, Welles's film provides a partial explanation for both the novel's and the film's disturbing elements while simultaneously protecting the audience's objective position.

Are all dream films that are connected with texts as reassuring? During the 1980s there was a brief spate of films dealing with children's relationships to dreams and dream worlds. Nearly all of these were based on books or stories, or had a text as the central motivating element of the narrative. *The Neverending Story, The Princess Bride, Labyrinth* and the TV series *The Storyteller* were based on the idea of a fantastic world being created through a child reading, or being told, a story with the camera functioning as the child's imagination. Darker themes concerning the wakening of childhood sexuality and the problematic relationship between children and adults appeared in **The Company of Wolves** (based on Angela Carter's story of the same name and her translation of Charles Perrault's 'Little Red Riding Hood'), *Dreamchild* (using excerpts from Lewis Carroll's *Alice* books), and *Paper House* (from Catherine Storr's children's novel *Marianne Dreams*). Of these I feel that **The Company of Wolves** and *Paper House* are especially significant because of the way they appear to use the text in an attempt consciously to engage with and neutralise the tenets of traditional Freudian psychoanalysis.

In the seventeenth century Charles Perrault collected traditional fairy tales, edited them and embellished them with morals. His version of 'Little Red Riding Hood' concludes with the wolf eating the girl, the message stating that there are 'also wolves who seem perfectly charming . . . who pursue young girls in the street and pay them the most flattering attentions. Unfortunately, these smooth-tongued, smooth pelted wolves are the most dangerous beasts of all'. The editing of the folk tales by Perrault involved the suppression of occasionally violent and sexual content and the 'adding of moral tags that temper their darkness'. In 1979 Angela Carter published the short story 'The Company of Wolves' as part of a collection of rewritten fairy stories. Based on Perrault's 'Little Red Riding Hood', Carter's tale presents the confrontation between the girl and the wolf as one between women's awakening sexual desire and that of men/ werewolves (creatures who 'would love to be less beastly if only they knew how'.) The eating of Little Red Riding Hood becomes a metaphor for sex; a consummation in which the desire of the girl allows her to confront the beast on equal, if not superior terms: 'She laughed at him full in the face, she ripped off his shirt for him and flung it into the fire, in the fiery wake of her own discarded clothing.' In this and other tales in the collection, Carter, while anxious to emphasise the validity of women's desire, suggests it is similar in nature and potential to oppressive male sexuality. She thereby implies that it is a mysterious power that women possess, free from the oppression of gender relationships. The film of *The Company of Wolves* adopts the same conclusion but, in reworking the tale as a quasi-Freudian dream, simultaneously reveals the inadequacy of this, and any, attempts to control the sexual 'darkness' of fairy tales.

In the film a young girl sleeps and, in her dreams, a number of narrative episodes are acted out. In her dream world the girl appears as a Little Red Riding Hood who lives in a Gothic style village. She periodically visits her grandmother who tells her to beware of men who are wolves in disguise. As in the story, the main narrative, which frames four minor tales, concludes with her meeting a handsome prince in the forest who turns out to be the (literal) wolf of the fairy tale. This encounter, which concludes with her turning into a wolf too, signifies the resolution between the young girl's awakening sexuality and the predatory sexuality of men.

What is being offered appears to be a parody of the Freudian dream work in which the dream symbols, instead of being scrambled images or 'puzzles' that represent unconscious wishes, turn out to be familiar literary images.
—John Collick

Surprisingly this theme is made obvious in a very deliberate way. The film is liberally sprinkled with very laboured references to sexuality as a seemingly dark and menacing power: the girl Rosaleen bites into an apple which contains a worm; a moth hovers near a candle; spiders fall onto her prayer book in church, and men whose eyebrows meet in the middle are, literally, wolves. The film constructs an elaborate framework of these, and other symbols. The problem with this web of signification is that it actually signifies very little, other than a string of familiar metaphors. What is being offered appears to be a parody of the Freudian dream work in which the dream symbols, instead of being scrambled images or 'puzzles' that represent unconscious wishes, turn out to be familiar literary images. The superficial symbolism of the movie gives it the appearance of a quasi-Freudian dream mystery which is then 'analysed'. Thus the ambiguous relationship between Rosaleen, the wolves and the imagery of the film is apparently resolved when Rosaleen turns into a wolf herself.

Many critics voiced dissatisfaction with this liberal humanist argument which they read as meaning 'if men are wolves then it doesn't really matter as women are capable of being wolves too'. It's interesting that this sequence is often described as if it marked the conclusion of the movie when, in fact, the film itself undercuts this somewhat glib conclusion and simultaneously topples the viewer from the comfortable position of the objective analyst. After Rosaleen has turned into a wolf she joins a pack of wolves who charge into the dream-equivalent of the house where the real Rosaleen is dreaming. In the final shots, as this Rosaleen wakes up, a wolf breaks through her bedroom window. The image has multiple associations: with male sexual violence, the seemingly fundamental uncontrollability of sexuality, and the process of dreaming itself (where unconscious thoughts erupt into dreams). On this level alone it undercuts the earlier resolution of the dream-narrative when Rosaleen becomes a wolf. At the same time the image makes explicit what has been implicit throughout the movie: that writing, filming and watching dreams (using the traditional Freudian methods of analysis to 'control' the unconscious) involve the adoption of inadequate and false positions of scientific objectivity. Rosaleen dreams and her dreams are enacted on the other side of the window which, in effect, functions like a cinema screen. Throughout the film the tales and images have tried to express, inadequately, some hidden meaning which is never revealed. A false, liberal and comforting conclusion is offered, and then effaced by the shot of the wolf bursting through the glass (which parallels the destruction of the audience's position of authority as the incomprehensible meaning of the film 'bursts' through the screen). The final sequence underscores the fundamental incomprehensibility of sexuality, texts and the film itself when subject to traditional Freudian analysis. When the wolf comes through the window the viewer/analyst is implicated in the relationship between the dream and its meaning: 'there is no language in which interpretation can itself escape the effects of the unconscious; the interpreter is not more immune than the poet to unconscious delusions and errors'. The repressed 'unconscious' tale that lurks behind Perrault's moral and Carter's conclusions, comes back to us, literally through the screen. . . .

What is original and special about *The Crying Game* is its execution, the mileage Jordan gets from the conventions he respects and those he upsets, and the complexity of its discourse on racial and gender issues.
—David Lugowski

A film that is based on a text about dreams, or which transforms a problematic text into a dream (as in Orson Welles's film of *The Trial*), is often very different from a film which tries to recreate the mechanics of a dream. Films that consciously imitate the processes of dreaming (for example, David Lynch's *Eraserhead*) are disturbing because they undercut the narrative coherence of cinema, simultaneously alienating the viewer from the image while underscoring film's similarity with the process of dreaming itself. No analysis is offered, the viewer is merely presented with absurd images that probably mean something else, but meaning is elusive. Films of dream-stories seem to confirm, rather than challenge, the orthodox belief in film as an impartial and scientific mode of representation. By framing the dream and contextualising it with the real world (even by merely stating 'the logic of this story is the logic of a dream'), the camera and the viewer are placed in the position of the analyst who, presented with a dream text, attempts to unravel its mystery and expose the true meaning (or problem) to the light of day. This tacit confirmation of the rationalist Freudian approach is underscored by the fact that films of dream-stories (as in the case of *Paper House* and *The Company of Wolves*) follow the narrative structure of the original tale. *Marianne Dreams,* Perrault's tale of Little Red Riding Hood and Carter's short story are, more or less, linear stories with clear resolutions. The films are largely the same, causality is affirmed, subjects remain coherent, there is no distortion or conflation of the body, no one's head falls off as in *Eraserhead.* Even *The Company of Wolves,* with its four sub-narratives, shows unchanging characters following a plot whose sudden mysteries can be as easily explained away by magic (or lycanthropy) as by dream-logic. Werewolves are an accepted part of orthodox fantasy and their appearance in a film does not radically interrogate an audience's preconceptions. It is only in the very last sequence of *The Company of Wolves* that the story breaks down (though this is partially redeemed by a moral spoken over the credits). Yet despite the distancing of both the unconscious itself and unpalatable Freudian theory, the security of the audience is not ensured. In both *Paper House* and *The Company of Wolves,* the audience are inserted into a simple, traditional Freudian

framework which is then undercut or challenged. In the case of *The Company of Wolves* the rejection of Freud as inadequate (i.e. through the use of a multitude of banal symbols that effectively mean nothing) takes on a radical slant when the wolf bursts through the window into the dreamer's bedroom. This ending implies that there is no safe, objective position from which to confront the unconscious, and that both the real Rosaleen and the quasi-analytical viewers cannot escape its disruptive powers. . . .

David Lugowski (essay date 1993)

SOURCE: "Genre Conventions and Visual Style in *The Crying Game,*" in *Cineaste,* Vol. XX, No. 1, 1993, pp. 31, 33, 35.

[*In the following essay, Lugowski asserts, "What is original and special about* The Crying Game *is its execution, the mileage Jordan gets from the conventions he respects and those he upsets, and the complexity of its discourse on racial and gender issues."*]

Much of the talk surrounding the considerable critical and popular success of writer-director Neil Jordan's latest film, *The Crying Game,* speaks of how unusual the film is: one critic went so far as to term it "unclassifiable," while Miramax executive Gerry Rich attributes its popularity to audience hunger for "unconventional films." Truth to tell, *The Crying Game* is nothing of the kind. It actually treads some well-worn territory. Like Jordan's last notable success, *Mona Lisa* (another effort, *The Company of Wolves,* unfortunately received very little attention), it is a neo-*film noir* named after a popular song from several decades back, dealing in a fairly conventional visual and narrative style with sexual obsession. Its basic plotline, the "Why am I falling in love with the lover of someone I killed?," cannot by any stretch of the imagination be considered original. Even the biggest of the film's twisty surprises may be anticipated by some viewers depending on their own knowledge and experience, and was in fact also the linchpin of the recent Broadway success, *M. Butterfly.* What is original and special about *The Crying Game* is its execution, the mileage Jordan gets from the conventions he respects and those he upsets, and the complexity of its discourse on racial and gender issues.

A black iron bridge grating frames the leisurely opening shot of a local fairground, hinting that something menacing is about to descend, which indeed it does, when the IRA kidnaps Jody (Forest Whitaker), a British soldier, in order to effect an exchange of prisoners. Jody is assaulted when he starts making out with Jude (Miranda Richardson), the IRA operative who has set him up, proving that naturalistic blondes in neo-*films noirs* cannot be trusted any more than their more artificially coiffed sisters from the Forties.

Despite the warnings of Jude and IRA group leader Peter (Adrian Dunbar)—do these names suggest perhaps a slyly ironic religious reference?—Fergus (Stephen Rea), the terrorist who first clouts Jody, becomes surprisingly friendly with his prisoner as the two men discuss such subjects as Jody's love for cricket and his lover Dil. Realizing that "it's not in [the IRA's] nature to let [him] go," Jody asks Fergus, his designated executioner, to find Dil after his certain death. It is one of the film's cutting ironies that Jody is killed not by the new friend unable to shoot him in the back, but by the British forces on their way to rescue him.

In one of the many identity switches which mark *The Crying Game,* Fergus adopts the name Jimmy when he relocates in London and finds work on a construction site which overlooks a cricket field, repeatedly evoking memories of Jody. Those memories intensify after Fergus locates Dil (Jaye Davidson) and finds pictures of Jody adorning her apartment. What begins as comfort mingled with attraction soon becomes full-fledged love on Fergus's part. As with every *film noir* character, however, Dil too has problems to solve and surprises to reveal. The film's heady mix of *hommes fatals* and *femmes fatales* proves almost too much for Fergus, who promptly runs into the bathroom and vomits when Dil unveils 'her' penis—the 'twist' which so many critics have dutifully avoided mentioning. Dil, however, isn't fazed: "Even when you were throwing up, I could tell you cared." Just how much Fergus cares is soon put to the test when Jude and Peter resurface, threatening to harm Dil if Fergus doesn't help them assassinate a prominent judge.

The film's execution of its many surprises does lend it a certain freshness, but to take only one of several earlier renditions of the same plot, consider Ernst Lubitsch's 1932 drama, *Broken Lullaby* (a.k.a. *The Man I Killed*). A WWI French soldier (Phillips Holmes) kills an enemy fighter, but the two are trapped in a foxhole overnight while the wounded German lingers in his arms. Realizing that wartime killing seems more like murder when it has a face to it, the young man visits his victim's family to beg forgiveness, but winds up falling for the dead man's fiancée (Nancy Carroll) and being all but adopted by his parents.

Sound familiar? Unlike Lubitsch, though, whose message is pacifism and whose tone is atypically somber, Jordan is wittier but his politics more ambiguous. His hero, unlike Lubitsch's, eventually reveals his role in the death of the beloved figure, but both men are ultimately impotent in the face of crisis. *The Crying Game's* final shootout takes place between Jude and Dil, while Fergus can only be called upon to sacrifice, taking the rap for Dil's killing of Jude. The old Hollywood Production Code would have loved the finale of

The Crying Game: while Lubitsch's hero is forgiven because his actions occurred in wartime, Fergus is punished as much for his earlier terrorist activities as for anything else. The question of what Dil is called upon to sacrifice is largely unclear, however, as are the motivations for the IRA activities. Such ambiguity, especially as it pertains to sex and gender roles, is both one of the great strengths of *The Crying Game* and symptomatic of its mainstream status.

The film's basic plot isn't the only antique on hand here; the soundtrack is, in fact, so full of golden oldies that one might justifiably wonder if the film is set in the Sixties or Seventies instead of the present day. A remake of "Stand by Your Man" closes the film, and, for those unfamiliar with Dave Berry's top five title song from the early Sixties, Jordan plays it several times at important moments, sung first by Kate Robbins, then by Berry himself, and finally by Boy George. In each case the gender of the singer is of exquisite importance vis-à-vis the power relations between the film's main characters. In true old movie fashion, even Dil, as 'female lead,' lip syncs the title song.

For all its play with gender roles, issues pertaining to race are also adroitly sketched in, as Jody speaks of being stationed at "one of the few places where they still call you a nigger to your face." More subtle, however, is Jude's reference to Dil as a "wee black chick" or the whiteness which the utopian space of the cricket field evokes. Perhaps most significant, though, is Jody's making out with Jude in the film's opening scene. When Jude resists and Jody asks, "Who gives a fuck?," she responds with, "You never know," leading him to the isolated spot where the kidnapping will occur. For a moment one gets the sense that it's not just the sight of a couple necking in public that might upset decorum but the sight of an interracial couple doing so. To some extent it is Jody's willingness to break this racial boundary which enables his kidnapping; ironically, it is his willingness to break other boundaries which later gives his side an ace up its sleeve.

The film's discourse on race extends beyond interracial relations to the construction of manhood. In one of the most memorable and economical shots, Fergus, covered in white dust from his London construction site, watches an all-white cricket match in the idyllic green field, wistfully recalling Jody. Though they may both have enjoyed the game, Jody and Fergus each were of a social class which would generally have been denied the privilege of playing on such a pristine pitch. The white dust foregrounds Fergus's whiteness as he casts off his 'black' Irishness yet, at the same time, recalls his incomplete bonding with the black soldier whose death he indirectly has caused. Fergus is also potentially a tragic clown, unable to follow through on his feelings, the butt of Jody's joke concerning what he didn't tell Fergus about Dil. (One of the most amusing shots in the film has

Fergus dreaming of Jody again, but instead of hurling a cricket ball, the dead man is now enjoying his joke.) The dust suggests a feminizing cosmetic as well, as Fergus is on the cusp of both an internal and a political makeover, where his very integrity, his manliness, so to speak, will be questioned.

The cleverly constructed screenplay makes considerable use of parallels and repetitions; indeed, in many ways the latter part of the film plays like an extended reversal of the opening third. Repeating Jude's earlier gesture of holding Jody's hand while he pisses, Fergus enables the bound Jody to lean forward so as not to wet himself. It is at once highly amusing and sweetly provocative that while Jude (at one time Fergus's lover) and Dil resist the roving hands of Jody and Fergus, respectively, Fergus, in helping Jody to piss, must take the other man's penis out of his pants. Fergus himself will be tied up by Dil later in the film after he reveals his role in Jody's death. In both cases, male bondage is caused by or juxtaposed with the IRA's activities. The workings of the political machine and the duplicitous actions and desires of woman are thus shown to render men helpless at crucial moments.

Dil cuts Fergus's hair when they first meet; Fergus will later cut the seductive hairdresser's locks when he attempts to disguise Dil as a 'man.' By this point, Dil, almost as confused as Fergus, can only wonder aloud, "Will you like me better this way?" These scenes bring the film's homoerotic play with gender roles around full circle: the clothing Fergus chooses for Dil is, in fact, Jody's white cricket uniform. Parallels which match up or break apart the film's many couples exist even among individual shots. Jordan's sensual use of a tilt and canted framing as a gun-toting Fergus gets Dil's picture out of Jody's pocket is echoed when the gun-wielding Jude attempts to kiss Fergus upon her reentry into his life.

In suitably *film noir* fashion, these parallels frequently serve to link sex with death. In one highly erotic scene, Fergus, while being fellated by Dil, sees the now-dead Jody clad in his cricket uniform. Later on, Jordan orchestrates cuts between Fergus, bound by Dil's underwear to the bedposts, and Jude and Peter angrily wondering why Fergus hasn't shown up for the planned assassination. As Fergus writhes orgasmically, Peter attempts the killing himself. Once the deed is done, we see a 'spent' Fergus lying back on the bed as he attempts to reason with the confused and angry Dil.

The success of *The Crying Game,* however, doesn't really reside in one's being fooled by appearances, reversals, or sudden plot twists. It lies, in part, with the remarkably cooperative attitude of the popular press in not giving away too many of the film's secrets. Rarely has the release of a film foregrounded to such an extent the truly textual nature

not of the projected celluloid strip alone, but rather of the entire film production and exhibition apparatus. One's experience of the film is utterly indissoluble from the hubbub surrounding it, and, in this case, that's a good thing.

The film does, in an academic sense, improve on a second viewing: one can more fully appreciate how carefully the film is put together. Although many viewers might be tempted to kick themselves for not noticing all the hints Jordan drops along the way (and how he cheats the *mise-en-scène* at the nightclub more than a little), a second viewing does reveal how lines as innocuous as "Thank you, handsome" and "She wouldn't suit you" suddenly take on great significance. If Jordan does rely rather heavily on the seemingly mimetic quality of mainstream realist cinema to shatter one's assumptions, it's at least good to note that they can still be shattered in this day and age. Or, if not shattered, at least bent a little bit.

This serious playfulness is a double-edged sword. In many ways *The Crying Game* is a perfectly *safe* sort of film in that its seemingly radical discourses are actually only likably liberal, its various loose cannons ultimately shown to be friendly fire. In true Hollywood fashion, questions of what seem to be the 'political' are collapsed into the realm of the 'personal.' The most obvious casualty is the film's treatment of the IRA; any sort of violent goings-on around the world would probably have sufficed equally well. The film suggests that Jude plays her soldier role only too well and, as a result, there's no love in her. When she reenters Fergus's life, Jude is able to transform threatening terrorist fervor to sexual proposition in a second.

Fergus, meanwhile, shows promise through the friendship he develops with Jody, and so he gets a second chance. He doesn't love Jody enough to save him, but he loves Dil enough to try harder and, in truly redemptive fashion, even goes to prison for a murder he didn't commit. One wonders, however, how much of the hero's actions are indeed motivated by love. The film clearly wants to play against the notion that 'biology is destiny,' and yet the social discourse surrounding Fergus's relationship with Dil is not fully explored. The result is that the film's coda, with Fergus retelling Jody's fable about a scorpion and a frog to Dil, is a little too pat, leaving one to wonder about the hidden significance of the glass barrier between the two men.

Like films ranging from *Tootsie, 9 to 5,* and *Victor/Victoria* through the more recent *Dances with Wolves* and *Malcolm X, The Crying Game* has a tendency to sometimes blunt its more likably ragged edges (the most obvious example is Jordan's reliance on the all-purpose cliché, "I can't help the way I am," at one particularly tense moment). If only for the shock so many nongay men feel when they must admit that they find Dil attractive, *The Crying Game* is, however, precisely the type of film that makes students of popular culture wonder if conventional form and liberal content can indeed promote social change.

Frann Michel (essay date 1993)

SOURCE: "Racial and Sexual Politics in *The Crying Game,*" in *Cineaste,* Vol. XX, No. 1, 1993, pp. 30, 32, 34.

[*In the following essay, Michel analyzes the pitfalls concerning gender, sexuality, and race that Jordan fell into when filming* The Crying Game.]

Complex, subtle, and beautifully acted, **The Crying Game** unmistakably evokes and disrupts conventional expectations about national, racial, and sexual boundaries. In achieving its impressive thematic and visual coherence, however, Neil Jordan's compelling film succumbs to some of the risks entailed in its ambitious project. Where its disruptions are insufficient or excessive, the film implies a conservative politics at odds with the screenplay's apparent intentions. Public discussion of those intentions and accomplishments has been limited, so as not to spoil the film for those who haven't yet seen it. But the engaging intricacy of the film demands a detailed consideration that is impossible without revealing the plot as well as the other means by which the film challenges customary views.

Repeatedly throughout the film, Ian Wilson's camera looks through windows and doorways; shots are framed by carnival booths, by furniture, by the architecture of a construction site, a bar, a stage. What we see is constructed by the frameworks available to us, foregrounding the film's interrogation of conventional boundaries and leading us to recognize and to challenge oppressive conventions of representation.

In the opening sequence, an Irish Republican Army group kidnaps a British soldier (Forest Whitaker). The facts that Jody is black and his IRA guard Fergus (Stephen Rea) is softhearted immediately disrupt conventional representations. A delicately calibrated relationship develops between Jody and Fergus: part kinship, part antagonism, part eroticism. On opposite sides of the war, the two men share analogous experiences of oppression, as well as the sense of being caught in structures larger than themselves.

In this first third of the film, the human face of the IRA provided by Fergus is supported by a more broadly sympathetic view of the group. Their motives for capturing Jody are comprehensible, defensive rather than aggressive. The disproportionate influx of British military might that ends the sequence makes clear, by contrast, that the IRA uses only the tactics available to the underdog. After Fergus escapes to a construction job in London and an assumed identity as "Jimmy," the justice of the Irish liberation movement is further underscored by the racism of his English boss who calls him by the Irish generic "Pat."

But the film's presentation of the IRA becomes increasingly unsympathetic, and, ultimately, trivializing. Fergus moves away from his political commitment and audience sympathies are likely to move with him: public issues yield to private narrative. Furthermore, the nationalist Jude (Miranda Richardson), who earlier lured Jody to his capture, now appears not only coldly ruthless, but also flippant. The IRA's planned assassination of "some judge" implies that the Army members are motivated not by articulated political strategy but by a cruel fondness for violence. After questioning the validity of national borders by displaying the brotherhood between IRA guard and British captive, the film goes on to abandon the anticolonialist critique that would make sense of the IRA.

Rather differently, in presenting the kinship between Jody and Fergus as both transnational and transracial, the film exploits (without fully subverting) conventional representations of racial otherness. The film twice exploits images of interracial sex, then subsequently relocates the transgressiveness of these images elsewhere, first in the abduction of Jody just as he begins making out with Jude, and later, in the revelation of Dil's secret just as she and Fergus begin making love. So, too, when Jody says that Jude is less his type of woman than his London girl-friend, Dil (Jaye Davidson), we are permitted, only temporarily, to hear this as a comment about the appropriateness of intraracial relationships. These conventional responses police the boundaries of race, and putting them in question offers a challenge to racist assumptions. Yet the fact that the film's two black or biracial characters are also sexual outlaws leaves unquestioned a conventional equation between racial and sexual otherness.

The representation of sexual otherness is, of course, the mesmerizing secret that most of the movie's reviewers dare not name. At Jody's request, Fergus looks up Dil in London. Instead of telling her about Jody's last thoughts of her, however, Fergus gently and gallantly woos Dil. When they are first about to go to bed together, Dil's robe opens to reveal a washboard flat chest and a small, flaccid penis. This is the information that reviewers avoid in an effort to evade the tenacious reassertion of sexual boundaries. To describe Dil as a transvestite, crossdresser, or drag queen is implicitly to describe her as 'really' a man, and thus effectively to preempt the audience's experience of watching and reading a character as a woman, only to have that reading challenged by a piece of information that is not part of our culture's definition of 'woman.' The surprise of the experience is presumably greatest for those who (like Fergus) walk into the film believing that there are always only two genders and that one can always tell them apart.

Indeed, this epistemological certainty is recuperated by those viewers who insist that Jaye Davidson is 'really' a woman wearing a prosthetic penis, or by those who insist that they could tell from the beginning (by the hands, or the jaw, or some other purported telltale feature) that Dil was 'really' a man. Either response by viewers asserts that there is a single, clear gender boundary, and that they cannot be deceived about where it lies. By avowing that gender is a stable and legible essence, such viewers disavow the film's demonstration that gender is a performance, and they refuse the conceptual reframings that the film provides.

That possibility of refusal leaves the question of the film's sexism up for grabs. To the extent that we come to perceive gender as a performance, we have undermined a central grounding of sexism: if femininity is always a masquerade, then inequality cannot be justified by appeal to women's 'natural' role. Yet, beside the discourse of performance, the film also mobilizes a discourse of nature. The film tells us and then demonstrates that characters act according to their natures and cannot help what they are. Through appeals to the natural basis of the conventionally 'unnatural,' however, such as Dil's natural femininity, even when dressed as a man, the film actually 'denaturalizes' conventionally held assumptions. But to the extent that the movie's subversion of naturalized gender is incomplete (as perhaps it must be at this point in our culture), the film enacts a cruel misogyny.

The relative stability of gender means that it matters that the only character in the film who is (presumably) without a penis is also a villain who maintains and manipulates boundaries. Jude is openly racist and aggressively sexual, and she uses that clearly-bounded sexuality to entrap Jody. Lacking the empathy of Fergus, the propensity for self-sacrifice of Peter Maguire (Adrian Dunbar), or the feminine sexual appeal of Dil (as Dil cattily points out and no one disputes), Jude is a heartless, selfish, unattractive bitch. Uninterested in the conventionally feminine concerns of appearance and romance, Jude dresses according to the needs of her politics, devoting herself to the public pursuit of violent nationalism.

Dil, by contrast, is indifferent to politics; she works as a hairdresser, wears sequined miniskirts, and decorates her apartment as a shrine to lost love. In addition, she displays an undemanding goodness compounded of the most painful elements of masochistic femininity. When Fergus first meets her, Dil is plagued by an abusive boyfriend; "I fix on anyone who's nice to me," she says. The film invites us to compare Jude with Dil—as women, as people in disguise, as sexual objects, as partners for Jody and Fergus—and Jude comes off much the worse for the comparison. In short, the only good woman is a man.

Inversely, the film also implies that the really gay man is a woman. The overtly sexual relationships between men in the film replicate heterosexual paradigms. Whether they parody or perfect those paradigms, the film's gay relationships offer no counter vision, and the invocation of AIDS through reference to Dil's "blood condition" flirts with a pathologizing of queer identity. The relationship between Jody and Fergus—both soldiers, both sexually paired with Jude as well as Dil—remains only covertly erotic.

Certainly the relation between the two men is eroticized: Jody persuades Fergus to remove his blindfold by insisting he has already seen Fergus's face; "You're the handsome one," Jody tells him. Jody also persuades Fergus to help him urinate, and smiles at Fergus's embarrassment at handling the prisoner's penis. The conceptual reframing effected by the frontal view of Dil's genitals seems to narrow the interpretive boundaries available to some critics, who read the kinship between Jody and Fergus solely as indicative of their sexual affinity. The film, in the final analysis, is not merely preoccupied with erotic quandaries, but demonstrates the way in which sexual politics reflect broader political concerns. But all these criticisms—of the movie's privatized individualism, racism, sexism, and homophobia—are made available by the film's willingness to take on such thorny issues. Balancing a thought-provoking exploration of serious political questions with a recurring lightness of tone and a redemptive romantic ending, *The Crying Game* is visually, intellectually, and emotionally engaging. If the film falls short of the radical innovations it sometimes promises, it nonetheless offers profound dislocations of vision: the chance to try to see anew.

Vanessa Place (essay date May-June 1993)

SOURCE: "The Politics of Denial," in *Film Comment,* Vol. 29, No. 3, May-June, 1993, pp. 84-86.

[In the following essay, Place discusses how the veiling phenomenon, difference, and uniformity are at work in The Bodyguard *and* The Crying Game.*]*

The good thing about middlebrow art is that it nicely reflects society's dull edge. Unlike the avant garde, it makes no particular pretense toward advancement; unlike absolute schlock, it doesn't wallow in the retrograde. Middlebrow art is feel-good art: the world may not be this pleasant yet, but we can spend a lot of money creating an accessible façade. And our current middlebrow ideal is a quiet, placid, Cokecommercial kind of world where race is irrelevant, gender immaterial, and sexuality beside the point.

But these fantasies are dangerous. We are awash in our own whitewash. Popular culture cuddles around the notion of love as the great leveler, promoting a false sense of individual social equality and carefully stacking the deck to prevent reality seepage. Today's mass media celebrate the myth of universal harmony and transcendent togetherness, to the exclusion of all contrary evidence. Love not only conquers all, it masks the domination.

The Bodyguard and **The Crying Game** are two recent examples of the veiling phenomenon at work. Though the films seem to broach that which is potentially and historically divisive from vastly different sociopolitical consciousnesses, both ultimately champion the negation of such differences and the redemptive power of pan-humanism. Each invites the audience to discount difference promising security in exchange for uniformity. The power of One.

The Bodyguard, starring Whitney Houston and Kevin Costner, is a love story of sorts between a black singer and her white bodyguard in which race is never mentioned. Promotional posters show Costner carrying Houston, her head buried in his shoulder, her face and her race hidden. Race, it is implied, is not a factor or even a fact. The film's studied blindness reaches an absurd height during a romantic dance sequence in which the newly infatuated couple sway lovingly in a regular down-home, sawdust-on-the-floor, mirror-above-the-bar, California country-western saloon, to the beaming approval of the all-white patrons. Not only do the locals fail to notice Houston's chromatically jarring presence—Houston herself doesn't seem to be aware that she is the lone African-American within spitting distance. No NWA here.

As *The Bodyguard* strenuously side-steps over racial questions, care also is taken to cipher and excuse some of the more problematic issues Houston and Costner's relationship might suggest. For example, Houston is the mother of a black child, darker-skinned than she, a child whose primary narrative function appears to be to reassure the audience that Houston is not exclusively a white man's woman. While the absence of a set racial reference is established as the preferred standard of sexual-social interaction, it is simultaneously belied by Houston's choice of Costner as romantic object. For Costner's character does not just happen to be white: Costner is aggressively Caucasian, a supercop to the short hairs whose deepest life wound was caused by his failure to prevent the Reagan assassination attempt. In another sort of Los Angeles, a streetwise black pop diva might not empathize so intently with our hero's Republican pain. ·

Houston is the employer, Costner the employee, escaping the

obvious connotation of exploitation signified by the white man—black woman paradigm. Yet the class ordering here allows us to come full circle: To avoid the appearance of recapitulating white male domination of black females, the black female is given apparent class superiority over the white male. But because of the male's official protector status, Costner is able to direct the parameters of their relationship and restrict Houston's movements—to continue in his historical role as master. Convention reappears, social order is restored, potentially disruptive difference defused. Glass, like race and politics, doesn't matter.

Sundry other points: The other figure allowed to orchestrate Houston's activities and personae is her white male—Eurotrash—manager. The suspense plot fields one white man as a red herring while another functions simply as a weapon at the disposition of the true would-be murderer, Houston's (black) sister. And of course *The Bodyguard* is a story of *doomed* love: for no readily discernible reason, at the end the couple part and the specter of miscegenation is swept away in a swirling 360° pan.

Despite readings of white bias in *The Bodyguard,* its most telling theme is that of racial indifference. By having Houston be supremely unconscious of race, the black character acts to negate racism. Both blacks and whites are thus racially comforted: if race is so insignificant as to be capable of being ignored, whites are absolved, blacks become liberated, and Rodney King is just a bad driver. The movie made a bundle, and long after its release the film's ubiquitous theme song continues to insistently perforate our collective consciousness, an unrelenting promise of transcendent, yet fruitless, colorblind passion. No one has stayed for dinner.

While *The Bodyguard* represents solidly middle middlebrow sensibilities, **The Crying Game** is on the tonier end of the popular spectrum. It too is a love story of sorts, between a white exiled IRA soldier (Stephen Rea) and the black lover (Jaye Davidson) of a black British soldier (Forest Whitaker) whose death he helped bring about. *The Bodyguard* wallows in blindness; *The Crying Game* revels in unveilings. Unlike *The Bodyguard,* *The Crying Game* is remarkable as it employs difference to create dramatic tension; it is a notable, and even noble, effort. Like *The Bodyguard,* **The Crying Game** holds out the promise of transcendence but delivers the reassurance of stasis.

The Crying Game's unveilings revolve around questions of nature and the ability to escape essence. At first, the film seems to aver that nature is individual, that one's nature is one's own, not conferred by color, nationality, sex, or sexuality. According to the fable Whitaker tells early in the film and Rea recapitulates at the movie's end, the world is made up of frogs and scorpions, givers and takers, prey and predators. But Whitaker's tale is given the lie by the other unveilings, and by that which is not unveiled.

Whitaker raises the specter of racial difference shortly after his kidnapping by the IRA and his literal unveiling (he had been hooded) by Rea. When the prisoner complains of being called a nigger by the Irish, Rea laughs and tells him not to take it so personally. Race is never again discussed between either Rea and Whitaker or Rea and Davidson, though Rea's continuing fight against anti-Irish sentiment suggests a generalized condemnation of ethnic bias. If the film has a racial message, it is that race is superficial, irrelevant to nature.

However, gender and sexuality, as represented by Davidson, are potentially disruptive forces of nature. Davidson is unmasked twice in the film: first, when Rea discovers that the beautiful black woman he has been seeing is a beautiful black man who has gendered himself female; second, when Rea cuts Davidson's hair and dresses Davidson in male clothes (Whitaker's, in fact), transforming the gendered-female male into a gendered-male man. While this multiplicity of unveilings shuffles the nature deck a couple of times, it changes nothing. Davidson is both man and not-man, and uncovering his true, inescapable nature simply involves another process of difference and denial.

As much as Davidson recasts femininity, gender is still portrayed as nature. The film's lone biological female, the rather unartfully named "Jude" (Miranda Richardson), betrays both Whitaker and Rea. She is a cold and methodical Eve, a "bitch" and a "whore," who is damned for her "tits and cute little ass" before being shot. Both she and Davidson are the sexual aggressors, conferring a sort of female sexual voracity on even male women. After Davidson's first unveiling, Rea talks of pretending that Davidson is a woman, and so she is. But Davidson is a *good* woman, devoted beyond death, a woman who gives her heart truly and well. Davidson is a woman like the men around her. In *The Crying Game,* the best man is a woman, and the best woman, a man. It's a man's world.

Much has been made about the film's secret: Davidson's first unveiling, the slow drift of the camera down her breasts to her penis. The transcendent trick is that the unveiling comes too late, for the audience has already pledged itself to Davidson as a heroine, and Rea and Davidson as a heroic couple. At the moment of Davidson's unveiling, the audience is forced to choose between either accepting her difference or going beyond the distinction. Both the film and the audience invariably opt for transcendence.

The penis, Whitaker assures Rea, is "just a piece of meat." Yet Rea and Davidson only have sex (the latter performing offscreen fellatio on the former) before Rea discovers Davidson's nature; afterward, strategically placed pillows and bedclothes attest to the chastity of their love. Again, this passion, no matter how transcendent, is going nowhere. *The Crying Game* brings its protagonists and audience to the brink of change, and then leaves them and us safely where we were all found. It's a buddy movie that plays its eroticism up front and to no avail.

Given that fictional characters are made, not born, rationales must exist for their racial and sexual configurations. The most optimistic explanation for the interracial relationship in *The Bodyguard* would be to assert that we have reached some sort of heightened state where race is only contextually significant. Because face was not important in the movie's narrative, there is no need for a racial exegesis of the film. And certainly it is tempting to believe that obliteration of racial distinction would lead to the elimination of racial bias. But this is foolish and naïve. Not just because race is not insignificant in *The Bodyguard,* but because for as long as racial differentiation exists, we will interpret that difference. And if we do not interpret difference consciously, we will do so unconsciously, subject to the effects of individual bias and cultural prejudice hidden in unconscious thought.

A more cynical interpretation of this phenomenon of denial is that difference is tolerable if it makes no difference. If race does not really matter, if the racial status quo remains the same, racial variety may be permitted. If homosexuality does not threaten heterosexuality, then homosexuality can be allowed. If a man is a man, even when he is a woman, women are no threat to men. Differences of gender, sexuality, or race are thus stripped of their real difference, of their potent difference, of the difference that gives strength and offense to the notion of difference.

And of course, by rendering socially defining qualities insignificant, other aspects of our current hegemony are maintained. For example, the myth of Horatio Alger-style individualism is conveniently perpetuated; triumphs and failures continue to be wholly self-created, and if at first you don't succeed, it must just be your fault. Additionally, the choice of African-Americans to act as representative Other in films like *The Bodyguard* is unsurprising. Caucasians view blacks both as the signifier of difference at its most extreme and as the most familiar oppositional symbol, allowing whites to play out racial transcendence with a historically insurmountable yet comfortable foe. It also simplifies things to keep racial relationships limited to a neat binary system of white and black, excusing us from addressing other racial or ethnic configurations.

The most pitiable explanation for these films is that they betray our anxious desire for universality: that in some way, we all want to be the same, to have the same hopes, fears, and dreams, to be able to understand and treasure one another without regard for difference. Universality is our remedy for our crimes of difference—for slavery, for the pogrom, for bashing, for rape. But universality is a tragic myth, and we cannot treasure what we do not recognize.

We must resist the urge for absolution. We cannot forgive ourselves, for our sins are not ours to forgive. Self-pardons are presumptuous and annoying. Pretending to universality of existence changes nothing, for negating difference merely robs us of the power of difference. In a world of One, difference continues to be problematic, a thing to be eliminated, decried, or ignored. But as difference can never be erased, it is difference itself that must be celebrated. Those who would have *The Crying Game* be a treatise on the omnipotence of true love cheat themselves of the effect of a black man's penis in a white man's face. We do not exist in a postmodern panisocracy in which all share equally in the spoils. Social constructions are not arbitrary or coincidental; as long as race and sex distinctions exist, we will construct around them. Universality just permits the building while cloaking the architects. If we are to begin to honor one another, it will be because of, not despite, our differences.

Leslie E. Gerber (essay date Summer 1993)

SOURCE: "The Virtuous Terrorist: Stanley Hauerwas and *The Crying Game*," in *Cross Currents,* Vol. 43, No. 2, Summer, 1993, pp. 230-35.

[*In the following essay, Gerber uses the work of Stanley Hauerwas to analyze the character of Fergus and his moral formation in Jordan's* The Crying Game.]

What startled me about *The Crying Game* was the way the film seemed to center on the very notions of character, virtue, and Christian moral formation that Stanley Hauerwas has been developing over the past two decades. Could this be? In a film devoid of any reference to the church? One about an IRA terrorist?

A friendship between enemies generates the film's movement. Fergus Hennessy is an Irish Republican Army "volunteer," determined to follow orders. Commanded to guard a tied-up hostage, Jody, he immediately exposes his own face, offers food, and initiates conversation. In a funny but oddly profound scene, Fergus must take the prisoner's penis out of his pants so he can urinate—an act which tests the limits of his compassion. Though the captive differs radically from himself (Jody is English, black, a soldier, and—presumably—a Protestant), Fergus finds him interesting and worthy of fellowship. Other guards avoid fraternization, but Fergus repeatedly yields to its charms.

Appointed to execute Jody, he requests permission to keep him company during his last night on earth. When the moment of execution arrives, Jody tries to run. This means that Fergus will have to shoot him in the back, but he simply cannot do it. Jody dies under the wheels of a British Saracen, and Fergus flees to London. He knows only that he must somehow atone for the death. He renounces his commitment to the IRA and—obedient to Jody's last request—he seeks out the dead man's girlfriend, Dil.

I think Stanley Hauerwas would urge us to speak of Fergus's excellence of character. Such excellence, he has argued, is manifested in an interdependent set of moral virtues—i.e., habits or dispositions of feeling, thinking, acting and receiving action. Courage is one important virtue, and Fergus richly displays it in a variety of situations. For Hauerwas, what we *believe* is infinitely less important than how we are formed; Fergus believes in the IRA, but he doesn't possess an IRA character. Hauerwas insists that moral goodness is not a property of particular *decisions*—Fergus makes few, if any—but rather shines through in the steady application of moral skills in all the small contexts of life.

Neil Jordan lovingly depicts the little ways in which Fergus is considerate and gracious: removing the choking black hood from Jody's face; thinking of things to talk about—listening, helping him smoke, remembering what he says. After his bursting bladder is relieved, Jody exults: "It's amazing how the small details of life take on such importance!" Fergus's habit of moral attention expresses this truth.

Another way of speaking about Fergus's nobility is to use Jody's word for him: gentleman. A "terrorist," he brings Dil flowers on their first date. Even in the brutal world of the IRA, he is mannerly. When the hood is first removed, Jody observes: "I was wrong about your looks. You're no pin-up." Fergus replies: "I could say the same about you, but I won't. We're too polite in these parts." Practicing etiquette in this way is not insignificant. It is an outward sign of an inner discipline. Especially in his essays on Trollope (for example, "Constancy and Forgiveness: The Novel as a School for Virtue"), Hauerwas has said much about the gentleman. And Thomas Shaffer—his former colleague at Notre Dame—has fruitfully applied Hauerwas's ideas to legal ethics, urging a restoration of the moral ideal of the gentleman in that field.

Stanley Hauerwas's writings emphasize the primacy of moral imagination and vision. Prior to "moral conduct" is *moral description.* Our vision of who and where we are determines our moral responses. "We can only act within a world we can see," he says in *Resident Aliens.* "Vision is the necessary prerequisite for ethics." Such an account sheds light on the war of names in *The Crying Game.* From beginning to end, Fergus disputes the labels, titles and characterizations others use. No sooner has Jody been captured than Fergus—over the others' objection—asks for his name.

Shortly thereafter he commits the sin of disclosing his own name. When, much later, he is assigned to murder an elderly English VIP, he wants his name too. The construction supervisor calls him "Paddy" and "Mick," while Dil is "your tart." Fergus always corrects these uses, just as he refuses Dil's endearing "Hon." "Don't call me that," he repeatedly insists. In London, he becomes "Jimmy," a new man, for whom the old descriptions have no meaning. His attentiveness to the particularity of persons makes him unable to describe them as "hostages" or "targets" or "the enemy."

Hauerwas persistently likens moral excellence to the mastery of a craft. "I often suggest that the most determinative moral formation most people have in our society," he says in *After Christendom,* "is when they learn to play baseball, basketball, quilt, cook, or lay bricks. Such crafts require apprenticeship, long practice, and initiation into a history of accomplishment by a master craftsman." The crafts providing Hauerwas with his most abundant examples are bricklaying (his father's profession) and baseball. In a sermon this year on the occasion of his father's funeral, Hauerwas said: "For the simple gentleness of my father was that which comes to those honed by a craft that gives them a sense of the superior good."

As it happens, Fergus is by trade a mason. In one of his rare moments of self-revelation, he quietly says, "I take pride in my work." We sense that his attainments as a mason and construction worker are somehow supportive of his profound moral skills. Put another way, Fergus's mastery of a complex set of craftsmanship practices inures him to the demands of well-doing in the moral life. Bricklaying, emphasizes Hauerwas, requires patience. Fergus exudes this quality in all he does, and, ultimately, even transfers it to Dil.

Jody is passionate about cricket. His father coached him from an early age, and he has become an expert bowler. The Irish love hurling (a form of field hockey), which Fergus argues is superior. In London, where he begins to take Jody's place in Dil's life, Fergus pays close attention to cricket; he does this, we sense, as a discipline of friendship. Jody's own moral excellence is connected to cricket's rigors. In Fergus's dreams, Jody is bowling (pitching) in his cricket uniform. When Fergus must disguise Dil, he has her dress in these very garments. Cricket thus becomes a symbol for virtue-in-friendship, as well as an emblem of Fergus's self-sacrifice. For in Jody's words, "cricket is a black man's game"; since it is also an English game, Fergus's investment in it becomes part of his graceful setting aside of racial and national barriers.

For Hauerwas, ethics is ultimately subservient to narrative.

The virtues find their point and motive in the practices and traditions of communities. The way to get at traditions, in turn, is to discover their master stories. What is Fergus's story? We might have expected him to rehearse the IRA narrative—three centuries of oppression, resistance, Easter Rebellion, and Bloody Sunday. But this clearly holds little attraction. For Fergus, the IRA merely stands for a worthy practical aim: the expulsion of the British Army from Northern Ireland. His real story—and perhaps that of Neil Jordan—is some version of the Christian story, a point that has eluded most of the critics who have written about the movie. While the story is invoked indirectly and circumstantially, in names and mumbled lines and refracted symbols, it is there.

We learn this only gradually. Jody, desperate for distraction in the hours before his execution, begs Fergus to tell him a story. What emerges is annoying. He whispers: "When I was a child . . . I thought as a child . . . and when I became a man I put away childish things." "What does that mean?" Jody irritatedly asks. "Nothing, nothing," Fergus responds. "Not a lot of use, are you, Fergus?" "No," he agrees. The significance of the allusion to Paul's hymn to love in 1 Corinthians only becomes apparent much later. In the meantime, Fergus's poor story is set against Jody's retelling of the fable of the scorpion and the frog.

In it, a scorpion implores a frog to carry him, a nonswimmer, across a river. The frog refuses, fearing a deadly sting. But the scorpion argues that since a sting would drown them both the frog has nothing to fear. Persuaded, the frog agrees and sets out. In midstream, however, the scorpion stings anyway. As they are going down, the frog cries out: "Why did you sting me, Mr. Scorpion? For now we both shall drown!" The scorpion replies: "I can't help it. It's in my nature." There are two types or natures, Jody moralizes, scorpions and frogs.

For Jody, the scorpion is the Irish and their IRA, quarrelsome killers "by nature." But he exempts Fergus, whom he recognizes to be "kind by nature." As the film develops, we come to see Fergus as the frog—trusting, of service, bearing others to safety. The IRA uses Fergus's devotion to Dil to sting him—to get him to undertake a suicide mission in London. But it is Dil whom he finally rescues, even though, as Jody had put it, "She's not your type." The way he allows himself *to become her type* is the most breathtakingly Christ-like dimension of the film.

Fergus may claim that his quoting Paul "means nothing," yet Jordan clearly intends to draw Christian elements close to the surface of his work. Early on, Jody implores Fergus, "Be a Christian, will ya?" Fergus is tempted and betrayed by a woman named Jude. His IRA unit commander is Peter. Dil's irksome friend is David. Dil quotes Ephesians 4:26: "Do not let the sun go down on your anger." More powerfully, in the final scene—recognizing that Fergus has taken her punishment on himself—she tosses off a paraphrase of John 15:13: "No greater love . . . as the Man says." Peter mashes a lighted cigarette on the back of Fergus's hand, giving him one of the stigmata. Though the wound is covered with a Band-Aid, because the camera lingers on it we remain aware of its presence.

Fergus is already a gentleman, a man of virtue, when we first meet him. But even the virtuous person needs conversion. We sense that something like this has happened by the end of the film. It began when Fergus, asked to provide a story, recognizes that he will not be able to kill Jody—will not be "a lot of use" to the IRA. At that moment, he put away childish things. The second half of the movie finds him acquiring the supernatural virtues with which Paul replaced childish things—faith, hope, and love. That it should be love of *someone like Dil*—this is the punch-in-the-gut, wonderful surprise Neil Jordan leaves us with.

Stanley Hauerwas is a church-centered theologian; that would seem to make his writings irrelevant to *The Crying Game.* For if the film is nothing else, it is testimony to the radically unchurched consciousness of modern British society. Yet if what I have said here has merit, those who admire Fergus (or Jordan) may be prompted to ask, "What accounts for this man?" What communities, narratives, disciplines, and moral saints explain him? To ask this is to raise a question about Jordan's own roots in Irish Catholicism. With *The Crying Game,* he has directed a magnificent film about one kind of contemporary saint.

Hawley Russell (essay date 1994)

SOURCE: "Crossing Games: Reading Black Transvestism at the Movies," in *Critical Matrix,* Vol. 8, No. 1, 1994, pp. 109-25.

[*In the following essay, Russell traces the crossing over of race, gender, and sexual categories by the character of Dil in Jordan's* The Crying Game, *and the cultural implications of our reading of Dil.*]

In Neil Jordan's 1992 film, *The Crying Game,* mainstream American moviegoers experience and participate in reviving latent cultural dreams of sexual and social taboo. A conspiracy not to disclose the film's "secret" spread like wildfire throughout the nation, adding fuel to the fire of transgressive appeal. Such appeal, however, goes beyond the observation that Dil, a black transvestite, surprises the viewer when "she" reveals "her" penis midway through the film.

Critics, both the official and the armchair varieties, skip over Dil's gendered blackness as if race and gender were mere complications secondary to the spotlighted event of the penis revelation. Haunted by this critical absence, I set out in this essay to examine how Dil, described by one movie critic as a "seductive, tough-talking, light-skinned beauty," seduces the viewer by physically embodying complicated and intertwined acts of racial and gender crossing. What interests me is how these crossings acquire transgressive appeal in a culture ridden with stereotypes of black female sexuality. It seems, after all, that the film's most attractive feature is the illusion that Dil is an accessible, exotic, racialized "feminine" body. Through the manipulation of the cinematic apparatus, racial and gender categories cross in and through Dil's overdetermined transgressive body.

While *The Crying Game* can be deconstructed on many levels, I am most intrigued by the ways in which American audiences consume the cinematic image of Dil, first as a black woman and later, during the film's climax, as a black gay male transvestite. To uncover some of the feminist meanings raised by these images, I consider the ways in which black feminist theorists have begun to deconstruct intersections between race and gender in popular culture. One might reasonably argue that black feminist theories developed in the United States have limited critical value in assessing *The Crying Game,* an Irish film. Unlike the cultural specificity of "blackness" in the United States, dominant discourse in Britain uses the term "black" to describe people of both Afro-Caribbean and Asian origin. Nevertheless, since I am limiting my inquiry to how the constructed image of Dil operates to revive latent cultural dreams among American moviegoers, American black feminist theories do offer critical tools for investigating possible ideological effects of Dil's transgressions. By exposing and deconstructing historically entrenched stereotypes of black female sexuality, these theorists revise cultural readings of black female images. The cinematic apparatus breathes life into such readings. Hence, deconstructing the cinematic image/experience of Dil's transvestism calls for yet another crossing, that of three usually separate fields of academic inquiry: film theory, black feminist theory, and cultural criticism.

In the realm of film theory, the work of theorists Jean-Louis Baudry and Laura Mulvey establishes a cinematic framework in which Dil's black feminist implications might be discussed. Baudry investigates how the cinematic apparatus successfully creates illusion in the eyes of the viewing subject by specifying the position of that subject. For Baudry, the subject is both a vehicle and a place where ideologies intersect. The subject is a space within the larger space of the closed, dark movie theater. And it is in the voluntary submission to be manipulated by the cinematic apparatus, our decision to "go to the movies," that we find ourselves "chained, captured, or captivated."

How do we come to desire certain kinds of cinematic submission while avoiding others? In this essay, I focus on particular cultural desires that may help to explain the tremendous commercial success of *The Crying Game* among American audiences. I argue that American moviegoers' desire to experience *The Crying Game* can be reduced to the erotic appeal of Dil's sexual, racial, and gender transgressions, all of which are exposed in the "revelation scene" when Dil reveals "her" penis. Baudry's formulation of the viewing subject as a vehicle implies a capacity for movement; the viewing subject might desire to move through Dil's body, both in an act of sexual transgression (and maybe aggression) and in a transcendence of the viewer's body. In teasing apart the layers of these transgressive impulses, I further posit that, viewed within the cultural terrain of the United States, this Irish film becomes mapped onto anxieties and erotic impulses which constitute latent and manifest cultural dreams uniquely American. Our collective cultural baggage is, to be sure, our most reliable "date" when we go in search of a good movie.

The idea of cultural dreaming, central to my analysis of Dil as a desirable crossed body, implies some notion of a collective body. After all, some *body* has to do the dreaming. Lisa Kennedy provides a useful definition of such a body in her article, "The Body in Question." Kennedy describes the collective body as "that phantasm with which I share blood, history, and hips. . . . Ambling, lumbering, hobbling in a monstrous mass, more male than female, urban than rural, angry than forgiving, the CB monster is reminiscent of some creature from a '50s sci-fi flick, bigger than a house." Here Kennedy makes the point that all notions of collective bodies are ultimately the work of our imagination. This is not to say that collective bodies do not exist; rather, they exist as imagined strategies for making sense out of the world around us. Film becomes a powerful instrument for unravelling this world: "Film because it feels extraordinarily powerful—all that money, and narrative, and pleasure— and because historically it is how America looks at itself."

The collective body I referred to above, the one who dreams, is a version of Kennedy's monstrous house with categorical racial, sexual, and gender rooms. Transgressive acts in this context translate into erotic and often shameful trips into rooms not of one's own. Such transgressive migrations occur as Baudry's viewing subject sits in the dark movie theater chained to the cinematic apparatus interacting with Dil, as well as in the frustrating attempts of the viewing subject to get outside her or his body. There are also various transgressions within the film and within the body of Dil—what we might call the "play within the play within the play." The metaphorical electrical wiring of this house/body becomes increasingly crossed and charged with sexual energy.

Baudry's reading of the cinematic apparatus sets this com-

plicated crossing in motion. He critically assesses the experience of being a cinematic subject bombarded with imposed ideology, an experience he calls a play of "reflection and projection." These mutually dependent processes support Kennedy's observation that film is the mirror of America's self. This play of reflection and projection creates the illusion of a closed, womb-like world that comforts in its denial of denial. Editing gives the illusion of continuity, denying the juxtaposition of temporally and spatially disconnected images. The film projector is hidden behind and above the viewer. The monocular vision of the camera specifies the ideological position of the subject, determining "the very spot it must necessarily occupy." Hence, no room for ideological squirming exists; we must sit still and play the role of ideological recipients or battlegrounds.

The artificial dream-like world constructed by cinematic experience makes cultural dreaming not only abundantly possible but also convenient. In about two hours, the viewer's cultural terrain is made readable. Baudry articulates this idea: "The world is no longer only an 'open and indeterminate horizon.' Limited only by the framing, lined up, put at the proper distance, the world offers up an object endowed with meaning, an intentional object, implied by and implying the action of the 'subject' which sights it." For the viewing subject who wants to make sense out of the vast American cultural terrain, there is something extremely comforting in the sort of readability offered by narrative cinema. Paradoxically, Baudry suggests that while subjects are "chained" and made to occupy specific subject positions, they also play an active role in constructing the ideological meanings of the images they see projected onto the screen. Baudry's rhetorical use of imposed ideology paints a picture of what being "chained" might look like. But inevitably, the subject actively creates and perpetuates a particular ideology.

With this passive/active model of the cinematic subject in mind, I read Dil as a body with intentional meaning, as a body that says something telling about American culture. Laura Mulvey points out in "Visual Pleasure and Narrative Cinema" that the mechanism by which cinematic objects are converted into meaningful objects in mainstream film has been, and continues to be, the male gaze. Through the monocular vision of the camera, the camera looks at and marks certain bodies as desirable feminized objects. Unlike the male protagonist, who looks back at the camera, feminized objects in the cinematic narrative look away from the camera. The viewer sees the "feminine" through the fixed, archimedean point of a male protagonist. Through this male gaze, the viewing subject is sutured, metaphorically stitched, to the culturally reflexive "perch" of phallocentrism.

In *The Crying Game,* the male gaze, specifically the white male gaze, is established through the white male protagonist, Fergus. Through Fergus, our suture point man, we engage with the constructed ideological meaning of Dil. The camera's monocular vision focuses on Dil as feminized spectacle. As a feminized object, Dil inhabits the cinematic space Mulvey describes as "to-be-looked-at-ness". Many aspects of Dil's image support this assertion. For instance, when Fergus finds Dil in London, "she" is working as a hairdresser. The camera establishes Dil's "to-be-looked-at-ness" in this initial meeting. Not only does "she" avoid looking into the camera, "she" avoids looking directly at Fergus (who at this point has changed his name to Jimmy). The first time we see Dil seeing Fergus in a sustained glance is in the reflection of the salon mirror as Dil begins cutting Fergus's hair. Even when Dil occupies this optimum vantage point (she stands behind him while he sits nervously), it is Fergus who uses the mirror to scrutinize Dil, not the other way around. Sutured to Fergus's gaze, we find Dil as someone who wants to be looked at.

This initial meeting of the male protagonist and his "woman" introduces Dil as a woman "still tied to her place as bearer of meaning, not maker of meaning." As a transvestite successfully passing as a woman, Dil carries meaning but cannot in any way be thought of as the maker of the ideological meaning that the viewer both projects and reflects onto "her" image. Passing as a woman, Dil occupies the cinematic space traditionally allotted feminized objects of desire in narrative cinema: "She is isolated, glamorous, on display, sexualised. But as the narrative progresses she falls in love with the main male protagonist and becomes his property, losing her outward glamorous characteristics, her generalised sexuality, her show-girl connotations; her eroticism is subjected to the male star alone. By means of identification with him, through participation in his power, the spectator can indirectly possess her, too."

When I, along with Fergus, first met Dil in Millies Hair Salon, I was struck by the ways in which "her" appearance not only adhered to Mulvey's narrative script but exaggerated it in a way that I have yet to witness in a mainstream popular film. Dil, depicted as a glamour queen, epitomizes the ultimate object of socially constructed heterosexual male desire: the "Cosmo girl," the supermodel of commodified advertiser-driven femininity. With her long hair, painted nails, tight red mini-dress, high-heeled shoes, and makeup, Dil is a socially perfected, glamorous object on display. And in keeping with Mulvey's narrative script of cinematic femininity, we find her isolated: working in a hair salon, abandoned. Photographs of her true love Jody, a black man, are found scattered about her apartment, exaggerating her isolation by communicating to the viewing subject that she has been abandoned, has lost the one dearest to her.

Mulvey's script, however, fails to account for the ways in which the cinematic apparatus transforms Dil's feminized blackness into deviant glamour. How do glamour and gendered blackness cross within a white, racist, capitalist patriarchy? bell hooks asserts that while black men in drag, gay or straight, subvert heterosexist representations of black manhood, they do so at the expense of perpetuating the prescription of glamour as fictional white womanhood. In her insightful critique of *Paris is Burning,* a quasi-documentary film depicting black gay drag culture in New York City, hooks notes, "What viewers witness is not black men longing to impersonate or even to become like 'real' black women but their obsession with an idealized fetishized vision of femininity that is white." Dil, too, exemplifies this problematic subversion that transgresses social categories but fails to challenge the larger social system.

While hooks's critique highlights an obvious but hidden ideological thread that links all forms of serious black male drag, Dil's transvestism differs from the cinematic construction of black transvestism in *Paris is Burning.* Whereas in *Paris is Burning* viewers see black and Hispanic men transform themselves into glamorous drag queens who could and did pass, **The Crying Game** introduces Dil as already transformed. The viewing subject is successfully manipulated into seeing Dil through Fergus's eyes as a "beautiful girl." Even if you notice that "her" makeup is a little heavy or that "her" hands seem to lack some requisite petiteness, it is impossible to sever yourself from cinematic suture; it is difficult not to see Dil as a glamorous feminine object.

But Dil's blackness complicates "her" feminized glamour. American cultural stereotypes of black women's exotic sexuality transform Dil's glamour into deviant glamour. Hortense Spillers's essay, "Interstices: A Small Drama of Words," provides useful tools for deconstructing the cinematic experience of Dil as an exotic and sexually deviant black woman. In her critical inquiry into culturally constructed mythology and latent dreams of black female sexuality, Spillers notes that, historically, black women's lack of access to public discourse has forced them into a "paradox of non-being." For Spillers, "sexuality is the locus of great drama—perhaps the fundamental one." And in this great drama, black women have been simultaneously "exposed" and "hidden." According to Spillers, "black women are the beached whales of the sexual universe, unvoiced, misseen, not doing, awaiting their verb. Their sexual experiences are depicted, but not often by them, and if and when by the subject herself, often in the guise of vocal music, often in the self-contained accent and sheer romance of the blues."

Spillers's claim that subjective articulation of black women's sexuality has often been expressed through singing the blues is applicable to Dil, who can often be found lipsynching "blue" songs at the Metro, a local pub. In one of her most glamorous scenes, Dil is viewed through Fergus's voyeuristic gaze, lipsynching the title song. The image of the black female singer, particularly the black female blues singer, is a familiar icon in American cultural dreaming. Whatever is mournful about her sexuality is, nonetheless, as Spillers reminds us, often romanticized by the art form of blues itself. While Dil's lipsynching is not an exact reproduction of the black female blues singer, the image of Dil as a singer of blue songs calls to mind this powerful American icon.

Our cinematic encounter with Dil as a mournful singer, a singer of blue songs, reinforces her role in the cinematic narrative as an object with the quality of "to-be-looked-at-ness." Dil's accessible exotification heightens this basic cinematic quality. Dil's light skin and long, loose hair reveal that "she" is not only black but probably also white. As a body with readable biracial features, Dil is black enough to be othered but white enough to be considered a realizable fantasy. In this sense, Dil not only facilitates visual access to a sexual taboo, she in fact embodies the taboo of miscegenation through her existence as a transvestite passing as biracial woman.

According to Spillers, the "sexual drama" of American popular culture casts black women as gateways to subcultures of sexual deviancy: "She [the black woman] became . . . the principal point of passage between the human and non-human world. Her issue became the focus of a cunning difference—visually, psychologically, ontologically—as the route by which the dominant male decided the distinction between humanity and 'other.'" One of the questions that Spillers's formulation raises is whether or not there is some temporal quality associated with black women *becoming* points of passage between the human and nonhuman worlds. Although I find Spillers's discussion of black women's constructed sexual reality to be an especially critical point, it seems that a more powerful and accurate assertion would simply state that black women *exist* as culturally constructed gateways into otherness.

The idea of black women as gateways to otherness is also discussed by Sander Gilman. In his analysis of nineteenth-century artistic and medical representations of black female sexuality, Gilman uncovers European cultural attempts to prove racial difference between blacks and whites by representing black women's bodies, and specifically their genitalia, as inherently different from those of white women. Black women, whose iconographic representative was the female Hottentot, were depicted as having larger labia minoria and a vaginal opening located differently from that of white women. Although this racist strategy aimed to distance white Europeans from black Africans, Gilman shows how this "othering" often represented white men's desire for racial transgression through sexual intercourse with black women. The black female icon was not just a metaphorical gateway to otherness, but the actual physical gateway: "The roots of this image of the sexualized female are to be found in the male observers, the progenitors of the vocabulary of

images through which they believed themselves able to capture the essence of Other."

Spillers's and Gilman's formulations of the social constructions of black female sexuality support the claim I introduced at the beginning of the paper: that as a constructed image of black womanhood, Dil serves as a gateway to a world of otherness, a world which mainstream American culture deems sexually deviant. The camera's monocular vision guides the viewer, gently and gradually, into a world of "sexual deviancy." Securely sutured to the male protagonist, we follow Fergus, who follows Dil, into the Metro. Gradually, it becomes clear to the specified subject that this pub is "different." Later we discover that the Metro is a world of gay men, lesbians, and transvestites who may or may not be gay or bisexual. In this sense, Dil exemplifies Spillers's formulation and takes it a step further. Not only does she, as a black woman, represent a point of passage into a world of otherness, she literally shows us the way.

In addition to Spillers and Gilman, Patricia Williams offers a critical tool for deconstructing Dil as a transvestite who successfully passes as a light-skinned black woman. In her essay, "On Being the Object of Property," Williams incorporates postmodern strategies to make sense of what she sees as black women's lack of subjectivity throughout American history. Williams's articulation of blackness as a quality that forces one to exist in the illusory present emerges as a powerful deconstructive angle. Since black women have not had access to public discourse, they have been cut off from history, and thus from the history of their constructed images. Williams describes herself as "spontaneously ahistorical," and "without documentation." The concept of spontaneous ahistoricity applies to Dil insofar as "she" is clearly constructed as someone without a history. We first see Dil as a photograph in a wallet. At this stage in the film, we have no clues about Dil's transvestism. "She" appears, smiling, in a photograph with Jody, her black male lover. "She" is strictly a representation, an image. Never do we learn about Dil's history. The camera discovers, or uncovers, Dil in the illusory present. The cinematic apparatus either deliberately erases Dil's history (i.e. his childhood, his parents, how old he is, where he comes from, when he started to dress as a woman), or passes over such details as if they were unimportant and unnecessary for our consumption of Dil's image through Fergus. In this respect, Dil exemplifies Williams's depiction of black women as extremely ahistoricized bodies. While history plays a critical part in constructing the stereotype we experience in Dil, the stereotype itself, by definition, has no historical narrative of "her" own.

After the viewer consumes Dil's black female sexuality through Fergus's gaze, the film's climax arrives with the revelation scene. This scene complicates my analysis of Dil's visual appeal. Mulvey's discussion of Freud's isolation of scopophilia, pleasure in looking at another person as an erotic object, as an instinctual drive independent of the erotogenetic zones, is particularly useful for "reading" Dil's revelation. According to Mulvey's reading of Freud, scopophilia is linked to the primal scene insofar as people carry into adulthood the curious desire to see if another person is lacking a penis. Scopophilia reinforces and makes concrete the perception of sexual difference; it is this aspect of scopophilia that controls "erotic ways of looking and spectacle." In *The Crying Game* the viewing subject is specified to identify with the assumption that Fergus has a penis, though we never actually see his genitalia. Through Fergus's gaze, Dil represents a lack of a penis: the castration wound. The interruption of this controlled sexual difference throws the viewing subject into a state of chaotic transgression.

Just as Fergus and Dil are about to "consummate" their mutual sexual attraction, the camera looks at Dil's feminized face and then pans down his naked body to reveal first the lack of developed breasts, a cultural sign of femininity. Continuing its pan, the camera then discovers that, instead of a castration wound, Dil has a penis. At this point in my own viewing of the film, I could hear around me the giggles and gasps of my fellow suture victims struggling in the dark theater. My friend asked, with an air of false hope, whether she had actually seen a penis when the camera panned down Dil's naked body. What could I say? It was chaos, just plain chaos! Freud's theory of scopophilia, which had seemingly stabilized sexual difference, falls apart in this scene. Fergus expresses shock and terror as he reads Dil's "femininity" turned "male." In a subtle play on Freud, Dil's naked body reveals another kind of wound which is not the result of castration: a tattoo on his right arm. As a self-inflicted wound and a work of art, Dil's tattoo masculinizes, makes aggressive, the body we had so far read as tragically "feminine" in its passivity. Whether or not the tattoo was an intentional marker of Dil's body, this symbol of artistic masochism adds a provocative dimension to the revelation scene. Identifying with Fergus, the viewing subject feels unsettled. Yet there seems to be something pleasurable in this violent disruption of the narrative. Physically manifesting the narrative rupture, Fergus hits Dil across the face, then rushes into the bathroom to vomit and cleanse his "dirtied" body with water. Still sitting in the bedroom, Dil lights a cigarette, a post-climactic sign, and pleads with Fergus, "I thought you knew." The likelihood that on some unconscious level, both Fergus and the viewing subject "knew" might explain the mixing of violence and pleasure during this scene. Here I'm suggesting what is by now surely a truism: that homophobia and homoeroticism are intimately linked.

In *Vested Interests: Cross-Dressing and Cultural Anxiety,* Marjorie Garber investigates how America's cultural obsession with racial boundaries affects pleasure in gender and sexual transgression. While it is clear to most people that the transvestite stands as a representation of gender instability, and thus sexual transgression, transvestism is also intertwined with the crossing of racial lines and boundaries. Garber analyzes the possible cultural meanings that black transvestism might hold for a society with deeply entrenched racial and gender categories. In American popular culture, Garber asserts, "What the 'black transvestite' does is to realize the latent dream thoughts—or nightmares—of American cultural mythology as the manifest content of American life." While this general statement can be interpreted on many levels, its significance for *The Crying Game* is that Dil's visual image states that not only gender boundaries but also racial lines are crossable. As Garber points out, American cultural stereotypes of black sexuality link the black transvestite inextricably to the dominant white culture's fears and fantasies of sexual taboo, namely the cultural nightmare of miscegenation.

Borrowing black poet and critic Sterling Brown's formulation of the six black literary stereotypes, Garber states that the contented slave, the wretched freeman, the brute Negro, the tragic mulatto, the local color Negro, and the exotic primitive are all figures for which transvestism can be read as a subtext. The readability of the black transvestite "below the surface" is consistent with the definition of transvestism. For instance, we read Dil as an effeminate and apparently castrated body incapable of sexual threat. Reading "below the surface," however, we discover evidence of possible sexual threat: a penis. Dil's transvestism also operates as transgression in the cinematic construction of Dil as a light-skinned black transvestite. As a biracial transvestite, Dil plays the stereotyped part of tragic mulatto in the play of American cultural dreaming. Garber observes that the transvestite as tragic mulatto was a common figure in nineteenth-century minstrel shows. Revealing many levels of crossing, white men "well-dressed and elegant [would portray] 'plantation yellow girls'—the tragic mulattoes of transvestism." To stretch Spillers's and Gilman's theories of black women's bodies as gateways to otherness, transvestism in minstrel shows might be read as an extreme form of crossing into the essentialized other. Instead of transgressing into otherness through sexual intercourse, these white men transformed their bodies into the very bodies of black women. Not only did they cross, they became crossed.

Dil's biracial appearance seems to enhance, if not establish, her erotic appeal. In a review of the film published in *The New Yorker,* Terrence Rafferty referred to Dil as "a seductive, tough-talking, light-skinned beauty." Rafferty's description of Dil provides critical insight into how her biracial appearance is inextricably linked to her erotic appeal. As a stereotype and, thus, a latent cultural dream, the tragic mulatto has existed as an erotic other/same in American popular culture. Just as the tragic mulatto has been constructed in opposition to the stereotype of the dark-skinned, over-weight Mammy deemed ironically "masculine" in her perceived asexuality, so Dil in her "feminine" biracialness is constructed in opposition to Jody, a dark-skinned, over-weight black man. This binary construction of stereotyped black female sexuality is made especially clear when Fergus looks at the juxtaposed photographs of Dil and Jody in Jody's wallet. Jody's dark skin emphasizes Dil's "lightness" and marks her as feminized spectacle. When Jody tells Fergus, "That's my girl," Fergus retorts, "She'd be anyone's girl!" Jody, a British soldier stationed in Northern Ireland, uses the photograph of Dil to establish with Fergus, an Irish Republican Army soldier holding him prisoner, an ostensibly heterosexual male bond based on "owning a girl." Ironically, director Neil Jordan also crosses gender and race to comment on British rule in Northern Ireland. By casting the imprisoned British soldier as a black man, feminized by his overweightness (his "softness"), Jordan debunks the hypermasculinized, white image of the typical British soldier portrayed in news accounts. But Jordan also takes critical jabs at Northern Ireland. As a prisoner, Jody's image can be read on two levels: first, he is a political prisoner of the IRA; and second, beyond this physical confinement, he is a prisoner of both British and Irish racism. Jody laments to Fergus that the British government has sent him to the only place in the world where they still call you "nigger" to your face.

Jordan's critique of racism takes on a particularized form within an American cultural framework. Contrasted with the image of Jody, who plays the part of a masculinized Mammy, Dil appears as a tragic mulatto, "feminine" in her perceived passivity and "tragic" fate of being caught between two racial worlds.

—Hawley Russell

Jordan's critique of racism takes on a particularized form within an American cultural framework. Contrasted with the image of Jody, who plays the part of a masculinized Mammy, Dil appears as a tragic mulatto, "feminine" in her perceived passivity and "tragic" fate of being caught between two racial worlds. And there are clear indications that Dil's erotic appeal is linked to her passivity. For example, when Fergus physically fights another man in order to establish Dil as his property, we catch a glimpse of Dil's prescribed helplessness: the tragedy of her hyperfemininity. What appears to be mutual sexual attraction between a black woman and a white man turns out to be one of the ways in which racial lines are crossed in our cinematic encounter with *The Crying Game*. At this point in the film, before Dil reveals "her" penis to Fergus and to us, we are under the illusion that the

latent dream we are experiencing is that of interracial heterosexual sex. And as I have pointed out, Dil's biracial body, the result of miscegenation, complicates this dream by turning the dream into an act of crossing into that which is already crossed.

Read on this level, the cultural dream is practically indistinguishable from commonly described sexual fantasies of desiring erotic encounters with racial others. According to this interpretation, can we distinguish Fergus's sexual attraction for Dil from, for example, Vivaldo's erotic impulse to cross into Harlem in James Baldwin's *Another Country,* or from any number of other literary or cinematic examples of eroticism based on racial otherness? Just as Baldwin's white male character, Vivaldo, in his search for exotic, erotic pleasure makes a premeditated physical crossing from his predominantly white neighborhood into Harlem, so we find Fergus making a premeditated physical crossing of the English Channel to meet Dil in London. As he tells his white friend in Ireland, "I need to go across the Water."

Indeed it is at this level of black/white sexual taboo that the film operates for the majority of our two-hour cinematic experience. Prior to Dil's revelation of "her" penis to Fergus, "she" passes as a light-skinned black woman, or as Fergus's white ex-lover, Jude, puts it, as "that wee black girl." The ideological meaning that we, along with the cinematic apparatus, construct at this point in the film has virtually nothing to do with transvestism. It is safe to say that while hints of transvestism might be flickering in the subject's gaze, Dil is, in effect, a black transvestite "passing."

So does *The Crying Game* just boil down to an interesting form of socially acceptable rebellion? While it may be just as simple as that, it is also as complicated as the multiple crossings between and among theoretical discourses I've examined in this paper. Reading black transvestism in this film calls for serious inquiry into the appeal of transgression. I have tried to open up a discussion that goes beyond a categorical discursive approach to deconstructing cultural productions. There is certainly more work to be done. Cultural productions like Dil force us to confront the messy inextricability of crossed categories of race, sex, and gender. As a reflection and projection of our latent and manifest cultural dreams, Dil emerges as a complicated cinematic construction with multiple readings and readabilities. After the lights go on and the credits roll, try not to forget: "she" was more than just another "wee black girl." Or was he?

Kristin Handler (essay date Spring 1994)

SOURCE: "Sexing *The Crying Game:* Difference, Identity,

Ethics," in *Film Quarterly,* Vol. 47, No. 3, Spring, 1994, pp. 31-42.

[*In the following essay, Handler argues that "because it takes inadequate account of the way difference has been and is always available as an occasion and an excuse for the inscription of power, the film* [The Crying Game] *ends up displacing the hierarchical relations that obtain between men and reinscribing them in the realm of sexual difference."*]

To what did Jordan's film **The Crying Game** owe its extraordinary success? Evidently the sheer fact of the film's vigorously promoted and initially well-kept secret drew crowds of the merely curious, but how were audiences affected once they were let in on it? Why did the film "work"—and get rewarded for its efforts by good box-office attendance, an Oscar, and general critical approval? Appending the missing part of Jordan's censored description (from an early interview) of the film's central predicament, we might well ask whether the story of a man who becomes humanized by a romantic relationship with another man who appears to be, and identifies as, a woman does not present a real challenge to normative convictions about the nature of sexual identity and preference. The film's success seems all the more remarkable for having coincided with the height of the furor over whether openly gay men and woman should be allowed to serve in the U.S. military, a debate which resulted in the airing of expressions of (sometimes violent) homophobia in the national media. We can begin to answer these questions by suggesting that the film attempts to remove difference from the realm of moral judgment by promoting a familiar and romantic brand of humanism.

The political-thriller plot (the kidnapping of a black British soldier by the I.R.A.) that inaugurates **The Crying Game** establishes a situation of maximum polarization. The film piles up binary oppositions in multiple registers with dizzying speed—male/female, black/white, Irish/British, and of course, cricket/hurling—then metamorphoses into an erotic thriller, the better to show that love and understanding can prevail over these deep, hierarchically organized divisions. It's crucial that this ideal gets fleshed out by a love story; the secret of Dil's sex forms the crux of the film's larger, structural, bait-and-switch: nationalism and racial difference become pretext and backdrop for a drama of sex, identity, and desire. The film could thus be said to substitute a "libidinal politics" for racial and national politics. But even granting that the film isn't ultimately very interested in politics as such, it is also equivocal on the relationship of its humanism to sexuality, identity, and difference. The film borrows from Orson Welles' *Mr. Arkadin* the parable of the scorpion and the frog, which Jody relates to Fergus near the beginning of the film, and Fergus then tells to Dil at the end. This story condenses **The Crying Game's** message and

moral impulse: the only difference that matters is the difference between frogs and scorpions—between those who give and those who take. But the film as a whole unwittingly reproduces the confusion inherent in the parable: paradoxically, though the telling of the story dramatizes a moment of choice between two ethical attitudes, "frog" and "scorpion" also seem to represent essential human identities (the scorpion can't help being destructive, the frog can't help being kind, because it's in their natures).

I will argue that because it takes inadequate account of the way difference has been and is always available as an occasion and an excuse for the inscription of power, the film ends up displacing the hierarchical relations that obtain between men and reinscribing them in the realm of sexual difference. What can be taken to be the film's genuinely anti-homophobic gesture is therefore purchased at an unacceptable price. Jordan's own account of **The Crying Game's** humanism intimates the inadequacy of its realization: the film dramatized only *Fergus's* accession to full humanity. In terms of the parable's ambiguous meaning, Fergus becomes an amphibious ("of a mixed or two-fold nature"; from the Greek, "living a double life") ethical being while the other characters become representatives of essential "natures" based on precisely those differences the film allegedly wants to overcome. **The Crying Game** unself-consciously essentializes sexual and racial difference to fix the identities of Jody, Jude, and Dil, in order to free Fergus to be all that he can be.

The Crying Game's treatment of homosexuality and homophobia comes closest to realizing its impulse to overcome difference. Although the film splits into two sharply differentiated parts, the change of theme from racial and national politics to libidinal politics is only apparent, since the homoeroticism of the bond between Fergus and Jody is of paramount importance from the start. The second part of the film works through the trauma of the short, violent "Irish" segment, in which Fergus's guard/prisoner relationship with Jody evolves from stark national and racial polarization to mutual articulation of the differences of race and nation, a process which permits the men to become united by a bond of deep sympathy before their relationship is brutally severed by Jody's death. The rest of the film develops the presumptively heterosexual, then potentially homosexual relationship between Fergus and Dil, a relationship in which the issues of race and nation seem to have become irrelevant, displaced onto a question of sex.

By luring us into desiring what is supposed to seem like a heterosexual love story while never ceasing to signal the fundamentally homoerotic component of Fergus's desire for Dil, the film forces us, with Fergus, to confront the continuity between male bonding ("normal," valorized by patriarchal culture, especially in the military) and male homosexuality (stigmatized, feared, repudiated). This culture strenuously insists on the absence of sexual desire in relationships between heterosexual men, and demands that men homophobically police themselves and each other for signs of incipient homosexuality. The debate over whether the military would allow its members to be openly gay provided only particularly blatant, and tragic, examples of the projective violence through which the repudiation of homosexuality is effected: the media coupled coverage of homophobic hate crimes, including murder, with accounts of macho soldiers' paranoid fantasies of sexually predatory gay men. It is not surprising, then, that in *The Crying Game* the desublimation of homoeroticism and the decomposition of Fergus's initially tough, aggressive masculinity go hand in hand. While ultimately, and importantly, Fergus does not explicitly experience homosexual desire, the film wants to show that he is a better man for overcoming violent homophobia. For Fergus to "lose himself" entails losing the armored, delusorily phallic ego of normative masculinity, thereby becoming lacking, feminized. As we will see, the problem feminization presents for Fergus's identity is ultimately solved by the film in a dubious manner. Nonetheless, *The Crying Game* valorizes a self-abnegating masculinity that can embrace what normative masculinity would seem most to abhor: the female-identified gay man.

The detumescence of Fergus's conventionally masculine identity begins in the first part of the film as he, reluctantly, forms a markedly homoerotic bond with his prisoner. Though he's never without his gun, Fergus's empathic response to Jody forbids him to use it as would the "tough undeluded motherfucker," the representation Jody makes of Fergus's "nature" as an Irish nationalist. "What the fuck do you know about my *nature?!*" Fergus retorts, and in fact Fergus refuses to dehumanize and brutalize Jody as the other I.R.A. members do. The turning point in their relationship occurs when Jody, whose hands are tied behind him, calls upon Fergus's good nature to help him urinate. Instead of refusing, Fergus reluctantly handles Jody's penis, and (as Jude does in the opening seduction scene) holds Jody's hands to assist him. Jody teases Fergus about his squeamishness: "For Christ's sake, man, it's only a piece of meat! It's got no major diseases!" The tension between them eases when Fergus participates in Jody's lighthearted treatment of the situation's overtones. Jody's sympathy with Fergus's discomfort—"It wasn't easy for you" ("as a straight man," we can add retrospectively)—relaxes Fergus's defenses: he bursts out laughing, "The pleasure was all mine!" "No, it was mine," Jody replies. Their shared joke makes a pleasure, if not a virtue, of necessity: their laughter promptly puts Fergus in conflict with the film's most aggressive male character, Peter, the I.R.A. leader.

The bond between Fergus and Jody becomes further solidified into what seems like a classic homosocial triangle through the exchange of Dil's picture: the "woman" becomes the point of convergence for the men's desire. Jody passes Dil along to Fergus for safekeeping, but instead Dil becomes the agent of Fergus's further diminution as a securely heterosexual man. In the "British" part of the film, far from mastering his homoerotic feelings by successfully sublimating them in heterosexuality, and mastering the trauma of Jody's death by assuming Jody's position vis-à-vis Jody's "woman," Fergus has to confront the fact that he has been loving and desiring a man without knowing it. Further, Fergus's obsession with Jody drives his pursuit of Dil: he constantly asks Dil, "What about your man?"; "Tell me about him?"; "Did he come here [the Metro] too?"; "Did he dance with you?"; "Did he ever tell you you were beautiful?" After he finds out Dil has a dick: "Did he know?" "*Absolutely,*" Dil replies. As if his insistent questions were insufficient indication of the homoerotic nature of Fergus's unconscious desire, his recurrent dreams of Jody bowling punctuate the progress of his romance with Dil. The first dream occurs after he meets Dil; the last, of Jody tossing the cricket ball with a satisfied look on his face, occurs after the revelation of Dil's secret; but, most extraordinarily, Fergus has his second vision of Jody in a waking state—*while* Dil appears to be giving him a blow job. After we see the convulsion of pleasure in his face, there is a cut to the picture the film will keep returning to, of Jody in his cricket uniform. "What would he think?" are the first words out of Fergus's mouth. Finally, under the necessity of protecting her from the I.R.A., Fergus eventually turns Dil *into* Jody, by cutting her hair, dressing her in the very cricket outfit of his dreams, and then taking her to a hotel for a "honeymoon." So that he won't have to tell her the truth, Fergus leads Dil to believe it's all because he really prefers her as a man. Dil treats as seduction what Fergus thinks he is doing merely to protect her, but the question of whether Fergus is *only* faking desire for her is begged by Dil's exclamation, "You want to make me like him!" i.e., Jody—the original object of Fergus's desire.

The Crying Game works very hard to put the viewer in Fergus's place by investing us in what looks like a heterosexual love story, at the same time that it continually invokes Jody's presence to triangulate the relationship. To the extent that we miss these cues by believing that Dil is a desirable woman, we are forced to participate, with Fergus, in the confrontation of the homoerotic/homosocial with the homosexual. The secret is therefore much more than a mere gimmick, even though it proved to be the film's most effective marketing device. The secret's revelation confronts the viewer with a homophobically unthinkable proposition—let it be represented by the castrato La Zambinella's proposition to the eponymous protagonist of Balzac's short story "Sarrasine," a man in love with what he believes is the perfect woman: "And if I were not a woman?" The question is no longer hypothetical after we've seen Dil's dick and discovered sexual similitude where we thought we were seeing sexual difference. Reaching beyond the moment of revelation and (gut-level) homophobic reaction, *The Crying Game* solicits the viewer's desire to continue an identificatory relationship with the romance between Fergus and Dil, thus asking us to partake in the process by which Fergus tries to get over homophobia.

Fergus and Jody are meant to be deeply sympathetic characters because they are both "gentlemen," as Dil puts it: that is, they are both gentle men, and what the film most values in them is their capacity for tenderness and empathy (though the conspicuous absence of these qualities in Jody's character when he's attempting to get sex from Jude in the opening scene anticipates my arguments about the film's treatment of women). Fergus gains a benign masculine identity insofar as he becomes like Jody: he knows about Dil and is able to love her as she is. Fergus's behavior bears out Jody's final assessments of Fergus's nature—"You're a kind person"; "You're my friend," Jody tells him. We must note, however, that although Dil persists to the end in casting Fergus as the man she loves, Fergus resists as assiduously the possibility of a sexual relationship with Dil after it's revealed that she's not the *woman* of his dreams. Fergus's sacrifice puts him safely behind bars, beyond the imminent possibility of sexual consummation. And so the question remains: To what extent is the "human being" in Fergus still defined by and confined to heterosexual masculinity?

From the melancholy grandeur of "When a Man Loves a Woman," which affectively saturates Percy Sledge's revelation that when a man loves a woman he becomes a dupe and a masochist, to the campy genderfuck of "Stand by Your Man" as styled by Lyle Lovett, *The Crying Game's* liminal moments provoke the questions "When a man loves a . . . *what,* exactly?" and "Who's the man?" The music underscores the film's deepest concerns: the film attempts to recuperate a masculine identity for Fergus by desublimating the homoerotic. However, the way in which the film constitutes this new masculine identity is problematic: Fergus's self-divestiture alters the content of masculine gender identity without challenging the binary and hierarchical structure of sexual difference that gender makes legible.

In order to understand *The Crying Game's* "libidinal politics," sex, sexual difference, and gender must be understood to have distinct but interrelated meanings. For the purposes of this argument, *sex* refers to anatomy—to the reproductive organs of human beings, conventionally categorized as either male or female. I am using the term *sexual difference* to describe a strictly ideological difference: the binary and hierarchical categorization of human beings as men and women, according to whether or not the body in question has or "lacks" a penis. By virtue of having penises, men can see themselves and are seen by others as whole, autonomous, and potent social agents, whereas women's supposed ana-

tomical lack inscribes them as deficient, inadequate, socially inferior. *Gender* (roles, traits) organizes the way sexual difference is lived socially and psychically through specific identities and characteristics marked as male or female. We might add that the meaning of *sexual preference*—the binary pair heterosexual/homosexual—obviously depends upon and reinforces the binary structure of sexual difference.

> *The Crying Game* draws on the cultural repertoire of racial and gender stereotypes to redistribute gender tropes, so that the bodies marked as *either* sexually *or* racially different from Fergus's become hyperbolically feminized.
> —*Kristin Handler*

This set of definitions allows us to see that *The Crying Game's* gender-bending fails to break the grip of sexual difference upon dominant notions of subjectivity. Fergus's experience challenges gender, not sexual difference: his transformation dramatizes a crisis in, but ultimately an enrichment of, *male* subjectivity. Fergus absorbs feminine gender attributes into his identity through the desublimation of homoeroticism, but the film doesn't want him to become too feminized: the film's refusal to slip from the homoerotic into the homosexual enjoins the border-policing function of heterosexuality, which naturalizes and reinforces sexual difference. But more decisively, Fergus's "nature" comes to be defined against the "natures" of Dil, Jude, and Jody. *The Crying Game* draws on the cultural repertoire of racial and gender stereotypes to redistribute gender tropes, so that the bodies marked as *either* sexually *or* racially different from Fergus's become hyperbolically feminized. The female term in the binary has to be fixed in order for the male term to become fluid *and still remain recognizably masculine.*

We might first consider, then, the degree to which *women,* both as agents and as victims, are erased by cultural representations (and, for that matter, theoretical accounts) which prioritize male feminization as the means of subverting phallic masculinity. Tania Modleski has argued that both "gender studies" criticism and popular films amply demonstrate "how frequently male subjectivity works to appropriate 'femininity' while oppressing women," with the result of consolidating male power. This argument has significant purchase on *The Crying Game,* which fails to question the hierarchical arrangement of sexual difference or the oppression of women by men, and is not at all interested in female subjectivity. On the contrary, the sole woman, Jude, is as her name suggests a Judas figure, and winds up a dead *femme fatale.* And though one might argue that Dil lives a female identity—and I will refer to the character as "she"—Dil challenges the relation of the sexed body to sexual difference (she asserts she *is* a "girl") without disturbing either the structure of sexual difference (there are men and women, she just happens to inhabit the wrong body) *or* the dominant configurations of gender (her feminine identity is highly conventional). Together Dil and Jude perform the limited range of simultaneously excessive and deficient—that is, normative—femininity.

How *do* we see Dil after we see her dick? I have said we see sexual similitude where we expect to see sexual difference, but it would be more accurate to say that we see a person with a penis: Dil always refers to herself as "she" and "a girl": "A girl has her feelings," she says to Fergus. "You're not a girl." "Details, baby, details," she replies. The representation of her character prompts the question, "Can a man *be* a woman at the level of the psyche?" The claim that drag is a subversive political act, a performance of gender that shows gender to be performative, has had much currency in the last few years, whether it's staked by academic theorists or stated far more succinctly by celebrity practitioner RuPaul, the 6' 7" black drag queen whose song "Supermodel" hit the top 40 dance charts when *The Crying Game* was a box-office success: "Every time I bat my eyelashes, it's a political act." *The Crying Game* represents male-to-female cross-dressing quite differently than do the champions of drag as political theater, in a way that reveals not only the arbitrary relations of both gender and sexual difference to the sexed body, but also the fundamental relation of gender and sexual difference to the psyche. For Dil to identify, rather than to masquerade, as a woman implicitly affirms the grip of sexual difference on *subjectivity,* even while the relationship of sexual difference to the *body* is denaturalized.

Biologically, if we can believe our eyes, Dil is a man; thus we could say that Dil, who desires other men, is gay. But Dil identifies and desires as a *heterosexual* woman. Once it's clear the Dil can only "be" a woman at the level of fantasy and desire, the "gay man" and the "woman" Dil simultaneously comes to represent are united by a shared condition of deviance from the male norm. As my discussion of race will indicate, not all men can lay claim to the phallus by virtue of having a penis; our definition of sexual difference might further be refined by the suggestion that the distinction sexual difference makes is not so much between men and women but between men and "not-men," the "nonmale" category being marked by femininity-as-lack. Thus, *The Crying Game re*naturalizes sexual difference through recourse to an amalgam of all-too-familiar feminine stereotypes.

The problem that Dil's character presents for the film's representational system becomes acute in *The Crying Game's* climactic sequence, where the representation of Dil as pathologically homosexual and feminine, and therefore as the site of an unpleasurable lack, is in tension with the film's demand that we—and Fergus—empathize with her pain. The sequence begins when Dil, drunk and furious, appears out of the darkness in the white cricket uniform Jody wears in Fergus's dreams. In the ensuing scenes, the accretion of stereotypical tropes around Dil's character becomes quite marked: far from being the cool, alluring, and self-possessed woman she once seemed to be, Dil's identity becomes inflected, or infected, by figures of pathological femininity: the pathetic queen, the hysterical, clingy, self-destructive woman. In place of the penis adequate to the phallus, she displays at this point the multiple lack of her homosexual/ transgendered/feminine identity.

At the same time, the film enlists our sympathy for Dil's rather histrionic performance: drinking and downing pills, she storms, weeps, faints, begs Fergus not to go. The morning after, Dil realizes that while she was drunk and drugged, Fergus told her he was responsible for Jody's death. She ties Fergus to the bed, ineffectually threatens to kill him, then collapses into his arms. Their dialogue reaches an emotional peak when Dil extorts Fergus's vows of love at gunpoint: "You like me now, Jimmy? [Fergus's alias in England]" "I like you, Dil." Still sardonic: "Give me a bit more, baby, a bit more." . . . "Tell me you love me." . . . "Love you, Dil." The scene resonates with the transformation of Fergus's coerced speech into a genuine response to Dil's demand for love and to his own feelings for her. "What would you do for me?" "Anything." She begins to break down. "Say it again." "I'd do anything for you, Dil," and as he utters them the words become utterly sincere, as he will prove by doing time for Dil. She frees his arm and puts it around her: "You'll never leave me?" "Never." "I know you're lying, Jimmy, but it's nice to hear it." The weight of Dil's desolation and of his responsibility for it hits Fergus with all the force of a love baffled but not destroyed by Dil's anatomical unfitness for this no-longer heterosexual relationship. He embraces her and begins to cry. "I'm sorry, Dil," he whispers. Enter Jude.

In the end, Dil blows Jude, not Fergus, away, as she realizes Jody's betrayal: "You was there, wasn't you? You used those tits and that ass to get him, didn't you!" Dil slips back into stereotype again—hear the "inadequate queen's" shrill resentment of the "real" woman—to the point of camp when she screams, "Tell me what she wore!" at Fergus. But Dil's demand demands an answer if we are to understand the relationship between the two versions of femininity modeled by the two "women."

Busch's comic speculation about Richardson's anatomy spotlights the metaphoric significance of Jude's role in *The Crying Game:* Jude doesn't have to have a dick, she *is* a dick. When Dil metamorphoses into one kind of feminine stereotype, her character continues to demand a sympathetic reading; Jude, in contrast, has an entirely antipathetic part to play from the start. After Jody tells the parable of the scorpion and the frog, and persuades Fergus to be merciful and take off the hood—"because you're kind, it's in your nature"— Jude comes into the greenhouse and insists that Jody be hooded again. When he protests, she smashes his face with the butt of the gun. "Women are trouble," Jody says, trembling and bleeding. "Do you know that?" "No," says Fergus. "Some kinds of women are." "She can't help it," Fergus replies. "It's in her nature," we might as well add, since he unconsciously repeats and reinforces the essentializing meaning of Jody's division of humanity into "those that give and those that take." Dil, on the other hand, is "no trouble at all": "I'm thinking of her now—you think of her too." It's not accidental that the sole woman in the film becomes the representative scorpion and that the untroublesome kind of woman turns out not to be one after all. If the film wants to divest its male characters of the phallus so that they can be human beings, it seems determined to relocate phallic masculinity at one of the culture's most overcrowded sites: the image of the *femme fatale,* the phallic woman. While I would not go so far as to say that "frog" and "scorpion" really mean "male" and "female" by the end of the film (largely because Dil continues to insist on her "feminine" identity), the fact is that the frog-identity becomes attached to feminized men while the scorpion emblematizes another arachnoid identity for the phallic woman, who has been more commonly described as Black Widow, Spider-Woman, Deadlier Than the Male.

The film's two sharply demarcated parts map out the process and purpose of Jude's demonization. Here, the answer to Dil's question, "Tell me what she wore!" takes on great significance. When the film begins, Jude looks like a woman trying to look girlishly "sexy": to pick up Jody, she wears, somewhat awkwardly, a tarty, lower-class version of the uniform of conventional femininity—short skirt, high heels, make-up, jewelry, coifed hair. Her appearance after Jody's capture reveals this outfit to be a costume. For the remainder of the "Irish" part of the film she is conspicuously and emphatically deglamorized: unkempt hair, shapeless clothing, flat boots, no make-up, no jewelry, no nonsense. This look isn't any more "natural" than the first, but it appears to be so because Jude is no longer wearing her gender as a sexual lure. Far from being the phallic female terrorist she is in London, here she seems subordinate to the men: at several points she's told by Peter, who is clearly the leader of the group, to make tea and shut up. Even Fergus, who the film rather off-handedly indicates is Jude's lover, interrogates her about her sexual transactions with Jody while shining a flashlight into her face. Though neither particularly developed nor very sympathetic, Jude's character initially has a degree of plausibility that she completely loses in the second part of *The Crying Game.* Undisguised in Ireland, she does not bear the burden of hyperbolically representing

Woman as Bitch, a burden massively laid on her by the rest of the film.

Whereas Fergus undergoes a humanizing diminution and feminization in London, Jude has acquired an inhumanly lacquered glamour. The visual tropes of film noir so thoroughly permeate the scene in which she materializes in Fergus's apartment that I assume Jordan is playing her transformation partly as a joke: dim blue light streams through venetian blinds but keeps in shadow the corner where Jude, arrayed in a helmet of shiny hair, tailored suit, and mask-like make-up, waits to trap the hapless Fergus. "I needed a tougher look," she says to her victim. Jude makes terrorism the scene of sexual seduction, in the style of the classic *femme fatale* whose murderousness is supposed to be the secret of her charm for the masochistic male, but Fergus doesn't respond well to her aggressive proposition ("Fuck me, Fergie," as she grabs his crotch). No matter, she's there on business—to force Fergus to undertake a suicide mission. When Fergus starts yelling at her to keep Dil out of it, Jude sneers at him, "Jesus, you're a walking cliché," and pulls a gun on him. She gives him the Judas kiss as she holds the gun to his head, then glides out of the room followed by her shadow, in exemplary noir style. "Keep the faith," she says.

The extreme change in register of Jude's character from minimally plausible I.R.A. terrorist to murderous phallic woman expresses *The Crying Game's* fantasy of Fergus's former lover after he has rejected her and her cause for the homoerotic, a fantasy which enforces sexual difference in such a way as to deny to Jude the humanity with which the film works to invest Fergus. Further, by becoming the phallic woman, Jude (who shares the name of the patron saint of lost causes) becomes the dumping ground for the rejected masculine identity that required Fergus to be hard, brutal, in the service of his country. Jude assumes the role of the terrorist in exaggerated and monstrous form, monstrous because her aggressivity is so inordinately gendered and sexualized. If, as in the first part of the film, Jude continued to represent a particular woman trying to emulate for the sake of her country's independence the warrior-ideal of the soldier-terrorist—an ideal the film repudiates as a species of toxic masculinity which enables people to torture and kill others in the name of freedom—the death of her character might have indicated that women can but should not, in the name of sexual equality, assume the same sadistic and delusorily "phallic" ego available to some men. Instead, Jude's transformation makes her represent first and foremost a fantasy of phallic womanhood, and her death at the hands of the "woman" with a penis places her terminally beyond the pale of *The Crying Game's* vision of humanity.

At the most perverse moment of *The Crying Game's* climax, Fergus lies tied to the bed between a castrating Scylla and a hysterically engulfing Charybdis, both of whose costumes—Jude's highly stylized and strangely askew *femme fatale* look, Dil's bad haircut and ill-fitting men's clothes—seem to outfit them for a drag, or horror, show of femininity. In the strait between them lies the narrow way to the salvation of masculinity. Jude and Dil function as complementary avatars of undesirable feminine identities, against which the human being within Fergus emerges as unambiguously masculine. By assigning "good" feminine attributes to Fergus, the film revises and reconstructs his male gender identity (Fergus's two doubles, the I.R.A. leader Peter and "Fuck Off!" Dave, Dil's *other* deluded suitor, respectively represent fatally and comically unreconstructed masculinity), while segregating Fergus from the implication of femininity in pathology and lack. In the end, Fergus and Jude are separated by sex and sexual difference; Fergus and Dil by gender stereotypes read through race, as we will see.

Why are Jody and Dil black? Jody and Fergus's conversation in the first part of the film stresses their different racial identities. When Fergus asks Jody what he's doing in Northern Ireland, Jody speaks of his experience of Irish racism: "So I get sent to the only place in the world where they call you nigger to your face. [Imitating Irish accent] 'Go back to your banana tree, nigger!' No use telling them I came from Tottenham." "You shouldn't take it personally," is Fergus's rather offhand response, to which perhaps, we could add: "Because your race is primarily understood and hated as a sign of your participation in the British occupation." (One interview with Neil Jordan noted that black British soldiers were the first people of color most Irish had ever seen.) But *The Crying Game* freights Jody's blackness with connotations far in excess of denoting that current British colonial occupation of Northern Ireland is enforced by the West Indian subjects of the former British Empire (during the conversation Jody indicates that he emigrated from Antigua). In the "Irish" segment, the film wants racial difference to signify a boundary transgressed between men who "find the human being" in each other in spite of the hierarchically organized differences which initially prevent them from recognizing each other's humanity. The reversal that occurs when Fergus goes across the water to "lose himself," as he puts it, suggests that Jody and Fergus in fact occupy analogous, though not identical, positions as England's colonial and racial others. When Fergus resurfaces in England as a day laborer, his Sloane-type employer, Deveroux, and the cockney foreman treat him as Pat-the-lazy-Irishman, and therefore as the object of their undisguised contempt: "Jim, Pat, Mick, what the fuck. Long as you remember you're not at Lords," Deveroux says when he sees Fergus imitating the motions of the cricket players on the field below. Just as Jody discovers that Ireland is the only place where "they call you nigger to your face," Fergus finds that to the upper- and lower-class Englishman alike, he's—what the Irish have been called since Carlyle—a white nigger.

If *The Crying Game* were not ultimately preoccupied with gender and sexual difference, the story of mutual recognition across the divide in Northern Ireland could be told in terms of national difference alone. The racial difference between Jody and Fergus functions as a difference in excess of national difference by being *visible in their bodies*. As I have argued, in the first part of the film the bond between the men is thoroughly homoerotic, but Jody's and Fergus's sexual and gender identity are meant to be legible as heterosexual and male. Gender and sexual identity become destabilized in the second part of the film through the unveiling of Dil's penis, but the difference between Fergus's and Dil's racial identities seems, at least on the surface, to be irrelevant. But because we have to reread Jody's character, Jody's relationship to Dil, *and* Fergus's homoerotic bond with Jody through Dil's visibly, sexually similar body, I would argue that Jody's *and* Dil's shared racial identity encodes their "different" sexuality: Jody's hidden sexual identity, which is not marked on his body, becomes openly displayed as Dil's penis.

Here the film may be construed as unconsciously invoking the racist trope Frantz Fanon describes in *Black Skins, White Masks,* the trope which makes "Black" hyperbolically represent "body" and "sex": "The Negro symbolizes the biological." Or, to paraphrase the sociologist Roger Bastide, once again, the question "race" provokes the answer "sex." Sex and sexual difference: *The Crying Game*'s big surprise, its "gimmick," is the unexpected sight of a black penis on the site of apparent femininity. Fanon again, on the European *imago* of the black: " . . . one is no longer aware of the Negro but only of a penis; the Negro is eclipsed. He is turned into a penis. He *is* a penis." Like the woman, the black man's different *body* could be said to pose a castrative threat to the white man, but like her, the social order poses him as already castrated. The "black rapist" fantasy, for example, imagines black male potency purely in the realm of animality; black masculinity is thereby deprived of the symbolic and cultural privilege the phallus represents. The black man is marked by lack of having a "different" body, a body fantasized as having a penis that can never be the phallus; thus, paradoxically, *the penis itself* signifies the black man's feminization.

Of course, *The Crying Game* asks us to value Jody and Dil's non-phallic masculinity, not to see them as monstrous penises: their characters are scarcely written and acted as the crude racist stereotypes Fanon discusses. Yet the film's treatment of racial difference remains disturbing. It's not just that the penises of black men represent "not having the phallus"; it's that race is no longer problematized as an explicit issue and simply drops out of the film once it has done a certain kind of representational work, which suggests that the film wants to inflect its discourse with that trope without acknowledging its racism. *The Crying Game* blunts its humanist impulse by calling on the representation of black men as deviant, as body, as lacking, to effect the further segregation of Fergus's sovereign subjectivity (of all the characters, he alone *chooses* his fate) from feminization. Jody, Dil, and Fergus are supposed to be united by a shared condition of feminization; but while the film reveals Dil's anatomical similitude to Fergus, it doesn't problematize the fact that Dil's body, marked by "non-white" hair and skin, reads as "black," as *more* similar to Jody's body than to Fergus's. By ceasing to interrogate race once sex has replaced it as a symbol of difference, the film offers Fergus, and through him, the white (not necessarily male) spectator/director, the ability to remain one body away from identification with the feminization Jody and Dil "naturally," that is, culturally, represent by being both black *and* gay.

Jody: Tell me something. [. . .]

Fergus: (*pauses, and recites slowly*) When I was a child, I thought as a child. But when I became a man I put away childish things.

Jody: What does that mean?

Fergus: (*pauses again*) Nothing.

Jody: (*bewildered, desperate*) Nothing? [. . .] Not a lot of use—are you, Fergus.

Fergus: Me? No . . . I'm not good for much.

It seems worth reiterating that *The Crying Game* presents a genuine, if limited, challenge to homophobia. By enlisting spectatorial identification with the more human and humane masculinity Jody and Fergus come to embody, the film addresses an unusually progressive message to us at the level of fantasy, identity, and desire. A libidinal politics which attempts to remake subjectivity in this way is necessary when the grip of bigotry on the imagination is—as the official "resolution" of the debate (which nonetheless continues) over the presence of gays in the military indicates—as profound as ever. However, the film's power as an instrument of moral suasion is debilitated by its reconstruction of white heterosexual male subjectivity, or humanity, in opposition to the other characters, who are required to represent essentially feminine identities. We might then return to the question of the film's success, and conclude that it provides for the comfort of the ideologically normative spectator (with whose interests all of us are supposed to identify) far more than might at first be apparent.

The contradictions in *The Crying Game*'s politics also return us to the film's only partial self-awareness about the meaning of its central parable. On one hand, the frog and the scorpion seem to represent essential human natures; on the other, the repetition of the story functions in the film's larger narrative to suggest that storytelling constitutes an intersubjective act in which people offer meaning to each other and affirm the possibility of *changing* human nature. Jody's story humanizes Fergus by modeling kindness as a self-sacrificing ethical attitude preferable to irrational self-destructive violence. That Fergus tells the story to Dil to explain why he's doing time for her indicates that, just as he has assumed Jody's political position as a prisoner of the enemy nation, so has he accepted Jody's moral position by *choosing* to be a frog.

The scene that illuminates both the power of storytelling and its limits as a response to the political and social context of *The Crying Game* occurs after Fergus asks to guard Jody during the night before Fergus is to execute him. The scene begins with Jody's anguished cries upon learning his fate. "Help me," he whispers, "Give me a cigarette." Fergus silently lights one for him and puts it in his mouth. This extraordinarily painful scene juxtaposes the terrifying image of Jody's mouth choking, speaking, under the black hood as he struggles with the knowledge of his imminent death. The hood frames the vulnerable mouth as grotesque, almost dehumanized flesh, but from that mouth comes a demand for meaning: "Tell me something. A story." Their subsequent conversation is quoted above: Fergus recites a verse from the famous passage on love in the first letter of Paul to the Corinthians ("In a word there are three things that last forever: faith, hope and love; but the greatest of them all is love").

Fergus fails Jody by being unable to communicate the meaning of the passage; but his failure emblematizes and follows from *The Crying Game*'s failure to convince us that love is the answer. Like *The Crying Game* itself, which dodges the political issues it raises in its rush to issues of sex and gender and which puts Jody's parable in the place of a substantive treatment of the armed conflict in Northern Ireland, Fergus can't give a meaning to Jody that would be adequate to his impending death at Fergus's hands. The possibility of acknowledging difference without repudiating commonality demands faith in an unessen-tialized universal humanity not prescribed by the hierarchically organized categories of gender, race, nation, etc. Because the film devotes insufficient attention to the particular ways identities are implicated in relations of domination and because it attempts to essentialize difference in the characters of Jody, Dil, and Jude, *The Crying Game* keeps that faith only with Fergus.

Jack Boozer, Jr. (essay date Winter 1995)

SOURCE: "Bending Phallic Patriarchy in *The Crying*

Game," in *Journal of Popular Film and Television,* Vol. 22, No. 4, Winter, 1995, pp. 172-79.

[*In the following essay, Boozer, Jr. analyzes how in* The Crying Game, *"Jordan emphasizes the construction of sexual difference in the context of political ideology and race, and the role of all three in cultural representation generally."*]

Irish writer-director Neil Jordan has set off a firestorm of serious critical response with his contemporary fable *The Crying Game.* Most of the film's tableaux are constructed around incendiary sexual seductions that deceive his positive characters and the unwary spectator into misreadings of the objects of desire. In particular, Jordan emphasizes the construction of sexual difference in the context of political ideology and race, and the role of all three in cultural representation generally.

The question for some observers has been whether *The Crying Game's* challenge to gender conventions goes far enough, or is sufficiently free of traditional patriarchal bias. Dual articles recently published in *Cineaste* find Jordan's film to be multitextured and engaging on several levels but go on to raise reservations about the ideological import of the film's nationalistic, gender, and racial discourses. Frann Michel's analysis interrogates the fact that "the only good woman in the film is a man," and David Lugowski asks whether the "conventional form and liberal content" of *The Crying Game* "can indeed promote social change." These are significant reservations, although both authors would probably agree that the engaging quality of the visual, intellectual, and emotional textures they find here also bears a more extended look. The essential concern that I find expressed in this film, as in Neil Jordan's other recent work *Mona Lisa,* seems to beg the question of a predominantly objectifying ideological debate: not because that debate is unimportant, but because Jordan grounds these narratives in personal, subjective terms that have viability at more intimate levels of human exchange.

In a professional newsletter devoted to *The Crying Game,* Harvey Greenberg pointedly observes, "Neil Jordan's special affinity for disaffiliated characters crushed in the vise of an utterly impossible love permeates *Mona Lisa, The Miracle,* and *The Crying Game.*" This theme of "impossible love" is very helpful as a framework for understanding Jordan's sexual and political thematics in his most recent film.

It is true that the only character in *The Crying Game* who represents a female biological position is Jude (Miranda Richardson). And she obviously suffers ethically in comparison with the effeminate transsexual Dil (Jaye Davidson). Jude chooses to sacrifice herself for the IRA cause, placing Irish nationalism not only above her sexual orientation but

above her humanity. Her religious devotion to a blanket political ideology simply makes her a mirror of the same kind of personal objectification encouraged by colonialist authority in general. Jude's projection of her personal desires through militant forms of political activism fixes her in the symbolic as a phallic woman. In David Lugowski's reading of this film as a neo *noir,* Jude is specifically identified as a femme fatale, although this view must take into account her specifically political idealism. Jude's politics are inconsistent with the greedy monetary aspirations of the traditional femme *noir.* Jude does "threaten masculinity" by using her sex to entrap Jody (Forest Whitaker) and to tease Fergus, but her IRA convictions remain the real touchstone of her coercive behavior. Her political terrorism freezes her into murderous dogma rather than seductive castration, which tends to override threats of mere sexual-economic betrayal.

In *The Crying Game,* seemingly private sexual and emotional desires are constantly intruded upon by the larger social symbolic of political positioning. Jude's sexual entrapment of Jody results in his political kidnapping and death, just as Fergus's consequent seduction of Jody's lover Dil is laden with political guilt and the desire for retribution. Political realities, including government enforcement, impinge upon private desire whatever a character's primary intent. By the same token, small demonstrations of persona consideration make the objectification inherent in political idealism appear hypocritical. When Fergus is comically forced to help his bound captive Jody free his penis for urination, Fergus must move his revolver to his other hand. This homophobic joke on the penis is really a joke on phallic power. The joke is short-lived, however, as the IRA's authority is quickly shifted to the faceless British army tank that crushes Jody's body in the roadway. The male genital (particularly in its most mundane body function) and the phallic logic of chauvinistic patriotism (Irish or British) are not necessarily synonymous, any more than Jude's femaleness necessarily exempts her from brutality.

The Meaning of Dil

The second and third acts of this symmetrical narrative take place in London, where the repercussions of the first act are played out. While the blond Jude becomes a brunette to disguise her otherwise singular political identity, Fergus, whose Gaelic name means "manly strength," experiences some alteration of his political and sexual convictions. He trims his hair, changes his name to Jimmy, and tries to put his IRA radicalism behind him. He must sort out the contradictory political/personal connections with Jody that now imprint his dreams. Having participated in Jody's capture and death, Fergus feels compelled to pursue Jody's legacy through an unusual association with Dil. His experience with Dil not only demonstrates how the political and sexual remain intertwined, but how constricted definitions of masculine and feminine heterosexuality support patriarchal hegemony.

Late in the film, for example, Fergus's violent paroxysms while tied to Dil's bed occur simultaneously with the death of his IRA leader Peter across town, who has just assassinated "some judge." The judge's respectability is in fact challenged by the fact that he dies at an apartment house where his mistress regularly entertains him. Peter's IRA martyrdom at the hands of the judge's bodyguards was to be Fergus's assignment, and one which Fergus meant to perform to protect Dil from threatened harm. But Fergus has been prevented by Dil's restraining hosiery from acting out his suicidal mission. Fergus must listen to Dil instead, who makes him give up his patriarchal power role as arbitrator of their destiny. Dil's act of bondage effectively snares Fergus not into sexual bliss, but into a masculinity that abjures phallic demonstrations of superiority.

Jordan seems to insist on the personal, not as a reductive alternative to the political, but as a necessary perspective on how the social invades the personal domain.
—Jack Boozer

In turn, Fergus's complex association with Dil threatens her self-absorbed, femininized passivity by inadvertently forcing Dil to confront the symbolic, sociopolitical realm of power. While Fergus's dramatic shearing of Dil's hair is a literal effort to disguise and protect her, it is also a metaphorical awakening of her assertive capabilities. This is confirmed by Dil's aggressive response to Fergus's confession of prior complicity in Jody's demise. Dil not only binds Fergus to her bed but stands over him with a pistol, prepared to kill them both. She gives notice that she will no longer tolerate others making decisions for her, whether politically or sexually motivated. Jordan seems to insist on the personal, not as a reductive alternative to the political, but as a necessary perspective on how the social invades the personal domain.

It is useful to note that Neil Jordan's tendency to foreground psychosexual problems of identity as primary to all sociopolitical crises is atypical of political thrillers generally. In Hollywood's *Three Days of the Condor* or, more recently, *Patriot Games,* for example, political discourses are played off against the constitution of the romantic couple, which ultimately justifies one nationality or ideological position over another. In these scenarios, no matter which side is glorified, authoritative patterns of violence and counterviolence assure that phallic logic remains intact. A 1984 British film, *Cal,* written and directed by Pat O'Connor, does go a bit further. Here, a sensitive and re-

luctant young IRA recruit has an affair with the widow of a man he has participated in killing, much as Fergus does in *The Crying Game.* But a positive solution for the protagonist Cal is made impossible by inescapable Irish political, religious, and class differences. The film places the constitution of the romantic couple at the mercy of all three of these oppositional platforms rather than having it support any one of them. *Cal* ultimately becomes just another plaintive version of the supremacy of ideology over romance that is as old as *Romeo and Juliet.* Thus, all three of these film thrillers fail to illuminate the way in which basic assumptions about gender might already play a key role in the configuration of larger political-economic beliefs.

The Crying Game, on the other hand, is a virtual treatise on how gender assumptions rooted in patriarchy contribute to the constant reproduction of mainstream ideology. In Jordan's wily narrative, Fergus's masculine desire is frustrated in the sociopolitical and romantic dimension so long as it is narrowly defined by the traditional limits that bind heterosexual desire to political meanings. It is the introduction of Dil's sliding sexual identity and her newfound assertiveness in relation to Fergus's increased feminization that begins to loosen the calcified tradition of sexual and political certitudes long bound to phallocentrism.

The performance of masquerade that Mary Ann Doane has claimed as the fate of woman's subjectivity in patriarchal culture, for example, also bears upon the security of the man's subjective position. Because the phallus as patriarchal force cannot exist in a void that speaks only power, it has depended upon a putatively weaker feminine "lack" to give it meaning and justification. But *The Crying Game* structures Fergus's fate in such a way that he realizes neither sexual fulfillment with, nor protective mastery over, the feminine Dil, which undermines and de-romanticizes the phallic mystique. Jordan insinuates the need for a broader basis of gender and sociopolitical organization.

Although *The Crying Game* provides no real validation of women characters per se, there is a validation of a hypothetically balanced femininity, albeit in the guise of the male transsexual. If biology is not necessarily destiny, then Dil is in the end a positive version of chosen subjectivity, whatever her physical makeup. In Dil's forced evolution from apolitical masochism to active self-determination, she does not change her claim to femininity but she does change the form it takes.

Kristin Handler's recent article, "Sexing *The Crying Game,*" builds an extensive argument for the way in which Jordan's film, while it presents "a genuine, if limited, challenge to homophobia," nevertheless "provides for the comfort of the ideologically normative spectator." She writes:

However, the film's power as an instrument of moral suasion is debilitated by its reconstruction of white heterosexual male subjectivity, or humanity, in opposition to the other characters, who are required to represent essentially feminine identities.

My question with Handler's complex argument primarily concerns her reading of Dil and Jody, which she collapses into a category of "feminine identities" alongside Jude. Handler shifts to a racial interpretation of victimization (à la Frantz Fanon) to explain how Dil and Jody are joined with the "phallic woman" Jude, noting simultaneously that the film fails to problematize Jody and Dil's racial similarity. Although it is true that Jody and Dil are both black and gay, and that this is a huge problem for mainstream culture generally, I am inclined to note that the issue is not whether the film chooses to address this as a problem, but how the film represents and places them in the narrative as characters. Does *The Crying Game* really only use them as feminized props "to effect the further segregation of Fergus's sovereign subjectivity (of all the characters, he alone *chooses* his fate) from femininization?"

It seems rather that Jordan's film constructs both Jody and Dil as characters capable of change. Jody's feminine and racial qualities are actually martyred in direct contrast to Jude's. And Dil does in fact choose her fate with Fergus/ Jimmy, moving from narcissistic masochism to direct confrontation (masculine strength?) in her sacrificial destruction of Jude. Jude certainly is a patriarchal scapegoat, clearly marked in angular wig and clothes as a neo femme fatale. But she is also a terrorist in the same devoted way that IRA group-leader Peter is. (Recall that Peter burns a wound into Fergus's hand with his cigarette butt.) Peter and Jude fit together in a category of ideological extremism that surpasses sexual difference. In contrast, Fergus, Jody, and Dil are closely aligned as positive characters, not because of their biology or even their mutual tendency toward the feminine, but because of their jointly discovered desire to disassociate themselves from fascistic phallocentrism. Dil is not simply the masochistic counterpart to the aggressive spider woman Jude, but a man/woman who is significant because her final choices, like those of Fergus, exceed the parameters of heterosexual, racial, and political dogma as it has been defined.

Jordan wants to assert the possibility of locating real alternatives for his characters no matter how alienated their circumstances may be. The point is not to show how Jody and Dil (as black and gay) might be beholden to Fergus's sensitivity, but how Fergus too must learn to respect their struggles without his patronage. The lesson for Fergus when Dil ties him to her bed is the value of receptivity to something other than phallic ultimatums and reactionary "final" solutions.

The larger theme implied by Fergus and Dil's unusual bonding and the character changes that result is underscored by the Aesop fable that Jody told to Fergus before his death. Fergus eventually retells this tale to Dil, who best seems to understand it. In Aesop's tale, the scorpion does in fact sting the frog as he crosses the water on the frog's back because it is in the scorpion's nature to do so, resulting in the death of both. A central issue for Jordan's characters is whether they can locate mutual interests beyond the learned political, gender, and racial roles that narrowly define "their nature."

Jordan hints not only that the only good woman or man is the one who can balance the traits of both without compromising either, but that the kind of society that might facilitate such gender flexibility must be pluralistic. Jordan clearly delineates how Fergus's initial phallic alignment moves toward the feminine with Dil's help, just as Dil's narcissism moves toward the masculine with the help of Fergus. It is not necessary for Fergus and Dil to share sex so long as they share mutual human respect. The real scorpion in *The Crying Game* is not the position of the feminine or the black or the gay, as Handler suggests, but the position of authority that insists upon a mythic tradition of sexual, racial, and/or political absolutes.

A comparison of this film with Jordan's previous work *Mona Lisa* is instructive here. Jordan's original draft of *The Crying Game* had a female character in the role of Dil, and she was to be like the abused call girl Simone in *Mona Lisa* (Jordan interview). Dil is in fact almost a clone of the mulatto beauty Simone (Cathy Tyson), not only in appearance but in her soft mannerisms. In the earlier film, too, Simone—to the great disappointment of her dull-witted admirer and friend George (Bob Hoskins)—turns out to be a lesbian, much as Dil shocks the lusting Fergus with her nude male body. George's criminal background and underworld connections to his big boss Mortwell (Michael Caine) also bear a resemblance to the underground political affiliation of Fergus. Furthermore, George and Fergus are both ultimately freed from their old structures of victimization with the help of their unusual mates.

These upbeat conclusions, therefore, far from condescending to feminism, squarely indict the excesses of patriarchy that place women into roles of prostitution, seduction, and terrorism in the first place. The central feminine characters, whether lesbian or transsexual, are made actively heroic in their ability to fight back. Simone and Dil's exemption from the status of heterosexual/romantic objects for George and Fergus frees them to deconstruct the illusion of romantic solutions that fall within the purview of traditional patriarchal narrative forms.

Simone shoots down her two male oppressors in the closing section of *Mona Lisa* and rescues herself and George, just as Dil finally murders Jude in self-defense and rescues herself and Fergus. However celebratory in phallic terms Simone and Dil's climatic aggression may be, the effect of its being carried out from a feminine perspective not only expands the definition of the feminine but alters the protective logic of the masculine position. It is not biology for either of the feminine heroines that is at issue, but rather the way sexual difference has been swallowed up by controlling systems of social organization. The conclusion of *Mona Lisa* has George walk off in a rediscovered relationship with his daughter, while Simone rescues her long-lost, drug-dependent lesbian lover. And in *The Crying Game,* Fergus serves prison time for his debt to Dil for the loss of Jody, while Dil offers her abiding support to Fergus despite his termination of their sexual activity. Male warrior codes of valor prove to have limited usefulness, just as do female codes of unquestioning devotion to the phallic signifier. Positive male characters are forced into more flexible, emotionally supportive roles, whereas positive feminine characters are pressed into becoming more assertive.

Jordan's representation of racial difference in these two narratives is not as thoroughly focused as the gender issues, although it is consistent with his narrative intentions overall. To briefly review the racial interrelationships in *Mona Lisa,* there is a black pimp who works for the highly successful white sexual panderer Mortwell, and together they enslave both the mulatto call girl Simone and her young, white prostitute friend. George, too, works for Mortwell, has served prison time for him, and is now given a job as Simone's chauffeur. George decides to help Simone find the younger prostitute, which gets them both in trouble, just as Simone eventually liberates herself and George from their sleazy white and black masters. A similar racial justification is provided for mulatto Dil's elimination of the white Jude in *The Crying Game,* as Jude participated in the seduction and death of Dil's black lover Jody.

The patterns of racial balancing in both films are somewhat offset by their one-way conclusions, which place white male protagonists with nonwhite females. But the final absence of either traditional sex-role definitions or of sexual consummation between these interracial pairs somewhat belies what might appear to be the confirmation of white, patriarchal authority. *The Crying Game*'s final image of the clear plastic prison wall separating Fergus from his loving visitor Dil may be read in both gender and racial terms as an institutional social barrier that currently may be breached only on a personal level that recognizes alternative forms of intersubjectivity. The Caucasian George and Fergus, who undergo the greatest character changes, demonstrate Jordan's primary concern with the obstacles that have been created by, and perhaps finally can be corrected by, changes in white

male perspectives that have dictated the course of Western society and culture.

Beyond Victimization

Both films are also instructive because of their emphasis on loneliness and marginal lifestyles. In *Mona Lisa,* there is a clear opposition involving the abusive pimp and the underworld sex king on the one hand, who represent violent greed, and George and Simone on the other, who have been severely exploited. These political-economic character oppositions, much like those in *The Crying Game,* are seen to have a basis both in abusive sexual and class roles and in the advancement of the specific character types who fill them. The black pimp and entrepreneur of sex Mortwell in *Mona Lisa,* like the sadistic IRA volunteers Jude and Peter, are negative because they are brutal psychological extremes created by a mainstream desire for profit and/or political domination. George and Fergus also have been low-level participants in these same outlaw communities, and yet both manage to discover a path of escape from vicious extremes. They accomplish this not by joining a highly suspect bourgeois society, but by forging personal, non-institutional alliances that do not mimic dominant culture. Their choices are not simply personal and arbitrary but represent specific pluralistic strategies in the face of forces that seem to have colonized every form of alternative meaning.

Mona Lisa and *The Crying Game* do present sadomasochistic structures of violence that are typical of contemporary society and its entertainment spectacles, although these narratives do not lose sight of political-economic realities by relying upon escapist resolutions. Jordan seems to mistrust institutional systems and mythic formulas of transcendent release, aiming his conclusions instead in the direction of honest, fundamental human associations that do not require sexual consummation as a payoff. This back-to-the-basics humanistic approach may be simplistic in light of the very real challenges cited by postmodernists regarding the overwhelming invasion of a dominant sign culture at all social levels and beginning in the earliest stages of childhood. But Jordan can hardly be accused of unawareness of the crises and conditions that exist. His focus simply emphasizes the microcosm of individual character development, of any possibility of finding a path through the circulating signifiers that pass for contemporary meaning and truth.

The significance of emergent consciousness for Jordan's positive characters need not be relegated to Lugowski's concern for "the reduction of ideology to the personal." Hollywood cinema's traditional obfuscation of sociopolitical realities through personal solutions does not seem to apply here. Rather, Jordan seeks out the frames of sexual, ideological, and racial oppositions in his last two films to show

how they can cancel themselves out as objectifying power struggles without changing anything substantive. Jordan's downtrodden central characters find themselves reaching out, often in spite of themselves, for any available human connection that will provide a hint of self-affirmation. Under the violent and obsessive tendencies of contemporary life, this seems to be the only possibility for subjectivity available to them as a first step.

Neil Jordan's interpersonal character contexts are enhanced by popular songs that take on thematic importance, almost as if the narratives were constructed out of the emotional meanings in the lyrics. The words of "Mona Lisa," sung ironically over the images of Jordan's 1986 film, seem to describe Jordan's own aesthetic self-awareness in both of his recent films: "Are you warm, are you real Mona Lisa, or just a cold and lonely, lovely work of art?" The dream of film art, like the dream of romance or political-economic liberation, can only offer so much through discourses still encumbered by the terms of alienation. In the song "The Crying Game," the sentimental longing of the "Mona Lisa" lyric is replaced by the expressed desire simply to be released from the repetitions of inordinate expectations that cohere around sexual romance in a politically frustrating simulational environment.

Jordan bonds these songs to the emotional tenor of his films not just as mood support but as tonal perspective. Mystery, longing, and heartbreak form the essence of his principal characters' experiences, which is reflected in the offbeat landscapes they inhabit. The opening shots of *Mona Lisa* and *The Crying Game* place the protagonists in relation to bridges, which suggest the turning points of departures and new beginnings, but also the sparse possibility of significant connections. In the latter film, for instance, Jody's gaping, bloody mouth protruding from under his depersonalizing prisoner's hood is like a vaginal wound that connects to Dil's London apartment, which she has turned into a womblike shrine to Jody. Fergus's guilt over Jody's death can only be absolved if he can traverse the Celtic Sea and the political and sexual forces that have separated him from a part of himself. His absolution is tied to a denial of traditional masculinity and the acceptance of the lack and alterity attributed to the feminine. This is the interior bridge he must cross over in the visual structures established by the text.

The nature of the violence that constantly invades the private worlds of the main characters in these films turns every setting into a potential trap. Jordan's visual topographies provide insecure middle spaces, like the sexual exploiter's house of one-way mirrors in *Mona Lisa* or, in *The Crying Game,* the club Metro or Fergus's London worksite, where he finds himself speaking through interpreters or breaking through walls like a chick hatching from a dark egg. These are indeed the margins of a world of grim consciousness, where the flood of dingy signifiers seems determined, if nothing else, to evacuate the personal, to strip the subject of a space or voice that can speak or sing anything but mistrust and pain.

Brutal abusers and the brutally abused make up the emotional poles of *The Crying Game* and *Mona Lisa,* whereas the heroes are lonely, scarred remnants picking their way blindly somewhere in between. As the abused call girl Simone laments to her much maligned driver George, "We don't control it, we can only swim in it!" Jordan chooses social victims like Simone and George or Fergus and Dil, and the squalid spaces that surround them, to catch their vitality and hunger for a way out. Their desperation is the very mark of their significance, making their tenuous grasp for simple connections all the more proof of the great odds against them.

In the examples of Jody, Fergus, and Dil, Jordan intimates a truer masculinity and femininity that does not reside in the genitals, much less in the phallic signification of power that dominates real and representational culture. These characters suggest a humor and ironic flexibility that resists a rigid phallocentrism bent on antagonistic alignments of difference that amount to rationalizations for control. As Dil so appropriately says to Fergus in response to his question, "But you're not a girl are you?"—"Details, Baby, details."

In contrast to the possessive savages in Jordan's tales who reflect larger cycles of ideological scapegoating and revenge, his protagonists maintain a thread of decency and the potential for change through their tough resiliency. They become joined in the unfolding narrative through a mutual recognition of shared need that contradicts the tendencies of patriarchy's restrictive patterns of gender, race, and politics, where the frog as well as the scorpion—locked in their "natures"—are sure to drown.

Does *The Crying Game* represent sexual consummation as "dangerous" and "repellent," as Norman Holland suggests in an otherwise perceptive article, or is it not the consummation in constant phallic recuperations of power that is repellent? When Fergus vomits after his discovery of Dil's penis, it is not because of Dil's sexual preferences, but because Fergus has allowed himself to be misled by surface appearances into a seemingly heterosexual seduction that included a climax from Dil's performance of fellatio. The value of not allowing oneself to be misled by the distortions of perpetual sexual and political seduction, while still trusting in the possibility of honest human connection, seems closer to the emphasis in Jordan's film.

As in *Mona Lisa,* Jordan is intent on linking issues of sexual identification and intimacy with those of knowledge and power. Mortwell's gaze of projection and control in the earlier film and Peter and Jude's in *The Crying Game* are filtered through George and Fergus, who finally recognize it for what it is. Fergus's politically inflected seduction of Dil is turned aside by its own penile (phallic) reflection in the object of its desire. Fergus may become momentarily ill over this discovery of what amounts metaphorically to the misrepresentations typical of sign culture, but his breakthrough is in his willingness finally to distinguish essential human needs from the ingrained social hierarchies that constantly enlist, objectify, and alienate them.

This is not to say, of course, that a satisfactory programmatic alternative to phallocentric structures is suggested in cultural artifacts like *Mona Lisa* or *The Crying Game.* Both George and Fergus are left in the end with alternative relationships that provide only temporary modes of release from the gender codes that reinforce dominant social authority. The basis for the real *ideological* crying game does not therefore disappear. But at least some of the interrelationships that constitute phallic patriarchy's sexual and political/racial seductions are made a little more clear.

Seán Farrell Moran (review date February 1997)

SOURCE: A review of *Michael Collins,* in *The American Historical Review,* Vol. 102, No. 1, February, 1997, pp. 248-49.

[*In the following review, Moran asserts that,* "Michael Collins *is a superior film that presents a legitimate interpretation of Collins's life and times.*"]

In the various controversies that swirl around Irish history, a few historical figures serve as ideological touchstones. One's opinions about them reveal much about how one views the nature of Irish politics and questions about Irish identity. Along with Patrick Pearse and Eamonn De Valera, perhaps no person serves this role so well as Michael Collins, arguably the founder of the Irish Republican Army and the soldier who won an independent Irish state at the cost of partition, civil war, and his own life.

Michael Collins is Neil Jordan's attempt to tell the tale of Collins from his participation as a minor player in the Easter Rising of 1916 through his major role in the Irish war of independence and the Irish civil war until his death at the hands of former comrades. The film is, however, less a historical biography than a cinemagraphic portrait of the myth of Michael Collins as well as a statement about the nature of things in Ireland since 1922.

Film is a wholly different thing from history. It must compress events, can make interpretive assumptions, and is not constrained by rules of evidence. Nonetheless, in many ways, *Michael Collins* is faithful to the past. The film's portrayal of period Dublin is masterful and has perhaps no rival in film history. While there are occasional errors in detail, the verisimilitude here is admirable despite the film's penchant for the now *de rigueur* use of gray and blue in period films. Crowd scenes in particular have been shot with an eye to the original photographs and films of many of these events and are done well.

Of course, there are the usual sins of commission and omission. The film dwells too much on Kitty Kiernan, who, in her role as the female personification of Ireland, is won over by Collins's willingness to endorse violence, but who also serves as the focal point of homoerotic tension between Collins and his friend Harry Boland. Some choices, such as Collins's seeming chastity, are of little consequence, while others, such as the execution of Ned Broy or the manner of Boland's death, are significant. Broy, only one of the intelligence contacts supplying information to Collins, accompanied him on his fateful trip to London, rejected the treaty that ended the war of independence at the cost of partition, eventually served as head of the Irish police, and died an old man. Boland, by contrast, was killed rather ignominiously when Free State soldiers found him half-dressed in a hotel room in Skerries. In both cases, the truth and its implications are far more interesting than what is presented in the film.

The film also presents its hero rather simplistically. Despite brilliant acting from Liam Neeson, Collins was a far more complex and interesting character than one finds here. He came by his patriotism as an teenage expatriate living and working in London, where he was swayed by the idea of an "Irish Ireland," and he came to the Irish Republican Brotherhood (IRB) through Gaelic games. He then learned the Irish language, and when Collins returned to Ireland in early 1916, he had come to believe, as many exiles do, with absolute certainty in the purity of a cause.

While imprisoned in Wales in 1916, Collins moved to establish his authority among his fellow prisoners. He then cultivated it through careful manipulation of his public image as a nattily dressed gunman with the mind of a banker and the tenderness of a serious Catholic. From 1917 onward, he worked tirelessly not only to gain Irish independence but to win leadership of the movement, holding key positions in both the IRB and the Irish Volunteers and alienating more than a few people in the process. His careful selection of IRB men to run in the 1918 general election was as much a tactic to secure control of the revolutionaries as it was an attempt to win a democratic mandate. If in democratic politics he could be manipulative, in matters military he was ruthless. The film actually goes easy on the British, where the Black and Tans deserved much of what they got. But

Collins's "squad," which dispatched the Cairo Gang, a British counterintelligence unit, also dispatched many an Irish civilian who had different notions of what it meant to be Irish, setting the stage for the ongoing conflict we have today.

The most glaring omission in this film, from both a historical and a dramatic perspective, is that of the peace negotiations in London. De Valera, as the film implies, sent Collins on the mission doomed to failure. But it was while he was in London that Collins, courted by English society, made his, and ultimately Ireland's, fateful compromise; without this, the story of his seizure of the middle ground is inexplicable.

In the end, the film casts Collins as a martyr for that middle ground. De Valera and his followers made the mistake of taking seriously the vision of Ireland for which Collins had so successfully fought, and it is not really clear in this film how they ended up on opposite sides. Nevertheless, *Michael Collins* is a superior film that presents a legitimate interpretation of Collins's life and times. Many critics in England and Ireland have been discomforted by the heroic portrayal presented here, and perhaps they should be. But almost any portrayal of Collins would bring to life that unresolved thing that is Ireland. The film suggests that the middle way, then and now, might not be what it seems to be.

FURTHER READING

Criticism

Badley, Linda. "Deconstructions of the Gaze." In her *Film, Horror, and the Body Fantastic,* pp. 101-23. Westport, CT: Greenwood Press, 1995.
> Asserts that in *The Company of Wolves,* Jordan and Angela Carter "represent female subjectivity and propose a female gaze."

Harmon, Maurice. "First Impressions: 1968-78." In *The Irish Short Story,* edited by Patrick Rafroidi and Terence Brown, pp. 63-77. Atlantic Highlands, NJ: Humanities Press Inc., 1979.
> Compares Jordan's work to that of his Irish contemporaries and asserts that he differs from other Irish writers in his view of character and in his style.

Shrimpton, Nicholas. "Cold Feet in Moscow." *New Statesman* 100, No. 2590 (7 November 1980): p. 30.
> Criticizes Jordan's *The Past* for being steeped in nostalgia.

Additional coverage of Jordan's life and career is contained in the following sources published by Gale: *Contemporary Authors,* **Vols. 124 and 130; and** *Contemporary Authors New Revision Series,* **Vol. 54.**

Edmund White

1940-

American novelist, dramatist, short story writer, essayist, and nonfiction writer.

The following entry presents an overview of White's career. For further information on his life and works, see *CLC,* Volume 27.

INTRODUCTION

With his first novel, *Forgetting Elena* (1973), Edmund White established a reputation as a new novelist of great promise. His elegant, self-conscious prose has been compared with that of Marcel Proust and Oscar Wilde, as have his decidedly homosexual viewpoint and sensibility. Like the work of F. Scott Fitzgerald, White's fiction frequently focuses on what he sees as the sad and shallow lives of the idle rich.

Biographical Information

White was born in Cincinnati, Ohio. His parents divorced when he was seven years old. His father remained in Cincinnati, and his mother began moving from city to city. White's mother was left in virtual poverty while his father remained relatively affluent. White had difficulty living between the two worlds of his parents, never really feeling a part of either of them. White attended Cranbrook, a boarding school outside of Detroit, Michigan, and then studied Chinese at the University of Michigan. Upon graduation, White moved to New York and worked for Time-Life books from 1962 through 1970. After leaving Time-Life he moved to Rome for a year, and in 1971 returned to New York and began working as a freelance writer and editor. He briefly worked for the *Saturday Review* and *Horizon* before he obtained a job teaching at Yale University. He later taught at Johns Hopkins and then Columbia University. In 1981 he became the executive director of the New York Institute for the Humanities. In 1983, White moved to Paris, using his Guggenheim Fellowship for support. He was a freelance writer for *Vogue* and other Condé-Nast publications while remaining in Paris. White returned to America and became a professor of English at Brown University in 1990. He returned to Paris in 1991, however, when his partner became sick with AIDS. His partner died of the disease in 1994. White himself is HIV positive and very conscious of his own mortality. He continues to live and work in Paris.

Major Works

White's first two novels, *Forgetting Elena* and *Nocturnes for*

the King of Naples* (1978) are entrenched in fantasy and poetic in tone. *Forgetting Elena* draws the picture of life on Fire Island, but it includes a fantastical prince and court. White's *Nocturnes for the King of Naples* lacks a conventional plot and character development. The novel contains several autobiographical elements, but many details of the protagonist's life differ from White's own, including having a rich playboy father. White's next novel, *A Boy's Own Story* (1982) is much more autobiographical than *Nocturnes for the King of Naples* and has a traditional form. The novel traces a young man's discovery of and acceptance of his homosexuality. With *Caracole* (1985) White returns to a more fantastic style as he portrays life in a high-powered city where greed and vanity rule. The story follows Gabriel as he is imprisoned by his father and then rescued by his uncle, Mateo. Mateo is a narcissist, but devotes himself to Gabriel's rehabilitation. The novel analyzes the relationship between sex and power, and focuses on heterosexual relationships. White tackles the same topic of sex and power in his *The Beautiful Room is Empty* (1988) but again turns to a more autobiographical style and centers on homosexual relationships. White's collection of short stories, *Skinned Alive*

(1995) takes on a darker theme than his earlier work. The stories center on living with and dying from AIDS. In addition to his fiction, White has written several nonfiction works, including *The Joy of Gay Sex* (1977), and his journalistic *States of Desire* (1980), a reportorial account of his journey across the United States in which he spoke to gay men openly and plainly about their experiences in American society. White's *The Burning Library* (1994) contains a collection of his essays on political and literary topics spanning 25 years.

Critical Reception

Many reviewers have commented on White's vacillation between realism and artifice. Phyllis Rose stated, "All literature looks in two directions, toward the world and back toward itself. It portrays the world (or gives the illusion of doing so) and creates a world of its own. More than most American writers, White is divided between these two impulses, old-fashioned realism and modernist artifice." Many critics complained that White's language is too stylized, especially in *Caracole*. Adam Mars-Jones said of White's style in *Caracole* that, "At his feeblest, White goes in for elegant variation saying 'adipose cummerbund' for *spare tyre* or having a character eat raven instead of crow. The sheer density of invention attests a bottomless terror of saying the obvious." Many reviewers lauded White for appealing to a universal audience, and for emphasizing the similarities that exist between gay and straight men. Clark Blaise asserted that "Mr. White's success lies in establishing two contradictory truths: gay men are very much like straight men; and gay men and straight men are fundamentally different. He does so by the meticulous reconstruction of the very texture of his sexuality. . . ." Critics have also praised White for his honest portrayal of desire and sexual relationships. Carter Wilson asserted, "Edmund White is to be envied not only for his productivity . . . but because he is a gifted writer who has staked himself a distinguished claim in the rocky territory called desire."

PRINCIPAL WORKS

Blue Boy in Black (play) 1963
When Zeppelins Flew [with Peter Wood] (nonfiction) 1969
The First Men [Dale Browne] (nonfiction) 1973
Forgetting Elena (novel) 1973
The Joy of Gay Sex: An Intimate Guide for Gay Men to the Pleasures of Gay Lifestyle [with Charles Silverstein] (nonfiction) 1977
Nocturnes for the King of Naples (novel) 1978
States of Desire: Travels in Gay America (nonfiction) 1980
A Boy's Own Story (novel) 1982
Caracole (novel) 1985

The Darker Proof: Stories from a Crisis [with Adam Mars-Jones] (short stories) 1987
The Beautiful Room is Empty (novel) 1988
Genet: A Biography (nonfiction) 1993
The Burning Library: Writings on Art, Politics, Sexuality (essays) 1994
Skinned Alive (novel) 1995

CRITICISM

Paul Bailey (review date 5 September 1980)

SOURCE: "Gay, Straight and Grim," in *Times Literary Supplement,* September 5, 1980, p. 964.

[*In the following review, Bailey discusses White's* States of Desire, *and how the book deals with the issue of bigotry against homosexuals.*]

I was living in America when Anita Bryant, a mediocre warbler of what are known in the music business as "inspirational" songs, began her campaign against male homosexuals in Dade County, Florida. In the spring of 1977, Bryant and her followers, united under the banner "Save Our Children", convinced the citizens of that clean, well-lighted place that they had several devils in their midst—in their schools, to be precise. As a result of Bryant's efforts, an ordinance which granted homosexual men and women certain basic freedoms was chucked out in the polling booths by an overwhelming majority. Later that year, similar ordinances were abrogated in Eugene, Oregon, Wichita, Kansas, and St Paul, Minnesota.

No less a person than the Almighty, it was revealed (on television, on radio, and in innumerable magazines and newspapers), had called upon this chanteuse of the chapel circuit to rescue the youth of America from the evil attentions of those hordes of limp-wristed pedagogues. God had spoken it seemed, and she was but obeying His instructions. I wondered at the time, and am wondering still, at the amazing limitations of the Holy Father's omniscience as revealed to Miss Bryant. Hasn't He heard about lesbians? Does He really believe (wrong word—*know*) that homosexual school teachers are interested only in seducing their charges? Is He unaware that heterosexual women indulge in fellatio? Has the diligent Linda Lovelace toiled in vain?

Anita Bryant's dangerous opinions have been widely disseminated throughout the United States. Her much-publicized antics have had an effect, however, that she probably never took into consideration when she laid her plans in the early days of 1977. She could not have known then of the success awaiting her nor that it would cause the homosexuals of America to unite in a way that they had not been united in before. She rapidly became the most conspicuous of the many public enemies of those she chooses to call perverted, and her position remains unchallenged in 1980; the dumbest hick in Hicksville is acquainted with her every utterance, her every move.

Edmund White's notably sane and sensible book is a response to the preachings of Bryant and her kind. **States of Desire** recounts how White travelled across America in search of people who would talk to him openly and honestly about the quality of their lives. He found them in Texas, in Oregon, in Kansas, in Georgia. He even found them in Salt Lake City. It was there, in the shade of the Mormon Tabernacle, that he chanced upon a man lacking those attributes of sanity and common sense so refreshingly apparent in the majority of the men he interviewed. "Harris" as White calls him, is visited by the Angel Michael, who tells him things that are distinctly at odds with what God tells His friend Anita.

Michael has let it be known to "Harris" that God first created woman in man—in Adam, prior to the departure of his rib. This creature is The Homosexual.

> Harris's great secret is that gays make up the lost tribe, the holy 144,000 who are superior to straights: the elect. God, who needed to hide his true people, put them under the yoke and has made them suffer over the centuries. But soon Armageddon will come and the gays will conquer the straights (among whom the Mormons are especially evil). After the battle has been won, gays will be quickened and will live here on earth in bliss—*all* the gays who have ever existed. A few of the gays will go to heaven. The straights will all be damned.

You only have to read the Bible properly, "Harris" asserts, to discover the truth of Michael's message:

> Christ and his disciples were all gay . . . Jacob was gay, Esau straight. . . . When the Lord tells Rebekah that "Two nations are in your womb" (Genesis 25:23), He is referring to the straight and the gay. . . . When Christ says in Matthew 19:5, "The two shall become one flesh," he is referring not to straight marriage but to the androgynous homosexual body. . . .

This sad, deluded human being lives chastely, out of fear that a heterosexual, "a son of Satan", masquerading as a homosexual, might tempt him into bed: he would then be "infected by evil" and would lose the chance to lead his brothers to victory in the coming cataclysm.

Edmund White writes about "Harris" with sympathy and tact. He is a shrewd questioner and an expert listener, a respecter of individuality. Unlike some of the men he questioned and listened to, he does not find it necessary to sit in judgment on his fellows. While in San Francisco, he visited David Goodstein, who publishes *The Advocate,* a magazine which contains a large number of advertisements from hustlers, as well as articles on Isherwood, Genet, and other notable writers and artists. Goodstein sounded off to White on the subject of Castro Street, in the heart of San Francisco's gay ghetto:

> The Castro Street group is a really *rough* culture. Their relationships are brief, they don't work but live off welfare, they hang out like teenagers, they drink too much, they take too many drugs, they fuck day and night, they are scattered—and of course radical politically. They act like kids in a candy store. . . . I oppose the gay obsession with sex. Most gay men have their lives led for them by their cocks. In return for ten minutes of pleasure they design the rest of the day.

It's alarming stuff, as White points out, coming from the owner of a paper that encourages male prostitutes to list their attractions in its pages. White goes on to say that he is always suspicious of those who denounce others for having too much sex. "At what point", he asks, "does a 'healthy' amount become 'too much'?"

What [White] demonstrates in his book is that there are many homosexuals who find it possible in spite of all the obvious difficulties, to function ordinarily and positively in parts of America not noted for their acceptance of gayness in any of its manifestations.

—*Paul Bailey*

Goodstein's notion that homosexual men are obsessed with sex is echoed, more elegantly, by Alfred Kazin in his autobiography *New York Jew,* when he expresses disgust for the gay life of his beloved city. (What was he thinking of when he was, as he confesses, following girls with pretty asses through the streets of Manhattan—Kafka?) Kazin's intolerance upsets me because he has been on the receiving end of intolerance himself, and knows where ignorance and bigotry lead. He must understand, as benighted Southern Baptists like Anita Bryant do not, that most homosexuals do not choose their desires. He must appreciate, as a man of imagination, the misery experienced by people who consider their feelings to be natural, but who are castigated by society when they try to satisfy those feelings.

On the evidence of *States of Desire,* Edmund White is the ideal person to challenge Alfred Kazin, James Dickey, Norman Mailer, and the other fag-haters of the American intelligentsia. What he demonstrates in his book is that there are many homosexuals who find it possible in spite of all the obvious difficulties, to function ordinarily and positively in parts of America not noted for their acceptance of gayness in any of its manifestations. He is splendidly and necessarily critical of those of his own kind who, in the service of a dubious masculinity, accuse the effeminate of betraying the gay cause. Their bogus butchness he regards with dismay—that aggressive hairiness, that determined maleness, has little to do with being a man. Men can afford to be feminine, to be vulnerable. They do not have to be seen, as it were, displaying their credentials. They do not need to flex imaginary muscles.

Edmund White has reason to feel dismayed by aggressive *machismo.* He writes of his Texan father:

> What he wanted in a son was someone brave, quiet, hardworking, unemotional, modest. I can remember once travelling to Mexico with him after I'd spent a year with my mother; I embarrassed him by being a know-it-all and by admiring the cathedrals with too much enthusiasm. He drew me aside and said, "A man doesn't say I love that building, he says I like it. Don't talk with your hands. . . ." He also told me that I should never wear a wristwatch, smoke a cigarette, or put on cologne—those were all sissy things. Men have pocket watches, smoke cigars, and wear witch hazel.

Edmund White is pleased to admit that he has been a sissy. His honesty about this aspect of his character, as indeed about others, is to be commended. He refrains from doing a whitewash job in order to satisfy sympathetic liberals. He even writes in defence of the men who frequent leather bars, who work out their sado-masochistic fantasies with obliging partners. These men, he argues, do not ignore the violent nature of much sexual activity. By releasing the violence in private, they are free to present to the outside world a peace of mind, a serenity, denied to the inhibited and repressed. White's argument makes sense to me. The lineaments of gratified desire are not restricted to the missionary position. How humane Mrs Patrick Campbell was when she observed that homosexuals were perfectly all right so long as they did not perform in the street and frighten the horses. The fulfilled fantasists are frightening no one but themselves. It is not only the horses who are safe with them.

If I have a serious criticism to make of *States of Desire,* it is that in its entirely admirable determination to stress that homosexuals are succeeding in living well in the United States, it somehow contrives to ignore the thousands who

are not. I am thinking of the poor blacks and hispanics in the big cities, the comparatively fewer poor whites. I recall a visit I paid two years ago to a gay bar in the shabbiest district of Oakland. The drinkers there, who included a pair of frantic hustlers, had desperation in common. The laughter was hysterical, and unnerving. Suddenly, a large, powerfully built black entered, and immediately launched into an aria of hatred against the police. "Those bastards have stole my husband", he shrieked. "They've run him in because they want to ball with him." The aria proceeded, becoming more explicitly obscene as he related each indignity his lover had endured. The words "my husband" were repeated constantly. Baldly accounted for, the scene sounds ridiculous, and indeed it did veer on the farcical—yet the man's lament was genuine; it had about it the urgency, the panic, the confusion of unbearable pain. James Baldwin has described such unhappiness, since from childhood he has been a frequent witness to it.

And I am thinking of those men and women who take their lives. In the rich and conservative state of North Dakota, where I lived for three years, there are frequent suicides—mostly married men in their late twenties and early thirties. The strain of having to conform, of having to play the role of devoted husband and doting father, causes them to accept death as the only possible solution to their problems. I met the parents of a young man who had killed himself. Their grief was unendurable because, had he told them, they would have supported him. But he could not tell them.

While living in North Dakota I took part in a forum on homosexuality. The other speakers included a psychiatrist from New York, and a lesbian counsellor and social worker from San Francisco. All who were involved felt that they were opening doors, helping to banish ignorance and prejudice, and—it was to be hoped—rescuing some distressed young people from possible self-destruction. My only regret is that I announced, with I suppose a certain smugness, that Britain was at last displaying tolerance and understanding towards homosexuals, that the bad old days were gone for good.

I was wrong—or, at least, not totally justified in my confident assertion. Since the unmasking of Anthony Blunt, a new wave of hysteria has broken out: the hoary cliché about homosexuals being untrustworthy has been expressed in a hundred different ways. The editor of *The Times* has entered the lists with a lengthy homily on the decline of the family. The *News of the World* has recently demanded of its reporters that they act as *agents provocateurs* at the YMCA hostel in Bloomsbury—no doubt they were young and handsome, not the usual flabby Fleet Street soaks. In the *Sunday Express* Sir John Junor has described a distinguished living writer as a "nancy", a word much favoured by the bigoted. And a serious magazine, the *Spectator,* has seen fit to publish an article, by Richard Ingrams, of unequalled odiousness, in which the satirist compares the long-lasting relationship between Benjamin Britten and Peter Pears to the anti-semitism of Richard Wagner. Britten's music is now diminished for Mr. Ingrams as a result of his discovery that Britten was gay.

"Gay", in fact, is a word that Britten would never have used about himself. It is not one that I care to use either—for reasons other than pedantry. Life is, by and large, a fairly grim business, for everybody, and terms like "gay" and "straight" tend to trivialize what should be grave concerns. Still, I appreciate why the word is used, and why it has—in its new form—taken its place in the language. Edmund White uses it confidently and proudly, with no apologies for its limitations. It contains a great deal of information about life in America, about those hundreds of good and decent human beings who are surviving in the face of superstition and intolerance. One final, niggling observation: White refers to the bigoted as "homophobes", who practice "homophobia", but doesn't "homophobia" mean "fear of the same"? It is a fear, a morbid and unhealthy fear, of difference, of a deviation from an obligatory norm, that such people suffer from. They are the truly diminished, and the diminishers.

Carter Wilson (review date 13 November 1982)

SOURCE: "Remembering Desire," in *The Nation*, Vol. 235, No. 16, November 13, 1982, p. 503-5.

[*In the following review, Wilson asserts that "In White's growing-up novel,* [A Boy's Own Story,] *the tale of the child's peregrinations in the treacherous land of desire is, finally, secondary to the 'story' of the adult's struggle to bring all to mind, to integrate his various selves by coming to love them.*"]

Edmund White is to be envied not only for his productivity (*A Boy's Own Story* is his fifth book in nine years) but because he is a gifted writer who has staked himself a distinguished claim in the rocky territory called desire.

The nameless hero of *A Boy's Own Story* grows up in the prosperous American 1950s with every advantage save one. Only son of a Texas millionaire, The Boy is coddled by black nannies, trained at the best private schools, whisked away each June to the toniest summer camps. "All of our daddy's dollars," he says, "were casters on which the furniture of our lives glided noiselessly."

What's wrong is something money can't do much to fix. It emerges as an intuition well before The Boy reaches the age of 7. In the midst of being beaten by his father with a belt, he recognizes in the man another child, no older than himself, but different, "less appeasable—a heartless boy." Soon the child understands more: that his father doesn't love him, that his older sister is more like the son the sire wanted, that he himself is a sissy, girlish, homosexual.

But *A Boy's Own Story* is not about a child's coming out to himself. Looking back, the adult narrator can discover in The Boy no particular heterosexual desire, though he does remember a real longing to shuck the burden of being different, to *turn out* straight, which is of course an entirely separate matter.

In the sweet, contemplative flow of the book, readers may not at first realize what radical assertions about sexuality White is making. Though the psychoanalytic experts now posit that the "arrest of sexual development" (Freud's phrase) that produces homosexuality takes place before the age of 3, few have given flesh to the idea's implications for the individual.

Even those born with silver spoons in their mouths may find childhood a trying time. The wise child learns to endure injustice, practices for grown-up life by oppressing those who are smaller and weaker and, above all, waits for childhood's end. But thirty years ago, a kid like The Boy (or me), who recognized the unacceptability of something which *felt* so much like his nature, had little reason to hope time alone would raise him out of his predicament. Even today, children who would devil themselves less if they knew of the adult gay subculture are kept ignorant of it and of the significant breakthroughs in society's attitudes toward homosexuality.

The Boy sets about manfully to become a man. But his world holds no men enough like him to serve as models. Even his desire for love sets him apart from a "real man" like his father, who accepts whatever love is given him but believes that only women actively go in search of it. The Boy seeks help: a psychiatrist pops diet pills and discusses the tangles of his own sexual life; a prep school faculty couple take him to bed for a three-way; a clergyman reminds him that homosexuality is a sin—and turns out to have been sleeping with the faculty husband all along.

What keeps *A Boy's Own Story* from being overwhelmingly sad is the presence of the man The Boy becomes. Content with himself sexually, the narrator is able to cherish and comfort The Boy, whose suffering and isolation gave him a "small, hard gland of bitter objectivity" the writer doesn't at all mind possessing. Among other things, it allows him an epicurean's slow exactness in summoning back the burning details of the few happy passionate encounters he did have as a youth.

In growing-up stories, the most difficult thing to prove is that the writer turned out O.K., because that sense must come from the writing itself. By the age of 14, The Boy has decided the style for rendering his life should be a "translation out of the crude patois of actual slow suffering . . . into the tidy couplets of brisk, beautiful sentiment." But then another possibility strikes him: "What if I could write about my life exactly as it was . . . show it in all its density and tedium and its concealed passion, never divined or expressed?"

The adult narrator of *A Boy's Own Story* remains conflicted. Often he yanks us from the middle of a painstakingly recalled moment to give the adult-embroidered version of the child's thought, as when he wonders if the bad smell his sister claimed emanated from him was really just "the terrible decaying Camembert of my heart?" This would be acceptable if the narrator were being ironic at The Boy's expense, but aside from the mildly self-mocking title, with its allusion to old-fashioned kiddie pulp, the grown-up never makes fun of the child. A 7-year-old seeing that his father's eyes "no longer had that veiled, compounded look of adults who stare at blank walls or get tangled up in the tulle of thought" calls attention to the writer rather than The Boy.

In his reportorial *States of Desire,* White said the ideal reader for his fiction was a "cultivated heterosexual woman in her sixties who knows English perfectly but is not an American"—which explained the problems I had with his last novel, the tumid, Baudelairean *Nocturnes for the King of Naples. A Boy's Own Story* is much less arty, partly because the European woman has been replaced as muse by The Boy's American father.

"I fear we shared nothing," the narrator says, "but I like to think that music spoke to us in similar ways and acted as the source and transcript of a shared rapture." There is nothing wrong with wanting to make music in fiction—it was one of Joyce's aims—or with trying to reunite rapturously with the father through reorchestrating the past in the consciousness of the present. These are, however, motives that yield more meditation than urgent storytelling. In White's growing-up novel, the tale of the child's peregrinations in the treacherous land of desire is, finally, secondary to the "story" of the adult's struggle to bring all to mind, to integrate his various selves by coming to love them.

Phyllis Rose (review date 16 November 1985)

SOURCE: "Moralists and Esthetes," in *The Nation,* Vol. 241, No. 16, November 16, 1985, pp. 526-28.

[*In the following review, Rose discusses the verbal stylization and psychological realism of White's* Caracole.]

Ford Madox Ford's *The Good Soldier* has been called the finest French novel written in English, but *Caracole* would be my nomination. Its epigraph from *The Charterhouse of Parma* suggests its literary ancestry. Like Fabrice del Dongo of *Charterhouse,* like Julien Sorel of *The Red and the Black,* Gabriel of *Caracole* is an innocent young man from the provinces who makes the move to the city that so fascinated nineteenth-century French novelists. No wonder. This narrative structure allows the author—along with his hero—to discover piece by relished piece the complexities and sophistications of a world by no means innocent. It worked for Stendhal and for Balzac, and it works for Edmund White. His hero learns about power and love and the ways in which they're connected. So do we. If you want to know about the dynamics of a small, closed social system and if Stendhal's Parma seems too remote, try White's portrait of an imaginary city, part Venice under the Austrians, part Paris and part New York of the intellectual coteries.

All literature looks in two directions, toward the world and back toward itself. It portrays the world (or gives the illusion of doing so) and creates a world of its own. More than most American writers, White is divided between these two impulses, old-fashioned realism and modernist artifice. His first novel, *Forgetting Elena,* was dazzlingly self-contained—a brilliant, original piece of fiction which created a world that never was. Well, perhaps there was a touch of Fire Island. But Fire Island with a prince, a court, a grand hotel where everyone gathers at night? It was White's distinctive accomplishment to produce the disquieting sense that you knew this world, these people, these feelings, despite their being placed in the middle of an uncompromisingly artificial narrative.

Nocturnes for the King of Naples, his second novel, detached itself even further from conventional plot and character development. As its title suggests, it is a series of lyric pieces, sometimes of breathtaking beauty. After that, White made the surprising move of writing a novel in a completely traditional form. *A Boy's Own Story,* a novel of growing up, is his most accessible book. The disquieting moments there (unlike the shocks of realism in the earlier novels) come with sentences of such precision and such careful elegance that you remember rudely that you have to do with art and not life.

Caracole seems a return to the mode of the earlier novels. Its lapidary style calls attention to the artifice and hardly encourages immersion in the fictional world White creates. (This style will always reach for "larder" when "cupboard" would do just as well). Nevertheless, psychological realism is as important in the book as verbal stylization. At times *Caracole* reads like one of those anatomies of love the French like to write—Stendhal's *On Love* or Roland Barthes's *Fragments of a Lover's Discourse:*

Edwige felt a physical aversion to Mateo that she couldn't hide and that, once she realized he was in love, she saw no further need to conceal. He had embraced several comforting fallacies. He believed that others love us for our merits and he struggled to prove his to Edwige, whereas the truth is that merit chills ardor. He believed that anyone he loved so well must sooner or later return his devotion, whereas the chief condition for devotion is that it not be reciprocal. He believed that if he insinuated himself into her friendship he'd eventually possess her love, whereas . . . affection tranquilizes passion.

White understands people well and tells us what he knows in balanced, epigrammatic sentences. He tells us that tastemakers in a great city idolize "either the tentative beginnings of youth or the absolute mastery of maturity," but have little patience for anything in between. He knows how "fame permits someone to be terse, since his remarks are sure to be heard, and beauty allows someone to be silent, since there is no danger of a beauty being ignored," and he understands that "the very sort of canned wisdom we hoot at in a public forum we greet as profound when someone lovely whispers it to us." In observations like this and in the dramatic encounters between the six main characters, *Caracole* offers a devastating panorama of life in a high-powered city where everyone is on the make in one way or another and where the mixture of greed and vanity is evident in most of the practices of love.

The opening sections are hard going. In a highly wrought novel, they are overwrought. Gabriel at Madder Pink, his family home, is bored, discovers sex, is imprisoned by his father, who bears him a mysterious grudge, is rescued by his uncle from the city and taken away. It is all very dreamy and archetypal. But with the move to the city, the novel seems to firm up. In the "capital," ruled by "conquerors," inhabited by sophisticated but powerless "patriots," *Caracole* puts down roots in reality.

White has created two splendid characters. One is Gabriel's uncle, Mateo, who rescues the boy from his father and arranges his rehabilitation. The other is Mathilda, the intellectual queen of the capital. (The beauty queen is Edwige, an actress, with whom Mateo is abjectly in love.) Portraits of female intellectuals are sufficiently rare that Mathilda ought to enter literature's gallery of great women characters.

Commanding in intellect, Mathilda fears that her "self," which she would be embarrassed to associate with her body but would not associate with her mind, is unlovable. When she and Gabriel are alone in her country home on the point of becoming lovers, she says, "I must bathe," and he understands that she means, "I am unworthy," at the same time that, in another way, she considers him unworthy of her. Few

writers have depicted this mixture of self-loathing and arrogance as well as White, and fewer have had the imagination to attribute such complexity to a woman. A moralist among esthetes, an esthete among moralists, Mathilda is never less than complicated. She is embarrassed by her wealth but likes beautiful objects, so she excuses them as ethnographic finds. All life is research to Mathilda. Her dandified son acts out the impulses she has forbidden herself. Too radical in thought to allow herself to respect the social conventions she in fact respects, she encourages Daniel to respect them for her. He functions partly as a companion, partly as a research assistant, going into low-life parts of town at night and bringing back prize pieces of reality to spread before her.

Mathilda loves the opera and always goes early, a habit she explains by invoking a "bourgeois anxiety" about being on time:

> To confess to "bourgeois anxiety" hinted at an appealing modesty—and concealed her real motive, which was to see and be seen. Although she presented herself as a withdrawn, morose intellectual, she had an infallible sense of theater.

Indeed, Mathilda, so much a product of her reading, has learned emotions either from novels or from even more melodramatic operas:

> The only emotions she could name, recognize and reproduce were the violent ones. As a result, she smiled ironically or with embarrassment at all her impulses toward expression, but there was no impulse that wasn't operatic in its irrationality and grandeur. When other people perceived her as being guarded, even sour, they mistook her choking back of instinct as contempt for instinct.

Mateo, who brings Gabriel back to life, is an aging Don Juan transformed by his disinterested love for his nephew. His friends are puzzled by the trouble he takes over the boy:

> If the boy had been a girl, a pretty adolescent girl, the public response might have appeared to be the same though it would have been entirely different. People would have rushed to congratulate him on his magnanimity in order to hush amused suspicions no one dared to voice but by which everyone felt titillated.

Thoroughly urban and urbane, Mateo enjoys "the game of trading favors and coercing courtesies" and finds the trade-off of influence for intimacy at which he is so adept "worldly, fair, even (if seen in the right light) cheerful." Yet he fears his specialized career of sexual conquest has left him unable to love, has "warped his responses as surely as some cultures stretch necks, lengthen earlobes or bind feet, distortions that cannot later be undone, that leave the victim incapable of a normal life." This courtly man is powered by a core of self-loathing which he structures his day to avoid. If he sees enough people and generates enough chatter, by evening he can manage to forget his fears enough to greet a stranger. But his terror of boring others ends by making him seem silly, and to Mathilda he is "someone so hounded by an inexplicable need to make it up to everyone that he'd ended by displaying a suspect courtesy matched only by his suspect compassion."

White's portrait of a narcissist taking on the care of someone else and helping his own soul in the process is done with tender and loving realism. I insist upon the psychological realism because of the strenuous artifice of so much of the book. White's work appeals to me precisely because of its unique mixture of artifice and realism, but for the same reason he is not everyone's cup of tea. Americans do not take readily to a lapidary prose style or to self-consciousness in literature at all. Over time, John Updike has established his commitment to golf-playing suburban reality, but at the start of his career even he was attacked for preciosity. Nabokov had to make his name synonymous with sexual perversion to neutralize his reputation for contrivance. If, as is the case with Edmund White, the writer has identified himself as homosexual, the offense is compounded and the work likely to be thought effete.

White's gorgeous style, his verbal intricacies and subtleties, will seem suspect to people brought up on Hemingway. The liaisons in this book will be seen as suspiciously heterosexual, forced and unearned, simply because the author is homosexual, just as people said the bickering couple of *Who's Afraid of Virginia Woolf?* was really a gay couple in drag—as though there were a difference between bickering gay couples and bickering straight ones. For this reason I could have wished the presentation of the book a little less gay. I wish it didn't have the title it has, smacking of Ronald Firbank and furbelows. I wish the beautiful young man by Piero della Francesca did not grace the cover. If I read the situation correctly, Americans will be too eager to dismiss White's work as merely gorgeous anyway.

Adam Mars-Jones (review date 14 March 1986)

SOURCE: "Passion, purity, innocence and (European) experience," in *Times Literary Supplement,* March 14, 1986, pp. 265-66.

[*In the following review, Mars-Jones lauds White's* Caracole *and says, "This suavely alien world can give intense and almost continuous pleasure."*]

Caracole is less a novel by the author of *A Boy's Own Story,* as the cover announces in justified eagerness to close a sale, than a novel by the author of *Forgetting Elena.* In that book, Edmund White described the experiences of a man who comes to consciousness in a sophisticated society, its physical details (shared houses, beaches, tea dances) suggesting an American resort, but its culture having a rigorous obliquity reminiscent of Imperial Japan's; each gesture in the world of that book had a prescribed meaning which the hero had to work out for himself, without ever admitting to being in the dark. It was the richest and most mysterious example of the amnesia novel, a sub-genre which includes Martin Amis's *Other People* and Eva Figes's *Nelly's Version.*

In *Caracole* the society is again a collage, but this time the sources are European. Venice and Paris are the most obvious models for the city in which most of the action takes place. A European setting, however gorgeously transformed by fantasy, is appropriate to the development of White's thinking: he sees experience as by nature European, that is, as layered and multiform, any seeming grossness being merely a ganglion of subtleties not yet teased into clarity. Even in its slang the book turns its back on America, and opts for pallid British forms: "tart", "twit", "trendiness", "infamous bounder" even.

The city is occupied by "the conquerors", who drain it of resources while paying lip-service to its cultural eminence. The six principal characters of the novel make various shifting compromises with the authorities, none of them identifying wholeheartedly with the invaders but all putting up no more than token resistance; they are certainly too sophisticated to throw in their lot with the patriots. Their lives intertwine in a plot that suggests operetta, but is carried off with considerable intensity and something very like conviction.

The story begins, though, far from the city, on a decayed estate called Madder Pink, where the teenager Gabriel tries to keep his collapsing family (mother fat and catatonic, father indifferent, children hungry) in some sort of rudimentary working order, and also carries on an affair with the tribal princess Angelica. These fifty pages are the least confident in the book, and give the novel an uncertain start. White inserts an occasional sentence of stylized spondees ("Just come day, go day", for instance) to enact the stopped flow of primitive life, but otherwise his style makes no concessions to a rural setting, where it is spectacularly out of place.

Any bumpkin can find things beautiful; an aesthete consults ideas of beauty. Such a temperament is likely to regard unmediated nature as downright sloppy, and if called on to represent it at any length will improve on it beyond all recognition. There are passages in the early part of *Caracole* where the sentences stretch on in their even glory as far as the eye can read, like virgin forests of topiary.

The social world of the country should present fewer difficulties; no human arrangement is actually unsophisticated, although dominant groups can sometimes succeed in dramatizing other groups as defective. It's only in a court or a city, nevertheless, where everything already represents a conscious choice on someone's part, that a ravishing rhetoric like Edmund White's can plausibly be housed in a character. But here in the country the point of view, nominally Gabriel's, can see in someone's ineptness "a charming rubato in the hesitation waltz of sincerity". Only in a city or a court is a taste for practical anthropology a part of the survival skills of the tribe; but here a tribesman attending Gabriel during his tribal marriage to Angelica, asked to explain a particular passage of ritual, shrugs and says: "'These ways . . . beautiful, no? I love the old ways. Very religious.' He kissed his bunched fingers with a loud smack: 'Very folkloric!'" The tone of the book can't accommodate this strayed Firbankian giggler. For his only other speech, a page later, the tribesman is a duly reformed character, purged of camp and using the ritual language of marital innuendo. He promises Gabriel much work for his broom, many juicy figs.

The most successful dramatization in the book of the contrast between city and country isn't in the first section at all, but in a splendid paragraph describing the Great Return to the People, when, one summer, intellectuals from the capital trooped into the fields to identify with the peasants and their labour. The noble experiment lasted barely a week. The city women offended the locals with their "pedantic licentiousness"; the farmers needed their sleep, but the intellectuals wanted to stay up all night, "flushed with compassion". They didn't realize they were consuming more food than they were producing "until they were unexpectedly greeted not with gratitude but a bill".

By burlesquing the assumptions of the intellectuals, and not approaching the country direct, White can prevent his prose from turning everything into a *fête champêtre*. Otherwise his version of pastoral is rather too much like one of those high-toned theatrical productions which feature real turf or real water on stage. His relentless *tours de force* of epiphanic description fit one of his descriptions of Gabriel: "he had succeeded in subjecting the involuntary to his will, a success that surely counted as a failure".

Caracole comes into its own from the moment that Gabriel is rescued from Madder Pink and moves in with his uncle Mateo in the capital. The major fascination of the book is its abstract worldliness; this may be a confected society, but its mechanics are convincing. Familiar elements stand out

disturbingly without the protective colouring of naturalness. Bohemians refuse to commit themselves even an hour in advance, their social lives being utterly expressive and impromptu, but turn up doggedly to every rout. Musicians at a reception mutate awkwardly from performers to servants as soon as they stop playing, "still amphibious, half guests, glasses of champagne empty in their hands and deliberately not refilled".

White has a particularly delicate perception of role-playing, of the way an identity must be built up from the registers available (many rewarding parts inevitably being pre-empted by others), and cannot be plucked from air. He insists, not on the coexistence merely, but the interdependence of real and factitious emotion.

White's literary personality dominates the book. Every sentence in a novel carries an implied promise, the promises in aggregate making up what we call readability. The plot of *Caracole* is soundly constructed, but its promise is not *Relax, I'm telling you a story,* but rather *Relax, I the writer am here in everything.* Every page, consequently, is a riot of nuance.

> **The plot of *Caracole* is soundly constructed, but its promise is not *Relax, I'm telling you a story,* but rather *Relax, I the writer am here in everything.* Every page, consequently, is a riot of nuance.**
> —*Adam Mars-Jones*

Not all of this prodigious activity can be laid to the account of the characters, though each of them has show-stopping arias of introspection. Gabriel, in particular, can seem like an *idiot savant,* his naive disclaimers recast in a style of lavish brilliance. There is in any case something odd about using him as an innocent eye, to whom the city's artificiality is patent, when *Caracole* so consistently portrays innocence as tactical. Perhaps the disparity between character and narrative voice should be invisible by convention, "like the hands of puppeteers", as the narrative voice observes in a slightly different context; but if so the convention should be evenly enforced, and not blurred by an intermittent psychological realism. White is something like a ventriloquist who cannot at the last moment bear the dummy on his knee to have tones less rounded than his own, since they are what he has spent his life perfecting.

The point of view shifts round, from Gabriel to Mathilda, the city's reigning intellectual, with whom he has an affair, to her son Daniel, tortured poseur, to the actress Edwige, with whom Gabriel also has an affair, but it is always most at home with Mateo. Mateo's life as a self-doubting socialite and anxious gallant is disrupted by Gabriel's arrival and the need to look after him. His avuncular feelings become deeply affectionate, and Gabriel returns them; but Mateo has also, unknown to Gabriel, set up Angelica in a little flat of her own, and after a period of intimate unease has become her lover.

Mateo's position, both in and out of society, both in and out of love, his manipulativeness always bound in with his altruism, brings out the best in Edmund White. His fondness for the character is signalled obliquely by an opening blast of irony, which never returns so rawly: Mateo is disappointed that Gabriel isn't handsome—he would have been flattered by a resemblance. The character has received the prescribed dosage of irony, and can now be taken seriously.

White in any case takes care to restrict the operations of irony. A charming passage describes how Gabriel sees irony looming darkly in everything his sophisticated uncle says, obliging Mateo to disengage from real and earned emotion out of politeness. At the crisis of Mateo's affair with Angelica a distinction is drawn, as a gloss on that little incidental smile that in highly conscious people accompanies a strong emotion", between cheap irony, which disowns experience, and the expensive kind that acknowledges it. Irony is too general a structuring element in the world to be a satisfactory response to it.

It is necessary for the book's balance, and even existence, for emotion to be refurbished as well as stripped. The ink in White's pen is not only a solvent but an emulsion. The habit of scepticism, as the narrative voice observes apropos of Mathilda, "like a design of oblique lines, needed to be placed against the grid of love's credulity".

Love in *Caracole* is "a progressive illness, one that starts as self-hallucination, an act of parody, and ends as a wholly real, involuntary malady that kills us or something vital in us". Love is an invented contract that binds no less for that. It must be said, though, that the rhetoric in the book that reinstates purities and passions is generally less successful than the rhetoric that breaks them down, which has a special brilliance—as if an acid was leaching glitter from the metals it attacked.

There is after all no overriding logic that insists on love presiding over the other illusions. One of the book's epigraphs, from *Middlemarch,* is bravely borrowed: "It is so painful in you, Celia, that you will look at human beings as if they were merely animals with a toilette, and never see the great soul in a man's face." The borrowing is brave because everything in Edmund White's literary personality concentrates on the way that behaviour is mediated by convention, precisely by a toilette; why should a soul make its appearance on a face, of all places?

In a recent and eloquent tribute to Christopher Isherwood, White pointed out the paradox of a man who as a matter of religious conviction disbelieved in the unity of human personality (described by White as "a useful illusion for a novelist") choosing as his literary form the dynamic portrait of an individual. Something similar happens in White's own case. He questions the unity of personality not on religious principle but from minute social observation. The moment when a character enters a fixed relationship with the world is always an ominous one in his writings. Edwige in *Caracole* is murdered, but she has never stopped negotiating her value, while Mathilda, becoming wholly the avenging lover, dies into a role she mistakes for an identity, taking a passing resemblance for a definitive portrait. It's significant that both this novel and *Forgetting Elena* end with the hero occupying, however accidentally, a public position, as if the book's freedom to speculate depended on its hero's non-alignment.

This amounts to an odd sort of Darwinism, as if evolution was the survival of the socially flexible. But there is no doubt, despite the book's attempt at musical balance, that White loads the dice in favour of Mateo and against Mathilda, whose portrayal has a certain sourness, both vague and pointed, as if she was a minor character in Fr Rolfe, being given a drubbing under cover of prose-poetry. Edmund White is nevertheless a full-time aesthete and only a part-time moralist, a busier bee than wasp.

In the long run, it is *Caracole*'s texture that will make friends, or lose them. Every melodic line is fully ornamented; the conceits are as vital to the progress of the book as they are in a Craig Raine poem, or a Tom Robbins novel, come to that. This style is more than most a matter of taste. White's rhetoric has a Jamesian fullness, but none of James's leisure; it has more in common, perhaps, with Proust. A sentence like this could easily find a home in *Caracole:*

> A quelques pas, un grand gaillard en livrée rèvait, immobile, sculptural, inutile, comme ce guerrier purement décoratif qu'on voit dans les tableaux les plus tumultueux de Mantegna songer, appuyé sur son bouclier, landis, qu'on se précipite et qu'on égorge à côté de lui.

The playful memorializing of a casual posture as characteristic.

At his feeblest, White goes in for elegant variation saying "adipose cummerbund" for *spare tyre* or having a character eat raven instead of crow. The sheer density of invention attests a bottomless terror of saying the obvious. It sometimes seems that this is a sensibility which would find anything as straight-forward as an oak an embarrassment, unless it had a galaxy of truffles stowed away in its roots—or failing that a patch of discoloured bark like a mole under an armpit.

White's rhetoric is sophisticated, but it is also highly specialized. A conceit in a Craig Raine poem taps energy from the incongruity of its materials, and teases the reader with apparent irrelevance for maximum, and delayed, impact; a conceit in a Tom Robbins novel conveys, rather complacently, the absurdity of comparing anything with anything else in a rich, unrepeatable world. White's conceits, by contrast, have a curiously homogenizing effect; they smooth out differences and seal similarities. When Gabriel imagines Angelica's heart, "as stately as a frog at night", the reader feels a twinge of hilarity and then thinks better of it, guiltily ignorant of frogs at night. When Mateo compares Gabriel with a potato, which, "washed, bruised, forgotten and cast under the sink, will sprout horribly in the dark, rampant with life since it is not only a comically banal vegetable but also a seed", the conceit elevates both potato and Gabriel, buoying them up in the same super-saturated medium.

When White's conceits overreach they go authentically gaga. Here is Gabriel reminiscing in the middle of coitus ("sting" is his countrified word for orgasm):

> Not that he himself was repelled by the odor, far from it. It was the smell of a stable, of his own long-ago stings in the thunder-box back at Madder Pink, the smell of steam lifting off those black sacs of roe he'd produced, that pair of blood sausages on a frosty morning in the echoing immensity of yet another day, as though time were a freezing mansion and he its caretaker bravely rubbing a fire into life with hard black and fluid white emissions, the *demideuil* of being human.

More often, the conceits retain a decorum which only the scenes of sexual exchange, notably successful in themselves and quite unlike the home life expected of a co-author of *The Joy of Gay Sex,* do anything to disrupt. Here is Gabriel with Angelica:

> He understood why people might give their favourite goddess eight arms and four faces. Those weren't enough but they did at least suggest the way a girl could crowd a hollow with herself—a pair of arms reaching out to clasp him as she turned her head away in profile, lips lifted, eyes downcast; another two hands to push her hair back from eyes that opened, brightening; two arms to hang at her sides and a face to lower in submission until he butted her side again and moaned and sank to the ground below her, frustrated and yearning; then one more glorious face to swim down towards his, her lips full, her breath fast and shallow, her last two arms

pressing his head against her one and only but wildly beating heart.

This is lovely, but also supremely calculated. The project may be passion, but the doing of it is scrupulous. The dizzy rhetoric describes exactly the promised eight arms and four faces, no more, no less; every extravagance is carefully budgeted, and the cadenza is also an inventory.

These quibbles are certainly churlish; but a reviewer is not merely a churl but a hired churl. There are things in *Caracole* that would win anyone over. This suavely alien world can give intense and almost continuous pleasure. Edmund White is a great dandy, and *Caracole* is a dandy novel.

Clark Blaise (review date 20 March 1988)

SOURCE: "Don't Give In to the Baggy Grown-Ups," in *The New York Times Book Review,* March 20, 1988, p. 7.

[*In the following review, Blaise asserts that White's* The Beautiful Room is Empty *"is packaged as an autobiographical novel, yet as a novel its flaws reduce its value and interest considerably."*]

The title of Edmund White's new novel, *The Beautiful Room is Empty,* derives from one of Kafka's nightmarish images of perfect symmetry. It seems to me part of a grand design, framed by an urgent and tragic necessity. Grand design because this book had its "prequel" in 1982 in *A Boy's Own Story* (set during the narrator's Midwestern childhood and adolescence), and this current volume breaks off in 1969, with the same narrator shouting "Gay Is Good!" on Christopher Street outside the just-raided Stonewall Inn. By the end of the first book, he had entered the gay life; by the end of the second, he has glimpsed the origins of gay politics and experienced the birth of a gay community. The specter of AIDS, much in the mind of anyone who reads these two books, had not yet surfaced. Neither had the sexual frenzy of the bathhouse 70's. (This book, in fact, opens on a note as innocent and reassuring as "Goodbye, Columbus": "I met Maria during my next-to-last year in prep school.")

As readers it is pleasant for us to think we might be at the inception of a planned series of intensely sexual experiences, a somber counterweight to John Updike's perennially greening Rabbit, or a gay-WASP retelling of Philip Roth's Zuckerman myth. The 70's and 80's in the life of gay America, as tumultuous and tragic a period as any we've experienced, demand their chronicler Edmund White (co-author of one monument to the gay liberation movement of the 70's, the now anachronistically titled *Joy of Gay Sex,* and the author of *States of Desire: Travels in Gay America,* plus three earlier novels) has the credentials for it.

This is, admittedly, putting the best possible interpretation on the enterprise. It's just as easy to observe that the form and content of this book are at odds, as they often are in matters of urgency. This book is packaged as an autobiographical novel, yet as a novel its flaws reduce its value and interest considerably. A novel is something considerably more than a personal narrative, wholly or partially imagined.

Material that *feels* autobiographical has to be dramatically recast. Unprepared, unmotivated conversions or revelations cannot appear as plot devices. In the course of this book and its predecessor, the narrator's favorite teacher is exposed (by letter) as gay; Maria, the apparently straight best female friend he thinks he loves, suddenly announces her lesbianism; the make-out king of his Michigan fraternity is at least bisexual; and, finally, the narrator's sister with her three children and suburban marriage—she's gay. Minor characters are far too often pure stereotypes: the blustery shrink who promises a cure of homosexuality turns out to be an alcoholic, pill-popping loony; the father is the essence of Babbittry; the mother resembles an aging coquette out of Tennessee Williams: "No *morphrodites,* for that's what they called homosexuals down South. No morphrodites in our bloodlines!"

Does it matter? Of course it matters. All readers want to know where the authority in a book is coming from, "real life" (the autobiography), the political agenda, or the artistic design. This book is a confusion of all three.

Yet Mr. White's success lies in establishing two contradictory truths: gay men are very much like straight men; and gay men and straight men are fundamentally different. He does so by the meticulous reconstruction of the very texture of his sexuality (much of it sordid, most of it unquotable in this review).

Anyone can identify with the narrator-as-wallflower. "It didn't occur to me that this shockingly intense pleasure could be sought after. If you're someone mainly eager to please others, you don't think much about your own pleasure." Much later he reflects, after years of dedicated iron pumping to eliminate a tendency to fat: "I was so glad I'd bothered to acquire a nice body, since it gave me something to offer every night to a different man. . . . I went to bed with anyone who wanted me." Two of the sturdiest heterosexual stereotypes, Don Juanism and nymphomania, fade before the fervid sexuality of this narrator. Of his years as a "John queen" in a University of Michigan men's room he writes, "I was alone with my sexuality, since none of these men spoke to me, nor did I even know their faces, much less their names." In describing his nightly cruising of the streets of Ann Arbor or Chicago, he writes, "The thrill came when one

bagged not another old fruit but a hot young college kid, for although I myself was at least young and in college, I already saw myself as vampire-cold, turned prematurely old as a punishment for vice. . . . I'd learned to feel nostalgia for my own youth while I was living it."

In other words, much—but not all—of this account of pre-AIDS male sexuality applies to most of the bachelor bulls of American puritanism, whatever their orientation. "Hets" can relate to the obsessive 50's and their rituals of picking up, making out, scoring, leering at centerfolds (size being a matter of anxiety to both camps). Any of us can relate to the soppy feelings of love, certain lines of which could be set to music: "Then he was gone. I put my lips where his had been on the coffee cup. I felt elated, because that was all I'd ever wanted, to be loved, and nobody ever had."

The promiscuity of the life, and the shallowness of each encounter, are rendered without apology, without reflection. But then Mr. White's narrator turns the tables, lest we be too quick to understand him. He acknowledges the deep sense of shame that accompanies his early "deeds in the dark," and perhaps we even approve the guilt he feels over his "malady." Then he launches a zinger:

> And yet something wild and free in me didn't want
> to give in to them, the big baggy grown-ups. No, if
> I were perfectly honest . . . I'd have to admit that
> there was a world run by women and feminized men
> (not effeminate but feminized men) that I wanted
> to escape, the world of mild suburban couples, his
> and her necks equally thick and creased, their white
> hair similarly cropped. The . . . slow wink of a drag
> queen looking back at me over her ratty fox
> neckpiece just before she turned the corner—these
> glimpses piqued my craving for freedom, despite
> my yearning after respectability.

So, according to Mr. White, gay men are "effeminate" and suburban straights are "feminized." Gay men are defined by their sex acts; straights are no less imprisoned by their sex roles. "We" would have the gay men "grow up" and quit acting out their narcissistic infantilism; "they" would have us act as sexually mature adults and quit sublimating our sex drives in child abuse, Super Bowls and mortgage payments.

With all the suspicion and downright fear that engulfs American "manhood" as it confronts one of its ancient fears, it's heartening to think that any reasonably tolerant heterosexual would be more likely to quarrel with the form than with the content of this book.

Brendan Lemon (review date 9 April 1988)

SOURCE: "An American Scrapbook," in *The Nation,* Vol. 246, No. 14, April 9, 1988, pp. 503-4.

[*In the following review, Lemon praises White's* The Beautiful Room is Empty, *but complains that "the ending's exhilarations [are] a diminishment of the power and beauty of what had gone before."*]

It was inevitable that the 1960s revival would produce a retrospective novel about gay life in New York City. Less fated, and more welcome, is that the task was assumed by an artist as gifted as Edmund White. *The Beautiful Room Is Empty* (the title comes from one of Franz Kafka's letters to Milena Jesenská) interweaves public and private events, and even more than its predecessor, *A Boy's Own Story,* encourages speculation that the author is offering us not just an autobiographical novel but a memoir *tout court.*

The unnamed narrator lifts facts from White's own dossier: year of birth (1940), Midwestern childhood, University of Michigan education, literary métier, current Parisian domicile and, of course, an appearance at the Stonewall riot, a badge as obligatory for an activist—and as often fudged—as attendance at Woodstock. More telling than this mere matching of facts is the author's fidelity to his master, Vladimir Nabokov, whose uncharacteristic "blurbissimo" advanced White's first novel, the icily brilliant *Forgetting Elena,* and who, in *Speak, Memory,* defined the purpose of autobiography as the tracing of thematic designs throughout a life.

Once again the main thread is the narrator's attempt "to love and be loved by men, yet remain heterosexual." It's a struggle perfectly attuned to the adolescent novel, which, since Fielding at least, has focused on the forging of identity, and it proves serviceable again here, in part because, although the book wraps itself in 1960s lore, much of its spirit remains mired in familiar familial repressions of the late 1950s. In *A Boy's Own Story,* the conflict was enacted inwardly, suffused with yearning, and flooded primarily with guilt; in *Beautiful Room,* the drama moves outward, oozes bald desire and acquires shame, a more public feature consonant with the new book's acts of furtive erotic expression.

White handles New York City street and subway cruising and collegiate lavatory sex not in the bloodless manner of the film *Prick Up Your Ears,* nor with the uninhibited glee of the spunky *Orton Diaries,* but with a mix of analysis and zeal characteristic of the author whose *Joy of Gay Sex* and *States of Desire: Travels in Gay America* remain uncanny monuments to the lost art of promiscuity and that art's classic age—the Bad Good Old Days: the 1970s. That his unbridled homoeroticism continues to provoke polite aversion in otherwise hale quarters might amuse White, for in his crisp Condé Nast journalism, and especially in his catty 1985 novel, *Caracole,* he delights in guying such exemplars of wealth, power and unyielding masculinity. This fascination continues in *Beautiful Room.* The narrator's fraternity brothers replay a weekend for each other on Monday morning, and "their reports contained no mention of feelings beyond nausea and highly localized lust ('I'm such a beaver man, just put a shaving brush to my lips when I'm asleep and I'll start munching')." Like his more patrician counterpart, Gore Vidal, White extracts gold from such base social ore most effectively when his gaze is trained on the mother lode: America.

For White's narrator, America is a world of stern fathers; the most heinous crimes are Communism, heroin addiction and homosexuality, and "talking about the self and its discontent, isolation, self-hatred, and burning ambition for sex and power" is forbidden. To escape these taboos the narrator befriends a leftist lesbian painter, Maria, the book's most vivid and exacting presence, and an ad exec/drug addict, Lou. In addition, the narrator, a nominal Buddhist who denies soul, will and self, turns to the quintessential American forum for talk: psychotherapy.

Dr. O'Reilly, *A Boy's Own Story's* cross-addicted analyst, reappears to guide the underclassman narrator, but like a star who, after a string of flops, returns to his career-launching part, his role has become a caricature. He introduces the narrator to Annie Schroeder, a bulimic patient:

> "Those stuffy Freudians would split a gut," he said, or rather mumbled, since the pills and alcohol slurred his speech. "But Annie's a good gal, though she's got a psycho for an old man, right out of Dostoevsky, and a mother who wants to be Annie's daughter." He clapped me on the shoulder with too much force. "A fine gal, Annie, but don't think I'm jealous. I'm not the avenging father."

O'Reilly scorns the narrator's reliance on intellect; in defense, the young man's resisting fancy takes flight, pouring forth a stream of interior, Quine-like definitions. "The mind a boat at sea rebuilding itself while under sail. The mind a rotting meat under expensive spices. The mind a pure spirit (the unsuspecting wife) under the sway of a murderous will (Bluebeard)." Readers grateful for the poetic intensity of White's language may also find themselves desirous, occasionally, of a word cop to direct the traffic in metaphors.

Much later, in New York, the shrink-shopping narrator learns to check his intellect at the door. He and his lover, Sean, like couples in tawdry French novels who renounce love to don collar and veil, enroll in "games people play" groups. In his assemblage the narrator encounters a Russian immigrant named Simon, whose repartee shows off White's ear for humor in dialogue even as Simon's relentless refrain ("I wanna hear about de goils") drives the young man to violence, thus ending the self-hating heterosexual quest.

Gays going straight is not the discarded literary theme of a decade ago; AIDS-related repression and attendant auto-homophobia have restored its aptness as a subject. White takes advantage of the shifting cultural wind: Like Maria's favorite opera, *Der Rosenkavalier,* he enrolls a bygone age—the 1960s—in his pursuit of commentary on more recent events. (He has composed three more overt tales about the AIDS era, collected, with several by Adam Mars-Jones, in **The Darker Proof.**) In **Beautiful Room,** White gets at the roots of modern gay self-loathing and its imperative: One must ingratiate oneself to society and its institutions, as well as to co-workers, family, even friends. With his boyfriend Sean, for example, as with the teen-age buddy Kevin in *A Boy's Own Story,* the narrator disavows what he has felt and experienced:

> One night as we were lying in bed, Sean said that that afternoon he had used a public toilet and walked in on an orgy.
>
> "Oh, how awful," I said.
>
> "What are they doing there?" he asked
>
> "What do you mean?"
>
> "Of course I know they're there for sex, but how can they do it? It's really subhuman."
>
> "Totally subhuman," I said.

The incongruence between inner avowal and public expression, of course, is the classic symptom of the Trilling syndrome: insincerity. White cleverly builds upon this quality in the Art of Fiction passages laced into the text. The clearest clue to his affect, however, may be contained at the end of Kafka's title-bestowing missive: "And don't demand any sincerity from me, Milena. No one can demand it from me more than I myself and yet many things elude me, I'm sure, perhaps everything eludes me."

Insincerity dogs almost all of **Beautiful Room's** characters eventually: William Everett Hunton, the prissy collegiate pal whose counterfeit sexual posing is matched by his fake name ("Some day when we're sisters I'll tell you my real name, but if you snitch on me I'll pull your braids and dip them in the inkwell"); the narrator's sister, who *contra natura* marries and settles in the suburbs before coming out, which convinces the narrator that "something—genetic or psychological—in our family . . . had made us both gay"; their mother, who frowns on her son's behavior and announces "I like *men,*" even as she grows more intimate with Maria. Maria, full of socialism, good sense and a University of Chicago-trained intellect, recants her pro-Moscow line and utters anachronistic slogans about the feminization of poverty.

> White's sad, stylish prose, his tonic mix of elegy and irony, the page-by-page proof that he is one of our most perceptive prose writers, overwhelms any serious caviling.
> —*Brendan Lemon*

If no character is endowed with what John Updike called "persuasive inertia," the quality that causes figures to linger long in the mind after the book is shut, it doesn't matter. White's sad, stylish prose, his tonic mix of elegy and irony, the page-by-page proof that he is one of our most perceptive prose writers, overwhelms any serious caviling. What's more, the idea that to respond to a novel we must "care" about its characters is hardly worth refuting. (As if we had always to *like* what we respect or admire or love.) And in a work this close to memoir, especially one which fulfills so beautifully its thematic premise, to ask for a well-wrought plot would amount to impertinence: "My plots are all scrapbooks," the author avers parenthetically.

And yet White's novel/memoir would be more satisfying, I think, had it "wrapped" less abruptly, at Stonewall. The narrator's *prise de conscience* has been inadequately prepared; the 1960s' second half, to most the more interesting years, are dispensed with in a few pages. And the remark dropped into the middle of the final scene, "I caught myself foolishly imagining that gays might someday constitute a community rather than a diagnosis," while thematically sharp, confers an awkward *roman à thèse* status on the entire enterprise. Perhaps the author wanted a way out, from community back to diagnosis, when he brings the story to the present. Perhaps community was too enticing a notion to leave out of his 1960s saga.

I may be alone in thinking the ending's exhilarations a diminishment of the power and beauty of what had gone before. Or it may be that under the current ravaged social and economic circumstances, few readers could greet liberation with the sound of more than one hand clapping.

Edmund White with Kay Bonetti (interview date 1990)

SOURCE: "An Interview with Edmund White," in *The Missouri Review,* 1990, pp. 89-110.

[*In the following interview, White discusses the autobiographical nature of his work and what he thinks about literature.*]

[*Bonetti:*] *Mr. White, can you fill us in on some background about yourself? Do* **A Boy's Own Story** *and* **The Beautiful Room Is Empty** *follow your own chronology?*

[White:] The books fairly reflect where I was and what I was doing. I was born in Cincinnati, Ohio. My parents got divorced when I was seven and my mother began to move from city to city while my father remained in Cincinnati. I was sent to a boarding school in Michigan, near Detroit, a school called Cranbrook, which appears as Eton in my books.

And you went to the University of Michigan?

I studied Chinese there, and when I graduated I moved to New York and worked for Time-Life Books from 1962 to 1970. Then I moved to Rome for a year, and when I came back, I became a freelance writer and editor, then worked briefly for *Saturday Review* and *Horizon*. I started teaching in the mid-seventies, first at Yale, then at Johns Hopkins, finally at Columbia and New York University. In 1981 I was the executive director of The New York Institute for the Humanities, which is an organization of smart people attached to New York University. Then in 1983, I moved to France, where I've been living ever since. Beginning in spring, 1990, I will be teaching at Brown University, where I've just been named a Professor of English with tenure.

There's a story in **The Darker Proof** *about a couple that move to Paris in an oblique response to the gay community and AIDS. Did you move to Paris for similar reasons?*

In a way I gave some of the events of my life to those characters, but the reasons were different. In my case, I won a Guggenheim, which allowed me to go for one year. I worked for *Vogue* and other Condé-Nast magazines as a journalist, so that allowed me to stay on. I could stay forever I suppose. I have a nice apartment and I make a decent living as a freelance American journalist writing from Paris.

Then why are you coming back to teaching?

I like teaching. I like the idea of a secure position. I'm positive for AIDS, and the statistics are rather grim, but if by some chance I do go on living I would like to have a retirement plan. I support my mother now, and if I weren't there, she would really be penniless.

Does your fiction sustain you economically?

If I weren't such a spendthrift and if I didn't have other people to support—my mother's not the only one—I could live very well from my fiction, but I'm a terrible spendthrift. I like to travel, and that takes money.

Is the narrator's job in **The Beautiful Room Is Empty** *similar to your job at Time-Life Books?*

Absolutely. In the sixties, which was the heyday of direct-mail sales of books, we were vastly overstaffed and the books made enormous amounts of money. I was accepted in a writer's trainee program where I learned lots of useful journalistic things—to change, edit, rewrite. We were so encouraged to say everything was the best, the biggest, the most, that it gave me a permanent horror of overstatement, which I think is also a useful tool for a serious writer. But I stayed too long. When I was thirty I thought, "If I continue here, I'll be here the rest of my life." So I just quit, took my profit-sharing, which was seven thousand dollars, a lot of money in 1970, and moved to Rome, where I lived for a year.

Were you working on fiction at that time?

I wasn't working on anything. I was just being a lazy bum. I write very little. I can go a year or even two years without blinking.

Yet you've put out quite a body of work.

Yes, but I write quickly when I write. Most writers write too much, they work too much, they live too little and they anguish too much. Especially American writers, who seem to feel guilty about being writers at all. It doesn't seem like a real job to them. In order to justify their existence in their own eyes, or in their friends' and family's eyes, they feel they must sit in an office and write eight hours a day. I don't think anybody writes well after two hours a day—really one—and anyway I tend to be a very old-fashioned writer who writes from inspiration.

During the years at Time-Life when did you write?

At night. After work. I wrote many, many plays and they were all very, very bad. The writing was dry, voices talking in a void, endless chattering dialogue. Then I wrote three or four novels, and they were all very bad. I think it's because I worked too hard in my twenties that I now don't believe in working hard.

Is that what you tell your students?

I do. Of course everybody's rhythms are different, but I do think that people should approach the page with a certain fear and trembling and a feeling that it's an important encounter. The problem with student writers is not that they write too little, but that they write too much. They crank it out. The ones who enjoy writing enjoy it because they usually have rather neurotic needs to write. It's a real psychological defense, but unfortunately that kind of compulsive writing, though it can sometimes be absolutely gripping can also be extremely dull. It's an experience that only the writer is having, not the reader. Writers should have a kind of wary distaste for the page, a feeling that when you engage with it, you should really be doing something that's interesting. That's compressed. That's beautiful.

You're in Washington, D.C. tonight to receive an award and give a lecture. Can you tell us a bit about that?

It's the first Bill Whitehead award, given by a group of gay people and lesbians in publishing called The Publishing Triangle. They have three or four hundred members and they've only just started. Bill Whitehead was a friend and my editor at E. P. Dutton for several years, and he freelanced the editing of *The Beautiful Room Is Empty* after he'd become ill and retired. Before he died of AIDS he suggested the topic of the book I'm working on now, a biography of Jean Genet.

I'm going to be talking about gay liberation and what that's meant in terms of gay publishing. This is the twentieth anniversary of the Stonewall uprising, which was the first time gay people, when faced with arrest during a bar raid, didn't run away into the night. They stayed behind and fought with the cops over a period of about three days. I participated in the riot, and it was a very exciting moment in my own life. It seems fitting that a publishing group should be giving its first award on the anniversary of that important occasion, even though the gay publishing movement did not begin right away.

One important book was published in 1971, called *Homosexual,* by Dennis Altman, but it really wasn't until 1978 that three gay novels came out: Larry Kramer's *Faggots; Dancer from the Dance,* by Andrew Holeran; and my *Nocturnes for the King of Naples.* Those three books gave the impression of a new wave, of a new movement coming along. Especially the first two. Mine was probably the least important of those three, as a publishing event.

How do you place the books by John Rechy, and Gore Vidal, and James Baldwin, and others that came along earlier?

They're all very important. Especially Christopher Isherwood's *A Single Man* and John Rechy's *City of Night,* in the sixties. The difference between the so-called gay writers like me and those earlier writers is that there is a tremendous network now of gay and lesbian bookshops throughout the United States with an enormous mail order business. It's a highly packaged, self-conscious, self-declared culture. Those guys back then were writing about rather lonely individuals combatting society. They were isolated by

the nature of things politically, and their position in publishing was always anomalous.

Do you see yourself as a writer who happens to be gay and deals with gay subject matter or as a gay writer?

It depends which country I'm in when somebody asks me. In France there is no such thing as a "gay writer" because there is no gay ghetto. Gays are so well integrated that nobody makes a fuss over his sexual orientation. In the United States we have nothing but ghettos. It's astonishing for a European to walk into an American bookshop and see books categorized by Women's Studies, Gay Studies, Children's Books. Literary fiction as such represents a tiny part of any particular bookshop, and even that small percentage is drifting more and more toward popular fiction. It all seems minimalist and regional and confessional.

I'm thinking as we talk that "gay literature" is more ghettoized than these other literatures.

The Beautiful Room Is Empty was number one on the bestseller list in England when it came out in hard cover last year. Here it would never be on any list. In England, I am a judge of the Booker Prize. Here I would never be asked to judge the Pulitzer. *The Beautiful Room Is Empty* came out first in England, then in Australia and New Zealand and only finally in the States. In those other countries I was interviewed by the major newspapers as a real writer who would be of interest to the general public, but when I arrived in America, the only people who were willing to interview me represented handouts distributed free in gay bars. In England I'm a famous writer, in America I'm a kind of funny ghettoized marginal writer. It's a peculiar experience.

Do you see yourself as writing primarily for a gay audience?

In my first few books I thought first of the general reader. With *The Beautiful Room Is Empty* I was more aware of writing for a gay reader primarily and then for general readers afterwards, because of AIDS, I think. In big cities, gay people have lost up to three quarters of their friends, which is an extraordinary experience for somebody who's not old to have to go through. Most gay people know they are HIV positive, which means that they have about a fifty percent chance of being dead within two years. It's an experience which gives an immediacy to your writing. That's something I tried to deal with in *The Darker Proof,* a collection of short stories that I wrote with Adam Mars-Jones, a very good young gay writer in England. We thought that AIDS had been treated too much from the point of view of experts, usually heterosexual, and discussed as though it were a kind of objective scientific condition, rather than an anguish to be lived through. We wanted to show the human side of this experience. We chose the story as a form, rather than the novel, because the novel has an inevitable trajectory to it. That is, you begin healthy and end sick and dead. We wanted to get into and out of the subject matter in a more angular and less predictable way.

I read that **The Beautiful Room Is Empty** *is part of a tetralogy. The idea of a writer being able to hold that much material in his head amazes me.*

Well, you can't claim that you know every last little thing, but the broad axes are clear. It's partly because I live my life as though it were a novel. As I'm experiencing it I see it in novelistic terms.

Now what do you mean by that? We're told that life is chaos. Art is discipline and order.

Yes, but I think everyone looks for the order in his or her own life. A novel is precisely that attempt to find a meaning or order. What is important to me is to find meaning with all the complexity left in. One of the things that makes a lot of new American fiction not very interesting is that though the books are shapely, they are shapely at the expense of complication. I like things to be complex.

A Boy's Own Story *is basically straight-on, as is* **The Beautiful Room Is Empty** *compared to the lush style of* **Forgetting Elena** *and* **Nocturnes for the King of Naples** *and* **Caracole.** *Any comments on that difference?*

In *Nocturnes for the King of Naples* I dealt with my youth in a rather fantastic way with an immensely rich playboy father who's not at all like my fairly dumpy and dour midwestern father. I dealt with some of the feelings of loneliness that I had as a child, some of my first longings for escape and sex and whatnot. All of that was in *Nocturnes* but given to an invented character, somebody who was small and blond and beautiful, whereas I am large and dark and not beautiful. It's as though I peeled away the fantasy layer, in a style that was extremely ornate and appropriate to that particular vision. Then I was ready to deal with the painful reality of my youth in a more direct way. If my goal now was to tell the truth, I wasn't going to disguise it with a style that was very rhetorical.

Are there any parts of **A Boy's Own Story** *that serve as an example of how reshaping "real experience" can fit the needs of the book?*

Of course the chronology itself—the real experiences were scattered over long periods of time, but I tend to group them in the book and shape them and simplify them. I wanted to have a boy who seemed believable, slightly shy, rather sympathetic and awkward. In real life I was much more self-as-

sured. I was a very successful student, well liked by the other kids, and wildly promiscuous sexually. Between the ages of twelve and sixteen I had hundreds of sexual partners.

In secret or openly?

I don't think it was really secretive. Most people knew that I was gay, but I didn't realize that. Thomas McGuane was in school with me, and he mentions in one of his interviews that he always knew I was gay and so did all the other boys. They thought it was amusing and it didn't bother them at all. Tom makes a brief appearance in one of my books, you know, but I won't give away his alias.

Are most of your characters based on real people, or do you often make them up?

Sometimes I'll take a character like Tex, whom I actually knew when I was twelve, thirteen, and revivify my memories by grafting on memories of somebody who's been more recently in my life.

In the epilogue to **States of Desire** *you say that you tend to examine people and individuals with a sociological eye as opposed to a psychological eye. Were you just talking about* **States of Desire** *or do you think that applies to you as a fiction writer, too?*

I think it's true of me as a fiction writer, but also as a biographer. For instance, in the book I'm working on now about Jean Genet, what's most interesting to me is to think of him as a child of the welfare system, a person who was in reform school and then in the army. Looking at the shaping power of these major institutions of French life excites me much more than wondering about his possible Oedipal feelings. I don't believe in psychoanalytic motivations of that sort. I believe that we're shaped by our class position. In my own case my father was a small entrepreneur who made a lot of money and then lost most of it during the time when small businessmen were being superseded by big corporations. That had an enormous impact on the way I perceived the world. When my mother was married to my father, she was well-to-do, a kind of society matron. After the divorce she was declassed and basically poor, and I along with her. I shuttled between living with my mother and sister in one room in a hotel to my father's house where there were ten bedrooms. I would spend my last five dollars as a tip for the maid, you know. I was sent to debutante balls by my father, but never with the right clothes. I was between two worlds socially. That probably created anxiety in me, but from a positive point of view, it made me more observant of society than a person who is either purely poor or purely rich would have been.

I was struck by the psychological versus sociological ques-

tion because after reading **A Boy's Own Story** *and* **The Beautiful Room Is Empty,** *the conclusion I came to as to why the narrator is gay seems to be the standard absent-father explanation.*

At least intellectually I reject the idea of there being any explanation of homosexuality. Just as there is no explanation of heterosexuality, and no one looks for one, so once you begin to look for an explanation of homosexuality, you're already involved in a medical discourse. It's true that I had an absent father and a domineering mother, but my father, when he was present, was extremely domineering too. He was not the usual feeble father that homosexuals are supposed to have. Whether that made me homosexual I have no way of knowing, and I certainly didn't choose those elements in order to illustrate a theory. I chose those elements because they were the ones that happened to have been allotted to me.

If you read **Forgetting Elena** *in the context of all of your other books, you can see oblique references to a homosexual culture, yet it's not a "gay book." Was that a conscious decision on your part?*

No. What happened was I had written a very autobiographical gay book in the sixties and I stole a few passages from it and the title for the book that was only recently published as **The Beautiful Room Is Empty.** That early book was very long, very self-analytical, very uncritical. It went to twenty-five publishers and was rejected by everybody. One reason it was rejected was because it was about a middle-class homosexual, and I think in the sixties, before gay liberation, publishers were prepared to publish books like those by Rechy or Jean Genet or William Burroughs about freaky people, drug-takers, pimps, prostitutes, marginal gay people. Such characters were colorful, they were strange, and they were certainly not you, dear reader. But it was more threatening to write about a person who was really quite like the presumably middle-class reader, except that he happened to be gay. Having had that book, which I believed in at the time, rejected by so many publishers, I thought, "Oh, the hell with it. No one's ever going to publish me. I'm going to write something purely for myself." So I wrote *Forgetting Elena* because it reflected my own taste in a way that nothing I had written up to then did. The idea of writing about a culture that had a surface democracy, but an actual hidden hierarchy, and where morality had been replaced by esthetics, where people no longer troubled themselves about what was good, but only about what was beautiful, fascinated me. It seemed to be true of how a certain group of highly privileged gay men were living in the seventies.

Yet homosexuality is never overtly mentioned or referred to in that novel.

There's very little that's explicit at all in that book. It's implicit.

Forgetting Elena *also ties into a theme that runs throughout your work, the position the homosexual is put into by the world of having to invent his identity because within the system there is no role model.*

All my books are about initiation into a society. I don't seem to be able to get beyond that as a theme. Although perhaps in recent stories I have begun to tackle other subjects. In *Caracole* I did deal with that initiation from both the point of view of the boy who's being initiated, Gabriel, and from the point of view of the adults who are doing the initiating. It's a painful process on both sides.

Gabriel is a figure that recurs in your work, essentially an amnesiac because he has no frame of reference for where he is and what's going on. He and Angelica are feral. They're strays, eating fried bread while their mysterious enormous mother drinks in the bedroom. Gabriel has no idea what they are doing to him until he finds himself locked in that blackened room in the cage.

I suppose these extreme experiences that I like to put my characters through dramatize a feeling that we all undergo, maybe in less evident forms. Everyone models his responses on the other person's cues, and social life is a kind of theatrical reciprocity and a constant improvisation. The self is a much more fluid thing than we imagine. If a psychiatrist nods while a patient is saying certain things, the patient will talk more about that subject with more enthusiasm. Whereas if the psychiatrist frowns the patient will become uneasy and talk less about it. You can shape and mold behavior by these Skinnerian techniques.

At the time that I wrote *Caracole,* I was also under the influence of the ideas of Michel Foucault, the French philosopher. I'm sure I didn't understand his ideas very well because I'm not really intelligent enough to, but what I gathered was that there are these large social codes that transect and shape all of our lives, and that the individual is only a locus where these lines of force cross. With Gabriel and Angelica I wanted to show two children who were as close to a state of nature—that is uncoded—as possible. They are brought to the city, and there they are very consciously and elaborately scripted with the ideas of our society, the codes, the laws of behavior and so on.

You have said that the unity of personality is a "useful illusion" for a novelist. Could you sort that out for me? What is meant by "unity of personality?"

Like the narrator in **The Beautiful Room Is Empty** *and A Boy's Own Story,* as a young person I read Max Muller's

Sacred Books of the East. One of the Buddhist ideas that seemed very true to me is that the "I," the self, the unifying principal that holds this collection of attributes together, is an illusion. What we really are is just a collection of random psychological states, predispositions, emotions, sentiments, and so on, not to mention bodily organs, more like a pile of objects than an actual unity of self. Buddhists feel that the most useful thing a person can do to escape pain and rebirth and suffering is to return the various elements to their origins, separate them out. Although I believe that philosophically, it's not a very easy way to write a novel. What makes a novel seem vivid to a reader is bright and easily recognizable characters.

The narrator of **The Beautiful Room Is Empty** *not only rejects the notion of unity of person but also says that he's come to distrust ideas: "every enthusiasm if genuinely embraced turns into folly or fanaticism." Some critics have taken you to task for that, but I wonder if the confusion might be in how people understand "idea."*

What I like about fiction is that it shows events as history does, but they are shaped by certain principles, certain ideas, but only ideas that are well implanted into actual experiences. They're always concrete and contextual. When William Carlos Williams says, "No ideas but in things," that is something I would agree with, and I think most writers would. The philosophical novelist, like Thomas Mann, is someone I tend to loathe and the very concrete novelist who has very few ideas, like Colette, is someone I tend to admire.

Yet you refer to yourself as being a very opinionated person. Now what is the difference between being opinionated and having ideas?

An essayist is someone who has thought about a subject deeply and knows what he thinks and reflects that in an essay. A novelist is somebody who has very divided feelings, but both sides of those feelings are held very strongly on particular questions. Fiction is finding which issues obsess you, but those obsessional issues are usually unresolved problems rather than neatly typed out position papers.

I'm interested to know how at this point in your life you feel about the "baggy grownups" that the narrator talks about in **The Beautiful Room Is Empty,** *especially in light of the homosexual community's response to AIDS. That response seems contrary to the attention to youth and physical beauty, the dread of growing old described in your books.*

The generation that came out and was liberated through Stonewall twenty years ago is now in its late forties. When AIDS came along a lot of gays in leadership positions suddenly had a whole new set of problems to deal with. It's true

that there's been an extraordinary amount of discipline and courage and dignity in the way the gay community has responded to AIDS. Once the viral nature of AIDS was understood and the means of transmission were fully clear, which was not until 1984, then the gay community made a very rapid change to safe sex behaviors, and if you think how hard it is to change sexual patterns, it's quite remarkable that people have been able to show this degree of coherence, discipline, and versatility. So, yes, I agree with all these things. On the other hand though, I don't regret the stand I appear to be taking in my books, in favor of youth and beauty, because art is about beauty, and young people are more beautiful than old people. I respond to physical beauty, and I agree with the Platonic notion that physical beauty, at least in the mind of the perceiver, is close to spiritual beauty.

Many readers have pointed out that one of the things you learn from reading an Edmund White novel is how alike gay men and straight men are, and how similar the dynamics of couples. Yet in the heterosexual world, the perception is that men become more handsome as they age, more vivid and more interesting, and women don't. How do you account for that?

I think almost all the differences can be accounted for by saying that the homosexual world is one in which you have basically male attitudes interacting with other male attitudes. In other words you are getting a kind of a laboratory-pure sample of how men act when they are both the subject and the object of desire. Just as lesbianism represents the laboratory-pure sample of how women would be if they weren't interacting with men. There was a study a few years ago of straight couples, lesbian couples, and gay couples, and they found that if you took a certain age group, the gay male couples were having sex three times a week, the straight couples were having sex twice a week and the lesbian couples were having sex once a week. So you can really see heterosexuality as a compromise between female and male psychology. In the same way, I think that women have been socialized to admire power, and older men tend to be richer and more powerful than younger men. Men have been socialized to admire a kind of flashy, youthful beauty that has a high status as an object. Thus the gay youth cult really has nothing to do with anything mysterious and unique to the gay community. All it has to do with is the nature of male socialization versus the nature of female socialization.

At what point in your life did you shake off the self-loathing about your homosexuality that you write so fully about in your two autobiographical novels, **A Boy's Own Story** *and* **The Beautiful Room Is Empty?**

A big turning point was when I decided to sign my name to **The Joy of Gay Sex.** It was a way of committing myself to gay life and to becoming a "gay writer." Another turning point came in my early thirties, when instead of choosing a straight woman therapist as I had oftentimes done before with the idea that I would eventually be able to go straight, I chose a gay male therapist, accepting the fact that I was probably going to stay gay and male and that I simply wanted to become better adapted to that position in life. I must say that AIDS reawakened and reactivated some of the long-buried feeling I had of self-loathing, and I think it has for many gay men. We live in a sex-phobic society, one that doesn't approve of pleasure in general, and of sex in particular. Something that seems a scourge directed towards people because of their sexual behavior certainly can't help—especially for a Puritanical society like ours—reawakening feelings of self-loathing that I think can be resolved but never extirpated.

Your books deal with love as passion, as obsession, and as an illness, yet love takes on a deeper and different dimension in concert with death and grief in **Nocturnes for the King of Naples.**

> **We live in a sex-phobic society, one that doesn't approve of pleasure in general, and of sex in particular. Something that seems a scourge directed towards people because of their sexual behavior certainly can't help—especially for a Puritanical society like ours—reawakening feelings of self-loathing that I think can be resolved but never extirpated.**
> **—Edmund White**

A lot of my own unresolved childhood and adolescent feelings of wanting to actually have sex with my father and live with him as a lover were reactivated in the writing of this book. It was an extraordinarily unhappy period of my life. In order to support my nephew and his girlfriend, I was writing college textbooks, including a thousand-page history of the United States, which I worked on every day—the whole thing had to be done in a year. I thought, "Well, I'll never write another word of fiction at this rate"—my expenses had gone from about ten thousand dollars a year to about forty thousand dollars a year because I suddenly had these two kids to send to private schools and so on.

Then John Ashbery told me that he'd been going to a Jungian psychiatrist who was supposed to help writers, and she suggested that he stay in bed and write longhand for half an hour every morning. I don't think he followed that advice, but I did. That's how I wrote that whole book. I wrote it out of a desire to find some small thing for myself, some small place in my life for myself and it was that little half hour in bed in the morning.

Quite a bit of criticism about this book picks up on the "I and thou," the philosophical and the theological implications.

I was interested in writing a book that would be Baroque in the literal sense of the word. The Baroque period was one when physical and spiritual love were mixed up with each other. It's hard to tell with the statues of Bernini whether Saint Theresa is having an orgasm or a vision. It's hard to tell whether certain poems addressed to God are ecstatic or visionary. I was also interested in the Sufi poets, and Saint John of the Cross. The original edition included a comment by Mary Gordon, the Catholic writer, who said that she felt that this book was a reinvention of devotional literature. I was quite pleased that she said that because I did want to suggest that this kind of wild, unreciprocated passion that I'd been talking about and the soul's longing for God are similar emotions. They are both emotions that lead you away from life and the world, that are life-denying in a sense.

The resolution seems to confirm that notion, yet it's the most ecstatically sensual and sensory book that you have written.

It's funny because it's one of those books that I feel goes beyond me. I know when I wrote the last chapter especially, I never felt quite so released as a writer, as though everything was available to me and I could touch on so many different things. I think I was really more interested simply in creating patterns which I knew were drenched with meaning than I was in sorting out what those meanings would be. It's as though you are flying blind, without signals, but aware that later maybe you'll understand it all. That old idea that the artist is a flute being played on by divine breath is a good metaphor for the puzzlement that I oftentimes feel when I'm writing, a kind of sureness about technique, but an unsureness about what it all is going to be interpreted to mean.

Do you see yourself as an American writer or a European writer?

I don't know. When I'm in Europe, I feel like I'm an American, and when I'm in America I feel like a European. Stendhal complained of Byron that he wanted the nobles to treat him like a poet and the poets to treat him like a noble. There's a way that you can waffle on this and have a kind of international schizophrenia, but I think there's a rich way in which you can use it if you're honest with yourself. *The Beautiful Room Is Empty* and **"Running on Empty"** are the most American things I've ever written. They are rather simple, straightforward, and seem to take a pleasure in the Americanness of America, and both of those I wrote in Paris. When I move back here, I don't know whether I'll be feeling as nostalgic for Paris or whether I'll have a kind of new and ecstatic enthusiasm for America. I imagine what I'll have is both an ecstatic *and* a critical response to America. That should be interesting.

Jonathan Dyson (review date 30 July 1993)

SOURCE: "Three times three," in *Times Literary Supplement,* July 30, 1993, p. 19.

[*In the following review, Dyson complains that, "The problem with* Trios *is that it plays as if real dramatic skill in writing and direction has not been applied."*]

Fresh from a biography of Jean Genet, Edmund White has presided over this revival of his 1990 three-hander, directed (as was that production) by Simon Usher and starring two of the original cast, Kelly Hunter and Robert Langdon Lloyd. But in fact the tone of this love triangle replayed in three different eras has much in common with the kind of sociological probing found in his life of the great *provocateur.* Visitors to this aircraft hangar of a theatre will see little of the humour and deftness of language which made such successes of White's autobiographical *A Boy's Own Story* and *The Beautiful Room Is Empty. Trios* is stuck firmly in the behavioural laboratory.

The starting point for each triangle is the same: a young woman (Hunter) is drawn from her marriage to an older husband (Langdon Lloyd) to have an affair with a younger man (played this time by newcomer Charles Edwards). In the first incarnation, the nineteenth-century society hostess rejects her suffocating marriage and elopes to the provinces with a dashing, penniless charmer. We then switch to an English country house in the 1920s where a deaf cook is tempted to seek solace from her brutal husband-chauffeur in the arms of the idealistic young houseboy planning to emigrate to Australia. And finally to a present-day open relationship in New York, where a striving young actress introduces her student lover to her washed-up artist husband.

The action darts back and forth between the three stories. "Dart" is the word: for every scene change the actors have to rush tables and chairs from one end of the long stage to the other and plunge themselves in and out of their period costumes. This is so cumbersome and time-consuming as to be comic, but the over-loud snatches of rock and country music played during these change-overs are just plain irritating. The effect is to drive a wedge between scenes when what we are presumably meant to be doing is considering their careful juxtaposition.

Evidently, the idea behind showing these stories being constructed is to reflect the play's central thesis that we all create fictions of ourselves and our relationships. For White in this play, love and all emotions are simply the constantly shifting products of time, place, prevailing social conditions and sexual instincts—"dressed up" and given spurious significance. Antony Lamble's sparse, uninspired set foregrounds this artificiality: three doors hang suspended in frames to the right and left and at the back, and beyond and between them we see the bricks and machinery of the theatre and the actors waiting their entrances and changing costumes.

The three stories of *Trios* are played out without much subtlety. The Victorian segment becomes something of a hammed-up *Anna Karenina* as the young lovers repent their hasty elopement and subsequent penury—the woman knowing society will not allow her to return to husband and son, the man aware he is locked in a doomed relationship. Only Edwards manages to snatch back some conviction here from bouts of lacklustre declaiming.

Meanwhile, below stairs, a generation on, the woman's social status as servant and wife and her disability mean that any kind of attempt to escape a violent marriage is not a realistic option and is likely to have disastrous consequences. A rather over-the-top Langdon Lloyd keeps the upper hand over a sharply, manically characterized Hunter—all nervous twitches and stifled shrieks—and a slightly sketchy Edwards.

Only in the modern section does White really seem to get the measure of his characters. Hippy Langdon Lloyd endearingly lollops around the stage and circles towards a growing attachment to the increasingly self-aware young student. Liberated modern woman, meanwhile, an unconvincingly physical Hunter, has the freedom to go elsewhere for sex and career progression. Here, White manages some convincing dialogue and humour—"I can never find Chicken Tarragon. It's listed under 'P'—Perfect Chicken Tarragon", exclaims Edwards over his cook book. And Hunter: "I want to love like in the olden days."

In his fiction and non-fiction books, White works with ideas similar to those in *Trios.* The pay-off in the books, however, is a beautiful style, with exact descriptions and imagery. The problem with *Trios* is that it plays as if real dramatic skill in writing and direction has not been applied.

Neil Powell (review date 1 July 1994)

SOURCE: "From celebration to elegy," in *Times Literary Supplement,* July 1, 1994, p. 13.

[*In the following review, Powell complains that, "As so often in the book,* [The Burning Library] *White's admirable capacity for sympathetic understanding not only inhibits his critical judgment but actually weakens the case being argued."*]

"Like any agile debater," confesses the student narrator of Edmund White's second autobiographical novel, *The Beautiful Room Is Empty,* "I could defend either side of the question, but I was too immoral to wonder which side was right." Within limits it's an entertaining and an engaging quality which for White becomes the literary dandy's irrepressible urge to try on new clothes, but it makes for some maddening contradictions and for the odd queasy moment when, beneath the loudest suit, there seems to be nothing but a tailor's dummy. In fact, this new collection of his essays spanning twenty-five years would have been a complicated, fragmented sort of book in any case, partly because its chronological range straddles the emergence of the AIDS crisis, and partly because of its symbiotic relationship with White's other writing—in particular with *States of Desire,* from which several chunks resurface verbatim in their original journalistic contexts.

States of Desire, jauntily subtitled *Travels in Gay America,* is a marvellous, often euphoric set of variations on the theme of the Great American Journey. White doesn't spend much time actually travelling; he just arrives, weary and hungry in equal measure, in a succession of places, each of which (even, incredibly, Salt Lake City) turns out to possess at least some degree of gay social life. Every so often, he digresses, in earnestly naive terms, into sexual politics or—for a memorable few pages—his Texan ancestry, interestingly concluding that "in old Texas what could not be named was unknowingly tolerated—a far cry from the half-informed Baptist bigotry of today". Mostly, though, that book was based on conversations with men he met on his travels, embellished with typically baroque touches and a winsome way with similes; Ned in Seattle, for instance, is "about as self-conscious as a mountain waterfall", even if the same can't be said of White's prose. In New York, he ponders an evolution of cultural styles from decadence through camp to the "new gay arts" but "cannot imagine a gay writer imitating the gray and brown abnegations of Joseph Conrad or the patient, dogged grumbling of late Céline". His stance is unblushingly upbeat, but that was how things seemed in 1980.

And that is how things seem for roughly half of *The Burning Library.* The earliest piece here, **"The Gay Philosopher"**, written in 1969 and previously unpublished, meshes both with *States of Desire* ("The nature of gay life is that it is philosophical") and with the adolescent recollections of *A Boy's Own Story,* but it is chiefly significant for recapturing that strangely distant moment in the year of the Stonewall riot when the case for creating a "militant gay group of activists" had still to be argued, when an end to police harassment and a ban on discriminatory laws could still strike

White as "far-fetched" demands; his youthful hedonism, culminating in the suggestion that "the promiscuity of many gay men is a vanguard experiment, a sort of trial run for the rest of the society", seems touchingly absurd. In 1977, addressing a university audience in Washington, DC, on "The Joys of Gay Life", he was still more optimistic, stressing the importance of friendship between gay people (though a statement such as "My old lovers have become close friends" rather raises the question "What, *all* of them?"):

> We gays derive spiritual sustenance and emotional continuity from our friendships—and that is what allows us to weather things so well. Some psychological studies have suggested that gays are, all in all, better adjusted than straights, and I think it is our gift for friendship that makes us so seaworthy.

Nothing in these earlier essays has been more cruelly transformed by time's ironies than that, for those who are most sustained by their enduring friendships must be those most devastated by loss.

White runs the risk of sounding, as he admits, "like a complete pollyanna", but his fulsomeness here is generous, sympathetic and forgivable—"silly like us", as Auden said. More questionable, if only because it depends on the kind of false equation which too often props up his shakier debating points, is his endorsement in **"Fantasia on the Seventies"** of the "gay leather scene" as "more honest—and because it is explicit less nasty—than more conventional sex, straight or gay": that attempt to foist an irrelevant moral value on to a simple preference is a stratagem altogether worthy of his student self. More convincing, temporarily at least, is the explanation of the respectable professional's leather *alter ego* proposed in a slightly later essay, **"Sado Machismo":**

> The children of the middle class grew up without seeing any signs of sexuality emanating from their daddies, those corporation drudges in bulky suits who never whistled at women or scratched their deodorized crotches. The only bare chests were those of construction workers; the only images of male raunch were of Marlon Brando astride his bike or caterwauling for Stella. There is no middle-class sexual style for men. What would it be based on? Golfing? Discussing stock options? Attending church? Downing highballs?

That certainly makes sense, and White's prose here has the tang it always takes on when he taps into his own lived experience; yet he only sets up the argument in order to trade it in for an anodyne theory about re-enacting "not our own private troubles but rather our society's nightmarish preoccupations with power, with might". Must pleasure be thus encumbered with sociological special pleading?

This unresolved tension between celebration and apologia becomes especially troublesome in the critical and analytical pieces. The essay on William Burroughs, for instance, begins in White's best down-there-on-a-visit style of reportage with some wonderfully grisly scene-setting, but when it comes to declaring his critical stance, he ducks the issue: "Nor can I disagree with his esthetics. He is against realistic novels, which he dismisses as 'journalism'." That seems a preposterous evasion or a mere untruth, for such a consummately elegant realist as White. An essay on Truman Capote, not improved by dreadful scissors-and-paste editing which attempts to interweave two separate short articles, reads even more oddly; here some sensible comments on the work—"One can imagine this purist cutting down Proust's usual three adjectives to the single limpid one, with a predictable loss of chiaroscuro and gain in brightness and resolution"—find themselves marooned in a rhapsodic muddle about the New York heat, Capote's frequent comings and goings, the altogether more charismatic arrival and departure of Robert Mapplethorpe.

Mapplethorpe, himself the subject of two other pieces, ensnares both White and his editor, David Bergman, as he has ensnared practically everyone who's dared to write about him. "What White values about Mapplethorpe's photographs", Bergman claims in his introduction, "is their obscenity—their refusal to submit themselves to domestication, to the social framework of the good and useful." But that is not what obscenity means; nor is it what White says. He admires Mapplethorpe's "irresponsibility", adding that "passion, like art, is always irresponsible, useless, an end in itself, regulated by its own impulses and nothing else"; yet this would equally support the notion of art's *responsibility* to ideals beyond the utilitarian, and the distant echo it so curiously seems to invoke is none other than E. M. Forster's eloquent case for the supreme uselessness of literature in *Aspects of the Novel*. Beyond White's masquerade of cultural iconoclasm lurks an endearingly conventional writer who reveres the "old model of communication" and who on two occasions records his admiration for Jane Austen (as well as for Barbara Pym, whom he regards as her modern counterpart). These are strange though actually not incomprehensible bedfellows for Mapplethorpe, whose cause might anyway be better served simply by noting that he was an extremely witty pornographer who also took some stunning pictures of flowers; White's subsequent "eulogy"—"All the time Robert seemed to be guarding a big secret, an amusing but tricky and intimate secret"—rather suggests that he wasn't remotely fooled by the grand theorizing prompted by his work.

The emergence of AIDS inescapably bisects the book and shadows the sunny assurance of its first half. In a way which now seems superficially shocking but which is in its chronological context wholly understandable, White's earliest reference to the "mysterious and usually fatal affliction" comes as a casual aside in a 1983 essay called, with grim retrospective irony, **"Paradise Found"**, which also contains his blandest affirmations of an "easygoing fraternity of sex and sociability"; much more shrewdly prescient (and, in the same piece, starkly contrasting) is an analysis of the way gay liberation modulated, or became corrupted, into gay consumerism:

> From the perspective of the present, we can now look back at the beginning of gay liberation and observe that it flowered exactly at the moment when gays became identified, by themselves and by their market, as a distinct group of affluent and avid consumers. . . . Unfortunately, today this rampant and ubiquitous consumerism not only characterises gay spending habits but also infects attitudes towards sexuality: gays rate each other quantitatively according to age, physical dimensions and income: and all too many gays consume and dispose of each other, as though the very act of possession brought about instant obsolescence.

It's a stern and uncharacteristically sour note for such a cheerful immoralist to strike.

But by the time we reach **"Esthetics and Loss"**, the predominant tone has deepened from celebration into elegy, approaching just that Conradian darkness which White's younger self couldn't imagine in a gay writer. This essay is one of his finest, with raw personal experience and writerly eloquence in an exact creative balance, and it catches the puzzling essence of a moment when "I, for one, feel repatriated to my lonely adolescence, the time when I was alone with my writing and I felt weird about being queer". Human life had suddenly become mysteriously and incurably evanescent in a way which would have been unthinkable five years earlier: "It's just like the Middle Ages", says White, though we might equally recall the impact, at once traumatic and creative, of syphilis on Renaissance England, a psychological effect memorably compared by A. P. Rossiter to that of myxomatosis on a thinking rabbit. White argues that a "writer or visual artist responds to this fragility as both a theme and as a practical limitation—no more projects that require five years to finish", which is possibly an over-literal view: the proximity of AIDS might just as well spur the urgency which dissuades the artist from deferring the start of the *magnum opus* until tomorrow. Thus, when he writes (in **"Out of the Closet, on to the Bookshelf"**), "The grotesque irony is that at the very moment so many writers are threatened with extinction gay literature is healthy and flourishing as never before", he accurately records but inaccurately interprets a phenomenon which is less a "grotesque irony" than an exact instance, of a kind understood by Shakespeare and his contemporaries, of the way in which art invariably works—with the dance of love and death as its oldest, most enduring theme.

Strangely and perhaps heroically, White sustains his equable stance of urbane generosity almost to the end of *The Burning Library*, only rarely revealing the kind of helpless fury which is provoked by a partly self-inflicted injury:

> In America gays have been ghettoized or so thoroughly identified with AIDS that their opinions on all other topics seem irrelevant to the public at large. Nor does such a public exist, since we're parceled out into so many special-interest, single-issue factions.

After so many well-tempered pages, this burst of impatience seems long overdue. Regrettably it doesn't spill over into the critical pieces, which end with an over indulgent essay on Hervé Guibert, who is mildly described as belonging to "a tough Continental line of writers": though he lacks the "charity and emotion" of Larry Kramer or Paul Monette and the "psychological realism and moral exactitude" of Adam Mars-Jones, he scrapes by on "rhetorical panache", which sounds like a poor third. As so often in the book, White's admirable capacity for sympathetic understanding not only inhibits his critical judgment but actually weakens the case being argued. Yet when he writes on a figure of unquestionable literary significance, such as Isherwood, he is reduced to tongue-tied reverence: *A Single Man* is indeed "one of the first and best novels of the modern gay liberation movement", but the claim is so blandly formulated that it reads curiously like an undervaluation. In taking his critical bearings from Arthur Symons—who, he says, "stood in an equally benign relationship to his subject and to his reader"—White runs the risk of his advocacy becoming indistinguishable from his goodwill.

Although the essays on literary subjects make up the weaker strand of *The Burning Library*, they nevertheless form an essential part of its untidy, intricate fabric. If the book seems unresolved, a patchwork of modulating and sometimes contradictory views, that indicates its fidelity to the peculiar quarter-century which it chronicles; it concludes with a typically passionate, ramshackle speech given in November 1993, in which White argues against "the whole concept of a canon" and for "the full implications of pluri-culturalism", upbeat to the end. It is a further measure of the age's strangeness that White's tolerant generosity should now seem so much more disquieting than his intermittent anger and despair.

Edmund White with Ryan Prout (interview date Fall 1994)

SOURCE: "From the Stonewall to *The Burning Library*," in *The Harvard Gay and Lesbian Review*, Vol. I, No. 4, Fall, 1994, pp. 5-8.

[*In the following interview, White discusses his career and his life as a gay writer.*]

Cambridge University scholar Ryan Prout interviewed the renowned author while Edmund White was in England last May. White's **The Burning Library,** *a collection of his major essays over a 25-year period, has just been published by Knopf. This event offered an occasion for Mr. White, who lives in Paris, to reflect on his work to date as well as his life as a gay writer and expatriate.*

[*Prout:*] *The most recent Cambridge University* LesBiGay Newsletter *describes you as a "queer hero" and suggests that you might be "A much better model for Cambridge grads than anything the present Cabinet has to offer." How do you feel about being read as a hero and about being a gay role model?*

[White:] I'm 54 years old now, and the rate at which time flies by can seem quite amazing, particularly if you don't have children and so you don't have this constant reminder that you're aging. Although it's now twenty-five years ago, it seems like only yesterday that the Stonewall uprising took place in 1969. Just by accident I was in that uprising and almost immediately after it took place I wrote a letter to Anne and Alfred Corn who were friends of mine living in Paris at the time. In this letter, which is reproduced in *The Violet Quill Reader,* I described the whole event as I saw it then in a kind of semi-comical way. I certainly had no idea that Stonewall was going to be a great turning point in gay history or history at all, or in my own life. But it *did* have consequences.

I moved to Rome right away, and when I came back a year later I joined a gay consciousness-raising group. I started off both as a writer and as a person thinking that my experience was so peculiar that it wouldn't mean anything to anybody, and now I've ended up seeing myself being almost banally representative of my generation of gay men. It seems to me as if almost everything I do reflects what everybody in my generation is doing, including being HIV positive.

I've avoided that question about being a hero because I don't have any sense of that at all. I think this is because, firstly, I live in France where there's no such thing as a really vital gay movement, and secondly, since I'm not very well known there anyway, I've been protected from the consequences of being a hero, if that's what I am.

I just watched again your interview with Jeremy Isaacs and from that I had the impression that you'd returned to America.

I did go back in 1991 to teach at Brown University. Then, when he became ill and we had no health care for my lover, Hubert Sorin, who just died about six weeks ago of AIDS, we had to move back to France, which was no hardship anyway. We wanted to be back. So I only stayed a year-and-a-half in America.

As **The Burning Library** *shows, you're someone who's deeply immersed in French culture and you've said that from an early age you had always dreamt of going to France. Why is that?*

It not only seemed like a great intellectual center, but I think, for me, it seemed like a place where bohemianism and intellectuality and a certain kind of glossy "high society" came together, and indeed they do. In other words, I think in America you find rather dowdy professors who can only talk about their own field and who have no general conversation and no notion at all that what they're doing might be of interest to nonspecialists, and then you have rich people who are very dull and never read a book, and then you have bohemians who are usually not very sure of themselves any more because they've been so overshadowed, if they're painters, for instance, by the marketplace. It's as if whatever bohemian values there were in America, let's say from the beginning of the century to about 1955 or 1960, got wiped out by the values of the marketplace. But in France, it seems to me that the strange confluence of these various elements still exists, a kind of worldly sophistication that joins with a real dedication to the arts and to reading and to making art, and especially to consuming art. I like that about France.

You've also given the impression in previous interviews that it's much easier to be gay in France because you don't have to be gay, that is, a gay life as such doesn't exist there. When I mentioned to a gay acquaintance that you had said this, he suggested that though that may be the case for a well known writer from abroad, it certainly isn't the case for French people themselves, especially those living in provincial France.

I don't think you need to be famous or a writer to have a very nice gay life in France—that is, a gay life of the kind that I like, which is one in which you're oftentimes integrated into the straight world. Now, when I go back to America and I attend an all-male dinner party, it always strikes me as weird. In France, what seems to be more usual, to give you an example, is the kind of dinner party I gave last night where I think all but one of the men was gay and all the women were straight. That seems to be what usually happens.

In your essay **"The Joys of Gay Life"** *you say that one of the advantages to being gay is that we're introspective. Comparing your approach to dealing with the AIDS crisis to, say, someone like Derek Jarman's, I wanted to ask you if an introspective attitude to HIV can enhance gay culture without reducing it to a single issue, which is what you say we must be careful to avoid.*

I was one of the five founding members of the Gay Men's Health Crisis in America as well as its first president. What I realized very quickly was that if I remained an AIDS activist I would never write another word. When I look at Larry Kramer I realize that he is a hero. He really has dedicated himself to AIDS activism, a choice which I think is a noble one and one which meant that there are quite a few books which he might have written which he hasn't. I made the other choice. I think what I've been trying to do with the Genet biography, for instance, is precisely to remind people that gay culture can be about things other than AIDS. I remember reading Richard Ellman's *Oscar Wilde* at a fairly early point in the AIDS crisis. It came to me as a wonderful breath of fresh air because I thought "It's great to be reminded of this important cultural hero who lived long before the AIDS era." Genet, though he died in 1986 and made one or two remarks about AIDS, basically never thought about it and it didn't touch his life.

When I heard you talking about the biography when it was published in this country, it struck me that the fact that you'd dedicated so much time to producing a work on the life of someone else was in its own way just as heroic a gesture as that of someone like Larry Kramer.

Thank you. Larry Kramer was somewhat vexed with me at the time although now I think he's forgiven me. He thought that if you were gay and were a writer or in any way a spokesperson you should feel obliged to talk about AIDS and nothing but AIDS one hundred percent of the time. But I had more the take that I think you're suggesting, which is that it was important that gay culture not be reduced to a single issue. Now I'm writing a novel in which I deal with both the 70's and the 80's, that's to say with the periods both before and after the outbreak of AIDS. So, I suppose there's a kind of natural trajectory to the book. But I'm not really writing it chronologically. I write about the earlier period and then I skip forward to the present. It's a kind of mélange of "before" and "after" because I feel that either period is unendurable alone. If you just wrote about everybody having lots of sex in the 70's and ended a book there, which is what I originally intended to do, I think it would be intolerable. And if you wrote a book only about everyone dying, I think that would also be pretty grim. Something that I do constantly in my own thoughts is to mix the two periods, and the book's form reproduces my own mental experience to produce what I hope will be an interesting approach.

When I first learned the title of the new anthology of your essays and critical work I was reminded of something that Bulgakov said, which was that the one thing that doesn't burn is a document. Would you say something about your views on writing and testimony?

I've heard various sources for the expression on which the title is based. An old French woman who's about 80 now told me that her mother used to tell her when she was a girl, "You must pay attention to what I'm saying because when I'm dead it's as though a library will have burned." And some French people say "*Quand une vieille personne meurt, c'est comme une bibiiothèque qui brûle.*" Other people have told me that the expression comes from Africa and yet other people ascribe it to a particular African writer but they can't remember which one. Marina Warner sent me a citation from a Caribbean woman poet whose use of the phrase suggested it was a local saying. But in any event, wherever it comes from, it seems to be quite a common expression. It suggests that the writer's job is to try to take down some of the experiences of other people before they all go up in flames. And I think, having lived through the AIDS era and having witnessed many of my friends leaving no testimonials behind, I have felt very strongly the oblivion of mortality and that the writer, maybe, can push that back a little bit, at least for a short time.

You once characterized the life cycle of Gay Liberation as being like a May fly's: "Oppressed in the 50's, liberated in the 60's, exalted in the 70's and wiped out in the 80's."

I think that was hasty. It hasn't really been wiped out at all. When I said that in 1988 or thereabouts, it was before I went back to America, and so I wasn't aware of the tremendously vital upsurge of gay culture there that had been stimulated precisely by AIDS activism. In France, Gay Liberation has pretty well died out. Like feminism and other liberation movements, it is subject to a rapid cycle of being "à la mode" and then "démodé." Now you find that in France if you say you're a gay liberationist people will sneer and ask, "How can you possibly do something so démodé?" Identification with the feminist movement provokes the same response. There is no feminism in France. Since they're completely forgotten there, French people can't believe that writers like Luce Irigaray or Hélène Cixous are famous in America. Even Julia Kristeva is seen differently depending on which country you're in. So, living in France I just wasn't aware that gay culture was alive and thriving in America. Now I am aware of it, but I'm not entirely happy with it, as the last essay in the book, **"The Personal is Political,"** suggests.

Obviously, chronology is important in the way the anthology is organized. One of the essays is about Goytisolo and, to ask a Goytisolian question, should we read the collection backwards or forwards? Which way are we going?

I suppose it depends on how much you've thought about these things. To some readers, the beginning could seem terribly basic and they'd want to skip ahead. It's interesting to me that young people, your age, whom I thought knew all about the history of gay liberation and would take it for granted, were surprised that as early on as the beginning of the 70's we were already thinking about all these same issues that are still being debated today. I think that when people see the early dates for some of those essays—**"The Gay Philosopher,"** for example—they're amused to notice that we were already debating gay identity in 1970.

What struck me in reading the early essays was just how late it was in terms of general modern history that things began to change so that 25 years later it would be acceptable for someone like me to say to the powers that be at Cambridge, for example, I want to study questions of homosexuality. I was surprised to realize in reading your essays that it's only such a short time ago that this would have been completely out of the question.

Yes, it's amazing how quickly things have evolved. But there are still many contradictions. My boyfriend Hubert was astonished that I was hired by Brown University because I was homosexual, and that in the same town where the university is located, Providence, Rhode Island, you could be beaten up for being homosexual. He said, "In France we would have neither one nor the other; there's no fag bashing but neither would you ever be allowed to talk about your personal life in the classroom." I think most French people still see homosexuality as being something strictly personal which you shouldn't mention one way or the other, just as you shouldn't mention how many mistresses you have if you're heterosexual.

You talk about writers like Marguerite Yourcenar and Nietzsche, who don't so much evolve as endlessly tease out themes set very early on in their lives. Do you see your own writing as evolutionary? What have been the most significant changes in the twenty-four years of writing covered by the anthology?

I think the evolving consciousness is reflected more in my fiction than in my non-fiction. My first two novels, **Forgetting Elena** and **Nocturnes for the King of Naples,** were, broadly speaking, *avant garde* or non-realistic novels. **Forgetting Elena** wasn't even openly homosexual, only covertly homosexual and **Nocturnes for the King of Naples** was similarly very exalted and poetic in its tone. I think it's only really with **A Boy's Own Story** that I began to write simply and autobiographically about my own experience and about homosexuality. I like to think that I kept in a lot of the complexities found in the earlier novels in treating that theme. A young writer today would probably start off with **A Boy's**

Own Story; and a lot of people assume it was my first novel, when in fact it was the fourth or fifth.

I think it took me quite a while to reach homosexuality as the primary subject matter of a novel. It was partly a question of my own need to undo a strictly personal reticence in talking about that material. I was able to do this in my writing. In *Nocturnes,* for instance, I dealt with the problems I had with my father on a fantasy level and translated them into extremely different terms that would have been unrecognizable to him. Then, in *A Boy's Own Story,* which I wrote after his death, I was able to tackle him as a subject much more directly, simply and factually. In the same way, I think *Caracole* was an attempt to look at the interrelationship between sex and power, but again on a fantasy level in a so-called heterosexual world. It's not a gay book. After *Caracole,* in *The Beautiful Room is Empty,* I was able to approach the same subject matter, sex and politics, sex and power, but homosexually and autobiographically.

In other words, I would say that oftentimes I seem to need to go through a stage of trying out new material on a fantasy level before I can deal with it autobiographically. But I like both kinds of writing. When I started off as a writer I was very impressed by a remark of Valéry's (Gide said the same thing in his *Journals*): He said that if you were a good writer you should lose with each new book the admirers you had gained with the preceding one; in other words, you should be radically changing each time you write. I felt that people would be dazzled by how virtuoso I was and how I never was repeating myself. But, in fact, everybody now discusses my *oeuvre,* tiny as it is, as though it's totally coherent, which surprises me because I don't see the coherence myself. But I'm happy that people discuss it at all.

From your later essays I have the impression that you think the essentialist-constructionist debate is fairly boring and stagnant. At the same time, though, there seems to be a conflict between positions within that debate in your own writing, a conflict which appears to be quite fruitful for you. Bergman writes that for you "The body is the only way we can have a sense of our being in the world," yet you yourself, when you're talking about the ad hoc-ness of gay living arrangements, for example, say that because these arrangements have no name they're almost invisible. The contest between an ontology of language and an ontology of the body seems to be an important one in your work.

It's funny because I was just talking to some French people about a similar contradiction that I think you can find in the work of Barthes. It seems to me that he's always holding out for the body as though it's something that you can oppose to the *doxa* and that doesn't seem to me to be rational. But now you're saying to me that I do the same and I think you're perfectly right. I suppose we all have some Edenic

notion of something that's going to be unmodified by culture, of something that remains primal and instinctual. Although we've all been trained not to think that way, what often happens is that the target is shifted in order to posit some new thing as the element which precedes culture, as that which is nature. David Bergman may find that process inflecting my writing, but I myself don't see it. What I find is more of an irrational attraction to beauty, to physical beauty. I think that I find beauty to be a self-evident value.

Last night I had a young German woman staying with me at my apartment in Paris. She's a Genet scholar, very Protestant and very German. When I said something about it being obvious that people would fall in love with somebody as beautiful as X she said "How can you say that!" She was quite outraged and she seemed to find that perspective almost immoral. I said, "But you're an artist, aren't you, and don't you respond to beauty?" "Yes," she said, "But intellectual beauty or artistic beauty." My response to that was to say, "But physical beauty is the *same kind* of beauty." I'm a Platonist in that sense, I guess. I do see a coherence between all forms of beauty. And I find it strange that American politically correct people should accuse me of being a "looksist"—that's their word—as though that were some terrible folly that needed to be eradicated. I have fallen in love with ugly people and I can probably find the beauty in most people. I can even be sexually indifferent to physical beauty but I will always respect it.

In **The Burning Library** *you talk about how those gay people are still imprisoned in so many ways. I wondered if you would expand on that idea and perhaps talk a bit about the differences between America and Britain where gay oppression is concerned.*

What happens, I think, is that there's a small group composed of people who are self-identified as gay, who are usually from a middle-class background, who have independent means and who step up the rhetoric. They will say "We must all be gay and in very evolved ways with a very high consciousness" and so on. The trouble with that elevated level of rhetoric is that it leaves behind in the dust the millions of people who are still coming out. I'm actually going out now with a 20-year-old Englishman who's from a working class background and he's completely tormented by the question of coming out. He flies into a terrible fit of anxiety if anybody suspects him of being gay. Of course, he chose the wrong person to go out with! Again and again I see this same battle being fought because a young gay man coming out today isn't being brought up by gay people. He's being brought up by working-class parents in, say, Hackney, so he's got to deal with their values and he's got to work through gay history all over again for himself.

I think we forget that the conservative values of society have to be faced again and again by each generation. It can be dangerous when gay leaders have evolved so far that they've lost touch with this very primary coming out experience. Some evolved and self-identified gay people are very bored with the whole idea of coming out because we've heard too much about it, but it will always be there as a theme.

You say quite defiantly at one point that nobody has the right to deny anybody else's feelings or his or her own account of them. Do you think the way that mainstream society reacts to gay people's experience of grief is another demonstration of how some people's feelings continue to be less respectable than others?

I started seeing a psychotherapist about four weeks before my lover died. He died six weeks ago and I'm still seeing the therapist. One of the things he keeps saying to me is that all the friends around me, most of whom are heterosexual, aren't letting me grieve in the way I want to grieve. He says they either think it's sacrilegious that I'm already going out with somebody else or they think that I'm not being sufficiently courageous if I break down and start crying. In other words, you have to follow the rhythm that the dominant environment dictates. My therapist said "To hell with them, you really have to grieve in the way that you want to and in the way that feels natural to you." I only cite my personal experience there because it's the one I know best, but maybe everyone who grieves finds that there's a program to it. Interestingly, I thought, the therapist told me, "Well, writing is a defense." I dwelt on that idea for a week and it occurred to me that perhaps it's true that writers are somehow able to distance their feelings through writing about them. But, on the other hand, if you are a writer you are obliged to be honest. You can't repeat the standard myths, like the one of the dead beloved that most people resort to. You have to keep even your resentments alive and you probably have to entertain the negative thoughts longer than most people would feel comfortable doing. In other words, if you're a writer I think you take into account and entertain for longer than anybody else would the feelings of abandonment and of anger that you have towards the person who's left you, by dying.

Do you think you will write about your partner?

I'm very eager to, actually, and I'm already taking lots of notes. Joe Brainard is a wonderful American writer who's about to die. He wrote something called *I Remember* which inspired Georges Perec to write a book called *Je me souviens.* Now I'm doing something I think of as "Je me souviens Hubert." This is simply a notebook for myself in which I put down all the things I remember about him. Just the little things, like the stories he would tell me about his aunt. But again, it's an example of *The Burning Library:* it's the details which count, which keep someone alive.

If you had to write a Ph.D. thesis on the works of Edmund White, what would it be about?

About somebody who was subjected to a tension arising from two very different sets of expectations: one set came from a literary community that wasn't particularly gay-identified and the other came from a gay community that wasn't particularly literary. I think the tension has been a fruitful one and an unusual one for a writer. It wasn't until Nabokov praised my first book that a lot of literary people who had previously shown no interest in my work and who certainly weren't interested in homosexuality began to think that I might be a writer worth watching. I was very aware of that. It took me years to get anything published at all, so I was enormously grateful to Nabokov for the interest that he had shown in my work because it got me started as a writer and I was already well into my thirties when that happened. The difficulties I'd had in getting started and Nabokov's interest were very real influences on the way I thought about the work that I was then in the process of doing.

On the other hand, after *Nocturnes,* I was already very much writing for a gay audience that had almost no books at that point. This was an audience eager for me to write in a kind of programmatic way, presenting positive gay heroes, something I always resisted. But I was aware of it. To me that is what would make an interesting thesis, to show somebody at the crux between a set of aesthetic expectations and a set of political expectations from two entirely different groups.

Morris Dickstein (review date 23 July 1995)

SOURCE: "Intimations of Mortality," in *The New York Times Book Review,* July 23, 1995, p. 6.

[*In the following review, Dickstein discusses White's* Skinned Alive *and asserts that, "In writing about AIDS yet keeping it at bay, he has turned a mortal threat into a surprising source of literary strength."*]

Among gay writers of his generation. Edmund White has emerged as the most versatile man of letters. A cosmopolitan writer with a deep sense of tradition, he has bridged the gap between gay subcultures and a broader literary audience. Besides five elegant novels, he has written a sex manual, a travel book about gay America, an award-winning biography of Jean Genet, a fine collection of literary essays and now a volume of mostly autobiographical stories that contains some of his best work.

Born in 1940, raised in the Midwest by parents originally form Texas, Mr. White spent two decades in New York before decamping to Paris in the early 1980's and his stories deal vividly with all three worlds—a young man growing up in Middle America, making his way uncertainly as an artist and homosexual in New York, and struggling with the depredations of aging and the AIDS virus as an expatriate in Europe. Yet over the years his style, his very conception of fiction, has changed even more strikingly than the settings he writes about.

Before the 1970's, when direct professions of homosexuality were taboo, writers from Oscar Wilde to Cocteau and Genet made their mark with works that were often theatrical, oblique, florid and artificial. The strategies of concealment many gay people used in their lives were turned into richly layered artistic strategies by gifted writers, choreographers, directors and set designers. For the writers, wit and paradox became more important than sincerity, since sincerity meant self-acceptance (which could be difficult) and self-exposure (which could be dangerous); style, baroque fantasy and sensuous detail were disguises that suited them far better than verisimilitude or realism. Oscar Wilde built a whole Nietzschean esthetic on "lying," and only devolved into plain speaking (in *De Profundis*) when his whole life had gone to pieces.

At a time when the confessional mode was in vogue and the plain style of Raymond Carver was on the horizon, Mr. White stepped forth as a mandarin esthete, winning applause from literary elders as different as Christopher Isherwood, Gore Vidal, Susan Sontag and Nabokov himself, who was little given to promiscuous enthusiasm.
—*Morris Dickstein*

Edmund White's early books were no exception. After years of working for Time Inc. while trying his luck as a playwright, he brought out two lushly conceived Nabokovian novels that were as elaborate as they were emotionally distant. At a time when the confessional mode was in vogue and the plain style of Raymond Carver was on the horizon, Mr. White stepped forth as a mandarin esthete, winning applause from literary elders as different as Christopher Isherwood, Gore Vidal, Susan Sontag and Nabokov himself, who was little given to promiscuous enthusiasm.

But great changes were in the air. A gay liberation movement had emerged from the Stonewall uprising of 1969, and Mr. White set out to report on it in vigorous, personal prose for *Christopher Street,* a gay magazine, and in *States of Desire: Travels in Gay America.* Thanks to the freer atmosphere, he argued in that book, the old stratagems of indirection and concealment were less necessary, though he

still wondered whether "art at its best should be evasive and quirky." Soon writers like Armistead Maupin and David Leavitt would be dealing with gay relationships in a surprisingly matter-of-fact way, as Gore Vidal and Tennessee Williams had begun to do in the late 1940's.

Mr. White's descent into journalistic writing and his cross-country encounters with gay liberation enlarged his sense of American life and dramatically altered his fiction. His next novel felt like finely honed personal history. Crisp and fresh in its language, unguarded in its autobiographical simplicity, *A Boy's Own Story* was a touching evocation of the childhood of a misfit. But its more raunchy sequel, *The Beautiful Room is Empty*—his entry into the "City of Night" / "Our Lady of Flowers" sweepstakes—put introspection aside for the shock value of cruising public toilets and masochistic self-abasement. Though beautifully written, it was frighteningly hollow.

Darkened by illness, the stories in *Skinned Alive* give up pornographic detail for emotional honesty. Nearly all belong to what Mr. White himself (in his Genet biography) calls "auto-fiction": edited memories that consciously blur the line between invention and recollection, novel and memoir, story and inventory. The stories have the slightly shapeless quality of real life and the haphazard way we tend to remember it. Where Mr. White's earlier novels were highly patterned and oblique, these loosely structured stories unfold casually; their drift conveys his sense of gay sexual relationships as impermanent. "I had never been happy in love," says a character who is clearly a stand-in for the author; fidelity is "as barbaric as female circumcision." Now the frantic hedonism of the 1970's is a distant rumor. Mr. White himself is H.I.V. positive, and many of the stories take on the elegiac tone of someone looking back over a life that's slipping through his fingers, reliving old pleasures and disappointments, conjuring up the people who really mattered to him.

The first piece, **"Pyrography,"** could be an outtake from *A Boy's Own Story.* It's a glimpse of the 1950's that sketches the emotional complications of a camping trip taken by a shy gay teen-ager with two straight buddies. In **"Reprise,"** an older boy whom the narrator had a crush on at the age of 14—which led his divorced parents to send him to a shrink to "cure" him—reappears 40 years later and goes to bed with him, just once. In **"Watermarked,"** the reprise takes place only in recollection. "I've written various versions of my youth but I've always left my first real lover," the story begins. "He's been stamped onto every page of my adult life as a watermark, though sometimes faintly."

Some longer AIDS stories avoid this breezy tone, but they are rarely somber. In one sense nearly all these pieces are AIDS stories, because it's the feeling of mortality that drives the writer to pull together his fugitive memories. But Mr.

White sidesteps the tragic note for a more bemused and rueful tone—a French tone, ironic, never at a loss, always worldly and knowing. **"Watermarked"** ends with a long letter to the old friend and lover, in which AIDS is merely the background music that will usher the two men from the stage. ("You and I are both positive and our prospects aren't exactly brilliant.") Call it denial. Or call it Mr. White's essayistic bent for intellectual comedy, his refusal to let the disease dominate his imagination.

But in the best stories, like **"Running on Empty," "Skinned Alive," "An Oracle"** and **"Palace Days,"** the author sometimes gives way to a sadness that reverberates more deeply than in anything else he has written. These are not AIDS stories but stories about people with AIDS, not so much wrestling with awful symptoms as coping with what remains of their lives. Writing some months ago in *The New Yorker*, Arlene Croce questioned whether the horrors of the disease, by eliciting a predictable pathos or rage, were not somehow inimical to art. The answer is simply that, like the grotesque inhumanities of the Holocaust, they make real art more elusive, a more terrible challenge. Mr. White wins this desperate wager by keeping AIDS darkly present yet peripheral to the Proustian endgame of living in the moment while reclaiming the past.

Skinned Alive is the right phrase for the painful, terminal exposure and hard-won candor of these stories. A sick man returns to visit his family in Texas, fearful of slipping back into their orbit if his illness worsens. Two men, no longer lovers but still living together, find they have each other when illness strikes all around them. A man goes to Greece to get over the death of his partner and falls desperately in love with a young Greek from whom he is buying sex, and who knows far better than he does that this feeling is a delusion. Abandoned by his French lover, a writer gives us a wickedly witty story about him, the story we're reading, complete with anatomical detail and cutting comparisons of French and American manners, in and out of bed. Though AIDS puts heavy pressure on these stories, each is essentially about people getting by, still playing the mating game or recalling the carefree way it was once played.

The sense of an ending gives the best of these stories an almost unearthly beauty. Though I was put off by the characters' "ideological horror of marriage as a model" and their "unreflecting appetite for pleasure," I was all the more moved by the sustaining quality of friendship in their lives. Mr. White's subject has always taken the permutations of desire and the impermanence of love, when AIDS exaggerates but friendship allays. Spending the last of many vacations with a dying friend, "Mark heard the radio and the typewriter, these faint life signals Joshua was emitting," Mr. White writes in **"Palace Days":** "He wanted to know how to enjoy these days without clasping them so tightly he'd stifle the pleasure. But he didn't want to drug himself on the moment either and miss out on what was happening to him. He was losing his best friend, the witness to his life. The skill for enjoying a familiar pleasure about to disappear was hard to acquire. . . . Knowing how to appreciate the rhythms of these last casual moments—to cherish them while letting them stay casual—demanded a new way of navigating time."

In passages like this, Edmund White the elegist, the essayist, the autobiographer and the novelist come together. These are fragments of memory, not tales with traditional beginnings and ends, but their anecdotal shape provides a much-needed narrative frame, and the constant presence of death gives the writing a heft and seriousness often missing before. This epidemic has heightened the immediacy of his work without washing out its human texture. In writing about AIDS yet keeping it at bay, he has turned a mortal threat into a surprising source of literary strength.

James Wood (review date 24 August 1995)

SOURCE: "Apologising," in *London Review of Books,* August 24, 1995, pp. 12-13.

[*In the following review, Wood discusses White's* The Burning Library *and* Skinned Alive.]

Edmund White has always struggled between appeasing the gods of his art and paying off the princelings of politics. Endearingly, and sometimes infuriatingly, he insists on doing both, and the result often leaves his pockets rather empty. Thus in his book of selected journalism, *The Burning Library,* he can move from a sublime celebration of Nabokov's 'greatness' to a demand that 'even the hierarchy inherent in the concept of a canon must be jettisoned.' It is how he is able, in a piece about Robert Mapplethorpe, to argue that 'passion, like art, is always irresponsible, useless, an end in itself, regulated by its own impulses and nothing else' and to propose in another that the best gay writing should be a combination of confession, reportage and witness.

His deepest aesthetic impulse, one suspects, is for a priestly withdrawal, surpliced in the vestments of concealment; but his heart, his politics and his obvious humanity keep him very much a senator of the loud city-state that is gay aesthetics and politics.

White's journalism is often strange because it appears to borrow crazy opinions without wanting to own them. Its pulse rate is slow. It is always humane, intelligent, but without serration. There is hardly a critical word for anyone in *The Burning Library.* Like his fiction, it is loose, free, occasionally idle and sometimes beautiful (White has a Nabokovian capacity for the splash of metaphor). Unlike his fiction, it has no talent for intimacy. His style is not very natural. The sentences refuse to lie down, and often he turns the page into a lecture hall. Even the best essay in the book, his fine celebration of Nabokov, has a kind of aural clatter: 'I may also seem to be saying that if *Lolita,* the supreme novel of love in the 20th century, is a parody of earlier love novels, we should not be surprised, since love itself—the very love you and I experience in real life—is also a parody of earlier novels . . . If I made such an assertion, or if I attributed it to Nabokov, I would be subscribing to the approach to literature and art advanced by Roland Barthes.' White's journalistic style is frequently lustreless, in striking contrast to the gloss of his fictional prose: 'In another passage the harsh power of clichés is invoked.' He can be pedagogical while being platitudinous: Christina Stead 'resists the evil reductionism of our culture and never "totalises" the self (an ugly but useful word)'; 'In great fiction the language is not only satisfying in itself, but it also fulfils larger purposes of design.'

This suggests that White is not a very natural critic, which matters little because he is so clearly a natural writer. His reports on gay identity and sexuality collected in this book are generally much more robust and engaging than his criticism of other writers. They tell a story—both personal and collective—of tentative beginnings, discovered confidence, sexual freedom and increasing politicisation. Aesthetically, the shift of the book is away from the high art of Nabokov towards a literature of witness and anti-canonical sweat. We watch a civilian militarise himself.

In the first piece in the book, **'The Gay Philosopher'**, written in the late Sixties, White provides a journalistic account, in effect, of the world of his autobiographical novel of childhood, *A Boy's Own Story,* when he writes of the damage done to homosexuals by society's determination to see their sexuality as an illness, a crime or a sin. White was 29, and had himself been in 'corrective' analysis. Obviously if homosexuals regard themselves as "sick" and most of them I know do, that belief cannot help but have a disastrous effect on their self-esteem.' He toys with a notion that only a few years later will become axiomatic, that of the homosexual 'as a member of a minority group, like the Jew or Negro or possibly the worker. Employing this metaphor can produce a whole range of fascinating insights.' Eight years later, in his essay **'Fantasia on the Seventies'**, White is appraising a decade in which, apparently, only half of the Sixties capital had made any interest: there is lots of sex, but political militancy has proved unsuccessful. 'Sexual permissiveness became a form of numbness, as rigidly codified as the old morality. Street cruising gave way to half-clothed quickies.' Life was psychically easier—'We don't hate ourselves so much,—but 'gay liberation as a militant programme has turned out to be ineffectual, perhaps impossible.' In

1983, as Aids is just beginning its destruction, White writes in **'Paradise Found'** that 'today, 14 years after the Stonewall Uprising and the beginning of gay liberation, there is a great deal more self-acceptance among gays, even a welcome show of arrogance.'

It is the last moment of political serenity in the book. By the late Eighties, the garden gates have been shut. White writes elegiacally that 'what seems unquestionable is that ten years ago sex was for gay men a reason for being. Not simple, humdrum coupling, but a new principle of adhesiveness.' But all this has disappeared, and White's aesthetics, politics, even diction, quicken their step. In literary terms, this is not always very attractive or coherent. In **'Aesthetics and Loss'**, written in 1987, White proposes a gay art about Aids which will 'witness to the cultural moment', and which must be tactful, angry and without humour, for 'humour, like melodrama, is an assertion of bourgeois values.' 'Cultural moment', 'bourgeois values'—White's language begins its theoretical apprenticeship. It has ceased to belong to him. When it is not in theoretical uniform, it is in ragged civvies. Attending, in 1991, an Out/Write Writers' Conference in San Francisco, he writes disapprovingly of canon formation, 'the process by which powerful critics select a few books to become classics, to be taught in college curricula and earmarked as the essential books of our civilisation'. 'Earmarked'—the word itself is telling.

The slide away from 'irresponsible' aesthetics towards responsible politics culminates in the last essay in the book, **'The Personal is Political'**, written in 1993. A coda was provided a few months ago in this journal, when White wrote about the importance of a new kind of gay writing—'autofiction'—which combines documentary witness and sexual confession, and which runs from Proust to the late novelist and autobiographer Hervé Guibert. Both essays propose a separatism: 'If previously I'd written for an older European heterosexual woman, an ideal reader who helped me to screen out in-jokes and preaching to the converted, I now pictured my reader as another gay man.' Of the new autofiction—a combination of 'an *apologia pro sua vita* and a sexologist's case history'—he notes that the 'defining characteristics . . . are that it is unapologetic, that it is addressed primarily to gay rather than straight readers, and that it conceives of homosexuals as an oppressed minority group rather than as victims of a pathology'.

These 'characteristics' are then filled with aesthetic gold and dropped to anchor the entire argument. The condition of this fiction is taken to be an aesthetic quality. The artist 'is a saint who writes his own life'. Confession is seen as in itself something good in art. Proust, for example, is praised for writing, in a documentary way, about cruising, male brothels and sadomasochism, and praised for halo-ing his own martyrdom: 'Proust recasts his own sexuality, conceals his Jewish origins and ascribes a social importance to himself that apparently he did not enjoy, but he nevertheless does not fail to portray himself as a martyr to love and to art.' Note how everything in Proust other than confession is made to seem a little sneaky ('conceals his Jewish origins') or aesthetically beside the point. White the artist, the unmolested soul, does not believe a word of this—or did not. In his essay on Nabokov, written ten years ago, he praised the 'deliciously slippery' concealments of Nabokov's autobiographical art, and praised in Proust not his quality of confession but its opposite: 'Many writers proceed by creating characters who are parodies of themselves or near-misses or fun-house distortions . . . One thinks of Proust, who gave his dilettantism to Swann, his homosexuality to Charlus, his love of his family to the narrator and his hatred of his family to Mlle Vinteuil . . . In this sense (but this strict sense only) every novel, including Nabokov's, is autobiographical.' It appears that the strictness has relaxed itself over the decade.

This is not the only contradiction in White's late position. In his essay **'Out of the Closet'**, written in 1991, he appeals to the idea of literary universality when he writes that AIDS has stimulated literary production by gay men because it has made them 'more reflective on the great questions of love, death, morality and identity, the very preoccupations that have always animated serious fiction and poetry'. But in his most recent journalism, universality is mocked.

White complains that minor gay art is called 'gay' while major gay art is called 'classic' or 'canonical'. There is muttering against the bourgeois recuperation of all dissident literatures (and of gay literature in particular) through an appeal to universalism . . . At this point it might be worth mentioning that whereas identification with an oppressed minority is seen as limiting ("gay writer") no limitation is assumed if the individual belongs to a dominant group ("white writer", or "heterosexual painter", for instance).'

But there is a difference between 'identification' with a group and 'belonging' to it—the very distinction White explores in an earlier essay when he writes that 'if one is gay, one is always in a crucial relationship to gayness as such, a defining category that is so full it is nearly empty . . . No straight man stands in rapt contemplation of his straightness unless he's an ass . . . No homosexual can take his homosexuality for granted.'

Theoretically, White simply runs from one side of the road to the other, apparently excited that he can interest crowds on both pavements. It makes little sense, yet one of the most attractive qualities of White's writing is its openness to self-contradiction. It is like a water-bed—if one argument is pushed too hard, another pops up somewhere else in the work (which makes it easy for critics . . .). In particular, and most important, his fiction has tended to disobey most of the theories he has been espousing in recent years—which is why he is an interesting writer and Hervé Guibert is not.

Indeed, when his fiction becomes either confessional or documentary—as in the second half of *The Beautiful Room is Empty,* and in some of the stories in *Skinned Alive*—it loses pressure, and becomes uninteresting. When White is documenting, he chokes on cognitive novelties. The strangeness of new encounters is taken to be sufficient for narrative; the descriptive bubble is lost in the exotic pool. This is noticeable elsewhere in writing about gay life—for instance, in the work of Gary Indiana—and tends to emerge as a kind of loose gossip. It may have something to do with the rapidity of certain encounters in gay life (White writes that 'the appeal of gay life for me was that it provided so many *glancing* contacts with other men'), but it is certainly not confined to gay writing, and may be typical of one kind of literary response to late 20th-century American bloat and detail (you can find it almost as an article of faith in the 'blankness' of mimetic apprehension in the work of Bret Easton Ellis and others).

A moment like this occurs in White's essay **'Fantasia on the Seventies',** when he visits a club

> where a go-go boy with a pretty body and bad skin stripped down to his jockey shorts and then peeled those off and tossed them at us. A burly man in the audience clambered up on to the dais and tried to fuck the performer but was, apparently, too drunk to get an erection. After a while we drifted into the back room, which was so dark I never received a sense of its dimensions, although I do remember standing on a platform and staring through the slowly revolving blades of a fan at one naked man fucking another in a cubbyhole.

There are similar scenes in *The Beautiful Room is Empty.* In a lesbian bar, 'a butch entered squiring a blonde whore tottering along on spike heels under dairy-whip hair.' This is certainly 'witness', but it is not literary creation. The language cedes its individuality, and rests on idle formulations ('pretty body', 'burly man') or on a ready-made public language ('butch', 'blonde whore').

Something similar occurs when White writes about sex. The language disappears, becomes familiar, shared, public. This is not, of course, an affliction confined to White (and White writes well about sex as often as he writes ordinarily about it) nor to gay writing. The problem with writing about sex in most fiction by men is that men apparently find it difficult to keep fantasy and wish-fulfilment out of such moments; and that men, apparently, have tediously similar fantasies. Sex is often unwittingly comic in contemporary literature because the act of greatest intimacy is revealed to be the least individual of all our activities, and hence the least private. Sex demonstrates our similarity to each other. Barthes famously said that 'I love you' is a quote; if so, sex is a kind of plagiarism.

All this emerges in White's work—as it does in most writers'—most obviously as repetition. For example, in at least three points in White's work, a hero stands in front of a man and drops his clothes 'in a puddle'. In *A Boy's Own Story,* the narrator imagines a sports teacher masturbating: 'his dark hand pulls open the pajama flap and grabs his penis, which in a moment is as hard as hickory.' In *The Beautiful Room is Empty,* the narrator, having dropped his clothes 'in a puddle', stands in front of a lover and sees 'the hickory-hard straining of this cock'. Elsewhere in the same book, the narrator imagines his 'rock-hard college boy erection'. In **'Pyrography'**, one of the new stories in *Skinned Alive,* we come across 'Howard's erection was so hard it hurt'; later, in the wonderful story **'Reprise'**, about a middle-aged man recalling a botched first love affair, we read: 'I'd been erect so long my penis began to ache, and I could feel a pre-come stain seeping through my khakis.'

White's sexual descriptions tend to resemble each other. There is a conformity. Intriguingly, he writes in one of his essays that so powerfully consuming was sex in the heyday of Seventies gay life that it made artistic activity seem unrewarding: 'Even so, sex was, if not fulfilling, then at least engrossing enough at times to make the pursuit of the toughest artistic goals seem too hard, too much work given the mild returns.' It may be that what White describes as a life-choice happens helplessly in literary terms, at the level of style. The powerful heat of sex burns away rival vapours; so engrossing—so fulfilling—is the evocation of sex that real creative notation disappears and melts into something close to pornography. Pornography, in that a ready-made public sex-language is preferred to an individual literary style; and the human being disappears: 'his stomach, so taut from all his sit-ups a dropped dime would have bounced on it'; 'I met a pretty Korean . . . He'd take it like a man, bite the pillow if I hurt him, and nothing had ever felt quite so good as those small taut muscles under the chamois-soft skin, the colour of cinnamon when it's sprinkled on cappuccino'; 'revealing strong tan calves above crisp ribbed athletic socks'; 'the next morning, lightly silvered in hangover sweat, he finally let me plunge into that strong ass, but not before he'd greased me up with KY'; 'that long flat stomach'; 'extra muscles, the long sexy kind—the interior ones gripping me now . . . The moment I looked at what I was doing to him, I could feel myself ready to explode.' In the new stories, the narrator of **'Reprise'** remembers his first love, 'that big tanned body' and recalls putting 'my slender calf against his massive one, my knobbly knee against his square majestic one'.

Most of the diction is from pornography not literature: 'nothing had ever felt quite so good'; 'ready to explode'; the reliance on the adjective 'sexy', and that telling obliquity 'that strong ass', where 'that' is substituting elegiacally for original descriptive work. Again, this is not a unique weakness of gay writing about sex. What is John Updike's offensive description of a woman as 'poignantly breastless' in *Roger's Version* if not a moment of heterosexual fantasy, simply inverted?

All one needs to do, to verify that such passages are weak stylistically, is compare them with the brilliance of White's non-sexual portraiture: 'a face sprouting brunet sideburns that swerved inward like cheese knives towards his mouth'. In this world the eccentric, the comic and the fallible are, unusually, allowed their place in the sexual: 'His jockey shorts had holes in them. Around one leg a broken elastic had popped out of the cotton seam and dangled against his thigh like a grey noodle'; 'so massive and quivering were her breasts and hips under the slip that the garment seemed to be the body of a vaudeville horse which at least two people were inhabiting.'

All White's writing has such moments—it is difficult to forget the scattered gorgeousness in his fiction. Clouds 'lit up like internal organs dyed for examination', a sun that 'pulsed feebly like the aura of a migraine that doesn't develop'. And my favourite from *The Beautiful Room is Empty,* as the narrator stands watching a city's lights come on from an apartment window: 'slowly constructing itself like coral under incoming tides of light'.

It is strange that a writer of this talent would exchange these precious stones for the rocks of 'anger'. In **'The Personal is Political'** White theoretically rewrites all his work, and suggests that it has always been political. He describes *A Boy's Own Story* thus: 'What I wanted to show was the harm psychotherapy had done to homosexuals and the self-hatred that was forced on a young gay man by a society that could conceive of homosexuality only as a sickness, sin or crime.' Does anyone reading that wonderful novel recognise inside it this glum silhouette? After all, one of its many comedies is that the young narrator priggishly *chooses* to undergo analysis because 'I wanted to overcome this thing I was becoming and was in danger soon of being, the homosexual.' Dr O'Reilly, the famous analyst selected, is not merely some appalling agent of the homophobic hegemony, but a comic creation who 'was not a good listener. He was always scooping up handfuls of orange diet pills and swallowing them with a jigger of scotch.' Were the book anything like White's retrospective description it would be not only dull but most certainly limited in appeal; this is precisely the difference between identification with a gay cause and belonging to gayness.

Skinned Alive shows us that for all his confusions, White has lost none of his artistry. In **'Running On Empty',** Luke, a sick translator, returns to his family in Texas. It is a world of conservative women—aunts, great-aunts, cousins. It is religious and rural. The story beautifully charts the awkwardness of Luke's homecoming. The artist in White sees the Southern Baptists with much comedy and tenderness. 'Then there were cheerful moments, as when Luke recounted the latest follies of folks in Paris. "Well, I declare," the ladies would exclaim, their voices dipping from pretended excitement down into real indifference. He was careful not to go on too long about a world they didn't know or care about or to shock them.' Luke's tact is matched by the author's: just as Luke tries not to shock his cousins, so the author respects their otherness.

> Other old ladies, all widows, stopped in to visit, and Luke wondered if Beth was ready to join grief's hen club. Girls started out clinging together, whispering secrets and flouncing past boys. Then there was the longish interlude of marriage, followed by the second sorority of widowhood; all these humped necks, bleared eyes, false teeth, the wide-legged sitting posture of country women sipping weak coffee and complaining about one another.

Note that 'weak coffee'. Luke, like White, is an HIV-positive artist from Paris. But White, in creating Luke, has done what Rilke did when he created Malte in his autobiographical *The Notebooks of Malte Laurids Brigge.* Rilke put it like this in a letter: 'Since you last heard of him Malte has grown into a figure completely detached from me and has acquired a being and an individuality which interested me more and more strongly the more they differentiated themselves from their author.' This is a long way from autofiction; but it is certainly art.

FURTHER READING

Criticism

Gerra, Michael. Review of *Our Paris: Sketches From Memory. The New York Times Book Review* (3 December 1995): 7, 49-50.
> States that "*Our Paris* isn't really a travel book—it's a valentine to a city most of us can only visit."

Gluck, Robert. "A Boy's Own Story." *Review of Contemporary Fiction* 16, No. 3 (Fall 1996): 56-60.
> Discusses White's *A Boy's Own Story* and how it was

different than anything that had been published previously.

Johnson, Diane. "The Midwesterner as Artist." *Review of Contemporary Literature* 16, No. 3 (Fall 1996): 69-72.
> Discusses how being a homosexual and a Midwesterner contributed to White's main topic of otherness.

Judt, Tony. Review of *The Selected Writings of Jean Genet,* by Edmund White. *The New York Review of Books* 40, No. 17 (21 October 1993): 8.
> Reviews White's *Genet: A Biography* and his *The Selected Writings of Jean Genet* and asserts that "Edmund White deserves unstinting praise for his painstaking efforts to unravel the threads that Genet so assiduously knotted and crossed in his various writings and interviews."

McCann, Richard. "Years Later, by the Pool: Looking Back at Edmund White's *Nocturnes for the King of Naples.*" *Review of Contemporary Fiction* 16, No. 3 (Fall 1996): 43-9.
> McCann discusses *Nocturnes for the King of Naples* as breaking away from the ordinary novel.

"Mixed Gay Chorus." *Women Artists News* 16 and 17, (1991/1992): 214-16.
> A group of writers, including Edmund White, debate the existence of a homosexual sensibility.

Picano, Felice. "Edmund White and the Violet Quill Club." *Review of Contemporary Fiction* 16, No. 3 (Fall 1996): 84-7.
> Discusses the work of Edmund White and the group of homosexual writers known as the Violet Quill Club, and their lack of acceptance in literary circles.

Pritchard, William H. "Fiction Chronicle." *The Hudson Review* XLIX, No. 1 (Spring 1996): 135-44.
> Argues that the stories in White's *Skinned Alive* "lack denouement and are severely limited in the subjects taken on."

Van Leer, David. "Beyond the Margins." *The New Republic* 207 (12 October 1992): 50-3.
> Discusses how three different anthologies, including White's *The Faber Book of Gay Short Fiction,* present gay literature.

Woods, Gregory. "Reaching a Loving Climax." *Times Literary Supplement* (21 June 1991): 20.
> Asserts that in *The Faber Book of Gay Short Fiction,* White "has succeeded in gathering a richly varied range of voices."

Additional coverage of White's life and career is contained in the following sources published by Gale Research: *Authors and Artists for Young Adults; Contemporary Authors*, Vol. 45-48; *Contemporary Authors New Revision Series*, Vol. 3, 19, and 36; *DISCovering Authors Modules: Popular Fiction and Genre Authors;* and *Major Twentieth-Century Writers.*

Richard Wilbur

1921-

(Full name Richard Purdy Wilbur) American poet, translator, critic, nonfiction writer, author of children's books, and editor.

The following entry provides an overview of Wilbur's career through 1997. For further information on Wilbur's life and works, see *CLC,* Volumes 3, 6, 9, 14, and 53.

INTRODUCTION

The former Poet Laureate of the United States from 1987-1988, Richard Wilbur is respected for the craftsmanship and elegance of his verse, which employs formal poetic structures and smoothly flowing language to pinpoint and poeticize individual moments in modern life. Wilbur's English translations of the works of French dramatists such as Molière and Racine are also widely praised and considered to be the definitive versions.

Biographical Information

Wilbur was born in New York City in 1921. The son of a commercial artist, Wilbur was interested in painting as a youth, but eventually opted to pursue writing, a decision he attributes to the influence of his mother's father and grandfather, both of whom were editors. Wilbur graduated from Amherst College in 1942 and Harvard University in 1947. During World War II he served in the Army, where he saw action in Italy, an experience that later helped form much of his poetry. Wilbur published his first book of poetry, *The Beautiful Changes and Other Poems,* in 1947, the same year he became a junior fellow at Harvard where he taught English until 1954. Wilbur went on to teach at Wellesley College, Wesleyan University, and Smith College. In 1987 he was named Poet Laureate of the United States, the second person to hold the position since its inception in 1986. Finding the bureaucratic responsibilities of the post too taxing, Wilbur opted not to serve a second year, and returned to writing and lecturing at various colleges and universities.

Major Works

Wilbur's first book of poems, *The Beautiful Changes and Other Poems,* contains several pieces that focus on his experience as a soldier in World War II and reflect his attempts to instill a sense of order to an existence full of destruction and chaos. Other poems describe natural phenomena and include meditations on spiritual and metaphysical topics, recurring themes in Wilbur's work. In *Ceremony and Other*

Poems (1950) Wilbur examines the relationship between the material world and the imagination, as he ponders mutability and death. Wilbur's next collection, *Things of This World* (1956), is widely regarded as containing his most mature work up to that point, and contains some of his most popular and critically acclaimed work, including "Love Calls Us to the Things of This World" and "A Baroque Wall-Fountain in the Villa Sciarra." Wilbur received both the National Book Award and the Pulitzer Prize in poetry for *Things of This World.* In *Advice to a Prophet, and Other Poems* (1961) Wilbur continued his lyricism and his command of various traditional poetic forms. *Walking to Sleep: New Poems and Translations* (1969), which won the Bollingen Prize, contains pastoral lyrics, an elegy, a Miltonic sonnet, tributes, narratives, and a riddle. In *The Mind-Reader* (1976), Wilbur examines characteristic concerns by employing witty language within tight lyrical structures. Wilbur's previously unpublished poems contained in *New and Collected Poems* (1988) include a tribute to W. H. Auden, a fable, observations on nature and the imagination, and a cantata on which he collaborated with composer William Schuman to honor the centennial of the Statue of Liberty. In *The Catbird's*

Song: Prose Pieces 1963-1995 (1997), Wilbur collects many of his nonfiction prose writings, including book reviews, criticism, and essays. Wilbur is also highly acclaimed for his translations. Of these he is best known for his versions of the Molière plays *The Misanthrope* and *Tartuffe,* having shared the Bollingen Prize for translation for the latter drama. His renderings into English of works by eminent French, Russian, and Spanish authors have been included in several of his poetry collections.

Critical Reception

While some critics have praised Wilbur's deft handling of formal conventions, others have asserted that his concern with form has led to thematic rigidity. Other commentators have noted that Wilbur's quiet conservatism is not likely to be well-received by an audience that expects poets to write personal and tormented explications of their own feelings rather than Wilbur's reserved metaphysical observations on nature. Thom Gunn wrote, after the publication of *Advice to a Prophet,* "The public prefers a wild and changeable poet to one who has pursued a single end consistently and quietly." Despite this bias, Wilbur's work has attracted wide admiration. Anthony Hecht commented on Wilbur's poem "Lying," "There is nobility in such utterance that is deeply persuasive, and throughout Wilbur's poetry we are accustomed to finding this rare quality, usually joined to wit, good humor, grace, modesty, and a kind of physical zest or athletic dexterity that is, so far as I know, unrivaled."

PRINCIPAL WORKS

The Beautiful Changes and Other Poems (poetry) 1947
Ceremony and Other Poems (poetry) 1950
Things of This World: Poems (poetry) 1956
Poems, 1943-1956 (poetry) 1957
Emily Dickinson: Three Views [with Louise Bogan and Archibald MacLeish] (criticism) 1960
Advice to a Prophet, and Other Poems (poetry) 1961
Loudmouse (juvenile) 1963
The Poems of Richard Wilbur (poetry) 1963
Prince Souvanna Phouma: An Exchange between Richard Wilbur and William Jay Smith (poetry) 1968
Walking to Sleep: New Poems and Translations (poetry) 1969
Opposites: Poems and Drawings (juvenile) 1973
Seed Leaves: Homage to R. F. (poetry) 1974
The Mind-Reader: New Poems (poetry) 1976
Seven Poems (poetry) 1981
New and Collected Poems (poetry) 1988
The Catbird's Song: Prose Pieces 1963-1995 (criticism, reviews, and essays) 1997

CRITICISM

Horace Gregory (review date Fall 1956)

SOURCE: "The Poetry of Suburbia," in *Partisan Review,* Vol. XIII, No. 4, Fall 1956, pp. 545-53.

[*Gregory is an American poet, critic, and translator whose works include* Rooming House *(1930) and* Medusa in Gramercy Park *(1960). In the following review, he praises the "charm" of Wilbur's poetry in* Things of This World, *but expresses reservations about its ability to retain a place in American literature.*]

The recent *Zeitgeist* in American culture is of suburban colors, manners, dress. Those who are currently publishing verse are affected by its daily habits and ambitions, and more than a few have mistaken its presence for a visitation of the Muse. The importance of the suburban *Zeitgeist* may not be enduring, but since the end of the Korean War, its influence has spread cross-country from the suburbs of Boston to the state of Washington, far beyond the toll-gates of large cities; and it can be heard and seen as vividly on a college campus as in Westchester or nearby Long Island. It is nourished by the magazines I find in my dentist's office: *The New Yorker, Life,* and *Time.* It may seem strange that popular culture should invade, and so thoroughly and quickly, the landscapes of academic life; it may not (I am sure it does not) represent academic thinking at its centers, yet on the fringes of the campus it is very much alive, geared to the speed of a two-toned—strawberry-pink and gingham-blue—station wagon. It is well known that most of the verse published today is brought forth in the temporary shelter of universities. Suburban culture has spread its wings over all the activities that surround the campus, and verse written in this atmosphere cannot help reflecting the surfaces of everyday experience.

Another factor influencing the spirit of the verse written today was the belated "discovery" of Wallace Stevens. Of course, he had been "discovered" long ago; but in the postwar years it was not only the wit and inventiveness of Stevens' work, it was the *image* of his success, both as an executive of an insurance company and as a poet, that caught and held the admiration of young men and women who wrote verse. It was rumored that he was rich, very rich, rich enough to escape all minor economic misfortunes and turns of chance. In the United States there has never been any sustained disrespect for wealth; roughness and the "homespun" manner are often enjoyed, but always with the hope of finding "a rough diamond" or "a heart of gold." So far as the best of Stevens' verse revealed him, he was a pluralist and a skeptic; and certain external features of his legend had become attractive to emulate. The new *Zeitgeist* quickly absorbed whatever it understood of this legend; then it acquired an air of "difference" from the forty years that separated it from the first publication of *Harmonium*. It disregarded conscious bohemianism and "sexual freedom," as well as the Left Wing politics of the 1930's, and the "academic" irony fashionable in the 1940's that was best represented by the little magazine *Furioso*.

The conventions of the new *Zeitgeist* were being formed. The more "advanced" younger poets had become instructors and lecturers and behind academic facades embittered laurels were being watered and cultivated; old-fashioned excess (if any) and toasts drunk to the memory of F. Scott Fitzgerald were reserved for holidays, or discreetly converted into weekend faculty cocktail parties. These younger poets began to use the word "elegance" in praising each other's writings, and if twenty years ago it had become fashionable to be "proletarian" in spirit, in the early 1950's, it had become a virtue to say that one could not live on less than ten thousand a year, that if one did not have hidden sources of wealth, it was a disgrace to live at all. Stevens' "elegance" was of mind and temperament, yet it was one that seemed easy to imitate in terms of the more garish advertising pages of *Harper's Bazaar, Vogue,* and *The New Yorker,* the kind of literature that for a brief, wholly deceptive moment makes the reader feel like a luxury product himself, ready to join the "International Set," to be severe with middle-aged, wealthy American patronesses in Rome, and to drink at Harry's Bar in Venice. The word "elegance," like so many transitory usages of language in the United States, has become the choice of copywriters to sell everything the suburban matron wears. One might suspect collusion between the poets of *Harper's Bazaar* and the shopkeepers of Westchester.

One effect of the suburban influence has been to revive a kind of writing that had been forgotten since 1914. What used to be called "magazine verse" forty years ago is back in print again, decorously written, and admirably fitted to fill empty spaces between fiction and feature articles. One might call it the *New Yorker* school of verse.

Though the offices of *The New Yorker* are in New York, its heart is in the suburbs. The magazine is certainly the handbook of the suburban matron throughout the country. *The New Yorker* publishes a quantity of light verse, which is nothing to be ashamed of; but light verse that lives beyond the moment is extremely rare. It is rare because poetic wit itself is a rarity; what often passes for it is something "cute," something coy, something pleasant, harmless, or naughty-bitter. It should be well-formed; and not—by the same poet—reiterated too frequently in the same phrases. The cutting edge too frequently wears dull. Large indiscriminate doses of it tend to cloy. These truisms are probably known in the offices of *The New Yorker* and regretted—therefore, it has

fallen back on publishing quasi-serious verse as well, constructed according to current formulas: certain verse forms used with enough caution to be recognized at once, certain images within the verses that recall the "happy-bitter" experience of childhood, the joy of collecting toys and the discovery that toys are perishable, the country places visited at home, the holiday from suburban security in Europe. The great discomfort in reading too much *New Yorker* verse is that the formula continually wears thin; it is not as cheering as it hoped to be—or as light and witty as Sandy Wilson's parody of the 1920's in his musical *The Boy Friend*. Reading too much *New Yorker* verse becomes a bore.

> **What Wilbur contributes to the verse of the *Zeitgeist* is an absolutely engaging personality with "the desire to please" between the lines of every stanza.**
> **—*Horace Gregory***

By these winding suburban roads I have come to Richard Wilbur's third book of verse, with its well-chosen title, ***Things of This World.*** It is a book that should utterly charm the *Zeitgeist*. It is undoubtedly the best of Wilbur's three books, and if his early reviewers have placed him among the better poets of his immediate generation, they have not been wrong. With the same care with which he has chosen his title he has selected poems for this volume; they are not too many, not too few; though he is in the *New Yorker* orbit he seems to float slightly beyond it. What Wilbur contributes to the verse of the *Zeitgeist* is an absolutely engaging personality with "the desire to please" between the lines of every stanza. This is "the something new" that he has offered to the *Zeitgeist*. Some of the recent poems reflect his travels in Italy; the first poem in the book, **"Altitudes,"** is among the best of written tributes to Emily Dickinson. His adaptation of Paul Valèry's **"Helen"** is written with excellent taste, restraint, and firmness; on second reading, more than half the poems in the book retain their charm. A second reading assures me that none of the poems would disturb the self-confidence of the young and smartly dressed suburban matron stepping from her station wagon on a sunny morning. She would probably enjoy most, wrinkling her forehead slightly—in the effort to recall her trips to Europe (on vacation from Radcliffe)—**"The Beacon,"** with its images of deep sea water, and **"Piazza Di Spagna, Early Morning"**; the girl in that poem must have been the way she looked when she spent three days in Rome. And since she has, of course, read Robert Frost, she would be delighted at hearing familiar Frostian accents in Wilbur's **"Digging for China."** She might even imagine that her own Junior, age three, would enjoy digging for China in New Jersey, and hope that he, twenty-five years later, would recall the scene as memorably as Richard Wilbur does.

But if one has a long memory for verse, which unfortunately I possess, further rereadings of Wilbur's verse bring doubts to mind. **"Piazza Di Spagna"** becomes a reduced, less memorable flutter of lines that recreate Eliot's "La Figlia Che Piange." There is also much pleasure in reading Wilbur's **"A Voice from Under the Table"**—until one remembers Phelps Putnam's "Hasbrouck and the Rose." Both the resemblance and the contrast between the two poems bring up embarrassing questions: Putnam's poem is direct; passionate young fools are drunk and talking aloud. In contrast to Putnam's, Wilbur's poem is overdressed and a shade pretentious—and his phrase, "God keep me a damned fool," rings false, false because Wilbur seems so expert at contriving certain of his lines. It well may be that he feels a necessity to reiterate his adaptation of Francis Jammes' "A Prayer to Go to Paradise with the Donkeys"—but one gains no other evidence from Wilbur's writing that he is foolish. These are my doubts—but I am also convinced that *Things of This World* will be regarded by many as the best single book of poems published this year; and I believe that Wilbur's charm should not be underrated. . . .

Charles R. Woodard (essay date Autumn 1977)

SOURCE: "Richard Wilbur's Critical Condition," in *Contemporary Poetry: A Journal of Criticism*, Vol. II, No. 2, Autumn 1977, pp. 16-24.

[*In the following essay, Woodard defends Wilbur's poetry against detractors who find his work "too happy."*]

Critical commentaries on Wilbur's poetry have come to seem rather highly stylized and predictable, like bullfighting. First there is the ritual praise of his technical virtuosity (music, diction, imagery, metrics), to show that the critic is not devoid of the appreciation of beauty, followed quickly by the disclaimers which establish his awareness of its irrelevance to contemporary life. Objections to Wilbur's poetry, to phrase them in the simplest terms, take the following forms: (1) He thinks too much. (2) He does not suffer enough.

Strictly speaking, it is not Wilbur's thought so much as his imagination that is derogated. Clearly we cannot condemn him for his epistemological interests if we are to permit them to Wallace Stevens. It is Wilbur's use of the things of this world, his chosen poetic province, which gets him into trouble; he is not tough enough with them, not sufficiently insistent upon their thinginess, but persists in allowing them to pass through his mind, where his recalcitrant imagination may act upon them. Back of such criticism there hover the dicta and practice of William Carlos Williams, whose followers put their faith in an objective "rendering" of reality or experience as little tampered with by mind as possible.

The chief emphasis is on outwitting the mind's insidious attempts to impose its own patterns on reality or to substitute them *for* reality—an end accomplished by limiting its reported activities to acts of perception or "prereflective cognition." It is as if the poet were arrested in his linguistic development on the verge of the invention of language, striving for an arrangement of shells on the shore from which we as readers are to deduce an idea, rather as Deism could deduce God's existence from an inspection of the natural world. Perhaps it is not quite so primitive as this; a better comparison would be the still-life tableau of such objects as apples, pears, and a freshly killed hare, except that the seemingly arbitrary grouping must "mean" something, without saying it. With a red wheelbarrow, glazed with rain, and white chickens, Williams takes us back to an approximation of pictographic writing. Thus the snares and delusions of discursive thought and emotive language are avoided, but only until we read an analysis of such symbols by one of Williams' exegetes. The reader is permitted to use his mind, we are tempted to say, but not the poet, except in the most rigorous "demonstrative" sense. It was Williams' insistence that there be no new wine in old bottles, and thus Wilbur is condemned for using older forms and conventions. Paradoxically, it is acceptable for Williams' imitators to put their wine in his old bottles, but Wilbur may not put his in Eliot's and certainly not in those of Pope and Donne. If wit and cleverness were not generally outside the laws governing the works of the Williams school, one of its members might write a satire on Wilbur, similar to that written by Dryden on Shadwell—no doubt it would be entitled "MacDonne."

The second complaint, which appears to have its origin in the vogue for "confessional" poetry, may at times be viewed as a result of the first; if Wilbur did not take refuge so habitually in his own mind, he would see the world for the pit of horror that everyone else knows it to be. Lowell and his followers, with their categories of "cooked" and "raw" poetry, take it as a priori that the good poet will suffer and, further, that good poetry consists precisely in the reporting of this suffering. Emotional Jacksonians, the critics who take this position, want no one whistling within hearing of their misery. They appear to view poetry as having some therapeutic function, but if poets are their physicians how can it profit them to be prescribed continuing doses of their own sickness? The answer must be that misery continues to love company; they want the assurance that the poet is not sunny or happy—that he is, in fact, exactly like themselves. They want it reaffirmed that man is beastly, the "human condition" hopeless. Thus assured, they may turn out the light and fall into dreamless sleep. In such a critical environment, Wilbur is a kind of Mauberley, born out of his due time in "a half-savage country, out of date"—a country with a taste, where a taste can be discerned, for meat not merely rare but raw.

The effect of such criticism is to confine poetry to immediate sensation and emotion. We appear to have reared a race of critics who go about with their tongues probing their aching teeth, hungering to see lepers, monstrosities, freaks, wounds, blood, madness. We require to be told that we are mad, or have at least the rich potential for going mad. We still, in some strange perversion of Victorianism, require our poets to be sages, but sages of a very rare and specialized breed, sages of suffering. Their hands display their stigmata, their wrists their slashes. The lurid path cut through our skies by the Welsh comet Dylan Thomas, Eliot's resigned nerveless suffering, Auden's frequent reminders of "the suffering to which we are fairly accustomed," Yeats even, with his cyclic cataclysms, our own grim expectations of life in the twentieth century, the dreadful tragedies of our younger poets—all these have led us to believe that the poet's role requires that he put the stamp of sincerity upon his work by stepping in front of an automobile or leaping off a bridge.

We seem, in fact, to have arrived, in recent years, at a kind of unwritten contract with our poets. Were it formalized, it might read more or less as follows: "You may be a poet, and we will reward you with grants and fellowships and readings if you are fashionable, and publish your doings in the papers, like those of football players and television performers, but never forget that it is your suffering for which you are being paid. We will begin to take most interest in your work precisely when it shows clearest symptoms of your breaking down. We want to know of every visit to a sanitarium, every cut, cuddled, and sucked thumb, your bouts with alcohol and depression, your flirtations with suicide. And then to prove your seriousness, you must write a final poem, in the form of a leap from a bridge or a pulled trigger. Then we will believe. Then we will establish a cult and proclaim you unreservedly a poet."

Confessional poetry may be quite as much a result of this attitude as its cause. The wounds! we cry, all the wounds, licked by so many bloody tongues. Knowledge is sorrow, but must art be pain? Must we now have suffering only, without catharsis? Unused to hearing confessionals, knowing only our own local pain, we are overwhelmed. This is what life is, we say, like the blind man laying hold of some part of the elephant. Granted that life is grim, that this may be, as Elizabeth Bishop said, "our worst century yet," must our poetry continue compulsively to rehearse this one obsessive fact? The mind's indwelling powers are capable of more; the vulture reminds the alert of Noah; another world opens through a hole in the floor. Even a man on the way to a madhouse may smile at a girl in the street.

Arnold criticized the Romantics for not knowing enough; another generation of critics condemns Wilbur for not suffering enough. He comes and sets up shop before us, dazzling us with displays of virtuosity such as to make him seem a creature from another world—or from another age, at the

very least. His technical skill is immense. His poems stand apart from him in the independent world of art; both he and they are like cats, licking their fur in total self-sufficiency, self-possession. It is almost as if he were too blessed with talent. We may be tempted to see him as a kind of happy fool, a "natural," into whose pockets apples fall as he dawdles cheerfully across the verdancy of an outmoded romantic landscape. "How graceful," we say, "but does he go through life without pain?" His poetry is a reminder that the tragic vision which we prize so highly in our poets need not rule out the "wit and wakefulness," the free play of the mind delighting in itself, which Wilbur proclaims as his own. "It's pretty," say Kipling's Philistines doubtfully, "but is it art?" "It's art," we say of Wilbur's poetry, shaking our heads with equal doubt, "but is it life? Does he not suffer?" He does not say, overtly, and thus we conclude that he *has* nothing to say. We might pay him the compliment, however, of thinking that he is perhaps not trying to say so much as to make, and with materials subtler than oyster-shells. The play of his mind, as shimmering and translucent as the spray of his fountains, may be a delight to the reader; if it is an equal delight to Wilbur, so much the better. It was once considered a virtue to suffer in silence; if Wilbur suffers, it is thus he does. Socialized suffering can only be ruinous; shared property dwindles; shared pain multiplies until every emotional reservoir is overflowing. The giver retains a full store, no matter how fully he burdens his recipients. It would be tragic indeed if we forced Wilbur, as the price of our adulation, to take to drink and end a suicide in some peaceful New England summer, and thus to become overnight another of our cult-heroes.

In lamenting man's tragic circumstance, however, and supposing that Wilbur is unaware of it, we do him a very real injustice. Apart from man's mortality, with its attendant suffering, there is perhaps no more tragic situation in his life than the discrepancy between the world he perceives and the world which he knows intellectually to exist. A study of Wilbur's poetry—we may confine ourselves to the collection *The Poems of Richard Wilbur* (1963)—shows how often the things of this world which he celebrates are shadowed by an awareness of this discrepancy. His little poem **"Epistemology"** states a theme implicit in much of his writing:

> I
> Kick at the rock, Sam Johnson, break your bones:
> But cloudy, cloudy is the stuff of stones.
> II
> We milk the cow of the world, and as we do
> We whisper in her ear, "You are not true."

This is not merely the cow of Berkeley's idealism but the cow of current science, without milking machines. Nothing can bridge the gap between appearance and the reality which we know to exist but cannot perceive. Wilbur for his poetry chooses the cow he can see and milk rather than some molecular cow which cloudily fails to abide our question. Nevertheless, he is far removed in his epistemology from Williams and his followers. Though he knows, as the title of one of his poems tells us, that "a world without objects is a sensible emptiness," his poetry is ironically informed with the further knowledge that a red wheelbarrow possesses no quality of redness and that the chickens in a barnyard are cloudy stuff indeed, as is his cow. His poetry itself, the milk from that cow, must thus partake of the general untruth of those things whose fragile beauty it celebrates; and that fragility is more moving than the traditional theme of mutability. The Williams school accepts without question the world as our senses give it to us, while rejecting the validity of any Wordsworthian recollection in tranquillity. It is as if Margaret Fuller had said, "I accept the universe, but I will not allow my mind to contaminate it." Wilbur permits the entry of mind into the reality-equation, and not without logic. If the world which the Williams school uses as the materials of poetry is "unreal," as scientifically viewed, then it is difficult to see that the senses are more reliable than the intellect for poetry or more valid than the imagination. How can the mind contaminate in any significant way a world which the mind knows already not to exist except as invisible particles awhirl in infinite immensities of space? Poets, after all, are not philosophers or scientists; their observations are neither methodologically nor logically immaculate. If on the other hand the world is "unreal" in philosophic terms, with no existence outside mind, then intellection is not only the order of the day—it *is* the day, and the night.

His poetry is a reminder that the tragic vision which we prize so highly in our poets need not rule out the "wit and wakefulness," the free play of the mind delighting in itself, which Wilbur proclaims as his own.
—*Charles R. Woodward*

We may, if we please, insist upon the validity of sensations and the "reality" of sensible objects; but such an assumption, in the context of modern scientific knowledge, is in itself a denial of the validity of the mind's operations; and thus we are returned to a primitive state of existence—a pre-cortical state, we are tempted to say—scratching or painting our visual perceptions on the wall of the cave. Such a state is not Wilbur's. In a world eternally in motion, where nothing is stable, where even atomic particles are beset with an uncertainty principle, the play of the individual mind, itself reducible to the activity of chemically generated electrical impulses, may be as good a model of reality as we have. If it imposes its own patterns on the outer world, perhaps that is not a calamitous event after all, since those patterns are a

part of that world. Beneath the sensible surface of Wilbur's world another threatens, like the crack in Auden's teacup, to open into unspeakable voids—"the buried strangeness / Which nourishes the known" ("**A Hole in the Floor**"). His is a landscape of ephemera, of "opulent bric-a-brac," mined country, touched with the fatal "seeming" of the Edenic pear in "**June Light,**" which constantly erodes the "truth and new delight" of the visible world. Each poem is a temporary victory over our knowledge of the nature of things; in each, like his juggler, he "has won for once over the world's weight," even as his prophet is being rehearsed to preach the "worldless rose" of an atomized earth ("**Advice to a Prophet**"). In this connection, Wilbur's tendency to concentrate on things rather than on dramatic situations (people), is perhaps not without its own sinister implications, as much a commentary by omission as Housman's excluding the fully adult and the aged from *A Shropshire Lad.*

Wilbur's concern is not mutability alone (although this too is a central theme) but the precariousness of a physical world which is known to be different from what our physical senses tell us it is, as we know that sand may be a component of glass, without being able to see it ("**Junk**"). A tension is set up between eye and mind. Wilbur must praise appearance even as he is being hoodwinked by it, because a molecular world is not a workable stuff for poetry, though it is always there, an undeniable adjunct to the assertions made by the poetry. His is not the too-solid flesh of Hamlet; things of summer growth "raise / Plainly their seeming into seamless air" ("**June Light**"); the erratic flight of birds suggests a world "dreamt" by "cross purposes" ("**An Event**"), and misty weather brings a fear of the loss of the physical world ("**A Chronic Condition**").

If Wilbur is to be criticized for being "too happy," for employing his mind too much, it might be well for those who do so to consider the poised fragility of his world as set against the "bloody loam," apparently eternal, which is the basis of Williams'. Both Williams and the confessional school appear to accept the sensible world at face value; in his later work Williams' world is poised between the mythic primal slime on the one hand and the momentary display of spirit on the other. The uneasy ground of Wilbur's poetry is the irreconcilable oppositions of appearance and knowledge. It is not immediately apparent that Williams' world is more "real," and thus more unhappy, than Wilbur's, or that it deals more rigorously with its facts and artifacts, since it does not show any inclination to question the evidence of the senses as the basis of its epistemology.

Between the two poles of sensation and knowledge, Wilbur's mind functions as mediator. Its graceful error may "correct the cave" of reality ("**Mind**"); it milks the cow of the world which it knows to be untrue. The perceived world, with its fine gauzy shimmer of fountains and its colored juggling balls, is equally a world of the fine shimmer and juggling of mind. His poetry constitutes a realm of its own, with its own truth, constantly reiterating that the mind's reflections are hardly less substantial or valid than the objects of its perceptions. If a critic, standing at the edge of one of Wilbur's displays, cries, "Unreal!" Wilbur need only allow a wider spin of the lariat to rope him into the scene whose existence he is denying. After all, Wilbur has denied it from the beginning.

Anthony Hecht (review date 16 May 1988)

SOURCE: "Master of Metaphor," in *The New Republic*, Vol. 3, No. 826, May 16, 1988, pp. 23-32.

[*Hecht is a Pulitzer Prize-winning American poet whose works include* A Summoning of Stones *(1954) and* The Hard Hours *(1968). In the following review, he offers an overview of major themes and techniques in Wilbur's work and praises his* New and Collected Poems.]

"The work of art is the object seen *sub specie aeternitatis*," observed Wittgenstein. And since today there are critics who maintain that art and criticism are indistinguishable from one another, it ought to follow that the critical work itself is seen from the same August perspective. Yet our experience of the history of criticism and the morphology of aesthetic theory fails conspicuously to support this view. Nothing is more familiar to us than the changes in the mode of taste that time itself seems to bring round in its course. Bach endured an eclipse of 200 years, and Richard Ellmann has recently told us that for the undergraduate Oscar Wilde, Keats and Swinburne (whom modern readers would only reluctantly identify with one another) were akin in the "effeminacy and languor and voluptuousness which are the characteristics of that 'passionate humanity' which is the background of true poetry." In the comparatively brief course of my lifetime, John Donne's reputation was virtually disinterred, and the Romantics are now enjoying a revival. And I suppose I should add that it must take a very curious and cultivated taste to enjoy reading criticism of Wordsworth as much as reading Wordsworth himself, though I have known such creatures. (They are desperate graduate students, and no less desperate professors.)

These ruminations are brought on by the publication of Richard Wilbur's *New and Collected Poems,* and by a wistful desire to arrive at a large and serene view of his accomplishment, the crowning of a long and distinguished career. (Just how distinguished is hard to assess, but apart from his many honors, awards, and appointments, I can note here that the 14th edition of Bartlett's *Familiar Quotations* contains 107 lines of his work.) I am already on record as a somewhat

defensive admirer of his, having reviewed his last book of poems, *The Mind-Reader* (1976). And while that review attempted to offer a view of his entire poetic career up to that point (apart from his translations of French drama), I have no desire now to serve up warmed-over views, or to engage again in the parochial and tribal battles that are often waged between rival schools and camps of current poetic taste. Wilbur's distinctions do not need to be set off by the infelicities of others, and his work is by now so well known, and so widely honored, that I can spare the reader a repetition of the formulaic terms of praise that have become the logos and labels of critical approval of his work.

This new work [*New and Collected Poems*] bears all the hallmarks of excellence that have stamped Wilbur's previous work: a kinetic imagination that is rare among poets, as well as an unusually rich and fertile gift for metaphor.
—Anthony Hecht

The new book presents all of his previous volumes in reverse order, concluding with his first book, *The Beautiful Changes and Other Poems* (1947)—the same order in which his poems were arranged in the, by now, familiar assemblage, *The Poems of Richard Wilbur,* which brought together everything from the first book to *Advice to a Prophet and Other Poems* (1961). The present volume reprints everything heretofore collected and adds to it the contents of two subsequent volumes, *Walking to Sleep: New Poems and Translations* (1969) and *The Mind-Reader,* and adds to them a volume of new poems with which this rich and impressive collection begins. This new work bears all the hallmarks of excellence that have stamped Wilbur's previous work: a kinetic imagination that is rare among poets, as well as an unusually rich and fertile gift for metaphor. I share with Aristotle a view of the importance of this gift, and cite him accordingly as follows:

> It is a great thing, indeed, to make a proper use of these poetical forms, as also of compound and strange words. But the greatest thing by far is to be a master of metaphor. It is one thing that cannot be learnt from others; and it is also a sign of genius, since a good metaphor implies an intuitive perception of the similarity in dissimilars.

When I try to make a mental list of the major English and American poets from, say, the turn of the century on, I find myself unable to come up with a single one who can match Wilbur in this regard. Each good poet, of course, has his own unique merits, his own vision, style, and idiom. And good poets do not cancel one another out; if we like Blake we are not thereby forbidden to like Marvell as well. But I can think of no other poet who could do what Wilbur does metaphorically in the following poem, **"An Event,"** from *Things of This World:*

> As if a cast of grain leapt back to the hand,
> A landscapeful of small black birds, intent
> On the far south, convene at some command
> At once in the middle of the air, at once are gone
> With headlong and unanimous consent
> From the pale trees and fields they settled on.
>
> What is an individual thing? They roll
> Like a drunken fingerprint across the sky!
> Or so I give their image to my soul
> Until, as if refusing to be caught
> In any singular vision of my eye
> Or in the nets and cages of my thought,
>
> They tower up, shatter, and madden space
> With their divergences, are each alone
> Swallowed from sight, and leave me in this place
> Shaping these images to make them stay:
> Meanwhile, in some formation of their own,
> They fly me still, and steal my thoughts away.
>
> Delighted with myself and with the birds,
> I set them down and give them leave to be.
> It is by words and the defeat of words,
> Down sudden vistas of the vain attempt,
> That for a flying moment one may see
> By what cross-purposes the world is dreamt.

There is a great deal that might be said about this poem, but I will confine myself to two observations. In its ingenious, philosophic course it plays with the pre-Socratic puzzle of "the One" and "the Many," a playfulness that is carefully carried out in such words as "their image" (which is both singular and plural), "singular vision" (s.), "divergences" (pl.), "alone" (s.), "images" (pl.), and "formation" (both s. and pl.). And then in the course of our progress we come to that matchless simile in answer to the question, "What is an individual thing?" "They roll / Like a drunken fingerprint across the sky!" There isn't a poet I can think of who would not have been overjoyed by a *trouvé* of that sort. It is breathtakingly vivid, accurate, and most astonishingly, *in motion.*

But Wilbur then proceeds to do what virtually no other poet would have the courage to do: he, in effect, throws it away. Or in any case declares that this is only one, and perhaps an imperfect, way to formulate what may in the end defy formulation. He allows the seriousness of his epistemological or metaphysical puzzle to take precedence over any incidental felicities that might be encountered along the way. This *sprezzatura* would be reckless in another poet. But Wilbur's

government of his enormous resources is what makes this poem (as well as many others) a triumph over its local details, and an amalgamation that is wonderfully greater than the sum of its parts. The Eleatic auditors of Zeno would have been delighted.

It seems worth adding that the theme of this poem—the delicate and necessarily imperfect attempt at an equation between the exterior world and the human faculties that apprehend and try to "render" it—is one that has preoccupied Wilbur almost from the first and figures beautifully in such an early stanza as this one:

> Sycamore, trawled by the tilt sun,
> Still scrawl your trunk with tattered lights, and
>   keep
> The spotted toad upon your patchy bark,
> Baffle the sight to sleep,
> Be such a deep
> Rapids of lacing light and dark,
> My eye will never know the dry disease
> Of thinking things no more than what he sees.

It's a theme that recurs in **"A Fire Truck," "The Mill," "Digging for China," "The Beacon," "A Plain Song for Comadre,"** and **"Altitudes."** In an era when a lot of supremely pompous things have been claimed for the omnipotence of language, it is refreshing in the work of so accomplished a poet to encounter an acknowledgment of "the defeat of words" in the face of the richness and multiplicity of an external reality that will always supersede and evade the limitations of our vocabulary, however well deployed. So there is to such poems a salutary and characteristic humility that is in itself attractive, and in turn points to something else about Wilbur's poetry that is worth remarking on, though I approach it with a certain tentativeness.

It has to do with the character of the man within or behind the poems; with how and to what degree that man gets expressed, if at all. This is a matter both delicate and controversial. There is an impressive body of modern thought that maintains there is no necessary connection between the work of art and the artist's nature, character, or history. Wilde, for one, maintained this view, and it seems implicit in Eliot's theory of the "impersonality" of art. It is a view Auden adopted in the stanzas he later deleted from his elegy to Yeats—the lines in which he declares:

> Time that is intolerant
> Of the brave and innocent,
> And indifferent in a week
> To a beautiful physique,
>
> Worships language and forgives
> Everyone by whom it lives;

Pardons cowardice, conceit,
Lays its honors at their feet.

The same view is expressed by Shaw in his preface to *The Doctor's Dilemma* in these words:

No man who is occupied in doing a very difficult thing, and doing it very well, ever loses his self-respect. . . . The common man may have to found his self-respect on sobriety, honesty, and industry; but . . . an artist needs no such props for his sense of dignity . . . The truth is, hardly any of us have ethical energy enough for more than one really inflexible point of honor. . . . An actor, a painter, a composer, an author, may be as selfish as he likes without reproach from the public if only his art is superb; and he cannot fulfill this condition without sufficient effort and sacrifice to make him feel noble and martyred in spite of his selfishness.

It is quite wonderful to think how widespread is this doctrine among some artists of very doubtful merit; and we are likely to find it so familiar that it will seem a curiously modern attitude, but it isn't. Plutarch reports in his *Life* of Pericles: "Antisthenes . . . when he was told that Ismenias played excellently on the flute, answered very properly, 'Then he is good for nothing else; otherwise he would not have played so well.'"

Yet this view is by no means universally shared, and it is generally felt that though precision in the matter is impossible, the work of art bears some important imprint of the spirit and inmost life of its maker. And so, by way of facing a puzzle that I have never comfortably resolved, I present two Wilbur poems, the first of them, **"Still, Citizen Sparrow,"** from a volume of 1950:

Still, citizen sparrow, this vulture which you call
Unnatural, let him but lumber again to air
Over the rotten office, let him bear
The carrion ballast up, and at the tall

Tip of the sky lie cruising. Then you'll see
That no more beautiful bird is in heaven's height,
No wider more placid wings, no watchfuller flight;
He shoulders nature there, the frightfully free,

The naked-headed one. Pardon him, you
Who dart in orchard aisles, for it is he
Devours death, mocks mutability,
Has heart to make an end, keeps nature new.

Thinking of Noah, childheart, try to forget
How for so many bedlam hours his saw
Soured the song of birds with its wheezy gnaw,

And the slam of his hammer all the day beset

The people's ears. Forget that he could bear
To see the towns like coral under the keel,
And the fields so dismal deep. Try rather to feel
How high and weary it was, on the waters where

He rocked his only world, and everyone's.
Forgive the hero, you who would have died
Gladly with all you knew; he rode that tide
To Ararat; all men are Noah's sons.

And now, in juxtaposition, a poem called **"A Wood,"** published in a volume nearly 20 years later:

Some would distinguish nothing here but oaks,
Proud heads conversant with the power and glory
Of heaven's rays or heaven's thunder-strokes,
And adumbrators to the understory,
Where, in their shade, small trees of modest
    leanings
Contend for light and are content with gleanings.

And yet here's dogwood: overshadowed, small,
But not inclined to droop and count its losses,
It cranes its way to sunlight after all,
And signs the air of May with Maltese crosses.
And here's witch hazel, that from underneath
Great vacant boughs will bloom in winter's teeth.

Given a source of light so far away
That nothing, short or tall, comes very near it,
Would it not take a proper fool to say
That any tree has not the proper spirit?
Air, water, earth and fire are to be blended,
But no one style, I think, is recommended.

These poems probably were not composed to be matched and mated, and yet they do form a pair by dint of theme and contrast. They are both symbolic poems in which some aspect of nature takes part in a little allegorical pageant, exhibiting human attitudes in a manner that we've become familiar with from poems like Robert Frost's "Spring Pools." And even though there was a long interval between their appearances, it is possible to think of them as a sort of diptych, as poems that face each other and quarrel in a friendly way, as do Milton's "L'Allegro" and "Il Penseroso"; though here we are prompted to wonder if the alternative postures presented by the two Wilbur poems are the consequence of a change of attitude on the part of the poet, or simply an attempt, as in Milton's case, to set up an antiphonal or dialogic relationship.

The question seems worth raising partly because there is something disturbing in the earlier, and in my view, the less successful, of these Wilbur poems. There is, for one thing, a curiously Jacobin flavor to the opening words and the title, suggesting the bloodthirsty resentment of some revolutionary leveler and vengeful egalitarian. The very first word, "Still," invites us to suppose that the speaker is now countering a long and detailed diatribe of condemnation with a word that means, "In spite of everything you say. . . . ." The *citoyen* is asked to admire his grotesque and more powerful rival and predator, whose ugliness, at a sufficiently great distance, will not be discernible. This powerful enemy "has heart to make an end" in that he finishes off his rivals, and in this way, it is claimed for him, "keeps nature new." I can't help feeling there is something frightful about this, and the more frightful in that we, and the *citoyen,* are being asked to admire and forgive it. In some way that is to me quite unpersuasive, this creature is identified as "the hero," and further identified with Noah, who, like the vulture, survives the hideous death of everyone else. Nothing is hinted about the merit of Noah and the wickedness of mankind to account for this introduction into the poem of a biblical story.

The poem seems to be about the elect who succeed and survive, in contrast to the masses who perish and are undeserving. Indeed, the biblical citation seems totally unexpected, and by no means easy to assimilate. There is a species of social Darwinism going on here "to which / The ripped mouse, safe in the owl's talon, cries / Concordance," in the words of Wilbur's poem **"Beasts."** I can't believe that this is a skewed or perverse reading of the poem, which seems to invite a sort of class distinction and exclusiveness. In any case, one cannot help feeling that the parable of the trees in **"A Wood"** is a great deal more charitable and generous than the parable of the birds in **"Still, Citizen Sparrow."**

This is the more striking in that, as opposed to the violence, insolence, and outright repulsiveness with which any number of poets now assault us, Wilbur's work has been characterized from the first by an admirable capacity to praise. "Obscurely yet most surely called to praise," begins one of his earliest poems. Long ago there used to be a commonplace belief that the end of art was precisely to delight ("Sounds and sweet airs that give delight and hurt not"). This did not mean, of course, that art was therefore purged of any taint of unpleasantness, presenting instead a dilute and sentimental version of existence, any more than Shakespeare's *The Tempest* is free from villainy. But, in Keats's formulation, "The excellency of every art is its intensity, capable of making all disagreeables evaporate"; by which, I assume, he means that even the most terrible matters could be redeemed by their assimilation into art.

Wilbur's poems have exhibited over the years an impressive capacity to confront the shocking, the appalling, the grotesque. Among his finest poems are the powerful dramatic monologues from which his last two books take their titles:

Walking to Sleep and *The Mind-Reader,* each of which deals with terrors of different sorts. It is an index, in fact, of Wilbur's growth as an artist that his emotional range has become increasingly ample over the years. If there could be said to be any characteristic limitations to his early work, they might be described as a sort of runaway mellifluousness, a Hopkinsian/Swinburnian/Tennysonian drench of language:

> A script of trees before the hill
> Spells cold, with laden serifs; all the walls
> Are battlemented still;
> But winter spring's winnowing the air
> Of chill, and crawls
> Wet-sparkling on the gutters;
> Everywhere
> Walls wince, and there's a steal of waters.
>
> Now all this proud royaume
> Is Veniced. Through the drift's mined dome
> One sees the rowdy rusted grass,
> And we're amazed as windows striken bright.
> This too-long spring will pass
> Perhaps tonight . . .

I don't mean that there's anything "wrong" with this, though it is perhaps a little more "mannered" than the later poems, and the calligraphy of the trees is less convincing than the fingerprint of that flock of birds in flight. Even here there is in "spells" a pun of the sort that will continue to inhabit Wilbur's poems throughout his career. His puns are serious and serviceable, and only occasionally comic; they are a major feature of his work, as are Shakespeare's "quibbles," which are the despair of translators. It was this sort of ambiguity and multivalenced power of words that led Tolstoy to his impatient dismissal of *King Lear* and his assertion that Shakespeare was "only playing with words." But, in a deeply serious way, that is actually what all good poets do: words are their only instruments to convey what is not easily conveyed by words alone. To resort to abusive epithets such as "artifice" or "dandy" is merely to embrace one convention and use it to bludgeon another that is equally valid.

Those who in past years have been stinting in their approval of Wilbur have pointed to his universally admired translations of classic French drama and have gone on to declare that this dated, formalized sensibility perfectly accords with his own tendencies to precision and stateliness. But I remember as an undergraduate reading Molière done, or rather, done in, by Louis Untermeyer in a translation that the veriest lout would recognize as doggerel. And since Wilbur's versions have become available there is no self-respecting production that would resort to another.

The linguistic gifts that have made possible these superb

translations from 17th-century French are also at work in the collections of lyric poems, which contain Wilbur's translations from French, Latin, Russian, Spanish, and Italian poems, dating from the fourth or fifth century to the work of his contemporaries. This latitude of sympathy for poets sometimes very idiosyncratic and different from one another (for example, Villon and Voltaire) is itself an expression of Wilbur's reach and suggests that like another American poet, he "contains multitudes."

The new poems that are now added to his six previous collections are as rich, varied, and accomplished as we have come to expect, and in addition he has risked, successfully, an admirable departure from his usual practice. Wilbur has written texts for musical settings before, and with great effect. Two very fine examples that come to mind are **"A Christmas Hymn"** and Pangloss's song about syphilis for the comic opera *Candide*. But now Wilbur has written a more extended text for a full cantata in celebration of the Statue of Liberty. It was written for the composer William Schuman, is divided into five sections, runs to a total of 102 lines, and is called **"On Freedom's Ground."** It seems to me to succeed wonderfully where anyone else I can think of would have failed. And the task was rife with potential pitfalls. There were the twin perils of jingoism and chauvinistic sentimentality on the one hand, and the symmetrical or compensatory danger of leaning over backward to avoid anything that looked suspiciously like "affirmation."

But over and above these was the problem of writing an extensive text for music. Many poets, and not a few composers, are likely to be obtuse in these matters. Poets incline to want to hang on to syntactical complexity and sinuousness, to resist end-stopped lines that these days are regarded as artificial, identified with 18th-century heroic couplets, verse epigrams, and plain lack of breath. Composers are sometimes too eager to find texts by poets of stature that are also short enough to set, and in consequence are likely to come up all too quickly with one of the more enigmatic and impenetrable of Emily Dickinson's poems, simply because it was written in the old hymnal quatrains, and thus seems eminently settable. Of modern poets Yeats may have been the most intuitive and plausible about writing for music, knowing somehow that he would have to simplify his ways if he wanted his auditors to grasp anything of what he wrote while having to attend to a vocal performance of music with accompaniment.

Wilbur has risked this kind of dangerous simplicity and straightforwardness, and has done so with great success. He has ingeniously made use of the device of the catalog, a genuine relief to a listener's need to follow the thread of an argument or a narrative, and he has cunningly and discreetly worked a famous phrase of Martin Luther King Jr.'s into the fabric of his text, where it is surely but unostentatiously reso-

nant. The cantata stands at the end of this new collection, separated from the rest and intended to be recognized for what it is: something written in a special, ceremonial, accessible idiom that will give the composer room to do some creative work of his own, and command some part of the listener's attention.

Before addressing the admirable new poems that open this volume I must confess that I am puzzled by a passage in one of Wilbur's loveliest and most celebrated poems, **"A Baroque Wall-Fountain in the Villa Sciarra."** After presenting a contrasting set of fountains, the poet returns to his *fons et origo* and asks:

> What of these showered fauns in their bizarre,
>   Spangled, and plunging house?
> They are at rest in fulness of desire
>   For what is given, they do not tire
> Of the smart of the sun, the pleasant water-douse
>   And riddled pool below,
> Reproving our disgust and our ennui
>   With humble insatiety.
> Francis, perhaps, who lay in sister snow
>   Before the wealthy gate
> Freezing and praising, might have seen in this
>   No trifle, but a shade of bliss—

But the account of Saint Francis on which these lines depend, and which comes from the anonymous *Little Flowers,* does not confirm what Wilbur says in his poem. The relevant passage goes this way:

> One winter day Saint Francis was walking with Brother Leo from Perugia to Saint Mary of the Angels, the Portiuncula. The very sharp cold made him suffer greatly, and he called to Brother Leo, who was walking ahead, and said: "Even though the Minor Brothers may set everywhere a fine example of holiness and edification, nevertheless write this down, and note carefully, that that does not make for perfect joy."

> And a little farther on Saint Francis called to him again: "O Brother Leo, even if the Minor Brothers should make the blind see, straighten crooked limbs, drive out demons, and make the deaf hear, the lame walk, the dumb speak, and—the greatest miracle—raise to life the four days dead, write that therein does not consist perfect joy."

After still more of these repudiations of what might have been thought the grounds for perfect joy, poor Brother Leo impatiently breaks out with "Father, I beg you, for God's sake, to tell me wherein lies perfect joy," and Francis answers as follows:

When we arrive at Saint Mary of the Angels, soaked by rain and frozen by cold, spattered with mud and tortured with hunger; if when we knock at the convent door, the porter comes angrily and says: "Who are you?" and we say: "We are two of your brothers"; and he says: "That is not true; you are a couple of tramps who go around fooling people and stealing the alms intended for the poor. So get out!" And when he won't open to us and he makes us stay outside till night, hungry in the snow and rain and cold—then if we bear all these rebuffs and cruel insults with patience, without answering back, and if we think with humility and charity that this doorkeeper really knows us, but God commands him to repulse us—then, O Brother Leo, write that there is perfect joy.

The new collection opens with a superb poem called **"The Ride,"** which continues a kind of obsessional theme that Wilbur has made characteristically his own: the poem that plays on the delicate and tenuous relationship between dream and waking. Readers of his work will know how this subject has preoccupied him in such poems as **"Love Calls Us to the Things of This World," "In Limbo," "Walking to Sleep," "For Ellen,"** and **"Marginalia,"** for example. The subtle changes between different states of consciousness are a rich source for poetry, and many of the best modern poets have worked the region with success, but none, I think, as successfully as Wilbur.

He also presents us with a translation of a poem by Joseph Brodsky called "Six Years Later," which Brodsky chose to open his most recent collection, *A Part of Speech*. It is a love poem of great formality, and with an ingenuity of metaphoric structure that is distinctly reminiscent of the poems of Donne. Brodsky was from very early in his career a great admirer of Donne, for whom he wrote an elegy. And it is no small accomplishment on Wilbur's part to have translated a poem from the Russian that allows the influence of the 17th-century poet to exhibit itself in a modern and modulated way.

I should add that Wilbur's translation, also included, of Apollinaire's "Mirabeau Bridge" is as miraculous in its poise and fragility as the original. There is a deftly funny poem called **"A Fable,"** which is a blithe commentary on American foreign policy, and a beautiful elegy for Auden. Again and again these poems take away the breath by the stunning aptness of simile or metaphor, and almost always of something in motion:

> Still, nothing changes as her perfect feet
> Click down the walk that issues in the street,
> Leaving the stations of her body there
> As a whip maps the countries of the air.

And in **"Trolling for Blues"** Wilbur returns to the subject of **"An Event,"** the problem of capturing in words or in the mind some fleeting hint of what is called "reality." This topic is also the focus of one of the very best, wittiest, and most thoughtful poems in the new groups, **"All That Is."** The poem begins with the mootness and growing obscurity of dusk, beautifully described, and with the uncertainty that this blurred hour engenders. As the night darkens the stars come out and we follow "a many-lighted bus" making its way through a city, and a passenger who has turned to the crossword puzzle, as have, at that hour, many others in the kitchens and parlors of their homes.

And somehow, strangely, suddenly, the poet invites us to raise our eyes above these heads bent over their puzzles to behold "a ghostly grille / Through which, as often, we begin to see / The confluence of the Oka and the Aare." We have moved wonderfully into a region of some obscurity, partly because of the approaching night, and partly because the language of crossword puzzles has, as it were, taken over. That grille we have focused upon is partly perhaps the gridwork of a celestial map, but much more surely the checkerboard of squares of a typical crossword puzzle in which we might find that two rivers, the Oka and the Aare, which in prosy geographical fact are located in Russia and Switzerland, can nevertheless form a confluence where their letters intersect. Their very names, perhaps, produce in the poet a kind of crossword reverie of exotic words, in which he giddily proceeds to indulge:

> Is it a vision? Does the eye make out
> A flight of ernes, rising from aits or aeries,
> Whose shadows track across a harsh terrain
> Of esker and arete? At waterside,
> Does the shocked eeler lay his congers by,
> Sighting a Reo driven by an edile?
> And does the edile, from his runningboard,
> Step down to meet a ranee? Does she end
> By reading to him from the works of Elia?

This charming fantasia of unanswered questions, this visionary excursion into the realm of the linguistically obscure, is not, in my view, the sort of text for which notes ought to be supplied or demanded. If it sends you, as it sent me, to the dictionary, and even to the Britannica, that is merely to acknowledge that the poet's mental life has gone off on a delightful toot of its own, and that we should take a puzzler's pleasure in tracking it down, just as he has attempted to trace, "Between the street-lamps and the jotted sky," a grille of crosswords that will resolve everything. There follows a passage I have not yet unravelled, in which the poet presents us with a vision of "A lambent god reposing on the sea, / Full of the knitted light of all that is." And he continues:

> It is a puzzle which, as puzzles do,

Dreams, that there is no puzzle. It is a rite
Of finitude, a picture in whose frame
Roc, oast, and Inca decompose at once
Into the ABCs of every day.
A door is rattled shut, a deadbolt thrown.
Under some clipped euonymus, a mushroom,
Bred of an old and deep mycelium
As hidden as the webwork of the world,
Strews, on the shifty night-wind, rising now,
A cast of spores as many as the stars.

Witty and complex and lovely as this poem may be, I nevertheless feel that another blank verse poem of meditation, titled **"Lying,"** is, at least in my present view of things, the best poem in the collection. It begins with distinct modesty this way:

To claim, at a dead party, to have spotted a
    grackle,
When in fact you haven't of late, can do no harm.
Your reputation for saying things of interest
Will not be marred, if you hasten to other topics.
Nor will the delicate web of human trust
Be ruptured by that airy fabrication.

The poem then goes on to speculate about what it is that prompts us to these little acts of mendacity. Perhaps, initially, an impatience or boredom with the dailiness, the sheer routine, of things, and even with the more miraculous of things, "the horse's neck / Clothed with its usual thunder," in an echo of the majestic words of God in the 39th chapter of the Book of Job. That biblical catalog of divine wonders is always before us, as are other, still more uncommon, wonders, "And so with that most rare conception, nothing."

Since evil is only the absence of good, and since Satan is the Prince of Lies, he makes his sinuous entrance into the poem with almost unperceived skill, as "the water of a dried-up well / Gone to assail the cliffs of Labrador." He then approaches us, "pretending not to be," and appears, in the words of Milton from the ninth book of *Paradise Lost,* as a "*black mist low creeping,*" which, when it rises, turns to a rainbow. But perhaps because of the invocation of Milton, the poem now finds itself confronting the axiom that art itself is a lie of sorts, and, in the words of Shakespeare's Touchstone, "The truest poetry is the most feigning." All of it is, according to Aristotle, a form of imitation, which is a kind of lie. Wilbur continues:

Closer to making than the deftest fraud
Is seeing how the catbird's tail was made
To counterpoise, on the mock-orange spray,
Its light, up-tilted spine; or, lighter still,
How the shucked tunic of an onion, brushed
To one side on a backlit currents, prints and prints

Its bright, ribbed shadows like a flapping sail.
Odd that a thing is most itself when likened: . . .

And now we have come to the very heart of metaphor itself. It is metaphor that allows us to contemplate a great deal that might otherwise be intolerable, and, like tragedy, it "Finds pleasure in the cruellest simile." We return to the catbird, which, like a mockingbird, or a poet, is distinguished as a mimic, gifted in the art of imitation. The bird's song is characterized as "a chant / Of the first springs," and as a "tributary / To the great lies told with the eyes half-shut / That have the truth in view: . . ." There follow three such lies, all of them masterpieces of the imagination. The first is the pagan tale of Chiron, who "Instructed brute Achilles in the lyre," another of Wilbur's serious puns. The second is the biblical image of faultless Eden, and the third the concluding sacrifice and valor of Roland:

who to Charles his king
And to the dove that hatched the dove tailed world
Was faithful unto death, and shamed the Devil.

There is nobility in such utterance that is deeply persuasive, and throughout Wilbur's poetry we are accustomed to finding this rare quality, usually joined to wit, good humor, grace, modesty, and a kind of physical zest or athletic dexterity that is, so far as I know, unrivaled.

Peter Harris (essay date Summer 1990)

SOURCE: "Forty Years of Richard Wilbur: The Loving Work of an Equilibrist," in *Virginia Quarterly Review,* Vol. 66, No. 3, Summer 1990, pp. 412-25.

[*In the following essay, Harris surveys major themes in Wilbur's poetry and explains how his work in* New and Collected Poems *forms a cohesive whole.*]

The publication of Richard Wilbur's *New and Collected Poems* brings under one cover his six previous books, plus 27 new poems and translations. Reading through four decades of work, comprising almost 250 poems, invitingly arranged in reverse chronological order, ringingly emphasizes the justice of his reputation as the master of his craft. His poetry celebrates the power of metaphorical language to divine the human implications of natural patternment, and it affirms the capacity of strict metrics to contain both the dictates of civility and the promptings of joy.

While Wilbur has extended his range of topic, theme, and metrical form, and while he has gradually become more direct, he has never found it necessary to alter the fundamental cast of his poetry as did, for example, Robert Lowell or James Wright. He has remained steadfast in his commitment to formalism, or, more precisely, to the indissolubility of form and value. Wilbur, like his mentor, Frost, has always been an equilibrist, up on the tightrope performing feats of association in the process of his search for an equilibrium between apparently opposed objects of desire. Most often, that opposition is construed in the poems as a yearning for a formal perfection beyond the depredations of time and an equally strong impulse to harrow the pleasures of the physical world. Put another way, the major theme in Wilbur's work reflects the central tension in Western metaphysics, between the ideal and the real, between being and becoming. At times, by virtue of his interest in essences, archetypes, and caught moments of perfection, Wilbur seems to express an informal neo-Platonism. For example, in **"Complaint,"** he has shown himself willing to explore—in good faith, seasoned with comic irony—Ficino's proposition that, "In reality, each love is that of the divine image and each is pure." Eden recurs several times in these poems, most recently in an almost nostalgic way, as the place "where we first mislaid / Simplicity of wish and will." And in the wonderful poem **"In Limbo,"** the speaker goes so far as to call himself "a truant portion of the all / Misshaped by time, incorrigible desire / And dear attachment to a sleeping hand."

> **The major theme in Wilbur's work reflects the central tension in Western metaphysics, between the ideal and the real, between being and becoming.**
> *—Peter Harris*

The spiritualizing side of consciousness has moments, in Wilbur's work, when it accepts its truancy into earthly existence only with a shudder. In **"Love Calls Us to the Things of This World,"** the soul, entranced by the angelic billowing of laundry on the line, somewhat shockingly describes mundane existence as "the punctual rape of every blessed day." For a moment, the soul hangs back from the onset of day and wishes for an existence comprised of shadowless felicity, "clear dances done in the sight of heaven." Only the heat of the sun reconciles the soul, in a mood of "bitter love," to accept that lovers will and must walk out in their fresh clothes "to be undone" and that even nuns must be clothed in "dark habits" to keep their "difficult balance." Finding that difficult balance between being and becoming, and between felicity and *gravitas,* is precisely Wilbur's forte. His work takes no particular position on formal religion, but it does seem to lean a bit, at times, in the direction of granting the archetypes a metaphysical rather than a merely psychological existence.

But the presence of metaphysical pathos in his work only

intensifies the poignancy of Wilbur's devotion to physicality. It would be hard to find a contemporary poet more evidently solicitous of the irreducible particularity of the natural world. His aesthetic appreciation of the visible world is suffused with wonder and a sense of kinship. While he is no Whitman seeking to liquefy and merge with the scent of lilacs or to ventriloquize the barbaric yawp of a spotted hawk, Wilbur's poetry has always affirmed, as he puts it in the title poem of his second book, that "ceremony never did conceal . . . How much we are the woods we wander in." As contemporary connections with the major literary figures of the American 19th century grow more tenuous, there is still perceptible in Wilbur a direct lineage, through Frost, back to Emerson's insistence that we can liberate ourselves, and create a liberating literature, by exploring the implications of the proposition that "natural facts are signs of spiritual facts."

Instances of the seminal reciprocity between nature and spirit abound in Wilbur. Opening the *New and Collected Poems* at random, I find, in **"Fern-Beds in Hampshire County,"** this characteristic surmise:

> Whatever at the heart
> Of creatures makes them branch and burst apart,
> Or at the core of star or tree may burn
> At last to turn
> And make an end of time.

The human, the natural, and the interstellar world are all of a piece in this passage, by virtue of the fact that their growth, their fission, is fueled by the fire of procreation which is also the fire of de-creation.

Because the end of time imagined in the **"Fern-Beds"** seems a remote astrophysical event, the poet speaks with understandable detachment, but Wilbur's voice can be considerably more urgent when considering the possibility that humankind may end time and destroy nature prematurely. He does this most memorably in his widely anthologized **"Advice to a Prophet,"** and, in the process, he shows his mastery of all the elements of poetry that interest him: the musical, the lyrical, the metaphorical, the descriptive, the dialectical, even the high rhetorical, to which he rises in the peroration that ends the poem:

> What should we be without
> The dolphin's arc, the dove's return,
>
> These things in which we have seen ourselves and
> spoken?
> Ask us, prophet, how we shall call
> Our natures forth when that live tongue is all
> Dispelled, that glass obscured or broken
>
> In which we have said the rose of our love and the

clean
Horse of our courage, in which beheld
The singing locust of the soul unshelled,
And all we mean or wish to mean.

Ask us, ask us whether with the worldless rose
Our hearts shall fail us; come demanding
Whether there shall be lofty or long standing
When the bronze annals of the oak-tree close.

The tendency to think of Wilbur as a cool formalist, detached, ironic, witty, has a basis in fact. But detachment and engagement are not necessarily opposites in poetry; moreover, there are any number of poems in the vein of **"Advice to a Prophet,"** poems that boil high emotionally, that verge on hymns, that passionately apostrophize, and most of all, that celebrate. In fact, Wilbur is, first and last, a celebratory poet, most often of the transient epiphanic glories of the natural world. And whether the subject is natural or human, the central value in his work is love.

Perhaps it is this combination of devotion to craft and a capacity for joyful love, Wilbur's form and value, that has kept his work so vital for so long. Though he is nearing 70, the 27 *New Poems,* as they are referred to in the table of contents [of *New and Collected Poems*], show him near the top of his powers. All the characteristic interests are here renewed: a preoccupation with the relationship between what lies within and what lies beyond our ken, a probing for implications in minute particulars in the natural world, an affirmation of the capacity of art to make the world seem more like itself through metaphor. What sign is there, then, of Wilbur's relationship to his advancing years? Congenitally optative, devoted to what survives rather than to what is lost, he has never been much attracted to the elegiac mode, and has been most comfortable treating death as an event in the cyclical process of renewal. This doesn't change in the *New Poems;* however, one may detect, if not a faint valedictory mood, at least an increased attention to what lies outside the light.

In the first poem, **"The Ride,"** the speaker, in a dream, rides through a nightscape of "shattering vacancies / On into what was not." Characteristically, though, the vacancies do not bother him; he survives them, and his main worry is how to keep alive the nocturnal mare that carried him through, and beyond, uncreation. Similarly in **"Alatus,"** dedicated to "R.P.W.," whom we must assume is the late Robert Penn Warren, the poet meditates on autumnal change. Such change is figured first as a battle which the leaves lose: "Their supply lines cut, / The leaves go down to defeat." But this un-Wilburian conceit gets overturned in favor of a celebration of time's brave condescension:

This time's true valor

Is a rash consent to change,
To crumbling pallor,

Dust, and dark re-merge.
See how the fire-bush, circled
By a crimson verge

Of its own sifting.
Bristles aloft its every
Naked stem, lifting

Beyond the faint sun,
Toward the hid pulse of things, its
Winged skeleton.

No getting tangled in the bare ruin'd choirs for Wilbur. In fact, no "nothing" for Wilbur. In **"Lying,"** a wonderfully supple aesthetic meditation, the poet denies ontological status to "nothing," referring to it instead as a "conception," albeit "most rare." Much as Borges denies "oblivion" in a sonnet Wilbur translated in *Walking to Sleep,* he finds "nothing" to be nothing in itself. Instead, it is "something missed," not gone in an absolute sense but redistributed elsewhere in the universe: "It is the water of a dried-up well / Gone to assail the cliffs of Labrador." This is the poetry of a man for whom wells are not forbidding cylinders of absence but vessels that can generally be counted on to spontaneously refill themselves from unfathomable sources. Whatever else he believes, Wilbur trusts that we all lie in the lap of an immense intelligence. "Step off assuredly into the blank of your mind," he counsels in **"Walking to Sleep,"** "Something will come to you." How so? By virtue of an imperial faith that more things wait on us than we can ever know: "As a queen sits down, knowing that a chair will be there, / Or a general raises his hand and is given the field glasses."

Given his bent toward affirmation, it is not so surprising that the saddest, most valedictory moment in the *New Poems* is not strictly Wilbur's own, but his masterful translation of Joseph Brodsky's "Six Years Later," which concerns a love relationship that endured while all manner of change and dissolution occurred in its environs. The poem, whose refrain is the increasingly poignant "So long had life together been," closes with the couple drifting away through the double door that their life had comprised, out "into the future, into the night." Wilbur has spent years rendering new English versions of Molière and, more recently and just as brilliantly, of Racine. He has few peers as a translator of poetry, and no one since Pound has made better use of translation for expanding the evident range of his or her poetic sympathies. It might even be said that his translations dovetail so well into his individual collections that they should be considered aspects of his vision. The uprooted Brodsky breathes in air of loss which is not Wilbur's own, but is one for which he has evident sympathy. The closest Wilbur himself comes to

Brodsky's pathos is in the gravely comic apocalypse of "Leaving," a poem about a moment of transformation brought by the descent of evening upon a garden party. As they leave the party, the speaker and his companion look back and discover that shadows have worked aesthetic magic:

> Curt shadows in the grass
> Hatched every blade,
> And now on pedestals
> Of mounting shade
>
> Stood all our friends—iconic,
> Now, in mien,
> Half-lost in dignities
> Till now unseen.

At the moment of departure, the archetypes intrude. Briefly the world becomes a stage, or gallery, which seems not less, but more, real than ordinary life. Wilbur's speaker is evidently moved but also embarrassed by having become iconic. He says he and his friends have "blundered into grand / Identities." It is important for Wilbur's sense of propriety that the dignities are not consciously assumed but rather revealed by an act of nature: "We had not played so surely, / Had we known."

After "Leaving," the *New Poems* primarily seek Wilbur's most familiar terrain, not the "outer dark," as he puts it in "Icarium Mare," but "a small province haunted by the good, / Where something may be understood." As it happens, rivers and oceans run through that province, and Wilbur goes a-fishing in them. In "Trolling for Blues," "Shad-Time," and "Hamlen Brook," Wilbur angles after metaphysical insight and aesthetic delight. "Hamlin Brook," the last of the new poems—excepting the somewhat disappointing libretto for the cantata, *On Freedom's Ground*—shows the poet in particularly fine and playful form. The issue the poem addresses might be described as one of gustatory epistemology: how do we "drink in" the instantaneous configurations that flow by us in such astonishing profusion? The opening of the poem might stand as object lesson to young poets about how to establish a dramatic situation, and the speaker's relation to it, with utmost economy and precision:

> At the alder-darkened brink
> Where the stream slows to a lucid jet
> I lean to the water, dinting its top with sweat,
> And see, before I can drink,
>
> A startled inchling trout
> of spotted near-transparency,
> Trawling a shadow solider than he.

The musical and descriptive delicacy of this passage matches the delicacy of the inchling itself. As in "Leaving," a shadow creates perspective by incongruity and, paradoxically, grants a substantiality to the young trout that the creature ordinarily lacks. The masterstroke is the unobtrusive use of the figuratively exact word "trawling" just where the sway of idiom would have us expect "trailing."

The poem goes on to detail the "flicked slew / Of sparks and glittering silt," as well as other minute glories in the stream before it pans back suddenly to show us, first, sky reflected on the water's surface and, then, birch trees which seem sublimely both to plunge and soar, "Toward where the azures of the zenith drown." After flirting with vertigo, the poet then springs the central question, "How shall I drink all this?" The concluding answer, for Wilbur is an answerer, shows a characteristic doubleness:

> Joy's trick is to supply
> Dry lips with what can cool and slake,
> Leaving them dumbstruck also with an ache
> Nothing can satisfy.

Wilbur affirms the importance of poems ending with a window and a door. Enough, and a thirst for more. A feeling of completion with no pretense that Hamlen Brook has been contained. The brook will clearly percolate onward, swelling, evaporating, re-emerging to assail the cliffs of Labrador.

If "Hamlin Brook" were, God forbid, to be Wilbur's last poem, it would be a fitting epitome. And *New Poems* would be a highly respectable finale. In poems I have not mentioned, it may be that Wilbur indulges his epigrammatic or hoary Horatian side a bit too fully, at least from the perspective of one who prefers his lyricism. But in reading backwards through Wilbur's collected poems, *New Poems* does not suffer much by comparison. That being said, *The Mind Reader* (1976) seems to me to edge out the others as Wilbur's best—or, at least, his most urgently moving—volume. I trust I am not merely displaying the vagrant prejudice of a crisis-burdened age toward the urgently personal in poetry, when I say I find "The Writer" and "Cottage Street, 1953," both in *The Mind-Reader,* if not the best, then the two most affecting poems that Wilbur has written. Part of the reason they hit with uncommon impact may be that Wilbur is usually so reticent. The reader, therefore, has the sense that, against certain ingrained commitments to preserving his privacy in the inevitably self-revealing vocation of poetry, Wilbur has, in these two poems, something quite private to which he simply must give public form.

Both poems are, of course, not mere autobiography but its transfiguration into something different, namely, poetry. Technically speaking, both are beautifully accomplished, though neither poem is particularly preoccupied with the pyrotechnic feats of metaphorical phrasing that leave us seeing stars in other of Wilbur's masterpieces, for example, **"On the Eyes of an SS Officer"** or **"A Baroque Wall-Fountain in the Villa Sciarra."**

"Cottage Street: 1953" draws no Frostian veil over its historicity. The poem is about Wilbur's agonizingly poignant encounter with Sylvia Plath soon after her penultimate suicide attempt. Inevitably, the poem breathes in an air of fatedness. Wilbur has been invited by the redoubtable Edna Ward to meet Plath and to serve her as a role model of the fulfilled poet, thereby lifting her spirits. Wilbur's description of this impossible situation is unforgettable:

> I am a stupid life-guard who has found,
> Swept to his shallows by the tide, a girl
> who, far from shore, has been immensely
>   drowned,
> And stares through water now with eyes of pearl.

What makes this stanza so distinctively rich is not the borrowing of Shakespeare's pearls, however apt that borrowing may be, but the paradoxical use of the word "immensely" in the phrase "immensely drowned." As we accede to the stanza's conceit of a seaside drowning, the details of its geography tempt us momentarily to forget it is not literal, until we come to "immensely," which reminds us we are considering not just a beach accident which has unceremoniously snuffed a consciousness, but a self-induced drowning of the soul which, horribly, the body has survived, though it wears an uncannily posthumous stare.

As a feat of narrative poetry, **"Cottage Street, 1953"** is electrified by the contrast between the speaker's sense of helplessness, which links him to Plath, and the tremendously purposive decorum of the speaker's verse form which links him to the character of Edna Ward who, by her commanding civility, is attempting to catalyze a resurrection of Plath's spirit. We do not discover whether, in the short term, Ward's efforts have any positive effect. We suspect they do not, though there is no suggestion that Ward is behaving shallowly or hubristically by inviting them to tea. On the contrary, she is being true to herself. The ending of the poem dramatizes the stunning contrast between the tempered armature of Ward's sympathetic grace and the phosphorous trail of Plath's descending comet:

> And Edna Ward shall die in fifteen years,
> After her eight-and-eighty summers of
> Such grace and courage as permit no tears,
> The thin hand reaching out, the last word love,
>
> Outliving Sylvia who, condemned to live,
> Shall study for a decade, as she must,

> To state at last her brilliant negative
> In poems free and helpless and unjust.

It is a tribute to Wilbur's sure-footed sense of justice that he can end the poem with the Johnsonian judgment that her poems, though brilliant, are "unjust" and yet be confident that his judgment neither stings nor condescends because it occurs in such an intensely sympathetic context.

It is precisely this same intensity of sympathy, or, if you will, love, which brings Wilbur's justly famous **"The Writer"** so indelibly alive. All well-written poems implicitly justify the act that brings them into being. It happens that **"The Writer"** explicitly justifies the act as well. It shows, in the context of Wilbur's relationship with his daughter, why the act of writing is, when scrupulously practiced, also an act of love, one that can be simultaneously personal and yet disinterested in an almost pure, Spinozan sense. Both love poem and *ars poetica,* its two modalities coalesce as perfectly as value and form ever do. Other poems of Wilbur's are more dazzling, will astonish us more with their Nijinskian or Michael Jordan-like air time, their liberating sense of difficulties overcome, their deceptively effortless articulation of ineluctable intricacy, but there is something uniquely moving about **"The Writer."** Wilbur is often a surprising poet, but the quality of surprise in this poem is so fine, so retrospectively inevitable, that the poem seems, as only the finest feats of craft do, to possess an authenticity beyond the reach of artfulness.

Other poems of Wilbur's are more dazzling, will astonish us more with their Nijinskian or Michael Jordan-like air time, their liberating sense of difficulties overcome, their deceptively effortless articulation of ineluctable intricacy, but there is something uniquely moving about "The Writer."
—Peter Harris

As with **"Cottage Street, 1953," "The Writer"** touches on the struggle of a woman writer, in this case Wilbur's daughter. As we eventually discover, the stakes of her struggle are also high, though, thankfully, her situation is infinitely less dire than Plath's. She is caught up in the strenuous business of creation, to which Wilbur is especially sympathetic because it is his daughter who is laboring and because he is acutely aware, from experience, how fraught writing can become at the junction of ink and page. The expository part of the poem is simply rendered; the poet is thinking of his daughter, who is upstairs writing a story. He figures her situation in nautical terms, the first of two conceits which carry the poem's freight. The sound of her typewriter reminds him of a "chain hauled over a gunwale" which, in turn, leads him to imagine her interior life as "a great cargo, and some of it heavy." There is nothing particularly surprising or distinctive about the opening section of the poem, which, as it turns out, is precisely the point.

The poem changes direction when the daughter's typewriter falls silent, implying an impasse in her search for the *mot juste.* The poet personalizes that pause, as if it were an implicit rejection of his too "easy" imagining of her life as a voyage. As her typewriter begins again with a "bunched clamor" and then once more ceases, he is carried by the winds of association to a more precise, more intense, more completely adequate analogy that lifts this poem to greatness. The on-again, off-again rhythm of his daughter's typing reminds him of the fitful struggle of a bird that had once strayed into her room:

> I remember the dazed starling
> Which was trapped in that very room, two years
>   ago;
> How we stole in, lifted a sash
>
> And retreated, not to affright it;
> And how for a helpless hour, through the crack of
>   the door,
> We watched the sleek, wild, dark
>
> And iridescent creature
> Batter against the brilliance, drop like a glove
> To the hard floor, or the desk-top,
>
> And wait then, humped and bloody,
> For the wits to try it again; and how our spirits
> Rose when, suddenly sure,
>
> It lifted off from a chair-back,
> Beating a smooth course for the right window
> And clearing the sill of the world.

The poem might have ended with the successful escape, and memorably. The strongly stressed set of adjectives describing the bird as a "sleek, wild, dark, / And iridescent creature" help objectify the struggle of creative energy to free itself through form. And the final phrase, "the sill of the world," makes clear that the issuance of the struggle is a moment of transcendence, the sudden sense of liberation that occurs the instant a stumbling block transforms itself into a stepping stone. But Wilbur has one more stanza for us, one that brings the largest implications of what has happened into even clearer relief:

> It is always a matter, my darling,
> Of life or death, as I had forgotten. I wish
> What I wished you before, but harder.

And here we have it, exposed through explicit statement, the fundamental impulse that drives Wilbur's scrupulous decorum. The finding of the right analogy for his daughter's situation is both the measure of the quality of his love and of the quality of his poem. Craftsmanship, in this instance, becomes a kind of exemplary categorical imperative with existentialist overtones: either we are exacting in our search for what is right and, thereby, affirm life or we are seduced by fatal ease and become, symbolically, unquickened. **"The Writer,"** a poem that begins as a caterpillar but becomes a butterfly, is only one example among many why, as long as we care about poetry, Richard Wilbur will be among the quick and not the dead, why he will remain a figure we turn to in order to renew the terms of our care, and not for poetry alone.

Richard Wilbur with Steve Kronen (interview date May-June 1991)

SOURCE: "Richard Wilbur: An Interview," in *The American Poetry Review,* Vol. 20, No. 3, May-June 1991, pp. 45-55.

[*Kronen is an American poet and critic. In the following interview, Wilbur discusses his influences, his thoughts on being poet laureate, and his opinions of contemporary poetry.*]

[*Steve Kronen:*] *For the past four or five years, there has been a range-war of sorts in the various journals between the so-called New Formalists and, ironically, the old free versers. What are your thoughts about this interchange?*

[Richard Wilbur]: I'm aware that there is something of that sort going on, and I was recently sent an article from *APR* by Ira Sadoff, in which he was engaging in one side of the controversy at considerable length. I don't follow all of the poetry periodicals, turning all the pages, but I know that there is a lot of talk about the New Formalism. Some of the young poets whom I know and think well of are associated, by people who engage in this sort of taxonomy, with the New Formalism. Of course it makes them nervous. No one wants to be defined simply in terms of whether he uses meter or not, whether he makes rhymes and stanzas. I think that the best of our poets who work in traditional forms, who make use of traditional forms, would rather be approached, as Mr. Sadoff said, in terms of their vision than in terms of their technical means.

I don't know that I can explain the resurgence of "form" except to say that a certain kind of extremely relaxed, personal and prosaic free verse poem may have run its course, may have tested itself about as much as it can, and that a number of poets now see it as a new and exciting thing to take advantage of the special capabilities of these old instruments—meter and rhyme. You run into people in poetry societies who attribute a kind of intrinsic sanity and goodness and even moral quality to received forms. I do think that that is nonsense. There's nothing essentially good about a meter in itself. And I think it is unfortunate for people to look back with nostalgia toward such poetic means, or to look towards the future in terms of them. They are really timeless. There is nothing particularly dated, is there, about a fundamental tool like a hammer? A hammer is neither of the past nor of the future. And that is how I think we should look at these things.

There was a while in the early part of this century when people like Eliot and Pound and Ford Madox Ford, who were very discriminating about many things, made that sort of error in their discussions of meter and rhyme. Timothy Steele has discussed this very well in a new book of his—*Missing Measures.*

People like Bill Williams used to say—as a matter of fact he said it to me—that a sonnet written nowadays was a curtsy to the court of Elizabeth I, that to write a sonnet was to commit yourself not only to 14 lines in iambic pentameter, but also to fall of necessity into old locutions, into tired diction. Well, that's not true. It was undoubtedly true of Williams that when he started out as a young poet, he tried to write in meter and rhyme and found himself being old fashioned and altogether too lovely, and therefore rightly moved away from those forms because he couldn't handle them. He couldn't, as Pound said, make them new. Well, we've made that kind of mistake in associating meters with ancient and tired diction and themes for a long time. There are people still making that mistake. And I shall be glad if an energetic movement, tendency, call it what you will, changes our minds about that, and makes it apparent to us that these tools can be used in the freshest way, and have nothing necessarily to do with whatever in the metrical poetry of the last century we would like to repudiate or not do again.

Many of the poets who published their first books in the last ten years or so studied under poets who themselves had written little or no verse in received forms. Can a poet, even if he or she chooses not to write in traditional forms get by without practicing it on studying formal prosody?

I guess my feeling about it is this: that poets who are any good and who do their homework—that is to say, who read the poetry of the English tradition right back as far as they can go, and respond to it—will have been keeping in touch with what can be done in so-called form, whatever their personal practice may have been. A few years ago, Brad Leithauser said in some publication that he thought that one of the many ruptures in culture brought on by the late fifties and sixties was loss of familiarity with meter, loss of the

ability to read confidently in meter, to know what metrical poetry was doing. I'm not so sure he was right. Not long ago the poet John Ridland, on the West Coast, offered some of my light verse poems, my children's poems called **"Opposites,"** to one of his writing classes. They're done in rhymed tetrameters, and after he showed them some of these poems and they talked a little about what they were doing, he said, all right, write some of these poems, write some opposites. Most of these young poets, Ridland told me, had not written in meter and rhyme before. He sent me some samples of their work and it was pretty good. They did know what tetrameters were and they could write them, just as people who have been watching waltzers for some time, but not waltzing themselves, can catch on pretty quickly.

I think, by the way—just to put in a parenthesis here, a response to one thing you said—I don't think that the study of prosody, the abstract study of prosody, is of any use to beginning poets. It's a bore. The use of prosodic terminology, it seems to me, is critical and not creative. We need sometimes, in order to talk about how a line of Gerard Manley Hopkins operates, to use terms like pentameter and talk about extra unstressed syllables, but heavens, I don't think anybody ever caught on the writing of meter by any means except infection.

About twenty-five years ago, you stated, "A good part of my work could, I suppose, be understood as a public quarrel with the aesthetics of Edgar Allan Poe. What are the aesthetics of Edgar Allan Poe and have you and Mr. Poe come to terms?

I think the people we quarrel with are always the people whom we're attracted to or people in whom we see something of ourselves. I like the thing that my friend Pierre Schneider said years and years ago; he said that "All satire is confession," and I do think that's true. If I denounce something in a poem, I denounce it because I understand it. And why do I understand it? I understand it because the reprehensible thing I'm pointing to it is something of which I'm capable or even guilty. So, in the case of Poe, I feel an attraction to him. And I think he was a genius and a great innovator in prose fiction, and in the exploration of states of mind and of the warfare that goes on in the soul. Those are the things that draw me greatly.

Is that the aesthetic to which you refer?

No, it's not. I think his poetry is the minor part of his work, and in his critical writing he distinguishes between prose fiction, in which a certain amount of what he calls truth is permitted, and poetry in which the sole object is beauty. And beauty consisted for him—I wish I could quote him exactly right now, I haven't been reading him of late, but I can paraphrase—it consisted for him in "a wild effort to reach the beauty above." Yes, that's how he put it. If poetry is forever renouncing this world and reaching out toward the beauty above, it means that it has a kind of destructive economy. Whatever of a mundane character poetry looks at, it is the business of poetry to destroy, to negate, so as to give the reader and the poet a sense of transcendence, a sense of embarkation toward the beyond. That's a rather exciting idea. It's like John Cage's theories, you know, exciting in themselves, desperately bad in their application.

Indeed, do you see as one of poetry's purposes to destroy and recreate?

No, I'm saying that's Poe's theory, that's Poe's view of poetry. There are various techniques in his work for negating, for putting to death almost everything that he mentions. Almost everything that isn't already hazy and of the spirit, he disintegrates in his poetry. He does this not only by verbal tricks, but also by the hypnotic, chanting character of his poems. They're there to put you to sleep, to put you perhaps into what seems a visionary condition. And I'm just too earth bound a person by nature, and on principle, to find that prescription satisfactory.

I think that we don't understand this world perfectly, and I think that it's reasonable to say that we live both here and in heaven. But we can't write poetry simply about heaven, we can't write poetry simply about transcendent things. We have to work with what's under our noses, and give the creation proper respect. So that's my war with Poe, I think. Have I been clear?

No ideas but in things?

Yes, I've always been fond of that expression, which of course is challenging and extreme. And would lead you away from using all abstract terms, all large concepts, make you embody everything in the Imagist object. It had marvelous results in Williams, and I know that he will always be one of my inspirers, but I wouldn't want to take on his program absolutely.

"Heaven in a grain of sand," to rephrase Blake here?

Yes, that mode of transcendence in which you see everything in itself and also see what is wonderful in it what has symbolic implications, what is divine in it. That's an aesthetic which appeals to me far more than Poe's.

Which was to negate that for the other world?

Yes, to negate the object. You never see any grains of sand in Poe. Never see much of anything.

Before Auden died, you said of him, "At the moment he's the best presence around, our most civilized, accomplished and heartening poet." And in your elegy to him you referred to his civil tongue and that he was the poet of all our cities. Is there anybody you would apply that description to now?

I think there are a number of very good, civilized poets among us. I don't think at the moment that I would vote for one as playing exactly the versatile and civilizing and encompassing role that Auden played. But of course, when I said that about Auden, he'd been at it for quite awhile. We'd had time to steep ourselves in his work, develop a long gratitude, apply to him words like "great," and I suspect that there are amongst us right now a number of poets of comparable stature doing a similar job, being in the broadest sense civilized. I don't think I want to reel off a list of names, though you or I could both think of poets of more or less my generation about whom I'd be inclined to say similar words of praise.

How about my generation?

I don't know the younger generation as well as I used to. For a long while there I was on the poetry board of the Wesleyan Poetry Program, of which I was an initiator, and I read (it seems to me) everything that was being written for many years, and was much in touch, and I'm less so now. All I know is that there are a lot of exciting young talents around. I know of a number of people in their thirties who seem awfully good to me. I don't think that I would right away apply to any of them the sort of praise I gave to Auden. You have to have had a long career before you're given that kind of gratitude. But there's a lot of reason for hope, indeed, enthusiasm.

You use the terms "civilized, accomplished, heartening" when talking about Auden. Do you see that as a function of poetry to civilize and hearten as a stay against anarchy or entropy?

Yes, certainly to civilize. It's a very unfortunate thing, I think, that we have taken off our poets a lot of the burdens that used to be on them. In the Soviet Union, they still look to the poet as a kind of conscience of the country.

An unacknowledged legislator, to wheel out another cliché?

Yes, kind of acknowledged, I think, some of them, as valuable social critics, not as protestors, not this dreary business of protesting. I think that the political role is one that we overdo. But the business of being the conscience of the nation, the conscience of the culture, that's something that the best Russian poets have always performed, sometimes, of course, to the point of protest. And then I think that poets, like all writers, should be continuators and custodians of our culture. I hate to apply the word "should" to poets, but let me say I'm grateful to writers who do that job, who don't simply sit in some room somewhere and complain of the draft and tell us that their dog is sick and that their father is dead. There's more to what poets can do and say than that. Heartening: when I speak of heartening, in connection with poetry, I don't think I mean poets should take on the job that the fireside poets gave themselves in the nineteenth century. So much of Bryant and Longfellow is kindly counsel, religious encouragement, a kind of noble hand-holding. I don't think that poetry is necessarily called on to do that at present. The heartening that a poet ought to do is to be as articulate as possible about his own life, his own feelings, and also about serious matters in which he's involved with the society in general. And so preserve us from inarticulateness. That's the heartening thing poetry does, I think, to have a great vocabulary and to use it as clearly as the subject permits.

When you think of Auden now, Auden the man, what do you think of?

I didn't know him very well. I had just a few encounters with him. When he published his book, *Nones,* I did a review of it for a little magazine published down at Johns Hopkins. And he wrote me a very pleasant letter saying that he had appreciated what I had said, that I'd caught his drift and that he wished that I had noticed that in his poem, "In Praise of Limestone," he had been using syllabics of 11 and 14. I hadn't noticed that. That was a species of encounter.

Later I met him at the Robert Frost's 85th birthday dinner in New York, at which Lionel Trilling gave the most interesting talk to which so many people objected. At that time, Auden and I discussed martinis and how hard it was to get a decent martini away from home. And at another time, when I was editing a series of paperback books of poetry for Dell, the Laurel series, I got Auden to agree to do one of the books and we had lunch together with an editor from Dell. And Auden was most amusing.

Did you want him to edit a book?

Yes, and he did, in fact, he did a beautiful job of editing a book of nineteenth-century English minor poets. But on that occasion at lunch, we went over English poetry from the beginning, at any rate, from Chaucer. And I would simply say, "Skelton" and he would say, "not bad at all." Or I would name some other name, and he would say, "a bore."

An example of the latter?

I don't remember which authors he considered bores. I should remember, because I kept making notes to think it over. But there were too many poets talked about. The ques-

tion was, what other authors we should represent in our series. And he was very arbitrary, he didn't give any arguments, but there was clearly spontaneity and conviction in what he said, and that was fun to do. The only other thing I remember about that luncheon was that toward the end of it, speaking of a common acquaintance, I said, well in view of such and such, I think I approve of him. And he said, "What did you say?" And I said, oh dear, that sounds a little smug, doesn't it? One doesn't approve of people. And he said no, certainly not (laughter) I think he did not much care for being judgmental.

He was so strong in his opinions, though I suppose that's different from being judgmental.

He was being strong in his aesthetic opinions, but as for judging people as people, I think that he had a good deal of the quality of mercy.

I suppose that's what you find so civilized in him?

That is one thing about him. I think that, although a lot of people have said that Auden's attending 8:00 mass every Sunday in his carpet slippers because his feet hurt, was mostly an aesthetic thing, that he enjoyed the pomp of it, the forms of it . . . many people have said that. But I don't think so really, I think that he was a serious, religious sensibility and a serious thinker about such matters. There's a strong moralistic element in Auden. I really think that he wanted to be good, and in fact, I could put in evidence certain of his poems like "Music is International" from that book *Nones,* which in a clever way does that most dangerous of things, he comes out in favor of kindness.

There was a period in mid to late-nineteenth century when Shelley fell out of favor and later Eliot more or less revived the reputations of Donne and Herbert. Are there any poets you feel have been overlooked, or the other way around, held in regard beyond their merits?

I'm sure that I could, given time, come up with some names on both sides of that I don't know whether I'm spoiling to devalue anybody right now, I'm very glad that Eliot changed his mind about John Milton. Because when people ask me what poet of another time I might like to be, I know that that's the answer. I'm very devoted to Milton except for *Paradise Regained,* which I can't stomach.

Why can't you?

I simply have never been able as they say, to "dig" it. It's never seemed to me to have the force and the verbal excitement and the technical glory of *Paradise Lost* or a lot of the early poems, the early short poems. I've been told by many people that when I grew up I would find that the severity of

Paradise Regained would appeal to me, the plainness. The plainness in some other poets very much appeals to me. In Shakespeare, who can write a very plain line, and in Dante, and in many another poet of lower degree. But *Paradise Regained* still seems to me impoverished rather than plain. I hope that I'll come around, because I'd rather like as many things as I can.

What is it in Milton that draws you so?

A superb architectural power, a power to build great verse paragraphs, to take a sonnet and make something massive and energetic out of it.

How does that differ from Shakespeare?

If you compare Shakespeare's sonnets, which are magnificent, with Milton's, I think that the big difference is that whereas Shakespeare works on the whole in delightful, restating quatrains, parallel quatrains, summed up by a final couplet, Milton comes near violating the sonnet form every time he takes it on, continually runs over the ends of the divisions and does this expressively and to some purpose.

He doesn't turn when he's supposed to turn?

He doesn't turn, he will run over into the next line, or he will stop short. What this does, I'm not the first person to say this, is to turn the sonnet into a great paragraph or sometimes two great paragraphs. Often a Milton sonnet will be one sentence, or two sentences. He simply had a great transforming influence on the sonnet. Very few people have taken up where he left off, but as with most forms and modes of writing, when Milton took the form on he transformed it— and well.

So I admire him as a genius in the building of verse structures and I respond greatly to his Baroque sensibility, it's full of concreteness. I know that Eliot indicted him for abstractness, but I find a great deal of the concrete in him, and especially in the muscularity of the movement of his lines. You can't read Milton with any enthusiasm without feeling that you're getting a good workout, a good physical workout, and I very much react to that in him. I react also to something that hasn't recently been noticed very much, to his playfulness. He's a man with an extraordinary linguistic knowledge, who wrote many Latin poems for example, and whose use of English is all full of etymological . . .

Little plays going on?

Lots of plays going on. There are many more jokes in Milton than is generally allowed. When I think of his etymological play, I always think of what the affable archangel Raphael says to Adam in the Garden, that if human beings will just

behave themselves they may be qualified to be transformed into higher creatures and to rise toward heaven by "gradual scale sublime." Now that's just full of Latin word play, *gradus,* and *scala,* and *sub limen.* Milton is just having a good time, a good lighthearted time with the Latin roots of English words. Probably to some of his readers that seems donnish, but to me it seems lighthearted and playful.

This seems to invoke Auden once more, that the poet's first requisite is to simply love playing with words.

I think so. It's serious play most of the time but it is play. And there's no harm in enjoying it to the point of laughter, even in the midst of the reading or the writing of a serious poem. I do think that that's something that was mislaid by many of our earnestly prosaic free verse poets in the sixties and seventies.

An overriding solipsism?

I don't know, I think that too many poets thought that they should, on some kind of principle, speak in the unadorned, unplayful, unclever language of the man on the next bar stool. Perhaps because, in the hands of such poets, the subject matter of poetry became so confessional, so merely personal, any great deal of wordplay struck them as a fancying up of their testimony. Maybe that was what was behind it. I confess, without naming any names, though I'm thinking of hundreds of people, that a lot of the poetry of the sixties and seventies has seemed to me extremely dull in its word choices.

Do you have Ginsberg in mind?

No, I'm not thinking of Ginsberg really. I'm not thinking of anyone of his degree of talent. It strikes me that there's a lot of verbal animation in his best work, in poems like "Howl." It may be that his kind of verbal play has become somewhat formulaic and repetitive in his later work, a kind of jargon. But no, he seems to have a lot more verbal life than the kind of anonymous person I'm speaking of has displayed in the last couple of decades. I'm talking about people who on principle want to talk like regular guys, and for whom to get anywhere above the level of ordinary bar stool discourse is to become too fancy, too arty.

Do you enjoy Frank O'Hara?

I don't read him very much. I read him somewhat during his very early days in Cambridge and I found him lively and amusing, not my kind of thing, but nevertheless I was glad he was there. I think that he belongs to some extent to a school, though I don't like to join those critics who put us all into schools. I used to enjoy, and still do, the work of people often associated with him, Kenneth Koch and John Ashbery. They had a lot of good jokes, a lot of playfulness.

Do you read Ashbery now?

Yes, I do. I find that, though I don't understand him very well, I am often fascinated by taking the trip through one of his poems and shifting from one kind of diction, one kind of literary awareness, one kind of implicit experience to another. I best understood him in one of his books, *Self-Portrait in a Convex Mirror,* I was delighted when that book came along because, though I've always liked Ashbery, known how bright he was, respected him as an artist, I had not fully enjoyed him until that time. I was able to write him a letter saying "good book."

I brought up Ginsberg not so much because he fulfilled the portrait you were painting, but when the Beats came along, it was such a divergence from what you and Shapiro and Lowell and the poets of your generation were doing that I just wonder what the effect was at that time?

I think it had different effects on different people.

On you.

On me. Well, I felt that there was a lot of PR in the Beat movement, so-called. Though Ginsberg was a truly talented person, and Gary Snyder a truly talented person, there was not really a lot of talent around amongst them. And their value was very greatly magnified by a lot of academic people who were really not specifically interested in letters whose approach to letters was very much American studies or sociological in nature. I don't mean to sound as if I were resentful of having been put in the shade by these fellows. I don't think I felt that. I was resentful of being classified by contrast to them. I thought it pretty silly that people like Allen Ginsberg and Gary Snyder who had their college and university degrees, some of them advanced, were thought to be wild fellows on the one hand, while others of us were classified as academic.

It sounds like you resent that designation.

I resent being put into that slot, because no one says "academic" in a kindly way. And distinctions like "cooked" and "raw" didn't seem to me to make very much sense either. So I was bothered not by the poets themselves, really, but by what silly critics began to do by way of organizing the American poetic scene.

When I went out to the West Coast in 1956, because I was dead broke and had to make some money reading poems up and down California, I went to San Francisco first, and Allen had just read his "Howl" for the first time and it had wowed

them as indeed was proper. And almost at once I began to feel that—well, I was someone who had hoboed up and down through California long before it had occurred to the Beat generation to wear blue jeans and ride on trains. I felt I now came there as an establishment figure in a gray flannel suit, reprehended for his academicism and his love of the past and his attachment to meters and all those reprehensible things.

Did you feel frustrated?

Not frustrated, bothered to be classified. Nobody wants to be classified, nobody wants to be limited by a classification. We all like to feel, though it's not true of any of us, that we can be all things, that in some way we can encompass all experience and find the right words. I was troubled to find myself, in the minds of some, a sort of regional specialist and a young fuddy-duddy.

About forty years ago Randall Jarrell wrote a rather scathing review of your work. I'm curious how that affected you at the time, what your relationship was with Jarrell before that, what your relationship was with him after that?

My relationship with Jarrell had been good before that and it was good after, actually.

Were you afraid to look at each other at the next party you were at together?

No. I remember the review, it was in the *Partisan Review.* It was the review of my second book, around 1950. He said some nice things in it. However, he got going very amusingly on the limitations of the book as he saw them, and I found myself laughing at these jokes that were at my expense; and at the same time I wrote him a letter saying come on Randall, it's all right you see me as having limitations, but why are all your jokes about me comparisons to girls and ladies, why do you say that my translation of *Beowulf* suggests Marie Laurencin's illustrations for the *Iliad,* and why do you say that I remind you of a nice southern girl who has been told that her accent is just charming and that she must persevere in it? There were a couple of other instances of that kind of thing. Do you think, I said to him, that there's anything essentially sissy in my poems? You seem to imply it by these comparisons. And he wrote back saying golly, I never meant anything of the sort, those were just the jokes that occurred to me.

That begs the question it seems to me. Why did those jokes occur to him? I wonder if he was being disingenuous.

I don't know. There was always an element of malice in him. He made very good negative jokes about people. But he never had it in for me before or after, and so I simply accepted what he said and was sorry I had written him at all.

We should never write letters to critics about the things they say. I felt foolish to have done so. I think that there may have been some truth in some of the things he said. At the same time, I explained to myself some of his emphases by the fact that Randall himself at that time was embarking on the writing of longish narrative poems, and so, my book having consisted largely of short lyrics, I said to myself, that's why he said I don't try for long gains. He feels that he himself is trying for long gains and he wishes I would. I suppose I tried to explain away some of his criticism. It really doesn't matter, and didn't matter greatly to me then. He and I remained friends, and my book was well enough received for me not to be blighted and to go ahead with my work. I think that the only thing that annoys me now about Randall's 1950 review is that people who write favorable essays on me always feel that they have to start by quoting that essay and then reacting against it. Jarrell's later critical treatment of me is very positive, but no one seems to quote it.

I want to ask you about some other people you knew forty years ago. "Cottage Street, 1953" portrays a Sylvia Plath, who has wished to die. This poem was written about twenty years after your meetings with Plath, and perhaps ten years after she took her life. Was her wish to die or hint thereof in any way evident to you back in 1953?

I saw Sylvia Plath a few times, very briefly, in my life. When I wrote that poem, I think I had perhaps a couple of meetings with her telescoped in my mind. Though the poem doesn't say so, doesn't say I'm trying to remember as well as I can, that's what I was doing. When she was an undergraduate at Smith, she once came to me and did an interview—for *Mademoiselle*. I believe, I think she also interviewed, at that time, Tony Hecht, and a couple of other then-young poets who were also teachers. I've some slight memory of her at that point, either then or at my mother-in-law's house. I remember her as very slumped and pale, and mute, and withdrawn. And my poem simply goes on that memory, whatever year it may derive from. It's a true memory, but I don't know where it belongs.

Some of the other poets who started publishing around the same time as you did, a little earlier than Sylvia Plath—Berryman, Lowell, Jarrell—also wished to die as it turns out and were granted their wishes. Looking back now, what do you remember?

I remember lots of the behavior of Lowell and Ted Roethke and of Berryman, and I know that it can be described as self-destructive.

Was that evident at the time?

The only person at that time in whom I really felt that I saw a desire to die was Dylan Thomas. We knew him during his trips around America. He stopped and saw us, and we gave or attended parties for him, things like that. I can remember him sitting on our couch and saying, "I am a used up, bottle-shaped rummy, who has been trading for years on his inspirations at age 18, and at the moment I'm riding high, but the world's going to see through me." He felt really quite desperate about himself, both as a person and as a writer at that time and so there was a kind of wish to die operating in him. I hasten to say that he was a terribly lively and entertaining man, and that such things were not what he talked about most of the time. Yet he had those drunken and lachrymose moments in which he felt he was played out and done for.

I never saw this in Lowell. Lowell seemed always to me—though he could be distressed by the onset of a bad state of mind, made glum by that—he seemed to me a man of great energy who was interested in continuing to make and to do. And no, I didn't see Roethke as self-destructive. For our generation, drinking a lot was standard behavior. Though God knows Berryman and Roethke overdid it. I don't think they thought they were trying to destroy themselves. I think they were wanting to have a hell of a time. And I think that for them, as often for me, drinking seemed to be something that poets did. Now, I never thought it inspired me to write poetry. No, never have I thought that I could write good poetry under the influence of booze. I don't even think Hart Crane did, but somehow it belonged then to the life of poetry. As it pretty much doesn't now.

Do you think they were trying to fulfill their own image of what a poet's supposed to be, including this kind of doomed, Byronic quality which eventually leads to death?

There was a little of that. I think. There were times at which I felt that Roethke, a marvelous fellow but not quite a jelled personality, was being Dylan Thomas. There were times when I thought he was conforming to that desperate and delightful pattern of behavior, and it's true that it was thought honorific in those days, since Thomas had done it, and since others had done it, to arrive late to your poetry reading a little drunk, a little untidy.

When I went for the first time to record my poems at Caedmon, a little bit after the Dylan days, the ladies at Caedmon said, "we'll be with you in a minute to make your recording, meanwhile wouldn't you like to have a few drinks," and they gave me a pint of whiskey. This was noon. I don't drink whiskey at noon, never have. That was the expectation at that time.

I always thought that one of the great expressions in English was Lil Armstrong's expression, on a record of hers, "Let's get drunk and be somebody." That's the way I think my generation felt about it, and we did not take a gloomy view of drink. It was something you did to laugh and raise hell, and blurt, and come out with surprising things. And it's too bad that that frayed people's nerves and hurt their health and led in some cases to the hospital and to death.

It didn't lead to death in you; why was your sensibility somehow different than some of your contemporaries?

I don't have enough insight into myself to answer that. No doubt it has to do with my genes, although I did once experience a depression of some depth and had to go into the hospital for it.

When was that?

In '85. My natural state of mind is a cheerful one. I've had a very lucky life. And I've been happily married. I've loved my children. All of the things that could hold you up have happened to me. So I think that I may have stayed away from self destruction for those reasons. I've had other things to do, and any undercurrent of self-destruction that's in my nature has never been allowed its head.

Have you any anecdotes about Berryman, anything that stands out?

I don't know that I can come up with any at this minute. I've told about the time Berryman and I, at a poetry conference in Washington, went to get Delmore Schwartz out of jail. That's on record in a biography of Schwartz.

Do you want to encapsulize that quickly?

Well, it's really a story more about Schwartz than about Berryman, except that I think it indicated a quality of Berryman which many people like his old friend William Meredith have spoken of, his great loyalty to people he regarded as friends and of whose work he approved. He was awfully choosy, indeed snobbish about other writers. But once he thought somebody was a good guy or a good girl and also a good writer, he really stuck with that person. And though Delmore Schwartz had been quite difficult with him at one time or another, when he heard that Schwartz was in trouble in Washington and in the jug for drunkenness and total destruction of a hotel room, he wanted at once to come to the rescue, and I went along to help. I saw at one or another time that kind of loyalty in his discourse, in his behavior. I always felt that though he had a very harsh tongue, it was utterly unlikely that he would ever say anything naughty about me behind my back. I felt that, yes, he had decided that I was okay and that he would always talk accordingly.

Howard Nemerov said something to the effect that he was happy to be the poet laureate but that he wasn't going to write any poems for the queen as it were. When you accepted the laureateship were there any expectations placed upon you and did you have any of your own?

I hadn't any expectations of my own, and certainly no expectation that I would fall into the writing of proper laureate poems. I knew that, if I took the job on, I would be expected to advise the Library as to who ought to record for its wonderful archive of poetry and fiction; and I knew that I would be expected to plan its lecture series, its series of readings and performances in poetry and fiction and drama. And I knew that there would be some ceremonial moments to it. Also, that I would undoubtedly find myself reading at schools and colleges and being visited by delegations of students, that kind of thing.

All that happened, and then there were more things that happened. There was an extraordinary influx of mail. You might not expect that, but from almost every state in the union there came letters from poets, or from people interested in poetry asking me all sorts of things, asking me to say whether they were good poets, to criticize their work, to suggest where they might publish, to identify remembered lines of verse, to give advice as to how poetry could be forwarded in one or another programmatic way.

I take it you felt rather inundated.

I did feel rather inundated. I faithfully answered all of my letters for months. That was both interesting and exhausting. Then, after a while, I threw up my hands and asked my two wonderful associates in the poetry office to screen the mail, and just give me what really needed answering.

As for the writing of poems, the main reason why I didn't take the job on for a second year was that I was inefficient in handling the various demands of the job—which included also, by the way, endless interviews by all the media. I was so inefficient in handling the demands that I wasn't getting any of my own writing done. I'm not very good at jumping on and off planes and writing poems in hotel rooms at night. And so I regretfully quit on it, although I had enjoyed a great deal of the experience.

I had written, in 1985 and 1986, the text of a cantata for the centenary of the Statue of Liberty at the request of the composer Bill Schuman. I had taken on that job, of course, with great horror. It seemed very unlikely that one could do anything fresh with that subject. But after a while I was challenged by it, and I was pretty well pleased by what I managed to turn out in the way of a text. And certainly pleased by Schuman's beautiful setting of it, which was performed at Lincoln Center in October of 1986. So I had done a laureate thing before I ever went to Washington, and didn't feel that I had to do any more. The situation was facilitated by the fact that Robert Penn Warren, the first person appointed as laureate, had stated that he damned well wasn't going to write any official poems.

Were you grateful for the precedent?

Yes, I was. I think that there's nothing wrong with writing poems that have a national political concern, and I did in fact write a poem in that year against the Strategic Defense Initiative; but I didn't write it as a laureate, I just wrote it as myself. Howard Nemerov has written, though, some occasional poems for Washington purposes. I think he wrote one which was read at the convening of Congress. Of course, he's very good at that. I liked very much a recent essay by Helen Vendler, in which she discussed Howard as a public poet. I think he's always been outstanding in this respect, in this and many others.

In your "A Miltonic Sonnet for Mr. Johnson on His Refusal of Mr. Peter Hurd's Official Portrait," you noted that Thomas Jefferson would have "wept to see small nations dread / the imposition of our cattlebrand," and you admonished Johnson for his "talk of vision" while being "weak of sight." And more recently, you wrote "A Fable" which you just referred to about Reagan's Star Wars. I wonder if you had any words for Reagan or Bush and any thoughts about the course of the U.S. over the last decade?

Of course, I have positions on all sorts of things that have arisen over the Reagan and Bush administrations, and I have very little admiration for Reagan's conduct in the Presidency, and I don't think that Mr. Bush is doing very well. I don't think I'm very likely to write a poem about Bush's stupidity in vetoing the Congressional bill which would have safeguarded Chinese students in America. That's a very special issue which I think I would only address if a happy phrase chanced to occur to me.

Feel free to elaborate right here.

I have my opinions on the matter, no more important than anybody else's. It's something on which I could imagine writing if the right slant came to me. I do think there's no point in writing poems on political subjects simply to go on record on the right side. Poetry had better be interesting always, it had better be fresh always, and so the sort of poem that simply says "don't drop the bomb" is of no interest to me.

There is one thing that I think would be useful for a poet to do. I almost wish that I had been asked to do some sort of song and dance for Congress. If I had, I might have taken the opportunity to be as simple as a poet is entitled to be. Our legislators naturally feel that the whole question of nuclear energy and nuclear arms is a complex one, and I think it's simple and I should have liked to say so. I should have liked to say to them, "Look here, haven't you watched people and seen how they behave, haven't you noticed that when people walk down the street, they bump into each other? Haven't you noticed how cars wrinkle each other's fenders? How utterly clumsy we all are and how high our insurance rates are? We're a fallible breed, and can we possibly afford to have energy sources which cannot be trusted to fallible hands? Can we possibly afford to have arms which cannot be entrusted to the irresponsible or the deranged or the drugged?" I don't have any Gary Cooper visions of what such a speech might accomplish. Nevertheless, I think that it might be useful in a public place to be as simple as that, because I think that something in almost all of one's hearers would respond.

I hope you do write it. You spoke of the Library of Congress before; in 1946 or 1947 there was a schism among poets as to whether Pound should be awarded the Bollingen Prize by the Library, which after all was a branch of the U.S. Government, after Pound's broadcasting for the Axis powers throughout the war. Pound's offense seemed especially egregious so soon after the war and the revelations of Nazi atrocities. More recently there was the Mapplethorpe flap with Helms and the NEA, and I was wondering if you can see any circumstances whatsoever when considerations other than those purely artistic should help determine such awards.

It's a really troublesome question, and yet I know where I have to stand on it. When I was in the Enlisted Reserve Corps in New York in 1942, waiting to go into the army, I had my short wave radio and my directional antennae rigged up down there on Christopher Street, and I used to listen to Ezra Pound's broadcasts from 2RO Rome. He did say all those things that he is said to have said, and they were primitive and disagreeable. And he also, in those broadcasts, showed a positive side, if one could get over the ugly things he was saying and note the positive side of it. He was rather touchingly pedagogical. That was something about him from beginning to end. He was a teacher, best when he was teaching literature, worst when he was teaching politics. He gave little incoherent lectures, and he gave, in fact, assignments. One of his assignments was to go and get Brooks Adams's *The Law of Civilization and Decay* and read it before the next broadcast.

I did that. I went up to the New York Public Library, took that book out, and read it, and it was a good book, most interesting. Nevertheless my reaction to his broadcasts was pretty negative. They did not have a great deal of redeeming artistic value to them. But as for the Bollingen Prize, I do think that he deserved it for the great art of his poetry, and I can't kick about that. Though I could not, I think, have given him warm personal congratulations. I feel the same way about these Mapplethorpes and—who's that other fellow, who photographed a crucifix through his own urine?

I can't remember his name. [Andres Serrano]

This fellow had been for some time, as I've learned, photographing this or that object through his own body fluids. And it just happened to occur to him, one day, to do a crucifix through his urine. I haven't seen the work on a museum wall, so unlike Jesse Helms, I'm not going to have opinions about the quality of the work sight unseen. I do feel that whatever's good about these artists, and whatever's the matter with them, I have to defend them because we can't have Jesse Helms messing with the freedom of art. I'm annoyed with people who abuse the freedom of art, and who say inhuman things in art. Yet I feel I have to stick by them. This photographer fellow was interviewed by the *Boston Globe* not long ago, and they did quite a whitewash on him and his artistic motives. I learned from that article, which dimly reproduced the offending photograph, that the title of the crucifix seen through urine was "Piss Christ." Now it seems to me that anyone who gives a photograph such a title is putting a chip on his shoulder and daring you to knock it off, and so I'm not going to join those apologists who say to offended parties, "Oh, how can you possibly be offended?" It was an offensive title, it was meant to offend, and to hell with the guy. Nevertheless, I have to be on his side.

The **New and Collected Poems** *begins with* **"A Ride."** *The poem seems particularly Frostian. Was this done consciously or in retrospect, unconsciously, or am I merely projecting my own agenda here?*

An English reviewer recently spoke of Frost in connection with that poem and then proceeded to say that the poem wasn't like Frost at all. I think it was the snow and the horse that put him in mind of Frost. I don't think it occurred to me. Although I'm a great admirer of Frost and once knew just about every line of Frost by heart, I don't think that it occurred to me that I might in any way be borrowing from him. One reason for that is that the poem proceeds directly from a dream I had. The poem tells, as clearly as I could tell it, what that dream was like. And it was not a dream about Robert Frost stopping by woods. It was a dream about a mysterious horse and terrible storm through which the horse carried me.

The poem also seemed as Poe-like as it did Frost-like because it had the dreamlike quality to it, that certain mystery around the edges.

Well, that is a thing that I've had in common with Poe. Poe is a great realizer of dream states. And I, who knows why, have always been interested in dreams. Just as John

Berryman was—he used to write down all his dreams in a notebook. Yes, I suppose whatever there is in me that responds to the dreamer in Poe is in that poem, and yet I don't think of it as a derivative poem. It seems to me one of my most direct. As you know, Steve, we do not on the whole have experiences and just go write them down. But this was one case in which, although to find words for things always changes them, I pretty much took an experience and stamped it on paper.

Twenty-five years ago you said your then earlier work was more decorative, which was expression of exuberance. And you said there was "less gaiety" in the then-more recent poems, that is, the poems that eventually became **Walking to Sleep.** *How would you characterize the difference in your work between then and now. Has it indeed become even less decorative, less gay?*

I think I've become plainer. This is the kind of thing which a nonwillful writer—I'm really not very willful with my work; I don't say "now I shall do such and such"—is not likely to be sure about. An outside critic, someone else, is more likely to be right about it. And yet I have a general impression that I've grown plainer, that to some extent as Yeats said, I've withered into the truth. I find more excitement now than I did as a young poet in the idea of saying something with the utmost simplicity, with perhaps an untranslatable degree of simplicity. As a translator, I know that the hardest lines to translate are those which are most simply put.

What about your poem **"Lying"**?

Of course, it's true that a number of people have found that poem very difficult. I wouldn't call it decorative, because decorative suggests the nonfunctional, the flossy, and I think that everything in that poem is trying to say something very hard. But it is a sort of torrential poem.

What do you mean by torrential?

A whole lot of data come at the reader very fast. They can be hard to assimilate, at whatever rate of hearing or reading, and I know that I took some pleasure in writing a poem that was going to be like that, that was going to be a bombardment of various instances. Perhaps I felt I could do that in honesty, because the poem is fundamentally simple and is simply saying throughout that all things are really of one nature, that all things are co-natural, that every comparison we might make, that every likening we might make, is justified because everything belongs to one creation. That's all the poem says.

Was it a job description of what the poet does?

I think so in great part although there is in our literature a lot of wonderful nonfigurative poetry. I think I would agree with Stevens that the central thing in poetry is metaphor. I'd agree with Mr. Aristotle that the specific poetic gift is for metaphor, comparison.

Donald Hall has stated that poetry itself is doing pretty well but poetry reviewing is in a bad way. How do you see the state of reviewing now? In this century, Eliot, Winters, and Jarrell all influenced the poetry of their day through their commentary. Do you see anyone fulfilling that function now? And though you've written much commentary, why don't we see any reviews from you?

I have written reviews in the past, but very little recently, that's true. I like to do reviews, they're challenging, and I think it's very important that there be good reviewing of poetry. I've been involved in other things of late, slacked-off on it. I do think that there are some fine reviewers going. I very much admired a review which came out last year in the *Times* by Richard Tillinghast. It seemed to me that he really grappled with what was going on in several books, had real insight, and some applicable criteria. There's a good piece by Alfred Corn in the latest *Poetry,* a very brainy job of reviewing and I like the work of William Logan, who very rightly, I think, received a reward from the Critic's Circle last year for his reviewing of poetry.

It's very hard for our reviewing media to find as much good poetry criticism as they would like to publish, and I think that's why the *Los Angeles Times,* a couple of years ago, said that it was going to cut down on its reviewing of poetry, and instead represent poetry by the reproducing of particular poems in its book section. Not a bad decision to make really, not at all as bad as some people took it to be. For a while there, everyone was belaboring the *Los Angeles Times,* because its decision was misunderstood. If you actually look at their admirable Book Review, they do still cover a number of important books of poetry, and every week there is a well chosen poem out of some recently published book, put there to speak for itself.

I don't think that poets on the whole make a direct and profitable reaction to being criticized. I've never learned how to do anything from any critic, and never been made either proud or ashamed of myself by a critic. I'm always gratified when somebody of great intelligence pays sustained attention to me in an article, whether or not he likes me. And yet that doesn't have anything to do with what I shall now write. I suspect that this is true of most poets.

Do you find that you write more for the page or the ear?

Nowadays, I know that I write with a fully developed awareness of the poem as designed for oral performance. When I'm writing a poem, I don't think of myself on an art museum stage reading to people, but I've done so many poetry readings now, enjoying them always and had so much to do with the theater through my translations of Molière and Racine, that I can no longer feel about poetry as I did when I was starting out. Then it was purely for the page, and I very often wrote lines that turned out to be not very pronounceable. When the age of the poetry reading came along I had to try to do them from a stage.

Can you think of any poem in particular that struck you that way?

No, I can't this minute, but I know that there are poems in my first book which would be hard to say aloud in this or that passage, there are clots of consonants or conjunctions of s's that would not do well in *bel canto.* They say that Tennyson used to write a couple of extra lines, if necessary, to avoid a conjunction of s's. Of course, he was very given to reading aloud. If you went to call on the great Tennyson, you had to listen to an hour of his verses sometimes. I've been educated in poetry as an oral art by giving poetry readings (which have become so popular since I began to write) and then I have also been very much involved with the stage. When I sit around translating Molière, I sound every line. Not, aloud, but I sound it in my head, and amongst two or three possible renderings of a line I choose the one that an actor would find best and most expressive to say. By now when I write, I write with sound and pronounceability and dramatic stress in mind. I know that there's a lot of poetry still being written which isn't of a highly oral character and I'm not telling anybody else what to do, but I place a very high value on speakability and dramatic force.

Do you think you came to that conclusion because of your translations which were meant for the stage?

They helped a great deal. I just drifted into this kind of awareness as a by product of my translations of seventeenth-century Classical plays. And also, I suppose, because I got mixed up in Broadway musical theater for awhile, and had to write for music, or with music. That conditioned me to some degree, I'm sure, not, however, a measurable degree. I can't really measure any of these effects. I never said to myself see here, Wilbur, poetry is an oral art. The awareness of the oral dimension of poetry just crept up on me.

Can you lose yourself in your translations in the same way you do with your original work?

Not in the same way, no. Because in a translation, quite obviously, one is leaning all the while on what someone else has said and meant. Of course you have to contemplate the original and you have to bring out of the original its deepest intention, if you can find it. But what you're bringing out when you write your own poetry is something you don't know yet, and something for which there is no original. There is a feeling of arbitrariness in writing a poem of one's own that doesn't belong to the translation art. If I'm translating Molière I'm trying to do well by something which already has its own deserved prestige. And which, if I do it properly in English, will emerge as an English classic. I don't have any of those feelings about producing a classic when I'm writing a poem of my own. I'm just getting something off my chest as clearly as I can.

Because you don't know where your own poem is going and you do know, more or less, where the translated piece is going, is it harder to maintain fervor while translating? Is it easier to keep a pitch of excitement when you're working on your own work as opposed to Molière, or whomever?

I think that's probably true. A poem—if you're at all serious as a poet—every poem is a terrible gamble. Though I find that whenever I start to write I have a pretty sure sense that there is a meaning to be found, that there will be an end to the poem. Nevertheless there's always a chance that it won't be there, the meaning, the end, or that I'll spoil it. And with translation, you never do feel that. Though you have to work with a grasp of the work as a whole in mind, it is a kind of moment by moment battle. To compare great things to small, it's a little bit like solving one corner of a crossword puzzle, to find a solution for some six-line speech in a Molière play.

You know one thing I've found—not in answer to your question, but something I've noticed in the last few days—if I translate a Molière play of 1,100 lines or 1,500 lines or something like that, I find that it's possible to render every thought that's in the original, to be faithful in a thought-by-thought manner to the original, not leaving anything out, and emerge with as many lines in the translation as there are in the play. I wouldn't feel any kind of emotional upset if I found myself writing four more lines than Molière had written, or four fewer. But it just happens that passing over from the Alexandrines of the original to the pentameter of my translations, I can conveniently reproduce each thought as it comes. I'm getting rhymes, too, in the process, and one thought that has occurred to me in the last few days is this: people are always speaking of English as a rhyme-poor language. Sometimes you hear poets say that rhyming is a bad idea, because we haven't enough rhymed sounds in the language, and therefore the use of rhyme compels us to say things we don't want to say. Well, it ain't so. I find that we have enough rhymes in English so that I can be faithful to each thought of Molière as I go along, and rhyme those thoughts as well. I think that's a considerable test of our language's resourcefulness in rhymed sounds, that this can be done if one is patient enough.

That's the fun of it, is it not, to find that rhyme, to work that puzzle out?

Yes, I think if the original is rhymed, good God, why put it into free verse or blank verse and destroy its economy, destroy the kind of punch it has in the original?

Do you enjoy working in French so as to take a break from the typical English pentameter?

If you speak of metrical waves the average Alexandrine comes out to be something like four humps, four waves of voice, and it's not at all as emphatic in its effect as a measure of our highly stressed language is. People have often asked whether I try to reproduce the rhythms and the sound patterns of Racine or Molière in English, especially they ask this about Racine, because he's considered so musical. Well you just can't, because a French rhythm just isn't like an English rhythm. You have to find a comparable English rhythm, and you have to find comparable English music. The effort to imitate French sounds in English verse is ludicrous.

In the same article in which you talk about Edgar Allan Poe and his aesthetic you used three poems of your own to demonstrate your aesthetics, "A Baroque Wall Fountain," "Two Voices in a Meadow," and "Love Calls Us to the Things of this World." Are these three poems still representative?

I think so, insofar as I know myself. I'm always quoting something that Edwin Muir said. He said, "If we could know ourselves, it would be a violation of ourselves." And I think that's true—at any rate, for the poet in connection with his art. It's not wise, it's not good economy, to be too analytically aware of one's own work and its themes. I got fairly explicit about my own work and its themes in that little piece you're referring to, because I'd been asked by Howard Nemerov to write a piece suitable for broadcast by the Voice of America; it seemed to me that what was called for was some very barefaced writing, and that I should be as open as possible about my concerns. I still wonder what that little essay sounded like when somebody broadcast it into a forest clearing in Kenya.

Of the poets of the last 50 years who do you think people will be reading 100 years from now?

I really can't speak about the people of 100 years from now. I don't have a gloomy view of the future. I hope there will be a future. I hope that poetry will still be a necessity to a lot of people then. As for how popular it will be, I cannot guess, really. Donald Hall's figures on poetry are extremely encouraging, very surprising to people who are accustomed to saying "of course, nobody reads poetry, of course people don't buy books of poetry." Well it appears they do read it, they do go out to hear it by the hundreds and they do buy it in the thousands. I'm glad of that. But what their tastes will be in 2090 I don't know. All I can say is that there are a lot of people whose poems seem to have a high quality and usefulness right now, and that I hope such usefulness will be perceived in the future. When I was hanging around the Library of Congress and giving a lot of interviews, I was often asked about the state of poetry, and the future of poetry, and I found myself saying that there were about fifty American poets I knew of whose next poem I would be interested in seeing. If others feel the same, that may indicate a good state of health for American poetry, and may give a good prognosis for the reading of poems in the next century.

Any poets now that you take particular pleasure in reading?

I continue to read, very often, poets of my own generation to whom I'm especially attached, Elizabeth Bishop, for example, I go back to her all the time.

What is it in Bishop that delights you?

A kind of lucidity. Some kind of cleanness of the language. Subtlety, humor.

Any particular poems of hers that you return to more than others?

The one I was saying to myself yesterday as I bicycled across Key West was the one called "Anaphora," from her first book, *North and South,* the one that begins "Each day with so much ceremony / begins . . ." and ends with the words "endless / endless assent," which as I told myself, riding along on my bicycle, means both *ascent* and *assent.* I never get tired of her work. I go back to Frost. I go back to Williams very often. Somehow Williams's work seems to have on it, as Robert Lowell once said of May Swenson—seems to have permanent fresh paint signs on it.

For me, there's a lot of wheat and chaff mixed in Williams.

Yes, there's lot of chaff. He's one of the few poets I can think of in the modern century who showed again and again that he didn't know what certain words meant. In this he's like Faulkner. Faulkner often didn't bother to look up a word in the dictionary. I can't give you an example, but it would be a long Latinate word.

Are we talking about Faulkner or Williams here?

Faulkner. Oh, I can give an example of Williams. Williams in his poem "Burning the Christmas Greens," which I love, at a certain point, when the greens go up in flame, cries out

"Recreant!" He thinks it means *recreating* and it doesn't, it means something like traitor. He should have looked that up.

Any young poets you're reading now?

I'm reading Stephen Mitchell right now.

His Parables and Portraits.

Yes, I enjoy his work. I'm very fond of the work of August Kleinzabler. Do you know his work?

Yes, Storm Over Hackensack *and his new one* Earthquake Weather *I think is the name.*

Yes. Really there is quite a list of fine young poets. It could go on quite a distance. I think I'd better not try to do it, because of the people I'd leave off.

How about poets before my generation or your generation. Milton as you mentioned, anybody else you keep returning to again and again?

Well I'd return to Herbert.

Herbert more than Donne? Why is that? What is it in Herbert?

Well I do, at times, to Donne. Elizabeth Bishop's favorite poet was George Herbert. They had many qualities of clear subtlety in common and there's a kind of sprightliness of soul in both of them which is very attractive to me. There's no end to poets. That's been something I've been grateful for all my life. I was very fond of Coventry Patmore; and who's that guy I'm trying to think of?

Clare.

Well, of course, of Clare. There's simply been a very wide range of poets and not only in English, but in other languages I dare to venture into in whom I delight and who are part of my impulse to write a poem to see if I can add one more poem. The reason I always recommend to young poets that they go out and get enamored of 50 or 100 poets is that, in my own experience, it is valuable never to have succumbed to one great influence. The only poet who ever seemed to me to threaten me with abolition was William Butler Yeats. I taught him for a while at Harvard. John Kelleher and I taught a seminar in Yeats.

What do you mean by "threaten you with abolition"?

He's a very idiosyncratic poet, and a very powerful one, and I found that while I was teaching him, reading him, and expounding him there were occasional false notes in my own poems, unconscious borrowing. His way of using the word "being" for example. He'll begin a phrase with "Being by Calvary's turbulence," you know that kind of thing. That's a specialty of his, nobody else can do that without falling into his language. And I've always felt that Dylan Thomas's poem "Do Not Go Gentle" was marred by his then-fashionable, then Yeatsian use of the word "rage" in it. It was a little too much a line of its time when he talked about "rage, rage against the dying of the light." Yeats had written so much about an old man's rage . . . A very overpowering influence. So I found myself not reading Yeats as much as I would have liked to do, just so that he would not get at me and queer my way of writing. Delmore Schwartz once said in the *Partisan Review,* in an essay on Hart Crane, that it was very nice that Hart Crane had happened once but that if he had become a major influence on American poetry it would have been a total disaster. I think that's true, he's an intoxicating poet. And we can't profit as poets from the people who intoxicate us.

John M. Green (essay date Summer 1991)

SOURCE: "Wilbur's Beasts," in *The Explicator,* Vol. 49, No. 4, Summer 1991, pp. 247-49.

[*In the following essay, Green analyzes and discusses the images and metaphors in Wilbur's poem "Beasts."*]

Richard Wilbur's **"Beasts"** depicts in striking imagery the anomalous place of man in Nature. This brilliant six-stanza lyric can be divided into three scenes: the harmonious world of Nature; the painful world of degenerating human nature; and the world of "superior" men who betray their calling and bring destruction on all the worlds. Man seems to be the only creature whose nature, form, and function are not fixed. Paradoxically, this freedom from definition leads him into obsessive thoughts and compulsive behavior. The vision of the poem is Calvinist.

In the first two stanzas, we are in a peaceful world, whose condition is reinforced by a motif of musical harmony. The elements of this motif are *major* (the major keys are happy ones), *plucked, lyric, dulcet,* and *concordance.* The water current "sleeps" (play on *sweeps*?) the sunfish. The deer's feet are "spotless," that is, immaculate, without the stain of sin, as well as unmarked. It is nevertheless a predatory world: the gull dreams in his "guts" of the fish that he has caught in the waves. And, most strikingly, the disembowelled mouse paradoxically sees the harmony of it all. Death is a feared occurrence, but a natural one; it is not horrifying. Hunting for survival is what beasts are supposed to do; their instincts make them behave this way. Their behavior is not immoral.

At the end of the second stanza, we switch to the world of man, entering a scene of much more horrifying "harm and . . . darkness." In this switch, we focus on the moon, which acts as a beneficent overseer in the first two stanzas, and even contributes its influence to the harmonious movement of the tidal waters ("the moon-plucked waves"). But in the world of man, the light of the moon is "warped in window-glass," a synecdoche for civilization.

Civilized man is still, uneasily, a prey to the influence of Nature; he is not completely at home in either world. Seeing himself as "above" the other animals, he nevertheless inevitably ("as always") slides back toward Nature. His painful situation becomes apparent; he can never fully revert to the animal. The werewolf is not an animal but a monster. The peacefulness of the world of Nature is closed to him. It holds a deep attraction, but consciously he draws back. Instead of "slumbering in peace," he turns his head away on "the sweaty bolster"—a pillow that is also a support, because it is manmade—trying to resist the inevitable metamorphosis into a monster. When the change takes place (as in the old Lon Chaney movies), his ears become "sharper" (more acute, as well as more pointed). Although *sharp* is another element in the motif of music, it represents not a full note, but something in-between.

In this sequence, "sponsors" suggests the godparents in the rite of baptism, in which the soul passes from the corruption of original sin to the innocence of sanctifying grace. Here the process is more-or-less reversed. Another word that reverberates is "minors," obliquely echoing "major" in the first line of the poem. The minor keys in music are melancholy. Another instance of verbal texturing is "panic," derived from Pan, god of Nature. Like the werewolf, he is an amalgam of man and beast. He is said not only to cause panic fear, but to send nightmares—like the werewolf's. The "degradation of the heavy streams" may be not only (polluted?) water flowing downhill and eroding the earth, but also the once-human bloodstream of the werewolf.

Next comes perhaps the most difficult phase of the poem. I am inclined to agree with Charles R. Woodard in his *Explicator* article in spring, 1978 (vol. 36, no. 3, 6-7) that the "suitors" are not scientists, as Donald L. Hill had maintained they were in *Richard Wilbur* (1967). Woodard holds that the more satisfactory reading would be to see them as "poets, philosophers, creators of myth, who have always been quite as much students of evil as suitors of excellence. . . ." But would the phrase not also suggest mystics, ascetics, and founders of religions, such as Christ and Buddha? In any case, their ambience is somewhat Platonic, inasmuch as they are at "high windows / Far from thicket and pad-fall." They are far from the beasts and the werewolf. Thus their vision is limited. In addition, they seem to undergo an experience similar to that of the werewolf: he "turned his head away" (presumably from human nature); they "turn from their work." Their work seems to have to do with "raising" man's nature by rejecting the body. (I do not see how their work could be "the contemplation of hell," as Woodard puts it.) Inasmuch as it is night, however, when the libido is in the ascendant, they are drawn, despite themselves, to contemplate what are for them projections of man's "baser" nature: the "painful / Beauty of heaven" (Venus), the "lucid moon" (Diana), and "the risen hunter" (Orion). All are aggressive (Venus also, through her archer son). In addition, man himself, as a product of evolution, can be seen as the "risen hunter."

As they turn from their work, the suitors "sigh" because they realize that their sublimated ideals are impracticable. As "suitors" they themselves are lovers, however Platonic. That is, they come to realize (as Plato himself did in the *Phaedrus*) that their drive for perfection originates in the libido. As a result, an uneasy amalgam of the intellectual/spiritual and the emotional/physical results, "making such dreams" as those that produce the chaos in the last stanza.

Another way of looking at the ordeal of the suitors is that they are experiencing what Freud calls "the return of the repressed." The physical/emotional rises up to play a largely unrecognized role in the dreams made by the suitors. It may be suggested that the work of the suitors—questionably perfecting themselves and mankind—is further perverted into a pursuit such as astrology (inasmuch as they are contemplating the heavens). Astrology is a perversion because it sees man as determined, and places the blame for his condition and actions on forces beyond his control. Compulsion rules.

But astrology is only a synecdoche. Any pseudo-science or dogma (Manifest Destiny, the Master Race, dialectical materialism, or the rightness of any orthodoxy) makes dreams that lead to the warlike chaos of the last stanza. Many religions, too, tend to create abstract beliefs and rules that hold up a "heavenly" standard of conduct, a standard that man consciously strives to attain, but which he unconsciously knows that he cannot. In the resulting "heartbreak," he projects his failure onto the external world in the form of violence. With the slippage of rationally sensitive control, men become sleepwalkers, in effect, and as Ralph Ellison maintains, there are few things in the world as dangerous as sleepwalkers (prologue to *Invisible Man*). When the "suitors of excellence" create their meretricious dreams, the inevitable ("as always") degeneration occurs. So finally, there is little to choose between the threat represented by the werewolf, and that represented by the suitors themselves. If anything, that of the werewolf is more limited in scope. In any case, "as always" connotes a tragic denial and fear of freedom.

Perhaps also the exaltation of the hunter-killer aspect of man represents the fatal compromise by men of intellect and taste (like the Poet in Giraudoux's *The Trojan War Will Not Take Place*) who feel that they must be "tough-minded" and construct apologias for the warriors. Christ and Buddha did not, but their doctrines were almost instantly so perverted. The result is that, instead of having pigeons (doves) on the "public statues" (themselves usually commemorating former wars) we have crows, scavengers of death. Ships are torpedoed ("fish" is Navy slang for a torpedo). Nature itself is troubled and out of control ("unbridled"). The contrast with the opening stanza is handled beautifully.

The poem is a reminder of Sartre's sardonic dictum, "We are condemned to freedom." Being human is a precarious undertaking.

Mohan Ramanen (essay date Fall 1991)

SOURCE: "Wilbur's 'The Writer'," in *The Explicator*, Vol. 50, No. 1, Fall 1991, pp. 58-60.

[*In the following essay, Ramanen explains Wilbur's use of form and contrasting imagery to create a unified poem.*]

Richard Wilbur's **"The Writer"** (*New and Collected Poems,* 1988), a poem about his daughter writing a story, is an outstanding example of the poet's method of setting up a poetic debate within the terms of a single meditative voice. The debate becomes an occasion for the demonstration of the deft formal control the poet has over stanza and line, point of view, diction, and imagery, which are all forged into a unity clinched by strong poetic closure.

Wilbur sustains through the poems what Brad Leithauser, speaking of formal verse, calls the "prosodic contract" that a poet enters into with the reader. The nature of the contract is clear from the pattern of three-line stanzas that the poem compares. The first and third lines of each stanza are shorter than the middle line, and there is no rhyme. The absence of rhyme is more than made up for by a strong narrative joining the stanzas together. The plot in the poem is one aspect of its unity, and this plot has its climax in a turning point precisely in the middle of the poem. The turning point and the momentum in the argument are achieved through imagery.

Wilbur organizes the poem in terms of two sets of images— the one natural, the other that of the whistling bird, the starling. The opening stanzas speak of the girl at the "prow" of the house, "where light breaks, and the windows are tossed with linden," writing a story. The poet pauses in the stairwell and listens to the sound of the typewriter, which resembles the commotion caused by "a chain hauled over a gunwale." The poet passes a benediction on the young writer who has a heavy cargo to carry, dealing as she is with the very stuff of her life. We expect the poet to develop the nautical imagery but he does not, preferring to announce a change in his attitude to the subject by moving on to the starling image.

The starling (*Sturnus vulgaris*), according to the *OED,* is a bird of gregarious habit and often nests near human habitations. Indeed, in America it is almost a pest. Wilbur's starling, in fact, has been trapped in the very room where his daughter is writing and escapes after great difficulty. The suggestion of a friendly singing bird trapped and seeking freedom fits the young writer's situation. The fable of the trapped starling is very literary indeed. Wilbur was perhaps aware of Sterne's use of it in *Sentimental Journey* and of Maria Bertram's reference to Sterne's use of it in *Mansfield Park,* for both instance the idea of confinement.

In any case Wilbur explains the change in his poem. The explanation is part of his poetic procedure of helping the reader along in his reading. Wilbur suggests that the nautical imagery is too simplistic, for the writer "pauses, / As if to reject my thought and its easy figure." The writer stops work, and the whole house seems to be considering the poet's "easy figure" and its appropriateness as a description of the writer. By this strategy Wilbur focuses on his own craft and on the crux of the debate in the poem as to what figure or image is the adequate one to describe the writer. Thus the poem about his daughter writing becomes a poem about his capacity to write about his daughter writing.

The change of imagery also means a change of point of view, but the shift does not disintegrate the unity of the poem. Indeed it underscores its unity because of the sense of one voice speaking and considering options and weighing choices. The same experience is rendered differently, more appropriately, but this could happen only because the first set of nautical images was tried out and found inadequate. The poet remembers the "dazed starling" in the room and how he and his daughter "stole in, lifted a sash / And retreated, not to affright it." The starling, after a long hour, rose from its "humped and bloody" state and flew out of the open window, but not before it had shown itself to be a "sleek, wild dark / And iridescent creature." The mellifluous accents of the poet's language now contrast with the heaviness of the nautical images. Both in mood and in diction the poet has now found an answering idiom for the idea of creative freedom that the writer represents. Significantly, it also release Wilbur's creative energies, for he, like his daughter, has been moving from captivity to freedom of the imagination and to the creative *jouissance* of adequate expression. This poetic triumph is best seen in the resolution of the poem into satisfying poetic closure:

It is always a matter, my darling,
Of life or death, as I had forgotten. I wish
What I wished you before, but harder.

Wilbur's narration allows for this kind of decisive ending. The debate about creativity, about what images are best suited for a description of it, and the subtle infusion of the poet's own creative conflicts into the poem make for a "sincerity" that has nothing to do with the sincerity of confessional exhibitionism. Wilbur's is the true voice of feeling, arrived at through a painstaking charting of the experience in formal terms. Such a method prevents flabbiness of thought and enables a poetry of almost Augustan strong sense.

Raymond-Jean Frontain (essay date Fall 1992)

SOURCE: "Wilbur's 'Advice to a Prophet'," in *The Explicator,* Vol. 51, No. 1, Fall 1992, pp. 55-59.

[*In the following essay, Frontain cites classical and biblical sources and influences of Wilbur's "Advice to a Prophet."*]

In **"Advice to a Prophet,"** the title poem in Richard Wilbur's 1961 collection, the poet addresses one of the most important social and political problems of the atomic/nuclear age—the danger of mankind's destroying itself and its planet. It also answers one of the most difficult questions addressed by the poets of his generation—namely, how to reach an alienated, uninterested, even apathetic audience grown deaf to the poet/prophet's voice of admonition and entreaty. The speaker's advice is that the anonymous prophet not emphasize the destruction that will result if the community continues on its present course; people have grown so incapable of imagining a world without them that the prophet's traditional scare tactics cannot serve any purpose. Rather, the prophet should employ a gentle, prophetic voice and, in a quiet celebration of passing beauty, remind the listeners of the poignant fragility of everything that is worth valuing in this world and thus of their own existence. Wilbur's **"Advice"** maps a new poetic program for an age no longer capable of being shocked out of its complacency by what Hungarian poet Endre Ady calls "the prophet's mad red rage / that storms against the seat of heaven."

The poem's opening line assumes the inevitable: "When you come, as you soon must, to the streets of our city. . . ." Conditions have become so extreme in the speaker's time that it is no longer a question of whether a prophet will come to upbraid them but simply of when. The tension that animates the poem is the urgency that animated the Hebrew prophetic oracles: the people's days are numbered; they are on the verge of horrible destruction and can be saved only if they heed the prophet's message and repent totally and immediately. In the Bible, the destructive wrath of Yahweh is figured variously as the smashing to the ground of an earthenware pot, as the sexual ravishing of an adulterous woman, and as the leveling of a proud city's walls by an invader's army. But Wilbur's speaker anticipates an even worse catastrophe: when the prophet arrives in this city, it will be too late for him to "proclaim . . . our fall" (line 3) or the fall of any single city, as the prophet will be confronted by the possible annihilation of the human race in an atomic war.

The question that the poem attempts to answer concerns the best tack for the prophet to take. Prophetic utterance, John Becker concludes, is "a perennial act of resistance against the complacency of the mind"; it aims to attack, and to "protest with the extravagant gestures" of the prophet's outrage the centers of political and social power. For this reason, as Abraham Heschel points out, Hebrew prophetic language is "luminous and explosive, firm and contingent, harsh and compassionate, a fusion of contradictions" as the prophet both alarms and urges his listener onward to recognition and reform. The prophet's channeling of "divine derision and scorn" makes prophecy intrinsically satiric.

But traditional prophetic utterance fails in the face of modern complacency. The prophet, when he finally gets to Wilbur's city, will already be "mad-eyed from stating the obvious" (2). One can recite statistics regarding the stockpiling of weapons and their destructive capacities, but people will no longer be persuaded. "Mad-eyed" suggests both the angry gaze of the prophet who speaks in an accusative mode and his going mad with frustration and despair because no one heeds. The enormity of the statistics and their constant repetition have the unintended effect of immuring the audience emotionally from the probability of their self-destruction. The problem, Wilbur's speaker understands, lies not in the people's unreasonableness, which paradoxically threatens to drive the prophet mad, but in their "slow, unreckoning hearts" that are "unable to fear what is too strange" (7-8). How to make those hearts "reckon"—in the dual sense of rationally computing the significance of the prophet's statistics and of accepting the consequences ("face the reckoning of") of their actions—forms the "advice."

Wilbur is, in effect, attempting to resolve the "Catch-22" that is inimical to prophecy: The only biblical prophet ever listened to by his audience was Jonah, whose narrative is a comic one. Jonah is acutely frustrated by the Ninevites' being so completely and immediately persuaded by his single-word oracle, "Repent." If people heed the prophet's warning and reform, then the doom that the prophet prophesies is averted, and no one will ever know if what the prophet threatened would have come to pass. People who scorn the prophet's message, on the other hand, do not live to acknowledge its authority, their deaths being that authority's proof. As Jesus sadly observed, a prophet is never respected in his own time or country (Mark 6:4), and, in classical tradition, Cassandra was condemned to foresee the future but never be believed by the people whom she tried to warn. The difference, perhaps even the scorn, of the people whom he would save leaves the prophet "mad-eyed from stating the obvious" and drives him or her to speak even more impassionedly, thus appearing crazed and further alienating the audience.

And thus the radically different form of address that Wilbur's speaker advocates: "Speak to us" (13); "Ask us, prophet" (26); and "Ask us, ask us whether" (33). The speaker advises the prophet to employ a gentle, questioning voice that can "call / Our natures forth" (26-27) in the root sense of to *educate* by "leading out" the knowledge that is an essential part of our humanity and by actualizing through use what the listener had only an implicit grasp of before. The prophet must be a gentle Socratic educator rather than a threatening, cajoling satirist.

Not only the prophet's voice but the message must change. If, as the speaker claims, the prophet's traditional threat of annihilation is rendered ineffective by human inability to see itself as anything but the center of creation, then the prophet must quicken the reckoning heart by rendering the possibility of death only too familiar. The exquisite beauty of Wilbur's poem derives from the complex, twofold program that is implied here. First, the prophet must show how transience is the very essence of all experience by speaking "of the world's own change." Thus, images of the white-tailed deer slipping into perfect shade of stillness, of the lark soaring just beyond the reach of human sight, and of the gliding trout suspended for just one moment in a rainbow of light represent the uncountable instances of nature holding in perfection for one brief moment before suffering inevitable eclipse. "The dolphin's arc" (24) recalls Cleopatra's eulogy for Antony, whose delights, she claims, "were dolphinlike, they showed his back above / The element they lived in" (5. 2. 88-90). The dolphin's momentary transcendence of its watery or mortal part makes its aerial soaring all the more joyous and intense. Everything in the world bespeaks change, allowing us finally to conceive of "the death of the [human] race."

But as Wilbur proclaims in what is perhaps his best-known poem, "Love calls us to the things of this world." People learn to love—that is, their hearts learn to reckon—only when they are faced with the loss of what they value most. In this, Wilbur is close to John Keats, whose goddess Melancholy

. . . dwells with Beauty—Beauty that must die;

And Joy, whose hand is ever at his lips
Bidding adieu; and aching Pleasure nigh,
      Turning to Poison while the bee-mouth sips.

Nature at its most fragile and beautiful is for Wilbur the "live tongue" that calls "our natures forth," the mirror that reflects back to us (by eliciting from us) our love and courage. Like the locust that sings during its most vulnerable stage of metamorphosis, nature teaches us to celebrate what is passing. And the song that nature gives voice to is "all we mean or wish to mean"—that is, the most significant or meaningful part of us, as well as the highest meaning that we can aspire to, the meaning that we cannot, on our own, find words to express but which we must rely upon the "live tongue" of nature to articulate.

Thus, if man destroys the world, the rose will have no place to grow, and our unreckoning hearts will finally have failed us. The prophet must make humans aware both of their own mortality and of how they hasten their eventual dissolution by the proliferation of atomic and nuclear weapons. By speaking of "The Beautiful Changes" in nature, the prophet holds up a mirror to human hearts, paradoxically strengthening and quickening them.

The root of the word *prophet,* the Greek *prophetes,* means "to speak for, or on behalf of." The colloquial oath that is sworn in lines 3 and 4 ("begging us / In God's name to have self-pity") seems only to emphasize the fact that it is not God who is speaking through the prophet, but Nature, that "live tongue" that "call[s] / Our natures forth." The biblical prophet, frenzied with righteous indignation and alienated from his fellows by the gift of divine inspiration, is out of place in the modern world, where people's solipsism prevents them from understanding the destructive consequences of their acts. Instead, the poet insists, the prophet must quietly direct his listener's or reader's attention to the details of a sacramental universe, one of "sensible fullness."

Samuel Hazo (essay date Fall 1992-Winter 1993)

SOURCE: "One Definite Mozart," in *Renascence,* Vol. XLV, No. 1-2, Fall 1992-Winter 1993, pp. 81-96.

[*Hazo is an award-winning American poet and critic. In the following essay, he surveys Wilbur's works and praises him as one of the greatest American poets.*]

Ever since I first began reading Richard Wilbur's poems in the late 1940's, I think I've read only one negative review of his work. It was not Randall Jarrell's somewhat patronizing critique of Wilbur's second book, *Ceremony.* It was a review of *The Mind-Reader* by Calvin Bedient in *The New Republic* (June 5, 1976). Bedient contended that Wilbur was too safe a poet—that he rarely took chances. The reviewer was not referring to subject matter; he was taking Wilbur to task for deliberately choosing to remain within the limits of traditional metrics and prosody and yielding to "moral complacency."

I mention this now because one of my themes in this appreciation will be to demonstrate that Richard Wilbur's refreshing and refreshened traditionalisms along the lines of metrics and prosody are not a weakness but a strength. And I make this statement as one not fully enthralled by that tradition as it is literally defined but fully supportive of Wilbur's achievements within it. To say smugly that he rarely took chances is to betray a superficial reading of Wilbur's work to date. The nuances of diversity and experiment are everywhere, and they serve to re-create rather than merely perpetuate the set patterns of quatrains, couplets, sonnets, pentameters, trimeters or the alliteratively linked linear segments that Wilbur adapted from the Anglo-Saxon scops. That he has done so with almost Elizabethan elegance is what has distinguished his poetry among that of all his contemporaries from the time of the publication of *The Beautiful Changes* in 1947 to the appearance of *New and Collected Poems* in 1988, for which he received his second Pulitzer Prize. That he has been criticized by some who lack his consistent virtuosity within the chosen disciplines that he has embraced and with which he feels most at home is perhaps inevitable. But to me this is not unlike criticizing a tennis player for playing tennis (also an activity governed by fixed rules) exceptionally well on, of all things, a tennis court. Even if one does not like the game or the rules, one at least can respect the talent of one who has mastered them, re-created them in his own style and advanced and enriched the tradition by performing well within its strictures.

> **To say smugly that he rarely took chances is to betray a superficial reading of Wilbur's work to date. The nuances of diversity and experiment are everywhere, and they serve to re-create rather than merely perpetuate the set patterns of quatrains, couplets, sonnets, pentameters, trimeters or the alliteratively linked linear segments that Wilbur adapted from the Anglo-Saxon scops.**
> **—Samuel Hazo**

On the other hand, the aforementioned reviewer may not have been impressed by how a poem by Wilbur reads, *i.e.,* how it evolves from first word to last word. Those who believe that poetry is a mere stream of consciousness or that the language of poetry is nothing but the language of associated meanings and not, as Maritain claimed, of "intelligenciated sense" or that poetry is a kind of imaginative ink blot whose destiny is simply to expand to the limits of exhaustion will assuredly not read Wilbur with pleasure. His work does not accommodate such frivolity. As a poet he has a definite syllogistic way of thinking; his poems have a beginning, a middle and an end. Not all of them follow the "If . . . but . . . therefore" mode of syllogistic logic, but a good many of them do, and the imprint of this way of thinking is characteristic of a mind that does not meander but concludes. Shakespeare's sonnets impress us with a similar way of thinking, which further accentuates my use of the adjective Elizabethan vis-à-vis Wilbur's style. Wilbur's poems seem to obey an inner imperative that is intellectual rather than emotional, or perhaps I should say emotionally intellectual. We sense that the poet is actually thinking through his feelings to their inevitable and ineluctable conclusion.

So much then by way of apologia. It is not my intention to defend Richard Wilbur against mere carping but to appreciate and admire his poetry that consistently rewards every moment of attention devoted to it. Rather than concentrate on Wilbur's evident technical virtuosity, I propose to focus on his artistic restraint, his genuine mirth, his sense of the tragic and his overall—for lack of a better word—felicity. By felicity I mean language that is happy with itself in the circumstances that this poet has created for it. As a rule Wilbur is such a felicitous poet except in those rare instances when he seems to *will* a poem into being because something rouses his indignation before his inspiration or talent can fully digest it. I will discuss this at greater length shortly.

To call Richard Wilbur a formalist, as he has been identified throughout his career, is simply to state that he writes within the established traditions of English and American poetics. But formalism is too pat a label to paste on any poet, and it clarifies little. (The same thing could be said about Anthony Hecht, Peter Taylor, and George Bradley.) Isn't it more helpful to speak about Wilbur's restraint as a poet, his peculiar aesthetic reserve that eschews the "let-it-all-hang-out" approach in favor of the minuscule detail that is capable of being the key to everything? For example, he does not flail at war's barbarity (which, as an infantryman in World War II, he must have seen at close quarters) but concentrates on the lonely sentry in **"First Snow in Alsace"** who is momentarily distracted by snowswirls and snow designs so that he ignores the whitening shell-holes, the snowdrifts on the ammunition stacks and, ineradicably, the "snowfall [that] fills the eyes / Of soldiers dead a little while." Nor in another poem called **"Place Pigalle"** does he moralize about the whores and stripshows but somehow intermingles the lust and loneliness of soldiers on leave from the front who search out "their ancient friends" with the poignancy of a midsummer night's dream-like respite from a war that makes murderers out of young men who might otherwise be lovers:

> Ionized innocence: this pair reclines,
> She on the table, he in a tilting chair,
> With Arden ease; her eyes as pale as air
> Travel his priestgoat face; his hand's thick tines
> Touch the gold whorls of her Corinthian hair.
>
> "Girl, if I love thee not, then let me die;
> Do I not scorn to change my state with kings?
> Your muchtouched flesh, incalculable, which
>   wrings
> Me so, now shall I gently seize in my
> Desperate soldier's hands which kill all things."

This poem illustrates Wilbur's restraint at its finest. The result is that the theme is strengthened by what is held back. I do not find this to be the case with **"On the Eyes of an SS Officer,"** which ends with this explicit final stanza:

> But this one's iced or ashen eyes devise,
> Foul purities, in flesh their wilderness,
> Their fire; I ask my makeshift God of this
> My opulent bric-a-brac earth to damn his eyes.

The rhetoric of hate is here, but the directness of its expression makes the poetry vanish. Wilbur does not suffer such lapses often, but they do occur. Perhaps this is because his basic optimistic and open nature does not easily transmute rage and indignation into the stuff of poetry. Dante, of course, could do it. Neruda did it when his inspiration and indignation fused; otherwise he simply versified a lot of personal propaganda. Wilbur is capable of the right indignations, which means he gets angry at the right times, but his moral umbrage often strips him of the restraint that is the fertile growing ground of his poetic talent, and the difference is immediately noticeable as in the aforementioned poem as well as in the concluding sestet of his **"A Miltonic Sonnet for Mr. Johnson on His Refusal of Peter Hurd's Official Portrait."**

> Rightly you say the picture is too large
> Which Peter Hurd by your appointment drew,
> And justly call that Capitol too bright
> Which signifies our people in your charge;
> Wait, Sir, and see how time will render you
> Who talk of vision but are weak of sight.

I suppose a case could be made for this poem as a re-creation of the Miltonic spirit in our time, but Wilbur's language has too direct an indebtedness to Milton for me to see it as more than an exercise in adaptation, despite the contemporaneity of the subject matter. The fact remains that Wilbur's formidable talent does not appear at its best when he is moved to write like this. It is not that one disagrees with his moral or political position (agreement or disagreement is not relevant here) but with the way it is stated. Knowing him less than casually, I would say that certain social or political issues affect him deeply and that he sincerely would like to take issue with guile or chicanery or plain wrongdoing through a poetic vision rather than through other means *i.e.,* speeches, letters, and the like. But such poems fail as poems more often than they succeed, despite his efforts to place them in a tradition of righteous anger, as with the just quoted Miltonic sonnet. Take his **"Speech for the Repeal of the McCarran Act"** as another example. Wilbur invokes Mercian figures as the basis for his central metaphor, but his rhetorical impulses still get the better of his poetic ones. In short, the style of his utterance in this hectoring vein seems to be adapted, not natural. And I attribute it to temperament. Some poets can make poems out of spleen; their poems seem a logical extension of their talent. But Wilbur's poems in this genre seem willed into existence; they lose in similitude what they gain in directness, and the poetry is in the similitude. I'll rest my case by quoting a few lines in evidence from a poem Wilbur wrote in 1970 entitled **"For the Student Strikers."**

> Go talk with those who are rumored to be unlike
>   you.
> And whom, it is said, you are so unlike.
> Stand on the stoops of their houses and tell them
>   why
> You are out on strike.
>
> It is not yet time for the rock, the bullet, the blunt
> Slogan that fuddles the mind toward force.
> Let the new sound in our street be the patient
>   sound
> Of your discourse.

Having expressed what is probably my only reservation about Wilbur's talent, I now feel free to praise. And I have no intention of being stingy in my praise of a man who, in poetic terms, is possibly the Mozart of our time. What Mozart achieved in music has a counterpart in Wilbur's achievement in poetry, particularly in his sense of symmetry, his uncanny precision of word choice and his almost infallible ear, his sense of humor as well as his sense of the tragic within a historical and literary tradition that he knows well and, finally, his basic Christian ethos and the worldview that it nurtures.

To speak of Wilbur's sense of symmetry means more than the appearance of the poem on the page, although even from that perspective the basic shape of a Wilbur poem gives one an immediate impression of entirety—an impression that a reading instantly confirms. His poems end in conclusions, not confusions. The conclusions may flow from an idea advanced early in the poem, or, as in **"Piazza di Spagna, Early Morning,"** the elaboration of a single image:

> ·I can't forget
> How she stood at the top of that long marble
>   stair
> Amazed, and then with a sleepy pirouette
> Went dancing slowly down to the fountain-quieted
>   square.
>
>   Nothing upon her face
> But some impersonal loneliness,—not then a
>   girl,
>   But as it were a reverie of the place,
>   A called-for falling glide and whirl;
>
>   As when a leaf, petal, or thin chip
> Is drawn to the falls of a pool and circling a
>   moment above it,
>   Rides on over the lip—
> Perfectly beautiful, perfectly ignorant of it.

He does something similar in **"A Glance from the Bridge."**

> Letting the eye descend from reeking stack
> And black facade to where the river goes,
> You see the freeze has started in to crack
> (As if the city squeezed it in a vise),
> And here and there the limbering water shows,
> And gulls colonial on the sullied ice.
>
> Some rise and braid their glidings white and spare,
> Or sweep the hemmed-in river up and down,
> Making a litheness in the barriered air,
> And through the town the freshening water swirls
> As if an ancient whore undid her gown
> And showed a body almost like a girl's.

The most regular poetic progressions in Wilbur's work appear in the riddle-poems or the what's-my-name poems that have been part of his writing from the very beginning (they spilled over delightfully into a book called *Opposites* whose meters challenge and rhymes please adult and young adult and children equally). These poems are not mere puzzles to be solved; they have about them a wit and whimsy that keep them enjoyable even after the solution is known. The poetry is in their very structure and resolution with each poem ending, as Yeats once said of good poems in general, like the snap-shut lid of a box. Here, for example, is one of the riddles of Symphosius—a three-liner describing coinage:

> First I was earth and deep in earth retired;
> Another name I gained when I was fired;
> I'm earth no more, but through me earth's
>   acquired.

Another example of Wilbur's sense of symmetry, though

somewhat atypical, is the following single image entitled **"Sleepless at Crown Point"**:

> All night, this headland
> Lunges into the rumpling
> Capework of the wind.

This symmetry in Wilbur's poetry is never imposed. It seems to proceed from the poetic seed out of which each poem grows, and Wilbur is artist enough (negatively capable enough, to use Keats's term) to go with the flow of this poetic energy until the poem has completed itself at his hands. If his poem were chairs or tables, one would always be convinced that their sutures and fastenings were secure and that they could stand on their own. At least this has been my experience. I know from my reading of his work over almost forty years that he has never permitted himself to release something that is not complete. At a time when some of his contemporaries regard opaqueness as a virtue and not a sign of immaturity, this is no small triumph. And, of course, Wilbur's ongoing concern with the exact meaning and connotation and sound of words is a further aspect of his talent that places him in direct (and, for me, happy) opposition to some modern poets described by E. M. Cioran in his recently translated and published *Anathemas and Admirations* as follows:

> Poetry is *threatened* when poets take too lively a theoretical interest in language and make it into a constant subject of meditation, when they confer upon it an exceptional status. . . . If we are truly to think, thought must adhere to the mind; if it becomes independent of the mind, exterior to it, the mind is shackled from the start, idles, and has but one source left—itself—instead of relying on the world for its substance or its pretexts. The writer must guard against reflecting obsessively upon language, must avoid making it the subject of his obsessions, must never forget that the important works have been created *despite* language. Dante was obsessed by what he had to say, not by the saying of it. (Cioran 105)

I do not think it presumptuous to claim that these words might have been written by Wilbur himself; in any case, I doubt if he would take violent exception to them. He is concerned with language the way a landscape painter is concerned with paint. He constantly searches for the right word as an artist might search for the right (the exactly right) color to express his vision. He identifies the song of bells, for example, as the "selfsame toothless voice for death or bridal." He alludes at just the right moment in **"The Melongene"** to the "purple presence" of an eggplant, and, presto, we see it. In **"Potato"** he is able to distill in two lines the essence of potato smell: "Cut open raw, it looses a cool clean stench,

/ Mineral acid seeping from pores of prest meal." His poetic obituary to Phelps Putnam (**"To an American Poet Just Dead"**) contains the "ssshh of sprays on all the little lawns" and an allusion to immortality as a "higher standard of living." In **"Driftwood"** he writes of "the great generality of waters" and the "warped" wood having the look of "excellence earned" by retaining "their dense / Ingenerate grain." In **"An Event"** he perceives in the zigzag of clouds of birds in flight "By what cross-purposes the world is dreamt." And **"A Baroque Wall-Fountain in the Villa Sciarra"** contains one of the best re-creations of the sound and sight of fountaining water that I have ever encountered in any literature:

> Happy in all that ragged, loose
> Collapse of water, its effortless descent
>
> And flatteries of spray.
> The stocky god upholds the shell with ease,
>   Watching, about his shaggy knees,
> The goatish innocence of his babes at play;
>
>   His fauness all the while
> Leans forward, slightly, into a clambering mesh
>   Of water-lights, her sparkling flesh
> In a saecular ecstasy, her blinded smile
>   Bent on the sand floor
> Of the trefoil pool, where ripple-shadows come
>   And go in swift reticulum,
> More addling to the eye than wine, and more
>
>   Interminable to thought
> Than pleasure's calculus. Yet since this all
>   Is pleasure, flash, and waterfall,
> Must it not be too simple? Are we not
>
>   More intricately expressed
> In the plain fountains that Maderna set
>   Before St. Peter's—the main jet
> Struggling aloft until it seems at rest
>
>   In the act of rising, until
> The very wish of water is reversed
>   That heaviness borne up to burst
> In a clear high, cavorting head, to fill
>
>   With blaze, and then in gauze
> Delays, in a gnatlike shimmering, in a fine
>   Illumined version of itself, decline,
> And patter on the stone its own applause?

It is in stanzas like these that one can detect how Wilbur's ear rarely fails him. The matching of sound and pace to the fall of fountaining water is so unobtrusively true that we actually hear as well as see the "wish of water" in the language.

I for one admire the subtlety here of Wilbur's musical sense much more than some of the onomatopoetic stanzas in **"On Freedom's Ground"** (Part IV) where he attempts to capture the rhythm of waltzes, polkas, cakewalks, and jigs. Subtlety gives way to the obvious, which is by definition a less suggestive alternative, and the result is verse. True, it is verse of a rather high quality, but it does not have the poetry of the aforementioned lines of the Villa Sciara fountain.

As he has grown older, Wilbur has not abandoned the formal hallmarks of his earlier style (as has Karl Shapiro, for instance) but adapted them to different subjects with the same jeweler's eye and musician's car for the right word in the right place at exactly the right moment. Poems like **"The Fire-Truck"** and **"The Undead"** from *Advice to a Prophet* (1961) testify to this as does the book's powerful title poem. Nor does Wilbur's basic style change in *Walking to Sleep* (1969) in such poems as **"For Dudley," "Playboy,"** and "A Late Aubade."

The poem called **"Shame"** in *Advice to a Prophet* is a happy aberration. True, the lines are basically iambic pentameter, but they are certainly not in the tradition of Pope's ten-syllabled pentameters. Wilbur hues to five-feet per line, but he plays fast and loose with the count, and the poem is the better for it because the fastness and looseness match the theme. This is one of the few poems in which Wilbur just lets himself go, and his sense of mild sarcasm, his basic good humor and his almost Rabelaisian swagger here and there (usually hidden to the point of invisibility) fuse and flourish to the plain delight of any fairminded person who reads the poem. Anyone familiar with the poem knows how the unspecified country of **"Shame"** achieves its ultimate and decisive victory over its occupiers. Wilbur informs us early in the poem that this is a nation with "no foreign policy," an unfathomable grammar, a national sense of its own unimportance and a geography "best described as unrelieved." The people's chief weapon seems to be self-deprecation wedded to self-disdain. Left alone, they turn these weapons upon themselves and manage thus to perpetuate their own mediocrity and undisguised mendacity. After all, this is a country whose "national product" is sheep and whose people truly believe that "they do not count" and who confirm this by announcing that the population total is "zero." Yet, their very vices make them invincible when they confront the "hoped for invasion" with "complete negligence" and "overwhelming submission." The result is that they conquer their conquerors by slowly imbuing them with their own vices:

> Their complete negligence is reserved, however,
> For the hoped-for invasion, at which time the
>   happy people
> (Sniggering, ruddily naked, and shamelessly
>   drunk)

> Will stun the foe by their overwhelming
>   submission.
> Corrupt the generals, infiltrate the staff,
> Usurp the throne, proclaim themselves to be
>   sun-gods,
> And bring about the collapse of the whole empire.

Further confirming Wilbur's sense of artistic restraint during the sixties were two touchstone poems—one from *Advice To a Prophet* (1961) and the other from *Walking to Sleep* (1969). The title poem from *Advice to a Prophet* is not a direct but a slantwise comment on the nuclear apocalypse, but Wilbur eschews the apocalyptic tone and pose so readily adopted by numerous other poets dealing with the same subject. He asks not to be informed about "the weapons, their force and range," nor does he want to be told for the zillionth time about the possible extinction of humanity ("Nor shall you scare us with talk of the death of the race"). Instead Wilbur considers the realizable desolation we would immediately know if certain specific animals and birds would disappear from the world as we know it. He is not speaking in general terms of the death of mankind but of finite, definite absences, and the sense of loss that the poem describes grows out of a consideration of these very absences:

> Though we cannot conceive
> Of an undreamt thing, we know to our cost
> How the dreamt world crumbles, the vines are
>   blackened by frost,
> How the view alters. We could believe,
>
> If you told us so, that the white-tailed deer will
>   slip
> Into perfect shade, grown perfectly shy,
> The lark avoid the reaches of our eye,
> The jack-pine lose its knuckled grip
>
> On the cold ledge, and very torrent burn
> As Xanthus once, its gliding trout
> Stunned in a twinkling. What should we be
>   without
> The dolphin's arc, the dove's return,
>
> These things in which we have seen ourselves and
>   spoken?
> Ask us, prophet, how we shall call
> Our natures forth when that live tongue is all
> Dispelled, that glass obscured or broken
>
> In which we have said the rose of our love and the
>   clean
> Horse of our courage, in which beheld.
> The singing locust of the soul unshelled,
> And all we mean or wish to mean.

The power of this poem derives from how we respond to these enumerated losses and the effect their absence will have on how we define ourselves. The extent of this loss is left to our imaginations. In terror as in art, less proves to be more, much more.

The poem entitled **"Running"** from *Walking to Sleep* is structurally a typical Wilbur poem—a series of introductory descriptions in each section, each ambience counterbalanced by the poet's reaction to it, the gradual evocation of the reality beneath the mere appearance asserting itself. All three sections of the poem deal straightforwardly with the joyful exhilaration of running or of observing runners in action. In the first section Wilbur remembers running in Caldwell, New Jersey, in 1933. The lickety-split run becomes an absolute in his memory—"Thinking of happiness, I think of that." Skipping the second section for a moment, we find in the third section a self-description—Wilbur running as an older man and coming upon two boys running in the opposite direction. As they prepare to pass one another, they rhyme for a moment simply as runners, and Wilbur senses the exhilaration of youth from that passing moment. But it is in the second section that we find the correlative that is (possibly) an inadvertent profile that Wilbur actually gives of himself. Watching marathon runners from the sidelines, Wilbur, now a non-participant, focuses on one of the runners in the pack:

> Dark in the glare, they seemed to thresh in place
> Like preening flies upon a window-sill,
> Yet gained and grew, and at a cruel pace
> Swept by us on their way to Heartbreak Hill—
>
> Legs driving, fits at port, clenched faces, men,
> And in amongst them, stamping on the sun,
> Our champion Kelley, who would win again,
> Rocked in his will, at rest within his run.

The style of Kelley's run is a perfect match for Wilbur's style as a writer—a man sure of his skills and strengths, secure within his own skin, husbanding his known resources and then pitting them against nothing but the challenge before him, confident that he is equal to it.

It may not seem important to some to identify humor as one of Wilbur's poetic assets, but I certainly believe it is. Levity is also a sign of a person with a sense of balance. Although Robert Lowell was and is a poet of genuine stature and was often regarded as a more cosmic poet than Wilbur in some quarters, one must look long and hard to find a Lowell poem with a smile on its face. This does not prevent us from taking Lowell seriously, despite Mark Van Doren's admonition that one should not take seriously someone who always takes himself and the world seriously. Nonetheless, a sense of lightness goes a long way to acquaint a writer's readers with his very humanity and not merely with his personal demons. Wilbur's humor, whether ribald enough to provoke a good guffaw or subtle enough to coax a good chuckle, is never mean-spirited or silly. Its aim seems to be pure fun whether it has a satirical edge or not. And this is true of his earlier poems (**"Superiorities," "Parable," "Museum Piece"**) as well as his later ones (**"Shame," "Matthew VIII, 28ff," "A Late Aubade," "The Prisoner of Zenda." "To His Skeleton"**). The spirit of humor in **"Matthew VIII. 28 ff,"** is a typical example:

> Rabbi, we Gadarenes
> Are not ascetics; we are fond of wealth and
>   possessions,
> Love, as you call it, we obviate by means
> Of the planned release of aggressions.
>
> We have deep faith in prosperity,
> Soon, it is hoped, we will reach our full potential.
> In the light of our gross national product, the
>   practice of charity
> Is palpably inessential.
>
> It is true that we go insane;
> That for no good reason we are possessed by
>   devils;
> That we suffer, despite the amenities which obtain
> At all but the lowest levels.
>
> We shall not, however, resign
> Our trust in the high-heaped table and the full
>   trough.
> If you cannot cure us without destroying our
>   swine,
> We had rather you shoved off.

The barely concealed criticism of the smugly rich in this poem somehow does not get in the way of the roystering, and by the time we get to the last line we are smiling our way into a good laugh.

To move from Wilbur's humorous poems to such masterpieces as **"The Writer," "Cottage Street, 1953,"** and **"Love Calls Us to the Things of This World"** is to realize that Wilbur is not a man who, like some of the confessionalists of his generation, eschews the lightsome in order to be "properly" glum. Not at all. His is a sensibility which permits him to respond to and then re-create in his poetry the light as well as the weighty, the smile as well as the frown. And who can deny that a complete vision of human life does, after all, include both?

Now to a consideration of the ethos of Wilbur's talent. That Wilbur has a theocentric view of life is traceable not only to those poems of his that have liturgical or theological themes, *i.e.,* **"A Christmas Hymn," "A Wedding Toast,"**

"For Dudley," "John Chrysostom," to name but a few of the many, but to a deeper and unmistakable spirituality that infuses his entire corpus and is unfeignable. Since tracing this thread is impossible in a short paper such as this, I will concentrate on only three poems since they represent to me the three salient aspects of this spirituality. The first is **"The Proof,"** a crypto-poem that is both a prayer and, in its succinctness, a further variation on his more telegrammic poems, *i.e.,* riddles etc. The second is **"Love Calls Us to the Things of This World"** a poem which, in its acceptance of the given world and its transfiguration of it, is as consummate a realization as I know of what the calling of poet as seer really means. And the third is **"Cottage Street, 1953,"** primarily because of all that stands behind the judgment of the final line.

The tone of **"The Proof"** (with tone defined as the author's attitude toward his subject, his audience, even toward himself) is as revealing of Wilbur's sensibility as the subject. From first word to last the author reveals himself as a trusting and humble man who is willing to abandon himself to the mercy and generosity of God. It is as if Wilbur has taken the Bible's injunction that fear of the Lord is the beginning of wisdom and made it the very soul of this poem. I have detected this same tone in numerous poems of Wilbur (and in some of his translations as well), and it is neither forced nor fictitious. Somehow one senses when one is in the presence of genuine feelings of this nature, and the feelings in **"The Proof"** impress me in this way.

> Shall I love God for causing me to be?
> I was mere utterance; shall these words love me?
>
> Yet when I caused his work to jar and stammer,
> And one free subject loosened all his grammar,
>
> I love him that he did not in a rage
> Once and forever rule me off the page,
>
> But, thinking that I might come to please him yet,
> Crossed out *delete* and wrote his patient *stet.*

This poem has the unmistakable resignation and deference of personal prayer. It is this deference that appears again and again in Wilbur's poetry—a deference to things as they are in their God-created or man-created uniqueness, a deference to the beautiful and its changes, a deference to love itself and a willingness to allow it the spaces it needs (which is the very proof of anyone's respect for love itself) to manifest itself and grow.

Perhaps no poem in all of Wilbur's writings affirms his wonder in the presence of God-created and man-created things than his much (and deservedly) anthologized **"Love Calls Us to the Things of This World."** Rather than quote the poem in its entirely since it is one of the most well known of Wilbur's works, I will allude only to the basic circumstance of the poem and how Wilbur, presumably the persona of the poem, finds in that circumstance a reason to affirm and bless it.

A sleeper is slowly coming awake. He imagines that the laundry hanging on a line outside his window is like a flight of seraphim. This angelic laundry seems to float and dance in the "false dawn" of semi-wakefulness.

> Now they are rising together in calm swells
> Of halcyon feeling, filling whatever they wear
> With the deep joy of their impersonal breathing.

But such a Platonic view has only a limited lease on the observer's life, and, no matter how much he wants the illusion to persist in defiance of the upcoming "punctual rape of every blessed day," he knows that the soul must descend "once more in bitter love / To accept the waking body." And, of course, form and function are destined to exist in consonance, which means that the laundry, which is destined for use as clothes, must come down from the "ruddy gallows." It must clothe thieves, lovers and nuns; the world must go on being the world. The fulcrum image of the lovers ("Let lovers go fresh and sweet to be undone") provides the ironic balance between thieves and nuns, since lovers go dressed only to that point where they must undo their clothes so that they can become lovers in fact. Regardless of the irony, the entire poem ends on the side of life and "the things of this world" where only love can humanize us, not in otherworldly but in this-worldly terms. Like Frost, Wilbur believes that "earth's the right place for love." Thus the "waking body" offsets the bitterness of its dream-ending moment of false bliss by quite literally blessing (what is an affirmation but a blessing?) the real world where theft, loving and devotion are ongoing and co-existent.

"Cottage Street, 1953" is Wilbur at his lyrical and perspicacious best. The setting could not be simpler—a tea on Cottage Street hosted by Edna Ward, Wilbur's mother-in-law. Present are Wilbur and his wife, Sylvia Plath and her mother. Wilbur admits to having been invited so as to serve as a role-model for the despondent Sylvia:

> It is my office to exemplify
> The published poet in his happiness,
> Thus cheering Sylvia, who has wished to die;
> But half-ashamed, and impotent to bless,
>
> I am a stupid life-guard who has found,
> Swept to his shallows by the tide, a girl
> Who far from shore has been immensely drowned
> And stares through water now with eyes of pearl.

The ongoing "refusal" of Sylvia Plath to do anything but drown is contrasted sharply with the quiet courage of Edna Ward, destined to die a decade and a half later (the poem was obviously written after 1968) but doing so with tearless dignity and speaking of love to and at the very end. Against the example of Edna Ward's graced and graceful end at the age of eighty-eight, Wilbur describes Sylvia Plath as one who in her despair seemed "condemned to live" and whose poem's "brilliant negative" was on balance "free and helpless and unjust." It is the mention of injustice that tells us how Wilbur perceives the lives of these two radically different women—the elder, a valiant example of keeping faith with life *in extremis;* the younger, a victim, not so much of life as of her twisted vision of it. Weighing Edna Ward's bravery against the spiritual self-betrayal of Sylvia Plath who, at the time of the writing of the poem had already taken her own life, Wilbur comes down on the side of justice—justice to life itself. This transmutes the poem into a double elegy, and, as elegies tell us more about life when it is touched by death than they tell us about death itself (since death is actually unknowable), they reveal the human values of the elegist. He pities Sylvia Plath; he is edified by Edna Ward.

This then completes the range of my appreciation of this immensely talented writer. (I should add that he is an equally talented reader of his own poems and translations. Whoever has listened to Richard Wilbur read his work has experienced what Wilbur himself once ascribed to the work of Degas—"Beauty joined to energy.") My few reservations, which I felt obliged to include in the spirit of absolute candor, are but quibbles in the balance. Far exceeding them is the wealth of poems by Richard Wilbur that will be part of our literature as long as it lasts. For that we can only be quick to praise and, above all, grateful.

Isabella Wai (essay date Summer 1996)

SOURCE: "Wilbur's 'A Baroque Wall-Fountain in the Villa Sciarra'," in *The Explicator,* Vol. 54, No. 4, Summer 1996, pp. 244-47.

[*In the following essay, Wai provides an analysis of Wilbur's poem "A Baroque Wall-Fountain in the Villa Sciarra."*]

In his book of word games for children **Opposites,** Richard Wilbur speculates about the relativity between objects, or between ideas, and between objects and ideas. In his poems, he uses contrasts to explore the relatedness of two conflicting inclinations: spiritual aspirations and mundane commitments. Wilbur approaches the intangible dimension of a real object through its tangible appearance. He tends to juxtapose one character or object against another, balancing each

against its "counterpoint." The opposed images show the inadequacy of one divorced from the other.

The rivalry between spiritual yearnings and a commitment to the imperfect world of objects inspires Wilbur's poem **"A Baroque Wall-Fountain in the Villa Sciarra."** The baroque fountain and its counterparts in St. Peter's Square represent two different views of happiness—participation in worldly pleasures and transcendence toward heavenly bliss. The poet favors a spirituality that is not world renouncing.

To comprehend His creation is to comprehend the Creator, Wilbur states:

> I think a lot of my poems, instead of saying "isn't this a marvellous world permeated by divinity," say instead "come on, let's not be too spiritual, let's get down *to* earth." That of course implies the possibility of being spiritual. That kind of attack on a too-unworldly spirituality could be seen as a way of affirming the possibility of any kind of spirituality.

The structure of many of Wilbur's poems is dialectical, corresponding to the rival claims of the actual and the ideal. His dialectics usually take the form of a succession of examples through which the poet examines the complexities involved in the conflict. The arrangement of the arguments is usually a juxtaposition of the thesis against the antithesis. Sometimes this is followed by a synthesis, which may be a poetic resolution ("difficult balance" in the poem **"Love Calls Us to the Things of this World"** [233-34]) or a paradoxical image ("light incarnate" in **"A World without Objects Is a Sensible Emptiness"** [283-84]). The religious allusion to St. Francis in **"A Baroque Wall-Fountain"** serves as a concluding argument.

The ornate Baroque wall fountain in a public garden of Rome, meticulously described in the first seven stanzas of the poem, is a scene of fallen Eden, of "saecular ecstasy." A stone cherub wears a bronze crown that is too big for its head. "A serpent has begun to eat" the cherub's feet. The water trickles down over the three shells in "effortless descent." The descent is "effortless," for it is in harmony with the natural law of gravity. Beneath the third scalloped shell live "a faun-ménage and their familiar goose." The presence of a serpent and the descent of water recall the Fall of Adam into the world of experience. The faun, expressing a possible view of happiness, accepts his condition with case.

The faun's "babes" are heirs to their parents' attitude toward life. The happiness of the faun-ménage consists in their total acceptance and enjoyment of what they are allowed. Sensuous delights are conveyed throughout the description of the wall fountain: the water is "Sweet," the flesh of the "fauness" is "sparkling," and the "ripple-shadows" are "More addling to the eye than wine."

Trickling down through the seven stanzas, the lengthy sentences imitate the downward movement of water from the stone cherub to the "trefoil pool," where "ripple-shadows come / And go in swift reticulum." Certain words are strategically placed at the beginning of a line to heighten the intensity of the fall or movement of the water. The word "Collapse," for example, sends the water, sustained by the adjective "loose" in the preceding line, plunging downward at full speed. And the phrase, "flatteries of spray" is a kinetic and graphic description of the water after "its effortless descent." The language suggests the dance of light and shadow associated with the music and patterns of splashing water.

Juxtaposed against the elaborate wall fountain are the plain Maderna fountains in St. Peter's Square. Compared with the wall fountain, they are less intricate in design, but more intricate in their expression of human ideals.

The Maderna fountains are depicted in one sentence, manifesting the effort that sustains the upward movement of the water in defiance of the natural law of gravity. Again Wilbur captures the kinetic motion of the water, "struggling" and balancing itself "aloft until it seems at rest / In the act of rising." Yet the world-renouncing struggle of the Maderna fountains toward spirituality seems to be indistinguishable from the desire for personal glamour. The words "cavorting" and "display" imply that the ascent itself is a showy performance, which is applauded by the descent of the water pattering "on the stones." The water of the main jet is only "at rest" after a glimpse of heaven and after self-glorification, whereas the fauns "are at rest in fulness of desire/For what is given."

The poet wonders whether men should model their lives on the "water-saints" who "display / The pattern of our areté" or on the "showered fauns" who "do not tire / Of the smart of the sun." It is through the example of St. Francis that the poet suggests a subtle, ambiguous resolution for the dilemma between the two human tendencies: restless spiritual yearning and "humble insatiety." Although St. Francis abstained from worldly pleasures, he might be enlightened by seeing the virtue of the fauns: their humbleness. The virtue of humility, according to the saint, can be the key to celestial riches. Yet this revelation that the saint may have experienced is only a possibility, and the "bliss" he "might have seen" only a "shade."

Unlike the fauns, who have fulfilled God's command to multiply, St. Francis at Sarteano scourged his recalcitrant body because of his desire for a family. But the saint differs from the water saints, whose struggle for spiritual bliss is tinted by a desire for secular applause. St. Francis believed that perfect joy consists in humility and acceptance.

St. Francis, who provides a contrasting parallel to both the water saints and the fauns, might have achieved a balance between the two sets of virtues: the fauns' humility and the water saints' aspiration toward transcendence. Yet the achievement of that balance would have been contingent upon his respect for and acceptance of "That land of tolerable flowers, that state / As near and far as grass/Where eyes become the sunlight. . . ." The word "flowers" recalls the title of the book *The Little Flowers of St. Francis.* Flowers ordinarily are emblems of the short duration of existence, but these flowers are "tolerable" because they are perceived as enduring. In St. Francis's case, the flowers are his virtues and his worldly religious accomplishments. The "eyes" or lights of the soul "become the sunlight," the life-giving force. And the "hand," meaning physical labor in general and the flower tender in particular, "Is worthy of water," which is associated with both Baptism and irrigation. The "tolerable flowers" (immortal mortality) are nourished by the lights of the soul and the sun and by water from both spiritual and physical sources. In this "dreamt land / Toward which all hungers leap, all pleasures pass," spirituality is world nourishing rather than world renouncing.

Isabella Wai (essay date Winter 1997)

SOURCE: "Wilbur's 'Ceremony'," in *The Explicator,* Vol. 55, No. 2, Winter 1997, pp. 98-99.

[*In the following essay, Wai provides a brief explication of Wilbur's poem "Ceremony."*]

In his poem **"Ceremony,"** Richard Wilbur treats the paradox that man and nature may seem to be in combat with each other yet are in some respects basically akin. The poem demonstrates his respect for ritualistic forms in both nature and society. "I think that a lot of one's feeling of union with natural things is unilateral," says Wilbur, "and yet I persist in feeling that nothing, right down to the stone, is irrelevant to us, is not part of a family."

"Ceremony" begins with Wilbur's response to a painting by Bazille, a nineteenth-century French-Impressionist painter:

> A striped blouse in a clearing by Bazille
> Is, you may say, patroness of boughs
> Too queenly kind toward nature to be kin.

The reader immediately senses the poet's awareness of man's

intrusion into nature and his perception of the contrast between civilization and wilderness.

Thus the girl in Wilbur's poem who seems to be "queenly kind," or supremely civil, must be alien to the wild, unruly life of the forest. But the second half of the first stanza contradicts this assumption. Although the formality of the girl's attire distinguishes her from the surrounding woods,

> . . . ceremony never did conceal
> Save to the silly eye, which all allows,
> How much we are the woods we wander in.

If the lady were without social mannerisms and formal dress and appeared instead as Sabrina the water nymph ("Let her be some Sabrina fresh from stream"), the nature-man distinction would be invisible in her. Without this contrast, Bazille's scene would have lost its meaning and form. "[F]resh from stream," closely associated with the sun and the fern beds, and having become "the flowers' cynosure." Sabrina is Nature herself, and Nature is she. The "nymph and wood" interpenetrate each other's being:

> Then nymph and wood must nod and strive to
>   dream
> That she is airy earth, the trees, undone,
> Must ape her languor natural and pure.

Yet their mingling of identities results in an absence of contrast and, consequently, a loss of vigor. Words such as "slowed," "[b]edded," "dream," and "languor" create an atmosphere of sleepiness and oppressive stillness.

The poet yawns. "Ho-hum." The idyllic scene associated with Sabrina is too pure or uniform and harmonious to provoke any creative impulse. Then the poet dispels the drowsiness and praises the "wit and wakefulness"—imaginationand dynamic contrast—embodied in the lady. The concluding stanza demonstrates that beneath the ceremonious appearance of "curtsey and quadrille," man and nature are akin. The lady's "social smile and formal dress" only "lightly"

hide her bond with the wild, unceremonious "tigers." Through the contrast between wild life and civilization, the presence of tigers and the lady's etiquette are more intensely felt. Wilbur shares Bazille's recognition of the interaction among objects in a certain environment and juxtaposes them with each other accordingly, to provide a surprising and revealing effect. Ironically, although the lady's social formality lends contrast to the forest, her stripes, resembling those of the tigers, reinforce the impression that she is part of "the woods" she "wander[s] in."

Like the lady, both Bazille and Wilbur feign. Bazille frames his response to reality in a painting, whereas Wilbur fables his interpretation of Bazille's impression in a poem, ceremoniously observant of restrictions of rhythm and rhyme.

FURTHER READING

Criticism

Bagg, Robert. "Merlin and Faust in Two Post-War Poems." In *Merlin versus Faust: Contending Archetypes in Western Culture,* edited by Charlotte Spivack, pp. 189-98. Lewiston, N.Y.: The Edwin Mellen Press, 1992.

> Analyzes Wilbur's poem "Merlin Enthralled" as exemplary of the search for meaning amid chaos in the tradition of war poetry.

Schwartz, Joseph. "The Concept of Historical Form in the Poetry of Richard Wilbur." *Renascence* 45, No. 1-2 (Fall 1992/Winter 1993): 35-48.

> Discusses Wilbur's "sense of history" evident throughout his work, but found particularly in his poem "Looking into History."

Turner, Alberta T. "About 'Cottage Street'." In *The Catbird's Song: Prose Pieces 1963-1995,* by Richard Wilbur, pp. 147-52. New York City: Harcourt, Brace, 1997.

> Interview in which Wilbur discusses his poem "Cottage Street, 1953."

Additional coverage of Wilbur's life and career is contained in the following sources published by Gale: *Contemporary Authors,* Vol. 1-4R; *Contemporary Authors Bibliographical Series,* Vol. 2; *Contemporary Authors New Revision Series,* Vols. 2 and 29; *Contemporary Literary Criticism,* Vols. 3, 6, 9, 14, and 53; *DISCovering Authors;* *DISCovering Authors: British; DISCovering Authors: Canadian; DISCovering Authors Modules: Most-Studied Authors, Poetry; Dictionary of Literary Biography,* Vols. 5 and 169; *Major Twentieth-Century Writers;* and *Something About the Author,* Vol. 9.

☐ Contemporary Literary Criticism

Indexes

Literary Criticism Series
Cumulative Author Index
Cumulative Topic Index
Cumulative Nationality Index
Title Index, Volume 110

How to Use This Index

The main references

> Camus, Albert
> 1913-1960 ...... CLC 1, 2, 4, 9, 11, 14,
> 32, 69; DA; DAB; DAC; DAM DRAM,
> MST, NOV; DC2; SSC 9; WLC

list all author entries in the following Gale Literary Criticism series:

BLC = *Black Literature Criticism*
CLC = *Contemporary Literary Criticism*
CLR = *Children's Literature Review*
CMLC = *Classical and Medieval Literature Criticism*
DA = *DISCovering Authors*
DAB = *DISCovering Authors: British*
DAC = *DISCovering Authors: Canadian*
DAM = *DISCovering Authors Modules*
  DRAM = *dramatists;* **MST** = *most-studied*
  authors; **MULT** = *multicultural authors;* **NOV** =
  novelists; **POET** = *poets;* **POP** = *popular/genre*
  writers; **DC** = *Drama Criticism*
HLC = *Hispanic Literature Criticism*
LC = *Literature Criticism from 1400 to 1800*
NCLC = *Nineteenth-Century Literature Criticism*
PC = *Poetry Criticism*
SSC = *Short Story Criticism*
TCLC = *Twentieth-Century Literary Criticism*
WLC = *World Literature Criticism, 1500 to the Present*
WLCS = *World Literature Criticism Supplement*

The cross-references

> See also CA 89-92; DLB 72; MTCW

list all author entries in the following Gale biographical and literary sources:

AAYA = *Authors & Artists for Young Adults*
AITN = *Authors in the News*
BEST = *Bestsellers*
BW = *Black Writers*
CA = *Contemporary Authors*
CAAS = *Contemporary Authors Autobiography Series*
CABS = *Contemporary Authors Bibliographical Series*
CANR = *Contemporary Authors New Revision Series*
CAP = *Contemporary Authors Permanent Series*
CDALB = *Concise Dictionary of American Literary Biography*
CDBLB = *Concise Dictionary of British Literary Biography*

DLB = *Dictionary of Literary Biography*
DLBD = *Dictionary of Literary Biography Documentary Series*
DLBY = *Dictionary of Literary Biography Yearbook*
HW = *Hispanic Writers*
JRDA = *Junior DISCovering Authors*
MAICYA = *Major Authors and Illustrators for Children and Young Adults*
MTCW = *Major 20th-Century Writers*
NNAL = *Native North American Literature*
SAAS = *Something about the Author Autobiography Series*
SATA = *Something about the Author*
YABC = *Yesterday's Authors of Books for Children*

Literary Criticism Series
Cumulative Author Index

Barea, Arturo 1897-1957 .... **TCLC 14**
    See also CA 111
Barfoot, Joan 1946- .... **CLC 18**
    See also CA 105
Baring, Maurice 1874-1945 .... **TCLC 8**
    See also CA 105; DLB 34
Barker, Clive 1952- .... **CLC 52; DAM POP**
    See also AAYA 10; BEST 90:3; CA 121; 129;
    INT 129; MTCW
Barker, George Granville 1913-1991 **CLC 8,**
    48; DAM POET
    See also CA 9-12R; 135; CANR 7, 38; DLB
    20; MTCW
Barker, Harley Granville
    See Granville-Barker, Harley
    See also DLB 10
Barker, Howard 1946- .... **CLC 37**
    See also CA 102; DLB 13
Barker, Pat(ricia) 1943- .... **CLC 32, 94**
    See also CA 117; 122; CANR 50; INT 122
Barlow, Joel 1754-1812 .... **NCLC 23**
    See also DLB 37
Barnard, Mary (Ethel) 1909- .... **CLC 48**
    See also CA 21-22; CAP 2
Barnes, Djuna 1892-1982 **CLC 3, 4, 8, 11, 29;**
    SSC 3
    See also CA 9-12R; 107; CANR 16, 55; DLB
    4, 9, 45; MTCW
Barnes, Julian (Patrick) 1946- **CLC 42; DAB**
    See also CA 102; CANR 19, 54; DLB 194;
    DLBY 93
Barnes, Peter 1931- .... **CLC 5, 56**
    See also CA 65-68; CAAS 12; CANR 33, 34,
    64; DLB 13; MTCW
Baroja (y Nessi), Pio 1872-1956 **TCLC 8; HLC**
    See also CA 104
Baron, David
    See Pinter, Harold
Baron Corvo
    See Rolfe, Frederick (William Serafino Austin
    Lewis Mary)
Barondess, Sue K(aufman) 1926-1977 **CLC 8**
    See also Kaufman, Sue
    See also CA 1-4R; 69-72; CANR 1
Baron de Teive
    See Pessoa, Fernando (Antonio Nogueira)
Barres, (Auguste-) Maurice 1862-1923 **T C L C**
    47
    See also CA 164; DLB 123
Barreto, Afonso Henrique de Lima
    See Lima Barreto, Afonso Henrique de
Barrett, (Roger) Syd 1946- .... **CLC 35**
Barrett, William (Christopher) 1913-1992
    CLC 27
    See also CA 13-16R; 139; CANR 11, 67; INT
    CANR-11
Barrie, J(ames) M(atthew) 1860-1937 **T C L C**
    2; DAB; DAM DRAM
    See also CA 104; 136; CDBLB 1890-1914;
    CLR 16; DLB 10, 141, 156; MAICYA;
    YABC 1
Barrington, Michael
    See Moorcock, Michael (John)
Barrol, Grady
    See Bograd, Larry
Barry, Mike
    See Malzberg, Barry N(athaniel)
Barry, Philip 1896-1949 .... **TCLC 11**
    See also CA 109; DLB 7
Bart, Andre Schwarz
    See Schwarz-Bart, Andre
Barth, John (Simmons) 1930- **CLC 1, 2, 3, 5, 7,**
    9, 10, 14, 27, 51, 89; DAM NOV; SSC 10

See also AITN 1, 2; CA 1-4R; CABS 1; CANR
    5, 23, 49, 64; DLB 2; MTCW
Barthelme, Donald 1931-1989 **CLC 1, 2, 3, 5, 6,**
    8, 13, 23, 46, 59; DAM NOV; SSC 2
    See also CA 21-24R; 129; CANR 20, 58; DLB
    2; DLBY 80, 89; MTCW; SATA 7; SATA-
    Obit 62
Barthelme, Frederick 1943- .... **CLC 36**
    See also CA 114; 122; DLBY 85; INT 122
Barthes, Roland (Gerard) 1915-1980 **CLC 24,**
    83
    See also CA 130; 97-100; CANR 66; MTCW
Barzun, Jacques (Martin) 1907- .... **CLC 51**
    See also CA 61-64; CANR 22
Bashevis, Isaac
    See Singer, Isaac Bashevis
Bashkirtseff, Marie 1859-1884 .... **NCLC 27**
Basho
    See Matsuo Basho
Bass, Kingsley B., Jr.
    See Bullins, Ed
Bass, Rick 1958- .... **CLC 79**
    See also CA 126; CANR 53
Bassani, Giorgio 1916- .... **CLC 9**
    See also CA 65-68; CANR 33; DLB 128, 177;
    MTCW
Bastos, Augusto (Antonio) Roa
    See Roa Bastos, Augusto (Antonio)
Bataille, Georges 1897-1962 .... **CLC 29**
    See also CA 101; 89-92
Bates, H(erbert) E(rnest) 1905-1974 **CLC 46;**
    DAB; DAM POP; SSC 10
    See also CA 93-96; 45-48; CANR 34; DLB 162,
    191; MTCW
Bauchart
    See Camus, Albert
Baudelaire, Charles 1821-1867 **NCLC 6, 29,**
    55; DA; DAB; DAC; DAM MST, POET;
    PC 1; SSC 18; WLC
Baudrillard, Jean 1929- .... **CLC 60**
Baum, L(yman) Frank 1856-1919 ... **TCLC 7**
    See also CA 108; 133; CLR 15; DLB 22; JRDA;
    MAICYA; MTCW; SATA 18
Baum, Louis F.
    See Baum, L(yman) Frank
Baumbach, Jonathan 1933- .... **CLC 6, 23**
    See also CA 13-16R; CAAS 5; CANR 12, 66;
    DLBY 80; INT CANR-12; MTCW
Bausch, Richard (Carl) 1945- .... **CLC 51**
    See also CA 101; CAAS 14; CANR 43, 61; DLB
    130
Baxter, Charles (Morley) 1947- **CLC 45, 78;**
    DAM POP
    See also CA 57-60; CANR 40, 64; DLB 130
Baxter, George Owen
    See Faust, Frederick (Schiller)
Baxter, James K(eir) 1926-1972 .... **CLC 14**
    See also CA 77-80
Baxter, John
    See Hunt, E(verette) Howard, (Jr.)
Bayer, Sylvia
    See Glassco, John
Baynton, Barbara 1857-1929 .... **TCLC 57**
Beagle, Peter S(oyer) 1939- .... **CLC 7, 104**
    See also CA 9-12R; CANR 4, 51; DLBY 80;
    INT CANR-4; SATA 60
Bean, Normal
    See Burroughs, Edgar Rice
Beard, Charles A(ustin) 1874-1948 **TCLC 15**
    See also CA 115; DLB 17; SATA 18
Beardsley, Aubrey 1872-1898 .... **NCLC 6**
Beattie, Ann 1947- **CLC 8, 13, 18, 40, 63; DAM**
    NOV, POP; SSC 11

See also BEST 90:2; CA 81-84; CANR 53;
    DLBY 82; MTCW
Beattie, James 1735-1803 .... **NCLC 25**
    See also DLB 109
Beauchamp, Kathleen Mansfield 1888-1923
    See Mansfield, Katherine
    See also CA 104; 134; DA; DAC; DAM MST
Beaumarchais, Pierre-Augustin Caron de 1732-
    1799 .... **DC 4**
    See also DAM DRAM
Beaumont, Francis 1584(?)-1616 **LC 33; DC 6**
    See also CDBLB Before 1660; DLB 58, 121
Beauvoir, Simone (Lucie Ernestine Marie
    Bertrand) de 1908-1986 **CLC 1, 2, 4, 8,**
    14, 31, 44, 50, 71; DA; DAB; DAC; DAM
    MST, NOV; WLC
    See also CA 9-12R; 118; CANR 28, 61; DLB
    72; DLBY 86; MTCW
Becker, Carl (Lotus) 1873-1945 ..... **TCLC 63**
    See also CA 157; DLB 17
Becker, Jurek 1937-1997 .... **CLC 7, 19**
    See also CA 85-88; 157; CANR 60; DLB 75
Becker, Walter 1950- .... **CLC 26**
Beckett, Samuel (Barclay) 1906-1989 **CLC 1,**
    2, 3, 4, 6, 9, 10, 11, 14, 18, 29, 57, 59, 83;
    DA; DAB; DAC; DAM DRAM, MST,
    NOV; SSC 16; WLC
    See also CA 5-8R; 130; CANR 33, 61; CDBLB
    1945-1960; DLB 13, 15; DLBY 90; MTCW
Beckford, William 1760-1844 .... **NCLC 16**
    See also DLB 39
Beckman, Gunnel 1910- .... **CLC 26**
    See also CA 33-36R; CANR 15; CLR 25;
    MAICYA; SAAS 9; SATA 6
Becque, Henri 1837-1899 .... **NCLC 3**
    See also DLB 192
Beddoes, Thomas Lovell 1803-1849 **NCLC 3**
    See also DLB 96
Bede c. 673-735 .... **CMLC 20**
    See also DLB 146
Bedford, Donald F.
    See Fearing, Kenneth (Flexner)
Beecher, Catharine Esther 1800-1878 **N C L C**
    30
    See also DLB 1
Beecher, John 1904-1980 .... **CLC 6**
    See also AITN 1; CA 5-8R; 105; CANR 8
Beer, Johann 1655-1700 .... **LC 5**
    See also DLB 168
Beer, Patricia 1924- .... **CLC 58**
    See also CA 61-64; CANR 13, 46; DLB 40
Beerbohm, Max
    See Beerbohm, (Henry) Max(imilian)
Beerbohm, (Henry) Max(imilian) 1872-1956
    TCLC 1, 24
    See also CA 104; 154; DLB 34, 100
Beer-Hofmann, Richard 1866-1945 **TCLC 60**
    See also CA 160; DLB 81
Begiebing, Robert J(ohn) 1946- .... **CLC 70**
    See also CA 122; CANR 40
Behan, Brendan 1923-1964 **CLC 1, 8, 11, 15,**
    79; DAM DRAM
    See also CA 73-76; CANR 33; CDBLB 1945-
    1960; DLB 13; MTCW
Behn, Aphra 1640(?)-1689 **LC 1, 30; DA; DAB;**
    DAC; DAM DRAM, MST, NOV, POET;
    DC 4; PC 13; WLC
    See also DLB 39, 80, 131
Behrman, S(amuel) N(athaniel) 1893-1973
    CLC 40
    See also CA 13-16; 45-48; CAP 1; DLB 7, 44
Belasco, David 1853-1931 .... **TCLC 3**
    See also CA 104; DLB 7

Besant, Annie (Wood) 1847-1933 ..... **TCLC 9**
See also CA 105
Bessie, Alvah 1904-1985 .... **CLC 23**
See also CA 5-8R; 116; CANR 2; DLB 26
Bethlen, T. D.
See Silverberg, Robert
Beti, Mongo ...... **CLC 27; BLC; DAM MULT**
See also Biyidi, Alexandre
Betjeman, John 1906-1984 **CLC 2, 6, 10, 34, 43; DAB; DAM MST, POET**
See also CA 9-12R; 112; CANR 33, 56; CDBLB 1945-1960; DLB 20; DLBY 84; MTCW
Bettelheim, Bruno 1903-1990 .... **CLC 79**
See also CA 81-84; 131; CANR 23, 61; MTCW
Betti, Ugo 1892-1953 .... **TCLC 5**
See also CA 104; 155
Betts, Doris (Waugh) 1932- ...... **CLC 3, 6, 28**
See also CA 13-16R; CANR 9, 66; DLBY 82; INT CANR-9
Bevan, Alistair
See Roberts, Keith (John Kingston)
Bialik, Chaim Nachman 1873-1934 **TCLC 25**
Bickerstaff, Isaac
See Swift, Jonathan
Bidart, Frank 1939- .... **CLC 33**
See also CA 140
Bienek, Horst 1930- .... **CLC 7, 11**
See also CA 73-76; DLB 75
Bierce, Ambrose (Gwinett) 1842-1914(?) **TCLC 1, 7, 44; DA; DAC; DAM MST; SSC 9; WLC**
See also CA 104; 139; CDALB 1865-1917; DLB 11, 12, 23, 71, 74, 186
Biggers, Earl Derr 1884-1933 .... **TCLC 65**
See also CA 108; 153
Billings, Josh
See Shaw, Henry Wheeler
Billington, (Lady) Rachel (Mary) 1942- **C L C 43**
See also AITN 2; CA 33-36R; CANR 44
Binyon, T(imothy) J(ohn) 1936- ...... **CLC 34**
See also CA 111; CANR 28
Bioy Casares, Adolfo 1914-1984 **CLC 4, 8, 13, 88; DAM MULT; HLC; SSC 17**
See also CA 29-32R; CANR 19, 43, 66; DLB 113; HW; MTCW
Bird, Cordwainer
See Ellison, Harlan (Jay)
Bird, Robert Montgomery 1806-1854 **NCLC 1**
Birney, (Alfred) Earle 1904-1995 **CLC 1, 4, 6, 11; DAC; DAM MST, POET**
See also CA 1-4R; CANR 5, 20; DLB 88; MTCW
Bishop, Elizabeth 1911-1979 **CLC 1, 4, 9, 13, 15, 32; DA; DAC; DAM MST, POET; PC 3**
See also CA 5-8R; 89-92; CABS 2; CANR 26, 61; CDALB 1968-1988; DLB 5, 169; MTCW; SATA-Obit 24
Bishop, John 1935- .... **CLC 10**
See also CA 105
Bissett, Bill 1939- .... **CLC 18; PC 14**
See also CA 69-72; CAAS 19; CANR 15; DLB 53; MTCW
Bitov, Andrei (Georgievich) 1937- ... **CLC 57**
See also CA 142
Biyidi, Alexandre 1932-
See Beti, Mongo
See also BW 1; CA 114; 124; MTCW
Bjarme, Brynjolf
See Ibsen, Henrik (Johan)
Bjornson, Bjornstjerne (Martinius) 1832-1910 **TCLC 7, 37**

See also CA 104
Black, Robert
See Holdstock, Robert P.
Blackburn, Paul 1926-1971 .... **CLC 9, 43**
See also CA 81-84; 33-36R; CANR 34; DLB 16; DLBY 81
Black Elk 1863-1950 **TCLC 33; DAM MULT**
See also CA 144; NNAL
Black Hobart
See Sanders, (James) Ed(ward)
Blacklin, Malcolm
See Chambers, Aidan
Blackmore, R(ichard) D(oddridge) 1825-1900 **TCLC 27**
See also CA 120; DLB 18
Blackmur, R(ichard) P(almer) 1904-1965 **CLC 2, 24**
See also CA 11-12; 25-28R; CAP 1; DLB 63
Black Tarantula
See Acker, Kathy
Blackwood, Algernon (Henry) 1869-1951 **TCLC 5**
See also CA 105; 150; DLB 153, 156, 178
Blackwood, Caroline 1931-1996 **CLC 6, 9, 100**
See also CA 85-88; 151; CANR 32, 61, 65; DLB 14; MTCW
Blade, Alexander
See Hamilton, Edmond; Silverberg, Robert
Blaga, Lucian 1895-1961 .... **CLC 75**
Blair, Eric (Arthur) 1903-1950
See Orwell, George
See also CA 104; 132; DA; DAB; DAC; DAM MST, NOV; MTCW; SATA 29
Blais, Marie-Claire 1939- **CLC 2, 4, 6, 13, 22; DAC; DAM MST**
See also CA 21-24R; CAAS 4; CANR 38; DLB 53; MTCW
Blaise, Clark 1940- .... **CLC 29**
See also AITN 2; CA 53-56; CAAS 3; CANR 5, 66; DLB 53
Blake, Fairley
See De Voto, Bernard (Augustine)
Blake, Nicholas
See Day Lewis, C(ecil)
See also DLB 77
Blake, William 1757-1827 . **NCLC 13, 37, 57; DA; DAB; DAC; DAM MST, POET; PC 12; WLC**
See also CDBLB 1789-1832; DLB 93, 163; MAICYA; SATA 30
Blasco Ibanez, Vicente 1867-1928 **TCLC 12; DAM NOV**
See also CA 110; 131; HW; MTCW
Blatty, William Peter 1928- **CLC 2; DAM POP**
See also CA 5-8R; CANR 9
Bleeck, Oliver
See Thomas, Ross (Elmore)
Blessing, Lee 1949- .... **CLC 54**
Blish, James (Benjamin) 1921-1975 . **CLC 14**
See also CA 1-4R; 57-60; CANR 3; DLB 8; MTCW; SATA 66
Bliss, Reginald
See Wells, H(erbert) G(eorge)
Blixen, Karen (Christentze Dinesen) 1885-1962
See Dinesen, Isak
See also CA 25-28; CANR 22, 50; CAP 2; MTCW; SATA 44
Bloch, Robert (Albert) 1917-1994 .... **CLC 33**
See also CA 5-8R; 146; CAAS 20; CANR 5; DLB 44; INT CANR-5; SATA 12; SATA-Obit 82
Blok, Alexander (Alexandrovich) 1880-1921 **TCLC 5; PC 21**

See also CA 104
Blom, Jan
See Breytenbach, Breyten
Bloom, Harold 1930- .... **CLC 24, 103**
See also CA 13-16R; CANR 39; DLB 67
Bloomfield, Aurelius
See Bourne, Randolph S(illiman)
Blount, Roy (Alton), Jr. 1941- .... **CLC 38**
See also CA 53-56; CANR 10, 28, 61; INT CANR-28; MTCW
Bloy, Leon 1846-1917 .... **TCLC 22**
See also CA 121; DLB 123
Blume, Judy (Sussman) 1938- ... **CLC 12, 30; DAM NOV, POP**
See also AAYA 3; CA 29-32R; CANR 13, 37, 66; CLR 2, 15; DLB 52; JRDA; MAICYA; MTCW; SATA 2, 31, 79
Blunden, Edmund (Charles) 1896-1974 **C L C 2, 56**
See also CA 17-18; 45-48; CANR 54; CAP 2; DLB 20, 100, 155; MTCW
Bly, Robert (Elwood) 1926- **CLC 1, 2, 5, 10, 15, 38; DAM POET**
See also CA 5-8R; CANR 41; DLB 5; MTCW
Boas, Franz 1858-1942 .... **TCLC 56**
See also CA 115
Bobette
See Simenon, Georges (Jacques Christian)
Boccaccio, Giovanni 1313-1375 .. **CMLC 13; SSC 10**
Bochco, Steven 1943- .... **CLC 35**
See also AAYA 11; CA 124; 138
Bodenheim, Maxwell 1892-1954 .... **TCLC 44**
See also CA 110; DLB 9, 45
Bodker, Cecil 1927- .... **CLC 21**
See also CA 73-76; CANR 13, 44; CLR 23; MAICYA; SATA 14
Boell, Heinrich (Theodor) 1917-1985 **CLC 2, 3, 6, 9, 11, 15, 27, 32, 72; DA; DAB; DAC; DAM MST, NOV; SSC 23; WLC**
See also CA 21-24R; 116; CANR 24; DLB 69; DLBY 85; MTCW
Boerne, Alfred
See Doeblin, Alfred
Boethius 480(?)-524(?) .... **CMLC 15**
See also DLB 115
Bogan, Louise 1897-1970 . **CLC 4, 39, 46, 93; DAM POET; PC 12**
See also CA 73-76; 25-28R; CANR 33; DLB 45, 169; MTCW
Bogarde, Dirk .... **CLC 19**
See also Van Den Bogarde, Derek Jules Gaspard Ulric Niven
See also DLB 14
Bogosian, Eric 1953- .... **CLC 45**
See also CA 138
Bograd, Larry 1953- .... **CLC 35**
See also CA 93-96; CANR 57; SAAS 21; SATA 33, 89
Boiardo, Matteo Maria 1441-1494 .... **LC 6**
Boileau-Despreaux, Nicolas 1636-1711 **LC 3**
Bojer, Johan 1872-1959 .... **TCLC 64**
Boland, Eavan (Aisling) 1944- .. **CLC 40, 67; DAM POET**
See also CA 143; CANR 61; DLB 40
Boll, Heinrich
See Boell, Heinrich (Theodor)
Bolt, Lee
See Faust, Frederick (Schiller)
Bolt, Robert (Oxton) 1924-1995 ..... **CLC 14; DAM DRAM**
See also CA 17-20R; 147; CANR 35, 67; DLB 13; MTCW

Bombet, Louis-Alexandre-Cesar
See Stendhal

Bomkauf
See Kaufman, Bob (Garnell)

Bonaventura .... NCLC 35
See also DLB 90

Bond, Edward 1934- CLC 4, 6, 13, 23; DAM
DRAM
See also CA 25-28R; CANR 38, 67; DLB 13;
MTCW

Bonham, Frank 1914-1989 .... CLC 12
See also AAYA 1; CA 9-12R; CANR 4, 36;
JRDA; MAICYA; SAAS 3; SATA 1, 49;
SATA-Obit 62

Bonnefoy, Yves 1923- .. CLC 9, 15, 58; DAM
MST, POET
See also CA 85-88; CANR 33; MTCW

Bontemps, Arna(ud Wendell) 1902-1973 C L C
1, 18; BLC; DAM MULT, NOV, POET
See also BW 1; CA 1-4R; 41-44R; CANR 4,
35; CLR 6; DLB 48, 51; JRDA; MAICYA;
MTCW; SATA 2, 44; SATA-Obit 24

Booth, Martin 1944- .... CLC 13
See also CA 93-96; CAAS 2

Booth, Philip 1925- .... CLC 23
See also CA 5-8R; CANR 5; DLBY 82

Booth, Wayne C(layson) 1921- .... CLC 24
See also CA 1-4R; CAAS 5; CANR 3, 43; DLB
67

Borchert, Wolfgang 1921-1947 .... TCLC 5
See also CA 104; DLB 69, 124

Borel, Petrus 1809-1859 .... NCLC 41

Borges, Jorge Luis 1899-1986CLC 1, 2, 3, 4, 6,
8, 9, 10, 13, 19, 44, 48, 83; DA; DAB; DAC;
DAM MST, MULT; HLC; PC 22; SSC 4;
WLC
See also AAYA 19; CA 21-24R; CANR 19, 33;
DLB 113; DLBY 86; HW; MTCW

Borowski, Tadeusz 1922-1951 .... TCLC 9
See also CA 106; 154

Borrow, George (Henry) 1803-1881 NCLC 9
See also DLB 21, 55, 166

Bosman, Herman Charles 1905-1951 . T C L C
49
See also Malan, Herman
See also CA 160

Bosschere, Jean de 1878(?)-1953 ... TCLC 19
See also CA 115

Boswell, James 1740-1795 . LC 4; DA; DAB;
DAC; DAM MST; WLC
See also CDBLB 1660-1789; DLB 104, 142

Bottoms, David 1949- .... CLC 53
See also CA 105; CANR 22; DLB 120; DLBY
83

Boucicault, Dion 1820-1890 .... NCLC 41

Boucolon, Maryse 1937(?)-
See Conde, Maryse
See also CA 110; CANR 30, 53

Bourget, Paul (Charles Joseph) 1852-1935
TCLC 12
See also CA 107; DLB 123

Bourjaily, Vance (Nye) 1922- .... CLC 8, 62
See also CA 1-4R; CAAS 1; CANR 2; DLB 2,
143

Bourne, Randolph S(illiman) 1886-1918
TCLC 16
See also CA 117; 155; DLB 63

Bova, Ben(jamin William) 1932- ..... CLC 45
See also AAYA 16; CA 5-8R; CAAS 18; CANR
11, 56; CLR 3; DLBY 81; INT CANR-11;
MAICYA; MTCW; SATA 6, 68

Bowen, Elizabeth (Dorothea Cole) 1899-1973
CLC 1, 3, 6, 11, 15, 22; DAM NOV; SSC 3,
28
See also CA 17-18; 41-44R; CANR 35; CAP 2;
CDBLB 1945-1960; DLB 15, 162; MTCW

Bowering, George 1935- .... CLC 15, 47
See also CA 21-24R; CAAS 16; CANR 10; DLB
53

Bowering, Marilyn R(uthe) 1949- .... CLC 32
See also CA 101; CANR 49

Bowers, Edgar 1924- .... CLC 9
See also CA 5-8R; CANR 24; DLB 5

Bowie, David .... CLC 17
See also Jones, David Robert

Bowles, Jane (Sydney) 1917-1973 CLC 3, 68
See also CA 19-20; 41-44R; CAP 2

Bowles, Paul (Frederick) 1910-1986CLC 1, 2,
19, 53; SSC 3
See also CA 1-4R; CAAS 1; CANR 1, 19, 50;
DLB 5, 6; MTCW

Box, Edgar
See Vidal, Gore

Boyd, Nancy
See Millay, Edna St. Vincent

Boyd, William 1952- .... CLC 28, 53, 70
See also CA 114; 120; CANR 51

Boyle, Kay 1902-1992CLC 1, 5, 19, 58; SSC 5
See also CA 13-16R; 140; CAAS 1; CANR 29,
61; DLB 4, 9, 48, 86; DLBY 93; MTCW

Boyle, Mark
See Kienzle, William X(avier)

Boyle, Patrick 1905-1982 .... CLC 19
See also CA 127

Boyle, T. C. 1948-
See Boyle, T(homas) Coraghessan

Boyle, T(homas) Coraghessan 1948-CLC 36,
55, 90; DAM POP; SSC 16
See also BEST 90:4; CA 120; CANR 44; DLBY
86

Boz
See Dickens, Charles (John Huffam)

Brackenridge, Hugh Henry 1748-1816N C L C
7
See also DLB 11, 37

Bradbury, Edward P.
See Moorcock, Michael (John)

Bradbury, Malcolm (Stanley) 1932- CLC 32,
61; DAM NOV
See also CA 1-4R; CANR 1, 33; DLB 14;
MTCW

Bradbury, Ray (Douglas) 1920-CLC 1, 3, 10,
15, 42, 98; DA; DAB; DAC; DAM MST,
NOV, POP; SSC 29; WLC
See also AAYA 15; AITN 1, 2; CA 1-4R; CANR
2, 30; CDALB 1968-1988; DLB 2, 8;
MTCW; SATA 11, 64

Bradford, Gamaliel 1863-1932 ...... TCLC 36
See also CA 160; DLB 17

Bradley, David (Henry, Jr.) 1950- .. CLC 23;
BLC; DAM MULT
See also BW 1; CA 104; CANR 26; DLB 33

Bradley, John Ed(mund, Jr.) 1958- ..CLC 55
See also CA 139

Bradley, Marion Zimmer 1930-CLC 30; DAM
POP
See also AAYA 9; CA 57-60; CAAS 10; CANR
7, 31, 51; DLB 8; MTCW; SATA 90

Bradstreet, Anne 1612(?)-1672LC 4, 30; DA;
DAC; DAM MST, POET; PC 10
See also CDALB 1640-1865; DLB 24

Brady, Joan 1939- .... CLC 86
See also CA 141

Bragg, Melvyn 1939- .... CLC 10
See also BEST 89:3; CA 57-60; CANR 10, 48;
DLB 14

Braine, John (Gerard) 1922-1986CLC 1, 3, 41
See also CA 1-4R; 120; CANR 1, 33; CDBLB
1945-1960; DLB 15; DLBY 86; MTCW

Bramah, Ernest 1868-1942 .... TCLC 72
See also CA 156; DLB 70

Brammer, William 1930(?)-1978 ...... CLC 31
See also CA 77-80

Brancati, Vitaliano 1907-1954 .... TCLC 12
See also CA 109

Brancato, Robin F(idler) 1936- .... CLC 35
See also AAYA 9; CA 69-72; CANR 11, 45;
CLR 32; JRDA; SAAS 9; SATA 97

Brand, Max
See Faust, Frederick (Schiller)

Brand, Millen 1906-1980 .... CLC 7
See also CA 21-24R; 97-100

Branden, Barbara .... CLC 44
See also CA 148

Brandes, Georg (Morris Cohen) 1842-1927
TCLC 10
See also CA 105

Brandys, Kazimierz 1916- .... CLC 62

Branley, Franklyn M(ansfield) 1915-CLC 21
See also CA 33-36R; CANR 14, 39; CLR 13;
MAICYA; SAAS 16; SATA 4, 68

Brathwaite, Edward Kamau 1930- CLC 11;
DAM POET
See also BW 2; CA 25-28R; CANR 11, 26, 47;
DLB 125

Brautigan, Richard (Gary) 1935-1984CLC 1,
3, 5, 9, 12, 34, 42; DAM NOV
See also CA 53-56; 113; CANR 34; DLB 2, 5;
DLBY 80, 84; MTCW; SATA 56

Brave Bird, Mary 1953-
See Crow Dog, Mary (Ellen)
See also NNAL

Braverman, Kate 1950- .... CLC 67
See also CA 89-92

Brecht, (Eugen) Bertolt (Friedrich) 1898-1956
TCLC 1, 6, 13, 35; DA; DAB; DAC; DAM
DRAM, MST; DC 3; WLC
See also CA 104; 133; CANR 62; DLB 56, 124;
MTCW

Brecht, Eugen Berthold Friedrich
See Brecht, (Eugen) Bertolt (Friedrich)

Bremer, Fredrika 1801-1865 .... NCLC 11

Brennan, Christopher John 1870-1932T C L C
17
See also CA 117

Brennan, Maeve 1917- ....CLC 5
See also CA 81-84

Brent, Linda
See Jacobs, Harriet

Brentano, Clemens (Maria) 1778-1842N C L C
1
See also DLB 90

Brent of Bin Bin
See Franklin, (Stella Maria Sarah) Miles

Brenton, Howard 1942- .... CLC 31
See also CA 69-72; CANR 33, 67; DLB 13;
MTCW

Breslin, James 1930-1996
See Breslin, Jimmy
See also CA 73-76; CANR 31; DAM NOV;
MTCW

Breslin, Jimmy .... CLC 4, 43
See also Breslin, James
See also AITN 1; DLB 185

Bresson, Robert 1901- .... CLC 16
See also CA 110; CANR 49

Breton, Andre 1896-1966CLC 2, 9, 15, 54; PC
15
See also CA 19-20; 25-28R; CANR 40, 60; CAP

See also BEST 89:1; CA 81-84; CANR 21; DLB 6, 173; MTCW

de Lisser, H. G.
See De Lisser, H(erbert) G(eorge)
See also DLB 117

De Lisser, H(erbert) G(eorge) 1878-1944 **TCLC 12**
See also de Lisser, H. G.
See also BW 2; CA 109; 152

Deloney, Thomas 1560-1600 .... **LC 41**

Deloria, Vine (Victor), Jr. 1933- ..... **CLC 21; DAM MULT**
See also CA 53-56; CANR 5, 20, 48; DLB 175; MTCW; NNAL; SATA 21

Del Vecchio, John M(ichael) 1947- .. **CLC 29**
See also CA 110; DLBD 9

de Man, Paul (Adolph Michel) 1919-1983 **CLC 55**
See also CA 128; 111; CANR 61; DLB 67; MTCW

De Marinis, Rick 1934- .... **CLC 54**
See also CA 57-60; CAAS 24; CANR 9, 25, 50

Dembry, R. Emmet
See Murfree, Mary Noailles

Demby, William 1922- . **CLC 53; BLC; DAM MULT**
See also BW 1; CA 81-84; DLB 33

de Menton, Francisco
See Chin, Frank (Chew, Jr.)

Demijohn, Thom
See Disch, Thomas M(ichael)

de Montherlant, Henry (Milon)
See Montherlant, Henry (Milon) de

Demosthenes 384B.C.-322B.C. ...... **CMLC 13**
See also DLB 176

de Natale, Francine
See Malzberg, Barry N(athaniel)

Denby, Edwin (Orr) 1903-1983 .... **CLC 48**
See also CA 138; 110

Denis, Julio
See Cortazar, Julio

Denmark, Harrison
See Zelazny, Roger (Joseph)

Dennis, John 1658-1734 .... **LC 11**
See also DLB 101

Dennis, Nigel (Forbes) 1912-1989 .... **CLC 8**
See also CA 25-28R; 129; DLB 13, 15; MTCW

Dent, Lester 1904(?)-1959 .... **TCLC 72**
See also CA 112; 161

De Palma, Brian (Russell) 1940- ...... **CLC 20**
See also CA 109

De Quincey, Thomas 1785-1859 .... **NCLC 4**
See also CDBLB 1789-1832; DLB 110; 144

Deren, Eleanora 1908(?)-1961
See Deren, Maya
See also CA 111

Deren, Maya 1917-1961 .... **CLC 16, 102**
See also Deren, Eleanora

Derleth, August (William) 1909-1971**CLC 31**
See also CA 1-4R; 29-32R; CANR 4; DLB 9; SATA 5

Der Nister 1884-1950 .... **TCLC 56**

de Routisie, Albert
See Aragon, Louis

Derrida, Jacques 1930- .... **CLC 24, 87**
See also CA 124; 127

Derry Down Derry
See Lear, Edward

Dersonnes, Jacques
See Simenon, Georges (Jacques Christian)

Desai, Anita 1937-**CLC 19, 37, 97; DAB; DAM NOV**
See also CA 81-84; CANR 33, 53; MTCW;

SATA 63

de Saint-Luc, Jean
See Glassco, John

de Saint Roman, Arnaud
See Aragon, Louis

Descartes, Rene 1596-1650 .... **LC 20, 35**

De Sica, Vittorio 1901(?)-1974 .... **CLC 20**
See also CA 117

Desnos, Robert 1900-1945 .... **TCLC 22**
See also CA 121; 151

Destouches, Louis-Ferdinand 1894-1961**CLC 9, 15**
See also Celine, Louis-Ferdinand
See also CA 85-88; CANR 28; MTCW

de Tolignac, Gaston
See Griffith, D(avid Lewelyn) W(ark)

Deutsch, Babette 1895-1982 ....**CLC 18**
See also CA 1-4R; 108; CANR 4; DLB 45; SATA 1; SATA-Obit 33

Devenant, William 1606-1649 .... **LC 13**

Devkota, Laxmiprasad 1909-1959 . **TCLC 23**
See also CA 123

De Voto, Bernard (Augustine) 1897-1955 **TCLC 29**
See also CA 113; 160; DLB 9

De Vries, Peter 1910-1993 **CLC 1, 2, 3, 7, 10, 28, 46; DAM NOV**
See also CA 17-20R; 142; CANR 41; DLB 6; DLBY 82; MTCW

Dexter, John
See Bradley, Marion Zimmer

Dexter, Martin
See Faust, Frederick (Schiller)

Dexter, Pete 1943- ... **CLC 34, 55; DAM POP**
See also BEST 89:2; CA 127; 131; INT 131; MTCW

Diamano, Silmang
See Senghor, Leopold Sedar

Diamond, Neil 1941- .... **CLC 30**
See also CA 108

Diaz del Castillo, Bernal 1496-1584 ... **LC 31**

di Bassetto, Corno
See Shaw, George Bernard

Dick, Philip K(indred) 1928-1982**CLC 10, 30, 72; DAM NOV, POP**
See also AAYA 24; CA 49-52; 106; CANR 2, 16; DLB 8; MTCW

Dickens, Charles (John Huffam) 1812-1870 **NCLC 3, 8, 18, 26, 37, 50; DA; DAB; DAC; DAM MST, NOV; SSC 17; WLC**
See also AAYA 23; CDBLB 1832-1890; DLB 21, 55, 70, 159, 166; JRDA; MAICYA; SATA 15

Dickey, James (Lafayette) 1923-1997 **CLC 1, 2, 4, 7, 10, 15, 47, 109; DAM NOV, POET, POP**
See also AITN 1, 2; CA 9-12R; 156; CABS 2; CANR 10, 48, 61; CDALB 1968-1988; DLB 5, 193; DLBD 7; DLBY 82, 93, 96, 97; INT CANR-10; MTCW

Dickey, William 1928-1994 .... **CLC 3, 28**
See also CA 9-12R; 145; CANR 24; DLB 5

Dickinson, Charles 1951- .... **CLC 49**
See also CA 128

Dickinson, Emily (Elizabeth) 1830-1886 **NCLC 21; DA; DAB; DAC; DAM MST, POET; PC 1; WLC**
See also AAYA 22; CDALB 1865-1917; DLB 1; SATA 29

Dickinson, Peter (Malcolm) 1927-**CLC 12, 35**
See also AAYA 9; CA 41-44R; CANR 31, 58; CLR 29; DLB 87, 161; JRDA; MAICYA; SATA 5, 62, 95

Dickson, Carr
See Carr, John Dickson

Dickson, Carter
See Carr, John Dickson

Diderot, Denis 1713-1784 .... **LC 26**

Didion, Joan 1934-**CLC 1, 3, 8, 14, 32; DAM NOV**
See also AITN 1; CA 5-8R; CANR 14, 52; CDALB 1968-1988; DLB 2, 173, 185; DLBY 81, 86; MTCW

Dietrich, Robert
See Hunt, E(verette) Howard, (Jr.)

Dillard, Annie 1945- . **CLC 9, 60; DAM NOV**
See also AAYA 6; CA 49-52; CANR 3, 43, 62; DLBY 80; MTCW; SATA 10

Dillard, R(ichard) H(enry) W(ilde) 1937- **CLC 5**
See also CA 21-24R; CAAS 7; CANR 10; DLB 5

Dillon, Eilis 1920-1994 .... **CLC 17**
See also CA 9-12R; 147; CAAS 3; CANR 4, 38; CLR 26; MAICYA; SATA 2, 74; SATA-Obit 83

Dimont, Penelope
See Mortimer, Penelope (Ruth)

Dinesen, Isak .... **CLC 10, 29, 95; SSC 7**
See also Blixen, Karen (Christentze Dinesen)

Ding Ling .... **CLC 68**
See also Chiang Pin-chin

Disch, Thomas M(ichael) 1940- ... **CLC 7, 36**
See also AAYA 17; CA 21-24R; CAAS 4; CANR 17, 36, 54; CLR 18; DLB 8; MAICYA; MTCW; SAAS 15; SATA 92

Disch, Tom
See Disch, Thomas M(ichael)

d'Isly, Georges
See Simenon, Georges (Jacques Christian)

Disraeli, Benjamin 1804-1881 ....**NCLC 2, 39**
See also DLB 21, 55

Ditcum, Steve
See Crumb, R(obert)

Dixon, Paige
See Corcoran, Barbara

Dixon, Stephen 1936- .... **CLC 52; SSC 16**
See also CA 89-92; CANR 17, 40, 54; DLB 130

Doak, Annie
See Dillard, Annie

Dobell, Sydney Thompson 1824-1874 **NCLC 43**
See also DLB 32

Doblin, Alfred .... **TCLC 13**
See also Doeblin, Alfred

Dobrolyubov, Nikolai Alexandrovich 1836-1861 **NCLC 5**

Dobson, Austin 1840-1921 .... **TCLC 79**
See also DLB 35; 144

Dobyns, Stephen 1941-....................... **CLC 37**
See also CA 45-48; CANR 2, 18

Doctorow, E(dgar) L(aurence) 1931- **CLC 6, 11, 15, 18, 37, 44, 65; DAM NOV, POP**
See also AAYA 22; AITN 2; BEST 89:3; CA 45-48; CANR 2, 33, 51; CDALB 1968-1988; DLB 2, 28, 173; DLBY 80; MTCW

Dodgson, Charles Lutwidge 1832-1898
See Carroll, Lewis
See also CLR 2; DA; DAB; DAC; DAM MST, NOV, POET; MAICYA; YABC 2

Dodson, Owen (Vincent) 1914-1983 **CLC 79; BLC; DAM MULT**
See also BW 1; CA 65-68; 110; CANR 24; DLB 76

Doeblin, Alfred 1878-1957 .... **TCLC 13**
See also Doblin, Alfred

See also CA 110; 141; DLB 66

Doerr, Harriet 1910- .... **CLC 34**
See also CA 117; 122; CANR 47; INT 122

Domecq, H(onorio) Bustos
See Bioy Casares, Adolfo; Borges, Jorge Luis

Domini, Rey
See Lorde, Audre (Geraldine)

Dominique
See Proust, (Valentin-Louis-George-Eugene-) Marcel

Don, A
See Stephen, SirLeslie

Donaldson, Stephen R. 1947- CLC 46; DAM POP
See also CA 89-92; CANR 13, 55; INT CANR-13

Donleavy, J(ames) P(atrick) 1926-CLC 1, 4, 6, 10, 45
See also AITN 2; CA 9-12R; CANR 24, 49, 62; DLB 6, 173; INT CANR-24; MTCW

Donne, John 1572-1631LC 10, 24; DA; DAB; DAC; DAM MST, POET; PC 1
See also CDBLB Before 1660; DLB 121, 151

Donnell, David 1939(?)- .... **CLC 34**

Donoghue, P. S.
See Hunt, E(verette) Howard, (Jr.)

Donoso (Yanez), Jose 1924-1996CLC 4, 8, 11, 32, 99; DAM MULT; HLC
See also CA 81-84; 155; CANR 32; DLB 113; HW; MTCW

Donovan, John 1928-1992 .... **CLC 35**
See also AAYA 20; CA 97-100; 137; CLR 3; MAICYA; SATA 72; SATA-Brief 29

Don Roberto
See Cunninghame Graham, R(obert) B(ontine)

Doolittle, Hilda 1886-1961CLC 3, 8, 14, 31, 34, 73; DA; DAC; DAM MST, POET; PC 5; WLC
See also H. D.
See also CA 97-100; CANR 35; DLB 4, 45; MTCW

Dorfman, Ariel 1942- ...... **CLC 48, 77; DAM MULT; HLC**
See also CA 124; 130; CANR 67; HW; INT 130

Dorn, Edward (Merton) 1929- ... **CLC 10, 18**
See also CA 93-96; CANR 42; DLB 5; INT 93-96

Dorris, Michael (Anthony) 1945-1997 ..C L C 109; DAM MULT, NOV
See also AAYA 20; BEST 90:1; CA 102; 157; CANR 19, 46; DLB 175; NNAL; SATA 75; SATA-Obit 94

Dorris, Michael A.
See Dorris, Michael (Anthony)

Dorsan, Luc
See Simenon, Georges (Jacques Christian)

Dorsange, Jean
See Simenon, Georges (Jacques Christian)

Dos Passos, John (Roderigo) 1896-1970 C L C 1, 4, 8, 11, 15, 25, 34, 82; DA; DAB; DAC; DAM MST, NOV; WLC
See also CA 1-4R; 29-32R; CANR 3; CDALB 1929-1941; DLB 4, 9; DLBD 1, 15; DLBY 96; MTCW

Dossage, Jean
See Simenon, Georges (Jacques Christian)

Dostoevsky, Fedor Mikhailovich 1821-1881 NCLC 2, 7, 21, 33, 43; DA; DAB; DAC; DAM MST, NOV; SSC 2; WLC

Doughty, Charles M(ontagu) 1843-1926 TCLC 27
See also CA 115; DLB 19, 57, 174

Douglas, Ellen .... **CLC 73**

See also Haxton, Josephine Ayres; Williamson, Ellen Douglas

Douglas, Gavin 1475(?)-1522 .... **LC 20**

Douglas, George
See Brown, George Douglas

Douglas, Keith (Castellain) 1920-1944T C L C 40
See also CA 160; DLB 27

Douglas, Leonard
See Bradbury, Ray (Douglas)

Douglas, Michael
See Crichton, (John) Michael

Douglas, Norman 1868-1952 .... **TCLC 68**
See also DLB 195

Douglas, William
See Brown, George Douglas

Douglass, Frederick 1817(?)-1895NCLC 7, 55; BLC; DA; DAC; DAM MST, MULT; WLC
See also CDALB 1640-1865; DLB 1, 43, 50, 79; SATA 29

Dourado, (Waldomiro Freitas) Autran 1926- CLC 23, 60
See also CA 25-28R; CANR 34

Dourado, Waldomiro Autran
See Dourado, (Waldomiro Freitas) Autran

Dove, Rita (Frances) 1952-CLC 50, 81; DAM MULT, POET; PC 6
See also BW 2; CA 109; CAAS 19; CANR 27, 42, 68; DLB 120

Dowell, Coleman 1925-1985 .... **CLC 60**
See also CA 25-28R; 117; CANR 10; DLB 130

Dowson, Ernest (Christopher) 1867-1900 TCLC 4
See also CA 105; 150; DLB 19, 135

Doyle, A. Conan
See Doyle, Arthur Conan

Doyle, Arthur Conan 1859-1930TCLC 7; DA; DAB; DAC; DAM MST, NOV; SSC 12; WLC
See also AAYA 14; CA 104; 122; CDBLB 1890-1914; DLB 18, 70, 156, 178; MTCW; SATA 24

Doyle, Conan
See Doyle, Arthur Conan

Doyle, John
See Graves, Robert (von Ranke)

Doyle, Roddy 1958(?)- .... **CLC 81**
See also AAYA 14; CA 143; DLB 194

Doyle, Sir A. Conan
See Doyle, Arthur Conan

Doyle, Sir Arthur Conan
See Doyle, Arthur Conan

Dr. A
See Asimov, Isaac; Silverstein, Alvin

Drabble, Margaret 1939-CLC 2, 3, 5, 8, 10, 22, 53; DAB; DAC; DAM MST, NOV, POP
See also CA 13-16R; CANR 18, 35, 63; CDBLB 1960 to Present; DLB 14, 155; MTCW; SATA 48

Drapier, M. B.
See Swift, Jonathan

Drayham, James
See Mencken, H(enry) L(ouis)

Drayton, Michael 1563-1631 .... **LC 8**

Dreadstone, Carl
See Campbell, (John) Ramsey

Dreiser, Theodore (Herman Albert) 1871-1945 TCLC 10, 18, 35; DA; DAC; DAM MST, NOV; SSC 30; WLC
See also CA 106; 132; CDALB 1865-1917; DLB 9, 12, 102, 137; DLBD 1; MTCW

Drexler, Rosalyn 1926- .... **CLC 2, 6**
See also CA 81-84; CANR 68

Dreyer, Carl Theodor 1889-1968 ..... **CLC 16**
See also CA 116

Drieu la Rochelle, Pierre(-Eugene) 1893-1945 TCLC 21
See also CA 117; DLB 72

Drinkwater, John 1882-1937 .... **TCLC 57**
See also CA 109; 149; DLB 10, 19, 149

Drop Shot
See Cable, George Washington

Droste-Hulshoff, Annette Freiin von 1797-1848 NCLC 3
See also DLB 133

Drummond, Walter
See Silverberg, Robert

Drummond, William Henry 1854-1907T C L C 25
See also CA 160; DLB 92

Drummond de Andrade, Carlos 1902-1987 CLC 18
See also Andrade, Carlos Drummond de
See also CA 132; 123

Drury, Allen (Stuart) 1918- .... **CLC 37**
See also CA 57-60; CANR 18, 52; INT CANR-18

Dryden, John 1631-1700LC 3, 21; DA; DAB; DAC; DAM DRAM, MST, POET; DC 3; WLC
See also CDBLB 1660-1789; DLB 80, 101, 131

Duberman, Martin (Bauml) 1930- ...... **CLC 8**
See also CA 1-4R; CANR 2, 63

Dubie, Norman (Evans) 1945- .... **CLC 36**
See also CA 69-72; CANR 12; DLB 120

Du Bois, W(illiam) E(dward) B(urghardt) 1868-1963CLC 1, 2, 13, 64, 96; BLC; DA; DAC; DAM MST, MULT, NOV; WLC
See also BW 1; CA 85-88; CANR 34; CDALB 1865-1917; DLB 47, 50, 91; MTCW; SATA 42

Dubus, Andre 1936- CLC 13, 36, 97; SSC 15
See also CA 21-24R; CANR 17; DLB 130; INT CANR-17

Duca Minimo
See D'Annunzio, Gabriele

Ducharme, Rejean 1941- .... **CLC 74**
See also CA 165; DLB 60

Duclos, Charles Pinot 1704-1772 .... **LC 1**

Dudek, Louis 1918- .... **CLC 11, 19**
See also CA 45-48; CAAS 14; CANR 1; DLB 88

Duerrenmatt, Friedrich 1921-1990 CLC 1, 4, 8, 11, 15, 43, 102; DAM DRAM
See also CA 17-20R; CANR 33; DLB 69, 124; MTCW

Duffy, Bruce (?)- .... **CLC 50**

Duffy, Maureen 1933- .... **CLC 37**
See also CA 25-28R; CANR 33, 68; DLB 14; MTCW

Dugan, Alan 1923- .... **CLC 2, 6**
See also CA 81-84; DLB 5

du Gard, Roger Martin
See Martin du Gard, Roger

Duhamel, Georges 1884-1966 .... **CLC 8**
See also CA 81-84; 25-28R; CANR 35; DLB 65; MTCW

Dujardin, Edouard (Emile Louis) 1861-1949 TCLC 13
See also CA 109; DLB 123

Dulles, John Foster 1888-1959 .... **TCLC 72**
See also CA 115; 149

Dumas, Alexandre (Davy de la Pailleterie) 1802-1870 ...NCLC 11; DA; DAB; DAC; DAM MST, NOV; WLC
See also DLB 119, 192; SATA 18

Dumas, Alexandre 1824-1895 **NCLC 9; DC 1**
See also AAYA 22; DLB 192
Dumas, Claudine
See Malzberg, Barry N(athaniel)
Dumas, Henry L. 1934-1968 .... **CLC 6, 62**
See also BW 1; CA 85-88; DLB 41
du Maurier, Daphne 1907-1989 **CLC 6, 11, 59;
DAB; DAC; DAM MST, POP; SSC 18**
See also CA 5-8R; 128; CANR 6, 55; DLB 191;
MTCW; SATA 27; SATA-Obit 60
Dunbar, Paul Laurence 1872-1906 . **TCLC 2,
12; BLC; DA; DAC; DAM MST, MULT,
POET; PC 5; SSC 8; WLC**
See also BW 1; CA 104; 124; CDALB 1865-
1917; DLB 50, 54, 78; SATA 34
Dunbar, William 1460(?)-1530(?) .... **LC 20**
See also DLB 132, 146
Duncan, Dora Angela
See Duncan, Isadora
Duncan, Isadora 1877(?)-1927 .... **TCLC 68**
See also CA 118; 149
Duncan, Lois 1934- .... **CLC 26**
See also AAYA 4; CA 1-4R; CANR 2, 23, 36;
CLR 29; JRDA; MAICYA; SAAS 2; SATA
1, 36, 75
Duncan, Robert (Edward) 1919-1988 **CLC 1,
2, 4, 7, 15, 41, 55; DAM POET; PC 2**
See also CA 9-12R; 124; CANR 28, 62; DLB
5, 16, 193; MTCW
Duncan, Sara Jeannette 1861-1922 **TCLC 60**
See also CA 157; DLB 92
Dunlap, William 1766-1839 .... **NCLC 2**
See also DLB 30, 37, 59
Dunn, Douglas (Eaglesham) 1942- **CLC 6, 40**
See also CA 45-48; CANR 2, 33; DLB 40;
MTCW
Dunn, Katherine (Karen) 1945- .... **CLC 71**
See also CA 33-36R
Dunn, Stephen 1939- .... **CLC 36**
See also CA 33-36R; CANR 12, 48, 53; DLB
105
Dunne, Finley Peter 1867-1936 ...... **TCLC 28**
See also CA 108; DLB 11, 23
Dunne, John Gregory 1932- .... **CLC 28**
See also CA 25-28R; CANR 14, 50; DLBY 80
Dunsany, Edward John Moreton Drax Plunkett
1878-1957
See Dunsany, Lord
See also CA 104; 148; DLB 10
Dunsany, Lord .... **TCLC 2, 59**
See also Dunsany, Edward John Moreton Drax
Plunkett
See also DLB 77, 153, 156
du Perry, Jean
See Simenon, Georges (Jacques Christian)
Durang, Christopher (Ferdinand) 1949-**C L C
27, 38**
See also CA 105; CANR 50
Duras, Marguerite 1914-1996 **CLC 3, 6, 11, 20,
34, 40, 68, 100**
See also CA 25-28R; 151; CANR 50; DLB 83;
MTCW
Durban, (Rosa) Pam 1947- .... **CLC 39**
See also CA 123
Durcan, Paul 1944-**CLC 43, 70; DAM POET**
See also CA 134
Durkheim, Emile 1858-1917 .... **TCLC 55**
Durrell, Lawrence (George) 1912-1990 **C L C
1, 4, 6, 8, 13, 27, 41; DAM NOV**
See also CA 9-12R; 132; CANR 40; CDBLB
1945-1960; DLB 15, 27; DLBY 90; MTCW
Durrenmatt, Friedrich
See Duerrenmatt, Friedrich

Dutt, Toru 1856-1877 .... **NCLC 29**
Dwight, Timothy 1752-1817 .... **NCLC 13**
See also DLB 37
Dworkin, Andrea 1946- .... **CLC 43**
See also CA 77-80; CAAS 21; CANR 16, 39;
INT CANR-16; MTCW
Dwyer, Deanna
See Koontz, Dean R(ay)
Dwyer, K. R.
See Koontz, Dean R(ay)
Dye, Richard
See De Voto, Bernard (Augustine)
Dylan, Bob 1941- .... **CLC 3, 4, 6, 12, 77**
See also CA 41-44R; DLB 16
Eagleton, Terence (Francis) 1943-
See Eagleton, Terry
See also CA 57-60; CANR 7, 23, 68; MTCW
Eagleton, Terry .... **CLC 63**
See also Eagleton, Terence (Francis)
Early, Jack
See Scoppettone, Sandra
East, Michael
See West, Morris L(anglo)
Eastaway, Edward
See Thomas, (Philip) Edward
Eastlake, William (Derry) 1917-1997 . **CLC 8**
See also CA 5-8R; 158; CAAS 1; CANR 5, 63;
DLB 6; INT CANR-5
Eastman, Charles A(lexander) 1858-1939
TCLC 55; DAM MULT
See also DLB 175; NNAL; YABC 1
Eberhart, Richard (Ghormley) 1904-**CLC 3,
11, 19, 56; DAM POET**
See also CA 1-4R; CANR 2; CDALB 1941-
1968; DLB 48; MTCW
Eberstadt, Fernanda 1960-................. **CLC 39**
See also CA 136
Echegaray (y Eizaguirre), Jose (Maria Waldo)
1832-1916 .... **TCLC 4**
See also CA 104; CANR 32; HW; MTCW
Echeverria, (Jose) Esteban (Antonino) 1805-
1851 .... **NCLC 18**
Echo
See Proust, (Valentin-Louis-George-Eugene-)
Marcel
Eckert, Allan W. 1931-...................... **CLC 17**
See also AAYA 18; CA 13-16R; CANR 14, 45;
INT CANR-14; SAAS 21; SATA 29, 91;
SATA-Brief 27
Eckhart, Meister 1260(?)-1328(?) ... **CMLC 9**
See also DLB 115
Eckmar, F. R.
See de Hartog, Jan
Eco, Umberto 1932-**CLC 28, 60; DAM NOV,
POP**
See also BEST 90:1; CA 77-80; CANR 12, 33,
55; DLB 196; MTCW
Eddison, E(ric) R(ucker) 1882-1945**TCLC 15**
See also CA 109; 156
Eddy, Mary (Morse) Baker 1821-1910**T C L C
71**
See also CA 113
Edel, (Joseph) Leon 1907-1997 .. **CLC 29, 34**
See also CA 1-4R; 161; CANR 1, 22; DLB 103;
INT CANR-22
Eden, Emily 1797-1869 .... **NCLC 10**
Edgar, David 1948-... **CLC 42; DAM DRAM**
See also CA 57-60; CANR 12, 61; DLB 13;
MTCW
Edgerton, Clyde (Carlyle) 1944- ...... **CLC 39**
See also AAYA 17; CA 118; 134; CANR 64;
INT 134
Edgeworth, Maria 1768-1849 ....**NCLC 1, 51**

See also DLB 116, 159, 163; SATA 21
Edmonds, Paul
See Kuttner, Henry
Edmonds, Walter D(umaux) 1903- ...**CLC 35**
See also CA 5-8R; CANR 2; DLB 9; MAICYA;
SAAS 4; SATA 1, 27
Edmondson, Wallace
See Ellison, Harlan (Jay)
Edson, Russell .... **CLC 13**
See also CA 33-36R
Edwards, Bronwen Elizabeth
See Rose, Wendy
Edwards, G(erald) B(asil) 1899-1976**CLC 25**
See also CA 110
Edwards, Gus 1939- .... **CLC 43**
See also CA 108; INT 108
Edwards, Jonathan 1703-1758 ..... **LC 7; DA;
DAC; DAM MST**
See also DLB 24
Efron, Marina Ivanovna Tsvetaeva
See Tsvetaeva (Efron), Marina (Ivanovna)
Ehle, John (Marsden, Jr.) 1925- ....**CLC 27**
See also CA 9-12R
Ehrenbourg, Ilya (Grigoryevich)
See Ehrenburg, Ilya (Grigoryevich)
Ehrenburg, Ilya (Grigoryevich) 1891-1967
CLC 18, 34, 62
See also CA 102; 25-28R
Ehrenburg, Ilyo (Grigoryevich)
See Ehrenburg, Ilya (Grigoryevich)
Ehrenreich, Barbara 1941- .... **CLC 110**
See also BEST 90:4; CA 73-76; CANR 16, 37,
62; MTCW
Eich, Guenter 1907-1972 .... **CLC 15**
See also CA 111; 93-96; DLB 69, 124
Eichendorff, Joseph Freiherr von 1788-1857
NCLC 8
See also DLB 90
Eigner, Larry .... **CLC 9**
See also Eigner, Laurence (Joel)
See also CAAS 23; DLB 5
Eigner, Laurence (Joel) 1927-1996
See Eigner, Larry
See also CA 9-12R; 151; CANR 6; DLB 193
Einstein, Albert 1879-1955 .... **TCLC 65**
See also CA 121; 133; MTCW
Eiseley, Loren Corey 1907-1977 .... **CLC 7**
See also AAYA 5; CA 1-4R; 73-76; CANR 6
Eisenstadt, Jill 1963- .... **CLC 50**
See also CA 140
Eisenstein, Sergei (Mikhailovich) 1898-1948
TCLC 57
See also CA 114; 149
Eisner, Simon
See Kornbluth, C(yril) M.
Ekeloef, (Bengt) Gunnar 1907-1968 **CLC 27;
DAM POET**
See also CA 123; 25-28R
Ekelof, (Bengt) Gunnar
See Ekeloef, (Bengt) Gunnar
Ekelund, Vilhelm 1880-1949 .... **TCLC 75**
Ekwensi, C. O. D.
See Ekwensi, Cyprian (Odiatu Duaka)
Ekwensi, Cyprian (Odiatu Duaka) 1921-**CLC
4; BLC; DAM MULT**
See also BW 2; CA 29-32R; CANR 18, 42; DLB
117; MTCW; SATA 66
Elaine .... **TCLC 18**
See also Leverson, Ada
El Crummo
See Crumb, R(obert)
Elder, Lonne III 1931-1996 .... **DC 8**
See also BLC; BW 1; CA 81-84; 152; CANR

25; DAM MULT; DLB 7, 38, 44
Elia
See Lamb, Charles
Eliade, Mircea 1907-1986 .... **CLC 19**
See also CA 65-68; 119; CANR 30, 62; MTCW
Eliot, A. D.
See Jewett, (Theodora) Sarah Orne
Eliot, Alice
See Jewett, (Theodora) Sarah Orne
Eliot, Dan
See Silverberg, Robert
Eliot, George 1819-1880 **NCLC 4, 13, 23, 41,
    49; DA; DAB; DAC; DAM MST, NOV; PC
    20; WLC**
See also CDBLB 1832-1890; DLB 21, 35, 55
Eliot, John 1604-1690 .... **LC 5**
See also DLB 24
Eliot, T(homas) S(tearns) 1888-1965 **CLC 1, 2,
    3, 6, 9, 10, 13, 15, 24, 34, 41, 55, 57; DA;
    DAB; DAC; DAM DRAM, MST, POET;
    PC 5; WLC 2**
See also CA 5-8R; 25-28R; CANR 41; CDALB
    1929-1941; DLB 7, 10, 45, 63; DLBY 88;
    MTCW
Elizabeth 1866-1941 .... **TCLC 41**
Elkin, Stanley L(awrence) 1930-1995 **CLC 4,
    6, 9, 14, 27, 51, 91; DAM NOV, POP; SSC
    12**
See also CA 9-12R; 148; CANR 8, 46; DLB 2,
    28; DLBY 80; INT CANR-8; MTCW
Elledge, Scott .... **CLC 34**
Elliot, Don
See Silverberg, Robert
Elliott, Don
See Silverberg, Robert
Elliott, George P(aul) 1918-1980 .... **CLC 2**
See also CA 1-4R; 97-100; CANR 2
Elliott, Janice 1931- .... **CLC 47**
See also CA 13-16R; CANR 8, 29; DLB 14
Elliott, Sumner Locke 1917-1991 .... **CLC 38**
See also CA 5-8R; 134; CANR 2, 21
Elliott, William
See Bradbury, Ray (Douglas)
Ellis, A. E. .... **CLC 7**
Ellis, Alice Thomas .... **CLC 40**
See also Haycraft, Anna
See also DLB 194
Ellis, Bret Easton 1964- .. **CLC 39, 71; DAM
    POP**
See also AAYA 2; CA 118; 123; CANR 51; INT
    123
Ellis, (Henry) Havelock 1859-1939 **TCLC 14**
See also CA 109; DLB 190
Ellis, Landon
See Ellison, Harlan (Jay)
Ellis, Trey 1962- .... **CLC 55**
See also CA 146
Ellison, Harlan (Jay) 1934- ... **CLC 1, 13, 42;
    DAM POP; SSC 14**
See also CA 5-8R; CANR 5, 46; DLB 8; INT
    CANR-5; MTCW
Ellison, Ralph (Waldo) 1914-1994 **CLC 1, 3,
    11, 54, 86; BLC; DA; DAB; DAC; DAM
    MST, MULT, NOV; SSC 26; WLC**
See also AAYA 19; BW 1; CA 9-12R; 145;
    CANR 24, 53; CDALB 1941-1968; DLB 2,
    76; DLBY 94; MTCW
Ellmann, Lucy (Elizabeth) 1956- ..... **CLC 61**
See also CA 128
Ellmann, Richard (David) 1918-1987 **CLC 50**
See also BEST 89:2; CA 1-4R; 122; CANR 2,
    28, 61; DLB 103; DLBY 87; MTCW
Elman, Richard (Martin) 1934-1997 **CLC 19**

See also CA 17-20R; 163; CAAS 3; CANR 47
Elron
See Hubbard, L(afayette) Ron(ald)
Eluard, Paul .... **TCLC 7, 41**
See also Grindel, Eugene
Elyot, Sir Thomas 1490(?)-1546 .... **LC 11**
Elytis, Odysseus 1911-1996 **CLC 15, 49, 100;
    DAM POET; PC 21**
See also CA 102; 151; MTCW
Emecheta, (Florence Onye) Buchi 1944- **C L C
    14, 48; BLC; DAM MULT**
See also BW 2; CA 81-84; CANR 27; DLB 117;
    MTCW; SATA 66
Emerson, Mary Moody 1774-1863 **NCLC 66**
Emerson, Ralph Waldo 1803-1882 .**NCLC 1,
    38; DA; DAB; DAC; DAM MST, POET;
    PC 18; WLC**
See also CDALB 1640-1865; DLB 1, 59, 73
Eminescu, Mihail 1850-1889 .... **NCLC 33**
Empson, William 1906-1984 **CLC 3, 8, 19, 33,
    34**
See also CA 17-20R; 112; CANR 31, 61; DLB
    20; MTCW
Enchi Fumiko (Ueda) 1905-1986 ...... **CLC 31**
See also CA 129; 121
Ende, Michael (Andreas Helmuth) 1929-1995
    CLC 31
See also CA 118; 124; 149; CANR 36; CLR
    14; DLB 75; MAICYA; SATA 61; SATA-
    Brief 42; SATA-Obit 86
Endo, Shusaku 1923-1996 **CLC 7, 14, 19, 54,
    99; DAM NOV**
See also CA 29-32R; 153; CANR 21, 54; DLB
    182; MTCW
Engel, Marian 1933-1985 .... **CLC 36**
See also CA 25-28R; CANR 12; DLB 53; INT
    CANR-12
Engelhardt, Frederick
See Hubbard, L(afayette) Ron(ald)
Enright, D(ennis) J(oseph) 1920- **CLC 4, 8, 31**
See also CA 1-4R; CANR 1, 42; DLB 27; SATA
    25
Enzensberger, Hans Magnus 1929- ..**CLC 43**
See also CA 116; 119
Ephron, Nora 1941- .... **CLC 17, 31**
See also AITN 2; CA 65-68; CANR 12, 39
Epicurus 341B.C.-270B.C. .... **CMLC 21**
See also DLB 176
Epsilon
See Betjeman, John
Epstein, Daniel Mark 1948- .... **CLC 7**
See also CA 49-52; CANR 2, 53
Epstein, Jacob 1956- .... **CLC 19**
See also CA 114
Epstein, Joseph 1937- .... **CLC 39**
See also CA 112; 119; CANR 50, 65
Epstein, Leslie 1938- .... **CLC 27**
See also CA 73-76; CAAS 12; CANR 23
Equiano, Olaudah 1745(?)-1797 **LC 16; BLC;
    DAM MULT**
See also DLB 37, 50
ER .... **TCLC 33**
See also CA 160; DLB 85
Erasmus, Desiderius 1469(?)-1536 ..... **LC 16**
Erdman, Paul E(mil) 1932- .... **CLC 25**
See also AITN 1; CA 61-64; CANR 13, 43
Erdrich, Louise 1954- ..... **CLC 39, 54; DAM
    MULT, NOV, POP**
See also AAYA 10; BEST 89:1; CA 114; CANR
    41, 62; DLB 152, 175; MTCW; NNAL;
    SATA 94
Erenburg, Ilya (Grigoryevich)
See Ehrenburg, Ilya (Grigoryevich)

Erickson, Stephen Michael 1950-
See Erickson, Steve
See also CA 129
Erickson, Steve 1950- .... **CLC 64**
See also Erickson, Stephen Michael
See also CANR 60, 68
Ericson, Walter
See Fast, Howard (Melvin)
Eriksson, Buntel
See Bergman, (Ernst) Ingmar
Ernaux, Annie 1940- .... **CLC 88**
See also CA 147
Eschenbach, Wolfram von
See Wolfram von Eschenbach
Eseki, Bruno
See Mphahlele, Ezekiel
Esenin, Sergei (Alexandrovich) 1895-1925
    TCLC 4
See also CA 104
Eshleman, Clayton 1935- .... **CLC 7**
See also CA 33-36R; CAAS 6; DLB 5
Espriella, Don Manuel Alvarez
See Southey, Robert
Espriu, Salvador 1913-1985 .... **CLC 9**
See also CA 154; 115; DLB 134
Espronceda, Jose de 1808-1842 .....**NCLC 39**
Esse, James
See Stephens, James
Esterbrook, Tom
See Hubbard, L(afayette) Ron(ald)
Estleman, Loren D. 1952- **CLC 48; DAM NOV,
    POP**
See also CA 85-88; CANR 27; INT CANR-27;
    MTCW
Euclid 306B.C.-283B.C. .... **CMLC 25**
Eugenides, Jeffrey 1960(?)- .... **CLC 81**
See also CA 144
Euripides c. 485B.C.-406B.C. **CMLC 23; DA;
    DAB; DAC; DAM DRAM, MST; DC 4;
    WLCS**
See also DLB 176
Evan, Evin
See Faust, Frederick (Schiller)
Evans, Evan
See Faust, Frederick (Schiller)
Evans, Marian
See Eliot, George
Evans, Mary Ann
See Eliot, George
Evarts, Esther
See Benson, Sally
Everett, Percival L. 1956- .... **CLC 57**
See also BW 2; CA 129
Everson, R(onald) G(ilmour) 1903- . **CLC 27**
See also CA 17-20R; DLB 88
Everson, William (Oliver) 1912-1994 **CLC 1,
    5, 14**
See also CA 9-12R; 145; CANR 20; DLB 5,
    16; MTCW
Evtushenko, Evgenii Aleksandrovich
See Yevtushenko, Yevgeny (Alexandrovich)
Ewart, Gavin (Buchanan) 1916-1995 **CLC 13,
    46**
See also CA 89-92; 150; CANR 17, 46; DLB
    40; MTCW
Ewers, Hanns Heinz 1871-1943 ..... **TCLC 12**
See also CA 109; 149
Ewing, Frederick R.
See Sturgeon, Theodore (Hamilton)
Exley, Frederick (Earl) 1929-1992 **CLC 6, 11**
See also AITN 2; CA 81-84; 138; DLB 143;
    DLBY 81
Eynhardt, Guillermo

Fitch, Clarke
   See Sinclair, Upton (Beall)
Fitch, John IV
   See Cormier, Robert (Edmund)
Fitzgerald, Captain Hugh
   See Baum, L(yman) Frank
FitzGerald, Edward 1809-1883 .... **NCLC 9**
   See also DLB 32
Fitzgerald, F(rancis) Scott (Key) 1896-1940
      **TCLC 1, 6, 14, 28, 55; DA; DAB; DAC;
      DAM MST, NOV; SSC 6; WLC**
   See also AAYA 24; AITN 1; CA 110; 123;
      CDALB 1917-1929; DLB 4, 9, 86; DLBD 1,
      15, 16; DLBY 81, 96; MTCW
Fitzgerald, Penelope 1916- ... **CLC 19, 51, 61**
   See also CA 85-88; CAAS 10; CANR 56; DLB
      14, 194
Fitzgerald, Robert (Stuart) 1910-1985**CLC 39**
   See also CA 1-4R; 114; CANR 1; DLBY 80
FitzGerald, Robert D(avid) 1902-1987**CLC 19**
   See also CA 17-20R
Fitzgerald, Zelda (Sayre) 1900-1948**TCLC 52**
   See also CA 117; 126; DLBY 84
Flanagan, Thomas (James Bonner) 1923-
      CLC 25, 52
   See also CA 108; CANR 55; DLBY 80; INT
      108; MTCW
Flaubert, Gustave 1821-1880**NCLC 2, 10, 19,
      62, 66; DA; DAB; DAC; DAM MST, NOV;
      SSC 11; WLC**
   See also DLB 119
Flecker, Herman Elroy
   See Flecker, (Herman) James Elroy
Flecker, (Herman) James Elroy 1884-1915
      TCLC 43
   See also CA 109; 150; DLB 10, 19
Fleming, Ian (Lancaster) 1908-1964 **CLC 3,
      30; DAM POP**
   See also CA 5-8R; CANR 59; CDBLB 1945-
      1960; DLB 87; MTCW; SATA 9
Fleming, Thomas (James) 1927- ...... **CLC 37**
   See also CA 5-8R; CANR 10; INT CANR-10;
      SATA 8
Fletcher, John 1579-1625 .... **LC 33; DC 6**
   See also CDBLB Before 1660; DLB 58
Fletcher, John Gould 1886-1950 .... **TCLC 35**
   See also CA 107; DLB 4, 45
Fleur, Paul
   See Pohl, Frederik
Flooglebuckle, Al
   See Spiegelman, Art
Flying Officer X
   See Bates, H(erbert) E(rnest)
Fo, Dario 1926- . **CLC 32, 109; DAM DRAM**
   See also CA 116; 128; CANR 68; DLBY 97;
      MTCW
Fogarty, Jonathan Titulescu Esq.
   See Farrell, James T(homas)
Folke, Will
   See Bloch, Robert (Albert)
Follett, Ken(neth Martin) 1949- ..... **CLC 18;
      DAM NOV, POP**
   See also AAYA 6; BEST 89:4; CA 81-84; CANR
      13, 33, 54; DLB 87; DLBY 81; INT CANR-
      33; MTCW
Fontane, Theodor 1819-1898 .... **NCLC 26**
   See also DLB 129
Foote, Horton 1916-**CLC 51, 91; DAM DRAM**
   See also CA 73-76; CANR 34, 51; DLB 26; INT
      CANR-34
Foote, Shelby 1916-**CLC 75; DAM NOV, POP**
   See also CA 5-8R; CANR 3, 45; DLB 2, 17
Forbes, Esther 1891-1967 .... **CLC 12**

See also AAYA 17; CA 13-14; 25-28R; CAP 1;
   CLR 27; DLB 22; JRDA; MAICYA; SATA 2
Forche, Carolyn (Louise) 1950- **CLC 25, 83,
      86; DAM POET; PC 10**
   See also CA 109; 117; CANR 50; DLB 5, 193;
      INT 117
Ford, Elbur
   See Hibbert, Eleanor Alice Burford
Ford, Ford Madox 1873-1939**TCLC 1, 15, 39,
      57; DAM NOV**
   See also CA 104; 132; CDBLB 1914-1945;
      DLB 162; MTCW
Ford, Henry 1863-1947 .... **TCLC 73**
   See also CA 115; 148
Ford, John 1586-(?) .... **DC 8**
   See also CDBLB Before 1660; DAM DRAM;
      DLB 58
Ford, John 1895-1973 .... **CLC 16**
   See also CA 45-48
Ford, Richard .... **CLC 99**
Ford, Richard 1944- .... **CLC 46**
   See also CA 69-72; CANR 11, 47
Ford, Webster
   See Masters, Edgar Lee
Foreman, Richard 1937- .... **CLC 50**
   See also CA 65-68; CANR 32, 63
Forester, C(ecil) S(cott) 1899-1966 ... **CLC 35**
   See also CA 73-76; 25-28R; DLB 191; SATA
      13
Forez
   See Mauriac, Francois (Charles)
Forman, James Douglas 1932- .... **CLC 21**
   See also AAYA 17; CA 9-12R; CANR 4, 19,
      42; JRDA; MAICYA; SATA 8, 70
Fornes, Maria Irene 1930- .... **CLC 39, 61**
   See also CA 25-28R; CANR 28; DLB 7; HW;
      INT CANR-28; MTCW
Forrest, Leon (Richard) 1937-1997 .... **CLC 4**
   See also BW 2; CA 89-92; 162; CAAS 7; CANR
      25, 52; DLB 33
Forster, E(dward) M(organ) 1879-1970 **CLC
      1, 2, 3, 4, 9, 10, 13, 15, 22, 45, 77; DA; DAB;
      DAC; DAM MST, NOV; SSC 27; WLC**
   See also AAYA 2; CA 13-14; 25-28R; CANR
      45; CAP 1; CDBLB 1914-1945; DLB 34, 98,
      162, 178, 195; DLBD 10; MTCW; SATA 57
Forster, John 1812-1876 .... **NCLC 11**
   See also DLB 144, 184
Forsyth, Frederick 1938-**CLC 2, 5, 36; DAM
      NOV, POP**
   See also BEST 89:4; CA 85-88; CANR 38, 62;
      DLB 87; MTCW
Forten, Charlotte L. .... **TCLC 16; BLC**
   See also Grimke, Charlotte L(ottie) Forten
   See also DLB 50
Foscolo, Ugo 1778-1827 .... **NCLC 8**
Fosse, Bob .... **CLC 20**
   See also Fosse, Robert Louis
Fosse, Robert Louis 1927-1987
   See Fosse, Bob
   See also CA 110; 123
Foster, Stephen Collins 1826-1864 **NCLC 26**
Foucault, Michel 1926-1984 . **CLC 31, 34, 69**
   See also CA 105; 113; CANR 34; MTCW
Fouque, Friedrich (Heinrich Karl) de la Motte
      1777-1843 .... **NCLC 2**
   See also DLB 90
Fourier, Charles 1772-1837 .... **NCLC 51**
Fournier, Henri Alban 1886-1914
   See Alain-Fournier
   See also CA 104
Fournier, Pierre 1916- .... **CLC 11**
   See also Gascar, Pierre

See also CA 89-92; CANR 16, 40
Fowles, John 1926-**CLC 1, 2, 3, 4, 6, 9, 10, 15,
      33, 87; DAB; DAC; DAM MST**
   See also CA 5-8R; CANR 25; CDBLB 1960 to
      Present; DLB 14, 139; MTCW; SATA 22
Fox, Paula 1923- .... **CLC 2, 8**
   See also AAYA 3; CA 73-76; CANR 20, 36,
      62; CLR 1, 44; DLB 52; JRDA; MAICYA;
      MTCW; SATA 17, 60
Fox, William Price (Jr.) 1926- .... **CLC 22**
   See also CA 17-20R; CAAS 19; CANR 11; DLB
      2; DLBY 81
Foxe, John 1516(?)-1587 .... **LC 14**
Frame, Janet 1924-**CLC 2, 3, 6, 22, 66, 96; SSC
      29**
   See also Clutha, Janet Paterson Frame
France, Anatole .... **TCLC 9**
   See also Thibault, Jacques Anatole Francois
   See also DLB 123
Francis, Claude 19(?)- .... **CLC 50**
Francis, Dick 1920-**CLC 2, 22, 42, 102; DAM
      POP**
   See also AAYA 5, 21; BEST 89:3; CA 5-8R;
      CANR 9, 42, 68; CDBLB 1960 to Present;
      DLB 87; INT CANR-9; MTCW
Francis, Robert (Churchill) 1901-1987 . **C L C
      15**
   See also CA 1-4R; 123; CANR 1
Frank, Anne(lies Marie) 1929-1945**TCLC 17;
      DA; DAB; DAC; DAM MST; WLC**
   See also AAYA 12; CA 113; 133; CANR 68;
      MTCW; SATA 87; SATA-Brief 42
Frank, Elizabeth 1945- .... **CLC 39**
   See also CA 121; 126; INT 126
Frankl, Viktor E(mil) 1905-1997 ..... **CLC 93**
   See also CA 65-68; 161
Franklin, Benjamin
   See Hasek, Jaroslav (Matej Frantisek)
Franklin, Benjamin 1706-1790 .. **LC 25; DA;
      DAB; DAC; DAM MST; WLCS**
   See also CDALB 1640-1865; DLB 24, 43, 73
Franklin, (Stella Maria Sarah) Miles 1879-1954
      TCLC 7
   See also CA 104; 164
Fraser, (Lady) Antonia (Pakenham) 1932-
      CLC 32, 107
   See also CA 85-88; CANR 44, 65; MTCW;
      SATA-Brief 32
Fraser, George MacDonald 1925- ...... **CLC 7**
   See also CA 45-48; CANR 2, 48
Fraser, Sylvia 1935- .... **CLC 64**
   See also CA 45-48; CANR 1, 16, 60
Frayn, Michael 1933-**CLC 3, 7, 31, 47; DAM
      DRAM, NOV**
   See also CA 5-8R; CANR 30; DLB 13, 14, 194;
      MTCW
Fraze, Candida (Merrill) 1945- .... **CLC 50**
   See also CA 126
Frazer, J(ames) G(eorge) 1854-1941**TCLC 32**
   See also CA 118
Frazer, Robert Caine
   See Creasey, John
Frazer, Sir James George
   See Frazer, J(ames) G(eorge)
Frazier, Charles 1950- .... **CLC 109**
   See also CA 161
Frazier, Ian 1951- .... **CLC 46**
   See also CA 130; CANR 54
Frederic, Harold 1856-1898 .... **NCLC 10**
   See also DLB 12, 23; DLBD 13
Frederick, John
   See Faust, Frederick (Schiller)
Frederick the Great 1712-1786 .... **LC 14**

See also AAYA 18; CA 73-76; CANR 15, 64;
CLR 20; DLB 161; MAICYA; MTCW; SATA
18, 69

Garner, Hugh 1913-1979 .... CLC 13
See also CA 69-72; CANR 31; DLB 68

Garnett, David 1892-1981 .... CLC 3
See also CA 5-8R; 103; CANR 17; DLB 34

Garos, Stephanie
See Katz, Steve

Garrett, George (Palmer) 1929-CLC 3, 11, 51;
SSC 30
See also CA 1-4R; CAAS 5; CANR 1, 42, 67;
DLB 2, 5, 130, 152; DLBY 83

Garrick, David 1717-1779 .... LC 15; DAM
DRAM
See also DLB 84

Garrigue, Jean 1914-1972 .... CLC 2, 8
See also CA 5-8R; 37-40R; CANR 20

Garrison, Frederick
See Sinclair, Upton (Beall)

Garth, Will
See Hamilton, Edmond; Kuttner, Henry

Garvey, Marcus (Moziah, Jr.) 1887-1940
TCLC 41; BLC; DAM MULT
See also BW 1; CA 120; 124

Gary, Romain .... CLC 25
See also Kacew, Romain
See also DLB 83

Gascar, Pierre .... CLC 11
See also Fournier, Pierre

Gascoyne, David (Emery) 1916- ...... CLC 45
See also CA 65-68; CANR 10, 28, 54; DLB 20;
MTCW

Gaskell, Elizabeth Cleghorn 1810-1865NCLC
5; DAB; DAM MST; SSC 25
See also CDBLB 1832-1890; DLB 21, 144, 159

Gass, William H(oward) 1924-CLC 1, 2, 8, 11,
15, 39; SSC 12
See also CA 17-20R; CANR 30; DLB 2; MTCW

Gasset, Jose Ortega y
See Ortega y Gasset, Jose

Gates, Henry Louis, Jr. 1950-CLC 65; DAM
MULT
See also BW 2; CA 109; CANR 25, 53; DLB
67

Gautier, Theophile 1811-1872 .. NCLC 1, 59;
DAM POET; PC 18; SSC 20
See also DLB 119

Gawsworth, John
See Bates, H(erbert) E(rnest)

Gay, Oliver
See Gogarty, Oliver St. John

Gaye, Marvin (Penze) 1939-1984 .... CLC 26
See also CA 112

Gebler, Carlo (Ernest) 1954-............ CLC 39
See also CA 119; 133

Gee, Maggie (Mary) 1948- .... CLC 57
See also CA 130

Gee, Maurice (Gough) 1931-............ CLC 29
See also CA 97-100; CANR 67; SATA 46

Gelbart, Larry (Simon) 1923-.... CLC 21, 61
See also CA 73-76; CANR 45

Gelber, Jack 1932- .... CLC 1, 6, 14, 79
See also CA 1-4R; CANR 2; DLB 7

Gellhorn, Martha (Ellis) 1908-1998 CLC 14,
60
See also CA 77-80; 164; CANR 44; DLBY 82

Genet, Jean 1910-1986CLC 1, 2, 5, 10, 14, 44,
46; DAM DRAM
See also CA 13-16R; CANR 18; DLB 72;
DLBY 86; MTCW

Gent, Peter 1942-.............................. CLC 29
See also AITN 1; CA 89-92; DLBY 82

Gentlewoman in New England, A
See Bradstreet, Anne

Gentlewoman in Those Parts, A
See Bradstreet, Anne

George, Jean Craighead 1919- .... CLC 35
See also AAYA 8; CA 5-8R; CANR 25; CLR 1;
DLB 52; JRDA; MAICYA; SATA 2, 68

George, Stefan (Anton) 1868-1933TCLC 2, 14
See also CA 104

Georges, Georges Martin
See Simenon, Georges (Jacques Christian)

Gerhardi, William Alexander
See Gerhardie, William Alexander

Gerhardie, William Alexander 1895-1977
CLC 5
See also CA 25-28R; 73-76; CANR 18; DLB
36

Gerstler, Amy 1956- .... CLC 70
See also CA 146

Gertler, T. .... CLC 34
See also CA 116; 121; INT 121

Ghalib .... NCLC 39
See also Ghalib, Hsadullah Khan

Ghalib, Hsadullah Khan 1797-1869
See Ghalib
See also DAM POET

Ghelderode, Michel de 1898-1962CLC 6, 11;
DAM DRAM
See also CA 85-88; CANR 40

Ghiselin, Brewster 1903- .... CLC 23
See also CA 13-16R; CAAS 10; CANR 13

Ghose, Zulfikar 1935- .... CLC 42
See also CA 65-68; CANR 67

Ghosh, Amitav 1956-.......................... CLC 44
See also CA 147

Giacosa, Giuseppe 1847-1906 .... TCLC 7
See also CA 104

Gibb, Lee
See Waterhouse, Keith (Spencer)

Gibbon, Lewis Grassic .... TCLC 4
See also Mitchell, James Leslie

Gibbons, Kaye 1960-CLC 50, 88; DAM POP
See also CA 151

Gibran, Kahlil 1883-1931 . TCLC 1, 9; DAM
POET, POP; PC 9
See also CA 104; 150

Gibran, Khalil
See Gibran, Kahlil

Gibson, William 1914- .. CLC 23; DA; DAB;
DAC; DAM DRAM, MST
See also CA 9-12R; CANR 9, 42; DLB 7; SATA
66

Gibson, William (Ford) 1948- ... CLC 39, 63;
DAM POP
See also AAYA 12; CA 126; 133; CANR 52

Gide, Andre (Paul Guillaume) 1869-1951
TCLC 5, 12, 36; DA; DAB; DAC; DAM
MST, NOV; SSC 13; WLC
See also CA 104; 124; DLB 65; MTCW

Gifford, Barry (Colby) 1946- .... CLC 34
See also CA 65-68; CANR 9, 30, 40

Gilbert, Frank
See De Voto, Bernard (Augustine)

Gilbert, W(illiam) S(chwenck) 1836-1911
TCLC 3; DAM DRAM, POET
See also CA 104; SATA 36

Gilbreth, Frank B., Jr. 1911- .... CLC 17
See also CA 9-12R; SATA 2

Gilchrist, Ellen 1935-CLC 34, 48; DAM POP;
SSC 14
See also CA 113; 116; CANR 41, 61; DLB 130;
MTCW

Giles, Molly 1942- .... CLC 39

See also CA 126

Gill, Patrick
See Creasey, John

Gilliam, Terry (Vance) 1940- .... CLC 21
See also Monty Python
See also AAYA 19; CA 108; 113; CANR 35;
INT 113

Gillian, Jerry
See Gilliam, Terry (Vance)

Gilliatt, Penelope (Ann Douglass) 1932-1993
CLC 2, 10, 13, 53
See also AITN 2; CA 13-16R; 141; CANR 49;
DLB 14

Gilman, Charlotte (Anna) Perkins (Stetson)
1860-1935 .... TCLC 9, 37; SSC 13
See also CA 106; 150

Gilmour, David 1949- .... CLC 35
See also CA 138, 147

Gilpin, William 1724-1804 .... NCLC 30

Gilray, J. D.
See Mencken, H(enry) L(ouis)

Gilroy, Frank D(aniel) 1925- .... CLC 2
See also CA 81-84; CANR 32, 64; DLB 7

Gilstrap, John 1957(?)- .... CLC 99
See also CA 160

Ginsberg, Allen 1926-1997CLC 1, 2, 3, 4, 6, 13,
36, 69, 109; DA; DAB; DAC; DAM MST,
POET; PC 4; WLC 3
See also AITN 1; CA 1-4R; 157; CANR 2, 41,
63; CDALB 1941-1968; DLB 5, 16, 169;
MTCW

Ginzburg, Natalia 1916-1991CLC 5, 11, 54, 70
See also CA 85-88; 135; CANR 33; DLB 177;
MTCW

Giono, Jean 1895-1970 .... CLC 4, 11
See also CA 45-48; 29-32R; CANR 2, 35; DLB
72; MTCW

Giovanni, Nikki 1943-CLC 2, 4, 19, 64; BLC;
DA; DAB; DAC; DAM MST, MULT,
POET; PC 19; WLCS
See also AAYA 22; AITN 1; BW 2; CA 29-32R;
CAAS 6; CANR 18, 41, 60; CLR 6; DLB 5,
41; INT CANR-18; MAICYA; MTCW; SATA
24

Giovene, Andrea 1904- .... CLC 7
See also CA 85-88

Gippius, Zinaida (Nikolayevna) 1869-1945
See Hippius, Zinaida
See also CA 106

Giraudoux, (Hippolyte) Jean 1882-1944
TCLC 2, 7; DAM DRAM
See also CA 104; DLB 65

Gironella, Jose Maria 1917- .... CLC 11
See also CA 101

Gissing, George (Robert) 1857-1903TCLC 3,
24, 47
See also CA 105; DLB 18, 135, 184

Giurlani, Aldo
See Palazzeschi, Aldo

Gladkov, Fyodor (Vasilyevich) 1883-1958
TCLC 27

Glanville, Brian (Lester) 1931- .... CLC 6
See also CA 5-8R; CAAS 9; CANR 3; DLB 15,
139; SATA 42

Glasgow, Ellen (Anderson Gholson) 1873-1945
TCLC 2, 7
See also CA 104; 164; DLB 9, 12

Glaspell, Susan 1882(?)-1948 .... TCLC 55
See also CA 110; 154; DLB 7, 9, 78; YABC 2

Glassco, John 1909-1981 .... CLC 9
See also CA 13-16R; 102; CANR 15; DLB 68

Glasscock, Amnesia
See Steinbeck, John (Ernst)

Glasser, Ronald J. 1940(?)-............... CLC 37
Glassman, Joyce
    See Johnson, Joyce
Glendinning, Victoria 1937-............. CLC 50
    See also CA 120; 127; CANR 59; DLB 155
Glissant, Edouard 1928-. CLC 10, 68; DAM
    MULT
    See also CA 153
Gloag, Julian 1930-........................... CLC 40
    See also AITN 1; CA 65-68; CANR 10
Glowacki, Aleksander
    See Prus, Boleslaw
Gluck, Louise (Elisabeth) 1943-CLC 7, 22, 44,
    81; DAM POET; PC 16
    See also CA 33-36R; CANR 40; DLB 5
Glyn, Elinor 1864-1943 .... TCLC 72
    See also DLB 153
Gobineau, Joseph Arthur (Comte) de 1816-
    1882 .... NCLC 17
    See also DLB 123
Godard, Jean-Luc 1930-................... CLC 20
    See also CA 93-96
Godden, (Margaret) Rumer 1907-... CLC 53
    See also AAYA 6; CA 5-8R; CANR 4, 27, 36,
    55; CLR 20; DLB 161; MAICYA; SAAS 12;
    SATA 3, 36
Godoy Alcayaga, Lucila 1889-1957
    See Mistral, Gabriela
    See also BW 2; CA 104; 131; DAM MULT;
    HW; MTCW
Godwin, Gail (Kathleen) 1937- CLC 5, 8, 22,
    31, 69; DAM POP
    See also CA 29-32R; CANR 15, 43; DLB 6;
    INT CANR-15; MTCW
Godwin, William 1756-1836 .... NCLC 14
    See also CDBLB 1789-1832; DLB 39, 104, 142,
    158, 163
Goebbels, Josef
    See Goebbels, (Paul) Joseph
Goebbels, (Paul) Joseph 1897-1945 TCLC 68
    See also CA 115; 148
Goebbels, Joseph Paul
    See Goebbels, (Paul) Joseph
Goethe, Johann Wolfgang von 1749-1832
    NCLC 4, 22, 34; DA; DAB; DAC; DAM
    DRAM, MST, POET; PC 5; WLC 3
    See also DLB 94
Gogarty, Oliver St. John 1878-1957TCLC 15
    See also CA 109; 150; DLB 15, 19
Gogol, Nikolai (Vasilyevich) 1809-1852NCLC
    5, 15, 31; DA; DAB; DAC; DAM DRAM,
    MST; DC 1; SSC 4, 29; WLC
Goines, Donald 1937(?)-1974 CLC 80; BLC;
    DAM MULT, POP
    See also AITN 1; BW 1; CA 124; 114; DLB 33
Gold, Herbert 1924-............ CLC 4, 7, 14, 42
    See also CA 9-12R; CANR 17, 45; DLB 2;
    DLBY 81
Goldbarth, Albert 1948- .... CLC 5, 38
    See also CA 53-56; CANR 6, 40; DLB 120
Goldberg, Anatol 1910-1982 .... CLC 34
    See also CA 131; 117
Goldemberg, Isaac 1945- .... CLC 52
    See also CA 69-72; CAAS 12; CANR 11, 32;
    HW
Golding, William (Gerald) 1911-1993CLC 1,
    2, 3, 8, 10, 17, 27, 58, 81; DA; DAB; DAC;
    DAM MST, NOV; WLC
    See also AAYA 5; CA 5-8R; 141; CANR 13,
    33, 54; CDBLB 1945-1960; DLB 15, 100;
    MTCW
Goldman, Emma 1869-1940 .... TCLC 13
    See also CA 110; 150

Goldman, Francisco 1954- .... CLC 76
    See also CA 162
Goldman, William (W.) 1931- ...... CLC 1, 48
    See also CA 9-12R; CANR 29; DLB 44
Goldmann, Lucien 1913-1970 .... CLC 24
    See also CA 25-28; CAP 2
Goldoni, Carlo 1707-1793LC 4; DAM DRAM
Goldsberry, Steven 1949- .... CLC 34
    See also CA 131
Goldsmith, Oliver 1728-1774LC 2; DA; DAB;
    DAC; DAM DRAM, MST, NOV, POET;
    DC 8; WLC
    See also CDBLB 1660-1789; DLB 39, 89, 104,
    109, 142; SATA 26
Goldsmith, Peter
    See Priestley, J(ohn) B(oynton)
Gombrowicz, Witold 1904-1969CLC 4, 7, 11,
    49; DAM DRAM
    See also CA 19-20; 25-28R; CAP 2
Gomez de la Serna, Ramon 1888-1963CLC 9
    See also CA 153; 116; HW
Goncharov, Ivan Alexandrovich 1812-1891
    NCLC 1, 63
Goncourt, Edmond (Louis Antoine Huot) de
    1822-1896 .... NCLC 7
    See also DLB 123
Goncourt, Jules (Alfred Huot) de 1830-1870
    NCLC 7
    See also DLB 123
Gontier, Fernande 19(?)- .... CLC 50
Gonzalez Martinez, Enrique 1871-1952
    TCLC 72
    See also HW
Goodman, Paul 1911-1972 ...... CLC 1, 2, 4, 7
    See also CA 19-20; 37-40R; CANR 34; CAP 2;
    DLB 130; MTCW
Gordimer, Nadine 1923-CLC 3, 5, 7, 10, 18, 33,
    51, 70; DA; DAB; DAC; DAM MST, NOV;
    SSC 17; WLCS
    See also CA 5-8R; CANR 3, 28, 56; INT CANR-
    28; MTCW
Gordon, Adam Lindsay 1833-1870 NCLC 21
Gordon, Caroline 1895-1981CLC 6, 13, 29, 83;
    SSC 15
    See also CA 11-12; 103; CANR 36; CAP 1;
    DLB 4, 9, 102; DLBY 81; MTCW
Gordon, Charles William 1860-1937
    See Connor, Ralph
    See also CA 109
Gordon, Mary (Catherine) 1949-CLC 13, 22
    See also CA 102; CANR 44; DLB 6; DLBY
    81; INT 102; MTCW
Gordon, N. J.
    See Bosman, Herman Charles
Gordon, Sol 1923- .... CLC 26
    See also CA 53-56; CANR 4; SATA 11
Gordone, Charles 1925-1995CLC 1, 4; DAM
    DRAM; DC 8
    See also BW 1; CA 93-96; 150; CANR 55; DLB
    7; INT 93-96; MTCW
Gore, Catherine 1800-1861 .... NCLC 65
    See also DLB 116
Gorenko, Anna Andreevna
    See Akhmatova, Anna
Gorky, Maxim 1868-1936TCLC 8; DAB; SSC
    28; WLC
    See also Peshkov, Alexei Maximovich
Goryan, Sirak
    See Saroyan, William
Gosse, Edmund (William) 1849-1928TCLC 28
    See also CA 117; DLB 57, 144, 184
Gotlieb, Phyllis Fay (Bloom) 1926- ..CLC 18
    See also CA 13-16R; CANR 7; DLB 88

Gottesman, S. D.
    See Kornbluth, C(yril) M.; Pohl, Frederik
Gottfried von Strassburg fl. c. 1210-. C M L C
    10
    See also DLB 138
Gould, Lois .... CLC 4, 10
    See also CA 77-80; CANR 29; MTCW
Gourmont, Remy (-Marie-Charles) de 1858-
    1915 .... TCLC 17
    See also CA 109; 150
Govier, Katherine 1948- .... CLC 51
    See also CA 101; CANR 18, 40
Goyen, (Charles) William 1915-1983CLC 5, 8,
    14, 40
    See also AITN 2; CA 5-8R; 110; CANR 6; DLB
    2; DLBY 83; INT CANR-6
Goytisolo, Juan 1931- . CLC 5, 10, 23; DAM
    MULT; HLC
    See also CA 85-88; CANR 32, 61; HW; MTCW
Gozzano, Guido 1883-1916 .... PC 10
    See also CA 154; DLB 114
Gozzi, (Conte) Carlo 1720-1806 .... NCLC 23
Grabbe, Christian Dietrich 1801-1836N C L C
    2
    See also DLB 133
Grace, Patricia 1937- .... CLC 56
Gracian y Morales, Baltasar 1601-1658LC 15
Gracq, Julien .... CLC 11, 48
    See also Poirier, Louis
    See also DLB 83
Grade, Chaim 1910-1982 .... CLC 10
    See also CA 93-96; 107
Graduate of Oxford, A
    See Ruskin, John
Grafton, Garth
    See Duncan, Sara Jeannette
Graham, John
    See Phillips, David Graham
Graham, Jorie 1951- .... CLC 48
    See also CA 111; CANR 63; DLB 120
Graham, R(obert) B(ontine) Cunninghame
    See Cunninghame Graham, R(obert) B(ontine)
    See also DLB 98, 135, 174
Graham, Robert
    See Haldeman, Joe (William)
Graham, Tom
    See Lewis, (Harry) Sinclair
Graham, W(illiam) S(ydney) 1918-1986C L C
    29
    See also CA 73-76; 118; DLB 20
Graham, Winston (Mawdsley) 1910- CLC 23
    .See also CA 49-52; CANR 2, 22, 45, 66; DLB
    77
Grahame, Kenneth 1859-1932TCLC 64; DAB
    See also CA 108; 136; CLR 5; DLB 34, 141,
    178; MAICYA; YABC 1
Grant, Skeeter
    See Spiegelman, Art
Granville-Barker, Harley 1877-1946TCLC 2;
    DAM DRAM
    See also Barker, Harley Granville
    See also CA 104
Grass, Guenter (Wilhelm) 1927-CLC 1, 2, 4, 6,
    11, 15, 22, 32, 49, 88; DA; DAB; DAC;
    DAM MST, NOV; WLC
    See also CA 13-16R; CANR 20; DLB 75, 124;
    MTCW
Gratton, Thomas
    See Hulme, T(homas) E(rnest)
Grau, Shirley Ann 1929- ..CLC 4, 9; SSC 15
    See also CA 89-92; CANR 22; DLB 2; INT
    CANR-22; MTCW
Gravel, Fern

Harmon, William (Ruth) 1938- .... **CLC 38**
See also CA 33-36R; CANR 14, 32, 35; SATA 65

Harper, F. E. W.
See Harper, Frances Ellen Watkins

Harper, Frances E. W.
See Harper, Frances Ellen Watkins

Harper, Frances E. Watkins
See Harper, Frances Ellen Watkins

Harper, Frances Ellen
See Harper, Frances Ellen Watkins

Harper, Frances Ellen Watkins 1825-1911
TCLC 14; BLC; DAM MULT, POET; PC 21
See also BW 1; CA 111; 125; DLB 50

Harper, Michael S(teven) 1938- ... **CLC 7, 22**
See also BW 1; CA 33-36R; CANR 24; DLB 41

Harper, Mrs. F. E. W.
See Harper, Frances Ellen Watkins

Harris, Christie (Lucy) Irwin 1907- **CLC 12**
See also CA 5-8R; CANR 6; CLR 47; DLB 88; JRDA; MAICYA; SAAS 10; SATA 6, 74

Harris, Frank 1856-1931 .... **TCLC 24**
See also CA 109; 150; DLB 156

Harris, George Washington 1814-1869 **NCLC 23**
See also DLB 3, 11

Harris, Joel Chandler 1848-1908 ... **TCLC 2; SSC 19**
See also CA 104; 137; CLR 49; DLB 11, 23, 42, 78, 91; MAICYA; YABC 1

Harris, John (Wyndham Parkes Lucas) Beynon 1903-1969
See Wyndham, John
See also CA 102; 89-92

Harris, MacDonald .... **CLC 9**
See also Heiney, Donald (William)

Harris, Mark 1922- .... **CLC 19**
See also CA 5-8R; CAAS 3; CANR 2, 55; DLB 2; DLBY 80

Harris, (Theodore) Wilson 1921- ..... **CLC 25**
See also BW 2; CA 65-68; CAAS 16; CANR 11, 27; DLB 117; MTCW

Harrison, Elizabeth Cavanna 1909-
See Cavanna, Betty
See also CA 9-12R; CANR 6, 27

Harrison, Harry (Max) 1925- .... **CLC 42**
See also CA 1-4R; CANR 5, 21; DLB 8; SATA 4

Harrison, James (Thomas) 1937- **CLC 6, 14, 33, 66; SSC 19**
See also CA 13-16R; CANR 8, 51; DLBY 82; INT CANR-8

Harrison, Jim
See Harrison, James (Thomas)

Harrison, Kathryn 1961- .... **CLC 70**
See also CA 144; CANR 68

Harrison, Tony 1937- .... **CLC 43**
See also CA 65-68; CANR 44; DLB 40; MTCW

Harriss, Will(ard Irvin) 1922- .... **CLC 34**
See also CA 111

Harson, Sley
See Ellison, Harlan (Jay)

Hart, Ellis
See Ellison, Harlan (Jay)

Hart, Josephine 1942(?)- **CLC 70; DAM POP**
See also CA 138

Hart, Moss 1904-1961 **CLC 66; DAM DRAM**
See also CA 109; 89-92; DLB 7

Harte, (Francis) Bret(t) 1836(?)-1902 **TCLC 1, 25; DA; DAC; DAM MST; SSC 8; WLC**
See also CA 104; 140; CDALB 1865-1917;

DLB 12, 64, 74, 79, 186; SATA 26

Hartley, L(eslie) P(oles) 1895-1972 **CLC 2, 22**
See also CA 45-48; 37-40R; CANR 33; DLB 15, 139; MTCW

Hartman, Geoffrey H. 1929- .... **CLC 27**
See also CA 117; 125; DLB 67

Hartmann, Sadakichi 1867-1944 ... **TCLC 73**
See also CA 157; DLB 54

Hartmann von Aue c. 1160-c. 1205 **CMLC 15**
See also DLB 138

Hartmann von Aue 1170-1210 ...... **CMLC 15**

Haruf, Kent 1943- .... **CLC 34**
See also CA 149

Harwood, Ronald 1934- .... **CLC 32; DAM DRAM, MST**
See also CA 1-4R; CANR 4, 55; DLB 13

Hasegawa Tatsunosuke
See Futabatei, Shimei

Hasek, Jaroslav (Matej Frantisek) 1883-1923 **TCLC 4**
See also CA 104; 129; MTCW

Hass, Robert 1941- ... **CLC 18, 39, 99; PC 16**
See also CA 111; CANR 30, 50; DLB 105; SATA 94

Hastings, Hudson
See Kuttner, Henry

Hastings, Selina .... **CLC 44**

Hathorne, John 1641-1717 .... **LC 38**

Hatteras, Amelia
See Mencken, H(enry) L(ouis)

Hatteras, Owen .... **TCLC 18**
See also Mencken, H(enry) L(ouis); Nathan, George Jean

Hauptmann, Gerhart (Johann Robert) 1862-1946 .... **TCLC 4; DAM DRAM**
See also CA 104; 153; DLB 66, 118

Havel, Vaclav 1936- ... **CLC 25, 58, 65; DAM DRAM; DC 6**
See also CA 104; CANR 36, 63; MTCW

Haviaras, Stratis .... **CLC 33**
See also Chaviaras, Strates

Hawes, Stephen 1475(?)-1523(?) .... **LC 17**

Hawkes, John (Clendennin Burne, Jr.) 1925- **CLC 1, 2, 3, 4, 7, 9, 14, 15, 27, 49**
See also CA 1-4R; CANR 2, 47, 64; DLB 2, 7; DLBY 80; MTCW

Hawking, S. W.
See Hawking, Stephen W(illiam)

Hawking, Stephen W(illiam) 1942- **CLC 63, 105**
See also AAYA 13; BEST 89:1; CA 126; 129; CANR 48

Hawthorne, Julian 1846-1934 .... **TCLC 25**
See also CA 165

Hawthorne, Nathaniel 1804-1864 **NCLC 39; DA; DAB; DAC; DAM MST, NOV; SSC 3, 29; WLC**
See also AAYA 18; CDALB 1640-1865; DLB 1, 74; YABC 2

Haxton, Josephine Ayres 1921-
See Douglas, Ellen
See also CA 115; CANR 41

Hayaseca y Eizaguirre, Jorge
See Echegaray (y Eizaguirre), Jose (Maria Waldo)

Hayashi Fumiko 1904-1951 .... **TCLC 27**
See also CA 161; DLB 180

Haycraft, Anna
See Ellis, Alice Thomas
See also CA 122

Hayden, Robert E(arl) 1913-1980 **CLC 5, 9, 14, 37; BLC; DA; DAC; DAM MST, MULT, POET; PC 6**

See also BW 1; CA 69-72; 97-100; CABS 2; CANR 24; CDALB 1941-1968; DLB 5, 76; MTCW; SATA 19; SATA-Obit 26

Hayford, J(oseph) E(phraim) Casely
See Casely-Hayford, J(oseph) E(phraim)

Hayman, Ronald 1932- .... **CLC 44**
See also CA 25-28R; CANR 18, 50; DLB 155

Haywood, Eliza (Fowler) 1693(?)-1756 **LC 1**

Hazlitt, William 1778-1830 .... **NCLC 29**
See also DLB 110, 158

Hazzard, Shirley 1931- .... **CLC 18**
See also CA 9-12R; CANR 4; DLBY 82; MTCW

Head, Bessie 1937-1986 .. **CLC 25, 67; BLC; DAM MULT**
See also BW 2; CA 29-32R; 119; CANR 25; DLB 117; MTCW

Headon, (Nicky) Topper 1956(?)- .... **CLC 30**

Heaney, Seamus (Justin) 1939- **CLC 5, 7, 14, 25, 37, 74, 91; DAB; DAM POET; PC 18; WLCS**
See also CA 85-88; CANR 25, 48; CDBLB 1960 to Present; DLB 40; DLBY 95; MTCW

Hearn, (Patricio) Lafcadio (Tessima Carlos) 1850-1904 .... **TCLC 9**
See also CA 105; DLB 12, 78

Hearne, Vicki 1946- .... **CLC 56**
See also CA 139

Hearon, Shelby 1931- .... **CLC 63**
See also AITN 2; CA 25-28R; CANR 18, 48

Heat-Moon, William Least .... **CLC 29**
See also Trogdon, William (Lewis)
See also AAYA 9

Hebbel, Friedrich 1813-1863 **NCLC 43; DAM DRAM**
See also DLB 129

Hebert, Anne 1916- **CLC 4, 13, 29; DAC; DAM MST, POET**
See also CA 85-88; DLB 68; MTCW

Hecht, Anthony (Evan) 1923- **CLC 8, 13, 19; DAM POET**
See also CA 9-12R; CANR 6; DLB 5, 169

Hecht, Ben 1894-1964 .... **CLC 8**
See also CA 85-88; DLB 7, 9, 25, 26, 28, 86

Hedayat, Sadeq 1903-1951 .... **TCLC 21**
See also CA 120

Hegel, Georg Wilhelm Friedrich 1770-1831 **NCLC 46**
See also DLB 90

Heidegger, Martin 1889-1976 .... **CLC 24**
See also CA 81-84; 65-68; CANR 34; MTCW

Heidenstam, (Carl Gustaf) Verner von 1859-1940 .... **TCLC 5**
See also CA 104

Heifner, Jack 1946- .... **CLC 11**
See also CA 105; CANR 47

Heijermans, Herman 1864-1924 .... **TCLC 24**
See also CA 123

Heilbrun, Carolyn G(old) 1926- ...... **CLC 25**
See also CA 45-48; CANR 1, 28, 58

Heine, Heinrich 1797-1856 .... **NCLC 4, 54**
See also DLB 90

Heinemann, Larry (Curtiss) 1944- .. **CLC 50**
See also CA 110; CAAS 21; CANR 31; DLBD 9; INT CANR-31

Heiney, Donald (William) 1921-1993
See Harris, MacDonald
See also CA 1-4R; 142; CANR 3, 58

Heinlein, Robert A(nson) 1907-1988 **CLC 1, 3, 8, 14, 26, 55; DAM POP**
See also AAYA 17; CA 1-4R; 125; CANR 1, 20, 53; DLB 8; JRDA; MAICYA; MTCW; SATA 9, 69; SATA-Obit 56

See also Gippius, Zinaida (Nikolayevna)

Hiraoka, Kimitake 1925-1970
See Mishima, Yukio
See also CA 97-100; 29-32R; DAM DRAM;
MTCW

Hirsch, E(ric) D(onald), Jr. 1928-.... CLC 79
See also CA 25-28R; CANR 27, 51; DLB 67;
INT CANR-27; MTCW

Hirsch, Edward 1950- .... CLC 31, 50
See also CA 104; CANR 20, 42; DLB 120

Hitchcock, Alfred (Joseph) 1899-1980CLC 16
See also AAYA 22; CA 159; 97-100; SATA 27;
SATA-Obit 24

Hitler, Adolf 1889-1945 .... TCLC 53
See also CA 117; 147

Hoagland, Edward 1932-................. CLC 28
See also CA 1-4R; CANR 2, 31, 57; DLB 6;
SATA 51

**Hoban, Russell (Conwell) 1925- . CLC 7, 25;
DAM NOV**
See also CA 5-8R; CANR 23, 37, 66; CLR 3;
DLB 52; MAICYA; MTCW; SATA 1, 40, 78

Hobbes, Thomas 1588-1679 .... LC 36
See also DLB 151

Hobbs, Perry
See Blackmur, R(ichard) P(almer)

**Hobson, Laura Z(ametkin) 1900-1986CLC 7,
25**
See also CA 17-20R; 118; CANR 55; DLB 28;
SATA 52

**Hochhuth, Rolf 1931-...CLC 4, 11, 18; DAM
DRAM**
See also CA 5-8R; CANR 33; DLB 124; MTCW

Hochman, Sandra 1936- .... CLC 3, 8
See also CA 5-8R; DLB 5

**Hochwaelder, Fritz 1911-1986CLC 36; DAM
DRAM**
See also CA 29-32R; 120; CANR 42; MTCW

Hochwalder, Fritz
See Hochwaelder, Fritz

Hocking, Mary (Eunice) 1921-......... CLC 13
See also CA 101; CANR 18, 40

Hodgins, Jack 1938- .... CLC 23
See also CA 93-96; DLB 60

**Hodgson, William Hope 1877(?)-1918 T C L C
13**
See also CA 111; 164; DLB 70, 153, 156, 178

Hoeg, Peter 1957- .... CLC 95
See also CA 151

Hoffman, Alice 1952- ... CLC 51; DAM NOV
See also CA 77-80; CANR 34, 66; MTCW

Hoffman, Daniel (Gerard) 1923-CLC 6, 13, 23
See also CA 1-4R; CANR 4; DLB 5

Hoffman, Stanley 1944- .... CLC 5
See also CA 77-80

Hoffman, William M(oses) 1939-..... CLC 40
See also CA 57-60; CANR 11

**Hoffmann, E(rnst) T(heodor) A(madeus) 1776-
1822 .... NCLC 2; SSC 13**
See also DLB 90; SATA 27

Hofmann, Gert 1931- .... CLC 54
See also CA 128

**Hofmannsthal, Hugo von 1874-1929TCLC 11;
DAM DRAM; DC 4**
See also CA 106; 153; DLB 81, 118

Hogan, Linda 1947-... CLC 73; DAM MULT
See also CA 120; CANR 45; DLB 175; NNAL

Hogarth, Charles
See Creasey, John

Hogarth, Emmett
See Polonsky, Abraham (Lincoln)

Hogg, James 1770-1835 .... NCLC 4
See also DLB 93, 116, 159

**Holbach, Paul Henri Thiry Baron 1723-1789
LC 14**

Holberg, Ludvig 1684-1754 .... LC 6

Holden, Ursula 1921- ....CLC 18
See also CA 101; CAAS 8; CANR 22

**Holderlin, (Johann Christian) Friedrich 1770-
1843 .... NCLC 16; PC 4**

Holdstock, Robert
See Holdstock, Robert P.

Holdstock, Robert P. 1948- ....CLC 39
See also CA 131

Holland, Isabelle 1920- ....CLC 21
See also AAYA 11; CA 21-24R; CANR 10, 25,
47; JRDA; MAICYA; SATA 8, 70

Holland, Marcus
See Caldwell, (Janet Miriam) Taylor (Holland)

Hollander, John 1929-........... CLC 2, 5, 8, 14
See also CA 1-4R; CANR 1, 52; DLB 5; SATA
13

Hollander, Paul
See Silverberg, Robert

Holleran, Andrew 1943(?)- ....CLC 38
See also CA 144

Hollinghurst, Alan 1954- .... CLC 55, 91
See also CA 114

Hollis, Jim
See Summers, Hollis (Spurgeon, Jr.)

Holly, Buddy 1936-1959 .... TCLC 65

Holmes, Gordon
See Shiel, M(atthew) P(hipps)

Holmes, John
See Souster, (Holmes) Raymond

Holmes, John Clellon 1926-1988 ......CLC 56
See also CA 9-12R; 125; CANR 4; DLB 16

**Holmes, Oliver Wendell, Jr. 1841-1935TCLC
77**
See also CA 114

Holmes, Oliver Wendell 1809-1894 NCLC 14
See also CDALB 1640-1865; DLB 1, 189;
SATA 34

Holmes, Raymond
See Souster, (Holmes) Raymond

Holt, Victoria
See Hibbert, Eleanor Alice Burford

Holub, Miroslav 1923- ....CLC 4
See also CA 21-24R; CANR 10

**Homer c. 8th cent. B.C.- ... CMLC 1, 16; DA;
DAB; DAC; DAM MST, POET; WLCS**
See also DLB 176

Honig, Edwin 1919-............................CLC 33
See also CA 5-8R; CAAS 8; CANR 4, 45; DLB
5

Hood, Hugh (John Blagdon) 1928-CLC 15, 28
See also CA 49-52; CAAS 17; CANR 1, 33;
DLB 53

Hood, Thomas 1799-1845 .... NCLC 16
See also DLB 96

Hooker, (Peter) Jeremy 1941- ....CLC 43
See also CA 77-80; CANR 22; DLB 40

hooks, bell ....CLC 94
See also Watkins, Gloria

Hope, A(lec) D(erwent) 1907- ...... CLC 3, 51
See also CA 21-24R; CANR 33; MTCW

Hope, Brian
See Creasey, John

**Hope, Christopher (David Tully) 1944- C L C
52**
See also CA 106; CANR 47; SATA 62

**Hopkins, Gerard Manley 1844-1889 ..N C L C
17; DA; DAB; DAC; DAM MST, POET;
PC 15; WLC**
See also CDBLB 1890-1914; DLB 35, 57

Hopkins, John (Richard) 1931-...........CLC 4

See also CA 85-88

**Hopkins, Pauline Elizabeth 1859-1930T C L C
28; BLC; DAM MULT**
See also BW 2; CA 141; DLB 50

Hopkinson, Francis 1737-1791 .... LC 25
See also DLB 31

Hopley-Woolrich, Cornell George 1903-1968
See Woolrich, Cornell
See also CA 13-14; CANR 58; CAP 1

Horatio
See Proust, (Valentin-Louis-George-Eugene-)
Marcel

**Horgan, Paul (George Vincent O'Shaughnessy)
1903-1995 .... CLC 9, 53; DAM NOV**
See also CA 13-16R; 147; CANR 9, 35; DLB
102; DLBY 85; INT CANR-9; MTCW;
SATA 13; SATA-Obit 84

Horn, Peter
See Kuttner, Henry

Hornem, Horace Esq.
See Byron, George Gordon (Noel)

**Horney, Karen (Clementine Theodore
Danielsen) 1885-1952 .... TCLC 71**
See also CA 114; 165

**Hornung, E(rnest) W(illiam) 1866-1921
TCLC 59**
See also CA 108; 160; DLB 70

**Horovitz, Israel (Arthur) 1939-CLC 56; DAM
DRAM**
See also CA 33-36R; CANR 46, 59; DLB 7

Horvath, Odon von
See Horvath, Oedoen von
See also DLB 85, 124

Horvath, Oedoen von 1901-1938 ... TCLC 45
See also Horvath, Odon von
See also CA 118

Horwitz, Julius 1920-1986................ CLC 14
See also CA 9-12R; 119; CANR 12

Hospital, Janette Turner 1942- .... CLC 42
See also CA 108; CANR 48

Hostos, E. M. de
See Hostos (y Bonilla), Eugenio Maria de

Hostos, Eugenio M. de
See Hostos (y Bonilla), Eugenio Maria de

Hostos, Eugenio Maria
See Hostos (y Bonilla), Eugenio Maria de

**Hostos (y Bonilla), Eugenio Maria de 1839-
1903 .... TCLC 24**
See also CA 123; 131; HW

Houdini
See Lovecraft, H(oward) P(hillips)

Hougan, Carolyn 1943-..................... CLC 34
See also CA 139

**Household, Geoffrey (Edward West) 1900-1988
CLC 11**
See also CA 77-80; 126; CANR 58; DLB 87;
SATA 14; SATA-Obit 59

**Housman, A(lfred) 1859-1936
TCLC 1, 10; DA; DAB; DAC; DAM MST,
POET; PC 2; WLCS**
See also CA 104; 125; DLB 19; MTCW

Housman, Laurence 1865-1959 .... TCLC 7
See also CA 106; 155; DLB 10; SATA 25

Howard, Elizabeth Jane 1923-...... CLC 7, 29
See also CA 5-8R; CANR 8, 62

Howard, Maureen 1930-........ CLC 5, 14, 46
See also CA 53-56; CANR 31; DLBY 83; INT
CANR-31; MTCW

Howard, Richard 1929- .... CLC 7, 10, 47
See also AITN 1; CA 85-88; CANR 25; DLB 5;
INT CANR-25

Howard, Robert E(rvin) 1906-1936 TCLC 8
See also CA 105; 157

NCLC 42
See also CDBLB 1832-1890; DLB 32, 55
MacBeth, George (Mann) 1932-1992**CLC 2, 5, 9**
See also CA 25-28R; 136; CANR 61, 66; DLB 40; MTCW; SATA 4; SATA-Obit 70
MacCaig, Norman (Alexander) 1910-**CLC 36; DAB; DAM POET**
See also CA 9-12R; CANR 3, 34; DLB 27
MacCarthy, (Sir Charles Otto) Desmond 1877-1952 .... **TCLC 36**
MacDiarmid, Hugh**CLC 2, 4, 11, 19, 63; PC 9**
See also Grieve, C(hristopher) M(urray)
See also CDBLB 1945-1960; DLB 20
MacDonald, Anson
See Heinlein, Robert A(nson)
Macdonald, Cynthia 1928- .... **CLC 13, 19**
See also CA 49-52; CANR 4, 44; DLB 105
MacDonald, George 1824-1905 .... **TCLC 9**
See also CA 106; 137; DLB 18, 163, 178; MAICYA; SATA 33
Macdonald, John
See Millar, Kenneth
MacDonald, John D(ann) 1916-1986 **CLC 3, 27, 44; DAM NOV, POP**
See also CA 1-4R; 121; CANR 1, 19, 60; DLB 8; DLBY 86; MTCW
Macdonald, John Ross
See Millar, Kenneth
Macdonald, Ross .... **CLC 1, 2, 3, 14, 34, 41**
See also Millar, Kenneth
See also DLBD 6
MacDougal, John
See Blish, James (Benjamin)
MacEwen, Gwendolyn (Margaret) 1941-1987 **CLC 13, 55**
See also CA 9-12R; 124; CANR 7, 22; DLB 53; SATA 50; SATA-Obit 55
Macha, Karel Hynek 1810-1846 .... **NCLC 46**
Machado (y Ruiz), Antonio 1875-1939**T C L C 3**
See also CA 104; DLB 108
Machado de Assis, Joaquim Maria 1839-1908 **TCLC 10; BLC; SSC 24**
See also CA 107; 153
Machen, Arthur .... **TCLC 4; SSC 20**
See also Jones, Arthur Llewellyn
See also DLB 36, 156, 178
Machiavelli, Niccolo 1469-1527**LC 8, 36; DA; DAB; DAC; DAM MST; WLCS**
MacInnes, Colin 1914-1976 .... **CLC 4, 23**
See also CA 69-72; 65-68; CANR 21; DLB 14; MTCW
MacInnes, Helen (Clark) 1907-1985 **CLC 27, 39; DAM POP**
See also CA 1-4R; 117; CANR 1, 28, 58; DLB 87; MTCW; SATA 22; SATA-Obit 44
Mackay, Mary 1855-1924
See Corelli, Marie
See also CA 118
Mackenzie, Compton (Edward Montague) 1883-1972 .... **CLC 18**
See also CA 21-22; 37-40R; CAP 2; DLB 34, 100
Mackenzie, Henry 1745-1831 .... **NCLC 41**
See also DLB 39
Mackintosh, Elizabeth 1896(?)-1952
See Tey, Josephine
See also CA 110
MacLaren, James
See Grieve, C(hristopher) M(urray)
Mac Laverty, Bernard 1942- .... **CLC 31**
See also CA 116; 118; CANR 43; INT 118

MacLean, Alistair (Stuart) 1922(?)-1987**C L C 3, 13, 50, 63; DAM POP**
See also CA 57-60; 121; CANR 28, 61; MTCW; SATA 23; SATA-Obit 50
Maclean, Norman (Fitzroy) 1902-1990 . **C L C 78; DAM POP; SSC 13**
See also CA 102; 132; CANR 49
MacLeish, Archibald 1892-1982**CLC 3, 8, 14, 68; DAM POET**
See also CA 9-12R; 106; CANR 33, 63; DLB 4, 7, 45; DLBY 82; MTCW
MacLennan, (John) Hugh 1907-1990 **CLC 2, 14, 92; DAC; DAM MST**
See also CA 5-8R; 142; CANR 33; DLB 68; MTCW
MacLeod, Alistair 1936-**CLC 56; DAC; DAM MST**
See also CA 123; DLB 60
Macleod, Fiona
See Sharp, William
MacNeice, (Frederick) Louis 1907-1963**C L C 1, 4, 10, 53; DAB; DAM POET**
See also CA 85-88; CANR 61; DLB 10, 20; MTCW
MacNeill, Dand
See Fraser, George MacDonald
Macpherson, James 1736-1796 .... **LC 29**
See also DLB 109
Macpherson, (Jean) Jay 1931- .... **CLC 14**
See also CA 5-8R; DLB 53
MacShane, Frank 1927- .... **CLC 39**
See also CA 9-12R; CANR 3, 33; DLB 111
Macumber, Mari
See Sandoz, Mari(e Susette)
Madach, Imre 1823-1864 .... **NCLC 19**
Madden, (Jerry) David 1933- .... **CLC 5, 15**
See also CA 1-4R; CAAS 3; CANR 4, 45; DLB 6; MTCW
Maddern, Al(an)
See Ellison, Harlan (Jay)
Madhubuti, Haki R. 1942- **CLC 6, 73; BLC; DAM MULT, POET; PC 5**
See also Lee, Don L.
See also BW 2; CA 73-76; CANR 24, 51; DLB 5, 41; DLBD 8
Maepenn, Hugh
See Kuttner, Henry
Maepenn, K. H.
See Kuttner, Henry
Maeterlinck, Maurice 1862-1949 .... **TCLC 3; DAM DRAM**
See also CA 104; 136; DLB 192; SATA 66
Maginn, William 1794-1842 .... **NCLC 8**
See also DLB 110, 159
Mahapatra, Jayanta 1928- .... **CLC 33; DAM MULT**
See also CA 73-76; CAAS 9; CANR 15, 33, 66
Mahfouz, Naguib (Abdel Aziz Al-Sabilgi) 1911(?)-
See Mahfuz, Najib
See also BEST 89:2; CA 128; CANR 55; DAM NOV; MTCW
Mahfuz, Najib .... **CLC 52, 55**
See also Mahfouz, Naguib (Abdel Aziz Al-Sabilgi)
See also DLBY 88
Mahon, Derek 1941- .... **CLC 27**
See also CA 113; 128; DLB 40
Mailer, Norman 1923-**CLC 1, 2, 3, 4, 5, 8, 11, 14, 28, 39, 74; DA; DAB; DAC; DAM MST, NOV, POP**
See also AITN 2; CA 9-12R; CABS 1; CANR 28; CDALB 1968-1988; DLB 2, 16, 28, 185;

DLBD 3; DLBY 80, 83; MTCW
Maillet, Antonine 1929- .... **CLC 54; DAC**
See also CA 115; 120; CANR 46; DLB 60; INT 120
Mais, Roger 1905-1955 .... **TCLC 8**
See also BW 1; CA 105; 124; DLB 125; MTCW
Maistre, Joseph de 1753-1821 .... **NCLC 37**
Maitland, Frederic 1850-1906 .... **TCLC 65**
Maitland, Sara (Louise) 1950- .... **CLC 49**
See also CA 69-72; CANR 13, 59
Major, Clarence 1936- **CLC 3, 19, 48; BLC; DAM MULT**
See also BW 2; CA 21-24R; CAAS 6; CANR 13, 25, 53; DLB 33
Major, Kevin (Gerald) 1949-..**CLC 26; DAC**
See also AAYA 16; CA 97-100; CANR 21, 38; CLR 11; DLB 60; INT CANR-21; JRDA; MAICYA; SATA 32, 82
Maki, James
See Ozu, Yasujiro
Malabaila, Damiano
See Levi, Primo
Malamud, Bernard 1914-1986**CLC 1, 2, 3, 5, 8, 9, 11, 18, 27, 44, 78, 85; DA; DAB; DAC; DAM MST, NOV, POP; SSC 15; WLC**
See also AAYA 16; CA 5-8R; 118; CABS 1; CANR 28, 62; CDALB 1941-1968; DLB 2, 28, 152; DLBY 80, 86; MTCW
Malan, Herman
See Bosman, Herman Charles; Bosman, Herman Charles
Malaparte, Curzio 1898-1957 .... **TCLC 52**
Malcolm, Dan
See Silverberg, Robert
Malcolm X .... **CLC 82; BLC; WLCS**
See also Little, Malcolm
Malherbe, Francois de 1555-1628 .... **LC 5**
Mallarme, Stephane 1842-1898 **NCLC 4, 41; DAM POET; PC 4**
Mallet-Joris, Francoise 1930- .... **CLC 11**
See also CA 65-68; CANR 17; DLB 83
Malley, Ern
See McAuley, James Phillip
Mallowan, Agatha Christie
See Christie, Agatha (Mary Clarissa)
Maloff, Saul 1922- ....**CLC 5**
See also CA 33-36R
Malone, Louis
See MacNeice, (Frederick) Louis
Malone, Michael (Christopher) 1942-**CLC 43**
See also CA 77-80; CANR 14, 32, 57
Malory, (Sir) Thomas 1410(?)-1471(?)**LC 11; DA; DAB; DAC; DAM MST; WLCS**
See also CDBLB Before 1660; DLB 146; SATA 59; SATA-Brief 33
Malouf, (George Joseph) David 1934-**CLC 28, 86**
See also CA 124; CANR 50
Malraux, (Georges-)Andre 1901-1976**CLC 1, 4, 9, 13, 15, 57; DAM NOV**
See also CA 21-22; 69-72; CANR 34, 58; CAP 2; DLB 72; MTCW
Malzberg, Barry N(athaniel) 1939- .... **CLC 7**
See also CA 61-64; CAAS 4; CANR 16; DLB 8
Mamet, David (Alan) 1947-**CLC 9, 15, 34, 46, 91; DAM DRAM; DC 4**
See also AAYA 3; CA 81-84; CABS 3; CANR 15, 41, 67; DLB 7; MTCW
Mamoulian, Rouben (Zachary) 1897-1987 **CLC 16**
See also CA 25-28R; 124
Mandelstam, Osip (Emilievich) 1891(?)-1938(?)

TCLC 2, 6; PC 14
See also CA 104; 150
Mander, (Mary) Jane 1877-1949 ... **TCLC 31**
See also CA 162
Mandeville, John fl. 1350- .... **CMLC 19**
See also DLB 146
Mandiargues, Andre Pieyre de .... **CLC 41**
See also Pieyre de Mandiargues, Andre
See also DLB 83
Mandrake, Ethel Belle
See Thurman, Wallace (Henry)
Mangan, James Clarence 1803-1849**NCLC 27**
Maniere, J.-E.
See Giraudoux, (Hippolyte) Jean
Manley, (Mary) Delariviere 1672(?)-1724 **L C 1**
See also DLB 39, 80
Mann, Abel
See Creasey, John
Mann, Emily 1952- .... **DC 7**
See also CA 130; CANR 55
Mann, (Luiz) Heinrich 1871-1950 ... **TCLC 9**
See also CA 106; 164; DLB 66
Mann, (Paul) Thomas 1875-1955 **TCLC 2, 8, 14, 21, 35, 44, 60; DA; DAB; DAC; DAM MST, NOV; SSC 5; WLC**
See also CA 104; 128; DLB 66; MTCW
Mannheim, Karl 1893-1947 .... **TCLC 65**
Manning, David
See Faust, Frederick (Schiller)
Manning, Frederic 1887(?)-1935 ... **TCLC 25**
See also CA 124
Manning, Olivia 1915-1980 .... **CLC 5, 19**
See also CA 5-8R; 101; CANR 29; MTCW
Mano, D. Keith 1942- .... **CLC 2, 10**
See also CA 25-28R; CAAS 6; CANR 26, 57; DLB 6
Mansfield, Katherine **TCLC 2, 8, 39; DAB; SSC 9, 23; WLC**
See also Beauchamp, Kathleen Mansfield
See also DLB 162
Manso, Peter 1940- .... **CLC 39**
See also CA 29-32R; CANR 44
Mantecon, Juan Jimenez
See Jimenez (Mantecon), Juan Ramon
Manton, Peter
See Creasey, John
Man Without a Spleen, A
See Chekhov, Anton (Pavlovich)
Manzoni, Alessandro 1785-1873 .... **NCLC 29**
Mapu, Abraham (ben Jekutiel) 1808-1867 **NCLC 18**
Mara, Sally
See Queneau, Raymond
Marat, Jean Paul 1743-1793 .... **LC 10**
Marcel, Gabriel Honore 1889-1973 . **CLC 15**
See also CA 102; 45-48; MTCW
Marchbanks, Samuel
See Davies, (William) Robertson
Marchi, Giacomo
See Bassani, Giorgio
Margulies, Donald .... **CLC 76**
Marie de France c. 12th cent. - .... **CMLC 8**
Marie de l'Incarnation 1599-1672 ...... **LC 10**
Marier, Captain Victor
See Griffith, D(avid Lewelyn) W(ark)
Mariner, Scott
See Pohl, Frederik
Marinetti, Filippo Tommaso 1876-1944**TCLC 10**
See also CA 107; DLB 114
Marivaux, Pierre Carlet de Chamblain de 1688-1763 .... **LC 4; DC 7**

Markandaya, Kamala .... **CLC 8, 38**
See also Taylor, Kamala (Purnaiya)
Markfield, Wallace 1926- .... **CLC 8**
See also CA 69-72; CAAS 3; DLB 2, 28
Markham, Edwin 1852-1940 .... **TCLC 47**
See also CA 160; DLB 54, 186
Markham, Robert
See Amis, Kingsley (William)
Marks, J
See Highwater, Jamake (Mamake)
Marks-Highwater, J
See Highwater, Jamake (Mamake)
Markson, David M(errill) 1927- .... **CLC 67**
See also CA 49-52; CANR 1
Marley, Bob ....**CLC 17**
See also Marley, Robert Nesta
Marley, Robert Nesta 1945-1981
See Marley, Bob
See also CA 107; 103
Marlowe, Christopher 1564-1593**LC 22; DA; DAB; DAC; DAM DRAM, MST; DC 1; WLC**
See also CDBLB Before 1660; DLB 62
Marlowe, Stephen 1928-
See Queen, Ellery
See also CA 13-16R; CANR 6, 55
Marmontel, Jean-Francois 1723-1799 . **LC 2**
Marquand, John P(hillips) 1893-1960**CLC 2, 10**
See also CA 85-88; DLB 9, 102
Marques, Rene 1919-1979 ..... **CLC 96; DAM MULT; HLC**
See also CA 97-100; 85-88; DLB 113; HW
Marquez, Gabriel (Jose) Garcia
See Garcia Marquez, Gabriel (Jose)
Marquis, Don(ald Robert Perry) 1878-1937 **TCLC 7**
See also CA 104; DLB 11, 25
Marric, J. J.
See Creasey, John
Marryat, Frederick 1792-1848 .... **NCLC 3**
See also DLB 21, 163
Marsden, James
See Creasey, John
Marsh, (Edith) Ngaio 1899-1982 **CLC 7, 53; DAM POP**
See also CA 9-12R; CANR 6, 58; DLB 77; MTCW
Marshall, Garry 1934- .... **CLC 17**
See also AAYA 3; CA 111; SATA 60
Marshall, Paule 1929-**CLC 27, 72; BLC; DAM MULT; SSC 3**
See also BW 2; CA 77-80; CANR 25; DLB 157; MTCW
Marsten, Richard
See Hunter, Evan
Marston, John 1576-1634**LC 33; DAM DRAM**
See also DLB 58, 172
Martha, Henry
See Harris, Mark
Marti, Jose 1853-1895**NCLC 63; DAM MULT; HLC**
Martial c. 40-c. 104 .... **PC 10**
Martin, Ken
See Hubbard, L(afayette) Ron(ald)
Martin, Richard
See Creasey, John
Martin, Steve 1945- .... **CLC 30**
See also CA 97-100; CANR 30; MTCW
Martin, Valerie 1948- ....**CLC 89**
See also BEST 90:2; CA 85-88; CANR 49
Martin, Violet Florence 1862-1915 **TCLC 51**
Martin, Webber

See Silverberg, Robert
Martindale, Patrick Victor
See White, Patrick (Victor Martindale)
Martin du Gard, Roger 1881-1958 **TCLC 24**
See also CA 118; DLB 65
Martineau, Harriet 1802-1876 .... **NCLC 26**
See also DLB 21, 55, 159, 163, 166, 190; YABC 2
Martines, Julia
See O'Faolain, Julia
Martinez, Enrique Gonzalez
See Gonzalez Martinez, Enrique
Martinez, Jacinto Benavente y
See Benavente (y Martinez), Jacinto
Martinez Ruiz, Jose 1873-1967
See Azorin; Ruiz, Jose Martinez
See also CA 93-96; HW
Martinez Sierra, Gregorio 1881-1947**TCLC 6**
See also CA 115
Martinez Sierra, Maria (de la O'LeJarraga) 1874-1974 .... **TCLC 6**
See also CA 115
Martinsen, Martin
See Follett, Ken(neth Martin)
Martinson, Harry (Edmund) 1904-1978**C L C 14**
See also CA 77-80; CANR 34
Marut, Ret
See Traven, B.
Marut, Robert
See Traven, B.
Marvell, Andrew 1621-1678**LC 4; DA; DAB; DAC; DAM MST, POET; PC 10; WLC**
See also CDBLB 1660-1789; DLB 131
Marx, Karl (Heinrich) 1818-1883 . **NCLC 17**
See also DLB 129
Masaoka Shiki .... **TCLC 18**
See also Masaoka Tsunenori
Masaoka Tsunenori 1867-1902
See Masaoka Shiki
See also CA 117
Masefield, John (Edward) 1878-1967**CLC 11, 47; DAM POET**
See also CA 19-20; 25-28R; CANR 33; CAP 2; CDBLB 1890-1914; DLB 10, 19, 153, 160; MTCW; SATA 19
Maso, Carole 19(?)- .... **CLC 44**
Mason, Bobbie Ann 1940-**CLC 28, 43, 82; SSC 4**
See also AAYA 5; CA 53-56; CANR 11, 31, 58; DLB 173; DLBY 87; INT CANR-31; MTCW
Mason, Ernst
See Pohl, Frederik
Mason, Lee W.
See Malzberg, Barry N(athaniel)
Mason, Nick 1945- .... **CLC 35**
Mason, Tally
See Derleth, August (William)
Mass, William
See Gibson, William
Masters, Edgar Lee 1868-1950 **TCLC 2, 25; DA; DAC; DAM MST, POET; PC 1; WLCS**
See also CA 104; 133; CDALB 1865-1917; DLB 54; MTCW
Masters, Hilary 1928- .... **CLC 48**
See also CA 25-28R; CANR 13, 47
Mastrosimone, William 19(?)- .... **CLC 36**
Mathe, Albert
See Camus, Albert
Mather, Cotton 1663-1728 .... **LC 38**
See also CDALB 1640-1865; DLB 24, 30, 140

See also CA 146

Minehaha, Cornelius
See Wedekind, (Benjamin) Frank(lin)

Miner, Valerie 1947- .... **CLC 40**
See also CA 97-100; CANR 59

Minimo, Duca
See D'Annunzio, Gabriele

Minot, Susan 1956- .... **CLC 44**
See also CA 134

Minus, Ed 1938- .... **CLC 39**

Miranda, Javier
See Bioy Casares, Adolfo

Mirbeau, Octave 1848-1917 .... **TCLC 55**
See also DLB 123, 192

Miro (Ferrer), Gabriel (Francisco Victor) 1879-
1930 .... **TCLC 5**
See also CA 104

Mishima, Yukio 1925-1970CLC 2, 4, 6, 9, 27;
DC 1; SSC 4
See also Hiraoka, Kimitake
See also DLB 182

Mistral, Frederic 1830-1914 .... **TCLC 51**
See also CA 122

Mistral, Gabriela .... **TCLC 2; HLC**
See also Godoy Alcayaga, Lucila

Mistry, Rohinton 1952- .... **CLC 71; DAC**
See also CA 141

Mitchell, Clyde
See Ellison, Harlan (Jay); Silverberg, Robert

Mitchell, James Leslie 1901-1935
See Gibbon, Lewis Grassic
See also CA 104; DLB 15

Mitchell, Joni 1943- .... **CLC 12**
See also CA 112

Mitchell, Joseph (Quincy) 1908-1996CLC 98
See also CA 77-80; 152; DLB 185; DLBY 96

Mitchell, Margaret (Munnerlyn) 1900-1949
TCLC 11; DAM NOV, POP
See also AAYA 23; CA 109; 125; CANR 55;
DLB 9; MTCW

Mitchell, Peggy
See Mitchell, Margaret (Munnerlyn)

Mitchell, S(ilas) Weir 1829-1914 ... **TCLC 36**
See also CA 165

Mitchell, W(illiam) O(rmond) 1914-1998CLC
25; DAC; DAM MST
See also CA 77-80; 165; CANR 15, 43; DLB
88

Mitford, Mary Russell 1787-1855 ...NCLC 4
See also DLB 110, 116

Mitford, Nancy 1904-1973 .... **CLC 44**
See also CA 9-12R; DLB 191

Miyamoto, Yuriko 1899-1951 .... **TCLC 37**
See also DLB 180

Miyazawa, Kenji 1896-1933 .... **TCLC 76**
See also CA 157

Mizoguchi, Kenji 1898-1956 .... **TCLC 72**

Mo, Timothy (Peter) 1950(?)- .... **CLC 46**
See also CA 117; DLB 194; MTCW

Modarressi, Taghi (M.) 1931- .... **CLC 44**
See also CA 121; 134; INT 134

Modiano, Patrick (Jean) 1945- .... **CLC 18**
See also CA 85-88; CANR 17, 40; DLB 83

Moerck, Paal
See Roelvaag, O(le) E(dvart)

Mofolo, Thomas (Mokopu) 1875(?)-1948
TCLC 22; BLC; DAM MULT
See also CA 121; 153

Mohr, Nicholasa 1938-CLC 12; DAM MULT;
HLC
See also AAYA 8; CA 49-52; CANR 1, 32, 64;
CLR 22; DLB 145; HW; JRDA; SAAS 8;
SATA 8, 97

Mojtabai, A(nn) G(race) 1938- CLC 5, 9, 15,
29
See also CA 85-88

Moliere 1622-1673 . LC 28; DA; DAB; DAC;
DAM DRAM, MST; WLC

Molin, Charles
See Mayne, William (James Carter)

Molnar, Ferenc 1878-1952 .. TCLC 20; DAM
DRAM
See also CA 109; 153

Momaday, N(avarre) Scott 1934- CLC 2, 19,
85, 95; DA; DAB; DAC; DAM MST,
MULT, NOV, POP; WLCS
See also AAYA 11; CA 25-28R; CANR 14, 34,
68; DLB 143, 175; INT CANR-14; MTCW;
NNAL; SATA 48; SATA-Brief 30

Monette, Paul 1945-1995 .... **CLC 82**
See also CA 139; 147

Monroe, Harriet 1860-1936 .... **TCLC 12**
See also CA 109; DLB 54, 91

Monroe, Lyle
See Heinlein, Robert A(nson)

Montagu, Elizabeth 1917- .... **NCLC 7**
See also CA 9-12R

Montagu, Mary (Pierrepont) Wortley 1689-
1762 .... **LC 9; PC 16**
See also DLB 95, 101

Montagu, W. H.
See Coleridge, Samuel Taylor

Montague, John (Patrick) 1929- CLC 13, 46
See also CA 9-12R; CANR 9; DLB 40; MTCW

Montaigne, Michel (Eyquem) de 1533-1592
LC 8; DA; DAB; DAC; DAM MST; WLC

Montale, Eugenio 1896-1981CLC 7, 9, 18; PC
13
See also CA 17-20R; 104; CANR 30; DLB 114;
MTCW

Montesquieu, Charles-Louis de Secondat 1689-
1755 .... **LC 7**

Montgomery, (Robert) Bruce 1921-1978
See Crispin, Edmund
See also CA 104

Montgomery, L(ucy) M(aud) 1874-1942
TCLC 51; DAC; DAM MST
See also AAYA 12; CA 108; 137; CLR 8; DLB
92; DLBD 14; JRDA; MAICYA; YABC 1

Montgomery, Marion H., Jr. 1925- .... **CLC 7**
See also AITN 1; CA 1-4R; CANR 3, 48; DLB
6

Montgomery, Max
See Davenport, Guy (Mattison, Jr.)

Montherlant, Henry (Milon) de 1896-1972
CLC 8, 19; DAM DRAM
See also CA 85-88; 37-40R; DLB 72; MTCW

Monty Python
See Chapman, Graham; Cleese, John
(Marwood); Gilliam, Terry (Vance); Idle,
Eric; Jones, Terence Graham Parry; Palin,
Michael (Edward)
See also AAYA 7

Moodie, Susanna (Strickland) 1803-1885
NCLC 14
See also DLB 99

Mooney, Edward 1951-
See Mooney, Ted
See also CA 130

Mooney, Ted .... **CLC 25**
See also Mooney, Edward

Moorcock, Michael (John) 1939-CLC 5, 27, 58
See also CA 45-48; CAAS 5; CANR 2, 17, 38,
64; DLB 14; MTCW; SATA 93

Moore, Brian 1921- CLC 1, 3, 5, 7, 8, 19, 32,
90; DAB; DAC; DAM MST

See also CA 1-4R; CANR 1, 25, 42, 63; MTCW

Moore, Edward
See Muir, Edwin

Moore, George Augustus 1852-1933TCLC 7;
SSC 19
See also CA 104; DLB 10, 18, 57, 135

Moore, Lorrie .... CLC 39, 45, 68
See also Moore, Marie Lorena

Moore, Marianne (Craig) 1887-1972CLC 1, 2,
4, 8, 10, 13, 19, 47; DA; DAB; DAC; DAM
MST, POET; PC 4; WLCS
See also CA 1-4R; 33-36R; CANR 3, 61;
CDALB 1929-1941; DLB 45; DLBD 7;
MTCW; SATA 20

Moore, Marie Lorena 1957-
See Moore, Lorrie
See also CA 116; CANR 39

Moore, Thomas 1779-1852 .... **NCLC 6**
See also DLB 96, 144

Morand, Paul 1888-1976 .... CLC 41; SSC 22
See also CA 69-72; DLB 65

Morante, Elsa 1918-1985 .... CLC 8, 47
See also CA 85-88; 117; CANR 35; DLB 177;
MTCW

Moravia, Alberto 1907-1990CLC 2, 7, 11, 27,
46; SSC 26
See also Pincherle, Alberto
See also DLB 177

More, Hannah 1745-1833 .... **NCLC 27**
See also DLB 107, 109, 116, 158

More, Henry 1614-1687 .... **LC 9**
See also DLB 126

More, Sir Thomas 1478-1535 .... LC 10, 32

Moreas, Jean .... **TCLC 18**
See also Papadiamantopoulos, Johannes

Morgan, Berry 1919- ....CLC 6
See also CA 49-52; DLB 6

Morgan, Claire
See Highsmith, (Mary) Patricia

Morgan, Edwin (George) 1920- .... **CLC 31**
See also CA 5-8R; CANR 3, 43; DLB 27

Morgan, (George) Frederick 1922- . **CLC 23**
See also CA 17-20R; CANR 21

Morgan, Harriet
See Mencken, H(enry) L(ouis)

Morgan, Jane
See Cooper, James Fenimore

Morgan, Janet 1945- .... **CLC 39**
See also CA 65-68

Morgan, Lady 1776(?)-1859 .... **NCLC 29**
See also DLB 116, 158

Morgan, Robin (Evonne) 1941- ....CLC 2
See also CA 69-72; CANR 29, 68; MTCW;
SATA 80

Morgan, Scott
See Kuttner, Henry

Morgan, Seth 1949(?)-1990 .... **CLC 65**
See also CA 132

Morgenstern, Christian 1871-1914 . **TCLC 8**
See also CA 105

Morgenstern, S.
See Goldman, William (W.)

Moricz, Zsigmond 1879-1942 .... **TCLC 33**
See also CA 165

Morike, Eduard (Friedrich) 1804-1875NCLC
10
See also DLB 133

Moritz, Karl Philipp 1756-1793 .... **LC 2**
See also DLB 94

Morland, Peter Henry
See Faust, Frederick (Schiller)

Morren, Theophil
See Hofmannsthal, Hugo von

See Clarke, Arthur C(harles)

O'Brien, Edna 1936- **CLC 3, 5, 8, 13, 36, 65; DAM NOV; SSC 10**
See also CA 1-4R; CANR 6, 41, 65; CDBLB 1960 to Present; DLB 14; MTCW

O'Brien, Fitz-James 1828-1862 ..... **NCLC 21**
See also DLB 74

O'Brien, Flann .... **CLC 1, 4, 5, 7, 10, 47**
See also O Nuallain, Brian

O'Brien, Richard 1942- .... **CLC 17**
See also CA 124

O'Brien, (William) Tim(othy) 1946- .**CLC 7, 19, 40, 103; DAM POP**
See also AAYA 16; CA 85-88; CANR 40, 58; DLB 152; DLBD 9; DLBY 80

Obstfelder, Sigbjoern 1866-1900 ... **TCLC 23**
See also CA 123

O'Casey, Sean 1880-1964**CLC 1, 5, 9, 11, 15, 88; DAB; DAC; DAM DRAM, MST; WLCS**
See also CA 89-92; CANR 62; CDBLB 1914-1945; DLB 10; MTCW

O'Cathasaigh, Sean
See O'Casey, Sean

Ochs, Phil 1940-1976 .... **CLC 17**
See also CA 65-68

O'Connor, Edwin (Greene) 1918-1968**CLC 14**
See also CA 93-96; 25-28R

O'Connor, (Mary) Flannery 1925-1964 **C L C 1, 2, 3, 6, 10, 13, 15, 21, 66, 104; DA; DAB; DAC; DAM MST, NOV; SSC 1, 23; WLC**
See also AAYA 7; CA 1-4R; CANR 3, 41; CDALB 1941-1968; DLB 2, 152; DLBD 12; DLBY 80; MTCW

O'Connor, Frank .... **CLC 23; SSC 5**
See also O'Donovan, Michael John
See also DLB 162

O'Dell, Scott 1898-1989 .... **CLC 30**
See also AAYA 3; CA 61-64; 129; CANR 12, 30; CLR 1, 16; DLB 52; JRDA; MAICYA; SATA 12, 60

Odets, Clifford 1906-1963**CLC 2, 28, 98; DAM DRAM; DC 6**
See also CA 85-88; CANR 62; DLB 7, 26; MTCW

O'Doherty, Brian 1934- .... **CLC 76**
See also CA 105

O'Donnell, K. M.
See Malzberg, Barry N(athaniel)

O'Donnell, Lawrence
See Kuttner, Henry

O'Donovan, Michael John 1903-1966**CLC 14**
See also O'Connor, Frank
See also CA 93-96

Oe, Kenzaburo 1935- **CLC 10, 36, 86; DAM NOV; SSC 20**
See also CA 97-100; CANR 36, 50; DLB 182; DLBY 94; MTCW

O'Faolain, Julia 1932- .... **CLC 6, 19, 47, 108**
See also CA 81-84; CAAS 2; CANR 12, 61; DLB 14; MTCW

O'Faolain, Sean 1900-1991 **CLC 1, 7, 14, 32, 70; SSC 13**
See also CA 61-64; 134; CANR 12, 66; DLB 15, 162; MTCW

O'Flaherty, Liam 1896-1984**CLC 5, 34; SSC 6**
See also CA 101; 113; CANR 35; DLB 36, 162; DLBY 84; MTCW

Ogilvy, Gavin
See Barrie, J(ames) M(atthew)

O'Grady, Standish (James) 1846-1928**T C L C 5**
See also CA 104; 157

O'Grady, Timothy 1951- .... **CLC 59**
See also CA 138

O'Hara, Frank 1926-1966 . **CLC 2, 5, 13, 78; DAM POET**
See also CA 9-12R; 25-28R; CANR 33; DLB 5, 16, 193; MTCW

O'Hara, John (Henry) 1905-1970**CLC 1, 2, 3, 6, 11, 42; DAM NOV; SSC 15**
See also CA 5-8R; 25-28R; CANR 31, 60; CDALB 1929-1941; DLB 9, 86; DLBD 2; MTCW

O Hehir, Diana 1922- .... **CLC 41**
See also CA 93-96

Okigbo, Christopher (Ifenayichukwu) 1932-1967 ... **CLC 25, 84; BLC; DAM MULT, POET; PC 7**
See also BW 1; CA 77-80; DLB 125; MTCW

Okri, Ben 1959- .... **CLC 87**
See also BW 2; CA 130; 138; CANR 65; DLB 157; INT 138

Olds, Sharon 1942- .... **CLC 32, 39, 85; DAM POET; PC 22**
See also CA 101; CANR 18, 41, 66; DLB 120

Oldstyle, Jonathan
See Irving, Washington

Olesha, Yuri (Karlovich) 1899-1960 ... **CLC 8**
See also CA 85-88

Oliphant, Laurence 1829(?)-1888 .. **NCLC 47**
See also DLB 18, 166

Oliphant, Margaret (Oliphant Wilson) 1828-1897 .... **NCLC 11, 61; SSC 25**
See also DLB 18, 159, 190

Oliver, Mary 1935- .... **CLC 19, 34, 98**
See also CA 21-24R; CANR 9, 43; DLB 5, 193

Olivier, Laurence (Kerr) 1907-1989 . **CLC 20**
See also CA 111; 150; 129

Olsen, Tillie 1913-**CLC 4, 13; DA; DAB; DAC; DAM MST; SSC 11**
See also CA 1-4R; CANR 1, 43; DLB 28; DLBY 80; MTCW

Olson, Charles (John) 1910-1970**CLC 1, 2, 5, 6, 9, 11, 29; DAM POET; PC 19**
See also CA 13-16; 25-28R; CABS 2; CANR 35, 61; CAP 1; DLB 5, 16, 193; MTCW

Olson, Toby 1937- .... **CLC 28**
See also CA 65-68; CANR 9, 31

Olyesha, Yuri
See Olesha, Yuri (Karlovich)

Ondaatje, (Philip) Michael 1943-**CLC 14, 29, 51, 76; DAB; DAC; DAM MST**
See also CA 77-80; CANR 42; DLB 60

Oneal, Elizabeth 1934-
See Oneal, Zibby
See also CA 106; CANR 28; MAICYA; SATA 30, 82

Oneal, Zibby .... **CLC 30**
See also Oneal, Elizabeth
See also AAYA 5; CLR 13; JRDA

O'Neill, Eugene (Gladstone) 1888-1953**TCLC 1, 6, 27, 49; DA; DAB; DAC; DAM DRAM, MST; WLC**
See also AITN 1; CA 110; 132; CDALB 1929-1941; DLB 7; MTCW

Onetti, Juan Carlos 1909-1994 ... **CLC 7, 10; DAM MULT, NOV; SSC 23**
See also CA 85-88; 145; CANR 32, 63; DLB 113; HW; MTCW

O Nuallain, Brian 1911-1966
See O'Brien, Flann
See also CA 21-22; 25-28R; CAP 2

Ophuls, Max 1902-1957 .... **TCLC 79**
See also CA 113

Opie, Amelia 1769-1853 .... **NCLC 65**

See also DLB 116, 159

Oppen, George 1908-1984 ...... **CLC 7, 13, 34**
See also CA 13-16R; 113; CANR 8; DLB 5, 165

Oppenheim, E(dward) Phillips 1866-1946 **TCLC 45**
See also CA 111; DLB 70

Opuls, Max
See Ophuls, Max

Origen c. 185-c. 254 .... **CMLC 19**

Orlovitz, Gil 1918-1973 .... **CLC 22**
See also CA 77-80; 45-48; DLB 2, 5

Orris
See Ingelow, Jean

Ortega y Gasset, Jose 1883-1955 ....**TCLC 9; DAM MULT; HLC**
See also CA 106; 130; HW; MTCW

Ortese, Anna Maria 1914- .... **CLC 89**
See also DLB 177

Ortiz, Simon J(oseph) 1941- ..**CLC 45; DAM MULT, POET; PC 17**
See also CA 134; DLB 120, 175; NNAL

Orton, Joe .... **CLC 4, 13, 43; DC 3**
See also Orton, John Kingsley
See also CDBLB 1960 to Present; DLB 13

Orton, John Kingsley 1933-1967
See Orton, Joe
See also CA 85-88; CANR 35, 66; DAM DRAM; MTCW

Orwell, George **TCLC 2, 6, 15, 31, 51; DAB; WLC**
See also Blair, Eric (Arthur)
See also CDBLB 1945-1960; DLB 15, 98, 195

Osborne, David
See Silverberg, Robert

Osborne, George
See Silverberg, Robert

Osborne, John (James) 1929-1994**CLC 1, 2, 5, 11, 45; DA; DAB; DAC; DAM DRAM, MST; WLC**
See also CA 13-16R; 147; CANR 21, 56; CDBLB 1945-1960; DLB 13; MTCW

Osborne, Lawrence 1958- .... **CLC 50**

Oshima, Nagisa 1932- .... **CLC 20**
See also CA 116; 121

Oskison, John Milton 1874-1947 . **TCLC 35; DAM MULT**
See also CA 144; DLB 175; NNAL

Ossoli, Sarah Margaret (Fuller marchesa d') 1810-1850
See Fuller, Margaret
See also SATA 25

Ostrovsky, Alexander 1823-1886**NCLC 30, 57**

Otero, Blas de 1916-1979 .... **CLC 11**
See also CA 89-92; DLB 134

Otto, Whitney 1955- .... **CLC 70**
See also CA 140

Ouida .... **TCLC 43**
See also De La Ramee, (Marie) Louise
See also DLB 18, 156

Ousmane, Sembene 1923- .... **CLC 66; BLC**
See also BW 1; CA 117; 125; MTCW

Ovid 43B.C.-18(?)**CMLC 7; DAM POET; PC 2**

Owen, Hugh
See Faust, Frederick (Schiller)

Owen, Wilfred (Edward Salter) 1893-1918 **TCLC 5, 27; DA; DAB; DAC; DAM MST, POET; PC 19; WLC**
See also CA 104; 141; CDBLB 1914-1945; DLB 20

Owens, Rochelle 1936- .... **CLC 8**
See also CA 17-20R; CAAS 2; CANR 39

Oz, Amos 1939-CLC **5, 8, 11, 27, 33, 54; DAM NOV**
   See also CA 53-56; CANR 27, 47, 65; MTCW
Ozick, Cynthia 1928-CLC **3, 7, 28, 62; DAM NOV, POP; SSC 15**
   See also BEST 90:1; CA 17-20R; CANR 23, 58; DLB 28, 152; DLBY 82; INT CANR-23; MTCW
Ozu, Yasujiro 1903-1963 .... CLC **16**
   See also CA 112
Pacheco, C.
   See Pessoa, Fernando (Antonio Nogueira)
Pa Chin .... CLC **18**
   See also Li Fei-kan
Pack, Robert 1929- .... CLC **13**
   See also CA 1-4R; CANR 3, 44; DLB 5
Padgett, Lewis
   See Kuttner, Henry
Padilla (Lorenzo), Heberto 1932- .... CLC **38**
   See also AITN 1; CA 123; 131; HW
Page, Jimmy 1944- .... CLC **12**
Page, Louise 1955- .... CLC **40**
   See also CA 140
Page, P(atricia) K(athleen) 1916- CLC **7, 18; DAC; DAM MST; PC 12**
   See also CA 53-56; CANR 4, 22, 65; DLB 68; MTCW
Page, Thomas Nelson 1853-1922 .... SSC **23**
   See also CA 118; DLB 12, 78; DLBD 13
Pagels, Elaine Hiesey 1943- .... CLC **104**
   See also CA 45-48; CANR 2, 24, 51
Paget, Violet 1856-1935
   See Lee, Vernon
   See also CA 104
Paget-Lowe, Henry
   See Lovecraft, H(oward) P(hillips)
Paglia, Camille (Anna) 1947- .... CLC **68**
   See also CA 140
Paige, Richard
   See Koontz, Dean R(ay)
Paine, Thomas 1737-1809 .... NCLC **62**
   See also CDALB 1640-1865; DLB 31, 43, 73, 158
Pakenham, Antonia
   See Fraser, (Lady) Antonia (Pakenham)
Palamas, Kostes 1859-1943 .... TCLC **5**
   See also CA 105
Palazzeschi, Aldo 1885-1974 .... CLC **11**
   See also CA 89-92; 53-56; DLB 114
Paley, Grace 1922-CLC **4, 6, 37; DAM POP; SSC 8**
   See also CA 25-28R; CANR 13, 46; DLB 28; INT CANR-13; MTCW
Palin, Michael (Edward) 1943- .... CLC **21**
   See also Monty Python
   See also CA 107; CANR 35; SATA 67
Palliser, Charles 1947- .... CLC **65**
   See also CA 136
Palma, Ricardo 1833-1919 .... TCLC **29**
Pancake, Breece Dexter 1952-1979
   See Pancake, Breece D'J
   See also CA 123; 109
Pancake, Breece D'J .... CLC **29**
   See also Pancake, Breece Dexter
   See also DLB 130
Panko, Rudy
   See Gogol, Nikolai (Vasilyevich)
Papadiamantis, Alexandros 1851-1911 T C L C **29**
Papadiamantopoulos, Johannes 1856-1910
   See Moreas, Jean
   See also CA 117
Papini, Giovanni 1881-1956 .... TCLC **22**

See also CA 121
Paracelsus 1493-1541 .... LC **14**
   See also DLB 179
Parasol, Peter
   See Stevens, Wallace
Pardo Bazán, Emilia 1851-1921 .... SSC **30**
Pareto, Vilfredo 1848-1923 .... TCLC **69**
Parfenie, Maria
   See Codrescu, Andrei
Parini, Jay (Lee) 1948- .... CLC **54**
   See also CA 97-100; CAAS 16; CANR 32
Park, Jordan
   See Kornbluth, C(yril) M.; Pohl, Frederik
Park, Robert E(zra) 1864-1944 ...... TCLC **73**
   See also CA 122; 165
Parker, Bert
   See Ellison, Harlan (Jay)
Parker, Dorothy (Rothschild) 1893-1967C L C **15, 68; DAM POET; SSC 2**
   See also CA 19-20; 25-28R; CAP 2; DLB 11, 45, 86; MTCW
Parker, Robert B(rown) 1932-CLC **27; DAM NOV, POP**
   See also BEST 89:4; CA 49-52; CANR 1, 26, 52; INT CANR-26; MTCW
Parkin, Frank 1940- .... CLC **43**
   See also CA 147
Parkman, Francis, Jr. 1823-1893 ... NCLC **12**
   See also DLB 1, 30, 186
Parks, Gordon (Alexander Buchanan) 1912-CLC **1, 16; BLC; DAM MULT**
   See also AITN 2; BW 2; CA 41-44R; CANR 26, 66; DLB 33; SATA 8
Parmenides c. 515B.C.-c. 450B.C. CMLC **22**
   See also DLB 176
Parnell, Thomas 1679-1718 .... LC **3**
   See also DLB 94
Parra, Nicanor 1914- ...... CLC **2, 102; DAM MULT; HLC**
   See also CA 85-88; CANR 32; HW; MTCW
Parrish, Mary Frances
   See Fisher, M(ary) F(rances) K(ennedy)
Parson
   See Coleridge, Samuel Taylor
Parson Lot
   See Kingsley, Charles
Partridge, Anthony
   See Oppenheim, E(dward) Phillips
Pascal, Blaise 1623-1662 .... LC **35**
Pascoli, Giovanni 1855-1912 .... TCLC **45**
Pasolini, Pier Paolo 1922-1975 . CLC **20, 37, 106; PC 17**
   See also CA 93-96; 61-64; CANR 63; DLB 128, 177; MTCW
Pasquini
   See Silone, Ignazio
Pastan, Linda (Olenik) 1932- CLC **27; DAM POET**
   See also CA 61-64; CANR 18, 40, 61; DLB 5
Pasternak, Boris (Leonidovich) 1890-1960 CLC **7, 10, 18, 63; DA; DAB; DAC; DAM MST, NOV, POET; PC 6; WLC**
   See also CA 127; 116; MTCW
Patchen, Kenneth 1911-1972 ... CLC **1, 2, 18; DAM POET**
   See also CA 1-4R; 33-36R; CANR 3, 35; DLB 16, 48; MTCW
Pater, Walter (Horatio) 1839-1894 ..NCLC **7**
   See also CDBLB 1832-1890; DLB 57, 156
Paterson, A(ndrew) B(arton) 1864-1941 TCLC **32**
   See also CA 155; SATA 97
Paterson, Katherine (Womeldorf) 1932-C L C

12, 30
   See also AAYA 1; CA 21-24R; CANR 28, 59; CLR 7, 50; DLB 52; JRDA; MAICYA; MTCW; SATA 13, 53, 92
Patmore, Coventry Kersey Dighton 1823-1896 NCLC **9**
   See also DLB 35, 98
Paton, Alan (Stewart) 1903-1988 CLC **4, 10, 25, 55, 106; DA; DAB; DAC; DAM MST, NOV; WLC**
   See also CA 13-16; 125; CANR 22; CAP 1; MTCW; SATA 11; SATA-Obit 56
Paton Walsh, Gillian 1937-
   See Walsh, Jill Paton
   See also CANR 38; JRDA; MAICYA; SAAS 3; SATA 4, 72
Patton, George S. 1885-1945 .... TCLC **79**
Paulding, James Kirke 1778-1860 ... NCLC **2**
   See also DLB 3, 59, 74
Paulin, Thomas Neilson 1949-
   See Paulin, Tom
   See also CA 123; 128
Paulin, Tom .... CLC **37**
   See also Paulin, Thomas Neilson
   See also DLB 40
Paustovsky, Konstantin (Georgievich) 1892-1968 .... CLC **40**
   See also CA 93-96; 25-28R
Pavese, Cesare 1908-1950 ... TCLC **3; PC 13; SSC 19**
   See also CA 104; DLB 128, 177
Pavic, Milorad 1929- .... CLC **60**
   See also CA 136; DLB 181
Payne, Alan
   See Jakes, John (William)
Paz, Gil
   See Lugones, Leopoldo
Paz, Octavio 1914-1998CLC **3, 4, 6, 10, 19, 51, 65; DA; DAB; DAC; DAM MST, MULT, POET; HLC; PC 1; WLC**
   See also CA 73-76; 165; CANR 32, 65; DLBY 90; HW; MTCW
p'Bitek, Okot 1931-1982CLC **96; BLC; DAM MULT**
   See also BW 2; CA 124; 107; DLB 125; MTCW
Peacock, Molly 1947- .... CLC **60**
   See also CA 103; CAAS 21; CANR 52; DLB 120
Peacock, Thomas Love 1785-1866 . NCLC **22**
   See also DLB 96, 116
Peake, Mervyn 1911-1968 .... CLC **7, 54**
   See also CA 5-8R; 25-28R; CANR 3; DLB 15, 160; MTCW; SATA 23
Pearce, Philippa .... CLC **21**
   See also Christie, (Ann) Philippa
   See also CLR 9; DLB 161; MAICYA; SATA 1, 67
Pearl, Eric
   See Elman, Richard (Martin)
Pearson, T(homas) R(eid) 1956- ...... CLC **39**
   See also CA 120; 130; INT 130
Peck, Dale 1967- .... CLC **81**
   See also CA 146
Peck, John 1941- .... CLC **3**
   See also CA 49-52; CANR 3
Peck, Richard (Wayne) 1934- .... CLC **21**
   See also AAYA 1, 24; CA 85-88; CANR 19, 38; CLR 15; INT CANR-19; JRDA; MAICYA; SAAS 2; SATA 18, 55, 97
Peck, Robert Newton 1928- ..... CLC **17; DA; DAC; DAM MST**
   See also AAYA 3; CA 81-84; CANR 31, 63; CLR 45; JRDA; MAICYA; SAAS 1; SATA

Redmon, Anne .... **CLC 22**
    See also Nightingale, Anne Redmon
    See also DLBY 86
Reed, Eliot
    See Ambler, Eric
Reed, Ishmael 1938-**CLC 2, 3, 5, 6, 13, 32, 60;**
    BLC; DAM MULT
    See also BW 2; CA 21-24R; CANR 25, 48; DLB
    2, 5, 33, 169; DLBD 8; MTCW
Reed, John (Silas) 1887-1920 .... **TCLC 9**
    See also CA 106
Reed, Lou .... **CLC 21**
    See also Firbank, Louis
Reeve, Clara 1729-1807 ....**NCLC 19**
    See also DLB 39
Reich, Wilhelm 1897-1957 .... **TCLC 57**
Reid, Christopher (John) 1949- .... **CLC 33**
    See also CA 140; DLB 40
Reid, Desmond
    See Moorcock, Michael (John)
Reid Banks, Lynne 1929-
    See Banks, Lynne Reid
    See also CA 1-4R; CANR 6, 22, 38; CLR 24;
    JRDA; MAICYA; SATA 22, 75
Reilly, William K.
    See Creasey, John
Reiner, Max
    See Caldwell, (Janet Miriam) Taylor (Holland)
Reis, Ricardo
    See Pessoa, Fernando (Antonio Nogueira)
Remarque, Erich Maria 1898-1970 **CLC 21;**
    DA; DAB; DAC; DAM MST, NOV
    See also CA 77-80; 29-32R; DLB 56; MTCW
Remizov, A.
    See Remizov, Aleksei (Mikhailovich)
Remizov, A. M.
    See Remizov, Aleksei (Mikhailovich)
Remizov, Aleksei (Mikhailovich) 1877-1957
    TCLC 27
    See also CA 125; 133
Renan, Joseph Ernest 1823-1892 ...**NCLC 26**
Renard, Jules 1864-1910 .... **TCLC 17**
    See also CA 117
Renault, Mary .... **CLC 3, 11, 17**
    See also Challans, Mary
    See also DLBY 83
Rendell, Ruth (Barbara) 1930- . **CLC 28, 48;**
    DAM POP
    See also Vine, Barbara
    See also CA 109; CANR 32, 52; DLB 87; INT
    CANR-32; MTCW
Renoir, Jean 1894-1979 .... **CLC 20**
    See also CA 129; 85-88
Resnais, Alain 1922- .... **CLC 16**
Reverdy, Pierre 1889-1960 .... **CLC 53**
    See also CA 97-100; 89-92
Rexroth, Kenneth 1905-1982 **CLC 1, 2, 6, 11,**
    22, 49; DAM POET; PC 20
    See also CA 5-8R; 107; CANR 14, 34, 63;
    CDALB 1941-1968; DLB 16, 48, 165;
    DLBY 82; INT CANR-14; MTCW
Reyes, Alfonso 1889-1959 .... **TCLC 33**
    See also CA 131; HW
Reyes y Basoalto, Ricardo Eliecer Neftali
    See Neruda, Pablo
Reymont, Wladyslaw (Stanislaw) 1868(?)-1925
    TCLC 5
    See also CA 104
Reynolds, Jonathan 1942- .... **CLC 6, 38**
    See also CA 65-68; CANR 28
Reynolds, Joshua 1723-1792 .... **LC 15**
    See also DLB 104
Reynolds, Michael Shane 1937- .... **CLC 44**

See also CA 65-68; CANR 9
Reznikoff, Charles 1894-1976 .... **CLC 9**
    See also CA 33-36; 61-64; CAP 2; DLB 28, 45
Rezzori (d'Arezzo), Gregor von 1914-**CLC 25**
    See also CA 122; 136
Rhine, Richard
    See Silverstein, Alvin
Rhodes, Eugene Manlove 1869-1934**TCLC 53**
R'hoone
    See Balzac, Honore de
Rhys, Jean 1890(?)-1979 **CLC 2, 4, 6, 14, 19,**
    51; DAM NOV; SSC 21
    See also CA 25-28R; 85-88; CANR 35, 62;
    CDBLB 1945-1960; DLB 36, 117, 162;
    MTCW
Ribeiro, Darcy 1922-1997 ....**CLC 34**
    See also CA 33-36R; 156
Ribeiro, Joao Ubaldo (Osorio Pimentel) 1941-
    CLC 10, 67
    See also CA 81-84
Ribman, Ronald (Burt) 1932- .... **CLC 7**
    See also CA 21-24R; CANR 46
Ricci, Nino 1959- ....**CLC 70**
    See also CA 137
Rice, Anne 1941- .... **CLC 41; DAM POP**
    See also AAYA 9; BEST 89:2; CA 65-68; CANR
    12, 36, 53
Rice, Elmer (Leopold) 1892-1967 **CLC 7, 49;**
    DAM DRAM
    See also CA 21-22; 25-28R; CAP 2; DLB 4, 7;
    MTCW
Rice, Tim(othy Miles Bindon) 1944- **CLC 21**
    See also CA 103; CANR 46
Rich, Adrienne (Cecile) 1929-**CLC 3, 6, 7, 11,**
    18, 36, 73, 76; DAM POET; PC 5
    See also CA 9-12R; CANR 20, 53; DLB 5, 67;
    MTCW
Rich, Barbara
    See Graves, Robert (von Ranke)
Rich, Robert
    See Trumbo, Dalton
Richard, Keith ....**CLC 17**
    See also Richards, Keith
Richards, David Adams 1950- **CLC 59; DAC**
    See also CA 93-96; CANR 60; DLB 53
Richards, I(vor) A(rmstrong) 1893-1979**C L C**
    14, 24
    See also CA 41-44R; 89-92; CANR 34; DLB
    27
Richards, Keith 1943-
    See Richard, Keith
    See also CA 107
Richardson, Anne
    See Roiphe, Anne (Richardson)
Richardson, Dorothy Miller 1873-1957**TCLC**
    3
    See also CA 104; DLB 36
Richardson, Ethel Florence (Lindesay) 1870-
    1946
    See Richardson, Henry Handel
    See also CA 105
Richardson, Henry Handel .... **TCLC 4**
    See also Richardson, Ethel Florence (Lindesay)
Richardson, John 1796-1852**NCLC 55; DAC**
    See also DLB 99
Richardson, Samuel 1689-1761 .... **LC 1; DA;**
    DAB; DAC; DAM MST, NOV; WLC
    See also CDBLB 1660-1789; DLB 39
Richler, Mordecai 1931-**CLC 3, 5, 9, 13, 18, 46,**
    70; DAC; DAM MST, NOV
    See also AITN 1; CA 65-68; CANR 31, 62; CLR
    17; DLB 53; MAICYA; MTCW; SATA 44,
    98; SATA-Brief 27

Richter, Conrad (Michael) 1890-1968**CLC 30**
    See also AAYA 21; CA 5-8R; 25-28R; CANR
    23; DLB 9; MTCW; SATA 3
Ricostranza, Tom
    See Ellis, Trey
Riddell, Charlotte 1832-1906 .... **TCLC 40**
    See also CA 165; DLB 156
Riding, Laura ....**CLC 3, 7**
    See also Jackson, Laura (Riding)
Riefenstahl, Berta Helene Amalia 1902-
    See Riefenstahl, Leni
    See also CA 108
Riefenstahl, Leni .... **CLC 16**
    See also Riefenstahl, Berta Helene Amalia
Riffe, Ernest
    See Bergman, (Ernst) Ingmar
Riggs, (Rolla) Lynn 1899-1954 ..... **TCLC 56;**
    DAM MULT
    See also CA 144; DLB 175; NNAL
Riis, Jacob A(ugust) 1849-1914 ..... **TCLC 80**
    See also CA 113; DLB 23
Riley, James Whitcomb 1849-1916**TCLC 51;**
    DAM POET
    See also CA 118; 137; MAICYA; SATA 17
Riley, Tex
    See Creasey, John
Rilke, Rainer Maria 1875-1926**TCLC 1, 6, 19;**
    DAM POET; PC 2
    See also CA 104; 132; CANR 62; DLB 81;
    MTCW
Rimbaud, (Jean Nicolas) Arthur 1854-1891
    NCLC 4, 35; DA; DAB; DAC; DAM MST,
    POET; PC 3; WLC
Rinehart, Mary Roberts 1876-1958**TCLC 52**
    See also CA 108
Ringmaster, The
    See Mencken, H(enry) L(ouis)
Ringwood, Gwen(dolyn Margaret) Pharis
    1910-1984 .... **CLC 48**
    See also CA 148; 112; DLB 88
Rio, Michel 19(?)- .... **CLC 43**
Ritsos, Giannes
    See Ritsos, Yannis
Ritsos, Yannis 1909-1990 .... **CLC 6, 13, 31**
    See also CA 77-80; 133; CANR 39, 61; MTCW
Ritter, Erika 1948(?)- .... **CLC 52**
Rivera, Jose Eustasio 1889-1928 ... **TCLC 35**
    See also CA 162; HW
Rivers, Conrad Kent 1933-1968 .... **CLC 1**
    See also BW 1; CA 85-88; DLB 41
Rivers, Elfrida
    See Bradley, Marion Zimmer
Riverside, John
    See Heinlein, Robert A(nson)
Rizal, Jose 1861-1896 ....**NCLC 27**
Roa Bastos, Augusto (Antonio) 1917-**CLC 45;**
    DAM MULT; HLC
    See also CA 131; DLB 113; HW
Robbe-Grillet, Alain 1922- **CLC 1, 2, 4, 6, 8,**
    10, 14, 43
    See also CA 9-12R; CANR 33, 65; DLB 83;
    MTCW
Robbins, Harold 1916-1997 ..... **CLC 5; DAM**
    NOV
    See also CA 73-76; 162; CANR 26, 54; MTCW
Robbins, Thomas Eugene 1936-
    See Robbins, Tom
    See also CA 81-84; CANR 29, 59; DAM NOV,
    POP; MTCW
Robbins, Tom .... **CLC 9, 32, 64**
    See also Robbins, Thomas Eugene
    See also BEST 90:3; DLBY 80
Robbins, Trina 1938- .... **CLC 21**

See also CA 128

Roberts, Charles G(eorge) D(ouglas) 1860-1943 TCLC 8
See also CA 105; CLR 33; DLB 92; SATA 88; SATA-Brief 29

Roberts, Elizabeth Madox 1886-1941 TCLC 68
See also CA 111; DLB 9, 54, 102; SATA 33; SATA-Brief 27

Roberts, Kate 1891-1985 .... CLC 15
See also CA 107; 116

Roberts, Keith (John Kingston) 1935-CLC 14
See also CA 25-28R; CANR 46

Roberts, Kenneth (Lewis) 1885-1957TCLC 23
See also CA 109; DLB 9

Roberts, Michele (B.) 1949-.............. CLC 48
See also CA 115; CANR 58

Robertson, Ellis
See Ellison, Harlan (Jay); Silverberg, Robert

Robertson, Thomas William 1829-1871NCLC 35; DAM DRAM

Robeson, Kenneth
See Dent, Lester

Robinson, Edwin Arlington 1869-1935TCLC 5; DA; DAC; DAM MST, POET; PC 1
See also CA 104; 133; CDALB 1865-1917; DLB 54; MTCW

Robinson, Henry Crabb 1775-1867NCLC 15
See also DLB 107

Robinson, Jill 1936-........................ CLC 10
See also CA 102; INT 102

Robinson, Kim Stanley 1952-.......... CLC 34
See also CA 126

Robinson, Lloyd
See Silverberg, Robert

Robinson, Marilynne 1944-.............. CLC 25
See also CA 116

Robinson, Smokey .... CLC 21
See also Robinson, William, Jr.

Robinson, William, Jr. 1940-
See Robinson, Smokey
See also CA 116

Robison, Mary 1949-.................... CLC 42, 98
See also CA 113; 116; DLB 130; INT 116

Rod, Edouard 1857-1910 .... TCLC 52

Roddenberry, Eugene Wesley 1921-1991
See Roddenberry, Gene
See also CA 110; 135; CANR 37; SATA 45; SATA-Obit 69

Roddenberry, Gene .... CLC 17
See also Roddenberry, Eugene Wesley
See also AAYA 5; SATA-Obit 69

Rodgers, Mary 1931-....................... CLC 12
See also CA 49-52; CANR 8, 55; CLR 20; INT CANR-8; JRDA; MAICYA; SATA 8

Rodgers, W(illiam) R(obert) 1909-1969CLC 7
See also CA 85-88; DLB 20

Rodman, Eric
See Silverberg, Robert

Rodman, Howard 1920(?)-1985 .... CLC 65
See also CA 118

Rodman, Maia
See Wojciechowska, Maia (Teresa)

Rodriguez, Claudio 1934-................ CLC 10
See also DLB 134

Roelvaag, O(le) E(dvart) 1876-1931TCLC 17
See also CA 117; DLB 9

Roethke, Theodore (Huebner) 1908-1963CLC 1, 3, 8, 11, 19, 46, 101; DAM POET; PC 15
See also CA 81-84; CABS 2; CDALB 1941-1968; DLB 5; MTCW

Rogers, Samuel 1763-1855 .... NCLC 69
See also DLB 93

Rogers, Thomas Hunton 1927- .... CLC 57
See also CA 89-92; INT 89-92

Rogers, Will(iam Penn Adair) 1879-1935 TCLC 8, 71; DAM MULT
See also CA 105; 144; DLB 11; NNAL

Rogin, Gilbert 1929- .... CLC 18
See also CA 65-68; CANR 15

Rohan, Koda .... TCLC 22
See also Koda Shigeyuki

Rohlfs, Anna Katharine Green
See Green, Anna Katharine

Rohmer, Eric .... CLC 16
See also Scherer, Jean-Marie Maurice

Rohmer, Sax .... TCLC 28
See also Ward, Arthur Henry Sarsfield
See also DLB 70

Roiphe, Anne (Richardson) 1935- . CLC 3, 9
See also CA 89-92; CANR 45; DLBY 80; INT 89-92

Rojas, Fernando de 1465-1541 .... LC 23

Rolfe, Frederick (William Serafino Austin Lewis Mary) 1860-1913 .... TCLC 12
See also CA 107; DLB 34, 156

Rolland, Romain 1866-1944 .... TCLC 23
See also CA 118; DLB 65

Rolle, Richard c. 1300-c. 1349 ...... CMLC 21
See also DLB 146

Rolvaag, O(le) E(dvart)
See Roelvaag, O(le) E(dvart)

Romain Arnaud, Saint
See Aragon, Louis

Romains, Jules 1885-1972 .... CLC 7
See also CA 85-88; CANR 34; DLB 65; MTCW

Romero, Jose Ruben 1890-1952 ..... TCLC 14
See also CA 114; 131; HW

Ronsard, Pierre de 1524-1585 ... LC 6; PC 11

Rooke, Leon 1934-.. CLC 25, 34; DAM POP
See also CA 25-28R; CANR 23, 53

Roosevelt, Theodore 1858-1919 ..... TCLC 69
See also CA 115; DLB 47, 186

Roper, William 1498-1578 .... LC 10

Roquelaure, A. N.
See Rice, Anne

Rosa, Joao Guimaraes 1908-1967 ....CLC 23
See also CA 89-92; DLB 113

Rose, Wendy 1948-CLC 85; DAM MULT; PC 13
See also CA 53-56; CANR 5, 51; DLB 175; NNAL; SATA 12

Rosen, R. D.
See Rosen, Richard (Dean)

Rosen, Richard (Dean) 1949- .... CLC 39
See also CA 77-80; CANR 62; INT CANR-30

Rosenberg, Isaac 1890-1918 .... TCLC 12
See also CA 107; DLB 20

Rosenblatt, Joe .... CLC 15
See also Rosenblatt, Joseph

Rosenblatt, Joseph 1933-
See Rosenblatt, Joe
See also CA 89-92; INT 89-92

Rosenfeld, Samuel
See Tzara, Tristan

Rosenstock, Sami
See Tzara, Tristan

Rosenstock, Samuel
See Tzara, Tristan

Rosenthal, M(acha) L(ouis) 1917-1996 . CLC 28
See also CA 1-4R; 152; CAAS 6; CANR 4, 51; DLB 5; SATA 59

Ross, Barnaby
See Dannay, Frederic

Ross, Bernard L.
See Follett, Ken(neth Martin)

Ross, J. H.
See Lawrence, T(homas) E(dward)

Ross, Martin
See Martin, Violet Florence
See also DLB 135

Ross, (James) Sinclair 1908- CLC 13; DAC; DAM MST; SSC 24
See also CA 73-76; DLB 88

Rossetti, Christina (Georgina) 1830-1894 NCLC 2, 50, 66; DA; DAB; DAC; DAM MST, POET; PC 7; WLC
See also DLB 35, 163; MAICYA; SATA 20

Rossetti, Dante Gabriel 1828-1882 NCLC 4; DA; DAB; DAC; DAM MST, POET; WLC
See also CDBLB 1832-1890; DLB 35

Rossner, Judith (Perelman) 1935-CLC 6, 9, 29
See also AITN 2; BEST 90:3; CA 17-20R; CANR 18, 51; DLB 6; INT CANR-18; MTCW

Rostand, Edmond (Eugene Alexis) 1868-1918 TCLC 6, 37; DA; DAB; DAC; DAM DRAM, MST
See also CA 104; 126; DLB 192; MTCW

Roth, Henry 1906-1995 ..... CLC 2, 6, 11, 104
See also CA 11-12; 149; CANR 38, 63; CAP 1; DLB 28; MTCW

Roth, Philip (Milton) 1933-CLC 1, 2, 3, 4, 6, 9, 15, 22, 31, 47, 66, 86; DA; DAB; DAC; DAM MST, NOV, POP; SSC 26; WLC
See also BEST 90:3; CA 1-4R; CANR 1, 22, 36, 55; CDALB 1968-1988; DLB 2, 28, 173; DLBY 82; MTCW

Rothenberg, Jerome 1931- .... CLC 6, 57
See also CA 45-48; CANR 1; DLB 5, 193

Roumain, Jacques (Jean Baptiste) 1907-1944 TCLC 19; BLC; DAM MULT
See also BW 1; CA 117; 125

Rourke, Constance (Mayfield) 1885-1941 TCLC 12
See also CA 107; YABC 1

Rousseau, Jean-Baptiste 1671-1741 ..... LC 9

Rousseau, Jean-Jacques 1712-1778LC 14, 36; DA; DAB; DAC; DAM MST; WLC

Roussel, Raymond 1877-1933 .... TCLC 20
See also CA 117

Rovit, Earl (Herbert) 1927-................ CLC 7
See also CA 5-8R; CANR 12

Rowe, Nicholas 1674-1718 .... LC 8
See also DLB 84

Rowley, Ames Dorrance
See Lovecraft, H(oward) P(hillips)

Rowson, Susanna Haswell 1762(?)-1824 NCLC 5, 69
See also DLB 37

Roy, Arundhati 1960(?)- .... CLC 109
See also CA 163; DLBY 97

Roy, Gabrielle 1909-1983 CLC 10, 14; DAB; DAC; DAM MST
See also CA 53-56; 110; CANR 5, 61; DLB 68; MTCW

Royko, Mike 1932-1997 .... CLC 109
See also CA 89-92; 157; CANR 26

Rozewicz, Tadeusz 1921- ...CLC 9, 23; DAM POET
See also CA 108; CANR 36, 66; MTCW

Ruark, Gibbons 1941- ....CLC 3
See also CA 33-36R; CAAS 23; CANR 14, 31, 57; DLB 120

Rubens, Bernice (Ruth) 1923- .... CLC 19, 31
See also CA 25-28R; CANR 33, 65; DLB 14; MTCW

See also CA 1-4R; 118; CANR 15, 33; DLBY 84; MTCW

Santoka, Taneda 1882-1940 .... **TCLC 72**

Santos, Bienvenido N(uqui) 1911-1996 . **C L C 22; DAM MULT**
See also CA 101; 151; CANR 19, 46

Sapper .... **TCLC 44**
See also McNeile, Herman Cyril

Sapphire 1950- .... **CLC 99**

Sappho fl. 6th cent. B.C.-...... **CMLC 3; DAM POET; PC 5**
See also DLB 176

Sarduy, Severo 1937-1993 .... **CLC 6, 97**
See also CA 89-92; 142; CANR 58; DLB 113; HW

Sargeson, Frank 1903-1982 .... **CLC 31**
See also CA 25-28R; 106; CANR 38

Sarmiento, Felix Ruben Garcia
See Dario, Ruben

Saroyan, William 1908-1981 **CLC 1, 8, 10, 29, 34, 56; DA; DAB; DAC; DAM DRAM, MST, NOV; SSC 21; WLC**
See also CA 5-8R; 103; CANR 30; DLB 7, 9, 86; DLBY 81; MTCW; SATA 23; SATA-Obit 24

Sarraute, Nathalie 1900- **CLC 1, 2, 4, 8, 10, 31, 80**
See also CA 9-12R; CANR 23, 66; DLB 83; MTCW

Sarton, (Eleanor) May 1912-1995 **CLC 4, 14, 49, 91; DAM POET**
See also CA 1-4R; 149; CANR 1, 34, 55; DLB 48; DLBY 81; INT CANR-34; MTCW; SATA 36; SATA-Obit 86

Sartre, Jean-Paul 1905-1980 **CLC 1, 4, 7, 9, 13, 18, 24, 44, 50, 52; DA; DAB; DAC; DAM DRAM, MST, NOV; DC 3; WLC**
See also CA 9-12R; 97-100; CANR 21; DLB 72; MTCW

Sassoon, Siegfried (Lorraine) 1886-1967 **C L C 36; DAB; DAM MST, NOV, POET; PC 12**
See also CA 104; 25-28R; CANR 36; DLB 20, 191; MTCW

Satterfield, Charles
See Pohl, Frederik

Saul, John (W. III) 1942- **CLC 46; DAM NOV, POP**
See also AAYA 10; BEST 90:4; CA 81-84; CANR 16, 40; SATA 98

Saunders, Caleb
See Heinlein, Robert A(nson)

Saura (Atares), Carlos 1932- .... **CLC 20**
See also CA 114; 131; HW

Sauser-Hall, Frederic 1887-1961 ..... **CLC 18**
See also Cendrars, Blaise
See also CA 102; 93-96; CANR 36, 62; MTCW

Saussure, Ferdinand de 1857-1913 **TCLC 49**

Savage, Catharine
See Brosman, Catharine Savage

Savage, Thomas 1915- .... **CLC 40**
See also CA 126; 132; CAAS 15; INT 132

Savan, Glenn 19(?)- .... **CLC 50**

Sayers, Dorothy L(eigh) 1893-1957 **TCLC 2, 15; DAM POP**
See also CA 104; 119; CANR 60; CDBLB 1914-1945; DLB 10, 36, 77, 100; MTCW

Sayers, Valerie 1952- .... **CLC 50**
See also CA 134; CANR 61

Sayles, John (Thomas) 1950- . **CLC 7, 10, 14**
See also CA 57-60; CANR 41; DLB 44

Scammell, Michael 1935- .... **CLC 34**
See also CA 156

Scannell, Vernon 1922- .... **CLC 49**

See also CA 5-8R; CANR 8, 24, 57; DLB 27; SATA 59

Scarlett, Susan
See Streatfeild, (Mary) Noel

Schaeffer, Susan Fromberg 1941- **CLC 6, 11, 22**
See also CA 49-52; CANR 18, 65; DLB 28; MTCW; SATA 22

Schary, Jill
See Robinson, Jill

Schell, Jonathan 1943- .... **CLC 35**
See also CA 73-76; CANR 12

Schelling, Friedrich Wilhelm Joseph von 1775-1854 .... **NCLC 30**
See also DLB 90

Schendel, Arthur van 1874-1946 ... **TCLC 56**

Scherer, Jean-Marie Maurice 1920-
See Rohmer, Eric
See also CA 110

Schevill, James (Erwin) 1920- .... **CLC 7**
See also CA 5-8R; CAAS 12

Schiller, Friedrich 1759-1805 . **NCLC 39, 69; DAM DRAM**
See also DLB 94

Schisgal, Murray (Joseph) 1926- .... **CLC 6**
See also CA 21-24R; CANR 48

Schlee, Ann 1934- .... **CLC 35**
See also CA 101; CANR 29; SATA 44; SATA-Brief 36

Schlegel, August Wilhelm von 1767-1845 **NCLC 15**
See also DLB 94

Schlegel, Friedrich 1772-1829 .... **NCLC 45**
See also DLB 90

Schlegel, Johann Elias (von) 1719(?)-1749 **L C 5**

Schlesinger, Arthur M(eier), Jr. 1917- **CLC 84**
See also AITN 1; CA 1-4R; CANR 1, 28, 58; DLB 17; INT CANR-28; MTCW; SATA 61

Schmidt, Arno (Otto) 1914-1979 ...... **CLC 56**
See also CA 128; 109; DLB 69

Schmitz, Aron Hector 1861-1928
See Svevo, Italo
See also CA 104; 122; MTCW

Schnackenberg, Gjertrud 1953- .... **CLC 40**
See also CA 116; DLB 120

Schneider, Leonard Alfred 1925-1966
See Bruce, Lenny
See also CA 89-92

Schnitzler, Arthur 1862-1931 **TCLC 4; SSC 15**
See also CA 104; DLB 81, 118

Schoenberg, Arnold 1874-1951 ...... **TCLC 75**
See also CA 109

Schonberg, Arnold
See Schoenberg, Arnold

Schopenhauer, Arthur 1788-1860 .. **NCLC 51**
See also DLB 90

Schor, Sandra (M.) 1932(?)-1990 ...... **CLC 65**
See also CA 132

Schorer, Mark 1908-1977 .... **CLC 9**
See also CA 5-8R; 73-76; CANR 7; DLB 103

Schrader, Paul (Joseph) 1946- .... **CLC 26**
See also CA 37-40R; CANR 41; DLB 44

Schreiner, Olive (Emilie Albertina) 1855-1920 **TCLC 9**
See also CA 105; 154; DLB 18, 156, 190

Schulberg, Budd (Wilson) 1914-.. **CLC 7, 48**
See also CA 25-28R; CANR 19; DLB 6, 26, 28; DLBY 81

Schulz, Bruno 1892-1942 **TCLC 5, 51; SSC 13**
See also CA 115; 123

Schulz, Charles M(onroe) 1922- .... **CLC 12**
See also CA 9-12R; CANR 6; INT CANR-6;

SATA 10

Schumacher, E(rnst) F(riedrich) 1911-1977 **CLC 80**
See also CA 81-84; 73-76; CANR 34

Schuyler, James Marcus 1923-1991 **CLC 5, 23; DAM POET**
See also CA 101; 134; DLB 5, 169; INT 101

Schwartz, Delmore (David) 1913-1966 **CLC 2, 4, 10, 45, 87; PC 8**
See also CA 17-18; 25-28R; CANR 35; CAP 2; DLB 28, 48; MTCW

Schwartz, Ernst
See Ozu, Yasujiro

Schwartz, John Burnham 1965- .... **CLC 59**
See also CA 132

Schwartz, Lynne Sharon 1939- .... **CLC 31**
See also CA 103; CANR 44

Schwartz, Muriel A.
See Eliot, T(homas) S(tearns)

Schwarz-Bart, Andre 1928- .... **CLC 2, 4**
See also CA 89-92

Schwarz-Bart, Simone 1938- .... **CLC 7**
See also BW 2; CA 97-100

Schwob, (Mayer Andre) Marcel 1867-1905 **TCLC 20**
See also CA 117; DLB 123

Sciascia, Leonardo 1921-1989 . **CLC 8, 9, 41**
See also CA 85-88; 130; CANR 35; DLB 177; MTCW

Scoppettone, Sandra 1936- .... **CLC 26**
See also AAYA 11; CA 5-8R; CANR 41; SATA 9, 92

Scorsese, Martin 1942- .... **CLC 20, 89**
See also CA 110; 114; CANR 46

Scotland, Jay
See Jakes, John (William)

Scott, Duncan Campbell 1862-1947 **TCLC 6; DAC**
See also CA 104; 153; DLB 92

Scott, Evelyn 1893-1963 .... **CLC 43**
See also CA 104; 112; CANR 64; DLB 9, 48

Scott, F(rancis) R(eginald) 1899-1985 **CLC 22**
See also CA 101; 114; DLB 88; INT 101

Scott, Frank
See Scott, F(rancis) R(eginald)

Scott, Joanna 1960- .... **CLC 50**
See also CA 126; CANR 53

Scott, Paul (Mark) 1920-1978 ...... **CLC 9, 60**
See also CA 81-84; 77-80; CANR 33; DLB 14; MTCW

Scott, Walter 1771-1832 .. **NCLC 15, 69; DA; DAB; DAC; DAM MST, NOV, POET; PC 13; WLC**
See also AAYA 22; CDBLB 1789-1832; DLB 93, 107, 116, 144, 159; YABC 2

Scribe, (Augustin) Eugene 1791-1861 **N C L C 16; DAM DRAM; DC 5**
See also DLB 192

Scrum, R.
See Crumb, R(obert)

Scudery, Madeleine de 1607-1701 .... **LC 2**

Scum
See Crumb, R(obert)

Scumbag, Little Bobby
See Crumb, R(obert)

Seabrook, John
See Hubbard, L(afayette) Ron(ald)

Sealy, I. Allan 1951- .... **CLC 55**

Search, Alexander
See Pessoa, Fernando (Antonio Nogueira)

Sebastian, Lee
See Silverberg, Robert

Sebastian Owl

See Thompson, Hunter S(tockton)
Sebestyen, Ouida 1924- .... **CLC 30**
    See also AAYA 8; CA 107; CANR 40; CLR 17;
    JRDA; MAICYA; SAAS 10; SATA 39
Secundus, H. Scriblerus
    See Fielding, Henry
Sedges, John
    See Buck, Pearl S(ydenstricker)
Sedgwick, Catharine Maria 1789-1867 **N C L C
19**
    See also DLB 1, 74
Seelye, John 1931- .... **CLC 7**
Seferiades, Giorgos Stylianou 1900-1971
    See Seferis, George
    See also CA 5-8R; 33-36R; CANR 5, 36;
    MTCW
Seferis, George .... **CLC 5, 11**
    See also Seferiades, Giorgos Stylianou
Segal, Erich (Wolf) 1937- ..**CLC 3, 10; DAM
POP**
    See also BEST 89:1; CA 25-28R; CANR 20,
    36, 65; DLBY 86; INT CANR-20; MTCW
Seger, Bob 1945- .... **CLC 35**
Seghers, Anna .... **CLC 7**
    See Radvanyi, Netty
    See also DLB 69
Seidel, Frederick (Lewis) 1936- .... **CLC 18**
    See also CA 13-16R; CANR 8; DLBY 84
Seifert, Jaroslav 1901-1986 .. **CLC 34, 44, 93**
    See also CA 127; MTCW
Sei Shonagon c. 966-1017(?) .... **CMLC 6**
Selby, Hubert, Jr. 1928-**CLC 1, 2, 4, 8; SSC 20**
    See also CA 13-16R; CANR 33; DLB 2
Selzer, Richard 1928- .... **CLC 74**
    See also CA 65-68; CANR 14
Sembene, Ousmane
    See Ousmane, Sembene
Senancour, Etienne Pivert de 1770-1846
    NCLC 16
    See also DLB 119
Sender, Ramon (Jose) 1902-1982**CLC 8; DAM
MULT; HLC**
    See also CA 5-8R; 105; CANR 8; HW; MTCW
Seneca, Lucius Annaeus 4B.C.-65 **CMLC 6;
DAM DRAM; DC 5**
Senghor, Leopold Sedar 1906-**CLC 54; BLC;
DAM MULT, POET**
    See also BW 2; CA 116; 125; CANR 47; MTCW
Serling, (Edward) Rod(man) 1924-1975**C L C
30**
    See also AAYA 14; AITN 1; CA 162; 57-60;
    DLB 26
Serna, Ramon Gomez de la
    See Gomez de la Serna, Ramon
Serpieres
    See Guillevic, (Eugene)
Service, Robert
    See Service, Robert W(illiam)
    See also DAB; DLB 92
Service, Robert W(illiam) 1874(?)-1958**TCLC
15; DA; DAC; DAM MST, POET; WLC**
    See also Service, Robert
    See also CA 115; 140; SATA 20
Seth, Vikram 1952-**CLC 43, 90; DAM MULT**
    See also CA 121; 127; CANR 50; DLB 120;
    INT 127
Seton, Cynthia Propper 1926-1982 . **CLC 27**
    See also CA 5-8R; 108; CANR 7
Seton, Ernest (Evan) Thompson 1860-1946
    TCLC 31
    See also CA 109; DLB 92; DLBD 13; JRDA;
    SATA 18
Seton-Thompson, Ernest

See Seton, Ernest (Evan) Thompson
Settle, Mary Lee 1918- .... **CLC 19, 61**
    See also CA 89-92; CAAS 1; CANR 44; DLB
    6; INT 89-92
Seuphor, Michel
    See Arp, Jean
**Sevigne, Marie (de Rabutin-Chantal) Marquise
de** 1626-1696 .... **LC 11**
Sewall, Samuel 1652-1730 .... **LC 38**
    See also DLB 24
Sexton, Anne (Harvey) 1928-1974**CLC 2, 4, 6,
8, 10, 15, 53; DA; DAB; DAC; DAM MST,
POET; PC 2; WLC**
    See also CA 1-4R; 53-56; CABS 2; CANR 3,
    36; CDALB 1941-1968; DLB 5, 169;
    MTCW; SATA 10
Shaara, Michael (Joseph, Jr.) 1929-1988**C L C
15; DAM POP**
    See also AITN 1; CA 102; 125; CANR 52;
    DLBY 83
Shackleton, C. C.
    See Aldiss, Brian W(ilson)
Shacochis, Bob .... **CLC 39**
    See also Shacochis, Robert G.
Shacochis, Robert G. 1951-
    See Shacochis, Bob
    See also CA 119; 124; INT 124
Shaffer, Anthony (Joshua) 1926- .... **CLC 19;
DAM DRAM**
    See also CA 110; 116; DLB 13
Shaffer, Peter (Levin) 1926-**CLC 5, 14, 18, 37,
60; DAB; DAM DRAM, MST; DC 7**
    See also CA 25-28R; CANR 25, 47; CDBLB
    1960 to Present; DLB 13; MTCW
Shakey, Bernard
    See Young, Neil
Shalamov, Varlam (Tikhonovich) 1907(?)-1982
    CLC 18
    See also CA 129; 105
Shamlu, Ahmad 1925-........................ **CLC 10**
Shammas, Anton 1951- .... **CLC 55**
Shange, Ntozake 1948-**CLC 8, 25, 38, 74; BLC;
DAM DRAM, MULT; DC 3**
    See also AAYA 9; BW 2; CA 85-88; CABS 3;
    CANR 27, 48; DLB 38; MTCW
Shanley, John Patrick 1950- .... **CLC 75**
    See also CA 128; 133
Shapcott, Thomas W(illiam) 1935- ... **CLC 38**
    See also CA 69-72; CANR 49
Shapiro, Jane .... **CLC 76**
Shapiro, Karl (Jay) 1913- ... **CLC 4, 8, 15, 53**
    See also CA 1-4R; CAAS 6; CANR 1, 36, 66;
    DLB 48; MTCW
Sharp, William 1855-1905 .... **TCLC 39**
    See also CA 160; DLB 156
Sharpe, Thomas Ridley 1928-
    See Sharpe, Tom
    See also CA 114; 122; INT 122
Sharpe, Tom .... **CLC 36**
    See also Sharpe, Thomas Ridley
    See also DLB 14
Shaw, Bernard .... **TCLC 45**
    See also Shaw, George Bernard
    See also BW 1
Shaw, G. Bernard
    See Shaw, George Bernard
Shaw, George Bernard 1856-1950**TCLC 3, 9,
21; DA; DAB; DAC; DAM DRAM, MST;
WLC**
    See also Shaw, Bernard
    See also CA 104; 128; CDBLB 1914-1945;
    DLB 10, 57, 190; MTCW
Shaw, Henry Wheeler 1818-1885 ..**NCLC 15**

See also DLB 11
Shaw, Irwin 1913-1984 **CLC 7, 23, 34; DAM
DRAM, POP**
    See also AITN 1; CA 13-16R; 112; CANR 21;
    CDALB 1941-1968; DLB 6, 102; DLBY 84;
    MTCW
Shaw, Robert 1927-1978 .... **CLC 5**
    See also AITN 1; CA 1-4R; 81-84; CANR 4;
    DLB 13, 14
Shaw, T. E.
    See Lawrence, T(homas) E(dward)
Shawn, Wallace 1943- .... **CLC 41**
    See also CA 112
Shea, Lisa 1953-................................. **CLC 86**
    See also CA 147
Sheed, Wilfrid (John Joseph) 1930-**CLC 2, 4,
10, 53**
    See also CA 65-68; CANR 30, 66; DLB 6;
    MTCW
Sheldon, Alice Hastings Bradley 1915(?)-1987
    See Tiptree, James, Jr.
    See also CA 108; 122; CANR 34; INT 108;
    MTCW
Sheldon, John
    See Bloch, Robert (Albert)
Shelley, Mary Wollstonecraft (Godwin) 1797-
    1851**NCLC 14, 59; DA; DAB; DAC; DAM
MST, NOV; WLC**
    See also AAYA 20; CDBLB 1789-1832; DLB
    110, 116, 159, 178; SATA 29
Shelley, Percy Bysshe 1792-1822 . **NCLC 18;
DA; DAB; DAC; DAM MST, POET; PC
14; WLC**
    See also CDBLB 1789-1832; DLB 96, 110, 158
Shepard, Jim 1956- .... **CLC 36**
    See also CA 137; CANR 59; SATA 90
Shepard, Lucius 1947- .... **CLC 34**
    See also CA 128; 141
Shepard, Sam 1943-**CLC 4, 6, 17, 34, 41, 44;
DAM DRAM; DC 5**
    See also AAYA 1; CA 69-72; CABS 3; CANR
    22; DLB 7; MTCW
Shepherd, Michael
    See Ludlum, Robert
Sherburne, Zoa (Morin) 1912- .... **CLC 30**
    See also AAYA 13; CA 1-4R; CANR 3, 37;
    MAICYA; SAAS 18; SATA 3
Sheridan, Frances 1724-1766 .... **LC 7**
    See also DLB 39, 84
Sheridan, Richard Brinsley 1751-1816**N C L C
5; DA; DAB; DAC; DAM DRAM, MST;
DC 1; WLC**
    See also CDBLB 1660-1789; DLB 89
Sherman, Jonathan Marc .... **CLC 55**
Sherman, Martin 1941(?)- .... **CLC 19**
    See also CA 116; 123
Sherwin, Judith Johnson 1936- ... **CLC 7, 15**
    See also CA 25-28R; CANR 34
Sherwood, Frances 1940- .... **CLC 81**
    See also CA 146
Sherwood, Robert E(mmet) 1896-1955**T C L C
3; DAM DRAM**
    See also CA 104; 153; DLB 7, 26
Shestov, Lev 1866-1938 .... **TCLC 56**
Shevchenko, Taras 1814-1861 .... **NCLC 54**
Shiel, M(atthew) P(hipps) 1865-1947**TCLC 8**
    See also Holmes, Gordon
    See also CA 106; 160; DLB 153
Shields, Carol 1935- ....**CLC 91; DAC**
    See also CA 81-84; CANR 51
Shields, David 1956- .... **CLC 97**
    See also CA 124; CANR 48
Shiga, Naoya 1883-1971 ..... **CLC 33; SSC 23**

See Spillane, Mickey
See also CA 25-28R; CANR 28, 63; MTCW; SATA 66
Spillane, Mickey .... **CLC 3, 13**
See also Spillane, Frank Morrison
Spinoza, Benedictus de 1632-1677 .... **LC 9**
Spinrad, Norman (Richard) 1940- .. **CLC 46**
See also CA 37-40R; CAAS 19; CANR 20; DLB 8; INT CANR-20
Spitteler, Carl (Friedrich Georg) 1845-1924 **TCLC 12**
See also CA 109; DLB 129
Spivack, Kathleen (Romola Drucker) 1938- **CLC 6**
See also CA 49-52
Spoto, Donald 1941- .... **CLC 39**
See also CA 65-68; CANR 11, 57
Springsteen, Bruce (F.) 1949- .... **CLC 17**
See also CA 111
Spurling, Hilary 1940- .... **CLC 34**
See also CA 104; CANR 25, 52
Spyker, John Howland
See Elman, Richard (Martin)
Squires, (James) Radcliffe 1917-1993 **CLC 51**
See also CA 1-4R; 140; CANR 6, 21
Srivastava, Dhanpat Rai 1880(?)-1936
See Premchand
See also CA 118
Stacy, Donald
See Pohl, Frederik
Stael, Germaine de 1766-1817
See Stael-Holstein, Anne Louise Germaine Necker Baronn
See also DLB 119
Stael-Holstein, Anne Louise Germaine Necker Baronn 1766-1817 ....
NCLC 3
See also Stael, Germaine de
See also DLB 192
Stafford, Jean 1915-1979 **CLC 4, 7, 19, 68; SSC 26**
See also CA 1-4R; 85-88; CANR 3, 65; DLB 2, 173; MTCW; SATA-Obit 22
Stafford, William (Edgar) 1914-1993 **CLC 4, 7, 29; DAM POET**
See also CA 5-8R; 142; CAAS 3; CANR 5, 22; DLB 5; INT CANR-22
Stagnelius, Eric Johan 1793-1823 . **NCLC 61**
Staines, Trevor
See Brunner, John (Kilian Houston)
Stairs, Gordon
See Austin, Mary (Hunter)
Stannard, Martin 1947- .... **CLC 44**
See also CA 142; DLB 155
Stanton, Elizabeth Cady 1815-1902 **TCLC 73**
See also DLB 79
Stanton, Maura 1946- .... **CLC 9**
See also CA 89-92; CANR 15; DLB 120
Stanton, Schuyler
See Baum, L(yman) Frank
Stapledon, (William) Olaf 1886-1950 . **T C L C 22**
See also CA 111; 162; DLB 15
Starbuck, George (Edwin) 1931-1996 **CLC 53; DAM POET**
See also CA 21-24R; 153; CANR 23
Stark, Richard
See Westlake, Donald E(dwin)
Staunton, Schuyler
See Baum, L(yman) Frank
Stead, Christina (Ellen) 1902-1983 **CLC 2, 5, 8, 32, 80**
See also CA 13-16R; 109; CANR 33, 40;

MTCW
Stead, William Thomas 1849-1912 **TCLC 48**
Steele, Richard 1672-1729 .... **LC 18**
See also CDBLB 1660-1789; DLB 84, 101
Steele, Timothy (Reid) 1948- .... **CLC 45**
See also CA 93-96; CANR 16, 50; DLB 120
Steffens, (Joseph) Lincoln 1866-1936 . **T C L C 20**
See also CA 117
Stegner, Wallace (Earle) 1909-1993 **CLC 9, 49, 81; DAM NOV; SSC 27**
See also AITN 1; BEST 90:3; CA 1-4R; 141; CAAS 9; CANR 1, 21, 46; DLB 9; DLBY 93; MTCW
Stein, Gertrude 1874-1946 **TCLC 1, 6, 28, 48; DA; DAB; DAC; DAM MST, NOV, POET; PC 18; WLC**
See also CA 104; 132; CDALB 1917-1929; DLB 4, 54, 86; DLBD 15; MTCW
Steinbeck, John (Ernst) 1902-1968 **CLC 1, 5, 9, 13, 21, 34, 45, 75; DA; DAB; DAC; DAM DRAM, MST, NOV; SSC 11; WLC**
See also AAYA 12; CA 1-4R; 25-28R; CANR 1, 35; CDALB 1929-1941; DLB 7, 9; DLBD 2; MTCW; SATA 9
Steinem, Gloria 1934- .... **CLC 63**
See also CA 53-56; CANR 28, 51; MTCW
Steiner, George 1929- ... **CLC 24; DAM NOV**
See also CA 73-76; CANR 31, 67; DLB 67; MTCW; SATA 62
Steiner, K. Leslie
See Delany, Samuel R(ay, Jr.)
Steiner, Rudolf 1861-1925 .... **TCLC 13**
See also CA 107
Stendhal 1783-1842 **NCLC 23, 46; DA; DAB; DAC; DAM MST, NOV; SSC 27; WLC**
See also DLB 119
Stephen, Adeline Virginia
See Woolf, (Adeline) Virginia
Stephen, Sir Leslie 1832-1904 .... **TCLC 23**
See also CA 123; DLB 57, 144, 190
Stephen, Sir Leslie
See Stephen, Sir Leslie
Stephen, Virginia
See Woolf, (Adeline) Virginia
Stephens, James 1882(?)-1950 .... **TCLC 4**
See also CA 104; DLB 19, 153, 162
Stephens, Reed
See Donaldson, Stephen R.
Steptoe, Lydia
See Barnes, Djuna
Sterchi, Beat 1949- .... **CLC 65**
Sterling, Brett
See Bradbury, Ray (Douglas); Hamilton, Edmond
Sterling, Bruce 1954- .... **CLC 72**
See also CA 119; CANR 44
Sterling, George 1869-1926 .... **TCLC 20**
See also CA 117; 165; DLB 54
Stern, Gerald 1925- .... **CLC 40, 100**
See also CA 81-84; CANR 28; DLB 105
Stern, Richard (Gustave) 1928- ... **CLC 4, 39**
See also CA 1-4R; CANR 1, 25, 52; DLBY 87; INT CANR-25
Sternberg, Josef von 1894-1969 .... **CLC 20**
See also CA 81-84
Sterne, Laurence 1713-1768 **LC 2; DA; DAB; DAC; DAM MST, NOV; WLC**
See also CDBLB 1660-1789; DLB 39
Sternheim, (William Adolf) Carl 1878-1942 **TCLC 8**
See also CA 105; DLB 56, 118
Stevens, Mark 1951- .... **CLC 34**

See also CA 122
Stevens, Wallace 1879-1955 **TCLC 3, 12, 45; DA; DAB; DAC; DAM MST, POET; PC 6; WLC**
See also CA 104; 124; CDALB 1929-1941; DLB 54; MTCW
Stevenson, Anne (Katharine) 1933- **CLC 7, 33**
See also CA 17-20R; CAAS 9; CANR 9, 33; DLB 40; MTCW
Stevenson, Robert Louis (Balfour) 1850-1894 **NCLC 5, 14, 63; DA; DAB; DAC; DAM MST, NOV; SSC 11; WLC**
See also AAYA 24; CDBLB 1890-1914; CLR 10, 11; DLB 18, 57, 141, 156, 174; DLBD 13; JRDA; MAICYA; YABC 2
Stewart, J(ohn) I(nnes) M(ackintosh) 1906-1994 .... **CLC 7, 14, 32**
See also CA 85-88; 147; CAAS 3; CANR 47; MTCW
Stewart, Mary (Florence Elinor) 1916- **CLC 7, 35; DAB**
See also CA 1-4R; CANR 1, 59; SATA 12
Stewart, Mary Rainbow
See Stewart, Mary (Florence Elinor)
Stifle, June
See Campbell, Maria
Stifter, Adalbert 1805-1868 **NCLC 41; SSC 28**
See also DLB 133
Still, James 1906- .... **CLC 49**
See also CA 65-68; CAAS 17; CANR 10, 26; DLB 9; SATA 29
Sting
See Sumner, Gordon Matthew
Stirling, Arthur
See Sinclair, Upton (Beall)
Stitt, Milan 1941- .... **CLC 29**
See also CA 69-72
Stockton, Francis Richard 1834-1902
See Stockton, Frank R.
See also CA 108; 137; MAICYA; SATA 44
Stockton, Frank R. .... **TCLC 47**
See also Stockton, Francis Richard
See also DLB 42, 74; DLBD 13; SATA-Brief 32
Stoddard, Charles
See Kuttner, Henry
Stoker, Abraham 1847-1912
See Stoker, Bram
See also CA 105; 150; DA; DAC; DAM MST, NOV; SATA 29
Stoker, Bram 1847-1912 **TCLC 8; DAB; WLC**
See also Stoker, Abraham
See also AAYA 23; CDBLB 1890-1914; DLB 36, 70, 178
Stolz, Mary (Slattery) 1920- .... **CLC 12**
See also AAYA 8; AITN 1; CA 5-8R; CANR 13, 41; JRDA; MAICYA; SAAS 3; SATA 10, 71
Stone, Irving 1903-1989 .. **CLC 7; DAM POP**
See also AITN 1; CA 1-4R; 129; CAAS 3; CANR 1, 23; INT CANR-23; MTCW; SATA 3; SATA-Obit 64
Stone, Oliver (William) 1946- .... **CLC 73**
See also AAYA 15; CA 110; CANR 55
Stone, Robert (Anthony) 1937- **CLC 5, 23, 42**
See also CA 85-88; CANR 23, 66; DLB 152; INT CANR-23; MTCW
Stone, Zachary
See Follett, Ken(neth Martin)
Stoppard, Tom 1937- **CLC 1, 3, 4, 5, 8, 15, 29, 34, 63, 91; DA; DAB; DAC; DAM DRAM, MST; DC 6; WLC**
See also CA 81-84; CANR 39, 67; CDBLB

See also CA 93-96; 25-28R; DLB 180

Tanner, William
See Amis, Kingsley (William)

Tao Lao
See Storni, Alfonsina

Tarassoff, Lev
See Troyat, Henri

Tarbell, Ida M(inerva) 1857-1944 . **TCLC 40**
See also CA 122; DLB 47

Tarkington, (Newton) Booth 1869-1946**TCLC 9**
See also CA 110; 143; DLB 9, 102; SATA 17

Tarkovsky, Andrei (Arsenyevich) 1932-1986
CLC 75
See also CA 127

Tartt, Donna 1964(?)- .... **CLC 76**
See also CA 142

Tasso, Torquato 1544-1595 .... **LC 5**

Tate, (John Orley) Allen 1899-1979**CLC 2, 4, 6, 9, 11, 14, 24**
See also CA 5-8R; 85-88; CANR 32; DLB 4, 45, 63; MTCW

Tate, Ellalice
See Hibbert, Eleanor Alice Burford

Tate, James (Vincent) 1943- ..... **CLC 2, 6, 25**
See also CA 21-24R; CANR 29, 57; DLB 5, 169

Tavel, Ronald 1940- ....**CLC 6**
See also CA 21-24R; CANR 33

Taylor, C(ecil) P(hilip) 1929-1981 .... **CLC 27**
See also CA 25-28R; 105; CANR 47

Taylor, Edward 1642(?)-1729 ..... **LC 11; DA; DAB; DAC; DAM MST, POET**
See also DLB 24

Taylor, Eleanor Ross 1920- ....**CLC 5**
See also CA 81-84

Taylor, Elizabeth 1912-1975 ..... **CLC 2, 4, 29**
See also CA 13-16R; CANR 9; DLB 139; MTCW; SATA 13

Taylor, Frederick Winslow 1856-1915 **T C L C 76**

Taylor, Henry (Splawn) 1942- .... **CLC 44**
See also CA 33-36R; CAAS 7; CANR 31; DLB 5

Taylor, Kamala (Purnaiya) 1924-
See Markandaya, Kamala
See also CA 77-80

Taylor, Mildred D. .... **CLC 21**
See also AAYA 10; BW 1; CA 85-88; CANR 25; CLR 9; DLB 52; JRDA; MAICYA; SAAS 5; SATA 15, 70

Taylor, Peter (Hillsman) 1917-1994**CLC 1, 4, 18, 37, 44, 50, 71; SSC 10**
See also CA 13-16R; 147; CANR 9, 50; DLBY 81, 94; INT CANR-9; MTCW

Taylor, Robert Lewis 1912- .... **CLC 14**
See also CA 1-4R; CANR 3, 64; SATA 10

Tchekhov, Anton
See Chekhov, Anton (Pavlovich)

Tchicaya, Gerald Felix 1931-1988 . **CLC 101**
See also CA 129; 125

Tchicaya U Tam'si
See Tchicaya, Gerald Felix

Teasdale, Sara 1884-1933 .... **TCLC 4**
See also CA 104; 163; DLB 45; SATA 32

Tegner, Esaias 1782-1846 .... **NCLC 2**

Teilhard de Chardin, (Marie Joseph) Pierre 1881-1955.................................. **TCLC 9**
See also CA 105

Temple, Ann
See Mortimer, Penelope (Ruth)

Tennant, Emma (Christina) 1937-**CLC 13, 52**
See also CA 65-68; CAAS 9; CANR 10, 38,

59; DLB 14

Tenneshaw, S. M.
See Silverberg, Robert

Tennyson, Alfred 1809-1892 ... **NCLC 30, 65; DA; DAB; DAC; DAM MST, POET; PC 6; WLC**
See also CDBLB 1832-1890; DLB 32

Teran, Lisa St. Aubin de .... **CLC 36**
See also St. Aubin de Teran, Lisa

Terence 195(?)B.C.-159B.C. **CMLC 14; DC 7**

Teresa de Jesus, St. 1515-1582 .... **LC 18**

Terkel, Louis 1912-
See Terkel, Studs
See also CA 57-60; CANR 18, 45, 67; MTCW

Terkel, Studs .... **CLC 38**
See also Terkel, Louis
See also AITN 1

Terry, C. V.
See Slaughter, Frank G(ill)

Terry, Megan 1932- ....**CLC 19**
See also CA 77-80; CABS 3; CANR 43; DLB 7

Tertz, Abram
See Sinyavsky, Andrei (Donatevich)

Tesich, Steve 1943(?)-1996 .... **CLC 40, 69**
See also CA 105; 152; DLBY 83

Teternikov, Fyodor Kuzmich 1863-1927
See Sologub, Fyodor
See also CA 104

Tevis, Walter 1928-1984 .... **CLC 42**
See also CA 113

Tey, Josephine .... **TCLC 14**
See also Mackintosh, Elizabeth
See also DLB 77

Thackeray, William Makepeace 1811-1863
NCLC 5, 14, 22, 43; DA; DAB; DAC; DAM MST, NOV; WLC
See also CDBLB 1832-1890; DLB 21, 55, 159, 163; SATA 23

Thakura, Ravindranatha
See Tagore, Rabindranath

Tharoor, Shashi 1956- .... **CLC 70**
See also CA 141

Thelwell, Michael Miles 1939- .... **CLC 22**
See also BW 2; CA 101

Theobald, Lewis, Jr.
See Lovecraft, H(oward) P(hillips)

Theodorescu, Ion N. 1880-1967
See Arghezi, Tudor
See also CA 116

Theriault, Yves 1915-1983 .... **CLC 79; DAC; DAM MST**
See also CA 102; DLB 88

Theroux, Alexander (Louis) 1939-**CLC 2, 25**
See also CA 85-88; CANR 20, 63

Theroux, Paul (Edward) 1941- **CLC 5, 8, 11, 15, 28, 46; DAM POP**
See also BEST 89:4; CA 33-36R; CANR 20, 45; DLB 2; MTCW; SATA 44

Thesen, Sharon 1946- ....**CLC 56**
See also CA 163

Thevenin, Denis
See Duhamel, Georges

Thibault, Jacques Anatole Francois 1844-1924
See France, Anatole
See also CA 106; 127; DAM NOV; MTCW

Thiele, Colin (Milton) 1920- ....**CLC 17**
See also CA 29-32R; CANR 12, 28, 53; CLR 27; MAICYA; SAAS 2; SATA 14, 72

Thomas, Audrey (Callahan) 1935-**CLC 7, 13, 37, 107; SSC 20**
See also AITN 2; CA 21-24R; CAAS 19; CANR 36, 58; DLB 60; MTCW

Thomas, D(onald) M(ichael) 1935- . **CLC 13,**

22, 31

See also CA 61-64; CAAS 11; CANR 17, 45; CDBLB 1960 to Present; DLB 40; INT CANR-17; MTCW

Thomas, Dylan (Marlais) 1914-1953**TCLC 1, 8, 45; DA; DAB; DAC; DAM DRAM, MST, POET; PC 2; SSC 3; WLC**
See also CA 104; 120; CANR 65; CDBLB 1945-1960; DLB 13, 20, 139; MTCW; SATA 60

Thomas, (Philip) Edward 1878-1917 . **T C L C 10; DAM POET**
See also CA 106; 153; DLB 19

Thomas, Joyce Carol 1938- .... **CLC 35**
See also AAYA 12; BW 2; CA 113; 116; CANR 48; CLR 19; DLB 33; INT 116; JRDA; MAICYA; MTCW; SAAS 7; SATA 40, 78

Thomas, Lewis 1913-1993 .... **CLC 35**
See also CA 85-88; 143; CANR 38, 60; MTCW

Thomas, Paul
See Mann, (Paul) Thomas

Thomas, Piri 1928- ....**CLC 17**
See also CA 73-76; HW

Thomas, R(onald) S(tuart) 1913- **CLC 6, 13, 48; DAB; DAM POET**
See also CA 89-92; CAAS 4; CANR 30; CDBLB 1960 to Present; DLB 27; MTCW

Thomas, Ross (Elmore) 1926-1995 ...**CLC 39**
See also CA 33-36R; 150; CANR 22, 63

Thompson, Francis Clegg
See Mencken, H(enry) L(ouis)

Thompson, Francis Joseph 1859-1907**TCLC 4**
See also CA 104; CDBLB 1890-1914; DLB 19

Thompson, Hunter S(tockton) 1939- .**CLC 9, 17, 40, 104; DAM POP**
See also BEST 89:1; CA 17-20R; CANR 23, 46; DLB 185; MTCW

Thompson, James Myers
See Thompson, Jim (Myers)

Thompson, Jim (Myers) 1906-1977(?)**CLC 69**
See also CA 140

Thompson, Judith ....**CLC 39**

Thomson, James 1700-1748 ... **LC 16, 29, 40; DAM POET**
See also DLB 95

Thomson, James 1834-1882 **NCLC 18; DAM POET**
See also DLB 35

Thoreau, Henry David 1817-1862**NCLC 7, 21, 61; DA; DAB; DAC; DAM MST; WLC**
See also CDALB 1640-1865; DLB 1

Thornton, Hall
See Silverberg, Robert

Thucydides c. 455B.C.-399B.C. ...... **CMLC 17**
See also DLB 176

Thurber, James (Grover) 1894-1961 .**CLC 5, 11, 25; DA; DAB; DAC; DAM DRAM, MST, NOV; SSC 1**
See also CA 73-76; CANR 17, 39; CDALB 1929-1941; DLB 4, 11, 22, 102; MAICYA; MTCW; SATA 13

Thurman, Wallace (Henry) 1902-1934**T C L C 6; BLC; DAM MULT**
See also BW 1; CA 104; 124; DLB 51

Ticheburn, Cheviot
See Ainsworth, William Harrison

Tieck, (Johann) Ludwig 1773-1853 **NCLC 5, 46**
See also DLB 90

Tiger, Derry
See Ellison, Harlan (Jay)

Tilghman, Christopher 1948(?)- .... **CLC 65**
See also CA 159

DLB 125; MTCW

Twain, Mark TCLC **6, 12, 19, 36, 48, 59; SSC 26; WLC**
See also Clemens, Samuel Langhorne
See also AAYA 20; DLB 11, 12, 23, 64, 74

Tyler, Anne 1941- . CLC **7, 11, 18, 28, 44, 59, 103; DAM NOV, POP**
See also AAYA 18; BEST 89:1; CA 9-12R; CANR 11, 33, 53; DLB 6, 143; DLBY 82; MTCW; SATA 7, 90

Tyler, Royall 1757-1826 .... NCLC **3**
See also DLB 37

Tynan, Katharine 1861-1931 .... TCLC **3**
See also CA 104; DLB 153

Tyutchev, Fyodor 1803-1873 .... NCLC **34**

Tzara, Tristan 1896-1963 ...... CLC **47; DAM POET**
See also CA 153; 89-92

Uhry, Alfred 1936-... CLC **55; DAM DRAM, POP**
See also CA 127; 133; INT 133

Ulf, Haerved
See Strindberg, (Johan) August

Ulf, Harved
See Strindberg, (Johan) August

Ulibarri, Sabine R(eyes) 1919-CLC **83; DAM MULT**
See also CA 131; DLB 82; HW

Unamuno (y Jugo), Miguel de 1864-1936
TCLC **2, 9; DAM MULT, NOV; HLC; SSC 11**
See also CA 104; 131; DLB 108; HW; MTCW

Undercliffe, Errol
See Campbell, (John) Ramsey

Underwood, Miles
See Glassco, John

Undset, Sigrid 1882-1949TCLC **3; DA; DAB; DAC; DAM MST, NOV; WLC**
See also CA 104; 129; MTCW

Ungaretti, Giuseppe 1888-1970CLC **7, 11, 15**
See also CA 19-20; 25-28R; CAP 2; DLB 114

Unger, Douglas 1952- .... CLC **34**
See also CA 130

Unsworth, Barry (Forster) 1930- .... CLC **76**
See also CA 25-28R; CANR 30, 54; DLB 194

Updike, John (Hoyer) 1932-CLC **1, 2, 3, 5, 7, 9, 13, 15, 23, 34, 43, 70; DA; DAB; DAC; DAM MST, NOV, POET, POP; SSC 13, 27; WLC**
See also CA 1-4R; CABS 1; CANR 4, 33, 51; CDALB 1968-1988; DLB 2, 5, 143; DLBD 3; DLBY 80, 82, 97; MTCW

Upshaw, Margaret Mitchell
See Mitchell, Margaret (Munnerlyn)

Upton, Mark
See Sanders, Lawrence

Urdang, Constance (Henriette) 1922-CLC **47**
See also CA 21-24R; CANR 9, 24

Uriel, Henry
See Faust, Frederick (Schiller)

Uris, Leon (Marcus) 1924- CLC **7, 32; DAM NOV, POP**
See also AITN 1, 2; BEST 89:2; CA 1-4R; CANR 1, 40, 65; MTCW; SATA 49

Urmuz
See Codrescu, Andrei

Urquhart, Jane 1949- .... CLC **90; DAC**
See also CA 113; CANR 32, 68

Ustinov, Peter (Alexander) 1921-........CLC **1**
See also AITN 1; CA 13-16R; CANR 25, 51; DLB 13

U Tam'si, Gerald Felix Tchicaya
See Tchicaya, Gerald Felix

U Tam'si, Tchicaya
See Tchicaya, Gerald Felix

Vachss, Andrew (Henry) 1942- ...... CLC **106**
See also CA 118; CANR 44

Vachss, Andrew H.
See Vachss, Andrew (Henry)

Vaculik, Ludvik 1926- ....CLC **7**
See also CA 53-56

Vaihinger, Hans 1852-1933 .... TCLC **71**
See also CA 116

Valdez, Luis (Miguel) 1940- ..CLC **84; DAM MULT; HLC**
See also CA 101; CANR 32; DLB 122; HW

Valenzuela, Luisa 1938- CLC **31, 104; DAM MULT; SSC 14**
See also CA 101; CANR 32, 65; DLB 113; HW

Valera y Alcala-Galiano, Juan 1824-1905
TCLC **10**
See also CA 106

Valery, (Ambroise) Paul (Toussaint Jules) 1871-1945 .... TCLC **4, 15; DAM POET; PC 9**
See also CA 104; 122; MTCW

Valle-Inclan, Ramon (Maria) del 1866-1936
TCLC **5; DAM MULT; HLC**
See also CA 106; 153; DLB 134

Vallejo, Antonio Buero
See Buero Vallejo, Antonio

Vallejo, Cesar (Abraham) 1892-1938TCLC **3, 56; DAM MULT; HLC**
See also CA 105; 153; HW

Vallette, Marguerite Eymery
See Rachilde

Valle Y Pena, Ramon del
See Valle-Inclan, Ramon (Maria) del

Van Ash, Cay 1918- ....CLC **34**

Vanbrugh, Sir John 1664-1726 LC **21; DAM DRAM**
See also DLB 80

Van Campen, Karl
See Campbell, John W(ood, Jr.)

Vance, Gerald
See Silverberg, Robert

Vance, Jack ....CLC **35**
See also Kuttner, Henry; Vance, John Holbrook
See also DLB 8

Vance, John Holbrook 1916-
See Queen, Ellery; Vance, Jack
See also CA 29-32R; CANR 17, 65; MTCW

Van Den Bogarde, Derek Jules Gaspard Ulric Niven 1921-
See Bogarde, Dirk
See also CA 77-80

Vandenburgh, Jane ....CLC **59**

Vanderhaeghe, Guy 1951- ....CLC **41**
See also CA 113

van der Post, Laurens (Jan) 1906-1996CLC **5**
See also CA 5-8R; 155; CANR 35

van de Wetering, Janwillem 1931- ...CLC **47**
See also CA 49-52; CANR 4, 62

Van Dine, S. S. .... TCLC **23**
See also Wright, Willard Huntington

Van Doren, Carl (Clinton) 1885-1950 T C L C **18**
See also CA 111

Van Doren, Mark 1894-1972 .... CLC **6, 10**
See also CA 1-4R; 37-40R; CANR 3; DLB 45; MTCW

Van Druten, John (William) 1901-1957TCLC **2**
See also CA 104; 161; DLB 10

Van Duyn, Mona (Jane) 1921- CLC **3, 7, 63; DAM POET**
See also CA 9-12R; CANR 7, 38, 60; DLB 5

Van Dyne, Edith
See Baum, L(yman) Frank

van Itallie, Jean-Claude 1936- ....CLC **3**
See also CA 45-48; CAAS 2; CANR 1, 48; DLB 7

van Ostaijen, Paul 1896-1928 .... TCLC **33**
See also CA 163

Van Peebles, Melvin 1932-.CLC **2, 20; DAM MULT**
See also BW 2; CA 85-88; CANR 27, 67

Vansittart, Peter 1920- ....CLC **42**
See also CA 1-4R; CANR 3, 49

Van Vechten, Carl 1880-1964 .... CLC **33**
See also CA 89-92; DLB 4, 9, 51

Van Vogt, A(lfred) E(lton) 1912-.........CLC **1**
See also CA 21-24R; CANR 28; DLB 8; SATA 14

Varda, Agnes 1928- ....CLC **16**
See also CA 116; 122

Vargas Llosa, (Jorge) Mario (Pedro) 1936-
CLC **3, 6, 9, 10, 15, 31, 42, 85; DA; DAB; DAC; DAM MST, MULT, NOV; HLC**
See also CA 73-76; CANR 18, 32, 42, 67; DLB 145; HW; MTCW

Vasiliu, Gheorghe 1881-1957
See Bacovia, George
See also CA 123

Vassa, Gustavus
See Equiano, Olaudah

Vassilikos, Vassilis 1933- .... CLC **4, 8**
See also CA 81-84

Vaughan, Henry 1621-1695 .... LC **27**
See also DLB 131

Vaughn, Stephanie ....CLC **62**

Vazov, Ivan (Minchov) 1850-1921 . TCLC **25**
See also CA 121; DLB 147

Veblen, Thorstein (Bunde) 1857-1929 T C L C **31**
See also CA 115; 165

Vega, Lope de 1562-1635 .... LC **23**

Venison, Alfred
See Pound, Ezra (Weston Loomis)

Verdi, Marie de
See Mencken, H(enry) L(ouis)

Verdu, Matilde
See Cela, Camilo Jose

Verga, Giovanni (Carmelo) 1840-1922T C L C **3; SSC 21**
See also CA 104; 123

Vergil 70B.C.-19B.C. .....CMLC **9; DA; DAB; DAC; DAM MST, POET; PC 12; WLCS**

Verhaeren, Emile (Adolphe Gustave) 1855-1916
TCLC **12**
See also CA 109

Verlaine, Paul (Marie) 1844-1896NCLC **2, 51; DAM POET; PC 2**

Verne, Jules (Gabriel) 1828-1905TCLC **6, 52**
See also AAYA 16; CA 110; 131; DLB 123; JRDA; MAICYA; SATA 21

Very, Jones 1813-1880 .... NCLC **9**
See also DLB 1

Vesaas, Tarjei 1897-1970 ....CLC **48**
See also CA 29-32R

Vialis, Gaston
See Simenon, Georges (Jacques Christian)

Vian, Boris 1920-1959 .... TCLC **9**
See also CA 106; 164; DLB 72

Viaud, (Louis Marie) Julien 1850-1923
See Loti, Pierre
See also CA 107

Vicar, Henry
See Felsen, Henry Gregor

Vicker, Angus

See also AAYA 12; BEST 89:4; CA 89-92; 121; CANR 34

Warner, Francis (Robert le Plastrier) 1937- **CLC 14**
See also CA 53-56; CANR 11

Warner, Marina 1946- .... **CLC 59**
See also CA 65-68; CANR 21, 55; DLB 194

Warner, Rex (Ernest) 1905-1986 ..... **CLC 45**
See also CA 89-92; 119; DLB 15

Warner, Susan (Bogert) 1819-1885 **NCLC 31**
See also DLB 3, 42

Warner, Sylvia (Constance) Ashton
See Ashton-Warner, Sylvia (Constance)

Warner, Sylvia Townsend 1893-1978 **CLC 7, 19; SSC 23**
See also CA 61-64; 77-80; CANR 16, 60; DLB 34, 139; MTCW

Warren, Mercy Otis 1728-1814 ...... **NCLC 13**
See also DLB 31

Warren, Robert Penn 1905-1989 **CLC 1, 4, 6, 8, 10, 13, 18, 39, 53, 59; DA; DAB; DAC; DAM MST, NOV, POET; SSC 4; WLC**
See also AITN 1; CA 13-16R; 129; CANR 10, 47; CDALB 1968-1988; DLB 2, 48, 152; DLBY 80, 89; INT CANR-10; MTCW; SATA 46; SATA-Obit 63

Warshofsky, Isaac
See Singer, Isaac Bashevis

Warton, Thomas 1728-1790 ..... **LC 15; DAM POET**
See also DLB 104, 109

Waruk, Kona
See Harris, (Theodore) Wilson

Warung, Price 1855-1911 .... **TCLC 45**

Warwick, Jarvis
See Garner, Hugh

Washington, Alex
See Harris, Mark

Washington, Booker T(aliaferro) 1856-1915 **TCLC 10; BLC; DAM MULT**
See also BW 1; CA 114; 125; SATA 28

Washington, George 1732-1799 .... **LC 25**
See also DLB 31

Wassermann, (Karl) Jakob 1873-1934 **T C L C 6**
See also CA 104; DLB 66

Wasserstein, Wendy 1950- ... **CLC 32, 59, 90; DAM DRAM; DC 4**
See also CA 121; 129; CABS 3; CANR 53; INT 129; SATA 94

Waterhouse, Keith (Spencer) 1929-. **CLC 47**
See also CA 5-8R; CANR 38, 67; DLB 13, 15; MTCW

Waters, Frank (Joseph) 1902-1995 .. **CLC 88**
See also CA 5-8R; 149; CAAS 13; CANR 3, 18, 63; DLBY 86

Waters, Roger 1944- .... **CLC 35**

Watkins, Frances Ellen
See Harper, Frances Ellen Watkins

Watkins, Gerrold
See Malzberg, Barry N(athaniel)

Watkins, Gloria 1955(?)-
See hooks, bell
See also BW 2; CA 143

Watkins, Paul 1964- .... **CLC 55**
See also CA 132; CANR 62

Watkins, Vernon Phillips 1906-1967 **CLC 43**
See also CA 9-10; 25-28R; CAP 1; DLB 20

Watson, Irving S.
See Mencken, H(enry) L(ouis)

Watson, John H.
See Farmer, Philip Jose

Watson, Richard F.

See Silverberg, Robert

Waugh, Auberon (Alexander) 1939- .. **CLC 7**
See also CA 45-48; CANR 6, 22; DLB 14, 194

Waugh, Evelyn (Arthur St. John) 1903-1966 **CLC 1, 3, 8, 13, 19, 27, 44, 107; DA; DAB; DAC; DAM MST, NOV, POP; WLC**
See also CA 85-88; 25-28R; CANR 22; CDBLB 1914-1945; DLB 15, 162, 195; MTCW

Waugh, Harriet 1944- .... **CLC 6**
See also CA 85-88; CANR 22

Ways, C. R.
See Blount, Roy (Alton), Jr.

Waystaff, Simon
See Swift, Jonathan

Webb, (Martha) Beatrice (Potter) 1858-1943 **TCLC 22**
See also Potter, (Helen) Beatrix
See also CA 117

Webb, Charles (Richard) 1939- .... **CLC 7**
See also CA 25-28R

Webb, James H(enry), Jr. 1946- .... **CLC 22**
See also CA 81-84

Webb, Mary (Gladys Meredith) 1881-1927 **TCLC 24**
See also CA 123; DLB 34

Webb, Mrs. Sidney
See Webb, (Martha) Beatrice (Potter)

Webb, Phyllis 1927- .... **CLC 18**
See also CA 104; CANR 23; DLB 53

Webb, Sidney (James) 1859-1947 .. **TCLC 22**
See also CA 117; 163; DLB 190

Webber, Andrew Lloyd .... **CLC 21**
See also Lloyd Webber, Andrew

Weber, Lenora Mattingly 1895-1971 **CLC 12**
See also CA 19-20; 29-32R; CAP 1; SATA 2; SATA-Obit 26

Weber, Max 1864-1920 .... **TCLC 69**
See also CA 109

Webster, John 1579(?)-1634(?) ... **LC 33; DA; DAB; DAC; DAM DRAM, MST; DC 2; WLC**
See also CDBLB Before 1660; DLB 58

Webster, Noah 1758-1843 .... **NCLC 30**

Wedekind, (Benjamin) Frank(lin) 1864-1918 **TCLC 7; DAM DRAM**
See also CA 104; 153; DLB 118

Weidman, Jerome 1913- .... **CLC 7**
See also AITN 2; CA 1-4R; CANR 1; DLB 28

Weil, Simone (Adolphine) 1909-1943 **TCLC 23**
See also CA 117; 159

Weinstein, Nathan
See West, Nathanael

Weinstein, Nathan von Wallenstein
See West, Nathanael

Weir, Peter (Lindsay) 1944- .... **CLC 20**
See also CA 113; 123

Weiss, Peter (Ulrich) 1916-1982 **CLC 3, 15, 51; DAM DRAM**
See also CA 45-48; 106; CANR 3; DLB 69, 124

Weiss, Theodore (Russell) 1916- **CLC 3, 8, 14**
See also CA 9-12R; CAAS 2; CANR 46; DLB 5

Welch, (Maurice) Denton 1915-1948 **TCLC 22**
See also CA 121; 148

Welch, James 1940- ..... **CLC 6, 14, 52; DAM MULT, POP**
See also CA 85-88; CANR 42, 66; DLB 175; NNAL

Weldon, Fay 1931-.. **CLC 6, 9, 11, 19, 36, 59; DAM POP**
See also CA 21-24R; CANR 16, 46, 63; CDBLB 1960 to Present; DLB 14, 194; INT CANR-16; MTCW

Wellek, Rene 1903-1995 .... **CLC 28**
See also CA 5-8R; 150; CAAS 7; CANR 8; DLB 63; INT CANR-8

Weller, Michael 1942- .... **CLC 10, 53**
See also CA 85-88

Weller, Paul 1958- .... **CLC 26**

Wellershoff, Dieter 1925- .... **CLC 46**
See also CA 89-92; CANR 16, 37

Welles, (George) Orson 1915-1985 **CLC 20, 80**
See also CA 93-96; 117

Wellman, Mac 1945- .... **CLC 65**

Wellman, Manly Wade 1903-1986 .... **CLC 49**
See also CA 1-4R; 118; CANR 6, 16, 44; SATA 6; SATA-Obit 47

Wells, Carolyn 1869(?)-1942 .... **TCLC 35**
See also CA 113; DLB 11

Wells, H(erbert) G(eorge) 1866-1946 **TCLC 6, 12, 19; DA; DAB; DAC; DAM MST, NOV; SSC 6; WLC**
See also AAYA 18; CA 110; 121; CDBLB 1914-1945; DLB 34, 70, 156, 178; MTCW; SATA 20

Wells, Rosemary 1943- .... **CLC 12**
See also AAYA 13; CA 85-88; CANR 48; CLR 16; MAICYA; SAAS 1; SATA 18, 69

Welty, Eudora 1909-. **CLC 1, 2, 5, 14, 22, 33, 105; DA; DAB; DAC; DAM MST, NOV; SSC 1, 27; WLC**
See also CA 9-12R; CABS 1; CANR 32, 65; CDALB 1941-1968; DLB 2, 102, 143; DLBD 12; DLBY 87; MTCW

Wen I-to 1899-1946 .... **TCLC 28**

Wentworth, Robert
See Hamilton, Edmond

Werfel, Franz (Viktor) 1890-1945 ... **TCLC 8**
See also CA 104; 161; DLB 81, 124

Wergeland, Henrik Arnold 1808-1845 **N C L C 5**

Wersba, Barbara 1932- .... **CLC 30**
See also AAYA 2; CA 29-32R; CANR 16, 38; CLR 3; DLB 52; JRDA; MAICYA; SAAS 2; SATA 1, 58

Wertmueller, Lina 1928- .... **CLC 16**
See also CA 97-100; CANR 39

Wescott, Glenway 1901-1987 .... **CLC 13**
See also CA 13-16R; 121; CANR 23; DLB 4, 9, 102

Wesker, Arnold 1932-.... **CLC 3, 5, 42; DAB; DAM DRAM**
See also CA 1-4R; CAAS 7; CANR 1, 33; CDBLB 1960 to Present; DLB 13; MTCW

Wesley, Richard (Errol) 1945- .... **CLC 7**
See also BW 1; CA 57-60; CANR 27; DLB 38

Wessel, Johan Herman 1742-1785 ...... **LC 7**

West, Anthony (Panther) 1914-1987 **CLC 50**
See also CA 45-48; 124; CANR 3, 19; DLB 15

West, C. P.
See Wodehouse, P(elham) G(renville)

West, (Mary) Jessamyn 1902-1984 **CLC 7, 17**
See also CA 9-12R; 112; CANR 27; DLB 6; DLBY 84; MTCW; SATA-Obit 37

West, Morris L(anglo) 1916- .... **CLC 6, 33**
See also CA 5-8R; CANR 24, 49, 64; MTCW

West, Nathanael 1903-1940 **TCLC 1, 14, 44; SSC 16**
See also CA 104; 125; CDALB 1929-1941; DLB 4, 9, 28; MTCW

West, Owen
See Koontz, Dean R(ay)

West, Paul 1930- .... **CLC 7, 14, 96**
See also CA 13-16R; CAAS 7; CANR 22, 53; DLB 14; INT CANR-22

West, Rebecca 1892-1983 ... **CLC 7, 9, 31, 50**

See Williamson, Jack
See also CA 17-20R; CANR 23
Willie, Frederick
See Lovecraft, H(oward) P(hillips)
Willingham, Calder (Baynard, Jr.) 1922-1995
CLC 5, 51
See also CA 5-8R; 147; CANR 3; DLB 2, 44;
MTCW
Willis, Charles
See Clarke, Arthur C(harles)
Willy
See Colette, (Sidonie-Gabrielle)
Willy, Colette
See Colette, (Sidonie-Gabrielle)
Wilson, A(ndrew) N(orman) 1950- .. **CLC 33**
See also CA 112; 122; DLB 14, 155, 194
Wilson, Angus (Frank Johnstone) 1913-1991
CLC 2, 3, 5, 25, 34; SSC 21
See also CA 5-8R; 134; CANR 21; DLB 15,
139, 155; MTCW
Wilson, August 1945- **CLC 39, 50, 63; BLC;**
DA; DAB; DAC; DAM DRAM, MST,
MULT; DC 2; WLCS
See also AAYA 16; BW 2; CA 115; 122; CANR
42, 54; MTCW
Wilson, Brian 1942- .... **CLC 12**
Wilson, Colin 1931- .... **CLC 3, 14**
See also CA 1-4R; CAAS 5; CANR 1, 22, 33;
DLB 14, 194; MTCW
Wilson, Dirk
See Pohl, Frederik
Wilson, Edmund 1895-1972**CLC 1, 2, 3, 8, 24**
See also CA 1-4R; 37-40R; CANR 1, 46; DLB
63; MTCW
Wilson, Ethel Davis (Bryant) 1888(?)-1980
CLC 13; DAC; DAM POET
See also CA 102; DLB 68; MTCW
Wilson, John 1785-1854 .... **NCLC 5**
Wilson, John (Anthony) Burgess 1917-1993
See Burgess, Anthony
See also CA 1-4R; 143; CANR 2, 46; DAC;
DAM NOV; MTCW
Wilson, Lanford 1937- **CLC 7, 14, 36; DAM**
DRAM
See also CA 17-20R; CABS 3; CANR 45; DLB
7
Wilson, Robert M. 1944- .... **CLC 7, 9**
See also CA 49-52; CANR 2, 41; MTCW
Wilson, Robert McLiam 1964- .... **CLC 59**
See also CA 132
Wilson, Sloan 1920- .... **CLC 32**
See also CA 1-4R; CANR 1, 44
Wilson, Snoo 1948- .... **CLC 33**
See also CA 69-72
Wilson, William S(mith) 1932- .... **CLC 49**
See also CA 81-84
Wilson, Woodrow 1856-1924 .... **TCLC 73**
See also DLB 47
Winchilsea, Anne (Kingsmill) Finch Counte
1661-1720
See Finch, Anne
Windham, Basil
See Wodehouse, P(elham) G(renville)
Wingrove, David (John) 1954- .... **CLC 68**
See also CA 133
Wintergreen, Jane
See Duncan, Sara Jeannette
Winters, Janet Lewis .... **CLC 41**
See also Lewis, Janet
See also DLBY 87
Winters, (Arthur) Yvor 1900-1968 **CLC 4, 8,**
32
See also CA 11-12; 25-28R; CAP 1; DLB 48;

MTCW
Winterson, Jeanette 1959-**CLC 64; DAM POP**
See also CA 136; CANR 58
Winthrop, John 1588-1649 .... **LC 31**
See also DLB 24, 30
Wiseman, Frederick 1930- .... **CLC 20**
See also CA 159
Wister, Owen 1860-1938 .... **TCLC 21**
See also CA 108; 162; DLB 9, 78, 186; SATA
62
Witkacy
See Witkiewicz, Stanislaw Ignacy
Witkiewicz, Stanislaw Ignacy 1885-1939
TCLC 8
See also CA 105; 162
Wittgenstein, Ludwig (Josef Johann) 1889-1951
TCLC 59
See also CA 113; 164
Wittig, Monique 1935(?)-.................... **CLC 22**
See also CA 116; 135; DLB 83
Wittlin, Jozef 1896-1976 .... **CLC 25**
See also CA 49-52; 65-68; CANR 3
Wodehouse, P(elham) G(renville) 1881-1975
CLC 1, 2, 5, 10, 22; DAB; DAC; DAM
NOV; SSC 2
See also AITN 2; CA 45-48; 57-60; CANR 3,
33; CDBLB 1914-1945; DLB 34, 162;
MTCW; SATA 22
Woiwode, L.
See Woiwode, Larry (Alfred)
Woiwode, Larry (Alfred) 1941- ... **CLC 6, 10**
See also CA 73-76; CANR 16; DLB 6; INT
CANR-16
Wojciechowska, Maia (Teresa) 1927-**CLC 26**
See also AAYA 8; CA 9-12R; CANR 4, 41; CLR
1; JRDA; MAICYA; SAAS 1; SATA 1, 28,
83
Wolf, Christa 1929- .... **CLC 14, 29, 58**
See also CA 85-88; CANR 45; DLB 75; MTCW
Wolfe, Gene (Rodman) 1931- **CLC 25; DAM**
POP
See also CA 57-60; CAAS 9; CANR 6, 32, 60;
DLB 8
Wolfe, George C. 1954- .... **CLC 49**
See also CA 149
Wolfe, Thomas (Clayton) 1900-1938**TCLC 4,**
13, 29, 61; DA; DAB; DAC; DAM MST,
NOV; WLC
See also CA 104; 132; CDALB 1929-1941;
DLB 9, 102; DLBD 2, 16; DLBY 85, 97;
MTCW
Wolfe, Thomas Kennerly, Jr. 1931-
See Wolfe, Tom
See also CA 13-16R; CANR 9, 33; DAM POP;
DLB 185; INT CANR-9; MTCW
Wolfe, Tom .... **CLC 1, 2, 9, 15, 35, 51**
See also Wolfe, Thomas Kennerly, Jr.
See also AAYA 8; AITN 2; BEST 89:1; DLB
152
Wolff, Geoffrey (Ansell) 1937- .... **CLC 41**
See also CA 29-32R; CANR 29, 43
Wolff, Sonia
See Levitin, Sonia (Wolff)
Wolff, Tobias (Jonathan Ansell) 1945-.. **C L C**
39, 64
See also AAYA 16; BEST 90:2; CA 114; 117;
CAAS 22; CANR 54; DLB 130; INT 117
Wolfram von Eschenbach c. 1170-c. 1220
CMLC 5
See also DLB 138
Wolitzer, Hilma 1930- .... **CLC 17**
See also CA 65-68; CANR 18, 40; INT CANR-
18; SATA 31

Wollstonecraft, Mary 1759-1797 .... **LC 5**
See also CDBLB 1789-1832; DLB 39, 104, 158
Wonder, Stevie .... **CLC 12**
See also Morris, Steveland Judkins
Wong, Jade Snow 1922- .... **CLC 17**
See also CA 109
Woodberry, George Edward 1855-1930
TCLC 73
See also CA 165; DLB 71, 103
Woodcott, Keith
See Brunner, John (Kilian Houston)
Woodruff, Robert W.
See Mencken, H(enry) L(ouis)
Woolf, (Adeline) Virginia 1882-1941**TCLC 1,**
5, 20, 43, 56; DA; DAB; DAC; DAM MST,
NOV; SSC 7; WLC
See also CA 104; 130; CANR 64; CDBLB
1914-1945; DLB 36, 100, 162; DLBD 10;
MTCW
Woolf, Virginia Adeline
See Woolf, (Adeline) Virginia
Woollcott, Alexander (Humphreys) 1887-1943
TCLC 5
See also CA 105; 161; DLB 29
Woolrich, Cornell 1903-1968 .... **CLC 77**
See also Hopley-Woolrich, Cornell George
Wordsworth, Dorothy 1771-1855 ..**NCLC 25**
See also DLB 107
Wordsworth, William 1770-1850 ..**NCLC 12,**
38; DA; DAB; DAC; DAM MST, POET;
PC 4; WLC
See also CDBLB 1789-1832; DLB 93, 107
Wouk, Herman 1915-**CLC 1, 9, 38; DAM NOV,**
POP
See also CA 5-8R; CANR 6, 33, 67; DLBY 82;
INT CANR-6; MTCW
Wright, Charles (Penzel, Jr.) 1935-**CLC 6, 13,**
28
See also CA 29-32R; CAAS 7; CANR 23, 36,
62; DLB 165; DLBY 82; MTCW
Wright, Charles Stevenson 1932- ... **CLC 49;**
BLC 3; DAM MULT, POET
See also BW 1; CA 9-12R; CANR 26; DLB 33
Wright, Jack R.
See Harris, Mark
Wright, James (Arlington) 1927-1980**CLC 3,**
5, 10, 28; DAM POET
See also AITN 2; CA 49-52; 97-100; CANR 4,
34, 64; DLB 5, 169; MTCW
Wright, Judith (Arandell) 1915- **CLC 11, 53;**
PC 14
See also CA 13-16R; CANR 31; MTCW; SATA
14
Wright, L(auroli) R. 1939- .... **CLC 44**
See also CA 138
Wright, Richard (Nathaniel) 1908-1960 **C L C**
1, 3, 4, 9, 14, 21, 48, 74; BLC; DA; DAB;
DAC; DAM MST, MULT, NOV; SSC 2;
WLC
See also AAYA 5; BW 1; CA 108; CANR 64;
CDALB 1929-1941; DLB 76, 102; DLBD
2; MTCW
Wright, Richard B(ruce) 1937- .... **CLC 6**
See also CA 85-88; DLB 53
Wright, Rick 1945- .... **CLC 35**
Wright, Rowland
See Wells, Carolyn
Wright, Stephen 1946- .... **CLC 33**
Wright, Willard Huntington 1888-1939
See Van Dine, S. S.
See also CA 115; DLBD 16
Wright, William 1930- .... **CLC 44**
See also CA 53-56; CANR 7, 23

Literary Criticism Series
Cumulative Topic Index

This index lists all topic entries in Gale's *Classical and Medieval Literature Criticism, Contemporary Literary Criticism, Literature Criticism from 1400 to 1800, Nineteenth-Century Literature Criticism,* and *Twentieth-Century Literary Criticism.*

Topic Index

Topic Index

Topic Index

Contemporary Literary Criticism
Cumulative Nationality Index

Nationality Index

Nationality Index

Nationality Index

Nationality Index

CLC-110 Title Index

487

Title Index

ISBN 0-7876-2033-5

90000

9 780787 620332